GULLS

OF EUROPE, ASIA AND NORTH AMERICA

GULLS

OF EUROPE, ASIA AND NORTH AMERICA

KLAUS MALLING OLSEN

ILLUSTRATED BY

HANS LARSSON

CHRISTOPHER HELM
LONDON

KMO dedicates this work to the late Claudia Wilds (1931–1997), a great friend
and inspiration for this work.
HL dedicates this work to Hugo Larsson (1931–2002), his beloved father.

Published 2003 by Christopher Helm,
an imprint of A & C Black Publishers Ltd.,
37 Soho Square, London W1D 3QZ

Reprinted with corrections 2004
Reprinted 2004, 2005

ISBN 0-7136-7087-8

A CIP catalogue record for this book is available from the British Library

A & C Black uses paper produced with elemental chlorine free pulp, harvested
from managed sustainable forests

www.acblack.com

A GMB Books production
Colour separations by René Pop

Printed in Italy through G. Canale and C. S.p.a.

10 9 8 7 6 5 4 3

CONTENTS

PREFACE

The publication of P. J. Grant's classic study *Gulls: a guide to identification* in 1982 heralded a passion for gull-watching for many people. At last, less experienced birdwatchers had a real chance to identify all the gulls of the Western Palearctic. It was not, however, until 1994 that I began working on this new gull identification book. In the meantime, I had met Hans Larsson, while he was working at Falsterbo Bird Observatory in the autumn of 1990. He eventually became involved in illustrating our joint books *Terns of Europe and North America* (1995b) and *Skuas and Jaegers of the World* (1997), both works proving his unsurpassed skills in illustrating flying as well as settled birds in a simple and clean manner — perfect for identification work. Hans was the ideal illustrator to work on the forthcoming gulls book.

As soon as the contract was signed, museum work started. Week after week was filled with extensive field studies and gull photography. Comparisons were made with sketches and photos from previous journeys, and I was especially happy that presumed Yellow-legged Gulls from northern Kazakhstan, studied and photographed in June 1989, perfectly matched the appearance of the few available skins of the form *barabensis* in the museum collections in Copenhagen and Tring; this was a gull that was almost unknown at the time to all but a few skilled gull fanatics! Before that, an unexpected and much-needed sighting of a Ross's Gull in Denmark, as well as numerous Glaucous and Iceland Gulls, had created a desire to write about their identification. As the work progressed, gulls became the focus of numerous field trips to the USA, most of Europe, including Iceland, the Azores and Madeira, Israel, Morocco, The Gambia, UAE, Pakistan, India, Nepal, New Zealand, China and Japan. Many tours were designed especially for seeing gulls, including a month-long trip to California in winter 2000 and a gull-tour to Japan in February 2001.

An enormous amount of new knowledge, published in long papers in birdwatching journals and magazines, was reviewed in detail and compared with our own results. This added much new and invaluable information, and caused us to recognise that gulls vary markedly throughout their ranges. For example, Herring Gulls just a few hundred kilometres apart do not necessarily resemble each other. Sometimes we felt that we were moving two steps forward and one step back, with Neil Young's wise words in our minds: 'I'm living here out on the beach, but these seagulls are still out of reach'.

The problems of gull identification go on, especially as new areas for study constantly emerge. We admit that, on some points, identification of the larger gulls is still in its infancy. It is our hope that this work will stimulate new generations of birdwatchers to take a closer interest in what is probably the most difficult subject in modern field identification. Gull watching will surely continue for decades, and new, important characters will certainly be discovered. For some, this book will only be the starting point.

ACKNOWLEDGEMENTS

During the preparation of this book, we have received much help from numerous birdwatchers, ornithologists and gull photographers. For stimulating discussions, important comments and loan of photographs we would like to thank: Kim Aaen, Frank Abrahamson, Peter Adriaens, Peter Alden, Jonathan Alderfer, Per Alström, Ruud Altenburg, Ole Amstrup, Björn Andersson, David Astins, Nicola Baccetti, R. Baradez, Graham Bell, John Bell, Per-Göran Bentz, Max Berlijn, Karel Beylevelt, Anders Blomdahl, David Boertmann, Jan Boshuizen, Pierrandrea Brichetti, Brynjúlfur Brynjúlfson, Andreas Buchheim, Mads Jensen Bunch, Lars Carlsson, Stieg Carlsson, Luis Carneiro, Carlos Carrapato, Mike Carter, Claes-Göran Cederlund, A. Charcier, Jan Hjort Christensen, Erik Christophersen, Hans Christophersen, Mark Cocker, Richard Coomber, David Cooper, John F. Cooper, Andrea Corso, Helder Costa, Kai Dallmann, Don DesJardin, Philippe J. Dubois, Michael Duckham, Barry Duffin, Michael Duffy, Jerzy Dyczkowski, Ayla Elkjær, Ola Ellestrom, Martin Elliott, Patric Engström, David Erterius, Zoltan Escedi, Knud Falk, Kim Fischer, Graham Foggitt, Dick Forsman, Alain Fossé, Gordon Frost, H.-J. Fünfstück, K. L. Garrett, Martin Gottschling, the late Peter J. Grant, Catarina Grengby, Morten Günther, Thomas Grüner, Marc Guyt, Percy Hadley, Andreas Hagerman, Joakim Hagström, Kaj Halberg, Lars Hansen, Fredrik Hansson, Ken Hatsuno, Håkon Heggland, Klaus Hein, Felix Heintzenberg, Andreas J. Helbig, Erik Hirschfeld, Charlie Holt, W. (Ted) Hoogendoorn, Julian R. Hough, Markku Huhta-Koivisto, David Hursthouse, John Idzikowski, Hiroshi Ikenaga, Ottavio Janni, Justin Jansen, Jens-Kjeld Jensen, Curt Johnsson, Morten Jørgensen, Alan Jortay, Eduardo de Juana, Matti Kapanen, Rolland Kern, Henrik Kisbye, Nils Kjellén, Alan Knox, Henrik

Knudsen, Peter Koch, Gert Groot Koerkamp, Yann Kolbeinsson, Volker Konrad, Daniel Kratzer, Andreas Bruhn Kristensen, Martin Kviesgaard, Ed Kwater, H. Lainer, Martin Langman, Knud Larsen, Lars Larsson, Mikkel Lausten, R. Vernon Laux, Anders Lindström, Leo Linnaerz, Birger Lønning, Jan Lontkowski, Johan Lorentzon, Richard Lowe, Sebastian Ludvigsen, Peter Lyngs, Mogens Majland, Sönke Martens, Ugo Mellone, Åse Mielow, Alf Tore Mjøs, Joseph Morlan, Peter Morris, Tomi Mukkinnen, Marc Moasso, Erik Mølgaard, Jan Kåre Ness, Dick Newell, Serge Nicolle, Boris Nikolov, Henrik Haaning Nielsen, Mikael Nord, Jyrki Normaja, Bård Nyberg, Lars Erik Nygren, Ivan Olsen, Kent Olsen, Lasse Olsson, Gerald J. Oreel, Steffen Ortmann, Troels Eske Ortvad, Phil Palmer, Alan Parkin, Robert Parsons, Johnny L. Pedersen, Keld T. Pedersen, Knud Pedersen, Mogens Ring Pedersen, Göran Pettersson, René Pop, Richard F. Porter, Christopher Randler, Brian Rasmussen, Martin Reid, George Reszeter, Michael Retter, Colin Richardson, John Richardson, Rose-Ann Rowlett, Kenneth Rude Nielsen, Markku Saarinen, Thomas Sacher, Kamma Sander, K. Sándor, Jan Eske Schmidt, Jevgeni Shergalin, Jonathan Simms, Mike Skakuj, Gunter de Smet, Uffe Gjøl Sørensen, Trond Sørhuus, Sven Splittorf, Alexander Stoehr, Rasmus Strack, Bruno Sundin, Werner Suter, Lars Svensson, Peter Szöke, Alan Tate, Kasper Thorup, Ray Tipper, Bjørn Olav Tveit, Rolf Uhlig, Jan Unoson, Morten Vang, Didier Vangeluwe, Markus Varesvuo, Morten Viker, Stephen Votier, P. Wallbridge, Mike Wallen, Arend Wassink, Ingo Weiss, Thure Wikberg, Rob Williams, Lars Witting, Arne Wolf, Tom Wurster, Pierre Yésou and Steve Young.

Hans Larsson additionally wishes to thank the following persons: Sven Splittorff, Lars Nilsson, Mikael Arinder, Jonas Rosqvist, Tommy Holmgren, Roine Strandberg, Lars Olsson, Jörgen Bernsmo, Richard Bergendahl, P-G Bentz, Falsterbo Fågelstation, Magnus Billqvist, Mattias Pettersson, Måns Hjernquist, Christian Cederroth, Cecilia Johansson, Stefan Cherrug, Svante Joelsson, Måns Sjöberg, Peter Larsson, Peter Elfman, Jan Danielsson, Richard Ek, Pierre Unge, Johan Lorentzon, Jesper Segergren, Hampe Lejon, Landsorts Fågelstation, Marie-Louise Kold, Mattias Nilsson, Jenny Gonzales, Karin Svensson, Dominika Polanska, Magnus and Mattias Ullman, Cecilia Cavefors, Bruno Wiebelt, Jan-Anders Hansson and Njutaren, Lars-Gunnar Lundqvist, Mattias Nordlund, Bo Holst, Alexander Hellquist, Björn Malmhagen, Johan Hammar, Lars Råberg, Niklas Holmqvist, Richard Ottvall, Lennart Nilsson, the late Hugo Larsson, Maty Jagne, Leif Hansson, Slys and Annica, Jörgen Israelsson, Björn Johansson, Ronny Johansson, Jesper Jönsson, Claes Larsson, Johannes Tallroth, Marcus Tallroth, Gustav Tallroth, Liselott Tallroth, Karl-Fredrik Sjölund, Sven Marling, Bo Petersson, Dan Mangsbo, Börje Monsén, Nicklas Nordbeck, Thomas Nyberg, Lars-Erik Nygren, Staffan Åkeby, Petter Ohlsson, Ben Slimane, Patrik Slimane, Mattias Olsson, Anders Wirdheim, Klas Rådberg, Johan Stenlund, Patrik Söderberg, Kent Söderberg, Nigel Redman, Magnus Unger, Uno Unger, Patric Österblad, Greger Flyckt, Martin Green, Daniel Green, Nicklas Lignell, Mats Rellmar, Hans-Åke Gustavsson, Staffanstorps Naturskyddsförening, Linda Stackerud, Zoegas, Micke på Drewex, Galleri Jacobsson, Anders Emgård, Stig Linné, Yvonne Linné, Åsa Kostenniemi, Lunds Konstskola, Jim Sundberg, Jonas Sundberg, Åke Andersson, Torbjörn Hegedüs, Jarl Lorensson, Patrik Werbaum, Henrik Hansen, Fredrik Hansson, Gert Ljungqvist, Bengt Bengtsson, Bo E. Pettersson, Paul Axelsson, Jens Frimer, Madeleine Bauer, Inge Flesjå, Lamin Sidibeh.

Special thanks go to Hadoram Shirihai, Harry Lehto, Henry J. Lehto, Don DesJardin, Paul Doherty, Hanne Eriksen, Jens Eriksen, Osao Ujihara, Michiaki Ujihara, Visa Rauste, Arnoud B. van den Berg, Antero Lindholm and Per Schiermacher-Hansen for supplying an extraordinarily large series of photographs. Antero Topp organised superb contact with several Finnish and Californian photographers.

For comments on species accounts we are especially grateful to Kenneth Bengtsson, Andrés Bermejo, Geoff J. Carey, Martin Collinson, Annika Forsten, Alvaro Jaramillo, Diederik Kok, Harry J. Lehto, Bruce Mactavish, Visa Rauste, Per Schiermacker-Hansen and Kevin Zimmer. We are extremely grateful to Jon R. King for his hospitality and for sharing his great knowledge of gulls during a month's gull-watching tour of California and Mexico in winter 2000.

Ger Meesters and René Pop kindly housed KMO during visits to the Netherlands, and made it possible for KMO to work. KMO also wants to offer special thanks to Gustav Rudebeck for 'Rudebeckstipendiatet 2001'! The late Claudia Wilds was a great friend and inspiration, and unselfishly housed KMO during several visits to Washington, DC.

We would like to thank personnel at the museums and skin collections we visited: Peter Colston and Robert Prys-Jones (NHM), Jon Fjeldså and Carsten Rahbek (UZM), Göran Frisk and Per Eriksson (NRK), Per-Göran Bentz (ZMO, MN), Christian Ås and Jan Lifjeld (ZMO), Sverker Wadén (MN), Pekka J. Nikander and Hannu Jännes (ZMH), René Dekker (NNH), C. J. (Kees) Roselaar (ZMA), Phil Angle (USNM), Raymond A. Paynter Jr. and Alison Pirie (MCZ), Bob Jones and Carla Cicero (MVZ), and Kimball L. Garrett and Kathy Molina (LACM).

INTRODUCTION

This book is a guide to the *identification* and *distribution* of the gulls of the Holarctic, and should be judged only as such. We describe and illustrate what the gulls of this region look like. We are fully aware of the enormous individual variation that exists in the larger gull species, but have attempted to account for the most typical individuals within certain populations. More advanced taxonomic aspects are considered to be beyond the scope of this general identification guide. The large gulls are discussed in detail in Yésou's excellent summaries (Yésou 2002, 2003).

In pursuit of our aims we have examined 7,000 gull specimens in the museums mentioned above, using measuring methods outlined below. We have been examining thousands of photographs, an endless number of references and—most importantly—living gulls in their natural habitats throughout most of the area under review for over 20 years. Special attention has been given to the plumage characters of birds of known age, as proved by ringing. We fully acknowledge that the inspiration of this work was Grant's classic *Gulls: a guide to identification* (1982), which itself was inspired by J. Dwight's *Gulls of the World* (1925).

1. Studying variation in gulls is great fun and makes you a better birder! Note the difference in timing of moult between summer and winter plumage in this flock of **Black-headed** and **Common Gulls**, and also how the different angles in a 'frozen' photograph reveal slight differences in primary pattern. Gulls are social birds, and often occur in mixed flocks containing several species. Many vagrants have been found by careful examination of flocks of the commoner species (can you spot the Herring and the Ross's Gulls in this photograph?). *George Reszeter.*

In questions of taxonomy, we follow del Hoyo *et al.* (1996) with the following differences:

Yellow-legged Gull We treat *Larus michahellis* as a seperate species from Caspian Gull *Larus cachinnans* based on differences in plumage, breeding biology, voice and the apparent absence of hybridisation in the possible contact zone in the western Black Sea. We treat the taxa *barabensis* and *mongolicus* as subspecies of Caspian Gull, although recent studies have indicated that *barabensis* may be closer to nominate *heuglini* of Heuglin's Gull and that *mongolicus* is probably a full species, related to Vega Gull *Larus vegae*.

Heuglin's Gull We treat *Larus heuglini* as a separate species from Lesser Black-backed Gull or Herring Gull on the basis of plumage differences, moult, migration and no proven hybridisation with the former.

Vega Gull We treat *Larus vegae* as a separate species from Herring Gull on the basis of isolation from other taxa, but are aware of the extensive hybridisation with the race '*taimyrensis*' of Heuglin's Gull.

American Herring Gull We treat *Larus smithsonianus* as a separate species from Herring Gull *Larus argentatus* on the basis of differences in first-year plumage, calls, recently established differences in DNA and geographical isolation.

Mew Gull We treat *Larus brachyrhynchus* as a separate species from Common Gull *Larus canus* on the basis of constant differences in all plumages as well as geographical isolation.

THE FORMAT OF THE SPECIES ACCOUNTS

The species accounts are organised into the following sections.

IDENTIFICATION. This covers field identification, stressing the most important structural specific characters, flight action, separation from similar species and a brief review of the various plumages. This section is intended to enable most observers to identify the species and their different age-types.

VOICE. This is described briefly, mentioning only the most typical calls.

MOULT. The data for this section is taken from a large number of skins, photographs, field notes and discussions with various authorities. The information has been supplemented with data from the relevant literature, cited under the different species or in the reference list.

DESCRIPTION. This is a detailed section, adding further information on the different ages and plumages. This section is intended mainly for those especially interested in small plumage details and correct ageing.

GEOGRAPHICAL VARIATION. When different subspecies occur, these are mentioned and described in a separate paragraph.

DISTRIBUTION AND MIGRATION. This section deals mainly with migration and winter distribution.

MEASUREMENTS. These were made by KMO and are presented in three columns: range of specimens measured, mean (in parentheses) and numbers measured. Wing length (carpal joint to tip of longest primary) is the maximum chord, with wing flattened and straightened against a ruler. Bill length is from feathering at the base of the bill to the tip. Bill depth at gonys is from the culmen to the gonydeal angle. Bill depth at the base of the bill is taken at the base of the upper mandible. Tarsus length is from the intertarsal joint to the distal end of the last undivided scale at the toe divergence. If measurements given in other sources add important information, notes are given. All lengths are in millimetres; all weights are in grams. The data is displayed as below, with averages in brackets and the far right column giving the sample size.

Wing

Adult male	387–460 (441.8)	16
Adult female	402–448 (424.9)	12
First-year male	418–447 (429.6)	5
First-year female	428,431	2

Mantle colour has been determined using the Kodak Grey Scale Color Separation Guide and the Grey Scale (large) CAT 152 7662 1995. The Grey Scale runs on a scale between 0 (white) and 20 (black). The method used was to place the Grey Scale over one of the scapular feather tracts and then hold it at different angles and in varying lights. No. 5 on the Kodak Grey Scale represents a Munsell-value of around 6.0, which is Light Neutral Grey (Smith's Colour Guide), and no. 7 represents Munsell 5.0 and Medium Neutral Grey in Smith's Colour Guide. If a colour tone falls between two shades, it is mentioned as (e.g.) 5.5. We found it difficult to establish exact values below 3. Measuring an exact value in the field is very difficult, but the method works very well on specimens and birds in the hand.

The following museum collections have been examined. LACM: Natural History Museum of Los Angeles County, Los Angeles, USA; MCZ: Museum of Comparative Zoology, Harvard University, Cambridge, Massachusetts, USA; MN: Malmö Naturmuseum, Malmö, Sweden; MVZ: Museum of Vertebrate Zoology, University of California at Berkeley, California, USA; NHM: Natural History Museum, Tring, UK; NNH: Nationaal Natuurhistorisch Museum, Leiden, Netherlands; NRK: Naturhistoriska Riksmuseet, Stockholm, Sweden; USNM: National Museum of Natural History, Smithsonian Institution, Washington DC, USA; UZM: Universitetets Zoologiske Museum, Copenhagen, Denmark; ZMA: Zoölogisch Museum (Instituut voor Taxonomische Zoölogie), Amsterdam, Netherlands; ZMO: Zoologisk Museum, Universitetet i Oslo, Norway.

GENERAL INFORMATION ON AGEING OF GULLS

During its lifespan, each gull goes through several plumage states. The length of time taken for a gull to reach full adult plumage differs. Most smaller gulls are 'two-year gulls', taking about 13–16 months to reach adult plumage, although first adult plumage often shows small traces of immaturity. This is typical for the majority of the 'hooded' gulls.

The medium-sized, 'three-year gulls' take one more year to attain fully adult plumage (25–28 months

2. Herring Gull, moulting from second-summer to third-winter. IJmuiden, Netherlands. 3 Jul 1994. *Klaus Malling Olsen*

after fledging). This is the case in a few 'hooded gulls' (Little, Pallas's), plus Slender-billed, Common, Ring-billed and Yellow-footed Gull, and some Lesser Black-backed Gull populations.

The large 'four-year gulls' show great variation in the time they take to develop into adult plumage. **Age-classes between first-summer and adult should be regarded as generalisations only.** The large gulls take at least 28–40 months to develop full adult plumage, although traces of immaturity remain frequent in later ages.

AGE TERMINOLOGY AND MOULT

Precise ageing of gulls is difficult apart from first-years and full adults. Most gulls go through several immature moults, and the appearance of the plumage is probably affected by both the general stage of the bird and whether the moult takes place early or late. For example, gulls which undergo body moult early often show more immature feather types than late moulters, and northerly gull species often have a more restricted moult. Common and Herring Gulls have been shown to retain traces of immaturity to a much older age than expected.

General ageing is, however, possible and is the basis for the information presented. It is worth attempting to ascribe an immature gull to a certain 'age-type'. Although the text, for the sake of clarity, gives 'precise' pronunciations such as 'second-winter', note that immature gulls moult more or less continuously, e.g. the 'moult to first-summer' in large gulls is in fact the first stages of moult to second-winter; 'first-summer' is thus an artificial term. From about 10 months of age, large gulls moult from first-winter to second-winter plumage; the hooded gulls, however, attain a first-summer plumage.

Juvenile is the first full plumage. In juveniles (and up to about one year of age) primaries are pointed, and from late winter browner through wear. In smaller/medium (and some larger) gulls, head and body (and some scapulars/coverts) are quickly moulted to **first-winter** plumage, where head and parts of the body become adult-like or—in larger gulls—more neatly dark-patterned than the juvenile. In most large gulls, moult into first-winter is restricted to mantle/scapulars and a variable number of head and body feathers. Sometimes juvenile plumage is retained, especially in Arctic breeders and certain long-distance migrants. The amount of moult is variable even within populations from the same areas, and the

3. Lesser Black-backed Gull adult moulting into winter plumage. During moult, which is at its most extensive at the time when primary moult has reached mid primaries, dark-mantled gulls may show 'abnormal' white patches in upperwing as a result of white bases to secondaries, exposed when greater coverts are shed. De Maasvlakte, Netherlands. 27 Aug 1993. *Klaus Malling Olsen*

coloration of the replacement feathers involved is also variable. It has, for example, been demonstrated that first-year Western Gulls which renew their juvenile scapulars into first-winter type by autumn develop brownish feathers (often noticeably darker than juvenile feathers), whereas those which moult later in winter develop greyer scapulars (Howell & Corben 2000a, Howell 2001). Variations in individual feathers within the same moult cycle have also been observed in other large gulls. In Caspian and Yellow-legged Gulls, the mantle, scapulars and coverts renewed in autumn are brown with extensive barring, whereas feathers renewed by late autumn and winter (although restricted in number) are greyer in ground coloration with narrower dark markings. The paler coloration of head and body feathers (especially hindneck and breast) during winter is caused by wear and bleaching of juvenile feathers. This is even true in gulls exchanging juvenile head feathers for new ones in autumn, as these too can wear to whitish in spring (Howell & King 1999, Howell 2001). Howell (2001) demonstrated that the moult strategies in first-years among European and North American gulls could be put into five main categories, shown below with some East Asian species added:

Group A Post-juvenile moult (moult into first-winter) extensive (complete or near-complete in Franklin's and Sabine's Gull), and moult into first-summer occurs: Laughing Gull *Larus atricilla*, Franklin's Gull *Larus pipixcan*, Mediterranean Gull *Larus melanocephalus*, Bonaparte's Gull *Larus philadelphia*, Brown-headed Gull *Larus brunnicephalus*, Saunders's Gull *Larus saundersi*, Black-headed Gull *Larus ridibundus*, Slender-billed Gull (?) *Larus genei*, Relict Gull (?) *Larus relictus*, Little Gull *Larus minutus*, Sabine's Gull *Larus sabini*, Ross's Gull, *Rhodostethia rosea*.

Group B Post-juvenile moult (into first-winter) moderate to extensive, but moult into first-summer lacking: Heermann's Gull *Larus heermanni*, Mew Gull *Larus brachyrhynchus*, Common Gull *Larus canus*, Grey-headed Gull *Larus cirrocephalus*, Ring-billed Gull *Larus delawarensis*, California Gull *Larus californicus*, Audouin's Gull (?) *Larus audouinii*, Pallas's Gull *Larus ichthyaetus*, Caspian Gull *Larus cachinnans* (except some *barabensis*), Herring Gull *Larus argentatus*, (some, especially subspecies *argenteus*), American Herring Gull *Larus smithsonianus* (some), Vega Gull *Larus vegae* (some), Yellow-legged Gull *Larus michahellis*, Lesser Black-backed Gull *Larus fuscus graellsii*, *Larus fuscus intermedius*, Heuglin's Gull *Larus heuglini* (some), Slaty-backed Gull *Larus schistisagus* (some), Glaucous-winged Gull *Larus glaucescens* (some), Western Gull *Larus occidentalis*, Yellow-footed Gull *Larus livens*, Kelp Gull *Larus dominicanus*, Great Black-backed Gull *Larus marinus* (some), Iceland Gull *Larus glaucoides glaucoides* and most *Larus glaucoides kumlieni*.

Group C Post-juvenile moult (into first-winter) limited (sometimes none, or moult delayed to winter), moult to first-summer lacking: Herring Gull (some), American Herring Gull (some), Vega Gull (some), Slaty-backed Gull (some), Glaucous-winged Gull (some), Great Black-backed Gull (some), Glaucous Gull *Larus hyperboreus*, Iceland Gull (especially nominate *glaucoides*), Thayer's Gull *Larus thayeri*, Black-legged Kittiwake *Rissa tridactyla*, Red-legged Kittiwake *Rissa brevirostris*.

Group D Post-juvenile moult (into first-winter/second-winter) extensive to complete, moult to first-summer apparently lacking: Lesser Black-backed Gull (nominate *fuscus*), Heuglin's Gull (some), Caspian Gull ('Steppe', race *barabensis*, some).

Group E Post-juvenile moult (into first-winter) and moult into first-summer lacking: Ivory Gull *Pagophila eburnea*.

Ageing points of **first-year** large gulls are: (1) pointed primaries with narrow pale fringes (becoming brown from late winter); (2) delicate pale and dark barring on greater upperwing-coverts; (3) dark eye; (4) narrow pale tip to bill normally restricted to upper mandible (but developing second-year pattern from March). First-winter gulls often show wear from late winter, with much-bleached upperwing (including brown and faded flight feathers) in contrast to better-marked mantle/scapulars, if these parts were renewed the previous autumn. In spring, many become extremely worn and faded, and may lose almost all dark patterning in the upperwing. Compare ageing of second-winter below.

Largely resident, mainly southern (and thus early-breeding) and short-distance migrant gull species can moult into first-winter both more extensively and up to several months earlier than medium- and long-distance migrants and late breeders (see also above). Most juvenile plumage in long-distance migrants is retained either until the winter quarters are reached (Sabine's Gull, Franklin's Gull, Heuglin's Gull, Lesser Black-backed Gull *fuscus*) or—in medium-distance migrant larger gulls—more or less all winter (Thayer's, Iceland, Glaucous, certain American Herring and Glaucous-winged Gulls). Brown-headed Gull and some Grey-headed Gulls moult upperwing-coverts and often secondaries/tail in first winter. Ivory Gull just has one yearly complete moult between spring and late summer.

In spring, a new head (and partial body) moult in the smaller (mainly hooded) gull species leads to **first-summer** plumage, in which there are at least traces of the adult hood, and many birds change the mid-tail in winter. The 'first-summer' plumage of larger gull species is an artificial term, describing various stages between very worn juvenile/first-winter plumage and the onset of second-winter plumage (Howell & King 1999, Howell 2001). In this work, we retain the phrase 'first-summer' for a first-year gull in spring/summer which has started, but not finished, the second complete moult (into second-winter), resulting in an identifiable plumage from late spring to summer. This term is unscientific, and should otherwise be called 'moult between first-winter and second-winter'. Moult in younger large gulls may be regarded as an almost continuous process (Howell & King 1999).

The complete moult to **second-winter** starts in spring with parts of the head, mantle/scapulars and inner primaries. **Second-winter** plumage is either (a) (*smaller gulls*) almost identical to the adult winter plumage, (b) (*medium-sized gulls* and Pallas's Gull) close to adult winter plumage or (c) (*large gulls*) either intermediate between first-winter and adult plumage or more like first-winter. In 'retarded' large gulls similar to first-years, ageing is best based on: (1) rounder primary tips, emphasised by broader, whiter fringes (as in older ages); (2) neater pattern on generally darker greater upperwing-coverts; (3) normally bicoloured eye; (4) broader pale tips to both mandibles. This plumage-type is the most variable in the large gulls.

In most gulls the onset of the complete moult takes place at the age of about 10 months, continuing for several months. It is earlier and slower than in adults. The first and last feathers to be moulted are the inner and outer primaries respectively. Primary moult is descendant, starting with the innermost primary (P1) and ending with outermost (P10). It takes place between late spring and early (small gulls) to late (larger gulls) autumn. Only one primary is moulted at a time, simultaneously in each wing, thus having less negative effect on flight ability, but P9–10 are normally in growth together, as P10 starts to grow when P9 is about half grown (see photo 4). At the onset of moult in the mid-primaries, moult of the secondaries and tail begins. On the hand, the coverts moult follows the primary moult, while on the arm, the median coverts are moulted as a group, followed by the greater coverts as a group and then the secondaries as a group. Below a missing feather group a dark panel is sometimes visible, created by the underlying, less worn part of the feathers of the underlying group. The tail normally starts in mid-tail; sometimes, the

4. Herring Gull adult, at last stages of complete moult into winter plumage. Note that P9 and 10 are growing, creating 'abnormal' wing-tip pattern (and in settled birds shorter wings than expected). North Jutland, Denmark. 30 Sep 1995. *Klaus Malling Olsen.*

whole tail or most of the secondaries are moulted at once. During moult, the gull is best labelled as 'first-summer moulting into second-winter'.

Subsequent moults follow a similar pattern, but are generally quicker. **Second-summer** plumage develops through a partial head and body moult in spring. As with first-years, second-summer plumage could be regarded as that of a bird in the early stages of moult into third-winter. Shortly thereafter the complete moult to **third-winter** plumage starts, as described above. Apart from in large gulls, the third-winter plumage is usually inseparable from adult plumage in the field. In larger gulls, it is basically similar to adult winter, but with traces of immature wing pattern, generally narrower white markings on the primaries, and duller bill with broader dark markings.

As moult is slow and feather wear influences the general look of the bird, there is a continuous change in the larger gulls throughout the year. A fresh winter-plumaged bird in autumn is surprisingly different from a worn bird in spring. This is especially true late in first-winter, as juvenile feathers wear more quickly than do feathers of older generations. Moult may also be delayed for physical reasons. Retarded birds may look strikingly different from what is to be expected.

Adult moults are similar. **Adult summer** is attained through partial moult before the breeding season (often from midwinter); **adult winter** moult starts on the breeding grounds and ends by late autumn. The timing of the adult moult to winter plumage is generally shorter than the immature moults. Exceptions are certain long-distance migrant gulls (Heuglin's, Lesser Black-backed Gull nominate *fuscus*), which delay most of their moult until reaching the wintering grounds. Ivory Gull moult is completed between spring and summer just once a year.

Northern populations of certain species moult later (up to several months) than southern ones; see under each species. We have found that weather conditions may affect timing of moult: following severe winters, Black-headed Gulls acquire their summer hoods 1–2 weeks later than they do after mild winters. Following early breeding seasons, onset of moult may be earlier than usual (pers. obs., S Scandinavia).

The smaller hooded gulls develop the hood in late winter and become pale-headed shortly after the end of the breeding season. An exception is Sabine's Gull, which mainly moults following its arrival on the wintering grounds. This late moult is common in long-distance migrant seabirds in the suborder Lari, such as skuas and terns. The larger gulls have a white head in summer, but spotted or streaked in winter.

The terms 'first-year', 'second-year' and so on are imprecise ones that follow the age cycle. A bird is 'first-year' up to one year of age, etc. This terminology is rarely used in identification chapters. The calendar year is sometimes useful. First calendar year is from fledging to 31 December, second calendar year from 1 January to 31 December, and so on.

An alternative terminology for naming age and plumages was introduced by Humphrey & Parkes (1959). Although not perfectly comparable, the alternatives are (for example):

First basic plumage (juvenile)
First alternate plumage (first-winter–first-summer)
Second basic plumage (second-winter)
Second alternate plumage (second-summer)
Basic plumage (winter adult = non-breeding plumage)
Alternate plumage (summer adult = breeding plumage)

In some species, such as Kelp Gull and Heermann's Gull, these terms work better than 'summer and winter' because of differences in breeding season from Northern Hemisphere gulls.

Some problems in moulting birds

In summer, many gulls look untidy owing to poor condition of the old plumage. When head-feathers are worn or moulting, the bill may look disproportionately large. If moult is delayed, most of the plumage often looks extremely bleached and untidy. Birds with extremely worn flight feathers fly with quicker, more-laboured wingbeats than in normal conditions. First-summer Black-legged Kittiwakes show this wear and flight at its extreme, but 'retarded' large gulls may also look extremely bleached and weakened.

During the moult of the greater coverts, the unmoulted darker secondaries of younger gulls may be exposed, creating an impression of all-dark greater coverts. This has confused some observers watching younger large gulls that lacked most of their greater coverts at one time, leaving the dark secondaries as a 'dark greater covert bar'. Similarly, older dark-winged gulls which have simultaneously moulted all their greater coverts expose the pale bases to the secondaries, leaving a pale bar on the midwing (easily seen in, for example, late-summer black-backed gulls – see photo 3, page 11).

Features such as primary projection, position of wing-tip in relation to tail-tip, and pattern of outer-wing are useful in fully grown birds, but more or less useless between late summer and late autumn, when the outer wing is growing; everyone who has tried to judge wing-tip position compared to tail-tip in large gull gatherings will have experienced this problem. For example, Iceland Gull normally has a long wing projection as a useful character to distinguish it from the shorter-winged Glaucous, but the lack of outer primaries in moulting Icelands has been known to frustrate observers (Hume 1980). Less well known is the fact that certain large gulls grow the whole tail at once, resulting in an unexpectedly short tail (and therefore seemingly extremely long wing-tip) in autumn. On the other hand, the exact pattern on certain outer primaries is much easier to assess when the bordering primary is missing. Preening birds often exhibit both upper and lower surfaces of the primaries well.

It should also be noted that vagrant gulls may differ slightly from their normal moult pattern. This has been demonstrated in Franklin's Gull in Europe and Australia (see that species). Southern Hemisphere gulls eventually settling in the Northern Hemisphere may adapt moult cycles similar to Northern Hemisphere gulls.

Wear and fading

The effect of wear is most obvious in spring and summer. White parts are more prone to wear than dark parts, and upperparts wear much quicker than underparts. In gulls with white primary tips, these are often almost worn off by spring.

Most extreme, however, are first-years, in which the feather quality is poorer than in adults. Brown juvenile parts may fade to whitish, and the dark pattern may disappear from mid-winter. This wear has often been linked with sun-bleaching or sand-blasting, as species spending most of their time in sunny conditions (e.g. along sandy shores) often have extremely pale and worn feathers, especially the unprotected greater coverts before moult in spring. But wear is also common in most medium-sized and large gulls from late winter (or in the Southern Hemisphere in Oct–Nov), and in retarded birds to summer or even later.

During wing moult the outer primaries, which are moulted last, are often conspicuously brownish-tinged and worn against fresh inner primaries, creating an unexpected wing pattern. This is even evident in adults with black markings on the wing-tip; worn unmoulted primaries are duller and browner than the black pattern in new feathers. During the moult of the outer wing, the primary pattern is very difficult to discern owing to growth of the outer primaries. This creates a strange outer wing pattern with restricted black compared to when the wing is fully grown.

The hybrid problem

Hybridisation is not infrequent in gulls. In certain populations a considerable proportion hybridise, this is particularly well-documented among Washington populations of Western and Glaucous-winged Gulls.

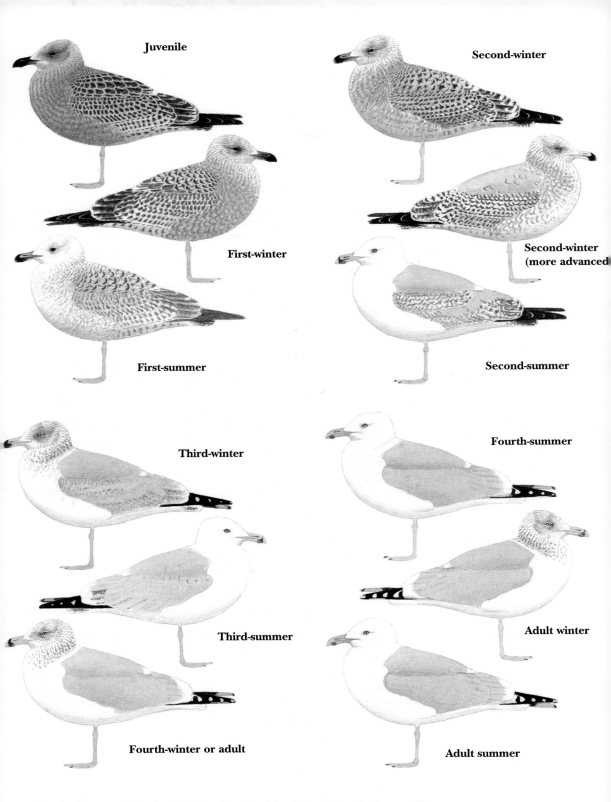

Juvenile

First-winter

First-summer

Second-winter

Second-winter (more advanced)

Second-summer

Third-winter

Third-summer

Fourth-winter or adult

Fourth-summer

Adult winter

Adult summer

Age development in Herring Gull, showing typical development in a 'four-year gull'.

Examples of hybrids in large gulls.

1   First-winter Glaucous-winged × American Herring Gull.
2   First-winter Western × Glaucous-winged Gull.
3   First-winter Glaucous-winged × Glaucous Gull.
4   First-winter Herring × Glaucous Gull. Similar to Herring Gull, but note pale primaries and pattern in
     upperwing resembling Glaucous Gull.
5   First-winter Herring × Glaucous Gull. Resembles Glaucous Gull, but note darker primaries and darker ter-
     tial centres.

5. Herring Gull, first-winter partial albino. Apart from white primaries, the rest of the bird is normal. Finland. *Henry Lehto*

6. Herring Gull, first-winter leucistic. Leucistic birds are frequent, especially among large gulls. Caused by unusual lack of dark pigmentation, the plumage gets pale and washed out; such birds are easily misidentified as Glaucous or Iceland Gulls, but note traces of dark in wing-tip and trailing edge of wings (normally darkest part of upperside in Herring Gull) as well as indications of solid dark tail-bar – typically the last feature to disappear in leucistic gulls. Identification of such birds might be complicated by hybridisation of e.g. Glaucous × Herring Gull. Netherlands. *Karel Beylevelt.*

This, and other known examples of hybridisation, are discussed in the text. Hybrids may clearly show characteristics of both parent species, but are often indeterminate and tricky to identify. Second- and third-generation hybrids are surely even more problematic.

Colour abnormalities: from white to dark

Albinism is rare but regular in gulls (*contra* Grant 1986b), and known for several species (see species accounts). 100% albinos are all-white with unusually pale bare parts. Partial albinos may show white feather parts in an otherwise normal plumage (see photo 5).

More commonly, leucistic individuals occur. These show reduced dark feather pigmentation and are therefore much paler than normal individuals. Such pale birds often cause identification problems, e.g. leucistic Herring Gulls may superficially resemble Glaucous-winged, Glaucous and Iceland Gulls, and it is only close inspection that reveals the presence of normal dark feather parts (although even these may be unusually pale). Also, leucistic gulls show normal-coloured bare parts. In the majority of cases, the most extensive dark area is in the tail-bar, if present (J. R. King *in litt.*; see photo 6).

7. Herring Gull, first-winter showing frequent aberrant bill. North Jutland, Denmark. 15 May 1995. *Klaus Malling Olsen.*

Melanism is even rarer than pure albinism, and results in unusually dark birds. It is mostly partial, and is known mainly in the smaller gulls.

Abnormally plumaged gulls are often in weaker condition than their conspecifics, and therefore, although not unknown in adults, most records of such birds refer to young birds. Typically the moult is strongly delayed compared to normal birds.

Oil pollution may lead to brown (but not black) discoloration of head and body plumage in gulls. Heavily oiled birds are unable to fly, but those with limited contamination may cause identification problems. There have been cases of large gulls with a dark 'mask', caused by cleaning oil from their feet. These have sometimes been misidentified as Pallas's Gulls, but the head pattern is 'wrong'.

Many smaller gulls may show a strong rosy or pinkish tinge to the body. This is probably caused by preen-gland oil being coated onto the feathers during preening (Grant 1986b), but possibly also by feeding on large quantities of crustaceans. A rosy tinge to the underbody is the rule in Ross's and Slender-billed Gulls, but also occurs regularly in other small species. Black-headed Gulls may show a striking rosy tinge, although rarely as clean as in Ross's; dull light enhances the rosy tinge, whereas strong sunlight makes it less conspicuous.

Abnormal bills

In the larger gulls abnormal bills are sometimes seen. The upper mandible may be almost twice as long as expected, and is sometimes strongly decurved and scimitar-shaped. Such birds are almost invariably first-years (Åberg 1979, H. & H. J. Lehto *in litt.*).

JUDGING SIZE AND JIZZ

In gulls, males are larger with a heavier, deeper bill and flatter head than females. The larger the species, the more obvious the difference is. Also, first-years are smaller than older birds. Therefore, in a given species, a first-year female may look unexpectedly small compared to an adult male (this difference is again most obvious in the larger species). This complex situation is the main reason for the inclusion of measurements of both adults and first-years in the species accounts. Try to use these measurements when comparing gatherings of gulls, preferably of several species.

Only by direct comparison—best in pairs—is sexing advisable. While general impression (jizz) and size, once learned, are very useful when identifying gulls (the jizz of a male and a female differs), the specific differences in jizz between closely related species are often overestimated and have led to some ques-

8. Putative hybrid Common × Mediterranean Gull. Hybridisation is frequent in gulls. In this summer-plumaged gull, a mixture of characters from Common and Mediterranean Gulls creates a plumage not illustrated in the field guides; hybrids might look like anything between the two involved species. A hybrid should always be considered when dealing with an unfamiliar plumage. It cannot be ruled out that this bird could be a hybrid Common × Black-headed Gull. Nord-Trøndelag, Norway. 7 Apr 1995. *Morten Vang.*

tionable identifications. For example, head and bill shape in the large gull complex have been introduced as characters separating Yellow-legged Gull from Herring Gull, and also within the Herring Gull subspecies, but the use of these characters often remains tentative. While certain individuals (especially large adult males and small first-year females) do show genuine differences, most may at first glance look identical. Be careful and patient and combine both jizz and feather details before a rare species is claimed: few other bird groups are as variable—or have so many individuals causing so many headaches among specialists—as the fascinating but frustrating larger gulls. No-one will ever be able to identify every large gull!

GREY AND BROWN TONES LOOK DIFFERENT UNDER DIFFERENT LIGHT CONDITIONS

The variation of grey or brown within a species is often large. When going through wintering flocks of Herring Gulls, one sees both very pale-backed and rather dark-backed birds, probably from different geographical areas. But also the effect of light is marked. In strong sunlight, grey tones become paler and are reduced. Adult Glaucous and Iceland Gulls then look much less 'pale' than expected against surrounding Herrings, and adult Mediterranean Gulls may not stand out as much in flocks of Black-headed Gulls. Also, if the upperparts are in strong sunlight, they look considerably paler than the unexposed parts (e.g. the coverts under certain conditions). On the other hand, poor light makes the grey parts look darker. Trying to assess the exact upperpart coloration in Herring Gull gatherings gives frustratingly different results on sunny and cloudy days!

A way to assess grey tones more precisely is through the Kodak Grey Scale (mentioned above). In the detailed descriptions, grey tones have been assigned by using the Kodak Grey Scale on skins.

Another problem is provided by brown tones, which look paler and colder in strong light from the tail-end, warmer and duller in bad light. While juvenile Sabine's Gull looks very dark brown in overcast conditions (with strong contrast to the white trailing edge of the inner wing), strong sunlight produces a much paler and greyer bird.

Against a pale background, dark birds look larger than against a dark background, while pale birds look smaller against a pale rather than a dark background.

JUDGING PHOTOGRAPHS

While the study of high-quality photographs is essential in assessing and establishing characters in gulls, some factors have to be taken into account, especially when judging upperpart coloration. The angle of the bird relative to the photographer, the light, film-types, equipment used and even processing methods may each result in subtly different tones of grey (King & Carey 1999, pers. obs.). For example, certain large adult gulls may show different shades of pallor from different angles or if the photograph was over- or underexposed. Such problems have made studies of large gulls from the Indian Ocean and Gulf States extremely difficult: a certain bird may in one photograph appear to be a perfect Heuglin's Gull (nominate *heuglini*), and in other photographs as pale as Caspian Gull *L. c. cachinnans*!

GULL TOPOGRAPHY

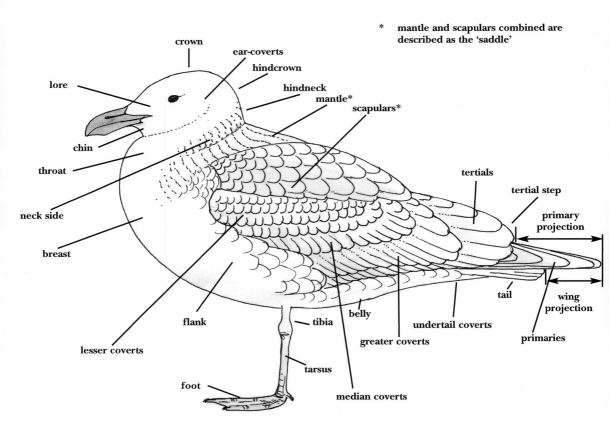

* mantle and scapulars combined are described as the 'saddle'

crown

ear-coverts

hindcrown

hindneck

mantle*

scapulars*

lore

chin

throat

neck side

breast

tertials

tertial step

primary projection

flank

tibia

belly

tail

wing projection

lesser coverts

tarsus

foot

median coverts

greater coverts

undertail coverts

primaries

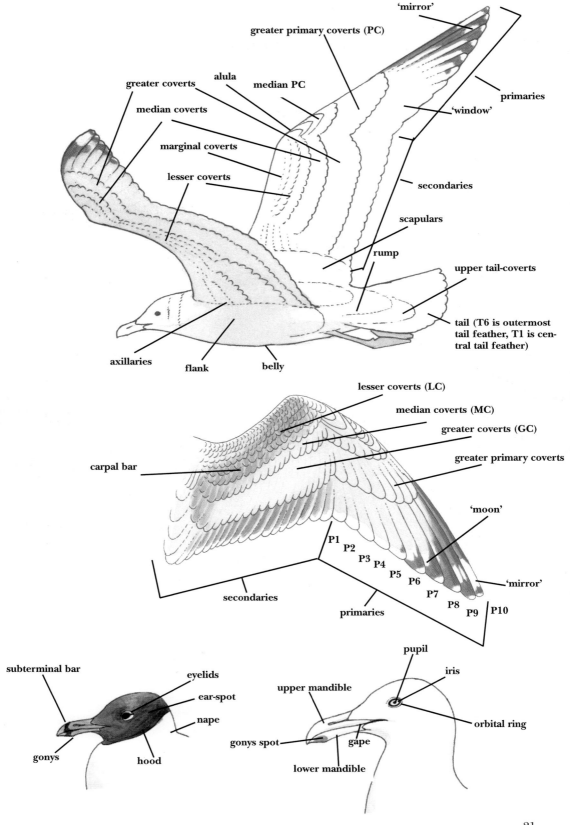

'mirror'

greater primary coverts (PC)

alula

median PC

primaries

greater coverts

'window'

median coverts

marginal coverts

lesser coverts

secondaries

scapulars

rump

upper tail-coverts

tail (T6 is outermost tail feather, T1 is central tail feather)

axillaries

flank

belly

lesser coverts (LC)

median coverts (MC)

greater coverts (GC)

greater primary coverts

carpal bar

'moon'

P1
P2
P3 P4
P5 P6
P7
P8 P9 P10

'mirror'

secondaries

primaries

subterminal bar

eyelids

ear-spot

nape

pupil

iris

upper mandible

orbital ring

gonys

hood

gonys spot

gape

lower mandible

COMPARISON OF LARGE GULL TAXA

L. glaucescens × *hyperboreus*

L. glaucescens

L. glaucescens × *occidentalis*

L. argentatus × *hyperboreus*

L. smithsonianus

L. schistisagus × *glaucescens*

L. hyperboreus barrovianus

L. hyperboreus hyperboreus

L. glaucescens × *smithsonianus*

L. glaucoides glaucoides

L. glaucoides kumlieni

L. thayeri

COMPARISON OF LARGE GULL TAXA

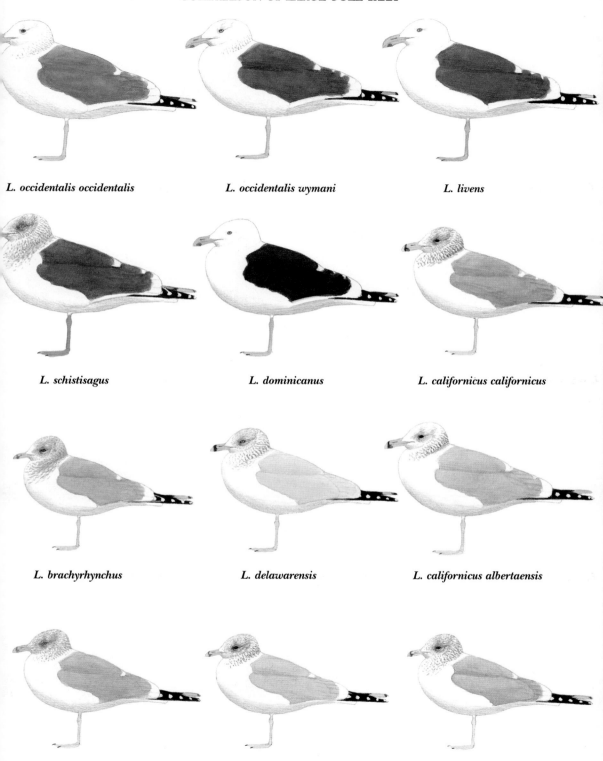

L. occidentalis occidentalis

L. occidentalis wymani

L. livens

L. schistisagus

L. dominicanus

L. californicus californicus

L. brachyrhynchus

L. delawarensis

L. californicus albertaensis

L. canus kamtschatschensis

L. canus canus

L. canus heinei

23

COMPARISON OF LARGE GULL TAXA

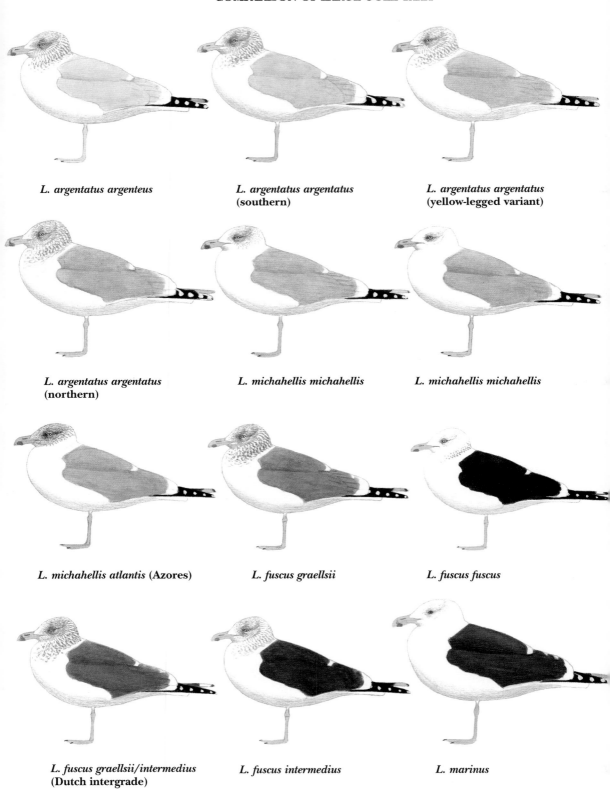

L. argentatus argenteus

L. argentatus argentatus
(southern)

L. argentatus argentatus
(yellow-legged variant)

L. argentatus argentatus
(northern)

L. michahellis michahellis

L. michahellis michahellis

L. michahellis atlantis (Azores)

L. fuscus graellsii

L. fuscus fuscus

L. fuscus graellsii/intermedius
(Dutch intergrade)

L. fuscus intermedius

L. marinus

COMPARISON OF LARGE GULL TAXA

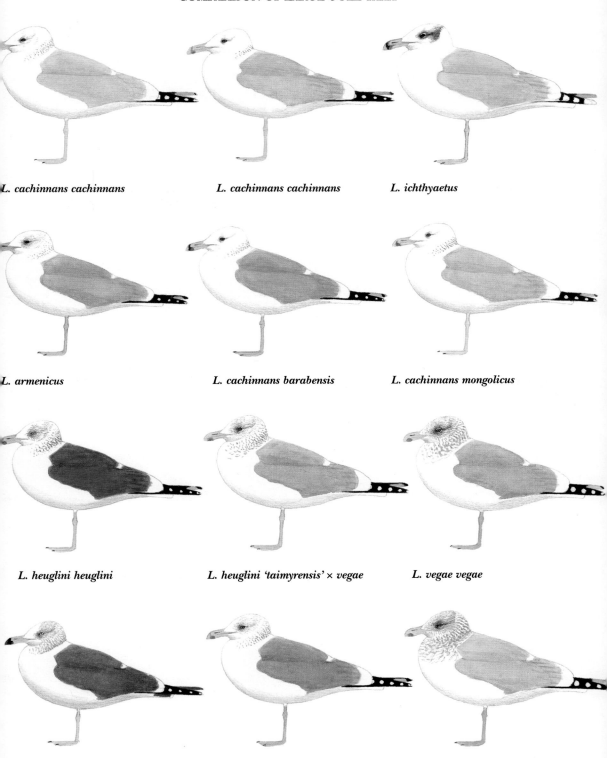

L. cachinnans cachinnans

L. cachinnans cachinnans

L. ichthyaetus

L. armenicus

L. cachinnans barabensis

L. cachinnans mongolicus

L. heuglini heuglini

L. heuglini 'taimyrensis' × vegae

L. vegae vegae

L. crassirostris

L. heuglini 'taimyrensis'

L. vegae 'birulai'

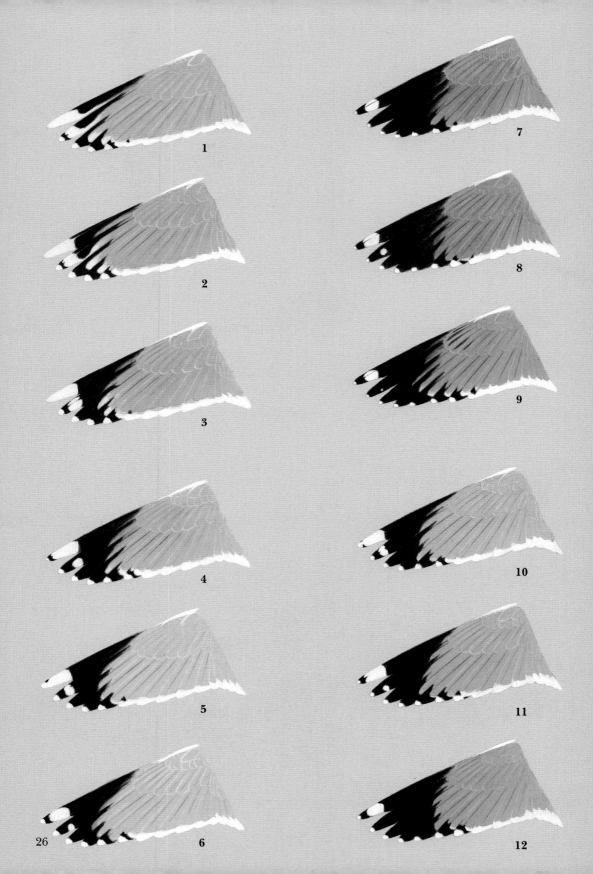

13

14

15

COMPARISON OF WINGTIP PATTERNS IN LARGE GULLS

Herring Gull. Much individual and geographical variation

1. *L. a. argentatus* – An example of very limited black markings, with Thayer's Gull-like pattern on P9-10 and often no black on P5. Note rounded pale tongues on P7-8. This pattern is dominant among north-westernmost breeders (Finnmark and NW Russia); wingtip sometimes has even less black than this. Compare American Herring on pp. 28-29.

2. *L. a. argentatus* – Another example of a lightly-marked bird, here with more extensive black in outermost primaries. Note P9 is almost identical to average Thayer's Gull.

3. *L. a. argentatus* – Typical wingtip pattern of S Scandinavian breeders. Note white tip to P10, large white mirrors on P9, and slight markings on P5. Pale tongues on mid-primaries eat into wingtip.

4. *L. a. argentatus* – More solid wingtip markings than in 3, with narrow black subterminal bar on P10. This pattern is also frequent in *argenteus*.

5. *L. a. argentatus* – Another common type from the south of the breeding range

6. *L. a. argenteus* – Note pale grey upperwing and more black/less white in wingtip than *argentatus*. P10 with white mirror (not tip), P9 with small white mirror, but P5 has solid black markings. Wingtip is similar to that of Yellow-legged Gull, but latter has much darker upperparts.

7-8. **Armenian Gull** – Clear-cut black wingtip lacking the pale tongues, and with white mirror on P10 only (occasionally to P9, as shown in 8).

9. **Caspian Gull** *L. (c.) barabensis* ('Steppe Gull') – Similar to Armenian gull, but note long pale tongues, eating into P6-9, and creating slightly streaked pattern. Compare with 7-8. Note extension of black onto P3. Primary coverts sometimes black-streaked.

10. **Yellow-legged Gull** *L. m. michahellis* – Black and white in wingtip similar to paler Herring *L.a. argenteus*, but note more solid black markings on P5. Usually P10 white mirror only, but sometimes has white tip as well. More extensive white on P10 is more frequent in E populations.

11. **Yellow-legged Gull** *L. m.michahellis* – Note white mirror on P10 and small white mirror on P9 (the latter often absent, especially in W population and NW African population).

12. **Yellow-legged Gull** *L. m. atlantis* – Black in wingtip more extensive than in *L. m. michahellis*, with white mirror on P10 only. Pattern similar to Armenian Gull.

13. **Caspian Gull** *L. (c.) barabensis* ('Steppe Gull') – Note long pale tongues eating into wingtip, and dark markings reaching P3 to create black trailing edge to outer wing.

14. **Caspian Gull** – Note long pale streaks eating into black in wingtip, broad white tip on P9, and dark markings on P5-7 with more black in outer web than inner web (compare Yellow-legged Gull). This extensive black is typical of E birds.

15. **Caspian Gull** – Often, western birds (*'ponticus'*) show very long and conspicuous pale tongues on all primaries, reducing black in wingtip. Note complete white tip on P10, large white mirror on P9, and solid but narrow markings on P5 (most pronounced in western birds).

16-17. **Heuglin's Gull** – Almost identical to Lesser Black-backed *L.f. graellsii*, but usually with white mirror on P10 only, and sometimes with faint darker markings on primary coverts.

18. **'taimyrensis'** – Regarded as a hybrid population of Heuglin's and Vega Gull. Upperwing more contrasting than in Heuglin's, with pale moons on P5-8. Often with larger white mirrors on P9-10.

16

17

18

27

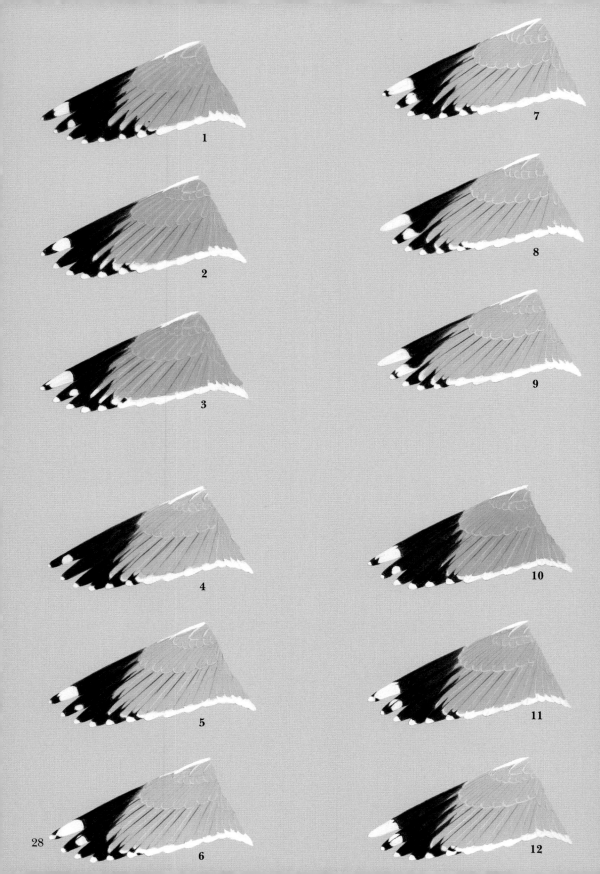

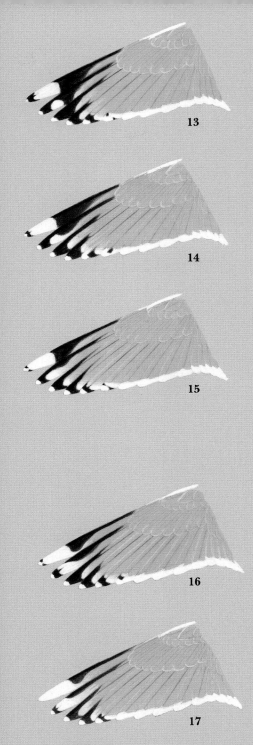

COMPARISON OF WINGTIP PATTERNS IN LARGE GULLS

1. Caspian Gull *L. (c.) mongolicus* **('Mongolian' Gull)** – White mirrors on P9-10, black reaching P4. Black covers 6-9 outer primaries.

2-3. Vega Gull – Similar to 'Mongolian' Gull and Herring Gull. Black covers 5-7 outer primaries.

4-6. American Herring Gull – W coast birds
There is a clinal variation in American Herring Gull, with W coast birds showing more black/less white in wingtip. Note white mirror on P10 (not reaching tip), small white mirror on P9, and P5 normally with solid black markings.

7-9. American Herring Gull – E coast birds
Most E coast birds show longer pale tongues in mid-primaries, broader white mirror (and often tip and base of inner web) on P10, more solid white mirror on P9, and generally broken, often indistinct (and sometimes absent) black markings on P5. Birds with most extensive white markings occur in NE part of breeding range, where many appear identical to N European Herring Gulls *L. a. argentatus.* A combination of extensive white on P10, long and pointed pale tongues ('bayonets') on P7-8 and black, W-shaped markings on P5-6 diagnostic against Herring Gull.

10. California Gull *L. c. californicus*
Note solid black wingtip with black reaching primary covert of P8, and white mirror on P10.

11-12. California Gull *L. c. albertaensis*
Many inseparable from *L. c. californicus* (10), but generally with longer pale tongues on P6-8. Black area in wingtip typically more angled than the squarely cut-off black area in *L. c. californicus.*

13. Thayer's Gull
Well-marked Thayer's Gulls show solid black markings on P9-10, similar to least well-marked American Herring Gull (see 6, above), but pattern more streaky.

14-15. Thayer's Gull
Outer wing appears streaky. Note that black on P9 often only covers edge of outer web. Black wingtip markings reach P5. Compare Kumlien's (Iceland) Gull.

16. Thayer's Gull
Outer wing appears streaked blackish. Note black extension on outer webs of P9-10, emphasising white mirrors. Shows blackish markings as far as P5. Upperwing darker grey than in Kumlien's (Iceland) Gull.

17. Thayer's Gull or Kumlien's (Iceland) Gull
This example could represent minimal dark streaking in Thayer's, with no dark markings on P5, or maximal dark streaking in Kumlien's.

18. Kumlien's (Iceland) Gull
There is large individual variation in this form, which is often regarded as a hybrid population between Thayer's and Iceland *L. g. glaucoides.* Kumlien's has dark grey, rarely blackish streaks in outer wing, with no dark markings on P5. Figure 18 shows maximum amount of dark. Figures 1-3 (page 30) show diagnostic frosty grey streaks of typical Kumlien's, with dark not reaching inner webs, and upper wing paler than in Thayer's. Figure 4 (page 30) shows minimal dark, but suggestion of patterning suggests Kumlien's rather than Iceland *L. g. glaucoides.*

1

2

3

4

5

6

7

8

9

10

11

30

12

13

14

15

16

17

COMPARISON OF WINGTIP PATTERNS IN LARGE GULLS

1-3. Kumlien's (Iceland) Gull
There is large individual variation in this form, which is often regarded as a hybrid population between Thayer's and Iceland *L. g. glaucoides*. Kumlien's has dark grey, not blackish streaks in outer wing, with no dark markings on P5. Figure 18 (page 29) shows maximum amount of dark. 1-2 show diagnostic frosty grey streaks of typical Kumlien's, with dark not reaching inner webs, and upper wing paler than in Thayer's. 3 shows minimal dark, but suggestion of patterning suggests Kumlien's rather than Iceland *L. g. glaucoides*.

4. Hybrid Glaucous-winged × Western Gull *L. o. occidentalis*
The dark primary pattern contrasts well with the inner wing.

5-6. Glaucous-winged Gull
Primary pattern concolorous or almost so with rest of the wing. Usually white mirror on P10 only.

7. Yellow-footed Gull
As dark as Western Gull *L. o. wymani*, with similar rounded white mirror on P10 only.

8. Western Gull *L. o. wymani*
White mirror on P10 rounded, often not reaching edge of inner web. Black markings on P5-6 covering both webs.

9. Western Gull *L. o. occidentalis*
White mirror on P10 usually squarer than in *wymani*, covering edges of inner web. Black markings on P5-6 narrower than in *L. o. wymani*, on P5 often as isolated spots.

10-12. Slaty-backed Gull
White moons on P5-8 appear as 'string of pearls', often connecting with white trailing edge to inner primaries. White moon may be almost absent on P8, as in figure 4.

13. Lesser Black-backed Gull *L. f. graellsii*
Dark grey upperwing contrasts somewhat with black wing-tip. P9-10 with white mirrors, sometimes covering tip on P10.

14. Lesser Black-backed Gull *L. f. intermedius*
Although there is a large overlap zone with *L. f. graellsii*, most *intermedius* have darker upperparts, similar to Great Black-backed (figures 16-17). On average has one more black primary than *L. f. graellsii*.

15. Lesser Black-backed Gull *L. f. fuscus* ('Baltic' Gull)
Upperwing velvety black, concolorous with wingtip. Usually with white mirror on P10 only.

16-17. Great Black-backed Gull.
Upperparts blackish-grey in slight contrast to black wingtip. Shows broad white tip to P10 and broad white mirror on P9. Figure 17 shows minimum amount of black on P9.

18. Kelp Gull
Upperwing almost as black as 'Baltic' Gull. White mirror on P10 (and sometimes a narrow mirror on P9). White trailing edge to wing broader than in any 'Baltic', thus similar to Great Black-backed Gull.

18

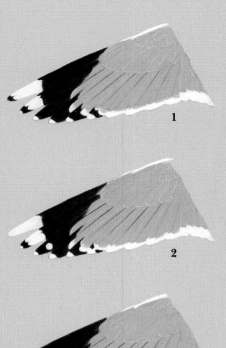

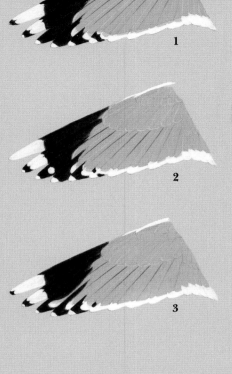

COMPARISON OF WINGTIP PATTERNS IN LARGE GULLS

1. Common Gull *L. c. canus*
Normal pattern shows large white mirrors on P9-10, creating rounded white spot in wingtip.

2. Common Gull *L. c. canus*
Certain males have white tip on P10 and additionally small white mirror on P8.

3. Common Gull *L. c. canus*
An unusual variant with extensive pale tongue on P8, which should be compared to Mew Gull (figures 7-9).

4. Common Gull *L. c. heinei*
As *L. c. canus*, but note narrower white trailing edge to inner primaries. Upperparts in many *heinei* slightly darker than in *L. c. canus*, therefore white moons in mid-primaries more conspicuous.

5-6. Common Gull *L. c. kamtschatschensis*
Generally darker grey than *L. c. canus* with more conspicuous white moons in mid-primaries.

7-9. Mew Gull *L. brachyrhynchus*
Figure 7 shows wing pattern almost identical to Common Gull. However, most show longer pale tongues on P7-8, with white moons falling level with white mirrors on P9-10. In some males, P9 has no black apart from small subterminal spot near tip – a pattern unknown in Common Gull.

1. BLACK-TAILED GULL

Larus crassirostris (Vieillot, 1818, Nagasaki, Japan)   **Plate 1, Photos 9–17**

IDENTIFICATION Length 46–48cm, wingspan 118–124cm. Black-tailed Gull is a medium-sized, dark-backed gull of the NW Pacific. It is slightly larger than Common Gull and shows a black tail or tail-bar at all ages. The overall impression, emphasised by its short tail, is of a graceful, small, round-headed 'large' gull with long, slender wings. When settled, looks attenuated with rounded head, slender bill, long wings and rather short legs. In flight it moves faster and more buoyantly than larger gulls; it is often very agile in hard winds, performing much gliding on angled wings. In light winds its flight is slightly slower than Common Gull. The dark upperparts and narrow wings often suggest a small Lesser Black-backed Gull or a white-headed Laughing Gull.

Adult Has blackish-grey upperparts with a black wing-tip (usually lacking mirror on P10), narrow but obvious white tertial-crescents and a white trailing edge to the wing. The tail shows a distinct black bar, among adult gulls only matched by Band-tailed Gull from South America. From below, the blackish primaries and grey secondaries contrast with the white coverts and body. The bill is yellow with a black subterminal bar and bright red tip. The eyes are pale and the orbital ring dark. The legs are yellow. In **summer** the head is white; in **winter** the hindneck shows brown streaks, sometimes strong enough to create a neck-bar.

Juvenile Dark greyish-brown with a paler face, pronounced white eyelids, paler lower belly and pale-scaled upperparts. The wing is dark with mid-brown coverts. It lacks a pale window on the inner primaries. The rump is white with dense dark spots. The tail is all dark. The underwing-coverts are dark brown in contrast to the paler flight feathers. Often shows pale 'double-comma' near wing-bend as in younger Pomarine Skua *Stercorarius pomarinus*. Bill pink with a clear-cut black tip, merging into the pale face. Legs pink.

First-winter Similar to juvenile, but pale face more obvious, often reaching the dark eyes and 'extending' to the pale bill-base. The mantle and scapulars are slate-grey with dark markings (often as shaft-streaks) and paler feather-edges. The brown nape to neck-sides is more contrasting than in juvenile. The lower underbody is pale. Resembles California Gull, but this species lacks conspicuous white eyelids, has darker-patterned underbody, and densely barred rump. Also, California generally has better-marked upperwing, with more conspicuous white bar along tips of greater coverts.

First-summer Similar to first-winter, but face paler off-white with paler grey wash to crown and ear-coverts. The brown hindneck creates a dark neck-boa, which contrasts with the pale bleached mantle. Has greyish or brownish breast-sides and flanks. Mantle/coverts often strongly bleached (sometimes whitish) through wear, but these parts piebald when new dark feathers occur. Flight feathers brownish through wear. Rump white with indistinct dark spotting. Bill and legs fleshy to pale green, the former with black tip.

Second-winter Intermediate between adult and first-year. Compared to adult winter it has stronger dark head-markings and traces of a brown breast-bar and flanks. Shows grey saddle and mid-wing bar (median coverts) against brown, dark-patterned lesser and greater coverts; saddle and new coverts often brown-tinged compared to adult. Wing-tip is browner with narrower white primary spots, looking all dark with wear. The broad black tail-bar almost reaches the tail-base, suggesting an all-black tail. The bill is pale grey with a blackish tip. The base may show a yellow or pinkish tinge. Legs dull yellow to fleshy.

Second-summer Similar to second winter, but head white.

Third-winter Similar to adult, but with a brown tinge to the primaries (which have narrower white tips), upperparts and secondaries, broader dark markings in the tail, duller bill and greyish tinge to the yellow legs.

VOICE A deep mewing *kaoo kaoo, kau-kau* or *yark-yark-yark*. Also a plaintive rasping mewing, higher than in Vega and American Herring Gulls (Higgins & Davies 1996, Sibley 2000).

MOULT The adult moult to **winter** plumage is complete Jun–Oct/Nov. P1 late Jun, P3–4 late Jul/early Aug, P4–7 late Aug, P7–9 mid–late Sep, P10 (late Aug–) mid-Oct–mid-Nov. Tail, secondaries and coverts late Jul–late Sep, lesser coverts generally last. Body from Jun, head from mid-Aug, often not finished before late Sep (skins MCZ). Moult to **adult summer** partial Jan–Mar, including head and body; >95% white-headed by mid-Feb (pers. obs. in Japan). Moult to **first-winter** partial late Jul–Jan, including head, neck, mantle, scapulars, rump, some tertials and sometimes some lesser coverts and inner median coverts. Starts with head, neck and upper breast (Il'icev & Zubakin 1990, King & Carey 2000). Moult to **first-summer** partial Dec–Jun, including parts of head. Moult to **second-winter** complete late Apr–Oct, thus earlier than in adults, starting with P1/inner median coverts late Apr. Moult has reached P2–3 late May and P7–9 late Aug. P10 early Sep–mid Oct. Secondaries and tail Jun/Jul–Sep/Oct. Head and body Jul–mid-Aug. Most median coverts renewed around mid Aug, as well as inner greater coverts and lesser coverts. Vagrants to Australia began moult to second-summer Aug–Sep, probably adjusting to austral seasons (Higgins & Davies 1996).

DESCRIPTION

Adult Upperparts dark slate (Kodak Grey Scale 8–10.5), often with slight brownish tinge. Primaries blackish, in small minority (males) P10 with 1–10mm indistinct mirror in one web only. P8–9 black. P7–4 with black markings near tips, on P4–5 often restricted to one web. P1–4 slightly paler than P5–10 (Kodak Grey Scale 9–11). Primaries with white tips, 1–3mm on P6–10, 5–7mm on P1–5. Secondaries and longest scapulars blackish with 15–20mm white tips. Underside of flight feathers sooty-grey, darkest on primaries. Marginal coverts white. Primary coverts sometimes with black drop markings. Underparts, underwing-coverts, rump and tail white; tail with black subterminal bar (in T1 28–60mm) and 15–20mm white tips; T6 white, sometimes with 13–23mm black subterminal bar

33

PLATE 1: BLACK-TAILED GULL *Larus crassirostris*

Medium-sized, E Pacific Gull, rare vagrant to N America and S Pacific Ocean. Slender with rounded head, long bill, accentuated rear and short legs. Recalls a small version of Lesser Black-backed Gull. In flight graceful with slender, angled wings. Handles severe winds well. The only Northern Hemisphere gull showing black tail or tail-bar in all ages.

1. **Juvenile** (Aug–Sep) Basically brown with darker saddle, heavily pale-scaled. Face pale and white eye-crescents conspicuous. Lacks pale barring on greater coverts as found in larger gulls. Tertials with narrow pale fringes. Bill pale flesh with clear-cut black tip. Legs fleshy.

2. **First-winter** (Sep/Oct–Mar/May) First-year rather dark gull with relatively unmarked upperwing, lacking pale window on inner primaries. Bill bicoloured, merging into pale face; rest of head, breast and flanks brown, belly normally paler, white eyelids conspicuous. Underwing with heavy dark markings. White rump contrasts with all-black tail. First-winters show paler mantle—with wear conspicuously so against brown hindneck and wings.

3. **First-winter** (Sep–Mar/May) Similar to juvenile, but mantle and scapulars paler with finer pattern (as streaks), creating pale saddle. Face paler and wing increasingly worn throughout winter.

4. **First-summer/second-winter** (Sep–Mar) Grey saddle and median covert bar against 'pale version' of first-year wing. Bill dull yellow with black tip.

5. **Second-winter** (Sep–Mar/Apr) Intermediate between first-year and adult. Shows grey saddle and median coverts, but rest of wing similar to first-year. Bill slightly paler and face whiter than in first-year, but black tail still prominent.

6. **Third-winter** (Sep–May) As adult, but primary coverts darker-centred, and tail-bar covers most of tail.

7. **Adult winter** (Sep–Feb/Mar) Wings dark slate with black tip. Normally lacks white mirror to P10. Complete black tail-bar conspicuous. Bill yellow with black and red tip. Shows dark hind-neck streaks in winter.

8. **Adult winter** (Oct–Feb/Mar) Shows dark slate-grey upperparts (coloured similar to Lesser Black-backed Gull race *graellsii*), narrow but conspicuous white tertial crescent and black wing-tip with narrow white primary tips. Bill yellow with black and red markings at tip, appearing tricoloured. Legs yellow. In winter with dark head-markings, most conspicuous on hindneck as dark neck-bar.

9. **Adult summer** (Feb/Mar–Sep) Head white, bill generally brighter-coloured than in winter.

2. First-winter

6. Third-winter

4. First-summer to second-winter

7. Adult winter

1. Juvenile

3. First-winter

5. Second-winter

8. Adult winter

9. Adult summer

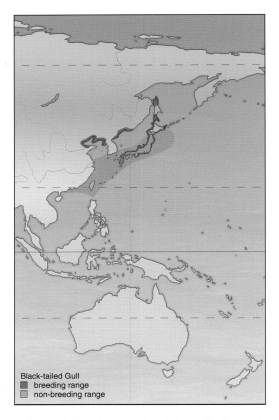

Black-tailed Gull
■ breeding range
■ non-breeding range

on innerweb (may be reduced to shaft-streak). Outer web white, sometimes slightly greyish-tinged. White eyelids above and below eye. Iris creamy, yellow or greyish-yellow. Orbital ring orange-red to brownish-red. Bill yellow to greenish-yellow with black subterminal bar and vermilion-red gonys-spot and tip. Legs yellow to greenish-yellow. **Adult summer** (Feb–Aug/Sep) Head white. Bill deep yellow with black subterminal bar and dark red tip. Orbital ring black or dark red. From late summer loses white tips to worn primaries and sometimes shows contrast between worn, brownish-tinged saddle (often even some coverts) and dark grey wings. **Adult winter** (Sep–Mar) Head white with grey, sooty or grey-brown ear-coverts and hindneck, creating a dark half-hood, most distinct bordering the hind-collar; sometimes as streaks or spots, especially around the eye (emphasising the white eyelids above and below eye). Chin, throat and upper breast often slightly dark-spotted. Bill yellow with greenish or greyish tinge. Has black subterminal bar 8–12mm wide on upper and 13–17mm wide on lower mandible, sometimes covering red gonys-spot. Bill-tip chrome-yellow to ivory, 10–14mm on upper and 6–8mm on lower mandible.

Juvenile (fledging–Sep/Oct) Head dark greyish-brown; hindneck, ear-coverts and neck-sides darker blackish-brown, sometimes as dark hind-collar. Forehead, lores, chin and throat paler greyish-brown with indistinct dark spots. Pale eyelids above and below eye narrow but conspicuous. Mantle, scapulars, lesser coverts, median coverts and tertials dark brown with broad sandy to pale brown

(with wear whitish) edges, creating scaly pattern. Tertials dark brown with pale edges restricted to distal part; rarely very narrow pale edges reach bases. Greater coverts brown (sometimes slightly paler than median coverts, especially at bases) with narrow but solid pale tips and edges (broadest on inner 50%) and sometimes faint dark subterminal markings. Rump and uppertail-coverts white with broad dark bars, spots or chevrons. Flight feathers sooty-brown, P1–5 and secondaries with narrow pale tips. Breast, flanks and upper belly dark brown, often forming a broad bar across the breast and upper belly. Central to lower belly and vent whitish. Underwing-coverts and axillaries sooty-brown with paler bases; greater primary coverts dark brown or pale with brown tips, often forming a pale 'double-comma' as in younger Pomarine Skua. Rarely, pale areas on underwing more extensive, with dark tips only to coverts/axillaries. Undertail-coverts whitish with row of dark chevrons along edges; central feathers white or only slightly dark-spotted. Tail brownish-black with 2–4(5)mm buffish tips and white extreme base. Iris dark brown. Bill pink, orange-yellow or yellow with 18–27mm black tip, usually reaching gonys; sometimes with narrow pale tip to upper mandible. Legs flesh, pink or fleshy-brown.

First-winter (Sep/Oct–Mar) as juvenile, but head paler and greyer; forehead, lores, chin and throat off-white. Crown and ear-coverts sometimes streaked greyish-brown. White eyelids above and below eye stronger. Hindneck and neck-sides brown, forming dark collar. Mantle and scapulars greyish-brown with dark spots, streaks or subterminal markings, broad sandy edges and grey bases; scapulars sometimes sandy with dark restricted to shaft-streaks/bases, creating pale line against darker coverts. Bare parts as juvenile, but pale on bill-tip often broader. Saddle much worn by spring, contrasting clearly with darker wings and hindneck (pers. obs. China, May).

First-summer (Apr–Sep) similar to first-winter, but head generally paler. Mantle/scapulars with grey admixed, often contrasting well with bleached off-white feathers. Rump and uppertail-coverts with finer dark markings. Underparts whitish with greyish-brown shading or patches on flanks and breast-sides, often joining collar. Wing mainly juvenile, but sometimes with a few grey median coverts admixed. Juvenile tail loses pale tips. Iris medium to dark brown, sometimes creamy. Bill pink to pale green with black tip; sometimes narrow red tip to one or both mandibles. Legs pale green, sometimes with a yellow or pinkish tinge.

Second-winter (Sep–Mar) A mixture between first-winter and adult. Compared to adult, head-markings usually more extensive with coarser brown spotting or shading, sometimes continuing onto breast. Upperparts similar to adult, but with slight brownish tinge and some brown wing-coverts (with narrow dark shaft-streaks and paler tips) admixed, especially median coverts and inner coverts. Tertials brownish-grey with broad pale edges. Tail-bar generally broader (max. 70mm on T1), often with slightly dark mottled division between black and white bases; normally including full bar on T6 (see adult). Primaries brownish-tinged with pale tips to P1–5 only, narrower than on adult. Lacks white on P10. Secondaries sometimes with brown subterminal markings. Primary coverts blackish with paler edges; dark most extensive on outer three, where it creates drop-spots. Underparts as adult, but often with slight brown to grey wash on breast-sides and flanks. Iris pale grey to brown. Orbital ring dark. Bill generally duller than in adult: bluish-grey with dull yellow, fleshy or pale green tinge, black subterminal bar and often red tip or gonys-spot (often only as indication); entire tip sometimes black. Legs greyish with dull yellow, greenish or fleshy tinge.

Second-summer (Mar–Sep) similar to adult, but with traces of immaturity such as brown-tinged tertials and darker cutting edges to bill. Wing often more worn than saddle. Legs pale yellow.

Third-winter similar to adult, but flight feathers brown-tinged with narrower white primary tips, upperparts with slight brownish tinge, primary coverts with dark drop markings and tail darker (T6 always black-marked). Bare parts less yellow than in adult.

Aberrants Leucistic adult known, showing pale grey saddle and almost whitish wing. Bill and legs normally coloured (Doherty & Oddie 2001).

DISTRIBUTION AND MIGRATION Population <350,000 pairs. Breeds colonially in the Sea of Japan on sandy and rocky shores, sea-cliffs and rocky islets. Coastal; often found in estuaries, bays and harbours. 100,000 pairs Russia (96% in Peter the Great Bay, of which 80,000 on the Furugelma Islands), 150,000 pairs in Japan, where most abundant large gull; otherwise breeds Sakhalin, China, Korea, E Siberia and the Kuril Islands (del Hoyo *et al.* 1996, Enticott & Tipling 1997).

Post-breeding dispersal to food-rich areas. Russian first-years move to coast of Tatar Strait. Birds from NW Honshu migrate to Pacific coast of Honshu, Hokkaido and S Sea of Okhotsk. Birds from Yellow Sea migrate to S and N along coast. Main wintering range lies in the Korea Straits, Sea of Japan and NE China coast. Small numbers occur further S off the Chinese coast to Hong Kong, where it is a scarce winter visitor.

Vagrant N America (>20, of which five Canada) S to New Jersey and California, E to Newfoundland and Rhode Island; also Kamchatka, Aleutians, Baja California, Philippines, Bougainville and Australia (Victoria) (Higgins & Davies 1996, Mactavish 1998, J. L. King pers. comm.).

MEASUREMENTS Lengths in mm; weights in g. Own data based on skins in MCZ, MVZ, NRK, UZM. E Siberia, Japan.

WING

Adult male	365–396 (380.7)	13
Adult female	352–385 (368.7)	17
Juv./first-winter	365–382 (371.0)	9

Note Il'icev & Zubakin (1990) give for adult: male 366–385 (mean 375, n=15), female 345–393 (mean 364, n=11). Higgins & Davies (1996) give for adult: male 350–393 (mean 393, n=9), female 331–394 (mean 367.5, n=10).

BILL

Adult male	44.4–53.8 (49.4)	13
Adult female	41.5–53.3 (47.4)	18
Juv./first-winter	42.8–51.4 (47.6)	9

Note Il'icev & Zubakin (1990) give for adult: male 46–59 (mean 49.5, n=19), female 43–49 (mean 46.5, n=16). Higgins & Davies (1996) give for adult: male 41.2–51.9 (mean 46.9, n=9), female 43.8–49.0 (mean 46.0, n=10).

BILL DEPTH AT GONYS

Adult male	13.2–16.1 (15.0)	13
Adult female	12.8–15.5 (14.2)	18
Juv./first-winter	10.7–14.3 (12.9)	9

BILL DEPTH AT BASE OF BILL

Adult male	14.8–17.2 (15.9)	13
Adult female	14.1–16.6 (15.0)	18
Juv./first-winter	13.1–16.7 (14.3)	9

GONYS LENGTH

Adult male	13.5–18.0 (15.1)	13
Adult female	12.4–15.7 (14.1)	18
Juv./first-winter	9.5–15.6 (13.1)	9

TARSUS

Adult male	51.2–58.6 (55.9)	13
Adult female	50.1–58.4 (53.2)	18
Juv./first-winter	51.2–59.2 (54.2)	6

Note Il'icev & Zubakin (1990) give for adult: male 52–59 (mean 55.1, n=19), female 48–57 (mean 52.2, n=16). Higgins & Davies (1996) give for adult: male 44.5–54.9 (mean 50.6, n=9), female 46.2–58.0 (mean 51.1, n=10).

Weight Adult: male 462–640, female 436–615 (Il'icev & Zubakin 1990, Higgins & Davies 1996).

BLACK-TAILED GULL Four-year gull. Medium-sized, shaped like Lesser Black-backed, but smaller and neater with rounder head, narrower bill and shorter tail. In flight long- and slender-winged. Handles hard winds well.

Adult has dark blackish-grey upperwing with blackish hand (normally lacking pale mirror to P10) and white trailing edge. Tail with broad black bar. Bill yellow with red and black tip, legs yellow. In **winter** (Sep–Mar) acquires brown-streaked hindneck.

First-year brownish-grey with broad white face merging into pale fleshy base to bill; bill black-tipped. White eyelids conspicuous. Upperwing brown with solid dark trailing edge. Tail blackish. Rump dark-spotted. By first-winter belly paler, mantle/scapulars grey with dark streaks or spots, from spring often contrasting with darker hindneck and wing. Underwing with dense dark patterning.

Second-year has adult-like mantle and most of wing, but with some brown coverts admixed. Tail-bar broader than in adult, often covering most of tail; rump white.

Third-year as adult, but with dark-streaked primary coverts and all-dark wing-tip lacking white primary tips of full adult and with broader black tail bar. Bill generally duller with more extensive dark markings.

Black-tailed Gull *Larus crassirostris*. **9. Juvenile**. Note very dark plumage with well-contrasting pale, black-tipped bill, pale face merging into base of bill and broad white scaling to mantle and scapulars. Hokkaido, Japan. 17 Aug 1997. *Harry J. Lehto.* **10. Juvenile**. A slightly darker bird with less prominent scaling to upperparts than 9. Hokkaido, Japan. 24 Aug 1997. *Harry J. Lehto.* **11. Juvenile**. Note dark, rather uniform wings including extensive dark coloration on underwing-coverts. All-dark tail contrasts with spotted rump. Japan. 15 Aug 1997. *Harry J. Lehto.* **12. 1st-summer moulting into 2nd-winter**. Paler face and more conspicuous white eyelids than in 1st-winter. Hokkaido, Japan. 25 Aug 1997. *Harry J. Lehto.*

Black-tailed Gull *Larus crassirostris*. **13. 2nd-winter.** Note pale face and white eyelids, making dark eye stand out. A few greyish-brown coverts intermix with otherwise rather uniform grey upperparts. Honshu, Japan. 7 Oct 2000. *Osao Ujihara*. **14. 3rd-winter or older**. Dark streaking in primary coverts and rather narrow white tips to inner primaries suggests 3rd-winter in otherwise adult plumage. Upperwings very dark with slightly paler mantle and innerwing. Honshu, Japan. 3 Mar 2001. *Osao Ujihara*. **15. Adult summer**. Elegant with rounded head, longish-looking bill and long wings reaching far beyond the short tail. Overall shape similar to Lesser Black-backed Gull *fuscus*. Honshu, Japan. 20 Sep 2000. *Osao Ujihara*. **16. Adult winter**. Note dark shading on hindneck (often as solid dark bar in the most well-marked birds). Bill greenish-yellow with scarlet and black tip. Honshu, Japan. Jan 2001. *Osao Ujihara*. **17. Adult summer**. Solid black tail-bar and broad white tips to rectrices typical for adults. Dark slate upperparts contrast with blackish wing-tips. Honshu, Japan. Feb 2001. *Paul Doherty*.

HEERMANN'S GULL
Larus heermanni (Cassin, 1852, San Diego, California)

IDENTIFICATION Length 45–50cm, wingspan 128–132cm. Heermann's Gull is a medium-sized, West Coast gull with dark plumage and red bill. It is the size of a Ring-billed Gull with sloping forehead, heavy bill, long dark legs and attenuated rear. In flight its dark plumage, blackish tail and long, slender wings give a skua-like impression. A few birds show white primary coverts, creating white wing-flashes, superficially similar to skuas, but placed 'wrongly'. Strongly coastal or offshore, it is found along beaches in small gatherings with other gulls. It is piratical, performing skua-like kleptoparasitism on birds up to the size of Brown Pelican *Pelecanus occidentalis*.
Adult Dark grey with contrasting white head and uppertail-coverts, the latter contrasting against the all-black tail. The greyish-brown mantle and coverts contrast with the dark flight feathers and the wing's broad white trailing edge. The eyes are dark and bill red with a black tip or terminal bar. In **summer** the head is white and most conspicuous against the dark plumage. In **winter** the head is greyish with white streaks or spots.
Juvenile is dark chocolate-brown with a pale-scaled mantle and often almost blackish face, which contrasts strongly with the orange to fleshy black-tipped bill. The rather uniform plumage varies little within the first year, but from around one year of age the hindneck is often slightly paler greyish-brown, the saddle becoming more uniform and coverts often fading to create a slightly paler midwing-panel. The uppertail-coverts are slightly paler greyish-brown than the mantle.
Second-year is similar to the first-winter but greyer and less brown, the head greyish-brown with a paler face (especially the cheek and throat), stronger pale eye-crescents and faint grey streaks. Mantle, coverts and rump are grey and the grey underbody is often faintly brown-tinged with paler barring. The tail and secondaries are dark with much narrower white edges than in adults. The bill is bicoloured with a yellow to orange-red base and broad black tip, covering the angle of the gonys. Second-year birds with plumage similar to the first-winter are aged by their uniform brownish-grey upperwing-coverts coloured as the mantle and blacker primaries with rounded tips. In **second-summer**, the head becomes cleaner white and the bill is usually as in the adult.
Third-winter as adult, but head dark-peppered and coverts, scapulars and parts of underbody tinged brownish. Primary coverts brown with faint pale mottling near the tips. Lacks broader white primary tips of adult and has narrower white trailing edge to inner wing. Tail tinged brownish. Bill as adult, but with orange-red base; in some similar to second-year.

VOICE Calls are a hoarse, nasal *av-av-av*, in a quick descending series. Described as a low hollow trumpeting (Sibley 2000). Also a single *ävh* and whiny calls.

MOULT (skins in LACM) **Adult** moult to winter plumage is complete Apr–Sep. P1 usually Apr, P3–5 Jun/Jul, P8 mid-Aug–early Sep, P9–10 usually late Sep. Winter head attained Jul–Sep. Body Jun–Sep, sometimes restricted to head and upper breast. **Adult** moult to **summer** plumage late Nov–Dec, including head and parts of body. **Juvenile** moult to **first-winter** partial Sep–Nov, including head and parts of body. Some coverts may be moulted. By early Feb, first-years have renewed most of mantle and scapulars and scattered coverts (0–50%; pers. obs., Mexico, Feb). Some show no or very little moult into Apr. Moult into **first-summer** partial mid-Jan–mid-Jul, including head, body and scapulars (Iron & Pittaway 2001). Moult to **second-winter** complete mid-Feb–Sep, generally earlier than in adult. P1 Apr, P5–6 June, P7–8 Jul/early Aug, P9–10 late Aug–mid-Sep. Secondaries early Jun–early Aug, tertials mid-May–June, median coverts mid-Feb–June, greater coverts early Apr–late Jun (Iron & Pittaway 2001). Head, body, rest of coverts and tail late May–Aug. Moult to **third-winter** similar to second-winter. Head winter-plumaged by mid-Jul–mid-Aug.

DESCRIPTION
Adult Head white shading into dark grey hindneck and underbody (Kodak Grey Scale 6–7). Mantle, scapulars, tertials and wing-coverts dark grey (Kodak Grey Scale 11–12), sometimes with slight brownish tinge. Flight feathers blackish with white tips (broadest on secondaries, narrower on P1–5 (max. 5mm)). P6–10 at most with very indistinct white tips. Primary coverts white in small percentage. Uppertail-coverts pale grey to whitish. Tail black with 7–17mm white trailing edge, gradually disappearing into breeding season. Underwing dark grey. White eyelids above and below eye. Iris dark, orbital ring red. Legs blackish. **Adult summer** (Dec–Aug) Head and neck white, shading into grey underbody. Bill bright red with black tip or Z-shaped subterminal bar (4–15mm on upper, 5–10mm on lower mandible); not reaching angle of gonys. Subterminal bars sometimes doubled. Extreme bill-tip white to creamy. **Adult winter** (Aug–Feb) Head and neck with dense spots or streaks and greyish tinge to crown, sometimes forming traces of dark hood, most conspicuous behind eye. Face, chin and throat often unpatterned whitish. Whole head sometimes dusky. Bill duller red than in adult summer and often with broader black tip (max. 21mm on upper mandible).
Juvenile (fledging–Oct/Dec) Head, mantle, scapulars, body and wing-coverts dark brown; wing-coverts and scapulars with varying (sometimes narrow) pale sandy to whitish fringes, 10% with faint paler subterminal markings on scapulars. Rump and uppertail-coverts (sometimes undertail-coverts) greyish-brown, with faint paler edges when fresh. Axillaries and underwing-coverts blackish-brown. Flight feathers and tail blackish-brown; secondaries, P1–5 and tail sometimes with inconspicuous pale edges. Eye dark. Gape pinkish. Bill greyish, pale flesh or yellowish-flesh with broad black tip broadest on lower mandible, where covers up to 50%, covering gonys. Legs greyish-black.
First-winter (Oct–May). Developed to a varying degree: sometimes no or very limited moult; some very worn on

coverts from Sep, others not before Apr. Similar to juvenile, but often with paler cheek/throat and slightly darker hood and face. Mantle and scapulars dark brown, from Feb contrasting somewhat with slightly bleached juvenile upperwing-coverts, which may be partly renewed Dec–Mar. Breast sometimes with faint paler feather-edges, usually disappearing from Apr. Bill generally with deeper orange to pink/rosy base (sometimes pale grey to greenish) from late winter. Broad black bill-tip better defined than in juvenile.

First-summer (May–Aug) similar to first-winter. but face often paler with coarser dark markings, especially on crown, neck and ear-coverts. Head may look darkish at distance. With wear, upperwing-coverts become paler greyish-brown than mantle (as do lesser coverts/median coverts following moult). Bill as first-winter, but on average brighter.

Second-winter (Sep–Mar) greyer, less brown than first-winter. Head and underbody greyish-brown with pale mottling and whitish cheek/throat, sometimes with greyish-brown, pale-mottled or -streaked hood contrasting with grey underbody and hindneck. Breast to belly often brownish-tinged. Most birds show thin but distinct white crescents above and below eye. Mantle, back, scapulars and upperwing-coverts brownish-grey; scapulars and tertials with neat pale fringes, creating crescents when perched. Flight feathers similar to juvenile, but blacker; secondaries and P1–4 with white tips. Tail slightly paler than in first-year with white trailing edge at most 5mm wide. Eye dark. Bill orange to red, often greenish-tinged at base. Shows broad black tip, 19–22mm wide on upper, 9.5–11mm on lower mandible, unlike adult covering entire angle of gonys. Sometimes inconspicuous pale tip to upper mandible or dark cutting edges. Greenish tinge to base has been noted (Iron & Pittaway 2001). Legs blackish- or bluish-grey.

Second-summer (Dec–Aug) as second-winter, but head paler, sometimes whitish with some dark shading, e.g. as grey tinge to crown or scattered grey spots on head. Worn coverts become brownish, contrasting well with fresh darkish grey.

Third-winter (Aug–Feb) as adult, but differs in: flight feathers and tail with brownish tinge, tips to P8–10 black, white tips to rectrices 4–11mm and white secondary tips narrower. White tips to scapulars merge more diffusely into greyish-brown bases. Head-markings generally coarser and body generally darker

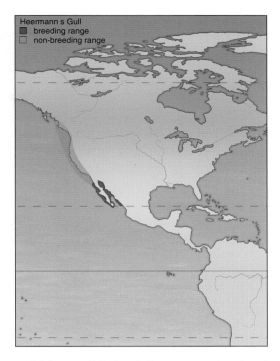

Heermann s Gull
■ breeding range
□ non-breeding range

and duller grey. Bill often duller or more orange-tinged than in adult, with complete black tip; may appear similar to second-year, but as in adults not covering angle of gonys.

Aberrants Regularly shows white primary coverts, but sometimes also parts of scapulars and underparts. A leucistic adult had pale greyish-brown underbody, pale grey upper median coverts, and brownish tail (skins in MVC, LACM; photo K. L. Garrett).

DISTRIBUTION AND MIGRATION 150,000 pairs (del Hoyo *et al.* 1996). Breeds late Jan–Mar on remote rocky coasts and islands with sparse vegetation in large colonies in the Gulf of California, Mexico. Eight colonies known; >90% of population on Isla Rasa (150,000 pairs in 1990s). Other large colonies (in pairs) 1,500 Cholluda, 4,000 Partida. In California, USA, 4–5 pairs in most years.

HEERMANN'S GULL Three-year gull. A characteristic dark gull of Baja California, spreading along American W Coast in non-breeding season. A dark gull, lacking any strong patterning. All-dark plumage prevents confusion with other gulls, and gives skua/jaeger impression, but it lacks white markings at primary bases (although sometimes shows white markings on primary coverts). Often kleptoparasitises terns as do skuas/jaegers. Legs dark.

Adult is dark sooty-grey. Wings are dark with white trailing edge to inner wing; rump grey and tail black with white edges. In **breeding** plumage (Dec–Aug), head white and bill coral-red contrasting well with dark plumage. In **non-breeding** plumage (Aug–Feb) head becomes darker with fine white streaks and spots.

First-year dark brown, in juvenile with narrow pale scaling on upperparts, but from first-winter saddle uniform dark brown; wings sometimes slightly paler through wear. Bill pale fleshy with dark tip.

Second-year similar to first-year, but sootier, less brown, with redder base to bill and white trailing edge to inner wing.

Third-year similar to adult, but in breeding season head often darker with fine white streaking, resembling adult non-breeding.

PLATE 2. HEERMANN'S GULL *Larus heermanni*

Breeding range restricted to Baja California and North Mexico, outside breeding season spreading along W North American coastline. Coastal, medium-sized dark gull. Rather heavy with long, broad wings; could be mistaken for skua/jaeger, and often parasitises other seabirds. Not uncommonly, shows white upper primary coverts, creating 'wrongly placed skua wing-patch'.

1.   **Juvenile** (Jul–Oct) Blackish-brown, with black flight feathers and tail, but bill fleshy with pale tips. Wings all dark, lacking any strong pale markings on either surface. Just shows narrow pale edges to upperpart feathers and coverts.

2.   **Juvenile** (Jul–Oct) Fresh juvenile, showing narrow pale fringes to upperparts and coverts on otherwise very dark brown plumage. Bill dull fleshy with black tip, legs long and blackish.

3.   **First-winter** (Oct–May) Similar to juvenile, but mantle and scapulars uniform sooty-brown, in light contrast to coverts (gradually more so with wear). Bill-base paler than in juvenile. Sits high on water when swimming.

4.   **First-winter** (Oct–May) Note all-dark appearance; wear produces slightly paler coverts. Tail black and rounded, lacking pointed central pair of rectrices of skuas/jaegers.

5.   **Second-winter** (Sep–Mar) Dark sooty-grey, often with brownish tinge. Shows narrow paler eye-crescents and brighter fleshy bill than in first-year, as well as narrow white tertial crescents.

6.   **Second-winter** (Oct–May) As dark as juvenile but appearing greyer, with broader white trailing edge to inner wing. With wear, coverts slightly paler than dark brown upperparts. Base of bill redder.

7.   **Third-winter** (Sep–Mar) Again very dark, but more greyish-tinged than first-year with red and black bill.

8.   **Third-winter** (Dec–Aug) Face paler and bill brighter than in second-winter, but head more uniform than in (most) adult winter and black tip to bill broader. May represent a variant within adult winter.

9.   **Adult winter** (Aug–Feb) Head streaked with grey; areas around bill (especially chin and throat) paler.

10.   **Adult summer** (Dec–Aug) Dark grey with conspicuous white head, white trailing edge to inner wing and red, black-tipped bill.

11.   **Adult summer** (Dec–Aug) Head white against dark grey body and wings. Bill red with black tip.

1. Juvenile

5. Second-winter

Third-winter

11. Adult summer

4. First-winter

2. Juvenile

3. First-winter

6. Second-winter

8. Third-winter

10. Adult summer

9. Adult winter

Sedentary or dispersive to C and S California, where autumn flocks of up to 7,500 Santa Cruz, 3,000 Monterey and 1,000 San Diego; In Washington state, flocks >3,000 noted Sep in El Niño years. Dispersal from post-breeding range from Dec. In California only scarce Jan–Mar, after which numbers start to build up again. Small numbers reach N to British Columbia, Canada, and S to Guatemala; and it is probably regular Arizona. Vagrant inland California, Great Lakes, Ohio, Oklahoma, Texas and Florida (Iron & Pittaway 2001).

MEASUREMENTS Lengths in mm; weights in g. Own data based on skins in LACM, MVZ, NHM, NRK, USNM, UZM. California, Mexico.

WING

Adult male	337–374 (359.1)	28
Adult female	329–357 (345.3)	37
First-year male	325–355 (343.2)	15
First-year female	312–338 (327.3)	22

BILL

Adult male	40.3–48.9 (44.4)	30
Adult female	38.2–44.8 (41.3)	39
First-year male	38.8–47.3 (43.3)	15
First-year female	37.3–42.5 (40.3)	22

BILL DEPTH AT GONYS

Adult male	11.8–15.1 (13.1)	30
Adult female	11.4–14.0 (12.7)	39
First-year male	11.1–15.0 (13.0)	15
First-year female	10.9–13.9 (11.6)	22

BILL DEPTH AT BASE OF BILL

Adult male	12.4–16.4 (14.7)	30
Adult female	12.4–14.6 (13.4)	39
First-year male	11.7–15.2 (13.2)	15
First-year female	11.2–14.5 (13.1)	22

GONYS LENGTH

Adult male	10.5–14.1 (12.0)	30
Adult female	10.1–13.5 (11.5)	39
First-year male	10.5–13.7 (11.6)	15
First-year female	9.9–12.2 (11.0)	22

TARSUS

Adult male	47.7–59.2 (53.9)	30
Adult female	46.8–56.0 (52.5)	39
First-year male	48.7–59.1 (53.6)	15
First-year female	46.6–54.8 (53.2)	22

Weight Adult: 417–670.

Heermann's Gull *Larus heermanni*. **18. Juvenile.** Blackish-brown, with faint pale scaling to upperparts. Suggests juvenile skua *Stercorarius*, but legs blackish and bill dark flesh with broad black tip. Santa Barbara, California, USA. Aug 1995. *Don DesJardin.* **19. 1st-winter.** Mantle and scapulars renewed into uniform type. Sonora, Mexico. 3 Feb 2000. *Klaus Malling Olsen.* **20. 1st-winter.** In flight younger birds appear very dark, with faintly contrasting paler rump. Sonora, Mexico. 3 Feb 2000. *Klaus Malling Olsen*

Heermann's Gull *Larus heermanni*. **21. 2nd- or 3rd-winter**. Similar to adult winter, but head darker and white tertial edges narrower. Black on bill-tip more extensive, covering entire gonys. Ventura, California, USA. Aug 1995. *Don DesJardin*. **22. 3rd-summer or adult**. As adult, but presence of fine dark head-streaks at a time when most full adults show uniform whitish-grey head suggests this bird may not be fully adult. Sonora, Mexico. 3 Feb 2000. *Klaus Malling Olsen*. **23. 3rd-summer or adult**. This bird shows broader head-streaks than 22. San Diego, California, USA. 6 Feb 2000. *Klaus Malling Olsen*. **24** (see p46)**. Adult summer**. Head whitish, strongly contrasting with dark grey body and deep red bill. Note narrow dark tip to lower mandible of 3rd-year or older, not reaching gonys angle. Ventura, California, USA. 18 Jan 2001. *Don DesJardin*.

Heermann's Gull *Larus heermanni*. **25. Adult winter**. In flight all-dark with whitish rump and narrow white trailing edge to inner-wing. Ventura, California, USA. 3 Nov 1996. *Don DesJardin*. **26. Adult winter** near end of primary moult. Underwing appears uniformly dark at any distance. Monterey, California, USA. Oct 1991. *René Pop*. **27** (previous page)**. Mixed flock** with 1st-, 2nd-, 3rd- and adult summer types. 1st-winter aged by dark brown plumage, but contrasting pale-edged coverts. Many 2nd-winters similar but with uniform coverts and brighter bill base. 3rd-summer type similar to adult but with less clean head pattern. Puerto Penasco, Sonora, Mexico. 3 Feb 2000. *Klaus Malling Olsen*.

3. WHITE-EYED GULL

Larus leucophthalmus (Temminck 1825, Red Sea coasts)

Plates 3–4, Photos 28–37

IDENTIFICATION Length 39–49cm, wingspan 100–115cm. White-eyed Gull is endemic to Red Sea. It is a slender, long-billed gull slightly larger than Black-headed Gull. Strictly coastal, it often flocks with Sooty Gull along the Red Sea coastline. Both gulls are dark with long, dark wings (including underwing) and full hoods, unlike other gulls extending as a bib onto the central breast. White-eyed is the smaller of the two; its head is smaller with a flatter forehead and much slenderer bill. Settled birds may give a shorebird-like impression, created both by the dark plumage and the long, drooping, dark bill. The bill has a narrow tip and lacks the bulbous tip and marked gonys-angle of Sooty. It has a sooty-grey head to breast, upperparts and underwing. Belly and tail are white and the legs yellow. In flight, its dark plumage recalls a skua, but the body and tail are shorter (the latter rounded), the rump white and the dark wings have a narrow white leading edge and broader white trailing edge. Flight similar to Black-headed, but quicker and with stiffer wingbeats. Often fishes by plunge-diving. Less of a scavenger than Sooty Gull. Sooty is larger, and structurally much more similar to a large gull. The head is notably heavier with a flatter crown and massive bill, looking bicoloured at long range. It has a bulkier body and longer legs. The body is darker greyish-brown (brown tinge lacking in White-eyed) and the legs are duller yellow than in White-eyed. The wings are similar to White-eyed, but the white leading edge is lacking or at most very indistinct.

Adult summer Has a jet-black hood penetrating to a point on the mid-breast. It has very prominent white eyelids—strong enough to suspect white eyes—but the eyes are in fact dark! A white hind-collar separates the hood from the greyer breast-sides to flanks. Bill dark red with a blackish tip—at any distance it looks rather uniform dark. Legs yellow, sometimes bright. In **winter** rather similar, but hood duller blackish-grey against paler forehead, chin and throat, and is often clearly white-streaked on chin, throat and upper breast; thus the bird may look 'half-hooded'. The hind-collar is generally greyer, bill brownish-red and legs duller.

Juvenile is dark with a blackish-brown head and paler face. The white eyelids are still conspicuous, although less prominent than in adult. Has greyish hind-collar and neck-sides, and brownish-grey breast (often also flanks); the belly is whitish. Upperparts are dark brownish-grey, generally with prominent pale scaling. Rump shows a narrow white V against the broad black tail. Bill blackish and legs greyish-brown. In flight, upperwing is rather uniform dark, with fainter paler inner wing, narrow pale wing-bars and white trailing edge to secondaries. Juvenile Sooty is larger and heavier with a much stronger and clearly bicoloured bill, paler and more uniform head, broader pale scaling to upperparts and broader pale wing-bars/trailing edge to wing. White rump-patch square, broader than the black tail. Legs grey.

First-winter similar to juvenile, but saddle uniform brownish-grey, contrasting with paler coverts, and dark half-hood more conspicuous. The forehead is white, in some contrasting with the dark-streaked crown. Breast-sides, flanks and back are dark grey, sometimes with a slight brownish wash, although never strong brown as in Sooty. On the upperparts the contrast becomes more striking with wear, as coverts fade to pale greyish-brown against the dark saddle. Bill dark.

First-summer as worn first-winter, but with a more prominent dark hood. The pale feather-edges to coverts and tertials are gradually lost with wear; the contrast between bleached coverts and dark saddle is then most striking. Tail-bar fades to brownish.

Second-winter similar to adult winter, but hood, breast, flanks and upperparts browner with contrast between new and old feathers. Black secondary bar broader, and white trailing edge narrower. Outer wing duller and more uniform, lacking clear white primary tips of adults, at most present on P1–3. Uppertail-coverts often a mixture of white and grey. Tail white with a broken dark bar. Bill greenish-grey, sometimes with a darker tip. Legs duller than in adult.

Second-summer similar to adult summer, but with duller, greyish hindneck to breast-sides and traces of dark on white tail. Bill brownish-red, darker and more uniform than in adult. Legs dull greyish-yellow.

VOICE Similar to Sooty Gull, but less harsh and deep. Long-call *kioow*, repeated 12–16 times; similar to Caspian Gull. Alarm call a *ke*, repeated 3–6 times; also *koup-koup-koup* (Urban *et al.* 1986, Lobley 1997).

MOULT Adult moult to **winter plumage** is complete following the breeding season; timing variable. P1–2 rarely from May, often from Aug, but sometimes Nov–Dec. In some, primary moult reaches P8–9 in early Dec. Attains winter head in Aug–Dec. Certain proportion of the population probably moult Apr–May (Grant 1986b). Moult to **adult summer** plumage partial Feb–Mar (Apr), including head, body and scattered coverts. Most have summer head late Mar (pers. obs. Israel); some still with white-spotted cheek and throat in May. **Juvenile** moult to **first-winter** partial Sep–Dec, including head and body; some still juvenile by Nov (skins in NHM). Subsequent moults similar to or slightly earlier than in adults. Birds moulting to second-winter Jun/Jul have renewed up to P5, T1–3 and had heavy moult in wing-coverts. Primary moult may be completed by Sep.

DESCRIPTION

Adult Primaries and outer primary coverts black, shading to grey inwards. P6–10 black, P1–5 blackish-grey with black outer web, blackish-grey inner web and narrow white tip and edges to outer part of inner web (up to 15mm on P1–3, often lacking on P3). Secondaries blackish-grey with white tips, creating white trailing edge to inner wing. Marginal coverts white, creating a thin but distinct leading edge to inner wing. Mantle, scapulars, wing-coverts and tertials dark grey to sooty-grey (Kodak

PLATE 3. WHITE-EYED GULL *Larus leucophthalmus*

Endemic to Red Sea. Strictly coastal. Small to medium-sized gull with long, slender, slightly drooping bill, at all ages appearing rather uniform. Dark gull, sharing dark wings (both surfaces) and white belly with Sooty Gull, with which it often gathers. Told from Sooty by smaller size, lighter build, narrower, fairly uniform bill and lack of clear brown plumage tones (instead being basically grey). When settled often resembles shorebird owing to narrow bill, small size and rather long, yellowish legs.

1. **Juvenile** (Aug–Nov) Brownish with narrow, all-dark bill, dark brown head with white crescents above and beyond eye, and brown, pale-fringed upperparts (variable; generally less heavily than in Sooty, but sometimes prominent). Legs dull yellow.

2. **First-winter** (Oct–Apr) From midwinter wing very worn. Head, breast and saddle dark grey, face and belly whiter. Note retained juvenile wing-coverts.

3. **Second-winter** (Jul–Mar) Medium grey with darker streaking above eye; looks half-hooded. Bill and white crescents above and behind eye similar to first-winter. Wing uniform grey, concolorous with mantle (compare first-winter).

4. **Adult winter** (Jan–Aug) Similar to adult summer, but head duller with variable (often very little) white streaking. White bar on neck-sides weaker and bill duller.

5. **Adult summer** (Feb–Aug) White-eyed and Sooty Gulls both show dark hood continuing as a black bib onto central breast. White-eyed shows coal-black hood, grey upperparts and broad white eyelids. Bill dull red with black tip, appearing dark and 'melting into head' at distance. Legs bright yellow.

1. Juvenile

2. First-winter

3. Second-winter

4. Adult winter

5. Adult summer

PLATE 4. WHITE-EYED GULL *Larus leucophthalmus*

In flight rather small with long, dark wings, appearing all dark with white belly at distance; closer views reveal narrow white trailing edge to wings. Head and neck short. Long, slender, darkish-looking bill seems separated from rather smallish-looking head. Often shows protruding breast against narrow head. Flight rather light, somewhat similar to Black-headed Gull.

1. **Juvenile** (Aug–Nov) Very dark when fresh, with pale-edged mantle, scapulars and coverts. Tail black, appearing broader than white U across rump.

2. **First-winter** (Oct–Apr) Head greyer with better contrast than in juvenile, and juvenile upperwing bleached, contrasting with grey saddle. Tail and its contrast as juvenile.

3. **Second-winter** (Jul–Mar) Compared to first-winter greyer with grey coverts, concolorous with saddle, better head contrast (but still mainly dark) and white tail with narrow, often incomplete black bar. Black secondary bar often broader than in adult, but white tips to inner primaries narrower.

4. **Adult winter** (Aug–Feb) Black hood duller owing to whitish streaking on forehead, chin and throat. Bill often duller than in summer.

5. **Adult summer** (Feb–Aug) Hood coal-black, extending onto throat. Bordered behind by white half-collar, again contrasting with grey breast to hindneck. Bill red with black tip.

6. **Adult summer** Note slender, dark wings and long, drooping bill, creating shorebird-like impression.

1. Juvenile

2. First-winter

3. Second-winter

4. Adult winter

5. Adult summer

6. Adult summer

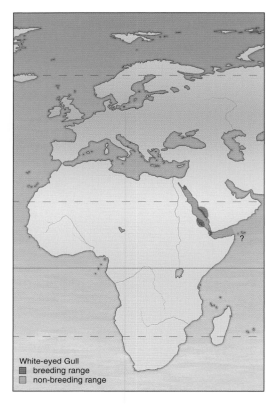

White-eyed Gull
■ breeding range
□ non-breeding range

Grey Scale 11–13); tertials with white tips. Underwing dark blackish-brown, primaries sometimes paler (but probably less underwing contrast than in Sooty). Outer greater coverts sometimes with narrow pale tips or shaft-streaks. Rump, belly, tail-coverts and tail white. Iris dark brown to brown, orbital ring black to red. Gape salmon-pink to fleshy. Bill crimson-red with a black tip (broadest on upper mandible, where maximum 18mm); angle to red basal part about 60 degrees, black not reaching gonys-angle as in Sooty. Extreme bill-tip sometimes pale. Legs bright yellow to greenish-yellow. Feet as legs, but sometimes with dusky mottling.

Adult summer (Jan–Aug) Has head and foreneck glossy black (Kodak Grey Scale 17–18) extending as dark bib to upper breast. Ear-coverts sometimes slightly paler. Prominent white eyelids above and below eye, broadest

at rear. Contrasting white half-collar on hindneck and neck-sides penetrates along hood to neck-sides, creating broad white patch, often slightly pointed towards ear-coverts (broader than in Sooty). Breast and sometimes flanks pale grey to slaty-grey; breast-centre often whitish. Bill red with black tip. Legs bright yellow.

Adult winter (Aug–Mar) Similar to adult summer, but head and foreneck duller, being white-flecked, most prominent on cheek and throat (sometimes forehead), which may be white. Hind-collar greyer, narrower and less well defined than in summer. Sides of neck greyish, sometimes continuing as narrow grey breast-bar. White primary tips gradually wear off during winter and spring. Bare parts duller. Base of bill brownish-red; bill looks rather uniform at a distance. Legs duller yellow, often with slight greenish tinge. With wear, head pattern more similar to adult summer.

Juvenile (fledging–Jun/Nov) Head brown, normally paler buffish-white on face, cheek, throat and sometimes crown. Head sometimes more uniform, but ear-coverts and eye-crescent dusky. White eye-crescents slightly narrower than in adult. Breast to flanks brownish; belly and undertail-coverts white. Mantle, scapulars, wing-coverts and tertials dark brownish-grey with pale buff, rather narrow edges; some have broader edges, creating a strong scaly pattern. Tertials often with blackish shaft-streaks and broader pale edges than rest of feathers on upperparts. Greater coverts sometimes darker forming dark triangle on closed wing, with only very faint paler tips and outer webs. Upper rump greyish, lower rump and uppertail-coverts white, creating white U; uppertail-coverts often dark-spotted. Flight feathers blackish with narrow white trailing edge to secondaries and P1–5 (which may be very slightly paler than secondaries and P6–10, forming indistinct white window). Underwing greyish-brown to brownish-black, on average duller and browner than in adult. Tail black with white terminal fringe and narrow white bases to inner webs of T5–6. Iris dark brown. Bill glossy black, sometimes with brown or grey base to lower mandible or paler tip to upper mandible. Legs greenish-grey to dark grey.

First-winter (Jun/Oct–Mar/Apr) similar to juvenile, but head generally with better-marked blackish mask from eye to nape, fine dark streaks on crown and slightly paler forehead, cheek and throat. Breast-bar and flanks brownish-grey. Mantle and scapulars brownish-grey, often contrasting well with wing-coverts (especially darker greater coverts). Uppertail-coverts and rump

WHITE-EYED GULL Three-year gull. Endemic to Red Sea. Superficially similar to Sooty Gull, but smaller and slenderer with uniform dark, very thin, drooping bill. Shares dark wings with white trailing edge to inner wing with Sooty, but is greyer, lacking brown tinges, and the leading edge of the inner wing shows narrow white line.

Adult has dark grey upperparts. In **summer** (Feb–Aug) hood glossy black extending onto upper breast as bib; shows prominent white eyelids. As in Sooty, hood is separated from body by broad white neck-sides. Bill red with black tip, looking uniform dark at any range. Legs yellow. In **winter** (Sep–Mar) hood less extensive and duller with prominent white streaks on foreparts.

Juvenile similar to Sooty, but head and upperparts concolorous dark brown, pale scaling on upperparts less prominent, tail dark with rump as narrow U towards back, and bill uniform dark.

First-winter as juvenile, but saddle uniform greyish, often in contrast to worn wings.

Second-year similar to adult, but with scattered brown upperpart-markings, darker bill and traces of dark tail-bar.

often with slight greyish tinge. Bare parts as juvenile.

First-summer (Feb–Jul) similar to first-winter, but hood darker and fuller. Tertials and wing-coverts become brownish-tinged and lose pale fringes through wear. Coverts normally in contrast to dark mantle. Tail-bar dark brown.

Second-winter (Jul–Mar) has hood brown to dull blackish, as in first-winter, but usually slightly darker with more contrasting whiter flecking, especially on cheek and throat. Upperparts similar to adult winter, but usually less clean grey with some brown-tinged feathers intermixed. Breast-bar and flanks brownish-grey, less clean than in adult; neck-sides duller greyish. P6–10, primary coverts, alula and secondaries blackish, P1–5 often very slightly paler. Narrow white fringes to tips of P3–4 and (broader) white tips to secondaries create narrower white trailing edge to inner wing than in adult. Upperwing-coverts dark grey with brownish tinge. Greater coverts generally darker than in adult. Uppertail-coverts white, often with greyish-brown tinge at tips. Tail white with some black or grey, forming variable, normally broken tail-bar. Bill brownish with black tip; sometimes with yellowish, brownish or dark red base. Legs dull yellow to greenish-grey.

Second-summer (Dec/Jan–Aug) as second-winter, but head similar to adult, although duller and often white-flecked on chin and throat. Neck-sides pale grey, less striking than in adult summer. Bill similar to adult, but base duller brownish-red - sometimes bill all-black.

Third-winter (Jul–Feb) similar to adult, but bare parts duller. Sometimes shows a few brownish-tinged upperpart feathers.

DISTRIBUTION AND MIGRATION Endemic to Red Sea, Gulf of Aden and NW Indian Ocean. 4,000–6,500 pairs in 1985, mainly in S part of range: several thousands Somalia (Aibat, Saad Din island off Zeyla) and Ethiopia, 1,000–2,000 mouth of Gulf of Suez and 200 Sudan. Other colonies small, rarely >50 pairs. Vulnerable; locally threatened by oil pollution and increasing human pressure. Breeds on inshore islands with rocks and sandy beaches late Jul–Sep.

Mostly sedentary, with some spread to whole Red Sea and Bitter Lakes, Eritrea, Somalia and Oman outside breeding season. Main range Red Sea between Suez and S Yemen: In Gulf of Suez max. 2,000 in Sep. In Yemen max. 200 Kutamah, 100 Al Kwawkhah, 100 Hodeidah and 80 Bab-el-Mandeb. At Eilat, Israel, population increased during the 1990s, now regular Mar–Oct, peaking late Mar–late Aug, max. day-count 84; most following strong southerlies. In Djibouti, max. 50 Obock. Regular Socotra where formerly breeding (Cornwallis & Porter 1982, Phillips 1982, Welch & Welch 1984, Brooks *et al.* 1987, Shirihai 1996b, Kirwan *et al.* 1996, del Hoyo *et al.* 1996, Porter *et al.* 1996b).

Vagrant E Africa (Kenya 1; claims Mozambique and South Africa not proven), UAE 3, Maldives (probably regular). In E Mediterranean 3 Israeli coast. Two records Greece in nineteenth century (Cramp & Simmons 1983, Urban *et al.* 1986, Lewis & Pomeroy 1989, Colston *et al.* 1992, Shirihai 1996b, Richardson & Aspinall 1997a & b, Grimmett *et al.* 1998; skins in AMNH, UZM).

MEASUREMENTS Lengths in mm; weights in g. Own data based on skins in AMNH, NHM, UZM, ZMO. Greece, South Arabia, Egypt and Sudan.

WING

Adult male	318–344 (333.5)	30
Adult female	311–334 (321.9)	12
First-year male	300–327 (313.8)	4
First-year female	297–323 (313.7)	6

BILL

Adult male	44.8–52.1 (48.9)	31
Adult female	41.5–47.4 (44.4)	12
First-year male	46.0–52.1 (48.1)	4
First-year female	42.4–45.7 (44.6)	6

BILL DEPTH AT GONYS

Adult male	10.6–11.7 (11.1)	30
Adult female	9.6–10.4 (9.9)	12
First-year male	9.6–10.3 (10.0)	4
First-year female	9.0–10.0 (9.7)	6

BILL DEPTH AT BASE OF BILL

Adult male	12.4–14.3 (13.2)	30
Adult female	10.1–12.3 (11.3)	12
First-year male	11.6–12.8 (12.3)	4
First-year female	11.3–12.4 (11.7)	6

GONYS LENGTH

Adult male	14.3–16.9 (15.4)	30
Adult female	12.8–14.2 (13.6)	12
First-year male	13.9–14.8 (14.1)	4
First-year female	12.3–15.0 (13.8)	6

TARSUS

Adult male	44.4–50.5 (47.8)	30
Adult female	43.6–46.4 (44.9)	12
First-year male	44.5–46.7 (45.4)	3
First-year female	44.6–46.5 (45.8)	5

Weight Egypt: males 325–413, females 275–355 (Urban *et al.* 1986).

White-eyed Gull *Larus leucophthalmus.* **28. Juveniles**. Long, dark and slightly downturned bill combined with small head, slender body and dark plumage makes identification easy. Tawila, Egypt. Sep 1992. *Hadoram Shirihai.* **29. Juvenile**. Note pale scaling, especially to scapulars, and pale U against dark tail. Tawila, Egypt. Sep 1992. *Hadoram Shirihai.* **30. 1st-winter**. Similar to juvenile, but mantle and scapulars of uniform colour, contrasting with pale-edged juvenile coverts. White eyelids broader than in juvenile. Note long, almost shorebird-like dark and drooping bill. Israel. 25 Feb 1986. *Volker Konrad.* **31. 1st-summer moulting to 2nd-winter**. Head similar to adult winter. Note dark tail-bar. Eilat, Israel. Aug 1990. *Hadoram Shirihai.* **32. 1st-summer moulting into 2nd-winter**. Note very worn and bleached outer primaries and active moult of greater coverts. Gulf of Suez, Egypt. 1 Jun 1985. *Arnoud B. van den Berg.* **33. 2nd-summer.** Similar to adult summer, but note dark tail-markings and broader black secondary bar than in adult. Gulf of Suez, Egypt. 10 Jun 1984. *Arnoud B. van den Berg.*

White-eyed Gull *Larus leucophthalmus*. **34. Adult summer**. Jet-black hood reaching upper breast as a bib – only shared with Sooty Gull. White-eyed easily identified by narrower and darker red bill, broad white eyelids and cleaner grey upperparts. Legs yellow. Gulf of Suez, Egypt. 10 Jan 1984. *Arnoud B. van den Berg.* **35. Presumed 2nd- and adult winter**. Outside breeding season hood duller with white spots or streaks, especially on chin and throat. Note the rather broad pale tertial edges of the adult compared to right-hand bird, which furthermore shows more extensive dark breast. Jeddah, Saudi Arabia. 15 Mar 1997. *Steve Young.* **36. Adult summer**. Note dark grey upperwing with blackish hand and white trailing and leading edges to wing. Sharm-el-Sheikh, Egypt. May 2001. *Andrea Corso.* **37. Adult summer**. Flying birds often appear deep-breasted with narrow head and shortish-looking tail. Dark underwings contrasts well with white belly and tail. Eilat, Israel. May 1994. *Markus Varesvuo.*

4. SOOTY GULL
Larus hemprichii (Bruch, 1853, Red Sea)

IDENTIFICATION Length 42–45cm, wingspan 105–118cm. Sooty Gull is a medium-sized gull with dark brown upperparts, blackish flight feathers and underwing, and white belly. Its large two-toned bill looks almost grotesque and is indeed proportionately heavier than in other gulls. The settled bird is stocky with a large head showing a flat crown and full neck, deep breast and long, slender wings. Relaxed bird looks neck-less, flat-crowned and 'masculine', recalling small, heavy-billed and long-legged Lesser Black-backed Gull. Flight lazy with slow elastic wingbeats similar to a large gull. Dark plumage and white rear body creates a skua-like impression. Often found in small parties along seashore. Scavenges, fishes by plunge-diving, usually close to surface, and may rob food from terns as skuas. For separation from White-eyed Gull, which often occurs alongside Sooty Gull in the Red Sea—and has similar dark plumage—see that species.

Adult summer Has dark brown hood and narrow white eyelids (rarely indistinct below). The hood extends down the breast in a bib, and is divided from the brown mantle by a broad white collar. It may be narrow on the hindneck, suggesting white neck-sides (especially when relaxed) against the sooty-brown breast-bar and flanks. Dark brown upperparts are relieved by a white trailing edge to the inner wing and a white rump/tail. Bill yellowish with dark tip and narrow red extreme tip. Legs yellow, often with greenish tinge.

Adult winter Similar, but hood duller and paler brown with whitish or pale-spotted chin and throat. Collar narrower or lacking; when present, normally greyish-tinged and separated from mantle by narrow, blackish border. Bare parts duller.

Juvenile pale brown with a white-scaled mantle, scapulars, tertials and to a lesser degree coverts. Head to breast pale buffish-brown, dark eye striking in pale head, again contrasting with brown upperparts and two white wing-bars created by white tips to median and greater coverts. Flight feathers darker, secondaries with white trailing edge. White rump and bases of tail create a broad square patch against the black tail-bar. Bill blue-grey with black ('dipped in ink') tip. Legs grey, paler than bill-base.

First-winter similar to juvenile, but mantle and scapulars uniform brownish in contrast to pale-edged juvenile wing-coverts, which by spring become worn and faded; from late winter replaced by fresh plumage.

First-summer similar to first-winter, but often with traces of adult-like hood and faded coverts, having lost most of their pale fringes.

Second-winter similar to adult winter, but white tail with incomplete or narrow dark bar against broad white tip, darker flight feathers (white primary tips restricted to innermost), narrower white trailing edge to wing, and paler, generally less defined hood. Upperparts duller, often with browner coverts intermixed. Bill pale with dark tip. Legs duller than in adults.

Second-summer similar to second-winter, but hood similar to adult summer, although duller and separated from mantle by narrower, often greyish collar. Bill often greenish-tinged.

Third-winter as adult, but hood generally with broader white spots and narrower white hind-collar.

VOICE Courtship call a repeated, goose-like *gar-gar*, a wailing *corr-ga* in rising scale. Long-call a loud, screaming *kioow*, repeated 12–16 times. Also a pained *owhaa*. Alarm call a rhythmical *ke* or *koup*, in staccato series of usually 3–6 notes. Attack call a hard *garkekkekk*. Voice harsher and deeper than in White-eyed Gull, like intermediate between White-eyed and Herring Gull (Walker 1981a & b, Urban *et al.* 1986).

MOULT Adult moult to **winter** plumage is complete following the breeding season (varying in different areas). In Red Sea, Persian Gulf and Makran coast generally moult P1–3 Oct, P8–10 Dec–mid Mar. Winter head acquired Oct–Nov (Cramp & Simmons 1983). E African birds (presumed breeders as moult differs from Red Sea population) generally moult later. Birds with P1 moulted Oct probably of northern origin. By Dec, some have not started primary moult, others reach P5–6 and have heavy moult in wing-coverts. Most moult P8–10 Mar–Apr. Secondaries and tail probably Dec–Feb (pers. obs. Kenya; skins). Moult to **adult summer** plumage partial, including head and body. In Red Sea, Persian Gulf and Makran, most have acquired summer head by Apr, when tail still in heavy moult (skins in NHM, Cramp & Simmons 1983, U. G. Sørensen pers. comm.). **Juvenile** moult to **first-winter** partial Nov–Feb, including head, body, and sometimes scapulars and some coverts. Moult to **second-winter** plumage complete (Feb)Mar/Apr/–Oct; timing variable, some having almost completed head and body moult and actively moulting coverts and flight feathers in Mar–Apr (may then reach P3–4) (Yemen, Egypt; photos in Grant 1986b). In Jun/Jul P4–5 renewed; retarded birds start primary moult in Jul. P6–7 late Jul, P9–10 Oct. Tail late Jun–early Aug, completed before flight feathers; some moults T4–6 Mar–mid-Apr (skins in NHM, UZM). Moult to **second-summer** plumage probably similar to adult moult.

DESCRIPTION
Adult Mantle, scapulars, inner wing-coverts and marginal coverts dark grey-brown (Kodak Grey Scale 10–13). Primaries, primary coverts and alula black, P1–4 sometimes dark grey-brown. P1–7 with white tips, generally broadest on innermost. Secondaries and tertials blackish with white edges, creating broad white trailing edge to inner wing. Rump, uppertail-coverts and tail white. Underwing dark with blackish-brown axillaries and coverts and greyish-brown flight feathers. Belly to undertail-coverts white. Iris dark brown, often with greyish tinge. Orbital ring and gape red to orange. Inner gape-line orange. Bill yellow to greenish-yellow with red tip and black subterminal bar (max. 20mm on upper mandible, with 60–70 degree angle to lower

mandible, on lower mandible covering gonys-angle). Extreme tip often yellow. Legs dull yellow to greenish-yellow.

Adult summer (generally Mar–Oct) Hood blackish-brown, extending to narrow, rounded bib on upper breast; shades to blackish on lower nape and bib (most striking with wear). Has narrow, sometimes prominent white eyelid above eye, sometimes a thin one below eye. Hood bordered by white half-collar from lower hind-neck to sides of neck (where up to 25mm; narrower and sometimes lacking on hindneck). A broad grey-brown breast-bar to flanks borders dark bib. With wear, upper-wing fades to dark brown, and white tips to P1–7 may disappear (but often retained on P1–3).

Adult winter (generally Aug–Mar) Similar to adult summer, but hood paler greyish-brownish with blackish border. White half-collar narrower and often greyish-tinged (max. 10mm, rarely incomplete or lacking). Chin and throat paler with faint brown spots. Bare parts generally duller than in adult summer with greyer bill-base and legs. Gape-line sometimes greenish.

Juvenile (fledging–Sep(Jan)) Head pale brown, shading to brown on nape and whitish on chin and forehead (which may show indistinct dark spots). Indistinct whitish eyelid above eye. Dark crescent in front of eye. Mantle and scapulars brown, inner wing-coverts pale brown and tertials darker brown with white to pale creamy-buff feather-fringes creating a scaly pattern. Median and greater coverts dark brown with white tips, creating two wing-bars. P6–10 and secondaries blackish, P1–5 sometimes slightly paler. P1–4 and secondaries with white tips. Marginal coverts dark. Rump and uppertail-coverts white to pale grey-brown. Breast and flanks pale brown with indistinct white mottling (sometimes creating dark breast-band) contrasting slightly with white belly and undertail-coverts. Underwing as adult. Rump and uppertail-coverts white, creating square patch, enlarged by white tail-base. Tail black with thin, white terminal fringes and white bases to inner webs of T6. Tail appears white-fringed when fully spread. Iris dark brown. Bill blue-grey to greyish-pink with black tip, covering up to 25mm on upper mandible, with 60–70 degree angle to lower mandible (dark covering gonys). Legs greyish, often with bluish or olive tinge (rarely blackish-brown).

First-winter (Aug/May–Jun) as juvenile, but breast-bar, flanks, mantle and scapulars uniform greyish-brown. Head sometimes pale greyish-brown. Wing and tail brown-tinged through wear. By late winter attains new coverts, which are uniform and darker than juvenile.

First-summer (Mar–Oct) as first-winter, but wings and tail heavily worn. Wing-coverts and tertials usually lose pale fringes. May show traces of darker hood.

Second-winter (Aug/May–Oct) Head similar to first-winter or slightly darker with paler chin and throat. Mantle, scapulars, breast-bar and flanks brown with greyish-brown adult feathers intermixed. Upperparts similar to adult winter, but secondary bar usually darker and broader with narrower, less distinct white trailing edge. White tips and fringes to P1–5 less prominent; often confined to P1–4. Tail white with variable black or grey subterminal spots: in some, tail still juvenile; in others, dark restricted to spots on 1–2 rectrices (espe-

cially T5–6; on T3–4 sometimes as U-markings), in contrast to broad white tips to all rectrices. T5–6 have dark shaft-streaks. Bill dull yellow to greyish-green with dark subterminal markings (10–15mm on upper mandible) and 10–15mm pale tip. Some have adult bills.

Second-summer (Mar–Oct) as second-winter; hood similar to adult summer, but duller, often with indistinct pale mottling, especially on chin and throat and narrower white hind-collar. Bill yellow with greenish, grey or bluish tinge and black tip, rarely red extreme tip to upper mandible. Legs as adult winter or greyer.

Third-winter (Aug–May) similar to second-years, but tail normally all white. Hood, white tips to P1–5, secondaries and bare parts as adult.

DISTRIBUTION AND MIGRATION Population 50,000–100,000 pairs. Breeds coasts and coastal islands Apr–Oct (Red Sea, Arabia). Outside breeding season marine, often associated with fishing activities and in sea-ports. Also scavenges. Gathers freely with White-eyed Gull. Largest colonies off Arabia (two colonies of 5,000 pairs), scarce Persian Gulf (100–120 pairs in UAE), Gulf of Aden (50–100 pairs), Socotra, eastern Red Sea N to Wadi El Gamal island and N to SW entrance of Gulf of Suez, Egypt and along E African coast S to Kenya (50–100 pairs) at Kiungu. Locally threatened by egg collection and oil pollution in Pakistan and the Gulf States. Recent breeding status in Pakistan uncertain (Cramp & Simmons 1983, Bundy 1986, Lewis & Pomeroy 1989, del Hoyo *et al.* 1996, Richardson *et al.* 1997).

Extensive spread Sep–Nov to wintering grounds along Indian Ocean coast from S Arabia to tropical E Africa S

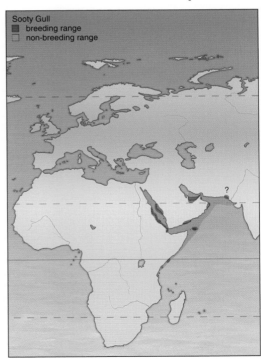

Sooty Gull
■ breeding range
□ non-breeding range

PLATE 5. SOOTY GULL *Larus hemprichii*

Occurs Red Sea and Indian Ocean around Arabia, E to N India and S to equatorial Africa. Strictly coastal, medium-sized, rather heavy, dark gull with large, bicoloured bill (appearing too large for the bird). Basically greyish-brown. Lacks conspicuous pale eyelids, and often such pattern restricted to above eye. In Red Sea often alongside the smaller, greyer White-eyed Gull, which lacks brown plumage tones and shows narrow, dark, drooping bill. Flying Sooty and White-eyed Gull have dark wings on both surfaces; appears heavier than White-eyed Gull with slower wingbeats and larger head, emphasised by heavy bill; flight similar to larger gull.

1. **Juvenile** (Aug–Jan/Feb) Greyish-brown with pale head, looking rather uniform. Bill greyish with distinct black tip. Upperparts prominently pale-scaled. Legs greyish. Pale head and heavy bicoloured bill are main differences from White-eyed Gull.

2. **First-winter** (Oct–Mar/Jun) similar to juvenile, but note greyish-brown saddle against retained (often strongly worn) juvenile wing. Head again pale, lacking contrast.

3. **Second-winter** (Jul–Mar) Head, breast and upperparts darker greyish-brown than in first-winter with wings concolorous with saddle. Shows variable dark tail-bar.

4. **Adult winter** (Oct–Apr/May) Hood brown in weak (but varying) contrast to pale collar along sides of neck. Hood and mantle of similar brown colour.

5. **Adult summer** (Mar–Sep/Oct) Hood blackish-brown, with only narrow white eyelids, often restricted to upper eyelid. The large bill is yellow with black and red tip. Upperparts and breast brownish.

1. Juvenile

2. First-winter

3. Second-winter

4. Adult winter

5. Adult summer

PLATE 6. SOOTY GULL *Larus hemprichii*

Medium-sized, rather heavy gull of Red Sea and NW Indian Ocean. Shape and flight like a small Lesser Black-backed Gull with rather large head and heavy, bicoloured bill. Wings dark, lacking any solid pale areas, strongly contrasting with white rump (and in older birds tail).

1. **Juvenile** (Aug–Jan/Feb) Brown with pale belly, rump and tail-base; shows black tail-bar narrower than white rump. Many show conspicuous pale head, with contrasting dark eye. Bill pale with distinct black tip.

2. **First-winter** (Oct–Jun) Similar to juvenile, but upperwing more worn and with fresh, darker greyish-brown saddle.

3. **Second-winter** (Jul–Mar) Dark brown upperparts and coverts; flight feathers blacker than in first-year and bill paler. Pale neck-ring starts to appear. Tail with dark markings.

4. **Adult winter** (Oct–Feb/May) Adult shows dark hood, continuing to breast-centre as bib. In winter, head pattern dull with varying white neck-ring, often narrow and incomplete.

5. **Adult summer** (Mar–Sep/Oct) Hood darker than in winter and neck-ring broader and cleaner white. Bare part coloration bright.

1. Juvenile

2. First-winter

3. Second-winter

4. Adult winter

5. Adult summer

to Mozambique. Red Sea population mainly resident. Large flocks at cold-water upwellings off S Arabia and along Arabian coastline. In UAE max. 1,600 Jan, Quanein island, and max. 5,000 summering, especially immatures. Max. 2,000 Dhofar. Very common Oman: flocks up to 5,000, especially late Oct–Dec and Apr. Commonest coastal gull Yemen: max. 7,800 Quisn, S Yemen, mid-Apr. Fairly common Socotra, Sind and Makran coasts, Pakistan. Scarce Kuwait and Bahrain (Bundy & Warr 1980, Walker 1981a & b, Cornwallis & Porter 1982, Bundy 1986, Kirwan *et al.* 1996, Porter *et al.* 1996b, Richardson & Aspinall 1997a, Grimmett *et al.* 1998).

Since 1950, increasing wintering Kenya, where max. 1,500 Malindi/Sabaki estuaries and several hundreds Tanzania–Mozambique frontier. Vagrant inland Kenya (three immatures, Lake Rudolf, Apr 1974). Return migration Apr–May. Rare N part of Red Sea and Gulf of Suez. In Sinai probably regular with max. 15 Nabq, Mar 1999. Red Sea birds believed to stem from small colonies at Tawila, Gubal and Gezira Ashrafi, N Red Sea. Vagrant Israel (four, Eilat), Jordan, Lebanon, India, Sri Lanka, Maldives (Cramp & Simmons 1983, Lewis & Pomeroy 1989, Grimmett *et al.* 1998, Shirihai 1999, U. G. Sørensen pers. comm. & photos).

MEASUREMENTS Lengths in mm; weights in g. Own data based on skins in MCZ, NHM, NRK, UZM, ZMO. Red Sea, Persian Gulf, Makran coast, Pakistan, Kenya, Tanzania and Somalia.

WING

Adult male	335–362	(354.2)	23
Adult female	320–351	(338.9)	23
First-year male	325–360	(342.1)	39
First-year female	305–343	(328.6)	30

BILL

Adult male	45.5–52.1	(49.2)	23
Adult female	41.9–51.7	(45.4)	23
First-year male	44.3–52.8	(49.0)	39
First-year female	40.5–49.1	(45.6)	30

BILL DEPTH AT GONYS

Adult male	12.6–13.9	(13.3)	23
Adult female	11.8–13.1	(12.3)	23
First-year male	11.5–13.8	(12.9)	39
First-year female	11.2–13.6	(12.2)	30

BILL DEPTH AT BASE OF BILL

Adult male	14.5–16.7	(15.7)	23
Adult female	12.7–15.2	(14.3)	23
First-year male	13.8–16.4	(15.2)	39
First-year female	13.4–15.6	(14.2)	30

GONYS LENGTH

Adult male	12.3–15.6	(14.0)	23
Adult female	11.8–14.6	(13.0)	23
First-year male	12.2–15.3	(13.8)	39
First-year female	11.2–14.9	(12.8)	30

TARSUS

Adult male	50.1–58.8	(53.7)	23
Adult female	48.8–55.2	(51.3)	23
First-year male	48.1–57.6	(53.4)	39
First-year female	46.6–54.8	(51.1)	30

Weight Kenya, Egypt: adult: male 496–640, female 400–522 (Urban *et al.* 1986).

SOOTY GULL Three-year gull. Breeds in Red Sea and along Arabian Peninsula to Persian Gulf and Pakistan. A medium-sized, dark gull with large, 'over-sized', bicoloured bill and dark wings including underwing.
Adult has dark brown upperwing with white trailing edge; hand fully dark. Bill yellow with red and black tip. In breeding season shows dark brown hood extending onto upper breast as bib, thus more extensive than in other hooded gulls apart from White-eyed. Neck-sides with extensive white elongated spot. Shows narrow white crescent above eye. In non-breeding season, head becomes duller brown and white neck-sides narrower and less extensive.
Juvenile has pale-scaled mid-brown saddle and coverts; flight feathers all dark. Head paler than body. Bill pale with black tip. Shows black bar on white tail. In **first-winter** saddle becomes uniform brown, and often contrasts well with worn juvenile wing.
Second-year similar to adult but head more uniform and paler, bill duller, traces of dark tail-bar present.

Sooty Gull *Larus hemprichii.* **38. Juvenile.** Robust with pale, rather square head, black eye and heavy, bicoloured bill with strongly curved tip. Upperparts prominently scaled. Compare White-eyed Gull, photos 28 and 29. Egypt. Sep 1992. *Hadoram Shirihai.* **39. 1st-winter.** Fresh mantle, scapulars and some wing-coverts (esp. median) uniform, in contrast to bleached juvenile coverts (often strongly so with wear). Oman. Apr 1997. *Steve Young.* **40. 2nd-winter.** Similar to adult winter, but typically lacks conspicuous pale half-collar. Oman. Apr 1997. *Steve Young.* **41. 1st-winter.** Juvenile parts of upperwing strongly worn, but in right-hand bird median coverts have been mainly renewed. Jeddah, Saudi Arabia. Mar 1997. *Steve Young.* **42. Adult moulting into winter plumage.** Head of winter plumage duller than in summer with less prominent white half-collar. Head browner than in White-eyed Gull, with just upper eyelid white. Tawila, Egypt. Sep 1992. *Hadoram Shirihai.*

Sooty Gull *Larus hemprichii*. **43. 2nd- and adult winters**. Jeddah, Saudi Arabia. Mar 1997. *Steve Young*. **44. Adult summer**. Note brownish-black head, white upper eyelid, diagnostic bill and brownish-tinged upperparts. Oman. Apr 1997. *Steve Young*. **45. Adult summer**. Note how the shape of the white half-collar changes as head moves (compare previous photo). Shinzi Island, Oman. Aug. *Hanne & Jens Eriksen*. **46. Adult summer**. In flight similar to White-eyed Gull, but with heavier head, bill and body. Lacks white leading edge to innerwing of White-eyed. Shaghaf Island, Oman. Aug. *Hanne & Jens Eriksen*. **47. Adult summer**. White belly and tail contrast strongly with dark underwing and head. Shaghaf island, Oman. Aug. *Hanne & Jens Eriksen*.

64

5. COMMON GULL
Larus canus (Linnaeus, 1758, Sweden)

IDENTIFICATION Length 40–45cm, wingspan 100–130cm. Common Gull is a medium-sized gull, being about 1.5 times the size of Black-headed. It is like a small, gentle Herring Gull with rounded head, neater bill, large dark eyes and rather narrow wings. The bill is rather weak with tapering tip and slightly broader base. Settled birds have a full breast and attenuated rear with long, narrow wings. Flies in a leisurely fashion with deep, powerful wingbeats and glides on slightly angled wings. Often gathers with other small gulls in ploughed fields and urban environments; only in icy conditions does it flock at sea-ports (more rarely rubbish tips) with larger gulls. It is similar to Ring-billed and Mew Gulls; adult vaguely recalls adult Black-legged Kittiwake; first-year recalls similar-aged Mediterranean Gull. See those species.

Adult Has bluish-grey upperparts, a prominent white trailing edge to the wing and a black wing-tip with broad white mirrors, evident even at long range. Settled birds have striking white tertial crescents and primary tips. Bill is yellow with a greenish tinge and often dark subterminal markings. Legs yellowish. In **summer** the head is white, bill sometimes with dark markings. In **winter** the head is dark-spotted or streaked with denser spotting on the hindneck. The bill is generally duller than in summer, in most with dark subterminal markings, typically appearing as a dark Z-shaped bar.

Juvenile is greyish-brown with pale-scaled upperparts and upperwing-coverts. Shows darker flight feathers with paler inner primaries creating a faint pale window. The tail is white with a clear-cut black bar. The underwing is pale with delicate dark scaling. Bill dark, legs fleshy. From Aug, head and body are moulted into **first-winter**, when head and mantle come to resemble the adult and the bill is bicoloured. Head, sides of breast and flanks have dark, usually distinct markings, creating a scaly pattern reaching the flanks and sometimes the undertail-coverts. The brownish-grey greater coverts contrast with the darker grey saddle. The legs are fleshy, greyish or greenish. In spring and **first-summer**, the upperwing-coverts wear to almost whitish and then contrast well with the grey saddle.

Second-winter similar to adult winter, but with darker wing-tip (including primary coverts) and smaller white mirrors, sometimes restricted to P10 and always small on P9. Folded wing-tip looks blackish and lacks the broad, pale primary tips of an adult. A small proportion retain dark markings on secondaries and tail. The bill usually has a broader black tip or bar than in the adult. The legs are greyish with a fleshy, yellow or greenish tinge. Birds with a complete black bill-band may appear similar to Ring-billed Gulls, which are slightly larger with paler grey upperparts, pale eyes and heavier bill.

Second-summer is similar to second-winter, but head, bill and body are similar to adult summer.

VOICE Vocal in breeding season. Most common call a mewing, elongated *glieoo* or *miieeuw*, mournful and high-pitched in spring and during breeding. Also a thin, nasal *keow*. Long-call is a series of mewing high *gleeu-gleeu-gleeu*, quicker and higher-pitched than in Ring-billed and Herring/American Herring Gull. When alert a rapid, nasal *yadadada*.

MOULT (*canus*, NW Europe) **Adult** moult to **winter** plumage is complete mid-May–mid-Oct. Head mid-Aug–Sep, starting with ear-coverts. Most coverts mid-Jul–mid-Aug, completing Sep–early Oct. P1 (mid-May)mid-Jun; 30–50% have renewed P1–3 early–mid-Jul (in N Germany P5 mid July), P4–5 early Aug, P6–8 late Aug, P9–10 late Sep–first half of Oct. Secondaries (late June)mid-Aug–late Sep, when P5–7 shed. Tail starts with T1–3 (late July)early Aug, completes early Sep. Moult to **summer** plumage partial Mar–May, including head and body. Most have summer head early Apr. **Juvenile** moult to **first-winter** partial Aug–Oct, including head, much of underparts, most/all of mantle, some (rarely all) scapulars, some back and rump feathers and rarely 1–2 median coverts. Mantle mostly grey by late Sep. Icelandic and Arctic birds generally moult later, retaining most of juvenile upperparts in autumn; by mid-Nov <50% of mantle new (skins in UZM, pers. obs. Iceland). Exceptionally, juvenile mantle and scapulars retained into May, the birds in question probably being offspring of late northern breeders (Holst & Ullman 1984, Grant 1986b, Eggenhuizen 1987, Hein & Martens 2002). See *heinei* under Geographical Variation.

Moult to **second-winter** completed Apr/May–early Sep, generally a month earlier than in the adult. P1 mid- to late May, P2–3 Jun; P6–8 late Jul/early Aug; P9–10 normally early–mid-Sep. Secondaries, coverts and tail (late May) Jul–Aug; median covert moult may start late May and is usually completed early Aug, before onset of moult of other coverts and P6–7. Lesser coverts moulted last. T1–2 mid-Jul. Completes tail moult late Aug; rarely, tail moult not started in Aug. Subsequent moults similar to adult, but in third-years on average slightly earlier (Hein & Martens 2002).

Moult in *kamtschatschensis* later than *canus/heinei*; **adult** moult complete Jul–Nov. P1 Jul, P9–10 mid-Oct–mid-Nov. Most adults still with winter head into mid-Apr (most *canus* white-headed from early Apr). **Juvenile** moult to **first-winter** later and often limited compared to *heinei*. Parts of juvenile plumage seemingly always retained in first-winter. Many retain juvenile (and rather fresh-looking) plumage into Nov, whereas others renew <50% of mantle/scapulars by this time. By Feb many still fresh-looking, only with scattered first-winter feathers on mantle and scapulars; at most, 70% of mantle/scapulars renewed (pers. obs. Japan, Feb; J. R. King pers. comm.). **Second-years** again moult later, often showing juvenile lesser and median coverts admixed with grey on upperparts into late autumn.

DESCRIPTION ssp. canus (NW Europe)
Adult Upperparts and upperwing medium grey with slight bluish tinge (Kodak Grey Scale 5–6(7)). P5–10

PLATE 7. COMMON GULL *Larus canus*

Medium-sized gull, abundant in N Europe and Asia. Breeds in shallow estuaries and lakes. Gathers in large flocks in estuaries, lakes and on ploughed fields. Round-headed with large dark eyes, rather small bill, lacking hooked tip (often appearing broadest at base), and short legs. Round-breasted with elongated hindparts. Superficially resembles larger gulls (such as Herring) in all ages, but note weaker bill lacking marked gonys-angle, dark eyes (together with rounded head producing gentle look) and unpatterned greater coverts. In all plumages rather similar to Mew and Ring-billed Gull.

1.   **Juvenile** (Jul–Sep) Greyish-brown head, breast and unpatterned greater coverts. Mantle and scapulars darker with pale edges. Bill dark. Legs fleshy.

2.   **First-winter** (Sep–May) By early autumn, juvenile head, breast and upperparts moulted into first-winter. Head white with darker spotting or streaking, sometimes reaching flanks and undertail-coverts. Shows contrasting bluish-grey saddle against juvenile wing with pale brownish-grey, unpatterned greater coverts. Bill with pale (greyish, greenish-grey or fleshy) base and black tip. Legs same colour as base of bill.

3.   **Late first-winter** (Mar–May) From late winter, worn juvenile wing often makes strong contrast to saddle. Pattern of coverts somewhat bleached, but generally well kept during first-winter. Dark head-markings gradually wear off during winter, but note also individual variation: some birds are unpatterned already from first autumn. Colour of base of bill and legs shown here reflect individual variation mentioned above.

4.   **Second-winter** (Aug–Apr) Similar to adult winter, but black ring around duller bill generally fuller and broader (but still appearing Z-shaped) in most cases. Primary coverts normally dark-marked (hidden by rest of wing-coverts here). Primaries with narrower white tips (and smaller white mirror on P10); some tertials may be dark-patterned.

5.   **Adult winter** (Sep–Apr) Bill yellowish with dark, Z-shaped ring around tip. Head with dark streaking, generally with longer streaks on hindneck. Upperparts bluish-grey with distinct white tertial crescents. Eye dark. Legs yellowish, normally with greenish tinge.

6.   **Adult summer** (Apr–Sep) Head white (offsetting dark eye, surrounded by red orbital ring). Bill and legs yellow; bill sometimes with faint grey markings.

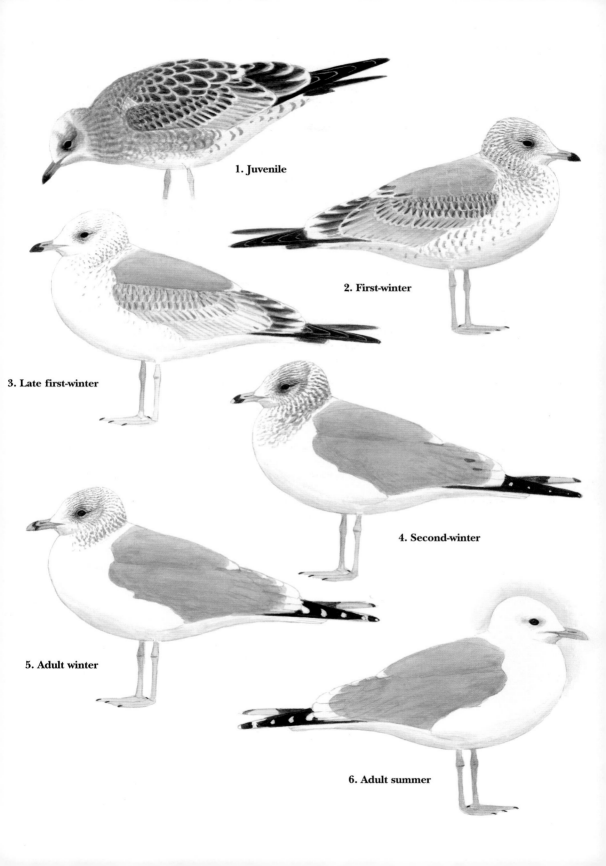

1. Juvenile

2. First-winter

3. Late first-winter

4. Second-winter

5. Adult winter

6. Adult summer

PLATE 8. COMMON GULL *Larus canus*

In flight like a round-headed miniature Herring Gull with narrower arm and much more graceful flight.

1. **Juvenile** (Jul–Sep) First-years greyish-brown with poor upperwing contrast, slightly paler window on inner primaries and distinct black tail-bar against unmarked white tail-base, creating strongly bicoloured tail. Underwing with varying dark markings, as bars with dark tips to coverts and axillaries. Rump often clean white, but sometimes with faint dark markings. Juvenile bill and body markings soon moulted into first-winter.

2. **First-winter** (Sep–May) Bill bicoloured and head white with dark streaks. Eye large and dark. Compared to 1, this bird shows less dark pattern on underwing.

3. **First-winter** (Sep–May) New bluish-grey saddle contrasts with browner wing—note especially contrast between saddle and brownish-tinged coverts. Bill bicoloured. Brown markings on head and body mostly faint. Tail white with black bar, appearing narrower than white tail-base.

4. **First-summer** (May–Sep) With wear, bluish-grey saddle in contrast to worn coverts. Head and body white. Bill yellow with black tip.

5. **Second-winter** (Aug–Apr) Similar to adult, showing bluish-grey upperwing with distinct white trailing edge. Compared to adult shows more dark on wing-tip, including dark primary coverts and white mirror on P10 only (occasionally a small one on P9). Primary pattern then similar to adult Ring-billed with paler grey upperwing including primary coverts. A small minority of nominate *canus* (but more *heinei* – see text) show faint dark markings on tail, lesser coverts and sometimes secondaries. Underwing unpatterned. Bill and head similar to adult winter, but with fuller black ring around bill. Again resembles the larger Ring-billed, but eyes dark, head rounder and bill weaker.

6. **Second-winter** (Aug–Apr) Most birds lack dark markings on tail of similar-aged Ring-billed, and P9 often with narrow white mirror.

7. **Adult winter** (Sep–Apr) Head with dark streaks, bill with narrow, irregular (Z-shaped) bar. Wing-tip solid black with large white mirrors on P9–10, creating large rounded spot on wing-tip. Upperparts bluish-grey with distinct white trailing edge to wing (often reduced on primaries in eastern race *heinei*).

8. **Adult summer** (Mar/Apr–Sep) Head white. With wear, black tip to P10 may disappear. Note, that some adult (older) males show white tip to P10 as well as less black in mid-primaries.

1. Juvenile

2. First-winter

4. First-summer

3. First-winter

5. Second-winter

6. Second-winter

8. Adult summer

7. Adult winter

PLATE 9. COMMON GULL *Larus canus kamtschatschensis* (Kamchatka Gull)

Common Gull gets larger and darker from west to east. The E Asian taxon *kamtschatschensis* (which may merit species status) is larger and heavier than *canus* from W and N Europe with longer, heavier bill. Structurally basically a Common Gull, lacking more angular head-shape and more parallel-edged, stronger-hooked bill of Ring-billed. In winter and first-year plumages generally more heavily marked than nominate *canus*. Plumage development generally slower. Adult normally with pale eyes.

1. **First-winter** (Jul/Aug–Jan) Generally heavier, more diluted markings than *canus*, often with a darker saddle: many first-years are still mainly juvenile by midwinter, or just with a few grey mantle and scapular feathers on otherwise juvenile upperparts. Dark markings on lesser and median coverts often less full, more triangular, as in Ring-billed Gull.

2. **First-winter** (Jul/Aug–Jan) Compared to *canus* underpart markings appear more diluted, and may look rather uniform greyish-brown at distance; upperwing contrast generally better defined and tail with broader black bar, often with narrow darker bars towards base, as in Ring-billed Gull.

3. **Second-winter** (Aug–Apr) Unlike *canus* generally has 'immature' markings such as brown-tinged, pale-edged coverts, dark markings on underwing and traces of dark tail-bar. Identified from Ring-billed by much darker grey upperparts.

4. **Second-winter** (Aug–Apr) Parts of or all coverts may be intermediate in pattern between first-year and adult, including dark tertial markings.

5. **Adult winter** (Sep–Apr) Compared to *canus* has more diluted dark head-markings, often creating hooded effect, and reaching breast-sides. Eyes often pale. Bill and legs generally brighter yellow than in *canus*.

6. **Adult winter** (Sep–Apr) Pattern similar to *canus*: note full black wing-tip with white mirrors on P9–10, creating large rounded white spot on wing-tip; on average, narrower white mirror on P9, upperparts a tinge darker than in *canus* with similar distinct white trailing edge on secondaries.

1. First-winter

4. Second-winter

5. Adult winter

2. First-winter

3. Second-winter

6. Adult winter

black, gradually reduced inwards to P5. P9–10 with white mirrors (on P10 50–70mm, on P9 20–50(60)), rounded, divided from black bases and tips; may show white tip to whole of or outer web of P10. A small proportion with 10–13mm white mirror on P8, mainly on inner web; often combined with largest mirrors on P9–10 and least black on P5, suggesting male. Dark outer web on P8 100–150mm, on P7 70–80mm, on P6 30–60mm; P6–8 with broad white inner webs to 60–80mm before tip. P5–7(8) with 10–20mm white 'moons' between black and grey. P5 normally with 20–25mm black subterminal spot, sometimes divided at shaft or restricted to black spot near tip of outer web; in <5% grey. P1–9 have white tips (may wear off in spring). P1–4, secondaries and tertials grey with whitish tips. Underbody, axillaries, underwing-coverts and tail white. Tail sometimes slightly forked (max. 10mm), but usually appears rounded. Male on average larger than female and generally with largest white mirrors on P9–10 (especially P9; in male 35–50mm, female 22–40mm), sometimes a white mirror on P8 and often no black on P5.

Adult summer (Mar–Sep) Head white. Orbital ring red. Iris dark brown, sometimes with chestnut tinge or silvery spots, creating slightly paler iris (exceptionally a pale greenish-yellow). Bill yellowish, often with a deeper yellow tip and sometimes a greenish-yellow base. May show thin dark subterminal spots or Z-shaped bar. Gape orange to fleshy. Legs yellow to greenish-yellow; generally deepest yellow in early breeding season.

Adult winter (Sep–Mar) Head white with fine dark streaks on crown and ear-coverts (sometimes forehead), more densely spotted on hindneck, in heaviest-marked birds creating ill-defined darker streaks on hindneck. Rear ear-coverts sometimes paler, creating pale area between ear-coverts and hindneck (see *heinei*). Rarely has denser dark streaks on crown suggesting slight cap. Thin white eyelids above and below eye. Often shows faint grey spot above and below eye or weak dark crescent in front of eye. Iris dark brown, often with a rufous or greyish tinge (appearing slightly two-toned at close range); rarely yellow to pale yellow (Grant 1986b, Koerkamp 1991, Malling Olsen 2003, D. Kok *in litt.*). Orbital ring dark brown. Bill duller than in summer, in >90% with broader, dusky, dark grey or blackish ring (or subterminal spots) around tip (Strangeman 1982, pers. obs.). Division between dark bars on upper and lower mandible Z-shaped, broadest on lower mandible (rarely equal on both mandibles, forming a complete ring). Bill-base sometimes greyish (esp. females); bill-tip often bright yellow, sometimes ivory. Legs yellowish, often greyish- or greenish-tinged.

Juvenile (fledging–Sep) Forehead, throat and nape whitish. Ear-coverts and crown streaked grey-brown, sometimes forming diffuse partial hood/dark ear-spot. Eye-crescents dusky. Thin white eyelids narrower than in adult; frequently lacking. Mantle and scapulars dark brown to greyish-brown with paler feather-fringes, creating a prominent scaly pattern; strongest on scapulars. Lower mantle sometimes clean grey. Rump and uppertail-coverts white, often with dark V-markings or spots, rarely as bars. Lesser coverts, median coverts and tertials brown with slightly darker shaft-streaks, rounded dark (sometimes blackish) centres and pale fringes; median coverts (especially outermost) frequently have more pointed centres. Greater coverts medium grey with slight brownish tinge, forming midwing-bar; inner and outer greater coverts sometimes slightly browner, the former frequently with uniform darker inner webs and the latter rarely with pale patterning, as in Ring-billed, or indistinct darker spots near tip. Outer greater primary coverts and P6–10 blackish-brown with narrow whitish tips. P1–5 slightly paler with dark grey outer webs and tips, and dark trapezoid-shaped spots at tips, with most dark in outer webs. Secondaries with white fringes and tips. P10 rarely with brownish-white mirror. Lower hindneck, flanks and breast uniform to slightly mottled grey-brown, flanks often with dusky spots (rarely slight V-markings). Belly and vent white, sometimes with faint dark spots, rarely mottled dark. Undertail-coverts white, frequently with dark V-markings along edges. Underwing-coverts and axillaries white with dark tips, forming evenly broad dark lines, sometimes narrow and indistinct; generally outer primary coverts have the most solid dark. Tail white with clear-cut brownish-black subterminal bar (30–50mm on T1). Rectrices with narrow pale tip. T6 white or with blackish-brown restricted to inner webs. Sometimes division between tail-bar and white tail less sharp or slightly dark-mottled, especially on T4–6 (see Ring-billed Gull). Orbital ring and iris dark brown. Bill blackish with diffuse dull flesh base, sometimes confined to lower mandible. Legs flesh.

First-winter (Sep–Apr) similar to juvenile, but head whiter with more distinct dark markings, reaching breast and flanks, as short streaks on crown and head; hindneck often more densely dark-spotted. Head pattern similar to adult winter, but generally denser, more diffuse and more brownish-tinged; frequently with white neck-sides and slight dark ear-spot. May show striking dark 'half-moon' in front of dark eye, making latter appear larger. Some only with narrow dark spots or streaks on head. Flanks often with dark spots or narrow V-markings. Central belly whitish, sometimes with scattered brown spots; rarely coarsely patterned. Mantle, back and scapulars blue-grey, in some with ill-defined paler fringes or very narrow dark shaft-streaks; scapulars rarely with faint brownish subterminal markings. Some (rarely all) juvenile mantle and back may be retained into spring. Dark markings on rump and uppertail-coverts less prominent than in juvenile. Bill pinkish, greyish or greenish-yellow with 11–16mm black tip, often broadest on lower mandible (from mid-winter, a few have very narrow pale bill-tips). Legs grey with pinkish to bluish (rarely greenish) tinge. With wear, wing-coverts paler brown with better-defined dark shaft-streaks and weaker median covert pattern (but normally obvious well into first winter; see Ring-billed Gull). Rarely develops traces of pale mirror on P10 (Grant 1986b, pers. obs.).

First-summer (Apr–Sep) as first-winter, but head white or with reduced dark streaking, rarely a faint darker ear-spot. Upperwing much faded: coverts off-white and P6–10 greyish-brown from late May; grey mantle makes good contrast to upperwing. Bill yellowish, often with greyish or pinkish tinge. Tip black, sometimes with paler extreme tip (prominent from Aug). Legs greyish with yellowish, bluish or fleshy tinge.

Second-winter (Sep–Mar) Head and body as adult winter, but generally with broader streaks on crown to ear-coverts and more defined dark spots on hindneck and breast-sides. Upperwing similar to adult winter, but black on forewing extends onto P5–7 and along leading edge, including primary coverts and alula (which have narrow white fringes). Outer median coverts often with dark shaft-streaks. Dark markings generally duller and browner than in adult, especially from midwinter. White mirrors on P9–10 smaller (in P10 30–50mm, in >95% covering both webs; on P9 8–25mm (rarely lacking). P8 lacks mirror. P5 with 20–35mm black tip. P4 normally with narrow black subterminal spot on outer web (lacking in adult); sometimes narrow dark subterminal markings on P3(2). White primary tips narrower than in adults; usually worn off by midwinter. May show some brown-tinged outer lesser coverts (rarer median or greater coverts) and small black spots on tertials. Brown-tinged coverts less frequent than in *kamtschatschensis* and Mew Gull. Secondaries and tail as adult, but a few birds show dark markings, typically as isolated spots (1–5% in W Europe midwinter, 1 of 300 in Great Britain in winter (Grant 1986b) though latter figure considered to be too low (Cade 1982)). Rarely, juvenile-like tail-bar present (Jörgensen 1982, Holst & Ullman 1984). Underwing white, sometimes with narrow dark fringes to lesser coverts and primary coverts. Eye as adult. Orbital ring sometimes pinkish from Feb. Bill blue-grey or grey-green (rarely pale yellow) with dark tip or subterminal bar, generally broader and more complete than in adult winter; tip often yellow. Legs blue-grey, fleshy or yellowish.

Second-summer (Mar–Oct) as second-winter, but head and body white or just with narrow dark spots or streaks. Black areas fade to brownish with wear.

Third-winter (Sep–Apr) as adult winter, but sometimes with small black spot or border on inner web of P4, black spot on alula and narrow dark shaft streaks to outer greater primary coverts. Legs as adult, but sometimes fleshy-tinged.

Subsequent plumages as adult. As in large gulls, traces of 'immaturity', such as dark markings on primary coverts and dark smudges on greater coverts, may occur in older birds as well, e.g. a six-year-old showed dark spots on upper primary coverts (H. J. Lehto *in litt.*; R. Strack and K. Pedersen pers. comm.; control of ringed bird).

Aberrants Adults with pale irides known (see above). Adult with reddish tinge to bill observed in Feb. A second-winter with an all-dark bill and unusually heavy dark head-markings, creating a darkish half-hood, was described from the Netherlands. A first-summer bird with a dark face covering the forehead between forecrown, bill and throat also known. A few first-years have broad white rounded terminal spots near tips of P6–10. An extremely patterned first-year bird showed uniform greyish-brown hindneck, breast-sides and breast and apparently all-dark tail; rump and undertail-coverts typical for *canus*; underwing pale with dark bars, similar to Ring-billed Gull. Leucistic birds white with pale grey mantle (as pale or paler than Glaucous Gull), whitish coverts and dark areas on the wings and tail (first-year) pale brown, often restricted compared to normal individuals. Albinos, both 100% with pale bare parts and part-albinos with many white wing-coverts, known. Rosy tinge to breast exceptional (Mauer 1984, Yésou 1985a, Hein & Martens 2002, H. J. & H. Lehto *in litt.*).

Hybrids For hybrids with **Black-headed** and **Mediterranean Gulls**, see these species. Hybridisation between Common and Ring-billed Gull has been suspected in Canada (Weseloh & Mineau 1986).

GEOGRAPHICAL VARIATION Three taxa.

L. c. canus (NW Europe to Baltic and coast of Russia east to Moscow and Kola Peninsula. Winters N, W and S Europe) described above. Wings on average shortest in S part of breeding range (see Measurements).

L. c. heinei (Russia E of range of *canus*; from E of Moscow and between Kanin Peninsula and basin of Lena River; occurrence further E poorly established (Dement'ev & Gladkov 1969). Winters Baltic to Black Sea and NW Europe, rarer Persian Gulf to Pakistan; recorded on migration E Asia and rarely in winter in Korea and Hong Kong (G.J. Carey *in litt*)) Very similar to *canus*. Intergrades common in W Russia, including both wing/tarsus length and plumage characters, making field identification impossible in all but large birds. Combination of *heinei* measurements and *canus* plumage characters common in Estonian breeders; many wintering birds from the Baltic have *canus* measurements combined with *heinei* plumage characters (Johansen 1961, Carey & Kennerley 1996, Bengtsson & Pedersen 1998, pers. obs., skins in UZM, ZMA). Ringing recoveries of Danish and Dutch winter birds from breeding areas of *heinei* (Russia, Kazakhstan; K. T. Pedersen *in litt.*) confirms occurrence in W Europe. Only birds showing a combination of *heinei* measurements *and* plumage characters are included in the summary below and measurement series.

L. c. heinei often has a fuller head (and thus sometimes a smaller-*looking* bill) than *canus*. Has 'hanging hand' habit (as in Iceland Gull) as a result of longer wings. On folded wing, tertials cover three (four) inner primaries (four in *canus*). Compared to *canus*, wing-tip generally more pointed: P10 (0)4–10mm longer than P9 (0–7mm longer in *canus*). Bill generally heavier and more parallel-edged. In the hand, males can be separated on a humerus length of 98.5 or more, ulna length of 112 or more and radius length of 198.5 or more, with females 95.5, 107 and 104 respectively (Kompanje & Post 1993). **Adult** Has smoky-grey upperparts (Kodak Grey Scale 6–8), lacking the bluish tinge of *canus*. Has narrower but (owing to darker ground colour of primary bases) more distinct white 'moons' between black wing-tip and grey primary bases. Upperparts gradually darker towards E of range. On average it has very slightly less white mirrors on P9–10 than *canus* (of no real use apart from extremes in the hand): on P10 40–60mm, sometimes with angled division to dark base, on P9 8–35 (45)mm, creating narrower, more triangular white spot on wing-tip, sometimes similar to Ring-billed and Herring Gull race *argenteus*; more frequently, adults have dark markings near the tip of P4. P1–5 grey, at most with very narrow white tips, but (owing to darker grey coloration) appearing more distinct (broader white in *canus*) and narrower than white trailing edge to inner wing. Bill generally deeper yellow than in *canus*, often with more complete dark subterminal bar even in summer (pers. obs., Kazakhstan and Siberia, Jun). Legs deeper yellow; may be similar to Lesser Black-backed Gull.

Head and underparts generally heavier marked in **winter/first-years**, sometimes forming complete dark-spotted necklace or large dark patch around eye (rare in *canus*). Rump and tail-base with heavy dark markings. **First-winter** similar to *canus*, but greater upperwing-coverts on average darker, deeper brownish-tinged, typically with weak dark subterminal spots; outer greater coverts gradually darker; sometimes similar to first-year Lesser Black-backed. Greater coverts may, however, be paler, offset by better wing contrast: lesser coverts generally darker brown than in *canus*, creating a stronger dark leading edge to the inner wing. Underwing similar to *canus*, but often paler with narrower, more distinct dark edges to coverts and axillaries; some with barred axillaries as in Eurasian Curlew *Numenius arquata*, others white (underwing then resembling first-year Ring-billed Gull). Dark tail-bar similar to *canus* (40–51mm on T1). May develop pale bill-tip from May, earlier than *canus*. **Second-winter** more often than *canus* has dark markings on lesser coverts, secondaries and tail (in about 10%; dark tail markings in 25% of Common Gulls in Finland, winter (Peltomäki 2000) suggests *heinei*). Size, wing-tip pattern and more heavily marked head and body in winter plumage invites confusion with Ring-billed Gull, but as dark as or darker than *canus* (Ring-billed paler than *canus*).

Moult generally later than in *canus*. Most adults still show winter head in mid-Apr, when S Scandinavian breeders are white-headed (pers. obs.). P1–2 late Jun. Moult to **first-winter** on average later (Aug–Nov); in late Sep no sign of moult to first-winter (Tove 1993). Most Oct–Dec birds show <50% new mantle feathers (all or most of mantle normally renewed in southern *canus*; moult of N *canus* similar (Bengtsson & Pedersen 1998). Most Finnish winter birds (showing *heinei* characters) retain >50% juvenile mantle late Dec. Primary moult probably slightly later than *canus*.

L. c. kamtschatschensis **Kamchatka Gull** (Kamchatka and Sea of Okhotsk to NE Siberia, where overlapping with *heinei*; intermediates Yakutia and Lena River region. Clinal division with *heinei* in Anadyr, Kolyma and Indirka. Populations from Anadyr and Alaseja sometimes treated as *kamtschatschensis*. Winters coastal E Asia, regularly S to Hong Kong; vagrant Alaska (Portenko 1939, Dement'ev 1940, Cramp & Simmons 1983, Tove 1993). A distinct (the largest) taxon, probably requiring fully specific status. Largest male approaches size of small Herring Gulls. Jizz-wise an over-sized *canus/heinei* with a more sloping forehead, flatter crown, deeper breast and slightly longer, deeper bill (as in *canus* with narrow base and gently hooked tip), which often looks long. Large, rounded head and narrow bill are main separation points from Ring-billed Gull. Eyes generally smaller than in *canus/heinei*.

Adult Upperpart colour similar to *heinei* or slightly darker (Kodak Grey Scale 6–9; rarely almost as dark as adult Black-tailed Gull). Primary pattern similar to *heinei*: white mirrors on P10 40–80mm, on P9 20–60mm; division from black base as in *canus*, but some with more angled division on outer web of P10 (as in Mew Gull; in *canus* and most *heinei* more rounded). P8 black grading to grey at base. Shows conspicuous white tongues on P5–7(8); rarely as prominent as in Mew on P8. P4 frequently with dark markings. As in *canus*, P1–5 have white tips, although in many matching the narrower tips of *heinei*, and in some as grey as in most *heinei*. P10 4mm >P9. Wing pattern from below as *canus/heinei*, but often with darker secondaries in better contrast to rest of underwing. Bill and legs similar to *canus/heinei*. Iris normally mid-brown to dark yellow, creating bicoloured eye. In **winter** head, breast-sides, breast and especially hindneck more densely dark-marked, similar to Ring-billed. Streaks around eye and on ear-coverts often narrow, in contrast to broader hindneck streaks, which may form distinct dark necklace, continuing to brown-washed neck- and breast-sides. The most strongly patterned birds look hooded with dense brown spotting on whole head. Iris varies: in some pale straw, matching Ring-billed (Carey & Kennerley 1996), in others mid-brown to dark to create a bicoloured eye; often darkish-looking (as in *canus/heinei*) at any distance. Bill similar to *canus/heinei*; dark bill markings often weaker (and more frequently lacking), and distal part of bill often warmer yellow.

First-years intermediate between *heinei* and Mew Gull. Compared to *canus* and *heinei* darker and more greyish-brown with extensive streaks, spots or washed-out markings on crown, ear-coverts, hindneck and underbody (especially at breast-sides around wing-bend, which may look washed or scaled). Flanks often extensively dark-spotted or barred, together with breast-sides and upper belly often the darkest areas on the underparts. Forehead, chin, throat and sometimes belly may be paler, thus barely differing from *canus/heinei*. Undertail-coverts white with extensive dark Vs or bars, sometimes reduced to along sides of tail-coverts, but in other cases creating distinct patterning or barring, similar to Mew. Lesser and median coverts with triangular dark centres and pale edges (as in Ring-billed). Greater coverts greyish-brown, sometimes darkening through distal part (especially innermost). Underwing-coverts have broader dark tips and axillaries than *canus/heinei*, creating much darker underwing; a small proportion are identical to *canus/heinei*. Rump and tail-coverts with dark spots or bars; sometimes complete barring across tail-coverts and rump as in Mew Gull, although dark bars generally narrower. Flight feathers similar to *canus/heinei*, but on average browner, primaries with more conspicuous white edges. Dark tail-bar as in *canus/heinei*, but usually broader (55–60mm on T1). Inner webs of rectrices (especially T4–6) may be dark-mottled, creating washed-out markings on edges of tail (as in Ring-billed, not seen in *canus/heinei*) and some have as extensive dark on tail as Mew (King & Carey 2000). White tail-tip generally broader than in *canus* and *heinei*. First-winter bill pinkish with clear-cut black tip, often similar to Ring-billed, but pink frequently dulled by grey tinge well into winter.

Juvenile plumage often mainly retained in first-winter;

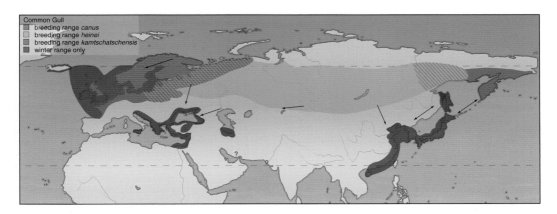

Common Gull
- breeding range *canus*
- breeding range *heinei*
- breeding range *kamtschatschensis*
- winter range only

just scattered first-winter mantle and scapular feathers present in rather fresh-looking juvenile plumage into Feb in most (pers. obs. Japan, Feb). Advanced birds have renewed most of mantle and scapulars Nov/Dec. Plumage development slower than in *canus/heinei* with more immature characters present in **second-winter**. This plumage often a mixture between first-year and adult. Compared to adult, white mirrors on P9–10 smaller (max. 40mm on P10; often lacking on P9) and dark subterminal markings on primaries reach P3. Mantle and scapulars grey, upperwing-coverts often a contrasting brownish-grey with faint pale edges. Most show scattered dark-marked secondaries/tertials, and dark barred uppertail-coverts and underwing (unlike *canus/heinei*, but similar to Mew and Ring-billed Gulls). Normally with traces of dark tail-bar. Iris often pale. **Third-winter** as adult, but sometimes with faint dark markings on primary coverts.

Note In many ways, *kamtschatschensis* represents 'the missing link' between *canus/heinei* and Ring-billed Gull, sharing size of the latter but most characters of the former (pale iris of adult and first-year plumage, however, are closer to Mew Gull); this was pointed out by Johansen (1961), who suggested specific status for *kamtschatschensis*. Stejneger (1885) regarded *kamtschatschensis* as an Asiatic representative of Ring-billed Gull.

DISTRIBUTION AND MIGRATION Around 1 million pairs (all taxa). Breeds on cliffs, islands, beaches, marshes, lakes, upland tundra and sometimes drier grassy areas, usually near water and often in dense colonies. Locally in towns. Winters along coasts, estuaries and inland, especially near agriculture and townships.

L. c. canus has expanded/increased its range to the W and expanded in the E since 1900. A local strong decline in Fennoscandia is probably linked to competition with the increasing Herring Gull population, forcing birds to move from the coast to inland areas. In Europe 450,000–550,000 pairs in the mid-1990s; stronghold W and N. Countries with the largest breeding numbers (in pairs): Great Britain 72,000, Denmark 25,000–30,000 (100,000 1940s, 60,000 1970s), Norway 150,000, Sweden 250,000 (145,000 1970–1980; in some areas recent decrease), Finland 42,000, Germany 18,000, Netherlands 6,000–7,900 (max. 11,500 pairs in

1980s), Russia 40,000–60,000, Estonia 17,000, Belarus 500–1,200, Faeroe Islands 500–1,000, Iceland 350–450. Small populations S to France (29–33 pairs 1998), C European lakes and Hungary. Recolonised Netherlands 1908, first bred Belgium 1924, Iceland, Poland and Germany 1955–1958, Switzerland 1966, Faeroe Islands 1980 (Møller 1978, Glutz von Blotzheim & Bauer 1982, Cramp & Simmons 1983, Hario 1985a, Malling Olsen 1992, Gjershaug *et al.* 1994, del Hoyo *et al.* 1996, Hagemeijer & Blair 1997, Väisinen *et al.* 1998).

Short- or medium-distance migrant, mainly within or close to breeding range S to N France and Adriatic Sea to E Mediterranean; scarce in Iberian Peninsula and S Mediterranean (in severe winters in W Europe more frequent in Iberia and S Mediterranean). Scandinavian, Finnish, NW and N German and Russian birds winter mainly between S Scandinavia (Waddenzee and Great Britain) and C France. Fewer reach Iberian Peninsula and Morocco. Some S Swedish, Finnish and German birds perform longer migrations to France, Iberia and Morocco. Some E Swedish birds and Finnish birds cross Europe in S/SE direction, with recoveries in Italy and Greece. Norwegian and NW Russian birds winter from E North Sea to Great Britain, especially N England, and to a lesser degree in the S Baltic Sea. Dutch birds are mainly sedentary. British and Faeroe/Iceland birds are sedentary or migrate to S England and Ireland. Ringing recoveries include birds from Iberian Peninsula and Denmark found in Great Britain, an Icelandic bird in Canada and a Kaliningrad bird in Faeroe Islands (Cramp & Simmons 1983, Kilpi & Saurola 1985, Bengtsson & Pedersen 1998). In winter 40,000–50,000 Denmark, 50,000 Kattegat. W Germany max. 30,000. Netherlands 80,000 at sea and 90,000–190,000 inland. In Great Britain 702,000 (423,000 England and Wales, 211,500 Scotland and 67,500 Ireland). France 73,000-100,000. In C Europe max. 2,000 Switzerland, 4,000 Bodensee and 5,000 Neusiedler See. Late arrival (mostly Nov, peak early Dec) suggests many *heinei* involved. Many in W Black Sea, e.g. in mid Jan 1997, 17,000 15 km from Cape Kaliakra, Bulgaria. Scarcer SE Europe, Ukraine, Mediterranean and NW Africa, especially first-years (Glutz von Blotzheim & Bauer 1982, Cramp & Simmons 1983, Schuster *et al.* 1983, Lack 1986, Jensen 1993, Khymyn 1993, Bijlsma *et al.* 2001, B. Nikolov, P. Yésou *in litt*).

Migration mainly coastal. S Scandinavian autumn

migration in two main waves. First includes Fennoscandian and Baltic breeders, in S Sweden/Denmark migration starting mid-Jun with second-years (peak late Jun–early Jul); adult vanguards mid-Jun, peak mid-Jul–early Aug. Juveniles scarce into Aug, peaking Sep–Oct, but often still abundant Oct when second wave of adults starts, peaking late Oct–mid-Nov; probably mainly Russian birds, including *heinei*. Peak counts in both waves >15,000 along main migration route in S Baltic (Öland and S Scania, Sweden) and 4,500 Alingsås, mid-Sweden; mainly adults, as juveniles spread more in all directions. Majority from latter wave overshoot first wave and continue to W Europe. Main adult arrival in W Baltic/North Sea Aug–Sep. Large roosts along migration route: in E Denmark max. flocks of 21,000, in N Denmark exceptionally up to 65,000 late Sep. In W Schleswig-Holstein 40,000–50,000 Sep–Oct, in Netherlands max. 70,000 Jul. Smaller numbers migrate from Baltic S and SW (SE) crossing C Europe for wintering area there (Glutz von Blotzheim & Bauer 1982, Cramp & Simmons 1983, Malling Olsen 1992, Breife *et al.* 1993, Jensen 1993, Dubois *et al.* 2000).

Spring migration C, W and N Europe begins mid-Feb, peaks Mar–mid-Apr (adult) to late Apr–mid-May (first-years). Arrives S Baltic breeding sites Mar. Most first-years summer away from breeding sites, e.g. >90% in C Europe in May.

Vagrant N to Spitsbergen, Bear Island, Greenland, and NE USA (regular, including bird ringed at Murmansk); also Morocco, Mauritania, Libya, Canary Islands, the Azores, Senegal (Vernon 1969, Glutz von Blotzheim & Bauer 1982, Cramp & Simmons 1983, Schuster *et al.* 1983, Urban *et al.* 1986, Boertmann 1994, Yésou & Triblet 1995).

L. c. heinei N Siberia and C Russia, winters between S Baltic, Mediterranean and Caspian Sea, to a lesser degree Middle East and Persian Gulf. Migrants ringed E Denmark, SW Sweden, N Germany, Netherlands and Great Britain recovered within range of *heinei*; one Danish bird in Kazakhstan. Generally scarce, but in some winters good numbers S Scandinavia and N Germany (in winter 2000/2001 50% of Common Gulls at Kiel, N Germany). Scarce E Mediterranean and N Black Sea, probably arriving after crossing Turkey or via Black Sea/Bosporus. E Mediterranean and Middle East population (mainly late Oct–Mar) show intermediate characters between *canus* and *heinei*, and probably involves both subspecies. In Greece regular early Nov–Mar; max. 1,055 Evros Delta. In Red Sea, Gulf States and eastwards population is more typical of *heinei*. Scarce Israel (20–50 annually) and Kuwait. Rare Pakistan. Some migrate S from Mongolia to wintering sites in China; E population migrates along E China coast Sep–Oct with a few reaching Hong Kong. At Beidaihe, Hebei Province, scarce migrant May (mainly immatures), commoner in autumn. Vagrant Syria, Persian Gulf, India, Nepal, Bhutan (Cramp & Simmons 1983, Osborn 1985, Nightingale & Hill 1993, Carey & Kennerley 1996, Shirihai 1996b, Handrinos & Akriotis 1997, Bengtsson & Pedersen 1998, Grimmett *et al.* 1998, van den Berg & Bosman 1999, Gantlett 1999, Hein & Martens 2002, G. Carey & K. Pedersen *in litt.*, pers. obs.).

L. c. kamtschatschensis winters E Asia between S Ussuriland, Japan and S China. Migrates along E China coast together with easternmost *heinei*, but later in autumn with peak Oct–Nov (del Hoyo *et al.* 1996, Carey & Kennerley 1996, P. Schiermacker-Hansen *in litt.*, pers. obs.).

MEASUREMENTS Lengths in mm; weights in g. Own data based on skins in AMNH, MCZ, MVZ, NHM, NRK, UZM, ZMA, ZMO. *L. c. canus* Denmark (breeders and wintering birds), Great Britain. *L. c. heinei* Dvine and Yenisei Rivers, W Europe, Middle East, Iran, Iraq, Lake Baikal. *L. c. kamtschatschensis* E Siberia, Kamchatka, China, Japan.

WING

L. c. canus		
Adult male	328–390 (363.7)	115
Adult female	322–376 (346.1)	82
First-year male	330–374 (357.6)	54
First-year female	328–361 (345.7)	46

COMMON GULL Three-year gull. Three forms breed across W Palearctic and E Asia. Generally becomes larger and darker towards E of range. A medium-sized gull with plumage pattern resembling larger gull, but has large rounded head, large dark eyes and rather narrow bill lacking marked gonydeal angle of larger gulls.

Adult has medium-grey upperwing with black tip and two large white mirrors on outer wing, creating rounded white spot. White leading edge to secondaries and white tertial crescents strong. Bill and legs greenish-yellow. In **summer** (Apr–Sep) head is white and bare parts brightest. In **winter** (Sep–Mar) head dark-spotted, often strongest on hindneck. Bill in majority with faint dark markings, creating dark Z on bill-tip.

Juvenile (Jul–Sep) greyish-brown with pale-scaled brown saddle, darkish bill and fleshy legs. Wing pattern resembles larger gull: upperwing greyish-brown with darker flight feathers and faint pale window on inner part of outer wing. Underwing dark-barred or spotted. Shows distinct black tail-bar against white or slightly dark-spotted rump.

First-winter (Sep–Apr/May) similar to juvenile, but head and body white with dark spotting as in adult. Bill bicoloured with black tip and grey, fleshy, greenish or yellowish base.

Second-year similar to adult, but black wing-tip fuller, as it includes primary coverts and the wing-tip has smaller white mirrors. Bill generally with broader, fuller black tip or ring. Legs duller. May show dark secondaries and traces of dark tail-bar; these immature features most frequent in E Asia (see Geographical Variation).

Note Barth (1968a) gives for Norwegian adult male 330–392 (mean 365, n=75), adult female 325–360 (mean 345, n=74). British breeding adult male 328–362 (mean 347.8, n=10), adult female 327–356 (mean 335.7, n=11). Danish breeding adults: male 346–380 (mean 362.1, n=57), female 322–376 (mean 348.1, n=34). Mean in Danish winter adult male 368.1, adult winter female 348.7, indicating wintering birds from farther N and E. Average for breeding males from Iceland and Faeroe Islands 348.0, for first-winters similar to Danish wintering birds (350.4) (skins in UZM). First-winters N Germany 330-385(mean 357, n=30) (Hein & Martens 2002).

L. c. heinei

Adult male	358–405 (383.8)	31
Adult female	359–396 (371.1)	26
First-year male	366–386 (375.1)	7
First-year female	357–377 (370.0)	7

Note Glutz von Blotzheim & Bauer (1982) give for adult male 362–410 (mean 386.4, n=50), adult female 348–395 (mean 371.8, n=54). Il'icev & Zubakin (1990) give for adult male 355–402 (mean 381, n=46), adult female 350–400 (mean 371.0, n=36). Hein & Martens (2002) give for adult 361–393 (mean 384).

L. c. kamtschatschensis

Adult male	366–412 (383.8)	43
Adult female	346–390 (366.0)	26
First-year male	345–388 (371.5)	22
First-year female	335–377 (366.2)	20

BILL

L. c. canus

Adult male	31.2–40.5 (36.1)	116
Adult female	29.0–37.0 (32.7)	85
First-year male	29.5–37.3 (33.7)	53
First-year female	28.0–35.3 (31.2)	46

Note Barth (1968a) gives for Norwegian adult male mean 36.3 (n=75), adult female mean 32.9 (n=73). Mean in Danish adult: male 35.9, female 32.0. Great Britain adult: male 34.9, female 32.3. Iceland and Faeroes adult male 33.6.

L. c. heinei

Adult male	35.5–44.4 (39.7)	30
Adult female	30.2–42.1 (34.6)	26
First-year male	30.9–39.4 (35.4)	7
First-year female	32.9–39.6 (35.6)	7

Note Glutz von Blotzheim & Bauer (1982) give mean for adult male 41.8, adult female 39.4. Il'icev & Zubakin (1990) give for adult male 32–43 (mean 38.4, n=46), adult female 31–40 (mean 34.8, n=36).

L. c. kamtschatschensis

Adult male	36.6–45.0 (40.0)	45
Adult female	29.5–44.8 (36.5)	27
First-year male	32.5–41.6 (37.1)	23
First-year female	32.1–41.9 (35.6)	15

BILL DEPTH AT GONYS

L. c. canus

Adult male	9.4–12.2 (10.9)	116
Adult female	8.8–10.4 (9.8)	85
First-year male	9.0–10.9 (10.0)	53
First-year female	8.3–10.4 (9.5)	47

L. c. heinei

Adult male	10.5–12.8 (11.5)	30
Adult female	10.1–11.2 (10.6)	26
First-year male	10.0–12.2 (10.7)	7
First-year female	9.5–10.7 (10.2)	7

L. c. kamtschatschensis

Adult male	10.3–13.3 (11.8)	43
Adult female	9.2–12.5 (11.2)	26
First-year male	9.5–12.4 (10.9)	23
First-year female	9.4–12.0 (10.4)	15

BILL DEPTH AT BASE OF BILL

L. c. canus

Adult male	10.5–13.2 (12.0)	115
Adult female	9.4–12.0 (10.6)	85
First-year male	9.3–12.4 (11.9)	54
First-year female	8.8–11.8 (10.4)	47

L. c. heinei

Adult male	11.6–13.8 (12.7)	30
Adult female	10.5–12.8 (11.9)	26
First-year male	11.4–13.9 (11.9)	7
First-year female	10.4–12.4 (11.4)	7

L. c. kamtschatschensis

Adult male	11.5–16.1 (13.7)	43
Adult female	10.4–15.8 (12.8)	26
First-year male	10.9–14.7 (13.0)	23
First-year female	10.0–13.5 (12.0)	15

GONYS LENGTH

L. c. canus

Adult male	10.0–13.2 (11.8)	115
Adult female	9.3–11.8 (10.7)	85
First-year male	8.4–12.8 (10.9)	53
First-year female	8.6–11.7 (10.4)	45

L. c. heinei

Adult male	10.3–13.6 (12.1)	30
Adult female	9.6–13.2 (11.6)	26
First-year male	9.9–12.7 (11.2)	7
First-year female	10.8–12.7 (11.6)	7

L. c. kamtschatschensis

Adult male	10.3–14.0 (12.2)	43
Adult female	10.4–13.0 (11.7)	25
First-year male	8.3–12.6 (11.3)	23
First-year female	9.1–12.3 (11.1)	15

TARSUS

L. c. canus

Adult male	43.8–56.8 (50.8)	115
Adult female	42.4–52.1 (47.1)	85
First-year male	44.7–53.7 (49.8)	53
First-year female	42.8–51.6 (47.3)	45

Note Barth (1968a) gives for Norwegian adult male mean 52.1 (n=75), adult female mean 48.6 (n=73). Average for Danish breeding males 50.0, for wintering males 51.2; adult breeding females 45.9, adult wintering females 47.3, indicating wintering birds from farther north and east of breeding range. Average for adult males from Iceland and Faeroe Islands 46.7 (n=4, skins in UZM).

L. c. heinei

Adult male	50.2–63.0 (56.8)	30
Adult female	46.0–60.9 (53.4)	26
First-year male	46.5–57.2 (51.2)	6
First-year female	45.9–56.3 (51.4)	7

Note Glutz von Blotzheim & Bauer (1982) give mean for adult male 60.2, adult female 57.0. Il'icev & Zubakin (1990) give for adult male 49–63 (mean 55.9, n=46), adult female 49–61 (mean 53.5, n=36).

L. c. kamtschatschensis

Adult male	49.0–61.1 (55.8)	43
Adult female	48.0–58.3 (53.0)	25
First-year male	47.2–59.7 (54.1)	23
First-year female	48.7–56.8 (51.8)	15

Weight *L. c. canus* adult: male 325–552, female 290–530, generally heaviest in N part of breeding range (Barth 1968a, Cramp & Simmons 1983, skins). First- and second-winters 322–540 (Denmark, skins in UZM, ZMO). *L. c. heinei* mean adult male 547.6, adult female 495.6 (Glutz von Blotzheim & Bauer 1982). First-winter female with low fat-score 375 g. Second-winter females 435–458 (skins in UZM). *L. c. kamtschatschensis* first-winter 583 (skin in MCZ).

Common Gull *Larus canus*; **48-62.** nominate unless otherwise mentioned. **63-74** Kamchatka Gull *L. c. kamtschatschensis*.
48. Juvenile. When fledging greyish-brown with prominent pale-scaled saddle and darkish bill. Haapsala, Estonia. 15 Jul 1998. *Harry J. Lehto.* **49. 1st-winter**, possibly ssp. *heinei*. Grey mantle, developed late in summer, contrasts well with juvenile wing, including slightly paler, brownish-tinged greater coverts. A large and rather heavily marked individual, suggesting *heinei*. Helsinki, Finland. 29 Dec 1997. *Harry J .Lehto.* **50. 1st-winter.** Note clear-cut black tail-bar against white rump and tail-base. Upperwing lacks strong contrast of several similar-looking species such as Mediterranean and Ring-billed Gulls. Damhussøen, Denmark. 14 Nov 1992. *Klaus Malling Olsen.* **51. 1st-winter.** White tail shows solid and clear-cut black tail-bar. Compare with Ring-billed Gull (photo 102). Copenhagen, Denmark. Feb. *Per Schiermacker-Hansen.*

Common Gull *Larus canus*. **52. 1st-winter**. Underwing-coverts and axillaries normally with rather prominent dark tips. Lynæs, Zealand, Denmark. 5 Jan 1997. *Klaus Malling Olsen*. **53. 1st-winter** ssp. *heinei*. Normally inseparable from *canus*. This bird shows narrower dark underwing markings than 52, but underwing still rather uniform. Compare with Mediterranean Gull photos 688 and 689. Chumunjin, South Korea. 11 Dec 2000. *Jon R. King*. **54. 1st-summer**. Note worn and bleached saddle and new coverts, evident from spring. Halland, Sweden. 29 May 1993. *Klaus Malling Olsen*. **55. 2nd-summer**. Compared to adult, 2nd-year shows less white/more black in wing-tip, including markings on primary coverts. Porkkala, Finland. 26 May 1995. *Henry Lehto*. **56. Adult summer**. Note gentle impression with large, dark eye centrally placed in rounded head. Greenish-tinged bill and legs. North Jutland, Denmark. June. *Hanne & Jens Eriksen*.

Common Gull *Larus canus*. **57. Adult winter**. Note faint streaking or spotting on head and narrow black ring ('Z-shaped' mark in profile) around bill. Note paler eyes of this bird and compare with Ring-billed (photos 108 and 109) and Mew Gull (photo 83). Compare Ring-billed Gull. IJmuiden, Netherlands. 11 Feb 1985. *Arnoud B. van den Berg*. **58. Adult winter**, probably ssp. *heinei*. A bird with unusual short and bright yellow bill as well as dark spotting on entire head. Turku, Finland. 6 Jan 1998. *Harry J. Lehto*. **59. Adult summer**. Note broad, rounded spot in wing-tip and prominent white trailing edge to wing. Ottenby, Öland, Sweden. 26 May 1993. *Klaus Malling Olsen*. **60. 3rd- or adult winter**. The rather narrow white markings on P9 and very narrow dark shaft streaks to outer greater primary coverts indicate 3rd-winter. White tips to inner primaries fainter than in 59, possibly indicating *heinei*. Copenhagen, Denmark. 29 Mar 1997. *Klaus Malling Olsen*. **61. Adult summer**. Storebælt, Denmark. June. *Hanne & Jens Eriksen*. **62. 1st-, 2nd-and adult summer** ssp. *heinei*. Compared to *canus*, may appear square-headed with slightly longer, more drooping wing-tip, but normally not identifiable in the field. Lake Baikal, Russia. Jun 1991. *Werner Suter*.

Kamchatka Gull *L.c. kamtschatschensis*. The largest taxon. Compared to *canus* and *heinei* slightly larger with squarer head and especially stronger bill, often longish-looking. **63. 1st-year (juvenile moulting into 1st-winter)** Many 1st-years are basically juvenile into mid-winter. This bird show a mixture of juvenile and 1st-winter mantle and scapulars. Dark centres to lesser and median coverts often more triangular (rounder in *canus*), thus closer to Ring-billed Gull. Choshi, Honshu, Japan. 9 Feb 1999. *Jon R. King*. **64. 1st-winter.** Well-marked individual with almost velvety underparts and strong dark barring on undertail-coverts. Choshi, Japan. Mar 2001. *Osao Ujihara*. **65. 1st-winter.** Note solid dark belly and underwing markings, typical for this taxon. Hokkaido, Japan. 10 Feb 2001. *Klaus Malling Olsen*. **66. 1st-winter.** Another typical individual. Hokkaido, Japan. 13 Feb 2001. *Klaus Malling Olsen*. **67. 2nd-winter.** Unlike *canus/heinei*, 2nd-year plumage typically shows good contrast between grey saddle and brownish-tinged, slightly patterned upperwing. Honshu, Japan. 4 Dec 2000. *Osao Ujihara*.

Kamchatka Gull *L.c. kamtschatschensis*. **68. 1st-winter**. Note long-billed appearance compared to *canus* and generally paler-tinged upperwing. Dark tail-bar generally broader than in *canus* and *heinei*. Honshu, Japan. Feb 2001. *Paul Doherty*. **69. 2nd-winter**. Grey saddle in some contrast with brown-tinged coverts. Dark markings in tail and secondaries often present at this age, unlike most *canus* and *heinei*. Choshi, Honshu, Japan. 13 Feb 2000. *Jon R. King*. **70. Adult summer**. Eye smaller than in *canus* and *heinei*. Magadan, East Siberia, Russia. 18 May 1999. *Ingo Weiss*. **71. Adult winter**. Eyes often pale unlike *canus* and *heinei*. Head markings generally more 'watered-down' and extensive. Choshi, Honshu, Japan. 12 Feb 1999. *Jon R. King*. **72. Adult winter**. Note faint brown hindneck spotting. Hokkaido, Japan. 10 Jan 2001. *Osao Ujihara*. **73. Adult winter**. Solid dark head-markings often appear as dark necklace. Choshi, Honshu, Japan. 11 Feb 1999. *Jon R. King*. **74. Adult winter**. Honshu, Japan. Feb 2001. *Paul Doherty*.

6. MEW GULL
Larus brachyrhynchus (Richardson, 1831, Northwest Territories, Canada)

Plates 10–11, Photos 75–85

IDENTIFICATION Length 38–41cm, wingspan 100–120cm. Alternative name Short-billed Gull.
Mew Gull is the Nearctic counterpart to Common Gull, from which it differs in structure, plumages and mitochondrial DNA (Zink *et al.* 1995). It is similar to Common Gull, but smaller with a rounder head and shorter, weaker bill with a more tapering tip. The wings are slightly longer. The very short bill makes it look even gentler than Common.
The range overlaps with Common Gull taxon *kamtschatschensis* and Ring-billed Gull. Both are larger, Ring-billed being largest with a heavier, more parallel-edged bill with a more hooked tip than Mew. Ring-billed shows a flatter crown and fuller, more angled hindneck, and as soon as the adult upperpart coloration is assumed it appears much paler than in Mew. From one year of age eyes are much paler. Common Gull *kamtschatschensis* has a rounded head, but longer (often thinner) bill and smaller eyes than Mew.
Adult Similar to Common Gull nominate *canus*, but with more white/less black on wing-tip; unlike Common, it has extensive white on P8, almost falling level with white mirrors on P9–10, and broader white tongues on P6–7. Some birds have a limited amount of white on P8 and smaller white tongues, with the wing-tip barely differing from Common. Also, a few Common—probably males—have a wing-tip pattern similar to Mew with an extensive white tongue on P8. At the other extreme certain Mew Gulls, probably males, show enough white on P8 (as well as P9–10) to exhibit a wing-tip similar to Thayer's Gull, see page 32. Bill yellow. Eyes mid-brown to yellow. Legs yellow-greenish. In **summer**, head is white and bill deep yellow. In **winter** head is brown-washed, always conspicuous on the hindneck, where often forming a dark half-collar. May show faint darker eye-mask and extensive markings from head spreading down to breast-sides. The pattern is more washed out than in Common with more extensive dark on breast sides than in Common *canus/heinei*. Bill greenish-yellow, generally with deeper yellow tip. If present, faint grey subterminal bar is weaker than the darker markings in Common. Legs greenish.
Juvenile brown with pale-scalloped back, dark bill and fleshy pink legs. Upperwing similar to Common nominate *canus*, but median coverts have more pointed centres and greater coverts sometimes show indistinct dark waving (as in Ring-billed and Common *kamtschatschensis*). Greater coverts brownish-grey. The primaries are dark brown with broader pale tips; in Common the primaries are blackish. Most importantly, the tail is brown and the rump heavily barred, creating an impression of these parts being the darkest part of the bird—a feature never seen in Common and Ring-billed. The pattern matches rump and tail of Thayer's Gull. Also, the undertail-coverts are distinctly barred and the belly is often extensively mottled dark, unlike the whiter, more sparsely spotted belly of Common. Underwing-coverts are mainly greyish-brown, as densely patterned as in Common *kamtschatschensis*.

First-winter attained from Aug, when mantle becomes (partly) grey, forehead paler and bill pale with black tip. Juvenile plumage may be more or less retained into midwinter; especially the extensive dark mottling and waving on head, hindneck, underbody and underwing is often partly retained, creating darker and more washed-out head and body than in Common or Ring-billed. Most still have extensive dark in underparts, but rear belly may be white. Mantle/scapulars normally a mixture of grey and pale brown (juvenile) feathers. Primaries have conspicuous pale fringes. Some advanced birds moult parts of upper wing-coverts in autumn, unlike Common and Ring-billed.
From midwinter, flight feathers and tail fade to brown and greater coverts fade to whitish, losing any dark pattern. This wear is more extensive in flight feathers and tail than in Common and Ring-billed. Grey mantle contrasts strongly with wing (similar to Ring-billed, frequent in Common *kamtschatschensis*, but rare in Common *canus/heinei* before Mar), especially striking in **first-summer** before it moults into second-winter. Legs fleshy, greenish or yellowish.
First-year Common and Ring-billed Gulls have a mainly white head and underbody with more distinct dark streaks or spots on the head (especially hindneck), breast and underbody, but just scattered dark spots, not bars, on belly, undertail-coverts and rump. The flight feathers are darker with narrower pale tips and bicoloured tail with extensive white base against blackish tail-bar. Underwing paler with more distinct dark rows; Ring-billed often shows an extensive whitish panel on underwing. Furthermore upper greater coverts cleaner grey and tail white with several, often broken dark bars. Only Common *kamtschatschensis* frequently shows a complete dark-barred rump and mostly dark tail, but it is larger. Other taxa have white tail with clear-cut dark bar. **Second-winter** similar to adult winter, but with brownish-black, more solid dark wing-tip (including primary coverts) and smaller white mirrors on P9–10. Compared to Common nominate *canus* and Ring-billed Gull, the plumage shows more 'immature' features: lesser coverts often brownish-tinged. Most show dark markings on secondaries, tail, axillaries and underwing-coverts. Tail varies from white to brown (as in first-years), but in most birds it is white with black spots, which may form a black tail-bar. Compared to adult, the bill is duller with a more solid black tip or subterminal bar. Legs are often grey with a fleshy to greenish tinge. **Second-summer** similar to second-winter, but head, bill and body as adult summer.
Third-winter as adult, but sometimes with indistinct dark markings on primary coverts and sometimes black P8.

VOICE Long-call similar to Common Gull with up to two distinct sections, introductory screechy longer notes, followed by repetitive notes. (A. Jaramillo *in litt*).

MOULT (skins in UZM, USNM, NHM, MCZ, MVZ,

PLATE 10. MEW GULL *Larus brachyrhynchus*

A Nearctic counterpart of Common Gull, breeding in NW North America, wintering along North American Pacific coastline to N Mexico. Similar to Common, but with shorter bill.
Smaller than Ring-billed Gull with rounder head, shorter and weaker bill, larger eyes and—in older birds—much darker grey upperparts.

1. **Juvenile** (Jul–Sep) Rather uniform greyish-brown with scaled, darker saddle, unpatterned greyish-brown greater coverts and greyish-brown underparts; undertail-coverts distinctly barred. Bill blackish. In plumage not too different from juvenile Thayer's, but much smaller with rounder head and short, weak bill (even compared to Ring-billed).

2. **First-winter** (Oct–Apr) Paler than juvenile, but still with extensive diluted dark markings on underbody. Saddle medium-grey, often with pale feather-fringes. Flight feathers and tail often brownish-tinged, former with pale edges. Head pattern diluted. Bill slightly bicoloured with fleshy base and black tip. Smaller, more round-headed than Ring-billed Gull with less streaking/more diluted markings on head and underbody and barred undertail-coverts; Ring-billed shows more distinct head-streaks and white underparts with fine chevrons or spots along flanks and on rump, as well as stronger, more contrasting bill pattern with paler pinkish base and more distinct black tip.

3. **First-summer** (Apr–Aug) Retained juvenile wing contrasts well with grey saddle. Underparts still diluted.

4. **Second-winter** (Aug–Apr) Upperparts as adult, but often with brown-centred lesser coverts, dark tertial and tail-markings, and only narrow white tips to primaries (sometimes non-existent). Bill duller with black bar or tip.

5. **Second-winter** More advanced individual, similar to adult winter, but note dark eye, faint grey markings on bill and only narrow white primary tips.

6. **Adult winter** (Sep–Apr) Head and hindneck with brownish diluted markings, often as 'woolly scarf' across hindneck. Brown head-markings often offset slightly by bicoloured eye in some individuals. Compared to Ring-billed Gull, bill much weaker and lacks strong black bar, head pattern more diluted, eyes darker and upperparts darker with more distinct white tertial crescents.

7. **Adult winter** Eye sometimes dark. This individual shows brighter yellow bill and legs than 6.

8. **Adult summer** (Apr-Sep) Head white, eyes dusky and orbital ring red. Bill unmarked yellow.

Juvenile

3. First-summer

2. First-winter

4. Second-winter

6. Adult winter

econd-winter

8. Adult summer

7. Adult winter

PLATE 11. MEW GULL *Larus brachyrhynchus*

In flight lighter with narrower wings than Ring-billed; similar to Common Gull. Head rounded with short bill.

1. **Juvenile** (Jul–Sep) Greyish-brown with weaker upperwing contrast than Ring-billed. Rump heavily barred and tail brownish-black (Common and Ring-billed show spotted rump, white tail and black tail-bar, very variable in Ring-billed, but tail never uniform dark). Underparts more diluted and underwing much more heavily marked than in Common and Ring-billed. Juveniles show brown head-markings extending onto body, scaled upperparts and all-dark bill.

2. **First-winter** (Oct–Apr) Face paler than in juvenile, and bill bicoloured; saddle grey with faint pale feather-edges. This individual shows paler tail-base than 1, but contrast never as strong as in Common and Ring-billed, and tail normally brownish-tinged, never strongly contrasting as rump brown-barred.

3. **Late first-winter** (Feb–Apr) With wear, upperwing contrast stronger, with much-faded flight feathers, tail and coverts in good contrast to grey saddle.

4. **Second-winter** (Aug–Apr) Similar to adult with conspicuous white trailing edge on dark grey upperwing, but with more black on wing-tip (in this illustration only P10 shows white mirror), including dark primary coverts. Normally shows traces of black tail-bar, and underwing still with dark pattern. These characters shared with larger, paler Ring-billed, but note diagnostic diluted brown head-markings and short bill.

5. **Second-winter** More advanced individual than 4 with unpatterned underwing, narrower dark markings on primary coverts and white mirrors on both P9 and P10.

6. **Adult winter** (Sep–Apr) Adult shows medium-grey upperwing with distinct white trailing edge as in Common, but unlike Ring-billed Gull, which is paler with indistinct white trailing edge. Typically shows broad white markings on mid-primaries onto P8, almost merging with large white mirrors on P9–10. This pattern is only rarely matched by Common and never by Ring-billed, which shows more complete black on outer wing and narrower white mirrors on P9–10. Note also yellow bill, at most with weak grey markings, and brownish diluted necklace.

7. **Adult summer** (Apr–Sep) Head white and bill yellow, lacking any dark markings. This individual shows – compared to 6 – more extensive black primary markings, more as in Common Gull. This is not too infrequent. Mirrors, however, still larger than in Ring-billed.

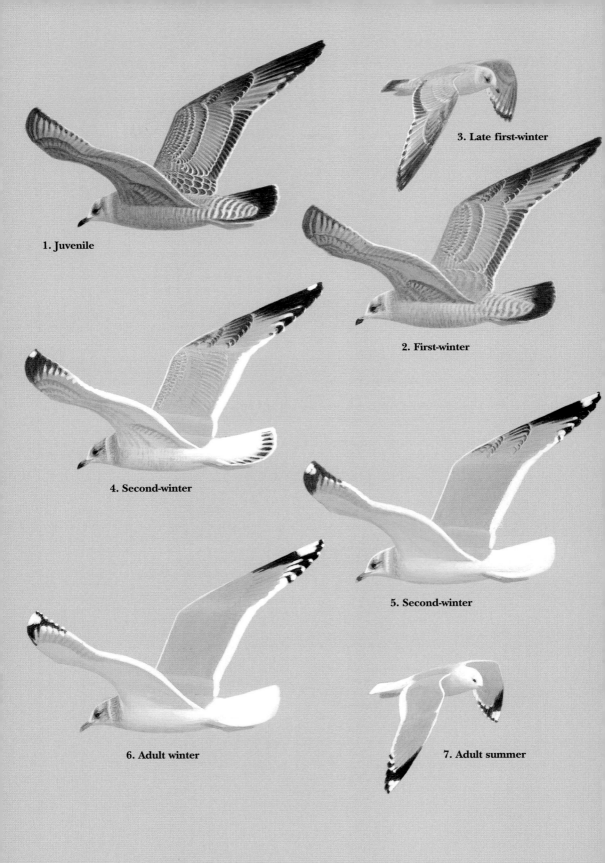

1. Juvenile

3. Late first-winter

2. First-winter

4. Second-winter

5. Second-winter

6. Adult winter

7. Adult summer

LACM) **Adult** moult to **winter** plumage complete following breeding season; generally later than Common; P1 late Jun, P2–3 generally late July. P5–6 mid-Aug, P7–8 late Aug–early Sep, P9–10 late Oct, but frequently into late Nov. Head and body late Jul–late Aug. **Juvenile** moult to **first-winter** partial late Aug–Nov, including head, much of underparts, 50–90(100)% of mantle/scapulars; a larger proportion than in Common nominate *canus* retains full juvenile plumage to Nov (Tove 1993); by Feb often a few juvenile mantle/scapular feathers still present. Moult to **second-winter** begins Apr–May, including head, underparts, rump and some mantle feathers; more extensive from late May. Moult to **second-winter** complete earlier than in adults, sometimes finished late Sep. Moult to **second-summer** and **third-winter** slightly earlier than in adults. A second-year had reached P6 late Jul.

DESCRIPTION

Compared to Common Gull slightly smaller with a more rounded head, weaker, parallel-edged bill with more gently tapering body and longer primary projection with 4–5(6) primary tips beyond tertials.

Adult Has, compared to Common Gull, a larger amount of white on P7–10; mirrors on P10 40–70 (100)mm before 10–15mm black tip. P9 with white mirror (15–50 mm; in 30–50° angle towards black bases on outer web); rarely most of inner web lacks black, creating pattern as in Thayer's Gull. P9 with extensive grey base. Shows 15–40mm conspicuous white tongues on P6–8. P5–8 with 15–60mm black subterminal spots, broadest on P8. Outer web of P8 with 90–115mm black; P8 rarely with isolated dark markings on inner web or with just indistinct white tongues, thus similar to Common Gull. Some show complete white inner webs on P5 often with black restricted to outer web. P4 sometimes with indistinct dark spot on outer web. P1–8 with 12–15mm white tips (disappearing with wear on P5–8). P10 0–6mm >P9. Some birds have wing-tip pattern similar to Common nominate *canus*. Grey on upperparts Kodak Grey Scale 5.5–7.5 (Johansen 1961, Tove 1993, Carey & Kennerley 1996, pers. obs.). Sometimes with narrow dark shaft-streaks on outer primary coverts (possibly younger adults). Bill and legs generally deeper yellow than in Common *canus/heinei*. Iris in >90% darkish: dull greenish-brown to olive, dull yellow, grey or dark amber, similar to or darker than Common *kamtschatschensis*. May appear bicoloured at closer range. A small proportion have pale eyes, but never whitish-yellow as in Ring-billed Gull (Carey & Kennerley 1996, pers. obs. California).

Adult summer (Apr–Sep) Head white. Bill deeper yellow than in Common nominate *canus*, lacking dark markings. Orbital ring orange-red to dark red. Rarely, legs and feet orange-yellow and bill reddish-orange.

Adult winter (Sep–Apr) Head, hindneck and breast-sides densely dark-mottled or -washed (rarely streaked), creating a grey-brown hood, sometimes as a dark cap, complete dark necklace, connecting with neck-sides; may show dark crescents in front of eye and washed-out dark ear-spot. Chin and throat less dark-patterned, sometimes white. Least-patterned birds have fine head-spots as in Common, but more often with traces of a grey ear-spot and crescent before the eye. Bill yellow to greenish-yellow, at most with very weak dark markings; in California late Jan–mid-Feb, 66% show no dark bill-markings, 28% a weak grey incomplete subterminal bill-ring, and 6% a complete but narrow grey bill-ring (pers. obs.). Orbital ring brown, dull red or rosy.

Juvenile (fledging–Aug/Nov) more like small first-year Thayer's than Common Gull. Head and body cleaner and darker greyish-brown than in Common and Ring-billed Gulls; rear belly often palest part of underbody. Most birds acquire pale forehead from Aug. Wing-markings paler and browner than in Common (apart from certain *kamtschatschensis*). Flight feathers dark brown with pale tips, creating a row of pale Vs on folded wing-tip. P10 rarely with small white mirror. Mantle, scapulars and tertials dark to greyish-brown with narrow pale edges; frequently paler subterminally or with darker shaft-streaks. Tail-coverts and rump heavily barred brown and white; bars of equal width. Tail dark greyish-brown; width of dark on T1 is 35–60mm. Base sometimes heavily dark-barred or mottled on pale grey background, diffusely divided from rest of tail by dark shading of tail-bar. Bases to T4–6 pale, but hard to observe in the field. Tail may show whitish edges and tips. Rarely, tail white with black bar (as in Common *canus/heinei* or certain Ring-billed; MCZ specimen 282339) or almost uniform brown, being darker than upperwing (J. R. King *in litt.*). Upperwing-coverts as Common *canus/heinei*, but median coverts sometimes with triangular centres as in Ring-billed and Common *kamtschatschensis* and generally broader pale edges. Greater coverts pale brown to grey, frequently with dark shading or bars. Underwing-coverts greyish-brown; greater underwing-coverts slightly paler with broad dark fringes. Coverts contrast slightly with paler surface of flight feathers. Bare parts as Common Gull.

First-winter (Aug/Nov–Apr) similar to juvenile, but forehead often whitish, crown spotted or streaked greyish-brown and chin/throat (sometimes neck-sides) pale greyish. Rest of head and underparts as juvenile, but sometimes with dark spot at rear ear-coverts and variable amount of white on underbody (especially central part). Mantle and scapulars mid-grey, sometimes with narrow dark shaft-streaks. A variable number of juvenile scapulars and lower mantle feathers retained in first-winter (Carey & Kennerley 1996; see also moult). Bill fleshy to greyish or yellow with diffusely marked darker outer 30–40% (as in first-year Iceland Gull nominate *glaucoides*); extreme tip sometimes pale. Legs as Common Gull, but more frequently yellow.

First-summer (mid-Feb–Jul) similar to first-winter, but grey saddle makes good contrast with very pale and faded coverts (especially greater coverts), which may form whitish midwing-panel; frequently whole outer wing whitish.

Second-year similar to adult, but normally with dark markings on secondaries, tail, tertials and sometimes lesser coverts, as in Ring-billed and eastern subspecies of Common (rarer in nominate *canus*, which see). P8–10 dark, duller and browner compared to adult with smaller white mirrors (on P10 10–60mm, on P9 0–30mm); pattern therefore more as adult Common *canus/heinei*. Compared to adult, shows more diffuse and irregular white tongues, broader dark subterminal markings on P4–5

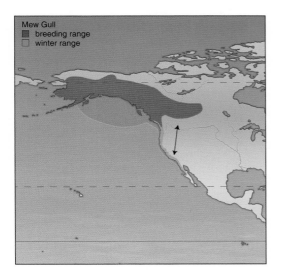

Mew Gull
■ breeding range
□ winter range

(28–39mm on T1), but otherwise with scattered black spots, sometimes creating black tail-bar similar to first-year Common Gull. Tail rarely as in first-year (Howell & McKee 1998, skins in MVC); 5–10% have white tail. Iris normally speckled brown, appearing darkish, but rarely pale as in a minority of adults. Legs pale greyish-green, often with bluish tinge. Bill similar to adult, but more frequently with dark subterminal markings to both mandibles and sometimes almost solid blackish tip.

Third-year as adult, but often with 'immature' traces such as browner tinge to primaries, dark shaft-streaks or faint brown markings on primary coverts, indistinct brown barring on uppertail-coverts and inconspicuous dark tail-markings; a few secondaries may be dark-marked. Wing-tip pattern as adult, but white tongue on P8 sometimes lacking.

DISTRIBUTION AND MIGRATION Population >10,000 pairs, mainly Alaska and NW Canada, probably Commander Islands. Coastal survey confirmed 1,700 pairs in 44 colonies, but at least three times that number along rivers. Breeding sites similar to Common Gull (del Hoyo *et al.* 1996).

Winters mainly along Pacific Coast S to Baja California with maximum counts of >10,300 Christmas Bird Count in California and 6,000 British Columbia; scarce Baja California. Irregular N Rocky Mountain region and Ontario. Very rare E North America. Scarce Commander Islands to Japan. Vagrant to most N American states, Hong Kong and Azores (Monroe 1988, 1989, Stepanyan 1990, Kwater 1992, Shitega 1993, Carey & Kennerley 1996). Claimed from Great Britain (Shepherd & Votier 1993).

MEASUREMENTS Lengths in mm; weights in g. Own data based on skins in AMNH, LACM, MCZ, MVZ, NHM, UZM. Canada, Alaska, Oregon and California. Included in adults are a few second-winters.

(frequently also on P3), narrower and less distinct white tips/edges to P1–8 (5–12mm; sometimes lacking with wear from midwinter). Primary coverts dark with pale edges. Tertials sometimes greyish-brown with broad white edges (Howell & McKee 1998). Upperwing-coverts otherwise as in adult, but often with brownish tinge on especially lesser coverts (as in Common Gull *kamtschatschensis*) and generally more prone to wear from midwinter. Underwing-coverts, axillaries and undertail-coverts often slightly dark-barred or spotted, typically as narrow, dark feather-fringes creating delicate scaly pattern similar to first-year Common *canus/heinei*. Breast often heavily dark-spotted, forming dark breast-bar, which may extend onto flanks and belly. Head-markings as in adult winter, but sometimes present in second-summer. Tail white, in most with some dark markings, in 5% as solid blackish bar

---

MEW GULL Three-year gull. A Nearctic counterpart to Common Gull, here treated as species separate from Common. Medium-sized with rounded head, large eyes and shortish bill, smaller and gentler than similar Ring-billed. From first-winter grey upperpart feathering darker than in Ring-billed.

Adult has medium-grey upperparts with distinct white trailing edge to inner wing and long white tongues in P5–8, almost falling equal to large white mirrors on P9–10. Some show restricted white markings, and may be similar to Common or even Ring-billed Gull. Shows prominent white tertial edges and scapular crescent. Eyes dark or slightly bicoloured, but never pale yellow as in Ring-billed. In **summer** (Apr–Sep) head white and bill yellow. In **winter** (Sep–Apr) head with washed-out brown waving or faint streaks, often densest and most solid on hindneck and breast-sides. Bill at most with faint grey markings.

Juvenile (Jul–Sep) has brownish head to underbody with distinct dark and solid bars on undertail-coverts. Upperwing similar to Common (less contrasting than in Ring-billed), but with browner outer wing. Rump densely dark-barred and tail almost solid dark. Underwing almost unpatterned dark. In **first-winter** (Oct–Apr) similar to juvenile, but saddle grey, contrasting with juvenile wing, which often shows paler midwing-panel through wear in late winter and spring. Head and underbody generally paler, but dense barring on lower body still prominent. Bill fleshy with black tip.

Second-year similar to adult, but with fuller dark wing-tip (including primary coverts) showing narrower white mirrors; coverts often brownish-tinged and secondaries and tail with dark markings – on tail often as black bar similar to Common and Ring-billed. Underwing often with faint dark markings. These immature markings shared with Ring-billed and eastern Common Gull *kamtschatschensis*.

WING		
Adult male	328–378 (357.4)	68
Adult female	328–369 (345.0)	78
First-year male	323–367 (351.5)	28
First-year female	313–357 (338.8)	57

BILL		
Adult male	31.3–40.3 (35.1)	68
Adult female	28.8–36.9 (32.7)	78
First-year male	29.7–37.3 (33.4)	28
First-year female	29.4–36.4 (32.1)	57

BILL DEPTH AT GONYS		
Adult male	9.0–11.2 (10.3)	68
Adult female	8.6–10.8 (9.5)	78
First-year male	8.6–10.4 (9.5)	30
First-year female	8.2–10.3 (9.1)	57

BILL DEPTH AT BASE OF BILL		
Adult male	10.3–12.6 (11.3)	68
Adult female	9.5–12.3 (10.4)	77
First-year male	9.9–12.0 (10.7)	29
First-year female	8.8–12.1 (10.2)	55

GONYS LENGTH		
Adult male	9.3–13.1 (11.7)	68
Adult female	9.3–12.4 (11.1)	77
First-year male	9.2–13.4 (11.2)	29
First-year female	8.3–12.6 (10.6)	58

TARSUS		
Adult male	45.0–54.2 (49.5)	68
Adult female	40.6–53.0 (47.0)	77
First-year male	44.4–53.9 (49.6)	29
First-year female	44.0–51.8 (47.3)	58

Weight Adult: male 376–493, female 326–394. Four first- to second-winter males 323–490; first-winter female 292, second-winter female 330 (skins in MCZ, MVC).

Mew Gull *Larus brachyrhynchus*. **75. Juvenile.** Overall impression pale greyish-brown, in plumage similar to Thayer's Gull, but much smaller. Note velvety brown, rather uniform head and underparts and mid-brown flight feathers. Anchorage, Alaska, USA. Jul 1989. *Ed Kwater.* **76. 1st-winter.** Slightly more spotted than 75, this individual resembles the larger and heavier Common Gull of taxon *kamtschatschensis*, but note very short bill, large eyes and rounded head. Santa Barbara, California, USA. 20 Nov 1995. *Don DesJardin.* **77. 1st-winter.** A worn individual, showing very good contrast between grey mantle and worn coverts. Note solid pale edges to primaries. Alameda Co., California, USA. 11 Mar 1999. *Jon R. King*

Mew Gull *Larus brachyrhynchus*. **78. 2nd-winter**. Breast-sides in this individual almost uniform greyish-brown, a pattern never seen in similarly aged Ring-billed and Common Gulls. Slight contrast between greyish-brown greater coverts and grey saddle, dark-centred tertials and lack of broad white primary tips ages this bird. Ventura, California, USA. 6 Jan 1997. *Don DesJardin*. **79. 2nd-winter**. A paler-headed individual, with diagnostic short bill and rounded head. Dark tail-markings often present in this age. Ventura, California, USA. 16 Feb 1995. *Don DesJardin*. **80. 2nd-winter**. Tail-bar unusually solid for this age. Dark-centred primary coverts and faint white mirror on P10 is age-diagnostic. California, USA. Jan. *Paul Doherty*. **81. Adult summer.** Similar to Common Gull, but note very long white mirror on P10. Alaska, USA. Jul 1989. *Ed Kwater*. **82. 2nd- and adult summer.** 2nd-summer bird with typical contrast between grey saddle and worn, paler coverts. Note extensive white in primaries of adult; white on P8 almost falls level with mirror on P9. Compare with photos 84 and 85. Alaska, USA. June. *Karel Beylevelt*.

91

Mew Gull *Larus brachyrhynchus*. **83. Adult winter**. Note diffuse head-pattern and short bill. Ventura, California, USA. Mar 1996. *Don DesJardin*. **84. Adult winter**. Note white 'string of pearls' in mid-primaries (broad white 'moons' on P5-8), white on P8 less typical than in photo 82. Point Reyes, California, USA. 30 Jan 2000. *Klaus Malling Olsen*. **85. Adult winter**. Compare wing-tip with 82 and 84. Ventura, California, USA. 12 Nov 1998, *Don DesJardin*.

7. AUDOUIN'S GULL

Larus audouinii (Payraudeau, 1826, Sardinia and Corsica)   **Plates 12–13, Photos 86–95**

IDENTIFICATION Length 48–52cm, wingspan 115–140cm. Audouin's Gull is restricted to the Mediterranean basin with winter quarters reaching the coastline of N and W Africa north of the equator. It is a medium-sized gull, 10–15% smaller, slenderer and more elegant than Lesser Black-backed and Yellow-legged Gulls. The head is also smaller with a long, sloping forehead and peak at rear-crown, creating an almost triangular head-shape. Shows prominent extension of feathering onto base of upper mandible. Bill stout and parallel-edged, shorter and slenderer than in larger gulls. Eyes and the long legs are dark. When settled, body is elongated with long, pointed wings, often held slightly lowered at rest as in Lesser Black-backed Gull. When alert, it stretches the neck and flattens the crown, vaguely recalling a large Slender-billed Gull. Flight is lighter and more graceful than in larger gulls, with much gliding along seashores on arched wings, the short arm being slightly raised, the long hand slightly lowered and tail folded. It is attracted by fishing activities, but also fishes itself by plunge-diving. May feed at night.

Adult has a dark coral-red bill with a black bar and paler tip. Upperwing pale grey (much paler than in Yellow-legged Gull), with only little contrast with white head. Wing-tip black with row of white spots along trailing edge, created by primary tips. Only shows a small white mirror on P10; outer wing looks all dark at a distance and forms a strong contrast with the very pale upperparts, which may look whitish in strong sunlight and sometimes slightly three-toned as in adult Black-legged Kittiwake. Contrast between wingtip and rest of wing very striking on the underwing. From spring to summer the white primary tips are gradually reduced by wear. Bill bright red, in breeding season sometimes darkening to create a blackish impression at a distance. Legs dark grey to greenish.

Juvenile looks like a small, smart and cleanly patterned Lesser Black-backed Gull. Head rather uniform grey-brown, with a variable – often striking – whitish face, which merges into the grey-brown head and underbody. The lower flanks often show a prominent darker patch, which contrasts well with the white lower belly and vent. Shows pale midwing-panel on underwing (and axillaries) against darker wing-linings and flanks. Upperwing similar to Lesser Black-backed with dark flight feathers and two whitish wing-bars. Shows broader white trailing edge to inner wing. Compared to Lesser Black-backed, scapulars, coverts and tertials colder greyish-brown, with more solid dark centres and narrower pale fringes, at most with indistinct pale barring. White uppertail-coverts create striking white U against nearly all-dark tail. Bill greyish with darker tip. Legs dark grey.

First-winter as juvenile, but mantle and scapulars grey with diagnostic but variable dark triangular centres (can be lacking on some feathers). Head whitish in contrast to dark streaks on neck and breast-sides, forming dark half-collar. May show dark eye-mask or streaks on rear-crown. Underparts more whitish. With wear, upperwing becomes paler, especially at midwing. Larg-

er first-year gulls all have fleshy legs. Lesser Black-backed is larger with more patterned head and upperparts. Underwing much darker, looking dark with paler flight feathers. First-year Yellow-legged and Armenian Gulls have larger head, stronger bill and no contrastingly darker flanks. In most, the underwing is darker with evenly darker-patterned coverts, although Armenian sometimes shows a paler midwing-panel similar to Audouin's. Upperparts especially on Yellow-legged warmer brown with pale panel on inner primaries (sometimes indistinct) and much more distinct pale barring on—at least inner—greater coverts. Black tail-band narrower and uppertail-coverts dark-spotted. In first-winter plumage, Lesser Black-backed, Yellow-legged and Armenian lack the pale grey scapulars with dark centres of first-winter Audouin's.

First-summer has white head and underbody, apart from varying brown spots and streaks on breast-sides, flanks and upper mantle, sometimes forming a darker 'shawl'. From midwinter the coverts are worn, and from Apr replaced by new grey, which often shows narrow dark centres, in flight often strongly contrasting with dark trailing edge to inner wing. Before moult to second-winter, juvenile greater coverts, flight feathers and tail are worn and faded. There is a conspicuous pale midwing-panel on upperwing, and the white U on the uppertail-coverts is less prominent than in first-winter. Bill pale with dark tip and cutting edges.

In **second-winter**, head similar to first-winter, but mantle, upperwing-coverts and inner primaries pale grey contrasting with blackish outer primaries, primary coverts and secondaries. Normally, lesser coverts and outer greater coverts have dark markings which seem to elongate dark wing-tip. When fresh, white tips to flight feathers and primary coverts are conspicuous. There may be a pale grey tinge to breast, belly and flanks, standing out against the whitish underwing. Uppertail-coverts and tail are white, latter with a variable dark band, sometimes reduced to indistinct and scattered dark spots on midtail. Bill greyish-green (sometimes reddish) with blackish sub-terminal bar and often paler tip. Legs dark grey.

Second-summer similar to second-winter, but head white and wing pattern faded. Fresh inner primaries pale grey, contrasting well with retained brownish outer wing and secondaries. Bill dull red, normally with greenish-tinged base.

Third-year similar to adult, but with dark-centred primary coverts, smaller white mirror on P10 (sometimes lacking) and often faint dark tail markings. Bill-tip sometimes black.

VOICE Long-call a series of hoarse, almost donkey- or goose-like tones, consisting of up to 30 units (about 1 per second). In flight sometimes a short *oog*, uttered in short series. Also nasal *gle-i-eh* and raw *arch* resembling call from Rook *Corvus frugilegus*. While feeding, a crying, moaning *ki-aou* (resembling crying child); at nest, a subdued *dog-dog* or *criek-criek* (Urban *et al.* 1986, Svensson *et al.* 1999).

PLATE 12. AUDOUIN'S GULL *Larus audouinii*

Restricted to the Mediterranean Basin with winter quarters reaching coastline of W Africa. Medium-sized, coastal gull, often associating with the larger gulls near fishing activities. Shaped like a small Lesser Black-backed with similar elongated hindparts, rather long legs and smaller head. Head-shape different with flatter forehead merging into rather long, parallel-edged bill. Eyes and legs always dark.

1.　**Juvenile** (Jul–Oct) Greyish-brown with prominent pale-scaled saddle, and dark, pale-edged wing-coverts. Shows no or only faint pale barring on greater coverts. Head unpatterned with dark eye surrounded by white eye-crescent, forehead a little paler. Bill dark with blackish tip. Flanks darker than belly.

2.　**First-winter** (Sep–Apr) Similar to juvenile, but head whiter and saddle pale grey with scattered dark markings, especially on scapulars, which may show diagnostic streaking. Bill greyish with black tip.

3.　**First-winter** (Mar–Oct) This plumage is a stage between first-winter and adult-like second-winter. During summer, shows bleached plumage compared to first-winter with new grey wing-coverts creating piebald pattern on upperwing. Note greyish-olive tinge to legs, typical of younger birds.

4.　**Second-winter** (Aug–Apr) Note bicoloured bill (sometimes more similar to adult), faint hindneck-streaking and grey legs. Upperparts similar to adult, but still with first-year-patterned coverts and tertials with dark streaks. Primaries with narrower white tips than in adult.

5.　**Second-summer** (Apr–Aug) As adult, but sometimes with dark-patterned tertials, primary coverts and tail feathers.

6.　**Third-summer** (Mar–Oct) Shows white head, and mainly white underbody (adult greyer underbody). Upperparts as in adult, pale grey with poorly marked tertial step; primaries with narrow white tips only. Legs grey. Bill coral-red with narrow dark ring around yellow tip. Eyes dark.

7.　**Adult summer** (Aug–Apr) Underbody often with greyer cast in some contrast to white head (also seen in summer). Bill brighter red, may look blackish at distance. This individual shows white primary tips at their broadest (fresh by autumn).

1. Juvenile

2. First-winter

3. First-winter

4. Second-winter

5. Second-summer

6. Third-summer

7. Adult summer

PLATE 13. AUDOUIN'S GULL *Larus audouinii*

In flight like a small Lesser Black-backed Gull with similar long wings, often held strongly angled and bowed when gliding. Performs much gliding along seashores. Head slenderer with long neck. Gathers at fishing activities, but also fishes for itself, sometimes with short dives.

1. **Juvenile** (Jul–Oct) Upperwing dark brown with blackish flight feathers and greater coverts, the latter showing pale edges to create wing-bar. Tail black against white rump. Underbody brownish with dark flanks. Underwing with large pale midwing-panel, created by unpatterned pale greater coverts.

2. **First-winter** (Sep–Apr) Similar to juvenile, but bill bicoloured, appearing slender, and underbody whiter with better contrast to darker lower flanks. Saddle grey with dark pattern especially on scapulars. With bleaching and wear, the juvenile upperwing gets less contrasting.

3. **First-summer** (Mar–Oct) Worn individual, showing contrast between fresh pale grey and worn brownish coverts. Note shape similar to Lesser Black-backed Gull with long pointed wings, showing conspicuous pale midwing-panel. Head pale with slender, bicoloured bill.

4. **Second-winter** (Aug–Apr) Upperparts and most of coverts grey, contrasting with dark outer wing and trailing edge. Black tail-bar narrower than in first-years. Bill red with black subterminal markings. Underparts basically as adult, but axillaries and underwing-coverts with faint dark markings.

5. **Third-winter** (Aug–Apr) Adult-like but with dark markings on primary coverts and, in this bird, a lack of white mirror on P10; note pale grey wings with black tip.

6. **Adult winter** (Aug–Apr) Adult shows very pale grey upperwing with faint white trailing edge and solid black wing-tip, with only narrow white mirror on P10; broader white tips to outer primaries, creating white spots along trailing edge to outerhand. Note whitish impression of most of wing from below contrasting well with black wingtip. Bill coral-red (with dark markings and yellow tip), eyes and legs dark.

7. **Adult summer** (Mar–Oct) Often very pale-looking—almost uniform pearly grey with full but rather narrow black wing-tip. Note long wings, short tail and red bill (which at distance may look blackish).

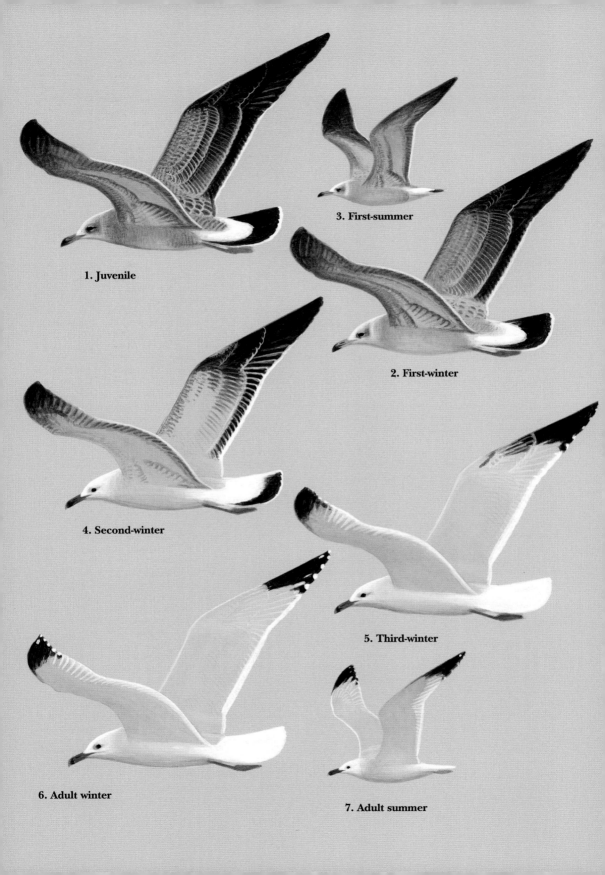

1. Juvenile

3. First-summer

2. First-winter

4. Second-winter

5. Third-winter

6. Adult winter

7. Adult summer

MOULT Adult moult to **winter** plumage is complete mid-May–Oct. Primaries Jun–Oct; P1–2 rarely delayed to late Sep. A bird from Germany had not yet started tail moult in Jul, all rectrices being very worn (Flore 1997). Coverts Jun–Aug, starting with median coverts, ending with outer greater coverts. Moult to adult **summer** plumage partial late Jan–Apr, including head and body. **Juvenile** moult to **first-winter** late Jun–Nov, including mantle and scapulars and (parts of) head and underbody. Timing varies; nape and mantle starts Jun–early Sep; most of moult finished late Oct; some juvenile feathers (especially scapulars) retained in first-winter. Moult to **first-summer** partial Jan–Apr, including head, body and some scapulars. This moult could be regarded as the first stages of moult into second-winter. Moult to **second-winter** late April–Oct starting with P1 and median coverts; in Jul primary moult has reached P4–6. Moult to **third-winter** similar to adult; in Jul P1–3 and most of mantle, scapulars and coverts may be renewed; secondaries often later. Birds from Aug moulted P9–10 and inner secondaries.

DESCRIPTION

Adult Head white; hindneck, nape and sometimes crown with pale grey wash as extension from mantle. Underparts off-white to pale grey, strongest on breast-sides and flanks. Upperparts and upperwings pale grey (Kodak Grey Scale 4–5, often with stronger bluish tinge). Rump, uppertail-coverts and tail white, with faint pale grey shade on rump and midtail. Scapulars and tertials pale grey with diffuse paler tips. Upperwing-coverts and P1–5 often with diffuse white fringes, median coverts and secondaries with white tips. P6–10 black, decreasing in extent inwards to small isolated subterminal marks on outer web of P6(5), forming clear-cut black wing-tip on both surfaces. P10 with 10–15mm white mirror on inner web. Primaries with max. 5–6mm white tips, reduced with wear from Mar, and often lacking from May. Underwing white to pale grey. May show very indistinct blackish shaft-streaks on outer 2–3 greater primary coverts (skins in NHM, probably younger adult). Iris dark brown. Orbital ring, mouth and gape red. Bill deep coral-red with 5–20mm black subterminal bar, sometimes irregular or as double bar (Barthel 1997). Tip yellow, orange or red. Legs dark grey, olive-grey or olive with yellow soles. Rather similar all year round. In **adult summer** (Mar–Oct), red base of bill sometimes darker, making bill look blackish at long range. A case of adult with bill pattern as in first-summer (King & Shirihai 1996) could be third-year. **Adult winter** (Aug–Apr) as adult summer, but generally with cleaner grey tinge to underbody and paler red base to bill. Sometimes with very faint and narrow grey streaks on ear-coverts, crown and hindneck.

Juvenile (fledging–Oct) Lores, forehead and forecrown whitish to pale brown, shading to uniform grey-brown on rest of head; ear-coverts sometimes faintly darker, creating a weak mask or emphasising whitish cap. Has dusky eye-crescents and thin white eyelids. Underparts smooth brown with darker rear flanks (often with faint whitish fringes) contrasting with whitish, lightly dark-spotted rear belly and vent. Undertail-coverts white, apart from brown-spotted lateral coverts. Mantle grey-brown with indistinct sandy to pale grey feather-fringes. Scapulars, lesser coverts and median coverts dark brown with pale fringes, creating scaly pattern (most prominent on scapulars); fringes of especially coverts narrow and even, with no notching. Greater coverts dark grey to brown with narrow pale edges and tips; sometimes with indistinct pale barring especially on innermost. Tertials blackish-brown with narrow pale fringes, generally broader at tips. Back and upper rump grey-brown with fine dark bars. Lower rump and upper-tail-coverts white, forming whitish U in contrast to dark tail and upper rump. Sometimes uppertail-coverts dark brown with pale fringes. May show slight dark spots on sides of rump. Secondaries blackish with broad white fringes. Primaries, alula and primary coverts dark brown. P1–4 sometimes slightly paler with indistinct darker subterminal spots (especially on upper surface). Underwing-coverts and axillaries with prominent, often broad, dark tips, creating streaked pattern or dark leading edge to underwing. Most of under primary coverts greyish-brown with darker tips. Axillaries, median coverts and sometimes greater primary coverts pale grey with dark tips, forming pale midwing-panel on underwing; dark tips of coverts often form dark bars. Tail from above black with whitish edges and base, from below with broader white bases; sometimes with narrow white fringe to outer web of T6. Inner webs of rectrices with whitish bases, visible on spread tail (especially from below). Iris dark brown. Bill blackish with dark grey to dull purple base, covering 50–75%. Extreme tip sometimes pale pinkish to whitish-yellow, especially when recently fledged. Legs dark grey, greenish-grey or dark olive-green.

First-winter (Sep–Apr) similar to juvenile, but head and underbody whiter with dark brown spots or streaks on hindneck and sometimes hindcrown, forming dark half-collar to breast-sides (sometimes also over upper mantle). May have stronger streaks around eye to ear-coverts, creating faint dark mask. Dark lower flanks retained, now in very good contrast to greyish-white breast to upper belly, which may show fine darker streaks or spots. Most of mantle and scapulars pale grey with blackish triangular (rarer anchor-shaped) marks, sometimes reduced to dark shaft-streaks. Median coverts paler, with wear forming pale midwing-panel. Scapulars with pale grey fringes. Tertials pale grey with narrow dark subterminal bars. With wear, upperparts generally become paler brown and may lose pale pattern. Bill greyish, often with greenish or fleshy tinge and black tip to cutting edges. Legs as juvenile.

First-summer (Mar–Oct) similar to first-winter, but head and underparts whiter; may show dark half-collar, sometimes conspicuous into Aug (Mackrill 1989a). Mantle and scapulars grey, often with scattered brown feather-centres. Normally shows grey inner wing-coverts (and also outer median coverts) with variable dark centres or shaft-streaks from May; grey 'spreads' over upperparts during summer as moult into second-winter progresses. From spring, retained juvenile greater coverts fade to create pale midwing-panel on upperwing. Tail dark brown, lacking white tips. Bill as first-winter, but base generally paler; sometimes with reddish- or yellowish-tinged base and black terminal band or tip. Bill normal-

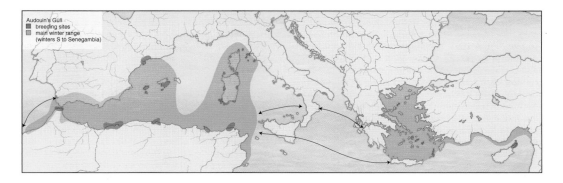

Audouin's Gull
■ breeding sites
■ main winter range
(winters S to Senegambia)

ly pale-tipped from Jun (Mackrill 1989a). Legs greyish, by late summer with an olive tinge.

Second-winter (Aug–Apr) Head white with dusky eye-crescents and often some dark streaks, spots or greyish-brown wash on lower hindneck and breast-sides. Under-body, axillaries and underwing-coverts white with faint dark markings on especially outer wing-coverts. Mantle, back and scapulars pale grey; mantle sometimes with brown spots. Inner wing pale grey with scattered brown coverts, many with brown shaft-streaks. Greater coverts pale or with blackish markings or shaft-streaks on especially outer ones; greater coverts sometimes brownish-tinged with pale fringes. Secondaries blackish with broad white tips. P1–5 pale grey, sometimes with broad white edges or weak dark subterminal markings. P6–10, alula and primary coverts blackish, often brownish-washed, especially at division from grey bases. P9–10 and their coverts black with white tips or fringes, soon disappearing with wear. Rump and tail white, the latter with a variable neat black subterminal band, normally limited to T1–4, but frequently even reduced to a few dark spots. Bill grey to reddish with a broad dark sub-terminal bar, most extensive along the lower mandible; tip normally pale. Iris dark. Orbital ring red.

Second-summer (Mar–Oct) similar to second-winter, but inner wing-coverts and P1–5 cleaner grey, and flight feathers, coverts and tail tinged greyish-brown. Bill bright to dull red, often with greenish-yellow tinge to base; black subterminal band on average broader than on adult; tip creamy to pinkish. Legs sometimes greyish-olive.

Third-winter (Aug–Apr) as adult winter, but with dark markings (mainly as shaft-streaks) on outer 3–5 greater primary coverts and sometimes alula. White mirror on P10 narrower, frequently lacking or inconspicuous; P(4)5–9 normally with black markings. White primary tips generally narrower and grey tinge to underparts weaker. Tail sometimes with weak grey subterminal band or tiny dark spots. Bare parts as adult; black bill-band generally broader, rarely covering tip.

Third-summer (Mar–Oct) as third-winter, but white primary tips reduced or lacking through wear from May.

DISTRIBUTION AND MIGRATION Population >22,000 pairs in 2000; increase from 1,000 in 1966. Breeds locally in often dense colonies, mostly on flat, sandy islets with short vegetation. In Ebro Delta on sandy peninsula. Population in pairs: Spain 15,100 (1994); 12,600 (1995), mostly in two colonies: Ebro Delta (0 1980, 10,500 2000; breeding success of about two chicks per pair yearly) and Chafarinas Islands (4,136 1994); also 825 Balearics. Elsewhere: Algeria 4,000, Tunisia 15, France 60–112, Italy 425–982, Greece 210 (rising from 40 in the late 1970s), Turkey 50, Cyprus 20. First breeding in Portugal in 2001 (11 pairs) (Cramp & Simmons 1983, Alvarez 1992, Collar *et al.* 1994, Tucker & Heath 1994, Pedrozzi & Ruiz 1995, Oro *et al.* 1996a & b, del Hoyo *et al.* 1996, Flore 1997, Oro *et al.* 2000, R. Tipper *in litt.*).

Vulnerable; dependent on conservation. Strongly dependent on fishing activities, often attracted to fish-

AUDOUIN'S GULL Four-year gull. Breeds mainly in Mediterranean, reaches W Africa in winter. Medium-sized with general jizz of larger gull; long, sloping forehead connects with strong, hooked bill. Breast is deep, rear parts slender, grey legs long. In flight elegant with long wings (especially hand); performs much gliding on angled wings.

Adult has pale grey upperwing with solid black tip, at most with small white mirror on P10, but with broad white primary tips, creating row of white lights on trailing edge to inner wing. Underparts often slightly greyish-tinged, but head white. Eyes dark. Bill coral-red with faint dark and yellow markings at tip. Little seasonal variation.

Juvenile (Jul–Sep) has greyish-brown head and body, and often contrasting pale forehead, this even conspicuous against dark bill. Upperwing dark with blackish flight feathers. Rump with narrow white U against broad dark tail. From below shows pale midwing-panel on underwing, contrasting with dark edges and dark flanks.

First-winter (Sep–Apr) as juvenile, but head white with grey streaks and saddle grey, often with dark spots or shaft streaks. Bill bicoloured.

Second-year similar to adult, but grey saddle and inner wing contrasts with dark outer wing and trailing edge to inner wing, and tail shows narrow black bar.

ing floats and upwelling; frequently fishes at night. A moratorium on inshore fishing in the 1991 breeding season and a ban on fishing in 1993 led to a serious decline in breeding success in the Ebro Delta. Local competition occurs with the Yellow-legged Gull, especially in the Chafarinas Islands; culling of Yellow-legged Gulls in Spain has had strong positive influence on the Audouin's population. Egg collecting probably a problem in the E Mediterranean. Protection should be given both to breeding sites and important migration stopovers (Witt 1977, 1982, Bradley 1986, Alvarez 1992, 1994, Paterson *et al.* 1992, de Juana & Varela 1993).

In winter spreads in the Mediterranean and NW Africa to main wintering areas in S Mediterranean and off NW Africa. SW migration past Gibraltar Jul–Oct, return passage Mar–Apr. In winter max. 824 Algerian coast Dec. Major roosts occur along the Moroccan coast, with 7,646 at Foum Assaka–Dakhla, Jan 1997, including 5,530 at Pointe d'Awfist. Scarcer further S, with max. numbers 456 Nouakchott, Mauritania, in Nov; 2% of population winters Senegal and The Gambia, e.g. 456 Dakar Nov–Dec 1995. Young birds spread most in winter: 82–85% wintering Algeria and Libya adults; 50–75% W Morocco. Away from breeding sites small numbers summer S Turkey marshlands and Atlantic, gathering from Jul in small groups. Regular in autumn at Zaranik, Egypt; max. 13 on 14 September 1996. Max. 30 winter in the Peloponnese, Greece. Regular at Canary Islands in winter. Irregular but increasing in Portugal, most Aug 1995 11 records of 61 birds (Cramp & Simmons 1983, Beaman 1986, de Juana *et al.* 1987, van der Have *et al.* 1989, Martins 1989, Bengtsson 1995, Costa *et al.* 1997, Enticott & Tipling 1997, Flore 1997, Handrinos & Akriotis 1997.
Vagrant W France several, Great Britain 1, Netherlands 1, Germany 1, Switzerland 5, Czech Republic 1, Georgia 1, Bulgaria 1, Sea of Marmara (several), Israel 17 (six Eilat), Sinai 3 (Glutz von Blotzheim & Bauer 1982, Beaman 1986, Hoogendoorn 1995b, Shirihai 1996a, Costa *et al.* 1997, Flore 1997, Walker 2003).

MEASUREMENTS Lengths in mm; weights in g. Own data based on skins in AMNH, MCZ, NHM, NRK, USNM, UZM. Mediterranean, N Africa.

WING

Adult male	392–423 (406.8)	18
Adult female	384–412 (394.8)	14
First-year female	393	1

BILL

Adult male	44.0–55.2 (50.2)	19
Adult female	40.7–51.8 (45.3)	16
First-year female	49.4	1

BILL DEPTH AT BASE OF BILL

Adult male	15.0–18.0 (17.2)	17
Adult female	14.9–17.0 (15.6)	14
First-year female	15.8	1

BILL DEPTH AT GONYS

Adult male	15.1–17.3 (15.5)	17
Adult female	13.5–15.5 (14.5)	14
First-year female	14.1	1

GONYS LENGTH

Adult male	13.9–17.3 (15.6)	17
Adult female	12.8–15.4 (13.9)	14
First-year female	12.0	1

TARSUS

Adult male	52.5–61.6 (58.7)	18
Adult female	51.7–59.9 (56.1)	16
First-year female	59.7	1

Weight Adult Jun–Jul: male 460–625, females 485–600. At hatching 500–600 (Cramp & Simmons 1983, skins in AMNH, NHM, USNM).

86

Audouin's Gull *Larus audouinii*. **86** (see page 100). **Juvenile**. The pale face, showing well here, is often striking in flight even at long range. Note long, sloping forehead and rather uniform head and underparts as well as practically unpatterned undertail-coverts. Ebro, Spain. Jul 1998. *Karel Beylevelt*. **87. Juvenile**. Dark flanks contrast well with pale midwing-panel on underwing. Ebro, Spain. July 1998. *Karel Beylevelt*. **88. Juvenile.** Note pale midwing-panel, dark flanks and pale belly. Isola De San Andrea, Italy. 30 Jun 2001. *Ugo Mellone*. **89. 2nd-summer**. Algarve, Portugal. 4 May 2000. *Ray Tipper*. **90. 2nd-, 3rd- and adult winter**. 2nd-winter shows dark secondary bar and extensive dark-patterned primaries, 3rd-summer is similar to adult, but outer primary coverts are dark-marked, and white primary tips narrower. Morocco. Nov 1992. *Markus Varesvuo*. **91. 2nd-summer.** Mantle and inner coverts grey, but secondaries and primary coverts are dark. Ebro, Spain. May 1993. *René Pop*.

Audouin's Gull *Larus audouinii*. **92. Adult summer**. Note faint grey tinge to breast-sides, coral-red bill and long, sloping forehead. White primary tips are worn off. Ebro, Spain. Jul 2000. *Kim Aaen*. **93. Adult summer** with 2nd-winter Yellow-legged Gull *Larus michahellis*. Compare size and structure with Yellow-legged Gull. Benidorm, Spain. 8 Sep 2001. *Trond Sørhuus*. **94. Adult winter.** Morocco. Jan 1995. *Markus Varesvuo*. **95. Adult summer.** Compare wing-pattern with 91, and note very narrow white mirror on P10 as well as pale grey upperparts, with faint pale trailing edge to wing, but in good contrast to black outerwing. Spain. May. *Per-Göran Bentz*

8. RING-BILLED GULL

Larus delawarensis (Ord, 1815, Philadelphia)   Plates 14–15, Photos 96–112

IDENTIFICATION Length 41–49cm, wingspan 115–135cm. Ring-billed Gull is similar to Common and Mew Gull, but on average larger and bulkier with thicker, more parallel-edged bill. Importantly, upperparts are much paler grey than in Common and Mew – similar to Black-headed, Herring race *argenteus*, American Herring or even Glaucous Gull. Compared to Common, the head is squarer with a flatter crown, fuller neck and more distinct peak behind the eye. The gape is generally longer and more down-curved, often penetrating to below the eye creating an angry look. Deeper breast and longer legs may give a plover-like impression combined with 'free and easy' gait. The heavier-billed birds (males) have bill longer than the distance from the bill-base to the eye (longer than any Common) and look – especially the pale-eyed adults – like miniature large gulls. Flight lighter than Herring, but heavier than Common. Wings proportionally longer than in Common Gull, with broader arm and more pointed hand.

Although large males, with their square head and broad neck as well as rather heavy, parallel-edged bill, are much more large-gull-like than Common and Mew Gull, small females may appear round-headed with rather narrow bills. In such birds, bill-shape is still important, being parallel-edged rather than (normally) broader at the base than on the rest of the bill even in heavy-billed Common. Note that Common Gull race *kamtschatschensis* is closest in size to Ring-billed, but jizz-wise is still a Common Gull. Grey feathers on upperparts of Ring-billed much paler than on any Common or Mew Gull.

Adult Has pale yellow eyes (surrounded by dark orbital ring) and a yellow bill with a full clear-cut black ring, evident even at distances when the pale eyes are hard to judge (dark orbital ring tends to 'obscure' pallor of eyes at longer ranges). The bill ring is normally broader than the width of the eye. The upperparts are pale grey and show only diffuse white tertial and rear scapular crescents and trailing edge to the inner wing. Mantle often a tinge darker than primary bases. Wing-tip similar to Herring race *argenteus*, with small white mirror on P10 (smaller than in Common, with a larger black tip). Bare parts yellow, especially in summer brighter yellow than in Common. Settled adults combine 'small Herring-gull head' with overall shape of Common, including long wing projection behind tail. In **summer**, head white and orbital ring orange to red. In **winter**, head dark-spotted, typically darker and more densely spotted than in Common or Mew Gulls, strongest on hindneck and around eyes. Neck-sides often white, sometimes strikingly so. Orbital ring blackish, like black glasses around the pale eyes.

Common and Mew Gulls have darker grey upperparts with a much more distinct white tertial crescents and trailing edge to the inner wing (the former mainly a character in settled birds). Their eyes are dark or darkish-looking, appearing large on the rounded head (Mew and Common race *kamtschatschensis* regularly show pale eyes, but never as whitish-yellow as Ring-billed). If present, bill-ring in Common is narrow and in form of Z-shaped bar, narrower than the width of the eye; only few Mew show dark inconspicuous markings on bill. White mirrors on outer primaries are larger, appearing as a rounded white spot, and white 'moons' on the mid-primaries are conspicuous (lacking or just faint in Ring-billed). California Gull is larger and slenderer with a longer, often four-coloured bill (red, yellow, black and ivory), dark eyes, and variable leg colour, generally with a greyer or greener tinge than in Ring-billed.

Juvenile Similar to Common Gull; see detailed description. Develops **first-winter** plumage from early autumn. Separation from Common can be tricky. Some (males) are larger with a squarer head and heavier, more parallel-edged bill than any Common; small females differ barely in jizz from average Common. Compared to Common *canus/heinei* and Mew Gulls, upperparts generally more contrasting and mantle always paler. There are nine important characters to look for.

(1) *Tail pattern* In Ring-billed most varying, but typically with less clear-cut tail-bar and usually extra tail-bands. 5–7% show clear-cut tail-bar as in Common (which shows little variation in tail-bar), but usually with grey tinge to T5–6. Tail exceptionally as dark as in Mew.

(2) *Greater coverts* In Ring-billed these are pale grey, concolorous with the mantle, normally with dark transverse bars on especially innermost greater coverts. In Common and Mew, greater coverts brownish-grey, paler and browner than mantle. This presents a useful character until wear in early spring makes greater coverts strongly bleached in Common and Mew Gulls.

(3) *Median coverts* Usually with triangular dark bases creating a weaker and more diffuse pattern than in Common (in which the centres of the median coverts are normally rounded); Mew and certain E Asian Common have median coverts closer to Ring-billed. Median coverts of Ring-billed wear quicker: from autumn, pale edges are often worn off and the pattern is diluted. In Common and Mew the strong pattern is retained better throughout the winter. A few Ring-billed have rounder centres as in Common

(4) *Bill* This is stouter, parallel-edged (i.e. rectangular) with a stronger-hooked tip, and strongly bicoloured, having a pinkish base and black tip, often recalling a first-year Glaucous Gull. Weaker bill of Common and Mew deeper at base than at more gently curved tip, and often with a less clear division between black and pale. Coloration in Common duller but variable (unlike Ring-billed): dull pink, pale yellow or grey with fleshy, yellow or greenish tinge.

(5) *Dark patterning on head and breast* In Ring-billed this is generally more extensive, with broader and denser streaks or spots and a more distinctly spotted hindneck. Flanks to undertail-coverts with broad blackish chevrons. Heavily marked birds may have crown, eye surroundings and sides of neck and breast so densely marked as to look almost uniform around wing-bend. White eye-crescents often conspicuous. Common is typ-

PLATE 14. RING-BILLED GULL *Larus delawarensis*

Common North American gull, found on lakes, in urban surroundings and estuaries, often in large flocks. Confident, attracted by human activities. Among Nearctic gulls, the commonest vagrant to Europe. Medium-sized gull with rather heavy head, full neck and rather strong, parallel-edged bill showing hooked tip. Jizzwise intermediate between Herring and Common/Mew Gulls: heavier with paler mantle than Mew and Common Gulls, and stronger bill.

1.   **Juvenile** (Jul–Oct) Head and underbody heavily patterned with dark spots, streaks or scales. Juvenile mantle and scapulars scaled. Medium and lesser coverts with somewhat pointed feather-centres. Greater coverts paler, sometimes with indistinct paler waving or bars (never in Common and Mew Gulls).

2.   **First-winter** (Sep–Apr) Similar to juvenile, but (most of) mantle and scapulars pale grey, often with indistinct markings. Head often whiter, head and body generally finer-patterned than in juvenile, but much variation. Most, however, show extensive dark spots or scales, often as dark chevrons, on head, breast and along flanks to rump. Mantle and greater coverts rather concolorous (in Common and Mew much better contrast between darker grey mantle and brownish-tinged greater coverts). Pattern on lesser and median coverts often diffuse from Nov, caused by wear; note pointed centres to lesser/median coverts (in Common centres rounder and pattern better retained throughout winter). Bill parallel-edged, distinctly contrasting: pink with black tip. Legs pinkish.

3.   **Late first-winter/first-summer** (Feb–Sep) An example of a less patterned individual with reduced dark markings on head and underbody compared to 2. With wear, juvenile pattern on coverts almost disappears and greater coverts may wear to very pale grey. Bill-tip often pale from late winter (from summer in Common Gull).

4.   **Second-winter** (Aug–Apr) Similar to adult, but with slightly darker eyes, often pinkish basal part of bill, fleshy tinge to legs and dark-centred tertials; note also slight dark tail-markings and, compared to adult, less white on wing-tip. Second-winter and older Ring-billed Gull identified from Common and Mew by paler grey upperparts, indistinct and narrow white tertial crescents and heavier bill with well-defined black ring of equal amount on both mandibles.

5.   **Adult winter** (Sep–Apr) Head markings stronger and much more distinct than in Mew and most Common. Eyes pale yellow, as pale as in Herring and American Herring Gull (darker, if not blackish in Common and Mew Gulls). Note pale grey upperparts with indistinct diffuse white tertial crescents. Bill yellow with complete black ring, appearing broader than width of eye (opposite in Common Gull; Mew with much less clear dark markings on bill, if any).

6.   **Adult summer** (Apr–Sep) Similar to adult Common Gull, but note pale eyes and complete black ring around bright yellow bill. Legs bright yellow. White tertial tips barely contrast with pale grey upperparts; in Common and Mew Gull, white tertial tips are contrasting and clean-cut against darker grey upperparts.

7.   **Adult summer** Even seen head-on, bill-ring most distinct. P10 with narrower white mirror compared to Common and Mew adult.

1. Juvenile

3. Late first-winter/
first-summer

2. First-winter

4. Second-winter

5. Adult winter

6. Adult summer

7. Adult summer

PLATE 15. RING-BILLED GULL *Larus delawarensis*

In flight like a small Herring Gull, or a large, broad-armed Common/Mew Gull. Flies more steadily with slower wingbeats than Common/Mew, like a small Herring.

1. **Juvenile** (Jul–Oct) Head and underbody heavily brown-spotted or -scaled well onto lower flanks and tail-coverts. Wing with paler midwing-panel and window on inner primaries, generally better contrasting than in Common and Mew Gulls. Underwing with dark edges to coverts and axillaries, but often with paler midwing-panel. Tail very variable, but generally with dark tail-bar and several narrower bars, broad white tips and edges or with greyish tinge, dulling contrast between white base and black tail-bar.

2. **First-winter** (Sep–Apr) Note pale grey saddle against juvenile wing, which may already appear worn from midwinter. Compare tail pattern with 1: this bird shows whiter base and better-defined black tail-bar. 5-10% may show tail and rump even less patterned, at distance creating white tail with distinct black bar as in Common Gull (see text for details). Note diamond-shaped dark subterminal spots to tips of P1-4 (generally more trapezoid-shaped in Common Gull). Head and body often similar to juvenile, but generally less patterned. Bill pink with black tip.

3. **First-winter** Some are virtually unpatterned on underwing, showing faint dark secondary rectangle and only faint dark edge to axillaries.

4. **Second-winter** (Sep–Apr) Similar to adult winter, but note dark-marked primary coverts and fuller dark wing-tip. Frequently with scattered dark-centred secondaries, and in >50% traces of black tail-bar. Underwing-coverts usually with dark markings. Bill duller than in adult.

5. **Second-winter** A more advanced individual than 4, only showing faint dark markings on primary coverts (and here narrow white mirror on P10).

6. **Adult winter** (Sep–Apr) Adult upperwing pale grey with less distinct white trailing edge than in Common and Mew Gulls. Wing tip black with rather small white mirrors on P9–10, creating triangular white patch. Lacks white 'moons' on wingtip of Common and Mew Gulls. Head rather heavily and distinctly marked. Bill yellow with conspicuous black ring.

7. **Adult summer** (Apr–Sep) Head white. Bill bright yellow with distinct black ring, reinforcing impression of heavier bill than in Common and Mew Gulls. Ring broader than eye.

First-summer (Feb–Aug)
Note strongly worn greater coverts contrasting with pale grey saddle, and 'extra' dark tail bar.

1. Juvenile

3. First-winter

2. First-winter

4. Second-winter

5. Second-winter

6. Adult winter

7. Adult summer

ically less extensively marked on head and underparts; more heavily marked Commons have more distinct streaks and paler flanks, at most with narrower and clearer-cut dark chevrons. Mew has a rather uniform, pale brown hindneck and underparts, and strongly brown-barred undertail-coverts. Both Common and Mew lack distinct white eye-crescents.

(6) *Tertials* Generally less full with narrower white edges than Common. Edges often with irregular pattern, at tips sometimes similar to Herring Gull. Often strongly worn from winter onwards (usually less so in Common).

(7) *Mantle* This is pale grey (as adult), often with broader dark and pale scaling than in all but extremely well-marked Common (evident into midwinter). Some have diagnostic dark subterminal spots, creating pattern similar to juvenile Red Knot *Calidris canutus*, or narrow dark shaft-streaks or spots intermixed. In Common and Mew mantle darker and normally cleaner grey, rarely with pale edges. Some Common populations (especially of *kamtschatschensis*) retain much of juvenile plumage in first-winter.

(8) *Underwing* This often shows a large pale midwing-panel: axillaries and greater coverts have narrower dark tips than Common. In midwinter, white on underwing contrasts well with dark secondaries, and underwing may appear as pale as in Mediterranean Gull. Most Common show more evenly dark pattern on underwing, and *kamtschatschensis* often has solid dark underwing-coverts; the same is true for most Mew Gulls.

(9) *Inner primaries* Dark subterminal markings to P1-4 diamond-shaped, concentrating along shaft. Common has trapezoid-shaped markings with more dark on inner than on outer web.

In **first-summer** many show pure grey saddle against strongly bleached upperwing with almost whitish midwing-panel. Bill and legs sometimes yellower. Bill-tip pale from late winter, giving space for the black bill-ring. Eye pale from one year of age.

ID pitfalls for first-years are small second-year Herring and American Herring with bill pattern similar to Ring-billed. In the large species, look for a grey mantle combined with much darker mottling or bars on coverts, broad white and irregular tertial-tips and more solid brown areas on the underwing-coverts. A combination of first-year-like wing pattern and pale eyes is frequent in Herring (in Ring-billed, first-year wing is always combined with dark eyes). Herring and American Herring are larger with a more sloping forehead, heavier bills (tips especially 'masculine' and bulbous-shaped), smaller eyes, longer legs and shorter wings with broader white primary edges and less wing projection beyond tail than in Ring-billed. Inner primaries often plain grey in second-year Herring; in first-year Ring-billed there are dark spots near the tips of the inner primaries. If present, red traces on gonys confirms Herring.

Second-winter similar to adult, but with darker outer wing, as primary coverts and alula are dark (pale grey in adult) and the white on the wing-tip is smaller, usually restricted to a small white mirror on P10 (second-year Common has a larger mirror on P10 and often a small one on P9). Has a darker wing-tip, lacking the white primary tips of adults. Traces of a dark tail-bar are the rule; many also show scattered dark on secondaries, dark

lesser covert bar and dark tips to some underwing-coverts. Such immature characters are rare in Common nominate *canus*, but more frequent in eastern taxa and Mew Gull. Bill often three-toned with grey-green or fleshy base, black ring and paler tip. Some develop the adult bill. Eyes usually pale, but some have eyes predominantly dark until second spring. Legs greyish (not bright yellow as in adult).

Second-summer as second-winter before moult into adult plumage, but head white and bill as adult.

Third-winter/summer as adult, but white mirror on P10 smaller and outer primary coverts with narrow dark markings.

VOICE Calls deeper, less mewing than in Common Gull: a mellow *kowk*. More similar to Herring Gull, but higher-pitched; intermediate between Herring and Common. Advertising call 2–4 short notes followed by a series of 5–7 hoarser calls, slightly penetrating in the middle (Glutz von Blotzheim & Bauer 1982, Urban *et al.* 1986).

MOULT (pers. obs. USA, photos and skins) **Adult** moult to **winter plumage** is complete May–Oct. P1 late May/early Jun; P7–8(9) Aug, P9–10 late Sep–mid-Oct(Nov). Head and body Aug–early Sep. Moult to adult **summer plumage** partial Mar–Apr, including head and body. Many still in winter plumage early Mar, the majority in summer plumage mid-Apr. **Juvenile** moult to **first-winter** plumage partial late July–Sep, including all or most of head and underparts, mantle, much of back and rump, most of scapulars and sometimes a few median coverts. Some in juvenile plumage into Nov (Lauro & Spencer 1980). Moult to **second-winter** completed (Mar)May–Oct. In Apr–May includes head, body and some wing-coverts (especially median and inner greater). Tertials from May. Often retains some juvenile scapulars until Jun–Jul. Occasionally T1–2 renewed; a bird from Mar had three new rectrices on one side of the tail. P1 from May, on average a month earlier than in Common Gull; reaches P5 late Jun; P7–8 early Aug; P8–10 late Aug–mid-Sep; primary moult usually completed late Sep (compare adult). Body, coverts and tertials from May; may retain few juvenile coverts to Oct. Secondaries and tail Jun–Jul (Mjøs & Solheim 1995), sometimes not before late Jul, but most in tail moult Jun (T1–2,6), completing early Sep. Moult to **second-summer** partial Feb–May, including head and body. Generally later than in adult; some still have winter head mid-Apr. Moult to **third-winter** complete Jun–Oct; similar to adult.

DESCRIPTION

Adult Head, underparts, underwing-coverts and tail white. Upperparts and upperwing pale grey (Kodak Grey Scale 3–4(5)). Primary pattern similar to Common Gull nominate *canus*, but white mirrors on P9–10 smaller – 22–42mm on P10, extending over both webs but with large black tip (in Common almost reaching tip of feather), 8–22mm on P9, frequently narrow oval-shaped spot only on inner web. Mirror on P9 increases with age, P8 exceptionally with white mirror. P6 with 12–40mm black subterminal spot, P5 with small dark subterminal spot on both webs (sometimes lacking). P10 5–7mm >P9. Normally just with inconspicuous white 'moons' between black tips and grey bases of primaries (sometimes lacking; rarely as distinct as in Common and Mew Gulls). Tips to P1–7, secondaries and tertials white; less contrasting than in Common, as division is weaker and narrower, and upperparts paler.

Adult summer (Mar–Sep/Oct) Head white. With wear, white primary tips reduced or lacking. Orbital ring red to orange-red. Iris pale yellow. Bill bright yellow to orange-yellow with 5–10mm clear-cut black ring of even width on both mandibles (rarely reduced to dark subterminal spots, especially in late breeding season). Bill-base often greenish-tinged, tip sometimes paler ivory. Gape orange. Legs bright yellow to greenish-yellow.

Adult winter (Aug/Sep–Mar/Apr) Head with dark spots, strongest on hindneck, nape and around eye, sometimes extending onto lower throat, sides of breast and upper flanks as narrower spots or scales. Crown often with narrow brown streaks. Often shows white 'half-moon' on lower ear-coverts contrasting with dark-spotted upper ear-coverts and hindneck. White eyelids broad, contrasting with grey around eye (more so than in Common); most evident in lower eye-crescent and from mid-eye level and behind. Bill and legs duller yellow than in adult summer; bill-base often greyish- or greenish-tinged, tip sometimes ivory. Bill-ring 9–12mm. Orbital ring blackish.

Juvenile (fledging–Oct) Head, neck, breast and flanks whitish with coarse dark brownish spots or streaks. Flanks and breast-sides with dark V-spots or scales, creating distinct barring, which may cover entire underparts (least on central belly). Sides of neck, breast and upper flanks sometimes almost uniform sooty-grey. Undertail-coverts white with dark bars, generally stronger than in Common. White eye-crescents as adult winter. Mantle and scapulars grey-brown with varying dark subterminal bars or crescents and pale edges. Lesser and median coverts with slightly pointed (rarely rounded) dark centres and sandy to whitish fringes. Greater coverts pale grey, usually with dark subterminal bars on inner 3–5 (rarely all, but on outermost normally restricted to dark subterminal bars near tip and base). All coverts rarely dark brown basally. Tertials and sometimes innermost greater coverts dark brown with narrow pale fringes, sometimes with irregular pale waving of fringe as in Herring, or with paler grey centres or dark 'tooth' onto pale tip. P6–10 and their coverts blackish-brown, the latter with narrow pale tips and sometimes grey subterminal spots on outer web. Inner primary coverts as outer or grey with dark shaft-streaks and subterminal fringes. P6–10 have grey on the inner webs, increasing inwards. P1–5 are pale grey with 10–20mm dark diamond-shaped subterminal spots. Rump and uppertail-coverts white with dark spots or bars. Tail whitish (often faintly greyish-tinged) with varying dark subterminal bar, typically broken by pale mottling or up to 2–3 dark 'extra-bars', e.g. as black spots on up to 8mm white tail-tip. Inner webs of rectrices sometimes dark. T1 with 22–40mm dark subterminal bar. T6 often pale grey to base or with indistinct dark mottling on inner part. 5–7% have tail similar to Common Gull, but generally with broader pale edges

and grey shading onto base of T5–6. Rarely, most of tail dark with pale restricted to indistinct spotting on outer web of T6. Variation in tail pattern very large; rarely are two individuals the same. Underwing similar to Common, but generally more contrasting with paler greater coverts, creating midwing-panel. Axillaries often with broad dark fringes, but sometimes whitish (especially in birds with almost unmarked greater coverts). Iris dark brown. Bill blackish with fleshy base; extreme tip rarely whitish. Legs flesh-pink, sometimes bluish-grey-tinged with greyish foot.

First-winter (July/Sep–Apr) as juvenile, but head and body whiter with more distinct grey-brown spots on lower hindneck and crescent marks on breast-sides and flanks. Mantle, scapulars and back pale grey with whitish feather-edges, disappearing with wear from midwinter. Some mantle feathers often with dark subterminal crescents, shaft-streaks or spots, creating uneven pattern. Juvenile mantle and scapulars often partly retained. Wing and tail as juvenile, but with wear (from late autumn), pattern on lesser and median coverts becomes weaker and dark areas browner. Sometimes shows striking contrast between worn brownish-centred lesser/median coverts and tertials towards rest of plumage (especially in birds with dark grey breast-sides) from autumn. Bill fleshy to pink with 12–22mm clear-cut black tip, often broadest on lower mandible; base rarely yellow or greenish-fleshy. Bill gets pale tip from (Nov–)Feb.

First-summer (Mar–Sep) as first-winter, but head and body whiter with fainter dark spotting; often lacking, but sometimes strong on crown and ear-coverts. Mantle, scapulars and sometimes all median coverts pale grey. From Jun much worn: retained juvenile coverts fade to whitish, tertials/inner wing-coverts to pale brown, flight feathers to browner and dark pattern often reduced or lacking. Eye dark. Bill yellowish or pink with yellow or greyish tinge and dark subterminal bar/paler tip. Legs as first-winter, but sometimes greyish-yellow.

Second-winter (Sep–Apr) Head, body and coverts similar to adult, but spots on hindneck often browner and coarser. Alula dark with white edges and tip. Outer 5–6 primary coverts dark (sometimes dark colour reduced to shaft-streak, when broadest near tip). Scattered coverts (especially median and greater coverts) may show dark shaft-streaks. Lesser and marginal coverts sometimes with dark spots. Tertials sometimes dark-centred/barred (but rarely all). Primaries similar to adult, but often slightly brownish-tinged, usually with small white mirror on P10 only (9–35mm on inner web; sometimes lacking). Dark on outer web of primaries covers 120–160mm on P8, 60–110 on P6–7 (on P7 often reaching primary coverts) and 20–35 on P5. P3–4 often with dark subterminal spots. Dark outer webs of primaries sometimes divided from paler bases by dark mottling. Dark markings on secondaries and tail, often creating irregular dark bars; in tail often asymmetrical or as isolated spots, most frequent on T1–4. Rectrices sometimes with dark shaft-streaks. >50% have traces of dark tail-bar: in Ontario 11% appeared white-tailed, 23% with complete tail-bar and the rest intermediate (Peltomäki 2000). 10–20% have dark secondary-markings. Underwing-coverts white, often with faint dark

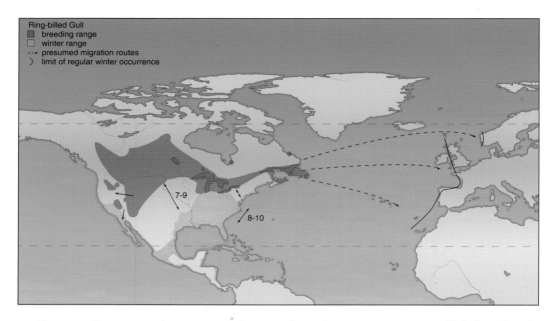

markings on median coverts and greater coverts. Eye on average darker brownish-yellow than in adult; sometimes dark as in first-years. Bill and legs similar to adult winter, but duller (more greyish- or greenish-yellow; rarely deep yellow). Bill-base often pink or fleshy and tip ivory to create a three-toned bill.

Second-summer (Mar–Oct) as second-winter, but head and body white with dark spots lacking or restricted to a few spots on hindneck. With wear, wing-tip browner. Bare parts as adult, but orbital ring generally duller red.

Third-winter (Mar–Sep.) as adult; black shaft-streaks on outer primary coverts, small white mirror on P10 (max. 25mm) and dark mottling in division between black and grey on P7–8 indicates this age.

Aberrants Partly albinistic birds have whitish wing-coverts and pale brown primaries. A first-winter with 'half' a tail-bar (being faded and reduced in one half) has been described (White & Kehoe 1992).

Hybrids Very rare. A probable hybrid **Ring-billed × Black-headed Gull** nested with a Ring-billed on Lake Ontario, New York, in 1982. A 'mystery' gull at Brigantine, Maryland, in 1974 was probably a **Ring-billed × Black-headed Gull** (Richards & Gill 1976, Weseloh & Mineau 1986). A putative hybrid **Ring-billed × Franklin's Gull** (Texas, Jan 2003) was slightly smaller and darker mantled than Ring-billed. Base of bill red, eyelids white against dark half-hood as in Franklin's. Upperwing pattern similar to Ring-billed with white mirror on P8, legs pale yellow-orange (M. Reid in litt.). A putative hybrid first-summer **Ring-billed × Common Gull** (England), similar to first-summer Common but with pale bill-tip and irregular tail-band (Kehoe 1992), could be an atypical Common Gull.

GEOGRAPHICAL VARIATION Negligible; considered least variable of N American gulls (C. Wilds *in litt.*).

Comparing mean measurements, birds from Ontario had on average a smaller bill but longer tarsus than those from Michigan (Ontario mean bill male 41.9, female 37.7, tarsus male 66.2, female 61.4; Michigan mean bill male 44.3, female 40.9, tarsus male 58.7, female 55.8) (Stugart 1977, Ryder 1978). W American first-years tend to show more complete white underwing-coverts and axillaries than those from E Coast (own. obs., California, Mexico, New Jersey, Massachusetts).

DISTRIBUTION AND MIGRATION Population 1.5–2 million pairs. Breeds on islands in freshwater lakes and on wet meadows, often in large colonies. Large decrease during late nineteenth century followed by a dramatic increase; in Great Lakes 500,000 pairs considered a pest to other breeding birds. Increase probably caused by increase in fish prey species. Examples of increases (in pairs) are Little Galoo Island, Ontario: 20,000 1950, 74,000 1981; Lake Huron and Lake Michigan 27,000 1960, 150,000 1974. Also an increase in New England. Small population in prairie regions. Range expansion taking place in USA; first bred Colorado 1985 (Ludwig 1974, Blokpoel & Tessier 1986, Lock 1988, del Hoyo *et al.* 1996, *Amer. Birds* 41: 308).

Leaves breeding colonies mid-July–early Aug, staying at Lake Erie and other lakes before further migration. Winter quarters reached from Sep. Migrates along rivers in interior USA to winter quarters in S USA, Great Lakes and St Lawrence River to coastal New Brunswick. Gatherings >200,000 Cleveland, 300,000 Lake Erie and tens of thousands in Appalachian region and Great Lakes, Oct–Dec, before freeze-up, eventually migrating over wide front to E coast, heading for Chesapeake Bay. In mild winters many stay, e.g. 30,000 Pennsylvania, 20,000 Illinois/Kentucky, >10,000 Ontario and >6,000 Appalachian Mountains. >10,000 winter in Florida with peaks every 5–6(10) years; >50% of winter population here from Great Lake regions. Also coasts and estuaries S to SE California, Greater Antilles and Mexico, where thousands winter (e.g. c.50,000 at night roost Salton Sea, Feb 2000). Main winter range for E population is N American Atlantic coastline between N Carolina and Florida. Max. 500,000 Cape Hatteras, N Carolina, late Dec/Jan, and max. 20,000 Virginia. W populations winter along the Pacific coastline S to Mexico and C America.

Spring migration late Feb–Apr, birds heading more directly towards breeding sites. Peak in New Jersey is in late Mar with max. day-counts of 5,000 at Cape May. Flocks of max. 20,000 in California. Casual in summer in Caribbean and in winter in Alaska; regular Hawaii (Southern 1974a & b, Nisbet 1978, Cramp & Simmons 1983, Hoogendoorn & Steinhaus 1990, Sibley 1993).

Increasing winter visitor to W Europe; first recorded Azores 1945, Spain 1951 and Great Britain 1973. Now regular Great Britain (most numerous Nearctic vagrant gull); influxes of first-years 1980/81, 1984/85 and 1986/87; often followed by left-overs: 65% first-years 1981, 44% second-years 1982, 66% adults 1983. Annual average for Great Britain 1958–1997 was 29, best year 1992 (103, mainly in SW). Most recorded in midwinter and spring; peak Mar–Apr, probably caused by birds heading N following wintering in areas further to S. Most summer records are second-years. Winter gatherings of max. 10 in W Ireland. Regular wintering France (max. 17 Jan–Mar 1999 and 25 Feb 2001), Iberian Peninsula (max. 18 Spain 1995/96; flocks of 10–15 on the Galician coast in the late 1990s), Azores (max. 50 1980 and flock of 56 Feb 2001), Madeira, Canary Islands and Morocco. Rare but regular Iceland (mainly spring–summer; 70 up to 2001) and Norway (29 up to 2000); indicates small migration route heading W from NE N America; summer occurrence probably a result of N migration following wintering E Atlantic. Vagrant Germany 6, Belgium 11, Netherlands 7, Denmark 1, Sweden 10, Faeroe Islands 2, Poland 5, Italy 2, Albania 1 and Bulgaria 2, Greenland 2, Senegal 1, S America 3, Galapagos 1 (Lack 1986, Small 1987, Hoogendoorn & Steinhaus 1990, Baillon & Dubois 1992, Poelmans 1992, BLIKI 1994, Boertmann 1994, Sørensen & Jensen 1994, Thrainsson & Péturson 1997, Mitchell & Young 1997, Nankinov 1998, van den Berg & Bosman 1999, Fraser et al. 1999a & b, SOF 2000, M. Elliott & A. T. Mjøs in litt.).

Increasing numbers of summering birds, often displaying to Common Gull (observed Great Britain, Netherlands and Sweden (in latter case 1993–99)) indicates that Ring-billed may establish itself as a breeding bird in W Europe. A bird ringed in Newfoundland spent several years in Norway and was eventually shot in Iceland (Mjøs & Solheim 1995).

MEASUREMENTS Lengths in mm; weights in g. Own data based on skins in AMNH, LACM, MCZ, NHM, NRK, USNM, ZMA, ZMO. North America, Mexico.

WING

Adult male	347–397 (378.2)	50
Adult female	335–385 (361.5)	46
First-year male	349–384 (367.4)	28
First-year female	326–384 (356.9)	51

BILL

Adult male	37.5–47.8 (41.3)	52
Adult female	34.6–43.0 (38.5)	49
First-year male	34.3–44.6 (39.5)	25
First-year female	33.6–43.9 (38.2)	49

BILL DEPTH AT GONYS

Adult male	12.9–14.8 (13.7)	51
Adult female	10.5–13.5 (12.6)	49
First-year male	10.5–14.2 (12.3)	29
First-year female	9.6–13.7 (12.1)	51

BILL DEPTH AT BASE OF BILL

Adult male	13.5–16.8 (14.9)	51
Adult female	11.6–15.0 (13.5)	49
First-year male	12.1–16.9 (13.4)	28
First-year female	11.1–15.5 (13.0)	51

RING-BILLED GULL Three-year gull. Nearctic, but regular migrant W Palearctic. Resembles a large, square-headed Common Gull with stronger, more parallel-edged bill (with stronger-hooked tip) and often much paler upperparts.

Adult has pale grey upperwing with only indistinctly paler trailing edge and tertial tips: wing-tip with smaller white mirrors than Common. Pale eyes and strongish bill create 'larger gull' impression. Bill with solid dark bar, looking broader than width of eye. Bare parts generally yellower than in Common. In **summer** (Apr–Sep) white-headed. In **winter** (Sep–Apr) head with coarse dark markings, generally stronger than in Common with more solid white area across neck-sides and dark spotting often penetrating breast-sides and flanks as dark chevrons.

Juvenile greyish-brown with scaled saddle. Upperwing similar to Common, but generally with more contrast between dark and paler areas (thus intermediate between Common and Mediterranean Gull). Most important, tail with varying dark bars, narrow extra bars or shading, only 5–7% with solid black tail-bar against white tail. Rump dark-spotted. Underwing often with solid pale midwing-panel. Bill fleshy with black tip, generally more strongly bicoloured than in Common, as bill broader.

First-winter (Sep–Apr) similar to juvenile, head and body to adult. Pale grey mantle almost concolorous with pale greater coverts; mantle and scapulars often with scattered juvenile feathers.

Second-year similar to adult, but dark wing-tip fuller, as dark reaches primary coverts, and the wing-tip is black (or with white mirror on P10 only). Most show traces of dark tail-bar, sometimes scattered dark secondaries and dark spotting on underwing. Bill often with greenish or fleshy tinge.

Third-year as adult, but sometimes with combination of few dark-streaked outer primary coverts and very narrow white mirror on P10.

GONYS LENGTH		
Adult male	11.2–14.0 (13.1)	51
Adult female	11.0–13.7 (12.3)	49
First-year male	9.8–13.9 (12.2)	28
First-year female	10.2–14.2 (12.1)	51

TARSUS		
Adult male	54.0–63.7 (57.9)	51
Adult female	50.0–61.2 (54.2)	49
First-year male	51.9–59.2 (55.6)	28
First-year female	48.3–58.1 (54.0)	51

Weight Adults 390–670, generally lighter in winter, when down to 331.8 in female. Juv./first-winter 288.6–496 (Glutz von Blotzheim & Bauer 1982, skins in ZMA).

Ring-billed Gull *Larus delawarensis.* **96. Juvenile moulting into 1st-winter**. A rather short-billed individual, resembling Common or even Mew Gull, but note dark-spotted head and underbody as well as faint pale barring on greater coverts and irregular pale edges to tertials. Alberta, Canada. 22 Jul 1999. *Jon R. King.* **97. Juvenile moulting into 1st-winter**. Bird with rather heavy bill, its pattern resembling Glaucous Gull. Often looks flat-crowned. Ocean City, Maryland, USA. 3 Oct 1994. *Klaus Malling Olsen.* **98. Juvenile moulting into 1st-winter**. Compare head and bill shape with 96–97 as well as with similar-aged Common and Mew Gulls. Ocean City, Maryland, USA. 3 Oct 1994. *Klaus Malling Olsen.*

Ring-billed Gull *Larus delawarensis.* **99. 1st-winter.** A round-headed and narrow-billed individual, in this respect resembling Common Gull, but note extensive dark spotting or scaling at breast-sides, and mantle being concolorous with greater coverts. Cape May, New Jersey, USA. 1 Oct. 1994. *Klaus Malling Olsen.* **100. 1st-winter.** A poorly marked individual. Note extensively worn coverts by mid-winter. Sonora, Mexico. 2 Feb 2000. *Klaus Malling Olsen.* **101. 1st-winter**. Note tail-pattern, typically with broad dark tail-bar surrounded by dark shading or several narrower bars – diagnostic from Common and Mew Gulls. Salton Sea, California, USA. 1 Feb 2000. *Klaus Malling Olsen.* **102. 1st-winter**. Individual with narrow tail-bar resembling Common Gull, but with grey shading in inner part. New Jersey, USA. 28 Jan 1985. *Arnoud B. van den Berg.* **103. 1st-winter**. Note pale midwing-panel, often striking in this species compared to Common Gull. Sonora, Mexico. 2 Feb 2000. *Klaus Malling Olsen.*

113

Ring-billed Gull *Larus delawarensis*. **104. 2nd-winter**. Similar to adult, but note faint dark tail-markings and uniform black primaries. Florida, USA. Oct. *Hanne & Jens Eriksen*. **105. 2nd-winter**. Traces of dark tail-bar present in >50% at this age. Massachusetts, USA. 11 Sep 1997. *Klaus Malling Olsen*. **106. 2nd-winter**. Unlike Common Gull *canus/heinei*, still shows extensive dark markings in underwing at this age. Sonora, Mexico. 2 Feb 2000. *Klaus Malling Olsen*. **107. Adult summer with Common Gull ssp. *canus*.** Note paler upperparts, fainter pale tertial tips and also fiercer expression than Common Gull, created by pale iris and fuller hindcrown. Halmstad, Halland, Sweden. 29 May 1993. *Klaus Malling Olsen*. **108. Adult summer**. Note that eye is small, but bill-ring extensive, often looking broader than eye, California, USA. 20 Feb 1997. *Don DesJardin*.

Ring-billed Gull *Larus delawarensis*. **109. Adult winter**. In winter extensive dark spots appear on the head, especially hindneck, and often on breast-sides. Note very pale eye surrounded by black orbital ring and broad, even ring around bill. Newport, California, USA. 31 Dec 1997. *Don DesJardin*. **110. 3rd-winters** are almost identical to adults, but generally with smaller white mirror on P10. Additionally, many third-winters show dark-streaked primary coverts. Sonora, Mexico. 2 Feb 2000. *Klaus Malling Olsen*. **111. Adult winter**. In flight often gives impression of a larger gull. Stratford, Connecticut, USA. Dec 1997. *Julian R. Hough*. **112. Adult winter.** Compared to Common Gull, lacks clear white spots between grey and black in primaries, as well as showing fainter white trailing edge and narrower white mirrors in P9-10. Belfast, Northern Ireland. Mar 1993. *René Pop*.

9. CALIFORNIA GULL

Larus californicus (Lawrence, 1854, Stockton, California) **Plates 16–17, Photos 113–128**

IDENTIFICATION Length 45–51cm, wingspan 122–140cm. California Gull is between Herring and Ring-billed Gull in size. It resembles Ring-billed but has a larger, slimmer and longer bill, smaller head, deeper breast and belly, more attenuated body and wings, shorter legs and dark eyes. The long wings are often lowered when settled. In flight it is slender with a deep breast, flat or slightly concave belly and narrow wings. California Gull takes four years to develop fully adult plumage as in larger gulls, making precise ageing difficult apart from first-year and adult. Two subspecies discernible (Jehl 1987b, King 2001), both rather similar; separation of *albertaensis* discussed under Geographical Variation.

Adult has dark grey upperparts with prominent white scapular and tertial crescents and trailing edge to inner wing. The clean-cut black wing-tip appears as a triangle with white mirrors on P9–10; on the otherwise white underwing the darker secondaries create a rectangle. Eyes are dark, surrounded by a red orbital ring. Bill yellow with red gonys-spot, dark markings and paler tip, often appearing four-coloured—a pattern unique in West Coast gulls. Often shows a long, reddish gape-line. Legs grey to yellow. In many ways resembles adult Armenian and Caspian Gull taxon *barabensis*. In **summer** head is white and bill greenish-yellow with dark markings normally restricted to lower mandible. Orbital ring red. Legs yellow, often with greenish tinge. In **winter** head has dark patterning, mainly as hindneck-streaks, creating a darker necklace which may reach breast-sides. Bill and legs duller and more variable than in summer, bill with broader dark subterminal bar and often ivory tip. Orbital ring sometimes dark.

May be confused with Ring-billed, which is normally slightly smaller with paler upperparts, a generally larger and bulkier head, shorter, blunter-tipped bill with a more complete black bill-ring, pale eyes and slightly longer, yellow legs. In settled birds, white crescent and tertial edges weaker and wings shorter with more evenly spaced white primary tips; in California, spacing between white primary tips more uneven, broadest on inner visible primary tips. In winter, Ring-billed has coarser dark head-markings, covering most of head and reaching breast to upper flanks.

Compared to American Herring, California Gull is smaller with rounder, smaller head, narrower bill and larger dark eyes situated more to the front of the head. The hindparts are narrower, wings longer and legs shorter. In most plumages it is darker than American Herring, often with grey legs showing a blue or greenish tinge not present in American Herring.

Juvenile has a dark brown head and underparts with a paler forehead, central belly and undertail-coverts, the latter brown-barred or mottled. The fresh juvenile plumage is often strongly cinnamon or buffish-tinged. The upperwing is dark with slightly paler coverts and 1–2 pale bars created by dark bases to the greater and median coverts; there is rarely a slight pale window on the inner primaries. The upperparts are dark brown

with indistinct mottled feather-edges. The greater coverts may be almost uniform dark, forming a dark midwing-panel, but some birds have entirely barred or mottled greater coverts, together with solid dark-centred tertials generally darker than rest of upperparts. Tail dark against the heavily barred rump. Underwing dark with slightly paler flight feathers. Bill blackish and legs fleshy.

In darkest birds, the dark overall plumage may approach first-year Heermann's, but lower belly and undertail-coverts are paler, bill often darker and legs fleshy, not dark.

First-winter similar to juvenile, but head generally paler with clearer dark hindneck spots and more conspicuous pale forehead. Mantle and scapulars grey to greyish-brown with variable dark streaks, subterminal bars or narrow spots. Bill develops pale base from Oct, and becomes fleshy with clear-cut black tip in winter, the pale base merging into the pale face. Legs fleshy to greenish-grey. Combination of bill, rather uniform head with pale blaze (and sometimes neck-sides), weakly mottled underbody, dark-streaked grey mantle, greenish-tinged legs and small size separates the plumage from other gulls. From late winter, pale mid-wing-panel on upperwing is developed through wear of median coverts, and the greater covert bar is more conspicuous. In **first-summer**, the head and underbody are whitish and retained juvenile feathers strongly faded.

Second-winter has white head and underbody with dark-streaked necklace and breast-sides, which may be barred. Saddle grey, in contrast to wing, which is similar to first-year, apart from darker greater coverts with fainter pale mottling (often restricted to innermost), creating brown carpal bar on inner wing. Parts of coverts renewed to adult type. Tertials with triangular dark centres and white edges. Compared to first-years, flight feathers darker with more conspicuous pale window on inner primaries, broader rounded white tips and rarely white mirror on P10. Rump white with barely any dark pattern, contrasting strongly with dark, white-edged tail. Underwing pale with dark tips to axillaries and coverts, creating dark rows. Bill duller than in adult with black subterminal bar or tip. Legs pale grey with bluish, green or fleshy tinge.

Second-summer similar to second-winter, but with more adult-type inner wing-coverts; often contrasting well with retained second-winter coverts. Bill yellowish-tinged.

Third-winter similar to adult, but with most of lesser and greater coverts of second-year type, dark-centred primary coverts and broken, blackish tail-bar. Wing-tip duller brownish-black with white mirror on P10 only; white primary tips narrower or lacking. May show a few dark-centred greater coverts and secondaries (rarely all) and black bill-tip.

Third-summer as adult, but before moult with age-characters of third-winter.

Fourth-winter as adult, but black on wing-tip duller with white mirror on P10 only, black shaft-streaks on primary coverts, traces of dark (often greyish) on tail, generally less yellow tinge to legs and blacker, more complete black ring around bill-tip.

VOICE Higher and quicker, more squeaky and hoarse than in American Herring Gull. A short, deep *gaaal* similar to call of Great Black-backed Gull. Long-call rapid, high and wheezy (Sibley 2000).

MOULT (ssp. *californicus*) **Adult** moult to **winter plumage** is complete mid-Jun–Nov. P1–2 mid-June, P4–6 late Jul–Aug, P10 late Oct–late Nov. Head Aug. Moult to **summer** plumage partial Feb–Mar, including head and body. By mid-Feb >95 % still have dark head-markings; last to be lost are hindneck streaks. By Apr, most have summer head, but often still a few dark streaks on ear-coverts and hindneck. **Juvenile** moult to **first-winter** partial Aug/Sep–Feb, including head and body, often restricted to mantle/scapulars. Moult slow with much individual variation. Mantle/scapulars generally Oct–Dec, but often with juvenile feathers admixed into Mar. Moult into **first-summer**, but complete into **second-winter** late Apr–Oct, starting with mantle/scapulars and P1, followed by head, body and coverts (starting late Apr–early Jun). P1 late Apr–early May, P4–5 mid-Jun–Jul, P7–8 Aug, P9–10 Sep–Oct. Some populations (probably *albertaensis*) have later primary moult, reaching P4–6 Sep–early Oct and P9–10 late Nov. Moult to **second-summer** partial Mar–May, including head and sometimes parts of underbody; could be regarded as start of complete moult into **third-winter**, which starts Mar–Apr with mantle and scapulars (>50% renewed May–Jun) and some wing-coverts. P1 usually from late Apr, but sometimes not before mid-Jun. P9–10 (early)mid-Sep–mid-Oct.

DESCRIPTION (*californicus*)
Adult Mantle, back, scapulars, tertials and upperwing-coverts dark blue-grey (Kodak Grey Scale 6–7.5), scapulars and tertials with prominent white edges. Secondaries with white tips, creating striking white trailing edge to inner wing. Primaries with grey bases and black outer parts/tips. P10 black with 32–45mm white mirror and 1–6 mm black subterminal bar near tip (often as isolated black spots; lacking in 9%, creating complete white tip of max. 55mm). P9 black with 5–25mm white mirror, sometimes oval-shaped or divided by black shaft-streak; a small proportion lack white mirror (King 2001). Black on outer web of P9–10 reaches primary coverts. P8 black (120–140mm on outer web, 70–100mm on inner); division between grey and black sometimes dark-mottled. Black on P8 reaches primary coverts in 56%; if base grey (max. 20mm), division between grey and black diffuse. P7 grey with 80–90mm black tip on outer and 40–60mm on inner web, running along shaft and reaching primary coverts in 84–95% (King 2001). P6 with 50–70mm black on outer web, 25–50mm on inner. P6–7 often with narrow white crescent-shaped division between grey and black. P5 with 10–35mm black subterminal bars near tip; sometimes restricted to black spot on outer web; may show black U-markings on both webs. Have narrow white tongues between black and grey, sometimes weak. P4 on

15–20% with black markings. Primaries with 8–15mm white tips, broadest on innermost. Tail, rump, underbody, axillaries and underwing-coverts white; from below, grey-centred secondaries create grey rectangle against white coverts. Bill yellow with red gonys-spot, black subterminal markings and often ivory tip. Gape red. Iris greyish-olive to dark brown, in birds with extensive amount of dark spotting appearing blackish; 10% with faint mottling, enough to create dull yellow eyes. Orbital ring red, yellow or violet-brown (Johnston 1956). Legs yellow, often with a greenish tinge; see under adult winter for variation.

Adult summer (Mar–Sep) Head white. Orbital ring red. Bill yellow with a red gonys-spot, often merging with narrow blackish subterminal bar (sometimes incomplete and restricted to lower mandible; rarely lacking); tip paler ivory to yellow. Legs yellow.

Adult winter (Oct–Apr) Head white with variable, often extensive brown streaks or spots, especially on hindneck, where they form a necklace in 98% of birds checked in California/Mexico late Jan–Feb, in 38% even with streaking on ear-coverts, and in 10% reaching crown. A minority show an evenly streaked head, and may appear hooded; <1% white-headed by early Feb (pers. obs.). Hindneck-streaks may reach breast-sides. Cheek, throat and foreneck sometimes with indistinct dark spots. Orbital ring dull red to black. Bill four-coloured: paler yellow than in summer plumage, with more complete black subterminal bar (max. 8mm), merging with reddish-orange to red gonys-spot. Tip ivory. Leg colour variable: from 207 adults mid-Jan–mid-Feb legs grey (37%), yellowish-grey (31%), greenish-yellow (18%), greyish-yellow (5%), bluish-yellow (4%) and yellow (3%); in <1% bright yellow or fleshy; seemingly larger percentage of yellow among N Mexican birds may be food-related (pers. obs., California and N Mexico).

Juvenile (fledging–Sep/Nov) Head and underbody greyish-brown to cinnamon, yellowish-buff, pale tan or dark brown. Warm coloration soon lost by wear. Forehead, lores and chin paler, often as pale blaze. Crown, ear-coverts, eye-mask and hindneck darker. Lower belly paler, often merging into dark-barred white undertail-coverts. Mantle and scapulars greyish-brown with sandy fringes, sometimes as dots along edges. Tertials pale brown to blackish-brown with pale edges, broadest on tips and sometimes mottled along edges; may show darker subterminal markings, paler subterminal spots or bars; rarely as broad as dark ones. Lesser and median coverts pale greyish-brown with dark brown bars or often indistinct spots. Greater coverts darker greyish-brown with narrow pale bars, normally restricted to inner ones, most distinct on inner 30% and broader white tips; greater coverts rarely lack barring. Primary coverts and flight feathers blackish-brown with 3–5mm white tips to secondaries and P1–8 (narrowest on P5–8). P1–5 with paler subterminal markings and inner webs, forming pale window, although less prominent than in American Herring, and darker outer webs and subterminal spots. Rump and uppertail-coverts white with broad dark bars. Tail blackish-brown, when fresh with 1–3mm pale tips to rectrices. Shows weak pale barring at bases of especially T4–6, reduced to weak pale

PLATE 16. CALIFORNIA GULL *Larus californicus*

Range restricted to W and C North America. Winters along Pacific coast. Structurally (and concerning plumage development) a small American Herring Gull with small rounded head, slimmer bill and slender body with accentuated rear, as wings rather long and narrow. Bill slender with parallel edges and only faint blunter tip or gonys-angle (both much stronger in larger gulls). Eyes dark, situated well forward in head. Often in large flocks, both in inland and coastal waters.

1. **Juvenile** (Aug–Sep) Head and underbody brown (with variable buff to cinnamon tinge), appearing waved with dark transverse barring on undertail-coverts. Covert-barring weaker than in American Herring Gull.

2. **First-winter** (Sep–Apr) Face pale, merging into pale fleshy bill (with black tip). Lacks pale eyelids. Wing and body otherwise similar to juvenile, but mantle and scapulars grey with varying dark subterminal streaks, spots or bars; pattern of scapulars especially variable: variant with subterminal bars shown; others show dark shaft-streaks, spots, some even uniform grey scapulars. Dark-centred greater coverts often stand out on wing.

3. **Second-winter** (Aug–Apr) Head and underbody white with brown markings, most extensive on hindneck (where forming brown neck-boa). Saddle and median coverts grey against dark-marked brownish other wing-coverts. Tail still mainly black. Plumage superficially similar to third-winter American Herring, which is larger and has paler upperparts, much stronger bill and pale eyes.

4. **Third-winter** (Oct–Apr) Similar to adult, but still with some brown-barred 'immature' coverts (especially greater), narrower white primary tips and duller bill. Leg colour variable, ranging from yellow to grey with greenish or bluish tinge to fleshy.

5. **Adult winter** (Oct–Apr) Adult shows dark grey upperparts with slight bluish tinge, upperparts being darker than in Ring-billed or American Herring. White tertial crescents broad and conspicuous. Bill four-coloured: yellow with red and black markings near tip and ivory tip. In winter head white with faint dark markings, but more contrasting brown hindneck-streaking, usually prominent enough to form conspicuous brown neck-boa. Gape red and long with somewhat downward extension to below eye. Eyes dark. Legs variable as in third-winter.

6. **Adult summer** (Apr–Oct) Compared to adult winter, head white and bill with narrow dark subterminal markings, but generally brighter red gonys-spot. White primary tips gradually worn off from spring. White spot on P10 usually separated from tip by black subterminal bar in nominate *californicus*, shown here (breeds Great Basin).

7. **Adult winter** race *albertaensis* (Northern Great Plains) Compared to *californicus*, slightly larger and paler grey with slightly longer bill and generally more white on wing-tip, including frequent whole white tip to P10. See text for details.

1. Juvenile

2. First-winter

3. Second-winter

4. Third-winter

5. Adult winter

6. Adult summer

7. Adult winter *albertaensis*

PLATE 17. CALIFORNIA GULL *Larus californicus*

In flight like a small American Herring Gull with smaller, rounder head, narrower bill and longer, narrower wings. Wingbeats quicker. Compared to Ring-billed Gull slightly larger with proportionately smaller head, longer and slenderer bill and fuller hand with blunter tip. Often in large flocks. Size and jizz similar to Black-tailed Gull (compare first year Black-tailed, Plate 1).

1. **Juvenile** (Aug–Oct) Head and body extensively brown, often with cinnamon to buff tinge. Face paler, but bill blackish. Upperwing rather uniform brown, lacking pale inner primary window (of Ring-billed and Herring Gulls), but often showing two whitish wing-bars formed by broad pale tips and edges to dark-based greater and median coverts. Rump heavily brown-barred, appearing brown against blackish tail. Axillaries and under-wing-coverts dark brown, slightly contrasting with paler flight feathers, but general impression of underwing much darker than in other similar-plumaged gulls.

2. **First-winter** (Sep–Apr) Similar to juvenile, but face and pinkish bill-base in contrast to black bill-tip and brown head. Underparts still mainly rather uniform brown. Mantle and scapulars grey with varying dark markings, sometimes faint, but normally as dark spots, crescent markings or streaks.

3. **Second-winter** (Aug–Apr) Mantle and some coverts grey. Wing greyer and less uniform than in first-years with slight pale window on inner primaries and paler coverts. Rump white. Tail usually with brown-black bar, covering >50% of tail surface. Underwing faintly dark-patterned. Head white with dark neck-boa.

4. **Second-summer** (Apr–Sep) An example showing traces of immaturity in otherwise adult plumage, such as dark secondary bar, brown-patterned lesser coverts and primary coverts and dark spots in tail.

5. **Third-winter** (Sep–Mar) Similar to adult, but with extensive dark markings on primary coverts and tail (often also secondaries), and more black on wing-tip; white mirrors on P9–10 smaller and white primary tips narrower; bill duller with more complete black markings.

6. **Adult winter** (Sep–Mar) Adult *californicus* shows medium grey upperwing with conspicuous white trailing edge and extensive black wing-tip with white mirrors on P9–10. Although there is much intergradation, certain birds of race *albertaensis* identifiable on larger size, slightly paler upperparts, often white tip to P10 and less black near tips of P5–8 (creating better-defined black trailing edge to midwing than in nominate). Four-coloured bill, dark eyes and distinctly streaked hindneck are all characters separating the species from Ring-billed and Herring Gulls.

1. Juvenile

2. First-winter

3. Second-winter

5. Third-winter

4. Second-summer

6. Adult winter

spots on T1–3, where sometimes lacking. T6 with 5–9 white spots along outer web (may be absent). Axillaries and underwing-coverts dark greyish-brown. Eye blackish. Bill black, quickly developing pale base (evident from Sep). Legs pale flesh to pink.

First-winter (Oct–Mar/Apr) similar to juvenile, but face paler and head-markings more distinct, on hindneck mostly as dark streaks, creating necklace. Mantle to scapulars with mix of greyish-brown to grey feathers and dark shaft-streaks or narrow subterminal spots/bars. Scapulars most variable: in some plain greyish, in others with black shaft-streaks, broader triangular markings or subterminal bars. Bill fleshy with 15–17mm black tip, upper mandible sometimes greyer; black tip to bill most extensive on lower mandible. Legs fleshy, often with slight bluish to greenish tinge. With wear, plumage paler greyish-brown and face whitish.

First-summer (Apr–Aug) as first-winter, but head to breast generally paler; belly often remains dark-patterned. Some grey (often paler-fringed) feathers intermix on mantle and scapulars as first parts of second-winter plumage. Wing-coverts (especially median coverts) worn and faded, creating pale midwing-panel, inner coverts often renewed paler, with narrow dark bars. Flight feathers and tail brownish through wear. Bill as first-winter, but normally greyish-tinged with pale tip. Legs pale flesh with greenish, greyish or bluish tinge.

Second-winter (Aug–Apr) Head paler than in first-years with more distinct dark spots on hindneck and breast-sides and dark streaks on ear-coverts, often as thin dark line behind eye. Mantle, scapulars and sometimes inner and median coverts grey, rest of wing-coverts greyish-brown, more uniform than in first-winter; most lack bars or mottling (but often with slight pale vermiculations on inner greater coverts). Coverts have pale greyish-brown fringes, on greater coverts creating faint pale wing-bar against rather dark bases. Tertials dark brown (often blackish on distal half) with broad white tips and edges, divided from dark, mostly triangular bases; division sometimes irregular. Primary coverts greyish-brown; paler than in first-years apart from outer. Secondaries blackish-brown with broad pale tips. P1–4(5) greyish with faint dark mottling, creating pale window against darker brown P6–10. P10 rarely with faint white mirror. P1–8 have narrow indistinct pale fringes. Uppertail-coverts and rump white, sometimes with indistinct dark mottling (especially along sides and on upper rump, where sometimes more extensive) in contrast to dark brown tail; extreme tail-base paler. T6 varies from white to dark, rarely with inconspicuous pale tips and mottling along edges (as in first-year, but pattern more vermiculated). Underbody pale brownish-grey to white with faint dark spots or streaks, often most extensive on belly and often barred on flanks; lower belly paler. Undertail-coverts white with narrower dark bars than in first-year (these sometimes lacking). Axillaries and underwing-coverts pale grey with dark tips and edges, creating dark rows or bars on underwing. Bill greyish, often with yellow to bluish tinge, and black tip or subterminal bar. Legs grey, often with yellow, fleshy or bluish tinge.

Large individual variability exists. 'Retarded' birds similar to first-years, but with more uniform greater coverts, grey feathers on both mantle/scapulars and inner wing-coverts; the contrast in first-years between fresher mantle/scapulars and the more worn coverts is lacking.

Second-summer (Apr–Sep) similar to second-winter, but head and underbody paler with fewer dark markings. Grey spreads to all inner wing-coverts. Bill yellow with black subterminal bar and normally reddish tinge to gonys.

Third-winter (Sep–Mar) similar to adult winter, but with dark-centred primary coverts and alula, more diffusely divided from brownish-tinged, black wing-tip. Often lacks white mirrors on P10; some show small white mirror (max. 25mm) on inner web. Unlike adult, P3–4 usually with narrow dark subterminal spot. White primary edges narrower. Upperparts may show traces of immaturity such as some black-centred greater coverts, dominance of second-year type lesser coverts and greater coverts, and incomplete blackish secondary bars and tail-bars (as dark spots, often broadest on central secondaries and T4–6); all secondaries rarely dark-centred. Tertials and coverts sometimes brownish-tinged. Bill and legs similar to second-winter, but bill usually yellow with broad black subterminal bar (rarely covering tip) and some red on gonys.

Third-summer (Apr–Sep) As third-winter, but head white and dark areas faded.

Fourth-winter (Sep–Mar) as adult, but lesser coverts, greater coverts and tail with dark markings, primary coverts often with dark shaft-streaks and P3–4 sometimes with dark subterminal spot. Black on wing-tip generally duller, white mirror normally restricted to P10 only. Tail often with indistinct dark markings, especially on T4–5. Bare parts as adult, but black subterminal bar on bill often more complete, and legs generally with less yellowish tinge (King 2001, pers. obs.).

GEOGRAPHICAL VARIATION Two taxa.

L. c. californicus (breeds Great Basin and adjacent areas from Washington and Montana S to California and E to Wyoming and Colorado; probably British Columbia) described above.

L. c. albertaensis (breeds N and E of nominate *californicus*; N Great Plains, from southern NW Territories S through Alberta into Montana, E to W Manitoba and North Dakota) larger than nominate with heavier, more parallel-edged bill and weaker gonys-angle. Generally bulkier with shorter projection of wings above tail, and on average shorter legs. Some (especially adult males) identifiable in the field, but many characters overlap with nominate (mirroring situation between Common Gull races *canus* and *heinei*). Racial identification should always be based on direct comparison between several individuals. Note also that appearance of hybrids in areas of presumed contact, particularly Montana, remains to be studied (King 2001).

Adult Has paler upperparts (Kodak Grey Scale 5–6.5 (probably palest Canada)), sometimes approaching American Herring and Ring-billed Gull. Black on wing-tip *in full adult* less extensive (and often comparable to Caspian Gull nominate race *cachinnans*, see p. 29). P10 often with complete white tip (29% versus 9% in nominate). Grey tongue on P10 continues 30–50% towards tip (max. 30% in nominate). P9 with white mirror, generally broader and squarer than in nominate (rarely <10mm); in 10% black on outer web of P9 does not reach primary coverts. P6–8 with deeper pale grey tongues, often whiter at distal end, where sometimes forming 'string of pearls'. Black on P7–8 normally does not reach primary coverts (in 15% on P8; grey base to P8 mainly >15mm) and is sharply divided from grey (in >90% of nominate, black reaches primary coverts; division between grey and black narrower and more diffuse, often as slight spotting). P7 with at least 50mm grey extension above primary coverts (<50mm in nominate); lacks diffuse black line along shaft almost to reach primary coverts of most nominate (but extension of black similar to fourth-year nominate). Distal edge of grey tongue on inner web of P7 longer than P5 (falls short of the tip in nominate); P5 grey, in 5–16% with black markings. P4 lack black markings. Black on wing-tip often L-shaped versus fuller black of nominate. Underwing with indistinct darker secondaries, not forming extensive rectangle of nominate. Moult to winter generally 2–3 weeks later than in nominate, reaching P5–7 by late Jul, P9–10 Oct/Nov (Jehl 1987b, King 2001). In **winter**, head-markings more extensive, sometimes similar to American Herring, with dark markings reaching chin and throat (rare in nominate).

First-years not subspecifically identifiable, although *albertaensis* is on average darker than the nominate. More research needed.

Note Separation of nominate and *albertaensis* based mainly on King (2001), who kindly submitted unpublished data for preparation of the text.

Aberrants Fourth-year-type part-albino white with weak dark pattern to P6, scapulars and tail.

Hybrids Hybridisation with American Herring Gull reported twice Colorado and one (probably) Wyoming (Winkler 1996).

DISTRIBUTION AND MIGRATION 200,000 pairs in

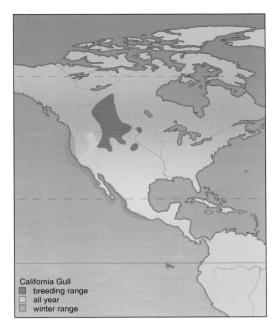

California Gull
- breeding range
- all year
- winter range

>100 colonies. Breeds in open, arid habitats, usually on low rocky islands in fresh and saline waters. Numbers reduced to 50,000 pairs in 1930, mainly by egg collecting, but increasing to 140,000 pairs in 1980 following protection (Conover 1983, del Hoyo *et al.* 1996). Extension of range linked with this increase. Largest colonies in Great Salt and Mono Lakes, Utah. Partly migratory, mainly moving north of breeding range following breeding season, gradually spreading S during winter. Common in all areas with sufficient food, such as towns, parks, estuaries, lakes and rivers.

At least 17,000 pairs of race *albertaensis* in Canada and 3,000 in Anaho Region, NW Territories.

Following the breeding season there is a strong westerly movement, with many younger *L. c. californicus* migrating N to Pacific NW, before moving S down Pacif-

CALIFORNIA GULL Four-year gull. An elegant W American gull, in size between Ring-billed and American Herring Gull; head small and rounded, bill slender and parallel-edged, hindparts long and slender and legs rather short.

Adult has pale grey upperwing with black wing-tip, white mirrors on P9–10 and white trailing edge to inner wing. Eyes dark. Bill yellow with black and red tip and ivory extreme tip. In **winter** (Oct–Apr) hindneck has dense brown streaks, sometimes spreading to head.

Juvenile (Aug–Sep) has greyish-brown to cinnamon head and underbody, heavily barred undertail-coverts and dark bill. Upperwing dark with all-dark primaries. Rump heavily brown-barred and tail dark brown. Underwing often extensively dark brown on coverts.

First-winter (Sep–Apr) similar to juvenile, but cinnamon wash soon lost and face paler; bill pale with black tip. Lacks prominent pale eyelids. Mantle and scapulars greyish with dark streaks or subterminal markings. Legs fleshy.

Second-year shows grey saddle and median coverts against brown upperwing similar to first-year, but with paler window on inner wing. White rump contrasts with all-black tail. Bill duller than in adult with more extensive black markings.

Third-year similar to adult, but black on wing-tip more extensive and primary coverts with dark markings. See Geographical Variation for differences between nominate *californicus* and race *albertaensis*.

ic coast to main winter areas in California and Mexico. *L. c. albertaensis* performs a leap-frog migration, wintering on average slightly more to the south than the nominate, mainly inland. However, nominate still dominates in whole area, accounting for >99% of birds in Sacramento and 90–95% at Salton Sea, California, and 70–80 % on the Sonora coast, Mexico (King 2001).

In late Jul flocks >8,000 Washington. Max. 26,000 Vancouver Island Sep. Winters mainly Pacific coast S to Baja California, Colima and N Mexico. Winter flocks of max. 13,000 California (Sacramento, Santa Cruz, Monterey Bay, Orange County). Saskatchewan breeders migrate W to coastal British Columbia and disperse S to Sinaloa. Max. 600 winter Mountain West Region. Scarce N from Alaska and S from Baja California. Casual winter visitor to American Mid-west, Colorado and C southern region (max. 21 per winter). Rare, but regular winter visitor Yukon, Quebec and Texas. Vagrant Virginia, Delaware and Florida, Hawaii, Japan. Birds recorded E of Chicago probably belong to the race *albertaensis* (King 2001, O. Janni *in litt.*).

MEASUREMENTS Lengths in mm; weights in g. Own data based on skins in LACM, MCZ, NHM, NRK, USNM, ZMO. Combined with Jehl (1987b). **Note** First-years all from California, not identified to subspecies.

WING

L. c. californicus		
Adult male	365–418 (393.8)	154
Adult female	341–395 (372.8)	209
L. c. albertaensis		
Adult male	385–431 (412.2)	48
Adult female	369–408 (391.3)	38
Subspecies undetermined		
First-year male	375–410 (388.7)	23
First-year female	353–392 (373.5)	29

BILL

L. c. californicus		
Adult male	40.5–59.2 (47.3)	153
Adult female	38.0–48.4 (42.7)	172
L. c. albertaensis		
Adult male	47.3–57.4 (53.0)	49
Adult female	41.2–52.0 (47.8)	38
Subspecies undetermined		
First-year male	43.3–50.8 (46.4)	23
First-year female	38.0–48.2 (42.1)	29

BILL DEPTH AT GONYS

L. c. californicus		
Adult male	13.7–18.8 (16.5)	149
Adult female	13.1–16.3 (14.9)	164
L. c. albertaensis		
Adult male	15.6–19.2 (17.7)	48
Adult female	14.8–17.0 (15.8)	36
Subspecies undetermined		
First-year male	14.2–17.2 (15.1)	23
First-year female	12.5–15.3 (13.7)	29

BILL DEPTH AT BASE OF BILL

L. c. californicus		
Adult male	14.3–16.5 (15.8)	28
Adult female	13.9–16.3 (15.2)	27
Subspecies undetermined		
First-year male	14.9–17.9 (16.0)	23
First-year female	12.8–16.0 (14.5)	29

GONYS LENGTH

L. c. californicus		
Adult male	11.2–13.6 (12.6)	28
Adult female	10.8–13.4 (12.3)	27
Subspecies undetermined		
First-year male	10.7–14.1 (12.6)	23
First-year female	9.8–13.8 (11.7)	29

TARSUS

L. c. californicus		
Adult male	47.7–65.0 (58.9)	140
Adult female	43.8–60.5 (54.8)	160
L. c. albertaensis		
Adult male	56.8–72.0 (63.1)	48
Adult female	52.8–65.1 (57.7)	36
Subspecies undetermined		
First-year male	55.3–60.8 (58.4)	23
First-year female	47.8–58.0 (54.4)	29

Weight *L. c. californicus* adult: male 490–885, female 432–695. *L. c. albertaensis* adult: male 653–1045, female 568–903 (Jehl 1987a & b).

California Gull *Larus californicus*. Unless otherwise stated, photos refer to ssp. *californicus*. **113. Juvenile.** When fresh, shows variable cinnamon to buff tinge to head and underbody, soon disappearing through wear. Santa Barbara, California, USA. Aug 1995. *Don DesJardin.* **114. Juvenile.** Darker individual than 113. Note pale forehead contrasting with browner head, also note lack of pale eyelids. Santa Barbara, California, USA. 27 Aug 1996. *Don DesJardin.* **115. Juvenile moulting into 1st-winter.** In 1st-winter shows strongly variable pattern in mantle and especially scapulars. Bill strongly bicoloured. Ventura, California, USA. Oct 1995. *Don DesJardin.* **116. 1st-winter.** Compare scapulars with 115. Santa Barbara, California, USA. 30 Oct 1998. *Don DesJardin,* **117. 1st-winter**. In flight often with conspicuous pale tips to greater coverts, forming pale wing-bar. Santa Cruz Island, California, USA. 19 Oct 1997. *Don DesJardin.*

California Gull *Larus californicus*. Unless otherwise stated, photos refer to ssp. *californicus*. **118. 1st-winter**. Underbody rather uniform. Undertail-coverts heavily dark-barred and tail dark. Note also very dark underwing-coverts. San Diego, California, USA. 12 Feb 2000. *Klaus Malling Olsen*. **119. Moulting into 2nd-winter**. Greater coverts more uniform than in 1st-winter, with finer vermiculations. Compare with 1st-years in photos 113-116. Santa Barbara, California, USA. Aug 1995. *Don DesJardin*. **120. 2nd-winter**. 2nd-winter shows combination of grey saddle and extensive barring in wing-coverts. Santa Barbara, California, USA. 30 Oct 1996. *Don DesJardin*. **121. 2nd-winter**. Grey saddle contrasts with wings, which in flight look similar to 1st-years. Tail still dark, at this age contrasting clearly with white rump. Orange Co., California, USA. 8 Jan 1986. *Harry J. Lehto*. **122. Moulting into 3rd-winter**. Santa Barbara, California, USA. Aug 1995. *Don DesJardin*. **123. 2nd-summer**. Note worn wing-coverts contrasting with grey saddle. Santa Barbara, California, USA. 7 May 1996. *Don DesJardin*. **124. 2nd-, 3rd- and adult summer**. Third year in flight looks similar to adult, but note narrow dark tail-bar. Ventura, California, USA. Aug. *Karel Beylevelt*. **125. Adult summer**. Extensive black wing-tip with white mirror on P10 typical for ssp. *californicus*. Orange County, California, USA. 8 Jan 1986. *Harry J. Lehto*. **126. Adult winter**. Shows varying, but often extensive dark streaks in hindneck. Note dark eye and 4-coloured bill, differing from American Herring, which is larger with pale eyes, more spotted head-pattern (though variable) and less patterned bill. Note leg colour, which ➤

in adults is extremely variable. Vancouver, Canada. Sep 1998. *René Pop*. **127. Adult winter and putative 1st-winter**. Immature in background probably 1st-winter with unusually narrow dark patterning to saddle, looking grey at distance, but note broad dark and pale bars in upperwing and dark barring in rump. The wing-tip of adult is typical for *californicus*. Orange Co., California, USA. 8 Jan 1986. *Harry J. Lehto*. **128. Adult summer** ssp. *albertaensis*. Compare wing-tip pattern with 125 and 127; in *albertaensis* less black, creating L-shaped black wing-tip with extensive pale tongues in mid-primaries. Alberta, Canada. 21 Jul 1999. *Jon R. King*.

10. GREAT BLACK-BACKED GULL
Larus marinus (Linnaeus, 1758, Gotland, Sweden)　　　Plates 18–19, Photos 129–145

IDENTIFICATION Length 61–78cm, wingspan 145–165cm. This is the largest gull. Males are often identifiable on size and structure alone, being much larger than Herring, with an extremely brutal appearance created by a combination of the small eyes positioned far back on the flat head and the heavy, parallel-edged (i.e. rectangular) and bulbous-tipped bill. The smallest females are only Herring Gull-sized, but have a larger head with a more angled forehead, flatter crown, smaller eyes, fuller hindneck, larger bill with a much more pronounced bulbous-shaped tip and longer, stouter legs with longer visible tibia. The wings are relatively shorter than Herring Gull with less projection above the tail. In flight the species appears stocky with powerful slow wingbeats, sometimes recalling *Haliaeetus* eagles, an impression reinforced by the long, heavy head and bill, full body and short tail.

Adult has blackish upperparts with a striking white wing-tip, as the tip of P10 is white and P9 has a large white mirror. The wingtips appear white when lit from tail-end; lit from head end and against pale background the white disappears and the wing-tip looks broad and rounded. White trailing edge to blackish upperwing conspicuous (although narrower in Slaty-backed and Kelp Gull). From below, the wing-tip appears black with broad white edges and tip. Bill and leg colour as Herring, but eyes darker yellow surrounded by a darker orbital ring. Adults are rather similar whole year; in **winter** head only indistinctly dark-streaked or spotted, looking white at distance. Bill often with faint dark markings. An ID pitfall is provided by the smaller Lesser Black-backed Gull race *intermedius*, which has same upperpart colour, but has slimmer, more pointed wings with a narrower white trailing edge and less white on the outer wing (on P10 the white mirror only rarely covers the tip). Greater has four white primary tips behind the tertials, Lesser usually five but narrower. In Lesser, the legs are shorter and yellow. Older immature Lesser may show fleshy legs, while similar-aged Greater may show limited white on the wing-tip compared to adult. Size and structure are then important; Lesser is smaller with rounder head and lighter bill; in winter Lesser shows much denser dark head-markings.

Slaty-backed Gull is slightly smaller with a less heavy bill, paler slaty upperparts and normally more restricted white wing-tip (in most P10 shows a mirror, not a tip), with a broader white trailing edge. There is often an obvious white 'string of pearls' on wing-tip, almost connecting with white tongue on P8, and from below the primaries look predominantly grey with black restricted to the tips. Kelp Gull is smaller with blacker upperparts, yellow to grey legs with a greenish tinge and a broad white trailing edge to wing as in Slaty-backed.

Juvenile similar to Herring, Yellow-legged and Heuglin's Gulls, but generally more contrasting 'black and white'. Slower rate of development indicated from early age. Size and proportions are main points, but these are less obvious in females, which may be surprisingly small. Compared to Herring it shows a heavier, black bill with a narrow pale tip. Head and underbody white, breast at most slightly dark-spotted. Acquires whitish forehead soon after fledging. Mantle and scapulars darker brown with more distinct pale fringes than in Herring, appearing chequered and contrasting somewhat with paler-patterned wing-coverts. Especially greater coverts pale with narrow dark bars—mostly narrower than pale bars and often creating pale panel against dark-centred secondaries, often evident in flight. Tertials blackish with irregular white edges and broad white tips. Primaries blackish, white tips to blacker outer primaries often broader than in Herring.

Juvenile Herring is a less contrasting greyish-brown with denser brown streaks on the head and breast, less distinct pale pattern to the upperparts and a dark-marked lower belly. Greater coverts generally with broader dark bars (mostly broader than or equal to pale bars, matching dark tertial centres). Most Herring acquire a pale bill-base from late autumn.

In flight, wing pattern similar to Herring, but inner primaries darker with weaker (if any) pale window, and the darker secondaries contrast better with the pale greater coverts. The dark tail-bar is typically weaker, appearing diluted with broader white bases and edge; the strong white edge to the tail-sides is a reliable specific character. The white rump makes a stronger contrast to the upperparts (and often to tail-bar!) than in Herring. Under-wing with weaker (if any) pale 'window' than Herring.

Juvenile Yellow-legged and Heuglin's Gulls share with Great Black-backed the pale head, black white-tipped bill and (in some Heuglin's) sloping forehead, but the upperparts are browner with darker greater coverts showing narrow pale bars (especially in Yellow-legged). Importantly, the black tail-bar is more solid and in better contrast to the white tail-base and rump (with pattern more similar to Common Gull).

First-winter similar to juvenile, but head and breast whiter. Mantle has darker transverse barring, contrasting well with juvenile wing, often with darker saddle reflecting eventual plumage development. Black bill retained into first spring.

'**First-summer**' generally shows a whiter head and underbody than in first-winter—an effect of wear. Upperparts have grey, dark-barred feathers, with wear contrasting with faded areas on wing and tail. Bill develops broader white tip and often paler base.

Second-winter varies. Most have whitish head with slight dark streaks (especially around eyes), pale-based bill with dark subterminal bar, white tip to both mandibles and sometimes scattered adult mantle feathers. Greater coverts generally darker than in first-years with only fine pale vermiculations, appearing buffish when fresh. Tail-bar less distinct than in first-winter. Many show slight pale mirror on P10. Eye becomes paler. Birds in similar plumage to first-years are aged by paler and rounded (not pointed) primaries, finer pale vermiculations on darker greater coverts, broader and more irregular white tertial-tips and pale-based bill with broader pale tip. Some first-year Yellow-legged *michahellis* are superficially similar (with similar large-looking pale head), but have slimmer hindparts, black bill, broader dark eye-mask, full black tail-bar and narrower V-shaped pale fringes to primaries.

Second-summer similar to second-winter, but head and underbody off-white, mantle and scapulars uniform black or just with scattered brown feathers. Wings and tail worn and faded; coverts may become whitish through wear. Some acquire adult-type blackish lesser and median coverts, contrasting strongly with bleached parts of wings. Bill varies from dark with paler base, black subterminal markings and rarely traces of red on gonys to dark with pale tip and smudgy paler base. Eyes generally darker than adult.

Third-winter similar to adult, but with scattered brown feathers on upperparts (especially coverts) and traces of dark tail-bar. White wing-tip markings narrower than in adult, with white mirror (not tip) on outer primary. Bill usually dull yellow with dull orange gonys-spot and traces of dark subterminal markings.

Third-summer similar to third-winter, but brown on upperwing-coverts fades, combined with new blackish feathers, creating piebald pattern. White primary tips reduced or lacking. Bill as second-winter, but often with extensive dark yellow behind nail.

Fourth-winter as adult but often with narrower white tip to P10 (usually broken by blackish subterminal markings near tip) and more extensive dark markings on bill; tail sometimes with a few dark-patterned feathers. Primary coverts darker than in adult.

Subsequent plumage as adult, but 'immature' features such as dark markings on bill and tail and immature-type wing-coverts (especially dark tips to under primary coverts) probably persist into higher ages than in other large gulls.

VOICE Usual calls are deeper, hoarser, slower and more cackling than in Herring Gull. While displaying, 'laughter' shorter and slower.

MOULT (pers. obs., S Scandinavia, skins; Ingolfsson 1970b, Cramp & Simmons 1983) Similar to Herring Gull, but slower in flight feathers. **Adult** moult to **winter** plumage is complete (Apr)mid-May–Dec/early Jan. P1 mid-May–mid-Jun (Iceland) to late Jun–early Jul (Scandinavia, W Europe); by Jul Iceland breeders have reached P4–5, Scandinavian P2–4. S Scandinavian birds reach P3–5 Aug, P6–8 Sep/early Oct and P9–10 (late Oct)mid-Nov–late Dec. (P10 often Jan; in 2–3% Mar–May.) Secondaries and tail generally start when primary moult has reached P4–6; secondaries from Jun; sometimes not before Sep. Tail Aug–Nov, sequence generally T4–5, 1–2,3, but often random; larger proportion than in other large gulls moult all rectrices simultaneously. Head and body Sep/Oct. Advanced birds may moult coverts from mid-May. Moult to adult **summer** partial Jan–Apr, including head and body; on upperparts, sometimes parts of mantle. Attains summer head by Mar. **Juvenile** moult to **first-winter** plumage partial (Aug)Sep–Jan, including mantle, scapulars and sometimes parts of the head and body. Often no sign of moult into Nov/Dec. Moult into **second-winter** complete Apr–Oct/Nov. P1 late Apr/early May. Up to P3

renewed late May, P4–6 late Jul/early Aug, P7–9 late Aug–mid-Sep, P10 (late Aug)Sep–early Nov. Mantle and coverts from mid-May, sometimes earlier. Moult to **second-summer** partial Dec–Mar/Apr, including head and body. Moult to **third-winter** complete late Apr–Nov; similar to moult to second-winter. Moult to **third-summer** similar to adult summer; little information available.

DESCRIPTION

Adult Head, underbody and tail white. Upperwings and back blackish-grey (Kodak Grey Scale 11–13), distal parts of primaries black. P9–10 black, P6–8 dark grey with black tips, decreasing inwards usually to subterminal mark on P5. P10 0–5mm > P9. P10 with white 50–80mm tip, often with faint dark spot on outer web. P9 with 25–55mm white mirror, usually with dark subterminal spot before 8–13mm white tip; often broken by black shaft-streak. Outer web rarely all black. P8 black, sometimes with max. 35 mm white mirror (in 10% of males; females with max. 10mm mirror in <1%) and/or with greyer bases to about 50mm from black tip. Sometimes with whitish tongues of max. 17mm on inner web, normally combined with largest amount of white on P9–10. P7 with black outer web and 23–40mm outer part of inner web, diffusely divided from dark grey base of inner web; often with 3–12mm white tongue. P6 dark grey with 10–28mm black outer web and 5–10mm white tongue; sometimes black distal part isolated from shaft. P5 dark grey, frequently with blackish-grey distal part, often restricted to dark spot near tip of outer web. Primaries with broad white tips, when fresh max. 20mm, but with wear almost disappearing on P6–10. Shows broad white tips to P1–5 and secondaries. Marginal coverts white. Underwing white with broad dark grey trailing edge, merging with blackish surface on outer primaries. Primary coverts frequently have narrow grey edges. White scapular-crescents narrow, white tertial-tips large and obvious. Iris pale greyish-yellow to amber. Orbital ring red to orange. Bill pale yellow with orange or red gonys-spot. Nostril oval-shaped or triangular: depth at distal edge 2.1–2.4mm, length 10.8–13.0mm. Legs flesh, sometimes with grey or creamy (rarely yellow or extremely orange) tinge (van Kreuningen 1980, de Heer 1982a, pers obs).

Male on average larger with heavier, squarer and parallel-edged bill. Female normally with curved inner part of lower mandible, emphasising bulbous shape to bill-tip (valuable also when sexing younger birds). Adults with broadest white markings on primaries and white mirror on P8 are almost invariably male (skins in UZM).

Adult summer (Feb–Sep) Head white. With wear, upperparts (especially coverts) acquire a brownish tinge and white primary-tips are reduced. Bill bright yellow with red gonys-spot. Legs sometimes with yellow (rarely orange) tinge.

Adult winter (Sep–Mar) Similar to adult summer, but head with dark eye-crescents and narrow brown streaks around eye, on ear-coverts, hindcrown and especially lower hindneck. Chin, throat and rump sometimes faintly streaked or spotted. Bill pale yellow (sometimes slightly tinged pinkish) with orange gonys-spot. May show faint dark markings on upper and sometimes lower mandible.

PLATE 18. GREAT BLACK-BACKED GULL *Larus marinus*

The largest gull. Generally larger than the Herring Gulls with heavier bulbous-tipped bill, flatter crown and squarer neck. Eyes dull, never pale yellow. Legs longer with larger amount of tibia visible; fleshy. Appears full-bodied with prominent tertial step and rather short wings, extending somewhat above tail. Basically coastal, breeding along seashores and on inlets, but outside breeding season often in small numbers in inland waters. Winters mainly along seashores, attracted by fishing activities. In many northern seaports common alongside Herring Gulls.
Plumage development slow; takes at least four years to attain full adult plumage, and often 1–2 years more, making precise ageing outside first-years and full adult difficult.

1. **Juvenile** (Aug–Nov) Similar to Herring Gull, but generally better marked with more chequered upperpart markings, better-contrasting dark coverts with whiter edges and broader pale barring on greater coverts, typically reducing dark covert-barring to isolated dark spots on inner greater coverts. Tertials blackish with broad white edges, often with paler subterminal markings. Primaries brownish-black with pointed tips. Edge to outer tail feathers white.

2. **First-winter** (Oct–May) Similar to juvenile, but upperparts acquire new, paler feathers with blackish subterminal markings; often contrasts well with paler juvenile wing. In winter, head mainly white and underparts only faintly dark-patterned. Bill black with faint paler tip. Compared to Herring, plumage better contrasting, never rather uniform greyish-brown at distance. Note especially white head against bulbous-tipped black bill, 'saddle' slightly darker than coverts (especially paler-patterned greater) and long legs with large amount of tibia visible.

3. **Second-winter** (Aug–Mar) Similar to first-winter, but bill with fleshy base and broader white tip on both mandibles. Fresh greater coverts often buffish-tinged, with more, finer bars than in first-year and tertials blacker with broader, more irregular white edges. Primaries blacker with rounder white tips, creating row of 'new moons' on wing-tip. May acquire a few blackish-grey upperpart feathers of adult type but generally shows fewer such feathers in second year than other large gulls.

4. **Second-winter** (Apr–Sep) Starts to attain adult-type upperpart feathers and some coverts of adult type (although often slightly paler than adult, with faint pale edges). Bill fleshy with black subterminal markings and broad white tip. Head and underbody sparsely dark-patterned.

5. **Third-winter** (Aug–Apr) Saddle and median coverts greyish-black, of adult type (but generally browner and duller), contrasting with lesser and greater coverts, which are brown with slight paler barring. Tertials with brownish-tinged centres and irregular white edges. Primaries black with narrower white tips than in adult, white mirror on P10 not reaching tip. Head white with faint dark streaking especially on hindneck, bill dull yellow with black subterminal markings; starts to show red on gonys by late winter/spring.

6. **Fourth- or adult winter** (Sep–Mar) In winter basically white-headed, but close inspection will reveal very fine narrow streaks around eye and short brown hindneck-streaks or -spots. Eyes dull yellow, typically appearing small and beady, set high and well back on head. Upperparts greyish-black with prominent white tertial crescents. Wing-tip black with broad white primary tips, the tip to P10 all white; variant shown here shows blackish subterminal markings on bill and very narrow black tip to P10, which in combination are signs of fourth-year (or young adult) rather than full adult.

7. **Adult summer** (Mar–Sep) Full adult shows broad white tips to two outer primaries, almost merging into one another. Tip of P10 wholly white. Upperparts greyish-black in very slight contrast to black on primaries; in North America the darkest-backed large gull, with fleshy legs (the smaller Lesser Black-backed Gull shows yellow legs and much less white on wing-tip; Kelp Gull slightly smaller with greenish legs and less white on wing-tip).

1. Juvenile

2. First-winter

3. Second-winter

4. Second-winter

5. Third-winter

6. Fourth- or adult winter

7. Adult summer

PLATE 19. GREAT BLACK-BACKED GULL *Larus marinus*

In flight heavy with broad, barrel-shaped body, short but full tail and long, broad, somewhat blunt-tipped wings. Wings placed well back on body. Head and neck well protruding. Flies ponderously with slow, eagle-like wingbeats.

1. **Juvenile** (Jul–Nov) First-year upperwing with dark primaries, at most with faint pale window on inner primaries; coverts paler, greater coverts pale enough to create good contrast to dark secondaries, dark trailing edge of wing thus narrower, but better contrasting than in Herrings. Rump and tail-base slightly dark-spotted, tail-bar rather narrow, most extensive on midtail. Tail edges mainly white, only with a few dark markings near tip. Underwing dark-patterned in contrast to paler flight feathers. Brownish juvenile head and body present into early winter, generally longer than in Herring.

2. **First-winter** (Oct–May) Compared to juvenile, head and underbody whiter; head contrasts with heavy, bulbous-tipped black bill. Compared to 1, this individual shows slight pale window on inner primaries, even paler greater coverts (isolating dark secondaries well from rest of wing) and tail with several narrow extra bars.

3. **Second-winter** (Aug–Mar) Rather similar to first-year, but mantle/scapulars darker, contrasting more with paler, more diluted upperwing pattern, showing paler edges to secondaries, slightly paler window on inner wing and blacker primaries, sometimes with faint brownish tinges; white mirror on P10 sometimes present. Tail-bar more diluted, but often blacker than in first-year. Bill paler-based with broad white tip.

4. **Third-winter** (Aug–Apr) Upperwing a mixture of adult and immature: shows greyish-blackish saddle and midwing-bar against browner lesser and greater coverts. Whole upperparts, however, brown-tinged, including black primary tip, just showing narrow white window. Tail with dark pattern, often as streaks. Underwing still with faint dark patterning. Bill dull yellow with red and black tip.

5. **Adult winter** (Sep–Mar) Adult shows greyish-black upperparts with slightly blacker wing-tip and broad white edge. White wing-tip reinforces impression of blunt-tipped wing; white wing-tip formed by extensive white on P9–10, much broader than in other dark-mantled gulls. White trailing edge to wing broader and more complete than in Lesser Blackback. Head white with faint dark streaking. Bill yellow with red gonys-spot.

6. **Adult summer** (Mar–Sep) Head white, bill brighter than in winter. Note long head with flat crown barely separated from heavy, blunt-tipped bill, small beady eyes (in white head looking dark), heavy body and short tail. Wing long and broad with full hand, white primary tips appearing light against greyish-black upperparts.

1. Juvenile

2. First-winter

3. Second-winter

4. Third-winter

5. Adult winter

6. Adult summer

Juvenile (fledging–Oct/Feb) Head white with narrow grey-brown streaks around and behind eye creating dark mask, and on hindneck often as broader spots or streaks. Chin/throat sometimes with faint dark spots. Has prominent dark eye-crescents. Breast to belly white with coarse dark spots (generally strongest on breast-sides, where sometimes streaked). Lower belly often whitish. Mantle and scapulars blackish-brown with pale internal markings and broad white to pale cinnamon edges, creating chequered pattern contrasting with paler-marked wing-coverts. Rump and uppertail-coverts whitish with dark streaks, spots or bars. Tail-base whitish, rest of tail highly variable, with black but somewhat diffuse waved or diluted bars and broad white edges and tips (typically forming weaker tail-bar than in congeners), but often with extensive dark spots on T1–3. T6 white with dark shaft-streak and drop-shaped spot near tip, more rarely with 2–3 narrow dark spots along edges. Inner wing-coverts barred as in juvenile Herring Gull, but in stronger contrast to darker mantle. Greater coverts pale with three dark bars or triangular subterminal spots. Pale bars typically (much) broader than dark; most evident on inner ones, often gradually weaker on outer, which in a small proportion are rather uniform darkish. Tertials blackish-brown with broad pale edges and tips, often strongly notched. Flight feathers blackish-brown with slightly paler P1–5, being greyish-brown with darker subterminal spots near tip and often whitish spots along edges of shafts on especially outer web; on some, P1–5 are almost as dark as P6–10. Primaries have slightly pointed white tips, creating row of narrow pale V-markings, disappearing with wear on P6–10 in first autumn, but retained throughout winter on P1–5. P10 5–6mm >P9. Axillaries and underwing-coverts greyish-brown with narrow transverse bars; sometimes more uniform dark axillaries, lesser coverts and median coverts contrast with paler greater coverts and flight feathers. Iris dark brown. Bill black with narrow white tip (3–8mm on upper, 0–6 on lower mandible). Legs fleshy, rarely with bluish tinge; feet often rosy (Glutz von Blotzheim & Bauer 1982).

First-winter (Sep–Mar) similar to juvenile, but head and upper breast whiter with narrower dark streaks (especially around eye and on hindneck); forehead normally white. May show dark ear-spot. Mantle and scapulars pale grey to buff with blackish subterminal bars or anchor-shaped spots; often intermixed with juvenile feathers. Bill similar to juvenile, but some develop paler base from early winter. Pale individuals have whitish underparts, narrower dark subterminal marks on upperparts and narrow dark covert-markings. With wear may bleach as described under Herring Gull, but rarely as extreme (an extremely pale spring bird shown by Grant (1989a) could to my eyes be partly leucistic, as the upperparts appear unmarked, which is atypical even in very worn birds).

First-summer (Mar–Aug) as first-winter, but head and underparts generally whiter. Mantle, back and scapulars grey with black subterminal bars and shaft-streaks. Upperwing and tail paler with wear. Bill black with smudgy, greyish- or fleshy-tinged base and pale tip to both mandibles. Eye dark.

Second-winter (Aug–Mar) Head white with dark streaks around eye and on lower hindneck, often as extensive as first-winter. Underbody white with coarse dark streaking on especially breast-sides and flanks; rump white. Mantle and scapulars acquire black or dark grey feathers, intermixed with others similar to first-winter. Lesser and median coverts grey-brown with pale edges and dark shaft-streaks or subterminal spots. Greater coverts darker than in first-years with finer, paler, more vermiculated bars (up to 8–10); on inner 30–50% sometimes patterned as in juvenile, but buffish-tinged when fresh. Tertials blackish with broad irregular white tip, subterminal bars or vermiculations. Flight feathers similar to juvenile, but primaries blackish-brown with rounded and more distinct (although narrow) white tips, emphasising rounded shape especially on innermost. P1–5 paler with blackish subterminal spots. P10 normally with diffuse brownish-white mirror of max. 40mm. P9 rarely with max. 8mm pale mirror. Tail white with variable blackish subterminal bar; similar to juvenile, but dark bars narrower and more vermiculated. Underwing-coverts and axillaries white with dark markings, most extensive on lesser coverts and primary coverts. Iris becomes paler. Orbital ring pale orange. Bill highly variable: black with diffuse pale base and tip or greyish-yellow with dark subterminal bar. Pale bill-tip broader than in first-winter; 10–20mm on upper, 7–10mm on lower mandible. Legs fleshy.

Second-summer (Mar–Sep) as second-winter, but head and underparts white with less dark streaking. Mantle, scapulars and normally some (all) lesser to median coverts blackish, often with brown admixed, especially in spring, before moult to third-winter. Wing and tail worn and faded; old coverts become rather uniform brown or even whitish with extreme wear, in strong contrast to black areas. Iris dark, rarely yellow from this age. Orbital ring yellow, orange or red, usually duller than in adult. Bill whitish or fleshy-yellow with variable black subterminal barring or patches; sometimes deeper yellow (especially behind nail) and, rarely, traces of red gonys-spot.

Third-winter (Sep–Apr) Head and underbody as in second-winter, but only with sparse, scattered dark patterning on underbody; rarely with rounded spots on hindneck. Upperparts as in adult, but mantle and scapulars usually duller greyish-black (sometimes looking slightly paler, with faint pale edges) with brownish tinge or a few browner-tinged feathers (mostly inner wing-coverts). Sometimes with a few brown, pale-patterned greater coverts similar to second-winter. Tertials as adult or paler, often brownish-tinged with dark subterminal markings near white tips, which may be rather irregularly patterned. Primary coverts often with brownish-grey tips. Underwing still rather heavily dark-marked, but in some mainly pale with dark restricted to lesser coverts. Compared to adult, shows duller black wing-tip with less white: P10 with max. 60mm white mirror, often with dark subterminal spot on tip of inner web. P9 dark or with 18–30mm white mirror (rarely lacking); P7–10 otherwise brownish-black. P6 normally with paler base. White primary tips 10–16mm, generally narrower than in adult. Tail white with faint dark subterminal bar, often broken and concentrated on T1–3; tail sometimes white with indistinct dark spots (especially on T6), grey shading to T1–4 or wholly white. Eye normally darker and browner than in adult. Bill greyish-flesh to dull yellow with varying black subterminal bar, strong yellow behind nail and red to orange gonys-spot; sometimes as adult. Legs fleshy.

Third-summer (Apr–Sep) as third-winter, but head and underparts white, patchy appearance on upperwing more pronounced and browner through wear and white primary tips reduced. New adult feathers often blacker than retained greyish-black of second-winter. Bill as adult, but sometimes with dark subterminal spot on upper mandible. Some hardly separable from second-summer.

Fourth-winter (Sep-Apr) as adult, but P10 sometimes with narrower white tip (often broken by black subterminal markings near tip) and upperparts sometimes with slight brownish tinge; primary coverts sometimes darker. Under primary coverts often with grey tips. Bill as adult, but often with dark subterminal markings especially on mandible.

Subsequent plumages as adult; a combination of several late immature characters indicates a younger adult, but much individual variation. Many take one more year to develop adult plumage than other large gulls.

Aberrants Leucistic adult shows pale grey upperparts (similar to adult Glaucous Gull), medium grey P9–10 and greyish-yellow bill with dark subterminal bar, combined with head and bill-shape of Great Black-backed (pers. obs., Sweden, Oct 1991). May be identical to 'albinistic' first-winter (white with black bill and fleshy legs) first seen 1984 and observed for subsequent 12 years S Sweden (Olsson 1983, Ullman 1983, Bruns 1985, Breife 1985).

Hybrids Glaucous × Great Black-backed Gull. Frequent Greenland. Adult has darker grey upperparts than Glaucous (similar to Herring Gull race *argentatus*). Pattern on P8–10 similar to adult Great Black-backed, but dark on outer web grey and dark on inner web reduced to near shaft. White tip to P9 divided in 45 degree angle from dark. Rest of primaries with reduced dark markings compared to Great Black-backed; sometimes similar to Glaucous-winged Gull, but with more extensive white on especially P9–10. An adult in winter plumage had broader dark head-markings than Great Black-backed. Wing 490–500 (including female with 500), bill 65.5–68.7, tarsus 79.2–81.0; mean measurements larger than in either parent species (skins in UZM, MCZ). For captive birds, see Lönnberg (1919). First-years often like ghostly Great Black-backed. Compared to latter, flight feathers dusky (not blackish) and tail-bar very narrow and faint. Covert-markings narrower. Bill often as heavy but with fleshy base, sometimes contrasting clearly to blackish tip and cutting edges (D. Boertmann, L. Witting & M. Kviesgaard *in litt.*, photos).

Adult (winter) **Great Black-backed × American Herring Gull** has dark grey upperparts similar to Lesser Black-backed Gull race *graellsii*. Crown, nape and sides of head with heavy, dark brown streaks similar to Herring (more streaked than adult winter Great Black-backed). P10 grey subterminally with max. 53mm white tip, often irregularly divided from black, extending around both webs. P9 with max. 21mm white mirror. Bill yellowish-white with greenish tinge and orange gonys-spot. Iris yellow with olive-brown or lightly fleshy-brown tinge. Orbital ring pale yellow. Legs and feet whitish-flesh. Wing 433–436, bill 51.3–57.0, bill depth at base 20.3–22, bill depth at gonys 21.2–21.5, tarsus 70 (in both) (Andrle 1972). Birds from Greenland had a similar wing pattern and head pattern, but head often with mixture of dark brown spots (from American Herring) and narrow blackish streaks (from Great Black-backed) (P. Grossman and D. Boertmann photos).

Suspected adult **Great Black-backed × Herring Gull** (Finland, Denmark, winter) was the size of a large Herring Gull, upperparts intermediate between Great Black-backed and Herring race *argentatus* (as dark as darkest Lesser Black-backed race *graellsii*), white tip to P10, black on outer wing as restricted as in average Herring *argentatus* and mainly white head (*DOF-Nyt 5/2:29*, H. Lehto *in litt.*).

GEOGRAPHICAL VARIATION Negligible. Birds from N part of breeding range heavier than in W Europe (Barth 1967, Cramp & Simmons 1983); measurements show large overlap and clinal variation.

Most N American adults have tawny-yellow eyes, generally darker than in Palearctic birds. Adults in S Carolina noted as white-headed in winter; in Newfoundland white or lightly streaked heads. Differences in other plumages unknown; certain first-years have shown dark, almost unpatterned outer greater upperwing-coverts, but still rarely (seemingly more frequent than in western Palearctic birds; further information required (pers. obs., B. Mactavish, A. B. Kristensen *in litt.*)).

DISTRIBUTION AND MIGRATION Population 200,000 pairs. Breeds on sandy islands and along rocky coasts; prefers flat-topped stacks. Local on salt marsh, lakes or urban areas. Opportunistic feeder, locally considered a threat towards other seabirds, especially eiders *Somateria*. In winter mainly coastal, but usually also occurs inland in small numbers.

Some spread in twentieth century, with expansion of breeding range to Spitsbergen and Iceland 1921, France 1925, Denmark 1930, Germany 1984, Netherlands 1993. Population stable or slightly declining Norway, Great Britain, Iceland and W Sweden, increasing Baltic, Denmark and France (Hagemeijer & Blair 1997).

European and Atlantic population in 2000 (in pairs): Great Britain 23,000; Iceland 15,000–30,000 (30,000–50,000 in 1970s); Spitsbergen 20–100 (in 1980); W and SE Greenland 3,000–5,000; France 4,000 (350 1970, 2,230 1988); Germany 1–10; Netherlands 10–15; Denmark 1,500–1,600 (464 1974); Norway 40,000; Sweden 15,000–20,000 (7,300 mid-1970s); Finland 2,800 (strong increase); European Russia 8,200–10,000 (4,100 Murmansk coast and some hundreds Gulf of Finland); Estonia 5,000 (Cramp & Simmons 1983, Risberg 1990, Gjershaug et al. 1994, Tucker & Heath 1994, del Hoyo et al. 1996, Hagemeijer & Blair 1997, Grell 1998, Väisinen et al. 1998, Dubois et al. 2000, Bijlsma et al. 2001, Lyngs 2003).

In N America it is increasing in numbers and extending

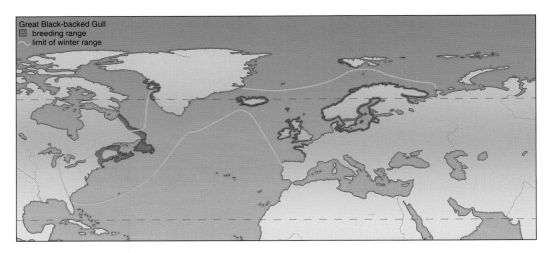

its breeding range. In New England 30 pairs 1930, 12,400 1972. First bred Maine 1928, Massachusetts 1931, New York 1940, Great Lakes 1954, New Jersey 1966. Breeds S to N Carolina. E North American population 17,415 pairs 1983. Summer flocks max. 800 Maryland. Vagrant W to Alaska (del Hoyo *et al.* 1996).

Migration variable: High Arctic populations completely migratory; sedentary in S part of breeding range. Populations of N Russia/N Norway leave breeding sites from Jul, migrating W to S along Norwegian coast to main winter areas in North Sea region; fewer Great Britain W to Ireland, even fewer S to Bay of Biscay, Iberian and Moroccan coastlines (recorded S to Casablanca) and W Mediterranean. Many W and S Norwegian birds migrate to NE England, where main arrival Sep (Cramp & Simmons 1983, Coulson *et al.* 1992, Lyngs 2003).

Migration in N Europe peaks Oct–Nov with flocks of hundreds S Scandinavia and max. 1500 Poland. Vanguards from Jul, flocks of hundreds (mainly younger birds) late Jul–mid-Aug; peak late Aug–Oct with flocks >3,000 in German Waddenzee. In S part of wintering range peak Nov–Feb with several thousands in Dutch Waddenzee.

NW European winter population 480,000. Baltic birds winter between Baltic and Kattegat/North Sea, mainly Danish Belts and Kattegat, where mingling with Danish, S Norwegian and W Swedish population. Danish winter population 3,000–4,000. Netherlands winter population 60,000–90,000 at sea and 4,000–16,000 along coasts. UK winter population c. 44,000, France 20,000. Some W Scandinavian birds migrate to North Sea S to English Channel. Scarce C Europe, mainly Oct–Apr; some N Scandinavian, Finnish and N Russian birds move east-south-east; ringing recoveries of Moscow birds from E Europe S to former Yugoslavia, Komi and Volga. Scarce, but increasing winter visitor E Europe to C European lakes and N Atlantic S to the Azores, occasional Morocco (Cramp & Simmons 1983, Jensen 1993, Rose & Scott 1994, Clarke 1999, Dubois *et al.* 2000, Bijlsma *et al.* 2001, Burton *et al.* 2003).

British population mainly resident, but some spread of especially younger birds to Ireland; few recoveries abroad E to Denmark and Norway and S to Biscay coast of France, Iberian Peninsula and Morocco. Faeroe and Iceland birds mainly resident; winter influxes to Faeroe Islands may be of both Icelandic and N Scandinavian origin; Iceland birds have been recovered in Great Britain (mainly W coast), Greenland (2) and Norway (1). Winter population around Iceland thought to be 50,000–80,000 birds. Greenland birds probably perform short-distance migration to S of breeding quarters. Birds from Murmansk, Iceland and Denmark recovered E Greenland in winter (Salomonsen 1967, Cramp & Simmons 1983, Lack 1986, Boertmann 1994, Petersen 1998, Lyngs 2003, Y. Kolbeinsson *in litt.*).

Spring migration Mar–Apr. Younger birds found between breeding and wintering areas, but many stay in winter quarters throughout summer, as indicated by several Danish recoveries of birds from Sweden and Finland summering in Denmark (Cramp & Simmons 1983).

Vagrant C and S Europe, E Mediterranean, Bulgaria, Turkey, Madeira, Canary and Cape Verde Islands, Mauritania, N and W Red Sea, Middle East to Persian Gulf (Glutz von Blotzheim & Bauer 1982, Martins 1989, Shirihai 1996b).

Wintering area of NE American population is the Atlantic seaboard, mainly between Newfoundland and New Jersey, with gatherings of up to 3,000 in autumn in Newfoundland and of 2,275 at Cape May, New Jersey, in winter. Increasing S of New Jersey, where formerly rare. Flocks of some hundreds noted Ontario and 1,000 Lake Erie, Mid-west. Scarce S to W Indies and Gulf of Mexico; vagrant West Coast of USA, Great Plains, Mexico and Japan (Cramp & Simmons 1983, Sibley 1993, Dunn 1997, Enticott & Tipling 1997, H. H. Nielsen *in litt.*).

MEASUREMENTS Lengths in mm; weights in g. Own data based on skins in NRK, UZM, ZMO. Norway, Sweden, Denmark, Faeroes, Iceland, Greenland.

WING

Adult male	465–520 (495.8)	95
Adult female	445–497 (471.4)	109
First-year male	438–510 (484.7)	61
First-year female	429–497 (466.5)	43
Second-year male	475–512 (491.5)	26
Second-year female	450–483 (468.3)	24

GREAT BLACK-BACKED GULL Four-year gull. A large Northern Hemisphere gull, breeding from NE North America E to N Russia. The largest gull, some males much larger than other gulls with flat crown almost merging into square, bulbous-tipped bill. Small eyes situated well back on head. Body heavy but wings short. Shows long, full, thick legs. Females smaller, more like Herring Gulls, but on average larger with more bulbous bill-tip (contrasting with narrower basal bill parts), squarer head and longer legs. Flight lazy; head protruding, wings broad with rounded hand and tail long; flight may recall eagle.

Adult shows greyish-black upperparts in slight contrast to black hand (as in Lesser Black-backed race *intermedius*). Shows full white tip to P10, large white mirror on P9 and broad white trailing edge to inner wing. Bill and fleshy legs similar to Herring Gull. In **winter** (Sep–Mar) head at most slightly dark-streaked; often shows dark markings on bill.

Juvenile more chequered black and white compared to Herring, thus more contrasting, less greyish-brown. Head whitish against massive black pale-tipped bill. Coverts contrasting, greater coverts mainly pale with narrow dark spots or bars. Tertials black with broad white tips. In flight wing darker than Herring with blacker flight feathers and only indistinct pale window on inner hand. Pale greater coverts often contrast strongly with dark secondaries. Tail white with diluted black bar, often appearing irregular and faint; tail with broad white edges.

First-winter (Oct–Apr) shows black chequered markings on saddle, often appearing darker than coverts (indicating later age development).

Second-year similar to first-year, but bill with broader pale tips and base, eye may start to become paler and upperparts with more vermiculated dark markings on greater coverts and tertials. May show scattered blackish feathers on upperparts.

Third-year similar to adult, but blackish saddle and midwing-bar contrast with browner lesser and greater coverts; bill has extensive dark markings and tail sometimes shows dark spots.

Note *In Arctic Russia larger: adult male max. 550mm, adult female max. 530 (Glutz von Blotzheim & Bauer 1982).*

BILL

Adult male	57.5–66.7 (63.1)	108
Adult female	53.9–64.5 (57.6)	121
First-year male	52.3–66.6 (59.7)	61
First-year female	49.4–62.1 (56.0)	43
Second-year male	57.0–66.5 (62.5)	31
Second-year female	52.4–61.5 (57.0)	24

Note *In Arctic Russia larger: adult male 55–87, adult female 51–76 (Glutz von Blotzheim & Bauer 1982).*

BILL DEPTH AT GONYS

Adult male	23.0–27.3 (25.1)	107
Adult female	20.0–25.4 (22.6)	120
First-year male	18.2–25.8 (22.1)	61
First-year female	18.0–22.2 (20.6)	43
Second-year male	21.9–26.3 (24.2)	29
Second-year female	19.6–22.8 (21.5)	26

BILL DEPTH AT BASE OF BILL

Adult male	22.5–28.2 (25.3)	107
Adult female	20.2–25.8 (22.3)	120
First-year male	18.3–26.7 (23.3)	61
First-year female	18.9–23.9 (21.5)	43
Second-year male	21.3–26.2 (24.5)	29
Second-year female	20.0–23.2 (21.8)	26

Note *Bill depth at middle part of the bill (the narrowest part of bill) normally >20mm, even in smallest birds (L. Svensson pers. comm.).*

GONYS LENGTH

Adult male	14.9–21.5 (18.2)	107
Adult female	14.2–19.5 (16.7)	120

First-year male	12.3–20.1 (16.3)	60
First-year female	11.6–19.3 (15.3)	43
Second-year male	16.0–21.6 (18.3)	29
Second-year female	14.4–18.4 (16.2)	26

TARSUS

Adult male	73.1–84.1 (78.8)	107
Adult female	66.5–78.7 (72.6)	120
First-year male	65.5–83.6 (76.8)	61
First-year female	68.6–81.9 (73.4)	43
Second-year male	72.8–83.6 (77.7)	29
Second-year female	66.8–77.8 (72.3)	26

Weight Adult Britain, S Scandinavia male 1,126–2,275, female 732–2,075. Murmansk, N Russia: male 1,380–2,272, female 1,033–2,085. **Juvenile** Murmansk; male 1,400–1,950, female 1,300–1,650. First-winter female Denmark 1,400. Second-winter male 1,550 (Harris 1964a, Glutz von Blotzheim & Bauer 1982, Cramp & Simmons 1983, skins in UZM, ZMO).

Note – *slight clinal variation across range: Wing adult male Scandinavia 465–517 (492.9, n=60), Iceland/Faeroes 482–508 (497.8, n=14), Greenland 485–520 (500.7, n=23). Wing adult female completely overlapping in Scandinavia, Faeroes and Iceland: 445–497 (470.9, n=94), Greenland 463–494 (473.8, n=19). Bill heaviest in Greenland birds: depth at base in adult male Scandinavia 22.5–27.0 (25.0, n=66), Iceland/Faeroes 24.0–27.7 (26.3, n=12), Greenland 24.4–28.2 (26.2, n=22), adult female Scandinavia 20.3–24.0 (21.9, n=82), Iceland/Faeroes 21.0–24.5 (22.9, n=20), Greenland 20.5–25.2 (22.9, n=19). Tarsus adult male Scandinavia 73.1–84.1 (78.3, n=45), Faeroes/Iceland 75.3–83.4 (79.9, n=45), Greenland 73.9–83.6 (79.3, n=22), adult female Scandinavia 67.2–78.2 (72.6, n=90), Iceland /Faeroes 68.6–76.6 (74.0, n=21), Greenland 69.2–78.7 (73.1, n=20).*

Great Black-backed Gull *Larus marinus*. **129. Juvenile**. Compared to most other gulls appears more chequered with a more strongly contrasting dark and pale pattern. Note black bill against large, squarish white head and broad white edges to juvenile mantle and scapulars. This individual shows unusually extensive dark-marked outer greater coverts. Newfoundland, Canada. 5 Nov 1998. *Bruce Mactavish*. **130. 1st-winter**. Similar to juvenile, but mantle and scapulars with dark barring or subterminal markings. Note more pale than dark inner greater coverts and broad white tertial tips. Skagen, Denmark. 9 May 1993. *Klaus Malling Olsen*. **131. 1st-winter**. Note the diffuse black tail-bar against broad white edges and tips to tail as well as lack of conspicuous pale window in inner primaries. Dark secondaries usually contrast well with greater coverts. Gilleleje, Zealand, Denmark. 14 Feb 1998. *Klaus Malling Olsen*. **132. 1st-winter**. Tail-bar in this individual more extensive than in 131, more similar to Herring Gull, but note extensive white edges to tail and rather uniform wing with conspicuous pale barring on greater coverts. Skagen, Denmark. 9 May 1993. *Klaus Malling Olsen*. **133. Juvenile**. Note barrel-shaped body, large, well-protruding head, strong, bulbous-tipped black bill and diffuse tail-pattern. Underwing markings similar to Herring Gull. Simrishamn, Scania, Sweden. 21 Sep ➥

1999. *Klaus Malling Olsen*. **134. Moulting into 2nd-winter** with similar-aged Herring Gull. Note larger size, longer legs and more contrasting plumage of Great Black-backed compared to Herring. Träslövsläge, Halland, Sweden. 12 Aug 1995. *Klaus Malling Olsen*. **135. Moulting into 2nd-winter.** Compare tertial and greater covert barring with 129-130. Turku, Finland. 27 Jul 1996. *Harry J .Lehto*. **136. 2nd-winter**. At this age, bill starts to develop pale base. Often shows dark saddle from young age. Hanstholm, Denmark. 25 Feb 1995. *Klaus Malling Olsen*. **137. 1st-winter and 2nd-summer**. Right-hand bird shows extensive dark on saddle contrasting with barred 2nd-winter wing. Compare with 3rd-summer, photo 138. Hirtshals, Denmark. 15 May 1995. *Klaus Malling Olsen*. **138. 3rd-summer**. Note piebald appearance with good contrast between black and paler upperpart feathers. Turku, Finland. 22 Jul 1996. *Henry Lehto*. **139. 3rd-summer**. At this age often most striking with black saddle and midwing-bar in contrast to rest of upperparts. Tail-bar still present with narrower dark markings than in earlier ages. Turku, Finland. Jul. *Harry J. Lehto*.

Great Black-backed Gull *Larus marinus*. **140. 4th-winter**. Similar to adult, but note duller bill with dark subterminal markings and slight brownish tinge to wing-coverts. The slow age development of this species makes accurate ageing difficult. Turku, Finland. 28 Nov 1996. *Henry Lehto*. **141. Adult summer**. Note very heavy, parallel-edged bill as indication of male, and also bulbous forehead, flat crown, small beady eyes and broad white tertial tips. Skagen, Denmark. 9 May 1993. *Klaus Malling Olsen*
142. Adult winter. Very heavy bill and flat crown obvious. In winter plumage head streaked faintly if at all, appearing white at distance. Hanstholm, Denmark. 11 Oct 1998. *Klaus Malling Olsen*. **143. Adult summer**. Note extensive white wing-tip with complete white tip to P10 and broad white mirror on P9. Thorsminde, Denmark. 8 Apr 1993. *Klaus Malling Olsen*. **144. Adult summer**. Against dark background white wing-tip most conspicuous. Note slight contrast between wing-tip and upperwing. Skagen, Denmark. 10 May 1999. *Klaus Malling Olsen*. **145. Adult moulting into winter plumage**. Note how growth of P9-10 creates unusual look to wing-tip. Ørhage, Denmark. 30 Sep 1995. *Klaus Malling Olsen*.

11. KELP GULL

Larus dominicanus (Lichtenstein, 1823, coast of Brazil)   **Plate 20, Photos 146–157**

IDENTIFICATION Length 54–65cm, wingspan 128–142cm. Kelp Gull is the Southern Hemisphere counterpart to the large, dark-backed gulls of the N. It resembles a heavy, stocky Lesser Black-backed *fuscus*, but has a much stronger bill with a prominent, bulbous tip and conspicuous deep gonys angle; smaller, beady eyes placed higher on larger, squarer head (similar to Western and Yellow-footed Gulls). The legs are longer with larger parts of tibia visible in settled birds. The chest is deeper and the wings are shorter with a rounder tip, in older birds with 2–3 white primary tips above tail (four beyond the tertials) and P10 concealed by P9. Large males may jizz-wise recall Great Black-backed Gull with heavy, blunt-tipped bill, bulbous forehead, flat crown, small eyes and very long legs, but the smallest females may be down to the size of Lesser Black-backed and may lack the very bulbous-tipped bill. Difference in moult, blacker upperparts and greenish-tinged legs should aid separation from Northern Hemisphere gulls.

Adult has black upperparts, in darkness just matched by Lesser Black-backed nominate *fuscus*. Shows broad white edges, especially trailing edge to arm, both at least as broad as in Great Black-backed Gull. Outer wing black with white mirrors on P(9)10 and narrow white tongues on mid-primaries. When it settles, it shows 4–5 narrow but prominent white primary tips above the tertials (distance between primaries lessening towards the outer primaries) and very broad white tertial and secondary crescents—the former as a broad white line on the folded wing. From below, the primaries are blackish against white coverts, but the black 'disappears' on the midwing as the white secondary tips are very broad. Bill yellow with red gonys-spot. Eyes vary from yellow to dark. Legs yellow with a greenish, olive or mustard tinge. White-headed all year. In **summer** (breeding) bill colour is strongest; in **winter** bill duller and paler with reduced (and sometimes no) red gonys-spot. May show very narrow dark spots or short streaks on hindneck, which at very close range may give other than a white-headed impression.

Lesser Black-backed nominate *fuscus* smaller and slenderer with a weaker bill, longer, narrower wings and shorter legs. However, certain large males approach Kelp Gull. The upperwing of *fuscus* is as black as in Kelp, but the white trailing edge and tertial tips are narrower and—as soon as the wing is fully grown—shows 5–6 visible primaries above the tertials. Legs shorter, thinner and yellow, lacking olive, green or strong grey tinge (in colour only matched by certain Malagasy Kelp). Other subspecies of Lesser Black-backed are paler, with some contrast between the black wing-tip and blackish upperwing, unlike the uniform black of Kelp. Great Black-backed even larger and paler with much larger amount of white on wing-tip (but narrower white trailing edge) and fleshy legs.

Juvenile similar to Lesser Black-backed, but stockier with fuller dark tail, different tail pattern, shorter, plainer wings, normally darker, deeper brown body and brownish legs. Generally better marked than Lesser Black-

backed. Overall dark brown with varying pale streaks or mottling on head, neck and underbody, often as conspicuous streaks on hindneck against paler collar. The uniform dark, rather conspicuous eye-mask often reaches the crown and, when it does so, is a main distinction from Lesser Black-backed, which has a white, finely dark-streaked crown and dark eye-mask. Upperparts very dark brown – mantle almost uniform, whereas scapulars have very narrow pale fringes. Coverts dark brown with pale edges, lesser coverts forming a dark wing-bar. Greater coverts dark brown with pale edges, forming conspicuous dark wing-bar as in Lesser Black-backed. Tertials have broader, more complete pale edges than Lesser Black-backed. Underwing-coverts solid dark, as in Lesser Black-backed. Tail dark brown with narrow white tip and spots along edges – as dark as in American Herring Gull and thus appearing darker than in most Lesser Black-backed, in which base is white; few Kelp match tail pattern of Lesser Black-backed. Legs darker and browner compared to the fleshy colour of Lesser Black-backed. Bill dark, heavy and bulbous-tipped.

First-winter similar to juvenile, but head, hind-collar and underparts paler, mainly by wear. Mantle paler greyish-brown with broader and weaker pale tips and edges, contrasting more strongly with wing. Often shows two generations of scapulars, the rear ones plain dark brown, the fore ones with broader, more diffuse markings. Underparts more distinctly dark-streaked with broad dark breast-bar against whitish lower belly. Rump often white, in strong contrast to dark tail. Bill often pale-tipped from May/Jun.

First-summer similar to first-winter, but head, neck and underparts whitish with scattered dark markings, shows dark past ocular line. Tertials worn and faded, contrasting well with fresh, adult-like saddle. Juvenile flight feathers and tail bleach to brown and lose pale tips. Outer primaries often with paler edges through wear. Legs greyish-pink, sometimes greyish-brown. Bill still mainly dark as in first-year, but often pink to yellow from base especially on lower mandible.

Second-winter rather variable. Typically with 'adult-type' feathers appearing paler slaty than in fully adult intermixed with brown. Head and underparts white, with dark eye-mask, conspicuous dark streaks (most prominent on head, hindneck and breast-sides), dark-spotted underbody and barred undertail-coverts. Many show extensive dark saddle and some coverts in contrast to brown, pale-edged feathers, and some also a blackish midwing-bar created by new median coverts. Scapulars slaty with pale brown tips. Tertials slaty with narrow white tips. Rump white, often dark-barred, but contrasting well with solid dark tail with just white edges and bases to outer rectrices; in some, the tail is white with only narrow black markings, which form an indistinct tail-bar. Underwing still with extensive dark markings. Flight feathers blackish with white generally confined to narrow trailing edge to secondaries. Bill yellow to fleshy with black subterminal bar and creamy tip; sometimes

141

PLATE 20. KELP GULL *Larus dominicanus*

Large, dark-backed gull of Southern Hemisphere. Recent northward spread has included regular occurrence Caribbean Sea and West African coastline. Has bred US southern states and Mauritania. Coastal, often in flocks.

Shape intermediate between Greater and Lesser Black-backed Gulls. Head large and square with rather heavy, bulbous-tipped bill, showing prominent and deep gonys-angle. Wing rather short and broad. Breeding in Southern Hemisphere means moult opposite to other gulls (but Northern Hemisphere moult score may be adopted in long-stayers).

1. **Juvenile** (Aug–Jan) Wings dark brown with blackish flight feathers; as in Lesser Blackback shows dark greater covert bar (and narrower white bar at tips of greater coverts). Rump white against dark tail, at most showing faint white mottling at base and very narrow white edges (more pronounced in race *vetula*). Broad, dark eye-mask reaches crown and contrasts with pale hind-collar. Underbody heavily brown-marked, with brown underwing-coverts.

2. **Juvenile** (Aug–Jan) Dark brown with narrow but prominent pale feather-edges. Very similar to Lesser Black-backed Gull, but larger and heavier with blunter bill-tip, shorter legs and shorter wings; appears more well-fed. Dark eye-mask reaches crown and contrasts with pale hind-collar. Underparts more extensive and patterned deeper brown. Tail mainly dark.

3. **First-winter** (Feb–Jul) Note dark grey mantle with dark markings, contrasting with brown coverts. Tertials with broad white edges. Head spotted with paler hind-collar. Bill dull fleshy with conspicuous bulbous, dark tip.

4. **Second-winter** (Feb–Jul) Wing rather similar to first-year but appears more unpatterned and duller greyish-tinged. Saddle dark grey with darker feather centres. Tail with broad blackish bar against white rump.

5. **Second-winter** (Feb–Jul) Head white against dark-patterned hind-collar, breast-sides and flanks. Saddle dull brownish-grey with faint darker centres. Dark greater coverts form darker midwing-panel.

6. **Second-summer/third-winter** Blackish saddle against brown and paler coverts. Tail still black, but often with all-white central tail feathers of adult type. Bill similar to adult, but with more extensive dark subterminal markings.

7. **Adult** Upperparts blacker than in all other except perhaps Lesser Black-backed Gull nominate *fuscus*, with broad white trailing edge—as broad as in Great Black-backed Gull. Wing-tip similar to Lesser Blackback with narrow white mirror on P10 only and narrow white primary tips; underwing appears bicoloured with broad black tip. Head appears white all year.

8. **Adult** shows yellow, often greenish-tinged legs. Shape rather close to Lesser Blackback, but head squarer, bill heavier (especially tip) and upperparts black with very broad and prominent white tertial crescents.

6. Second-summer/third-winter

1. Juvenile

4. Second-winter

3. First-winter

7. Adult

2. Juvenile

5. Second-winter

8. Adult

black with pale tip and base; rarely red gonys appears from this age. Legs brown, greyish-green or pinkish. Blackish saddle (and midwing-bar if present) against brown wings is typical for birds in Nov–Jan, but in Northern Hemisphere gulls of similar age only present in May–Jul.

Second-summer similar to second-winter, but with sparser dark markings on head and underparts and wholly black saddle/median coverts in strong contrast to worn parts. Bill bright yellow with narrow dark markings, sometimes as adult, but duller. Eye yellow with dark spotting.

Third-winter similar to adult winter, but usually with brown streaks or spots on head, breast and sometimes belly, brown tinge to upperparts and generally dark-patterned tail. Flight feathers with narrower white tips, and often with all-black outer-wing, lacking white mirror (although frequent in certain populations). Underwing often with dark spotting. Bill duller with dark subterminal markings and deeper red gonys-spot. Legs grey with bluish or greenish tinge.

Third-summer as third-winter, but head and underparts normally white; worn upperparts may show strong brownish tinge against all-black saddle.

VOICE A repeated *ee-ah* and various yelping and raucous calls; similar to Lesser Black-backed but deeper and hoarser than Yellow-legged or American Herring Gull. Call a 2–3 syllable, staccato, repeated *kwee-ah*. Long-call noisier and higher than Yellow-footed, lower than Western, in S Indian birds close to Caspian Gull (Urban *et al.* 1986, Higgins & Davies 1996, Sibley 2000, Pineau *et al.* 2001, Jiguet *et al.* 2002).

MOULT (ssp. *dominicanus*: Higgins & Davies 1996, Jiguet *et al.* 2001). As a Southern Hemisphere breeder, the timing of moult is the reverse of Northern Hemisphere birds, and this is important to consider when identifying out-of-range birds. Note, however, that Kelp Gulls in Northern Hemisphere may adopt moult cycles similar to Northern Hemisphere gulls, as has been observed in US and Mexican adults. Moult also varies somewhat geographically: Antarctic birds are several weeks ahead of South American populations, in which the northernmost birds moult slightly later than southern ones. **Adult** moult to **winter** plumage is complete following breeding season Dec/Mar–May/Jul, lasting about four months. In Australian and New Zealand populations the moult starts with P1 mid-Jan/Mar, in few % late Nov; two (sometimes three) primaries are often moulted simultaneously. Birds from Madagascar grow P4–5 in late Feb/early Mar. The primary moult is finished May–mid-Jul. Secondaries/tail start when primary moult reaches P5–6, tertials shortly after. Moult to **summer** plumage partial mid-Jul–late Oct, including head and body. Juvenile moult to **first-winter** partial early Mar–Sep, including most of head and body; rarely some marginal coverts. Starts with lower neck and upper back; ends with forehead and breast. Moult is sometimes confined to a few feathers on head and underparts, and a few (especially S Indian Ocean birds) do not moult in their first winter, and appear 'fully juvenile' into Sep. Moult to **second-winter** (Sep/Nov– Mar/Apr) starts with

mantle, scapulars and rump and is followed by the coverts, starting with median coverts (and some inner lesser coverts). Flight feathers start on average a month after onset of head/body moult; lasts 3–4 months. Primary moult begins Oct–Nov, at a time when many scapulars and mantle feathers have been moulted, and ends Feb/Apr. Moult to **second-summer** partial Mar–Apr often including head, body and median coverts and some tertials. Moult to **third-winter** complete Oct–early Jun, although P10 may grow mid-Apr. Moult to **third-summer** restricted to head, neck and underparts.

DESCRIPTION (ssp. *dominicanus*)
Adult Head, underbody, underwing-coverts, rump and tail white. Upperparts black, similar to Lesser Black-backed Gull nominate *fuscus* (Kodak Grey Scale 13.5–15), becoming brownish-tinged with wear (Jan–Mar). Primaries black, P10 with 35–60mm white mirror (rarely entire tip), P9 in 8–35% with 14–30mm white mirror, often broken by black shaft-streak. P7 black with grey shading across inner web *c*.45mm from tip. P5–6 blackish. P(4)5–7 with white tongues on inner webs. P1–4 greyish-black. P5–10 with pure black markings. Flight feathers with white tips, broadening inwards; from 2–5mm on P10 to 30–35mm on P1–4 and secondaries. Marginal coverts and some lesser coverts white, forming white leading edge to wing, 50% the width of trailing edge. Scapulars and tertials with 15–20mm white tips. Underside of flight feathers grey-black, darkening to black on outer wing, creating a strong contrast with the white axillaries/coverts; greater primary coverts often grey-spotted. Eyes pale yellow, creamy with variable dark spotting (see Geographical Variation; dark eyes predominate in S African populations). Orbital ring orange-red to red. Bill yellow to orange-yellow with red gonys-spot and often creamy tip to upper mandible. Gape orange. Legs yellow.

Adult summer (Aug–Mar) Head white. White primary tips gradually wear off, often absent on P8–10 by Jan–Mar, when upperparts become brownish-tinged with wear. Bill bright yellow, often with orange tinge. Gonys-spot and orbital ring bright red (latter sometimes orange-red). Legs greenish to greenish yellow or mustard-yellow.

Adult winter (Feb–Jul) Head white, but sometimes with faint dark spots or streaks on hindneck, especially just after post-breeding moult. Bill straw-yellow to yellow with greenish, olive or bluish tinge; sometimes lacking yellow. Gonys-spot dull red. Bill-tip often creamy-yellow. Legs greyish (duller than in summer), olive-grey or straw-yellow, often with bluish or greenish tinge (Urban *et al.* 1986, Higgins & Davies 1996).

Juvenile (fledging–Jan) Head dull dark brown with pale buff or creamy streaks along feather-edges. Chin and throat off-white with fine greyish-brown streaking. Often with rather uniform dark eye-mask, reaching crown. Neck dark brown with off-white to creamy feather-edges, creating conspicuous streaking. Mantle and scapulars dark greyish-brown with distinct creamy to buff edges (sometimes paler subterminally), creating a scaly pattern. Longest scapulars with brownish-grey shading to tips. Tertials brown with broad white tips and narrower, sometimes irregular edges and white notches. White on outer web may not reach coverts. Lower back slightly paler with broader pale feather-edges. Rump and upper-tail-coverts white with irregular dark brown diamond- or chevron-shaped spots, sometimes as barring similar to a juvenile skua *Stercorarius*; generally more dark-patterned than rest of body, sometimes mainly dark brown. Flight feathers brownish-black. P1–4 with narrow pale brown tips and sometimes slightly paler inner webs. Secondaries have pale brownish-grey tips, sometimes off-white. Greater coverts dark brown; outer almost uniform dark, inner with brown mottling and broader off-white to creamy tips, edges, notches and bars. Lesser and median coverts dark brown with creamy, often irregular edges, generally broadest and most irregular on innermost. Marginal coverts, primary coverts and alula dark brown. Underparts brown to off-white with variable, often dense mottling or streaking (sometimes creamy) on breast and flanks; rear flanks often with dark bars contrasting with off-white, only indistinctly dark-spotted belly. When fresh, underparts often with slight grey to olive wash. Underwing-coverts dark brown with paler centres; greater coverts and underside of flight feathers paler greyish-brown. Tail blackish-brown with irregular white tips; bases of rectrices sometimes pale-barred, but usually little or no barring visible beyond tail-coverts. T6 with 3–4 narrow white spots along outer edge; in some with more extensive white spotting even at bases of T4–5. White at tail-base seemingly most prominent in S American and Antarctic birds (Jiguet *et al.* 2001). Bill black, often with greyish tinge. Gape pink. Iris dark brown. Orbital ring dark grey. Legs pink, grey, pale grey or brownish-grey.

First-winter (Feb–Jul) similar to juvenile, but head (especially hindneck) whiter with more distinct dark streaking, heaviest around eye and ear-coverts (forming dark mask) and across nape. Sometimes lacks streaking on forehead, lores, chin and throat. Eye-crescents dark. Neck white, hindneck darker. Differences from juvenile mainly affected by wear. Mantle and scapulars grey-brown with indistinct darker subterminal bars and broad buffish to creamy fringes; fading to whitish with wear. Rump white with brownish-grey barring or spotting, sometimes mainly white. Underparts generally whiter with more distinct dark breast-bar and more regular flank-barring. Most of belly off-white. With wear, flight feathers and tail become brownish and lose pale tips. Bill as juvenile. Legs brown with olive or yellow tinge. Bill develops yellow tip from May/Jun.

First-summer (May–Feb) as first-winter, but head, neck and underparts generally whiter. Rump/tail-coverts whiter with restricted dark spotting. Bill sometimes with olive-grey base to lower mandible (and in S America bases of both mandibles) (Jiguet *et al.* 2001). Shows pale tips to both mandibles. Legs grey with olive, blue or fleshy tinge.

Second-winter (Feb–Jul) Head and underbody similar to first-winter, but more variable: some with restricted dark spotting, others with heavy dark streaks around eye and on ear-coverts (sometimes as faint ear-spot, otherwise as eye-mask), weaker on crown and nape. Hindneck white, forming white collar. Chin and throat white, latter with short dark streaks. Mantle, scapulars, back and median coverts (sometimes inner lesser coverts) slate-grey to greyish-black (but normally paler than in full adult), paler (often brownish) towards fringes and tips. Often intermixed with first-year feathers. Rear scapulars and tertials slate with grey and pale marbling near the mainly narrow white tip. Lesser and greater coverts pale brown, inner lesser coverts sometimes with weak paler bars or vermiculations on outerwebs. Rump and upper-tail-coverts white with varying brown pattern, ranging from indistinct spots to extensive bars. Flight feathers brownish-black with rounded tips. P1–4 often palest, creating slight, never conspicuous, pale window on outer wing; P1–4 with narrow white tips, P10 rarely with narrow white mirror. Secondaries have broader white tips. Greater primary coverts with pale brown tips or mottling. Underwing varies from dark as in first-year to white with narrow dark feather-edges on axillaries, lesser and median coverts. Greater coverts mainly white. Underbody white with brownish-grey streaks on upper breast, and variable (sometimes no) darker spots or bars on flanks, vent and belly (most extensive on lower belly). Undertail-coverts white with brown bars. Tail varies from similar to first-year (but with more white barring or even streaking near tail-base, on T1–2 and along edges and base of T6) to white with narrow, broken dark tail-bar; exceptionally white from this age (Higgins & Davies 1996). Eyes pale brown to brown. Bill pink, creamy or straw-yellow with blackish subterminal bar and sometimes cutting edges. Red gonys-spot sometimes present, but duller than in adult. Legs grey, sometimes with green, olive, pale yellow or pinkish tinge.

Second-summer (Aug–Feb) similar to second-winter, but head and underparts generally whiter. Head white or with darker spots or streaks, strongest on ear-coverts and hindneck. Underbody with scattered dark markings. Upperparts slate-black, often with brown tinge or some brown feathers intermixed. Slate-black median coverts often form conspicuous wing-bar. Scapulars slate-black with broad white tips; similar to adult, but division from dark base often more irregular. Rump and uppertail-coverts white, sometimes with narrow dark streaks. Eye brownish-yellow with darker freckling. Orbital ring yellow to orange. Bill yellow with narrow dark subterminal markings; sometimes uniform yellow or as adult. Legs olive with grey or pale grey tinge.

Third-winter (Feb–Jul) similar to adult, but head with fine dark streaks or mottling on especially ear-coverts and hindneck. Head and upper breast sometimes more extensively dark-marked. Often shows dark spotting on flanks, belly and tail-coverts. Upperparts similar to adult, but slightly duller and often brownish-tinged (especially scapulars). Tertials often with irregular division between white tips and slate-black base. Flight feathers black, similar to adult, but often lack white mirrors on P9–10 (see Geographical Variation). P3–10 with pure black markings. White primary tips generally narrower than in adult. P(3)4–6(7) often with narrow white moon on inner webs. White trailing edge to wing often irregular. Underwing similar to adult, but often with few dark markings on especially primary coverts. Tail usually with brown waving near shaft-streaks, especially on T1–2, but sometimes white. Iris generally as in adult. Bill usually paler with smaller (or no) red gonys-spot and dark subterminal markings. Orbital ring yellow to orange-yellow.

Legs greyish with dull yellow, bluish or greenish tinge.

Third-summer (May–Feb) as third-winter, but head and underparts normally white; worn upperpart feathers brown in contrast to fresh slaty-black. Bare parts similar to adult, but bill often with dark subterminal markings. Orbital ring orange-red.

Fourth-winter as adult winter, but head sometimes slightly dark-spotted.

GEOGRAPHICAL VARIATION At least two, probably four, subspecies (Brooke & Cooper 1979, Jiguet 2002).

L. d. dominicanus (Australia, New Zealand, Antarctica and S America) Described above. The longest-winged birds are found in Patagonia and E South America, Antarctic birds have the shortest bill (Jiguet 2002), the smallest in Madagascar and S Indian Ocean. In S Indian Ocean **adult**, white mirrors to both P9 and 10 frequent, and white tip to P10 more regular; white mirror in P9 present in up to 35% from new Zealand; noted in 19% from North Island, 28% from S Island (own obs. Nov–Dec 2002); birds from Falklands, S Georgia, Antarctica, Madagascar and S America generally show mirror only on P10, although a few S American birds also show an indistinct one on P9. For bare parts, see detailed descriptions. **First-year** birds from Indian Ocean are darkest on head, underparts, tail and bare parts. Many S American birds develop pale base to both mandibles, sometimes rather bright (Jiguet *et al.* 2001). **Second-years** generally palest in S America and Antarctic, with broadest pale base to bill, covering both mandibles. A rare type, known from S Indian Ocean, has a very dark head and underparts with strongly contrasting pale collar. Birds from S Indian Ocean and New Zealand frequently show white mirror on P10. Second-years from Chile invariably show greenish-grey legs

(Jiguet *et al.* 2001). **Third-year**. Most such birds from S Indian Ocean show narrow white mirror on P10 (rarely on P9), lacking in birds from S America and Antarctica.

L. d. vetula **Cape Gull** (Southern Africa) similar to *dominicanus* but slightly larger (on size matched by certain birds from Antarctica). In **adult**, iris dark, speckled dark to olive-brown or pale yellow, thus eye appears dark in field (but dark iris also frequent in S American birds, especially from Chile). Orbital ring orange, turning yellow in non-breeding season (Jiguet 2002). Compared to *dominicanus*, shows generally narrower white moons on mid-primaries, often restricted to P5 (obvious) and P6 (almost imperceptible). Normally shows white mirror on P10 only; said to show narrower white tertial crescents and trailing edge to wing, but further information needed. Orbital ring yellowish-orange in breeding season, otherwise pale yellow. Legs generally with more olive tinge than in other populations, never bright yellow (Murphy 1936, Brooke & Cooper 1979, Dunn 1997, Jiguet *et al.* 2001). **First-years** similar, but tail often fuller blackish-brown and rump more densely dark-spotted. **Second-years** generally more advanced than most *dominicanus*, often showing more uniform upperparts and more mottled slate-grey wing-coverts (Jiguet *et al.* 2001). Second-year shows mainly black bill with dull yellow base to lower mandible (Jiguet *et al.* 2001). Second- and **third-year** similar to nominate, but third-year usually lacks white mirrors on P9–10, and white moons on mid-primaries.

Note: Jiguet (2002) proposed division into two further subspecies:

Kerguelen Kelp Gull *L. d. judithae* (Kerguelen, Crozet and probably Heard, Marion and Prince Edward Islands). Smaller than other subspecies with short, deep bill. **Adult** Orbital ring vermilion red. Eyes invariably

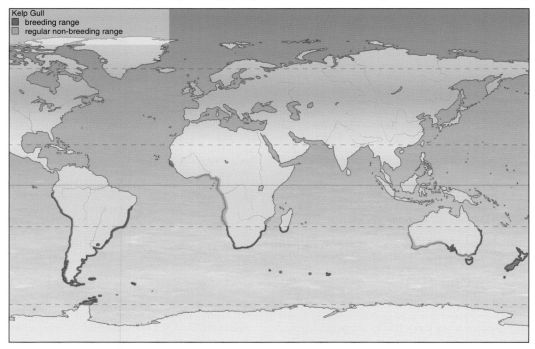

Kelp Gull
■ breeding range
■ regular non-breeding range

KELP GULL Four-year gull. Southern Hemisphere gull. Blackish upperparts of adult shared with
Lesser Black-backed nominate *fuscus*, but Kelp is larger and bulkier with broader wings, shorter
projection of primaries behind tail and much heavier, strongly bulbous-tipped bill.
Adult has blackish upperwing with broad white trailing edge and white mirror to P10. Upperparts
darker than in other gulls apart from nominate Lesser Black-backed. Legs greyish to greenish.
Remains white-headed throughout year.
First-year dark brown with extensive dark mask from eye to crown; dark wing lacks pale window.
Rump barred and tail blackish.
Second-year acquires black saddle and some coverts, contrasting strongly with brownish remainder
of wing.

pale, yellow to ivory. P9-10 always with white mirrors, and
P10 often with white tip (max. 50mm, P5-7 with white
moons. Very rarely with white mirror in P8. **Juvenile-
immature** Very dark in head and body, often still very
dark into third year. Wing 362-428mm, bill 71.8-
50.5mm.
Malagasy Kelp Gull *L. d. melisandae* (Madagascar).
Smaller than *veluta*, with slimmer bill. **Adult** has smaller
white moons in mid-primaries, lacking altogether in P6-
7. White mirror to P10 small, max. 10mm. Pale greenish-
yellow eyes, legs bright yellow.
Aberrants Albinos and leucistic individuals have been
recorded. A few adults show white-spotted greater primary coverts (Higgins & Davies 1996).

Hybrids Adult hybrid **Kelp × American Herring** (based
on offspring from small colony in Louisiana, USA) have
upperparts intermediate between the two (thus similar
to Lesser Black-backed Gull race *graellsii*), black on wing-
tip larger than in American Herring with white mirror
to P10 only, and in winter some dark spotting on head,
strongest on hindneck. Legs often dull greyish.

DISTRIBUTION AND MIGRATION 1,085 million
pairs. Breeds in a wide variety of habitats, but mostly
coastal, preferring rocky islands, beaches and lava fields,
in Madagascar desert lakes. Breeds mainly Oct–Mar,
generally earliest in S Africa; in Senegambia, breeding
noted May–Jun. Coastal, gathering in harbours and rubbish dumps. Recent range expansion and locally strong
increase, e.g. now >1 million pairs New Zealand. In Australia first bred 1958, since when it has greatly increased;
mostly confined to S part. A colony of 1,275 nests noted
in Tasmania early 1990s. Other populations (in pairs)
50,000 S America/Falklands; 11,200 South Africa (mainly Cape Province); 2,000 Namibia; 5,000–20,000 Antarctica; 4,000–8,000 Iles Kerguelen; colonies of some hundreds on many Southern Ocean islands. Also
Madagascar and Mozambique (scarce) (Erard *et al.*
1984, Urban *et al.* 1986, Higgins & Davies 1996, del Hoyo
et al. 1996, Harrison *et al.* 1997, Jiguet 2002).
In South Africa non-breeding dispersal towards coastline in Atlantic and Indian Ocean coastline N to
Maputo, Mozambique, Bazaruto Island; also recorded
Beira; probably regular (but overlooked) Angola,
Gabon and Gulf of Guinea. Regular Senegal (9 pairs
bred 2000; previously bred 1980, 1983). In Australia,
non-breeders disperse N to Queensland, along S coast
and rarely to N Australia. Antarctic population migratory, leaves breeding sites following breeding, and wintering between N edge of the pack ice and extreme S

America. Falkland, South Georgia and Crozet archipela-
go breeders resident with short-distance movements
within the area, leaving coldest parts in winter. Some S
American birds move N; usually only short-distance
migrant N of equator, with Ecuador and Brazil around
Rio de Janeiro as northernmost regular sites. Rarer further N, but now regular and increasing in West Indies,
from 1980 followed by several N American records
(Texas, Indiana and N to Maryland) and since 1989
there has been a small breeding colony in Louisiana (six
pairs 1995; hybridisation with American Herring recorded) (Milon *et al.* 1973, Crawford *et al.* 1982, del Hoyo *et
al.* 1996, Dunn 1997, Harrison *et al.* 1997, Lehman
1999).
Vagrant Mexico, Tristan da Cunha, E Africa N to Malindi, Kenya and W Africa N to Gambia and Mauritania.
Sole WP record adult Mauritania Apr–Sep 1997 and
again May–Jun 1998, Nov 1998 and Jun 1999 (always in
a pair with Yellow-legged Gull; the pair incubated an egg
in May–Jun 1998, (Erard *et al.* 1984, Mulder & Ridder
1985, Haase 1996, Higgins & Davies 1996, Barlow *et al.*
1997, van den Berg & Bosman 1999, Pineau *et al.* 2001.
Ridgley & Greenfield 2001).

MEASUREMENTS Lengths in mm; weights in g. Own
data based on skins in LACM, USNM, UZM, ZMO, combined with Dwight (1925), Escalante (1970), Urban *et al.*
(1986), Higgins & Davies (1996), plus live birds (Jehl
1987b). *L. d. dominicanus*, New Zealand, South America;
L. d. vetula, South Africa. Also see Jiguet 2002 for further
details.

WING

L. d. dominicanus

Adult male	400–448 (427.4)	57
Adult female	373–428 (404.5)	55
First-year male	392–430 (410.8)	24
First-year female	320–412 (387.4)	23

*Note S American birds said to be slightly shorter-winged than
those from New Zealand (but see Jiguet 2002): for S American
birds adult male 403–431 (415.7) (n=22), female 363–404
(392.1) (n=10).*

L. d. vetula

Adult male	419–452 (429.0)	13
Adult female	395–438 (414.0)	25

BILL

L. d. dominicanus

Adult male	49.0–59.0 (53.9)	57

Adult female	44.5–53.0 (49.2)	55
First-year male	46.0–54.0 (50.3)	26
First-year female	39.0–51.5 (45.4)	24

Note S American birds: Adult male 46.0–57.0 (51.8, n=19), female 45.7–53.0 (48.8, n=10). Jehl et al. (1978) give for S Georgian adult male 45.3–51.0 (47.8, n=8), female 41.3–43.6 (42.0, n=7).

L. d. vetula

| Adult male | 54.0–61.5 (57.4) | 13 |
| Adult female | 50.0–54.5 (52.5) | 25 |

BILL DEPTH AT BASE OF BILL

L. d. dominicanus

Adult male	18.5–23.5 (20.1)	64
Adult female	16.5–21.0 (17.9)	59
First-year male	15.5–20.0 (18.4)	26
First-year female	14.0–19.3 (16.5)	24

BILL DEPTH AT GONYS

L. d. dominicanus

Adult male	18.7–23.5 (21.8)	57
Adult female	18.0–21.5 (19.6)	55
First-year male	18.0–21.5 (19.4)	24
First-year female	15.5–19.5 (17.8)	23

Note S American adult male 18.7–21.0 (20.2, n=7), female 18.5–21.3 (18.8, n=4).

GONYS LENGTH

L. d. dominicanus

| Adult male | 13.4–18.4 (16.3) | 12 |
| Adult female | 13.2–15.3 (14.3) | 10 |

TARSUS

L. d. dominicanus

Adult male	60.0–72.5 (66.7)	57
Adult female	53.0–70.0 (60.4)	55
First-year male	58.0–70.0 (64.6)	24
First-year female	57.5–64.5 (60.9)	23

Note: S America adult male 60.8–72.3 (62.3) (n=19), female 56.0–70.0 (63.0) (n=10).

L. d. vetula

| Adult male | 66.0–75.5 (68.6) | 13 |
| Adult female | 60.5–70.0 (65.1) | 25 |

Weight *L. d. dominicanus* Male 950–1,388, female 540–1,020, *vetula* adult male 1,060–1,096, adult female 870–970 (Urban *et al.* 1986, Higgins & Davies 1996).

Kelp Gull *Larus dominicanus*. **148. 1st-winter and adult** ssp. *dominicanus*. In adults, most ssp. shows just a small white mirror to P10. Note broad white trailing edge to wing, broader than in the black-backed gulls of the N hemisphere. Jizz might recall Great Black-backed Gull. In 1st-winter note all-black tail and barred rump, as in most North American Gulls, but unlike the Black-backeds. Upperwing strongly recalls Lesser Black-backed. Note paleness of head and underbody of many S American birds. Chile. Nov 2000. *Don DesJardin.*

Kelp Gull *Larus dominicanus*. **146. Juvenile** ssp *judithae*. Note very dark, rather uniform brown overall impression in this ssp. Kerguelen. Mar 1998. *Didier Vangeluwe*. **147 1st-winter** ssp. *vetula*. Plumage similar to Lesser Black-backed Gull of ssp. *graellsii*, but note deeper bill and squarer head, fuller body and shorter wings. Swakopmund, Namibia. 30 Mar 1999. *Arnoud B. van den Berg*. **149. 1st-winter** ssp. *dominicanus*. General impression often paler in S American birds than in other populations. Note dark line through eyes on rather pale head. Paracas, Peru. Mar 2001. *Marc Guyt*. **150. Moulting into 2nd-winter**, ssp. *dominicanus*. Many show dark eye-mask and crown, creating more extensive dark area than in Lesser Black-backed. Port Stanley, Falklands. 1 Feb 1990. *René Pop*. **151. 2nd-winter** ssp. *vetula*. Compare pattern of this age with 1st-year. Dark eye-line connects with darker ear-coverts to form mask. Bill tip bulbous, much more so than in any Lesser Black-backed Gull. Swakopmund, Namibia. 30 Mar 1999. *Arnoud B. van den Berg*. **152. 2nd-summer** ssp. *dominicanus*. Black saddle contrasts with worn wing. From this age many - especially S American birds - turn white-headed. Coquimbo, Chile. Nov. *Hanne & Jens Eriksen*.

Kelp Gull *Larus dominicanus*. **153 3rd-winter** ssp. *vetula*. Eye dark-patterned or even entirely dark in this ssp. Swakopmund, Namibia. 30 Mar 1999. *Arnoud B. van den Berg*. **154. 2nd-summer** ssp. *dominicanus*. A rather slender individual, recalling Lesser Black-backed Gull, but note distinctly bulbous bill-tip. Chile. Nov 2000. *Don DesJardin*. **155. Adult** ssp. *dominicanus*. Eyes often pale in this ssp., creating beady-eyed look similar to Great Black-backed Gull. Note short wings and very broad white tertial crescents. Chile. Nov 2000. *Don DesJardin*. **156. Adult** ssp. *vetula*. An especially flat-crowned and long-legged individual, jizzwise similar to Great Black-backed Gull, but note greenish tinge to legs and even darker upperparts. Swakopmund, Namibia. 30 Mar 1999. *Arnoud B. van den Berg*. **157. Adult** ssp. *dominicanus*. Black flight feathers create extensive area of blackish in underwing, matching Lesser Black-backed Gull *fuscus*. Coquimbo, Chile. Nov. *Hanne & Jens Eriksen*.

12. GLAUCOUS-WINGED GULL

Larus glaucescens (J. F. Naumann, 1840, North America) **Plates 21–22, Photos 158–182**

IDENTIFICATION Length 60–66cm, wingspan 137–150cm. A large, bulky, pale gull of the northern Pacific coasts, sharing size and shape with Western Gull. In W North America it behaves as a pale northern counterpart to Western Gull (with which it often settles and, in Washington state area, extensively hybridises). It has small dark beady eyes placed high on head (often very striking in males) and a heavy, bulbous-tipped bill. Compared to Western, Glaucous-winged generally has rounder head with fuller feathering at base of upper bill and less bulbous bill-tip. The wings are rather short and broad with more curved outer primaries than in other large gulls and relatively longer secondaries—a shape shared just with Western. In settled birds, 2–3 primary tips extend beyond tail-tip. The plumage is pale, in many ways rather similar to Glaucous Gull, but the wing-tip is either concolorous with the rest of the wing or slightly darker with a diffuse but well-defined pattern. Size varies: whereas the largest males are almost the size of Great Black-backed Gull, small females are closer in size to Herring (and even Thayer's) Gulls.

Although pure individuals are relatively straightforward to determine, identification is complicated by the species' extensive hybridisation with Herring, Western, Glaucous and Slaty-backed Gulls (see hybrids below).

Adult has grey upperparts, varying from pale as in American Herring to dark as in Mew Gull. Wing-tip is concolorous with rest of wing or slightly darker with white mirror to P10 only; close inspection reveals grey pattern on P5–10, mirroring the black pattern of American Herring and Western, but greyer, less extensive and clear-cut, rather than black and well separated from rest of wing-tip as in American Herring. Often shows conspicuous white 'string of pearls' on upperwing. The palest birds have wing-tip superficially similar to Glaucous, but still with slightly darker markings and white mirror on P10 (often inconspicuous from below), unlike the unmarked whitish of Glaucous. Unlike American Herring and Glaucous eyes are dark, surrounded by pink orbital ring. Legs pink to purplish. In **summer**, head white and bill bright yellow with red gonys-spot. In **winter** head brown-mottled or washed. Glaucous-winged shows the most conspicuous 'thumbprint'-shaped markings of any large gull, appearing rather uniform at distances where most Herring and Glaucous continue to look spotted or streaked. These markings often form a rather complete hood, reaching breast-sides, where they are divided from the grey wing by a white wedge (similar to *Actitis* sandpipers.). Bill duller than in summer, often with narrow dark markings such as a Z-shaped bar.

Juvenile has the most unmarked plumage of all large gulls, being greyish-brown with almost concolorous upper- and underparts. Scapulars and tertials have more solid greyish-brown centres, the coverts broader dark (but still diffuse) barring. Flight feathers greyish-brown, concolorous with upperparts or at most a tinge darker on outer primaries and secondaries. On folded wing the pale primary tips create a row of Vs. Flight feathers moderately translucent, from below often appearing similar to Glaucous, reinforced by dark coverts, which creates a distinctly bicoloured underwing. The greyish-brown tail looks uniform, at close range with indistinct pale barring at base and along edges. The tail and densely dark-barred rump often appear as the darkest areas of the upperparts. Bill black; legs dull fleshy, generally darker than in other large gulls. Plumage rather similar to Thayer's, which is smaller and neater with a rounder head, larger, more centrally placed eye and longer wings, with outer primaries darker than upperparts (mainly caused by darker outerwebs). Western, American Herring and Slaty-backed Gulls are darker with blackish tails and outer wing and denser head pattern.

First-winter as juvenile, but wear creates a paler head (especially forehead and hindneck) in contrast to darker velvety ear-coverts and mask. Hindneck often with more conspicuous brown mottling. Otherwise rather uniform with flight feathers and upperparts rather concolorous, but from midwinter primaries often paler through wear, appearing slightly paler than rest of plumage as in Glaucous Gull, and sometimes whitish. Also from midwinter coverts fade to whitish, but from Apr new dingy brown, weakly marked upperpart feathers intermix, creating piebald pattern.

First-year Glaucous is paler and browner with finer, more restricted dark markings; best told by pink, black-tipped and less bluntly tipped bill, but also shows pale-barred tertials and coverts and whitish flight feathers, primaries typically paler than body. Tail and rump never darkest part of bird, but rump-barring more distinct and pale tail shows fine dark markings. Head pattern generally better marked apart from in very pale-headed birds (which should not create any ID problems). Legs paler and brighter flesh-pink.

'First-summer' attained by wear in head and body. From spring moults to second-winter wich is lightly paler than first-winter; silvery-grey overall with new grey (sometimes sooty) mantle feathers appearing from May. Head and underpart-markings paler and browner than in first-year, sometimes similar to adult winter, but still with large amount of greyish-brown especially on underbody. Mantle and scapulars with varying amount of grey (rarer on coverts and tertials). Coverts and tertials dingy brown with very weak darker markings, often slightly barred. Darker greater coverts often form midwing-bar on upperwing. Outer primaries and some (especially inner) secondaries might be slightly darker than rest of wing. Rump whitish, often with strong dark barring, but now in strong contrast to dull brown tail, which is similar to first-years. Bill bicoloured, mostly dark grey with characteristic pale base and edges, leaving solid dark area on central bill. Legs dull greyish-pink.

Second-summer paler than second-winter with grey saddle against bleached wing-coverts. Bill pale with broad black subterminal bar and whitish tip.

Third-winter similar to adult, but with some brownish-tinged wing-coverts admixed. Primary pattern more diffuse with brownish tinge, and white primary tips narrower, appearing as small, indistinct triangles. Inner sec-

PLATE 21. GLAUCOUS-WINGED GULL *Larus glaucescens*

Large, robust North Pacific gull. Structurally similar to Western (with which it hybridises extensively British Columbia to Washington). Larger than American Herring and Vega Gulls with large, square head, flat forehead and heavy, bulbous-tipped bill (often appearing deeper at tip than at base). Feathering on forehead thick. Small dark eyes, normally situated high in head, create 'evil' expression. Body stocky and wings short; 2–3 exposed primaries extend beyond tail. Shows prominent tertial step and short, somewhat rounded hand. Size varies; large males as average Great Black-backed, small females slenderer with rounder head (but still small, beady eyes). Abundant along American W Coast, often associated with Western Gulls. Coastal.

1. **Juvenile** (Aug–Nov) Greyish-brown with plumage pattern weaker and more washed out than in other similar-sized gulls. At distance rather uniform-looking greyish-brown with black bill and eye and dirty pink legs. Body and wings are concolorous. Primaries show narrow pale edges.

2. **First-winter** (Sep–May) Generally as juvenile, but fades on especially head (and particularly hindneck), and develops a few second-generation feathers on mantle and scapulars, with washed-out pattern typical for the species.

3. **Late first-winter** A late winter/spring individual showing conspicuous bleaching to head and body. Note dark, deep bill and high-situated dark eyes. Some pale birds are at this time of year rather similar to Glaucous Gull, but note all-dark bill and wing-tip concolorous with rest of plumage.

4. **Second-winter** (Aug–Mar) Superficially similar to first-year, but bill starts to develop pale base and tip, the saddle is more or less grey and the coverts even fainter-patterned than in first-year, often with uniform grey median coverts. The primaries are rounder, their shape rather easy to see because of their pale edges. Legs dirty pink, greyer and duller than in other large gulls.

5. **Third-winter** (Aug–Mar) In this plumage a mixture of adult (mainly grey upperparts, broad white edges to tertials and secondaries) and second-year type. Note bicoloured, fleshy black-tipped bill and slightly brownish tinge to primaries, which have narrower white tips than adult. The very typical diluted 'thumbnail' markings on head and breast are developed from this age. Note also the white line in wing, created by white secondary tips.

6. **Adult or fourth-winter** (Sep–Apr) Note extensive brownish diluted hood (consisting of transverse 'fingerprint' markings) often penetrating onto breast-sides, and isolated from wings by white breast-sides. Adult uppersides pale grey with very broad tertial and secondary tips, creating complete white line. Primaries concolorous with upperparts or a tinge darker. Bill in winter often with dark subterminal markings (here extensive enough to suggest fourth-winter).

7. **Adult winter** (Sep–Apr) Note, compared to 6, less extensive head-markings, but typically has transverse bars of 'anchor-markings' on neck-sides.

8. **Adult summer** (Feb–Sep) Dark eyes, heavy drooping bill and short grey wing-tip (with only 2–3 primaries above tail-tip) in combination identify the species—even in a rather weak-billed, round-headed bird as shown here.

. Juvenile

2. First-winter

4. Second-winter

3. Late first-winter

5. Third-winter

6. Adult or
fourth-winter

8. Adult summer

7. Adult winter

PLATE 22. GLAUCOUS-WINGED GULL *Larus glaucescens*

In flight a robust, rather broad- and short-billed gull with large, protruding head, barrel-shaped body and long tail. The conspicuous broad wings are given emphasis by the relatively longer secondaries compared to other gulls other than Western and Yellow-footed. See text for hybrids.

1. **Juvenile** (Aug–Nov) Note uniform greyish-brown impression: flight feathers and adjacent upperparts concolorous, primaries at most a trifle darker (on outer webs and near tips). Rump heavily brown-barred (brown bars typically broader than paler). Tail uniform; only at very close range a slight pale mottling may be observed. Bill black.

2. **Juvenile/first-winter** (Nov–Apr) From below, flight feathers are pale, contrasting well with darker body and coverts. May—especially with wear from midwinter—look similar to Glaucous Gull, but note black bill, more diffuse undertail-covert markings and longer, darker tail (may look paler from below).

3. **First-winter** (Sep–Apr) Similar to juvenile, but with few new mantle and scapulars and paler head caused by wear. This rather pale individual shows the typical uniform greyish-brown tail, which—together with the barred rump—may be the most distinctive feature of first-years, and often the darkest part of the bird.

4. **Second-winter** (Aug–Mar) Superficially similar to first-year, but note variable amount of grey on mantle and scapulars and even less patterned plumage. Rump conspicuously paler than the still juvenile-looking tail. The almost uniform overall appearance, combined with shape and size, usually makes ID simple.

5. **Third-winter** (Aug–Mar) Rather similar to adult, but note extensive dark tail-markings, slight brown tinge to coverts, full dark bill-markings and less defined, smaller pale mirror to P10. From this age often shows slight 'string of pearls' on wing-tip. Note, however, again the uniform look of the wing with coverts and flight feathers concolorous.

6. **Fourth-winter** (Aug–Mar) As adult: some individuals show scattered dark tail-markings at this age. Primary tip representative of adult: primaries concolorous with or only a tinge darker than rest of wing, and with mirror on P10 only.

7. **Adult winter** (Sep–Mar) Note extensive diluted dark head-markings and diagnostic wing pattern with primaries concolorous with rest of wing; this individual shows white mirrors on P9–10 and 'string of pearls' on primaries, created by extensive pale areas on inner webs.

8. **Adult summer** (Mar–Sep) From below, adults are almost uniform with white mirror to P10 as the most eye-catching feature. Note especially the pale bases to all flight feathers, resulting in a very pale and clean-looking underwing.

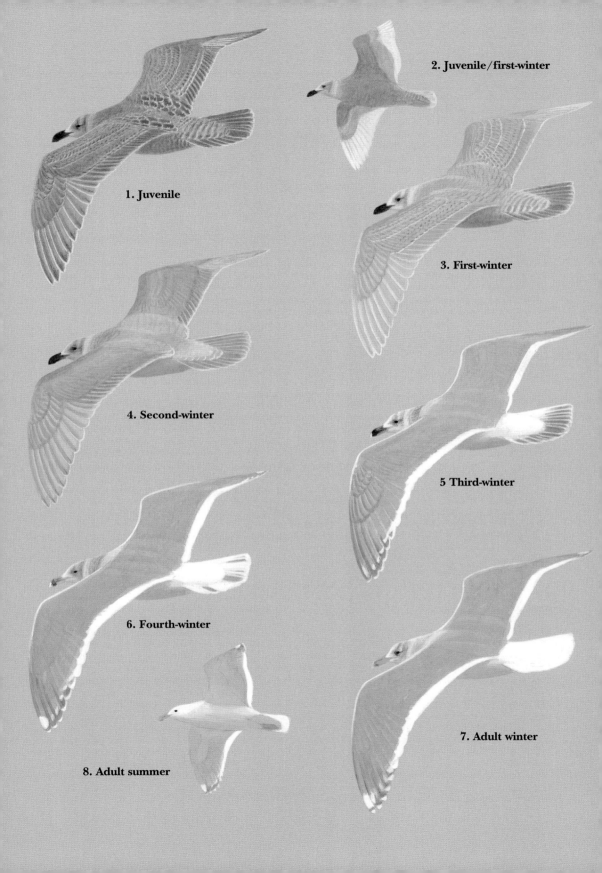

1. Juvenile

2. Juvenile/first-winter

3. First-winter

4. Second-winter

5 Third-winter

6. Fourth-winter

7. Adult winter

8. Adult summer

ondaries typically brownish-tinged. Often with scattered dark markings on underbody and underwing. Tail often with narrow grey markings. Bill dull fleshy to yellow with broader black subterminal markings, often concentrated on mid-bill, leaving pale edges, but sometimes as complete black ring around bill-tip. Retarded birds more like second-years, showing larger amount of brown on upperwing and extensive dark on tail. Such birds aged by uniform grey secondaries with broad white tips and brownish-grey primaries with white mirror to P10.

Third-summer as adult, but with characters of third-winter. Narrower white primary tips wear off, making wing-tip more uniform. Bill as third-winter, but dark markings smaller.

VOICE A moaning, rather deep, slow *aah-aah-aah* is the most frequently heard call outside breeding season; slightly flatter and hollower than in Western. Long-call of Washington state populations similar to Western, but slightly higher-pitched with longer notes. Long-call of Siberian populations lower and slower, similar to Slaty-backed Gull (Sibley 2000), in Vancouver and California, longer, lower-pitched and more drawn-out compared to Western Gull (A. Jaramillo *in litt.*)

MOULT Adult moult complete to **winter** plumage May/mid-Jun–Nov. P1 late May/Jun, P4–6 Jul, P5–7 Aug, P7–9 mid–late Sep, P10 Oct–Nov. Head and body mid-Aug–Sep. Winter head attained late Sep. Moult to **adult summer** partial mid-Feb/Mar–early Apr, including head and various parts of body. Head late Mar–early Apr. **Juvenile** moult into **first-winter** limited, including various parts of head and body late Oct–Mar (exceptionally from Aug), but often restricted to scattered mantle and scapulars; occasionally 1–2 coverts. Timing and extent of moult highly variable; residents or short-distance migrants moult earlier and more extensively than northern long-distance migrants. Some had completed moult at a time when others have just started; some still juvenile by mid-Mar. Moult into **second-summer** complete (Apr)May–Nov. P1 May, P3–6 mid-Jul/early Aug, P7–8 late Aug, P10 late Sep. Mantle/scapulars and tail from Jun. Subsequent moult similar to adult (skins in NHM, MCZ, MVZ, LACM, Il'icev & Zubakin 1990, King & Howell 1998, Howell & King 1999, pers. obs. California).

DESCRIPTION

Adult Upperparts medium grey (Kodak Grey Scale 4–7(8)), on average darkest in N and E populations (Alaska to Japan). Birds with upperparts >9 in Kodak Grey Scale probably hybrids with Western Gull race *occidentalis*. Head, body, rump and tail white. Primary pattern basically like Western Gull, but much paler (1–2 steps darker than rest of upperwing judged from Kodak Grey Scale) and slightly more washed out with larger extension of white on P10. Dark pattern on P6–10 mid-to pale grey (Kodak Grey Scale 5–8 (with slightly paler inner vanes); birds with 8–12 probably of hybrid origin); often 'frosty', concolorous with or barely darker than rest of upperparts. P10 with 40–50mm white mirror, often reduced to weak spot on inner web, some with grey cast

to whole outer web. Birds with uniform grey P10 probably younger adults. P9 greyish, in 10% with up to 20mm white mirror, mainly on inner web, but rarely as on P10 or with entire pale inner webs, creating Thayer's Gull pattern. Very rarely with indistinct white mirror on P8. P5–8(9) in most with 3–15mm white tongues, most extensive on outer webs, creating white 'string of pearls'. P5–8 with darker outer web or 6–40mm subterminal bar, most extensive on P8; P5 sometimes with dark subterminal spot. P4 in 10% (mainly males?) with indistinct dark subterminal spot. P1–4, tertials and secondaries grey with white tips. White primary tips 10–15mm on P6–10, 20–30mm on P1–5 and secondaries. With wear white primary tips gradually wear off and dark on primaries becomes browner. Iris dark brown, tawny or olive with dark peppering. Eye looks dark in field, but is in 5% dirty yellow (J. R. King pers. comm.). Orbital ring red, pinkish or purple. Bill yellow with orange gonys-spot. Gape pink to purple. Feathers at base of bill full, extending in 45° angle towards lower cutting edge of upper mandible to 5–10mm before triangular nostril. The nostril often appears 'open' in front; depth at distal part 2–4mm, length 13–15mm. Bill-tip bulbous; depth of bill generally deeper at gonys-angle than at base, most conspicuous in males (see Measurements). Legs purple to deep pinkish, rarely orange.

Adult summer (Mar–Sep) Head white, orbital ring bright purple. Bill yellow with orange to bright red gonys-spot.

Adult winter (Sep–Mar/Apr) Head with buff to greyish-brown barring, mottling or waving ('fingerprint markings'), strongest on ear-coverts, hindcrown and neck, creating hooded appearance; often penetrates to breast-sides, leaving white wedge against grey forewing. Forehead and lores sometimes slightly streaked. Bill brownish-yellow to dull yellow with greyish-tinged orange gonys-spot, in 75% with narrow black subterminal markings: as Z-shaped ring or dark bars on both mandibles. Bill sometimes pinkish-tinged, especially at base. Orbital ring pinkish, duller than in summer.

Juvenile (fledging–Nov/Mar) Head pale greyish-brown with slightly paler forehead, neck-sides, chin and throat. Hindneck and neck-sides (sometimes forehead) show diffuse whitish streaks. Lores and ear-coverts velvety brown. Underbody pale greyish-brown. Undertail-coverts white with distinct brown bars, rarely inconspicuous darker waving. Mantle and scapulars greyish-brown with narrow, often indistinct pale bars and fringes, sometimes restricted to narrow buff spots along edges. May show darker subterminal markings, sometimes as 'holly-leaf' centres (Ebels *et al.* 2001). Rump and uppertail-coverts pale with brownish barring, often broader than pale bars; sometimes indistinctly pale-waved. Tertials and outer greater coverts greyish-brown with irregular sandy to off-white fringes, often with dark markings or spots along outer webs, rarely pale subterminal bars. Inner greater coverts sometimes with slight pale barring near tips and edges. Lesser and median coverts pale greyish-brown with brownish subterminal bars and pale fringes. Primary coverts greyish-brown, slightly darker than primary bases. Flight feathers greyish-brown (darkest on outer webs), concolorous with or slightly darker than rest of upperparts, except secondaries, which may form darker panel; inner web to P1–4 and secondaries often slightly paler. Primaries with complete pale fringes. P1–5 and secondaries sometimes with faint dark arrowhead-markings near tips. Underwing-coverts greyish-brown, lesser coverts sometimes darker. Primary coverts sometimes paler with darker tips forming narrow 'comma'. Underside of flight feathers paler than coverts. Tail greyish-brown with pale fringes and sometimes inconspicuous pale mottling or bars (up to 4–5 indistinct pale spots on outer webs to T4–6; T6 with narrow, often complete pale outer web. Tail often darkens towards tip. Iris dark. Bill black, sometimes with pale extreme tip to upper mandible. Legs dull fleshy- to brownish-grey, rarer grey or bubblegum-pink.

First-winter (Nov–Apr) as juvenile, but head paler, often with faint grey mask to face and spots on hindneck in contrast to paler neck-sides. Paler breast often contrasts with darker belly. Scattered new feathers on mantle and scapulars pale greyish-brown with faint pale mottling, brown anchor-markings and weak pale edges. Bill may develop narrow pale base, especially to lower mandible, and narrow pale tip (max. 5mm). From Jan entire plumage bleaches to paler, in late spring even whitish on greater coverts (and sometimes primaries) in contrast to darker secondaries and tail. From Mar primaries may bleach to off-white and any plumage pattern disappears; then looks silvery-grey with black bill.

First-summer (Apr–Sep) intermediate plumage between first-year and second-winter. Similar to first-year but head, body and upperwing even paler through wear, often appearing whitish in contrast to new greyish (or even sooty) second-winter mantle and scapulars. Bill black with paler base and broader pale tip.

Second-winter (Aug–Mar) similar to first-winter, but generally paler. Upperparts more uniform, lacking any strong pale barring on wing-coverts (at most very indistinct pale spots on inner greater coverts); greater coverts sometimes dark, forming midwing-panel, sometimes paler greyish-brown with very fine pale vermiculations. Mantle and scapulars mainly grey, often with white edges. Tertials greyish-brown, often with paler mottling especially on distal part. Primary coverts greyish-brown. Flight feathers slightly paler and cleaner grey than in first-year, primaries with rounder, broader pale edges. Inner secondaries normally brownish-tinged. Tail pale greyish-brown with faint brown mottling, especially on outer web of T6. Rump white, sometimes with brown barring, rarely extensive. Bill black with paler base; black and pale sometimes of equal amount with black mostly concentrated to mid-bill; white bill-tip usually evident. Legs as first-year.

Second-summer (Apr–Sep) as second-winter, but bleached wing often contrasts well with grey mantle and new median coverts of third-winter. Bill pale with dark tip or subterminal bar. Iris dark.

Third-winter (Aug–Apr) similar to adult, but wing-coverts and sometimes tertials brownish-washed (often partly); greater coverts may show pale vermiculations. Primary coverts greyish-brown with pale edges. Dark primary pattern brown-tinged and less distinct, with smaller off-white 20–25mm mirror on P10; P9 normally lacks mirror. Compared to adults, primaries have narrower, more triangular white tips. Underbody has

greyish-brown intermixed, especially on belly to under-tail-coverts, in latter as mottling. Tail usually with greyish-brown subterminal bar or indistinct grey spots, especially at bases of rectrices. Often similar to second-winter, but base finer pale-mottled and T5–6 pale with scattered dark spots; T1–3 may be uniform greyish-brown. Bill pale with broad black subterminal bar, sometimes restricted to dark spot on upper mandible. 'Retarded' birds similar to second-winter, but grey secondaries have broad white tips, and primary pattern similar to adult, including white mirror on P10 (Ebels *et al.* 2001).

Third-summer as adult summer apart from details outlined under third-winter; upperparts still with some brown mottling. Pale primary tips typically worn off. Bill as third-winter.

Fourth-winter (Sep–Apr) as adult, but sometimes with brown tinge to alula, primary coverts, greater coverts and tail.

Hybrids In W North America, Glaucous-winged hybridises with American Herring, Glaucous and Western Gull race *occidentalis*. In E Asia hybridises with Slaty-backed Gull, but probably to a lesser extent. Apparently hybridisation with all other similar-sized gulls possible (pers. obs., J. R. King *in litt.*).

Hybrid **Glaucous-winged × Western Gull** *occidentalis* common in overlap zone between Puget Sound and N Oregon. In small breeding area in Washington state between Juan de Fuca and Oregon, at least 70% hybrids (Bell 1997). Hybrids spread in winter S to California, with almost equal amounts of Western, Glaucous-winged and hybrids at Point Reyes N of San Francisco, although fewer reach further south: of 22,500 Western, Santa Cruz, California, Dec, 212 were considered hybrid Glaucous-winged × Western. Regular S to Baja California. Hybrids mostly coastal (Hoffman *et al.* 1978, Bell 1997, *Amer. Birds* 41: 324, R. Stallcup & J. R. King *in litt.*). Hybrids are identified on characteristic jizz (shared between Glaucous-winged and Western) combined with 'wrong' plumage pattern for pure specimens. Outer wing (especially underside) never blackish as in Western. **Adult** variable. Upperparts generally darker grey than in Glaucous-winged (Kodak Grey Scale mainly 7–8.5) and darker wing-tip (Kodak Grey Scale mainly 10–12), mirroring pattern of Western, but less clearly divided from grey, and outer webs of P9–10 grey, rarely as black as in pure Western and not reaching primary coverts. Usually only white mirror on P10. From below, shows dark-based flight feathers. Unlike Western, winter head pattern often extensively brown-washed (but may be white from Jan). Said often to show more white on wing-tip than either parent species, underside of outer wing appearing white with dark streaks on P6–10. Shows no or very inconspicuous white tongues between black and white on P5–6. Orbital ring pink as in Glaucous-winged, yellow as in Western, but may be whitish. Some show yellow eyes.

Often similar to male American Herring Gull, but bill heavier with broader bulbous tip, eyes dark, situated higher on head, head squarer and generally more washed out and less streaked in winter. Also has less clearly offset, blackish wing-tip with white mirror on P10 only (also seen in some W American Herring) (Hoffman *et al.* 1978, Tove & Fischer 1988, Bell 1997, Dunn 1997, Sibley 2000, Ebels *et al.* 2001, J. R. King pers. comm.).

First-year often similar to Glaucous-winged, but generally with contrasting darker flight feathers and tail; may show diffuse pale window on inner primaries. Bill dark, but often with pale base especially to lower mandible. Plumage generally coarser-patterned and darker than in Glaucous-winged with darker, more distinct pale bars on wing-coverts, darker centres to pale-edged scapulars and sometimes slightly barred upperpart feathers, lacking clean appearance of Glaucous-winged. Flight feathers (especially secondaries and P6–10) and tail dark greyish-brown with more conspicuous pale primary fringes. Scapulars often blackish-brown with pale edges. Tertial centres more solidly dark with irregular pale waving along edges (as in American Herring, but paler; often paler than wing-tip). First-winter scapulars often with darker bases and subterminal bars. Greater coverts often with much plainer, darker brown bases than in Glaucous-winged (where bases often show whitish spots and waving). Body moult as in Glaucous-winged, thus later than in Western (which see and compare) (King & Howell 1998).

Certain hybrids have contrasting pale outer wing, especially from below, resembling Thayer's with similar dark trailing edge. Identified *with care* from Thayer's by size and structure; small female hybrids are especially tricky, but bill usually longer with heavier tip. Plumage generally darker and colder brown with more weakly patterned upperparts. Primaries generally duskier, sometimes lacking pale fringes of first-year Thayer's. All intergrades through Western Gull exist. Second- and third-winters often tricky, mainly told *with care* by coloration of intermixed adult feathers; often combine darker upperparts and blackish-looking wing-tip of Western with extensive brown head patterning of Glaucous-winged.

Glaucous-winged × American Herring Gull (mainly S coast of Alaska, wintering regularly S to N Mexico) typically smaller with rounder head and narrower wings than Glaucous-winged (many may be misidentified as 'oversized' Thayer's Gulls). **Adult** has pale grey upperparts with wing pattern intermediate between the two: on some, wing-tip has grey, rather diffuse pattern (as in Glaucous-winged), but often contrasting blackish, with white mirror on both P9 and P10, although often small on P9. Many show broad white tongues on outer webs of P5–10, creating streaked wing-tip as in Thayer's Gull. White tongues on primaries generally broader than in (West) American Herring, often appearing as 'string of pearls'. Unlike Glaucous-winged, may show pale eyes and, in winter, distinct dark head-streaking. Upperparts paler grey than in Glaucous-winged × Western hybrids. **First-years** often similar to Western, but with paler-based bill, slimmer than in Glaucous-winged with more parallel edges and less bulbous tip; hindneck often streaked and P6–10 slightly darker than in pure Glaucous-winged. *Main ID pitfall is Thayer's*, as many are almost identical in plumage: Hybrid Glaucous-winged × American Herring generally larger with stronger bill (not dove-like head with weak bill of many Thayer's) and

often strong gonys-angle unlike Thayer's. Has 'blocky' head with small beady eyes. Finely marbled greyish-brown head and underbody, often with streaked hind-neck unlike Thayer's. Also, scapulars patterned finer and more diffusely; Thayer's shows greyish-brown scapulars with tendency to darker anchor-markings towards tip. Compared to Thayer's, pale window on inner primaries often more distinct, similar to American Herring. Underside of primaries pale greyish-brown, lacking silvery tinge of Thayer's (and with more extensive blackish tips than in Glaucous-winged). Settled birds heavier with stronger bill and flatter crown, broader tertial step and shorter primary projection; shows 2–4 pale primary tips behind tail (>4 in Thayer's). Legs normally duller, not bright pink. Like Thayer's, most retain juvenile plumage well into winter (King & Howell 1998, Ebels *et al.* 2001, A. Jaramillo *in litt.*, J. R. King pers. comm., pers. obs. California and Mexico).

Glaucous-winged × Glaucous Gull (locally common in certain Arctic breeding areas—in W Alaska (Seward Peninsula) up to 50% of population hybrids, also locally common E Bering Sea: Strang 1977, Ebels *et al.* 2001). Mainly resident; rare S of native range, but some reach Japan and California. Large and pale, but may show every intergradation of appearance between their parent species. Most look like 'pure' species with wrong pattern. **Adult** pale grey, often with outer wing pattern of Glaucous-winged (Kodak Grey Scale around 5), but less or no dark on P5–6. More Glaucous-like birds show whitish primaries with narrow grey markings on up to six outer primaries, especially near tips, in settled birds looking like narrow grey spots on white wing-tip. May show head-streaking in winter. Unlike Glaucous, eyes often darkish. **First-year** varies. Some Glaucous-like, but with broader, darker and crisper markings on mantle, scapulars and wing-coverts, darker-tinged flight feathers (especially secondaries; primaries sometimes as pale as in Glaucous) and tail, the latter often appearing uniform greyish-brown without the delicate markings of Glaucous, but sometimes with paler base. Bill varies from mainly dark with bulbous tip (as in Glaucous-winged) to Glaucous-like, but generally duskier pink with broader, more diffuse black tip and darker cutting edges. Some show bill pattern identical to Glaucous. Darker birds combine plumage of Glaucous-winged with pink, black-tipped bill of Glaucous (even second-years). Measurements (n=1, MCZ 282317) wing 448mm, bill 68.6mm, tarsus 72.8mm, weight 1,372g. A **second-winter** had paler primaries than upperparts, but broader dark subterminal spots at tips of P6–10 than Glaucous.

Glaucous-winged × Slaty-backed Gull (small proportion of breeding birds along N and E coasts of Kamchatka and Commander Islands; reach S to Japan in winter). Compared to Glaucous-winged, head generally rounder with weaker bill. **Adult** upperparts darker grey than Glaucous-winged with blacker wing-tip, showing good contrast between upperparts and wing-tip, unlike in Slaty-backed. Primary pattern blackish to dark grey, often with indication of broad white tongues on P5–7(8) recalling 'string of pearls' of Slaty-backed. Shows broad white tertial crescents, connecting with white bar at secondary tips. Winter head pattern coarser with denser spots or streaks than in Glaucous-winged and often dark

Glaucous-winged Gull
□ breeding range
⌒ limit of winter range

eye-mask. Eyes often pale. Legs often rosy-tinged, generally more so than in Glaucous-winged. Better documentation needed of plumage and bare parts of younger birds (King & Carey 1999, Ebels *et al.* 2001, pers. obs., Hokkaido, Japan, Feb 2001).

GEOGRAPHICAL VARIATION Moderate. Birds from W America described above. Populations from E Asia (Commander Islands to Japan) generally darker with longer wings. **Adults** in Japan have slightly darker upperparts and wing-tip than in W America, the darkest approaching W Coast hybrid Glaucous-winged × Western Gull in upperpart coloration. Japanese winter birds on average shows deeper raspberry-pink legs than W American birds (could be food-related). In N American adult male mean wing length 442.5 (n=36), in Commander Islands/Japan mean 445.4 (n=5); further information required in other sexes/ages.
First-years in E Pacific (Japan) generally darker but more variable than W American birds, some appearing almost uniform sooty and very weakly pale-marked in field; darkest part usually the dark greyish-brown tail, but sometimes primaries greyish-brown with narrower pale edges than described above. Could be misidentified as Slaty-backed Gull, but are on average greyer with greyish-brown, pale-edged flight feathers. Tail not conspicuously darker than upperparts. Slaty-backed generally smaller with weaker bill, rounder head, more centrally placed eyes. Plumage browner with more clearly streaked head and breast, often contrasting pale mid-belly and blackish-brown underwing-coverts, flight feathers (often paler subterminally on outer wing) and tail (own data and pers. obs., California, Japan; J. R. King pers. comm.).

DISTRIBUTION AND MIGRATION 250,000–300,000 pairs. Breeds on small, flat, rocky or vegetated islands, in bays, estuaries and meadows, by lakes, on cliffs, on buildings and near human settlements; exceptionally inland. General increase and expansion in both S and N. In Alaska 135,000 pairs in >600 colonies; on the Commander Islands 2,000–3,000 pairs (del Hoyo *et al.* 1996).
Mainly migratory; common winterer in Alaska and British Columbia (max. 45,000), but also S along Pacific Coast to California, scarce to Baja California; rare to Yukon, C American states E to Utah and Illinois. First-year performs the longest migration. Hybrid Glaucous-winged × Western Gull common between Washington and California - see above. Some dispersal to Bering Sea into pelagic N Pacific and Japan; in Hokkaido rather common in winter, scarce S to Tokyo. Stragglers reach E and S China. Vagrant Hong Kong, Hawaii, Morocco (Jan 1995); Canary Islands (Feb 1992). Record from Switzerland of bird ringed in SW Canada considered unsatisfactory (Dennis 1986, Bakker *et al.* 2001, *Brit. Birds* 92: 73; *Birding World* 9:237). For occurrence of hybrids with Western Gull, see above.

GLAUCOUS-WINGED GULL Four-year gull. Breeds NW coast of America and in NE Asia; hybridises freely with Western Gull in Washington State area, but hybridisation reported with other gulls within its breeding range (see Hybrids in main text). Shape and size similar to Western Gull, but much paler and more uniform with wing-tip basically similar to rest of plumage.
Adult has pale grey upperwing with wing-tip concolorous, or almost so, with rest of wing. Has white mirror to P10 and broad white spots on outer wing extending almost to P9–10; from below wing-tip mainly white with narrow dark trailing edge to outer wing and greyer bases to flight feathers. Eye darkish; sits high in head and well to rear. In **winter** (Sep–Mar) head brown-washed, often extensively to include breast-sides; weak 'fingerprint' markings create rather solid, unstreaked head pattern even at rather close range.
First-year rather uniform mid-brown, appearing clouded and lacking any strong pattern. Bill dark. In flight, may give impression of being as white-winged as Glaucous, but easily separated by more solid brown tail, all-dark bill and wing-tip concolorous with rest of wing.
Second-year rather similar to first-year, but bill with paler base and tip (often isolating large dark patch on mid-part) and saddle grey. Rump white, tail greyish-shaded.
Third-year similar to adult, but coverts still with extensive brown areas intermixed with grey, primaries with narrower white tips and bill duller with faint broader dark markings.
Fourth-year similar to adult, but bill duller with more solid dark markings.

MEASUREMENTS Lengths in mm; weights in g. Own data based on skins in LACM, MCZ, MVZ, NHM, NNH, UZM, ZMA. North America, Aleutians, Japan. *Note Only birds with coloration matching Kodak Grey Scale as mentioned under detailed descriptions are included.*

WING

Adult male	398–480 (445.0)	51
Adult female	392–470 (435.0)	47
First-year male	412–465 (437.0)	26
First-year female	390–450 (416.0)	25

BILL

Adult male	49.0–64.3 (57.5)	40
Adult female	46.4–62.2 (54.1)	56
First-year male	51.1–61.9 (56.3)	26
First-year female	48.7–62.8 (53.9)	35

BILL DEPTH AT GONYS

Adult male	18.5–24.4 (21.0	40
Adult female	16.4–21.2 (19.4)	51
First-year male	17.4–21.0 (18.9)	26
First-year female	15.2–22.3 (18.3)	35

BILL DEPTH AT BASE OF BILL

Adult male	18.5–24.7 (20.8)	41
Adult female	16.6–22.0 (19.1)	52
First-year male	17.7–22.4 (20.0)	26
First-year female	16.3–23.6 (19.0)	15

GONYS LENGTH

Adult male	13.6–20.8 (17.0)	41
Adult female	12.5–18.2 (15.9)	52
First-year male	14.2–17.9 (16.0)	26
First-year female	11.6–17.5 (15.3)	35

TARSUS

Adult male	59.8–78.0 (67.8)	41
Adult female	58.4–73.9 (65.0)	53
First-year male	59.2–78.0 (68.0)	26
First-year female	62.1–73.9 (65.5)	35

Weight (W USA between Alaska and California): Adult male 1,160–1,690, female 820–1,300; heaviest at start of breeding season. First-year male 1,020–1,372, female 920–1,018; juvenile late Aug 900 (skins in MCZ, MVZ, LACM).

Glaucous-winged Gull *Larus glaucescens*, **158. Juvenile/1st-winter.** The most diffusely patterned of all large 1st-year gulls. Note greyish-brown overall impression, long sloping forehead, black bill and beady eyes sitting high in head. Tertials with solid greyish-brown centres. California, USA. 17 Jan 2001. *Don DesJardin.* **159. 1st-winter.** A slightly darker individual with darker tinge to tertials and flight feathers. Note conspicuous pale edges to primaries and velvety appearance of body, lacking strong dark markings. Ventura, California, USA. 24 Nov 1986. *Don DesJardin.* **160. 1st-winter.** New 1st-winter mantle and scapulars almost unpatterned. E Pacific 1st-years often slightly darker-tinged than those from W America. Note long sloping forehead with extensive feathering at base of upper mandible and very short wing-projection. Hokkaido, Japan. 10 Feb 2001. *Klaus Malling Olsen.* **161. 1st-winter.** Superficially similar to Glaucous. Note black bill (not pink with black tip), wholly unpatterned tail and dark-streaked primaries. Appears barrel-shaped and short-winged in flight. Hokkaido, Japan. 12 Feb 2001. *Klaus Malling Olsen.*

Glaucous-winged Gull *Larus glaucescens*. **162. 1st-winter**. A rather pale and uniform individual. Note primaries concolorous with rest of wing. Oakland, California, USA. 26 Jan 2000. *Klaus Malling Olsen*. **163. 2nd-winter.** Note pale bill-base and rounded shape to primaries compared to 1st-years, as well as more uniform coverts. Point Reyes, California, USA. 30 Jan 2000. *Klaus Malling Olsen*. **164. 2nd-winter.** Many birds shows underwing-pattern resembling Glaucous, but note more densely-marked ear-coverts and darkish-looking bill. Hokkaido, Japan. 12 Feb 2001. *Klaus Malling Olsen*. **165. 2nd- or 3rd-winter**. Due to slow age development and diffusely patterned plumage many are difficult to age with certainty. Note uniform impression typical for the species. Hokkaido, Japan. 10 Feb 2001. *Klaus Malling Olsen*. **166. 3rd-winter.** Note extensive fingerprint markings on head and breast-sides typical for Glaucous-winged. The rather dark primaries and tail-markings may however suggest hybrid Glaucous-winged × Slaty-backed Gull. Akkeshi, Hokkaido, Japan. 10 Feb 2001. *Klaus Malling Olsen*.

Glaucous-winged Gull *Larus glaucescens*. **167. 4th- or adult winter**. Extensive dark markings on fleshy-tinged bill as well as rather narrow pale primary tips suggest a 4th-year rather than full adult. Oakland, California, USA. 26 Jan 2000. *Klaus Malling Olsen*. **168. 4th-winter.** As adult, but note dark-patterned primary coverts. Hokkaido, Japan. 12 Feb 2001. *Klaus Malling Olsen*. **169. 3rd-summer**. As adult, but note narrow white primary tips compared to full adult. Northwest USA, 10 Jul 1997. *Per Schiermacker-Hansen*. **170. Adult winter**. Note diffuse greyish-brown markings in head and breast-sides. Hokkaido, Japan. 12 Feb 2001. *Klaus Malling Olsen*. **171. Adult winter**. A rather short-billed individual. Wing-tip and upperparts almost concolorous. Sonora, Mexico. 3 Feb 2000. *Klaus Malling Olsen*. **172. Adult summer**. Note wing-tip is concolorous with rest of wing, with white mirror on P10 and a weaker mirror on P9. Northwest USA. 10 Jul 1997. *Per Schiermacker-Hansen.*

162

Hybrid Glaucous-winged Gull × Western Gull 173. Adult summer Compare with 172 and note dark P9-10, indicating hybrid origin. NW USA, 10 Jul 2000. *Per Schiermacker-Hansen.* **174. 1st-winter.** Similar to Glaucous Gull, but dark wing-markings broader and clearer, tertials with narrow pale fringes and wing-tip darker than mantle. Oakland, California, USA. 26 Jan 2000. *Klaus Malling Olsen.* **175. 1st-winter.** Note primaries darker than tertials (never seen in either pure Western or Glaucous-winged Gull). Note also slightly piebald appearance to underbody. Santa Barbara, California, USA. 28 Aug 1996. *Don DesJardin.* **176. 2nd-winter.** Here, dark tail-bar and extensive dark in wing-tip excludes Glaucous-winged, but still too pale for pure Western. Point Reyes, California, USA. 30 Jan 2000. *Klaus Malling Olsen.* **177. 3rd-winter.** Typical combination for hybrids are pale grey upperparts, but much darker (although rarely black) wing-tip, creating plumage more similar to American Herring. Note long, bulbous-tipped bill and small beady eye sitting high in head are typical for Western and Glaucous-winged. Head-pattern in hybrids rarely as extensive as in Glaucous-winged. Point Reyes, California, USA. 30 Jan 2000. *Klaus Malling Olsen.* **178. 4th- or adult winter.** Compared to 177, this bird shows slightly darker upperparts and primaries, but slightly more extensive (but still diffuse) head-pattern. Point Reyes, California, USA. 30 Jan 2000. *Klaus Malling Olsen.* **179. Adult winter.** This bird is very similar to Glaucous-winged Gull, and might represent 2nd-generation hybrid. Wing-tip (too dark for Glaucous-winged) is the only visible characteristic that differs from Glaucous-winged. Point Reyes, California, USA. 30 Jan 2000. *Klaus Malling Olsen.*

Hybrid Glaucous-winged Gull × American Herring Gull 180. 1st-winter. This not infrequent type resembles Thayer's Gull, and some are very tricky to identify. Note that mantle and scapulars have been moulted, creating contrast with coverts, whereas Thayer's typically will appear juvenile into late winter. Head too streaked for Thayer's and Glaucous-winged Gulls. Sacramento, California, USA. 29 Jan 2000. *Klaus Malling Olsen*. **181. 1st-winter**. Combines more elegant jizz and size of American Herring with flat crown and extensive pale in outerwing of Glaucous-winged, just outer primaries being extensively dark. Sonora, Mexico. 4 Feb 2000. *Klaus Malling Olsen*.

Putative hybrid Glaucous-winged × Slaty-backed Gull 182. Adult. In the field this bird appeared darker than surrounding Glaucous-winged with smallish head, bicoloured eyes and less heavy bill, showing conspicuously darker primaries with extensive 'string of pearls' in flight. Kushiro, Hokkaido, Japan. 10 Feb 2001. *Klaus Malling Olsen*.

13. WESTERN GULL

Larus occidentalis (Audubon, 1839, Cape Disappointment, Washington, USA)

Plates 23–24, Photos 183–204

IDENTIFICATION Length 62–66cm, wingspan 135–140cm. A large, American W Coast gull, usually the only dark-mantled large gull within its range, making identification straightforward in birds more than 1.5 years of age. Very common along W Coast, often in flocks with Glaucous-winged Gull, with which it hybridises freely in Washington state area (for ID of hybrids, see Glaucous-winged Gull under Hybrids).

Western Gull is stocky with a domed forehead, very heavy, bulbous-shaped bill (often broader at tip than base) with prominent gonys-angle and eyes placed high on head. The head peaks behind the eyes and the hind-crown slopes. In flight stocky with relatively short but broad wings, showing protruding head and rather long tail; shape similar to Glaucous-winged, or in males even to Great Black-backed Gull. Settled birds are compact and short-winged with prominent tertial step; 2–3 primary tips project beyond tail. Two subspecies.

Adult has dark grey upperparts and black wing-tip with white mirror to P10 occasionally also P9. Broad white tertial crescents merge into a white line at secondaries, which are long as in Glaucous-winged. From below, outer primaries blackish and secondaries grey. Eye varies from dark to pale. Legs pink, but at onset of breeding season sometimes slightly yellow-tinged. Northern *occidentalis* has paler upperparts but generally darker eyes than *wymani* and faint dark head-markings in winter; from Monterey area and S, breeding population consists of race *wymani*, which is slightly darker, looks white-headed all-year round and generally has paler eyes. For other ages, see Geographical Variation. Could be confused with Slaty-backed Gull, which is more elegant with rounder head-shape, less heavy bill and eyes placed more centrally on head. Adult Slaty-backed has slightly paler slaty upperparts, broader mirror to P10 and white mirror on P9, white 'string of pearls' on outer wing (at most very faint in Western and normally on mid-primaries only) and broader white trailing edge to wing, most conspicuous in flight; settled birds show similar broad white tertial edges and drooping 'skirt' of Western. In winter, Slaty-backed shows heavy, dark brown head-streaking, often strongest around the pale eyes to create oval-shaped eye-mask – a pattern lacking in Western or in Western × Glaucous-winged Gull hybrids. The legs are generally rosier than in Western. To S, Western Gull reaches Gulf of California, the range of Yellow-footed Gull (which see). The dark upperparts invite confusion with Lesser Black-backed Gull, which is smaller and slenderer with a weaker bill, paler eye more centrally placed on head, more streaked head in winter, longer wings and bright yellow legs.

Juvenile very dark and uniform, appearing sooty- to blackish-brown. Head and underparts lack streaked pattern. Mantle, scapulars and wing-coverts only show narrow, inconspicuous pale fringes or markings, mostly on mantle and scapulars, which have narrow whitish fringes. Greater coverts dark-based, forming solid dark rectangle on midwing, often striking in flight against white wing-bars created by paler tips to greater coverts and secondaries. Flight feathers dark, at most with very faint pale window on inner primaries but conspicuous white trailing edge to inner wing. In flight, very broad white trailing edge to wing, more distinct than in any other West Coast gull. Underwing-coverts and axillaries dark brown, creating strongly two-toned impression against paler flight feathers. Hindparts very dark: rump pale brown with dense dark bars or mottling against black tail. Bill black. Legs fleshy.

First-winter as juvenile, but with greyish-brown feathers intermixed on head, breast, mantle and scapulars. These greyer areas contrast with brown juvenile wing, which gets worn from midwinter. May attain dark eye-mask against paler, lightly streaked crown and neck-sides, caused by wear of head feathers. Develops pale base to bill from midwinter.

ID pitfalls in first-years provided by the darkest American Herring Gulls, which are warmer brown and have a narrower bill (usually paler base from autumn), eyes placed more centrally on paler and generally more streaked head, paler bars on greater coverts (often lacking at bases), conspicuous pale window on inner primaries and more distinctly barred rump, but much less striking pale trailing edge to wing. Saddle barred. First-winter often acquires pale head and pink bill-base. First-year Slaty-backed rather similar, but on average paler with slightly lighter build: tail paler brown (not blackish), and primaries medium brown with paler bases, showing up as pale mid-area on outer wing against darker trailing edge (larger, more diffuse area than 'window' of palest Western). From below, most Slaty-backed show paler, mostly unpatterned belly against darker flanks and breast, the latter often creating a breast-bar; in Western underparts darker and more uniform, at most with paler lower belly. Bill in Slaty-backed usually dark, at most with narrow pale line on lower mandible; if present pale areas of Western more diffuse and covering both mandibles. Legs of Slaty-backed generally deeper pink (even rosy) than greyish-pink of Western. By spring, Western ('first-summer') is worn. Then attains whitish head and body, and usually shows obvious dark eye-mask. Bleaching and wear create whitish patches on upperwing, in some contrast to grey saddle, brownish flight feathers and tail. Sometimes difficult to identify from Glaucous-winged (and especially hybrids with latter, which see), but generally with more obvious dark saddle.

Second-winter has dull grey saddle combined with darkish wings and tail similar to first-year. Head and body paler than in first-year; most show distinct dark eye-mask and ear-coverts, better-defined dark hindneck-streaks and scattered dark-patterned underparts, especially flanks and belly. Upperwing-coverts rather plain greyish-brown. Compared to first-years, tertials and secondaries blacker with broader white edges, inner primaries paler (creating slight 'window') and underwing-

PLATE 23. WESTERN GULL *Larus occidentalis*

Large West Coast gull, in shape similar to much paler Glaucous-winged Gull (with which it hybridises extensively in Washington area). Compared to American Herring slightly larger with flatter crown, heavier, more blunt-tipped bill, fuller body and shorter wings: 2–3 primary tips above tail-tip. Eyes dark, sitting high in head as in Glaucous-winged.
Coastal, occurring in flocks (often with other large gulls) in estuaries, beaches and ports.

1. **Juvenile** (Aug–Oct) Dark brown, rather uniform with velvety brown head and underbody. Upperparts with dark brown feather-centres. At most shows inconspicuous paler barring on greater coverts. Bill blackish, at most with faint fleshy tinge to lower mandible.

2. **First-winter** (Sep–May) Similar to juvenile, but with a (highly variable) number of dark grey feathers on head, breast, mantle and scapulars, often 'surrounding' brown, worn upperwing. The uniform, rather dark and nondescript appearance of this individual is typical of northern race *occidentalis*.

3. **First-winter** (Sep–May) Compared to 2, this bird has limited its moult into first-winter to mantle and scapulars against greyish-brown on head and underparts. Paler hindneck often occurs from midwinter, caused by wear.

4. **Second-winter** (Aug–Mar) Head and underbody with whiter undertone than first-year, appearing finer-marked, often diluted although rarely approaching cross-barring of Glaucous-winged. Saddle and some coverts renewed into adult type. Coverts otherwise similar to first-year but even finer-barred, appearing uniform at any distance. Bill fleshy with black tip and cutting edges.

5. **Second-winter** (Aug–Mar) As in first-winter, moult variable. This individual shows grey saddle against 'immature' wings. The contrasting greyish, diluted or cross-barred hood shown here occurs in certain individuals, and may betray traces of hybridisation with Glaucous-winged Gull.

6. **Third-winter** (Aug–Mar) Similar to adult, but with stronger brown head-markings, traces of brown-tinged coverts, dark-marked tertials, narrower white primary tips and dark subterminal markings on bill.

7. **Adult winter** *wymani* (Feb–Sep) Upperparts dark grey. Head in winter sometimes very lightly brown-streaked. Eyes darkish, but sometimes paler. Note broad white tertial crescents continuing into solid white line, created by white tips to long secondaries (as in Glaucous-winged Gull). Legs fleshy.

8. **Adult summer** *occidentalis* (Sep–Mar) As winter, but with all-white head and narrow white primary tips. Note rather pale upperparts; ssp. *wymani* is slightly darker above than *occidentalis* and generally with paler eyes. Head in winter at most with very faint brown spots on hindneck. Both races show orange orbital ring. For *wymani*, see page 23 and photos 201/203.

166

1. Juvenile

2. First-winter

3. First-winter

4. Second-winter

5. Second-winter

6. Third-winter

7. Adult winter *wymani*

8. Adult summer
occidentalis

PLATE 24. WESTERN GULL *Larus occidentalis*

In flight heavy with rather broad, short, blunt-tipped wings, accentuated by long neck, flat crown and long, bulbous-tipped bill. Tail rather long. Flies slow and rather ponderously. Flight impression similar to Glaucous-winged Gull.

1. **Juvenile** (Aug–Oct) Dark brown, appearing rather uniform. Upperwing dark, lacking pale window on inner primaries, but showing two dark bars, caused by dark-centred greater coverts and dark secondaries, and whitish wing-bars, caused by pale tips to greater coverts and secondaries. White trailing edge to inner wing more conspicuous than in other West Coast gulls. Rump very heavily brown-barred, barely contrasting with mantle, and in moderate contrast to blackish-brown tail.

2. **First-winter** (Sep–May) First-years show dark brown underwing-coverts in contrast to paler primaries, often with underside of hand pale, with black primary tips only. Underbody dark, undertail-coverts heavily dark-barred.

3. **First-winter** (Sep–May) Similar to juvenile, but (parts of) head and mantle grey with pale edges. With wear, pale hind-collar more distinct and wings and rump browner.

4. **Second-winter** (Aug–Mar) Grey saddle against wings; pattern similar to first-year but with even fainter pale barring on greater coverts. Often shows traces of pale window on inner primaries. Rump white, conspicuous against black tail. Head white with brown patterning, bill pale with black tip. Underwing heavily dark-marked.

5. **Third-winter** (Aug–Mar) Upperparts and (to a varying degree) coverts grey; grey inner primaries form pale window against black outer wing, including primary coverts and secondaries. Tail with black markings, often appearing as isolated streaks or spots.

6. **Fourth-winter** (Aug–Mar) Similar to adult, but with more extensive dark head-markings, dark subterminal markings on bill and primary coverts, narrow black tail-markings and often smaller white mirror on P10.

7. **Adult** From below, underwing white with grey flight feathers and black wing-tip, only with narrow white mirror on P10 (sometimes P9). Note characteristic elongated shape with long neck. Flat head, heavy bill and long tail. Wings rather broad and short with blunt tip.

8. **Adult summer** *occidentalis* (Feb–Sep) Adult upperwing dark grey (blackish-grey in *wymani*) with black tip, small white mirror on P10 and broad white trailing edge.

168

1. Juvenile

2. First-winter

3. First-winter

4. Second-winter

5. Third-winter

7. Adult

6. Fourth-winter

8. Adult summer

coverts a mixture of dark and pale, often as well-defined dark and pale bars. Rump white, in strong contrast to blackish tail, which now may show white feather-bases. Bill dusky to fleshy with broad black tip or subterminal bar. Eyes intermediate between first-year and adult, in nominate *occidentalis* darkish-looking in field; some *wymani* pale-eyed at this age.

Second-winter Slaty-backed Gull shows darker slaty-grey saddle, often striking against pale, often strongly worn coverts, pale eye (often creamy or whitish, much paler than in any Western) and more distinct head-streaking, especially as oval-shaped area around pale beady eyes. The legs are often strongly rosy-pink, brighter than in Western. In flight, bases to primaries paler than tips, creating broad, rather diffuse pale area on outer wing, very different from the basically dark outer wing of Western.

Second-summer similar to second-winter, but coverts fade to whitish in clear contrast to dark saddle, flight feathers are faded, head whiter and bill usually deeper yellow with narrower black subterminal bar and sometimes red gonys-spot.

Third-winter similar to adult, but with brownish tinge to upperwing-coverts and wing-tip, broader and more diffuse blackish wing-tip (at most with small mirror on P10 and no white tips of P8–10), dark primary coverts, some darker secondaries and usually faint dark tail-bar. Bill anywhere between second-summer and adult.

Fourth-winter as adult, but often with dark markings on primary coverts, underwing-coverts and tail, smaller white mirror on P10, narrower white primary tips and narrow dark subterminal markings on bill. Head sometimes with slight dark spotting, extending onto breast-sides.

VOICE Similar to American Herring Gull, but slightly lower, quicker and drier, with more clipped notes. Flying adult often gives deep, gruff *oowa* or *kwaow*, differing from high, clear notes of American Herring (Sibley 2000). Calls higher than Yellow-footed.

MOULT (*L. o. occidentalis*) Adult moult to **winter** plumage complete May–Nov. P1–2 mid-May–mid-Jun; primary moult has reached P3–4 late Jun–late Jul, P5–7 Aug–early Sep, P7–8 late Sep–mid-Oct, P9–10 (early)late Oct–Nov. Secondaries and tail late Aug–Sep. Winter head assumed Aug (when primary moult reaches P5–7); rarely not before early Nov. Onset of moult earliest in S population. In California P1 shed late May, in Oregon latter half of Jun (skins in MVZ).

Juvenile moult to **first-winter** partial Aug–Apr, including parts of upperparts, head and body. Moult often continuous for entire period, but might be reduced or suspended in winter. Starts with anterior scapulars and some upper back feathers Sep–Oct, finishing with head and longest scapulars Mar–Apr (Howell & Corben 2000a, Howell 2001). Rarely 1–2 inner wing-coverts moulted. Northern populations have more restricted moult and may basically be juvenile into midwinter apart from scattered upperparts and mantle feathers. Moult into **second-winter** complete late Apr–Oct, earlier than in adults. P1 May, up to P5 late Jun, P3–5(8) mid–late Jul, P8 late Aug, and P9–10 late Sep–early Oct.

Mantle/scapulars from May, coverts generally Jul, although median coverts sometimes from May. Primary moult timed between first-years and adult (skins in LACM, MVZ). Subsequent moults similar to adults.

DESCRIPTION, ssp. *occidentalis*
Adult Mantle, scapulars and upperwing-coverts dark grey (Kodak Grey Scale 7.5–9.5). Very slightly paler to N: in British Columbia 7.5–9, in Oregon 8–9, in California 8.5–9.5(10) (Bell 1996, skins in LACM, MVZ). Has black pattern on outer wing, reaching primary coverts onto P8–9. P10 black with 35–45mm white mirror (normally reaching edge of inner web; division from black on inner web straight in 75%; rounded in 25%) and narrow dark subterminal bar near extreme tip. P9 with black tip and in small minority with narrow white mirror on inner web. P8–5 with gradually less black. P6 with 40–58mm black on outer web, 28–40mm on inner web, and 10–15mm white tongue between black and grey on inner web. P5 with 10–25mm black on outer 7–11(20)mm on inner web; usually with 7–12mm white tongues on both webs. P4 sometimes with dark subterminal spot near tip; P1–4 otherwise dark grey. Primaries with white tips, broadest on P1–5, where up to 14mm when fresh; white primary tips usually evident into Mar. White tips to secondaries broader, forming white trailing edge to wing. Underside of P10 blackish. Underside, axillaries, underwing-coverts, rump and tail white. Iris darkish-looking, but ground colour may be pearly-grey, pale yellow or yellowish-brown, obscured by normally extensive dark flecking. Orbital ring yellow to orange-yellow, rarely orange or dull purple. Bill yellow with red gonys and whitish tip. White feathering at upper mandible penetrates in 45–60° towards cutting edges, ending 7–11mm before nostril. Gape orange-red. Depth of bill at gonys up to 2–3mm broader than at base. Nostril depth at proximal edge 2.0–2.5mm, length 10–12mm, appearing oval-shaped. Legs fleshy to pink.

Adult summer (Jan/Feb–Aug) Head white. Bill deep yellow, often orange-tinged. Legs sometimes with slight yellow tinge to upper tarsus and toes from late Jan; in Mar some have yellow-orange tarsus, but webs remain pink (King 1999, pers. obs.).

Adult winter (Sep–Feb) Head white with variable dark wash – in heaviest-marked birds somewhat similar to Glaucous-winged – or with narrow spots on especially ear-coverts and hindneck, sometimes also breast-sides and face. Bill yellow with orange to red gonys-spot and sometimes dark subterminal markings; bill often creamy- or pinkish-tinged at base.

Juvenile (fledging–Sep/Oct) Head and underbody greyish-brown to sooty-grey with faint paler waving or mottling especially on neck and hindneck; face and lower belly sometimes slightly paler. Undertail-coverts pale with narrow dark bars or mottling. Mantle, back and scapulars dark brown with narrow pale buff to whitish fringes. Tertials greyish-brown with narrow white to sandy fringes, often restricted to pale edges to tip; sometimes with distal part paler. Upperwing-coverts dark greyish-brown with faint pale fringes; when fresh sandy, sometimes with slightly darker shaft-streaks or subterminal spots. Greater coverts dark greyish-brown,

outer mostly uniform but gradually paler barred or waved on innermost near tips, leaving solid dark area at bases, creating dark rectangle on upperwing (but rarely all greater coverts pale-barred). Flight feathers dark brown, darkening to blackish on P6–10; P1–5 rarely with slightly paler inner webs. Fresh primaries have narrow pale tips, creating row of pale V-spots on folded wing. Secondaries with white tips. Primary coverts blackish-brown with narrow pale fringes. Underwing-coverts and axillaries brownish-black, bases to greater coverts and flight feathers slightly paler. Rump and uppertail-coverts whitish with broad but diffuse brown or buffish barring or waving. Tail black to dark greyish-brown with narrow pale tips to rectrices. T6 at most with 3–4 pale spots on outer web or slight pale mottling at base. Bill black, sometimes with fleshy tinge to base of lower mandible and narrow pale tip to upper mandible. **First-winter** (Sep–Apr) similar to juvenile, but (parts of) mantle and scapulars brownish-slate or greyish-brown with dark shaft-streaks, creating streaky pattern, indistinct pale fringes and often grey bases. Rump sometimes more strongly dark-barred in some contrast to mantle. Compared to juvenile, head more contrasting: cheek, throat and hindneck often paler with broad dark streaks or spots, crown and neck-sides often lightly streaked; paler head pattern mainly caused by wear, but sometimes with extensive grey feathering intermixing with retained juvenile plumage. Underbody with scattered grey feathers. Bill develops pale base from Dec; in late winter bill sometimes fleshy with dark culmen, cutting edges (lower mandible) and tip. In spring, upperparts (especially greater coverts) paler through wear and by spring plumage often very worn ('first-summer'): head and underside dusky-white with irregular greyish-brown blotching, upperwing-coverts faded (greater may fade to whitish). Flight feathers and tail bleach brownish.
Second-winter (May–Mar) Head whitish with dark shading, mottling or spotting, especially around eye (forming dark mask), on ear-coverts and hindneck. Underbody white with dark spots or mottling especially on belly and flanks, sometimes solid white; on breast-sides sometimes delicate bars. Undertail-coverts sometimes with faint dark markings. Mantle, back and scapulars dark grey, duller than adult and often with faint pale edges and dark subterminal spots or shaft-streaks; contrasts with first-year-type upperwing, often with few grey median coverts and inner coverts. Greater coverts greyish-brown with whitish fringes (at most with very faint pale mottling). Tertials blackish with strong whitish mottling at tips; some inner tertials sometimes grey as in adult. Flight feathers similar to first-winter, but tips rounded, P1–5 generally paler greyish-brown (often with darker subterminal spots near tips). P6–10 and secondaries blacker with broader whitish tips. A minority show narrow white mirror on P10. Scapular-crescents and tertial edges white, in the latter often irregular against black bases. Rump white with faint dark spots or streaks. Tail brownish-black with white fringes and faint pale mottling at base; rarely T1–2(4) white with varying dark markings. Axillaries and underwing-coverts either similar to first-year or paler with broad dark tips, looking blotchy. Bill greyish with fleshy to yellow tinge and

black tip or subterminal markings, sometimes covering >50% of bill as solid dark central part surrounded by pale, or as black distal part and broad ivory tip (broadest on upper mandible). Legs greyish-pink. Eyes on average paler than in first-year (dark amber); may attain adult colour, but rarely as pale.
Second-summer (Apr–Sep) as second-winter, but head and underparts whiter and retained upperwing-coverts often worn, in strong contrast to dark grey mantle and fresh grey median coverts. Head white with varying dark eye-mask or dark crescent in front of eye. Flight feathers and tail-markings paler and browner. Rump white with indistinct dark waving. Bill yellow with black subterminal bar (sometimes tip black), often orange to red tinge to gonys and whitish tip. Orbital ring yellow. Iris medium brown to pale yellow or pale blue-grey.
Third-winter (Jun–Apr) similar to adult winter, but sometimes with faint dark mottling around eye, grey spots or waving on hindneck. Some wing-coverts brown-tipped (generally more solid on greater coverts) and blackish on outer wing more extensive. Division between grey bases to blackish-brown P6–10 more diffuse than in adult. P10 usually black, sometimes with narrow white mirror. Outer secondaries sometimes dark-centred. Primary coverts and alula brownish-black with paler edges. Tail white with variable grey to blackish marking, forming indistinct dark tail-bar, normally broken and restricted to T1–4. Underwing-coverts with dark markings, sometimes as regular dark and pale bars. Bill yellow with black subterminal bar, sometimes just narrow and restricted to upper mandible, and whitish tip; orange to red often appears on gonys. Bill sometimes as second-winter.
Third-summer (Apr–Aug) similar to third-winter, but head and underparts cleaner white. Bare parts similar to adult, but bill sometimes with faint dark subterminal mark, dusky-pinkish ground coloration and yellow tip and gonys. Outer primaries browner through wear.
Fourth-winter (Sep–Feb) as adult, but primaries with narrower white tips and mirror to P10 (where restricted to inner web), tail with scattered dark spotting on especially T4–5, some brownish-tinged wing-coverts, darker centres to primary coverts, some dark on underwing and generally darker eyes and more solid dark bill-markings.

GEOGRAPHICAL VARIATION Two subspecies.
L. o. occidentalis (between Central Washington and Monterey Peninsula, California) described; for extensive hybridisation with Glaucous-winged Gull, see that species.
L. o. wymani (W Coast, generally S of San Francisco) slightly lighter build with less heavy bill, often deeper at tip. **Adult** has darker upperparts (Kodak Grey Scale (9)9.5–10.5(11)). Black pattern on wing-tip similar to nominate *occidentalis*, but black on P6–10 more extensive, generally covering one primary more and on P7–8 reaching primary coverts. White mirror on P10 (max. 30mm) generally more rounded and less frequently reaching edge of inner web in <90% (mirror shape rounded on outer web in 66%, more or less straight in 34%, but rarely as straight as in nominate). In 5–10%, small white mirror to P9. P4–5 have more equal amount

of black on both webs (23–50 on P5, 15–23 on P4) (in old males sometimes reduced to faint subterminal spot on outer web or even lacking); nominate normally shows more black on outer than inner web. Have narrower whitish tongues; on P4–6 3–8mm on innerwebs only. Primaries often moderately worn from Dec, only with moderate white tips (earlier than in nominate, which by direct comparison shows broader white primary tips in winter caused by later moult; see below). White-headed most of year; in late summer to early winter sometimes with fine dark spots around eyes and on hindneck; appears white-headed from Feb, when many nominate still show dark head-markings. Eyes greyish to brownish-yellow with variable amount of dark spotting (as nominate) but sometimes paler medium yellow to whitish. Legs may show slight yellow tinge from late Jan, especially on upper tarsus and toes, but sometimes on entire tarsus Feb–Mar. This, however, rarely matches Yellow-footed Gull (Dunn 1997, skins in LACM, MVZ, J. R. King pers. comm., pers. obs. in San Diego, California). **Juvenile/first-winter** similar to nominate, but generally more contrasting: head darker (especially mask to hindneck to form sooty-black half-hood), but cheek and throat paler. Breast dark brown, often in some contrast to paler (but still dark-patterned) belly. Mantle and scapulars greyish-brown with dark shaft-streaks, sometimes mantle feathers with more solid dark centres intermixed. Flight feathers, tail, tertials and greater coverts darker than in nominate, with more conspicuous dark barring or patterning on upperparts, e.g. often slight buff barring to distal part of all greater coverts. Underwing with darker brown lesser coverts (sometimes median coverts) than nominate, appearing more strikingly two-toned. **Second-years** often more 'adult-looking' compared to nominate. Sometimes similar to adult, but primaries brownish, only rarely with white mirror to P10, wing-coverts brownish-tinged, tail normally with dark pattern and bill duller with dark subterminal markings. Head often with dark vermiculations (as nominate), even in third-winter. **Moult** generally earlier and more advanced than nominate. **Adult** moult into **winter** generally one month earlier than nominate; P1 late May–mid-Jun; P5–6(8) generally Aug, P7–8 Sep, P9–10 (Aug)late Sep–mid-Oct. Head mid–late Sep. Moult into **adult summer** partial or very limited, including (some of) head Jan–Feb. **Juvenile** moult into **first-winter** partial late Aug–Feb, including mantle, scapulars and scattered feathers on head and upper body (especially breast-sides). Moult to **second-winter** Mar–Oct, earlier and more advanced compared to nominate with larger amount of adult feathers, including mantle, scapulars and a variable number of (sometimes almost all) wing-coverts. P1 and wing-coverts from late Apr. Birds which have renewed T1–2 and inner tertials noted from early Feb. P8–10 late Aug–mid-Sep (skins in LACM, MVZ; J. R. King pers. comm.).

Hybrids See Glaucous-winged Gull.

DISTRIBUTION AND MIGRATION 32,000 pairs. Breeds on rocky islands with some cover and gravelly beaches, often near sea-lions *Zalophus californianus*.

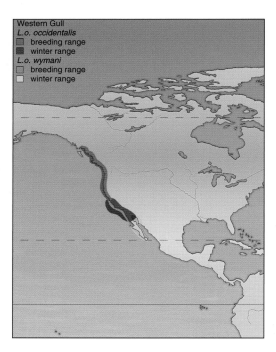

Western Gull
L.o. occidentalis
☐ breeding range
■ winter range
L.o. wymani
☐ breeding range
☐ winter range

Strictly coastal all year. Locally common. *L. o. occidentalis* breeds mainly N of Monterey Peninsula, *wymani* south from here. From mid-1980s increase of breeding range California. 13,000 pairs (40% of population of nominate) breed SE Farallon Island, where present and defending territories all year; winter max. 25,000. *L. o. occidentalis* mainly sedentary with mid-Jul gatherings up to 5,000 California N of San Francisco, but with some dispersal along entire Californian coast among younger birds which head N after fledging (A. Jaramillo *in litt.*) *L. o. wymani* migratory, with post-breeding movements to N to British Columbia, E to Anchorage and S to Baja California, where flock of max. 500. At Santa Cruz, California, 20,000–30,000 winter. Generally, young *occidentalis* perform the longest migration, summering to the north in fish-rich waters; site varies from year to year depending on food supply. Accidental Alaska, W Mexico S of Baja California, and inland USA.

MEASUREMENTS Lengths in mm; weights in g. Own data based on skins in LACM, MVZ, NHM, NRK. *L. o. occidentalis* California (S to San Francisco), Oregon, British Columbia. *L. o. wymani* California S of Monterey (mainly Los Angeles area), breeding season.

WING

L. o. occidentalis		
Adult male	405–440 (422.1)	27
Adult female	388–422 (405.3)	35
First-year male	418–432 (423.0)	3
First-year female	394–425 (404.9)	8
L. o. wymani		
Adult male	405–448 (426.5)	38
Adult female	380–423 (404.0)	35

172

WESTERN GULL Four-year gull. Abundant along American W Coast. Stout, heavy-billed and flat-crowned, with short wings (3–4 primary tips behind prominent tertial step). Long secondaries create broad- and short-winged impression in flight.

Adult has blackish-grey upperwing, slightly paler in N nominate *occidentalis* (which hybridises extensively with Glaucous-winged Gull). Wing-tip black with white mirror to P10; wing-tip from below appears solid dark (unlike Slaty-backed). Eye situated high in head; darkish, but in southern race *wymani* paler yellow. Legs fleshy, at onset of breeding season sometimes slightly yellowish-tinged, but never as bright yellow as in Yellow-footed. In **winter** (Sep–Mar) at most shows faint dark head-streaking, most prominent on hindneck, and most frequent in northern *occidentalis*.

First-year dark with faintly mottled head and underbody; upperwing dark, at most with faint paler inner primaries, but white tips to greater coverts and secondaries form broad white wing-bars. Rump heavily barred and tail all dark.

First-winter mantle and scapulars mainly dark; poorly marked and never appearing barred. Bill with paler base from midwinter.

Second-year has dark, adult-like saddle and parts of innerwing, fleshy-based and dark-tipped bill, and white rump against black tail. Underwing-coverts dark against white (sparsely dark-spotted) underbody.

Third-year similar to adult, but with brown-tinged wing-coverts and narrower (if any) white primary tips.

Juv./first-winter ♂	390–420 (414.0)	9
Juv./first-winter ♀	372–414 (393.7)	7

BILL

L. o. occidentalis		
Adult male	49.7–62.2 (57.0)	27
Adult female	47.2–59.1 (52.7)	35
Juv./first-winter ♂	53.2–57.0 (55.3)	3
Juv./first-winter ♀	49.2–56.4 (52.5)	8
L. o. wymani		
Adult male	53.5–58.8 (56.3)	42
Adult female	46.9–54.2 (51.3)	37
Juv./first-winter ♂	47.8–55.0 (52.1)	9
Juv./first-winter ♀	46.5–53.4 (49.0)	8

BILL DEPTH AT GONYS

L. o. occidentalis		
Adult male	18.7–23.4 (21.4)	27
Adult female	17.2–22.0 (19.4)	35
Juv./first-winter ♂	19.5–20.8 (20.0)	3
Juv./first-winter ♀	17.0–20.4 (18.3)	8
L. o. wymani		
Adult male	19.0–22.1 (20.4)	42
Adult female	17.0–19.7 (18.3)	37
Juv./first-winter ♂	16.7–19.1 (18.2)	9
Juv./first-winter ♀	14.5–18.9 (16.8)	8

BILL DEPTH AT BASE OF BILL

L. o. occidentalis		
Adult male	18.4–23.0 (20.8)	27
Adult female	16.9–22.7 (18.8)	35
Juv./first-winter ♂	18.8–20.6 (19.8)	3
Juv./first-winter ♀	17.0–21.6 (18.8)	8
L. o. wymani		
Adult male	18.0–21.6 (19.5)	42
Adult female	16.6–19.5 (17.7)	37
Juv./first-winter ♂	16.3–18.8 (17.7)	9
Juv./first-winter ♀	15.2–18.1 (16.5)	8

GONYS LENGTH

L. o. occidentalis		
Adult male	14.0–18.3 (16.0)	27
Adult female	14.0–18.8 (15.2)	35
Juv./first-winter ♂	14.8–15.8 (15.2)	3
Juv./first-winter ♀	13.9–16.6 (14.9)	8
L. o. wymani		
Adult male	14.3–18.5 (16.2)	42
Adult female	13.0–15.8 (14.6)	37
Juv./first-winter ♂	12.5–15.2 (14.1)	9
Juv./first-winter ♀	10.7–16.3 (13.8)	8

TARSUS

L. o. occidentalis		
Adult male	62.7–73.3 (68.9)	27
Adult female	57.8–70.2 (64.1)	35
Juv./first-winter ♂	66.8–69.0 (68.2)	3
Juv./first-winter ♀	62.1–70.6 (65.6)	8
L. o. wymani		
Adult male	61.8–72.1 (68.3)	42
Adult female	58.9–65.4 (62.4)	37
Juv./first-winter ♂	60.0–69.3 (66.9)	9
Juv./first-winter ♀	59.2–63.2 (62.4)	8

Weight *L. o. occidentalis* British Columbia, Oregon, breeding adult: male 1,050–1,400, female 860–1,070; lighter at onset of breeding season, when females down to 850. First-year male 1,096, female 846. *L. o. wymani* California S of San Francisco breeding adult: male 1,013–1,250, female 800–1,030. First-year male 960 (skins in LACM, MVZ).

Western Gull *Larus occidentalis*. **183. Juvenile** ssp. *occidentalis*. Note dark greyish-brown head and underbody, being rather uniform and dark in ssp. *occidentalis*. Compared to darker-patterned American Herring, bill much stronger, eyes smaller and situated higher in head, and wing projection shorter. Oregon, USA. Oct 1991. *René Pop*. **184. 1st-winter** ssp. *occidentalis*. Note dark-centred 1st-winter mantle feathers, thus not creating barring (unlike American Herring). Point Reyes, California, USA. 30 Jan 2000. *Klaus Malling Olsen*. **185. Juvenile** ssp. *wymani*. Note dark head but paler hindneck, indicating *wymani*. Ventura, California, USA. Jul 1995. *Don DesJardin*. **186 1st-winter**. Rather short-billed individual; note typical spotted to streaked mantle. Dana Point, California, USA. 6 Feb 2000. *Klaus Malling Olsen*. **187 1st-winter**. Note dark flight-feathers and greater covert bases, leaving white wing-bar at tips of greater coverts. Rump heavily barred in this age. Monterey, California, USA. 4 Oct 1987. *Harry J. Lehto*.

Western Gull *Larus occidentalis.* **188. 1st-winter.** Very broad white trailing edge to innerwing well illustrated here. Dana Point, California, USA. 6 Feb 2000. *Klaus Malling Olsen,* **189. 2nd-winter.** Note very dark underwing-coverts and dense dark pattern on underbody. Monterey, California, USA. Oct 1987. *René Pop.* **190. 2nd-winter** ssp. *occidentalis.* Pale upperparts suggest this ssp. Compared to 1st-winter more contrasting with pale base to bill, whiter underbody, extensive grey saddle and white rump. Santa Barbara, California, USA. 2 Jan 1996. *Don DesJardin.* **191. 2nd-winter** ssp. *occidentalis.* White rump against black tail evident. Note broad, white trailing edge to wing. Point Reyes, California, USA. 30 Jan 2000. *Klaus Malling Olsen.* **192. 2nd-winter.** Compare with 1st-winter Yellow-footed Gull (photo 209) and note differences in bill pattern as well as fresher appearance of 2nd-winter plumage compared to 1st-winter. Dana Point, California, USA. 6 Feb 2000. *Klaus Malling Olsen.* **193. 2nd-winter** ssp. *wymani.* Note white underbody contrasts well with dark underwing-coverts, and compare Yellow-footed Gull photo 210. Dana Point, California, USA. 12 Feb 2000. *Klaus Malling Olsen.*

Western Gull *Larus occidentalis*. **194. 2nd-summer** ssp. *wymani*. Dark saddle indicates this ssp. Saddle contrasts well with worn coverts. Santa Barbara, California, USA. 7 May 1996. *Don DesJardin*. **195. 3rd-winter**. Similar to adult, but note extensive black bill markings, brownish-tinged coverts and just narrow white primary tips. Ventura, California, USA. 18 Nov 1995. *Don DesJardin*. **196. 3rd-winter.** Note just small white mirror on P10 and dark markings in tail at this age. Dana Point, California, USA. 6 Feb 2000. *Klaus Malling Olsen*. **197. Moulting into 3rd-winter**. Underwing-coverts predominantly white from this age. Monterey, California, USA. 3 Oct 1987. *Harry J. Lehto*. **198. Adult, 3rd-winter and 1st-winter** ssp. *occidentalis*. Note heavy, bulbous-tipped bill, small eyes sitting high in head and short wing-projection. Point Reyes, California, USA. 30 Jan 2000. *Klaus Malling Olsen*. **199. Adult winter** ssp. *occidentalis*. Point Reyes, California, USA. Note rather pale upperparts in this ssp. 30 Jan 2000. *Klaus Malling Olsen*

Western Gull *Larus occidentalis*. **200. Adult summer** ssp. *occidentalis*. At onset of breeding season, yellowish cast may show in legs. California, USA. 12 Mar 1999. *Jon R. King*. **201. Adult summer** ssp. *wymani*. Upperparts darker than in *occidentalis*, head white all year. Santa Barbara, California, USA. 7 May 1996. *Don DesJardin*. **202. Adult winter** ssp. *occidentalis*. Note suggestion of 'string of pearls' in outerwing, reminiscent of Slaty-backed Gull, which would show rounder head, shorter bill, broader white mirror on P10 as well as white window in P9. Compare upperparts with 203. Mendocino Co., California, USA. 13 Dec 1999. *Jon R. King*. **203. Adult winter** ssp. *wymani*. Note darker upperparts than 202. Mirror on P10 generally more rounded, less square than in *occidentalis*. San Diego, California, USA. 6 Feb 2000. *Klaus Malling Olsen*. **204. Adult winter** ssp. *wymani*. Small percentage show narrow white mirror to P9. Note very broad white trailing edge to wing. San Diego, California, USA. 12 Feb 2000. *Klaus Malling Olsen*.

14. YELLOW-FOOTED GULL

Larus livens (Dwight, 1919, San José Island, Lower California)

Plates 25–26, Photos 205–214

IDENTIFICATION Length 55–72cm, wingspan 150–155cm. Yellow-footed Gull is endemic to Baja California and N Mexico, with a pre-breeding spread to Salton Sea, California. In its normal range, usually simply told on range alone since it is the area's only large gull with blackish upperparts (apart from rare Western). It is similar to Western Gull race *wymani*, but slightly larger with more elongated forehead and chunkier, deeper-based bill with heavier, bulbous tip. Appears longer-legged with 'swan-neck' similar to Caspian Gull *cachinnans*. Acquires adult plumage a year earlier than Western (and most other large gulls). Legs become yellow from late in first-winter.

Adult similar to Western *wymani*, but with yellow legs (pink in Western), slightly darker upperparts and white head all year. By late winter, upperparts get dull brownish-tinged with wear and white primary tips narrow, often lacking from Apr, when Western appears fresher, with slight bluish tinge to fresher upperparts, generally broader white primary tips and fleshy legs (at most slightly yellow-tinged).

Juvenile similar to Western, but more contrasting: head greyish-brown, often with greyish mask or half-hood against white hindneck and underparts, the latter at most with dark spots on breast-sides, flanks and edges of undertail-coverts. The mainly white underparts contrast strongly with dark brown underwing-coverts. Mantle and scapulars blackish with strong pale scaling. Rump and uppertail-coverts mainly white in strong contrast to blackish tail. Wing pattern slightly more contrasting than in Western, with blackish outer wing and secondary bar, darker greater covert bases and stronger pattern to lesser and median coverts. Normally with weak pale window on inner primaries. Bill black, legs pink. Juvenile Western Gull is darker and browner with more evenly and strongly dark-patterned underbody—a key feature from Yellow-footed. Western also shows dark-marked rump and uppertail-coverts and less contrasting wing pattern. Juvenile American Herring Gull also differs by darker underparts, heavily marked rump and uppertail-coverts and paler window on inner primaries, in addition to structural differences, especially lighter, less bulbous-tipped bill.

First-winter acquires paler head with dark streaks (most on ear-coverts and hindneck, often forming slight dark mask). Some have dense streaks on hindneck, creating necklace. Mantle and scapulars brownish-grey to dark slate with pale fringes and dark shaft-streaks, often creating partly streaked pattern. White scapular-crescents and broad white tips to new, fresh tertials often eye-catching. Some coverts renewed to greyer type. Bill blackish with dull flesh base to upper mandible and paler yellow inner 50% of lower mandible; this tricolour is diagnostic against Western Gull. Eyes often begin to grow pale from midwinter, when legs may become yellowish. First-year Western has duller fleshy bill with greyish-pink, not yellow, base to lower mandible. Also, both belly and rump are dark-spotted, appearing more uniform.

Second-year Western is similar to first-year Yellow-footed, but has darker primaries with rounded tips, broader white edges to all tertials, strong dark markings on underbody (especially flanks and belly; rarely cleaner white as Yellow-footed), cleaner grey saddle and never yellow-tinged legs. The bill is usually dull fleshy on both mandibles.

Moult to second-winter earlier than in Western. By spring (first-summer) Yellow-footed develops blackish-grey saddle (and, later, inner wing-coverts, starting with median), creating contrast with bleached, almost whitish juvenile coverts and brownish juvenile primaries and tail. Combination of adult-type and juvenile feathers unique among Nearctic large gulls (in Palearctic shared with Lesser Black-backed race *fuscus*, Heuglin's Gull, Pallas's and Audouin's Gulls). Legs normally dull yellow, rarely fleshy.

Second-winter similar to adult, but with narrow dark head-streaks, brownish tinge to upperwing-coverts and less clear primary pattern without pale tips and white mirror to P10. Underwing-coverts and tail with some dark. Bill yellow to pink with black tip. Legs dull yellow. Similar to third-winter Western Gull, but with yellow legs and more black on bill and tail.

Second-summer similar to second-winter, but wings more bleached, head white and bill yellow with dark subterminal markings and often red gonys-spot.

Third-year as adult, but sometimes aged by slightly brownish-tinged upperparts, narrow black tail-markings and narrow dark subterminal bill-markings.

VOICE Deep, hoarse *gruff-gruff, hoar-hoar-hoar...* or *wouf-wouf-wouf...*, deeper, slower and more nasal than in Western, sometimes recalling 'laughter' of Caspian Gull. A harsh *gee-a-eer* may recall call of Caspian Tern *Sterna caspia*. Long-call consists of rapid notes, lower than in Western and lacking rough first segment of each phrase (Sibley 2000).

MOULT (skins in LACM, MVZ, photos, pers. obs. in Mexico) At least 2–3 months earlier than in Western Gull.

Adult moult to **winter** plumage complete in Apr–Oct, earlier than in Western *wymani*. Starts with P1 Apr. Reaches P5–7 Jul, P7–8 Aug, P10 Sep–Oct. Head and body Jul–Aug, secondaries normally finished shortly before moult of P9–10. Moult to **adult summer** limited to parts of head and body, Nov–Mar.

Juvenile moult to **first-winter** mid-Jul–Oct, including head, body, some tertials and often some inner wing-coverts. Mantle, scapulars and tertials from Sep/Oct. Moults directly into **second-winter**, complete moult, (Jan)Mar–Sep, starting with parts of head, body, mantle and scapulars and some tertials and coverts from Jan. By late May, most show active covert moult. Wing-moult earlier than in Western: P1–2 Mar/Apr (sometimes simultaneously), P9–10 Sep (rarely late Jul). Secondaries and tail from mid-Jul.

Moult to **second-summer** partial, including head and some body feathers; similar to adult, but perhaps slightly earlier. Moult to **third-winter** complete Mar–Sep, reaches P6–7 mid-Jul.

DESCRIPTION
Adult Similar to Western Gull *wymani*, but upperparts slightly darker slate (Kodak Grey Scale 10–11). P10 with 30–50mm white mirror (on average largest in males, where sometimes almost reaching tip), which is often straight-lined at inner parts and often, unlike most Western *wymani*, extends to outer web. P9 rarely with narrow white mirror on outer web. Other primaries similar to Western *wymani*. P5 with max. 30mm black subterminal spot and narrow white 'moon' on inner web. P4 sometimes with black subterminal spot, especially on outer web. Tertials and scapulars with 15–22mm white tips, generally broader than in Western *wymani*. Iris pale greyish, olive-grey or bright yellow. Orbital ring chrome-yellow, on average deeper in colour than in Western *wymani*. Bill yellow to orange-yellow with red gonys-spot. Legs and feet yellow. Nostril length 7.5–11.5mm, depth at proximal edge 2.5–3mm.
Adult summer (Nov–Jul) Head white. Bare parts at their brightest in summer.
Adult winter (Jun–Dec) As adult summer, but head sometimes with very faint dark markings and legs generally duller yellow.
Juvenile (fledging–Sep) Head, hindneck and breast-sides whitish to greyish-brown, often with dark eye-mask/hood reaching crown, and distinct dark streaks on neck- and breast-sides (often as strongly spotted breast-band or traces of neck-boa). May show faint dark crown-streaks, sometimes reaching forehead. Breast sharply divided from white belly to undertail-coverts, barring being restricted to flanks and sides of undertail-coverts. Mantle, back and scapulars blackish with whitish to pale buff fringes, sometimes restricted to mottling along edges. Tertials blackish with pale fringes, mostly restricted to broad, pale tips; often with some mottling in division between dark and pale and greyish-brown subterminal markings on distal parts. Upperwing-coverts dark greyish-brown with extensive, but rather diffuse dark subterminal markings ('anchors' near tips) and pale fringes. Greater coverts blackish-brown with faint pale barring or mottling on distal parts, most conspicuous on inner greater coverts. Flight feathers blackish-brown with white tip to P1–5 and secondaries; P1–5 sometimes slightly paler, forming pale 'window' in flight. Rump and uppertail-coverts white, the former with slight dark mottling or barring along edges. Underwing-coverts dark brown. Tail black with narrow pale tips and mottling along outer web of T6. Iris dark. Bill black. Legs fleshy.
First-winter (Oct–Jan) Similar to juvenile, but head and breast with dark streaking restricted to ear-coverts (often as faint dark mask), hindneck and breast-sides. Mantle, back and scapulars a mixture of juvenile feathers and new blackish-grey feathers (dull with dark shaft-streaks; on scapulars with broad white fringes, shaped as triangles near tip). Some inner wing-coverts renewed to dark grey, against faded juvenile coverts; some tertials renewed to black with conspicuous broad white

Yellow-footed Gull
■ breeding range
--- N limit of non-breeding occurrence

fringes. Iris pale from Jan. Bill black with dull fleshy culmen and base to upper mandible and dull yellow inner 50% of lower mandible; yellow often present as streak along cutting edges. Legs fleshy to dull yellow.
Moults directly into **second-winter** from spring. During transition stages in late spring and summer, head and underbody merely have fainter dark mottling. From spring, mantle, back and scapulars gradually sooty-black contrasting strongly with worn whitish upper-wing-coverts (especially greater coverts). The worn upperwing-coverts are gradually restricted as moult progresses; from Jun–Jul fresh dark coverts dominate. Tertials dark with broad pale tips, covering up to 40% of feather-tip. Eye often becomes paler. Bill yellow to pink with black tip; sometimes 50% of bill black, including cutting edges; in others reduced to dark subterminal bar. Legs flesh to dull yellow.
Second-winter (Aug–Mar) Similar to adult, but hind-neck often densely dark-spotted, upperwing-coverts brownish-tinged, primaries brownish-black with 2–3mm indistinct pale edges; P10 (usually) and P9 (always) lack white mirror. Primary coverts dark brown with pale tips to edges. Tertials brownish-black with irregular whitish edges. Underwing-coverts with dark markings, especially on median coverts and axillaries. Tail with some

179

PLATE 25. YELLOW-FOOTED GULL *Larus livens*

Large gull with range restricted to Baja California and N Mexico. Summer visitor to Salton Sea, California, otherwise coastal. Breeds on islands; visits fishing ports and beaches outside breeding season. In all plumages resembles Western Gull, but generally 'lankier' with even broader bill-tip and longer neck. Plumage development generally a year in advance of Western Gull.

1. **Juvenile** (Jun–Sep) Head very dark, contrasting with pale hindneck. Breast brown-marked but belly whitish.

2. **First-winter** (Jul–Oct) Already rather contrasting. Head and underbody mainly white, wing worn and mantle/scapulars moulted to grey. Bill blackish with yellowish-flesh base to lower mandible. In this individual, juvenile wing retained, resulting in strongly worn wing and tertials by early winter. Note long neck held in 'swan-neck posture' and very broad bulbous-shaped bill-tip. Legs fleshy, but from first-winter often with faint yellow tinge.

3. **First-winter** (Jul–Oct) This and 4 show variations in first-winter. Head white with faint dark mask, isolated from hindneck by paler neck-sides. Underparts mainly white, often unmarked from midwinter, but in some with faint brown markings on breast-sides and flanks. Central belly unmarked. New tertials with broader white edges and darker centres than in juvenile. Primaries slightly brownish-tinged with pointed tips. Bill blackish with fleshy base to upper mandible and greyish-yellow basal 50% of lower mandible, creating slightly three-toned bill. Legs often slightly yellowish-tinged. (In this plumage similar to second-winter Western, which is identified by blacker primaries with rounder white edges, fleshy base to both mandibles, saddle and wing-coverts of same generation, and always fleshy legs; also, most second-winter Western still show some extensive markings on belly.) Many first-winter Yellow-footed moult some wing coverts, which then contrast with worn primaries.

4. **First-winter** (Jul–Oct) A more advanced individual than 3, showing clearer contrast in bill, whiter underparts and yellowish-tinged fleshy legs.

5. **Second-winter** (Mar–Sep) Generally as adult, but coverts slightly brownish-tinged or with scattered brown markings, bill fleshy (often with yellow tinge) with extensive black sub-terminal markings, black tail and much narrower white primary tips than in adult.

6. **Second-summer** (Nov–Jul) As adult, but tail and bill with some dark markings.

7. **Adult** Appears white-headed all year. Eyes and orbital ring bright yellow. Upperparts blackish-grey, similar to Western Gull *wymani* or slightly darker, generally with narrower white primary tips and broader white tertial crescents Legs bright yellow. Generally bill-tip even broader than in Western. Pale eyes often small and beady.

1. Juvenile

2. First-winter

3. First-winter

4. First-winter

5. Second-winter

6. Second-summer

7. Adult

PLATE 26. YELLOW-FOOTED GULL *Larus livens*

Size and shape similar to Western Gull (and Glaucous-winged Gull). A large gull with elongated shape, longer neck and longer tail than American Herring, but wings broader, shorter and rounder.

1. **Juvenile** (Jun–Sep) Similar to Western Gull: brown with blackish flight feathers (lacking pale window on inner primaries) and dark wing-bars created by dark centres to greater coverts and secondaries; shows pale wing-bars created by pale tips to greater coverts and secondaries. Tail black. Compared to Western rump paler, appearing whitish with faint barring.

2. **Juvenile/first-winter** (Jun–Oct) Underwing similar to Western, but belly contrastingly pale.

3. **First-winter** (Jul–Oct) Rather good contrast between pale and dark. Head whitish with faint dark mask. Bill blackish with fleshy base to upper mandible and yellowish base to lower mandible. Upperwing worn, slightly contrasting with new, greyer saddle with paler feather-edges. Shows white rump and hindneck; tail black. Underbody mainly white and unmarked. See Plate 25 for discussion of ID from second-winter Western Gull.

4. **Second-winter** (Mar–Sep) Mantle, scapulars and coverts grey, primary coverts black-marked, flight feathers blackish, only with faint pale window on inner primaries. Rump white against black tail. Bill fleshy with black tip.

5. **Adult** Elongated shape with long head, bulbous-tipped bill and long tail. Underwing white with grey flight feathers and black tip with white mirror to P10. Similar to Western Gull, but legs bright yellow.

6. **Adult summer** (Jan–Jul) Adult upperwing blackish-grey, similar to Western Gull race *wymani*, but a tinge darker. As in Western, wing-tip black with white mirror on P10 only.

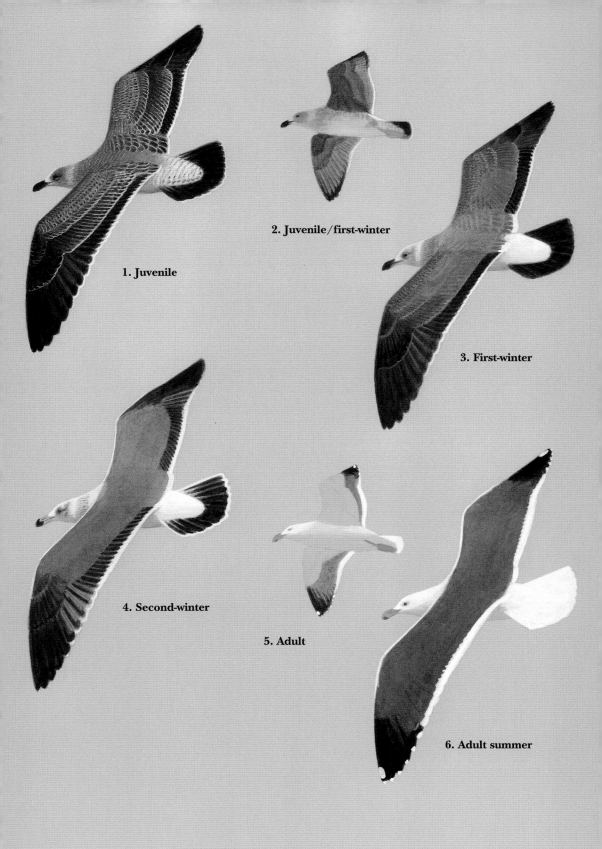

1. Juvenile

2. Juvenile/first-winter

3. First-winter

4. Second-winter

5. Adult

6. Adult summer

YELLOW-FOOTED GULL Three-year large gull, resembling Western. Range restricted to Baja California with non-breeding spread to Salton Sea, California. Large and long-necked with flattish forehead and massive, bulbous-tipped bill.

Adult has blackish-grey upperwing with white mirrors to P(9)10 and broad white trailing edge to wing. Resembles Western race *wymani*, but legs bright yellow. Head remains white throughout the year.

First-year resembles second-year Western, but from winter breast to underparts cleaner white and bill dark with faint fleshy tinge to base of upper bill, and broader yellowish base of lower. Moult more advanced and earlier than in Western. Legs turn yellowish from this age.

Second-year similar to adult, but with dark markings on tail and extensive dark tail-markings.

Third-year as adult apart from faint dark markings on tail and bill.

black, often as subterminal bar, especially on T4–6, in which tips and bases always white. Iris normally dull brown to yellow. Bill yellow with black tip to subterminal markings; upper mandible sometimes fleshy-tinged. Legs yellow, generally duller than in adult; rarely fleshy (skins in LACM).

Third-winter (Mar–Sep) Similar to adult, but often with narrow dark streaks behind eye and on hindneck, and usually still dark bill-markings. Before moult, wing-coverts and flight feathers brownish-tinged.

Third-summer As adult, but with very slight brown tinge to upperparts and very scattered dark markings on bill and tail.

DISTRIBUTION AND MIGRATION Endemic to Baja California and N Mexico. Total population 3,600 pairs in 11 colonies (each 200–600 pairs) on sandy or rocky islands with little or no vegetation. Some post-breeding dispersal to Salton Sea, where first arrives June. Numbers peak Jul–Aug with hundreds. Most leave Sep; but few (max. 10–20) winter; most have left by early Jan (Western Gull is very rare here). Very scarce Californian coast S to Sonora and Guerrero. Main winter area Mexican part of Baja California, where flocks of max. 220 Dec–Jan; most leave for breeding sites by early Feb. Following breeding season prior to movements N to Salton Sea flocks of max. 500 Colorado River (del Hoyo *et al.* 1996, Dunn 1997, M. Jørgensen *in litt.*, J. R. King & K. L. Garrett pers. comm., pers. obs.).

MEASUREMENTS Lengths in mm; weights in g. Own data based on skins in LACM, MCZ, MVZ, NHM. California, Mexico.

WING

Adult male	387–460 (441.8)	16
Adult female	402–448 (424.9)	12
First-year male	418–447 (429.6)	5
First-year female	428, 431	

BILL

Adult male	53.2–60.9 (58.5)	16
Adult female	49.7–60.3 (53.8)	12
First-year male	54.6–60.2 (57.2)	5
First-year female	53.7, 55.8	

BILL DEPTH AT GONYS

Adult male	18.1–23.8 (21.6)	16
Adult female	17.8–21.4 (19.9)	12
First-year male	19.5–21.9 (21.0)	5
First-year female	18.4, 21.2	

BILL DEPTH AT BASE OF BILL

Adult male	16.9–25.5 (21.3)	16
Adult female	17.5–22.3 (19.4)	12
First-year male	19.9–22.7 (20.9)	5
First-year female	17.3, 22.5	

GONYS LENGTH

Adult male	15.0–18.7 (16.7)	16
Adult female	14.2–17.8 (15.6)	12
First-year male	14.3–17.0 (16.2)	5
First-year female	14.4, 16.0	

TARSUS

Adult male	62.6–75.0 (70.5)	16
Adult female	59.3–71.2 (64.8)	12
First-year male	65.7–71.7 (68.9)	5
First-year female	67.4, 66.8	

Weight Non-breeding birds 930–1,300 (skins in LACM).

Yellow-footed Gull *Larus livens.* Photos 205-214 all Puerto Penasco, Sonora, Mexico. 2-4 Feb 2000. *Klaus Malling Olsen*
205-208. 1st-winter. These three individuals show the typical, very bulbous-tipped bill with broad black tip, fleshy base to upper mandible and yellow-tinged lower mandible. This three-toned effect is not seen in Western Gull, 2nd-years of which otherwise resemble Yellow-footed. Also note whitish underbody, faint dark mask and grey saddle contrasting with barred coverts. Note pointed juvenile primaries; similarly plumaged 2nd-year Western are blacker with rounder tips. **209**. **1st-winter**. Similar to 2nd-year Western in showing extensive grey saddle and white rump against black tail, but note bill pattern and juvenile flight feathers. Compare with photo 192. **210**. **1st-winter**. Dark in underwing contrasts well with white underbody.

Yellow-footed Gull *Larus livens*. **211 & 212. 3rd-winter**, same individual. Age development one year quicker than in Western. In 3rd-year very similar to adult, but note dark markings on bill as well as on tail. **213. Adult**. Similar to Western Gull ssp. *wymani*, but note bright yellow legs. **214. Adult**. Wing-pattern as Western Gull ssp. *wymani*.

15. GLAUCOUS GULL

Larus hyperboreus (Gunnerus, 1767, northern Norway)   **Plates 27–28, Photos 215–244**

IDENTIFICATION Length 62-70cm, wingspan 140–160cm. An arctic counterpart to Herring Gull, but in all plumages paler and more uniform, with wing-tips paler than rest of wing. In gull flocks, Glaucous Gull looks like a ghost, especially in flight. Plumage almost identical to Iceland Gull *glaucoides* (see below), from which ID is best based on size and structure.

Glaucous is among the largest gulls, but with large size variation: the largest males are as big as Great Black-backed Gulls, but females may be smaller than male Herring. It is a powerful and 'fierce-looking' gull with heavy, parallel-edged bill, sloping forehead and peak of crown behind level of small, beady eye. In largest males, head appears triangular, but small birds with raised crown-feathers often look unexpectedly, round-headed. Bill length >50% of head length. Body heavier and wings shorter than in Herring. Has prominent tertial step and short primary projection beyond tail: less than bill length or distance between tips of longest tertial and tail-tip in all but small first-year females. In flight, barrel-shaped with flat head and long, often slender-looking bill, frequently held slightly lowered. Wing is broad with long arm but short hand, latter compounded by the translucency of the primaries when bird lit from the head or side. The flight is lazy, recalling Great Blackback, but rarely as 'eagle-like'. Often aggressive towards other gulls.

The main ID problem is Iceland Gull of nominate race *glaucoides*, in which plumages are almost identical to Glaucous. Iceland Gull is smaller than Herring with smaller, domed head, larger eyes, and weaker, less hooked bill (<50% of head length), creating gentle Common Gull look, enhanced by deep 'pigeon-breast', short legs and long primaries, with wings projecting well beyond tail: typically >bill length or distance between tip of longest tertial and tail-tip. Only a few first-year female Glaucous look similar, with unexpectedly short bill and long wings (projection above tail = bill length), but they have larger, squarer head, smaller 'evil' eyes, stronger bill with well-marked gonys-angle and fuller tertials. Flight of Iceland lighter, and its neat shape – with small, rounded head, deep breast and narrow wings with arm and hand of equal length and width– is often striking. Handles hard winds as well as kittiwakes with long glides on angled wings and agile manoeuvres. Unlike the heavier Glaucous feeds with elegant surface dips, often together with small gulls. Also see Glaucous-winged Gull,

Adult has pale grey upperwings with broad, white edges to flight feathers; upperwing pattern similar to adult Little Gull. In **summer** head white. In **winter** (autumn–April) head brown-patterned, often creating hooded appearance. Bare parts similar to Herring, but orbital ring yellow to orange and legs often deeper pink.

Iceland *glaucoides* similar but often even paler, and in winter, head often weaker marked on especially chin to breast. Unlike Glaucous, orbital ring red and bill often slightly olive-tinged. Certain Herrings with restricted dark wing-markings are problematic – especially during moult of outer primaries in late autumn; closer inspection discloses black on primaries. See Hybrids below and Aberrants under other large gulls.

First-year retains most or all juvenile plumage in first winter. It is pale brown with neat brown pattern, pale, translucent flight feathers and pale, poorly marked tail. Head and body creamy to dark brownish-grey. Darkest birds seen head-on may look darker than Herring Gulls, but are finer marked and even at close range show rather uniform head and underbody (Herring has dark-spotted head and underbody even at long range). When settled, wing-tip pale against darker body – the reverse of all gulls except Iceland race *glaucoides* and some Glaucous-winged. Upperparts, including tertials, show fine barring; at most pale and dark markings are of equal width, pale often dominating. Importantly, bill bubblegum-pink with neat black 'dipped-in-ink' tip, looking like a matchstick. Head poorly marked, with white eyelids surrounding small dark eye creating 'pig-like' impression. Underwing two-toned with darker coverts and paler, translucent flight feathers. Brown-barred undertail-coverts contrast well with unpatterned underparts and pale tail.

First-year Iceland Gull identified from Glaucous by size, structure and bill pattern: in Iceland, broader black tip fades into paler base (brown/greyish with greenish or yellowish tinge, in a few with pink base), which covers inner 50% only (more in Glaucous); ground pattern often similar to Glaucous, but darker feather-bases create more contrasting pattern. Many Iceland have cleaner pale hindneck and often weak grey bars over neck and above eye, but lack pale eye-ring. Plumage on average more greyish. Brown bars on tail-coverts generally weaker, but tail-markings often stronger. Flight feathers and tail slightly more variable. Some have better-marked, narrow tail-bars and more conspicuous dark chevrons on primary tips than any Glaucous.

Apart from worn (and still black-billed) Glaucous-winged, no other similar-sized gull has wing-tip paler than upperparts. In spring, primaries and tail of other large gulls may bleach to become concolorous with upperparts. The 'matchstick-bill' of Glaucous is diagnostic: other similar-plumaged large gulls with bicoloured bill have dirtier base and darker cutting edges.

'First-summer' (from late winter) similar to first-winter, but head whitish and worn upperwing creamy-white with scattered darker feathers – first traces of second-winter plumage – intermixed (especially on scapulars). Lacks clean, even pattern of birds up to late winter, and may develop some greyish upperpart feathers, although bleaching mostly caused by wear, not moult. From Apr, bill may develop yellowish tinge and pale tip, and eyes become paler. May in spring be mistakenly aged as second-year, but has pointed, not rounded primary tips, and secondaries often show faint dark chevrons.

PLATE 27. GLAUCOUS GULL *Larus hyperboreus*

Large Arctic gull, in size between Herring and Great Black-backed Gull. Heavy with flat crown and rather long bill with somewhat bulbous tip and marked gonys-angle. Appears full-bodied and stocky with clear tertial step and full chest. Centre of gravity around mid-body. Wings rather short, with short projection above tail (shorter than bill length). Certain small females (especially first-years) rounder-headed with slightly longer wings. Very pale primaries lack any solid dark markings; in settled birds, wing-tip distinctly paler than rest of plumage.

1. **Juvenile/first-winter** (Aug–Apr) Rather uniform pale buff with wing-tip paler than rest of plumage. Undertail-coverts distinctly brown-barred. Upperparts and wing-coverts with narrow browner markings, tertials pale-centred with whitish edges. Head plain-looking with white eyelids. Bill pink with clear-cut black tip. This individual is particularly dark and strongly patterned. Only moults (if any) limited number of especially upperpart feathers into first-winter.

2. **Juvenile/first-winter** (Aug–Apr) A typically patterned individual, showing pale 'tea-with-milk' coloured plumage and whiter primaries, accentuating short primary projection.

3. **First-winter** (Feb–Aug) Some individuals, especially of eastern race *pallidissimus* (but even frequent in other populations), appear almost white with wear, only showing faint brown markings on upperparts and coverts, thus looking 'older' than 1 year. Aged by dark eye and often complete black bill-tip (although first-winters may develop pale bill-tip from Mar).

4. **Second-winter** (Aug–Apr) Similar to first-year, but less regularly patterned. Head often better marked. Eye bicoloured. Bill duller pink with pale tip and black subterminal ring. Primaries often slightly brown-tinged, but still paler than body.

5. **Second-winter/third-winter** (May–Sep) As moult progresses, new grey feathers of adult type occur on upperparts and wing-coverts.

6. **Third-winter** (Aug–Apr) Upperparts and a large number of coverts pale grey, some coverts browner with paler edges. Tertials grey with narrower white edges than adult. Eye pale. Bill fleshy (to yellow) with dark subterminal markings. Face whiter than in most second-winters (but matched by many).

7. **Adult winter** (Sep–Apr) Adult upperparts very pale grey with broad white tips to tertials and primaries. In winter shows extensive, diffuse brown head-markings, sometimes more streaked than shown here, forming incomplete brown hood.

8. **Adult summer** (Apr–Aug) Head white. Eyes pale yellow, orbital ring yellow.

3. First-winter

1. Juvenile/first-winter

2. Juvenile/first-winter

4. Second-winter

5. Second-winter/ third-winter

6. Third-winter

7. Adult winter

8. Adult summer

PLATE 28. GLAUCOUS GULL *Larus hyperboreus*

In flight heavy with barrel-shaped body, rather long neck and long bill. Wings broad, often appearing short as primaries translucent. Wing-tip paler than rest of plumage, reinforcing 'ghostly' appearance of species. Tail always lacks darker tail-bar, appearing diluted in younger birds. Flight slow and ponderous, similar to Great Black-backed Gull in all but the smallest birds.

1.	**Juvenile/first-winter** (Aug–Apr) Pale buffish overall appearance, lacking any strong dark markings. Faintly patterned wing contrasts with paler flight feathers, which often show narrow dark arrowhead-markings near tips, diagnostic of first-year. Body often darker than wings. Rump heavily brown-barred; tail with only indistinct browner waving. Bill long and pink with black tip.

2.	**Juvenile/first-winter** (Aug–Apr) A fainter-marked individual than 1, showing whitish wing-tip and broad white edges to rather uniform tail. Note shortish-looking wing reinforced by pale, translucent primaries.

3.	**Late first-winter** (Mar–Aug) Some appear almost white with wear, with flight feathers white in slight contrast to underwing-coverts. Note dark eyes and first-winter bill coloration. Such very pale birds may look almost whitish and are often erroneously aged as second-years; close inspection reveals pointed primaries and often narrow dark markings on secondaries (pale second-years have rounder primaries and no dark secondary markings). Plate shows the elongated, barrel-shaped body, long neck and long 'matchstick' bill typical of the species. Such very pale birds are most regular in E Asian race *pallidissimus*, but occur in all populations.

4.	**Second-winter** (Aug–Apr) Similar to paler-type first-winter, but less regularly patterned on upperwing and lacking dark markings on secondaries. Eye starts to become pale at about one year of age. Bill develops pale tip.

5.	**Third-winter** (Aug–Apr) Similar to adult, but still with brown-tinged lesser and greater coverts, grey tail-markings and fleshy to dull yellow bill with extensive black markings.

6.	**Adult winter** (Aug–Apr) Adult upperwing pale grey with broad white tips to flight feathers, lacking any dark markings. Head in winter often extensively brown-patterned, sometimes appearing as brownish hood.

7.	**Adult** Upperwing pattern recalls that of much smaller adult Little Gull.

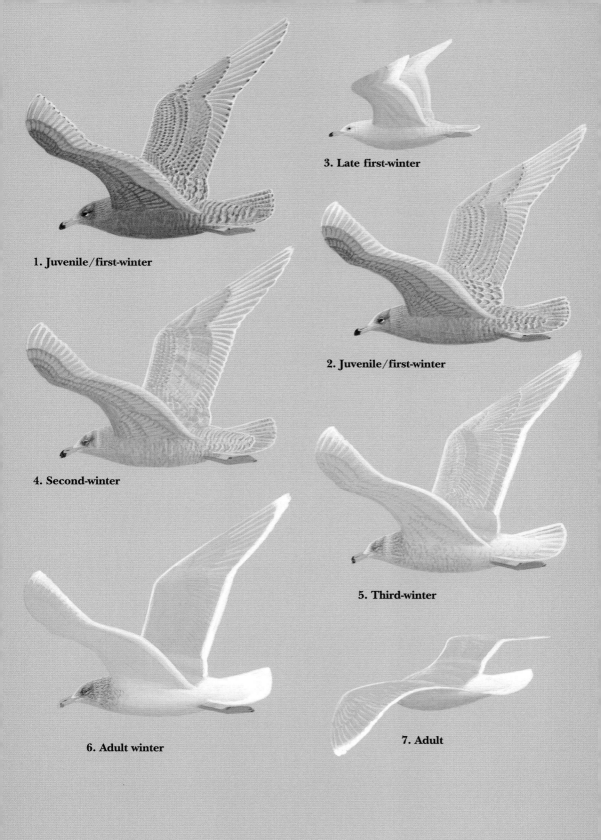

1. Juvenile/first-winter

3. Late first-winter

2. Juvenile/first-winter

4. Second-winter

5. Third-winter

6. Adult winter

7. Adult

Second-winter/summer similar to first-summer, but generally paler and more unevenly patterned, often with few adult mantle feathers. 'Retarded' birds similar to first-spring birds; aged by darker, more finely (pale) vermiculated greater coverts (often darker than rest of upperwing), flight feathers all pale with rounded (not pointed) primary tips (no dark chevrons at tips of many first-years). Bill generally less clean pink with broader pale tip, and thus black bill-ring; some second-years have unique combination of adult mantle and first-winter-like bill. Eye mostly pale, often surrounded by dark mask.

Third-winter similar to adult winter, but with some browner wing-coverts (especially lesser underwing-coverts and greater upperwing-coverts), tertials and greyish tinge to tail. Bill greyish-yellow with black bar and sometimes adult-like gonys-spot.

Third-summer similar to third-winter, but head and underbody whiter, and upperparts mainly grey apart from few dark-mottled coverts, tertials and rectrices. Bill as adult, but often with dark subterminal markings.

Fourth-winter as adult winter; some have fleshy-tinged bill with dark markings on both mandibles.

VOICE Long-call similar to Herring Gull, but slightly hoarser. Call a two-part *k-lee*, higher and weaker than in Herring Gull.

MOULT Adult moult to **winter plumage** complete Jun–Nov. P1 (late Apr) early Jun. Most reach P3–6 mid-Jul–mid-Aug, P5–8 late Aug–early Sep. P9–10 (late Sep) late Oct–Nov, rarely into late Feb (Kay 1947, skins in UZM, ZMA, pers. obs.). Secondaries from late Jul, starting when primary moult reaches P5–7; inner- and outermost secondaries simultaneous; exceptionally a few secondaries moulted Apr before onset of primary moult. Tail late Jul–Sep/Oct. Head and body from mid-Jul; head generally mid-Aug–late Sep. Coverts Sep–Oct, starting with lesser coverts, which are mainly renewed by early Sep.

Adult moult to **summer plumage** partial late Feb–Apr, including head and body.

Juvenile plumage normally retained in **first-winter;** at most a few head, mantle and scapulars renewed autumn–winter. Complete moult to **second-winter**, starting Mar–May with P1–2, forehead and mantle. Most of head, body, tertials and coverts moulted Jun–late Jul; lesser coverts often not before mid-Sep. Primary moult slower and earlier than in adult; P1–2 late Mar–May(late Jul), P5–7(8) generally late Jul–early Aug, P9–10 mid-Sep–Oct(early Nov). Secondaries and tail from mid-Jul, secondaries sometimes from mid-May; some renew most secondaries and rectrices simultaneously.

Moult to **second-summer/third-winter** similar to adult, but generally earlier with P1 often shed Apr. Some still show traces of winter head by Apr, when most adults are in summer plumage.

DESCRIPTION

Adult Upperparts pale grey (Kodak Grey Scale 2–3(4)) with white tips to flight feathers, creating broad white tip and trailing edge to wing. Marginal coverts, under-

parts and tail white. Iris pale yellow. Orbital ring chrome-yellow to orange, rarely pinkish-tinged or red. Bill yellow with orange-red gonys-spot, rarely extending to upper mandible; extreme tip often ivory. Bill length:bill depth at gonys 2.7–3.1. Legs greyish-flesh to bright pink; pink sometimes reduced to toes (Veysey 1971).

Adult summer (Mar–Sep) Head and body white. With wear, upperwing-coverts become slightly brownish-tinged contrasting with fresh grey feathers. Bill bright yellow with red to orange-red gonys.

Adult winter (Oct–Mar) Head white with varying dark brown to buff streaks and spots on head and upper breast, often forming traces of dark hood or reaching upper flanks. Bill paler yellow (rarely with pinkish tinge to upper mandible). Gonys-spot paler orange than in summer.

Juvenile (fledging–Mar) Head brownish-grey to pale buff, paling to whitish on chin, forehead and some-times neck-sides. Diffuse brown head-streaks vary from narrow to broad, especially on hindneck. Eye-crescent dusky. White crescents above and below eye create a pale eye-ring. Mantle, scapulars, back and upperwing-coverts pale buff to pale greyish-brown with neat pat-tern of brown bars, U- or V-spots, strongest on lower scapulars; darkest birds with even buff and brown bars (especially in birds acquiring some fresh scapulars in first winter). Tertials pale with dark bars; in darkest birds sometimes with uniform but diffuse grey centres. Rump pale with dark bars or mottling; typically con-trasting with pale, poorly marked tail. Upperwing-coverts pale buff to greyish-brown with neat dark bars, strongest on greater coverts; barring progressively less conspicuous on outer wing. Primary coverts greyish-brown with narrow pale edges and bases. Flight feathers grey-brown, buffish or whitish; in all but the darkest paler than rest of upperparts; sometimes with dusky chevrons near tip. Primary shafts whitish to greyish-yellow. P10 0–8mm >P9. Tail pale grey to buff with vary-ing greyish marbling or vermiculations. Palest birds have almost unmarked white tail, darkest almost unbarred mid-grey. Buff centres to T1–3(4) with up to 10 narrow grey bars or notches on T5–6; tips and edges whitish. Underbody buff to brownish-grey, generally darker than upperparts (especially belly) with weak darker mottling, strongest on breast-sides and flanks. Darkest birds appear sooty at distance. Undertail-coverts pale with medium to dark brown transverse bars, often distinct. Axillaries and underwing-coverts greyish-brown, slightly pale-mottled and often darker than underbody; often contrast strongly with pale, translucent flight feathers. Orbital ring brown. Iris dark brown. Bill pink with 20–30mm black tip (rarely includ-ing few mm of a dark line along lower cutting edges). Bill length:bill depth at gonys 2.8–3.3(3.5 in few females). Gape flesh. Legs pale pink to rosy, sometimes purplish (H. J. Lehto *in litt.*).

Some grow a few **first-winter** feathers on mantle and scapulars, being similar to juvenile, but averaging paler buffish with narrower, but stronger dark markings.

With wear (sometimes as early as Jan, normally from Mar) some individuals become whitish with reduced darker markings, and some intermix new pale grey feathers on mantle and scapulars. Dark birds retain plumage better and still look like autumn juveniles in May, although dark on wing and tail is often faded. If initially present, dark V-spots on secondaries still retained.

'First-summer' (Mar–Sep) is worn first-winter, becoming bleached. Head and body whitish to pale buff with indistinct darker mottling or streaks. Mantle and scapulars whitish with irregular and inconspicuous dark barring, almost disappearing with wear. Rarely acquires a few grey feathers (especially on upper row of scapulars). Axillaries and underwing-coverts sometimes moulted to whitish type. Wing and tail often whitish through wear. Bill similar to juvenile, but extreme tip pale from (Jan) Mar and base yellowish-tinged. Iris dark to medium brown, rarely dull yellow.

Second-winter (Aug–Mar) Head and underbody whitish to pale buff, often with darker eye-mask. Sometimes similar to first-years, but dark markings narrower and less regular (especially on hindneck and breast-sides); rarely with extensive grey-brown mottling on head and especially underbody, which may show pinkish-buff tinge (Hume 1980). Mantle and scapulars mostly white with less intricate buff mottling or indistinct barring than in first-year; may have some (rarely all) adult-type grey mantle and scapulars (often white-fringed) or few, very worn juvenile feathers. Tertials pale grey to whitish with 1–2 narrow dark Us near tip, rarely greyish-brown with pale vermiculations. Upperwing as juvenile or paler buff with weaker/no covert-barring. Greater coverts whitish to greyish-buff with indistinct darker mottling or pale vermiculations; often restricted to innermost, and often slightly darker than rest of upperwing. Most advanced birds may show a few adult-type grey inner median coverts. Primary coverts off-white with pale brown mottling. Flight feathers pale buff to white, paler than in adult with rounded tips, lacking dark chevrons; in exceptionally dark birds primaries grey with faint pale edges as in first-year Thayer's; P10 normally white. Tail pale greyish-brown with fainter, weaker markings than juvenile, looking more uniform. Tail-covert barring paler and narrower than in first-years. Underwing-coverts as juvenile or whitish with darker tips, creating dark rows; axillaries sometimes unmarked white. Iris pale grey-green, yellow or whitish, rarely medium brown, looking dark in field. Bill pink to yellowish-flesh with black subterminal bar and white tip; sometimes as juvenile. Legs fleshy.

Second-summer (Mar–Sep) As second-winter, but head and underparts pale buff or whitish. Mantle and scapulars mostly pale grey. Wings and tail whitish to pale buff with scattered brown markings; may become very pale through fading and wear. Iris pale yellow. Orbital ring sometimes yellowish. Bill as second-winter, but white tip generally broader and black bill-ring more conspicuous.

Third-winter (Oct–Apr) Head as adult winter, but often with stronger dark eye-mask. Underparts usually with indistinct brown mottling, but sometimes heavy on belly. Mantle, scapulars and median coverts pale grey, often with slight brownish cast; scapulars sometimes with patches of white. Rump white or faintly dark-mottled. Upperwing varies from adult-like to like bleached

second-winter, typically with irregular whitish patches in grey areas and some brown coverts. Greater coverts often slightly darker than rest of upperwing with faint brown freckling. Other coverts and tertials sometimes with narrow brown bars. Primaries off-white, pale grey or pale buff; sometimes as adult. Tail-coverts white, usually brown-barred or with a brownish tinge. Tail white to pale grey, often with faint brown tinge. Underwing as second-winter but usually with narrower dark bars, especially on lesser coverts; rarely as in juvenile. Bare parts similar to adult winter, but bill usually duller greyish-yellow with black to brown subterminal marks or cutting edges; may lack orange-red gonys-spot.

Third-summer (Feb–Sep) As third-winter, but head and underparts white or only faintly dark-streaked. Brown markings on upperwing and tail faded and inconspicuous.

Fourth-winter (Oct–Mar) As adult, but with a few, scattered pale brown feathers, notably on tail and tail-coverts. Bill often with fleshy tinge, frequently with dark subterminal markings on both mandibles.

Fourth-summer (Mar–Oct) As adult, but some still with dark subterminal spots near tip of upper mandible.

Hybrids Hybrid **Herring or American Herring × Glaucous Gull** ('Nelson's Gull') frequent Iceland, especially in the southwest, and regular in Kola Peninsula, Mackenzie Delta, Canada, and NE Canadian districts, where the two species meet; hybridisation also known Greenland. Mainly resident, but several observed S to Great Britain and Scandinavia (Ingolfsson 1970a, Madge 1978, Sutherland 1983, Spear 1987, Boertmann 1994, H. Kisbye, H. J. & H. Lehto *in litt.*, pers. obs.). Snell (1991c) questioned hybrid origin of Iceland population, claiming that it refers to large pale Herring Gull founders from N Europe; this countered by Ingolfsson (1993). A weakness in these discussions is that no information is given on first-year birds, which are less like adults of the involved species. First-years with genuine characters from both species are regular in N Europe; a number of such observed in Iceland (pers. obs., McGeehan & Garner 1997). We maintain hybridisation as the explanation of large gulls showing perfect combinations of characters from the two species.

Observations of hybrids W Europe coincides with peak time for Glaucous/Iceland Gull. Russian populations probably more migratory, as hybrid numbers from Finland relatively large (H. J. & H. Lehto *in litt.*).

Plumage development in Herring Gull (including leucistics) often ignored when attributing hybrid Glaucous × Herring status to certain birds; some 'hybrids' may simply be pale Herrings. When confronted with a possible hybrid, it is essential to search for Glaucous characters—especially bill pattern, size and markings on wing-tip and tail, as palest Herring and American Herring show reduced dark markings, which could be mistaken for signs of hybrid origin. Also, very short primary projection should be looked for.

Adult Similar to Glaucous, but with varying darker wing-tip; darkest birds similar to Herring, and often not identifiable the field. However, most have broader white mirror on P9 (covering both webs), broader pale markings on inner webs, broader white tongues, generally reduced dark markings on outer webs of P6–8, and rarely dark markings on P5; blackish primary pattern on outer webs of P7–10 may recall Thayer's Gull (but frequent in northern populations of Herring nominate *argentatus* and E Coast American Herring (Barth 1968a, Jonsson & Mactavish 2001, skins in ZMO, H. Heggland, H. & H. J. Lehto *in litt.*).

Most typical hybrids have pale grey streaks on outer web of P7–10 to form pattern as in Iceland race *kumlieni*: grey primary-markings darker than upperparts, appearing 'frosty-grey' or slightly brownish-tinged with broad white edges to P7–10 (small minority of all large gulls in Iceland in autumn—pers. obs.). Some show unique pattern of dark restricted to narrow, dark grey streaks on outer webs of P8–10. See Ingolfsson (1970b, 1993) for detailed discussion. Note that faint dark markings to P9–10 occur in Glaucous race *barrovianus* (see below).

First-years show all intergrades between the two, and many—especially several generation hybrids—are not safely identifiable. As a minimum, claimed hybrids must combine head-shape, size, bill pattern and the delicate plumage pattern of Glaucous with greyish-brown flight feathers and tail-bar: many are simply 'Glaucous Gulls with darker wing-tip and tail-bar' often showing short primary projection of Glaucous. Primaries mainly mud-brown with pale edges, inner webs and sometimes dark arrow marks (like Glaucous, but often broader, forming row of dark spots on spread wing, dark on outer web often reaching base) or greyish-brown with pale edges as in Thayer's Gull. Rarely as dark as Herring: usually just P7–10 dark, whereas paleness of P1–7 forms broader but more diffuse pale 'window' than in Herring. Tertials with greyish-brown (often narrow) centres, faint dark subterminal bars and irregular pale edges/tips, broader than in all but the palest Herring. Head and underbody generally cleaner than Herring. Often with white eyelids, greyish tinge around eye, grey shading on hindcrown, darker flanks and barred rump/tail-coverts as in Glaucous. Tail has pale brown to greyish bar (often narrow) and broad pale tip; tail typically appears as 'ghost' version of Herring's (in hybrids with American Herring sometimes all dark). Bill often similar to Glaucous, but sometimes duller with dark cutting edges; in some closer to Herring.

Darker hybrids are more like Herring Gull with darker bill and stronger dark markings on coverts, tertials, secondaries and outer primaries. Many inseparable from pale or leucistic Herring, but head and underbody paler and less streaked, and wing-markings usually paler; tertial-centres, flight feathers and tail-bar mid-brown. Often shows pale eye-ring and small beady eye of Glaucous, and black bill-tip sharply divided from fleshy base, as indication of typical bill of Glaucous.

Certain small birds hard to tell from Thayer's Gull owing to Thayer's-like tail of American Herring; wing sometimes as Thayer's, but normally underside of primaries brownish-tinged, not silvery as in Thayer's (Sutherland 1983, Ullman 1992, Millington & Garner 1999, H. J. Lehto *in litt.*, J. R. King pers. comm.). See also under Thayer's Gull.

Second-winter more problematic, but large size combined with pale, black-tipped bill (appearing clean without dark cutting edges, and with grey tinge) indica-

tive; also paler grey mantle, finer covert-barring, narrow brown centres to tertials, mid-brown flight feathers and tail-bar, and dark transverse barring on undertail-coverts.

Presumed **third-winter** had pale grey mantle as Glaucous Gull, very pale wing with grey restricted to outer two primaries; P10 grey with broad white tip, pale yellow, dark-tipped bill and weak, grey tail-bar. On water, appeared typically Glaucous-shaped with wing-tip barely projecting beyond tail. Another was similar to Herring, but with just P9–10 pale greyish-brown with entire white edges, four outer primary-coverts pale brown; had irregular grey pattern on whole central tail (pers. obs., Denmark and Iceland).

For hybridisation with Glaucous-winged and Great Black-backed Gull, see those species. See also Herring Gull under Aberrants.

Aberrants Albino all white (or with few grey mantle feathers) with greyish-yellow legs. First-winter leucistic bird had white plumage but normal bare parts (H. J. Lehto *in litt.* & photos, pers. obs. Iceland, skin UZM 16689).

Certain adults may show a very faint grey cast to outer web of P10 and indistinct dark U-shaped subterminal spots near tip to P9–10 (*Birding World* 10: 275, Snell 1993). Could be darkest variant or hybrid (probably with Herring Gull), but this feature is regular in race *barrovianus* (skins in MCZ; see Geographical Variation).

GEOGRAPHICAL VARIATION Three subspecies recognised here. No clear variation in N Atlantic; measurements Greenland and Spitsbergen identical in all series (see below).

L. h. hyperboreus (N America towards Arctic Sea to Taimyr, Siberia) described above.

L. h. barrovianus (Alaska; winters NW America S to California) smaller than *hyperboreus*, with relatively longer wings and legs but smaller, 'compressed' bill. Size, long wings and poor tertial steps create jizz similar to Iceland Gull especially in females, but head typical for large gull (with small eyes; bill heavy with well-marked gonys-angle). Jizz-wise, certain small females combine Herring Gull head on Iceland Gull body. **Adult** upperparts as nominate *hyperboreus* or darker (Kodak Grey Scale 3–4.5(5)).Otherwise as nominate, apart from: small minority show faint dark wash to outer webs of P8–10, and a bird also had pale grey outer web to P10 with 65 mm white tip. Orbital ring yellow as in nominate, but sometimes red or violet-brown. Iris dark-speckled in Aleutian populations, probably as a result of hybridisation with Glaucous-winged Gull, as only 2% Glaucous in study area pure, rest with traces of dark grey pattern on wing-tip (Banks 1986, Ingolfsson 1970a, Strang 1977, Zimmer 1991, skins).

Adult moult generally three weeks earlier than in nominate. Primary moult has reached P2–4 late Jun, P5–7 late Jul–mid-Aug, P8–9 late Aug, P10 late Oct (de Korte 1972, skins in MCZ).

Juvenile/first-winter as nominate, but many darker and more coarsely marked; mantle and tertials often with stronger brown bars than in all but exceptionally pale nominate (1%). Uppertail-coverts often strongly dark-

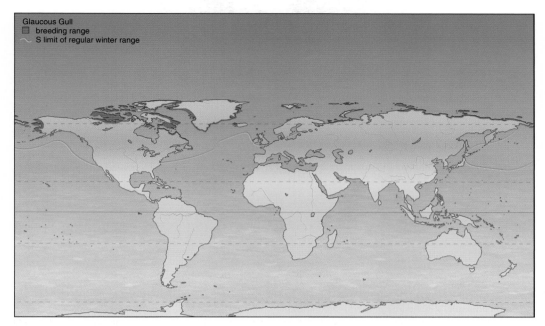

mottled and tail darker, similar to Thayer's Gull; more coarsely dark-barred than in nominate. Primaries often with darker outer webs, appearing concolorous with upperparts, thus darker than in nominate. Bill as nominate, but dark tip on average broader. In **second-year** dark pattern on P9–10 and tail often present.

L. h. pallidissimus (E Siberia between Taimyr and Bering Sea) largest and palest race. Similar to nominate, but wings on average longer, projecting further beyond tail-tip. Probably much intergradation with nominate in overlap areas. No or very little differences in upperpart coloration found on skins from Siberia, but majority in Japan, Feb, paler than all but palest nominate. **Adult** on average paler than nominate with less sharply defined primary tips (merging into pale grey primary bases) and weaker head-streaking. **First-year** generally paler and less marked than nominate, many appearing whitish with only weak brown markings. Legs and sometimes bill generally more strongly rosy-tinged, sometimes raspberry-pink especially on legs (pers. obs., Japan, Feb). **Second-year** often very pale compared to other races, with much less dark patterning on upperparts, especially on greater coverts, which are generally much paler and less patterned than in other populations.

Note *L. h. 'leucerectes'* (Greenland, Iceland, N Canada) said to be paler than nominate (Banks 1986). We found no evidence of this during extensive skin studies and comparison with birds from other parts of the N Atlantic; compared to European birds, N American birds generally less marked, and very pale first-years commoner (B. Mactavish, J. Hough & O. Janni *in litt.*).

DISTRIBUTION AND MIGRATION Total population >100,000 pairs. Breeds on cliffs facing or near coast of Arctic, often near human settlements, gull or goose colonies. In winter coastal, often in fishing harbours.

W Palearctic population (in pairs) >20,000, of which 8,000 Bear Island, 1,000–10,000 Spitsbergen, Iceland 8,000–15,000 (50% increase 1970–1990, since stable) and European Russia 4,000–7,000. Greenland 30,000–100,000 (mainly W Greenland). E Palearctic population 10,000–50,000. Alaska 15,000. Tens of thousands North Canada (Cramp & Simmons 1983, del Hoyo *et al.* 1996, Hagemeijer & Blair 1997).

Partly migratory, wintering within/S of breeding range from edge of ice across Holarctic. Adults turn up at breeding sites late Apr–May (northernmost breeding sites occupied latter half of May). Leave breeding sites Sep–mid-Oct, remaining near breeding range (younger birds until freeze-up). W Greenland birds sedentary, winter population 300,000; E Greenland population mainly migratory, wintering mainly Iceland (winter population 30,000–50,000 birds) with some reaching Great Britain/North Sea. Most W Palearctic birds sedentary or perform short-distance migration to coasts of N Norway. Spitsbergen/Jan Mayen populations mostly move SW, with ringing recoveries from Faeroe Islands, Iceland, SW Norway and E/SW coast of Greenland; Iceland population partly migratory spreading to UK, Faeroe Islands and a few further away (Cramp & Simmons 1983, Boertmann 1994, Lyngs 2003).

Scarce winter visitor (>80% first-years) N and W Europe, mainly Dec–Apr; especially Jan–Mar, with return migration Feb–May. In Great Britain more widespread than Iceland Gull. Max. 500 winter, mainly in N. In Ireland average 70 per year. British influxes often correspond with gales from N and E and influxes of Iceland Gull, the latter indicating Greenland origin of some birds; influxes following N to E gales may indicate birds of N Russian origin. In N Norway max. 200 Varanger. In Sweden 50–100 yearly (equal numbers Baltic and W coast; best year Öland 20); in Denmark

GLAUCOUS GULL Four-year gull. Almost as big as Great Black-backed Gull (thus bigger than Herring), generally with short wings (wing-projection beyond tail-tip shorter than bill length), full body and long bill. Plumages very pale with virtually unmarked pale wing-tip. Flight similar to Great Blackback. Shows long arm but rather short hand, emphasised by paleness and translucency.

Adult has pale grey upperwing with white tips to primaries, most prominent on inner ones, whereas wing-tip almost whitish. Bill yellow with red gonys-spot, legs fleshy. In **winter** (Sep–Apr) head with dense brown streaking.

First-year pale buffish to greyish-brown with whitish wing-tip, narrow dark spots to secondaries and faintly pale brown tail-markings. Upper- and undertail-coverts brown-barred, on underparts creating contrast to velvety body. Head rather unmarked with narrow white eyelids. Bill long and pink with clear-cut black tip. Eyes dark. In spring often heavily worn, almost whitish.

Second-year rather similar to first-year, but bill-tip pale and pattern of upperparts more uneven; may show few grey feathers on saddle. Secondaries and primaries unmarked and pale. Eye starts to become paler.

Third-year similar to adult, but still with scattered brown markings on coverts, greyish tinge to tail and solid dark markings on duller bill.

Fourth-year similar to adult, but often with scattered browner markings on coverts and normally dark markings on both mandibles. See text for Geographical Variation.

30–100, mainly fishing harbours N Sea/Kattegat; max. 28 Bornholm, Baltic, in one year. In Baltic peak Feb–Apr, probably birds of NE origin. Best year in Finland 114. Scarcer S to France and Poland (where regular). A few immatures summer in N and W Europe.

Recent decline in numbers in N and W Europe from around 1990 may be caused by more fishing activities (including cleaning of fish) out at sea, leaving less food in fishing harbours (Glutz von Blotzheim & Bauer 1982, Dean 1984, Hirschfeld & Ullman 1985, Lack 1986, Rigbäck 1988, Risberg 1990, Malling Olsen 1992, Lange 1995).

Vagrant C and E Europe S to Mediterranean, N Red Sea (Israel 1), Black and Caspian Seas; Atlantic S to Canary Islands (>5) and Morocco (6).

Canadian birds winter S to New York and mid-Atlantic states. >208 Ontario 1986/1987; scarcer S of New York. In Newfoundland thousands with largest concentrations of max. 1,270 St John, Jan–Feb. Vagrant S USA, Mexican Gulf, Bermuda.

L. h. barrovianus breeds Alaska (>15,000 pairs) and winters between Aleutians and California (where scarce); vagrant Baja California, Mexico and Hawaii. *L. h. pallidissimus* winters E Asian coast S to Japan, more irregular E China. Gatherings of hundreds in each active fishing harbour in Hokkaido in severe winters. Vagrant S to Hong Kong.

MEASUREMENTS Lengths in mm; weights in g. Own data based on skins in LACM, MCZ, MVC, NHM, UZM, ZMA, ZMO. *L. h. hyperboreus* Greenland, Spitsbergen, Jan Mayen, Iceland, Faeroes and NW Europe; *L. h. barrovianus* Alaska, California, Japan; *L. h. pallidissimus* Amur, Siberia, Japan. Juv./first-winter from early Sep when fully grown.

WING

L. h. hyperboreus		
Adult male	445–501 (472.3)	107
Adult female	408–469 (450.6)	125
First-year male	435–493 (466.8)	57
First-year female	422–472 (446.9)	40
L. h. barrovianus		
Adult male	436–484 (459.8)	26
Adult female	414–467 (445.2)	26
First-year male	436–480 (454.9)	11
First-year female	427–468 (446.8)	17
L. h. pallidissimus		
Adult male	461–498 (473.1)	18
Adult female	436–472 (452.1)	16
First-year winter	435–492 (459.9)	9

BILL

L. h. hyperboreus		
Adult male	56.8–69.1 (62.8)	95
Adult female	50.2–64.0 (57.1)	123
First-year male	53.9–65.2 (58.1)	60
First-year female	48.9–62.6 (54.3)	40
L. h. barrovianus		
Adult male	53.3–65.5 (59.7)	26
Adult female	49.0–63.4 (54.1)	27
First-year male	48.1–64.3 (52.8)	11
First-year female	46.2–61.5 (52.5)	17
L. h. pallidissimus		
Adult male	57.3–70.0 (64.1)	18
Adult female	56.3–63.2 (59.7)	16
First-year	51.4–62.1 (57.3)	9

BILL DEPTH AT BASE OF BILL

L. h. hyperboreus		
Adult male	20.4–25.4 (23.0)	91
Adult female	18.8–24.9 (20.5)	109
First-year male	18.8–24.7 (21.4)	60
First-year female	16.6–22.6 (19.3)	40
L. h. barrovianus		
Adult male	17.7–24.0 (21.6)	26
Adult female	18.2–22.5 (19.9)	25
First-year male	17.7–21.2 (19.2)	11
First-year female	17.0–21.9 (18.6)	17

BILL DEPTH AT GONYS

L. h. hyperboreus

Adult male	18.7–23.7 (21.9)	94
Adult female	17.0–22.3 (19.7)	110
First-year male	16.8–23.0 (19.5)	60
First-year female	15.2–21.2 (17.9)	40

L. h. barrovianus

Adult male	18.8–23.0 (21.0)	26
Adult female	17.0–21.1 (18.8)	26
First-year male	16.6–19.9 (17.7)	10
First-year female	16.4–20.7 (17.7)	17

GONYS LENGTH

L. h. hyperboreus

Adult male	15.4–21.0 (18.0)	85
Adult female	13.5–19.4 (16.6)	100
First-year male	12.3–19.4 (16.5)	59
First-year female	12.3–18.3 (15.5)	41

L. h. barrovianus

Adult male	14.7–18.9 (16.5)	26
Adult female	13.2–19.3 (16.3)	26
First-year male	12.6–17.4 (15.3)	11
First-year female	13.2–17.5 (14.7)	17

TARSUS

L. h. hyperboreus

Adult male	64.5–76.5 (71.1)	96
Adult female	61.1–74.0 (65.8)	123
First-year male	62.4–77.0 (70.4)	60
First-year female	59.9–73.1 (65.8)	40

L. h. barrovianus

Adult male	67.2–75.0 (71.8)	26
Adult female	60.7–72.5 (66.3)	26
First-year male	61.9–72.6 (68.8)	11
First-year female	61.2–70.2 (66.6)	17

L. h. pallidissimus

Adult male	67.2–81.0 (74.9)	18
Adult female	66.9–75.0 (71.0)	16
First-year	65.8–75.0 (70.0)	9

Weight *L. h. hyperboreus.* Breeding adults: male 1,000–2,215, female 964–1,830 (Greenland, Iceland, Spitsbergen, Murmansk and Novaya Zemliya); exceptionally, third-year male 2,659. Canadian breeders: male 1,765–2,125, female 1,375–1,525. Greenland and Spitsbergen first-summer 1,050–1,373, second-winter males 1,659–1,926, female 1,186–1,520 (Ingolfsson 1970b, de Korte 1972, Cramp & Simmons 1983, skins in UZM, ZMA, ZMO). *L. h. barrovianus* adult male breeding 1,379, 1,428 (skin LACM).

Glaucous Gull *Larus hyperboreus.* **217. Juvenile/1st-winter** ssp. *pallidissimus.* Note parallel-edged bill, small beady eye, prominent tertial step and short wing-projection. This very pale individual typical for this ssp. Hokkaido, Japan. 12 Feb 2001. *Klaus Malling Olsen*

215

216

218

219

198

Glaucous Gull *Larus hyperboreus*. Photos refer to ssp. *hyperboreus*, unless otherwise stated.

215. Juvenile/1st-winter with Herring Gull, Note larger size, pink, black-tipped bill and paler wing-tip than rest of plumage, compare to Herring Gull in background. IJmuiden, Netherlands, 4 Feb 1983. *Arnoud B. van den Berg.* **216. Juvenile/1st-winter**. A particularly dark-patterned individual, appearing unpatterned at medium range. Note pink, 'dipped-in-ink' bill. Pembrokeshire, Wales, Great Britain. Jan 1997. *David Astins.* **218. Juvenile/1st-winter** ssp. *pallidissimus*. A slightly smaller, more long-winged individual than 216, probably female. Note white eyelids and typical bill-pattern. Hokkaido, Japan. 12 Feb 2001. *Klaus Malling Olsen.* **219. Juvenile/1st-winter** ssp. *pallidissimus*. These three individuals show almost the complete range of variation at this age. Hokkaido, Japan. 12 Feb 2001. *Klaus Malling Olsen.* **220. Juvenile/1st-winter** ssp. *barrovianus*. This ssp. is the smallest, often appearing similar to Iceland Gull. This individual is particularly small, round-headed and short-billed, inviting confusion with Iceland, but note small eye and short wing-projection. Compare photos 246-247. California, USA. 21 Feb 1999. *Don DesJardin.* **221. Juvenile/1st-winter**. Note barrel-shaped body, long bill and translucent flight-feathers. Turku, Finland. 23 Jan 1993. *Henry Lehto.* **222. Juvenile/1st-winter.** Wing-tip and tail appear the palest parts of the bird unlike all other gulls apart from Iceland Gull *glaucoides*. Turku, Finland. Jan 1993. *Henry Lehto.* **223. Juvenile/1st-winter** ssp. *pallidissimus*. Note barrel-shaped body, faint barring on rump and the two narrow black spots, created by eye and bill tip against pale background. Hokkaido, Japan. 12 Feb 2001. *Klaus Malling Olsen.* **224. Juvenile/1st-winter** ssp. *pallidissimus*. A large, flat-crowned individual with heavy bill. From below, barring in undertail-coverts the only well-patterned part of the bird. Hokkaido, Japan. 9 Feb 2001. *Klaus Malling Olsen.* **225 1st-winter** By late winter often bleached with contrasting new, better marked scapulars. Turku, Finland. 23 May 2000. *Harry J. Lehto.*

199

Glaucous Gull *Larus hyperboreus*. Photos refer to ssp. *hyperboreus*, unless otherwise stated. **226. 2nd-winter**. Note unevenly patterned plumage, pale tip to greyish-flesh bill and pale eyes of this age. Turku, Finland. 23 May 2000. *Henry Lehto*. **227. 2nd-winter**. Note pale eye and bill-tip as well as more uneven plumage pattern than in 1st-years. IJmuiden, Netherlands. 5 Feb 1983. *Arnoud B. van den Berg*. **228. 2nd-winter**. Some birds at this age look similar to worn and faded 1st-winters, but note pale eye and rounder primaries than in 1st-years. Hokkaido, Japan. Feb 2001. *Klaus Malling Olsen*. **229. 2nd-winter** Flight feathers cleaner than in 1st-years, lacking dark subterminal spots to secondaries - and sometimes primaries - found in many 1st-years. Finland. March. *Henry Lehto*. **230. 2nd-winter**. ssp. *pallidissimus*. Upperwing more unevenly patterned than in 1st-years. This heavy, deep-bellied bird looks short-winged, exaggerated by translucency of primaries. Hokkaido, Japan. 12 Feb 2001. *Klaus Malling Olsen*.

Glaucous Gull *Larus hyperboreus*. Photos refer to ssp. *hyperboreus*, unless otherwise stated. **231. moulting into 3rd-winter**. Note mixture of slightly barred and clean grey feathers in upperparts. Spitsbergen, Norway. Aug 1992. *Ger Meesters*. **232. 4th- or adult winter** ssp. *pallidissimus*. Greyish tinge and narrow dark subterminal markings in bill suggest this age in an otherwise adult plumage. Hokkaido, Japan. 12 Feb 2001. *Klaus Malling Olsen*. **233. Adult summer**. Note white wing-tip concolorous with tail, thus paler than upperparts. A rather round-headed and narrow-billed individual, suggesting female. Spitsbergen, Norway. 28 Jun 1999. *Jan Eske Schmidt*. **234. Adult winter**. By winter, head becomes densely brown-spotted, creating hooded appearance. Note very pale, staring eye surrounded by brown. Zeeland, Netherlands. Jan 1996. *René Pop*.

Glaucous Gull *Larus hyperboreus.* Photos refer to ssp. *hyperboreus,* unless otherwise stated. **235. Adult winter** ssp. *pallidissimus.* Note typical structure of Glaucous Gull, especially flat crown, small eyes, long legs and short wing-projection, creating shape similar to Great Black-backed Gull. Hokkaido, Japan. 9 Feb 2001. *Klaus Malling Olsen.* **236. Adult winter,** putative ssp. *barrovianus.* A very small bird with very long wings, suggesting Iceland Gull, but note square head, smallish-looking eyes and bill too long for Iceland Gull. This bird was much smaller and somewhat darker in upperparts than accompanying *pallidissimus.* Kushiro, Hokkaido, Japan. 9 Feb 2001. *Klaus Malling Olsen.* **237. 4th-winter.** Note pale grey upperwing bordered by white as in adult (this bird 4th-winter judging by dark pattern on bill). Blåvandshuk, Denmark. 7 Mar 1998. *Klaus Malling Olsen.* **238. Adult winter** ssp. *pallidissimus.* Note clean white underwing with broad white, translucent tips to primaries. Hokkaido, Japan. 12 Feb 2001. *Klaus Malling Olsen*

Putative hybrid Glaucous Gull × Glaucous-winged Gull
239. 1st-winter. General plumage pattern suggests Glaucous, but note darker tinge to primaries, more extensive dark centres to mantle and more extensive dark in bill, including cutting edges (unlike any Glaucous). Kushiro, Hokkaido, Japan. 9 Feb 2001. *Klaus Malling Olsen*

Hybrid Glaucous Gull × Herring Gull
240. 1st-winter. Note bill as in Glaucous, coverts and tertial pattern intermediate between Glaucous and Herring, and dark primaries and tail-bar from Herring. Helsinki, Finland. 2 Mar 1997. *Henry Lehto*. **241. 1st-winter.** Bill and undertail-covert barring from Glaucous combined with solid dark tail-bar and dark primary tips from Herring, although latter shows broad translucent area at bases unlike Herring. Hanko, Finland. 3 Mar 1997. *Henry Lehto*. **242. 1st-winter** Note extensive, but pale brown tail-bar, and indications of dark secondary bar - both as in Herring, but much paler. Although this theoretically could be shown by leucistic Herring, the Glaucous Gull-like tail and rump strongly indicates hybrid origin. Hanko, Finland. 3 Mar 1997. *Harry J. Lehto*. **243. 2nd-winter**. Glaucous Gull bill pattern combined with seemingly too-dark tertials, greater coverts and primaries. This bird could represent a very dark Glaucous. Short wing-projection fits Glaucous. Turku, Finland. 28 Dec 1997. *Henry Lehto*. **244. Adult, probably 'arctic'** *argentatus*. Adult showing minimum amount of black in wing-tip, suggesting hybrid, but probably Arctic Herring with least amount of black in tip. Turku, Finland. 4 Apr 1998. *Harry J. Lehto*

16. ICELAND GULL

Larus glaucoides (B. Meyer, 1822, Greenland)

Plates 29–32, Photos 245–283

IDENTIFICATION Length 52–60cm, wingspan 125–145cm. A medium-sized arctic gull, smaller than Herring and Glaucous Gull with smaller, more rounded head, larger eyes and shorter, weaker bill. The first impression is of a large gull with the head of Common Gull! The breast is deep and the rear accentuated, as the long wings reach several cms beyond the tail (equivalent of bill length or longer). The legs are short, with little of tibia visible. Large males have more sloping forehead, heavier bill and proportionately shorter wings. Although sometimes approaches Herring Gull in size, it lacks latter's brute masculine look. In flight elegant with slender wings (hand clearly longer than in Glaucous), short, rounded head and deep breast. Handles hard winds well, and may perform much shearwatering in hard head-winds. Often feeds agilely, snapping up food directly from sea. See Glaucous Gull for further differences and treatment of ID from that species.

Two forms: Iceland Gull nominate *glaucoides* (in plumages almost identical to Glaucous Gull) and Kumlien's Gull *kumlieni*, which is thought to have evolved from hybridisation with Thayer's Gull (Dwight 1925, Weir *et al.* 2000). Kumlien's is a highly variable taxon with hardly any two birds being identical, giving meaning to treating it as a hybrid population appearing over a very wide zone – probably with a narrow hybridisation zone with *glaucoides* to the East and Thayer's Gull to the West. It is suggested that its name should be put in brackets (Yésou 2002). While we fully agree with the explanation of its origin, we maintain to treat *kumlieni* as a valid taxon, given its often distinct plumage, while this from a taxonomic view may be considered dubious, it seems better from an ID point of view.

Adult *glaucoides* has pale grey upperparts with broad white trailing edge to wing. Bill yellow, often with an olive tinge and reddish gonys-spot. Eyes pale with reddish orbital ring. Legs pink. In **summer**, head is white; in **winter** brown-spotted or streaked.

Kumlien's Gull *kumlieni* has pale grey upperparts, and darker grey shading to outer webs of P6–10, varying from very inconspicuous to (in small minority) almost as blackish and extensive as in Thayer's Gull (which see for fuller discussion on ID). Most birds have narrow grey lines on outer webs of primaries and faint darker markings on P6–7. In settled birds, wing-tip on most is frosty-grey with row of white Vs. Unlike nominate, many have darkish iris, often heavier bill and sometimes more sloping forehead creating head- and bill-shape between nominate and the herring gulls. Winter head pattern generally more diluted and sometimes more extensive than in nominate. Certain large pale gulls (leucistic birds or hybrids, especially Herring × Glaucous Gull, American Herring × Glaucous-winged and Glaucous × Glaucous-winged) have wing-tip similar to *kumlieni*; large-gull structure and size, pale eye, orbital ring colour and pattern on surface of primaries (like bleached wing-tip of Herring Gull) should prevent misidentification.

Juvenile/first-winter *glaucoides* similar to Glaucous Gull, but the shorter bill has broader black tip grading into paler base. The base may be fleshy, but not the bubblegum-pink of Glaucous. Plumage generally greyer, and head often with pale hind-collar against dark shadings above and behind eye. For further differences, see Glaucous.

Palest *kumlieni* identical. Many *kumlieni* however identifiable by *combination* of black bill and dark leading edge to outer primaries (rarely dark trailing edge similar to Thayer's Gull and many *Sterna* terns). When settled, pale-fringed primaries often slightly darker than upperparts and at least some primaries have dark V-markings (sometimes restricted to inner ones, unlike Thayer's Gull—J. R. King *in litt.*). Some have darker outer webs to P6–10, creating vague 'venetian blind' pattern, others have rather plain brown-washed primaries, concentrating along the shafts. (*Glaucoides* has much paler primaries, these typically being the palest part of the bird and only rarely with indistinct dark V-markings.) Some *kumlieni* show slightly dark outer webs of primaries, but markings are coarser, and their overall paleness suggests a very pale gull. With wear, outer primaries may lose dark markings and appear whitish, thus similar to *glaucoides*. Tail in *kumlieni* often with dark-shaded subterminal bar, matched by darkest nominate, which normally has pale, faintly mottled tail or several narrow subterminal bars. Head and body of *kumlieni* often darker greyish; normally paler buffish in *glaucoides*. For fuller discussion, see Geographical Variation.

Second-winter similar to first-winter, but bill pale with black subterminal bar. Head and underbody paler, often with dark mask offsetting pale eye. A few birds with grey, adult-type mantle and scapulars, creating grey saddle, often seen from Dec, more often than in Glaucous; but individual variation is large. *Glaucoides* has whitish flight feathers and paler pattern to greater coverts and tail and weaker rump-barring than first-year. *Kumlieni* similar, apart from pale brown outer webs to P7–10, often in strong contrast to rest of flight feathers. From below primaries look white and translucent, emphasising dark tips and innerwebs to P10. Mantle mostly grey against paler wings, which from spring become much worn and faded; may show some median coverts of adult type. Tail-bar as first-year, but generally more solid brown with less marbling, and even outer primaries sometimes with slight greyish or pale brown cast.

Second-summer/third-winter nominate has grey mantle and some inner wing-coverts. Wings and tail off-white, tail often slightly greyish-tinged. *Kumlieni* carries indication of adult primary pattern. Bill duller than in adults, usually with traces of dark subterminal spots intermixed with reddish gonys-spot, but sometimes similar to adult.

Third-summer/fourth-winter similar to adult, but with brown-tinged coverts (especially primary coverts), dark subterminal spots on yellow bill and sometimes traces of weak dark markings on undertail-coverts.

VOICE Similar to Herring Gull, but shriller.

MOULT *Glaucoides* and *kumlieni* very similar (skins in AMNH, MCZ, USNM, UZM, ZMA), apart from tendency for *kumlieni* to moult larger parts of mantle/scapulars in first-year, and for adult to complete primary moult later; see below.

Adult moult to **winter** plumage complete May–Nov. P1–2 May–Jun, P5–7 mid-Jul–Aug, P8–10 Sep–mid-Oct; some still growing P(8)9–10 mid-Nov. *L. g. kumlieni* generally moults later, with 50% growing P10 by Nov, finishing late Nov as in American Herring Gull (B. Mactavish *in litt.*). Secondaries late Jul–mid-Oct. Tail early Aug–mid-Oct. Head and body Sep–mid-Oct. Faster, but later moult than in Glaucous (Andresen & Thomas 1986) not supported by own studies. **Adult** moult to **summer** plumage partial from late Jan, including head and body. Most show summer head late Mar; rarely winter head present into May.

Juvenile plumage retained to Mar, or moult restricted to very few mantle and scapulars feathers (J. R. King *in litt.*). For *kumlieni* see below. Moult to **second-winter** is complete (late Mar) Apr–Oct, starting with P1–2 and followed by head, body, mantle and scapulars. P6–7 moulted by late Aug, P9–10 by Sep/early Oct. Flight feather moult earlier and slower than in adults; one had finished primary moult early Aug. Subsequent moults similar to adult, but generally earlier, starting with P1 in Mar (third-winter-type from late Feb had shed P1).

DESCRIPTION

Adult *glaucoides* Mantle, scapulars and upperwing pale grey (sometimes paler than in Glaucous Gull: Kodak Grey Scale 2–3.5) with broad white tips to flight feathers. Primaries lack dark markings and streaks of *kumlieni*. Head, body, tail and marginal coverts white. P10 0–10mm >P9. Iris pale yellow, orbital ring pinkish-brown to red. Bill yellow, often with olive tinge. Gonys-spot red to orange-red. Legs pinkish.

Adult summer ((Feb)Mar/Apr–Aug/Sep) Head white. Orbital ring purple-red and bill deep yellow into mid-summer. Legs pink to rosy-pink.

Adult winter (Sep–Mar) Head white with brown to buff streaks to head, sometimes upper breast (generally less than in Glaucous Gull; often densest on crown and hindneck). Bill duller yellow and more frequently olive-tinged than in summer, especially at base. Orbital ring dull purple-red to red, often darkish-looking in field (reinforcing Common Gull look). Legs greyish-flesh to pink.

Juvenile (fledging–(Dec)Mar) Head light brownish-grey to greyish-buff, fading to whitish on chin, forehead and hindneck. Brown streaks fine and inconspicuous, but sometimes denser above eye and neck, creating pattern similar to washed-out winter Black-headed Gull. Eye-crescent dusky. May show inconspicuous whitish crescents above and below eye, but only rarely pale eye-ring. Mantle, scapulars, tertials and upperwing-coverts pale greyish to buff with intricate brownish bars, marbling or V-shaped spots, strongest on lower scapulars and greater coverts; on average neater and denser than in Glaucous (especially on distal part of tertials); pale birds have weak, scattered markings. Primary coverts often slightly darker with pale edges and narrow dark subterminal markings near tip. Rump white with brown bars; in many paler than in Glaucous. Primaries and secondaries grey-brown to whitish-buff (concolorous with or paler than upperparts) with broad paler tips, forming pale wing-tip in settled birds; often with narrow dark chevrons near tip (generally more prominent than in Glaucous). Shafts white to pale yellow. The darkest-patterned birds may show darker grey outer web to P6–10 and slight pale edge to tips of P6–10 (often together with darker-than-average plumage and more solid dark on tail—intermediates with *kumlieni*?). P10 6–12mm >P9. Tail pale grey or buff with variable amount of dark marbling or diffuse pattern, several grey subterminal bars or one broad grey subterminal bar, bordered by white tips and tail-sides. Some have stronger dark barring on outer tail than any Glaucous, barely different from rump-barring. Underbody brownish-grey to buff with faint dark barring on breast-sides and flanks; belly often darkest. Small minority with denser dark spots on whole underbody. Undertail-coverts pale with pale brown bars. Axillaries and underwing-coverts greyish-brown with indistinct dark mottling contrasting with pale flight feathers; greater coverts often paler and greyer than lesser/median. Iris dark brown. Bill variable: in <2% whole bill is blackish, but normally with paler (dark brown to grey-brown, greyish-yellow or olive-grey) basal 30–45%; in <5% the basal region is fleshy or pink. Division from black tip normally more definite than in Glaucous, with black penetrating along cutting edges. Precise bill pattern may be hard to judge according to darkish coloration of base; birds with pale bill patterned more like Glaucous. Gape flesh. At fledging, bill generally darker. Legs pale flesh, at fledging often with slight grey cast, especially around knee. Legs then generally darker than in Glaucous Gull (C. Johnson *in litt.*).

First-winter (Oct–May) Most retain juvenile plumage; birds renewing parts of plumage have head and body (especially hindneck) paler, in some almost whitish. If renewed, new mantle to scapulars whiter with coarser, more irregular barring. From Jan/Feb most fade to whitish apart from scattered brownish feathers. May develop pale bill-tip from Mar (rarely late Dec).

First-summer (Mar/Apr–Sep) as first-winter; plumage differences caused by bleaching. Head and body whitish to pale buff with reduced dark pattern. Mantle and scapulars whitish with irregular and inconspicuous brown barring. May develop a few grey feathers on mantle and inner median coverts. Wing and tail very faded, may look whitish when dark pattern disappears with wear. Bill as in first-winter, but base often yellow and tip pale.

Second-winter (Aug–Apr). Head and body whitish to pale buff, sometimes with coarser brown streaks or mottling, especially around eye and on hindneck. Mantle and scapulars whitish with buffish pattern or bars, typically irregular and less distinct than the cleaner, uniform first-year pattern. Normally with 40–90% grey on mantle and scapulars; in most advanced 100%; lacking in retarded birds. Upperwing plainer pale buff to whitish, lacking regular barring on coverts and tertials of juveniles; may be pale, with very indistinct pale brown patterning confined to inner coverts (Grant

PLATE 29. ICELAND GULL *Larus glaucoides glaucoides*

Breeds Greenland only, wintering coastally with good numbers reaching Iceland, and smaller numbers W Europe and American E Coast. Medium-sized to large Arctic gull, plumage almost identical to Glaucous but normally smaller (even than Herring Gull) with small, rounded head and short bill, recalling Common Gull. Lacks strongly marked gonys-angle, and shows larger eyes than Glaucous, enhancing gentle Common Gull impression. Breast deep but wing long, with primary projection equal to or longer than bill. Centre of gravity around breast. Legs short, emphasising elongated shape. Breeds on cliffs.

1. **Juvenile/first-winter** (Aug–Apr) Plumage as Glaucous Gull (though often greyer), but head-markings on average stronger with faint dark-shadowed crown and ear-coverts, only faint or no white eyelids and paler hindneck. Bill with broad black tip merging into slightly paler base (varies from dark as tip to, more commonly, paler fleshy, grey or greenish). Wing-tip white, sometimes with faint dark arrowhead-markings. Undertail-coverts barred. Eyes dark; large-looking. Moult (if any) into first-winter very limited.

2. **Juvenile/first-winter** (Aug–Apr) A typically patterned individual. Note faint dark shading on head, diffuse bill-contrast, rounded head with centrally placed eyes and long primary projection above tail, together with short legs emphasising accentuated rear.

3. **First-winter** (Feb–May) With wear, some birds appear almost white, with only faint brown upperpart-markings. Note characteristic elongated shape and rounded head with short bill.

4. **Second-winter** (Aug–Apr) Somewhat variable. Compared to first-winter more unevenly patterned, often with darker-centred primaries. Bill contrast similar to Glaucous Gull (but this also seen in certain first-years). Eye bicoloured.

5. **Second-winter** (Aug–Apr) A more advanced individual than 4, showing grey saddle against faintly brown-patterned coverts (greater coverts often slightly darker).

6. **Third-winter** (Aug–Apr) Similar to adult, but some coverts faintly brown-patterned and bill duller yellow with solid dark markings.

7. **Adult winter** (Aug–Apr) Adult shows pale grey upperparts and broad white tips to tertials and primaries. Plumage identical to Glaucous Gull, but head markings often fainter (and often more streaked). Bill greenish-yellow.

8. **Adult summer** (Apr–Aug) Head white. Bill yellow (often slightly greenish-tinged). Eyes pale yellow. Orbital ring red.

3. First-winter

Juvenile/first-winter

2. Juvenile/first-winter

4. Second-winter

5. Second-winter

Third-winter

7. Adult winter

8. Adult summer

PLATE 30. ICELAND GULL *Larus glaucoides glaucoides*

Plumage almost identical to Glaucous Gull. Smaller (smaller even than Herring Gull) with short, rounded head and short bill, creating head similar to Common Gull. Breast deep. Wings longer and narrower than in Glaucous Gull (but may appear short owing to pale translucent primaries). Arm broader than the long hand. Flight more elegant than Glaucous Gull, often agile with quick turns in hard winds. May pick food from surface.

1. **Juvenile/first-winter** (Aug–Apr) Similar to Glaucous, but on average slightly greyer, in some with grey, pale-edged primaries. Mostly lacks any strong tail-markings, but some show browner tail-bar. Bill dark and dark eyes large-looking. Darkest birds may appear rather uniform pale.

2. **Juvenile/first-winter** (Aug–Apr) A typically patterned individual with wing-tip paler than rest of plumage. Pale hindneck bar often conspicuous.

3. **First-winter** (Aug–Apr) Note short, rounded head with large eyes and mainly dark, short bill, recalling Common Gull. Primaries translucent, appearing white.

4. **Second-winter** (Aug–Apr) Similar to first-winter, but mantle greyish-tinged with fainter dark markings; wing often more irregularly patterned and bill fleshy with black tip. Tail uniform brownish-grey.

5. **Third-winter** (Aug–Apr) Similar to adult in showing pale grey upperwing with white tips to primaries and secondaries, but note duller bill with dark subterminal markings and greyish tinge to tail.

6. **Adult winter** (Aug–Apr) Adult upperwing pale grey with white edge, appearing uniform (lacking any dark pattern). Head with faint brownish pattern. Compared to Glaucous, white tips to outer primaries are on average broader, creating a broad white, clear-cut wing-tip.

7. **Adult summer** (Apr–Aug) Head white. Note uniform, very pale wing with translucent primaries, also rounded head with short bill, creating gentle expression as in Common and Mew Gull. Wing-tip rounder than in first-years.

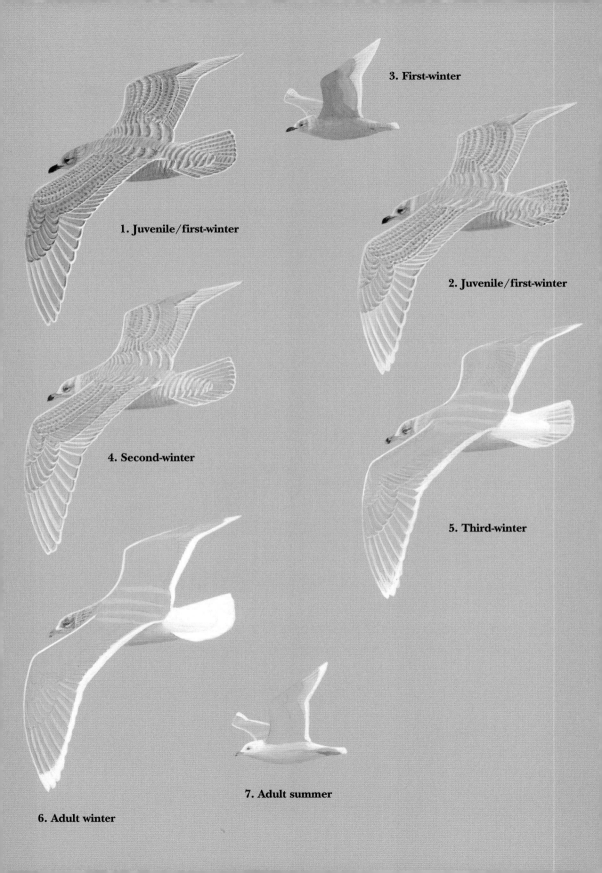

1. Juvenile/first-winter

2. Juvenile/first-winter

3. First-winter

4. Second-winter

5. Third-winter

6. Adult winter

7. Adult summer

PLATE 31. KUMLIEN'S GULL *Larus glaucoides kumlieni*

Now widely regarded as hybrid population between Iceland *glaucoides* and Thayer's Gull. Breeds Baffin Island. Winters NE North America, scarce along E American Coast. Vagrant to W Europe. Basically as Iceland Gull nominate *glaucoides*, and many indistinguishable, but most with darker markings on primaries.

1. **Juvenile** (Aug–Apr) Very similar to Iceland *glaucoides*, but most identifiable on combination of black bill, slightly darker, greyer plumage with more coarsely dark upperpart markings, darker tertial centres and pale greyish-brown primaries with solid white edges.

2. **Juvenile/first-winter** (Sep–Apr) The majority moult parts of mantle and scapulars in first-winter (rare in Iceland *glaucoides*) and grow greyer feathers with narrower dark markings (but much variation). Grey cast to outer webs of outer primaries creates less uniform white wing-tip than in nominate *glaucoides*, which at most shows narrow dark arrowhead-markings on primary tips. Bill mainly black throughout first-winter (in *glaucoides*, most show paler base to bill).

3. **First-winter** (Jan–May) Worn first-winter, appearing identical to certain, more frequent, very pale Iceland *glaucoides*.

4. **Second-winter** (Aug–Apr) Similar to first-winter, but more unevenly patterned with bicoloured bill, showing fleshy base and black tip/cutting edges; bill generally more extensively dark-marked than in Iceland *glaucoides*. Note pale greyish-brown, white-edged primaries, appearing slightly darker than tertials. Eyes often dark (much rarer in similar-aged Iceland *glaucoides*).

5. **Second-winter** Develops grey saddle and parts of coverts. Wing-tip pattern like that of adult but generally with more extensive and browner-tinged dark markings.

6. **Third-winter** (Aug–Apr) Similar to adult, but with brown-patterned lesser and greater coverts and narrower white tips to grey primaries. Eye often still dark at this age (and even later). Bill fleshy with black subterminal markings.

7. **Adult winter** (Aug–Apr) Shows grey upperparts (a tinge darker than average nominate *glaucoides*) and much varying grey on primaries (often very faint, only covering outer webs of outermost primaries). Head generally more diluted with more extensive brown markings than in Iceland *glaucoides*. Eye often darkish-looking (at this age invariably pale yellow in nominate *glaucoides*). Legs often deeper pink.

8. **Adult summer** (Apr–Aug) Head white. Orbital ring reddish. Eyes vary from yellow to dark.

1. Juvenile

2. Juvenile/first-winter

3. First-winter

4. Second-winter

5. Second-winter

6. Third-winter

7. Adult winter

8. Adult summer

PLATE 32. KUMLIEN'S GULL *Larus glaucoides kumlieni*

In flight similar-shaped and -sized to nominate *glaucoides*; many first-years indistinguishable, but most with darker markings on wing-tip.

1.   **Juvenile/first-winter** (Aug–Apr) First-years are pale brownish-grey, in typical birds with slightly darker outer webs to outer primaries and more solid pale brown tail-bar than in nominate *glaucoides*. Note also slightly darker-centred secondaries and blackish bill.

2.   **Juvenile/first-winter** (Aug–Apr) Compared to nominate *glaucoides*, wing-tip does not appear paler than inner wing, as outer primaries greyish-brown with pale edges. Tail often slightly bicoloured. A typically patterned individual.

3.   **First-winter** (Aug–Apr) Pale birds indistinguishable from nominate *glaucoides*, although black bill is rule (rare in nominate *glaucoides*). Often with slightly greyish tinge to outer primaries, slightly contrasting with whiter inner primaries and sometimes secondaries.

4.   **Second-winter** (Aug–Apr) From this age, dark primary markings get stronger. Compared to first-winter rump whiter in better contrast to pale brown tail.

5.   **Third-winter** (Aug–Apr) A typical individual, showing brownish-grey striped pattern on outer wing (as outer webs of 3–5 outermost primaries darker than inner webs). Tail still with grey bar, contrasting with white rump. Bill still with extensive black markings, and upperwing slightly brownish-tinged.

6.   **Adult winter** (Aug–Apr) Adult shows many variable grey markings on up to five outer primaries, ranging from faint grey on outer webs of P9–10 to more complex grey pattern, as shown here. Compare especially Thayer's Gull (see pp. 29–30). Upperparts paler grey than in Thayer's and wing-tip pattern only rarely appears darker; but birds with blacker primary markings reaching P5 better left undetermined. Head-markings generally slightly more streaked than in Thayer's, appearing intermediate between nominate *glaucoides* and Thayer's Gull.

7.   **Adult winter** (Aug–Apr) Compare the less extensive primary markings on this individual with 6. This represents a diagnostic type, as Thayer's Gull shows blacker, more complete markings reaching P5–6 (see also pp. 29–30 and 230–31).

8.   **Adult summer** (Apr–Aug) In summer head is white. This bird has grey primary pattern only covering outer webs of P1–3 and narrow dark markings near tips; on underwing, dark pattern reduced compared to view from above. The least-patterned Kumlien's Gull only shows very faint grey cast to outer webs of 1–2 outer primaries, hardly visible at any distance.

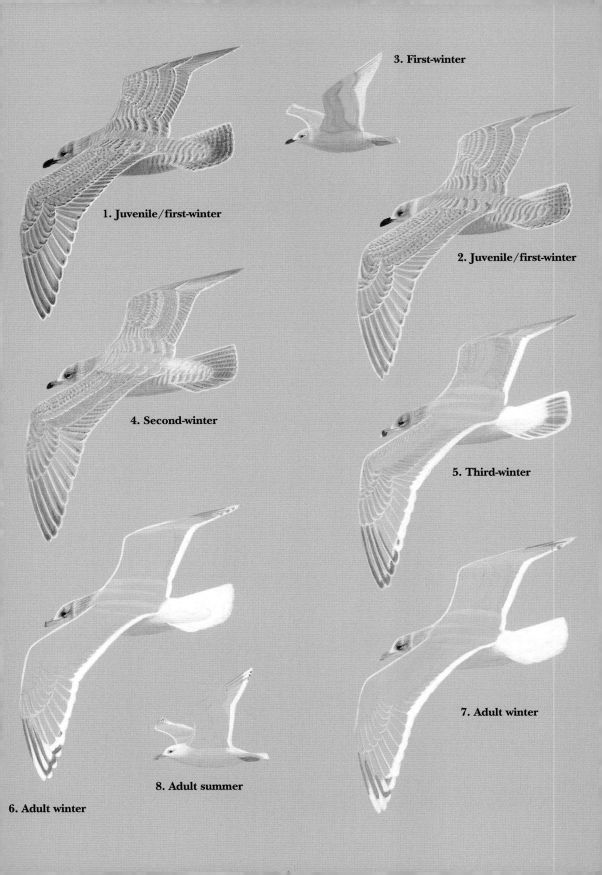

1. Juvenile/first-winter

2. Juvenile/first-winter

3. First-winter

4. Second-winter

5. Third-winter

6. Adult winter

7. Adult winter

8. Adult summer

1986b) or with some grey median coverts of adult type. Others have slight contrast between darker bases to lesser and median coverts and slightly darker, more uniform greater coverts. Axillaries and underwing-coverts similar to first-year, but generally paler with neater dark pattern. Primaries and secondaries pale and plain, as in pale first-winters. Tail and tail-coverts grey to pale grey with fainter brown markings than in first-year and without distinct barring; sometimes with weak, uniform or broken grey tail-bar in T(1–2)4–6. Iris normally pale, often as in adult. Bill yellowish, greenish, fleshy-yellow, grey or dull pink with black subterminal ring and whitish tip; tip rarely black (Dean 1988, Breife *et al.* 2003).

Second-summer (Apr–Aug) As second-winter, but head and underparts whitish to pale buff. Mantle and scapulars with varying amount of grey, typically as pale grey mantle, against whitish upperwing and tail. Iris pale. Orbital ring sometimes reddish from this age. Bill as second-winter.

Third-winter (Sep–Apr) Similar to adult winter, but underparts often with weak dark mottling. May show patches of white on scapulars and/or faintly dark-mottled rump and tail-coverts. Lesser coverts, median coverts and tertials whitish with weak buff bars or patterning. Greater coverts pale brown, often with pale vermiculations. Flight feathers and tail white, sometimes with pale brown intermixed, giving patchy, faded look; on tail often as delicate brown freckling (Grant 1986b). Upper- and undertail-coverts white, usually with scattered brown spots or bars; sometimes brownish wash more extensive. Bill similar to adult, but usually with black subterminal marks, often as isolated dark spots; may lack orange or red gonys-spot.

Third-summer (Mar/Apr–Aug/Sep) as third-winter, but head and underparts white or faintly spotted or streaked; sometimes with faded brown areas on wing and tail, strongest on underwing-coverts. Bill often as adult, but frequently with dark subterminal spot.

Fourth-winter/summer as adult, but sometimes with pale brown wash to wings and tail, some dark spotting on underwing-coverts (especially lesser coverts), few dark bars on undertail-coverts and narrow dark subterminal marks on bill.

Hybrids

Hybrid **Thayer's × Kumlien's Gull** claimed from Nunawat, formerly NW Territories. These taxa probably hybridise freely in overlap range. Hybrids show all intergrades between the two forms (Gaston & Decker 1985, Snell 1989, Zimmer 1991).

GEOGRAPHICAL VARIATION Two taxa.

L. g. glaucoides **Iceland Gull** Greenland, winters N Atlantic, mainly Iceland; scarce, but regular N and W Europe, NE Canada and New England (Cramp & Simmons 1983, Zimmer 1991). Described above.

L. g. kumlieni **Kumlien's Gull** S Baffin Island to NW Quebec. Winters N American E coast. Vagrant NW/W Europe. Similar to nominate, but with variable grey to blackish pattern on wing-tip (in some almost impossible to judge).

Adult has pale grey upperparts (Kodak Grey Scale

(2)3–4(5)). Primary pattern highly variable (Fjeldså & Jensen 1985, Zimmer 1991, Weir *et al.* 1995, B. Mactavish *in litt.*, pers. obs.; *contra* Grant 1986b): in least-marked birds (small minority of Newfoundland birds) just faint greyer pigmentation along outer webs (Kodak Grey Scale 5) of P10–(9); white tip to P10 60–80mm. 50–70% Newfoundland birds have 'frosty' to dark grey markings on P6–10 (Kodak Grey Scale 8–9, on darkest 12–13): P10 with narrow dark streak along outer web and sometimes dark spot or complete dark bar near tip. P9 normally with 5–8mm grey subterminal mark, isolating white tip from grey on outer web. P8 often has broadest dark markings; up to 80 mm on outer web and 20mm on inner web. Often with dark subterminal markings near tip of P(6)7–9, on P7 max. 25mm on outer and 12mm on inner web. P5 rarely with dark markings on outer web. Rarely shows grey outer webs and tips to P6–9. Darkest birds with blackish-grey pattern on outer wing may be Kumlien's × Thayer's hybrids or even 'pale Thayer's' (skins in MCZ). In folded wing, greyish outer webs create grey wing-tip against pale spots and tips. In **winter**, head generally slightly denser dark-patterned than in nominate, especially on hind-neck and breast-sides (often diluted as in Thayer's), in some reaching upper flanks. Iris generally darker than in nominate: golden-yellow, greyish-yellow, amber, dark olive or rarely brown, often dark-spotted (birds with most black spots giving impression of an all-dark eye) (Zimmer 1991, B. Mactavish *in litt.*). Orbital ring reddish-purple (summer) to duller reddish-grey/greyish-mauve (Millington 1993). Bill often greenish- or olive-tinged at base.

Juvenile/first-winter highly variable. Pale birds inseparable from *glaucoides*, dark birds very similar to certain Thayer's Gulls. Many darker greyish-brown with more solid dark markings than any *glaucoides*, especially on wing-tip. From extensive study (skins, photos and live birds, Greenland and N Atlantic—Zimmer 1991, Garner *et al.* 2000, B. Mactavish *in litt.*) characters indicating *kumlieni* from nominate *glaucoides* are:

Medium greyish-brown outer webs and dark subterminal markings to P6–10, from below creating brownish trailing edge. From above, dark outer webs create darker outer wing than in *glaucoides*, appearing concolorous with inner wing and typically plain, with brown wash centred along primary shafts, spreading onto both webs, generally darkest on middle part of outer web. The darkest birds show pale brown or grey primaries with pale tips as in Thayer's Gull, but often with pale covering edges, not just tips as in Thayer's, which typically has inner primaries paler than outer primaries (as broad window). Many have dark V-markings on wing-tip, sometimes on all primaries, but in paler birds restricted to P1–5. *Glaucoides* has primaries paler than rest of upperparts, often uniform (but this seen in worn *kumlieni* from midwinter), and at most with weak dark chevrons. May show narrow but distinct dark subterminal crescents on inner primaries as in juvenile *Calidris* waders. Sometimes P1–5 slightly paler than P6–10. Note that from mid-Feb brown primary wash of most *kumlieni* disappears, leaving outer wing very similar to average nominate.

Normally pale brownish-grey tail-bar or tail-centres with

pale mottling on T4–6 (rarely T1–3), at bases of most or all rectrices and darker internal markings on midtail; tail-bar contrasts with paler, dark-barred uppertail-coverts. Dark tail-bar present in 15% *glaucoides*, in 80–95% *kumlieni* (Zimmer 1991, pers. obs.). Tail-bar of *kumlieni* often rather uniform, just with faint pale (often broken) mottling at tip of tail and along edges of T1–2, whereas tail-bar of *glaucoides* typically consists of narrow bars melting together. Thayer's usually has darker, mud-brown tail-bar with pale mottling restricted to base and edges of rectrices.

Stronger greyish tinge to generally darker, denser-patterned head and body, including broader, darker spots or subterminal crescents on mantle, scapulars and sometimes wing-coverts, sometimes forming irregular pattern. Thayer's typically darker with broader dark eye-mask and longish-looking lores.

Most *kumlieni* have black bill with slightly paler brown base, but this becomes gradually paler by midwinter. Small minority have bicoloured bill with pale inner 60%. Most *glaucoides* have bicoloured bill, some pale with black tip, small minority black-billed.

Tertials sometimes medium brown with pale spotting or mottling along edges; intermediate between nominate and Thayer's Gull. *Glaucoides* (and many *kumlieni*) have pale tertials with narrow brown bars. In Thayer's tertial centres more solid mud-brown, recalling pattern of American Herring Gull.

Darkest birds have slightly darker secondaries in contrast to pale inner primaries and coverts. In Thayer's Gull, contrast is stronger, in nominate absent.

Primary projection probably never as grotesquely long as in many *glaucoides*.

Moult into **first-winter** generally more advanced compared to *glaucoides*; mantle and scapulars from Oct/Nov. Fifteen Newfoundland birds Jan–Feb had renewed 10–80% of scapulars, most 40–60% (B. Mactavish *in litt.*).

Subsequent ages ID from *glaucoides* easier with increas-

ing age in darker-patterned birds, as adult dark primary pattern indicated. Note that overall impression of wing in nominate is less uniform than in first-years.

Second-winter/summer Pale-winged *kumlieni* inseparable from *glaucoides*, but most have brown to grey outerweb to up to 5–6 outer primaries and brownish tinge to distal part of P5, on folded primaries creating darker, pale-edged wing-tip. Normally shows darker, more contrasting grey tail-bar than first-years (rare in *glaucoides*), contrasting well with whitish rump; tail-bar present mostly in birds with darker primaries. Bill bicoloured, with black covering 40% and pale covering 60%, more rarely in equal amounts or blackish (in *glaucoides* pale with narrower black ring; matched by some *kumlieni*), and tip usually black (rare in *glaucoides*). Eyes often darkish, appearing bicoloured, but only rarely whitish-yellow as in many nominate. Identification from Thayer's tricky as wing-tip pattern may be similar, but Thayer's usually darker with outer wing pattern covering P6–10 (mostly more restricted and paler in *kumlieni*; may in some cases indicate hybrid origin). *L. g. kumlieni* lacks strong, darkish secondary bar of Thayer's Gull; normally has paler tertials with barred or marbled dark markings, in most appearing paler than primaries, and often with pale eyes. Birds with just one atypical character better left unidentified.

Third-winter/summer Adult primary pattern usually well developed, although sometimes fainter, slightly brownish-tinged and sometimes with brown subterminal marking on P5. Bill often with greenish-yellow tinge and black markings.

Note An undescribed taxon of large pale gull might occur in N Russia: Along west coast of Novaya Zemlya, Aug 1993, Glaucous Gulls were accompanied by smaller, tamer adults not yet in moult, which had a brighter eye-ring and yellower iris; they were accompanied by smaller, grey immatures. In 1994 a pair of these birds was found nesting in Cape Zhuralev. The female had a

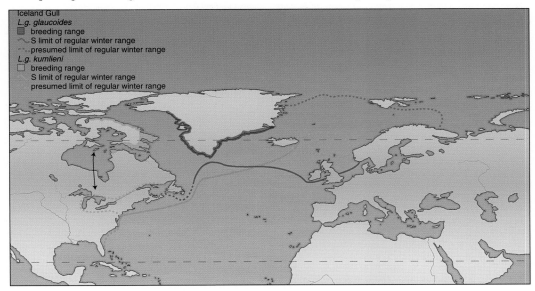

Iceland Gull
L.g. glaucoides
□ breeding range
～ S limit of regular winter range
···· presumed limit of regular winter range
L.g. kumlieni
□ breeding range
 S limit of regular winter range
 presumed limit of regular winter range

ICELAND GULL Four-year gull. Resembles Glaucous in plumages, but generally smaller than Herring Gull with smaller head, larger eyes and shorter, weaker bill creating head similar to Common Gull. Shows long primary projection beyond tail (longer than bill length), only matched by small female first-year Glaucous. In flight more elegant with longer hand, more protruding breast and rounder head. Flight often agile, may fish together with smaller gulls. Active flight often similar to Common Gull. Two taxa. Nominate *glaucoides* (breeds Greenland, winters mainly N Atlantic) is in all plumages very similar to Glaucous Gull, but **first-year** has mainly dark bill with vaguely paler base, generally stronger dark head-markings and greyer overall appearance, and adult often has greenish-tinged bill. Shares white wing-tip and lack of tail-bar with Glaucous. *Kumlieni* (Baffin Island, winters mainly NE North America) often similar, but **adult** shows grey markings on up to 5 outer primaries, often as frosty grey streaks on wing-tip; younger bird generally with more dark streaking on wing-tip and more solid dark markings on tail; *kumlieni* is a highly variable form.

bright lemon iris, orange orbital ring and measurements 'similar to large Iceland Gull' (but no details given). Such birds were even found at four sites in Novaja Zemlya in 1994, but not in 1995 (V.N. Kalyakin/W.R.P. Bourne, in Hagemeijer & Blair 1997).

DISTRIBUTION AND MIGRATION *Glaucoides* endemic to Greenland, where probably <80,000 pairs. Breeds on steep cliffs along rocky coasts, mainly in W, where northernmost colony recorded at 74°30´N; in smaller numbers in SE to Ammassalik at 66°N. Breeding population heavily hunted: >20% of population taken for food each year. Up to 1860 breeding range included western High Arctic Canada, but since about 1900 restricted to Greenland. May have bred in nineteenth century Jan Mayen; may occasionally breed N Russia and NE Baffin Island; see note above (Boertmann 1994, Hagemeijer & Blair 1996, Enticott & Tipling 1997, Weir *et al.* 2000).

Most of S and W population sedentary with autumn migration Oct–Nov. Spring migration late Mar–early May; N and E population spreads in winter N to Thule, NW Greenland. Greenland winter population 300,000. Most stay within Greenland; of 641 recoveries of birds ringed in Greenland only seven were away from W Greenland (1 Iceland, 1 Faeroes, 1 Scotland, 1 NE England, 1 SW Norway, 1 SE Greenland and 1 Labrador). Many birds from E Greenland population move to Iceland: vanguards arrive mid-Sep, peak from late Oct, most gone by May, adults from late Mar; a few immatures summer. Iceland winter population 5,000-10,000; most numerous late Mar–Apr. Scarce Norway, N and W Europe; mainly first-years, often in influxes linked with severe winters in Greenland or decline of fishing industries in N Atlantic, mainly Feb–early May. In Great Britain mean winter numbers 70–100 (>300 in influxes); most Scotland (50–70 annually; exceptionally >300 1993 (172 Feb), and Ireland (yearly average 12; influx max. 75). Annually 9–24 Denmark, 2–15 Sweden. In Netherlands 90 up to 1998. Few to France. Vagrant Baltic E to Finland (12), C and S Europe E to Italy (4) and Greece and W to the Azores. Regular, but scarce NE America S to New England, where degree of overlap with *kumlieni* unknown. Vagrant S to Georgia, Nebraska and Florida (some probably *kumlieni*). Also Japan and claims from W USA (Glutz von Blotzheim & Bauer 1982, Lack 1986, Malling Olsen 1992, Murray 1994, Handrinos & Akriotis 1997, Petersen 1998, van den Berg & Bosman 2001, McGowan & Kitchener 2001, Lyngs 2003, SOF 2003, J.

R. King & B. Mactavish, M. Retter *in litt.*).

Kumlieni breeds S Baffin Island to NW Quebec. Population probably around 10,000 pairs. Winters S to Hudson Bay and maritime provinces. Most winter Gulf of St. Lawrence and Newfoundland, where flocks >9,000 noted. Also in New Brunswick (thousands) and New England, with gatherings of c.100 Massachusetts (especially Nantucket) in Mar. Scarcer between Labrador (where common before freeze-up), at Lake Michigan (2-400 winter), E Great Lakes (97% of 1,392 'Iceland Gulls' in 14 years) and along E American coast S to South Carolina, but with an increase during twentieth century. Vagrant between British Columbia and California (where birds with *kumlieni* characters regular). Scarce but regular in winter, Greenland (mid-Aug–early May; one summering in colony of nominate near Nuuk, 2001) and Iceland (e.g. 20, 1998/1999, most in SW Iceland). Influx Faeroe Islands winter, 1982/1983, including at least 38 adults; 14 first-years undocumented. In Great Britain 78 into 1998, most Jan–Mar; now considered regular. Also Norway few, Sweden 2, France 1. Most identified birds adults (Fjeldså & Jensen 1985, Zimmer 1991, Colston *et al.* 1992, Boertmann 1994, 2001, Rogers 1998,1999, Weir *et al.* 2000, G. Péturson & I. Idzikowski *in litt.*, J. R. King & S. Sørensen pers comm., *Ornithos* 5: 166).

MEASUREMENTS Lengths in mm; weights in g. Own data based on skins in AMNH, MVZ, NHM, NNH, NRK, USNM, UZM, ZMA, ZMO. *glaucoides* Greenland, Iceland, Norway, W Europe. *kumlieni* New Brunswick, Newfoundland, Baffin Island, Greenland, Iceland. Included in adults are a few second-/third-winters.

WING

glaucoides		
Adult male	395–443 (419.4)	50
Adult female	379–428 (403.0)	53
Juv./first-winter ♂	394–442 (415.7)	41
Juv./first-winter ♀	378–430 (398.5)	47
kumlieni		
Adult male	398–442 (418.8)	24
Adult female	380–430 (404.7)	26
Juv./first-winter ♂	393–441 (460) (422.9)	11
Juv./first-winter ♀	375–426 (407.5)	16

***Note** Weir et al. (1995) gave for adult male 398–439 (mean 419.4, n=13), adult female 384–417 (mean 399.9, n=16).*

First-winter male 440, first-winter female 395–415 (mean 406.8, n=4), second-winter male 407–432 (mean 422.7, n=7), second-winter female 388–415 (mean 400.1, n=7), third-winter female 395–423 (mean 408.9, n=7).

BILL

glaucoides

Adult male	39.9–53.5 (44.1)	53
Adult female	36.3–50.0 (42.0)	53
Juv./first-winter ♂	37.5–52.0 (42.4)	41
Juv./first-winter ♀	35.2–49.7 (40.7)	48

kumlieni

Adult male	41.9–50.6 (45.2)	21
Adult female	38.8–44.8 (41.9)	25
Juv./first-winter ♂	42.0–49.7 (44.8)	11
Juv./first-winter ♀	39.0–50.0 (41.9)	16

Note *Weir* et al. *(1995) gave for adult male 43–52 (mean 47.7, n=13), adult female 39–47 (mean 43.9, n=16), first-winter male 47.3, first-winter female 40.1–47.5 (mean 43.6, n=4), second-winter male 46.9–49.0 (mean 48.1, n=7), second-winter female 41.6–48.0 (mean 43.9, n=7), third-winter female 42–47 (mean 44.5, n=6).*

BILL DEPTH AT GONYS

glaucoides

Adult male	14.4–17.3 (15.9)	52
Adult female	12.5–16.0 (14.7)	53
Juv./first-winter ♂	12.3–18.0 (14.2)	41
Juv./first-winter ♀	10.8–17.2 (13.6)	48

kumlieni

Adult male	14.8–17.3 (16.1)	22
Adult female	13.8–17.3 (15.3)	26
Juv./first-winter ♂	14.6–16.0 (15.3)	11
Juv./first-winter ♀	12.5–15.9 (14.2)	16

BILL DEPTH AT BASE OF BILL

glaucoides

Adult male	14.6–18.4 (16.5)	52
Adult female	12.9–17.3 (15.0)	53
Juv./first-winter ♂	12.6–18.8 (14.8)	42
Juv./first-winter ♀	11.7–17.7 (14.6)	48

kumlieni

Adult male	15.5–17.8 (16.5)	22
Adult female	14.0–17.6 (15.6)	24
Juv./first-winter ♂	15.3–17.0 (16.0)	11
Juv./first-winter ♀	14.2–16.6 (15.0)	16

GONYS LENGTH

glaucoides

Adult male	11.1–16.4 (13.2)	52
Adult female	10.4–15.6 (12.6)	53
Juv./first-winter ♂	10.8–14.7 (12.6)	42
Juv./first-winter ♀	8.6–15.5 (12.1)	48

Note *Weir* et al. *(1995) gave for adult male 15.6–17.8 (mean 16.7, n=2), adult female 15.0–17.7 (mean 16.0, n=8).*

kumlieni

Adult male	12.5–16.4 (14.3)	22
Adult female	10.5–14.5 (12.9)	25
Juv./first-winter ♂	12.7–15.3 (14.0)	11
Juv./first-winter ♀	12.2–15.2 (13.3)	16

Note *Weir* et al. *(1995) gave for adult male 14.0–18.1 (mean 16.1, n=5), adult female 14.5, first-winter male 18.4, first-winter female 13.5–16.3 (mean 14.9, n=2), second-winter male 14.0–14.4 (mean 14.2, n=3), third-winter female 14.2–15.4 (mean 14.8, n=2).*

TARSUS

glaucoides

Adult male	53.7–67.5 (58.0)	51
Adult female	48.8–60.2 (54.2)	53
Juv./first-winter ♂	49.4–62.2 (55.9)	41
Juv./first-winter ♀	47.8–60.9 (53.9)	48

Note *Cramp & Simmons (1983) gave for adult male 50.7–65.7 (mean 58.1, n=28), adult female 49.6–59.6 (mean 55.4, n=23). Glutz von Blotzheim & Bauer (1982) gave for adult male 50–65.5 (mean 58.8, n=20), adult female 51–60 (mean 55.4, n=14). Weir et al. (1995) gave for adult male 56–65 (mean 59.0, n=5), adult female 50–60.6 (mean 55.3, n=14).*

kumlieni

Adult male	51.8–63.5 (58.1)	22
Adult female	50.1–63.7 (55.1)	25
Juv./first-winter ♂	53.9–64.7 (59.3)	11
Juv./first-winter ♀	52.9–63.5 (56.0)	16

Note *Weir* et al. *(1995) gave for adult male 47.4–64.0 (mean 58.4, n=16), adult female 39–47 (mean 43.9, n=14), first-winter male 47.3, first-winter female 40.1–47.5 (mean 43.6, n=4), second-winter male 55.5–65 (mean 60.0, n=7), second-winter female 51–58 (mean 55.6, n=7), third-winter female 53.5–61 (mean 57.1, n=6).*

Weight *glaucoides* Adult male Iceland, Faeroes and Shetland 530–970, adult female 480–1,039 (Fjeldså & Jensen 1985, Weir *et al.* 1995), Scotland November 863. First-winter females 620–735, first-summer female in primary moult 460, third-winter female 730 (Glutz von Blotzheim & Bauer 1982, Cramp & Simmons 1983). *kumlieni* (Faeroes, winter): adult male 750–970, adult female 530–820, first-winter female 720–760 (skins in MCZ, UZM, Fjeldså & Jensen 1985, J.-K. Jensen *in litt.*).

Iceland Gull *Larus glaucoides glaucoides*. **245. Juvenile/1st-winter**. Compare with Glaucous Gull, photo 216, and note especially rounded head and short bill similar to Common Gull and very long hindparts with long wing-projection. Pembrokeshire, Wales, Great Britain. Feb 2000. *David Astins*. **246. Juvenile/1st-winter.** A rather faded and whitish-looking individual. Note deep breast, rounded head and very long wing-projection. Bill predominantly dark, only rarely as pale pink with clear-cut black tip as in Glaucous. Thorsminde, Denmark. 4 Mar 2000. *Klaus Malling Olsen*. **247. Juvenile/1st-winter**. Note overall shape and the large eye. In this bird the pale base to bill is more similar to Glaucous, but black on bill-tip more extensive. Compare with photo 220. Helsinki, Finland. 30 Dec 1990. *Henry Lehto*. **248. Juvenile/1st-winter**. Appears deep-breasted and long-winged with especially long hand. Like Glaucous very pale with primaries and tail typically being palest parts. Thorsminde, Denmark, 4 Mar 2000. *Klaus Malling Olsen*. **249. Juvenile/1st-winter**. Note rounded head and short neck. Head and body in darker end of range, wing-tip therefore even more contrastingly pale. Glommen, Halland, Sweden. Mar 2001. *Lasse Olsson*. **250. Juvenile/1st-winter**. Note long wings and rounded, dove-like head. As in Glaucous, barred undertail-coverts most densely patterned part of underparts. Skagen, Denmark. 16 Mar 1997. *Knud Pedersen* **251. 1st-winter**. Becomes much bleached with wear, losing almost any dark pattern and then appears similar to 2nd-winter, but note dark eyes and extensive dark on bill. Legs very short. Grindavik, Iceland. 27 May 1999. *Harry J. Lehto*. **252. 1st-winter**. Note whitish primary tips against darker coverts. West Jutland, Denmark. Mar 2000. *Klaus Malling Olsen*. **253. 1st-winter with Glaucous Gull**. Glaucous Gull is larger, with longer body, head and bill compared to the small, compact, round-headed Iceland Gull. Reykjavik, Iceland. 27 May 1999. *Harry J. Lehto*. **254. 2nd-winter**. Pale eyes age-diagnostic, but this bird (in retarded moult) otherwise is similar to certain paler 1st-winters. IJmuiden, Netherlands. Jan 1980. *René Pop*. **255. 2nd-winter**. A rather dark-patterned individual, inseparable from paler types of *kumlieni*. Pas-de-Calais, France. 12 Sep 1992. *Arnoud B. van den Berg*.

251

252

253

254

255

Iceland Gull *Larus glaucoides glaucoides*. **256. 2nd-summer moulting into 3rd-winter.** Note adult wing-pattern from 3rd-winter against worn and unmoulted outer primaries. Bill still with extensive dark on tip. Nesseby, Finnmark, Norway. Aug. *Håkon Heggland.* **257. Juvenile and 2nd-winter.** Compare more uneven wing-pattern of 2nd-winter in foreground with more regular and coarser markings of juvenile in background. Sandgerdi, Iceland. 10 Oct 1994. *Klaus Malling Olsen.* **258. 3rd-winter.** Dark markings on dull bill in otherwise adult plumage indicates this age. Norway, Feb. *Jan Kåre Ness.* **259. Adult winter.** Winter head pattern typically fainter than in Glaucous Gull. Skagen, Denmark. 27 Mar 1999. *Knud Pedersen.* **260. Adult winter.** Note small head and long wings with broad white, translucent tips. Great Britain. Feb. *Henry Lehto.*

Kumlien's Gull *Larus glaucoides kumlieni.* **261. Juvenile/1st-winter.** This form shows the largest individual variation found in any gull - ranging from as pale as in Iceland Gull of nominate form to as dark as Thayer's Gull, and is widely regarded as a hybrid between Iceland Gull and Thayer's Gull. Upperparts show denser pattern than *glaucoides* with larger number of renewed mantle feathers by mid-winter. Note darkish-looking bill and darker wing-tip pattern than in *glaucoides*. Compare these impressions. 261 and 263 show typical individuals. Newfoundland, Canada. 8 Dec 1999. *Bruce Mactavish.* **262. Juvenile/1st-winter.** The palest *kumlieni* are inseparable from *glaucoides*, and frequent in *kumlieni* wintering in main winter range. Newfoundland, Canada. Feb 1999. *Bruce Mactavish.* **263. Juvenile/1st-winter.** Note dark pattern in tail and wing-tip as well as all-dark bill. Newfoundland. 3 Feb 1995. *Bruce Mactavish.* **264. 1st-winter.** Note faint, but extensive tail-bar consisting of several narrower bars. Hartford, Connecticut, USA. Feb 1998. *Julian R. Hough.* **265. Late 1st-winter.** A much worn bird, just showing a few 1st-winter mantle feathers. Inseparable from *glaucoides*. Newfoundland, Canada. 22 Apr 2000. *Bruce Mactavish.*

261

262

263

264

265

Kumlien's Gull *Larus glaucoides kumlieni*. **266. Late 1st-winter**. Cape Tormentine, Canada. 21 May 1994. *Arnoud B. van den Berg*. **267. 2nd-winter**. More distinct pattern in primary tips occurs from this age. Compare pattern with juvenile in background. Newfoundland, Canada. Nov 1998. *Bruce Mactavish*. **268. 2nd-winter**. Many show pale grey saddle at this age, combined with barred coverts. Note grey-shaded primaries with broad white edges. Newfoundland, Canada. 30 Nov 1998. *Bruce Mactavish*. **269. 2nd-winter**. Bill often with extensive dark markings at this age, unlike typical 2nd-winter *glaucoides*. Newfoundland, Canada. 26 Nov 1996. *Bruce Mactavish*. **270. 2nd-winter.** Bill sometimes almost completely dark at this age. Note grey primary tips surrounded by white. Newfoundland, Canada. 7 Nov 1999. *Bruce Mactavish*.

222

Kumlien's Gull *Larus glaucoides kumlieni.* **271. 2nd-winter.** Note tail and primary pattern, which excludes any *glaucoides.* Note adult in background. Newfoundland, Canada. 13 Jan 1993. *Bruce Mactavish.* **272. 2nd-winter.** Note dark tail-bar against pale rump, and streaked pattern to outer primaries. Newfoundland, Canada. 13 Jan 1993. *Bruce Mactavish.* **273. 3rd-winter.** Note extensive dark markings on bill in otherwise adult-like plumage. Wing-tip pattern typical for *kumlieni.* Newfoundland, Canada. 23 Dec 1999. *Bruce Mactavish.* **274. 3rd-winter.** A more moult-retarded bird, showing areas of barred coverts and tertials. Newfoundland, Canada. 15 Dec 1998. *Bruce Mactavish.* **275. Adult winter.** Note darkish eye unlike *glaucoides* as well as dark grey primary pattern. Newfoundland, Canada. 10 Jan 2000. *Bruce Mactavish.*

Kumlien's Gull *Larus glaucoides kumlieni*. **276. Adult winter**. A pale-eyed individual, with very faint grey pattern in outermost primaries. Newfoundland, Canada. 6 Dec 1993. *Bruce Mactavish*. **277. Adult winter**. Pale grey wing-tip with broad white tips, combined with Common Gull-like shape and long wings makes identification of certain individuals straightforward. Newfoundland, Canada. 9 Dec 1996. *Bruce Mactavish*. **278. Adult winter**. Compare with 279 and note that eyes might be as pale as in *glaucoides*. Newfoundland, Canada. Nov 1998. *Bruce Mactavish*. **279. Adult winter**. Eyes sometimes all-dark unlike *glaucoides*, but identical to majority of Thayer's Gull. Newfoundland, Canada. 20 Dec 1998. *Bruce Mactavish*.

Kumlien's Gull *Larus glaucoides kumlieni*. **280. Adult winter**. Note dark slate pattern in outer 5 primaries. Similar to Thayer's Gull, which shows blackish pattern to 6 outermost primaries and more extensive dark coloration in outer 2 primaries. Compare photos 299-302. Newfoundland, Canada. 13 Jan 1993. *Bruce Mactavish*. **281. Adult + 3rd-winter**. Note wing-tip pattern variation. Newfoundland, Canada. 13 Jan 1993. *Bruce Mactavish*. **282. Adult winter**. Some *kumlieni* just show faint dark markings in outer primaries, and are thus easily separated as soon as the larger hybrids with Glaucous Gull are excluded. Newfoundland, Canada. 13 Jan 1993. *Bruce Mactavish*. **283. Adult winter**. An example of a bird with the least amount of dark markings in wing-tip, but still outside the range of the totally unmarked adult *glaucoides*. Halland, Sweden. Feb 2000. *Lasse Olsson*.

225

17. THAYER'S GULL

Larus thayeri (W. S. Brooks, 1915, Buchanan Bay, Ellesmere Island)

Plates 33–34, Photos 284–302

IDENTIFICATION Length 57–64cm, wingspan 137–148cm. A medium-sized Nearctic gull, often regarded as a subspecies of Iceland. Taxonomic status not fully clarified; specific status retained here (following del Hoyo *et al.* 1996, AOU 1998). By contrast with Iceland *kumlieni* it shows a rather constant wing pattern and distinctive first-year and adult plumages. While many *are* readily identifiable, showing combination of Iceland Gull size/jizz and American Herring Gull plumage, a number of ID factors must be taken into account, especially given the large (but still unclarified) gull hybridisation along the American W Coast, and the still incompletely understood variation in Iceland race *kumlieni*.

Thayer's is smaller than American Herring with a more rounded head, shorter bill with gently rounded tip and less pronounced gonys-angle. The eyes are larger and usually dark. These features, plus the deep breast and shorter legs create a jizz similar to Iceland Gull. Wing-tip projection falls between American Herring and Iceland Gull. In flight similar to Iceland with similar deep breast. Although size and structure important, it must be noted that large male Thayer's and female American Herring are closer to each other especially in head-/bill-shape, but American Herring rarely approaches gentler look of Thayer's.

Largest ID problems are (a) Kumlien's Iceland, (b) small female American Herring Gull and (c) some American W Coast hybrids. While Glaucous-winged × Western hybrids may have plumage almost identical to Thayer's, they are larger with heavier, bulbous-tipped bill (with better-marked gonys-angle), smaller, beady eyes placed higher on head, and shorter wings. *Most problematic are small American Herring × Glaucous-winged hybrids* (which see under Glaucous-winged): ID must involve all specific characters, and any bird with just one atypical character is better left unidentified.

Adult has grey upperparts, similar to or a shade darker than American Herring. The outer wing has less extensive blackish, as most of inner webs are pale, often melting into white mirrors at P10 and P9 to create blackish streaks on upperwing. There is regularly a black subterminal bar behind white mirrors on P9–10. Most show full dark subterminal bar on P5 (but often incomplete and frequently lacking). From below, primaries are translucent with dark trailing edge to P6–10 (pale inner webs shading to dark outer webs), creating unique combination of 'Herring upperwing and Glaucous underwing'. In settled birds, tail-tip falls between outermost 3–4 exposed white primary tips. Eye varies from dark through dark-spotted to almost as pale as in Herring, and is surrounded by purple to pinkish-red orbital ring. Bill often greenish-tinged in winter. Legs pale raspberry, usually darker and brighter than in American Herring. In **summer**, head is white. In **winter**, brown-washed head creates brownish hood and neck-sides,

often forming solid areas on especially hindneck and neck-sides. Bill greenish-yellow with paler tip of upper mandible, but at most faint subterminal markings.

American Herring Gull generally larger with flatter forehead, more angled hindneck, shorter wing and longer legs. The bill is heavier with more pronounced gonys-angle. The upperparts are similar to Thayer's, but the wing-tip is more extensively dark (jet-black), looking more fully black with isolated white mirrors, just rarely with extension of white mirror onto inner webs of P9(10). Adult shows very pale eyes, shared with just a minority of Thayer's, set off by yellow to orange orbital ring. The bill is generally yellower with dark subterminal markings, and the legs generally duller fleshy.

Tricky large gulls resembling Thayer's derive from American Herring × Glaucous Gull and American Herring × Glaucous-winged hybridisation. These are large with shorter wings (tail-tip falling between outermost 2–3 exposed white primary tips), lack greenish tinge to bill, and have deeper, more solid dark primary pattern with dark well visible even from below, though some match Thayer's on this aspect. In hybrid Glaucous-winged × American Herring other Glaucous-winged characters often evident, such as even more washed-out head pattern in winter, greyish primary pattern with white mirror on P10 only, larger, deeper-yellow bill with much more swollen tip, more sloping forehead and smaller eye situated higher on head. The upperparts are generally darker than in Thayer's. Most problematic are certain Glaucous-winged × American Herring hybrids in which wing-tip may look almost identical to Thayer's, although with more extensive dark on P9–10, normally traces of yellow in orbital ring and more solid dark markings on bill. Certain Herring Gull and American Herring Gull of northern populations may show wing-tip pattern similar to Thayer's Gull, but normally have more extensive black on wing-tip with larger amount of visible dark from below. The orbital ring never matches the dark purplish-tinge of Thayer's and the eyes are pale. These Herring Gulls are normally the largest within their species, so most should be identifiable on structure.

Iceland race *kumlieni* is similar in size and structure to Thayer's, but on average with rounder head and finer bill. More important, the upperparts are paler grey and adult wing-tip pattern greyer and more limited, with most of inner webs being white. Note that younger adult *kumlieni* may show more dark on wing-tip, thus matching Thayer's. But any fully adult of these gulls with both black subterminal band on P10 and complete dark subterminal bar on P5 is Thayer's (Howell & Elliott 2001, own study of skins). The grey zone is represented by birds showing complex blackish-grey wing-tip (including dark grey outer web to P9–10) onto white mirrors and dark markings onto P5–6, a pattern seen in a small minority of *kumlieni* (as well as in putative hybrids between the two). Such birds are impossible to identify outside their normal range, but are few (more regular Great Lakes): the average *kumlieni* – with their narrow grey streaks on wing-tip, extensive white inner webs to primaries, and pearly grey upperparts – are readily identifiable. In more *kumlieni* than Thayer's the eyes are pale as in the herring gulls, but eye coloration is a rather unreliable feature.

First-year combines gentle jizz of Iceland with plumage of pale, washed-out American Herring. Bill black, but from Dec often with dull purple base. Often shows unmarked dark eye-mask, pale face and longish-looking lores. Plumage mud- to greyish-brown, paler and often frostier than in Herring and appearing velvety, lacking streaks especially on head of American Herring and their hybrids with Glaucous-winged. The palest birds are as dark as *kumlieni*. Wing and tail pattern are most important: outer webs of primaries and secondary centres brown, slightly darker than rest of upperparts, including greyish-brown-centred tertials, concolorous with or just slightly darker than rest of upperparts. Folded wing-tip brown with pale fringes, creating rows of chevrons. Pale and worn spring birds have wing-tip concolorous with rest of upperparts; most have outer primaries and secondaries slightly darker than rest of plumage (like washed-out American Herring). In flight, wing-tip pale with dark streaks – from below translucent silvery with dark tern-like trailing edge, a pattern only matched by the darkest *kumlieni*, very pale/worn American Herrings and some hybrids. Some have dark spots or streaks near tips of inner primaries. Brown secondary bar appears solid, as a dark rectangle, despite secondaries having pale edges/inner webs. Tail mainly brown, normally darker than rest of upperparts and appearing rather uniform. If present, mottling restricted to bases of P4–6 with midtail being uniform (see *kumlieni*). The brown, pale-edged mantle and scapulars often show diagnostic darker U-markings (or shaft-streaks), not present in American Herring. Legs generally dark rosy-pink, darker than in American Herring.

Juvenile plumage retained into midwinter. If any moult takes place, mantle and scapulars of **first-winter** contrasts with juvenile coverts. Head brown and bill black; from midwinter, face becomes paler and bill often develops pale lower mandible.

Iceland *kumlieni* generally has rounder head and longer wings than Thayer's. Plumage generally paler with pale, normally well-barred tertials, pale secondaries and paler wing-tip with dark outer webs to P6–10. Folded wing-tip paler with dark restricted to V-markings on outer primaries and sometimes dark shading behind tip. Tail-bar paler grey, typically narrower and slightly pale-mottled, especially on outer rectrices; often appears unpatterned on midtail (unlike most Thayer's). Bill often blackish, but more frequently with paler base than in Thayer's, and some have bicoloured bill. See Iceland Gull *kumlieni* for finer ID points. Note that second-winter Iceland nominate *glaucoides* may show pale head with dark mask as in first-winter Thayer's Gull, but has bicoloured bill, some pale grey on mantle, uneven upperpart pattern and often pale eyes.

First-year American Herring is usually larger with less gentle expression, and is more uniform greyish-brown with darker flight feathers (unlike Thayer's, outer primaries solid dark from below apart from in worn birds from midwinter), tertials and tail. Fresh primaries have narrow white tips, disappearing in early winter but often present well into spring in western populations. From Dec, bill normally bicoloured and head often white in strong contrast to brown body. First-year Western, Glaucous-winged and their hybrids are normally larger with stronger, bulbous-tipped bill and flatter crown. In hybrids, bill, primary- and tail pattern may be as in Thayer's: generally, Thayer's has broader white Vs on primary tips (often covering entire fringe in congeners). Trickiest are small female hybrids, which may be similar in jizz to Thayer's, but plumage generally darker and colder brown with weak dark upperpart-markings. Tail sometimes paler-mottled at base. Hybrid Herring × Glaucous Gull larger than Thayer's; plumage may be similar but bill normally with strong Glaucous influence: pink with black tip.

In spring plumage appears bleached, sometimes with uniform pale primaries without obvious pale fringes. Seems to moult directly into second-winter, so bleaching is caused by wear instead of moult.

Second-winter similar to first-winter, but head and underbody paler and mantle grey in contrast to pale brown, slightly mottled upperwing. Darker secondary bar, P6–10 and solid brown tail-bar (often darker and more solid than in first-winter). Bill acquires broader pinkish base and dark tip or subterminal bar. Eyes dark, but in 10% pale (J. R. King *in litt.*). Certain birds similar to first-years, but with fainter pattern in tertials and secondaries (A. Jaramillo *in litt.*) Identification at this age from larger gulls based on characters outlined under first-winter. Glaucous-winged Gull typically remains black-billed and has dingier brown overall plumage; Iceland and American Herring Gulls become pale-eyed (apart from certain *kumlieni*) from age of one year.

Second-summer as second-winter, but head, body and coverts fade to whitish, thus grey saddle more conspicuous and flight feathers/tail very bleached, although brownish pattern should still be apparent.

Third-winter similar to adult, but primary pattern is washed-out brownish, white normally restricted to mirror on P10, some tertials are brown-centred and primary coverts darker. Secondaries and tail often with grey shading; when present, grey tail-bar contrasts well with white rump. Bill similar to adult, but generally paler pinkish with traces of black markings and orange gonys-spot.

Third-summer/fourth-winter similar to adult, but pattern on wing-tip slightly browner and more diffuse and primary coverts dark. May show weak dark barring on undertail-coverts, dark spotting on tail and dark spots on bill.

VOICE Long-call very like American Herring, but a little higher pitched (J. R. King and A. Jaramillo *in litt.*).

MOULT (skins in AMNH, LACM, MCZ, USNM, UZM, pers. obs., Howell & King 1999).
Adult moult to **winter** plumage complete May–Dec. P1–4 May–Jun, P5 late Jun–early Jul, P6–7(8) late Jul–late Aug, P7–9 Sep, P9–10 mid-Oct–late Dec (mid-Jan). Head and body Sep.

PLATE 33. THAYER'S GULL *Larus thayeri*

A medium-sized to large N American gull, breeding in N Canada. Winters along American W Coast S to N Mexico, vagrant to Japan and W Europe. Structurally rather similar to Iceland Gull; compared to American Herring smaller and gentler-looking with more rounded head, weaker bill lacking marked gonys-angle, and slightly longer wings. Coastal, occurring with other gulls along beaches and in seaports. Plumages often similar to American Herring, but also to Iceland race *kumlieni,* and certain American Herring × Glaucous-winged Gull hybrids. Range of overlap with Iceland *kumlieni* poorly known, and not yet fully understood.

1. **Juvenile** (Aug–Apr) Normally retains most of juvenile plumage into first-winter. Darkest birds dull greyish-brown, appearing rather uniform velvety on head and underbody. Juvenile mantle, scapulars and tertials mud-brown with paler edges; tertial centres concolorous with upperparts and paler than dark brown wing-tip, which shows narrow white edges, creating line of white arrowheads. Tail greyish-brown to dark brown. Bill black, often with slight greyish-red base from midwinter.

2. **Juvenile/first-winter** (Dec–Apr) Some moult limited into first-winter, showing narrower brown markings on mantle and scapulars. Note anchor-shaped dark markings on scapulars, velvety grey head and underbody and broader pale bars on greater coverts. Tertials in this individual paler than in 1, paler than wing-tip.

3. **First-winter** (Dec–Apr) Some become paler throughout winter, although rarely so pale as in Iceland. Legs often raspberry-pink.

4. **Second-winter** (Aug–Apr) Paler head and upperparts than first-years, mantle often a mixture of greyish-brown and dark-centred feathers. Tertials with brown centres, contrasting with darker wing-tip, as in first-year showing broad white feather-edges. Bill fleshy with black tip and cutting edges.

5. **Second-winter** (Aug–Apr) A more advanced individual, showing grey saddle (and some coverts) against finely patterned greyish-brown coverts. Tail and wing-tip markings similar to first-year but, with wear, primaries often paler, sometimes appearing whitish on outer primaries. Legs raspberry-pink. Eyes dark.

6. **Third-winter** (Aug–Apr) Similar to adult winter, but bill duller with dark subterminal markings, upperwing with some greyish-brown feathers admixed, tail still grey-patterned and wing-tip with narrower white primary tips.

7. **Adult winter** (Aug–Apr) Adult shows mid-grey upperparts (typically darker than American Herring and Iceland Gulls) and blackish wing-tip with broad white primary tips (black and white often seemingly in equal amount). Head-markings more diluted than in Iceland and American Herring, often creating solid, darkish hood. Bill greenish-tinged yellow. Eye very variable, but often dark.

8. **Adult summer** (Apr–Aug/Sep) Head white. Eye usually dark, but 10% show paler yellow iris. Orbital ring purplish-red. Legs deep raspberry-pink.

Juvenile

3. First-winter

2. Juvenile/first-winter

4. Second-winter

5. Second-winter

6. Third-winter

7. Adult winter

8. Adult summer

PLATE 34. THAYER'S GULL *Larus thayeri*

Smaller, with rounder head and shorter bill than American Herring, similar-shaped to Iceland Gull.

1.　**Juvenile** (Aug–Apr) Greyish-brown with solid darker outer webs to outer primaries, in some contrast to paler inner primaries, creating pale window on outer wing. Secondaries dark-centred. Rump heavily dark-barred and tail greyish-brown, appearing uniform at distance (but may show faint pale markings along edges and at base). Bill black. A rather dark but typical individual.

2.　**Juvenile/first-winter** (Aug–Apr) A paler individual, appearing similar to Iceland Gull *kumlieni*, but with darker outer webs and tips to outer primaries, more solid dark secondary bar and broader, more uniform greyish-brown tail.

3.　**First-winter** (Aug–Apr) Underwing with pale silvery-grey flight feathers, showing dark trailing edge to outer primaries (recalling pattern of underwing in many terns); this pattern rarely shared with Iceland *kumlieni*. Head and underparts more uniform than in *kumlieni*, appearing velvety, but often with paler hind-collar through wear in first-winter. Note neat proportions and rounder head with weaker bill than in American Herring, which furthermore shows browner, more solid dark wing-tip, better contrasting with pale inner primaries.

4.　**Second-winter** (Aug–Apr) Similar to first-year, but inner primaries paler, tail with broader pale base; rump paler with narrower greyish-brown bars. Mantle often grey and bill bicoloured.

5.　**Third-winter** (Aug–Apr) Upperwing grey with brown-centred primary coverts and slightly more diffuse, brownish-tinged pattern on primaries compared to adult. Tail still with extensive grey bar. Bill fleshy with black subterminal markings.

6.　**Adult winter** (Aug–Apr) Adult shows slightly darker grey upperparts than American Herring and Iceland Gulls with blackish-grey streaking on outer wing, covering 5–6 outer primaries. Pattern streakier, less solid (and often slightly paler, not pure black) than in American Herring. In winter head with extensive brown markings.

7.　**Adult winter** (Aug–Apr) Compared to 6, this individual shows less extensive dark markings on outer wing, covering only 5 outer primaries and more extensive white on P9–10; these features are shared by Iceland Gull *kumlieni*, but markings darker, almost black (see also pp. 29–30).

8.　**Adult summer** (Apr–Aug) Head white in summer. On underwing, dark pattern less extensive than on upperwing, appearing as dark streaks, sometimes confined to trailing edge of wing.

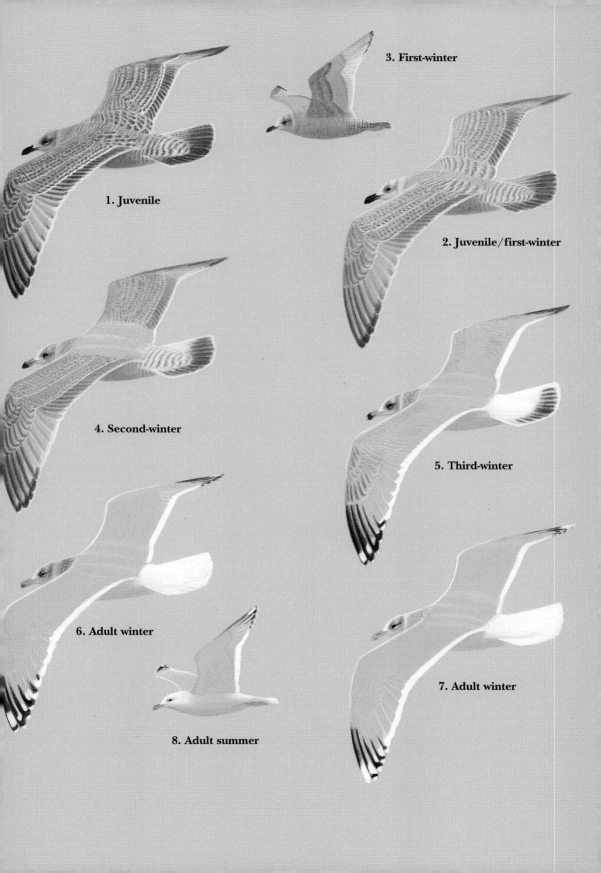

1. Juvenile

3. First-winter

2. Juvenile/first-winter

4. Second-winter

5. Third-winter

6. Adult winter

7. Adult winter

8. Adult summer

Adult moult to **summer** plumage partial Mar–May, including head, and some feathers on body and (sometimes all) coverts. Most have winter head when leaving wintering sites, attaining white head late Mar, but winter head may be present into early May.

Juvenile retains juvenile plumage into late winter/early spring (as in long-distance migrant American Herring Gull), but moult later and more restricted. >90% retain juvenile head, body, mantle and scapulars to late Dec/Jan; may moult a few scapulars (sometimes minor parts of head, mantle, back, rump and underparts) from Dec. Most into Mar had just moulted mantle/scapulars (in most advanced 60–90%) and just 1–5% of feathers on head, neck, chest and flanks. Some still juvenile (and not very heavily worn) Mar/Apr, when head/body moulted directly into **second-winter.** Subsequent moults probably similar to adult moult, but generally earlier. Typically, moult to **second-winter** including most of mantle. Primaries Mar–early Sep.

DESCRIPTION

Adult Mantle, scapulars and upperwing medium grey (Kodak Grey Scale 4.5–6), generally a shade darker than American Herring, and sometimes with a bluish tinge. P10 0–10mm >P9. Primaries with 10–25mm white tips. P5–10 with dusky to slaty-black markings (Kodak Grey Scale 14.5–17 on outer webs, with wear browner). P10 with 35–70mm white tip or mirror, sometimes extending along inner web to meet grey base. P9 with 20–40mm white mirror, often merging into white on inner web, forming complete extension of mirror across inner webs, narrowest across black extension of outer web behind white mirror (known as '*thayeri* pattern'). Outer web with 85–110mm black distal part. P8 pale grey with blackish outer web and 25–110mm blackish to inner web. Shows large white tongue on inner web between grey bases and black tip. P7 grey with 40–70mm black subterminal spot on outer web, 20–30mm on inner web near tip; white tongue between black and grey as on P8. P6 grey with 25–40mm black subterminal spot near tip, often reduced to outer web only. P5 grey with varying black subterminal spot; from 20mm on both webs to just faint dark marking near tip of especially outer web; lack of dark markings on P5 seen in 25% (Howell & Elliott 2001). P1–4 and secondaries grey with distinct white tips, P4 rarely with dark markings. Marginal coverts white. White tertial fans deeper and wider than in American Herring. Underparts, rump and tail white. Iris variable, generally darker than American Herring Gull. Iris colour of 283 birds Dec–Mar was: five uniform dark brown, 35 medium brown, 63 pale brown/honey-coloured, 74 dusky, greenish, dark yellow or amber with extensive dark spotting, 49 pale greenish or yellowish with brown markings, 44 pale greenish or yellowish with little or no brown mottling, 13 pale yellow, as in American Herring Gull. Eye-coloration may vary geographically; more research needed (King & Howell 1999, Howell & Elliott 2001). Orbital ring dark red, purple or deep pink. Bill yellow with red to orange-red gonys-spot and often ivory tip. Nostril narrow and slit-like; depth at distal edge 1.1–1.7mm, length 9.9–11.8mm. Legs raspberry-pink to purplish.

A slight variation in wing-tip pattern noted (see also Howell & Elliott 2001); probably age- or sex-related, with oldest males generally showing least dark.

Adult summer (Feb/Mar–Sep) Head white. Bill bright yellow to orange-yellow with red gonys-spot. Orbital ring purple.

Adult winter (Sep–Apr) Head white with brown to buff streaks or mottling, creating brownish hood, often including chest and upper breast. Pattern denser and more waved than in most American Herring, especially on breast-sides; similar to Glaucous-winged. Bill, orbital ring and legs duller than in summer; bill often with greenish-yellow base contrasting with yellow tip of upper mandible; 10% with faint dark subterminal markings (Howell & Elliott 2001). Orbital ring dark pink.

Juvenile (fledging–Feb) Head and underbody brown to greyish-buff, shading to whitish on chin, lores and forehead. Feathering around eye often darker uniform, forming eye-mask; sometimes with dark streaks or smudging around eye. Eye-crescent dusky. Mantle, back and scapulars greyish-brown with dark subterminal markings and sandy to whitish fringes (frosty when fresh), creating chequered or scaly pattern; scapulars often with darker subterminal crescents near tip and dark shaft-streaks. Tertials greyish-brown with pale fringes, broadening towards tips; sometimes with paler subterminal spots and dark subterminal crescents behind tip, rarely bars; in extreme cases matching Iceland *kumlieni* (may be hybrid character). Upperwing-coverts greyish-brown with dark spots, centres or chequering and whitish tips; central and inner greater coverts usually chequered (Garner & McGeehan 1998). Greater coverts sometimes pale with indistinct dark bars or dots, as in Great Black-backed Gull. Primary coverts greyish-brown with slightly paler inner webs. Rump white with dense brown bars, often broader than pale bars, as in American Herring. Primaries greyish-brown to dark brown with broad pale chevrons at tips, from below appearing silvery. P10 6–8mm up to 6–10mm >P9. P6–10 with dark brown to greyish-brown outer webs/tips and pale inner webs/fringes surrounding tip; P1–5 paler with inconspicuous darker outer webs, subterminal spots and sometimes tips. Primary coverts grey-brown with broad pale edges. Secondaries greyish-brown with paler fringes. Tail greyish-brown to brown, often with slight pale mottling near bases of rectrices (especially T4–6) and pale tips to all rectrices. T6 varies: some have white outer web to T6, others faint dark mottling and broader white spot near tip; darkest-patterned birds have dark outer web with 2–5 small pale spots on basal part (sometimes similar pattern on T4–5). Outertail sometimes with paler brown 'extra bar' behind tip; tail looks rather uniform in field. Underbody pale greyish-brown, appearing velvety, but sometimes with faint dark bars or spots on breast-sides and flanks or dense dark spots on whole underbody. Undertail-coverts whitish with brown bars. Axillaries and underwing-coverts greyish-brown with indistinct dark mottling. Iris dark brown. Bill black, rarely with grey to fleshy base to lower (sometime both) mandible; sometimes with extreme pale tip to upper mandible. Gape flesh. Legs fleshy to pinkish.

First-winter (Jan–May) as juvenile, but head and body (especially forehead and hindneck) generally slightly paler and dusky eye-mask more conspicuous. From midwinter, new mantle and scapulars greyish with brown bars or spots, forming irregular barring. From Feb/Mar coverts (especially greater coverts) and primary tips fade. Bill black, from Jan normally with dull purplish or greyish base and from Mar with pale tip (J. R. King *in litt.*).

'First-summer' (Apr–Sep) as first-winter, but head and body whitish to greyish-buff with reduced dark pattern. Mantle and scapulars with irregular and inconspicuous brown bars. Wing and tail fades to pale brown. Bill-base fleshy to pink and tip pale.

Second-winter (Aug–Mar) Head and body whitish-pink, usually with extensive brownish-grey smudging and mottling around head, hindneck and especially belly. Mantle, back and scapulars grey; sometimes a few pale, slightly barred feathers of first-year type present. Rarely entire upperparts consist of creamy, heavily brown-barred feathers (J. R. King *in litt.*). Lower scapulars, wing-coverts and tertials pale brown (at most with indistinct darker patterning with broad pale fringes), creating washed-out look. Rump whitish, sometimes with a few dark markings. Flight feathers similar to juvenile/first-winter, but dark areas often darker brown, darker than rest of upperparts. Tail with white base and solid dark subterminal bar, usually blacker than in first-years. Iris dark brown to golden-brown; rarely yellow (King & Howell 1999). Bill pink with variable black subterminal markings, sometimes covering most of bill. Extreme tip often ivory.

Second-summer (Mar–Sep) as second-winter, but head and underparts whitish to pale buff. Mantle and scapulars usually grey, creating strong saddle against bleached upperwing-coverts. Outer primaries, secondaries and tail may bleach to pale greyish-buff. Orbital ring sometimes reddish as in adult. Bill similar to second-winter, but base may become yellow.

Third-winter (Sep–Apr) similar to adult winter, but underparts and tail-coverts often with some dark mottling and tertials with some dark markings. Wing pattern similar to adult, but brownish and more diffuse;

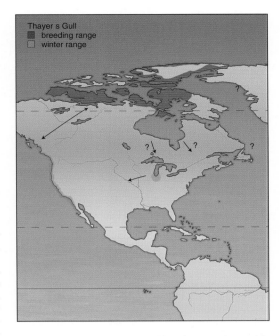

Thayer s Gull
■ breeding range
□ winter range

often with white mirror on P10 only, sometimes with pale on inner web of P9 much reduced. Primary coverts dark-patterned. Upperwing-coverts often with brownish wash, sometimes faintly brownish-flecked. Tail white, often with uneven greyish to blackish spots or patches, sometimes forming irregular subterminal bar. Bill as adult, but usually greener (sometimes greyish-yellow or pinkish) with black subterminal marks, often as complete bar.

Third-summer (Mar–Sep) as third-winter, but head and underparts white or faintly spotted or streaked, and faded brown areas on wing and tail. Bare parts often as adult.

Fourth-winter/summer as adult, but sometimes with pale brown wash to wings and sometimes tail and narrow dark subterminal marks on bill.

THAYER'S GULL Four-year gull. Breeds Arctic N America, winters mainly along American W Coast. Size and structure similar to Iceland Gull (and many difficult to identify from latter's darker race *kumlieni*), but some with flatter forecrown, heavier bill and slightly shorter wings, thus more like American Herring.

Adult has slightly darker upperparts than Iceland Gull (and even American Herring) and blackish markings on wing-tip reaching P5 as full dark bar. Pattern from above streaked, with white mirrors on P9–10 usually prominent, as white inner webs to P9–10 often broken by black subterminal markings. From below, underwing white with dark trailing edge to outer hand. Eye varies from pale (as in Iceland) to dark. Legs pinkish, often with a rosy tinge. In **winter** (Oct–Mar) head with brownish waving or streaks, often prominent on neck- and breast-sides. Bill often greenish-tinged in winter.

Juvenile (Jul–Feb) greyish-brown, appearing velvety on head and underbody with faint pale scaling on upperparts, on scapulars often with dark subterminal bars. Upperwing with darker outer webs to P6–10 and dark secondaries. Settled birds show brown, pale-edged primaries; tertials slightly darker. Rump heavily dark-barred against rather uniform mud-brown tail. Bill dark, but develops paler base from midwinter. Only moult limited into **first-winter**, at most scattered feathers on mantle and scapulars.

Second-year similar to first-year, but with grey saddle and pale, black-tipped bill.

Third-year similar to adult, but wing-tip brownish (often with more extensive dark than in adult) and bill duller with more extensive dark markings.

Hybrids Hybridises with Iceland *kumlieni* to an unknown degree; reported from Southampton Island, islands of N Hudson Bay, and S Baffin Island (Gaston & Decker 1985, Snell 1989). More research needed concerning current situation.

DISTRIBUTION AND MIGRATION Total population 4,000–6,000 pairs. Breeds Banks Island to N Hudson Bay and arctic NE Canada. Range extension since 1900; formerly, breeding restricted to west Canada High Arctic, but since then expanded throughout High Arctic Canada (Weir *et al.* 2000). Formerly bred Thule, N Greenland (1920s and 1930s; since then rare summer visitor). Largest population Foxe Basin, Frozen Strait/Lyon Inlet. Breeds on sea-cliffs. Outside breeding season founds in fishing harbours, rubbish dumps, freshwater lakes and flooded land, and sometimes on fields, behaving like Ring-billed Gull.

Long-distance migrant. Following breeding season migrates S to W, reaching Pacific coast of Alaska (first-years also Chukchi Sea), eventually heading S to main wintering range around British Columbia and Washington. Generally, adults winter more to the N than younger birds. Pacific winter population 20,000; max. 2,000 Victoria (British Columbia) and N Baja California, where flocks up to 120 Dec–Jan; mainly immatures. Rather common Great Lakes, e.g. 800–1,000 Lake Michigan, common S to 120 miles S of Chicago. Probably regular E coast S to New Jersey, and Japan (where a few recorded each year). Irregular Louisiana. Vagrant SE USA, Mexican Gulf, Korea, Pribilofs and W Palearctic (for latter see below) (Monroe 1988, 1989, Brazil 1991, Zimmermann & Jones 1991, del Hoyo *et al.* 1996, Weir *et al.* 2000, Boertmann 2001, J. R. King, I. Idzikowski, M. Retter & A. Jaramillo *in litt.*).

In W Palearctic vagrant: Ireland 4 (1 adult and 3 first-years), Norway 1, Iceland 1, Denmark 1 (Wilson 1990, McGeehan & Garner 1997, McGeehan & Millington 1998, Lonergan 1999, Mjøs & Garner 2000, Y. Kolbeinsson *in litt.*); further British claims not accepted—possible hybrid Thayer's × Kumlien's or very dark Kumlien's (Kilbane 1989, Hogg 1991).

MEASUREMENTS Lengths in mm; weights in g. Own data based on skins in AMNH, LACM, MCZ, MVZ, NHM, NNH, NRK, USNM, UZM, ZMA, ZMO. Canada, W USA, Greenland. Included in adults are a few second-winters.

WING

Adult male	402–442 (419.9)	40
Adult female	384–430 (403.3)	51
First-year male	387–424 (406.5)	15
First-year female	365–414 (390.4)	21

BILL

Adult male	46.8–55.5 (50.5)	38
Adult female	44.0–54.2 (47.8)	57
First-year male	40.5–50.0 (45.8)	15
First-year female	38.3–48.3 (42.8)	20

BILL DEPTH AT GONYS

Adult male	15.6–18.8 (17.5)	38
Adult female	14.4–18.5 (15.8)	57
First-year male	12.3–16.4 (14.3)	15
First-year female	9.8–16.0 (13.5)	20

BILL DEPTH AT BASE OF BILL

Adult male	16.8–20.4 (18.4)	38
Adult female	14.1–18.8 (16.6)	57
First-year male	13.4–18.5 (15.8)	15
First-year female	10.9–16.6 (14.1)	20

GONYS LENGTH

Adult male	13.2–16.4 (14.9)	38
Adult female	11.4–16.8 (14.0)	57
First-year male	8.6–16.4 (12.1)	15
First-year female	9.2–14.7 (11.7)	20

TARSUS

Adult male	58.8–68.8 (62.6)	38
Adult female	52.1–68.6 (58.4)	57
First-year male	57.5–62.4 (61.1)	14
First-year female	48.8–60.8 (56.6)	20

Weight Two adult females 712–1,002. First-winter female 1,000, second-winter female 770 (skins in MCZ, USNM).

Thayer's Gull *Larus thayeri*. **284. Juvenile.** Size and jizz similar to Iceland Gull, but note darker, more velvety overall impression with stronger dark markings on upperparts and darker tertial centres and primaries. Often appears like a small and pale American Herring Gull. Ventura, California, USA. 20 Dec 1997. *Don DesJardin.* **285. Juvenile.** Note tertial centres paler than primaries as well as all-dark bill. Santa Barbara, California, USA. 4 Jan 1993. *Don DesJardin.* **286. Juvenile** (pale individual) with similar-aged Glaucous-winged Gull. Although the plumages of the two species are rather similar, the jizz differs strongly. Port Hueneme, California, USA. 17 Jan 2001. *Don DesJardin.* **287. Juvenile moulting into 1st-winter.** Most retain mainly juvenile plumage throughout winter, with scattered new mantle feathers from mid-winter. Note slender bill, rather large eyes and long-winged appearance compared to American Herring. Tertials concolorous with mantle, paler than primaries. Sacramento, California, USA. 29 Jan 2000. *Klaus Malling Olsen.* **288. Juvenile/1st-winter.** A rather pale individual, similar to Iceland Gull *kumlieni*, but note uniform-looking dark tail and darker wing-tip, with narrow pale edge along tips. San Diego, California, USA. 12 Feb 2000. *Klaus Malling Olsen*

Thayer' s Gull *Larus thayeri.* **289. Juvenile.** A rather dark and typical individual with wing-pattern similar to Herring. Note velvety, uniform-looking underparts and paler chin, throat and neck-sides. Hanstholm, Denmark. 19 Feb 2002. *Kent Olsen.* **290. Juvenile/1st-winter.** Note uniform tail and dark secondary bar. Compare tail and wing-pattern to Iceland *kumlieni* photo 264. Oakland, California, USA. 26 Jan 2000. *Klaus Malling Olsen.* **291. Juvenile/1st-winter.** Tail and rump pattern as a pale version of American Herring Gull. Point Reyes, California, USA. 30 Jan 2000. *Klaus Malling Olsen.* **292. 1st-winter Thayer's or Kumlien's Gull.** A tricky, pale individual. While tail-pattern looks good for Thayer's Gull, albeit with rather extensive pale bases to rectrices, wing-pattern looks paler, within range of *kumlieni*, but also within Thayer's. Connecticut, USA. Feb 1998. *Julian R. Hough.* **293. 1st-winter.** Note silvery cast to undersurface of primaries. Lake Natoma, California, USA. 29 Jan 2000. *Klaus Malling Olsen.* **294. 2nd-winter with 2nd-winter American Herring Gull, small bird.** Jizz very similar, but compare differences in pattern on underparts, coverts, tertials and primaries. Point Reyes, California, USA. 26 Jan 2000. *Klaus Malling Olsen.* **295. 2nd-winter.** Often similar to 1st-years, but note grey saddle. Compare with *kumlieni*, photos 271-272. California. USA. Feb. *Paul Doherty.* **296. 3rd-winter.** Wing-tip similar to adult, but with more diffuse pattern. Note extensive dark tail-markings. California, USA. Feb. *Paul Doherty.* **297. 3rd-winter.** As adult, but note slight dark pattern on primary coverts. California, USA. Feb. *Paul Doherty.* **298. Adult winter.** Note plumage similar to American Herring, but note rounded head, darkish-looking eye and rather slender, greenish-tinged bill. In background, juvenile and adults. Point Reyes, California, USA. 30 Jan 2000. *Klaus Malling Olsen.*

236

295

296

297

298

Thayer' s Gull *Larus thayeri*. **299. Adult winter**. Note pattern of especially P9-10. Background: Mew Gull. Point Reyes, California, USA. 30 Jan 2000. *Klaus Malling Olsen*. **300. Adult winter**. Point Reyes, California, USA. 30 Jan 2000. *Klaus Malling Olsen*. **301. Adult winter**. 6 outermost primaries show dark pattern. Compare Iceland Gull *kumlieni*, photos 280-282. P9-10 with more extensive dark coloration than in *kumlieni*, and white mirrors. California, USA. Feb. *Paul Doherty*. **302. Adult winter**. California, USA. Feb. *Paul Doherty*.

18. AMERICAN HERRING GULL

Larus smithsonianus (Coues, 1862, North America)   **Plates 35–36, Photos 303–321**

IDENTIFICATION Length 53–65cm, wingspan 120–150cm. The Nearctic counterpart of Herring Gull. Based on DNA, call, first-year plumages and geographical isolation, it is here treated separately from Herring. Sound recordings of American Herring played to Herring Gulls in W Europe elicited no response (Frings *et al.* 1958, Crochet 1998, Crochet *et al.* 2002).

American Herring is similar to Herring *argentatus*, thus often slightly larger and heavier with stronger bill, smaller head and flatter forehead than Herring Gull *argenteus*. There is a geographical variation in size and structure. The largest, flattest-crowned birds with the heaviest bills and the strongest legs are found in the NE of the range, where some recall Glaucous Gull in jizz. Many West Coast birds are rather small and neat with slender, narrow and parallel-edged bill, the tip being gently curved. In such birds the appearance is similar to Vega Gull.

Compared to Glaucous, Glaucous-winged and Western Gull, American Herring is slimmer with a rounder head, more centrally placed eyes and slenderer bill with less clear gonys-angle, and narrower tip. The head often peaks on the crown well behind eyes. When settled shows 3-4 equally spaced primary tips beyond tail. Identification from Herring often straightforward in first-years, but otherwise extremely difficult, and for older birds often impossible.

Adult similar to Herring Gull. The wing-tip is black with white mirror (sometimes tip) on P10 and sometimes P9. Compared to Herring *argenteus*, American Herring shows longer grey tongues on P5–8 (as in most Herring *argentatus*) extending beyond tertial tips in settled birds. The tongues are often striking in E Coast birds— when they are strongest they appear as 'string of pearls' as in Vega and Slaty-backed Gulls. Unlike most Herring *argentatus*, American Herring shows solid black markings on P5–6 (but see Geographical Variation). Certain NE American Herring combine extensive extension of white in P10 (with dark restricted along edges to divided dark bar behind tip) with narrow, but complete black W-markings on P5 (exceptional in Herring, in which dark markings on P5 incomplete in birds with large amount of white in outer primaries). Black markings on primary coverts and tertials sometimes present in adult (very rare in Herring). Orbital ring orange-yellow and eyes pale. Legs pink. In **summer** white-headed with strong orange-yellow bill and bright red gonys-spot. Some develop slight yellow tinge to tarsus at onset of breeding season. In **winter** head strongly brown-streaked/spotted, often as dark hood and mask against pale 'fish-eyes'. Head-markings vary from faint brown streaks to more solid, dark brown markings or streaks, forming conspicuous dark hood and breast-sides, most notable in E Coast populations. Winter head generally more washed out, less streaked than in Herring, with clear streaks mostly confined to hindneck and neck-sides. Bill duller, often with rather solid dark subterminal markings. Gonys spot smaller and more orange than in Herring.

Juvenile similar to Herring, but head and underbody more uniform, in some velvety dark brown. Rump extensively dark-barred on both surfaces and tail often all dark. In most typical birds, all-dark tail contrasts little with rump. Birds which combine uniform brown underbody with clearly barred rump and all-dark tail are easy to identify, the darkest looking like oversized Heermann's Gull. Close inspection of tail should reveal narrow pale bars along tail-edges and base in the majority, and a few birds show limited white mottling at tail-base, matching Herring race *argenteus* with the broadest tail-bar (Herring shows clearer contrast between dark tail-bar and pale tail-base and rump). Flight feathers dark with pale window on inner primaries, the latter dark-spotted, as in Herring or broader, as a larger number of primaries have pale inner webs; in the darkest birds it is almost lacking. Some are similar to Herring and Vega Gulls (especially W Coast birds) in being colder greyish-brown with more distinct head-streaks (normally confined to neck-sides), but tail/rump still diagnostic. Greater coverts often have solid dark centres, contrasting with faint pale bars near tips creating pale wing-bar in flight, similar to pattern of Lesser Black-backed Gull. In many birds, greater coverts have even dark and pale bars as in Herring, especially in W Coast birds, which may also show mainly white barring with 2–3 rows of dark dots, creating pattern similar to Great Black-backed, Vega Gull and Caspian Gull *mongolicus*. Juvenile mantle and scapulars dark, with narrow, often indistinct pale edges and notches to edges, especially in W Coast birds, retained well into winter. Tertials often solid dark, merely with narrow pale markings at tip, but in some notched with irregular pale edges (generally narrower than in Herring). Underwing-coverts darker and more uniform than in Herring and in better contrast to paler flight feathers, as in Lesser Black-backed and Yellow-legged race *atlantis*. Some show pale 'string of pearls' on outer wing, as in Vega and Slaty-backed; others just have the trailing edge to hand dark as in Thayer's. The bill is black, but may show paler base from fledging.

First-winter develops from autumn. Similar to juvenile, but (parts of) mantle and scapulars renewed. New feathers are dark-barred, and often intermix with retained juvenile feathers, especially scapulars. The head generally becomes paler, in strong contrast to solid dark ('woolly scarf') markings on hindneck and upper mantle. A few become white-headed in winter, in good contrast to rather uniform brown body. New feathers on breast-sides and flanks grey. In birds with brown juvenile plumage there is often a good contrast between these new grey feathers and retained brown (as in Laughing and Western Gull). Many also have darker leading edge to wing in contrast to paler median coverts, forming dark U around wing-bend, not dissimilar to winter Sanderling *Calidris alba*. In many, bill becomes pinkish with black tip as in Glaucous Gull; others remain dark-billed throughout first-winter. The easiest birds to identify are those with pink, black-

PLATE 35. AMERICAN HERRING GULL *Larus smithsonianus*

Abundant North American large gull; the Nearctic counterpart to Herring Gull. Vagrant E Pacific and Europe. A large 'masculine' gull with moderately rounded head (often looking smallish with flat crown), powerful bill, centrally placed eyes, full body and moderately long wings. Usually shows obvious tertial step; 4–5 primary tips reach beyond tail-tip. Less heavy than Western, Glaucous-winged and Great Black-backed Gulls, which show larger head with flatter crown, stronger, bulbous-tipped bill, smaller eyes situated higher in head, longer legs but shorter wing projection above tail (2–3 primary tips). Abundant, occurring in large flocks along sea-coasts, estuaries, garbage dumps and seaports. Attracted by human activity such as fishing ports. Flight rather slow with slow, powerful wingbeats.

1. **Juvenile** (Aug–Nov/Dec) Juveniles highly variable. Very dark, almost chocolate-brown birds, as shown here, are most frequent in E North America. They are identifiable alone on very dark, almost uniform brown head and body combined with dark-looking tail and heavy brown barring on rump and undertail-coverts (similar to juvenile Pomarine Skua/Jaeger *Stercorarius pomarinus*). Note also dark coverts and tertials, with only narrow white barring at tips.

2. **First-winter** (Oct–Apr) Darker birds retain most of darkish-looking plumage, but become slightly paler (noticeable on hindneck) with wear. New mantle and scapulars grey with dark subterminal markings of variable extent.

3. **First-winter** (Oct–Apr) A paler individual with greyish-brown head and underbody. While head, especially in W coast birds, may appear slightly streaked (thus similar to Herring and Vega Gulls), underbody still solid brown, appearing velvety, and tail all dark, with only faint pale spots along edges. Undertail-coverts distinctly dark-barred. Greater coverts and tertials in this individual patterned as much as Herring and Vega Gulls. Bill starts to become pale from late autumn.

4. **Worn first-winter/first-summer** (Dec–Jul) With wear, plumage gets paler and covert-markings fade to brown. Such pale birds less frequent along E Coast than W Coast. Almost identical to Herring Gull, but with more diluted pattern to underbody. Best identified on all-dark tail and transverse bars on rump and undertail-coverts. May show densely dark-spotted necklace.

5. **First-winter** (Oct–Apr) Some birds in winter develop almost uniform pale head against velvety brown body. Compare extent of markings on coverts with 2–4 and 6, especially dark-based greater coverts, which may form a dark line on midwing; also note the variation in markings on mantle and scapulars. Some acquire pink bill with black tip, as in first-year Glaucous Gull, in late autumn.

6. **Second-winter** (Aug–Apr) Some are greyer with tendency to slight barring on underparts. Head-markings are generally more diffuse and diluted than in Herring. Note darker midwing-bar caused by dark centres to greater coverts.

7. **Second-winter** (Oct–Apr) Shows variable amount of grey in mantle and scapulars (generally more than in Herring Gull nominate *argentatus*); sometimes none. Coverts more finely-patterned with larger number of pale bars than in first-year (but still looking darkish against paler lesser and median coverts). Underbody still rather diffusely grey-patterned. Wing-tip and tail similar to first-year; note blacker primaries with rounder white edges. Eye pale. Bill fleshy with dark subterminal markings. Hindneck dark-spotted.

8. **Third-winter** (Aug–Apr) Similar to adult, but with greyish-brown markings on greater coverts and tertials, narrower white primary tips, broad dark tail markings and more solid dark on bill.

9. **Fourth-winter** (Aug–Apr) Most similar to adult, but note dark markings on tertials, narrower white primary tips, dark tail markings and more solid dark markings on bill (which at this age often appears similar to adult). Note brown-patterned half-collar, strongest on neck-sides.

10. **Adult winter** (Sep–Mar) Adult shows pale grey upperparts with rather prominent white tertial crescents and black wing-tip with white tips (generally narrower than in Herring). Often shows white tip on P10. Head pattern variable, but often diffuse; others show densely brown-spotted 'hood' and neck-sides; generally strongest in E North America; many W American birds show narrower, more even brown streaks, similar to Vega and Herring Gulls. Gonys spot brighter and broader than in winter. Slight dark subterminal markings on bill regular (rarer among Herring Gull). Orange gonys spot narrow. Legs fleshy.

11. **Adult summer** (Sep–Mar) Head white. Eyes pale, orbital ring yellow. Gonys spot brighter than in winter.

1. Juvenile

2. First-winter

3. First-winter

Worn first-win-
first-summer

5. First-winter

6. Second-winter

7. Second-winter

9. Fourth-winter

10. Adult winter

8. Third-winter

11. Adult summer

PLATE 36. AMERICAN HERRING GULL *Larus smithsonianus*

Rather large and stocky with moderately broad wings. Shape similar to Herring Gull.

1. **Juvenile** (Aug–Nov/Dec) Some birds very dark chocolate-brown (especially E Coast birds). Upperwing brown with blackish flight feathers (but normally pale window on inner primaries, although often faint in darker birds). Underbody velvety brown with distinctly barred undertail-coverts. Underwing-coverts solid dark against slightly paler flight feathers, appearing rather dull. Rump heavily brown-barred; at distance, rump brownish-looking in only slight contrast to upper-parts. Tail blackish, with only faint pale spotting along edges. Even the darkest Herring Gulls show more mottled, less clean underbody and underwing-coverts. Problematic, dark-tailed Herring Gulls (mainly *argenteus*) have narrower dark (and irregular) bars or spots on rump/upper-tail-coverts, and paler hind-belly. Tail has paler base and spotting along edges.

2. **First-winter** (Aug–Apr) A pale-headed individual with whitish head and pink, black-tipped bill contrasting well with browner underbody. Wing pattern in this individual more like Herring Gull, but note barred rump, all-dark tail, denser dark necklace and darker, more uniform greater coverts.

3. **Second-winter** (Aug–Apr) A 'retarded' individual, similar to first-year, but with stronger pale win-dow on inner primaries. Head rather dark, but with pale hind-collar, most evident with wear from mid-winter. Axillaries may be slightly paler than underwing-coverts. Rump and tail with slightly more pale at tail-base than 1 and 2 (often with pale spots along edges of T6). Such birds often show a pale grey saddle surrounded by dark wings, hindneck and tail.

4. **Second-winter** (Aug–Apr) Upperwing generally more contrasting than in first-year with paler coverts (but more solid brown greater coverts), distinct pale window on inner primaries and darker secondaries/outer primaries. Mantle and scapulars varying grey. Rump white against extensive black tail, with only white at base (but rump often still distinctly barred). At this age and third-winter often very contrasting, as adult parts very pale grey; a pattern shared with Herring Gull race *argenteus*. Compared to *argenteus*, American Herring shows more extensive dark on hindneck and underwing, broader blackish tail-bar (entire tail may appear dark, but this is known in *argenteus* too) and often browner (less grey) window in inner primaries. Also, greater coverts show fine barring.

5. **Third-winter** (Aug–Apr) Similar to adult, but with browner greater coverts, blacker wing-tip with smaller white mirror on P10, dark-patterned primary coverts and extensive black in tail (appear-ing irregular). Such dark immature markings are much more regular than in similar-aged Her-ring Gulls.

6. **Fourth-winter/summer** As adult, but with dark markings on primary coverts and smaller white mirror on P10.

7. **Adult winter** (Sep–Mar) Head in winter often with strong brown markings, creating hooded appearance, often strongest on neck-sides. Adult upperwing pale grey with white trailing edge. Wing-tip black with small white mirrors on P9–10, black tip extending to P5. Large grey 'tongues' on P5–8 almost reach trailing edge. Some NE birds combine long pale tongues on P9-10 ('*thayeri*-pattern') with complete, but narrow black W markings on P5; Herring with similar pattern on P9-10 at most shows incomplete black markings in P5 (mainly restricted to outer web); W Coast birds lack white 'moons' on primaries.

1. Juvenile

2. First-winter

3. Second-winter

4. Second-winter

5. Third-winter

6. Fourth-winter/summer

7. Adult winter

tipped bill combined with white head, dark-spotted hindneck, brown underbody and strongly barred rump and all-dark tail.

Herring best identified by extensive white base to tail, isolating dark as dark tail-bar, showing pale tips and edges. Bases of tail feathers and rump/undertail-coverts are white with dark spots. Rarely, Herring (especially *argenteus*) closer to American Herring in showing mainly dark tail. White tail-bases and white pattern along tail-sides will still be more extensive than in typical American Herring (which may show narrow white spots on tail-sides as well as limited white at tail-base), and an all-dark tail combined with heavy dark barring on rump should exclude Herring. Herring normally more streaked on head and blotchy brown on underbody, dissimilar to the uniform look of American Herring. Furthermore, shows broader pale edges to tertials (more often leaving 'oak-leafed' centres), more even amount of pale and dark barring on greater coverts (creating less solid wing-bar), more consistent pale and brown barring on mantle/scapulars and less solid hindneck-markings. Most problematic Herring are as dark as darkest American Herring, with dark markings on mantle, scapulars, greater coverts and tertials as in American, but still with more pale at tail-base and along edges of tail, more streaked head, dark blotching on underparts, paler hind-belly and narrower dark markings on rump and undertail-coverts. New feathers on breast-sides and flanks are less contrasting, caused by paler, more spotted underbody. A few are tricky enough to be left unidentified, see also Glaucous × Herring hybrids.

Lesser Black-backed Gull smaller and more elegant with smaller, more rounded head, longer, slenderer hindparts and shorter legs. Mantle, scapulars, greater coverts and tertials may strongly suggest American Herring, but tail-coverts (especially under) are whiter with dark pattern restricted to dark spots, most conspicuous along sides. Lacks the pale inner wing window of American Herring (but latter with weak window exists). Unlike American Herring, retains black bill in first-winter.

First-summer similar to first-winter, but head and underparts paler through wear and bleaching. Flight feathers and tail bleach to brownish.

Second-winter highly variable, generally with more immature markings than Herring. Many have grey saddle contrasting with otherwise '1st-year'-type plumage. Head and underbody, still looking rather uniformly dark albeit with some dark blotching. Hindneck often conspicuously dark-marked, sometimes solid. Mantle and scapulars a mixture of grey and barred feathers thus appearing less clean than most Herrings; wing basically as first-year. Contrast between dark and grey areas generally strong, creating piebald appearance. Underwing often with as extensive dark as in first-years, but some show white axillaries against solid dark coverts—a combination unknown in Herring. Birds with retained dark primary coverts against white coverts get dark carpal patches as in Rough-legged Buzzard *Buteo lagopus*. Black tail still conspicuous; tail-coverts at first barred, but dark barring gradually lost over winter. Bill fleshy with black tip or subterminal markings.

Second-summer basically similar to Herring, but tail-coverts extensively dark-barred (with mare dark than pale) and tail often mainly black (rarely matched by certain Herring *argenteus*); greater coverts and tertials generally darker with more solid centres than in Herring.

Third-winter similar to adult, but upperparts still with extensive traces of greyish-brown and fine pale vermiculations (especially greater coverts and tertials), tail still with traces of dark (sometimes as line of distinct black spots, as in second-year Ring-billed Gull) and often broad, rather solid black tail-bar. Underwing still extensively dark-marked. Bill with extensive black subterminal markings; sometimes greenish-tinged.

Third-summer Herring at this age similar, and most not identifiable. However, many show solid black markings at the base of 2–3 mid-tertials, distinct black margins to secondaries (in Herring vermiculated brown). Tail-bar of Herring more vermiculated, lacking solid black markings of American (Lonergan & Mullarney 2004).

Fourth-winter as adult; seemingly more birds in adult plumage show black markings on primary coverts as well as narrow black tertial spots in this age (and even in otherwise adult plumage) than Herring (Lonergan & Mullarney 2004).

VOICE Similar to Herring, but somewhat drier, deeper and quicker: *ci-auww*, often combined with deep, cackling *gag-ag-ag-ag*. Also a single-noted *klooh* and hollow, low *kaaw*. Compared to Western, long-call higher, clearer and more disyllabic.

MOULT (Dubois 1997a, Howell & King 1999, skins in LACM, pers. obs.) Moult to winter plumage similar to or slightly earlier than in Herring Gull.

Adult moult to **winter** plumage complete mid-May–Dec. Starts with P1 late May (SE populations), P1–2 early Jun (British Columbia); P3–5 late Jul, P5–6 mid-Aug. E Coast birds reach P(5)7–9(10) late Sep–mid-Oct. W Coast birds later: adult from California reaches P6–8 mid–late Sep, P8–10 early Nov; one bird grew P10 late Dec (one partial albino P10 early Jan). Texas birds moult much the same way as W Coast birds. Head from late Aug; almost 100% have head-streaks mid-Sep, New England.

Adult moult to **summer** plumage partial, including head and some body feathers late Feb–early Apr, generally earliest in S populations. New Jersey breeders become white-headed from Feb. 99% of Newfoundland winter population retains head pattern into late Feb (attains white head in Mar). In California/Mexico none of >1,000 in Jan–mid-Feb had traces of summer head or intense yellow tinge to bare parts; migrants in California in Mar–Apr still with winter head, and traces of winter head still present in some breeders at Lake Superior in late May. By contrast, few adults from Virginia, mid-Feb, had attained summer head.

Juvenile moult to **first-winter** partial Sep–Feb. Moult depends on length of migration, with resident populations moulting earlier and more extensively than long-distance migrants. On E Coast (New England–New Jersey) moult includes parts of head, body, mantle, scapulars and sometimes rump Aug–Jan, sometimes few coverts from Sep. 70% late Sep–mid-Oct showed obvious sign of moult and by Nov most of mantle/scapulars replaced; <10% had moulted <10% of mantle/scapulars by Nov–late Jan. Sometimes no traces of moult into midwinter in birds from N breeding sites. In Great Lakes, moulting residents joined in autumn by northern birds, still in juvenile plumage (Howell & King 1999, Mullarney & Lonergan in press, A. Jaramillo *in litt.*). In Californian wintering birds very little trace of moult; >50% still juvenile early Dec, 30% late Jan. By Jan–mid-Feb moult restricted to parts of mantle, scattered scapulars and sometimes few feathers on head and body (especially breast-sides). Moult starts with scapulars and mantle; 20–30% of scapulars and (in 10–20%) max. 50% of mantle/scapulars renewed before moult starts in other parts (Howell & King 1999), but some renew parts of mantle before scapulars (pers. obs.); 60–90% of scapulars and mantle renewed by Mar. Next to be moulted are parts of chest-sides, lores, crown, ear-coverts, sides of neck and hindneck; then nape and upper hindneck, which may be retained during winter; many only moult 1–5% head and underbody in first winter, and no feathers on belly (Howell & King 1999). Moult to **second-winter** complete; starts with scattered feathers on head, body, and sometimes mantle (Jan)Mar–May, mostly from late Apr, finishing Sep/Oct. Primaries moulted earlier than in adults, P1 early–mid-May, P8 mid–late Sep; see Herring Gull. **Second-summer** partial, including head, body and scapulars Jan–Apr. Subsequently moults as adult.

DESCRIPTION

Adult As Herring Gull, but upperparts paler grey with slight bluish tinge (Kodak Grey Scale (3)3.5–6; see Geographical Variation). Black wing-tip similar to Herring *argentatus*: P10 black with 25–50mm white mirror, in some reduced to inner web, in others almost reaching tip, or whole tip white (especially NE populations). White mirror at 45° angle to black on outer web, often with straight 90° division on inner web; a few have rounded mirror. P9 black, in some with max. 25mm white mirror, often restricted to inner web; black reaches primary coverts in majority of W Coast birds (75% California), much fewer in E Coast birds, especially from N part of range. Small minority, especially NE coast birds, show white inner web almost reaching white mirror, creating 'Thayer's Gull pattern'. Outer web with 100–120mm black. P8 with 50–150mm black outer web (ending 30–55mm before primary coverts), 20–55mm black inner web and varying white tongue, especially on inner web. P7 with 50–70mm black on outer web (ending 35–65mm before primary coverts), 20–65mm on inner web and up to 10mm tongue. P6 grey with 25–75mm black on outer and 35–60mm on inner web; white tongue as P7, but usually on both webs. P5 with 10–35mm black on outer 15–30mm black on inner web—as bows or W (in most broader and more complete than in Herring, similar to Yellow-legged Gull, where rarely as 'bow-like'). Old males may lack dark markings on P5; see also Geographical Variation. P4 sometimes with faint dark subterminal spot, normally on outer web only. P3 rarely with indistinct dark subterminal spot on outer web (7% Massachusetts—Lonergan & Mullarney 2004). Primaries with max. 18mm white tips.

Eyes as Herring. Orbital ring yellow, chrome-yellow or orange. Gape yellow. Bill as Herring, but red gonys-spot generally smaller, rarely reaching upper mandible. Nostril triangular or oval: depth at distal edge 1.2–1.5mm, length 8–11.2mm (skins in LACM, MVC, NHM, USNM). Bare parts otherwise as Herring Gull.

Adult summer (Feb/Mar–Sep) Head white. By (late Jan)Feb–Mar, bill generally orange-yellow with brighter red gonys-spot. Legs pinkish to greyish-flesh, rarely grey. When attaining breeding condition, *c.*1% acquire yellow legs (some already with faint yellow tinge to upper tarsus from Feb (King 1999, pers. obs.)).

Adult winter (Sep–Mar) Head with extensive dusky streaks or spots, densest around eye (forming slight eye-mask) and on breast-sides; markings sometimes covering entire head and upper breast to create hooded appearance, most frequent in some E Coast birds, which may be as dark brown and washed out as in *atlantis* race of Yellow-legged. Conversely, most W Coast birds and those from Texas show head-markings mainly concentrated as dense brown spots on hindneck and weaker streaks on crown, ear-coverts and neck-sides. Bill pale yellow, often with fleshy to greenish tinge and dark markings retained to May, often as narrow bow behind gonys spot. Gonys spot orange, often on lower part of bill only (thus more restricted than in Herring Gull).

Juvenile (fledging–Sep/Jan) Head and underparts dark chocolate-brown to greyish-brown with weak streaks or spots, appearing velvety. Crown sometimes pale-spotted. Chin/throat, neck-sides and hindneck often with brown streaks. Mantle and scapulars generally darker brown than Herring with more distinct but narrower pale edges (or notches). Upperwing-coverts dark to mid-brown with dark subterminal spots and pale edges. Median and lesser coverts sometimes darker, forming dark leading edge to wing (or bend around wing) in birds with pale-patterned coverts. Greater coverts usually dark or muddy brown with uniform dark centres and narrow pale barring on distal part (especially outer coverts); in some with even pale and dark barring (as in typical Herring) or whitish with 2–3 rows of narrow dark spots, as in Great Black-backed, Vega and certain Caspian Gulls race *mongolicus* (W Coast birds), in such birds forming paler midwing-panel. Primary coverts often with pale edges. Tertials blackish-brown with pale narrow fringes, in most as irregular pale notches, in some as straighter pale edges, broadest near tips (and often restricted to tips as in Lesser Black-backed Gull). Flight feathers as Herring: P1–5 pale greyish-brown with dark subterminal spots, creating pale window (sometimes weak, especially E Coast birds), dark subterminal markings usually more extensive than in Herring, but, in some, even P6–7 have pale inner webs, 'enlarging' pale window. Pale edges to P6–10 generally narrower (especially E Coast birds), but more distinct according to darker ground coloration of P6–10. Edges rarely paler, creating row of pale Vs (mainly W Coast birds). Underwing-coverts and axillaries rather uniform dark brown to greyish-brown, similar to Lesser Black-backed, Yellow-legged race *atlantis* and Kelp Gull, thus more solid dark than in Herring. Most coverts dark-tipped or -edged; bases to all coverts and axillaries sometimes paler. Rump and undertail-coverts dark brown to greyish-brown with narrow pale bars or waving, often similar to rump-barring of juvenile Thayer's Gull or Pomarine Skua *Stercorarius pomarinus*, in darkest birds more diffuse with dark predominant; in a minority with more white/less dark, and dark more as spots as in Herring. Tail brownish-black to dark brown (darkish in field) with faint pale mottling to bases of T(3–4)5–6, sometimes barring to bases of all rectrices as in Thayer's Gull; very rarely with more solid white base as in some Herring *argenteus* (Dubois 1997a, Howell & King 1998, J. R. Hough *in litt.*, pers. obs.). T6 with 4–5 pale spots, usually on outer web only; rarely lacking. Bare parts as Herring. Bill black, from Nov developing fleshy base to lower mandible.

First-winter (Sep/Jan–Apr) similar to juvenile, but head generally paler, especially forehead, chin and throat, and some develop whitish-looking head, with merely indistinct dark spotting and darker eye-mask, contrasting well with brown underbody; lower belly sometimes paler. Some show distinct dark streaks on crown, ear-coverts and hindneck, and dark dots on lores, from late Jan sometimes conspicuously so; chin and throat white with indistinct dark spots or streaks. Hindneck to upper mantle often solid brown, creating necklace. Most of plumage as juvenile, but mantle and sometimes scapulars acquire first-winter feathers similar to Herring; dark markings generally more anchor-shaped, triangular or even greyish; two generations of scapulars sometimes present Sep–Nov (unlike Herring), the lower juvenile, the upper paler with more distinct dark barring (Mullarney 1990, Dubois 1997a, pers. obs.). With wear, darker median coverts and lesser coverts contrast well with paler greater coverts in paler-patterned birds. Primaries bleach to brown from midwinter, and lose pale fringes from late Dec, although still evident into May in some W populations. Underbody usually a mixture of brown irregular blotching and paler greyish, by midwinter sometimes strikingly so. Bill usually bicoloured from Nov with dark tip/cutting edges and dull fleshy base, in many pink with black tip similar to Glaucous Gull. Acquires broader pale tip from Apr.

'First-summer' (Mar–Sep) best identified from Herring by mainly dark tail (often brownish-tinged through wear) and distinct dark-barred or -washed rump. May develop grey mantle feathers, max. 30% by summer. Lower belly often white. Bill fleshy to pink with dark tip and sometimes cutting edges, in some dark with faint pale base and tip. Plumage often strongly bleached from May.

Second-winter (Sep–Mar) like same-aged Herring Gull (which see for detailed description), but head and underbody generally more coarsely and extensively dark-patterned, appearing more diffuse. Hindneck to upper mantle more solid dark. Mantle and scapulars a mixture of grey and barred feathers (sometimes no grey). Grey feathers often with fine white edges and narrow black shaft-streaks, barring more diffuse, less regular than in Herring. Greater coverts dark greyish-brown with very fine vermiculations, but in some uniform mud-brown and concolorous with secondaries (Herring has more well-marked, paler coverts in better contrast to secondaries). Lesser and median coverts sometimes grey, and then in very good contrast to

greater coverts bar. Tertials with solid black centres and broad white edges, often irregular and restricted to tips. Rump and tail-coverts on both surfaces extensively dark-barred (more dark than pale), but pattern gradually lost throughout winter, and in late winter and spring rump mainly white. P6–10 and secondaries dark with narrow white tips. P1–5 paler, creating pale window; browner and more subdued than in Herring with more conspicuous dark subterminal spots. Underwing often solid dark on wing-coverts and axillaries, as in first-years, but sometimes paler except for primary coverts (in which dark feathers may form carpal patch as in Rough-legged Buzzard *Buteo lagopus*). Some show unique combination of white axillaries and dark coverts. P10 lacks white mirror. Tail with extensive black sometimes covering whole tail, white in most restricted to fine vermiculations at bases of T3–6 and spots along outer web of T6. Some show larger amount of white at tail-base and along edges of T6.

Birds more similar to first-years aged by finer pale vermiculations on greater coverts, paler base to bill, bicoloured eye (appearing intermediate between first-year and adult) and different primary pattern (see Herring).

Certain birds show unusual bill pattern: pink with black subterminal markings, only narrow on lower mandible where giving way to yellow tip.

Second-summer (Mar–Sep) as Herring (which see for detailed description), but generally with broader dark tail-markings; unlike Herring, tail often all darkish-looking at distance.

Third-winter (Sep–Apr) as Herring (which see for detailed description), but some have wholly uniform brownish-grey greater coverts, creating strong panel against very pale grey coverts and P1–5. P10 sometimes with small white mirror. Secondaries with black margins. Tertials (especially middle ones) sometimes with black markings near bases. Tail sometimes still as second-winter; mainly dark with pale edges and tips. Black pattern more as solid spots than the vermiculations of Herring, thus similar to Ring-billed Gull (Mullarney & Lonergan in press). Some show grey saddle/median coverts and darkish-looking tail. Bill yellow to greenish-tinged with dark subterminal markings.

Third-summer (Mar–Sep) as Herring, but if present dark pattern on tail may reach tail-base (unlike Herring); dark markings on primary coverts probably more solid on average.

Fourth-winter (Sep–Feb) as adult, but often with dark streaks or spots to outer primary coverts (more frequent than in Herring) (skins in LACM). Tertials sometimes with black spots. Primaries usually as adults, but sometimes duller and browner with less sharp division between dark and pale. Underbody sometimes with dark markings. May show faint dark markings on T1–2. **Note** 'Immature' markings such as black markings on tertials and primary coverts are more frequent in otherwise adult birds than in Herring Gull (Lonergan & Mullarney 2004).

GEOGRAPHICAL VARIATION Slight and clinal. Generally largest and heaviest to NE, especially Newfoundland.

Adult There is a clinal variation, from darkest birds in E Coast states and NW British Columbia to paler across N, central and W coast part of range. Upperwing Kodak Grey Scale: Newfoundland 3.5–4.5, C USA 5–6, Lake Superior 4.5–5.5, California (3)4–5.

Primary pattern differs slightly between populations, with clinal variation from more white/less black in NE and E populations towards more black/less white, but more solid white tongues on P5–7 in W Coast populations (fainter in E Coast birds, where mostly confined to inner wedges; rarely lacking). P10 in E Coast birds often with large white mirror (30–50mm), in males sometimes covering tip. White tip to P10 noted in 61% Newfoundland, 14% Massachusetts, 0% in Niagara and 0% California in winter (Jonsson & Mactavish 2001, pers. obs.). Sometimes, black on wing-tip reduced to create wing-tip pattern as in Thayer's Gull, Caspian Gull ('*ponticus*') and certain Herring *argentatus* with pale grey inner webs joining white mirror on P9–10 (1% E Coast, 5–10% Newfoundland). Lake Superior birds had white mirror 25–30mm, usually with 45° angle to black on outer web and straight division on inner; white usually reaches edges. In Californian birds white mirror on P10 20–40mm and rounded, often not reaching edges. P9 with white mirror in >85% Newfoundland, 70–80% Massachusetts to Virginia (larger proportion in winter, as many northern populations occur here), 36% Lake Superior, 20–25% California/northern Mexico, 10% Niagara (Jonsson & Mactavish 2001, Adriaens & Mactavish in press, pers. obs.).

P5–6 generally with broader black markings in W Coast birds (in the majority as 15–20mm solid black bar on both webs; rarely lacking); in E Coast birds mostly as narrow black crescents; lacking in 10–20%. Solid or complete band to P5 present in 96% Niagara, 73% in Newfoundland, where often narrower (Jonsson & Mactavish 2001, Adriaens & Mactavish in press), restricted to one web and normally surrounded by white. P4 in 25% E Coast and 35% Niagara Falls birds with black markings (mainly outer web), in 50% in W Coast; 7% only in Massachusetts and 2% Newfoundland noted. Dark markings on P3 a feature of adult W Coast birds.

E Coast and NE populations show longer white tongues in mid-primaries, 'eating' into black wing-tip, which looks hollowed out. The tongues which are pointed ('bayonet'-shaped) may be nearly the same length on P7–8, and even on P10 there is often a long white tongue on the inner web almost reaching the white mir-

ror; in Newfoundland birds, the black division between mirror and tongue is typically narrower than the mirror. In W Coast birds (and Niagara Falls autumn birds) black on wing-tip is generally more extensive with shorter white tongues (creating black wedge on wing-tip) and underside of P10 is mainly black. P5 has narrow black markings (often as W on both webs). Newfoundland birds show on average broader white primary tips than populations from Niagara and W Coast (Sibley 2000, Jonsson & Mactavish 2001, Lonergan & Mullarney 2004, pers. obs., skins in AMNH, LACM, NHM, USNM, UZM).

Birds with the least amount of black on P9–10 also show least amount of black on P(4)5–6. Black on wing-tip is probably age-related, but also relates to sex, as male shows less black on wing-tip than female.

Winter E Coast adults often with very densely dark brown spots or waving on head and hindneck, forming partial hood extending to breast as solid dark bib (matched by certain Yellow-legged Gulls race *atlantis*). This type rarer on W Coast, where winter head pattern paler brown and finer: soft mid-brown streaks, spots or waving on especially ear-coverts, hindneck and breast-sides, often isolated from grey wing by white extension behind brown on breast-sides (as in Glaucous-winged Gull or even *Actitis* sandpipers). This pattern matched by wintering birds from Texas, which also had wing pattern closest to W Coast birds, apart from tendency to show more white on P9–10 than breeders from New England.

Size similar in all populations, but on average W birds (British Columbia, California) have longer wings and legs: mean measurements in some samples are Wing British Columbia adult male 451.2, adult female 430.8; Great Lakes adult male 448, female 422.4; Michigan adult male 432.2, female 405.5; E Coast adult male 443.4, female 428.5; Tarsus adult male E Coast 65.0 (n=23), W Coast 67.4 (n=16), adult female E Coast 61.5 (n=16), adult female W Coast 62.1 (n=16) (Stugart 1977, Fox *et al.* 1981, own data). Average bill in E Coast birds adult male 54.9, in W Coast 55.9, but no difference found in females. Nostril shortest and most 'open' (oval-shaped) in Great Lakes breeders (6–10mm), generally longer and more slit-like in Pacific breeders from British Columbia (8–12mm). As there is an extensive overlap in all measurements, all own data are combined below.

First-years The darkest chocolate-brown birds with

AMERICAN HERRING GULL Four-year gull. The Nearctic counterpart of Herring and Vega Gull. **Adult** similar to both; shows paler grey upperwing than Vega. Wing-tip black with white mirrors to P9–10 and rather conspicuous white tongues on mid-primaries. Unlike Herring normally shows extensive black markings on P5. See Geographical Variation. In **winter** (Sep–Mar) head brown-patterned, in many E Coast birds very densely, creating impression of solid dark hood reaching breast-sides; this rarer on W Coast, where head often with most extensive dark streaks on hindneck. Often shows dark subterminal bill-markings.

First-year either like Herring and Vega Gull or darker brown with more waved pattern on head and underbody, more solid dark centres to coverts and tertials and distinct dark bars on upper- and undertail-coverts. Tail dark, at most with faint white spots along edges and near base. In paler birds, tail/rump pattern offers best clues, also denser dark hindneck-streaks, creating solid dark scarf; some become pale-headed, but retain solid brown underbody.

Second- and third-year as corresponding age of Herring and Vega, but dark tail-bar and pattern on rump often retained in second-year, and hindneck often with denser dark markings.

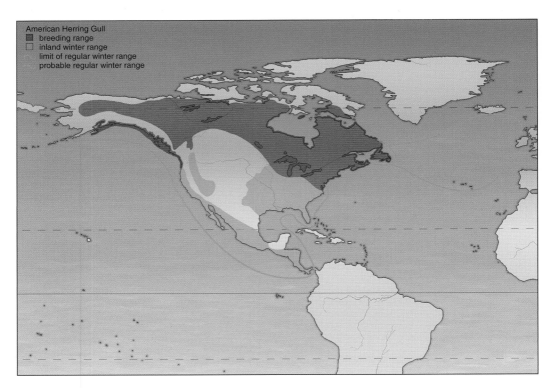

darkest wing-covert pattern, faintest pale window on inner primaries (rarely lacking) and darkest underwing-coverts are found in E, e.g. dominating in New England (just 10–15% on W Coast). Birds from Great Lakes somewhat paler. All intergrades exist towards paler greyish-brown birds with more distinct head-streaks (similar to Herring, apart from rump/tail pattern), this paler form dominates along W Coast. Greater coverts most variable (see above); birds with mainly whitish greater coverts and just 2–3 dark spots (as in Great Black-backed Gull) occur along W Coast. Midwest to W populations generally with more extensive pale markings in tail and rump.

Moult to first-winter differs geographically; later and less extensive on W than on E Coast. W Coast birds (California, Mexico) mainly juvenile into midwinter, starting moult Jan or later. By mid-Jan–mid-Feb only scattered feathers on head and underbody renewed, but up to 30% on mantle and often some scapulars (Howell & King 1999, own. obs.). On E Coast, moult more extensive, including head, body, mantle and scapulars and often some coverts (unlike Herring) Sep–Nov. Birds in New England at that time may – unlike Herring – show two generations of scapulars. Some at this time, however, have not started moult (Dubois 1997a, pers. obs.). Age development seemingly quicker in W population, where on average more second-winters develop a pure grey saddle.

Aberrants Partial **albinistic** 3–4 year old had up to 50% of upperpart feathers white admixed with grey. P5–10 all white in one wing, P8–10 in other wing (where P4–7 had markings as in normal bird, but browner). Head with 'normal' dark winter pattern. Dark markings on some tail feathers coloured normally (skin LACM 1091).

Hybrids Hybrid **American Herring × Glaucous Gull** fairly common in some Arctic breeding areas. **Adult** basically like pale American Herring, but with slightly paler (rarely black) primary pattern with larger amount of white on wing-tip (e.g. broad white tip to P10, long whitish tongues on P9–7 and broad white primary tips. In settled birds, wing-tip greyish-black with broad white tips, almost as broad as visible amount of dark. Certain small birds (females) may create ID problems with Thayer's and Iceland Gull race *kumlieni*, but head usually larger and bill heavier with more evident gonys-angle. Compared to Thayer's, upperparts paler grey. **First-year** generally paler than American Herring with paler brown outer primaries, almost clean white inner primaries, pale brown secondaries and tail, and sometimes narrower, more distinct brown rump and tail-covert barring. Bill usually pink with black tip, but sometimes with dark cutting edges and grey smudging basally. May appear in juvenile plumage throughout winter.

For hybridisation with Glaucous-winged Gulls, see that species.

DISTRIBUTION AND MIGRATION Population around 150,000 pairs. Habitat similar to Herring Gull. Marked increase in New England: 4,000–8,000 pairs 1901, 90,000 1972; local decline (Great Lakes) until 1980. Mainly sedentary, but N population leapfrogs southern to main wintering areas in E and S USA, Great

Plains and Ontario: 180,000 late 1960s followed by slight decrease. Peak Dec–Jan with max. gatherings of 75,300 New York, 65,000 Ontario, 50,000 Pennsylvania/ Virginia, 23,640 Cape May (New Jersey) and 20,000 in other parts of winter range. Well spread in Pacific area in winter, but much scarcer here than on E Coast; often inland. Scarce W Indies (where casual in summer) and C America; casual S to Venezuela.

Vagrant W Palearctic: Great Britain 37 up to 2000, the majority in Ireland where annual Feb–Mar; Azores (incl. 11 Jan/Feb 2003 and Feb 2004), France 4, NW Spain 2 (one ringed in New Brunswick recovered Bay of Biscay), Portugal 6, Norway 1, Iceland 8 (probably overlooked). Probably regular Greenland (Drury & Kadlec 1974, Møller 1978, Dennis 1981, Boertmann 1994, Batty *et al.* 2003, Rogers 2003, Hoogendoorn *et al.* 2003, Lyngs 2003, Y. Kolbeinsson *in litt.*).

MEASUREMENTS Lengths inmm; weights in g. Own data based on skins in AMNH, LACM, MVC, NHM, UZM, ZMA. North America.

WING LENGTH

Adult male	421–468 (446.1)	36
Adult female	412–450 (429.7)	36
First-year male	404–471 (438.0)	14
First-year female	395–438 (416.4)	19

Note Fox et al. *(1981) gave for Great Lakes adult: male 420–475 (n=69), female 385–450 (n=84).*

BILL

Adult male	48.3–62.1 (55.5)	39
Adult female	44.2–57.7 (51.8)	33
First-year male	47.7–60.7 (54.1)	15
First-year female	44.6–55.4 (49.3)	19

BILL DEPTH AT GONYS

Adult male	17.2–22.1 (19.4)	39
Adult female	13.8–21.6 (17.7)	33
First-year male	16.0–19.8 (17.7)	14
First-year female	13.8–18.1 (16.3)	19

BILL DEPTH AT BASE OF BILL

Adult male	18.2–22.0 (20.1)	39
Adult female	16.7–21.5 (18.5)	33
First-year male	17.4–20.0 (18.7)	14
First-year female	15.6–19.4 (16.9)	19

GONYS LENGTH

Adult male	13.1–18.9 (15.8)	39
Adult female	12.9–17.8 (15.0)	33
First-year male	13.9–19.9 (15.9)	14
First-year female	10.0–17.2 (14.0)	19

TARSUS

Adult male	58.3–75.5 (66.0)	39
Adult female	55.3–66.5 (61.8)	33
First-year male	58.5–73.5 (64.8)	14
First-year female	53.5–66.6 (60.0)	19

Weight Great Lakes adult: male 797–1,650, female 600–1,240 (n=84). Massachusetts adult early Jun 823–1,180, female 780–1,075 (skins in LACM, NHM). First-year 950 (Fox *et al.* 1981).

American Herring Gull *Larus smithsonianus.* **303. Juvenile.** Note velvety chocolate-brown plumage, typical for E coast juveniles. Martha's Vineyard, Massachusetts, USA. 14 Sep 1997. *Klaus Malling Olsen.* **304. Juvenile moulting into 1st-winter.** Note 1st-winter mantle feathers. Greater coverts generally with more extensive dark barring than in Herring Gull and tertials with narrower pale edges. Ocean City, Maryland, USA. 3 Oct 1994. *Klaus Malling Olsen.*

American Herring Gull *Larus smithsonianus.* **305. Juvenile moulting into 1st-winter.** Birds from W Coast generally paler greyish-brown and more streaked, less uniform than those from E Coast, but much individual variation. San Diego, California, USA. Note narrow pale spotting in tail-sides. 6 Jan 1996. *Don DesJardin.* **306. 1st-winter.** New 1st-winter mantle feathers noticeable against worn coverts. By winter head often becomes pale against dark underbody. Sonora, Mexico. 2 Feb 2000. *Klaus Malling Olsen.* **307. 1st-winter.** A characteristic individual, easily identifiable on combination of pink, black 'dipped-in-ink' bill, pale head and velvety brown underbody. Note distinct barred undertail-coverts. Point Reyes, California, USA. 30 Jan 2000. *Klaus Malling Olsen.* **308. 1st-winter.** Note dark tail against barred rump, the latter appearing brown in the field caused by barring. A dark E Coast individual showing chocolate-brown underbody, very dark underwing-coverts and just slight pale window in inner primaries. Cape May, New Jersey, USA. 4 Oct 1994. *Klaus Malling Olsen.* **309 Juvenile.** Another dark individual with all-dark tail and barred rump, like a dark 1st-year Thayer's Gull rather than Herring. Newfoundland, Canada. Late Sep 1998. *Bruce Mactavish.*

American Herring Gull *Larus smithsonianus*. **310. 1st-winter.** A paler, more Herring Gull-like bird, but note extensively dark tail and distinctly barred rump. Note, however, that tail bases and sides have pale pattern, but the extensive dark is only matched by a very few Herrings. Compare photo 338. Sonora, Mexico. 3 Feb 2000. *Klaus Malling Olsen*. **311. 2nd-winter.** In general develops more solid grey saddle in 2nd-winter than Herring Gull. Underbody still velvety rather than streaked or spotted as in Herring. Ventura, California, USA. 11 Nov 1995. *Don DesJardin*. **312. 3rd-winter.** Note rather large amount of dark in tertials and tail compared to similar-age Herring. New Jersey, USA. 26 Jan 1995. *Arnoud B. van den Berg*. **313. 3rd-winter.** New inner primaries often strikingly paler than greater coverts. This also seen in Herring *argenteus*, but rare in *argentatus*. Virginia, USA. 3 Oct 1994. *Klaus Malling Olsen*. **314. 3rd-winter**. Compare wing-pattern with 313. Also note densely dark-patterned hindneck, creating solid dark necklace. Greater coverts uniformly dark in contrast to rest of innerwing. Tertials with extensive dark markings. Martha's Vineyard, Massachusetts, USA. 14 Sep 1997. *Klaus Malling Olsen*.

315

316

317

318

319

American Herring Gull *Larus smithsonianus.* **315. 3rd-summer**. Note heavy bill and flat forehead, similar to Herring *argentatus*. Massachusetts, USA. Jun 1995. *Don DesJardin.* **316. 4th-winter.** Dark markings in bill more extensive than in adult. Note very dense dark brown spots in head, breast-sides and especially hindneck. Rhode Island, USA. 11 Sep 1997. *Klaus Malling Olsen.* **317. 4th- or adult winter.** Note conspicuous dark streaks on hindneck. Sonora, Mexico. 2 Feb 2000. *Klaus Malling Olsen.* **318. Adult winter**. The densely dark-spotted breast-sides, isolated from forewing by white wedge, recall pattern of winter Glaucous-winged, but note spotted rather than diffuse pattern. Bill more slender with less bulbous tip than Glaucous-winged. The most well-marked parts are the breast-sides. Eyes pale. Sonora, Mexico. 4 Feb 2000. *Klaus Malling Olsen.* **319. Adult summer**. Dark markings on bill are often present into May. Larger, heavier-tipped bill (bill and head shape often similar to Glaucous Gull, especially in eastern males). These are probably a pair, the male (right) looks flatter-crowned with larger, heavier-tipped bill. Connecticut, USA. Mar 1997. *Julian R. Hough.* **320. Adult winter**. Compare extent of black in outer wing with 321. In general, head paler-streaked, less dark-spotted in W Coast birds than E Coast birds, but much individual variation. Sonora, Mexico. 2 Feb 2000. *Klaus Malling Olsen.* **321. Adult**. In N and E populations, wing shows more white/less black than in W. Note long, pale tongues in mid-primaries and narrow black W in P5. Newfoundland, Canada. Apr 1997. *Bruce Mactavish.* **322. Adult winter**. Note variation in wing-tip pattern and compare with Herring Gull (especially photos 358 and 366-367). Note (in American Herring Gull) the more pointed pale extensions in mid-primaries and more extensive black markings on P5-6 (on P5, often thin W-shaped). Newfoundland, Canada. 6 Dec 2000. *Bruce Mactavish.*

253

19. HERRING GULL

Larus argentatus (Pontoppidan, 1763, Denmark)   **Plates 37–38, Photos 323–369**

IDENTIFICATION Length 55–67cm, wingspan 125–155cm (both measurements largest in N populations). Herring Gull is, together with its close relatives Vega and American Herring Gulls, abundant in the Northern Hemisphere. Its opportunistic behaviour makes it one of the most numerous seabirds in Europe, and it is a key species in large gull ID; everywhere within its range it exhibits a notoriously wide individual variation. It is fierce-looking with a square head (peaking behind eye), heavy bill and small, beady eye. It has moderately long wings, a rather full body and usually a prominent tertial step. The male is larger with a heavier, more bulbous-tipped bill, flatter forehead and squarer neck than the female, which may appear round-headed with a rather short bill. The flight is steady with rather slow, powerful wingbeats. Forms large flocks at rubbish tips and fishing harbours. Two subspecies; *argentatus* from N Europe is generally larger and heavier than *argenteus* from Great Britain and W Europe, but there is a large zone of intergrades between Denmark and W Europe, and in these areas subspecies identification often impossible.

Adult has grey, slightly bluish-tinged upperparts. The wing-tip is black with white mirrors. In most *argentatus* the mirrors form a white triangle, as white includes tip of P10, and there is a large mirror on P9 as well as white tongues between grey and black in mid-primaries. To the north *argentatus* becomes darker on upperparts and shows reduced black on wing-tip, in some Arctic breeders enough to create whitish wing-tip with limited amount of black. *Argenteus* has paler grey upperparts and more black/less white in tip, as white mirror on P10 often does not include tip, and there are at most very inconspicuous white tongues in mid-primaries. Adult has yellow or even whitish eyes, surrounded by fleshy orbital ring to create beady look. The bill is yellow with red gonys-spot and the legs are fleshy, but in Baltic population many show yellow legs; see section following "adult winter".

Adult winter (Sep–Jan) has strongly brown-streaked or -spotted head, often creating dark hood and mask against pale 'fish-eyes'. The pattern is strongest Sep–Nov, as dark markings gradually wear off during autumn and early winter. During late stages of primary moult (Oct–Dec), wing-tip short and rounded with reduced black—nominate *argentatus* then often seems to lack black on wing-tip.

In Baltic some populations show a large percentage of yellow-legged birds. Such could be misidentified as Yellow-legged Gulls, but the following five points of comparison can help resolve the problem. (1) Herring is rather heavy with evenly rounded head, moderately strong bill and rather short primary projection; appears full-bodied. Yellow-legged is more elegant with larger, squarer head, heavier bill and more protruding breast, but longer, slenderer hindparts with larger primary projection. (2) Winter head pattern (Aug/Sep–Jan)—Herring coarsely dark-spotted or streaked on whole head, often creating dark half-hood that reaches sides of breast. Yellow-legged shows whiter head with finer streaks restricted to around eyes and on crown, head appearing whitish in autumn, when it is heavily dark-marked in Herring. (3) Fresh primaries in most Herrings have broad white tips, on P5–6 often merging with white tertial edges; equal amount of black and white in folded adult wing. Yellow-legged shows narrower white primary tips, and the white in tips of P5–6 does not merge with tertial edges. The hand in settled bird shows more black than white. (4) Herring shows extensive white on P9–10, on P10 often covering tip, and just narrow black markings on P5. Typically shows conspicuous white tongues in mid-primaries. Yellow-legged has more black, less white on wing-tip: white on P9–10 often narrow, on P10 typically a rounded window, which does not reach tip. Shows extensive black markings on P5, but no or just very faint white tongues on mid-primaries. (5) Eyes and orbital ring normally very pale in Herring: eyes whitish to pale yellow, orbital ring fleshy to yellow or orange. In Yellow-legged, eyes a tinge darker and orbital ring red to orange-red (though this is matched by many yellow-legged Herring Gulls).

Attains white **adult summer** head from Dec/Jan, at a time when bill becomes strong orange-yellow, gonys-spot bright red, and some develop slight yellow tinge to tarsus. The intensity of bare part coloration is strongest in early breeding season (Mar–May).

Juvenile overall greyish-brown, appearing rather featureless compared to other juvenile large gulls. In flight shows a conspicuous pale window on outer wing, which breaks the dark trailing edge. Dark secondaries then show up as dark rectangle along trailing edge of wing. Pale window is generally much stronger than in other large gulls, apart from American Herring and Vega Gulls. Mantle and scapulars are dark brown with faint pale scaling. Greater coverts have 4–5 even-width alternating dark and pale bars; some have broader dark than pale bars especially on outer coverts. Tertials vary, but are typically notched brown with irregular 'worm-bitten' pale edges reaching onto greater coverts. Underwing-coverts dark, in contrast to paler flight feathers, especially inner primaries, which also from below form a pale window. Tail has dark brown bar, pale edges and dark-spotted base, merging into dark-spotted tail-base, rump and tail-coverts. Bill black, but may at fledging already develop paler base.

First-winter similar to juvenile, but mantle and scapulars paler with dark transverse markings and often appear barred. During winter, these parts increasingly contrast with worn coverts. Head paler and less heavily marked through wear, and some birds appear white-headed at long range; close inspection should disclose dark spotting on forehead. Breast to belly become patchier. Bill mainly pale-based diffusing into darker tip, but some retain black bill into spring.

There is much individual variation. Although the rather weakly contrasting, brownish birds dominate, some are more like Lesser Black-backed, Yellow-legged or even Caspian Gull (which see for fuller discussion). These (most frequent E Baltic Sea) may show a combination of some of the following: black bill, pale head, almost uniform flight feathers (with much less window than expected), reduced pale barring on greater coverts (especially outer) and narrow pale edges to tertials (but covering entire inner web).

At the palest end of the range are birds with much broader paler barring on coverts, dark restricted mainly to pale tertials and broad pale edges to primaries, creating possible confusion with Glaucous or even Iceland Gull. At the darkest end of the range, rare very dark brown birds look very like American Herring Gull of the 'dark E Coast type' (which see for fuller discussion), but close inspection should reveal more extensive white at the base of the tail feathers, as well as along tail-sides. By Mar–Jun, head and body become paler, and retained juvenile wing feathers very worn and faded; flight feathers may bleach to colour of rest of upperparts, and dark pattern on tertials, coverts and tail is almost lost. Birds then look superficially similar to Glaucous and Iceland Gull, but mantle and scapulars still show dark barring in strong contrast to worn wing. This, together with untidy look, should prevent misidentification.

'First-summer' similar to first-winter, but head and underparts paler through wear, plumage strongly bleached and dark on secondaries, outer primaries and tail becoming brownish. Usually starts complete moult into second-winter by Apr/May, but retarded birds delay moult several months and become almost whitish.

Second-winter rather similar to first-winter, but normally more contrastingly pale and dark: head and underbody paler, outer primaries darker with rounded but narrow white edges, and pale window becomes more prominent, especially on the pale-mantled race *argenteus*. Greater coverts darker with finer pale vermiculations. Saddle with a mixture of greyish and barred feathers, grey ranging from all (mostly *argenteus*) to none (many nominate *argentatus*), sometimes showing a few grey median coverts (esp. *argenteus*). Rump white, in strong contrast to blackish tail-bar, being blacker and often more extensive than in first-years. Underwing pale with better-defined dark rows. Eye usually intermediate between first-year and adult. Bill almost invariably more bicoloured than in first-year, with broader pale tip and paler fleshy base against dark markings. Some show distinctly bicoloured bill, recalling bill of first-year Glaucous Gull.

Birds with plumage similar to first-winter are best identified by rounded shape of blacker outer primaries, more vermiculated greater covert markings, blacker tertials with broader, more irregular white tips, darker secondaries, paler eyes and solid white bill-tip.

Second-summer similar to second-winter, but head and underparts whiter. Advanced birds show grey on mantle/scapulars and new median coverts. Some birds have greater coverts darkest, forming dark carpal bar in midwing. Most show pale eyes, although many still not as whitish as in adult. Bill normally still without red gonys-spot.

Third-winter similar to second-winter (advanced birds similar to adult), but dark wing-tip larger, as (brownish-tinged) outer primaries have reduced white mirrors and tips and primary coverts are dark-centred. A varying number of wing-coverts brown or barred (in nominate *argentatus* often extensive). Traces of dark tail-bar often present. Bill mostly similar to second-winter, but by spring of fourth calendar year some develop red gonys-spot.

Third-summer similar to adult summer, but with flight feathers of third-winter and often extensive brown on coverts. Primaries have narrower white tips than adult. Bill may show dark markings.

Fourth-winter rather similar to adult, but dark brown markings on primary coverts, tertials, wing-coverts and on both mandibles indicate this age; dark markings on upper mandible are often especially seen in older birds.

VOICE Vocal. Commonest call a pale *ki-auww*, often combined with a deeper, cackling *gag-ag-ag* or *gau gau*. In breeding season ('song') a mournful, slow version of the call: *kyjAAh–kyjAAh…*

MOULT (nominate *argentatus*, S Scandinavia; pers. obs.) **Adult** moult to **winter** plumage complete mid-May–Dec. Starts with P1 (mid May–early Jul), latest in northern and eastern breeders. In E Denmark, P1 shed mid-late May; P3–5 late Jul, P5–6 mid-Aug, P(5)6–8(10) late Sep, P8–9 mid-Oct. P10 completed in 15–20% late Oct, in 50% early Dec and in 90% late Dec. Northern population generally later, with P1 shed normally late May, but sometimes not before mid-Jul, and P10 sometimes not completed until late Jan. This also noted in small minority Danish wintering birds, probably of N Scandinavian origin. Primary moult in Baltic Sea generally later; in Gotland, small minority reaches P8–9 late Oct (Jonsson 1998c). W populations (including W Denmark) generally complete moult earliest; P9–10 mid-Sep/mid-Oct–late Nov (Glutz von Blotzheim & Bauer 1982, pers. obs.). Inner secondaries simultaneously with P5–8 from (mid-May) early Aug. Tail Aug–Oct. Head and body mid-Jul–Oct, starting with median coverts. Head usually from late Aug. By mid-Sep >95% have some dark head-streaks (especially around eye); full winter head usually developed first half Oct.

Adult moult to **summer** plumage partial mid-Dec–Feb, including head and parts of body. Many white-headed from mid-Jan (rarely Dec): in Kattegat 75–90%, W Baltic Sea 50–75%, Finland 25–50% late Jan/mid-Feb. Northern breeders retain winter head into Mar (pers. obs., H. J. Lehto *in litt.*).

Juvenile moult to **first-winter** partial late Aug–Apr, including head, body, mantle and sometimes rump. Starts with lower scapulars and lower mantle late Aug–Sep, rest of mantle usually Oct. Suspends moult Nov–Feb, most obvious in large birds, probably of northern origin. Rarely, (1 in 200 or fewer) moults a restricted number of coverts (Jonsson 1998c, A. Forsten *in litt.*, pers. obs.).

Moult to **second-winter** complete Apr–Oct. Head and body from late April/May, mantle and scapulars mainly from late May. Primaries earlier than in adults; P1–2 (Mar)Apr, P5–8 Jun–mid-Jul, P7–9 Aug; P9–10 mid-late

PLATE 37. HERRING GULL *Larus argentatus*

Abundant large gull of W and N Europe. Breeds in colonies along coasts and on inlets, gathering in large flocks outside breeding season where food available, noticeably at rubbish dumps and fishing harbours.

Legs fleshy to pink; in E Baltic a small percentage of yellow-legged birds.

1. **Juvenile** (Jul–Oct) Rather uniform greyish-brown with diffuse streaks on head and underparts. Mantle and scapulars dark brown with pale edges, often leaving oak-leafed centres. Tertials variable, but majority with oak-leafed brown centres and complete paler edges, at outer webs reaching greater coverts. Greater coverts usually with even dark and pale barring. Wing-tip brownish-black with narrow pale edges. Bill at first dark, but in majority soon becoming paler-based. Legs fleshy.

2. **First-winter** (Oct–May) Renews mantle and scapulars throughout first-autumn. These feathers rather variable, but usually with dark subterminal markings, creating slight barring. Through wear, head (especially hindneck) and underbody become paler, and retained juvenile wing bleaches, producing some contrast to mantle and scapulars. Bill usually paler-based from Sep.

3. **First-winter** (Oct–May) Large individual variation. Some birds show paler head and breast, but still brown-mottled underparts and brown markings on undertail-coverts. Tertials in this individual with broader dark centres, but still with pale outer webs reaching greater coverts (which here are more finely dark-marked than 2 and 4).

4. **Second-winter** (Sep–Apr) Some similar to first-winter in showing broader dark markings on mantle and scapulars; but broad white tip to bill, more diffuse pattern to greater coverts, and broader white tips to tertials and primaries (the latter appearing rounded, showing white 'new moons').

5. **Second-winter** (Sep–Apr) Rather variable, but in majority slightly paler than in first-winter with mantle and scapulars a mixture of grey and dark-marked feathers, and finer, more vermiculated markings on greater coverts. Wing-tip blacker with rounder white primary tips (as 'new-moons') than in first-winter. Eye becomes paler from about 10 months of age. Bill fleshy with dark subterminal markings and pale tip.

6. **Third-winter** (Sep–Apr) More similar to adult, but note greyish-brown, slightly mottled tertials and parts of coverts, slight dark tail-markings and duller bill with black subterminal markings. Late in this plumage red starts to occur at gonys.

7. **Fourth-winter** (Sep–Mar) Similar to adult, but primaries generally with narrow white tips and bill still with extensive black subterminal markings.

8. **Adult winter** *argenteus* (Sep–Jan/Feb) Upperparts very pale grey. Black on wing-tip more extensive than in nominate *argentatus*; showing white mirror on P10, often not reaching tip. Black outer web of outer primaries usually reaches primary coverts. In winter, Herring Gull shows extensive brown head-streaking, sometimes creating slightly hooded appearance. Eye very pale. Legs pink.

9. **Adult winter** *argentatus* (Sep–Jan) As 8, but generally darker on upperparts with more extensive white on wing-tip; in most with complete white tip to P10, and often white and black on primaries of equal amount, white tips to P6–7 often merge into broad white tertial tips. Black on outer primaries does not reach primary coverts. Head markings in Baltic Sea populations often weaker and less distinct on breast-sides, more streaked than shown.

10. **Adult summer** *argentatus* (Jan–Aug) Head white. Bill bright yellow with red gonys-spot. Orbital ring fleshy to reddish.

1. Juvenile

2. First-winter

3. First-winter

4. Second-winter

5. Second-winter

7. Fourth-winter

8. Adult winter *argenteus*

6. Third-winter

9. Adult winter *argentatus*

10. Adult summer *argentatus*

PLATE 38. HERRING GULL *Larus argentatus*

Large gull of N and W Europe. In flight rather heavy with moderately long wings. Often in large flocks.

1. **Juvenile** (Jul–Oct) Brownish with brown-mottled head, underparts and underwing-coverts, the latter in some contrast to paler flight feathers. Upperwing with pale window on inner primaries, where dark confined to near tips. Shows dark brown tail-bar and pale edges to tail, rump moderately spotted; contrast between tail-bar and tail-base/rump thus never strong.

2. **First-winter** (Oct–May) Underwing two-toned with paler window on inner primaries mirrored on underwing. Some show darker trailing edge to outer wing. Head and underbody whiter through wear during first-winter, but underbody retains dense brown spotting.

3. **First-winter** (Oct–May) Similar to juvenile, but mantle and scapulars grey with dark subterminal markings, and head, especially hindneck, paler through wear. Bill with fleshy base from autumn.

4. **Second-winter** (Sep–Apr) Some rather similar to first-winter, but note dark, rather uniform greater coverts and broad white bill-tip (not shown on illustration).

5. **Second-winter** (Sep–Apr/May) Wing pattern similar to first-winter, but pale window on inner primaries stronger, and mantle/scapulars of same generation as coverts (in this individual grey). Some show pale mirror on P10. Rump white, thus better contrasting with blacker tail-bar than in first-winter. Bill variable, often fleshy with black subterminal markings. Underwing still with brown patterning.

6. **Third-winter** (Sep–Apr) Similar to adult, but with more extensive black on wing-tip, as primary coverts are black and white mirrors on P9–10 smaller. Shows variable black markings on tail. Bill duller than in adult with dark subterminal markings.

7. **Fourth-winter** (Sep–Apr) As adult, but sometimes with dark markings on primary coverts and black markings to bill.

8. **Adult summer** *argentatus* (Jan–Aug) Adult shows grey upperwing and black wing-tip, in *argentatus* with white on P10 normally covering entire tip.

9. **Adult winter** (Sep–Jan). Note differences in wing-tip pattern and paler upperparts of *argenteus*.

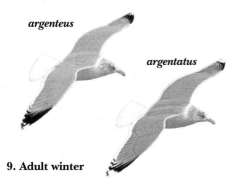

argenteus

argentatus

9. Adult winter

Juvenile *argentatus*

1. Juvenile

2. First-winter

3. First-winter

4. Second-winter

5. Second-winter

6. Third-winter

7. Fourth-winter

8. Adult summer
argentatus

Sep (mid-Nov). Coverts from Apr–May; mantle, lesser and greater coverts usually before mid-Jul, but greater coverts rarely not before early Aug. Head mid-Aug–Oct; many white-headed into late Sep.

Moult to **second-summer** partial Jan–Apr, including head and some or all body feathers and scapulars; sometimes some median coverts from May.

Moult to **third-winter** complete mid-Apr–Oct. Similar to adult, but earlier; P1 (sometimes T1–2) often mid-Apr, P9–10 mostly Oct–Nov. Coverts from mid-Apr–Jun.

DESCRIPTION ssp. *argentatus*

Adult Upperparts grey with slight bluish tinge (sometimes lacking) and clear-cut white trailing edge; shade of grey varies (Kodak Grey Scale (4)5–7(8)), darkest in N populations, palest in Atlantic W Europe, where many match paleness of race *argenteus*. Black in primaries Kodak Grey Scale 17–19 (when fresh). P10 black with white tip (max. 72mm in males, 65 in females), often with 1–5mm dark spot near tip of (especially) outer web; less frequent as complete bar (compare *argenteus* below). Birds with least amount of black show extensive pale tongues on inner webs to P8–10 'eating' into white tip, leaving only limited amount of black on inner web. P9 black with max. 36mm white mirror, in *c.* 25% restricted to inner web (in male rarely whole tip (max. 60mm) white with faint dark markings on inner web), in settled birds generally covering black on P10 to create broad white wing-tip. Outer web with 100–120mm black, not reaching primary coverts; inner web sometimes white apart from narrow blackish stripe near tip. P8 with 45–140mm black outer web, 20–85mm black inner web and max. 10mm white tongue between grey and black (broadest on inner web). P7 with 50–70mm black on outer, 18–40 on inner web and up to 10mm tongue on inner web. P6 grey with 18–39mm black subterminal spot on outer web and 10–25 on inner web, where sometimes lacking; white tongue as on P7, but usually covering both webs. P5 grey, in 30% with indistinct dark subterminal spots, mostly on outer web, but, in a few birds, covering both webs. P4 grey; 2% with dark subterminal markings. Primaries with max. 20mm white tips when fresh; P1–3 and secondaries grey with white tips (extremely rarely, black on wing-tip reaches P3 as very narrow dark marking on outer web, H. Lehto *in litt.*). P10 1–8mm >P9. Rest of plumage white.

Black on wing-tip gradually reduced towards N of breeding range. Birds with least black wing-tip markings (N Norway; in winter reaching S to Baltic/S Scandinavia and Great Britain, where represented by <1% in winter) sometimes referred to as 'Thayer's Gull-type'. In least black-patterned birds, black on P9–10 restricted to outer webs (mostly with more dark on inner webs than Thayer's). Often lacks dark subterminal markings on P5–6; some with only streaks on wing-tip. Narrow dark streaks in P7-10, restricted to outer webs. Upperparts darker than average nominate *argentatus*; rarely paler. All intergrades towards 'normal' birds exist, but variation between W and N Norwegian birds poorly documented. See also hybrids and yellow-legged adults below (skins in UZM, ZMO, Barth 1968a & b, Hume 1978a, Golley & Elliot 1993, Jonsson 1996, 1998c, Hario

1997, H. Heggland *in litt.*, pers. obs.).

Bill yellow with red to orange gonys-spot (normally restricted to lower mandible, but may reach upper mandible). Bill size: depth of gonys 1.75–2.5mm. Nostril triangular to oval: depth at distal edge 1.4–2.6mm, length 9.5–13.8mm; generally most oval-shaped in Baltic populations, in W Denmark narrower (depth >2mm rare). Orbital ring yellow, dull orange or greyish-pink, sometimes red to bright orange (frequent in yellow-legged birds). Iris whitish with creamy, lemonish or yellow tinge, rarely dark-peppered; exceptionally rarely dark (<1 of 5,000 in Finland—H. J. Lehto *in litt.*). Legs pinkish to greyish-fleshy; sometimes yellow, varying from greyish-yellow to bright yellow (thus similar to Yellow-legged Gull); yellow most frequent in late winter and early spring before onset of breeding season (at time when bill turns bright yellow); many show pinkish feet and yellow or yellowish tarsus (5–20% Denmark Feb–Mar), but small minority extensive yellow on both tarsus and feet. For yellow-legged birds, see also Geographical Variation below.

Adult summer (Jan–Sep) Head white. By late Jan–Mar, bill generally orange-yellow with bright red gonys-spot; tarsus sometimes yellowish-tinged. With wear, white primary tips reduced to narrow triangular spots, but never lacking in full adults. Eye might darken slightly before onset of breeding season; in mid–late Jan iris colour of 222 birds recorded: pale yellow to creamy in 217, dark greyish-yellow in two and brownish in three (pers. obs.).

Adult winter (Sep–Feb) Head with extensive dusky streaks or spots, densest around eye, occasionally covering whole head and upper breast to create hooded appearance (rarely as strong as in Yellow-legged Gull race *atlantis*). Dark patterning generally reduced with age; a small minority white-headed throughout winter (apparently birds aged >15 years—Klein 1994). Bill pale yellow with orange gonys-spot; often with indistinct dark markings especially on upper mandible. Base of bill sometimes with very faint fleshy tinge; may show greenish tinge Sep–Jan, especially in Baltic populations.

Juvenile (fledging–Sep/Jan) Head and underparts greyish-brown with heavy streaks or spots; forehead and hindneck paler, but usually dark-streaked. Eye-crescents dark grey, ear-coverts dark-spotted. <1% with more uniform greyish-brown to brownish-grey head and breast. Mantle and scapulars grey-brown with paler fringes, sometimes as pale spots along edges. Rump and tail-coverts white with dark brown streaks or spots, contrasting slightly with mantle and lower belly. Wing-coverts pale brown with dark subterminal markings, on greater coverts 3–5 bars of even width; may be mainly dark with narrower pale bars as in Yellow-legged Gull race *michahellis* (especially outer greater coverts), rarely mainly white as in Great Black-backed Gull. Alula and median primary coverts dark with pale edges, rarely pale with dark patterning. Tertials blackish-brown with oak-leaf centres and solid pale fringes, in most as irregular notches along entire edge; usually show darker subterminal bars, rarely on white background; 10% have tertials more solid dark with regular pale fringes as in Yellow-legged and Caspian Gulls, but white edges reach base (base dark in congeners; this occurs in <0.5% Herring). Palest birds (probably of Arctic origin) may show very pale tertials with dark reduced to centre or narrow subterminal barring, and very broad pale edges. P6–10 blackish-brown with 1–2mm pale tips (2–3mm on P8–3), emphasising pointed shape of juvenile feathers; edges rarely paler, creating row of pale Vs, strongest on inner webs, and slightly paler bases. P1–5 paler with dark subterminal markings, in most creating obvious pale window; rarely indistinct, as whole outer webs dark. P10 5–12mm >P9. Pale tips to P9 and P10 create pale 'double-spot' at wing-tip. Underwing-coverts and axillaries dark greyish-brown with narrow pale patterning in contrast to paler flight feathers, especially inner primaries. Rump and undertail-coverts white with dark spots or irregular bars. Tail white to brownish-white with greyish-brown bars. Has dark brown to blackish-brown tail-band of varying width, showing white tips and edges, but sometimes slight, broken or as several bars, reduced to T1–4. Tail-band generally covers <50% of tail (width at T1 50–80mm). T6 white with scattered dark pattern, in most with 2–3 spots on outer web. Iris dark brown. Bill blackish; sometimes with fleshy base to lower mandible. Pale tip to upper mandible 3–8mm, lower 0–5mm. Nostril as adult. Bill-shape similar to adult, but sometimes with more gently curved tip as in Caspian Gull. Legs flesh to greyish-flesh, rarely pinkish.

First-winter (Sep–Mar) similar to juvenile, but head generally paler through wear, especially forehead, chin and throat. Often shows dark eye-mask. Mantle and scapulars pale buff with 2–3 brown to sooty subterminal bars, sometimes triangular, anchor- or diamond-shaped markings, from midwinter in contrast to worn upperwing. Primaries may lose pale fringes from late Dec and pale to brown from midwinter. Underbody usually a mixture of brown irregular blotching and paler areas. Bill usually bicoloured from Dec with dark tip/cutting edges and dull fleshy base. Broader pale bill-tip developed from Mar.

Large individual variation. Certain birds almost white-headed with blackish bill, denser dark upperpart-markings and inner primaries, solid dark-centred tertials with narrow pale edges and more solid dark tail-band. Such birds mainly of Baltic origin, represented in winter by max. 5% in Denmark and 15% in Finland (see below under 'Yellow-legged Herring Gulls').

By (Mar)late Apr–late May upperwing often strongly bleached; coverts, tertials and flight feathers may lose most dark or pale markings; secondaries, P6–10 and dark on tail becomes brown (but never palest part of plumage as in Glaucous/ Iceland Gulls). Fresher mantle and scapulars then in clear contrast to upperwing. With wear, exposed primary parts may become paler: appear as row of diffuse paler chevrons on folded wing-tip, from below creating impression of pale primaries with faint darker tips, in head-view from below sometimes showing wing-tip similar to Thayer's or even Iceland Gull race *kumlieni*. This sometimes shown from Jan, commoner in spring (Hedgren & Larsson 1973, pers. obs.).

'**First-summer**' (Mar–Sep) similar to first-winter, but head (especially hindneck), rump and underbody paler through wear, and juvenile wing-coverts faded (sometimes to whitish late spring; birds with broader darker subterminal markings on mantle become darker as pale feather-edges wear off). May develop grey mantle feathers (<5% of mantle Apr, max. 20% late May, but some geographic variation in amount of grey, with least in Finland) as first step of complete moult into second-winter. Bill usually bicoloured with fleshy base in contrast to darkish cutting edges and tip; some have dark bill similar to juvenile, but with broader pale tip. Iris turns olive-grey, greyish-brown or dull yellow from Apr, but some still dark-eyed well into autumn.

Second-winter (Sep–Mar) Head white with extensive dark streaks; sometimes whitish with few streaks. Underbody and rump whitish with variable, sometimes few, dark streaks or spots, on undertail-coverts often reduced to dark V-spots along edges as in first-year Caspian/Yellow-legged Gull. Mantle and scapulars vary from patterned as first-winter (the rule in Baltic populations) to grey; <5% with wholly grey 'saddle', but then often with dark spots and paler edges. Tertials barred black/white or with strong whitish subterminal markings; normally dark bars are narrower than pale, especially at tip. Inner wing-coverts similar to juvenile, but paler with narrower dark bars, sometimes with a few greyish-tinged coverts (especially median coverts) intermixed. Greater coverts greyish-brown with fine paler barring (5–10 indistinct bars) or vermiculations, sometimes indistinct; few inner coverts rarely grey. P6–10 brownish-black; rarely with indistinct white mirror on P10 and indication of white tongues of adults. Primaries with distinct whitish fringes, emphasising rounded shape (compare juvenile). P1–4(5) grey with dark shaft-streaks and subterminal markings; pale window stronger than in first-years. P10 0–9mm >P9. Secondaries dark brown with irregular pale fringes; sometimes whitish with dark outer webs. Underwing-coverts similar to juvenile or whiter with dark restricted to feather-tips creating more regular dark lines, in 10% white with dark restricted to narrow markings on lesser coverts and primary coverts. Tail white with variable black band, generally narrower but blacker than in first-years, on T1 40–50mm; often with white intermixed; white tips and edges to tail wider. T6 with dark subterminal bar near tip, sometimes with a few dark spots along outer web. Iris grey to yellow with olive or brownish tinge; rarely as pale as in adult, or as dark as in first-years. Bill very variable: in majority flesh with black tip or subterminal bar (13–19mm), dark cutting edges and pale tip (5–11mm on upper, 4–7mm on lower mandible). Rarely similar to first-winter Glaucous Gull, but only exceptionally bubblegum-pink. Bill sometimes dark with pale distal part. Legs fleshy.

Second-summer (Mar–Sep) similar to second-winter, but head and underbody usually white; belly often dark-spotted. Mantle, scapulars and often median coverts grey, sometimes greyish-brown or brown-tinged with dark subterminal markings. Dark areas on wing and tail fade to whitish, in contrast to new grey feathers of third-winter plumage. White fringes to P1–7 often evident into late May (compare first-years). Bare parts similar to second-winter; bill dull yellow with dark subterminal markings (13–19mm dark bar on upper, 4–7mm on lower mandible).

Third-winter (Sep–Apr) Head and underbody similar to adult winter, but sometimes with scattered brown and grey spots on underbody, especially on breast-sides and flanks. Mantle, scapulars, median coverts and most of lesser coverts and greater coverts brownish-mottled to grey (grey dominates in most advanced birds); usually brown markings on inner wing, strongest on lesser coverts; greater coverts sometimes similar to second-winter, creating darker midwing-bar. Sometimes lacks grey on coverts. Primary coverts greyish-brown with pale edges. Primaries similar to adult, but browner with smaller white mirror on P10 (28–50mm), rarely lacking. P9 dark, in small minority with indistinct white mirror on inner web. Division between dark tip and pale bases diffuse or slightly mottled. P5 with 15–27mm dark subterminal bar, sometimes up to 50mm on inner web. Some have P5 grey. P4 sometimes with dark markings. Primaries with 10–15mm white tips; often worn off on P5–10 by mid-spring. P1–2 normally as adult. Underwing, usually with some dark markings especially on lesser and primary coverts; on a few birds extensively dark as in first-years. Upper- and undertail-coverts white, usually with scattered dark markings, especially along edges. Tertials dark grey with irregular pale edges and darker vermiculations; rarely as in adult (but exceptional in race *argentatus* – A. Forsten *in litt.*). Tail white with varying dark subterminal markings, often reduced to isolated black spots, streaks or vermiculations in T1–4; T5–6 often with very scattered dark markings; sometimes similar to second-winter. Tail might be white from this age. Bare parts similar to second-winter, but bill often paler yellow (from spring) with narrower dark subterminal spots or bar (5–16mm on both mandibles), normally covering gonys; rarely >50% of bill dark. As in second-winter, some have dark bill with broad pale tip (opposite to Glaucous Gull). Develops red in gonys from spring of fourth calendar year (K. Bengtsson *in litt.*). Legs as adult or slightly duller.

Retarded third-winter similar to second-winter with grey saddle, dark/pale-patterned coverts, all-dark outer primaries, and secondaries/tail. Tail, however, generally has finer dark vermiculations, especially towards base. Bill greyish-brown with indistinct darker subterminal bar and paler yellow tip to mandible (Bengtsson 1998).

Third-summer (Mar–Sep) similar to third-winter, but head and underparts white or with limited dark spots or streaks, especially on belly and primary coverts. With wear (summer), brown on wing-coverts fades to whitish and white primary tips wear off. Orbital ring reddish-brown. Bill generally as adult, but sometimes with weak dark subterminal bar on both mandibles.

Fourth-winter (Sep–Feb) similar to adult, but most show brownish tinge to outer primary coverts (sometimes restricted to dark shaft-streaks), a few dark-patterned wing-coverts and brown or grey mottling on largest alula (white or pale grey in adult). Wing-tip brownish-tinged black with (compared to adult) restricted white mirrors, on P10 30–60mm, on P9 10–25mm, and more diffuse division between dark and grey at primary bases. Tail sometimes with faint dark mottling to T1–4. Dark subterminal bill-markings generally broader, covering both mandibles (max. 12mm); in fully adult normally restricted to narrow 'new moon' on upper mandible. 'Retarded' birds of this age similar to third-winter (Monaghan & Duncan 1979).

Fourth-summer (Feb–Sep) as adult apart from wing-markings of fourth-winter until moult.

Fifth-winter (Oct–Feb) as adult; a minority with darker

centres to 1–4 outer greater primary coverts (sometimes as dark shaft-streaks), and sometimes dark-mottled alula.

Note Detailed description based on extensive skins in NHM, NRK, UZM, ZMO, many of which are ringed birds of known age. There is no rule without exceptions, and especially not so in Herring Gull: e.g. a bird in its eighth summer had a 35mm white mirror on P10 and dark shaft-streaks on outer three greater primary coverts, on inner web as drop-shaped spot (skin UZM 68062). Birds of 5–8 years of age may still show characters typical of 3–4 years, especially brown-tinged primary coverts and dark bill-markings. Adult may show dark bill-markings (proven up to 17 years of age), mainly in winter, but regular from July (H. J. Lehto *in litt.*).

GEOGRAPHICAL VARIATION Slight and clinal in W Europe (see race *argenteus* below); intergradation evident in W Europe between English Channel, some N British populations and SW Denmark (own studies and skins).

L. a. argentatus (Germany, Scandinavia, Baltic Sea, Finland) described above. Gradually becomes larger in wing and bill length towards N (see below). Adults in populations in N Norway and along White Sea coast to Murmansk Coast differ from southerly populations in having darker bluish-grey upperparts, but reduced black on wing-tip (especially on P9–10, and on P5–6 where dark markings may be lacking). 53% show white tip to P10; pale tongue on P10 small or narrow. Certain birds show limited enough black pattern on wing-tip to suggest Thayer's Gull or hybrid Glaucous × Herring Gull. Frequently shows yellowish tinge to legs (28 out of 180) (Barth 1968a, 1975, Jonsson 1998c, H. Heggland & A. Forsten *in litt.*, pers. obs., skins in ZMO), but this not supported by field studies in N Norway may–Jun 2002, where just one of 3000 adults showed yellow legs (U.G. Sørensen, pers. comm., pers. obs.)

Adult in **E Baltic/S Finland** (probably also Belarus and along S Baltic coastline W to Schleswig-Holstein) as western population, but frequently with yellow or yellowish-tinged legs, in Finland 5–54.5% in spring/summer, in Christianø, Bornholm, Denmark 6%, but varying from year to year. In other respects similar to other populations, apart from slight tendency for slightly paler upperparts (Kodak Grey Scale 4.5–6), on average more black on P5, covering both webs in 30% (Adriaens & Mactavish in prep.). Orbital ring often red to reddish-orange. Head-streaking in winter finer on average than in Kattegat/Atlantic populations. First-years frequently rather more contrasting, with white head, black bill and darker wing, than more westerly populations, but pale window on inner primaries usually still obvious. Pale markings on tertials and greater coverts often reduced, thus often similar to Yellow-legged and Caspian Gulls, which see.

Note Birds with mainly yellow legs formerly distributed in bogs of E Baltic states and W Russia, with 100% yellow-legged adults Lake Saimaa, Finland, up to 1950s. Following increase and range expansion of westerly population in the 1960s, yellow-legged colonies were eventually invaded by pink-legged birds, resulting in hybridisation and the extinction of the yellow-legged type. The yellow-legged populations in E Baltic and

Russia could also be a result of simultaneous meeting between Herring and Yellow-legged/Caspian Gulls following expansion of breeding range.

Birds with yellow legs in winter present in <1% of population in Great Britain, 2–8% in Denmark.

Yellow-legged populations from Baltic Sea sometimes referred to as '*omissus*' (Voipio 1954, Stegmann 1960, Barth 1968a & b, Franzmann 1973, Glutz von Blotzheim & Bauer 1982, Mierauskas *et al.* 1992, Hario 1997, Jonsson 1998c, A. Forsten, A. Lindholm, H. Lehto & H. J. Lehto *in litt.*).

L. a. argenteus (Netherlands, N France, Great Britain and N Atlantic islands; winters W Europe between S Scandinavia and Iberia). Generally slightly smaller with more rounded head, less deep breast and shorter legs than *argentatus*; identification on structure alone not recommended owing to differences between males and females, but sometimes possible in small females; only a few males look as powerful and 'fierce' as many nominate *argentatus*. Nostril generally more slit-like, as depth at distal edge 1.1–2.0mm (compare nominate *argentatus*).

Adult differs from nominate *argentatus* by combination of generally paler grey upperparts (Kodak Grey Scale 3–5.5; rarely as pale as Glaucous Gull) and more black on wing-tip: P10 black with 30–35mm white mirror; in *c.*20% with white tip, max. 65mm, most frequent in birds from Ireland, Scotland and Iceland; in S Germany and England 13–20% with white tip to P10, in Faeroe Islands 14–20%. P6 with max. 45mm black subterminal spots on both webs (rarely reduced to outer web), P5 with dark, often narrow subterminal markings (lacking in 10% – M. Collinson *in litt.*); P4 in 14% British birds with black subterminal mark. White tongues on P3–5 weak or lacking. P10 0–6mm >P9. White tertial crescents generally less distinct. Orbital ring orange-yellow to dull orange; in winter sometimes brown. Eyes pale yellow to pale cream. Bill usually yellow with bright red gonys-spot, generally brighter coloured than in *argentatus* throughout winter.

Largest in N and W part of range: Wing Scotland, Ireland adult male 404–443 (425.8, n=20), adult female 395–421 (409.3, n=20). Netherlands, England adult male 395–429 (416.8, n=21), adult female 382–420 (399.5, n=23). Bill adult male Scotland, Ireland 50.6–61.0 (54.5, n=20), England, Netherlands 44.3–54.1 (50.6, n=23), adult female Scotland, Ireland 44.3–54.1 (48.6, n=20), England, Netherlands 44.4–50.8 (47.8, n=22). Tarsus adult male Scotland, Ireland 59.9–69.3 (64.4, n=21), England, Netherlands 58.0–66.6 (62.9, n=22), adult female Scotland, Ireland 56.4–65.6 (61.4, n=20), England, Netherlands 53.3–68.6 (58.7, n=22) (Coulson *et al.* 1982, Grant 1986b, Garner & Quinn 1997, skins).

Moult to winter plumage in southern breeders averages one month earlier than in nominate *argentatus*. Primary moult starts with P1 late Apr–May, reaches P3–5 early Jul, P7–8 late Sep–mid-Oct, P9–10 late Oct–early Nov. Winter head assumed Aug–Dec; most in summer plumage early Jan–Feb. Northern populations from Atlantic islands, however, have later moult than southern populations; in such birds probably as late as in same-latitude *argentatus*.

Large area of overlap between nominate *argentatus* and *argenteus* between SW Denmark and N Netherlands, to a lesser degree also N and E Britain (in winter occurs regularly S to Belgium). Measurements in Dutch population intermediate between *argentatus* and *argenteus*. Breeders from W Denmark slightly paler than Norwegian birds (Kodak Grey Scale 4–5 in W Denmark). Many birds in overlap area combine dark upperparts of *argentatus* with wing-tip of *argenteus*, or very pale upperparts and wing-tip of *argenteus*; also among wintering birds North Sea/Kattegat, where '*argentatus*' with *argenteus* wing-tip account for up to 10% (pers. obs., skins in UZM; also Glutz von Blotzheim & Bauer 1982).

Juvenile/first-winter very similar to *argentatus*, and generally not identifiable in field. *L. a. argenteus*, however, seems to vary less, may appear cleaner brown on head and underparts, and generally shows broader dark tail-bar and spotting at tail-base and rump. Underwing frequently darker, appearing solid dark brown on underwing-coverts and axillaries. Said to show narrower pale tips and edges to rectrices, only narrow pale edges to primary tips (often worn off from Dec), and 2–4 dark (and often narrower) bars on greater coverts (Golley & Elliot 1993), but much individual variation. Tail-bar normally solid, and in some covering most of tail, leaving impression of darkish-looking tail in field as in American Herring: close inspection reveals extensive white patterning especially on T6 with dark tip and 3–5 dark bars on outer web. Tail variation, however, as large as in nominate *argentatus*, some showing broad paler tips/edges and white 'extra bars'. Birds with white head in winter rare (versus *argentatus*). A greater proportion retain dark bill in winter than *argentatus* (Golley & Elliot 1993). In southern population moult into first-winter starts mid-late Aug, thus generally earlier than in *argentatus*. Rarely includes some coverts. In contrast, Iceland birds mainly juvenile into early Oct (pers. obs.). Some show very worn upperwing-coverts from Jan – earlier than *argentatus*.

Second-winter similar to *argentatus*, but a larger proportion develop complete grey saddle and median coverts, sometimes also inner lesser and greater coverts; as these areas are pale grey, they contrast more strongly with brown and dark areas in plumage (generally darker than in *argentatus*). Head generally paler (sometimes white) and dark tail-bar on average broader and fuller, in some creating extensive blackish-looking tail. Paler window on inner wing usually stronger, lacks white mirror in P10. Moult slightly earlier; 50% shed P1 late Apr; P4–6 moulted late May and P9–10 late Aug (Cramp & Simmons 1983).

Golley & Elliott (1993) mention that full adult plumage is acquired more rapidly than in nominate *argentatus*. While certain second-winters look like third-winter *argentatus*, age development is affected by individual variation in both subspecies.

Aberrants *Leucism* Very pale birds with reduced dark pigmentation most frequent among **first-years**. Younger birds superficially similar to Glaucous, Glaucous-winged and Iceland Gull, but often look untidy and very worn from midwinter and especially spring. Most creamy-white to white with reduced dark patterning on body and coverts, and very faint brownish outer primaries (dark often reduced to P7–10, sometimes only on outer webs), secondaries and tail-bar; dark parts in flight feathers exclude Glaucous and Iceland Gulls (but not hybrid Glaucous × Herring). Often shows darker eye-mask in first winter (Hedgren & Larsson 1973). Bare parts normal. Flight action often quicker than usual, the result of poor plumage condition. Separation from Glaucous and Iceland Gull not too difficult, as these have paler wing-tip than rest of the delicately scaled, buff or creamy-tinged plumage. Survival rate of such birds probably low, explaining the very rare occurrence of older birds (Hedgren & Larsson 1973, Ullman 1983, pers. obs.). **Adult** shows grey and reduced primary-markings and pale upperparts (Kodak Grey Scale 2–3), inviting confusion with Iceland *kumlieni* and Glaucous-winged Gull. The former is smaller and neater with jizz as in Iceland Gull, the latter have dark eyes situated high on head, broader bulbous bill-tip and white mirror on P10 only. Note that poor condition of leucistics may cause delayed moult (Jukema 1987, pers. obs.).

Albinism True albinos all white, often with atypically pale bare parts. Some very pale leucistics show normal bare parts (such as mainly dark bill and eyes in first-year) (Hedgren & Larsson 1973, Walker 1991a, pers. obs.). First- year plumage is mostly seen between late summer and spring, suggesting that survival of atypically pale large gulls is low. The quick wear of such birds produces an untidy look at a time when other pale gulls (e.g. Glaucous and Iceland) look rather fresh.

Partial albinos show normal plumage with parts being all white, e.g. white outer primaries. The same white parts may occur in subsequent years (Bentz 2000, H. & H. J. Lehto *in litt.* & photos). Melanistics are known.

Hybrids For hybridisation with Glaucous, Yellow-legged and Lesser Black-backed Gull, see these species.

DISTRIBUTION AND MIGRATION Breeds in colonies on islands, from coastal cliffs, sandy islands and dunes to gravel pits and buildings; also lakes up to 2,000m altitude. Winters mainly along coasts, but dependent on rich food sources. Plentiful at fishing ports and refuse dumps.

Total population 700,000–850,000 pairs. Dramatic growth twentieth century following protection from persecution and egg-collecting, and with increasing availability of refuse. Increase dramatic 1910–1975 with 15–20-fold increase in Denmark and Germany and five-fold increase in the Netherlands; increasing rate 13–14% annually Britain and the Netherlands to 1970s. In some areas arrested by preventative measures; in Britain decrease of 50% 1969–1987 owing to combination of culling, botulism and salmonella, reduction of food availability through better refuse disposal management, and improved utilisation of commercial fishing. In Saltholm, Denmark, colony of 43,000 in 1979 reduced to 7,000 in year 2000.

Population around 2000 and development in some countries (pairs): Great Britain 206,000 (334,000 1969–1970); Ireland 51,970 late 1960s; Iceland

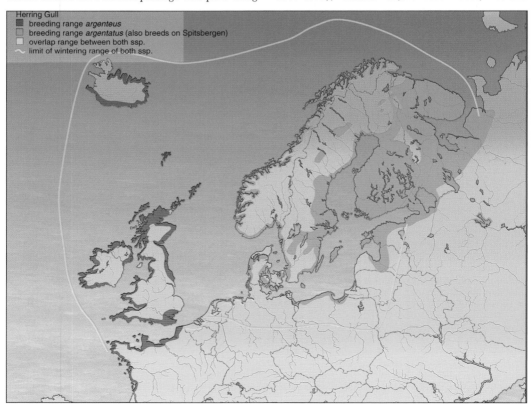

Herring Gull
- breeding range *argenteus*
- breeding range *argentatus* (also breeds on Spitsbergen)
- overlap range between both ssp.
- limit of wintering range of both ssp.

10,000–15,000 (colonised 1925); Netherlands 67,000 (10,000 1925–1930, 15,000–20,000 1957, 62,000 1979, 90,000 1980s); Belgium 1,300 (first bred 1959); France 74–77,000 1997/98 (decrease from 87–89,000 in 1987/88); Germany 50,000 (W Germany N Sea coast 3,000 1906, 21,148 1977; some hundreds Baltic coast; E Germany 1,500–1,700 (rare early twentieth century)); Denmark 55,000–58,000 (3,000 1920, 17,000 1960, 62,300 1975); Norway 150,000–200,000 (260,000 1970; colonised Spitsbergen 1950); Sweden 60,000–100,000 (population stable from mid-1970s); Finland 28,300; Poland 2200; Switzerland 5–6 1979; Estonia 40,000; Lithuania 300–350; Russia 6,700 (Murmansk coast) and 1,300 (White Sea); Poland small population (Chabrzyk & Coulson 1976, Glutz von Blotzheim & Bauer 1982, Risberg 1990, Lloyd et al. 1991, del Hoyo et al. 1996, Hagemeijer & Blair 1997, Grell 1998, Petersen 1998, Väisinen et al. 1998, Bijlsma et al. 2001, Faber et al. 2001, Faber & Neubauer 2002, P. Adriaens & P. Yésou in litt.).

Sedentary or short-distance migrant, first-years generally most dispersive. In winter sparsely reaches Iberian Peninsula; a few Mediterranean. N population (N Norway, N Russia and N Finland) mostly migratory, leap-frogging over S populations. Winters to Great Britain and France.

Breeding sites left from Aug. In Sep gatherings up to 50,000 Schleswig-Holstein/Dutch Waddenzee and 20,000 NW Jutland, Denmark. Main migration Swedish Baltic mid-Sep–Nov, peak days >10,000 Öland; smaller migration across Swedish Great Lakes to Kattegat. N German migration peak from Oct/Nov, largest numbers there Jan–Mar (Goethe 1963, Cramp & Simmons

1983, Gruber 1995). White Sea and N Norwegian birds migrate directly to Baltic or westwards. Murmansk birds follow Norwegian coastline to main wintering areas N Sea and English Channel S to France and W to Faeroe Islands. Of 99 recoveries of N Norwegian birds Oct–Feb, 23% from Netherlands, Belgium and France, 23% from Great Britain. Populations from E Baltic States and Finland mainly stay within Baltic region in winter with dispersal to Kattegat. A few reach further S, as far as Adriatic and Lake Garda. Italy.

In N and W Europe 2.7 million birds winter; most are attracted by refuse tips, where gatherings reach 20,000. Danish winter population 500,000; in Kattegat area 100,000. In Great Britain increase early Dec, peak Dec–mid-Feb, including nominate argentatus, which normally leaves Jan–Feb; 275,632 1983, rising to 376,775 in 1993; max. 45,000 London area. In Netherlands around 100,000 winter along coasts and 60,000 offshore. In Germany, e.g. Ruhr 10,000; in France 300,000; in Iceland 15,000–25,000 (Glutz von Blotzheim & Bauer 1982, Coulson et al. 1984b, Lack 1986, Dean 1987, Breife et al. 1993, Jensen 1993, Rose & Scott 1994, Grell 1998, Bijlsma et al. 2001, Burton et al. 2003, P. Yésou in litt.).

S Scandinavian population sedentary or short-distance migrants, wintering mainly S Norway, Kattegat, Skagerrak and W coast of N Europe S to Belgium/Great Britain, where probably scarcer than N population. Baltic birds move W and SW to winter quarters in W Baltic N to Stockholm and S to Denmark and S to E coast of Baltic, to a lesser degree N Sea. Wismar (Germany) birds mainly go SW to Ruhr. S Scandinavian, W European and British population sedentary or disper-

---

HERRING GULL Four-year gull. Abundant N and W Europe. Similar to American Herring and Vega Gull. Most abundant Northern European large gull. Stocky and full-bodied with prominent tertial step, rather short wings, and strong bill with pronounced gonydeal angle. Eyes small, situated centrally in head.

Adult has pale grey upperwing with contrasting black wing-tip; white mirrors on P9–10 (often including wing-tip), but only narrow, often incomplete dark markings on P5 (W European race argenteus generally paler grey with fuller black wing-tip than N and E nominate argentatus). Bill yellow with red gonys-spot. Eyes whitish to pale yellow, orbital ring pale. Legs fleshy to pink (some populations within nominate argentatus show yellow legs). As **summer** plumage is attained (Jan–Jul) bill often orange-yellow and tarsus sometimes tinged yellowish in late winter, at this time the white summer head is acquired. In **winter** (Aug–Jan) head with dark streaks or spots, densest around eye and on hindneck: pale eye then conspicuous. Bill at most with faint dark markings.

Juvenile (Jul–Oct) rather uniform greyish-brown, upperwing with pale window on inner hand, between dark outer wing and secondaries. Underwing dark-patterned, contrasting with paler flight feathers. Rump dark-spotted, dulling contrast to dark brownish-black tail-bar. Greater coverts dark- and pale-barred, especially on inner ones. Underbody densely dark-patterned. Tertials with oak-leafed centres and broad, irregular pale edges. For individual variation see text.

First-winter (Oct–Apr) similar to juvenile, but head generally paler, bill-base paler, underparts blotchier. Mantle and scapulars paler and greyer with more distinct dark bars or markings, as winter progresses in contrast to worn and brown (eventually paler) wing.

Second-year similar to first-year, but eye paler, bill-tip solid pale, base of bill paler fleshy to yellow and pale markings on greater coverts fainter, more as vermiculations. Tertials blacker with broader white edges. Primaries blacker with broader white tips. Often shows grey intermixed in saddle. Rump generally whiter and pale window on inner hand generally stronger.

Third-year similar to adult, but with fuller dark wing-tip, as primary coverts have dark markings, and there are narrower white mirrors on P9–10. Often with scattered dark markings on coverts and tail; bill normally with solid black markings; red gonys-spot starts to turn up in spring of fourth calendar year.

Fourth-year as adult, but often with narrow dark shaft-streaks to primary coverts, some dark marking on bill and broader dark markings on P5–7.

sive, moving in all directions; British and Dutch birds have reached S to Portugal, E to Denmark/Poland and W to Greenland. E German birds have reached C Europe and N Italy. Ringed birds from Finland and Poland have been recovered Italy and Greece. Iceland and Faeroe birds sedentary, but some recoveries from W Great Britain, Denmark and E Greenland (Fritze 1976, Glutz von Blotzheim & Bauer 1982, Cramp & Simmons 1983, Petersen 1984, Flensted 1985, Handrinos & Akriotis 1997, Dubois *et al.* 2000).

S breeding sites settled from late Jan. Spring migration of northern population Mar–Apr.

Vagrant Mediterranean E to Israel (1) and Egypt (1). Also NE America, where regular wintering Newfoundland.

MEASUREMENTS Lengths in mm; weights in g. Own data based on skins in AMNH, NHM, UZM, ZMA, ZMO. *L. a. argentatus* N Norway, S Scandinavia. *L. a. argenteus* Great Britain, Faeroes, Iceland. Juvenile/first-winters from late Aug when fully grown. Included in adults are second-years+, which have measurements identical to adults.

WING LENGTH

L. a. argentatus		
Adult male	418–480 (445.3)	127
Adult female	394–455 (424.5)	141
First-year male	417–462 (442.2)	50
First-year female	392–435 (417.8)	43
L. a. argenteus		
Adult male	395–460 (424.5)	45
Adult female	381–427 (404.3)	59
First-year male	381–444 (422.4)	22
First-year female	375–418 (397.4)	22

Note Harris & Jones (1969) give for British adult male 399–455 (mean 426, n=129), adult female 382–418 (mean 406, n=116), juv./first-winter male 406–435 (mean 416), juv./first-winter female 373–418 (mean 395).

BILL

L. a. argentatus		
Adult male	49.0–64.9 (56.5)	127
Adult female	44.6–59.1 (50.1)	139
First-year male	46.2–57.9 (52.7)	50
First-year female	44.7–52.9 (48.8)	43
L. a. argenteus		
Adult male	46.4–63.9 (53.9)	53
Adult female	44.4–55.8 (49.3)	63
First-year male	44.1–53.6 (49.5)	22
First-year female	44.2–50.9 (45.3)	22

Note Harris & Jones (1969) give for British adult male 49.0–64.4 (mean 54.6, n=148), adult female 43.0–56.2 (mean 50.0, n=130), juv./first-winter male 50.0–59.8 (mean 55.2, n=10), juv./first-winter female 44.0–63.0 (mean 49.2, n=6).

BILL DEPTH AT GONYS

L. a. argentatus		
Adult male	16.2–21.9 (19.9)	127
Adult female	15.5–20.9 (17.7)	143
First-year male	15.9–19.8 (18.0)	50
First-year female	14.8–18.3 (16.4)	43

Note Coulson et al. *(1981) found gonys depth to increase with age. This to some degree fits our own data of birds of known age; average in birds 10 years or older larger than in other series (skins in UZM).*

L. a. argenteus		
Adult male	16.9–21.3 (19.3)	63
Adult female	15.0–19.5 (17.2)	64
First-year male	14.2–18.9 (16.7)	22
First-year female	13.3–17.0 (15.7)	22

BILL DEPTH AT BASE OF BILL

L. a. argentatus		
Adult male	17.2–22.3 (19.9)	117
Adult female	15.4–20.7 (17.8)	129
First-year male	15.8–21.1 (19.0)	50
First-year female	15.3–18.6 (17.0)	43
L. a. argenteus		
Adult male	17.1–21.1 (18.4)	53
Adult female	15.0–19.3 (17.3)	53
First-year male	14.7–19.9 (17.8)	22
First-year female	13.8–17.3 (16.3)	22

GONYS LENGTH

L. a. argentatus		
Adult male	13.6–20.0 (17.2)	127
Adult female	12.3–18.3 (15.2)	141
First-year male	13.2–19.3 (15.8)	50
First-year female	12.9–16.6 (15.0)	43
L. a. argenteus		
Adult male	13.3–18.1 (16.4)	52
Adult female	11.9–16.9 (15.2)	54
First-year male	12.6–17.9 (15.0)	22
First-year female	10.9–16.4 (14.3)	22

TARSUS

L. a. argentatus		
Adult male	62.0–75.2 (67.1)	131
Adult female	55.1–69.8 (62.4)	142
First-year male	59.4–70.3 (66.7)	48
First-year female	55.8–68.0 (60.9)	43
L. a. argenteus		
Adult male	56.4–70.3 (64.1)	52
Adult female	53.3–68.6 (59.6)	63
First-year male	54.5–66.7 (62.6)	22
First-year female	52.9–64.2 (58.5)	22

Note Harris & Jones (1969) give for British adult male 55–71 (mean 63, n=126), adult female 52–69 (mean 58, n=112), juv./first-winter male 57–68 (mean 62, n=14), juv./first-winter female 53–63 (mean 60, n=6).

Weight *L. a. argentatus* N Norway/N Russia adult male 755–1,495, adult female 717–1,385; Finland adult male 1,040–1,300, adult female 780–1,100 (Hario 1986), juv./first-winter female 750–910; Bohuslän, W Sweden, adult male 975–1,525, adult female 800–1,375; Denmark adult male 973–1,310, adult female 830–1,450, first-year male 898–965, first-winter female 1,040–1,350; Germany adult male 890–1,365, adult female 720–1,080; Texel, Netherlands, first-years 565–1,275; heaviest midwinter (Glutz von Blotzheim & Bauer 1982, Cramp & Simmons 1983, skins in UZM, ZMO). *L. a. argenteus* Britain adult male 725–1,150, adult female 600–975 (Glutz von Blotzheim & Bauer 1982, Cramp & Simmons 1983).

Note: slight clinal variation in size:
N Norway:

WING

Adult male	427–478 (448.4)	25
Adult female	415–438 (424.3)	21

BILL

Adult male	52.2–65.2 (56.9)	25
Adult female	49.2–58.0 (51.5)	21

TARSUS

Adult male	62.5–75.0 (67.5)	25
Adult female	57.1–68.1 (62.2)	21

Finland, Estonia:

WING

Adult male	445–475 (458.0)	6
Adult female	417–439 (427)	7

BILL

Adult male	53.9–59.6 (57.2)	6
Adult female	50.1–52.6 (51.1)	7

TARSUS

Adult male	67.0–72.0 (69.2)	6
Adult female	57.3–66.8 (60.6)	7

Denmark (breeding birds):

WING

Adult male	418–469 (439.4)	54
Adult female	394–446 (419.5)	56

BILL

Adult male	43.9–60.8 (55.5)	57
Adult female	44.6–59.8 (50.2)	56

TARSUS

Adult male	61.6–73.6 (66.7)	52
Adult female	53.6–70.4 (62.8)	55

W Germany:

WING

Adult male	409–454 (431)	80
Adult female	385–440 (412)	80

BILL

Adult male	48.0–59.5 (54.5)	80
Adult female	43.9–55.6 (50.1)	80

TARSUS

Adult male	57.0–72.0 (65.9)	80
Adult female	52.5–67.0 (61.2)	80

(Barth 1968a, 1975, Glutz von Blotzheim & Bauer 1982, Cramp & Simmons 1983, pers. obs. and skins).

Sobortsk, White Sea

TARSUS

58.8–75.0 (rarely <70mm)

(Skovgaard 1932).

Herring Gull *Larus argentatus*. **323. Juvenile** ssp. *argentatus*. A typical, rather uniform juvenile with dark saddle, showing irregular pale dots on feather edges. Møn, Denmark. Jul 1990. *Per Schiermacker-Hansen.* **324. Juvenile** ssp. *argenteus*. While the plumage variation among both subspecies is considerable, these particular birds are clearly paler and greyer-tinged than 323. Note the tendency for *argenteus* to look slightly rounder-headed and narrower-billed than *argentatus*. IJmuiden, Netherlands. 27 Aug 1993. *Klaus Malling Olsen.*

Herring Gull *Larus argentatus*. **325. 1st-winter** ssp. *argentatus*. Note new, barred mantle feathers present from around Sep in 1st-years. In photo 325-333, compare especially differences in barring on tertials and greater coverts. On tertials, pale edges often irregular, leaving dark 'hollow-leaf' centres, but sometimes with more regular pale edges similar to Lesser Black-backed, Yellow-legged and Caspian Gulls. Greater covert pattern varies from equal amounts of pale and darker barring to predominantly dark. Ørhage, Denmark. 6 Oct 1995. *Klaus Malling Olsen*. **326. 1st-winter** ssp. *argentatus*. A dark individual with extensively dark tertial-centres and predominance of dark barring on greater coverts. Compare American Herring, and note colder-tinged grey-ish-brown overall impression and densely spotted rather than rather uniform underbody as well as spotted (not barred) ➡

undertail-coverts. Turku, Finland, 6 Nov. 1998. *Harry J. Lehto.* **327. 1st-winter** ssp. *argentatus.* While mantle and scapulars appear barred in most, some, especially birds of NE origin, show broader dark markings and more spotted feathers. Turku, Finland. 9 Jan 1999. *Harry J. Lehto.* **328. 1st-winter** ssp. *argentatus.* A rather pale bird with unusually pale tertial centres and pale-edged primary tips. With wear, saddle contrasts well with worn coverts. Copenhagen, Denmark. 9 Mar 2001. *Klaus Malling Olsen.* **329. 1st-winter** ssp. *argentatus.* Note extensive pale area at base of bill and rather pale head. Underbody spotted. Compare American Herring photos 305-307. Turku, Finland. 28 Dec 1997. *Harry J. Lehto.* **330. 1st-winter** ssp. *argentatus.* This and 333 are examples of birds with extensive pale coloration along tertial edges and on greater coverts, the latter matching Great Black-backed, Vega and Mongolian *L. cachinnans mongolicus.* Turku, Finland. 28 Dec 1997. *Harry J. Lehto.* **331. 1st-winter** ssp. *argentatus.* Turku, Finland. 28 Dec 1997. *Harry J. Lehto*

269

Herring Gull *Larus argentatus*. **332. 1st-winter** ssp. *argentatus*. Note the unusual white head of upper bird, which furthermore has darkish bill and broad dark tertial centres. Such rather contrasting birds occur regularly among *argentatus* in the Baltic Sea. Turku, Finland. 16 Jan 2000. *Harry J. Lehto*. **333. 1st-winter**. Frequently, very pale individuals may show indistinct pattern on upperparts including tertials, and conspicuous pale fringes to primaries, inviting confusion with the paler large gull species. Datteln, Germany. 24 Dec 1999. *Martin Gottschling*. **334. 1st-winter** ssp. *argentatus*. In flight, note conspicuous pale window in inner primaries in both ssp, leaving dark secondaries as an isolated rectangle on innerwing. The rump is less patterned than in most birds, leaving contrast to dark tail-bar similar to e.g. Yellow-legged Gull, but note extensive pale edges and tips to tail feathers. Helsinki, Finland. 21 Mar 1993. *Klaus Malling Olsen*. **335. Juvenile** ssp. *argentatus*. Note extensive spotting on rump and tail-base, dulling contrast to dark tail-bar and typical 1st-year wing-pattern. Simrishamn, Scania, Sweden. 8 Aug 1999. *Klaus Malling Olsen*. **336. Juvenile,** probable ssp. *argenteus*. Note rather extensive and broad tail-bar, often present in western breeders. Rotterdam, Netherlands. 27 Aug 1993. *Klaus Malling Olsen*. **337. Juvenile** ssp. *argenteus*. A very typical 1st-year Herring, appearing rather uniform greyish-brown with conspicuous pale window in inner primaries and densely dark-spotted rump to tail-base. Note that birds with rather broad tail-bars show tendency to broader dark areas in mid-tail than along tail-sides, contrary to American Herring. Le Portel, France. 12 Sep 1997. *Arnoud B. van den Berg*. **338. Juvenile** ssp. *argenteus*. Dark tail-bar strong enough to create impression of an all-dark tail occurs in ssp. *argenteus*. Such birds are easily misidentified as American Herring Gull, but note the much fainter barring on a whiter rump compared to American Herring Gull as well as extensive pale sides to tail. (photo 308-310). Borgarnes, Iceland. 9 Oct. 1994. *Klaus Malling Olsen*. **339. Juvenile** ssp. *argentatus*. A pale individual with atypical,

but not too infrequent, tail-pattern. Scania, Sweden. 8 Aug 1999. *Klaus Malling Olsen*. **340. 1st-winter** ssp. *argentatus*. A very unusual individual, which might be a hybrid with Glaucous, or just an abnormally patterned bird. Helsinki, Finland. 21 Mar 1993. *Klaus Malling Olsen*. **341. 1st-winter** ssp. *argentatus*. Rather dark bird with heavy dark spotting on underbody. Møn, Denmark. 26 Oct 1992. *Per Schiermacker-Hansen*. **342. 1st-winter** ssp. *argenteus*. A very dark bird with unusual broad dark tail-bar and predominantly (but still blotchy) dark brown plumage. Similar to American Herring, but with more extensive pale at base of tail and along edges of T6. Compare with photos 308-310. Scheveningen, Netherlands. 20 Nov 1998. *Arnoud B. van den Berg*. **343. 1st-winter** ssp. *argentatus*. From below, Herring Gull shows extensive, rather diffusely patterned underwing-coverts and axillaries and often rather pale primaries, tipped dark. Note also broad white tips to edge of tail and densely dark-spotted undertail-coverts. Finland. 24 Jan 1998. *Henry Lehto*.

Herring Gull *Larus argentatus*. **344. 1st-summer** ssp. *argentatus*. Actually, 1st-summer is a synonym for late 1st-winters. Note how dark wing-pattern may almost disappear through wear and fading, and primaries develop broad white edges. Finland. 12 May 1998. *Henry Lehto*. **345. Moulting into 2nd-winter**, ssp. *argentatus*. Halland, Sweden. 12 Aug 1995. *Klaus Malling Olsen*. **346. 2nd-winter** ssp. *argentatus*. Although many 1st-winters of esp. this ssp. develop another generation of barred mantle and scapular feathers, this bird is aged by pale eyes, by coarser markings on greater coverts, broader, more complex tertial pattern and rounder white tips to blacker primaries. Gilleleje, Denmark. 12 Jan 1997. *Klaus Malling Olsen*. **347. 2nd-winter moulting into 2nd-summer** ssp. *argentatus*. Compare with 345. Finland. 15 May 1998. *Henry Lehto*. **348. Moulting into 2nd-winter**, ssp. *argen-* ➡

349
350
351
352
353
354

teus. 2nd-year tail often looks more extensively black than in 1st-years. This individual rather similar to 1st-year, but note active wing moult and coarser dark upperpart markings. Pas-de-Calais, France. 30 Aug 1993. *Klaus Malling Olsen.* **349. 2nd-winter** ssp. *argenteus.* Many *argenteus* develop grey saddle against barred upperwing, and are as such easily aged. Great Britain. 21 Feb 1990. *Harry J. Lehto.* **350. 1st-winter moulting into 2nd-winter** ssp. *argenteus.* Certain *argenteus* have dark axillaries and underwing-coverts as seen in American Herring, Lesser Black-backed and Yellow-legged ssp. *atlantis.* Rotterdam, Netherlands. 4 Jul 1994. *Klaus Malling Olsen.* **351. 3rd-winter** Underparts somewhat similar to adult, but note browner primaries with smaller white mirrors, brown tail-bar and still extensive dark markings on underwing-coverts. Skagen, Denmark. 16 May 1995. *Klaus Malling Olsen.* **352. 3rd-winter** ssp. *argentatus.* Many birds at this age show a mixture of characters related to each plumage. Grey saddle against dark-barred coverts and large amount of dark in tail should suggest 2nd-winter, but the rather extensive grey on other coverts and broader white tips to new primaries point towards 3rd-winter. Turku, Finland. 6 Nov 1998. *Harry J. Lehto.* **353. 3rd-winter** ssp. *argentatus.* Note grey saddle and large amount of grey in coverts, contrasting with darker-centred outer primary coverts. Hanstholm, Denmark. 25 Feb 1995. *Klaus Malling Olsen.* **354. 3rd-winter** ssp. *argentatus.* Some of this age-type still show darker-barred greater coverts. Helsinki, Finland. 21 Mar 1993. *Klaus Malling Olsen.*

Herring Gull *Larus argentatus*. **355. 3rd- summer** ssp. *argentatus* of yellow-legged type. Dark markings on tail and coverts and black-ish bill markings are signs of immaturity. Møn, Denmark. 2 May 1999. *Klaus Malling Olsen.* **356. 4th-winter** ssp. *argentatus.* Dark markings on dull-looking bill in otherwise adult plumage indicates this age. Møn, Denmark. 20 Jan 1990. *Per Schiermacker-Hansen.* **357. 4th-summer** ssp. *argentatus.* Wing-tip pattern in *argentatus* varies, but compared to *argenteus* has more white in wing-tip. Note broad white tip to P10 and black just reaching P6. Turku, Finland. 24 Apr 1996. *Harry J. Lehto.* **358. 4th-summer** ssp. *argen-tatus.* Compare wing-tip with 357, and note lack of dark pattern on P5 and broad white primary tips typical for ssp. *argen-*

tatus. Turku, Finland. May. *Harry J. Lehto*. **359. Adult summer** ssp. *argentatus*. Note equal amount of black and white in wing-tip and fleshy legs. This bird shows a rounded head and narrow bill, indicating female. Compare male in 360. West Jutland, Denmark. April 1993. *Klaus Malling Olsen*. **360. Adult summer** ssp. *argentatus*. Compare especially large bill with 359, indicating male. Note pale orbital ring and broad white tip to P10. Öland, Sweden. 22 May 2000. *Klaus Malling Olsen*. **361. Adult winter** ssp. *argentatus* of yellow-legged type. Note coarse brown head-markings, typical for Herring (cf. Yellow-legged Gull). Møn, Denmark. 20 Jan 1990. *Per Schiermacker-Hansen*. **362 Adult summer** ssp. *argentatus*. Møn, Denmark. 4 Mar 1990. *Per Schiermacker-Hansen*. **363 Adult (or 5th) winter** ssp. *argentatus*. Note coarse dark spotting on head and breast-sides, emphasising whitish, evil-looking eyes. Outer primaries missing, caused by moult. Esbjerg, Denmark. 10 Oct 1995. *Klaus Malling Olsen*.

Herring Gull *Larus argentatus*. **364. Adult winter** ssp. *argentatus*. Note head-streaking creating slightly hooded appearance. Møn, Denmark. 25 Nov 1990. *Per Schiermacker-Hansen*. **365. Adult summer** ssp. *argenteus*. The black on the wing-tip, more extensive than in *argentatus*, is noticeable here; note esp. small white mirror, not broad white tip to P10 and extensive black in wing-tip reaching P5 as narrow bar (see American Herring Gull, photo 321). However, upperparts rather dark, matching *argentatus*. Many birds in W Europe show intermediate characters between the two subspecies so assignment to race should be cautious in any other than birds showing all racial characters. IJmuiden, Netherlands. 4 Jul 1994. *Klaus Malling Olsen*. **366 Adult summer** ssp. *argentatus*. Note rather narrow black primary markings of this ssp. with just very faint dark markings on P5. Turku, Finland. 13 Jul 1998. *Henry Lehto*.

Herring Gull *Larus argentatus*. **367. Adult summer** ssp. *argentatus* Compare wing-tip pattern with 365 as well as with American Herring, photo 321. Turku, Finland. 15 May 1998. *Henry Lehto*. **368. Adult summer** with wing-tip intermediate between *argentatus* and *argenteus*. IJmuiden, Netherlands. 4 Jul 1994. *Klaus Malling Olsen*. **369. Adult summer** ssp. *argentatus* of arctic type. Note restricted amount of black in wing-tip compared to 'southern' *argentatus* with black pattern appearing as streaking rather than solid black tip. More white on P7-9 especially striking. Vardø, Finnmark, Norway. Jul 1998. *Håkon Heggland*.

20. YELLOW-LEGGED GULL

Larus michahellis (Naumann, 1840, coast of Dalmatia)   **Plates 39–40, Photos 370–417**

IDENTIFICATION Length 52–58cm, wingspan 120–140cm. Yellow-legged Gull is the Mediterranean and mid-Atlantic counterpart of Herring Gull. In areas of overlap with Herring and Caspian Gulls there is very little or no hybridisation with either. There are several differences in jizz, plumage and calls, and the treatment of Yellow-legged Gull as a separate species from Herring and Caspian Gull is fully supported by genetic studies (Yésou 1991b, Klein & Buchheim 1997, Faber *et al.* 2001, Crochet *et al.* 2002, Yésou 2002).

The widespread taxon *michahellis* is similar to Herring *argentatus*, but generally it is more powerful, elegant and deep-breasted with a larger head, more bulbous forehead, flatter crown and fuller, squarer neck. Bill generally stronger with blunter, more strongly curved tip, in largest males approaching Great Black-backed Gull. Breast deeper, but hindparts slenderer, emphasised by less prominent tertial step. Settled birds have longer wings: fully grown primaries project 5–7cm beyond tail (3–6 in Herring). Often gives impression of being 'Herring Gull in front, Lesser Black-backed Gull behind'. Legs slightly longer with longer visible tibia. Structural differences most evident in males of SW Mediterranean birds, birds from Atlantic coastline of Iberian/N Africa being generally smaller with flatter forehead and shorter legs. Eastern populations often neater with slenderer bill; may approach Caspian Gull (which see).

Adult Similar to Herring *argentatus*, but upperparts generally darker grey, lacking bluish tinge of most Herrings. Shows distinct white trailing edge to inner wing, which, combined with smoky-grey upperparts, recalls Common Gull races *canus/heinei*. Has more black/less white on wing-tip than Herring nominate *argenteus*: white mirror on P10 narrower, thus similar to average Herring race *argenteus*. Often lacks white mirror on P9. Shows extensive black subterminal bar on P5; if present in Herring, it is narrower and mainly restricted to outer web. Some E Mediterranean/Black Sea Yellow-legged show more white on wing-tip, approaching Herring nominate *argentatus* and Caspian nominate *cachinnans*, sometimes with white tip to P10 and only narrow black markings on P5. When fresh, folded wing shows 4–5(6) evenly spaced white primary tips beyond tertials, narrower than black exposed primary bases (evident with wear). Inner visible primaries have white tips surrounded by black, not merging into white tertial edges as in most Herring *argentatus*. In flight, fuller black wing-tip and darker secondaries create underwing intermediate between Herring and Lesser Black-backed, sometimes close to latter's race *graellsii*. On upperwing, some have paler primary bases, creating slightly three-toned 'Black-legged Kittiwake' impression. Legs yellow. Bill as Herring but, unlike Herring, red gonys-spot often reaches upper mandible. Eye darker yellow; orange to blood-red orbital ring (often broader than in Herring) adds to darker-eyed look than in Herring. Head white, in **winter** (Jul–Nov) often with fine dark streaks around/behind eye and on crown only. Most Herring

have entire head coarsely dark-spotted Oct–Jan, often as dark hood (see *atlantis* below), making pale eyes staring.

Juvenile intermediate between Herring and Lesser Black-backed, but generally more 'colourful' and contrasting, with whiter head and dark mask in contrast to black bill and whitish, grey-brownish-tinged underbody with whitish lower belly to undertail-coverts, the latter with dark spots along sides. Flight feathers blackish-brown, often with slightly paler inner primaries, but not as strong as in Herring. Greater coverts intermediate between Herring and Lesser Black-backed: outer dark-centred grading to paler barring on inner ones, which are often as distinctly barred as on Herring. Tertials dark, with pale tips only, at edges often irregular as in Herring, but centres darker and more solid. Underwing pale greyish-brown, generally better patterned than Herring, but in many as darkish-looking; the contrast between pale belly and dark underwing often striking. Rump and tail-base white (with weak dark spots) contrasting well with solid black tapering tail-bar, at distance similar to first-year Common Gull. Often shows pale wedge on lower back as in Caspian Gull.

Moults mantle, scapulars and coverts from Jul/Aug. earlier than Herring (see Moult). When direct comparison with Herring made, coverts, tertials and primary tips generally more worn and warmer brown. In **first-winter (autumn)** nominate *michahellis* acquires whitish head and underbody with dark eye-mask, combined with black bill (creating impression similar to first-year Mediterranean), dark streaks or spots on hindneck and often streaked crown. Breast (especially sides) dark-spotted against white head and belly; rear-flanks just above tibia often with more conspicuous dark chevron-markings. Tertials and coverts become worn and partly lose pale fringes, thus looking cleaner and warmer brown from Sep. Upperwing then in strong contrast to new grey scapulars and, in many, also inner coverts, with double transverse bars, anchors or broad dark spots. Barred first-winter feathers occur later in Herring and Lesser Black-backed (earliest from late Aug), but contrast not evident before midwinter, and there are no new coverts in Herring (frequently a few in Lesser Black-backed). In autumn appears three- or four-toned: warm-brown upperparts and greyish-patterned scapulars contrast with white head and underbody (especially in E populations). Bill black, at most with paler base to lower mandible.

First-year Herring less contrasting and colder greyish-brown with more densely but evenly dark-patterned head, broader pale bars on greater coverts and less contrast between fresh mantle/scapulars and coverts. Tertials in most 'oak-leafed', with pale edges reaching coverts. Lacks pale wedge on densely spotted lower back. Underparts more coarsely dark-patterned (especially belly), which only exceptionally are unmarked white. Underwing-coverts generally more uniform dark. Tail-bar often narrower and browner against dark-spotted tail and rump. Bill usually pale-based from late

278

autumn. Some *argentatus* trickier with pale head, black bill, browner upperparts and tertial/greater covert pattern approaching Yellow-legged: in such birds look for more densely dark-spotted underbody (especially belly), pale tertial edges reaching coverts and all dark-spotted/barred undertail-coverts. Certain male Yellow-legged approach jizz of Great Black-backed, with which they share black (and large) bill, white head and rather uniform dark flight feathers, but Great Black-backed is generally larger with denser pale upperpart-markings, much broader pale bars on greater coverts, broad and irregular white tertial tips and much weaker dark tail-bar (never strong blackish) against broad white tail-edges. Some second-winter Herring and Great Black-backeds similar to first-winter Yellow-legged, but with pale bill-tip (and normally base), uniform-looking greater coverts, with only indistinct pale marbling, no contrast between mantle and upperwing-coverts and blacker new primaries with broader whitish edges (not brownish and pointed as in first-year). See Lesser Black-backed Gull and Caspian Gull for fuller discussion of main characters.

'**First-summer**' as first-winter, but becomes paler and less patterned through wear, with scattered second-winter feathers turning up on upperparts from late spring. Unmoulted parts on upperwing often strongly bleached, especially greater coverts. Legs may start to get yellow from late May (Garner & Quinn 1997). From Apr/May, moult into **second-winter**, where mantle, scapulars and inner greater coverts become grey or weaker-patterned than in first-winter. Head white with fine streaks on crown and nape, often heavier on hindneck and breast-sides, dark eye-mask and sometimes white border to lower ear-coverts. Greater coverts often greyish-brown with narrow faint irregular bars. Tertials dark with whitish tips, irregularly barred near tip. Grey mantle contrasts with white rump and tail-base. Tail white with black bar, suggesting Common Gull. Underwing whitish with scattered, sometimes solid dark markings. Eye often still dark. Bill blackish with paler base and tip. Legs fleshy to yellowish.

Herring Gull paler and less 'adult', with only scattered grey mantle feathers, fainter tail-bar, broader white tips and edges to tertials, and darker-patterned underwing. Eyes often pale and bill normally more strongly bicoloured.

Second-summer similar to adult, but bill often as adult; combination of dominantly adult head/bill and upperparts with brown primaries and traces of dark in tail is the rule (combination exceptional in similarly aged Herring (L. Larsson *in litt.*). Legs yellowish.

For subsequent ages, see detailed description.

Third-year similar to adult, but with less extensive white mirrors in wingtip, dark-centred primary coverts, traces of dark tail-bar and dark markings in bill.

VOICE Somewhat similar to Lesser Black-backed Gull, deeper and hoarser than Herring Gull: *woouw* or *grou-uw*. Long-call consists of 14–25 elements (8–14 in Herring Gull) (Mierauskas *et al.* 1992); differs strongly from Caspian Gull, which see.

MOULT Occurs from a few weeks to three months ear-lier than in Herring Gull; in Black Sea 2–4 weeks earlier, in C Europe 1–2 weeks (Garner & Quinn 1997, Jonsson 1998c, A. Forsten *in litt.*, pers. obs. in Slovakia, Hungary, Bulgaria, France, Portugal).

Adult moult complete to **winter plumage** late Apr/early Jun–early Nov, earliest in S Mediterranean populations (in most birds studied, Sicily, Apr–early May, most had shed P1). P1–2 May, P(3)5–6 late Jul/early Aug, P6–8 mid-Aug; P9–10 late Sep–mid-Oct (late Nov). Secondaries and tail moulting heavily latter half of Aug–Sep, completed early Oct. Winter head assumed late Jul–mid-Aug, generally earliest in W populations. (exceptionally, N American vagrant has not completed primary moult before late Jan—Mactavish 1995).

Adult moult to **summer plumage** partial Oct/Nov–Mar, including head and body. Many white-headed from Oct/Nov.

Juvenile moult to **first-winter** partial, including head, body and often inner wing-coverts (especially median and inner greater coverts) mid-Jul–Oct, starting with mantle and scapulars, in E part of range from Jul, where 50–75% of mantle/scapulars moulted late Aug. Scapulars and parts of coverts Aug–Oct; in NW France early Oct >95% had moulted mantle and scapulars, but 3% still juvenile, and 60% showed no sign of covert moult; 37% had moulted max. 50% of lesser coverts and some inner greater coverts and 3% >50% of coverts; 10% had moulted one inner tertial and 30% had renewed some tertials by Jan; 75–80% in Spain and Switzerland had renewed some coverts Dec–Feb (Jonsson 1998c, Schweizer 2003). Head Sep–Oct. Covert moult more restricted in E populations, where sometimes none until spring.

Moult to **first-summer** partial; sometimes few feathers moulted from midwinter, but mainly from Apr, including head, body and some or rest of wing-coverts; could be regarded as first steps of moult into **second-winter,** which is complete between Apr and Sep. May attain greyish mantle and scapulars from Apr, followed by inner greater coverts. Primaries Apr–late Aug/Sep (Oct), normally reaching P2–3 late May, P6–8 late Jul–mid-Aug. Birds finishing primary moult by late Jul/early Aug have been noted (Garner & Quinn 1997, A. Forsten *in litt.*).

Moult to **second-summer** (Dec)Jan–May partial, including head and body, continuing with complete moult into **third-winter**, which on average is earlier than in adult; birds from late Jun had renewed up to P5–6, some coverts and parts of tail.

DESCRIPTION

Adult Upperparts medium grey, like darker Herring race *argentatus* (Kodak Grey Scale 5–7), but lacking bluish tinge. Wing-tip with more black than Herring *argentatus*, more similar to race *argenteus*. P10 black with 20–55mm white mirror. Tip black, less frequently reduced to dark spots on one or both wedges, more rarely white (11% E populations). Grey inner web runs <50% out to the tip, rarely 75%, especially in E of range (Jonsson 1998c). P9 black, in 50–68% with 6–21mm white mirror, often restricted to inner web. P8–6 with 25–42mm black subterminal markings, gradually less extensive inwards; often with faint white tongues, espe-

PLATE 39. YELLOW-LEGGED GULL *Larus michahellis*

The 'Herring Gull' of the Mediterranean basin and W Black Sea. Reaches N and W Europe in autumn; winter range includes NW Africa. Compared to Herring Gull, shows larger, squarer head, flatter crown and fuller hindneck, but slenderer rear-parts.

1. **Juvenile** (Jul–Aug/Sep) Greyish-brown with whitish face and dark eye-mask. Breast and flanks brown-mottled, but belly and central undertail-coverts pale. Mantle and scapulars dark brown with pale edges, creating scaly pattern. Tertials with solid dark centres and pale edges (often slightly 'oak-leafed' at tips only), white on outer web not reaching greater coverts. Inner greater coverts distinctly barred, but outer gradually darker, often creating slight dark rectangle in folded wing. Bill black. Legs fleshy.

2. **First-winter** (Sep–May) Mantle and scapulars renewed by Sep (in Herring Gull on average a month later). New mantle feathers, scapulars (and some inner coverts) grey with dark subterminal markings, often with finer dark subterminal anchors than in Herring. Retained juvenile coverts contrast somewhat to new feathers. Tertials blackish with white edges to tips and distal part of outer web only. Head with white face and solid dark mask, similar to first-year Mediterranean Gull. Bill remains black in first year. Note fine dark markings to sides of tail-coverts only and dark scaling in flanks.

3. **First-winter** (Sep–May) A paler individual than 2. In addition to new mantle and scapulars, many also renew some coverts (as in Caspian Gull and unlike Herring Gull). Tertials moderately worn from autumn. From Sep, most show white underparts with dark spotting to breast-sides and flanks only. Note also strongly hooked black bill and solid dark mask, compared with Caspian Gull, although some show slightly paler base especially to lower mandible from winter.

4. **Second-winter** (Jul–Feb) An early second-winter individual. Dark rectangle on greater coverts especially striking in this rather pale-patterned individual. Next generation tertials with broader white edges than in first-year. Bill with broad pale tip. Retarded birds later in second-winter may look like this individual.

5. **Second-winter** (Sep–Mar) Individual which has attained mainly grey saddle and median coverts (and some tertials). Wing still with brown, pale-vermiculated lesser and greater coverts, the latter appearing more diluted than in first-winter. Primaries blacker with rounder white tips. Dark eye-mask still conspicuous. Bill dull flesh with extensive dark subterminal markings. Develops pale eye from about one year of age. Legs start to attain yellowish tinge.

6. **Third-winter** (Sep–Mar) Similar to adult, but with more extensive dark markings on bill, and often dark markings on tertials and indistinct pale primary tips. Legs pale yellow.

7. **Adult winter** (Aug–Nov/Dec) Adult shows grey upperparts, generally darker and lacking slight bluish tinge of Herring Gull. Shows more black on wing-tip than Herring with narrower white primary tips and white mirror on P10. Head often with fine brown streaking especially on crown and ear-coverts. The illustrated bird shows maximum amount of streaking. Some show narrow blackish markings on upper mandible. Legs dull yellow. Herring Gulls with yellow legs (frequent N Norway and Baltic Sea) normally show more extensive brown head-markings, often as spots covering whole head, bluish tinge to upperparts and broader white primary tips, often merging into white tertial tips.

8. **Adult summer** (Dec–Jul/Aug) Head white. Orbital ring red. Extensive red gonys-spot often reaches upper mandible, unlike Herring Gull. Legs bright yellow.

9. **Adult winter** *atlantis* from Azores, showing darker upperparts than *michahellis* and heavily dark-spotted head between autumn and mid-winter, creating hooded appearance.

9.

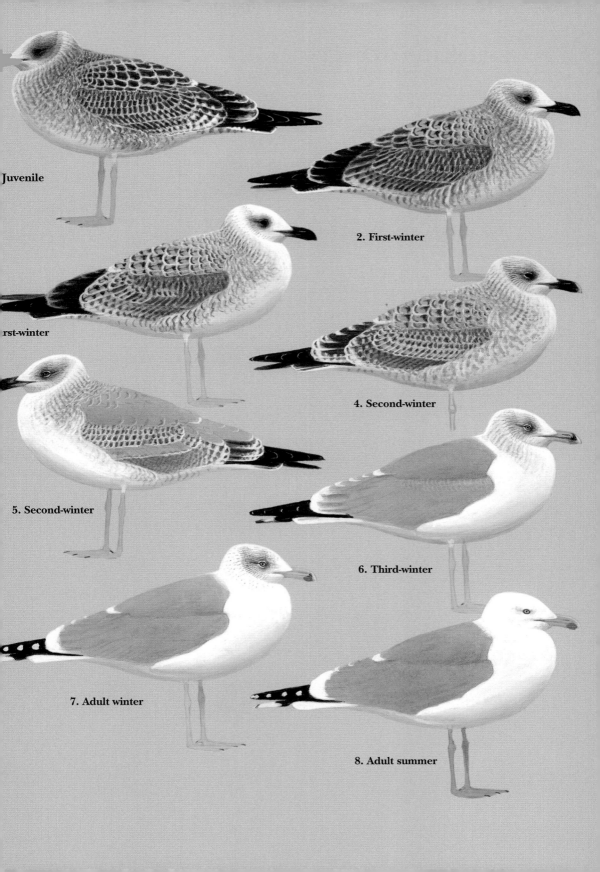

Juvenile

2. First-winter

rst-winter

4. Second-winter

5. Second-winter

6. Third-winter

7. Adult winter

8. Adult summer

PLATE 40. YELLOW-LEGGED GULL *Larus michahellis*

In flight similar to Herring Gull, but slightly narrower-winged, hence recalling Lesser Black-backed Gull.

1. **Juvenile** (Jul–Sep) Compared to Herring Gull more contrasting without or with only slight (from wear) pale window on inner primaries, darker outer greater coverts (creating dark rectangle), better contrast between solid black tail-bar (with white edges) and white, faintly dark-spotted rump (rump and tail more as in Common Gull). Often shows pale wedge on lower back in contrast to dark tertials. Underwing generally more finely dark-marked than in Herring Gull. Head with white face and dark mask, underbody at first with brown spotting.

2. **First-winter** (Sep–May) Mantle and scapulars (and often some wing-coverts) renewed. Head and underbody whiter than in juvenile, white body in good contrast to brown-marked underwing-coverts. Black bill and dark eye-mask contrast well to pale head. Rump and tail-base white in very good contrast to blackish tail-bar.

3. **Second-winter** (Aug–May) Grey saddle (and often median coverts) contrasts well with brownish wing, white rump and black tail-bar: combination of all-grey saddle and solid black tail-bar the rule; very rare in Herring Gull. Underwing still with extensive dark markings. Head often white with faint dark mask, in contrast to brown hindneck-markings. Lacks pale mirror on P10.

4. **Second-summer** (May–Aug) Note grey mantle and inner wing combined with solid black tail-bar.

5. **Third-winter** (Aug–Apr) Similar to adult, but with more extensive dark on wing-tip, as primary coverts dark and white mirror on P10 much smaller. Shows variable black tail-bar, often broken. Bill dull yellow with extensive dark markings.

6. **Adult winter *michahellis*** (Aug–Mar) Adult shows medium-grey upperwing (cleaner grey than in Herring) and black wing-tip with white mirrors on P9–10 narrower than in Herring. Lacks white 'moons' between black and grey in mid-primaries of Herring nominate *argentatus*; unlike typical Herring, black markings solid on P5. White trailing edge to inner wing stronger than in Herring. Underwing with extensive grey rectangle on secondaries. Faint head-streaking usually present in winter.

7. **Adult summer *atlantis*** (Dec–Jul/Aug) Head white. Note solid black wing-tip with smaller white mirrors than 6. This wing-tip matches ssp. *atlantis* but is seen in many *michahellis* too.

1. Juvenile

4. Second-summer

2. First-winter

3. Second-winter

5. Third-winter

6. Adult winter *michahellis*

7. Adult summer
atlantis

cially on inner web (in nominate *argentatus* tongue longer and more obvious, covering both webs). P5 with 10–35mm black subterminal bar of even amount on both webs; rarely reduced to indistinct dark spot on outer web. On folded wing, P5 falls beneath outer tertial. P4 rarely with faint greyish-black subterminal bar/spot in one web only. P3–1 grey, P3 rarely with faint darker subterminal marking. Primaries with 5–10mm white tips when fresh. Orbital ring dark red to reddish-orange, rarely brown. Eyes dull greyish-yellow to bright greenish-yellow, exceptionally brown or dark (Gruber 1995, Garner & Quinn 1997, Millington & Garner 1999, skins). Bill orange-yellow to bright yellow with red gonys-spot. Nostril triangular; depth at distal edge 1.8–2.5mm, length 9–12.1mm. Bill depth at gonys (2.5) 2.6–3.0(3.1). Legs bright yellow to duller yellow-greyish; rarely fleshy but never bright pink. In Hungary mid-Aug, tarsus in 12% bright yellow, in 25% yellowish, in 55% greyish-yellow, in 8% grey, in 3% fleshy-grey (pers. obs.). See Caspian Gull.

Adult summer (Oct/Nov–Jun) Head white. With wear, white primary tips reduced to faint spots. Legs yellow to orange-yellow. Blood-red gonys-spot often penetrates to upper mandible. Legs bright yellow.

Adult winter (Jul/Aug–Dec) Head white with fine brown streaks, from few to rather extensive behind and around eye, especially ear-coverts to nape, where rarely more drop-shaped or streaked (especially E populations). Forehead white. Head streaks in >90% Sep–Oct (Burneleau 1987, Garner & Quinn 1997). Bill duller yellow, often with ivory tip and faint dark subterminal markings. Legs yellow to dull yellow, less frequently creamy; about 50% acquire bright yellow legs from late autumn. Legs rarely fleshy in E populations.

Juvenile (fledging–Sep/Oct) Head dull greyish-brown with darker streaks, strongest around eye and on ear-coverts (forming darker eye-mask) and broadest on hindneck, sometimes continuing onto breast-sides. Mantle, back and scapulars dark brown with buffish fringes or notches, in best-marked leaving 'holly-leaf' dark centres, most evident on rear scapulars. Lesser and median coverts dark brown (often rusty-tinged) with narrow pale edges. Greater coverts generally intermediate between Herring and Lesser Black-backed: dark brown with faint pale bars, darkening progressively outwards to mostly solid dark centres on outermost; however, 30–50% of inner greater coverts may show pale bars as in Herring (most frequent in eastern part of range, where small minority show bars to all greater coverts as in Herring) and very few with dominance of pale, similar to Great Black-backed (photo in Neubauer & Millington 2000: 463). Two inner greater coverts often all dark (Garner & Quinn 1997); inner coverts often moulted to first-winter type in autumn unlike in Herring and most Lesser Black-backed. Primary coverts dark brown; lesser primary coverts and alula often paler. Tertials dark brown with pale tips and edges restricted to distal part; normally lacks irregular pattern as in typical Herring, but often with 1–2 indentations towards tip (Dubois & Yésou 1984). Pale tertial edges in all but extremes not reaching inner greater coverts (opposite to Herring). Tertials rarely with dark shaft-streaks or anchor-markings, inner tertials often solid brown, with dull buff or dark brown tip. Flight feathers black, fading to blackish-brown in autumn, sometimes with paler inner webs to P1–5, creating slightly pale window (most obvious in E populations). Uppertail-coverts and rump white with a few dark bars or spots. Tail white with blackish-brown subterminal bar (50–55mm in T1) and narrow pale tips to all rectrices. T6 white with dark distal part of inner webs (up to 50%); outer web white or with 2–3(5) narrow dark bars to broader dark spot near tip (as on inner web). Underwing-coverts greyish-brown with narrow pale bars and rather well-marked dark tips (especially on lesser and median coverts); generally better contrasting than in Herring. In E of range (Aegean Sea and E) underwing in 5% paler as on average Caspian Gull. Undertail-coverts whitish with dark bars or spots, in most restricted to sides. Bill blackish. Legs greyish to dull flesh.

First-winter (Aug/Sep–Mar) similar to juvenile, but head whiter with more striking dark eye-mask and sometimes lightly dark-streaked or -spotted crown; streaks rarely cover whole of head behind eye, in contrast to whitish, unpatterned lores, forehead, cheeks, throat, neck-sides and often hindneck/breast-sides. Underbody white, often with dark spots, generally finer than in Herring. Flanks normally dark-spotted, sometimes as chevrons. Mantle, scapulars and new inner coverts pale grey, gingery or creamy with 1–2(3) dark spots or bars; often narrower than pale bars, but sometimes as full as in Herring; outer bar often anchor-shaped. Bill black, often with pale tip and sometimes with fleshy-grey base of lower mandible (or rarely both mandibles). Cutting edges dark.

Juvenile wing worn from Aug–Sep, appearing gingery or rusty-brown in contrast to fresh greyer/dark markings on mantle and scapulars. With wear (from Apr), may lose most of pale feather-edges on upperparts, including tertials: wing-coverts (especially greater coverts) often very pale, forming pale midwing-panel. Mantle may be whitish-grey with reduced dark markings.

First-summer (Mar–Sep) at first intermediate between worn first-winter and second-winter. From Apr/May with grey on mantle and scapulars, later grey inner median coverts and greater coverts. Many have variegated upperparts with light bars to mantle and scapulars. Eyes often dark. Bill blackish with variable paler base and broad pale tip to both mandibles. Legs fleshy, from May sometimes with yellowish tinge.

Second-winter (Aug–Feb/Apr) Head whitish with fine dark streaks on crown and nape and coarser spotting on hindneck and breast-sides. Often shows dark eye-mask and pale border to darker ear-coverts. Mantle, back, scapulars and some coverts (especially inner and median coverts) brownish-grey to grey (often duller than in adults and with dark markings); retarded birds develop first-winter-type upperpart feathers. Other coverts with broader dark bars than in Herring Gull, looking uniform at distance, and reaching paler mantle. Tertials black to dark brown with pale edges, often irregular at tip; sometimes shows complete pale tertial edges. Flight feathers blackish-brown; P1–4 normally with paler inner webs and sometimes paler notching on outer webs (photo 17, Klein & Gruber 1997); P10 lacks white mirror. Underbody and underwing white with scattered dark markings, especially along leading edge of wing and on primary coverts. Tail white with broad blackish subterminal bar; T6 white or with narrow dark markings; entire tail sometimes as first-year. Eye medium yellow to brown, darker than in adults. Bill blackish, sometimes with olive to yellow base, darkening towards tip. Tip often pale, sometimes strikingly so on both mandibles. May develop slight reddish gonys-spot. Legs fleshy or dull yellow.

Second-summer (Mar–Sep) similar to second-winter, but head white with narrow dark eye-mask and dark spots on hindneck to breast-sides. Advanced birds similar to adult summer, but with scattered dark upperpart markings and dark in tail. Legs with yellow tinge, especially tarsus; feet often fleshy.

Third-winter (Aug–Mar) similar to adult (unlike most Herring Gull), but dark head-markings generally stronger, especially in front of eye. Upperparts duller grey. Outer primary coverts dark or dark-shafted. Primaries with less white (just faint mirror on P10) and more frequent dark markings on P4. Underwing-coverts with some dark markings. Tail white with narrow, normally complete, dark bar. Iris often medium brown, looking dark at distance. Bill similar to adult, but with dark subterminal markings and red gonys spot. Legs fleshy to dull yellow.

Third-summer (Mar–Sep) similar to third-winter, but head white or with faint grey wash around eye.

Fourth-winter (Aug–Mar) similar to adult, but sometimes with dark markings on primary coverts, tail and bill (Gruber 1995).

GEOGRAPHICAL VARIATION *L. m. michahellis* (Iberia from Gibraltar and Golfo de Cadiz S of Berlanga; Mediterranean, Black Sea NE to S Romania and W to Anatolia) described above. Gradually larger and darker towards SW part of range: mean wing length, adult male N Africa 457.6mm (10), Italy 451.1 (12). Bill N Africa 57.6 (10), Italy 54.5 (12). Series in females too small for comparison; birds with wing >470mm all from Italy–N Africa (own data).
In Balkans and the Bosporus, said to show intermediacy with Caspian Gull, but no details given (Cramp & Simmons 1983); see below. For putative hybrid Yellow-legged × Caspian Gull, see hybrids below. Adults from W Mediterranean often show white mirror on P10 only. Birds from E part of range (Italy, Aegean Sea and Black Sea) on average with more white on P9–10; often white tip to P10 (rare in W Mediterranean) and white mirror on P9. In adult winter, sometimes with dark spots or streaks on hindneck as in Caspian. Other plumages similar; few first-winters in Black Sea populations have narrower bill, paler underwing (axillaries and especially greater underwing-coverts) and paler inner primaries than birds from W Mediterranean/N Africa; closer to Caspian Gull, but head pattern (especially dark-eye mask) and greater coverts/tertial pattern typical of *michahellis*; problematic birds better left undetermined (pers. obs. in Morocco, Sicily, Lesbos, Bosporus, Hungary, Bulgaria, E Mediterranean; skins; A. Corso *in litt.*).
L. m. 'lusitanius' ('*cantabricans*') Birds from W Iberia (between Berlanga and Basque Country) differ slightly from *michahellis*. DNA sequences intermediate between *michahellis* and *atlantis* (A. Bermejo & D. Liebers *in litt.*). While some are like *michahellis*, others resemble Herring Gull (based on extensive photo series kindly submitted by R. Baradez) and a description of those populations is therefore given. Generally smaller than *michahellis* (two Portuguese first-winter females with wing 411, 413mm). Heavy-billed with flat forehead, 'snaky' neck, slender hindparts and short legs. **Adult** has 23–57mm white mirror on P10, mostly divided from tip by narrow dark subterminal markings; 60–74% have white mirror on P9. Compared to *michahellis* shows narrower black markings on P5, but in 35% indistinct even on P4. Upperparts generally slightly darker (Kodak Grey Scale 6.5–8). As it breeds generally one month later than in *michahellis*, moult later too. By Jul most have reached P1–3; P8–9 by Nov, when secondaries and tail often not started, and upperparts very worn. Moult finished Dec. White-headed Jul–Jan or just with scattered dark markings especially on hindneck. In Aug–Nov generally with broader and more complete dark head-markings than *michahellis*. Bare parts as *michahellis*, but generally brighter; orbital ring reddish-orange to orange; extensive red gonys-spot reaches upper mandible. **First-year** similar to *michahellis*, but underparts closer to Herring, including densely spotted breast to belly, with only vent whitish, and on average more solid dark underwing-coverts and axillaries (often uniform sooty-brown as in *atlantis*). Head generally more heavily streaked, especially around crown and nape, thus similar to Lesser Black-backed. Juvenile mantle and scapulars dark brown (paler than in Lesser Black-backed). White tertial fringes sometimes cover entire edge. Greater coverts often entirely pale-barred on distal part, but basal part often uniformly dark as in *atlantis*; in some, outer greater coverts more uniform as in *michahellis* or barred through as in Herring. Often shows pale window (as in Herring) on inner primaries. Rump and tail-base heavily dark-spotted. Undertail-coverts entirely dark-spotted (unlike pale centres of *michahellis*). Tail often with broader white edges than *michahellis*. Outer web of T6 white with 2-3 dark spots. Bill black but sometimes with paler base to lower mandible from Jan. Age development generally less advanced than *michahellis*, thus closer to Herring Gull. In **second-year**, mantle and scapulars sandy with dark markings, with limited amount of grey compared to *michahellis*. Greater coverts often pale with 3–4 narrow dark bars, differing from *michahellis*. Often retains dark underwing-coverts and axillaries, but some closer to *michahellis*. Breast to belly often densely dark-spotted. Bill mainly dark, just with small amount of yellow on lower mandible. Primary moult has normally reached P6–7 by Jul. **Third-year** again closer to Herring than to *michahellis*, retaining larger parts of immature plumage; upperparts with large amount of grey admixed with brown markings especially on greater coverts and tertials, and extensive dark markings in underwing-coverts. By Jul, primary moult has reached P5–6.
Long-call and mew-calls sharper and higher-pitched than *michahellis* with fewer harmonics (Teyssèdre 1983, 1984, A. Bermejo pers. comm.). In Galicia, NW Iberia as above, but some slight differences noted. **Adult** with

less black on wing-tip (more frequent with white tip to P10 and pale spot on both webs of P9) than average *michahellis*. Upperpart colour often slightly paler (Garner & Quinn 1997, pers. obs. in Portugal). Legs yellow, sometimes with greyish or fleshy tinge in winter. Noted as fleshy in 5–10%, Galicia, Aug; probably third-summers (Stegemann 1991, Yésou & Dubois 1993). **Adult winter** with head pattern retained into Jan–Feb (A. Bermejo *in litt.*). However, most juveniles normally have dark centres to greater coverts and tertials as in *atlantis*. Populations from NE Iberia larger. In plumage close to Herring Gull, but slightly longer-winged. Compared to *michahellis* slightly smaller and slimmer with shorter legs and **adult** upperparts similar to *michahellis*; primary pattern similar but less frequent with white tip to P10; 51% with white mirror to P9 (A. Bermejo *in litt.*). Legs bright yellow, orbital ring red.

First-year often dingier than *michahellis*, especially on underparts. Head and base of tail more densely patterned, recalling Herring Gull. Pattern on greater coverts and tertials similar to Herring.

Second-year has most of mantle/scapulars grey (as saddle) against wing pattern mostly like first-year: generally second-year is a year in advance of Herring, thus more like *michahellis*.

L. m. atlantis **Atlantic Gull** (Azores, probably also Madeira, Canary Isles, Atlantic coastline between N Iberia and Morocco). Sedentary, with some spread to NW Africa and sub-Saharan W Coast in winter; possibly straggler to N America (Wilds & Czaplak 1994). Adult and first-year plumages differ from other subspecies, being closer to Lesser Black-backed Gull race *graellsii*, of which it is sometimes regarded as a sedentary form (Dwight 1925). The darkest taxon. The darkest, most extreme birds with densest head-streaking in winter plumage found in the Azores; birds from Madeira and Canary Islands more like *michahellis* and often regarded as *michahellis*. While we fully accept that only Azores birds should be regarded as true *atlantis*, we include here information from Madeira/Canary Islands, preferring to keep these birds under *atlantis* until more is known about differences between the populations from different areas.

Atlantic Gull is on average smaller and more compact than nominate *michahellis*. Head squarer, forehead often flat, and bill stockier with generally longer gonys-angle. Wings and legs relatively shorter. Nostril, compared to *michahellis*, generally deeper at distal edge (*c.* 2mm) and shorter (9–11mm). Bill length:bill depth at gonys 2.6–3.0. Long gape-line sometimes downcurved.

Adult In the Azores has dark slate upperparts similar to Lesser Black-backed Gull race *graellsii* (Kodak Grey Scale 7–9); more varying in Madeira, where some as nominate *michahellis*. Certain Canary Island adults as dark as Azores birds. Upperparts sometimes with faint olive tinge. P9–10 black, P10 with 32–45mm white mirror, rarely covering one or both webs to form white tip (Madeira). White mirror on P9 in 10% of Canary Island/Madeiran populations, <2% in the Azores (pers. obs.). Division between grey and black on P6–7 sharp, on inner web diffuse. P6 with 30–50mm black subterminal bar, P5 with 20–33mm black subterminal bar and narrow white tongues restricted to inner web. On P5–6

often most black on outer web, as in most Caspian Gull nominate *cachinnans*. P4 grey, in 75% with dark subterminal spot, most frequent on outer web where max. 22mm. P3 in 10% with dark markings, max. 9mm on outer web. Wing-tip black on both surfaces. In winter (Aug–Nov/Dec), head more strongly patterned than in *michahellis*, similar to Herring and Lesser Black-backed, but streaking even denser around eye and below gape, but fainter on hindneck. Azores (and a few Madeiran) birds have even stronger head-spotting and look dark-hooded at distance; hindneck sometimes unstreaked. Head is mainly white with narrow dark streaks around eye and well-scattered brown spots on crown, hindneck and ear-coverts (Madeira and Canary Islands populations). Bill in winter dull yellow with orange gonys-spot and sometimes dark subterminal bar. In summer similar to *michahellis*, but lighter orange-yellow. Iris pale creamy to pale yellow (as in Herring), thus paler than in *michahellis*, but sometimes dark-freckled. Legs yellow; a few cases of pink-legged birds from the Azores known (Dubois 2001).

Juvenile (Azores) closer to Lesser Black-backed Gull than to *michahellis*, as plumage is dark chocolate-brown. Head and underbody with dense dark streaks or spots; often rather uniform brownish, recalling American Herring. Saddle chocolate-brown with pale feather-fringes (Azores/Madeira). In Canary Islands sometimes paler with more chequered pale spotting along edges. Upperwing rather uniform dark, at most with faint pale window on inner primaries (a larger proportion in Madeira/Canary Islands have paler inner primaries). Greater coverts blackish with slight pale barring or waving near tips to *all* greater coverts (more obvious than in *michahellis*, similar to American Herring). Tertials similar to *michahellis*: dark with white to sandy edges and tips, often irregular near tip (where sometimes narrow dark 'extra' bar). Often pale spot near bend of upperwing. Underwing-coverts dark brown, occasionally with gingery tinge; darker and more uniform than in *michahellis* and Herring; closer to some Lesser Black-backeds, American Herring and Kelp Gulls, but sometimes paler-barred. Tail and rump similar to Lesser Black-backed; tail with broad dark bar, covering 55–80mm on T1. T6 usually with white, dark-spotted outer web, grading into paler base (rarely as dark as in American Herring); sometimes closer to Herring nominate *argentatus* and Yellow-legged. 1–2mm white tips to rectrices. Rump and uppertail-coverts more strongly dark-barred than in *michahellis*, again often similar to American Herring. Dark streaks or spots on head, body and underparts extensive into first-winter; usually has whitish forehead, throat and lower belly. Breast-sides to flanks often dark greyish-brown, sometimes reduced to spotting. Under-tail-coverts white with dark V-markings, often crossing the whole of each feather (unlike typical *michahellis*); in others only along edges as in most *michahellis*. Eye dark, but may already become paler in first-winter. Bill black with 0–5mm pale tip. Legs fleshy, many with darker spotting on upper tarsus and on feet (Dubois 2001)—a character unknown in other Palearctic gulls (but frequent in Kelp Gull).

First-winter similar to juvenile. Many seem to retain most of juvenile plumage in winter, moulting directly into second-winter. Some attain new brownish-grey mantle/scapulars in late summer. Wing strongly worn from Feb/Mar.

First-summer similar to first-winter, but head and underbody whiter. Many show dark eye-mask and spots to entire breast and belly; lower belly often white. Some develop grey on mantle and coverts (especially inner ones).

Second-winter similar to first-winter, but usually with grey saddle and paler head with broad, dark mask surrounding whitish eye. Barring on wing-coverts weaker, creating almost uniform dark impression, especially on greater coverts; pattern less contrasting than in first-year. Mantle and scapulars uniform grey, in some sandy with 2–3 dark bars. Tail and tail-coverts similar to first-winter, but rump usually white. Underwing-coverts dark but with scattered pale areas. Bill black with pale tip or bicoloured with fleshy base and tip. Eyes medium brown to whitish.

Third-winter somewhat similar to adult, but outer primaries and their coverts and secondaries dark, contrasting well with grey inner primaries. P10 may show narrow white mirror (P. J. Dubois *in litt.*). Head often as strongly dark-patterned as in adult, creating dark hood at distance. Upperparts (including upper lesser and median coverts) dark grey intermixed with brown. Underwing mainly white with unmoulted darker coverts in strong contrast. Shows traces of dark tail-bar (sometimes complete). Bill bi- or tricoloured: base pinkish, isolated from yellow tip by broad blackish subterminal bar, frequently covering >50% of bill.

Moult Slightly earlier than in *michahellis*; **adult** moult P1 mid-May, P7–8 late Jul–early Sep, P9–10 mid-Sep–mid-Oct. Head and body from late Jul, tail and secondaries late Jul–Sep. Most show winter head and heavy moult in secondaries and tail late Aug–early Sep.

Moult from juvenile to first-winter non-existent, or restricted to parts of mantle and scapulars Sep–Nov. Often juvenile plumage moulted directly into second-winter. Moult into **second-winter** complete. Reaches P5, coverts and tail by early Jul (pers. obs. in Azores and Madeira; skins in NHM, UZM).

Moult to third-winter similar to adult, but on average earlier, being finished late Jul–Aug.

Hybrids Hybrid pairs of nominate *michahellis* × Herring Gull reported W France (2) and Great Britain. Hybrid pairs with Lesser Black-backed Gull known W Iberia, W France, Netherlands (regular), Germany and Great Britain. Young known from Netherlands and Germany (Yésou 1991, Garner & Quinn 1997, Ogilvie *et al.* 2001, Cottaar 2004, *Limicola* 11: 266, A. Bermejo *in litt.*).

Probably hybrid second-winter Herring Gull nominate *argentatus* × Yellow-legged nominate *michahellis* combined upperparts (with much grey) and dark primaries of *michahellis* with head-streaks and yellow bill with dark subterminal markings (photo 30, Klein & Gruber 1997). Putative adult hybrid Yellow-legged Gull *michahellis* (or Herring) × Caspian Gull nominate *cachinnans* reported from Poland (two males). These showed darker mantle than nominate *cachinnans* with broad black markings on P5, and relatively steep forehead and long, deep bill. Legs pale yellow or pale pink. Iris yellow with some brown spotting; measurements closer to Caspian than to Yellow-legged (for details, see Faber *et al.* 2001). has paired with Kelp Gull in Mauretania 1997/98 (Pineau *et al.* 2001).

Aberrants A second-winter leucistic from Spain was similar to leucistic Herring; had just moulted inner four primaries Nov. Juvenile with white subterminal markings on primary coverts and primary tips known. Leucistic adult with white P7–10 and secondaries noticed from Cies Island, Spain. Melanistics are known (Garcia 1987, Rufray & Cramus 2002, A. Bermejo & E. de Juana *in litt.*).

DISTRIBUTION AND MIGRATION Breeds sea-cliffs and rocky islands, coastal wetlands and cultivation, often with high cover. Locally on roofs in towns and seaports (Bulgaria, Istanbul); frequently inland. Mediterranean breeding sites occupied Nov–Feb (Isenmann 1973, 1976, Cramp & Simmons 1983, Albrecht 1986b, Goutner 1992, Nankinov 1992a, Gruber 1995, Klein & Buchheim 1997).

L. m. michahellis (Mediterranean, Aegean Sea and Black Sea to Romanian and Turkish coastline; C Europe to about 52°N). Total population 150,000–200,000 pairs (including W Iberian population). Late-1990s (in pairs): Iberian Atlantic coastline between S Portugal and Basque country 83,000 (most 46,000 Galicia, Cantabrian coast 10,000 and Portugal 22,510); Gibraltar 10,000–30,000; Mediterranean Spain >18,500 (Catalonia 8,140); Balearics 7,700; France 40,000–45,000 (incl. 4,200 Corsica, Mediterranean coast 25,447, Marseilles 3,400–3,600); strong increase in France; 1970 9,000, 1980 25,000. Recent spread along French Atlantic coast N to Normandy (80 pairs late 1990s), where breeding alongside Herring with very limited or no hybridisation, and to inland France N to Alsace. 8,750 Sardinia; Italy 40,000–50,000 (recent spread; 4,767 Sicily); Croatia 30,000; Greece 15,000; Bulgaria 4,274 in 1992 (also Romanian Black Sea coast); Lebanon small colonies; Israel 20–25; Mauritania 10; Morocco 6,325; Algeria 2,500; Tunisia 600–700; Libya some hundreds; Egypt small colonies. Scarce C and N Europe: small population Switzerland and S Germany (e.g. 250 pairs Lake Neuchatel late 1990s). Small population inland Poland, Austria since 1987 and Slovakia since 1984. Bred Netherlands 1994 (but several cases of mixed pairs with Herring and Lesser Black-backed) and Great Britain irregular since 1995. (Guyot & Miege 1980, Carrera *et al.* 1981, Guyot 1981, Glutz von Blotzheim & Bauer 1982, Cramp & Simmons 1983, Bercena *et al.* 1984, Beaubrun 1989, Nankinov 1992a, Cottaar & Verbeek 1994, Gruber 1995, Vercruijsse 1995, Meininger *et al.* 1996, Shirihai 1996b, del Hoyo *et al.* 1996, Hagemeijer & Blair 1997, Ramadan-Jaradi & Ramadan-Jadari 1997, Rumbao 1997, van den Berg & Bosman 1999, Ogilvie *et al.* 2001, Dubois *et al.* 2000).

Atlantic–Cantabrian population was isolated from the Mediterranean population until twentieth century, when expansion and increase started (A. Bermejo *in litt.*).

Increase less dramatic than in Herring (but strong in France), as mainly fish-eater, not as highly opportunistic. Mainly sedentary. Population of France, Iberia and NW

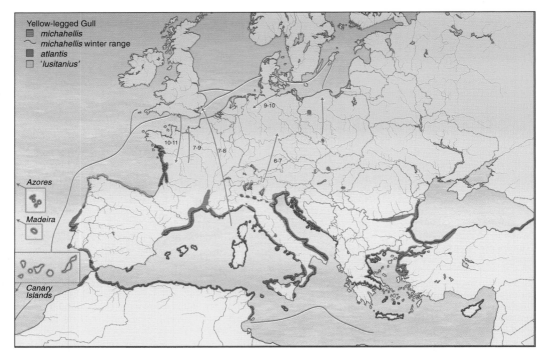

michahellis
michahellis winter range
atlantis
'lusitanius'

Azores

Madeira

Canary
Islands

Africa stays in Mediterranean or disperses to W Atlantic coast; W Mediterranean and Atlantic populations mainly sedentary. Autumn census of 10,000–12,000 moulting adults Ebro Delta, S Spain. In winter 180,000 around Iberian Peninsula, of which 30,000 NE Spain (Gerona–Valencia) and 9,000 Galicia, NW Spain. In France 123,000 (96% in Mediterranean), 60,000–100,000 Italy, of which 15,000–20,000 Sicily; 12,000 Algeria, 2,340 N Egypt (latter not separated from Caspian Gull). Balkan and Adriatic population sedentary or dispersing N/NW to River Danube (Isenmann 1973, 1976, Gallissa 1987, Glutz von Blotzheim & Bauer 1982, Meininger & Sørensen 1992, A. Corso *in litt.*).

SW European, Adriatic and E Mediterranean birds disperse N-W Jul–Oct. Some reach N, W and C Europe. Earliest influxes to C Europe (first- and second-years) Apr; in May mainly adults and from Jul larger influxes of all ages. In C Europe commonest large gull Jul–Sep. Starts to leave C Europe late Aug/early Sep; mostly left by early Nov; a very few winter. Max. 5,000 Lake Neusiedler See, Austria, 10,000 Lakes Geneva and Neuenburger; 500 Bodensee, 100 Limburg, Netherlands, 100 S Poland. Small numbers present throughout the year, mainly immatures. Spread to W European, British and Baltic S Coast and S Scandinavia proved by ringing recoveries of Italian, N Adriatic and inland France/S Germany birds to N and W Europe N to N and E Denmark and Sweden and W to Great Britain in autumn/winter. N Iberian birds recovered Great Britain and France. Increase W Europe since 1980 correlated with expansion and range extension along French Atlantic coast. In Great Britain first record 1971. Vanguards mid-Jun (adults), numbers rising to first peak mid–late Jul (max. 36 Dungeness). First-years from early Aug. Along River Thames, Essex,

peak late Aug–mid-Oct (mainly adults) >500 Mucking; decrease from late Oct until dispersal Dec. Similar peak time French Atlantic coast/Belgium: late Jul–mid-Aug, most gone late Oct; sometimes late peak, e.g. 191 on 8 October 1997, Nieuwpoort-de-Pann, Belgium. Along French W coast sometimes outnumbers Herring (20,000 along Atlantic coast). In Netherlands scarce all year, but most are seen Jul–Sep, adults preceding juveniles. Recoveries from Netherlands and Belgian ringing programmes reveal origin of W European late-summer birds to be Mediterranean (between Spain and Italy).

In S Scandinavia scarce Jul–Nov; outnumbered there by Caspian Gull. Regular S Sweden (especially Scania) and S Denmark. In Sweden 216 records up to 2001, annually Jul–Nov (peak Sep), maximum 86 Scania, Öland and Gotland autumn 2000. In Denmark scarce in the S. especially SW Jutland (Waddenzee), but regular in the Baltics. e.g. 1990-97 138 Møn. In S Scandinavia vanguards here from mid-Jun, numbers rising Aug to peak Sep. N and W Europe mostly abandoned in winter, except for Germany (especially Niedersachsen and Nordrhein-Westfalen) and Netherlands (max. >50 Limburg Dec 1998). A few winter N to Denmark. Scarce SE Baltic Sea (Géroudet 1968, 1989, 1992a, Nicolau-Guillaumet 1977, Herroelen 1981, Grant 1983, Schuster *et al.* 1983, de Mesel 1990, Dubois & Stawarczyk 1991, Dvorak 1991, Yésou 1985, 1991b, Dennis 1992, 1995, Gruber 1995, Walker 1995, Garner & Quinn 1997, van den Berg & Bosman 1999, Bijlsma *et al.* 2001, SOF 2003, K. Fischer, Z. Eckedi, K. Sándor, P. Schiermacker-Hansen & J. Jansen *in litt.*).

Occurrence in Red Sea area uncertain; at most scarce. Birds with *michahellis* characters have occurred S to Yemen.

YELLOW-LEGGED GULL Four-year gull. The counterpart to Herring Gull in Macronesia, Iberia, Mediterranean and W Black Sea. Similar to Herring, but head often larger and squarer and bill generally larger and heavier; hindparts slenderer than in Herring.

Adult has darker grey upperparts and fuller black wing-tip than Herring with white mirrors on P(9)10 and solid black markings onto P5. White tongues on mid-hand narrower, but white trailing edge to inner wing more distinct than in Herring. Legs invariably yellow to bright yellow. Red bill-marking frequently reaches upper mandible. Head white, in **winter** (Sep–Dec) often with narrow dark streaks around eyes and on crown.

First-year similar to Herring, but better contrasting. Upperwing darker with little or no pale window on inner hand; greater coverts barred on inner ones as in Herring, but outer 50% often unbarred, creating dark rectangle in folded wing. Tertials dark with white edges and markings normally reduced to distal parts. Head and underbody white. Conspicuous dark eye-mask and black bill suggests giant Mediterranean Gull.

First-winter mantle and scapulars grey to pale brown with dark barring; together with some inner wing-coverts attained from Sep. Tail white with solid dark bar, appearing similar to Common Gull. Underwing-coverts dark, in contrast to white belly.

Second-year similar to adult, but only rarely with white primary to P10 and underwing still heavily dark-patterned. Many show grey saddle combined with solid black tail-bar (more rarely in similar-aged Herring).

Third-year similar to adult, but with some dark markings on coverts (especially primary coverts), tail and underwing; bill with blackish subterminal markings and white on P9–10 less extensive.

Atlantic Iberian birds sedentary or with limited dispersal, as indicated by recoveries from France (1) and Great Britain (1). Vagrant Norway (2), Finland (2), Iceland (3).

L. m. atlantis (Azores, Madeira and Canary Islands) Total population >8,000 pairs (6,000 Madeira/Desertas and 2,000 Azores) (Hagemeijer & Blair 1997). Probably also breeds along Iberian and Moroccan coastline. Sedentary; some local movements involved. Some birds from W African coast S to Senegambia, Guinea and Nigeria said to show characters of *atlantis*; more research needed. Vagrant Canada/N America S to N Carolina (5), Ireland (Cramp & Simmons 1983, Dubois 2001, Cornell *et al.* 1995, Mactavish 1995, Lewis 1996, Gantlett 1999, V. Rauste *in litt.*)

MEASUREMENTS Lengths in mm; weights in g. Own data based on skins in AMNH, MCZ, NHM, NNH, NRK, USNM, UZM, ZMA. *Michahellis* Mediterranean and N Black Sea. *Atlantis* Canary Islands, Madeira, the Azores.

WING

L. m. michahellis		
Adult male	425–472 (449.3)	36
Adult female	415–472 (436.0)	19
First-year male	415–447 (432.7)	8
First-year female	408–450 (429.6)	8

Note Adults, Camargue, S France, 418–485 (mean male 465, female 440; n=160) (Isenmann 1973); Spanish Mediterranean 411–478 (mean 451, n=107); Spanish Atlantic and Cantabria 337–452 (mean 421, n=57) (A. Bermejo in litt.).

L. m. atlantis		
Adult male	426–453 (439.6)	19
Adult female	408–445 (421.3)	17
First-year male	408–446 (427.7)	6
First-year female	391–420 (411.0)	5

BILL

L. m. michahellis		
Adult male	51.6–59.9 (54.4)	36
Adult female	48.0–55.9 (52.2)	19
First-year male	48.8–56.8 (52.7)	8
First-year female	43.0–54.5 (49.0)	9

Note Adults, Camargue, S France, male 56–65 (mean 61, n=80), adult female 50–61(65) (mean 56, n=80) (Isenmann 1973); Spanish Mediterranean 46–67 (mean 56, n=107); Spanish Atlantic and Cantabria 46–64 (mean 55, n=57) (A. Bermejo in litt.).

L. m. atlantis		
Adult male	49.6–57.0 (53.4)	18
Adult female	45.5–54.1 (49.1)	17
First-year male	47.8–56.5 (52.5)	5
First-year female	44.5–51.4 (47.6)	4

BILL DEPTH AT GONYS

L. m. michahellis		
Adult male	17.0–21.5 (19.5)	36
Adult female	16.6–20.9 (18.0)	19
First-year male	15.9–18.7 (16.9)	8
First-year female	14.5–18.5 (16.8)	9

L. m. atlantis		
Adult male	16.7–20.6 (19.1)	18
Adult female	16.4–19.1 (17.4)	16
First-year male	17.0–20.1 (18.5)	5
First-year female	15.6–17.7 (16.8)	4

BILL DEPTH AT BASE OF BILL

L. m. michahellis		
Adult male	17.5–22.4 (20.0)	36
Adult female	16.7–21.9 (18.5)	19
First-year male	17.0–19.0 (18.2)	8
First-year female	15.2–18.5 (17.2)	9

L. m. atlantis

Adult male	18.3–21.1 (19.8)	18
Adult female	16.0–19.9 (17.8)	16
First-year male	16.5–19.6 (18.3)	5
First-year female	15.8–18.3 (16.9)	4

GONYS LENGTH

L. m. michahellis

Adult male	13.8–18.9 (16.0)	36
Adult female	13.0–17.1 (14.9)	19
First-year male	14.0–16.6 (15.4)	8
First-year female	11.6–16.1 (14.7)	8

Note Spanish Mediterranean 16.0–22.6 (mean 19.5, n=107); Spanish Atlantic and Cantabria 11.7–20.7 (mean 18.0, n=57) (A. Bermejo in litt.).

L. m. atlantis

Adult male	14.4–17.8 (16.3)	18
Adult female	13.5–16.9 (15.3)	16
First-year male	14.2–18.7 (16.4)	5
First-year female	14.4–15.9 (15.0)	4

TARSUS

L. m. michahellis

Adult male	60.2–73.8 (67.6)	36
Adult female	58.3–72.6 (63.2)	19
First-year male	62.5–68.8 (66.4)	8
First-year female	59.6–68.9 (65.2)	9

Note Adults, Camargue, France: male 65–80 (mean 72, n=80), female 60–75 (mean 67, n=80) (Isenmann 1973); Spanish Mediterranean 51.6–79.5 (mean 64.6, n=107); Spanish Atlantic and Cantabria 55.4–75.0 (mean 64, n=57) (A. Bermejo in litt.).

L. m. atlantis

Adult male	61.3–68.6 (65.5)	18
Adult female	56.6–63.9 (61.4)	17
First-year male	58.6–68.5 (65.3)	5
First-year female	56.6–67.1 (60.3)	4

Weight *L. m. michahellis* S France adult male 1,040–1,500, adult female 800–1,400 (Isenmann 1973); Spanish Mediterranean 550–1,225; Spanish Atlantic and Cantabria 420–1,600 (A. Bermejo *in litt.*).

Yellow-legged Gull *Larus michahellis*, ssp. **michahellis** unless otherwise stated. **370. Juvenile.** Note broad pale edges to mantle feathers, creating prominent pale scaling. These parts will soon moult into 1st-winter. Evros, Greece. 17 Jul 1990. *Per Schiermacker-Hansen.* **371. Juvenile moulting into 1st-winter.** Compare Herring and Caspian Gulls, and note especially the heavy bill showing prominent gonys angle compared to Caspian, and also dark mask and bill. Plumage otherwise similar to Caspian, but barring in inner greater coverts typically more prominent. New 1st-winter mantle feathers barred. Note pale face against black bill and eye-mask as well as scaly flanks. Constanza, Romania. Late Aug. *Peter Szőke.* **372. 1st-winter.** Most of saddle renewed. Black bill and mask conspicuous. Note tertial pattern similar to Caspian, but often with more irregular, better contrasting edges, thus closer to Herring. Note that pale edges do not reach base of greater coverts. White underbelly to undertail-coverts visible. Møn, Denmark. 13 Sep 1995. *Per Schiermacker-Hansen.* **373. 1st-winter.** As Caspian, most appear white-headed with greyer, 1st-winter saddle against brownish wings with scattered new coverts. Note that some inner coverts have been renewed (as in Caspian, unlike Herring Gull). Møn, Denmark. 22 Oct 1995. *Per Schiermacker-Hansen.* **374. 1st-winter.** Note white face against heavy black bill, dark eye-mask and more uniform upperwing than in Herring with less conspicuous pale window in inner primaries ➠

(P2–4 with pale areas). Extensive black tail-bar conspicuous. Hannover, Germany. 20 Sep 1998. *Annika Forsten*. **375. 1st-winter** with Caspian Gull ssp. *cachinnans*. Note broader bill with bulbous tip and well-marked gonys angle of Yellow-legged compared with the slimmer bill of 2nd-winter Caspian. Mamaia, Romania. 12 Oct 2000. *Annika Forsten*. **376. 1st-winter.** Upperparts darker than in 374, closer to Lesser Black-backed, but note less prominent dark greater coverts and narrower tail-bar, in good contrast to less dark-spotted tail-base and uppertail-coverts. Pas-de-Calais, France. 10 Oct 1999. *Klaus Malling Olsen.*

Yellow-legged Gull *Larus michahellis,* ssp. *michahellis* unless otherwise stated, **377. Juvenile**. Type '*lusitanius*'. Compared to *michahellis*, this type generally coarsely-marked on underparts, underwing-coverts and rump, closer to *atlantis*, but pale window in inner primaries resembles Herring. Peniche, Portugal. Aug 1998. *Rémy Baradez.* **378. 1st-winter.** Dark bill present throughout 1st-winter. Note dark eye-mask and whitish underbody and, in this individual, underwing-coverts. More typical birds show darker underwing-coverts in good contrast to white underbody at this age. Agadir, Morocco. 6 Jan 1993. *Klaus Malling Olsen.* **379. 1st-summer.** Worn in spring before moult into 2nd-winter. Constanta, Romania. 5 Apr. 1999. *Annika Forsten.* **380. 2nd-winter.** Paler than 1st-years, with prominent white tertial edges. Møn, Denmark. 12 Sep 1995. *Per Schiermacker-Hansen.* **381. moulting into 2nd-winter** '*lusitanius*'. West Iberian birds often show more extensive spotting from head to breast-sides, in this bird prominent on breast-sides. Peniche, Portugal. Aug 1998. *Rémy Baradez.* **382. 2nd-winter.** Grey saddle contrasts with otherwise rather 1st-year-like ➡

plumage. Note almost complete lack of pale window in primaries. Pas-de-Calais, France. 10 Oct 1999. *Klaus Malling Olsen.*
383. 2nd-winter or retarded 3rd-winter. Compare individual differences in age development with 382. Mamaia, Romania. 15 Oct 2000. *Annika Forsten.* **384. 2nd-winter moulting into 2nd-summer.** 2nd-winters still show extensive dark tail-bar, contrasting with almost white rump and grey saddle. Constanta, Romania. 31 Mar 1999. *Annika Forsten.* **385. 3rd-winter and adults** type '*lusitanius*'. Peniche, Portugal. Aug. *Rémy Baradez.* **386. 3rd-winter.** Similar to adult, but note more extensive black wing-tip including primary coverts, and traces of dark in tail and scattered brown-patterned upper wing-coverts. Mamaia, Romania. 12 Oct 2000. *Annika Forsten.*

Yellow-legged Gull *Larus michahellis*, ssp. *michahellis* unless otherwise stated. **387. Adult winter** in threatening posture. Compare Caspian Gull (photo 449). Pas-de-Calais, France. 9 Oct 1999. *Andreas Buchheim.* **388. Adult summer**. Upperparts darker compared to Herring. Worn primaries lose white tips. Legs bright yellow. Berlenga, Portugal. Apr 1996. *Luis Carneiro.* **389. Adult summer.** Compared to Herring head squarer with flatter crown and fuller hindneck; hindparts more elongated, with more black, less white in primary tips. Note also cleaner grey upperparts lacking bluish tinge. Many Baltic Herrings show yellow legs. Møn, Denmark. 29 Jan 1997. *Per Schiermacker-Hansen.* **390. Adult winter**. Head with narrow dark streaks, mainly around eye and on crown between late summer and early winter. Portugal. Oct 1991. *Markus Varesvuo.* **391. Adult summer**. Note narrow white mirror on P10, and dark primary markings onto P4. Constanta, Romania. 5 Apr 1999. *Annika Forsten.* **392. Adult summer** with Herring Gull. Note differences in head-shape with Yellow-legged showing squarer head than the rounder-headed Herring to the left. Eye slightly darker in Yellow-legged, surrounded by red, not fleshy orbital ring. Maasvlakte, Netherlands. Feb 1988. *René* ➧

Pop. **393. Adult** type *'lusitanius'.* Unlike typical *michahellis*, this form has narrower, sometimes absent black markings in P5, as in Herring. Note lack of white mirror to P9 as frequent in western Yellow-legged Gulls. Peniche, Portugal. Aug 1998. *Rémy Baradez.* **394. Adult summer**. Note small white mirrors on P9-10 and black reaching P5. Compare Herring 364-369 and Caspian Gull 449–453. Lesbos, Greece. 27 Apr 2002. *René Pop.* **395. Adult summer**. Greece. 30 Jun 1990. *Per Schiermacker-Hansen*

Yellow-legged Gull *Larus michahellis*, ssp. *michahellis* unless otherwise stated. **396. Adult.** Compare wing-tip with photos 364-369. Same bird as 389. Møn, Denmark. 29 Jan 1997. *Per Schiermacker-Hansen.* **397. Adult.** Complete white tip to P10 rare, and probably in males only. Greece. 30 Jun 1990. *Per Schiermacker-Hansen.* **398. Adult.** White mirror on P10 only most frequent in W populations. Estoril, Portugal. 25 May 2001. *Klaus Malling Olsen.* **399. Adult summer.** Rarely, even western populations show white tip to P10, probably males only. Compare Herring, photos 365-368. Gibraltar. Feb 1991. *Markus Varesvuo.*

Yellow-legged Gull *Larus michahellis*, ssp. *atlantis.* **Note:** It has been recommended only to label birds from the Azores *atlantis* – see Yésou 2002 for review. Here forms from both Azores and other parts of Macaronesia are shown. **400. Juvenile.** Compared with Mediterranean and Black Sea birds, this Madeiran juvenile is much more coarsely dark-patterned on the underparts and head. Madeira, Portugal. 11 Aug 1998. *Klaus Malling Olsen.* **401. 1st-winter.** Overall darker and less contrasting than birds from Mediterranean and eastwards. Gran Canaria, Canary Islands, Spain. 20 Feb 1998. *Harry J. Lehto.*

Yellow-legged Gull *Larus michahellis,* ssp. *atlantis.* **402. Juvenile Lesser Black-backed Gull** *graellsii.* Included in this section to show direct comparison with Yellow-legged. Note the overall darker appearance, being very close to *atlantis,* but also the much slenderer hindparts of Lesser Black-backed. Tenerife, Canary Islands, Spain. 15 Sep 1998. *Harry J. Lehto.* **403. 1st-winter.** Underwing-coverts and axillaries very dark in Atlantic breeders, as in Lesser Black-backed and American Herring Gulls. Tenerife, Canary Islands, Spain. 17 Feb 1998. *Harry J. Lehto.* **404. 1st-winter.** Atlantic breeders show virtually no pale window in inner primaries. Lack long-winged and elegant look of most Lesser Black-backed. La Palma, Canary Islands, Spain. 10 Sep 1998. *Harry J. Lehto.* **405. 1st-winter.** Dark mask and underparts pattern as well as underwing much more extensive than in Mediterranean populations. Tenerife, Canary Islands, Spain. 17 Feb 1998. *Harry J. Lehto.* **406. Juvenile moulting into 1st-winter**. Note extensive dark pattern on head, neck-sides and underwing typical for *atlantis,* and compare 405. Sao Miguel, Azores, Portugal. 2 Sep 1996. *Klaus Malling Olsen.*

Yellow-legged Gull *Larus michahellis*, ssp. *atlantis*. **407. 1st-summer moulting into 2nd-winter.** Madeira, Portugal. 10 Aug 1998. *Klaus Malling Olsen.* **408. 2nd-winter.** Very extensive dark head-pattern emphasises the very pale eyes of many *atlantis* of this age. Breast to belly extensively dark-patterned, note lower belly white. Sao Miguel, Azores, Portugal. 4 Sep 1996. *Klaus Malling Olsen.* **409. 1st-winter.** Note more heavily patterned head to underbody compared to *michahellis*. Tenerife, Canary Islands, Spain. 20 Feb 1998. *Harry J. Lehto.* **410. 2nd-summer.** Most inseparable from Mediterranean birds. Tenerife, Canary Islands, Spain. 27 Feb 1999. *Harry J. Lehto.* **411. 3rd-summer.** Tenerife, Canary Islands, Spain. 17 Feb 1998. *Harry J. Lehto.* **412. 3rd-summer.** Tenerife, Canary Islands, Spain. 17 Feb 1998. *Harry J. Lehto.* **413. Adult.** Eye-mask often heavier and fuller in winter-plumaged birds in Atlantic populations. Gran Canaria, Canary Islands, Spain. 15 Sep 1998. *Harry J. Lehto.* **414. Adult winter.** Inseparable from *michahellis*. Madeira, Portugal. 10 Aug 1998. *Klaus Malling Olsen.* **415. Adult winter.** Very dense dark head-spotting, creating hooded appearance, is the rule in Azores birds, much less frequent, although not unknown in populations from Madeira. Sao ➡

412

413

414

415

416

417

Miguel, Azores, Portugal. 31 Aug 1996. *Klaus Malling Olsen*.
416. Adult summer. Compared to Mediterranean and especially Black Sea populations, wing-tip generally with slightly more black, appearing more solid and square-cut, and generally with white on P10 only, although very little white visible even on P9 here. Tenerife, Canary Islands, Spain. 26 Feb 1999. *Harry J. Lehto*. **417. Adult summer**. Note underwing pattern with solid black tip, white mirror on P10. Grey secondaries and inner primaries contrast with white underwing-coverts. Tenerife, Canary Islands, Spain. 20 Feb 1998. *Harry J. Lehto*.

21. ARMENIAN GULL
Larus armenicus (Buturlin, 1934, Lake Sevan, Armenia)

IDENTIFICATION Length 52–60cm, wingspan 120–140cm. A distinct large gull, closely related to Yellow-legged Gull (of which recently treated as a 'weak semispecies' (Liebers *et al.* 2001). It breeds in Central Turkey and Armenia and winters in E Mediterranean with some spreading to northern Red Sea.

Compared to Yellow-legged Gull, Armenian is slightly smaller with rounder head, darkish eyes and shorter, stubbier bill. Male often shows flattish front, heavy bill and angular hindneck, creating impression barely differing from 'average large gull'; female indeed looks round-headed, steep-fronted and short-billed, almost like Ring-billed and Common Gull. Compared to larger gulls, belly is flat and hindparts as elongated as in Caspian Gull. A minor difference, sometimes visible at close range, is that distance between feathers at base of bill and nostrils is shorter than in Yellow-legged and Caspian. Nostrils are triangular—broad in front and narrow at rear—and thus easier to observe in field (Caspian shows slit-like nostrils). In flight stockier than Yellow-legged and Caspian Gulls with flat belly.

Very similar to Caspian Gull race *barabensis* ('Steppe Gull'), which has more gently curving tip to slenderer bill, but in plumage is almost identical (see below for small differences in adult wing-tip).

Adult has dark eyes and yellow bill, in winter with dark ring, together with rounded head often creating Ring-billed Gull impression. Upperparts darker than in Yellow-legged, as both darker grey and with more complete black, clear-cut wing-tip, extending onto outer 3–4 primary coverts; usually with white mirror to P10 only. From below, wing-tip similar to the complete blackish of Caspian Tern *Sterna caspia* with black on P10 covering >90%. Secondaries appear as dark rectangle against white underwing-coverts. White trailing edge to upperwing is broad on secondaries, narrow on inner primaries. Bill has blackish markings. Legs are yellow.

Barabensis may appear almost identical, but normally shows slenderer bill, less black on wing-tip (in P10 black covers 30–50%), and much more pronounced pale tongues on outer wing, extending onto bases of P9–10. Legs are normally duller and there is generally a larger extension of red on gonys, more often reaching upper mandible even in winter.

In **summer** (from Mar), head white and bill bright yellow with prominent gonys-spot, dark markings (sometimes lacking) and ivory tip, appearing four-coloured. In **winter**, head faintly dark-streaked with coarser spots on hindneck and complete black bar around bill obscuring red gonys-spot, which may be entirely absent; bill often similar to Ring-billed Gull.

Juvenile paler than Yellow-legged, generally with coarser dark head-streaks and paler upperparts; see first-winter.

First-winter intermediate between Herring and Yellow-legged Gull, often first suggested by small size, gentle look and short, blunt-tipped bill. Bill black as in Yellow-legged, but head, breast and flanks often more heavily streaked in autumn, approaching Herring, but neater.

These parts become whitish from winter, leaving dark neck-streaks as the most striking head pattern. The greyish-brown upperwing shows paler inner primaries, as in Herring creating pale 'window' against broad dark tip. Greater coverts mostly well-barred throughout as in Herring. Tertials dark with pale tips and fringes, often appearing notched and reaching coverts (rare in Yellow-legged, the rule in Herring). Uppertail-coverts and tail-bases white, contrasting with solid black-brown tail-bar as in Common Gull races *canus/heinei*. Mantle and scapulars grey with fine anchor-shaped markings or bars. Underwing pale brown with fine dark markings, normally paler than in Yellow-legged, sometimes as pale as in *barabensis*, with prominent pale midwing-panel/axillaries.

From late autumn, greyish-looking with coverts (especially greater) often very pale, creating obvious pale midwing-panel. Whether caused by wear (Grant 1987b) or typically first-year plumage is open to question.

First-summer similar to first-winter but, with wear, flight feathers become browner and dark upperwing-markings may disappear.

Second-winter similar to first-winter, but normally with coarser hindneck streaking, grey saddle, paler grey inner primaries, darker secondary bar and more strongly pale-patterned tertials. Outer primaries all dark, only rarely with indistinct pale mirror on P10. Underwing paler with finer dark markings, similar to first-year Common Gull. Bill yellow with black tip. Legs may become yellowish.

Second-summer much as second-winter, but very worn.

Third-winter similar to adult, but with dark primary coverts, often all-dark outer primaries and generally broader dark bill-bar (in some covering most of bill).

VOICE Shrill and hoarse; less melodious than in Herring Gull, reminding some observers of Common Gull. Long call hurried and excited as in Caspian Gull but, unlike this taxon, does not spread in 'albatross-posture' during display (Meininger & Sørensen 1992, Filchagov 1993, Liebers & Helbig 1999).

MOULT Adult moult to **winter** plumage complete Jul–Dec, at least a month later than in Yellow-legged nominate *michahellis*. Primary moult starts with P1 (late Jun)late Jul–Aug, P8–10 Nov–early Dec; head Oct–Nov (Cramp & Simmons 1983, P. Schiermacker-Hansen *in litt.*, pers. obs.). Moult to **adult summer** partial Feb–Mar, including head and body.

Juvenile moult to **first-winter** partial Sep–Oct including head, body and some wing-coverts. Subsequent moults similar to adult, but earlier; most second-years have renewed P2–4 early Jun. In Jul P5–7, mantle, scapulars, median coverts and T1–2 (Cramp & Simmons 1983, P. Schiermacker-Hansen *in litt.*).

DESCRIPTION
Adult Similar to Yellow-legged Gull, but upperparts slightly darker (Kodak Grey Scale 7–8.5) and wing-tip

with more black/less white, invariably reaching P4. P10 black with 22–31mm white mirror; lacks pale tongue on inner web of *barabensis*. P9 with 112–177mm black outer web; in 20–45% with indistinct white mirror on inner web. P8 with 80–137mm black outer web, P7 with 62–79 (in one specimen 140)mm black outer web diffusely divided from grey base. P6 with max. 100mm black outer web. P5 with 28–52mm, P3–4 with max. 22mm black subterminal bar (mostly outer web on P3–4). 10% show faint dark markings on P3. Lacks white tongues on mid-primaries of *barabensis*. Primary coverts rarely with black shaft-streaks or drops. Tertials and usually scapulars with indistinct white tips. Eye greyish-brown to dark brown, in 10% paler silvery-brown or yellow with slight dark pigmentation (especially Feb–summer); rarely pale yellow or pale grey (see below). Orbital ring scarlet-red to orange. Gape orange to scarlet. Legs yellow. Nostril triangular; similar to Yellow-legged Gull *michahellis*. Bill length:bill depth at gonys 2.8–2.9.

Adult summer (Mar–Aug) Head white. With wear, loses most of white tips to primaries. Iris variable; among 173 Tuz Gölü and Van Gölü, pale in 14%, medium dark-spotted in 42%, dark in 44%. Bill dirty yellow to orange-yellow with red gonys-spot, sometimes penetrating to upper mandible. Black to dark grey markings on bill (especially upper mandible) in >99%, but just faint in 5%; covers both mandibles in *c*.50% (Filchagov 1993, Liebers & Helbig 1999; *contra* Frede & Langbehn 1997, who mention that bill normally lacks dark markings during breeding season, but this probably caused by slight geographical variation). Extreme tip to bill whitish. Legs pale yellow to orange-yellow, sometimes with greyish tinge.

Adult winter (Aug–Feb) Head white with narrow brown streaks and coarser dark streaks on hindneck and breast-sides. Bill bright yellow with black subterminal bar (9–12mm on upper mandible, 10–15 on lower), in most obscuring red gonys-spot, which may appear as isolated, dark red spot. Extreme bill-tip often ivory. Eyes dark, darker than in summer; rarely yellow. Legs yellow to greenish-yellow.

Juvenile (fledging–Sep) Head and underparts pale with dark streaks, especially around eye; hindneck, breast-sides and flanks dark-spotted. Upperparts often with salmon-pink tinge (Frede & Langbehn 1997). Mantle and scapulars greyish-brown with pale edges. Tertials dark brown with broad pale tips and narrow pale edges, often irregular along entire edges as in Herring; sometimes paler brown basically. Lower back dark-barred. Lesser and median coverts greyish-brown with pale edges. Greater coverts medium brown with pale barring, usually extensive in >50% (sometimes all) to form paler midwing-bar as in Herring. Flight feathers blackish-brown; inner primaries often paler, forming pale window similar to Herring; evident against dark outer primaries. Axillaries and underwing-coverts pale with fine greyish-brown barring; lesser coverts and some median coverts often with browner centres; axillaries and covert-bases often pale. Primary coverts darker. Lower belly pale. Undertail-coverts with dark spots, often restricted to edges as in Yellow-legged and Caspian Gull. Tail white with brownish-black bar and pale edges; often bordered by slight dark mottling. T6 with

white, slightly dark-mottled edges. Bill black. Eye dark-brown. Legs fleshy.

First-winter (Aug–Apr) Head and body as juvenile, but head generally with narrower dark streaks (especially around eye) and fewer brown streaks or spots on hindneck. Breast and flanks as juvenile; flanks sometimes greyish-tinged (Satat & Laird 1992). Mantle and scapulars pale greyish-brown with narrow darker subterminal bars. Wing generally paler than in congeners, especially greater coverts and P1–5. May show paler lesser primary coverts. From midwinter, dark in flight feathers, tertials and tail brownish through wear. Bare parts as juvenile, bill sometimes with slightly paler brown base.

First-summer (Apr–Aug) Similar to first-winter, but coverts often strongly bleached, especially median coverts and greater coverts.

Second-winter (Aug–Apr) Head white with faint greyish-brown streaks, especially around eyes. Hindneck often densely dark-spotted. Mantle and scapulars variable; in most mainly grey, but retarded birds acquire pale, dark-barred feathers similar to first-winter. Tertials pale grey with dark subterminal markings. Wing similar to first-winter, but generally paler; greater coverts usually greyish-brown with pale vermiculations or barring, outer greater coverts sometimes darker basally. May show some grey median and a few lesser and greater coverts. Flight feathers dark brown, P1–5 with paler inner webs creating obvious pale window. Underwing white with some dark tips to coverts, especially lesser and primary coverts. Tail white with black to brown bar similar to juvenile. Bill sometimes as first-winter, but usually yellowish (sometimes deep yellow) with dark tip and cutting edges. Legs mostly yellow.

Second-summer (Mar–Aug) Similar to second-winter, but mantle, scapulars and some coverts of adult type, primary coverts and P5–10 blackish (former with pale edges). Bill as second-winter or adult.

Third-winter (Aug–Mar) Head white. Hindneck with dark spotting. Upperparts similar to adult, but coverts (especially primary coverts) with scattered dark markings. Bill deep yellow with black tip or subterminal bar; sometimes dark with pale tip. Legs yellow to greyish-yellow.

Hybrids Hybridises with Yellow-legged Gull *michahellis* at Beysehir, S Turkey, where certain birds show overlapping characters between the two taxa (Liebers & Helbig 1999).

DISTRIBUTION AND MIGRATION 23–25,000 pairs 2000. Very local breeder in dense colonies in reedbeds and along stony and grassy shores of mountain lakes. 98% of entire population restricted to four colonies. In Armenia 11,000–13,000 in two lakes (mainly Lake Sevan and formerly Arpilich, but only 15 pairs 1999). Local persecution by local inhabitants, including harvesting of eggs. Turkish population estimated 2,400 pairs 1999, mainly Van Gölü (2,000 pairs) and Tuz Gölü (500 pairs). In Iran 4,000–5,000 pairs at one lake; may breed Georgia. Strong decrease 1930–1960, since when a dramatic increase, but recently a local strong decrease (Kasparek 1992, Filchagov 1993, del Hoyo *et al.* 1996, Liebers & Helbig 1999, Rufray 2000).

PLATE 41. ARMENIAN GULL *Larus armenicus*

Breeds Central Turkey to Armenia, winters E Mediterranean, especially Israel and N Egypt. Closely related to Yellow-legged Gull. Smaller than Yellow-legged with shorter bill, appearing stubby. Hindparts slender.

1. **First-winter** (Aug–Apr) Similar to Yellow-legged Gull, but with more conspicuous pale window on inner primaries (similar to Herring) and broader pale markings on greater coverts. Underparts similar to Yellow-legged, but head whiter with fainter dark mask and underwing generally paler with pale midwing-panel against darker lesser coverts and secondaries. Rump white against blackish-brown tail-bar.

2. **First-winter** (Aug–Apr) Head and underbody with more extensive dark markings than in Yellow-legged, head plainer with fainter dark mask. Greater coverts similar to Herring Gull with rather even distribution of brown and white bars, reaching outer greater coverts (compare Yellow-legged). Tertials dark with narrow pale edges, as in Yellow-legged not reaching greater coverts.

3. **First-winter** (Aug–Apr) Worn individual, showing almost white head, but still with fine darker markings on underbody (as in Herring Gull). Mantle and scapulars grey with varying dark, often rather narrow markings. Worn brown wing—often with much-worn and faded greater coverts—contrasts well with mantle and scapulars. Bill develops paler base from midwinter.

4. **Second-winter** (Aug–Apr) Generally paler than first-winter with grey saddle, grey median coverts and white rump. Shows extensive black tail-bar. Bill fleshy with black subterminal markings. Underwing almost unpatterned white.

5. **Second-winter** (Aug–Apr) Head and underbody mainly white. Mantle, scapulars and median coverts grey in contrast to brown, pale-patterned lesser and greater coverts. Tertials with solid white tips and edges. Bill fleshy with extensive dark subterminal markings. Legs become yellowish.

6. **Third-summer** (Mar–Aug) Similar to adult, but with more extensive dark wing-tip, as P10 only shows indistinct white mirror and primary coverts are dark-marked. Varying but often indistinct dark markings on tail.

7. **Adult winter** (Aug–Mar) Adult shows dark grey upperwing, generally darker than Yellow-legged with narrower white trailing edge to inner hand. Black on wing-tip more extensive, covering on average one primary more, and white mirror restricted to P10. From below, triangular black wing-tip solid. Head with indistinct brown streaking. Bill bright yellow with black subterminal markings, often obscuring red on gonys.

8. **Adult summer** (Mar–Aug) Similar to Yellow-legged Gull, but bill usually with extensive black markings (although some lack this), eye dark and white primary tips narrower. Legs bright yellow.

1. First-winter

6. Third-summer

4. Second-winter

7. Adult winter

3. First-winter

2. First-winter

5. Second-winter

8. Adult summer

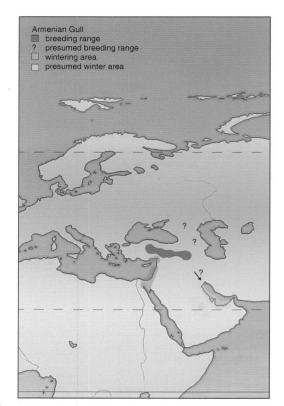

Armenian Gull
▨ breeding range
? presumed breeding range
☐ wintering area
☐ presumed winter area

Winter records Black and Caspian Seas and Gulf States poorly documented; probably very scarce; noted from Oman (where probably scarce winter visitor), UAE, Bahrain and N Indian Ocean. The uncertain status in those regions is caused by occurrence of the very similar *barabensis* (Madge 1992, Jonsson 1996, Frede & Langbehn 1997, Garner 1997, Richardson & Aspinall 1997a & b, Yésou & Hirschfeld 1997, M. Skakuj *in litt.*). Highly unlikely to occur in N, C and W Europe, where claims probably refer to Caspian Gull races *cachinnans* or *barabensis*.

MEASUREMENTS inmm. From Buzun (1993), combined with few measured skins in NHM.
Note Birds labelled 'armenicus' in NHM mainly from Gulf Area, Pakistan, and probably Aden, judged from measurements mislabelled barabensis. *These birds are referred to as* armenicus *by Cramp & Simmons (1983), who give measurements, but are excluded in this work following my studies at NHM, and are referred to under Caspian Gull* barabensis.

WING

Adult male	411–458 (439.8)	18
Adult female	385–436 (417.8)	24
First-year female	389	

BILL

Adult male	48.1–56.5 (52.3)	18
Adult male	41.3–50.6 (46.3)	24
First-year female	41.2	

BILL DEPTH AT GONYS

Adult male	16.8–20.1 (18.6)	18
Adult female	15.3–17.4 (16.4)	24
First-year female	14.6	

Note
Bill depth at base of bill *in one adult female 16.6, in one first-year female 15.1.* **Gonys length** *in one adult female 11.7, in one first-year female 12.3 (own data).*

TARSUS

Adult male	64.3–73.7 (68.7)	18
Adult female	57.7–68.0 (63.9)	24
First-year female	59.8	

Weight Adult: male 785–960, female 605–900 (Cramp & Simmons 1983, Buzun 1993).

Partly migratory. Probably migrates along large rivers and in deltas of Turkey; noted on passage Cyprus (Kraft 1994, Thiede 1995), arriving from Aug (50% first-years) at main wintering area along Mediterranean coast of Israel, where estimated 60,000 winter. Main arrival Oct–Dec. Found mainly in fishponds and artificial lakes N of Tel Aviv. Peak numbers 20,000 Beit Shean valley and 15,000 in Haifa and Ma'agan Michael areas respectively; *c.* 1,000 winter Suez. Much scarcer, but increasing S Israel, e.g. 147 Eilat winter 1989/90. Many resident. Main return migration late Mar; 200–400 oversummer (Shirihai 1996b, Rufray 2000).

Smaller numbers winter N Egypt (44 second-winter 1989/1990), mostly Mediterranean coast; also Bardawil Lagoon, Suez area and Great Bitter Lakes. Scarce, rivers and deltas of S Turkey; probably Lebanon/Jordan. Vagrant Sicily (Bourne 1988, Meininger & Sørensen 1992, A. Corso *in litt.*).

ARMENIAN GULL Four-year gull. Confined to inland lakes of Turkey and Armenia, winters E Mediterranean. Slightly smaller than Yellow-legged Gull.
Adult has slightly darker upperwing with fuller black wing-tip, appearing as black triangle on wing-tip; shows one white mirror. Eyes dark; bill yellow with black and red pattern and whitish tip, appearing four-coloured (but may lack dark markings apart from red gonys-spot in summer). Legs yellow.
First-year intermediate between Herring and Yellow-legged Gull, showing combination of whitish head and underbody from Yellow-legged with well-patterned pale and dark greater covert bar and pale window on inner wing of Herring. Underwing with pale midwing-panel. At all ages ID from 'Steppe Gull' (Caspian race *barabensis*) tricky, but shows shorter, heavier bill with bulbous tip, not slenderer with gentler-curved tip. See main text.

Armenian Gull *Larus armenicus*. **418. 1st-winter**. Note rather neat appearance, lack of clear dark eye-mask of Yellow-legged and broad barring on all greater coverts. Israel. Feb. *Hadoram Shirihai*. **419. 1st-winter**. Note the rather broad, short and rounded bill-tip compared to Caspian *barabensis* photo 457. Rounded head and rather short bill sometimes gives Common Gull-like impression. Israel, Feb. *Hadoram Shirihai*. **420. Flock of mixed ages**. Note greater covert-barring of 1st-winters. Compare Caspian Gull ssp. *barabensis* photo 457. Israel. Feb. *Hadoram Shirihai*.

Armenian Gull *Larus armenicus*. **421. 1st-winter**. Upperwing often more similar to Herring than to Yellow-legged Gull caused by extensive pale barring on greater coverts and pale window in inner primaries. Israel. Feb. *Hadoram Shirihai*. **422. 1st-winter**. Pale underparts with greater coverts creating pale midwing-panel. Ma'agan Michael, Israel. 29 Dec 1996. *Harry J. Lehto*. **423. 2nd-winter**. Grey saddle against barred upperwings and broad, distinct black tail-bar diagnostic at this age. Ma'agan Michael, Israel. 29 Dec 1996. *Harry J. Lehto*. **424. Adult winter**. Note bright four-coloured and blunt-tipped bill, and dark eyes. Ma'agan Michael, Israel. 29 Dec 1996. *Harry J. Lehto*. **425. Adult winter**. Solid, square-cut black wing-tip, with white mirror just to P10 and extensive black on P6-9. Hindneck slightly dark-streaked early autumn to mid-winter. Ma'agan Michael, Israel. 29 Dec 1996. *Harry J. Lehto*. **426 Adult summer**. Note extensive black in wing-tip, and compare this and 425 to Caspian *barabensis* photos 467-470. Van Gölü, Turkey. 30 May 1985. *Volker Konrad*.

Armenian Gull *Larus armenicus*. **427. Adult summer**. Van Gölü, Turkey. Note that by late June, primary moult has just started, on average one month later than in Yellow-legged Gull. 30 Jun 1987. *Per Schiermacker-Hansen*. **428. 3rd-winter**. Extensive black bill markings as well as lack of white primary tips indicates this age. Kfar Ruppin, Israel. Jan 2001. *Felix Heintzenberg*. **429. Adult summer**. Wing-tip often looks all back at distance. Van Gölü, Turkey. 30 May 1983. *Volker Konrad*.

22. CASPIAN GULL

Larus cachinnans (Pallas, 1811, Caspian Sea)

Plates 42–46, Photos 430–483

IDENTIFICATION Length 56–68cm, wingspan 137–145cm. Large gull of E. Europe to Asia. In Black Sea areas overlaps with Yellow-legged, but breeds on low isolated islands and islets in deltas, while Yellow-legged uses cliffs and roofs with no proven interbreeding (Klein & Buchheim 1997); putative hybrids reported from Poland (Faber *et al.* 2001; see Yellow-legged Gull 'Hybrids').

In Caspian Gull we include the taxa *barabensis* (now mainly treated as a subspecies of Heuglin's Gull) and *mongolicus* – now generally regarded as subspecies of Vega Gull; both may eventually attain fully specific status; see Geographical Variation.

Description and comparison below with other large gulls refers to taxon *cachinnans*.

With experience, jizz (and call) offers the best basis for identification. Caspian is typically lanky with curiously small head, slender body and long, slender legs – these structural differences are most marked in first-years. Although the size of Herring and Yellow-legged Gulls, it appears lighter and slenderer with a smaller, pear-shaped head, long sloping forehead, angled hindneck and long neck. Eyes small, usually darkish and beady, placed higher, more forward on head than in Herring/Yellow-legged. Bill slender with parallel edges, gently drooping tip and weak gonys-angle (in males often pronounced, enhanced by slenderness of bill; gape often long). Breast often surprisingly protruding in relaxed birds; body slender with flat back lacking clear tertial step and flat belly angled behind legs, which are long with large amount of visible tibia. Primary projection long (apart from in wing-moult): distance tail-tip–wing-tip greater than longest distance tertial-tip–tail-tip (equal to or slightly longer than in Yellow-legged, equal to or shorter than in Herring). Long wings often held close to ground.

Large males may look like narrow-billed and slender Pallas's Gulls, small females like oversized Slender-billed Gulls, with bill too long and slender and head too small for a large gull. Shows rather large variation jizz-wise; round-headed and short-legged females may look like a different species from larger males.

Has a relaxed, buoyant flight with boat-shaped body (protruding breast and lower belly against flat middle belly) and long arm; may look hump-backed. Often lowers bill. Fishes agilely, surface-dipping or plunge-diving. Aggressive against other gulls, defending food with 'albatross-posture' with half-spread wings and stretched neck while uttering hoarse laughter similar to Jackass Penguin *Spheniscus demersus* or sea-lion *Otariidae*. This behaviour is shared with Yellow-legged Gull and Heuglin's Gull, but unlike these species, it also occurs when 'long-calling'.

Adult has grey upperparts similar to or paler than Herring nominate *argentatus*, but softer, lacking bluish tinge. Head white, in Jul–Oct often with soft brown hindneck-streaks and sometimes narrow darker streaks around eye. Compared to Yellow-legged, wing-tip has more white/less black, often similar to Herring *argentatus* with complete white tip to P10 and white mirror to P9, shows diagnostic streaky pattern in mid-primaries with long white tongues to inner webs of P6–8. Shows black markings on P5

(inner webs of P5–6 often with more black than outer webs; if present, normally only on one web in Herring). White markings most conspicuous in western populations, Underwing looks very pale with pale secondaries. Legs dull grey with fleshy or yellow tinge. Bill often greenish-tinged (and in winter often with dark subterminal markings). The orange gonys-spot rarely reaches upper mandible. The eyes are darkish. In Herring Gull gatherings in autumn found by combination of jizz, small white head, dark eyes (high on head), greenish-tinged bill, soft grey upperparts and paler, greyish legs with weak yellow or fleshy tinge. Small females, with their dark eyes and greenish bill, may recall oversized Common Gulls with disproportionately long bill. Herring Gull, apart from its typical 'masculine' jizz, has cleaner yellow bill, coarser dark head-markings (setting off pale eyes) and bluish-tinged upperparts; some Baltic Herrings may show stronger yellow legs than average Caspian.

Yellow-legged generally has jizz of Herring, with more black on wing-tip (white on P10 only rarely covering tip; lacks streaking on mid-primaries), usually darker upperparts, darker secondaries from below, deeper yellow legs and pale eyes. Some Black Sea birds have jizz more like Caspian, but usually with heavier, bulbous-tipped bill, and more black/less white on wing-tip. If present, autumn head-streaking strongest around eyes and in crown.

Juvenile/first-winter has whitish head (but see juvenile under detailed description below), black bill, dark, pale-fringed tertials ('thumb nailed', restricted to tip) and indistinct diluted pale pattern on greater coverts (especially inner). Solid dark bases and broad white tips to greater coverts, secondaries and tertials create dark and pale bars in spread upperwing. Underwing mainly white. Tail-base white against black tail-bar (often narrow) and mainly pale underparts, including underwing, central belly and undertail-coverts.

Important characters for first-winter Caspian from Yellow-legged, Herring and certain pale-patterned Lesser Black-backed Gulls nominate *fuscus* are:

1 Small, elongated head with flat crown, slender black bill without pronounced gonys-angle, flat belly and long legs with considerable length of tibia visible. Some females barely differ from other large gulls, have small head and slender bill lacking bulbous tip. Herring and Yellow-legged heavier with larger, bulbous-tipped bill, rounder belly and shorter legs. Lesser Black-backed has more rounded head, shorter bill, shorter legs and the darkest plumage among these confusing species, and is fresh in autumn when most Caspian are worn.

2 In first-winter four-toned: head and underbody white, wings brown, (first-winter) mantle and scapulars grey with varying dark streaks, dots and bars and bill black. In Aug–Sep, head almost white in strong contrast to brown hindneck. In most birds, coverts then bleached and in contrast to fresher mantle (in other large gulls not before later in autumn; earliest – from Sep – in Yellow-legged).

3 Underwing often mainly white with fine pale greyish-brown markings. Yellow-legged and Herring Gulls have strong but diffuse brownish pattern on coverts/axillaries against paler flight feathers. Small minority Yellow-legged, Herring, Lesser Black-backed nominate *fuscus* and Heuglin's Gulls similar, but underwing with fine pale grey bars lacking solid white areas. Also, some Caspian have faintly brown-barred axillaries and underwing-coverts (especially lesser).

4 Head at first pale brown with darker eye-mask and variable amount of streaking on head, breast and upper flanks. By late Aug–early Oct head becomes white with fine dark streaks around eye and broader brown spots on hindneck and neck-sides, creating necklace. Often with faint pale eye-ring around small beady eye. Yellow-legged similar, but dark pattern strongest around eye forming dark eye-mask (which, together with black bill, recalls Mediterranean Gull). Herring greyer-brown, normally with coarser dark markings on entire head, damping the contrast between head and body. Herring with paler head shows more of a brown tinge. Lesser Black-backed and Heuglin's have more densely streaked head, darker eye-mask and often contrasting paler neck-sides/hindneck.

5 In late summer, dark-spotted breast-bar strong against whitish head and underbody, but lost from Sep, when head and underparts are white, although breast-sides may still show dark markings. Some Yellow-legged similar. In Herring, Lesser Black-backed and Heuglin's breast to belly has coarser dark markings, creating dark-patterned underbody into late winter – a main character for birds otherwise similar to Caspian.

6 Bill black, long and slender, with gently tapering tip to upper mandible and only a weak gonys-angle (often absent in female); all but large males lack bulbous tip and strong gonys-angle of most Yellow-legged and Herring Gulls. Bill mostly acquires paler base and sometimes tip in autumn, but some remain black in winter. Although many Herrings are similar, most acquire stronger-bicoloured bill in late autumn. Yellow-legged remains black-billed into first-summer.

7 Tertials blackish (soon becoming brown through wear) with broad white tips and narrower pale edges, typically restricted to outer 50%, leaving solid dark bases; pale tips may appear 'thumbnailed'. Pattern of Yellow-legged similar, but typically with broader, often notched edges. Herring very variable: tertials in most greyish-brown with oak-leaf centres, irregular pale waving and broader white tips; 10% (especially Baltic birds) more like Caspian, but pale edges reach onto coverts (rare in Caspian). Tertials of Lesser Black-backed and Heuglin's often similar to Caspian, but generally blacker with narrower paler edges. In Caspian, tertials often already very worn from autumn (never in confusing species, especially Lesser Black-backed and Heuglin's, in which tertials are fresh-looking into winter), and frequently 1–2 tertials have been exchanged for fresh new ones.

8 Greater coverts dark, gradually becoming paler towards tip to create broad pale wing-bar; combined with pale tertial and secondary tips forming rather evenly broad pale and dark bars on upperwing. Inner 50% often with diffuse grey barring or waving; less on outer 50%, which in folded wing may form darker rectangle. Yellow-legged more strongly pale-barred on inner 50% greater coverts, often similar to Herring, grading into darker outer coverts forming darker rectangle on folded wing; most lack 'extra' pale wing-bar of most Caspian (and Lesser Black-backed/Heuglin's). In Caspian, upperwing pattern thus similar to Lesser Black-backed, but lesser and median coverts paler, and often both tips and edges of greater coverts pale (when fresh creating white-streaked pattern at bases). Most Herring have pale and dark bars of equal width; all four species may show darker, faintly pale-barred and tipped greater coverts, often darkening on outermost.

9 Juvenile scapulars and coverts greyish-brown with pale edges (sometimes as notching) and often darker anchor-shaped markings/bases. From Aug, first-winter mantle and scapulars greyish with faint dark subterminal spots, triangles or anchor-markings, mostly with distinct dark shaft-streaks. Markings typically narrow and delicate, differing from the stronger, broader and more irregular markings of Herring and Lesser Black-backed Gull. Scapulars may be all-grey, creating diagnostic grey line, but rear scapulars often darker with irregular edges. New feathers in strong contrast to worn coverts from Sep (later in confusion species, only some Yellow-legged are similar).

10 Tail white with solid black bar. Similar to Yellow-legged, but tail-bar fuller and more even (generally with less white in T6/tips to rectrices) and tail often with narrow dark 'extra' bars. Herring Gull has browner tail-bar with broader whitish edges, less contrasting with denser dark barring on tail-base and their coverts. Lesser Black-backed has blackish tail with just pale barring at base, Heuglin's has broader black tail-bar than (most) Caspian.

11 Undertail-coverts pale with line of dark arrow-markings along sides; sometimes also with indistinct grey spots in central ones. As Yellow-legged nominate *michahellis*; first-year Herring and Lesser Black-backed have more even waving, barring or spots on all undertail-coverts; note that second-year Herring has pattern of first-year Caspian.

12 Legs often long and slender with clearly visible tibia (longer than in Herring), grey to pale 'plastic pink', generally paler than in congeners.

13 White area around alula in majority shared with Yellow-legged; rare in first-year Herring.

14 Often with pale window on inner primaries, but less striking than in Herring as entire outer webs are dark, creating streaky 'venetian blind' pattern (in Herring inner primaries pale, just with dark area near tip of inner web). Window generally weaker in Yellow-legged and Heuglin's Gulls; normally absent in Lesser Black-backed. In first spring primaries conspicuously more worn than congeners.

15 Most birds have pale wedge on lower back, broadening towards tail-base (similar to Curlew *Numenius arquata*) and contrasting with dark-centred tertials. This also seen in Yellow-legged, but lacking or inconspicuous in Herring and Lesser Black-backed.

Acquires first-winter mantle/scapulars (grey with dark pattern) and often scattered coverts (especially median and inner) and tertials from Jul. If present in late Sep, renewed coverts and tertials diagnostic of Caspian (and Yellow-legged), and thus a main character from Herring, which acquires new mantle feathers from Oct/Nov, but

PLATE 42. CASPIAN GULL *Larus cachinnans cachinnans*

Breeds on flat sandy bars from N Black Sea and eastwards to Central Asia. Following breeding season some spread to W, C and N Europe, occurring alongside other large gulls. Compared to Yellow-legged and Herring smaller-headed with longer neck, slenderer, more parallel-edged bill, deeper breast, slenderer hindparts (with characteristic 'hanging-belly' behind legs) and long, thin legs. Dark eyes situated well forward in head. In direct comparison differences often surprisingly striking.

1. **Juvenile** (Jul–Aug) Head greyish-brown with white forehead, paler hindneck and dense brown streaking on hindneck and breast-sides, contrasting with whitish breast, belly and central undertail-coverts. Mantle and scapulars greyish-brown with pale edges, creating scaly pattern. Greater coverts greyish-brown basally, at distal part with diluted pale (normally rather indistinct) pattern. Shows broad white tips to greater coverts. Tertials dark brown with pale tips, not reaching greater coverts. Bill black. Legs pale fleshy.

2. **First-winter** (Sep–Apr) Often contrastingly four-coloured. White head in contrast to brown neck-streaks, faint white eyelids, white underbody and brown juvenile wing, already worn from Sep. Mantle and scapulars grey with varying dark markings (bars, streaks or diamond-shaped spots, typically rather narrow); rear scapulars often dark-spotted. Tertials with white edges, often 'thumbnail'-shaped against dark bases. Markings on undertail-coverts restricted to edges. Bill may start to become pale at base from autumn, but some remain black-billed throughout first-winter. Note long, pale bubblegum-pink legs.

3. **First-winter** (Sep–Apr) Worn individual. Most birds renew some inner coverts in first autumn, in some contrast to juvenile worn coverts. Greater coverts in this individual pale greyish-brown with extensive white tips and edges, creating streaky pattern. Head and underbody white. Hind neck with dark streaks, forming necklace.

4. **Second-winter** (Sep–Apr) 'Retarded' bird resembling first-winter. Aged by lack of contrast between mantle/scapulars and coverts, more finely vermiculated greater coverts, more solid and complex white edges and tips to tertials, and blacker wing-tip with rounder white tips. If present, dark markings on mantle and scapulars finer than in all but a few first-winters. Bill fleshy with dark subterminal markings and cutting edges. Bill with pale base and tip.

5. **Second-winter** (Sep–Apr) Mantle and median coverts grey (often with faint dark markings), lesser and greater coverts browner with faint white markings. Head white against dark hindneck-streaking.

6. **Second-summer** (Apr–Aug) Tail-bar still obvious.

7. **Third-winter** (Aug–Apr) Similar to adult, but with duller bill, showing more extensive dark markings, parts of upperwing still with brown, pale-marked coverts, tertials with dark centres, primaries with narrower white tips (and white mirror to P10), tail with faint dark markings and legs often pale fleshy.

8. **Adult winter** (Aug–Apr) Adult shows grey upperparts of similar colour tone to Herring Gull, but lacking bluish tinge; generally paler than Yellow-legged Gull. Head white with narrow dark hindneck-streaks. Eyes darkish-looking. Bill yellow with greenish tinge, and often slight dark subterminal markings. Legs greyish with faint fleshy (greenish or yellowish) tinge. Most western birds '*ponticus*' show white tips to P10.

9. **Adult summer** (Apr–Aug) Head white. Eye darkish-looking (but in adult usually bicoloured). Legs pale yellow, greyish or pale pink.

Juvenile

. First-winter

2. First-winter

4. Second-winter

Second-winter

6. Second-summer

7. Third-winter

8. Adult winter

9. Adult summer

PLATE 43. CASPIAN GULL *Larus cachinnans cachinnans*

In flight lighter than Herring and Yellow-legged Gull with long, narrow wings, small, slender head, long, slender bill and deep breast.

1. **Juvenile** (Jul–Sep) First-years show brown upperwing with faint pale window on inner primaries (appearing streaky) and dark bases to greater coverts and secondaries, both being paler-tipped to create two dark and two pale wing-bars (as in Lesser Black-backed Gull). Broad pale wedge on lower back connects with white tail-base. Shows solid black tail-bar (and often an indication of narrow extra bars). Underwing mainly white (but some variation), in juvenile contrasting with browner head and body.

2. **First-winter** (Sep–Apr) From Sep shows good contrast between grey, dark-marked mantle and scapulars and brown, worn wing (with scattered new coverts). Note broad pale bars on upperwing as well as contrasting blackish, solid tail-bar. Underwing mainly white, only with faint dark markings, appearing concolorous with white underbody. Head white against brown hindneck-bar. Bill blackish. Inner primary coverts often pale.

3. **First-winter** (Sep–Apr) White head in contrast to brown hindneck-streaking. Note narrow bill and small head, sometimes recalling Slender-billed Gull. Wing faded, often already strongly so from autumn, in good contrast to fresh mantle, scapulars and inner coverts.

4. **Second-winter** (Sep–Apr) Grey saddle contrasts with white rump and dark tail-bar. Compared to first-year inner primaries paler (creating better-defined pale window), and P10 often with narrow white mirror. Underwing white, only with faint dark markings.

5. **Third-winter** (Sep–Apr) Similar to adult, but with darker wing-tip, mirror only on P10 and dark-marked primary coverts. Tail with scattered black markings, Bill dull yellow with dark subterminal markings.

6. **Adult winter** (Sep–Mar) Adult shows grey upperparts, similar to Herring Gull nominate *argentatus*, but lacking bluish tinge. Wing-tip black with long white tongues eating into black on wingtip, most obvious on mid-primaries; black markings reach P5, markings on P5–6 often triangular with most black in outer webs. Tip to P10 often white in western type '*ponticus*'. Head white most of year, in winter often with faint brown neck-streaks. Bill greenish-yellow, often with dark markings. Eye darkish.

7. **Adult summer** (Mar–Sep) Compare wing-tip pattern with Yellow-legged and Herring Gull, including more black on outer than on inner webs of P5–6. Bill bright yellow with orange to red gonys-spot. This bird shows maximum amount of white at tips of P10-9. Many birds from E part of breeding range (Caspian Sea) show more black/less white in wingtip as well as generally darker grey in upperparts. Bill often as bright as in Yellow-legged and Herring Gulls.

1. Juvenile

3. First-winter

2. First-winter

4. Second-winter

5. Third-winter

6. Adult winter

7. Adult summer

PLATE 44. 'MONGOLIAN GULL' *Larus (cachinnans) mongolicus*

Breeds on lakes in Central Asia, isolated from other large white-headed gull taxa. Winters E and SE Asia. Appears heavier than Caspian Gull nominate *cachinnans* with larger, fuller head and more blunt-tipped bill with well-marked gonys-angle. Jizz similar to Vega Gull, with which winter range overlaps.

1. **Juvenile** (Aug–Oct) Upperwing similar to Vega Gull with stronger pale window on inner primaries than in Caspian *cachinnans* and broader pale bars on all greater coverts. Secondaries dark, forming wing-bar against pale greater coverts. Tail white with dark bar, on average narrower than in Vega Gull. Underbody and underwing densely brown-marked.

2. **Juvenile** (Aug–Oct) Rather pale greyish-brown. Mantle and scapulars dark with pale edges, creating scaly pattern; often in contrast to paler-edged coverts. Greater coverts with even pale and dark bars, similar to Herring Gull. Tertials dark-centred with pale tips and edges, unlike nominate *cachinnans* reaching greater coverts. Whole underbody with greyish-brown markings. Head greyish-brown with paler hindneck and whitish face. Bill black.

3. **First-winter** (Oct–May) Head and underbody white. Coverts often very pale and faded. Mantle and scapulars grey with fine dark subterminal markings, often as anchors. Bill black.

4. **Second-winter** (Aug–May) Mantle and scapulars grey with dark subterminal markings. Upperwing paler than in first-year with more distinct pale window on inner primaries, similar to Vega Gull. Underwing mainly white, only with faint dark markings. Tail-bar narrow, often diluted.

5. **Third-winter** (Aug–Apr) Similar to adult, but with stronger dark hindneck-streaks, duller bill and dark subterminal markings on both mandibles. White mirror on P10 generally narrower and tertials and primary coverts with faint dark markings.

6. **Third-summer** (Apr–Sep) Similar to adult, but with fuller dark wing-tip, including primary coverts and traces of dark tail-bar.

7. **Adult winter** (Aug–Apr) Acquires mainly white head throughout year, in winter only with faint and indistinct streaks on hindneck (shown at its maximum here). Bill often with dark subterminal markings, even in summer.

8. **Adult winter** Shows grey upperwing, darker than in nominate *cachinnans* with broader white trailing edge to inner wing and more solid black wing-tip, black markings reaching P4–5. White mirror or tip to P10. This individual shows maximum amount of hindneck-streaking.

9 . **Adult summer** (Apr–Aug) Upperparts darker grey than in nominate *cachinnans*. Eye varies from pale to dark. Legs vary from fleshy to yellow.

1. Juvenile

6. Third-summer

4. Second-winter

3. First-winter

8. Adult winter

2. Juvenile

5. Third-winter

7. Adult winter

9. Adult summer

PLATE 45. 'STEPPE GULL' *Larus (cachinnans) barabensis*

Breeds steppes of Central Asia (Kazakhstan), wintering between Persian Gulf and western India; status in Red Sea less certain. Generally smaller than nominate *cachinnans*. Closely related to Heuglin's Gull, and identification not yet fully understood.

1.   **First-winter** (Oct–Mar) Compared to nominate *cachinnans* has more extensive brown markings on head and underbody and generally broader dark markings on upperparts. Coverts and tertials similar to nominate *cachinnans* and Heuglin's Gull.

2.   **First-winter** (Oct–Mar) An individual showing white head and underparts similar to nominate *cachinnans*. As in nominate, moult into first-winter normally includes some inner coverts; but in autumn moult generally later and more restricted compared to *cachinnans*; similar-aged Heuglin's Gull is fresher-looking, often still juvenile into midwinter. In late winter moult more advanced than in nominate. Bill often bicoloured from midwinter.

3.   **First-summer** (Mar–Sep) Often moults mantle, scapulars, tertials and parts of upperwing into almost adult type in first-winter, in contrast to worn juvenile primaries.

4.   **Second-winter** (Sep–Apr) Similar to adult, but bill dull fleshy with dark subterminal markings, tertials dark-marked and wing-tip black with faint pale primary edges.

5.   **Adult summer** (Mar–Sep) Adult shows darker upperparts than nominate *cachinnans* and taxon *mongolicus*, matching Heuglin's Gull race *taimyrensis* and Armenian Gull. As in Armenian, bill often four-coloured (yellow with red and black markings and pale tip). Eyes often dark, but in some pale. Legs bright yellow (sometimes grey or fleshy).

6.   **Adult winter** (Sep–Mar) Head white with faint brown hindneck-streaks. Bill four-coloured. Very similar to Armenian Gull, but bill slenderer with more curved tip.

First-winter

2. First-winter

3. First-summer

4. Second-winter

5. Adult summer

6. Adult winter

46. 'STEPPE GULL' *Larus (cachinnans) barabensis*

Smaller and more elegant than nominate *cachinnans*, very similar to Heuglin's Gull race *'taimyrensis'*.

1. **First-winter** (Sep–Mar) Upperwing similar to nominate *cachinnans* or Heuglin's Gull: brown with faint pale window on inner primaries and dark greater coverts and secondaries, both pale-tipped to produce two pale wing-bars. Underbody with coarser brown markings than in nominate and underwing generally darker. Many indistinguishable from darker (eastern) *cachinnans*.

2. **First-winter/summer** (Dec–Aug) Unlike nominate *cachinnans*, often moults large parts of mantle, scapulars and coverts into grey type from Dec, and additionally a variable number of secondaries; by late first-winter thus more advanced than nominate. Tail still juvenile. Underwing in this individual paler with finer brown markings, matching darkest-patterned nominate.

3. **Second-winter** (Sep–Apr) Similar to adult, but with dark-marked primary coverts, small white mirror on P10 and scattered dark tail-markings. A few secondaries often dark-centred.

4. **Second-summer** (Mar–Sep) Some still show extensive dark tail-bar into second summer.

5. **Adult winter** (Sep–Mar) Adult shows rather dark grey upperwing, but black tip still evident and strongly contrasting with rest of upperparts. Black wing-tip solid with black markings often reaching P3, and small white mirror (sometimes tip) to P10. Primary coverts sometimes dark-streaked (as in all eastern white-headed gulls this streaking in adults is much more frequent than in large gull species from western parts of W Palearctic and North America). Note strongly bicoloured bill.

6. **Adult summer** (Mar–Sep) Head white. Some show white mirror to P9. Note large extension of black at primary tips, reaching P3–4.

1. First-winter

4. Second-summer

2. First-winter/summer

Second-winter

5. Adult winter

6. Adult summer

very rarely moults various coverts. In contrast >90% Caspian from Nov have renewed some coverts, especially inner median and lesser (P. Schiermacker-Hansen *in litt.*, pers. obs.). Earliest moulting populations already show strongly bleached wings in Aug–Sep, which is not the case in confusing species.

While most first-years readily identifiable, it should be stressed that certain Herring nominate *argentatus* (especially Baltic birds) appear white-headed/black-billed in winter with fuller black tertial centres, whiter breast and stronger black tail-bar. Such birds best identified on a combination of larger, squarer head, stronger, bulbous-tipped bill, heavier body, shorter legs, more uniform dark upperwing lacking pale bar on greater coverts (but normally with paler window on inner primaries). Underwing and lower belly darker. Finer points discussed above. Bleached first-year Herrings in spring may be problematic, showing whitish head to underbody (including central body and undertail-coverts) and washed-out pattern on greater coverts/tertials through wear. As in other cases, jizz is often the main character. This is also the case in autumn, when distant second-year Herring and Great Black-backed may look white headed/dark-billed with fresh grey, dark-barred mantle resembling Caspian. Closer view reveals that mantle, scapulars and coverts are in same condition, lacking contrast between first-winter mantle/scapulars and worn juvenile coverts. Furthermore, greater coverts normally look darker with more but finer pale bars; tertials are blacker with broader white edges; and fresh primaries black with broader, rounder white tips ('new moons') – not the browner and pointed primaries of first-year gulls.

First-summer very pale with white head. Bill rather pale with black subterminal bar. Mantle grey with some reduced dark pattern compared to first-winters, and in strong contrast to those juvenile coverts that were not renewed in autumn (if juvenile coverts retained, they look extremely bleached from midwinter). Lesser coverts often dark, creating U around wing-bend (sometimes evident in first-winter). For identification of similar-aged Heuglin's Gull, see that species. Compare Herring Gull.

Second-winter has white head, underparts and underwing. From Sep mantle, scapulars and some (especially median) upperwing-coverts grey, the former often with dark shaft-streaks (broadening towards tip), the latter cleaner greyish than in first-winter. Secondaries, primary coverts and usually outer coverts dark-centred. Inner primaries paler against blackish wing-tip; often with white mirror on P10. Black tail-bar narrow and washed out, sometimes reduced to dark markings. Bill greenish-yellow with dark (often broad) bar and pale tip. Legs greyish. Generally 'more adult' than similar-aged Herring Gulls, the latter basically similar to first-winter, with no or very little grey on scapulars.

Second-summer similar to second-winter. May develop orange gonys-spot and slight yellow tinge to legs.

Third-winter similar to adult, but with darker wing-tip (including primary coverts), smaller white mirror to P10 and broken tail-bar, narrow and normally restricted to sides of tail. Sometimes shows a few dark-patterned tertials and wing-coverts. Has dark spots on hindneck. Compared to adult, bill duller greenish-yellow with broader black subterminal bar, covering both mandibles.

Fourth-winter as adult, but normally with complete dark subterminal bar on bill.

VOICE When defending feeding territory a hoarse, staccato laughter or mooing, comparable to sea-lion, Jackass Penguin or ass. Higher-pitched than in Yellow-legged: when excited uttered as *ääcchhh-äch-äch-äch-achacha* with a laughter-like quality, often slowing down towards the end; sometimes as single braying note. All calls lower than in Herring (Jonsson 1996, Garner & Quinn 1997, Klein & Gruber 1997, Small 2001, Klein & Buchheim 2003). In race *barabensis* either similar to or more like Lesser Black-backed and Heuglin's Gulls (Panov & Monzikov 2000, J. Dyczkowski *in litt.*).

MOULT ssp. *cachinnans* (pers. obs. in Hungary, Bulgaria, Scandinavia; skins; Jonsson 1996, 1998c, Garner 1997, Klein & Buchheim 1997). Generally 3–5 weeks earlier than Herring Gull, 2–3 weeks earlier than Yellow-legged Gull *michahellis* of E population.

Adult moult to **winter plumage** complete May–Sep (Nov). Primary moult starts with P1 early Apr, has reached P6–8(9) mid–late Aug and P9–10 mid-Sep–early Oct (mid-Nov–early Dec mentioned from UAE, Garner 1997), suggesting later moult in E populations, although misidentification for *barabensis* could be involved). Head and body Aug.

Juvenile moult to **first-winter** partial, including head, body, mantle and scapulars late Jul–mid-Sep; mantle and scapulars often completed by late Aug, but some still juvenile into early Sep. Often also moults some coverts (especially median and inner greater), scapulars and inner tertials; coverts from mid-Aug (up to 90% S Baltic birds had moulted some coverts by late Nov). Some from S Hungary and Romania Jan–late Mar had just renewed a few coverts. Covert-moult only progresses slowly, if at all, in winter (Schiermacker-Hansen 1998, Larsson 1999a, Bakker *et al.* 2000, Z. Eczedi *in litt.*, pers. obs.). Moult to **first-summer** at most restricted to a few feathers on head, body, mantle and lower scapulars Jan–Mar. However, birds staying S in winter range often moult extensively into second-winter from Feb–Mar. Moult to **second-winter** complete (Feb)Mar–Sep, on average a month earlier than in adults. Starts with P1 and median coverts late Mar/Apr, reaching P5 by Jun/Jul; max. 50% of coverts moulted into adult type. Subsequent moults similar to adult, but sometimes earlier; a bird moulting into third-winter had renewed P8 early Sep (A. Forsten *in litt.*).

Moult to **summer plumage** partial, including head and body Nov–Jan; most white-headed from Jan.

DESCRIPTION ssp. *cachinnans*
Size as Herring/Yellow-legged Gull. Differs structurally as outlined above, and as outlined below.

Adult Pattern of black on wing-tip: P10 with black outer web and whitish inner web before black marking behind 45–70mm white tip; whole inner web sometimes white or just with narrow dark subterminal markings, e.g. as 8–10mm subterminal bar before tip. In N Black Sea (type locality of '*ponticus*') 60–74% had all-white tip to P10 (max. 75mm), 14% traces of black near tip and 7% complete black bar. Many have whitish inner web and shaft against black outer web, isolating black subterminal marking near tip, creating unique wing-tip pattern compared to Herring. To E of range, generally shows more black/less white on P10 (in N Caspian Sea, most show dark subterminal bar near tip). P9 blackish with white inner web and 12–50mm white tongue; rarer as isolated white spots; 2% with white inner web reaching tip as in adult Thayer's and certain northern Herring nominate *argentatus*; width between tip/mirror and whitish tongue 70–98mm (in Yellow-legged nominate *michahellis* 96–140mm). P8 grey with 130–150mm black outer web, 60–80mm black inner web before 10–15mm white tip. P7 grey with 75–100mm black subterminal spot on outer web, 35–55mm on inner web and 7–10mm white tip. P6 grey with 25–35mm black, often most on outer web. Dark markings on P6–7 normally broader on inner than on outer web, separated from grey bases by white tongues. P5 grey with faint black markings (in 10% only small spot on outer web). P4 grey, in some (10–25% in Black Sea, up to 50% in E populations) with 10–15mm black spot on outer web, rarely also inner web; normally broken by white shaft. Upperparts paler than in Yellow-legged, as pale Herring nominate *argentatus* or even *argenteus* (Kodak Grey Scale (4)5–6.5) (Kohl 1959, Mierauskas *et al.* 1991, Shirihai 1996b, Liebers & Dierschke 1997, Jonsson 1998c, Gibbins 2003).

Gape bright orange to blood-red. Iris dark brown, dull yellow-brown or pale greyish-yellow with dark speckling; eye typically looks dark at distance, rarely as pale as in Herring. In Ukrainian breeders, eyes pale in 55%, medium in 28% and dark in 17%; seemingly a larger percentage of pale-eyed birds towards the E of breeding range. Orbital ring orange, in 2–3% red; red normally combined with dark eyes. Legs greyish with yellow (rarely bright) to fleshy-pink tinge. In Ukrainian colonies pale or greyish-yellow (88%), deep yellow (12%). In Hungary, Aug, 2–3% dull yellow, 12% greyish-yellow, 25% grey, 61% greyish-flesh. Birds with fleshy legs have fleshy to yellow feet. Bill parallel-edged and rather slender, lacking strongly curved tip to upper mandible and pronounced gonys-angle; a few males with more strongly curved upper mandible as in Herring/Yellow-legged. Nostril long and slit-like (triangular and broader in Yellow-legged and Herring): depth of nostril at distal edge 1.2–2.2mm, length 9.0–13.5mm. Bill greenish- to greyish-yellow with orange to red gonys-spot; rarely reaches upper mandible and sometimes incomplete or even lacking. Often with dark gonys markings. Bill length: bill depth at gonys all ages (2.0)2.9–4.0 (Liebers & Dierschke 1997, Schiermacker-Hansen 1998, Schiermacker-Hansen & Tofte 1999, Gibbins 2003, pers. obs.).

Adult summer (Nov–Aug) Head white. Bare parts brighter yellow in early breeding season.

Adult winter (Jul–Nov) Head white, often with brown streaks or spots on nape and hindneck and thin but dense grey streaks on crown and around eyes. Bill dull olive-yellow to yellowish-green, sometimes fleshy-tinged at base. Most have black subterminal markings on both mandibles, creating ring around bill. Eyes normally darker than in summer. Bill yellow to greenish-yellow. Gonys-spot dull red to reddish-orange. Most have dark subterminal bar (as bows), sometimes restricted to lower mandible; may obscure gonys-spot.

Juvenile (fledging–Aug) Head creamy-white with dark eye-mask and streaks, broadest on hindneck, where often present as dense brown spots or drops. Has narrow white eyelids above and below eye, emphasised by grey shading or streaks around eye. Mantle, scapulars, lesser coverts and median coverts greyish-brown to brown with buff to creamy edges (sometimes restricted to dots) and sometimes darker anchor-markings and bases (Jonsson 1998c). Lower scapulars often darker-centred. Lesser coverts with dark centres, creating spotted pattern. Greater coverts blackish-brown with pale tips and edges, normally with faint pale barring or waving (most on inner 50%); generally more uniform, indistinct or diluted than in Yellow-legged and especially Herring. Pale tips typically fade into dark bases; rarely greater coverts almost uniform greyish-brown, just with broad diffuse paler edges. Tertials blackish with whitish tips and distal edges, as white 'thumbnail'; rarely, narrow white edges reach base of outer web. Lower back, uppertail-coverts and rump white with dark spots. Flight feathers dark brown with P1–5 often with pale grey inner webs, creating slight pale 'window' with streaky pattern ('Venetian blind'). Primaries pale-based from below. Pale primary tips narrower than in most Herrings, soon disappearing with wear. Underbody whitish with dark spots to streaks on breast and flanks, forming dark breast-bar against white head and central underbody. Mid-breast often unmarked white. Undertail-coverts white with dark V-markings restricted to sides; rarely faint in central ones. Underwing-coverts and axillaries whitish with dark feather-tips and edges, sometimes barred or mottled greyish-brown (especially lesser coverts and axillaries); in birds with dark lesser coverts this offsets pale mid-wing-panel. More rarely darker-patterned, more like Yellow-legged or even Herring Gull. Primary coverts often with dark tips or centres, creating dark comma or carpal-patch against pale primary bases. Tail white with clear-cut black subterminal bar, on average broader than in Yellow-legged (but sometimes broader in E populations). Sometimes with indistinct dark spots, rarely 1–2 'extra bars' creating tail pattern as in adult male Rough-legged Buzzard *Buteo lagopus*. T1 with 40–65mm black bar, outer web of T6 white with 2–5 dark spots (rarely white). Bill black, sometimes with pale tinge to nail. Legs pale fleshy to pale pink.

First-winter (Aug–Apr) similar to juvenile, but head white with brown to cinnamon-brown streaks on neck, hindneck and breast-sides. Underbody with sparser dark spotting than juvenile; central breast to belly usually white. Mantle and scapulars pale brown or grey with slight brownish tinge, narrow dark shaft-streaks or anchor-markings (similar to Curlew Sandpiper *Calidris ferruginea*, especially lower scapulars). Dark markings often squarer, as 'diamond spots'. Pale ground colour quickly fades to greyish. Edges pale. With wear, dark markings reduced to create adult-looking grey scapulars; contrast to juvenile upperwing; some inner coverts usually replaced by new feathers, being grey with dark subterminal markings. Back often pale grey with narrow dark shaft-streaks. Flight feathers often wear to brownish, similar to Herring in colour (Klein & Gruber 1997). From (Oct) Nov/Dec bill often with pinkish or greenish-yellow base to lower or both mandibles and pale tip. Rarely, bill greyish-flesh with black tip and cutting edges. Legs as juvenile or brighter 'plastic-pink'.

First-summer (Mar–Sep) similar to first-winter, but with varying grey saddle in strong contrast to worn and bleached upperwing-coverts (from Mar often whitish through wear). Head/underbody generally whiter with weaker dark markings, strongest on breast-sides. Bill black to yellowish with dark tip and cutting edges.

Second-winter (Aug–Apr) Head white with dark spots or drops on hindneck and sides of neck, sometimes creating complete breast-bar. Mantle, scapulars and inner coverts (especially median coverts—sometimes all—and inner greater coverts) pale grey, often with narrow black shaft-streaks or anchor-markings, broadening towards tips. Lesser coverts and median coverts otherwise brown with greyish edges. Greater coverts darker greyish-brown with faint paler barring or mottling on outer 50%. Tertials blackish with whiter subterminal outer part often as irregular barring; sometimes with pale spots in dark centres. Secondaries blackish with broad white edges. P1–5 grey with darker inner webs and subterminal spots, outer primaries blackish, P10 sometimes with faint white mirror. Normally shows dark markings to P3–4. Underwing white with faint dark markings, mostly on primary coverts and tips of lesser/greater coverts. Rump white. Tail white with narrow black bar, often vermiculated towards base or intermixed with pale spots. Bill greyish-flesh to greenish-yellow with black subterminal bar and pale tip; rarely with dark basal parts as in Yellow-legged; generally with more dark from autumn (Jonsson 1998c). Eyes dark. Legs greyish with fleshy, rarely greenish-yellow tinge.

Second-summer (Apr–Sep) similar to second-winter, but head and breast with reduced dark markings; upperwing strongly worn and bleached with some new grey coverts (especially inner and median) and tertials.

Third-winter (Aug–Apr) similar to adult, but outer wing darker with white mirror on P10 only, often dark markings on P3 and dark-centred primary coverts. Often with scattered darker coverts (especially outer greater coverts) and tertials, the latter often with blackish spot at base. Shows incomplete blackish secondary and tail-bar; T1–3 mostly white. Eyes dark, but in a minority pale. Bill greenish-yellow with black subterminal bar and sometimes orange gonys-spot, generally duller than in adult.

Third-summer (Apr–Sep) similar to third-winter, but head as adult summer.

Fourth-winter (Aug–Apr) as adult, but sometimes with faint dark markings on primary coverts and bill; bill rarely greyish-tinged.

GEOGRAPHICAL VARIATION Three subspecies.

Caspian Gull *L. c. cachinnans* (N Black, Caspian and Azov Seas to Lake Aral and E to Lake Balkash and Lake Saisan, Kazakhstan; recent spread to Moscow area, Poland and Germany. Winters within S part of breeding range, in Persian Gulf E to Indian subcontinent and probably sparsely N Red Sea. Regular late summer to autumn, fewer in winter in N, C and W Europe. Detailed treatment above. Clinal variation between Black and Aral Seas comparable to similar situation in Herring Gull nominate *argentatus* between N Norway and S Baltic.

Supposed race '*ponticus*' (N Black Sea) the palest end of the cline with most white on wing-tip in adult. Compared to Caspian Sea and birds wintering in Arabia, adult generally has slightly paler upperparts. Has full white tip to P10, long white tongue from base of P10 along inner webs towards tip, and generally longer bill.

In E populations a larger percentage shows paler eyes and gradually becomes darker on upperparts with on average more black, less white on wing-tip; white on P10 usually restricted to mirror. P6-9 with more solid black areas and shorter pale tongues into black on wing-tip. P4-5 often with dark markings. First-years generally with more extensive dark markings on underwing (but central hind-wing still pale) and more restricted coverts moult than western birds; many retain wholly juvenile wing into mid-Nov. In Nov–Dec, generally with denser brown streaks on ear-coverts and hindneck, occasionally forming traces of half-hood. (Stegmann 1934a, Garner & Quinn 1997, pers. obs, UAE). Bill generally brighter and more 'multi-coloured', resembling race *barabensis*; many are indistinguishable from latter.

L. c. barabensis **'Steppe Gull'** (SW Siberia to SE Urals, Baraba and Kulunda Plains) Breeds steppe/lake margins surrounded by extensive reedbeds or on small birch-grown islets. Recent spread N to Moscow area. Could co-exist with Heuglin's Gull north of known range. Probably also N Kazakhstan (where birds showing mixed characters with *cachinnans*). Winters mainly Indian Ocean between Arabian and Persian Gulf and W India; small dark birds sometimes observed in Baltic and Europe could be this taxon.

This distinct taxon has been considered a subspecies of either (1) Caspian Gull (Johansen 1960) or (2) Heuglin's Gull, as a southern representative of Heuglin's *taimyrensis*, having developed as a result of introgression by nominate *cachinnans* genes into Heuglin's Gull population when the latter expanded its range southwards. At MtDNA level not genetically different from Heuglin's Gull (Panov & Monzikov 2000, Liebers *et al.* 2001, Yésou 2002). Area of overlap with Heuglin's and nominate *cachinnans* unknown; certain latter from area E of Caspian Sea similar to *barabensis*, whereas birds from N Kazakhstan have wing-tip of *barabensis* but characters from *cachinnans* (Yésou 2001a & b, Yésou 2002).

Barabensis generally slightly smaller than *cachinnans* with a more rounded head (forehead still flattish-looking), shorter, narrower bill, smallish-looking eye and shorter legs. Has lighter body, often looks flat-crested and flat-backed with poorly marked tertial step. Shape and adult plumage close to Armenian Gull (which is very slightly smaller), apart from head-shape and slenderer, less blunt-tipped bill. Bill proportions: nostril slit-like: length 10.5–12.5mm, depth at distal edge 1–2mm; noted as triangular (Garner 1997, photos UAE, W India; skin UZM). Bill length:bill depth at gonys 2.8–3.5. Wings shorter than in Armenian Gull, with short primary projection. P10 8–9mm <P9. It should be noted, that the full range of ID features between *barabensis* and eastern *cachinnans* as well as from paler Heuglin's Gull. '*taimyrensis*' is not fully understood.

Adult Has darker grey upperparts (Kodak Grey Scale 7–8.5) and fuller black wing-tip than *cachinnans*, approaching Armenian or Heuglin's Gull; often brownish-tinged (more than in Heuglin's Gull). Upperparts generally darkest to the N of range, in areas close to breeding sites of Heuglin's Gull, matching Heuglin's race *taimyrensis*. Conspicuous white trailing edge to wing, but narrow (sometimes lacking) white scapular and tertial crescents. Wing-tip black with more black/less white than in *cachinnans* (apart from certain eastern *cachinnans*); in some as Heuglin's *taimyrensis*. P10 with >50% black and 17–54mm white mirror (in <1% covering whole tip; probably males) and pale grey base to lower surface, as wedge to inner web along 30–50% of distance of visible part (Garner & Quinn 1997). P8–9 black, P9 in 10–44% (mainly males) with 3–19mm white mirror, mostly confined to inner web. On P5–7 40–80mm black subterminal markings, with narrow white tongues. Black primary-markings often reach P3(2). May show dark-streaked primary coverts (but not noted among 200 adults Goa, India; rare in adult Armenian and Yellow-legged (Jonsson 1996, Garner & Quinn 1997, skins, photos & own. obs.), but this is regular among all 'older subadult' large gulls, especially E Asian (pers. obs., skins). Bare parts generally brighter than in (western) *cachinnans* (see below for summer and winter). Gape orange to scarlet. Eye yellow (rarely silvery) with varying dark pigmentation (0–80%), in some creating darkish-looking eyes in field. Orbital ring orange to dark red. Legs variable; yellow, orange-yellow or greyish-flesh, generally deeper yellow than *cachinnans*. Bare parts brightest Feb–Apr; in Goa, India, Feb, legs in 36% bright yellow, 45% dull yellow, 14% fleshy and 4% grey; in N Kazakhstan, Jun, equal proportions of fleshy, grey and yellow (rarely bright) legs. In flight, underside of flight feathers grey against white coverts (as Armenian and Yellow-legged; unlike most *cachinnans*). White trailing edge to wing broadest on inner primaries (Garner & Quinn 1997).

Adult summer (Feb–Aug) Has white head and deep yellow bill with broad red gonys-spot, often reaching upper mandible (as subterminal bar). A varying number with black markings; 18 of 29 Saltaim Lakes (Filchagov 1993), but only 2 of 12 Malye Chany, 360km from former site. Markings most evident on upper mandible. Orbital ring orange-red with yellow or red tinge. Legs bright yellow, feet sometimes with orange tinge; in southern part of range (N Kazakhstan) seemingly more variable; paler and duller yellow to fleshy and thus similar to *cachinnans* (Panov & Monzikov 2000, pers. obs.).

Adult winter (Sep–Feb) Often shows narrow dark streaks on ear-coverts and coarser dark spots or streaks on hindneck. Bill generally paler than in summer, often four-coloured: yellow with grey or greenish tinge, black subterminal markings (in >80%, often broadest on lower mandible), red gonys-spot (sometimes reaching upper mandible) and pale yellow to ivory tip. Legs yellow in most, but often with grey, rarer fleshy tinge. >95% white-headed Feb.

Juvenile and immatures similar to nominate *cachinnans*, but never as pale and four-coloured as W *cachinnans*. ID from eastern *cachinnans* still poorly understood. Apart from in autumn, almost impossible to identify from similar-aged Heuglin's Gull; in autumn mantle and scapulars renewed into brown, dark-barred type at a time when Heuglin's still in mainly juvenile plumage. In **first-winter**, bill often yellow with black tip; in 10% black. Head usually with dark markings, especially on ear-coverts and crown. Underwing generally darker than in *cachinnans*, especially axillaries and lesser coverts; paler median and greater coverts often form pale midwing-panel similar to Audouin's Gull; others almost as pale as most *cachinnans*, but less 'clean'. Bases of outer primaries dark (pale in *cachinnans*). Head and body sometimes more heavily streaked than in *cachinnans*), which, especially on breast-bar and spotted or barred flanks retained well into winter. Mantle and scapulars darker greyish-brown with broader dark dots or triangles than in most *cachinnans*; sometimes solid dark feather-bases; some have narrow dark markings as in *cachinnans*, but on a darker, dirtier grey background. Tertials dark-centred with rather broad, irregular edges as in Heuglin's or even Herring Gull. May lack pale wedge on lower back shown by most *cachinnans*. Dark tail-bar often broader than in *cachinnans*, rarely covering most of tail. T1 with 50–72mm black bar. T6 with white outer web and faint dark spotting. Tail-base and rump generally more heavily spotted than in *cachinnans*. Juvenile feathers often worn from Mar.

First-summer/second-winter from Jan–Feb. In first winter often moult mantle, scapulars and many coverts, especially median and greater, into grey adult type. These parts may, however, also be moulted into grey with faint dark subterminal markings or barred type (probably when moulted in autumn), which, especially on scapulars, are strongly black-barred on buff to grey background, or more uniform brownish-grey with weaker pattern. Parts (sometimes all) of secondaries may be renewed into black type, in contrast to unmoulted brown primaries and their coverts. Tail rarely white. Legs fleshy. Bill dull yellow with broad black subterminal bar, rarely black. Note that moult into first-summer is similar to Heuglin's Gull, occurring from midwinter; bears some resemblance to the usual extensive moult of first-year Lesser Black-backed Gull nominate *fuscus*.

Second-winter similar to *cachinnans*, but some have more solid dark primary coverts and better-patterned black-barred scapulars and coverts contrasting well with new grey feathers. Tail-bar varies: may be absent, but sometimes as in first-year. Bill similar to first-summer, but sometimes with traces of red gonys-spot.

Third-winter as adult, but often with scattered dark tail-spots, dark primary coverts, a few dark-centred outer secondaries and black subterminal markings always reaching P2–3.

Moult L. c. barabensis **Adult** moult to **winter plumage** 1–2 months later than in *cachinnans* (one month later than in Armenian) as breeding season later; 1 month earlier than Heuglin's and Lesser Black-backed Gull nominate *fuscus*. P1 from late May. By Sep has reached P4–6, by Nov P7–9. Usually suspends moult during migration. Completes primary moult (mid-Oct)mid-Dec–Jan (1–2% mid-Feb) (Garner & Quinn 1997, Yésou & Hirschfeld 1997, Jonsson 1998c, P. Schiermacker-Hansen *in litt.*, pers. obs. in Goa, India). Moult to **summer** plumage Feb, including head and body. Most are white-headed by mid-Feb (compare Heuglin's Gull).

Juvenile moult to **first-winter** from Sep/Oct, starting with mantle and scapulars, sometimes followed by coverts and tertials from Nov; onset of moult generally later than in western *cachinnans*. Seemingly, actively moults in winter. Moult to **first-summer** similar to first-year Heuglin's Gull. Starts Jan–Feb, including head, body, mantle and scapulars and often some wing-coverts, especially median coverts. Usually moult some (sometimes all) inner secondaries and rarely tail Jan–Feb. Some moult P1–3 in winter (pers. obs. in Goa, India, mid-Feb).

Subsequent moults similar to adult, but sometimes slightly slower with earlier onset and later completion: some second- and third-winters reach P9–10 early Jan.

Mongolian Gull *L. c. mongolicus* (C Asia from SE Altai to NE Mongolia and W part of NW China; winters SE and E Asia). Here treated as subspecies of Caspian, but more closely related to Vega Gull. Could attain full specific status based on differences from *cachinnans* and *barabensis* in plumage, breeding season, migration routes and winter quarters. Preliminary mitochondrial DNA analysis (Crochet 1998) showed that *mongolicus* differs from *cachinnans*. Genetically closer to Vega Gull, thus probably a good species, but alternatively could become regarded as subspecies of Vega Gull (Buturlin & Dement'ev 1934, Barth 1968a, Filchagov *et al.* 1992a & b, Kennerley *et al.* 1995, Crochet 1998, Yésou 2001a, 2002).

On average larger and heavier than nominate *cachinnans* with a rounder head and heavier, parallel-edged bill and in males longish-looking with fuller chest and slightly shorter wings. May look flat-backed with prominent tertial step. Smallish eye shared with *cachinnans*, but well back on head. Shape and jizz similar to Heuglin's and Vega Gull; compared to both shows flatter forecrown, and compared to Vega slightly longer wings. Bill length:bill depth at gonys 2.7–3.1.

Adult White-headed, in Nov–Mar/Apr at most with very faint narrow dark streaks around eyes and on hindneck, sometimes more extensive (G. J. Carey *in litt.*). Upperparts grey (Kodak Grey Scale 5–6); as *cachinnans* or darker, similar to Vega Gull or palest Heuglin's Gull race *taimyrensis*. The palest birds (from Lake Baikal) approach Herring race *argenteus* in paleness with similar bluish tinge; the darkest birds are found NW Mongolia. White trailing edge to inner wing stronger than in *cachinnans*, and white tertial and scapular crescents larger. Wing-tip with more black than in *cachinnans*, thus closer to Vega Gull. P10 with white mirror and pale grey tongue of 9–15(20)cm; in darkest birds reduced, being similar to race *barabensis* and Vega Gull. Has rather large white mirrors on P9–10: P10 with 13–47mm (in 5–10% covering tip of P10, which covers max. 62mm of tip) and 5–25mm black subterminal bar behind tip. P9 with 4–39mm mirror; in 68% covering both webs, mainly as two isolated spots; 10–15% lack white mirror on P9. Rarely shows indication of white mirror on P8. P8–6(5) similar to *cachinnans*: has black subterminal markings (most on outer web) and 5–10mm white moons between grey and black, most on inner web (may be absent on outer—rarely both—webs). P4 usually with blackish subterminal spot (max. 16mm) on outer web. P(2)–3 often black-marked in younger adults. Primary coverts in 25–30% with dark shaft-streaks. From below, flight feather bases as white as coverts, contrasting well with blackish underside of outer primaries. Legs pale flesh to bright yellow (rarely orange-yellow), thus variable; no colour dominant in any population; birds with different leg colour pair freely. In Baikal area and Mongolia grey in 22–40%, yellow in 13–27% (differing within colonies and from year to year; in small minority bright yellow), pink in 21–46% and flesh in 4–10%; 'yellowish-flesh' in 6–30% (Pyzhianov & Tubitsyn 1992). In Baikal 11.9% flesh to pink, 49.9% yellowish-flesh, 3.9% pale yellow, 1.3% bright yellow; many birds have most extensive yellow around knee and lower tarsus, whereas feet fleshy; in extreme cases, legs flesh and feet orange-yellow (Yésou 2001a). More birds yellow-legged at onset of breeding season; wintering birds in Hong Kong have mainly yellowish-flesh legs. Iris dull yellow, in palest birds pale yellow or even whitish, but usually peppered with grey (from pale bluish-grey to greyish-brown), sometimes enough to create darkish-looking eyes in field. Eyes pale in 54% Baikal, 68% NE Mongolian birds. Orbital ring vermilion-red, brightest in breeding season. Bill usually with orange to red gonys-spot, normally restricted to lower part of lower mandible, falling 2–3mm short of upper mandible. Bill usually with dark subterminal markings especially on upper mandible; in summer 30% with dark markings, usually separated from each other, but in 1% creating complete black ring around bill. Gape bright orange. Nostril as nominate *cachinnans* (Madge 1983, 1985, Kennerley 1987, Pyzhianov & Tubitsyn 1992, Yésou & Filchagov 1993, Kennerley *et al.* 1995, Yésou 2001a, pers. obs. in Siberia).

First-year similar to Herring and Vega Gulls, inner primaries pale with dark subterminal spots on outer webs near tip, creating pale window. Primaries with variable pale edges, sometimes creating pale row of Vs. Greater coverts barred pale and dark. Pale bars typically broader than dark; similar to Great Black-backed and certain Vega Gulls. Juvenile mantle and scapulars blackish-brown with broad white edges, creating strong scaly pattern. Juvenile head and underparts rather cold-tinged and heavily dark-spotted or -streaked with traces of dark eye-mask and broad hindneck-streaking.

First-winter often very pale, appearing 'white-powdered'. Head and underbody white with scattered dark markings, most extensive on lower belly; often with narrow dark chevrons on lower flanks. May show narrow dark eye-mask. Mantle and scapulars pale grey with narrow black subterminal markings (sometimes reduced to spots), from Nov in strong contrast to bleached, very pale juvenile wing with indistinct pattern. Bill blackish, sometimes with narrow pale base from Nov. Underbody white, sometimes with dark spotting especially on breast and flanks, belly often clean white. Tertials similar to Herring and Vega Gull with dark (sometimes oak-leafed centres), pale-notched tips and complete white edges. Rump and tail-coverts white, sometimes with dark spots, especially along sides; undertail-coverts as *cachinnans*. Tail white in contrast to narrow black tail-bar (narrower than in Vega and Heuglin's Gull). T6 white, mostly with 1–3 narrow dark spots. Often shows narrow dark bars or waves adjacent tail-bar. Fresh rectrices have white tips. Underwing pale with delicate fine barring on coverts and axillaries, in paler birds approaching *cachinnans* with paler greater coverts (sometimes median coverts, creating pale mid-wing-panel against darker lesser coverts).

Second-year similar to Herring, but with purer grey saddle, whiter rump and tail-bases and cleaner black tail-bar; upperwing-coverts often strongly bleached by May in strong contrast to darker outer primaries and dark-centred secondaries; inner primaries very pale.

Third-year may show white mirror-spots on P9–10 (40 and 10mm respectively).

Moult *L. c. mongolicus* About a month later than nominate *cachinnans*. More information required. **Adult** moult P1–2, immatures P3–4 mid-Jun, P5–6 mid–late Aug, P9–10 Oct–Nov. Head, body and upperparts strongly worn mid-Aug Lake Baikal (P. Yésou *in litt.*, pers. obs.). **Juvenile** moult of mantle and scapulars to **first-winter** Sep–Nov.

Aberrants Leucistic known from Poland.

Hybrids Interbreeding with Yellow-legged known from Poland (see Yellow-legged Gull) (Faber *et al.* 2001).

DISTRIBUTION AND MIGRATION *L. c. cachinnans* breeds sandy dunes, islands, steppe lakes and along rivers. Russian population 25,000–30,000 pairs (20,000 Ukraine). Recent spread via large C European river systems N to Hungary, Belarus, Czech Republic, S Germany (rare), S Poland (180 pairs) and Russia N to Moscow (Dubois *et al.* 1990, Gruber 1995, Hagemeijer & Blair 1997, Faber *et al.* 2001, *Brit. Birds* 92: 73).

Main winter area Black/S Caspian Seas and the Gulf States. Very scarce Ukraine and SW Black Sea coast. Some winter S Russian lakes and rivers. Autumn migration Kazakhstan Sep; Israel mid-Jul–mid-Nov, scarce into Dec, peak Jan–Feb; Israeli winter population increasing: max. 7,360 adults Shifdan, late Feb 1997. In Sicily hundreds Dec–Jan. Common in Persian Gulf and UAE, where sometimes outnumbered by *barabensis* (from late

Nov) and Heuglin's Gull (Oct–early Nov); in some years max. 20–30% *cachinnans* in gull gatherings. Vanguards early Jul (adults and juveniles). Scarce S to Socotra, probably S Red Sea and E to Indian subcontinent, where mainly *barabensis* winters. Return migration mid-Feb–mid-Jun. On Israeli Mediterranean coast peak Mar–Apr; scarce Eilat; max. 23 per spring (Cramp & Simmons 1983, Shirihai 1996b, Richardson & Aspinall 1997b, Jonsson 1998c, M. Skakuj & A. Corso *in litt.*, pers. obs.).

Following breeding, many move NW and W (probably following Volga, Donau and Dnjepr) to C, W and N Europe; ringing recoveries of Black Sea (Ukraine, Asov) birds from S Scandinavia, Germany W to Heligoland, Netherlands, France, Italy, Hungary , Poland and Israel. In Hortobagy, E Hungary, scarce late Jul (mainly adults), numbers rising late Aug–Oct, when outnumbering Yellow-legged *michahellis* (which dominates to late Aug and thereafter gradually disappears); peak mid-Sep. In Poland similar pattern. In Warszawa more numerous than Herring in autumn, with flocks of several hundreds. In N and W Europe vanguards mid-Jul (including juveniles), increasing mid-Aug. Often immature peak late Aug; general peak late Aug–Oct, sometimes with another peak late Oct/mid-Nov. Most left by Dec. First-years dominate; increasing numbers of older birds from mid-1990s. In Baltic Sea, largest numbers occur between E Denmark Öland, Sweden and Poland. Regular N to Gotland and N Jutland, Denmark. Scarce wintering westwards to Great Britain, E Netherlands and S Scandinavia, in Central Europe outnumbering Yellow-legged in winter, e.g. late Nov–early Jan 1997/1998 max. 170 Ruhr and >2,000 Sachsen/Mecklenburg, Germany, 75 Netherlands (40 Limburg) and min. 25 Zealand, Denmark Oct 1998–Feb 1999. Locally common wintering in the

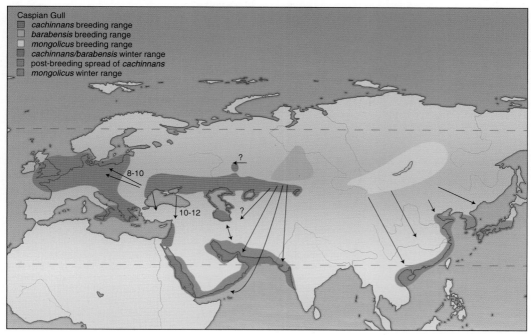

Caspian Gull
- *cachinnans* breeding range
- *barabensis* breeding range
- *mongolicus* breeding range
- *cachinnans/barabensis* winter range
- post-breeding spread of *cachinnans*
- *mongolicus* winter range

8-10

10-12

Netherlands, especially Limburg/Oost Maarland (>100) and C Europe (to C and S Germany). In S Poland dominant in wintering gull flocks, and in S Hungary flocks of max. 300–400 winter; some hundreds Sicily and Adriatic Sea. Scarce W to France (where annual). 20% of 'yellow-legged gulls' summering Niedersachsen thought to be this species (the rest Yellow-legged). Return migration Feb–Mar. Vagrant Finland (8), Norway (4), Ireland (1), Luxembourg (Nicolau-Guillaumet 1977, Larsson 1995, Cederroth 1995, Gruber 1995, Ebels *et al.* 1996, Jonsson 1996, Garner *et al.* 1997, Klein & Gruber 1997, Larsson & Lorentzon 1998, Schiermacker-Hansen 1998, van den Berg & Bosman 1999, Faber & Neubauer 2002, *Brit. Birds* 92: 73, *Dutch Birding* 22: 50, Z. Escedi, M. Cocker, A. Corso, K. Sándor, I. Dyczkowski & A. T. Mjøs *in litt.*, pers. obs. in Hungary, S Scandinavia).

L. c. barabensis (breeds SE Urals to N Kazakhstan). Population unknown. Breeds steppe/lake margins surrounded by reedbeds or on small birch-grown inlets with high open areas of sand, usually in small colonies (max. 200 pairs). Abundant in gatherings of hundreds Kurgashja, N Kazakhstan, Jun (Panov & Monzikov 2000, pers. obs.). Migratory. Main wintering area Persian Gulf and Oman, where numerically dominant large wintering gull in flocks of max. 2,000 with main arrival probably from late Nov–Dec (C. Richardson, pers. comm.); also Arabian Peninsula S to S Red Sea, Socotra and Indian Ocean coasts to W India (probably S to Sri Lanka). Of 300 large gulls Goa, India, Feb, >90% *barabensis*. Few SE Mediterranean, N Red Sea and Hong Kong.

Arrives at breeding sites mid-Apr–mid-Jun. Breeds about one month later than *cachinnans*.

Spread into N and W Europe suspected as 'birds showing characters of Armenian Gull' noted there; unusually small, dark birds observed Moscow, Poland, Sweden, Denmark since 1990s. Vagrant Maldives (Kennerley *et al.* 1995, Grimmett *et al.* 1998, Panov & Monzikov 2000, M. Skakuj & R. F. Porter *in litt.*, pers. obs.).

L. c. mongolicus breeds C Asia from SE Altai to Transbaikalia, NE Mongolia and Hulan Nor, China. Population 19,000–22,000 pairs in three separated populations: 750–1,200 W Mongolia, 7,200 Lake Baikal and Transbaikalia to NE Mongolia and 7,500–10,000 Hulan Nor, China. 16 adults nesting, Jun 2003 Udyl Lake, Ussuria, at 52.3 °N, 140.27 °E, tentatively attributed to this taxon. Small isolated population on W coast of South Korea. Migrates SE to winter range in coastal E Asia between Japan and Hong Kong, also Yangtze River inland at least as far as Po Yang Lake. Birds ringed Lake Baikal recovered Sea of Japan and Vladivostok; no recoveries W of Indochina. Migrates along E Chinese coast autumn (often in hundreds per day), to a lesser degree in spring. Unlikely to occur in Indian Ocean; claims from India, Pakistan and Persian Gulf unreliable (Kennerley *et al.* 1995, del Hoyo *et al.* 1996, Yésou & Hirschfeld 1997, Yésou 2001a, J. Jansen, E. Mølgård *in litt.*).

MEASUREMENTS Lengths in mm; weights in g. Own data based on skins in MCZ, NHM, NRK, USNM, UZM. *Cachinnans* Aral, Russia, Pakistan, Persian Gulf. *Mongolicus* Baikal, China. *Barabensis* Baraba Plains, Kirgizia, N Mongolia, UAE, Aden, Iraq (includes NHM series of '*armenicus*', eventually identified as *barabensis* on the base of measurements and detailed skin notes). Included in *barabensis* are measurement series given by Panov & Monzikov (2000).

WING

L. c. cachinnans		
Adult male	428–480 (454.1)	30
Adult female	410–458 (429.9)	26
First-year male	425–451 (438.3)	4
First-year female	408–430 (420.7)	4

Note *Dement'ev & Gladkov (1969) give for adult 418–482 (n=51, mean male 449, female 433). In Black Sea, mean in male 464.5, female 440.8 (Panov & Monzikov 2000).*

CASPIAN GULL Four-year gull. Breeds in several forms from C Europe across Black and Caspian Seas to steppe lakes of C Asia. Nominate *cachinnans* described here. Compared to Herring Gull, slenderer with smaller head, slenderer, parallel-edged bill (lacking marked gonydeal angle) and smaller eyes sitting well forward in head. Neck is long, breast well protruding and hindparts slender. Often shows pronounced 'hanging-belly' behind long, thin legs.

Adult with wing pattern similar to Herring, including white tip to P10, but white tongues on primaries longer, often creating streaked wing-tip, and P5 with extensive black markings. Head white (in autumn at most with faint brown hindneck-streaks), eye often darkish-looking. Bill often greenish-tinged. Legs grey with fleshy to faint yellow tinge.

First-year from autumn white on head and body with dark markings reduced to spots on hindneck, fainter on breast-sides, flanks and edges of undertail-coverts. Bill and eye black in white head. Upperwing brown with solid dark bars across bases of secondaries and greater coverts (as Lesser Black-backed); sometimes faint pale window on inner hand. Tertials dark with white tips, often appearing slightly crescentic. Shows pale wedge on lower back, reaching white tail-base, which contrasts with solid blackish tail-bar (often with narrow extra bars). Underwing often mainly white. First-winter mantle and scapulars greyish-brown with dark streaks or crescents; mantle, scapulars and some inner coverts renewed from Aug–Oct when parts of plumage already worn.

Second-year has grey upperparts, contrasting with browner lesser and greater coverts, solid dark wing-tip (sometimes with white mirror to P10) and whitish head, underbody and underwing. Shows traces of dark tail-bar.

Third-year as adult, but black on wing-tip generally fuller, and there are often dark markings on primary coverts, tail and bill. For taxa *barabensis* and *mongolicus* see detailed descriptions.

L. c. mongolicus
Adult male	443–470 (459.1)	6
Adult female	442–460 (448.5)	6
First-year female	450	

Note *Yésou (2001a) gives for 42 adults (Lake Baikal, Jun) 432–494 (458.4).*

L. c. barabensis
Adult male	428–457 (437.5)	15
Adult female	385–442 (419.4)	19
First-year male	378–415 (398.3)	3

BILL
L. c. cachinnans
Adult male	50.7–63.5 (56.3)	30
Adult female	48.0–59.5 (51.9)	26
First-year male	51.5–60.2 (55.5)	4
First-year female	49.2–53.2 (51.5)	4

Note *Mean in Black Sea males 62.1, female 56.3; Caspian Sea adult male mean 60.0, female 53.1 (Panov & Monzikov 2000).*

L. c. mongolicus
Adult male	49.3–62.0 (56.0)	6
Adult female	51.3–60.0 (55.1)	6
First-year female	50.4	

Note *Yésou (2001a) gives for 42 adults (Lake Baikal, Jun) 48.0–61.7 (54.9).*

L. c. barabensis
Adult male	47.1–61.2 (55.0)	12
Adult female	45.7–55.1 (48.8)	23
First-year male	43.0–49.8 (46.0)	3

BILL DEPTH AT GONYS
L. c. cachinnans
Adult male	16.2–21.0 (18.1)	30
Adult female	14.9–20.0	26
First-year male	16.0–18.3 (17.2)	4
First-year female	15.0–16.0 (15.5)	4

L. c. mongolicus
Adult male	17.2–21.3 (18.9)	6
Adult female	17.4–19.9 (18.6)	6
First-year female	15.7	

Note *Yésou (2001a) gives for 42 adults (Lake Baikal, Jun) 16.6–22.1 (19.0).*

L. c. barabensis
Adult male	16.4–18.8 (17.8)	14
Adult female	13.5–18.6 (15.9)	23
First-year male	15.4–15.8 (15.6)	3

BILL DEPTH AT BASE OF BILL
L. c. cachinnans
Adult male	16.8–21.0 (19.2)	30
Adult female	14.0–19.6 (17.3)	26
First-year male	17.9–19.3 (18.5)	4
First-year female	14.5–16.5 (15.7)	4

L. c. mongolicus
Adult male	17.7–21.9 (20.1)	6
Adult female	17.1–21.2 (18.9)	6
First-year female	17.6	

L. c barabensis
Adult male	16.8–19.0 (18.1)	7
Adult female	15.5–18.2 (16.6)	12
First-year male	16.9–17.1 (17.0)	3

GONYS LENGTH
L. c. cachinnans
Adult male	14.1–17.6 (15.8)	30
Adult female	12.9–17.5 (15.5)	26
First-year male	14.7–16.7 (15.6)	4
First-year female	10.7–15.6 (13.9)	4

L. c. mongolicus
Adult male	14.2–16.8 (15.5)	6
Adult female	13.6–16.2 (14.9)	6
First-year female	14.6	

L. c. barabensis
Adult male	12.4–16.3 (14.5)	7
Adult female	11.4–15.1 (13.7)	12
First-year male	13.2–13.8 (13.6)	3

TARSUS
L. c. cachinnans
Adult male	65.8–77.0 (69.9)	30
Adult female	58.7–73.8 (64.0)	26
First-year male	65.7–69.9 (67.5)	4
First-year female	57.2–66.1 (61.1)	4

Note *Mean Black Sea male 72.3, female 66.9; Caspian Sea male 70.2, female 65.6 (Panov & Monzikov 2000).*

L. c. mongolicus
Adult male	62.0–72.3 (68.6)	6
Adult female	62.0–70.9 (65.6)	6
First-year female	65.5	

Note *Yésou (2001a) gives 63.2–79.3 (68.9).*

L. c. barabensis
Adult male	61.2–73.0 (67.3)	15
Adult female	58.2–69.1 (62.4)	23
First-year male	60.9–65.4 (62.7)	3

Weight *L. c. cachinnans* adult male 750–1,193, female 680–1,037; Volga Delta to N Black Sea adult male 1,045–1,500, female 809–1,147; Caspian Sea adult male 750–1,193, female 700–1,050 (Dement'ev & Gladkov 1969, Panov & Monzikov 2000). *L. c. mongolicus* (Mongolia) adult male 1,150–1,580, female 850–1,100; Lake Baikal 880–1,590 (Cramp & Simmons 1983, Yésou 2001a). *L. c. barabensis* 680–1,170; breeding adult: male 900–1,070, female 680–950 (Yésou & Hirschfeld 1997, Panov & Monzikov 2000).

Caspian Gull ssp. *cachinnans*. **430. Juvenile**. Note greyish-brown mantle and scapulars, paler than in Yellow-legged Gull. These feathers are soon moulted into 1st-winter. Møn, Denmark. 16 Aug 1993. *Per Schiermacker-Hansen*. **431. 1st-winter**. Note slender bill, lacking both strongly hooked tip and pronounced gonys angle. By autumn appears white on head and underparts. 1st-winter mantle, scapulars and some innerwing-coverts grey with dark anchor-markings. Tertials dark with white edges, not reaching coverts. Møn, Denmark. 22 Oct 1995. *Per Schiermacker-Hansen*. **432. 1st-winter**. Often appears four-coloured with black bill and wing-tip, white head and underparts, grey saddle and darker brown coverts. Note diffuse pale barring on greater coverts and long-winged appearance. Møn, Denmark. 2 Nov 1992. *Per Schiermacker-Hansen*. **433. 1st-winter** (left, with Herring Gull). Compare the two species, and note especially the smaller head with slenderer bill, slimmer body, bulging hindbelly, longer legs and more contrasting plumage of Caspian compared to the browner Herring Gull. Bornholm, Denmark. 17 Oct 2001. *Klaus Malling Olsen*.

Caspian Gull ssp. *cachinnans*. **434. 1st-winter**. Note broad pale wing-bars, large amount of new coverts and faint pale window in innerhand, being obscured by dark outerwebs to P1-5. Møn, Denmark. 30 Nov 1991. *Per Schiermacker-Hansen*. **435. 1st-winter**. Note black tail-bar and narrower dark extra bars in white tail, slender dark bill and dark neck-boa. Møn, Denmark. 18 Sep 1993. *Per Schiermacker-Hansen*. **436. 1st-winter**. White head contrasts strongly with grey mantle and dark wings. Several narrow, dark bars in tail typical. Gilleleje, Denmark. 14 Feb 1998. *Klaus Malling Olsen*. **437. 1st-winter**. Note predominantly white underwing. Møn, Denmark. 22 Sep 1991. *Per Schiermacker-Hansen*. **438. 1st-winter**. Some birds have darker underwing-covert markings, but note pale, unmarked belly and central undertail-coverts. Møn, Denmark. 5 Nov 1991. *Per Schiermacker-Hansen*

Caspian Gull ssp. *cachinnans*. **439. 1st-winter** (eastern *cachinnans* or possibly *barabensis*). Note the predominantly pale-looking underwing, typical for Caspian Gull, as well as unmarked white undertail-coverts and solid black tail-bar. Red Sea. Mar. *Kaj Halberg*. **440. Moulting into 2nd-winter**. Head more slender with eyes placed further forward on head than in Herring Gull. Note broad pale tip to bill and dark-centred tertials. Esbjerg, Denmark. 11 Oct 1995. *Klaus Malling Olsen*. **441. 2nd-winter**. At this age, most show partly uniform grey saddle, but still extensive dark-centred tertials. Primaries blacker than in 1st-winter and bill pale at base and tip. Germany. 4 Dec 1999. *Martin Gottschling*. **442. 2nd-winter**. Tail-bar often broader, but more diffuse at this age compared to 1st-years. Mamaia, Romania. 12 Oct 2000. *Annika Forsten*. **443. 2nd-summer moulting into 3rd-winter**. Shape of this bird very typical, appearing slender with small head, well-protruding breast and slender hindparts, as well as long legs. Hindneck faintly streaked. Skagen, Denmark. 3 Aug 2000. *Knud Pedersen*.

Caspian Gull ssp. *cachinnans*. **444. 3rd-winter/summer**. Similar to adult, but primary coverts dark and white mirror on P10 much smaller. Bill with solid dark markings on both mandibles. Red Sea. Mar. *Kaj Halberg*. **445. 3rd-summer**. Note lack of pale primary tips and dark bill-markings at this age. Eye dark in predominantly white head. Israel. Feb. *Hadoram Shirihai*. **446. 4th- or adult winter**. Extensive dark markings on bill as well as full brown streaks on hindneck indicate this age. Evros, Greece. 2 Dec 1998. *Didier Vangeluwe*. **447. Adult moulting into winter plumage** with Herring Gull. Note the smaller, whiter head, darkish-looking eyes, greenish-tinged bill and paler, greyer legs of Caspian compared to Herring. Kåseberga, Scania, Sweden. 28 Sep 2000. *Klaus Malling Olsen*. **448. Adult winter** with Herring Gulls. Note more slender bill, white head with small, dark and beady eyes, longer legs and more black in wing-tip than in Herring. Complete white under-surface to tip of P10 shown. Herring bulkier with short-er, stronger legs and more extensive head-streaking as well as paler eyes. Katwijk, Netherlands. 7 Nov 1998. *Marc Guyt*.

Caspian Gull ssp. *cachinnans*. **449. Adult** in threatening posture (this "albatross-posture" is diagnostic, and differs strongly from similar posture of Yellow-legged Gull (compare photo 387). Also note the limited amount of black in wing-tip. The broad white bases to all primaries show up very well in this posture. Germany. 30 Nov 2000. *Andreas Buchheim.* **450 Adult winter.** Note the broad white tip to P10 as well as long white tongues in the white outer wing. Shifdan, Israel. Feb. *Hadoram Shirihai.* **451. Adult moulting into winter plumage.** Note long white tongues in mid-primaries and dark markings onto P5. P9-10 growing, the former showing complete white tip. Mamaia, Romania. 15 Oct 2000. *Annika Forsten.* **452. Adult.** Note white underwing, white tip to P10 and large white mirror on P10. Long white tongues in primaries visible even from below. Shifdan, Israel. Feb. *Hadoram Shirihai.* **453. Adult.** Note how white tongues in primaries create streaked pattern in spread wing. Shifdan, Israel. Feb. *Hadoram Shirihai.*

Caspian Gull ssp. *cachinnans*. **454. Adult**. Note narrow black markings in outer wing. Bochum, Germany. 10 Nov 2000. *Martin Gottschling*. **455. Adult** of 'eastern type'. Compared to most birds in the western part of the range, eastern birds show on average more black/less white in wing-tip, more similar to *barabensis* and Yellow-legged Gull, but more extensive white tongues in mid-primaries. Baluchistan, Iran. Feb 2000. *Philippe J. Dubois*. **456. Adult** of 'eastern' type, showing more extensive black in wing-tip than 450-454, including dark sub-terminal bar on P10, as well as brighter bill coloration. Many very similar to Steppe Gull *barabensis* and often not separable, but in most *barabensis*, black markings in primaries include P4 and white tongues in primaries shorter, resulting in fuller black wing-tip. Red Sea. Mar. *Kaj Halberg*.

'Steppe Gull' (Caspian Gull ssp. *barabensis*). **457. 1st-winter**. Very similar to especially eastern *cachinnans*, but coarser dark spotting on flanks and generally broader dark markings on fresh mantle and scapulars as well as generally more restricted wing-coverts moult at this age suggests *barabensis*. Ras Al Hadd, Oman. Oct. *Hanne & Jens Eriksen*.

'Steppe Gull' (Caspian Gull ssp. *barabensis*). 458 1st-winter *cachinnans* or *barabensis*. Many birds are almost identical to *cachinnans*. Compared to the similar Heuglin's Gull, typically worn with new mantle and scapulars at a time when Heuglin's Gull appears fresh and in predominantly juvenile plumage. Bahrain. Nov 1995. *Mike Skakuj*. 459. 1st-winter with adults. Note jizz similar to *cachinnans*, but adults generally darker on upperparts and almost invariably with yellow legs. Note variation in underwing of the two flying 1st-years, generally appearing more heavily dark-marked than *cachinnans*. Note two 1st-winter Pallas's Gulls in flock. Goa, India. 14 Feb 1999. *Klaus Malling Olsen*. 460. 1st-winter moulting. Moult in 1st-winter includes secondaries in *barabensis*, but this is also found in Heuglin's Gull and Lesser Black-backed *fuscus*. Goa, India. 14 Feb 1999. *Klaus Malling Olsen*. 461. 1st-summer. Very similar to *cachinnans*, but note fresh tertials and many wing-coverts; this moult is as extensive as in many Heuglin's Gulls. Northern Kazakhstan. Jun 2001. *Max Berlijn*. 462. 2nd-winter. Often rather similar to adult at this age, but note dark outer secondaries and tail-bar. Goa, India. 1 Jan 1998. *Per Schiermacker-Hansen*.

'Steppe Gull' (Caspian Gull ssp. *barabensis*). **463. 2nd-or 3rd-winter.** Immatures show dark neck-streaks against white head, extensive dark markings on bill and black primaries just with narrow pale edges. This bird could be an advanced 2nd-winter, but overall appearance similar to adult suggests 3rd-winter. Ras Al Hadd, Oman. 18 Oct 1995. *Hanne & Jens Eriksen*. **464. 3rd-winter.** Note extensive dark markings on primary coverts as well as smaller white mirrors on P9-10 than adult. Jizz of settled 1st-winters similar to *cachinnans*, but head often slightly larger-looking and bill generally shorter. Goa, India. 1 Jan 1998. *Per Schiermacker-Hansen*. **465. 3rd- and adult summer**. Note upperpart coloration, darker than in *cachinnans* and similar to paler extreme of Heuglin's Gull. Compare with photos 582–588. North Kazakhstan. Jun 2001. *Max Berlijn*. **466. Adult winter.** Note four-coloured bill, rather dark upperparts and fresh primaries, moulted at a time when darker and somewhat larger Heuglin's Gull still shows moult in outer wing. UAE. Jan 1998. *Steve Young*.

'Steppe Gull' (Caspian Gull ssp. *barabensis*). **467. Adult summer**. Jizz similar to *cachinnans*, but darker upperparts, generally deep-er yellow legs and more extensive markings on stronger coloured bill are all *barabensis* characters. However, many such birds are almost identical to eastern *cachinnans*, and better left unidentified. UAE. Jan 1998. *Steve Young*. **468. Adult summer**. Quesh Island, Iran. Feb 2001. *Philippe J. Dubois*. **469. Adult winter**. Note more extensive black wing-tip than *cachinnans*, lacking long white tongues eating into wing-tip. P10 normally with white mirror only. Black markings in primaries reach at least P4. Ras Al Hadd, Oman. 15 Oct 1995. *Hanne & Jens Eriksen*. **470. Adults** (flock - note Heuglin's Gull ssp. *heuglini* in background). Black wing-tip well separated from grey upperparts. Note that by mid-Feb birds have renewed all primaries. In background centre, a Heuglin's Gull - identified on darker upperparts with less of a contrast between black wing-tip and paler upperparts, as well as by growing P10 - can be seen. Goa, India. 14 Feb 1999. *Klaus Malling Olsen*.

336

'Mongolian Gull' (Caspian Gull ssp. *mongolicus*). **471. Juvenile.** Note the very broad pale bars in greater coverts as well as extensive pale tertial edges with irregular pattern, differing strongly from other taxa within Caspian group. Compare other taxa as well as Great Black-backed and Vega Gulls. Lake Baikal, Russia. 16 Aug 1997. *Gert Groot Koerkamp.* **472. 1st-winter.** Typically "frosty" pale in winter. Note narrow dark markings in grey mantle/scapulars and pale greater covert bars broader than dark ones. Underparts more heavily marked than in *cachinnans*, similar to Vega and Herring Gulls. Honshu, Japan. 5 Jan 2001. *Osao Ujihara.* **473. 1st-winter.** Bill-shape, with hooked tip and well developed gonys angle, resembles Herring and Vega Gulls, and is different from the more slender bill of *cachinnans*. Note frosty appearance, extensive pale markings on greater coverts, broad pale tertial edges and very faint upperparts markings. Honshu, Japan. Feb 2001. *Osao Ujihara.* **474. 1st-winter.** Note very narrow dark tail-bar, white undertail-coverts with dark chevrons along edges and extensive dark markings on flanks and hindneck. Honshu, Japan. Jan 2001. *Osao Ujihara.* **475. 1st-winter.** Head- and bill-shape more similar to Vega and Herring Gulls than to *cachinnans*, dark-spotted hindneck and pale upperwing with contrasting dark secondaries. Chumunjin, South Korea. 11 Dec 2000. *Jon R. King.* **476. 1st-winter.** The underwing of 1st-year birds is typically very pale (similar to *cachinnans*) - as shown here - but can be darker. Dark tail-bar narrow. Lake Baikal, Russia. 16 Jun 1989. *Klaus Malling Olsen.*

477

478

'Mongolian Gull' (Caspian Gull ssp. *mongolicus*). **477. 2nd- and adult summers**. Upperparts generally darker than in *cachinnans*, thus similar to *barabensis* or Vega Gull. Ojij Noor, Mongolia. Aug 2000. *H-J. Fünfstück.* **478. Adult summer**. Note large white wing mirrors on P9-10. Lake Baikal, Russia. Jun 1992. *Pierre Yésou.* **479. Adult summer**. Jizz often as Vega and Herring Gulls with similar strong bill. Extensive white mirrors on P9-10, on P10 often covering entire tip. Note very pale eyes of settled birds, in some matching Vega and Herring Gulls unlike *cachinnans* and *barabensis*. Ojij Noor, Mongolia. Aug 2000. *H-J. Fünfstück.*

479

'Mongolian Gull' (Caspian Gull ssp. *mongolicus*).
480. Adult summer. A slight variation in upperpart coloration noticeable here. Legs vary from yellow to fleshy, and eyes from dark to pale. Lake Baikal, Russia. Jun 1992. *Pierre Yésou*. **481. Adult.** Black reaches to P5. Note short pale tongues eating into black on P6-8. Lake Baikal, Russia. Jun 1992. *Pierre Yésou*. **482. Adult**. Many show almost complete white tip to P10. Black markings reach P4. Lake Baikal, Russia. Jun 1992. *Pierre Yésou*. **483. Adult winter**. Note just faint head-streaks in winter, and compare with Vega Gull, photos 492-494. Tokyo, Honshu, Japan. Feb 2001. *Osao Ujihara*.

23. VEGA GULL

Larus vegae (Palmén, 1887, Northeastern Siberia)

IDENTIFICATION Length and wingspan as for Herring Gull. A large gull of NE Asia, sometimes regarded conspecific with Herring Gull (Filchagov 1994), and to many European birdwatchers, the similarity between Vega Gull and Herring Gull is striking. Taxonomic status unclear. We treat it here as a full species, but more research needed. Apparent sympatry with Heuglin's Gull over huge areas provides evidence of specific status (Kennerley *et al.* 1995), although hybridisation with Heuglin's seems extensive. Probably closely related to Caspian Gull taxon *mongolicus*.

Size and shape similar to Herring, American Herring and Heuglin's Gull: front-heavy with rounded head and heavy bill with pronounced gonys-angle, but often more gently curved upper mandible. Eye sits slightly higher and more forward on head than in American Herring. In flight similar to Herring and American Herring, but outer wing slightly narrower. See also Slaty-backed Gull.

Adult similar to Herring Gull, darkest birds to Heuglin's '*taimyrensis*'. Wing-tip shows small white mirrors on P9–10; there are dark markings on P5–6 and obvious white tongues in mid-primaries, in flight sometimes creating 'string of pearls' as in Slaty-backed Gull (but situated closer to primary tips) and some western American Herring, with palest birds at northern part of range and darkest to the W (Western Taimyr) and the E (Chutki Peninsula). Upperparts dark grey, similar to Herring *argentatus*, thus darker than in American Herring. Compared to American Herring, Vega shows broader white tertial, scapular crescents and trailing edge to inner wing. In folded wing four outer primaries have well-shaped white tips. Late moult means that white primary tips are still obvious by May, but also that white primary tips have mainly been worn off by Aug–Sep, when American Herring shows at least inner primaries fresh with broad white tips. In winter, head moderately to heavily streaked, ranging from full brown spots covering head and breast-sides to faint streaks, most extensive on hindneck. Eye varies from pale (as in American Herring) to dark-spotted or dark. Orbital ring red. Legs fleshy, pink or rosy, generally brighter than in American Herring, but to W part of range yellow. See Geographical variation. '*Birulai*' sometimes said to show yellow legs; see Geographical Variation.

Vega is very like Caspian race *mongolicus*, which shows black in 6–9 outer primaries (5–7 in Vega) and has mainly white head, at most with faint brown streaks on hindneck in winter. Many *mongolicus* have paler upperparts than Vega.

Heuglin's Gull generally darker (but paleness sometimes matched in pale '*taimyrensis*'), with yellow legs and later moult into winter than in Vega Gull. See below for hybrids.

Juvenile/first-winter similar to American Herring Gull with obvious pale window on P1–5, heavily dark-patterned head, often with faint darker eye-mask and brown-patterned underparts; E birds often paler-headed with pale face and dark neck-streaks, but some show enough solid dark head-markings to appear hooded. Overall more greyish-tinged and generally paler with more distinct streaks or spots than American Herring. Mantle and scapulars of first-winter often paler grey with finer, narrower dark anchor-markings, appearing barred in the field. Tertials variable, in many similar to typical Herring, but pale edges often narrower and more regular. Dark tail-bar broad against white tail-base, being slightly narrower than in Heuglin's; unlike both, typically with more white than black mottling in T6, contrasting well with white tail-base. While this is a good ID feature from American Herring, a few birds show almost as extensive dark tail as American Herring. Many have densely dark-barred rump, but just in well-marked birds as strong as in American Herring. Greater coverts vary from dark with narrow pale bars (especially on outer) to very pale with 2–3 narrow bars as in Great Black-backed, Caspian *mongolicus* and the palest Heuglin's Gulls. In such birds, they contrast strongly with dark secondaries. Underwing with extensive brown on coverts in contrast to paler flight feathers. Bill first blackish, but from Dec mostly pale-based.

Many show predominantly juvenile, rather fresh-looking plumage well into winter, and are never strongly abraded before Jun.

Heuglin's Gull has browner and darker upperparts with weaker or no pale window on inner primaries, broader dark tail-bar, less extensively patterned juvenile coverts and tertials. Underbody often paler, resulting in a more contrasting bird. Head smaller and more elongated. Wings longer. Unlike Vega often replaces some coverts in first-winter (King & Carey 2000).

Caspian Gull *mongolicus* heavier with deeper chest, more angular head with flat forehead, smaller eye situated further back on head, deeper bill and slightly longer wing. Often appears flat-backed with obvious tertial-step. Plumage paler and more greyish-tinged with narrower dark markings on mantle and scapulars and often mainly pale greater coverts, and dark tail-bar narrower. Underwing generally paler. By first-winter typically paler with finer pattern and more abraded wing.

First-summer has grey saddle and median coverts, strongly contrasting with almost whitish, bleached juvenile coverts (especially lesser and greater). Mantle, scapulars and median coverts often with delicate darker bars. Underbody with dense dark mottling. Bill often pale-tipped.

Second-winter acquires grey back and some (especially median) coverts, the latter finely dark-barred; greater coverts sometimes more as first-years. Broad black tail-bar similar to first-year, but blacker and in better contrast to white rump.

Second-summer has whitish faded coverts against grey saddle and dark outer primaries. Very pale plumage matches similar-aged Slaty-backed Gull (which see).

Third-summer similar to adult, but white mirror on P10 and primary tips smaller or lacking, primary coverts dark and traces of tail-bar often visible.

VOICE Similar to Herring Gull. Also a laughing *ha-ha-ha*.

MOULT Adult moult to **winter plumage** complete Jul–Jan(Feb). Starts with P1–2 early Jul, P3–5 usually Aug, P5–6(9) mid-Sep–Oct, P7–8 late Nov, P9–10 late Dec–Feb. Most finish primary moult by early Jan, but most advanced birds late Nov (Kennerley *et al.* 1995, King & Carey 2000). Winter head assumed mid-Sep.
Moult to **adult summer** partial, including head and body mid-Feb–Mar(early Apr).
Moult to **first-winter** often restricted to parts of mantle and scapulars; although some have renewed whole mantle and scapulars by midwinter, many still show juvenile plumage Feb. No moult of tertials and coverts in first-winter. Information on immature moult limited: first-years have shed P1–2 mid-May, second-years P5 mid-Aug. Moult into second-winter from Jun, starting with (adult type) mantle, scapulars and median coverts. A few third-years still grow P9–10 mid-Feb (skins in MCZ, pers. obs. in China and Japan).

DESCRIPTION

Similar to Herring Gull, but differs in: bill shape sometimes similar to Caspian Gull; nostril obvious; depth at distal edge 1.5–2.3mm, length 11–14mm.
Adult Upperparts grey to darker grey (Kodak Grey Scale (5)6–7(8)), approaching darkest Herring nominate *argentatus* or Heuglin's '*taimyrensis*'; palest in NE part of range (5,5–7). Wing-tip similar to western American Herring. Compared to Herring race *argenteus* white mirror on P10 usually broader (25–60mm, often covering whole tip) with angled division to black base. P9 black with 5–30mm white mirror, most extensive on inner web (may be absent on outer); some show '*thayeri*-type' P9 with white mirror on inner web sometimes almost reaching tip; in 10% lacking. P8 blackish; sometimes grey base of inner web reaches 50% towards tip; black on P8 does not reach primary coverts. Shows conspicuous white tongues on P5–6(8), normally covering both webs. P6 with 5–28mm black subterminal spots on both webs; often as two crescents; sometimes lacking. P4–5 may show black to greyish-black subterminal markings, mainly on outer web; markings usually more solid than in Herring nominate *argentatus* and more wedge-shaped, with 45° angle towards shaft. White primary tips evident into early summer. Outer primary coverts often with dark shaft-streaks. Bare parts similar to Herring Gull. Iris yellow to pale yellow, mostly with some dark spotting, which may create impression of dark eye. Orbital ring red. Legs pink to pale flesh, occasionally with pale blue or pale yellow tinge; by late winter and spring sometimes raspberry-pink. In W part of range legs bright yellow; see Geographical Variation below.
Adult summer (Mar–Sep) Head white. Bill sometimes orange-yellow with blood-red gonys-spot.
Adult winter (Sep–Mar) Head white with variable, often fine greyish-brown streaks and more solid dark spots or streaks on hindneck to breast-sides, often isolated from grey forewing by white wedge as in Glaucous-winged. Whole head sometimes more densely spotted, including narrow dark spots on forehead, chin and throat.

Juvenile/first-winter similar to Herring Gull with greyish-brown upperparts, solid pale window on inner primaries (as in Herring dark restricted to drop-shapes near tips of P1–5), greyish-brown underwing-coverts and pale-notched tertials (latter variable with some only showing pale edges to outer part, in others more solid dark with narrow pale edges). Juvenile mantle often pale with only feather-bases dark brown, gradually merging into paler greyish-brown distal part; often with narrow dark anchor-markings before pale edges. First-winter mantle pale grey to pale buff with delicate narrow dark anchor-markings. Greater coverts generally with narrower pale barring, often lacking on outer 50%, but on some greater coverts pale with 2–3 dark bars. Rump and tail-coverts generally with better developed dark barring, in densest-marked birds similar to American Herring. Tail-bar blackish-brown, often broad (60–75mm on T1). Usually with equal amount of pale and dark mottling on T6, but sometimes dominance of dark merging into dark mottling (thus similar to 'banded' type of American Herring); rarely outer web white, with just two narrow dark bars. Plumage usually fresh into midwinter; juvenile plumage might be retained to Jan.
Some show head and underbody similar to American Herring, but on average more densely dark-spotted with paler hindneck and central belly against darker flanks. If present, first-winter mantle and scapulars with dark centres, narrow dark anchor-markings and broad pale edges, sometimes as dark shaft-streaks. Tertials greyish-brown with irregular pale edges and bars (similar to Herring nominate *argentatus*; centres sometimes solid dark and pale edges straighter). First-winter head sometimes with contrasting pale hind-collar and clean pale face. Bill develops pale base from Dec/Jan.
First-summer has whitish head and rump in strong contrast to medium-grey mantle, scapulars and median coverts (latter often dark-barred). New fresh feathers on mantle and median coverts are first part of second-winter plumage. Breast to belly densely dark-spotted. Retained juvenile wing-coverts usually strongly bleached. Tail-bar broad and conspicuous. Bill bicoloured with pale tip.
Second-winter has mantle, scapulars and coverts grey (first median coverts, grey spreading across wing as soon as fresh lesser and greater coverts are acquired). Tertials dark with broad pale edges and mottling as in Herring. Tail-bar blackish, usually less complete than in first-years, appearing waved and normally restricted to 55–60mm dark on T1–3. Retained juvenile upperwing-coverts usually strongly bleached by midsummer.
Third-winter similar to adult, but normally with reduced white mirror on P10, narrower white primary tips, dark markings on primary coverts, dark-washed tail-bar (often extensive) and dark subterminal markings on bill.
Hybrids Hybridises with Heuglin's Gull, Slaty-backed Gull and Glaucous-winged Gull where ranges overlap.
Hybrid **Vega Gull × Heuglin's Gull '*taimyrensis*': Adult** winter (Japan) has fine head-streaks (mainly confined to nape and around eyes), upperpart colour generally darker than in Vega Gull, as in '*taimyrensis*' (some identical to Vega) with more extensive black on wing-tip.

PLATE 47. VEGA GULL *Larus vegae*

E Asian counterpart of American Herring and Herring Gull, which it resembles at all ages. Habitat as Herring Gull.

1. **First-winter** (Sep/Oct–Apr) Overall brown with conspicuous pale window on inner primaries, as in Herring and American Herring Gulls. Rump and tail-base white with scattered dark spotting. Tail with broad dark bar, sometimes covering most of tail as in American Herring. White tips to tail feathers often broad. Head and underbody brown-mottled or -streaked, thus better patterned than average American Herring Gull.

2. **Second-winter** (Aug–Apr) Compared to first-years with paler wing, clearer pale window on inner primaries and contrasting grey saddle. Tail-bar conspicuous against white rump. Bill fleshy with black tip.

3. **Third-winter** (Aug–Apr) Similar to adult, but with more extensive black on wing-tip (including primary coverts), traces of black tail-bar and duller bill with dark subterminal markings.

4. **Adult winter** (Sep–Mar/Apr) Adult shows grey underwing, generally darker than American Herring and often with indication of white 'string of pearls' on mid-primaries. Wing-tip otherwise black with white mirrors on P9–10; black on outer wing extends to dark markings on P5–6. In winter head densely streaked, either covering most of head or restricted to hindneck, creating brown necklace.

5. **Juvenile** (Jul–Sep) Head and underbody brown, rather faintly marked. Mantle and scapulars dark brown with pale edges, creating scaly pattern. Greater coverts normally with equal amount of pale and dark barring throughout (similar to Herring Gull). Tertials dark with complete pale edges, undertail-coverts dark-spotted.

6. **First-winter** (Sep–Apr) Mantle and scapulars renewed, creating greyish-brown, dark-barred saddle against juvenile wing. Scapular markings normally as delicate anchor-markings (in American Herring and most Herrings dark markings are broader and more diffuse). Compared to juvenile, head and underbody paler. Develops pale base to bill from late autumn. This individual shows broader pale than dark bars on greater coverts, similar to Caspian Gull race *mongolicus* (or Great Black-backed Gull). Note brown wash and well-marked patterns to upperparts and upperwing, compared to Slaty-backed and Caspian race *mongolicus*.

7. **Second-winter** (Aug–Apr) Mantle and scapulars mainly grey against brown-patterned wing, with finer, more diffuse pattern than in first-year. Bill fleshy with black tip. Eye bicoloured, although not as pale as in adult.

8. **Adult summer** (Mar–Aug/Sep) Adult shows grey upperparts, black wing-tip and rather narrow white primary tips. Legs pink, sometimes raspberry-pink. Eye often darkish-looking.

9. **Adult winter** (Sep–Mar) Head with variable brown spotting and streaking, often restricted to hindneck. Markings generally stronger than in Caspian Gull race *mongolicus*, but weaker – streakier – than in most American Herring Gulls.

1. First-winter

3. Third-winter

2. Second-winter

4. Adult winter

5. Juvenile

6. First-winter

7. Second-winter

8. Adult summer

9. Adult winter

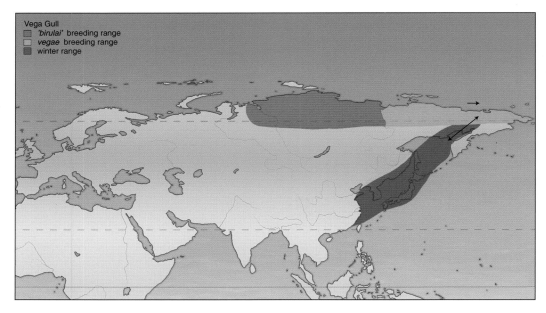

Vega Gull
- 'birulai' breeding range
- vegae breeding range
- winter range

Legs creamy-yellow with a pinkish tinge, more rarely yellow. Eyes mainly pale. Resembles Lesser Black-backed Gull race *graellsii*. Compared to Vega Gull often with smaller bill, longer wings, more rounded head, paler eyes and darker upperparts (King & Carey 2000). Moult later than Vega Gull; primary moult reaches P3–4 Nov and P9–10 Jan/Feb, intermediate between Vega and '*taimyrensis*' (J. R. King pers. comm.). ID of hybrids in younger plumages largely unknown.

Hybridisation with Glaucous and Glaucous-winged Gull suspected from Japan, such birds combining Vega characters with paler inner webs to P6–10 and dark eyes. Further details required (J. R. King *in litt.*).

For hybridisation with Slaty-backed Gull, see that species.

GEOGRAPHICAL VARIATION (western population sometimes treated as subspecies '*birulai*') In western part of range (W Taimyr to NW Yakutia) legs in breeding season vary from bright yellow to fleshy; legs always pink in eastern part of range, yellow only in western part of range.

Palest mantled birds appear at northernmost part of range, darkest to the W (western Taimyr but large part of population here suspected to be hybrids with Heuglin's Gull) and to the E (Chukci Peninsula). Western birds generally with more black in wingtip (smaller white mirror in P10, more extensive black in P4-5). In winter usually whiter with dark restricted to hindneck streaks.

DISTRIBUTION AND MIGRATION Population unknown. Breeds islands and sea-cliffs in High Arctic. *Vegae* winters from breeding sites to NW Pacific S to Japan, (where often in large flocks) along S Chinese coastline to Korea. A few reach Hong Kong, where many are probably hybrids (G.J. Carey & J. R. King *in litt.*). More research needed. Some post-breeding wandering to N Alaskan coast, but no other reliable observations from North America. '*Birulai*' probably winters mainly in Japan (del Hoyo *et al.* 1996, Filchagov *et al.* 2001).

VEGA GULL Four-year gull. An E Asian counterpart to Herring and American Herring Gulls, with which it shares size and shape.

Adult has grey upperparts (darker than in American Herring) with black wing-tip, showing two white mirrors; dark markings reach P4–5. Legs fleshy, eyes pale, bill yellow with red gonys-spot. In **winter** (Sep–Mar) head with varying brown streaks, sometimes extensive, but in others confined to hindneck.

First-year greyish-brown with pale window on inner wing as in Herring and American Herring. Tail with dark bar and dark spotting at base; sometimes tail-bar almost covers tail, but edges usually with extensive pale markings. Head streaked or spotted, similar to Herring and many American Herring. In first-winter mantle and scapulars pale with delicate barring of narrow dark anchor-markings; greater coverts often mainly pale with narrow dark bars.

Second-year rather similar to first-year but saddle with large amount of grey, pale window on inner hand more conspicuous, and dark tail in better contrast to white rump.

Third- year similar to adult, but some coverts brown-marked and bill tip with extensive dark markings.

MEASUREMENTS Lengths in mm; weights in g. Own data on *L. v. vegae* from skins in MCZ, MVZ, NRK, USNM. Alaska, E Russia, Sakhalin, Kamchatka, Kuriles, China, Korea, Japan.

WING

Adult male	424–475 (452.4)	29
Adult female	414–468 (441.5)	23
Juv./first-winter	416–458 (435.9)	12

BILL

Adult male	50.8–61.7 (56.6)	30
Adult female	47.3–59.5 (53.6)	24
Juv./first-winter	45.9–57.7 (52.4)	12

BILL DEPTH AT GONYS

Adult male	17.6–21.8 (19.8)	30
Adult female	16.2–19.7 (18.2)	24
Juv./first-winter	15.0–18.3 (17.2)	12

BILL DEPTH AT BASE OF BILL

Adult male	18.4–22.2 (20.5)	30
Adult female	17.6–21.3 (19.1)	22
Juv./first-winter	12.5–20.5 (17.9)	12

GONYS LENGTH

Adult male	14.3–19.6 (16.3)	30
Adult female	12.4–16.6 (15.2)	18
Juv./first-winter	12.9–16.6 (15.2)	12

TARSUS

Adult male	60.2–74.2 (68.9)	30
Adult female	59.5–73.5 (65.0)	23
Juv./first-winter	60.4–71.6 (65.6)	12

Weight Alaska breeding adult male 1,318–1,368. Winter Korea male 1,343 (second-winter), adult female 1,083–1,158 (skins in MVZ).

484

Vega Gull *Larus vegae*. **484. 1st-winter**. Note similarity to Herring Gull, including densely dark-spotted underparts, complete pale edges to irregularly pale-edged tertials and broad pale and dark bars on greater coverts. Compare Mongolian Gull, photos 471–473 and American Herring Gull, photos 303–307. Choshi, Honshu, Japan. 13 Feb 1999. *Jon R. King.*

Vega Gull *Larus vegae*. **485. Juvenile moulting into 1st-winter**. Moult often limited to parts of mantle and scapulars in 1st-autumn, thus less extensive than in Mongolian and many American Herring. Ibaraki, Honshu, Japan. *Hiroshi Ikenega.* **486. 1st-winter**. Note narrow dark transverse bars on 1st-winter mantle and scapulars and by mid-winter just moderately worn with all juvenile wing. Pale barring on greater coverts and complete, broad white edges to tertials differs from the more extensively dark-marked feathers of American Herring. Hokkaido, Japan. 12 Feb 2001. *Klaus Malling Olsen.* **487. 1st-winter**. Many develop paler head in winter, especially behind ear-coverts, but rarely as extensive as in American Herring. Hokkaido, Japan. 14 Feb 2001. *Klaus Malling Olsen.* **488. 1st-winter.** Large and conspicuous pale window across inner primaries recalls Herring and some American Herring Gulls. Note solid dark tail-bar, but narrower than in American Herring, as bases to rectrices are pale. Hokkaido, Japan. 12 Feb 2001. *Klaus Malling Olsen.* **489. 1st-winter.** Note greyish-brown overall appearance with pale window in inner primaries and broad, but somewhat diffuse dark tail-bar. Choshi, Honshu, Japan. 13 Nov 1999. *Jon R. King.* **490. 1st-summer**. Actually worn 1st-winter. Vega Gull at this age typically shows very worn and pale bleached wing-coverts in strong contrast to grey saddle. Chukotka, E Russia. Jun 1992. *Werner Suter.* **491. 1st-summer**. Note large pale areas in upperwing, caused by worn and bleached coverts. Chukotka, E Russia. Jun 1992. *Werner Suter.* **492. 2nd-winter**. Grey saddle and brown-patterned lesser and greater coverts. Note extensive dark spotting and streaking on hindneck to breast and along flanks. Ibaraki, Honshu, Japan. *Hiroshi Ikenega.* **493. Adult summer**. Legs fleshy to pink in eastern part of range. Note similarity to Herring Gull, but generally narrower white primary tips. Chukotka, E Russia. Jun 1992. *Werner Suter.* **494. Adult winter**. In winter most develop coarse dark spots and streaks on head, sometimes with more distinct brown streaks on hindneck. Compare Mongolian and American Herring Gulls, the pattern of this Vega Gull being matched by many - especially W coast American Herring. Hokkaido, Japan. 12 Feb 2001. *Klaus Malling Olsen.*

491

492

493

494

495

496

497

498

499

Vega Gull *Larus vegae*. **495. Adult winter**. Note variation in head-pattern, which normally consists of broad dark spots or streaks. Many appear pale-faced in winter. Ibaraki, Honshu, Japan. *Hiroshi Ikenega*. **496. Adult summer**. Wing-tip pattern recalls Herring Gull, but on average with dark coloration on one more primary, and more conspicuous white moons between grey and black in primaries. Anadyr, East Russia. Jul 1993. *Werner Suter*. **497. Adult summer**. Note smaller amount of white in wing-tip of this individual, indicating younger adult. Anadyr, East Russia. Jul 1993. *Werner Suter*. **498. Adult summer**. Note dark coloration in primaries to at least P5. Anadyr, East Russia. Late Jun 1992. *Hanne & Jens Eriksen*. **499. Adult, putative hybrid Vega Gull × Heuglin's Gull** '*taimyrensis*'. Note yellowish-tinged fleshy legs and rather dark upperparts, indicating origin from western part of range, where extensive hybridisation with Heuglin's Gull occurs. Tokyo, Honshu, Japan. 25 Feb 2991. *Ken Hatsuno*.

24. SLATY-BACKED GULL

Larus schistisagus (Stejneger, 1884, Bering Island, Kamchatka)

Plates 48–49, Photos 500–526

IDENTIFICATION Length 61–66cm, wingspan 145–150cm. A large gull from N Asia, the only large dark-backed gull in its breeding range. It is stocky with rounded head, rather straight thick bill (at most with poorly marked gonys-angle) and rather strong but often shortish-looking pink to rosy legs. Alert birds often stretch the neck and adopt characteristic pot-bellied appearance. Wings are rather short in settled birds. In flight heavy with full neck, broad arm, but rather short pointed hand and often slender hindparts. Males may approach jizz and size of Great Black-backed or Glaucous Gull, smallest females Herring and Vega Gull. In all ages, outer wing pattern offers best clues; wing-tip appears streaked with pale line of dots, as primaries (apart from P9–10) have pale inner webs and mid-primaries broad white tongues, a pattern only matched to such a clear degree by certain hybrid gulls (Glaucous-winged × Western Gull, Glaucous-winged × American Herring Gull). Western Gull of the paler-mantled subspecies *occidentalis* shows heavier bill with more bulbous tip and squarer head, with eyes sitting higher on head. American Herring and Vega are slightly smaller and less heavy with slimmer bill and generally longer wings. Adult upperparts are much paler than in Slaty-backed and wing-tip darker.

Adult has slaty upperparts, slightly darker than Western Gull nominate *occidentalis*. Wing-tip diagnostic: black with pale inner webs to primaries and large white tongues, forming 'string of pearls' which gently tapers away towards wing-tip. This is obvious in head- or side-view from below, and dark tips to outer primaries as dark trailing edge to outer wing. P10 and sometimes P9 have white mirrors; 5–7% have white tip to P10. Shows broad white trailing edge to inner wing, broader than in other large gulls apart from Great Black-backed and Kelp, which have blackish upperparts. The trailing edge merges with white tips to P1–5 in flight. In settled birds, broad white scapular and tertial crescents are most noticeable, tertial crescents connecting to slightly narrower but striking white line on secondary tips. Wing-tip in settled birds similar to Western Gull, with 4–5 white primary tips beyond tertials, and 2–3 beyond tail-tip. In some there is a slight gap between inner two and exposed outer 2–3 primaries. Eyes pale (sometimes dark-peppered), surrounded by purple to deep pink orbital ring. Legs raspberry to rosy or pink.

In flight the adult wing pattern is striking. Caused by grey inner webs to primaries, the underside of the wing-tip looks mainly grey with black limited to tips, and the conspicuous white 'string of pearls' dulled somewhat by pale surroundings.

In **summer**, bill similar to Vega and American Herring, but generally paler orange-yellow. In **winter**, bill duller; base of bill often pinkish from Aug, and frequently bill shows narrow dark subterminal markings. Head and breast-sides heavily brown-spotted or -streaked, often with dense streaks around eye forming elongated dark mask, narrowing in front of pale eye. Legs pink, often raspberry-pink to rosy.

The rather dark upperparts make confusion with Western Gull highly probable. Western of similar size, but head heavier, bill with more bulbous tip, eyes are smaller and darker, and placed further back and higher on head, and wing-tip is more solid black with white mirror on P10 only and black wedges to all primaries; at most shows 'string of pearls' in mid-primaries and – from below – much fuller black hand than Slaty-backed. Furthermore, upperparts are less bluish-tinged, legs duller flesh and head mainly white in winter.

Vega and American Herring Gull generally smaller with paler grey upperparts (darkest in Vega) and more solid black wing-tip, typically lacking pale streaks and line of spots: the character is not foolproof, as some Vega and American Herring show limited black on wing-tip, and some Slaty-backed lack white subterminal spot on P8. Hybrid Western × Glaucous-winged Gull with outer wing similar to Slaty-backed identified in winter by weaker, greyer, dark head-markings – more diffuse rather than spotted or streaked, squarer head with eyes places higher on head, and bulbous tip to heavier bill.

Juvenile dark to greyish-brown with washed-out brown patterning and pale-scaled saddle; rear scapulars often with paler subterminal areas. In some, pale hindneck contrasts with darker ear-coverts and crown. Underbody brown, appearing velvety, but lower belly often pale, isolated from darker breast-bar, flanks and rather uniform dark underwing-coverts. Undertail-coverts with scattered dark markings only. Wing-tip brown with pale inner webs and edges as in first-year Thayer's, but P9–10 often uniform; mid-primaries with dark spots near tip, forming dark trailing edge to outer wing – from below striking in head-view. The primary pattern mirrors the 'string of pearls' of adults, but pale tongues on P6–10 prominent. In flight, the hand often appears mid-brown with darker edges, and thus pale 'window' on inner wing of Vega and American Herring appears non-existent or at least very weak. Secondaries create dark trailing edge to inner wing and show white tips. Coverts brown, lesser coverts with pale edges, greater coverts with indistinct pale diluted markings and broader whitish tips. Outer greater coverts may be paler or darker than inner ones, but lack any strong barring. Tertials brown with rather straight and often narrow pale edges; notching and irregular pattern reduces to tips, typically slightly paler than wing-tip but darker than mantle. Tail black to dark brown, together with dark-barred or -spotted rump creating dark 'rear' typical for W American gulls, but unlike Vega Gull. Tail sometimes with fine white mottling at base and along edges, just visible at close range. Bill black. Legs pink.

First-winter similar to juvenile, but generally with paler chin, throat and hindneck, isolating dark head as hood,

PLATE 48. SLATY-BACKED GULL *Larus schistisagus*

Large dark-backed gull of East Asia, reaching Alaska yearly; in North America otherwise vagrant. Winters E Asia to Japan. Coastal, occurring in large flocks where food available, such as fishing ports and dumps. A compact, rather short-legged gull with strong bill and small beady eyes situated centrally but high in head.

1. **Juvenile** (Aug–Nov) Head and body greyish-brown, often lacking any strong barring. Mantle and scapulars mid-brown with pale notchings. Coverts and tertials with diffuse pale patterning compared to Vega Gull, on greater coverts barring mainly on inner coverts and along edges. Primaries dark, varying from dark brown to black, often with broader pale tips and edges than in Vega Gull. Bill black.

2. **First-winter** (Sep–Apr) Generally greyish-brown with diluted covert pattern. Mantle and scapulars grey with dark shaft-streaks or subterminal markings, appearing much weaker and unbarred compared to Vega Gull. Head paler than in juvenile through wear. Bill starts to develop fleshy base.

3. **First-summer** (or pale first-winter) Some appear very pale with much-bleached coverts already from midwinter. Primaries and tail bleach to brown. Similar to Glaucous-winged Gull, but less 'evil-looking', with better-marked mantle and scapulars.

4. **Second-winter** (Aug–Apr) Retarded birds similar to first-winter, but bill paler-based, eye bicoloured; tertials and greater coverts with finer pale vermiculations, and primaries darker with broader white tips.

5. **Second-winter** (Aug–Apr) Slaty-grey saddle often in very good contrast to pale-patterned wing-coverts, which soon fade to whitish.

6. **Third-winter** (Aug–Apr) Similar to adult, but with scattered brown, pale-marked coverts, narrower black subterminal bill-markings and narrower white wing-tips.

7. **Adult winter** (Sep–Mar) Adult shows slaty-grey upperparts with broad white tertial edges melting into white secondary tips. Legs fleshy to rosy or raspberry-pink. Head dark-streaked or -spotted, often with denser dark streaking around and behind eye, creating dark streak through eye. Eyes pale, often as pale as in Herring Gull. Bill often with narrow dark markings on upper mandible.

8. **Adult summer** (Feb/Mar–Sep) Head white. Slaty-grey upperparts often slightly bluish-tinged. Legs deep pink or raspberry-pink. Orbital ring pinkish-red.

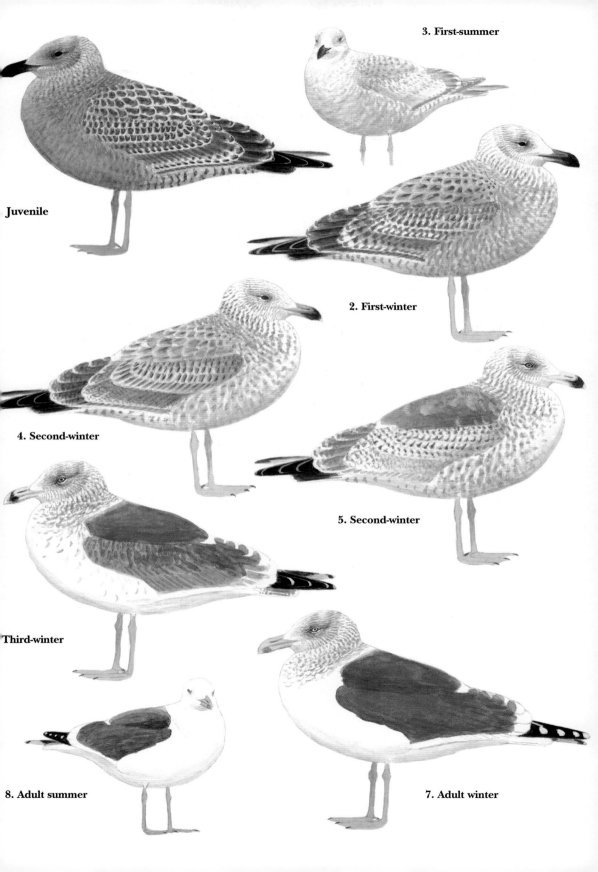

Juvenile

3. First-summer

2. First-winter

4. Second-winter

5. Second-winter

Third-winter

8. Adult summer

7. Adult winter

PLATE 49. SLATY-BACKED GULL *Larus schistisagus*

In flight rather short-winged with full body; appears bull-necked. Outer wing sometimes narrowish-looking.

1.   **Juvenile** (Aug–Nov) Rather uniform greyish-brown. Shows pale window on inner primaries merging into gradually increasing amount of dark on outer primaries; wing panel thus more diffuse, but broader than in Vega Gull and American Herring Gull; often shows indication of adult 'string of pearls' on wing-tip. Tail all dark in some contrast to muddy dark-spotted rump.

2.   **First-winter** (Sep–Apr) Underwing contrasting: coverts muddy-brown, contrasting with paler flight feathers; shows dark trailing edge and indication of string of pearls on wing-tip. Breast and flanks often contrast with paler belly and undertail-coverts (not shown here).

3.   **First-winter** (Sep–Apr) Wing soon appears bleached, often with very weakly patterned, pale greater coverts, creating pale midwing-bar. First-winter saddle grey with dark streaks or feather-centres.

4.   **Second-winter** (Aug–Apr) Slaty-grey saddle contrasts well with pale, often diffusely patterned upperwing. Pale pattern on outer wing stronger than in first-years with pale inner webs on primaries almost reaching trailing edge to wing. Rump white in strong contrast to still dark-looking tail. Underwing contrast often very strong with dark coverts, pale silvery flight feather bases and dark trailing edge to hand.

5.   **Third-winter** (Aug–Apr) Saddle still contrasts somewhat to paler-patterned upperwing. Outer primaries grey with dark outer webs and tips; shows white window to P10 and indication of 'string of pearls' of adult. Tail still with broad dark markings.

6.   **Adult winter** (Sep–Mar) Adult shows slaty-grey, bluish-tinged upperwing with broad white trailing edge 'melting' into white 'string of pearls' on outer primaries, reaching P8, and connecting with white mirrors on P9–10. The 'string of pearls' shown here is sometimes less complete, as P8 frequently lacks white markings. Head heavily dark-streaked or spotted in winter.

7.   **Adult summer** (Feb/Mar–Sep) Head white in summer. Note characteristic wing-tip pattern, often strong when seen from below. Underside of flight feathers slaty-grey, contrasting with both white coverts, broad white trailing edge (which blends into white 'string of pearls' onto P8) and black pattern on wing-tip.

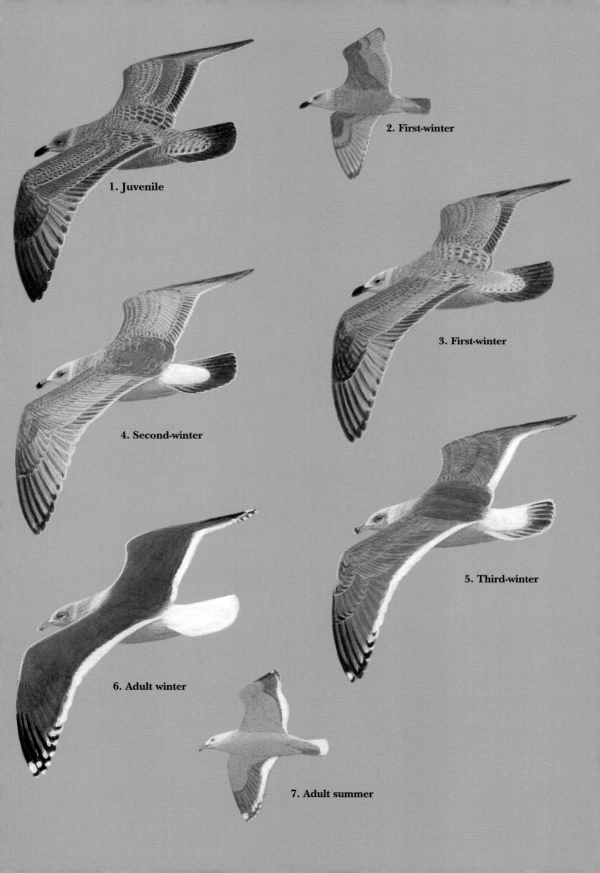

1. Juvenile

2. First-winter

3. First-winter

4. Second-winter

5. Third-winter

6. Adult winter

7. Adult summer

half-hood or even mask. Mantle and scapulars with scattered new grey to greyish-brown feathers, showing blackish triangles, fine blackish anchor-markings, subterminal bars or shaft-streaks and pale tips. Juvenile wing often fades quickly from first-autumn, being strongly worn from Feb. Bare parts as juvenile, but base of bill and sometimes line along lower mandible may be dull fleshy and legs often rosy.

First-year Vega Gull browner with paler head and blackish wing-tip in better contrast to paler window. Lacks pale inner webs and line of spots on outer wing. Mantle and scapulars look barred, as dark subterminal bars are stronger. Greater coverts more strongly patterned, with more distinct pale and dark bars in better contrast to darker secondaries. Tertials blackish with pale notching along sides, concolorous with wing-tip. Rump whitish with dark barring against whitish tail-base and broad black tail-bar.

From Feb/Mar juvenile coverts and rump fade to almost whitish in contrast to dark tail and subterminal markings on inner primaries. Some show brown outer primaries, appearing concolorous with, or sometimes paler than, tertial centres. Separated from American Herring and Vega Gulls by solid brown tail and paler brown flight feathers with obvious streaked and 'dotted' appearance to outer wing. Eye becomes paler from Feb. By **first-summer** white-headed and often with very bleached wing. Bill often appears bicoloured, but some remain black-billed. During moult in summer shows very good contrast between bleached areas and fresh dark feathers of second-winter.

Second-winter varies. Most have whitish head and body with strong dark spots or streaks (mirroring elongated dark eye-mask surrounding pale eyes of adult) and lower belly normally pale. Outer wing and tail similar to first-winter, but blacker, the primaries being round-tipped with narrow white edges. Outer webs of outer primaries darker, but inner primaries paler, thus forming more contrasting pale window than in first-years. Saddle with mixture (sometimes predominance) of slaty, pale-edged feathers and browner ones, patterned as in first-winter. Saddle often contrasts well with paler, often whitish wing-coverts, which may be intermixed with slaty feathers. Greater coverts sometimes mud-brown, appearing uniform or with fine whitish vermiculations. Secondaries black, and may appear darkest part of wing. White rump contrasts well with dark tail. Underwing shows varying brown edges to especially lesser and median coverts, but often whitish greater coverts and axillaries, creating whitish midwing-panel, which again contrasts with silvery-based flight feather bases to create three-coloured underwing. Bill pale with variable black bar.

Second-summer acquires dark slate saddle (often only partial) in strong contrast to mainly whitish coverts and inner primaries, which again contrasts with dark, pale-streaked and -spotted outer wing. Darkest of upperparts are inner secondaries followed by new inner primaries. Tertials, tail and outer primaries faded brownish. Head and underbody mainly white; hindneck sometimes dark-spotted. Bill yellow to flesh with variable black markings. Eye pale.

Second-summer Vega Gull often similar, but wing-tip

darker, lacking pale streaks and spots, and tail white with black bar.

Third-winter similar to adult, but upperwing a mixture of slaty and brown, often with mainly brown greater coverts. Wing-tip with smaller, indistinct (or lacking) white mirror on P10/9 and narrower white tips. White trailing edge to inner wing narrower. Tail with variable dark markings. Some show complete dark bar, others black spots. Underwing mainly white, but often with dark markings on lesser and median coverts similar to second-winter (but generally narrower). Bill duller than in adult with dark subterminal markings. Red gonys-spot starts to appear from Feb. Legs as adult.

Third-summer similar to adult, but before moult with wing pattern similar to third-winter.

Fourth-winter as adult, but sometimes with dark mottling on underwing-coverts and generally broader dark subterminal markings on bill.

VOICE Similar to Siberian Glaucous-winged Gull: deep, hoarse series and an eager *hap-hap*. Long-call lower and slower than in Western Gull (Sibley 2000).

MOULT Adult moult to **winter plumage** from May; up to P4 renewed Jul, P5–7 late Aug, P9–10 (late Sep) Oct–Nov. Head sometimes from Jul; most still have summer head early Sep. Coverts and tail Aug–Sep. Moult to **adult summer** partial (Jan)Feb–Mar, including head and body. In Japan mid-Feb small minority white-headed (pers. obs.).

Juvenile moult to **first-winter** Oct–Feb. Moult limited to parts of mantle and scapulars, and probably a few head and body feathers. May occasionally renew a few wing-coverts and inner tertials. Moult to **second-winter** complete, starting with P1, mantle and scapulars late May–Jun. P5–7, tail, secondaries and coverts Aug, P9–10 late Sep–Oct (Cornier & Savard 1994a & b, pers. obs.). Moult to **third-winter** similar to adult, but slightly earlier; P6–8 Aug.

DESCRIPTION

Adult Mantle, scapulars, back and upperwing blackish-grey to dark slate (Kodak Grey Scale (10)11–12(14)), generally slightly darker than Lesser Black-backed Gull race *graellsii* and with more bluish tinge. Primaries with black outer webs and dark grey inner webs. P10 with 30–60mm white mirror, normally separated from tip by dark subterminal bar; 6% show fully white tip (pers. obs. in Japan). P9 dark grey, darkening to black towards tip, in 78% with 20–40mm white mirror, normally restricted to inner web. P8 dark grey with paler inner web: 52% show white tongue near tip, connecting with white tongues on P5–7. P7–5 dark grey with pale inner webs and 10–35mm white tongues before black subterminal spot behind white tip. P5 with narrow black subterminal spot, sometimes restricted to one web. P4 rarely with slight dark subterminal spot. P1–8 with pale inner webs. Primaries and secondaries with 15–25mm white tips, covering 15–20% of width of inner wing. Underside of primaries silver with blacker tips to P5–10 and white 'string of pearls', created by white tongues mentioned above. Underbody, axillaries and underwing-coverts white. Iris creamy, yellow to brownish-yellow, in 30% dark-freckled (sometimes enough to create darkish-looking eyes). Orbital ring purple to purplish-pink, in small minority red. Gape fleshy-pink. Bill yellow with red to orange gonys-spot and paler tip. Base of upper mandible often slightly pinkish-tinged. Legs pink to rosy, rear tarsus often with purplish tinge.

Adult summer (Jan–Aug) Head white. Bill deep yellow with red gonys-spot.

Adult winter (Sep–Feb/Mar) Head to breast-sides with greyish-brown to warm brown spots or streaks. Markings strongest around eyes, where often forming elongated dark patch, narrowing before and behind eyes, but sometimes continuing as narrow line across hindneck. Often reaches upper breast. Bill duller than in summer, in most with pinkish tinge at basal parts; sometimes base greenish-tinged. Some 25–30% show narrow dark markings especially on upper mandible. Legs raspberry-pink, rosy or deep pink, more rarely fleshy; in Japan (Feb 2001) 65% showed raspberry legs, 30% deep pink and 5% fleshy legs (pers. obs.).

Juvenile (fledging–Nov/Feb) Most variable. Head and underbody greyish-brown to dark brown with diluted dark streaks on head and longer streaks on neck to breast; belly often paler with more distinct brown bars. Hindneck and sides of neck paler; often contrast with uniform dark upper mantle. Lores and ear-coverts often uniform dark, forming eye-mask. Mantle and scapulars dark brown to greyish-brown with darker subterminal crescents and pale fringes or notches. Tertials dark to mid-brown (often intermediate in colour between primaries and mantle, thus paler than primaries) with pale fringes, often waved or mottled at tips and sometimes darker subterminal markings; bases often solid dark. Upperwing-coverts pale brown with indistinct darker vermiculations near pale tips, greater coverts dark brown with indistinct pale mottling, strongest near tips of inner 30%, and often solid dark bases. Some 10% with stronger pale tinge or bars on all coverts or paler bases to especially outer greater coverts (as in Glaucous-winged), in flight contrasting with dark secondaries. Primary coverts darker brown with pale fringes. Rump brownish with indistinct pale barring or mottling, dark and pale bars often of even width. Primaries dark brown to brown with varying, often prominent Vs at tips. P9–10 uniform, P5–8 with paler inner webs to near tip and narrow pale fringes; may show slight white tongues as indication of adult wing-tip pattern. P1–4 paler with dark subterminal markings at tips. Secondaries blackish-brown to mid-brown with paler inner webs and rusty tinge to outer web. Underwing-coverts brown in strong contrast to paler flight feathers. Undertail-coverts white with scattered dark spots or waving. Tail blackish to blackish-brown with narrow pale fringes and tips, and pale vermiculations on inner 50%. T6 dark or with inconspicuous pale mottling on outer web and pale base; sometimes pale mottling near bases of T4–5. Iris dark. Bill black, sometimes with pale tip to upper mandible. Legs pink.

First-winter (Nov–Apr/May) similar to juvenile, but mantle and scapulars intermixed with grey to pale brown with paler fringes and narrow dark subterminal markings (often anchor-shaped, but sometimes as dark triangles; but regularly restricted to black shaft-streaks).

Head generally paler especially on chin/throat, hindneck and rear ear-coverts; may show dark ear-spot. May appear hooded. Sometimes with slight brown breast-streaks. Coverts, rump, flight feathers and tail bleach strongly from midwinter, sometimes Nov, when P1–5 become paler with more obvious dark subterminal markings. Tertial centres may then appear darker than primaries. Legs fleshy to pink, sometimes with darker upper tarsus.

First-summer (Apr–Sep) as first-winter, but coverts (especially greater coverts) and rump fade to whitish; flight feathers and tail bleach to brown. New upperpart feathers dark, creating piebald pattern. Bill often acquires pale base/tip and eye becomes paler.

Second-winter (Aug–Mar) Head and underparts whitish with irregular dark markings, especially around eye, on rear ear-coverts and weak dark streaks on hindneck, sides of neck and breast. Underbody whiter with more contrasting dark markings on especially breast and flanks (sometimes mid-belly). Mantle and scapulars mud-brown to brownish-slate, often with dark shaft-streaks, indistinct paler subterminal areas and pale edges. From late winter with adult-type slaty feathers intermixed, sometimes on most of mantle/scapulars and some inner median coverts. Upperwing-coverts plain greyish-brown with pale edges, often strikingly pale from midwinter. Lesser coverts darker with broad pale edges and sometimes dark shaft-streaks. Greater coverts mud-brown, sometimes with narrow and washed-out pale bars. Tertials mid-brown with broad pale tips and edges; division between pale tip and dark base varies from slightly dark-mottled to 2–3 bars near tip. P6–10 and tail much as first-winter, but P1–5 paler, creating pale window blending into paler bases of P6–8(9). Primaries blackish-brown with broader pale edges than in first-years. Secondaries mid-brown to blackish-brown with paler tips and edges. Tail usually with broader pale base and more obvious dark barring or mottling, especially at T3–6. T6 white with black subterminal markings or greyish tinge. Tail rarely blackish. Rump white, sometimes with very faint brown bars, contrasting strongly with tail. Under lesser and median coverts dark brown, greater coverts and axillaries often whitish, in contrast to silvery-brown flight feathers, creating three-toned look. In birds with narrow dark feather-edges on coverts, underwing appears pale with line of dark rows. Bill pale fleshy to greyish-yellow with 15–18mm dark subterminal bar and extensive pale tip, generally broadest on lower mandible; division from pale base often Z-shaped. Iris mid- to pale brown, sometimes yellow. Legs pink to raspberry-pink, more rarely greyish-flesh.

Second-summer (Mar–Sep) Head, underparts and rump white, breast and upper belly sometimes mottled darker. Mantle and scapulars dark slate, contrasting strongly with worn, almost whitish wing-coverts (especially greater coverts). Inner secondaries dark. Rest of flight feathers and tail faded and brownish. Bill yellowish with dark subterminal markings and, rarely, red gonys.

Third-winter (Sep–Mar) similar to adult, but wing-coverts a mixture of slate and brown; lesser coverts sometimes paler with darker mottling, greater coverts rather uniform dark brown. Primaries with narrower

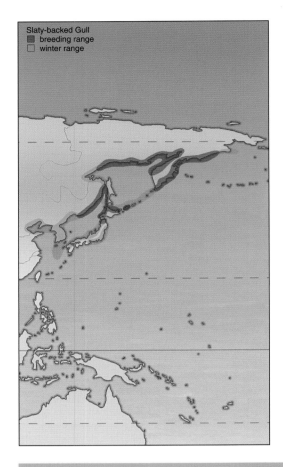

Slaty-backed Gull
- breeding range
- winter range

pale tips, often restricted to P1–6. Lacks or shows small white mirror on P10 (max. 30mm); sometimes also on P9. White 'moons' and division between grey, white and black less distinct. White tips to secondaries often narrower. Underwing similar to second-winter, but dark normally reduced. Tail white with irregular dark markings forming weak, often incomplete dark tail-bar. Bill much as adult, but normally with broad dark subterminal markings, especially on lower mandible.

Third-summer (Mar–Sep) similar to third-winter, but bill often as adult.

Fourth-winter as adult, but primary coverts often with dark shaft-streaks and bill with more complete dark markings on both mandibles, sometimes creating black ring before ivory tip.

Hybrids Hybrid **Slaty-backed × Vega Gull** known from Koriak, Kamchatka and Japan (Haffer 1982, J. L. King *in litt.*). **Adults** have paler upperparts than Slaty-backed Gull; further details required. For hybridisation with Glaucous-winged Gull, see that species.

GEOGRAPHICAL VARIATION Very small. Northern population tends to be larger and possibly have darker adult upperparts than southern (King & Carey 1999); further details required.

DISTRIBUTION AND MIGRATION Population 100,000 pairs. Breeds on (top of) low sea-cliffs, on rocky islands and along sandy shores; also inshore coastal waters.
In Kamchatka 47,000–111,000 pairs in >200 colonies, the largest Ptichem Island, NE Kamchatka. Hokkaido population small, but increasing.
Sedentary with some dispersing into Bering Sea, Sea of Japan and, much more rarely, S to coast of China and Taiwan. In Hokkaido, Japan, the most abundant gull in

SLATY-BACKED GULL Four-year gull. Breeds NE Asia, wintering S to Hong Kong; vagrant NW North America. Slightly stockier than Vega and American Herring Gulls, with short legs. In flight compact with broad arm and slenderer hand. At all ages shows extensive pale areas on inner webs of primaries, often creating pale 'string of pearls' on wing-tip. Adult has dark slate upperwing with black outer webs to wing-tip and broad pale tongues on mid-primaries, mostly extending onto P8 and almost joining white mirrors on P9–10. White 'string of pearls' curves gently towards wing-tip, and is prominent from both above and below; from below hand looks greyish with restricted black compared to other large gulls. Eyes pale, legs pink to rosy. Bill yellow with red gonys-spot. In **winter** (Sep–Mar) head with extensive dark streaks, most conspicuous around the pale eyes forming elongated dark eye-mask. Bill often with dark markings.

First-year greyish-brown, appearing rather velvety with dense streaking on head and breast. Upperwing faintly dark-patterned, thus lacking clear barring on mantle and scapulars and clear pattern on uniformly pale brown greater coverts, which often become very pale on outermost. In flight shows extensive pale inner webs to primaries, creating broad but diffuse pale window almost reaching outer wing. Rump barred against unpatterned brownish tail. Folded wing-tip brown with pale edges.

Second-year develops slate mantle in contrast to pale coverts (often strikingly paler in midwinter). Head densely streaked as in adult, bill dull fleshy to yellow with broad dark markings. Tail dark against white rump. Shows extensive pale inner wing but darker outer webs to flight feathers. Underwing often mainly pale with dark rows and extensive grey bases to flight feathers; underwing often strikingly three-toned.

Third-winter similar to adult, but some coverts brown-tinged and bill markings usually more extensive.

Fourth-year as adult apart from dark streaks on primary coverts and sometimes faint dark tail- and bill-markings.

winter with numbers in icy winters reaching 10,000–15,000 in largest fishing ports (pers. obs., Feb 2001). Non-breeding and winter birds scarce but regular in W Alaska. Small numbers summer Pribilof Islands (max. 8 St. Paul 1 June 1988); vagrant N North America, mainly between S Alaska and Oregon; scattered records from Ontario, Quebec, Missouri, Texas and Hawaii (Zimmermann & Jones 1991, del Hoyo *et al.* 1996, King & Carey 1999).

MEASUREMENTS Lengths in mm; weights in g. Own data based on skins in MCZ, MVZ, NHM, NRK, UZM. Kamchatka, Kuriles, Amur, Japan and Alaska.

WING

Adult male	426–479 (453.2)	21
Adult female	406–457 (435.1)	17
Juv./first-winter	400–447 (431.7)	9

Note *Il'icev & Zubakin (1990) give for adult male 408–467 (438, n=46), adult female 391–455 (417, n=31).*

BILL

Adult male	51.4–64.6 (57.8)	21
Adult female	48.4–61.1 (53.0)	20
Juv./first-winter	48.2–58.3 (53.6)	9

Note *Il'icev & Zubakin (1990) give for adult male 53.7–64.1 (62.0, n=46), adult female 48.0–59.4 (53.8, n=31).*

BILL DEPTH AT GONYS

Adult male	19.3–23.7 (20.9)	21
Adult female	17.2–22.0 (18.9)	19
Juv./first-winter	16.6–20.7 (18.5)	9

BILL DEPTH AT BASE OF BILL

Adult male	19.0–24.3 (21.7)	21
Adult female	17.5–21.8 (19.3)	19
Juv./first-winter	17.7–21.0 (19.2)	9

GONYS LENGTH

Adult male	13.3–18.9 (15.9)	21
Adult female	12.5–16.5 (14.9)	20
Juv./first-winter	11.2–15.9 (14.5)	9

TARSUS

Adult male	66.9–75.8 (69.9)	21
Adult female	60.5–68.6 (64.3)	20
Juv./first-winter	60.5–71.3 (66.7)	9

Note *Il'icev & Zubakin (1990) give for adult male 64.6–86.0 (73.9, n=46), adult female 59.8–78.9 (67.7, n=31).*

Weight Average 1,350 (Sibley 2000).

501

Slaty-backed Gull *Larus schistisagus.* All photos are from **Hokkaido, Japan** unless otherwise stated. **501. 1st-winter.** Note diffuse pattern on mantle, scapulars and coverts, strong bulbous bill and small, beady eye situated rather centrally in head. Tail brown and rump densely dark-spotted. 9 Feb 2001. *Klaus Malling Olsen*

Slaty-backed Gull *Larus schistisagus*. All photos are from **Hokkaido, Japan** unless otherwise stated. **500. Juvenile.** Note rather uniform, greyish-brown overall impression, the scaled juvenile saddle being the best-patterned part of the bird. Lacks any strong barring on greater coverts. 24 Aug 1997. *Harry J. Lehto.* **502. 1st-winter.** A slightly paler individual with slightly more well-marked mantle feathers. Note almost white and unpatterned greater coverts. 9 Feb 2001. *Klaus Malling Olsen.* **503. Juvenile.** Note large amount of pale in outer wing with just primary tips being extensively dark, as well as spotted rump against all-dark-looking tail. 24 Aug 1997. *Harry J. Lehto.* **504. 1st-winter.** Note diffuse, but broad pale window in inner and mid-primaries, brown wing-tip and brownish tail-bar, against paler bases to tail. Choshi, Japan. 11 Nov 1999. *Jon R. King.* **505. Juvenile.** Underwing rather dark, in this dark-bodied bird emphasising darkness of underparts. 24 Aug 1997. *Harry J. Lehto.* **506. 1st-summer.** As in Vega Gull, many become strongly bleached in 1st-summer. Note new dark mantle feathers in very strong contrast to bleached feath-

ers. 24 Aug 1997. *Harry J. Lehto.* **507. 2nd-winter**. Note grey, diffusely pale edges to mantle feathers and scapulars, almost unpatterned greater coverts and broad pale primary tips. 12 Feb 2001. *Klaus Malling Olsen.* **508. 2nd-winter**. A more advanced bird, showing slaty saddle against paler, very diffusely-patterned wing-coverts. Primaries often brownish-tinged. 12 Feb 2001. *Klaus Malling Olsen.* **509. 2nd-winter**. 10 Feb 2001. Note short-legged appearance and pale-edged mantle and scapulars. *Klaus Malling Olsen.* **510. 2nd-winter**. Similar to 1st-winter, but note age-diagnostic mantle and scapulars. Tail-bar often prominent into 2nd-summer. 10 Feb 2001. *Klaus Malling Olsen.* **511. 2nd-winter**. Underwing characteristic with rather pale flight feathers apart from dark tips to outer primaries, rather pale mid-wing panel but darker lesser coverts. Underbody heavily dark-spotted. 12 Feb 2001. *Klaus Malling Olsen.*

Slaty-backed Gull *Larus schistisagus*. All photos are from **Hokkaido, Japan** unless otherwise stated. **512. 3rd-winter**. Mantle, scapulars and most of coverts of adult are slaty-dark, but still with some barred coverts. White primary tips narrower than in adult, bill duller with extensive dark markings. Very pale eyes surrounded by elongated dark mask. 10 Feb 2001. *Klaus Malling Olsen.* **513. 3rd-winter**. Note variation in bill pattern at this age. 10 Feb 2001. *Klaus Malling Olsen.* **514. 3rd-winter**. Note narrow, but distinct dark mask around whitish eye, pointed before and behind eye emphasising impression of small, half-closed eyes at distance, typical from 3rd-winter on. Similar to adult, but with extensive dark markings in bill and tail and a few barred coverts. This individual is more advanced than 513. 12 Feb 2001. *Klaus Malling Olsen.* **515. 4th-winter**. Note slaty upperwings and pale 'string of pearls' in primaries. Traces of dark tail-bar in otherwise adult plumage suggests 4th-winter. 10 Feb 2001. *Klaus Malling Olsen.* **516. 4th-winter or adult**. Rather small white mirrors and extensive black on P8 suggests younger adult. 10 Feb 2001. *Klaus Malling Olsen.* **517. Adult summer** Note pink legs, slaty upperparts and very broad white tips to tertials and secondaries. Magadan, East Russia. 18 May 1999. *Ingo Weiss.* **518. Adult winter**. Note faint grey mask around very pale eyes. 12 Feb 2001. *Klaus* ➡

360

Malling Olsen. **519. 4th- or adult winter**. Dark bill markings on rather dull bill suggests 4th-winter, but otherwise adult. Note diffuse dark streaks on head and hindneck, and pink or rosy legs. 12 Feb 2001. *Klaus Malling Olsen.* **520. Adult winter**. Note very broad white tertial tips continuing onto white secondary tips to create extensive white area in settled birds. Eye surrounded by narrow dark mask. 12 Feb 2001. *Klaus Malling Olsen.* **521. Adult moulting from summer to winter**. As in other dark-mantled gulls, shows extensive pale areas in upperwing when coverts are missing; compare photo 3. 25 Aug 1997. *Harry J. Lehto.*

Slaty-backed Gull *Larus schistisagus*. All photos are from **Hokkaido, Japan** unless otherwise stated. **522. Adult winter**. Note white 'string of pearls' in outer wing, reaching P8. White trailing edge to inner wing and inner primaries very broad, in outer wing merging into 'string of pearls'. 9 Feb 2001. *Klaus Malling Olsen*. **523. Adult winter**. Note 'string of pearls'. 9 Feb 2001. *Klaus Malling Olsen*. **524. Adult winter**. Many adults show more extensive black in wing-tip than 522, thus 'string of pearls' less conspicuous. Still, broad white trailing edge to inner primaries connects with white pearls in mid-primaries. 9 Feb 2001. *Klaus Malling Olsen*. **525. Adult winter**. Note dark grey surface to flight feathers, white 'string of pearls' and black on wing-tip. 12 Feb 2001. *Klaus Malling Olsen*. **526. Adult winter**. Note narrow dark eye-mask and characteristic three-coloured effect of underwing. This bird shows large white mirrors on P9-10, almost connecting with extensive white 'string of pearls' in P8 and inwards. 9 Feb 2001. *Klaus Malling Olsen*.

362

25. LESSER BLACK-BACKED GULL
Larus fuscus (Linnaeus, 1758, Sweden)

Plates 50–53, Photos 527–562

IDENTIFICATION Length 49–57cm, wingspan 118–150cm. A dark-backed, slender version of Herring Gull, with more rounded head and slightly thinner, less blunt-tipped and slightly drooping bill. Certain male *graellsii* as large and heavily built as Herring. The wings are longer, narrower and more pointed. Relaxed birds often lower wings slightly. In fully grown wing, projection beyond tail exceeds distance between longest exposed tertial and tail-tip (about equal in Herring). Jizz differences most evident in the Baltic subspecies *fuscus* ('Baltic Gull') – the most elegant taxon with the roundest head, rather weak, but sometimes longish-looking bill and long, narrow wings. It differs furthermore from western populations in plumage, moult and migration. Unlike other taxa there has been a strong decline in recent decades and it should be considered vulnerable.

Coexists with Herring with high degree of success in W Europe, including some large, mixed colonies. All taxa feed over deep sea with short dives or surface-picking, similar to kittiwakes, but also on rubbish dumps and in fishing harbours with other large gulls.

Adult has dark slate (race *graellsii*) to sooty-black (race *intermedius*) upperparts and contrasting black wing-tip with small white mirrors on P9-10. The dark underside of the flight feathers creates a darker area which is only weak in the palest *graellsii*. Legs are yellow. Attains strongly dark-spotted head in **winter** (from Sep–Oct), but 5–10% remain white-headed or almost so in winter (especially *intermedius*). In Aug–Oct, wing-coverts moulting, often creating white upperwing-bar, as pale covert bases are exposed.

Baltic nominate *fuscus* has velvety-black upperparts with no or just very little contrast to wing-tip. Moults later into winter plumage, most leaving N Europe in summer plumage, with only inner primaries renewed. Any adult Lesser Black-backed with dark-spotted head and heavy secondary and tail moult in Aug–Sep in Northern Hemisphere is not *fuscus*. In winter, bill often with dark subterminal markings.

Juvenile similar to Herring Gull, but darker with blackish flight-feathers, normally lacking pale 'window' in inner primaries, present in almost every Herring, but sometimes indicated in Lesser Black-backed races *intermedius* and *graellsii*. Two solid dark wing-bars, created by dark centres to greater coverts and secondaries, evident in flight. Greater coverts sometimes as dark as flight feathers, but often with 2–3 pale bars, most evident on inner ones. Mantle and scapulars blackish-brown with scaly pattern, kept well into autumn when Herring either has pale edges worn off or has moulted to barred first-winter feathers. Head dark-streaked with broad dark eye-mask and black bill. Underbody pale brown with extensive dark spots on breast, flanks and upper belly. Underwing darker than in Herring with almost blackish-brown axillaries, lesser and median coverts. Tail black with narrow

white bases and spots along edges of outer tail feathers. Rump white with dense dark spotting, penetrating to upper mantle as slight paler wedge against darker scapulars. In flight, dark enough to be mistaken for juvenile skua (especially Pomarine *Stercorarius pomarinus*, with which it shares size and dark overall plumage).

When settled, more contrasting than Herring with darker upper- and rear parts: dark greater covert bar often creates dark rectangle, and this combined with blackish tertials (with narrow white edges only) and primaries create blackish rear. Pale-patterned birds with pale bars to all greater coverts and broader, more irregular pale tertial tips similar to Herring, but Herring has paler brown tertials and flight feathers, the former normally with broader, irregular pale edges throughout their entire length, the latter with broader pale tips.

Yellow-legged generally larger with larger, more squarish head, being whiter with distinct dark mask (as in Mediterranean winter), and the rear parts are generally fuller. In autumn, most Yellow-legged have attained new saddle and some coverts at a time when most Lesser Black-backeds are juvenile. These parts are pale with distinct, often narrow, dark markings (often anchor-shaped), not matched by the darker and fuller markings of Lesser Black-backeds. Yellow-legged has whiter underbody with hardly any dark on breast, belly and central undertail-coverts. Tertials and greater coverts as Lesser Black-backed, but in some the pale markings are more extensive, similar to Herring. Generally has less dark inner primaries than Lesser-Black-backed. Rump and tail-base are whiter with finer dark spotting than on Lesser Black-backed, and the tail-bar is usually narrower and more clear-cut. Underwing is generally paler with better-marked dark rows.

Juvenile nominate *fuscus* sometimes identified on combination of rounder head, longer wings and more contrasting plumage than races *intermedius* and *graellsii*: darker upperparts/paler underparts with blacker, more white-edged mantle/scapulars. Greater coverts and tertials more often dark-based (as in Caspian nominate *cachinnans*). Underbody and undertail-coverts often unmarked white, as in Caspian and Yellow-legged Gulls. Rump generally whiter with narrower dark spots. Underwing-coverts vary, in some pale, similar to Caspian nominate *cachinnans*.

First-winter retains most of juvenile plumage throughout autumn, but head and upper breast become whiter, and white edges to mantle may wear off, creating slight darker saddle against juvenile wing. However, dark-spotted belly is retained and head-streaks are mostly distinct. From late autumn, new mantle and scapulars dark to greyish-brown with browner bases and narrow pale fringes, and these, together with juvenile wing, emphasise darker upperparts than in Herring and Yellow-legged Gulls.

In nominate *fuscus*, mantle feathers generally darker

363

PLATE 50. LESSER BLACK-BACKED GULL *Larus fuscus fuscus* (Baltic Gull)

Baltic Gull is mainly restricted to the Baltic Sea, and winters in E Africa. Compared to Lesser Black-backed Gull race *graellsii/intermedius*, it is a more elegant bird with a smallish-looking head, slenderer bill and more attenuated rear with very long primary projection beyond tail. The legs are rather short.

1. **Juvenile** (Aug–Nov/Dec) Greyish-brown, often with pale belly and central undertail-coverts in some contrast to breast and flanks. Mantle and scapulars dark brown with pale feather-edges, creating scaly pattern, although pale on outer webs often broken by dark. Greater coverts dark, on inner greater coverts often with pale barring. Tertials solid dark-centred with narrow pale tips and outer edges, not reaching greater coverts. Long hand appears blackish with very narrow or no pale tips. Often shows broad dark eye-mask. Bill black. (Races *graellsii/intermedius* generally browner with darker pattern on belly similar to patterning on breast and flanks.)

2. **Juvenile** (Aug–Nov/Dec) A paler, more contrasting bird with paler face and hindneck, more solid pale feather-edges to blackish mantle and scapulars, and pale belly, but with darker greater coverts, creating solid dark rectangle on folded wing. Tertials may be slightly notched at tips. Migrates south in mainly juvenile plumage. Often strikingly dark and pale compared to races *graellsii/intermedius*; see also very similar-looking Heuglin's Gull.

3. **First-winter** (Nov–Mar) As juvenile, but mantle and scapulars here renewed, first-winter feathers slightly paler brown with diffuse blackish and broad subterminal markings. Head and underbody generally paler than in juvenile, mainly caused by wear.

4. **First-winter** (Dec–May) An individual with slightly browner pattern in mantle and scapulars. Tertials and wing-coverts renewed, the former with broader and less regular pale tips than juvenile. Bill may start to develop pale base.

5. **First-summer** (Mar–Oct) By late spring parts of mantle and parts of coverts renewed to adult-like blackish type, although often slightly brownish-tinged and therefore looking slightly paler, frequently with paler edges. Often similar to second-summer of races *graellsii/intermedius*, but long primaries normally all dark and belly cleaner pale. Bill fleshy with blackish subterminal markings and cutting edges.

6. **Second-winter** (Nov–Apr) Basically as adult, but head-markings generally stronger, bill duller with black subterminal markings and coverts brownish-tinged. Shows narrower pale tertial tips and almost black primaries, at most with very narrow white tips.

7. **Adult winter** (Oct–Mar) Adult upperparts black with no contrast between upperside and primaries; primaries with only narrow white tips, soon reduced by wear. Head in winter plumage white or with fine streaks around eyes and on hindneck. Legs yellow.

8. **Adult summer** (Mar–Sep) Head white. Bill bright yellow with red gonys-markings. Legs bright yellow. White primary tips often worn off. Compare races *graellsii/intermedius*.

1. Juvenile

2. Juvenile

3. First-winter

4. First-winter

5. First-summer

6. Second-winter

7. Adult winter

8. Adult summer

PLATE 51. LESSER BLACK-BACKED GULL *Larus fuscus fuscus* (Baltic Gull)

In flight long- and slender-winged with pointed hand and smallish-looking head.

1.   **Juvenile** (Aug–Nov/Dec) Upperwing dark, lacking pale window on inner primaries (but some-times slightly indicated). Shows dark greater coverts and secondaries, both with whitish tips, cre-ating white lines on upperwing. Tail with broad blackish bar, reaching mid-rump; tail base and rump white with slight dark mottling. Face and hindneck contrasts with darker eye-mask; pale belly contrasts with brown-marked breast and flanks. Undertail-coverts often white with dark spotting reduced to sides. Underwing often with solid pale areas, especially on midwing. Bill black.

2.   **First-winter** (Nov–Mar) Very dark brown upperwing. Mantle and scapulars dark with inconspicu-ous pale patterning. Rump often white, contrasting with broad blackish tail-bar. This individual shows rather uniform dark axillaries and underwing-coverts, matching many representatives of races *graellsii/intermedius*; note pale, almost unmarked belly.

3.   **First-summer** (Mar–Oct) Moult extensive compared to other large gulls, apart from Heuglin's Gull and certain Caspian Gull race *barabensis*, although a few *intermedius* may be similarly advanced. Mantle and scapulars blackish and all flight feathers in this individual renewed in win-ter. This advanced moult is unique to *fuscus*, and although individually variable, it always includes some flight feathers in first-winter. Broad blackish tail-bar contrasts with white rump.

4.   **First-summer** (Mar–Oct) Compared to 3, this individual has only moulted parts of secondaries and inner primaries (arrested moult), the latter contrasting somewhat with browner juvenile and worn outer primaries. Bill pink with black tip.

5.   **Second-summer** (Mar–Oct) Similar to adult, thus age development on average one year quicker than in races *graellsii/intermedius*. Compared to adult, shows some black marking on tail and bill, and indistinct white window on P10. Black upperparts often slightly brownish-tinged.

6.   **Adult winter** (Oct–Mar) Adult upperwing black with no contrasting wing-tip. Shows white mirror on P10 (and sometimes a narrow one on P9), white primary tips narrower than in *graellsii/inter-medius*. In winter head white, often with narrow dark streaks around eye and on hindneck.

7.   **Adult summer** (Mar–Sep/Oct) Head white, bill bright yellow with red gonys-spot. Note concolor-ous black upperparts and long, narrow hand.

1. Juvenile

4. First-summer

2. First-winter

3. First-summer

5. Second-summer

6. Adult winter

7. Adult summer

PLATE 52. LESSER BLACK-BACKED GULL *Larus fuscus graellsii* and *L. f. intermedius*

W Europe and N Atlantic coastline to Lofoten (Norway) and N Atlantic Islands. Scarce breeder Greenland and E North America; increasing visitor to North America, mainly along E Coast and Great Lakes. Winters between Great Britain and W Africa. Slightly smaller than Herring Gull with slightly longer wings, rounder head and weaker bill, but structural differences not always evident.

1. **Juvenile** (Aug–Oct) Rather uniform dark brown with blackish mantle and scapulars, showing pale edges which create scaly pattern. Shows extensive dark mask and black bill. Greater coverts blackish-brown with pale tips and edges, sometimes with broader pale bars especially on innermost. Tertials black with narrow white tips and edges, the latter not reaching greater coverts. Primaries blackish. Compare Herring Gull. Similar to nominate *fuscus*, but browner with more evenly distributed brown pattern on underbody and more solid brown markings on undertail-coverts.

2. **Juvenile moulting into first-winter** (Oct–Jan) As juvenile, but new mantle and scapulars (here partly) paler brown with more distinct dark subterminal markings than in nominate *fuscus*. Sometimes few inner coverts renewed as well in autumn (almost unknown in Herring Gull). Note dark rectangle on wing created by solid dark outer greater coverts, dark eye-mask and sometimes white face. Bill may start to become pale at base.

3. **First-winter** (Oct–Apr) With wear, new mantle and scapulars contrast slightly with worn wing. Head and underbody often paler with wear from midwinter, but dark eye-mask retained. With wear, pale tips to tertials may almost disappear.

4. **Advanced first-summer–second-winter** (May–Apr) Unlike nominate *fuscus*, first-summer mantle and scapulars greyish-brown with dark markings and pale edges. New tertials with broader, less regular edges than in first-winter. Greater coverts slightly paler and more uniform caused by finer pale vermiculations. Primaries with narrow white tips. Bill often mainly dark into second-winter.

5. **Second-winter *graellsii*** (Aug–Apr) Mantle, scapulars, median coverts and inner tertials dark slaty-grey, contrasting with brown, pale-marked lesser and greater coverts. Head, breast-sides and flanks with extensive brown markings. Bill fleshy with black tip and cutting edges.

6. **Third-winter *graellsii*** (Aug–Apr) Basically as adult, but bill duller with solid black markings and white primary tips narrower. Parts of upperwing slightly brownish-tinged. Legs still fleshy (often into third-summer). Head with extensive dark markings, sometimes creating impression of hood.

7. **Adult winter *graellsii*** (Aug–Mar) Upperparts dark slaty-grey, contrasting with blackish wing-tip (with white tips), with black commonly reaching P4. Most show extensive dark head-markings, but face normally whitish. Compare Yellow-legged Gull, in which head-markings in nominate *michahellis* less extensive, more as streaks than spots, but in subspecies *atlantis* often similar or even stronger, especially on face. Legs yellow.

8. **Adult winter *intermedius*** (Aug–Mar) Upperparts darker blackish-grey than in *fuscus*, similar to Great Black-backed Gull. Head generally more finely marked than in race *graellsii*, often as fine as in *fuscus*. A few individuals are wholly white-headed in winter.

9. **Adult summer *graellsii*** (Sep–Mar) Head white, bill bright yellow with red gonys-spot. Orbital ring red around pale yellow eye. Legs bright yellow.

1. Juvenile

2. Juvenile moulting into first-winter

3. First-winter

4. Advanced first-summer–second-winter

5. Second-winter *graellsii*

6. Third-winter *graellsii*

7. Adult winter *graellsii*

8. Adult winter *intermedius*

9. Adult summer *graellsii*

PLATE 53. LESSER BLACK-BACKED GULL *Larus fuscus graellsii* and *L. f. intermedius*

Compared to Herring Gull slightly smaller and more elegant, with narrower, more pointed wings.

1. **Juvenile** (Aug–Oct) Upperwing dark with blackish flight feathers (sometimes weak pale window on inner primaries) and solid dark centres to greater coverts. These and secondaries pale-tipped, creating two pale wing-bars. Shows broad dark tail-bar and spotted uppertail-coverts. Underwing-coverts and axillaries typically dark brown, appearing rather uniform and contrasting slightly with paler flight feathers. Head and underbody brown, including belly; undertail-coverts dark-spotted throughout. Compare Herring Gull, Yellow-legged Gull and Lesser Black-backed Gull nominate *fuscus*.

2. **First-winter** (Oct–Apr) As juvenile, but mantle and scapulars greyish-brown with blackish subterminal markings and pale edges. Face, hindneck and underbody often paler through wear, and rump generally whiter in better contrast to broad dark tail-bar.

3. **First-winter** Note dark upperwing with solid dark greater coverts, appearing pale-tipped to create pale wing-bar. Extensive dark eye-mask contrasts with pale face and hindneck. Bill black.

4. **Second-winter** *graellsii* (Aug–Apr) Mantle, scapulars and parts of median coverts slaty-grey, rest of wing similar to first-winter. Extensive dark tail-bar still present. Bill with paler base. Underwing still with extensive dark patterning.

5. **Third-winter** *graellsii* (Aug–Apr) Upperwing similar to adult, but only with narrow white mirror to P10 and dark-patterned primary coverts. Tail with scattered dark markings. Bill fleshy with black markings. Underwing still with scattered dark markings.

6. **Adult winter** *graellsii* (Sep–Mar) Upperwing dark slaty-grey with black tip, white mirrors to P9–10 and rather narrow white trailing edge. In winter with extensive dark head pattern.

7. **Adult winter** *intermedius* (Sep–Mar) Upperwing darker than *graellsii*, similar to Great Black-backed Gull. Outer primaries black in slight contrast to rest of upperwing (compare Lesser Black-backed Gull nominate *fuscus* – Baltic Gull). Head-marking generally finer than in *graellsii*.

8. **Adult summer** *graellsii* (Mar–Aug) Black primaries in some contrast to slaty-grey upperwing, but still mainly a dark-backed gull. Head white and bill bright yellow with red gonys-spot.

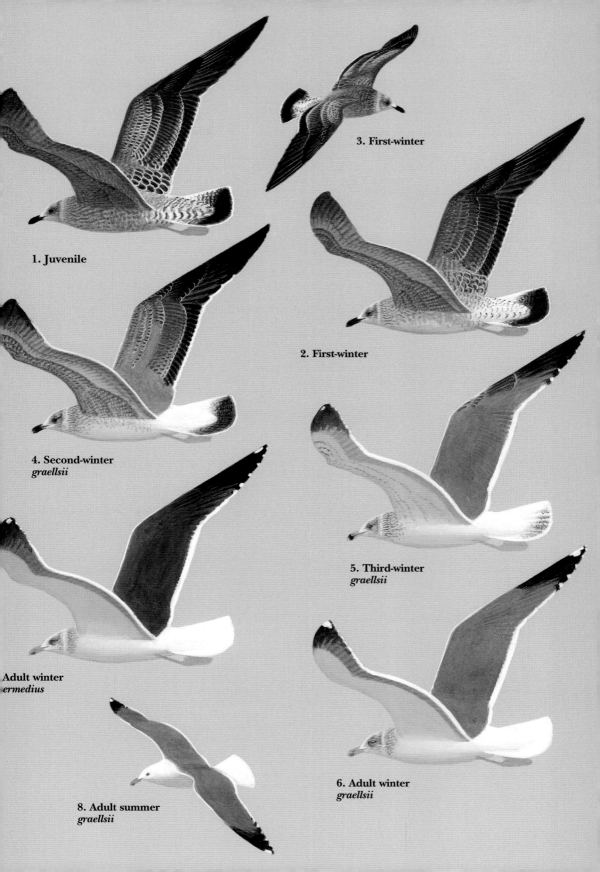

1. Juvenile

3. First-winter

2. First-winter

4. Second-winter
graellsii

5. Third-winter
graellsii

Adult winter
ermedius

6. Adult winter
graellsii

8. Adult summer
graellsii

with, if any, more diffuse dark anchor-markings. Bill black, often with slightly paler base. Unlike *graellsii* or *intermedius, fuscus* often moults flight feathers and tail from Jan–Feb, and acquires partly brownish-black upperparts, especially mantle, scapulars and median coverts. This moult generally most advanced in birds migrating N in their first summer, but otherwise moult is very variable (M. Hario *in litt.*). Bill often bicoloured.

First-summer *graellsii/intermedius* similar to first-winter, but more uniform dark through wear, with some adult-type feathers on mantle and scapulars. Rump white in strong contrast to black tail-bar. Bill black or pale-based, but sometimes strongly bicoloured. Nominate *fuscus* more advanced with blackish to dark-brown upperparts, whitish head and bicoloured bill.

Second-winter has extensive adult-type feathering on mantle, scapulars and coverts. Greater coverts and flight feathers blackish-brown. Tail with broad black band against white base, often creating impression of a mainly black tail. Bill yellow with clear-cut black tip, but sometimes darker with diffuse pale base.

Second-summer has head/body similar to adult, but flight feathers brownish-black, lacking white spots on P9–10 (although white often present on P10 in *fuscus*). Wings faded, in slight contrast to uniform dark saddle, but some have renewed all upperwing-coverts as well to adult-type (P. Adriaens *in litt.*). Nominate *fuscus* with more uniform black upperparts (see Geographical Variation). Tail generally with dark markings before moult into third-winter. Bill yellow with black subterminal bar and sometimes red gonys-spot. Legs may start to acquire yellow.

Third-winter as adult winter, but wings more brownish-tinged and white mirror present on P10 only (may be absent). Shows dark-streaked primary coverts. Some still show traces of dark tail-bar (especially in midtail) and black bill-bar.

Third-summer as adult summer, but with traces of immaturity outlined under third-winter.

VOICE Similar to Herring Gull, but deeper and hoarser.

MOULT *Larus fuscus graellsii/intermedius* (S part of Scandinavia, W Europe, Morocco; pers. obs., skins).

Adult moult complete to **winter** plumage late May–Dec. Head and body mid-Aug–mid-Oct. Primaries start late May – early Aug, earliest in S populations. In Norway, Denmark and W Europe primary moult starts late May–mid-Jun, reaches P2–4 Jul, P3–6 late Aug–early Sep, P7–9 mid–late Oct; P10 (mid-Oct)early Nov–Dec(early Jan). In Faeroe Islands, 40% have not started primary moult mid-Aug, while others have reached up to P4; a few *graellsii* reach moult of P9 late Sep. Latest to finish moult are N breeders, which grow P9–10 by Feb(early Mar), thus matching *fuscus*. (Also noted in Texan autumn birds, M. Reid *in litt.*). Coverts and tail Aug when primary moult has reached P4–6. Secondaries generally later, starting when primary moult reaches P6–7.

Moult to **adult summer** plumage partial late Jan–Mar, including head and body. P1–2 sometimes late Feb. Head usually winter-plumaged into Feb–Mar.

Juvenile moult to **first-winter** partial (late Aug)Sep

–Dec, including head and body (sometimes just partly), mainly following arrival in winter quarters, but mantle and scapular feathers sometimes from late Aug/Sep, while still near breeding sites. Some wing-coverts (especially inner and median coverts) often renewed in autumn (unlike Herring); sometimes scattered tertials. Moult to **first-summer** partial Jan–Jul, including head and body. Could be regarded as first steps of complete moult into second-winter. In Portugal, >50% of coverts and some tail feathers moulted May (A. Forsten, P. Adriaens *in litt.*).

Complete moult to **second-winter** May–Oct. P1 (mid-Apr)mid-May; P3–7 mid-Jun–mid-Jul, P9–10 early Oct (frequently only reaches P6–7 by late Sep). Body, tail and inner coverts Jun–Aug.

Moult to **second-summer** partial Jan–Apr, including head and body. Moult to **third-winter** similar to adult, but sometimes earlier (one 20 October had reached P9: skin in ZMA).

For moult in Baltic *fuscus*, see Geographical variation.

DESCRIPTION

(*graellsii, intermedius*). For *fuscus*, see Geographical Variation.

Adult Head and underbody white. Eye yellow. Orbital ring red. Legs yellow. Bill length:bill depth at gonys 2.9–3.3.

L. f. graellsii (Spain, France, Great Britain, Atlantic islands) Upperparts pale slaty-grey (Kodak Grey Scale 8–10(11)); P10 black with 16–50mm white mirror, sometimes restricted to outer web or greyish-tinged; tip sometimes white or broken by dark subterminal bar up to 13mm near tip. Male on average with largest amount of white to P9–10; tip to P10 sometimes white; max. 60mm. P9 black, sometimes with grey distal inner web; 35–40% of Dutch and <50% of British population with 10–23mm white mirror (especially males), often divided by black shaft-streak or restricted to inner web. P8–7 black distally with grey inner web to 80–90mm before tip; often black in intergrade areas with *intermedius*. P6 grey with 18–40mm black bar, P3–5 grey or with up to 25mm black subterminal spots, often confined to one web. P3–6 often with 3–6mm white tongues on inner webs, sometimes 10mm on both webs. P4 normally with very faint black subterminal markings. Mainly lacks black subterminal spot on P3. P1–9 with white tips, when fresh up to 15mm on P1–6, 10–12mm on P7–9. P10 0–12mm >P9. Primary coverts sometimes with dark shaft-streaks, broadening into drop-shapes at tip. Some have limited amount of pale on wing-tip, matching *intermedius*; in populations between Netherlands and SW Denmark/Scotland subspecific status uncertain according to large percentage of birds with intermediate characters and large area of clinal variation. Dutch birds generally as *graellsii*, but slightly darker.

L. f. intermedius grades into *graellsii*, but in darkest birds upperparts blackish-grey to sooty-grey (Kodak Grey Scale 11–13), gaining slaty, or in darkest birds brownish tinge with wear. On average with one black primary more than in *graellsii*. P8–10 much as *graellsii*, but white mirror on P10 often smaller: in adult male 22–58mm (S Scandinavia); sometimes covering whole tip. In female 10–38mm on inner web; rarely lacking. P9 black, in

18–22% (Norway) and 25–35% (Denmark) with 9–35mm white mirror on inner (rarely both) webs. Sometimes basal part of inner web of P8–9 grey (as in all *graellsii*). P3–6 normally with broader black subterminal spots than *graellsii* (on average 40–45mm on P5–6) and very narrow, indistinct white tongues on inner webs only, barely visible in field. P6 rarely black as *fuscus*. Unlike *graellsii*, P2–3 often with indistinct black subterminal spot on outer web. Primary tips, length of P9 compared to P10 and bill proportions as *graellsii*.

Danish breeders on average with broader black subterminal spots on P8–5. In Anholt, Kattegat, 1% match *fuscus* in blackness, 1% *graellsii* in paleness (Barth 1966). This represents individual variation matched by W Swedish *intermedius*. Grant (1986b) mentions birds in Great Britain as dark as *fuscus*, but status unclear according to individual variation.

Descriptions below refer to *graellsii* and *intermedius*.

Adult summer (Mar–Aug) Head white. Iris yellow. Orbital ring red. Bill bright yellow with blood-red gonys-spot, in 1% extending to upper mandible. Legs bright yellow, rarely orange-tinged (especially Apr–May); exceptionally, fleshy with yellow restricted to foot only (Debruyne 1982, pers. obs.). With wear, white primary tips reduced or lacking.

Adult winter (Sep–Mar) Head white with varying amount of brown spots or streaks, densest around eye to form dark eye-mask and on hindneck; streaks on forehead narrow or appearing as spots. Often with cleaner white lower ear-coverts, isolating head-streaking from dark spots on hindneck/breast-sides. The heaviest dark-patterned birds have hooded appearance (most frequent in pale-mantled *graellsii*); 5–10% white-headed in winter, mostly dark *intermedius* types (pers. obs. in Denmark, Great Britain, France, Morocco). Bare parts generally duller than in summer; bill and legs dull paler yellow, red gonys-spot reduced, bill often with dark subterminal markings. Some with bright bare parts into Oct (especially *graellsii*). Orbital ring often dull red. Legs dull yellow.

Juvenile (fledging–Nov) Head and underbody greyish-brown with darker eye-mask, dense streaks on head and upper breast and dark spots on underbody; flanks often barred. Lower belly may be whiter. Mantle and scapulars brownish-black with buff to whitish edges, creating scaly pattern; edges may show pale notching. Lower scapulars with narrow pale fringes, often broadening at tips leaving dark 'hollow-leaf' centre or with brown V- or U-markings (obvious with wear from Oct). Rump and tail-coverts whitish with dense dark spots or bars (rump rarely mainly white). Upper back sometimes with greyish wedge (weaker than in Yellow-legged/Caspian Gull). Upperwing-coverts dark brown with narrow pale edges. Greater coverts dark brown to blackish-brown with narrow pale edges and pale tips, creating wing-bar; inner 50% (rarely all) sometimes with 2–3 pale bars or irregular edges as in Herring. Tertials blackish-brown with narrow pale edges restricted to around tip; in *graellsii* sometimes paler sooty-brown with complete pale edges or slight waving and notching at tips (as in Herring and Yellow-legged nominate *michahellis*). Flight feathers blackish; P1–5 at most with narrow pale inner webs adjacent to broad, elongated sub-

terminal spots on outer webs and tips; most evident in western *graellsii*, where sometimes create slight pale window. Primaries with narrow pale edges, disappearing from autumn with wear. P10 2–2mm >P9. Axillaries, lesser coverts and sometimes median coverts on underwing dark brown to blackish-brown with narrow indistinct paler barring. Greater coverts brownish-grey with diffuse dark bars. Tail blackish-brown with white, dark-barred base (black in T1 35–62mm). T6 black with fine pale notching along edge, often as 2–4 isolated pale spots. Tail rarely as dark as in American Herring. Bill black. Nostril oval-shaped; depth at distal edge 2.0mm, length 8.6mm. Eyes brown. Legs fleshy.

First-winter (Nov–Apr) similar to juvenile, but head whiter (especially forehead and sides of neck) with denser dark spots or streaks and less prominent ear-patch. Breast to belly dark-spotted, belly often prominent in contrast to paler breast/head. Mantle and scapulars dark sooty- or greyish-brown with blackish anchor-markings and narrow pale edges; pattern often distinct. Often intermixed with juvenile feathers. Rarely acquires a few adult-type scapulars. Sometimes attains a few new inner coverts. Pattern less streaked and normally (but not always) darker than in Herring Gull. Wing and tail slightly browner with wear; from midwinter loses pale tips to primaries. Iris dark, sometimes greyish-brown from Apr. Bill often acquires slightly paler base and narrow pale tip to upper mandible (3–6mm; 0–2mm on lower). Legs fleshy to pink.

First-summer (Jan–Jul) Head and underbody white with dark spots or streaks on head, hindneck and breast-sides. Underwing strongly dark-patterned in contrast to body. Mantle, scapulars and most of coverts greyish-brown with broad blackish bars or anchor-markings, brownish bases and pale tips (rarely, a few adult-type feathers are present). Greater coverts dark brown with indistinct pale barring, most on inner 50%. Median coverts often dark brown to slaty with broad pale tips and edges. Retained first-winter scapulars and greater coverts mid-brown with dark subterminal markings near tips, in some contrasting with darker new, less patterned feathers. Tertials blackish with narrow white edges around tips; sometimes dark subterminal markings. New flight feathers (of second-winter) blackish. Iris dark to greyish-brown. Bill greyish to yellow or flesh with broad dark subterminal bar, sometimes covering most of bill-tip and cutting edges; sometimes dark. Extreme bill-tip white on both mandibles. Legs fleshy. In heavy moult Jun–Jul.

Second-winter (Aug–Mar) Head and underbody white with dusky streaks, densest around eye, crown, lower hindneck, breast-sides and flanks; central belly to rump white, latter with dark V-shaped spots. Mantle, scapulars, tertials and normally some coverts (especially median coverts) of adult type, but sometimes paler. Coverts otherwise dark brown with narrow pale fringes, greater often with fine pale vermiculations. Tertials as adult or with irregular white edges and notching. Flight feathers blackish; T1–4 sometimes slightly paler with dark shaft-streaks and subterminal markings. Underwing variable; in some similar to juvenile (but with broad pale areas), in others white with scattered dark markings. Tail white with some black feather-centres, often forming incomplete tail-bar, but sometimes full; more washed out than in first-year. Iris bicoloured, but darker than adult. Bill dark to yellow with distinct black tip or subterminal bar.

Second-summer (Mar–Sep) similar to second-winter, but head and underbody white, with only scattered dark patterning. Mantle, scapulars and median/inner coverts adult, but usually with scattered brown-barred or mottled feathers, contrasting well with retained, faded, medium- to greyish-brown, pale-edged coverts. Flight feathers old, faded dark brownish, contrasting with new P1–2 of adult type (especially *graellsii*). Tail a mixture of white and dark-patterned feathers, ranging from all-white to having more complete dark bar. Rump and uppertail-coverts white, at most with scattered dark markings. Iris yellow to amber, rarely dark. Legs fleshy or dull yellow, sometimes bright yellow. Bill yellow with varying red gonys-spot and black subterminal bar/tip, sometimes as adult.

Third-winter (Sep–Apr) Similar to adult winter, but sometimes with dark spots or streaks on underbody and underwing. White mirror on P10 weaker or lacking (max. 13mm, often diffuse and brownish-tinged). Lacks mirror on P9. Often with brown freckling on inner wing, especially lesser coverts, inner greater coverts and tertials. Primary coverts with dark shaft-streaks. Under-wing-coverts with dark markings; sometimes piebald pattern created by mixture of white axillaries/greater coverts and dark lesser coverts/median coverts. Tail usually with faint dark bar, sometimes all white. Iris as adult, but often darker; in small minority all dark. Bill as adult, but usually with faint black subterminal bar. Legs yellow, yellowish-flesh or even greyish with fleshy tinge.

Third-summer (Mar–Oct) similar to adult; upperwing as third-winter, but faded and patchy brown areas more obvious. Often lacks white primary tips through wear, more so than in adult. Bare parts as adult, but often with (sometimes extensive) dark subterminal markings on bill; legs rarely fleshy.

Subsequent ages as in other large gulls, ageing difficult in field in immature stages. Dark shaft-streaks on primary coverts may be present in full adults (up to 12 years of age). White mirrors on P9–10 generally smaller in younger adults.

Aberrants An albinistic first-winter white, just with faint grey wash to two outer primaries (skin in NRK). Unusual fourth-winter bird reported with all-dark primaries, black eye and dark, pale-tipped bill (Morgan 1989). A 'melanistic' adult, with pale grey instead of white on head and underbody, is held in the museum of Oulu, Finland (H. Lehto *in litt.*).

Hybrids Hybrid **Herring Gull × Lesser Black-backed Gull** known from Britain, France, Netherlands, Belgium, Denmark and Iceland. Adult very similar to Yellow-legged Gull nominate *michahellis*, but head more rounded, less square. Upperparts Kodak Grey Scale 6–8; unlike Yellow-legged, upperparts often slightly bluish-tinged. In primaries, tip to P10 either as mirror or white tip up to 61mm. P9 with 20–30mm white mirror. P7–9 with pale grey inner webs before black tip. Black subterminal bar on P5 similar to Yellow-legged,

but may show broader black markings on outer than on inner web. Also shows long white tongues on P4–6 and sometimes black subterminal markings on P4. Orbital ring and gape orange-yellow to reddish-orange. Legs yellow to fleshy. Darker hybrids probably indistinguishable in field from Heuglin's Gull (especially *taimyrensis*). In four birds (Netherlands, Denmark) adult wing male 429–442mm, female 407–414mm; bill male 51.8–52.9mm, female 48.3–49.1mm; bill depth at gonys male 18.1mm, female 16.7mm; bill depth at base of bill male 18.5mm, female 17.9mm; gonys length 9.5–15.0mm; tarsus male 63–68.0mm, female 57.4–61.4mm. Weight female 900 g (Harris & Jones 1969, Garner & Quinn 1997, H. J. Lehto & M. Wallen *in litt.*, skins in NNH, UZM, photos).

Mixed pair Lesser Black-backed *intermedius* and Yellow-legged Gull *michahellis* with breeding attempt known from Germany, England and Netherlands (Cottaar & Verbeek 1994, Cottaar 2004, M. Collinson *in litt.*).

GEOGRAPHICAL VARIATION Large and partly clinal in races *graellsii* and *intermedius*; may represent only one clinal taxon *graellsii*, the situation in N and W Europe paralleled by the (albeit more complex) clinal variation within and between Herring Gull races *argentatus* and *argenteus*.

L. f. graellsii The palest race, especially S and W England, Irish Sea and Faeroe Islands (where largest).

L. f. intermedius (S to C Norway (Runda and Ankra), Kattegat and N to W Denmark) Rather constant in upperpart coloration within mentioned range. Many from SW Denmark paler, matching *graellsii*, especially in Waddenzee area, where pale-backed birds normally occur in 'pure' pairs. Great variation in large Dutch colonies near Rotterdam, with all intergrades between very dark and very pale birds, the majority in the darker range of *graellsii* (and thus nicknamed 'Dutch intergrades'); Belgian and Scottish population similar; also noted Lofoten, N Norway.

Norwegian breeding birds (N to Runde and N Ankra) (in mm): adult male 410–458 (433), adult female 385–435 (410). Bill adult male 50.2–58.4 (54.4), adult female 46–53.5 (45.4). Weight (in g) adult male 750–1,045, adult female 580–875 (Haftorn 1971). Sample of 40 males and 40 females from S Norway and W Sweden: wing adult male mean 437.9, female 413.3, bill adult male mean 53.0, adult female 48.5 (skins in ZMO). Danish breeding birds (20 males, 19 females): wing adult male 416–443 (428.6), adult female 392–426 (409.3); bill adult male 47.3–56.4 (53.0), adult female 45.5–52.4 (48.9); tarsus adult male 63.0, adult female 58.7. Weight adult male 778–985 g, adult female 650–930 g (May, skins in UZM). Netherlands breeding birds (12 males, 17 females): mean wing adult male 433.5, adult female 409.0. Bill adult male 53.6, female 48.9, tarsus adult male mean 63.0, adult female 57.8 (skins in ZMA).

Baltic Gull L. f. fuscus (Breeds Baltic Sea in Finland, Sweden; very scarce N Norway between Tarva and Finnmark, locally Russian White Sea (Onezhskii Bay and Kandalaksha Bay); disappeared from Kola Peninsula.

Long-distance migrant, wintering between Black Sea and E Africa. Claimed hybridisation between *intermedius* and *fuscus* (Cramp & Simmons 1983) not supported (Gruber 1999; skins). No known contact areas. Jizz often characteristic. The smallest and most elegant taxon. Compared to *graellsii* and *intermedius* slenderer and more graceful with smaller, more rounded head, smaller, more slender bill, more pointed wings with longer hand. Primary projection >150% of length of exposed tertials (equal to distance from bill-tip to rear corner of eye), leaving 4–5 exposed primary tips beyond tail. Legs slightly shorter, often with very little tibia visible. In flight wings look long, slender and pointed with short arm. Settled birds sometimes comparable to a slender, narrow-winged Iceland Gull, younger birds sometimes to short-legged Caspian Gull.

Adult Has velvety-black to greyish-black upperparts with little or no contrast to wing-tips (upperwing Kodak Grey Scale 13–17; wing-tip 17–18). Lack of contrast diagnostic; a few paler birds overlap with darkest *intermedius*. With wear, upperparts slightly brownish-tinged. Compared to other taxa, white primary tips much narrower, often disappearing with wear. P10 with 5–40mm white mirror, often restricted to around shaft. In a few males, entire tip to P10 white; some (probably younger) females lack white mirror. 5–16% (especially males) have white mirror on P9 (skins and photos; Hario (1986) gives 22%). P6–7 rarely with faint slaty tinge on inner web (creating diffuse division between grey and black); more frequent on P1–5. P5–7 with very narrow whitish tongues, restricted to outer web and often lacking. P4 with complete black outer web, P2–3 with black subterminal markings. P10 (0)3–15mm >P9. Bill length:bill depth at gonys 3.0–3.6. Measurements in mm: N Norway (Tarva–Finnmark) adult breeding (54 males, 71 females): wing: male 416–462 (433), female 395–430 (412); bill: male 49.4–55.3 (52.1), female 44.4–52.2 (47.8). Denmark adult breeding (16 males, 31 females) wing: male 404–453 (430.5), female 394–430 (410.3); bill as Norwegian birds (Haftorn 1971, skins).

Adult summer (Mar–Oct/Nov) As *graellsii* and *intermedius* but with blacker upperparts. Retains bright yellow legs into late Sep when duller in many *intermedius*. Moult to **winter** plumage similar to Heuglin's Gull, unlike *graellsii* and *intermedius*. Normally with moult restricted to P1–2 and scattered upperpart feathers Aug–Sep, when >75% *graellsii* moult head/body and primary moult reaches P3–6. See Moult.

Adult winter (Oct–Mar) Head white with narrow brown streaks on crown and ear-coverts, and sometimes broader dark spots/streaks on lower hindneck. Most patterned birds show traces of dark hood (M. Hario *in litt.*). Most show dark subterminal markings on bill into spring.

Juvenile/first-winter Similar to *graellsii*, but often more contrasting 'black and white', in juvenile with colder greyish tinge. Many (25%) have whitish head and underbody: belly, foreneck, chin, throat, neck-sides and central breast often almost unmarked; thus combined with dark eye-mask and sometimes narrow white eyelids appears similar to Yellow-legged nominate *michahellis* or Caspian Gull. Some, however, rather dark-headed with brownish head-markings (especially mask) contrasting

with whitish neck-bar. Undertail-coverts white with dark markings often restricted to along edges as in Yellow-legged and Caspian Gulls. Juvenile mantle/scapulars and coverts generally blacker with more distinct and narrower whitish edges, creating strong scaly pattern; notched edges (as in *graellsii/intermedius*) rare; dark notches normally reach feather-edges. Often fresh-looking into late Oct. First-winter mantle/scapulars dark slate with diluted pattern: diffuse blackish wedge in centre and weak pale edges (compare *graellsii/intermedius*), but a few have varying, often thin, anchor-markings or shaft-streaks. Lower scapulars generally heaviest marked. Greater coverts brownish-black with narrow white tips and edges, creating streaked pattern on outer greater coverts (rarely lacking; edges frequently worn off by winter); some have pale-barred greater coverts as in many *graellsii/intermedius*. Tertials black with narrow white tips and distal part of edges; often similar to Yellow-legged Gull, but some with pale notching along edges. Rump whitish, contrasting well with black tail-bar. Axillaries and underwing-coverts as *graellsii/intermedius*; but in some much paler, approaching Yellow-legged or Caspian Gull nominate *cachinnans*, although never white. Flight feathers and tail blackish; primaries with narrower pale tips than *graellsii/intermedius*, sometimes lacking. Bill black, but soon acquires pale base. In first-winter, bill often fleshy-pink with black tip.

Moult limited in autumn (normally including a few mantle feathers), but almost complete late winter, including all secondaries and P1–3 (see Heuglin's Gull). Takes one year less to develop adult plumage compared to *graellsii/intermedius*, as in Heuglin's Gull (Jonsson 1998b, Gruber 1999, Rauste 1999, pers. obs.).

First-summer Head and underbody white with variable dark brown streaks and spots, usually concentrated around eyes, on hindneck, breast-sides and flanks. Many have pure white head and underparts. Mantle, scapulars and some coverts (especially median coverts) a mixture of blackish and dark brown feathers (the latter covering typically >50% of feathers) with variable pale edges and sometimes black subterminal markings/shaft-streaks (rarely anchor-like pattern). Usually some all-black feathers present, especially on scapulars; greater coverts sometimes with faint brown bars/vermiculations. Tertials blackish with broad white tips and edges and dark waving at tips, sometimes similar to adults. Older feathers brownish in strong contrast to new ones. Underwing generally with narrower dark markings and 'cleaner' white areas than in first-years, especially on midwing. Most flight feathers renewed late winter (60–70% Finnish summer birds have renewed all – Rauste 1999), new primaries dull brownish-black (lacking bluish tinge of adults) with narrow white edges in contrast to juvenile's, which are browner. Secondaries blackish-brown with broad white tips. Flight feathers normally moulted prior to spring migration. Tail rather fresh, being moulted late in winter (Jonsson 1998b, pers. obs.): white with variable dark bar, in some as broad as in juvenile, in others narrower and more diluted. Iris dark to brown, rarely distinctly pale. Bill varies from blackish to – more commonly – pale (grey, pink, yellow, olive or bluish-grey) with black tip and cutting edges. Extreme tip pale on both mandibles. Gonys rarely starts to develop red spot. Most advanced show bill similar to adult, but with dark subterminal ring. Legs fleshy to grey, often with bluish or yellow tinge.

Advanced birds rather similar to adult, and should be separated with care from second-summer birds and adults. Certain birds are very similar to Heuglin's nominate *heuglini* (V. Rauste *in litt.*), which see.

Second-winter similar to adult, but usually with some greyer or browner coverts contrasting with black saddle, dark markings on underwing-coverts and variable, often incomplete dark tail-bar. Saddle often slightly paler than in adult. Outer wing black; if present, narrow white mirror on P10 only. Bill with black subterminal bar; rarely mainly black.

Second-summer similar to adult, but with dark markings on bill and tail, often browner outerwing with no white mirror on P10 and abraded tertials with narrower white tips. Hindneck sometimes weakly brown-spotted. Unlike adult, usually with two generations of primaries: birds which arrest primary moult in spring (before northward migration) have new blackish inner primaries contrasting with abraded greyish-brown outer primaries.

The least advanced also show brownish-tinged scapulars, and can strongly resemble advanced second-year birds. Usually separated by pale yellow iris, deeper yellow bill with deeper red gonys, and isolated dark markings on bill, usually restricted to small spot near tip of upper mandible, and usually two generations of non-juvenile primaries (V. Rauste *in litt.*). Iris as adult, but in 10% darker. Bill as adult or duller; normally with dark markings. Legs dull yellow to greyish-flesh.

Third-winter/fourth-summer as adult; birds with a few immature characters such as brownish-tinged wing, faint dark markings on bill and tail probably this age; better classified as 'older subadults' only.

MOULT *L. f. fuscus* (Baltic Sea)

Moult in *fuscus* very different from *graellsii/intermedius*.

Adult moult to **winter** plumage complete Jun/Jul–Dec, in Northern Hemisphere limited to P1–2(4) mid-Jul–Aug, and suspended before southward migration; mainly in summer plumage when leaving breeding areas, apart from scattered upperpart feathers, and often P1–2(4) Jul–Sep (12–34% Finland, 60% Gotland, but probably different populations). Primary moult suspended during migration and resumed in winter quarters. Up to P4 renewed Oct–Nov. P8–9 Jan–Feb, P9–10 first half of Mar (small minority mid-Apr during migration). Head and body Nov–Dec (Feb) (Hario 1984, 1986, Jonsson 1998b, Gruber 1999, Rauste 1999, V. Rauste & M. Hario *in litt.*, pers. obs.).

Moult to **adult summer** partial Mar–early Apr, including head and body, in 20% P1–3 moulted simultaneously with P9–10 before northward migration.

Juvenile moult to **first-winter** partial, but only very restricted near breeding sites, and many still in juvenile plumage Nov–Dec. May renew scattered mantle and scapulars late Aug–Sep. Moult often very quick in winter quarters. A wintering bird from Denmark (Feb) had just renewed a single mantle feather, otherwise in juvenile plumage (pers. obs.)

Moult to **first-summer** very variable. Often complete (unlike *graellsii/intermedius*), but sometimes partial, restricted to mantle, scapulars, tertials and (90% of) coverts and tail Jan–Apr. Most, however, moult flight feathers Feb–May (Jun) before northbound migration (60–70% in Finland in summer had mainly fresh flight feathers). Birds which suspend primary moult, with up to P8 renewed before northbound migration, resume flight feather moult in summer quarters. Most Finnish birds have renewed all rectrices and flight feathers by Jun (Rauste 1999, M. Hario, A. Forsten & V. Rauste *in litt.* & photos). Unlike other gulls, the most advanced birds are more than one primary moult cycle ahead of the least advanced. Sometimes two active waves can be simultaneously active in Aug (V. Rauste *in litt.*). Retarded birds moult much more restricted—to scattered upperpart feathers (sometimes no coverts) and odd tertials. More information needed when establishing moult progress in those staying in winter quarters. Very few *intermedius/graellsii* similarly advanced (P. Adriaens *in litt.*).

Moult to **second-winter** complete from May/Jul. Flight feathers moulted again from Jul (70–80% start flight feather moult during first-summer/autumn and complete in winter). P1–5 often moulted again in spring of third calendar year as indication of next moult cycle, resulting in two generations of primaries in spring. Some show a mixture of three primary generations. It remains to be clarified how the variation is connected to the very variable moult situation in spring of second calendar year. In spring often renews entire tail, although sometimes partial, or even completely unmoulted into summer (Jonsson 1998b, Rauste 1999, A. Forsten & V. Rauste *in litt.*).

Moult to **second-summer** partial, including head and underbody.

DISTRIBUTION AND MIGRATION Population 250,000–300,000 pairs (all ssp.). Breeds along sea coasts and on islands, locally on islands in lakes and rivers, on moors and buildings.

Large increase in *graellsii/intermedius* since the 1940s with extension of breeding range from 1920s to Iceland, France, Netherlands and Germany; Denmark 1940, 1970s to Spain and Portugal (first bred 1975), since mid-1990s probably mid- and S Baltic and recolonisation of France. Fairly capable of managing competition from Herring Gull, in the Netherlands having outcompeted it through greater manoeuvrability. However, local decrease (Scotland, Norway) since 1980s attributed to changes in fishing practices and competition from Herring and Great Black-backed Gulls.

L. f. graellsii/intermedius Population (in pairs) mid-1990s: Great Britain 86,000 (45,291 1969–1970); Germany 9,000; Netherlands 58,300 1998 (increase from 81 1960, 610 late 1960s, 11,000 late 1970s and max. 57,000 1990–1997); France 23,000 (200 1920, 13,000 1978); Spain 250–300 (75 1980; colonisation of Ebro Delta 1983); Portugal 1–3; Germany 100; Denmark 4,400; Norway 25,000–36,000; Sweden 75,000 (mid-1970s 29,000); Faeroe Islands 9,000; Iceland 25,000–30,000 (10,000 1970; first record 1913). Mentioned breeding

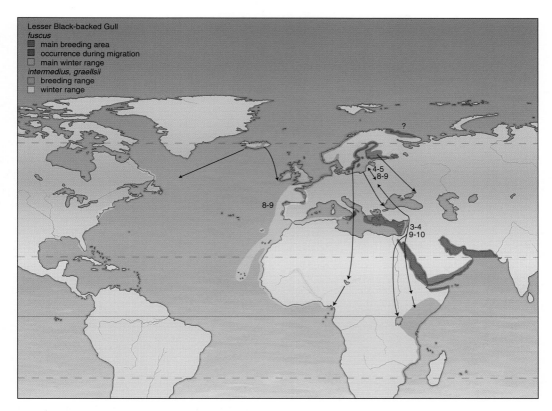

Senegambia 1980 (Cramp & Simmons 1983, Urban *et al.* 1986, Risberg 1990, Noordhuis & Spaans 1992, Rheinwald 1993, Gjershaug *et al.* 1994, del Hoyo *et al.* 1996, Hagemeijer & Blair 1997, Grell 1998, Dubois *et al.* 2000, Bijlsma *et al.* 2001).

Has invaded N America (first record 1934); slow increase until mid-1970s, since when a large growth in numbers. Reached Hudson Bay 1969, Florida and Colorado 1970s and California 1978. Increasing numbers recorded along Atlantic coast between Newfoundland and Florida/Bermuda; scattered records throughout the continent W to California, N to Alaska and S to Texas. Regular Great Lakes. Most noted Oct–Jan; small numbers of immatures summer. Of 717 Ontario, 185 spring, 36 summer, 336 autumn and 160 winter. CBC 1992/93 160, of which 143 between Newfoundland and Texas, 11 the Midwest, three Bermuda and one each Kentucky and Tennessee. Max. 100 New York–N Carolina, 40 Bucks County, Pennsylvania, 35 Pompano, Florida (10 April 1993) and 29 Ontario. Numbers steadily rising since then. In Caribbean very rare Nov–Apr, wintering in very small numbers. New World birds match both *graellsii* and *intermedius* (E Coast S to Florida and Ohio) (Post & Lewis 1995a & b, Ebels 2002, A. B. Kristensen & M. Reid *in litt.*).

In Greenland first record 1850; max. 10 pairs since 1990 W Greenland, where increasing summer vagrant. In summer 2001, 43 birds at one site. Faeroe Islands and British birds recovered Greenland (Boertmann 1994, Lyngs 2003, M. Kviesgaard *in litt.*).

Most of European population migratory, using many stopovers en route. Autumn migration starts with non-breeders late Jun; breeding birds leave from late Jul. In Denmark migration peak mid-Jul–early Oct; gatherings up to 1,500 along W coast and migration Kattegat of hundreds. In W Europe peak late Aug–early Oct; in Netherlands 16,000 coastal waters, 19,000 offshore and 5,500 Limburg. Scarcer interior (W) Germany and E to SE/S coast of Sweden; vagrant Eastern Baltic Sea. Migration peak N Spain/Morocco late Aug–Sep/Oct. Winter quarters reached from Aug; main exodus Oct Morocco. Largest numbers Lagos, Nigeria, Nov–Mar. European migration mainly coastal, but W Africa suggestions of inland migration along large rivers to Gulf of Guinea.

Main wintering range for N/NW European and younger British birds is Atlantic coastal shoreline between France and Mauritania, of which 115,000 Iberian Peninsula, 120,000–130,000 France. Very common wintering along NW African coastline, e.g. 22,000 Tan Tan Plage, S Morocco, in Jan and 24,000 midwinter Mauritania. Quite common W Mediterranean, but scarce E to Sicily (*intermedius*; 1% *graellsii* Sicily). Around Strait of Gibraltar (where 15,000–20,000 winter) and in Portugal mainly *graellsii*; majority in Morocco closer to *intermedius*, but ringing suggests both British and Scandinavian birds winter there. 83% of African recoveries of British birds first-years. Many reach further S on African coast: common Senegal Oct–Mar (max. 3,550 Jan, 90% adult), Lagos and Niger (Nov–Feb); scarcer S to Gulf of Guinea and Lake Chad. British population winters sparsely W Mediterranean, where more Scandinavian birds present, although these largely winter in same areas as *graellsii*. British population mainly migratory up to 1940–1950s, since mainly sedentary or short-distance migrant. Numbers rising from 310 England/Wales 1950 to 60,830 1993. British/Irish winter population around 70,000 (80% adult), largest numbers at inland reservoirs. Pure *graellsii* dominates, but in S England many *intermedius*. Scarce wintering Scotland. Iceland and Faeroe populations mainly winter Irish Sea to Bay of Biscay. Scarce, but increasing in winter NW Europe N to S Norway. Scarce E Mediterranean (Hickling 1977, 1984, Glutz von Blotzheim & Bauer 1982, Cramp & Simmons 1983, Davenport 1985, Lack 1986, Urban *et al.* 1986, Gallissa 1987, Finlayson 1992, Malling Olsen 1992, Post & Lewis 1995a & b, Bijlsma *et al.* 2001, Burton *et al.* 2003, A. Corso, J. Jansen & A. Forsten *in litt.*).

Parts of British winter population in Iberia move N from Sep (mainly immatures). Spring migration from late Feb, at Gibraltar peaking Feb–Mar (mainly adults), with immatures largely Apr–May. Most adults have left Morocco late Mar, but migration continues into late Apr. Mar–Apr gatherings Bay of Biscay at time of immigration into N and W European colonies. In offshore Danish waters, max. 40,000 gather spring; peak Danish W coast late Apr–mid-May, from land max. 700 Skagen, N Jutland. First half of April max. 3,200 at certain sites Limburg (Baker 1980, Glutz von Blotzheim & Bauer 1982, Lack 1986, Finlayson 1992, Malling Olsen 1992, Grell 1998, Dubois *et al.* 2000, J. Jansen *in litt.*).

Vagrant Africa S of Nigeria, California, E Mexico, Venezuela, French Guiana; probably Persian Gulf.

L. f. fuscus Total population max. 20,000 pairs; maybe <10,000; strong decrease in whole breeding area alarming; may be considered threatened. Breeds Finland and Baltic Sea W to Danish Isle of Bornholm and Hanö Bukt, Sweden; scarce N Norway S to Tarva; very local N Russia (Onezhskii and Kandalaksha Bay) and Poland. Recent strong decrease caused mainly by poor reproductive rate. In Finland up to 70% chicks die from disease, and many taken by Herring Gulls. Despite prudent feeding by parents, the chicks fail to digest. The liver fails to function, and the final cause of death is sepsis. High PCB loadings in the liver of Finnish breeders – absorbed from pesticide-treated grasshoppers in winter quarters – is probably a promoting factor, although grasshoppers presumably only a secondary food in winter quarters after fish offal (Hario & Rudbäck 1996,1999, Hario *et al.* 2000, M. Hario & M. Collinson *in litt.*).

Population (in pairs) Finland 5,200–5,700 (20,000 in 1960s, 6,200 1986 E to Karelia; has disappeared from many areas, especially from coast; 2,000–3,000 pairs Karelia); Norway 300–400 (strong decrease: 3,000 in 1970s, now rare in Finnmark, and might have disappeared from Norway); Sweden 4,000–5,000 (mainly Stockholm area and Gotland; strong decrease in S part of range); Estonia 250–300; Russian White Sea max. 350 and Gulf of Finland 1,267; Denmark 7–15 Bornholm/Christiansø 2001 (1,000 1930–1950, since when decrease to 100 1972, 20 1980s). Disappeared during

1920s from most of Kola Peninsula. Irregular NE Germany (Haftorn 1971, Møller 1978, Glutz von Blotzheim & Bauer 1982, Cramp & Simmons 1983, Bevanger & Thingstad 1990, Risberg 1990, Gjershaug *et al.* 1994, Juvaste 1994a & b, Christensen & Søby 1998, Väisinen *et al.* 1998, A. Forsten & H. J. Lehto *in litt.*).

Mainly coastal, but also breeds in inland lakes. Generally avoids tundra habitat, occupied by Heuglin's Gull. Long-distance migrant. Leaves breeding areas Jul–Sep. S Baltic Sea migration peaks Sep–early Oct; max. 500 Björn, Uppland and Christiansø, Bornholm and 3,500 Baltic coast of Poland. Migrates S/SE crossing E Europe between E Germany and St Petersburg along large river systems, generally without stopovers, although small numbers settle at C European lakes. Migration then heads for W Black Sea and E Mediterranean. At Bosporus, day-counts >1,000 late Sep. Some N Norwegian birds follow more easterly migration route, as shown by recoveries Oct–Nov. NW Black Sea and Sea of Azov. In Israel, migration peaks late Sep–early Oct. Mainly coastal; max. 1,100 along Mediterranean coastline. Much scarcer Eilat than in spring. Many stop over at Lake Chad.

Birds from W part of breeding area (Baltic islands of Denmark, N Norway) generally move more to S across European mainland to mid-Mediterranean (recoveries C Europe, Mediterranean between France and Egypt). Recoveries of Finnish birds Niedersachsen (Germany), Bulgaria, Netherlands, France, Portugal, Valencia (Spain) and NW Africa (7) indicate that a few follow more W migration route; recoveries from Netherlands not fully documented, as they could refer to Herring Gull. From Netherlands 11 accepted records up to and including 2001. Two records Belgium (Winters 1999, Wiegant *et al.* 1999, van der Vliet *et al.* 2001, 2002, Yésou 2002, V. Rauste *in litt.*).

Main wintering area E Africa, where common Oct–Apr along coast and W Rift Valley Lakes (e.g. max. 1,000 Lake Turkana, Kenya). Winters further S to Zambia, Malawi, Natal, Mozambique and S Africa, but scarce S of equator. A few move further S and W and cross the Sahara Desert; in winter recoveries of Swedish and Finnish birds from Chad, Niger, DR Congo and Angola; small numbers to Mozambique and occasionally S Africa. Some (especially first-winters) reach W Africa to Mali, Gulf of Guinea and Ghana, meeting *graellsii/intermedius*. Five recoveries of Swedish and Danish birds Nigeria and Cameroon. Also Israel (4,000–6,000 mid-1980s), Red Sea (max. 200 in Jan. N Yemen); scarce Persian Gulf (10–60 Oman yearly). Status between Arabian Gulf and India uncertain; migration up to 2000 mentioned Dhofar, but probably mainly Heuglin's Gull. Scarce E Mediterranean W to Italy/Algeria; 800–1,000 Sicily; probably some hundreds Greece. Small numbers C European lakes; very rare but regular wintering S Baltic Sea (Glutz von Blotzheim & Bauer 1982, Cramp & Simmons 1983, Schuster *et al.* 1983, Meininger & Sørensen 1992, Deutsch *et al.* 1996, Shirihai 1996b, Hoogendoorn & van Scheepen 1998, Jonsson 1998b, Wiegant *et al.* 1998, Gruber 1999, A. Corso *in litt.*).

Return migration Feb–late Jun. In Eilat, Israel, peak late Mar–early Apr and another wave late Apr, on average 20,000 each spring (max. 27,361 in 1983; max. day-count 5,200 24 March 1984); in peak period 95–99% adult; younger birds scarce, peaking late Apr–May. From there, migrates N in dense flocks at great height to cross desert before reaching E Mediterranean along Israeli coastline, where numbers equal to Eilat (max. 5,000 Ma'agan Michael early Apr). Some head N to Sea of Galilee, where flocks of several hundred settle. Along Lebanese coastline max. 1,300 8 April 1997. In Greece peak late Mar–early Apr. In spring much commoner E Mediterranean and along Black Sea coast than in autumn. Arrives Baltic Sea breeding sites from late Mar, mainly mid-Apr; northernmost population on average one month later. Most immatures arrive from early May, second-years from early Jun (Glutz von Blotzheim & Bauer 1982, Shirihai 1996b, Handrinos & Akriotis 1997, Busuttill & Flumm 1998, A. Forsten *in litt.*). Most first- and second-years summer in winter quarters, but many migrate N to E Mediterranean, Red Sea and Arabia. At least 5–10% first-years reach Finland; during summer 2000, 130 recorded Tampere (Cramp & Simmons 1983, Hoogendoorn & van Scheepen 1998, Tuomainen 1998, Rauste 1999, Koskinen *et al.* 2001). Vagrant Cocos-Keeling Island, Indian Ocean, Seychelles, Madagascar, Nepal, Goa (India), Sumatra (Cramp & Simmons 1983, Inskipp & Inskipp 1985, G. Frost *in litt.*).

MEASUREMENTS Lengths in mm; weights in g. Own data based on skins in NHM, NRK, UZM, ZMA, ZMO. *Fuscus* breeding birds N Norway, N Russia, Baltic. *Intermedius* S Norway, Kattegat area, Netherlands. *Graellsii* (Faeroe Islands, Great Britain). See also Geographical Variation above for details.

WING

L. f. fuscus

Adult male	404–455 (430.3)	63
Adult female	393–436 (410.1)	78
Juv./first-winter male	368–430 (404.9)	7
Juv./first-winter female	389–431 (404.8)	7

Note Haftorn (1971) gives for N Norwegian birds (Tarva-Finnmark) adult male 416–462 (433, n=54), adult female 395–430 (412, n=71).

L. f. intermedius

Adult male	414–452 (432.6)	56
Adult female	390–435 (410.5)	69
Juv./first-winter male	379–431 (410.9)	13
Juv./first-winter female	378–428 (396.7)	20

L. f. graellsii

Adult male	397–456 (424.4)	61
Adult female	383–432 (404.5)	21
Juv./first-winter male	388	1
Juv./first-winter female	388,400	2

Note Harris & Jones (1969) give for adults from Anglesey adult male 417–446 (430, n=30), adult female 394–430 (409, n=50).

BILL

L. f. fuscus

Adult male	47.3–56.0 (52.0)	63
Adult female	42.0–53.6 (46.2)	78
Juv./first-winter male	40.4–53.0 (47.6)	7
Juv./first-winter female	41.1–47.9 (43.7)	7

L. f. intermedius

Adult male	47.3–58.0 (52.9)	54
Adult female	45.1–54.3 (48.6)	63
Juv./first-winter male	48.1–53.1 (49.2)	13
Juv./first-winter female	40.3–47.5 (45.0)	21

L. f. graellsii

Adult male	47.4–57.2 (52.8)	60
Adult female	45.5–53.5 (48.0)	37
Juv./first-winter male	41.8	1
Juv./first-winter female	41.0, 44.8	2

Note *Harris & Jones (1969) give for adults, Anglesey adult male 49.0–60.0 (55.6, n=30), adult female 45.5–54.9 (50, n=50).*

BILL DEPTH AT GONYS

L. f. fuscus

Adult male	13.6–17.8 (16.0)	62
Adult female	(11.2)13.2–17.0 (14.7)	78
Juv./first-winter male	12.0–15.0 (13.7)	7
Juv./first-winter female	11.4–15.0 (13.2)	7

L. f. intermedius

Adult male	14.8–18.2 (16.9)	53
Adult female	13.9–17.3 (15.3)	63
Juv./first-winter male	13.3–17.0 (15.0)	13
Juv./first-winter female	12.0–16.4 (13.7)	21

Note *Averages of S Norway, Kattegat and Netherlands populations identical, even regarding depth at base of bill.*

L. f. graellsii

Adult male	15.2–19.5 (17.6)	60
Adult female	14.0–17.8 (15.9)	38
Juv./first-winter male	12.0	1
Juv./first-winter female	13.9, 14.5	2

BILL DEPTH AT BASE OF BILL

L. f. fuscus

Adult male	14.4–19.3 (17.5)	63
Adult female	13.6–18.4 (16.1)	78
Juv./first-winter male	13.4–17.7 (15.5)	7
Juv./first-winter female	13.2–16.8 (14.4)	6

L. f. intermedius

Adult male	15.9–20.1 (17.9)	52
Adult female	15.1–18.1 (16.3)	63
Juv./first-winter male	14.8–17.8 (16.1)	13
Juv./first-winter female	12.9–16.4 (14.9)	21

L. f. graellsii

Adult male	16.8–21.1 (19.0)	60
Adult female	15.0–19.5 (17.0)	21
Juv./first-winter male	15.5	1
Juv./first-winter female	15.7, 16.4	2

GONYS LENGTH

L. f. fuscus

Adult male	12.1–17.2 (14.6)	63
Adult female	11.3–16.6 (13.6)	78
Juv./first-winter male	10.8–16.5 (12.6)	7
Juv./first-winter female	9.9–13.8 (11.6)	6

L. f. intermedius

Adult male	12.8–17.4 (15.2)	53
Adult female	12.4–16.5 (14.2)	63
Juv./first-winter male	11.0–15.6 (13.1)	13
Juv./first-winter female	10.3–15.4 (12.5)	21

L. f. graellsii

Adult male	12.7–17.7 (15.1)	60
Adult female	12.5–16.5 (14.4)	38
Juv./first-winter male	8.8	1
Juv./first-winter female	10.2, 13.8	2

TARSUS

L. f. fuscus

Adult male	55.0–66.4 (61.0)	63
Adult female	53.6–62.4 (56.4)	78
Juv./first-winter male	54.7–62.8 (58.7)	7
Juv./first-winter female	54.5–61.2 (58.3)	6

L. f. intermedius

Adult male	58.4–68.0 (62.6)	53
Adult female	51.8–65.2 (58.4)	63
Juv./first-winter male	55.4–65.6 (62.2)	13
Juv./first-winter female	51.7–64.1 (58.3)	13

L. f. graellsii

Adult male	56.3–68.7 (64.2)	60
Adult female	55.2–66.8 (59.8)	38
Juv./first-winter male	56.3	1
Juv./first-winter female	55.5, 62.6	2

Note *Harris & Jones (1969) give for adults from Pembrokeshire, Anglesey, adult male 56–70 (65.0, n=26), adult female 55–68 (60.0, n=35). Faeroe specimens have heavier bill than in other samples, but material restricted.*

Weight *L. f. fuscus* adult: male (N Norway and Baltic) 620–1,095, female 452–885; first-summer male 965, female 910 (skins in NRK, UZM, ZMO). *L. f. intermedius* (S Norway and Kattegat) adult: male 757–1,025, female 535–835. Netherlands adult: male 716–958, female 471–810, juv.: male 750–965, female 391–910 (skins in NRK, UZM, ZMA, ZMO). *L. f. graellsii* Pembrokeshire and Anglesey (Wales), adult: male 770–1,100, female 620–908. A male from Faeroe Islands 688 (Harris & Jones 1969, skins in UZM).

Lesser Black-backed Gull, ssp. **Baltic Gull,** *Larus fuscus fuscus.* **527. Juvenile.** Combination of slender outline, rather fresh dark and pale contrasting upperparts, just faint pale edges to tertials, long blackish wing-projection and dark mask and bill provides species identification. *Fuscus* is the lightest and most long-winged taxon. Note contrast between pale underparts (in mid-belly almost unmarked) and almost black-and-white patterned saddle, this contrast often pronounced in *fuscus.* Lahti, Finland. 26 Aug 1999. *Visa Rauste.* **528. Juvenile moulting into 1st-winter.** Moult usually restricted to a few mantle and scapular feathers by autumn. Note rather diffuse pattern of new mantle feathers and compare with photos 402 and 549. Helsinki, Finland. Late autumn. *Harry J. Lehto.* **529. Juvenile.** *Fuscus* often appears flat-headed and slender-billed, in 1st-years sometimes recalling Caspian Gull. Note almost unmarked belly, slender black bill and short legs. A single, new 1st-winter scapular shows, with washed-out pattern typical for Baltic Gull. Suissalo, Turku, Finland. 7 Sep 1997. *Tomi Muukkonen.*

381

Lesser Black-backed Gull, ssp. **Baltic Gull**, *Larus fuscus fuscus*. **530. Juvenile**. Note dark flight-feathers and solid dark bar across greater coverts. White tail contrasts strongly with solid black tail-bar. Tampere, Finland. 19 Aug 2000. *Annika Forsten*. **531. Juvenile**. Note complete black primaries, lacking any pale window as well as long, slender wing with long, pointed hand. This individual shows more dense dark pattern in the rump than 530. Helsinki, Finland. 14 Aug 1997. *Visa Rauste*. **532. Juvenile**. Many 1st-year *fuscus* have extensive pale parts of underwing. Note white, unmarked belly and central undertail-coverts, thus similar to Yellow-legged and Caspian Gulls. Helsinki, Finland. Nov 1995. *Markus Varesvuo*. **533. Juvenile**. Note pale central area in underwing, differing from more solid dark underwing in *intermedius* and *graellsii*, as well as white undertail-coverts. Hanko, Finland. 5 Oct 1996. *Harry J. Lehto*. **534. 1st-winter**. Note dark, rather diffuse pattern of new mantle and scapulars. Note also extensive moult in wing-coverts. Wing still appears rather fresh by autumn. Shifdan, Israel. Feb 1995. *Hadoram Shirihai*. **535. 1st-spring/summer**. Mantle, scapulars, tertials and wing-coverts of slaty-type, with pale edges. Outer primaries still juvenile. Turku, Finland. 5 Jun 1998. *Harry J. Lehto*.

Lesser Black-backed Gull, ssp. **Baltic Gull**, *Larus fuscus fuscus*. **536. 1st-spring/summer**. A more adult-looking example of a 1st-summer bird. Note slightly pale edges to blackish saddle feathers and median coverts, and fresh primaries. Oulu, Finland. 2 Jun 1997. *Henry Lehto.* **537 1st-spring/summer**. All flight feathers and tail-feathers have been renewed by winter. Tampere, Finland. 4 Aug 1998. *Annika Forsten.* **538. 2nd-summer**. Age development in this taxon generally one year quicker than in *intermedius* and *graellsii*. By 2nd-summer, basically as adult, but note lack of white primary tips, faint pale edges to mantle and scapulars, and faint dark subterminal markings on bill. Kuopio, Finland. 2 Jul 1998. *Harry J. Lehto.*

Lesser Black-backed Gull, ssp. **Baltic Gull,** *Larus fuscus fuscus*. **539. 1st- or 2nd-summer**. Age development varies individually. Note complete dark tail-bar, indicating 1st-summer, but also only faint dark markings on underwing-coverts and adult-patterned bill, indicating 2nd-summer. Kuopio, Finland. 2 Jul 1998. *Harry J. Lehto*. **540. Adult summer**. Note very long wing-projection and only very faint white primary tips. Upperparts velvety black, concolorous with wing-tip. Note short yellow legs and rather long and slender bill. Kuopio, Finland. 9 Jul 1998. *Harry J. Lehto*. **541. Adult summer**. The most common wing-pattern, black with just a small white mirror to P10 and lack of large white primary tips, resulting in black, pointed hand. Kuopio, Finland. 7 Jul 1998. *Harry J. Lehto*. **542. Adult at onset of moult to winter plumage.** Note slender outline, solid black upperparts and extensive dark undersurface to all flight feathers. Retains summer plumage by autumn or just moults inner primaries from late summer. Main moult takes place in winter quarters. Simrishamn, Scania, Sweden. 20 Sep 1999. *Klaus Malling Olsen*.

Lesser Black-backed Gull of ssp. *graellsii/intermedius.* **543. Juvenile.** Similar to Herring Gull, but slightly better-contrasting with darker eye-mask and more distinct pale edges to darker upperpart feathers, more extensive dark in greater coverts, narrower pale tertial edges not reaching greater coverts and longer black primaries. The dense, well scattered brown spotting on entire underparts differs from most *fuscus.* Esbjerg, West Jutland, Denmark. 10 Oct 1995. *Klaus Malling Olsen.* **544 Juvenile.** Some birds show greater covert barring more similar to Herring Gull, but note blackish primaries, vaguely with pale edges, more chequered mantle and darker mask around eye. Many birds have not started moult into 1st-winter at this time, when most Herrings are well advanced, but individual variation is large. IJmuiden, Netherlands. 27 Sep 1998. *Harry J. Lehto.* **545. Juvenile.** Note more elegant and slender appearance than Herring Gull. Note paler forehead and hind-collar, enhancing dark eye-mask, long, slender hindparts, just narrow white tertial tips and solid dark greater-coverts bar. Head rounded and bill rather short in this bird, indicating female. Heligoland, Germany. 6 Oct 1993. *Arnoud B. van den Berg.* **546. Juvenile.** Note dark flight-feathers lacking pale window, dark mid-wing bars created by dark greater coverts and secondaries, and solid black tail-bar against white rump. Similar to many Yellow-legged Gulls, but bill smaller and plumage still juvenile. Most Yellow-legged at this time would have renewed mantle, scapulars and a number of inner wing-coverts. Pas-de-Calais, France. 11 Oct 1999. *Annika Forsten.* **547. Juvenile.** Note wing-pattern outlined above. Tail-bar at its broadest, recalling American Herring Gull, but note much paler, less patterned and spotted, not barred, rump. IJmuiden, Netherlands. 27 Sep 1998. *Harry J. Lehto.* **548. Juvenile.** Note dark underwing-coverts, more solid than in Herring and Yellow-legged *michahellis* Gulls. Portugal. Oct 1991. *Markus Varesvuo.*

385

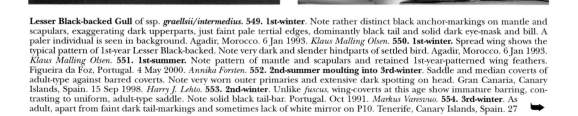

Lesser Black-backed Gull of ssp. *graellsii/intermedius.* **549. 1st-winter.** Note rather distinct black anchor-markings on mantle and scapulars, exaggerating dark upperparts, just faint pale tertial edges, dominantly black tail and solid dark eye-mask and bill. A paler individual is seen in background. Agadir, Morocco. 6 Jan 1993. *Klaus Malling Olsen.* **550. 1st-winter.** Spread wing shows the typical pattern of 1st-year Lesser Black-backed. Note very dark and slender hindparts of settled bird. Agadir, Morocco. 6 Jan 1993. *Klaus Malling Olsen.* **551. 1st-summer.** Note pattern of mantle and scapulars and retained 1st-year-patterned wing feathers. Figueira da Foz, Portugal. 4 May 2000. *Annika Forsten.* **552. 2nd-summer moulting into 3rd-winter.** Saddle and median coverts of adult-type against barred coverts. Note very worn outer primaries and extensive dark spotting on head. Gran Canaria, Canary Islands, Spain. 15 Sep 1998. *Harry J. Lehto.* **553. 2nd-winter.** Unlike *fuscus*, wing-coverts at this age show immature barring, contrasting to uniform, adult-type saddle. Note solid black tail-bar. Portugal. Oct 1991. *Markus Varesvuo.* **554. 3rd-winter.** As adult, apart from faint dark tail-markings and sometimes lack of white mirror on P10. Tenerife, Canary Islands, Spain. 27 ➡

Feb 1999. *Harry J. Lehto.* **555. Adult summer** ssp. *graellsii.* Note dark grey upperparts, contrasting somewhat to black primaries. General appearance more like Herring Gull than *fuscus.* Hafnafjordur, Iceland. 30 May 1999. *Harry J. Lehto.* **556. Adult winter** ssp. *graellsii,* with Yellow-legged Gull. Note dark grey upperparts with some contrast to wing-tip, rounded head and - in left individual - coarsely marked winter head of Lesser Black-backed. In comparison, Yellow-legged has paler upperparts more similar to Herring Gull, squarer head with flatter crown and just fine dark streaks concentrated around eyes. IJmuiden, Netherlands. 29 Oct 1982. *Arnoud B. van den Berg.* **557. Adult summer.** Many Dutch birds are at the darker end of the *graellsii*-range, thus appearing as paler *intermedius,* which has upperparts as dark as Great Black-backed. Maasvlakte, Netherlands. Apr 1987. *René Pop.* **558. Adult summer** matching ssp. *intermedius.* Upperpart colour as dark as Great Black-backed, thus fitting *intermedius* of Kattegat Area. Maasvlakte, Netherlands. 4 Jul 1994. *Klaus Malling Olsen.* **559. Adult winter** ssp. *graellsii.* Note coarse head-markings, sometimes forming traces of dark hood - most commonly found in *graellsii.* Portugal. Feb 1991. *Markus Varesvuo.*

560

561

562

Lesser Black-backed Gull of ssp. *graellsii/intermedius*. **560. Adult summer** ssp. *intermedius*. Note slight contrast between black wing-tip and rest of surface of flight feathers. Gothenburg, Bohuslän, Sweden. 8 May 1993. *Klaus Malling Olsen*. **561. Adult summer**. Wing-tip darker than rest of wing, but never as conspicuous as in Herring and Yellow-legged Gulls. White mirror on P10 only. Texel, Netherlands. 7 Apr 2002. *René Pop*. **562. Adult summer** ssp. *graellsii*. Some show small white mirror in P9. Note slender, long-winged appearance of this species. Texel, Netherlands. 7 Apr 2002. *René Pop*.

26. HEUGLIN'S GULL

Larus heuglini (Bree, 1876, North Siberia)

IDENTIFICATION Length 53–70cm, wingspan 138–158cm. Breeds in North Russia, in areas overlapping with Herring and Lesser Black-backed Gull with no interbreeding, as the species are found in different habitats (Filchagov & Semashko 1987, Stepanyan 1990), with Heuglin's breeding in lone pairs or small colonies in tundra-like habitat along coasts and rivers and on lakes, although it frequently scavenges on dumps. Nevertheless, the taxonomic status of Heuglin's Gull is still unclear; it is treated here as a full species, but by late 2003 AERC will treat it as conspecific with Lesser Black-backed Gull. Here *'taimyrensis'*, the larger and paler type occuring in E part of breeding range is mentioned in inverted commas, as it is now considered a hybrid between Heuglin's and Vega Gull.

Heuglin's Gull is the size of Lesser Black-backed Gull or slightly larger, and could be described as a large version of Lesser Black-backed nominate *fuscus*, sharing the latter's neat, elongated shape and small, rounded head, relatively fine bill, rather slender legs and short tail. Males have flatter crown, heavier, more bulbous-tipped bill and fuller legs. Certain males have jizz close to Yellow-legged or even Great Black-backed Gull, but never so grotesquely heavy-billed or small-eyed. Alert birds stretch neck, causing breast to protrude.

Compared to most other large gulls, plumage development seems to be 'one year in advance', as in Lesser Black-backed nominate *fuscus*.

Adult similar to Lesser Black-backed Gull races *graellsii/intermedius*, and most indistinguishable in field. Many Lesser Black-backeds are heavier with more rounded head and heavier bill (but not in ssp *fuscus*); most Heuglin's are slenderer with smaller head, slimmer bill and longer legs. Identification least complicated in autumn, as Heuglin's retains most of summer plumage prior to autumn migration from breeding grounds, with at most 1–2 inner primaries moulted, and with summer plumage still present. At this time, *graellsii/intermedius* have moulted into dark-patterned head and show heavy wing-moult: differences in moult timing are therefore better clues than plumage markings, but it should be stressed that certain Lesser Black-backeds show delayed moult in autumn. In Heuglin's, moult into winter plumage occurs Jun–Mar, in *graellsii/intermedius* May–Jan. Eyes normally pale, but in 10% with dark peppering, in rare cases enough to create dark eye in field. Minor characters for Heuglin's Gull are tendency for more frequent dark markings on primary coverts, white mirror mainly restricted to P10 (and often set further behind than in Lesser Black-backed) and generally more distinct grey tongues in inner webs of P3–8. In summer, bill yellow, rarely as bright as in Lesser Black-backed and more often with dark markings at tip. Red gonys-spot generally more restricted, not reaching upper mandible. Legs yellow, often with pinkish tinge. In **summer**, head white. In

winter (late autumn–Mar) slightly dark-streaked with coarser dark spots or streaks on hindneck, creating dark necklace. Pattern sometimes includes crown and ear-coverts. Bare parts duller, bill with irregular dark subterminal bar, thus looking three-coloured, but coloration rarely bright.

As a result of late moult, Heuglin's Gull has winter head and rather fresh white primary tips well into spring when other large gulls have summer head and moderately worn primaries. White primary tips may almost wear off by midsummer.

'*Taimyrensis*' generally paler; may approach colour of Caspian race *barabensis*. Compared to nominate *heuglini*, slightly larger with larger head, deeper, duller bill, larger eyes, longer legs and broader white trailing edge to inner wing. Legs often pinkish (see Geographical Variation).

Juvenile resembles heavy Lesser Black-backed Gull nominate *fuscus* with similar dark eye-mask and brown, pale-scaled juvenile mantle and scapulars retained into late autumn (most other large gulls gradually acquire first-winter mantle and scapulars from mid-autumn). While some birds are browner and more uniform than Lesser Black-backed nominate *fuscus*, most are inseparable on the basis of plumage alone. Typical birds are heavier with stronger bill, paler overall plumage with less dark-marked head and body (especially belly) and stronger dark eye-mask. The upperparts are colder and greyer-brown, in better contrast to dark flight feathers. Unlike nominate *fuscus*, inner primaries often show faint pale window. Juvenile upperpart feathers generally have broader, fuller pale edges than *fuscus*, and greater coverts generally have more pale patterning against narrower dark barring, sometimes mainly buffish or whitish with 2–3 rows of narrow, dark triangles, as in Great Black-backed or even Vega and Caspian Gull race *mongolicus*. There is, however, much variation in greater covert pattern, and birds with almost all-dark greater coverts are frequent. The blackish tertials have narrow white edges. Rump and tail-base are white with dark spots, in strong contrast to black tail-bar, which on average is narrower than in nominate *fuscus*, extending to tail-sides and tips of tail-coverts; unlike Lesser Black-backed, rump and tail may appear similar to Common Gull. Underwing varies from dark as in Herring Gull to almost as pale as in Caspian Gull (again shared with certain Lesser Black-backed nominate *fuscus*), but not as clean palish-looking, since axillaries and lesser coverts are finely barred. Bill black, sometimes faintly pinker at base.

Scaled juvenile upperparts present into winter and still fresh-looking by Dec. The darkest birds then look rather rich brown with dark covert-markings stronger as pale edges wear off. Note that juvenile plumage shows complete overlap with Lesser Black-backed nominate *fuscus*, making field identification of birds outside breeding grounds almost impossible.

PLATE 54. HEUGLIN'S GULL *Larus heuglini*

Heuglin's Gull is a northern counterpart of Lesser Black-backed Gull, breeding in the Arctic tundra of Russia. It resembles Lesser Black-backed, but is on average larger and slightly heavier, often with more squarish-looking head and slightly larger bill; jizz sometimes similar to Yellow-legged Gull or even Great Black-backed Gull. Winters Indian Ocean and E Pacific (*'taimyrensis'* only).

1. **Juvenile** (Aug–Nov/Dec) Greyish-brown, generally greyer with broader pale feather-edges on upperparts than Lesser Black-backed Gull nominate *fuscus*, including full whitish edges to mantle and scapulars. Greater covert bar variable from pale with narrow dark bars to almost uniform dark with narrow pale feather-edges and tips (latter making birds resemble Lesser Black-backed). Tertials dark with narrow pale tips and outer webs, latter not reaching greater coverts. Plumage fresh in autumn, retained well into winter.

2. **Juvenile** A paler bird, but with covert pattern darker, resembling Lesser Black-backed Gull nominate *fuscus*. Head generally whiter with more restricted dark mask, and underbody often even more faintly dark-marked.

3. **First-winter** (Dec–Mar) With wear, head and underbody bleach to whitish. New mantle and scapulars pale grey with distinct dark subterminal markings (these areas darker and more diffuse in Lesser Black-backed Gull nominate *fuscus*).

4. **First-winter–summer** (Dec–Oct) Some birds at this age almost white on head and underbody with pink, black-tipped bill. This bird has renewed tertials and wing-coverts, which have blacker centres but broader white edges than in first-winter.

5. **First-summer (spring)** (Mar–Oct) Most birds at this age have renewed parts of mantle, scapulars and coverts into more uniform, adult-looking grey (with pale edges) and parts of flight feathers. Head white with faint dark streaks concentrated on hindneck.

6. **Second-winter** *heuglini* (Nov–Apr) Similar to adult, but with brown-tinged coverts and indistinct white primary tips. Shows dark subterminal markings on bill. Head pattern also seen in adult winter.

7. **Adult winter** *'taimyrensis'* (Oct–Apr) often regarded as a hybrid between Vega Gull and Heuglin's Gull *heuglini*. Upperparts dark grey, paler than *heuglini*. Legs yellow. In winter head and hindneck-streaking generally stronger than in nominate *heuglini*. Pale upperparts and strong head-markings are features of Vega Gull, yellow legs are from *heuglini*.

8. **Adult summer** *heuglini* (Apr–Oct) Very similar to Lesser Black-backed Gull race *graellsii*, and spring–summer not identifiable from latter. However, retains summer plumage (at most with 1–4 inner primaries renewed) in autumn before southward migration Sep–Oct, a time where *graellsii* shows more advanced primary moult and is actively moulting its coverts, secondaries and tail feathers. In winter Heuglin's only has streaking on hindneck and around eyes, whereas *graellsii* shows dense spots on whole head from late Sep.

1. Juvenile

2. Juvenile

3. First-winter

4. First-winter–
summer

5. First-summer
(spring)

6. Second-winter
heuglini

7. Adult winter
'*taimyrensis*'

8. Adult summer
heuglini

PLATE 55. HEUGLIN'S GULL *Larus heuglini*

Very similar to Lesser Black-backed Gull races *graellsii/intermedius*, in first-year also nominate *fuscus*, and many not safely identifiable.

1. **Juvenile** (Aug–Nov/Dec) Upperwing almost identical to Lesser Black-backed Gull, especially nominate *fuscus*: like latter, retains juvenile plumage into winter quarters. In general, inner primaries slightly paler and underwing more often paler, with only faint dark marking, often appearing as fine dense streaks. Overall impression more greyish. Importantly, tail-bar narrower, generally reaching distal part of uppertail-coverts (mid-part in *fuscus*).

2. **First-winter** (Dec–Mar) Palest birds paler than Lesser Black-backed Gull nominate *fuscus*; note especially narrower dark tail-bar and whitish underwing, in palest birds (shown here) more similar to Caspian Gull nominate *cachinnans*. However, *cachinnans* has renewed most of mantle and scapulars as well as some inner coverts by Sep–Oct, when Heuglin's still in juvenile plumage. First-winter shown here occurs at earliest from Nov, showing similar fine markings on grey mantle and scapulars as in Caspian races *cachinnans* and *barabensis*. ID from latter still not fully understood.

3. **First-spring/summer** *heuglini* (Mar–Oct) By spring, parts of mantle, scapulars and coverts renewed into grey type, similar to adult, but sometimes paler, and almost always with some pale edgings. Also renews some flight feathers (esp. inner primaries) and tail, the latter with blacker centres and more vermiculated base than in first-year; contrasts with white rump. Underwing shown here is typical. Bill fleshy with black tip. Head and underbody white with faint dark hindneck-streaks.

4. **Second-winter** *heuglini* (Nov–Apr) Grey spreads to large parts of wing, but some parts patterned as in first-year. Pale inner primaries may create pale window, and P10 sometimes with white mirror. Parts of tail white.

5. **Third-winter** *heuglini* (Nov–Apr) Similar to adult, but with dark markings on primary coverts (narrow dark shaft-streaks often present in adult). Head white with faint dark hindneck-streaks and sometimes darker streaking around eyes.

6. **Adult winter** *heuglini* (Nov–Apr) Very similar to Lesser Black-backed Gull race *graellsii*, but normally with white window on P10 only. Head pattern with finer streaks, not broader spots of *graellsii*, and winter plumage acquired later; following arrival at winter quarters, whereas from Sep/Oct *graellsii* shows more than half of primaries renewed and heavy moult in rest of plumage. At this time, Heuglin's has moulted P1–4 at most.

7. **Adult summer** '*taimyrensis*' (Apr–Oct/Nov) Regarded as a hybrid between Vega Gull and Heuglin's Gull *heuglini*. Paler than nominate *heuglini*; many match Yellow-legged Gull or even darkest Vega Gull. Black wing-tip better contrasting than in *heuglini*, and more often with white mirror on P9.

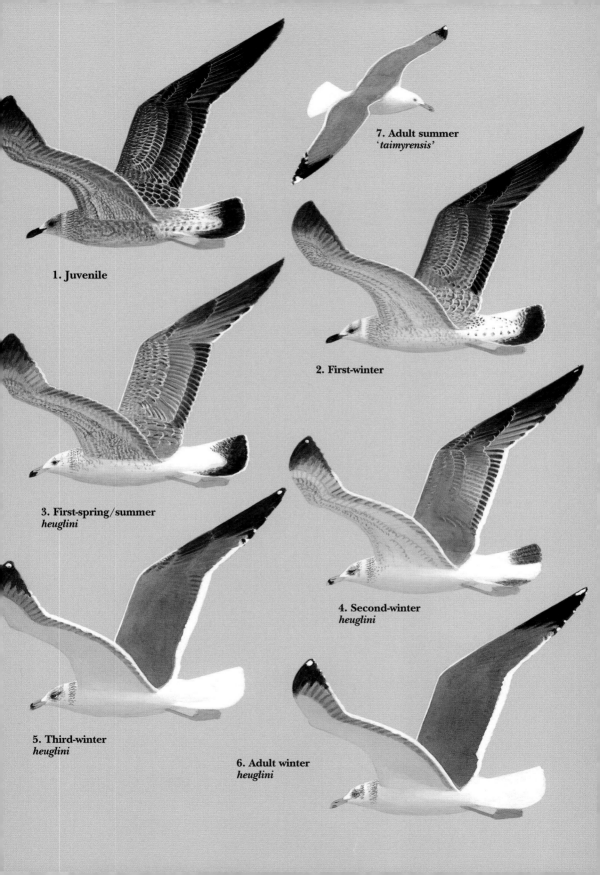

1. Juvenile

7. Adult summer
'taimyrensis'

2. First-winter

3. First-spring/summer
heuglini

4. Second-winter
heuglini

5. Third-winter
heuglini

6. Adult winter
heuglini

On wintering grounds moults into **first-winter**, where head becomes white, but ear-coverts and crown often retain brown markings, which contrast well with white hindneck and neck-sides. New first-winter mantle and scapulars (rarely some inner coverts) are pale brown with distinct black bars or anchor-markings (unlike the fainter, darker pattern of Lesser Black-backed nominate *fuscus*; some match *fuscus*). Others moult mantle and scapulars directly into adult or first-summer type, creating combination of grey saddle and juvenile-patterned wing (including pointed primaries) in spring. Bill normally bicoloured from midwinter.

The plumage during and shortly after spring migration (**first-spring**, Apr–mid-Jun) is rather characteristic and usually easy to identify among Herring Gull and Lesser Black-backed nominate *fuscus*; note that darker birds can be similar to Lesser Black-backed race *graellsii* and *fuscus*, and paler birds to Caspian Gull.

Head and underparts are white, at most with weak streaking especially on hindneck. Scapulars and new wing-coverts are rather pale brownish-grey, often whitish near tips, with dark pattern usually restricted to thin, dark shaft-streaks, although broader anchor-markings may be present. Juvenile wing-coverts (ranging from none to all) often look rather fresh. A few darker grey feathers of adult type may be present, and in most-advanced birds such dark feathers create dark saddle of almost adult type, creating a unique contrast to juvenile, still rather dark primaries. Tertials are either juvenile or grey with broad white edges. During summer, gradually acquires more adult-type mantle, and some coverts (especially median, of which sometimes all) intermixed with old, brown, pale-fringed feathers. Rump white, contrasting strongly with black tail-bar. Bill pale with black tip, often similar to first-year Glaucous Gull; rarely dark. Eyes dark, rarely pale. Legs greyish-pink, often with blue-grey tinge in tibia.

Identification of first-spring Heuglin's from Caspian Gull sometimes very tricky, although some individuals should cause no real problems. Main difference is structure, as almost all Caspian have small head with long, parallel-edged bill, slender, elongated body and long legs (described in more detail under Caspian); although certain Heuglin's may superficially look similar, they are much more compact. If the bird is heard, the typically laughing 'sea-lion' call of Caspian versus the deeper, hoarser call of Heuglin's should confirm identity. In more problematic birds, look for all-dark inner primaries of Heuglin's (normally with slightly paler window in Caspian, although matched by some Heuglin's). If there has been any flight feather and/or tail moult in winter, this is a strong indication for Heuglin's: Caspian normally moults P1 by May, when Heuglin's shows no active moult. Heuglin's should show a much broader tail-bar than Caspian, lacking the narrow zone of fine bars inside the main bar typical of most Caspian. First-winter coverts of Heuglin's are much fresher in spring, and even juvenile coverts never look so strongly bleached as in typical Caspian. Also look for underwing: rather uniform dark underwing-coverts are seen in many Heuglin's (never in Caspian), but both species may show whitish underwing-coverts. Many Heuglin's show rather dark, fresh scapulars,

always appearing paler in Caspian. Head usually all white in Caspian, often extensively streaked in Heuglin's. Adult-type upperpart feathers – if present – are conclusive, being dark slate in Heuglin's (but often paler than in adult), pale grey in Caspian.

Certain dark Heuglin's may even look similar to Lesser Black-backed Gull, although latter normally a smaller, lighter bird. Scapulars and wing-coverts usually differ strongly: in Heuglin's these feathers are pale grey with narrow dark shaft-streaks, while on Lesser Black-backed (especially nominate *fuscus*) they are darker with much more diffuse shaft-streaks (a very few *L. f. fuscus*, however, match Heuglin's in this respect). Many Heuglin's show two 'blocks' of lesser and greater coverts, the inner ones being fresher. In *L. f. fuscus* new and older coverts are often mixed, producing a 'piano keyboard pattern'.

Compared to most other large gulls, plumage development 'one year in advance' as in *L. f. fuscus* (Jonsson 1998b, *contra* Shirihai 1996b).

ID of older immature Heuglin's from Lesser Black-backed Gull races *graellsii/intermedius* based on combination of white head (with streaking restricted to hindneck), paleness of scapulars, rump and underwing, and late onset of primary moult. Second-winter *graellsii/intermedius* have even and coarser head pattern, darker pattern on underbody, darker and less distinct scapular pattern and generally darker bill. Generally moult earlier, with moult more advanced in autumn than in Heuglin's.

Second-winter similar to adult, but wing-tip uniform dark (often brown-tinged; rarely with small white mirror on P10) with dark markings on all primaries, inner primaries slightly paler and some secondaries dark brown. Normally a few brownish coverts intermix with sooty-grey upperparts. Greater coverts and tertials often ashy-brown with indistinct pale spotting or waving. Primary coverts brown with pale edges. Underwing white with dark rows. Tail white, normally with black in some feathers (especially T5–6); some have complete blackish tail-bar. Bill pale with black tip or subterminal bar. Legs pinkish or with slight yellowish cast. Less advanced birds closer to first-summer.

Second-summer as adult, but with variable amount of brown wing-coverts, dark streaks on hindneck and broken dark tail-bar. Outer wing uniform; normally lacks white mirror on P10. Legs sometimes greyish-pink, bill often with black subterminal bar.

Third-winter/summer similar to adult in respective plumages, but wing-tip blacker, white mirror on P10 at most faint. Some still with dark tail-markings. In summer often with dark streaks on hindneck, dark subterminal markings on bill and greyish-fleshy tinge to legs.

VOICE Deeper and stronger than Herring and Lesser Black-backed Gull: a nasal *gagaga* (Lindholm 1997).

MOULT (*L. h. heuglini*) Similar to Lesser Black-backed Gull nominate *fuscus*; later than in *graellsii/intermedius*.
Adult moult to **winter** plumage complete. Starts with P1–4 on breeding grounds mid-Jun–Aug; By mid-Jun, 2–5% have moulted P1. On Russkyi Zavarot peninsula, P1 shed between late Jun and late Jul (Buzun 2002).

Moult suspended prior to long-distance migration, and by early Sep most have only reached P4. At stopover sites in Romania, P6 reached by mid-Oct; P5–7 generally Nov. However, by mid-Nov small minority (failed breeders?) complete primary moult. In Oman early–mid-Nov, moult has reached P4–8 (P4 7%, P5 18%, P6 30%, P7 33%, P8 12%). P9–10 Jan–early Mar(Apr). Secondaries start when moult reaches P4–6 or later; sometimes not completed Apr. Tail in heavy moult Nov. Head mid-Oct–Dec. 50% in Oman have head-streaks from mid-Nov (Rauste 1999, V. Rauste & P. Schiermacker-Hansen *in litt.*; photos)

Moult to **summer** plumage partial Feb–Apr, including head, body, tertials and some coverts. Head moult may start Jan (when the most advanced may show summer head), but in Mar >85% still show winter head pattern. May attain winter head into mid-Apr.

Juvenile moult to **first-winter** partial, but mostly extensive Nov–Mar, following arrival on wintering grounds. Moult includes head and in 50% some mantle and scapulars (rarely all); these parts sometimes moulted directly into adult-like type (see moult to first-summer). Most moult some coverts and tertials, the most advanced (10–20%) all coverts and tertials (apart from primary coverts and some outer greater coverts), 10–20% do not moult any coverts or tertials. 10–20% moult some (rarely all) secondaries. Most do not moult any primaries; 5–10% some inner primaries (rarely more than five) and <1% all primaries winter–early summer. Tail partly moulted in 50% (Eskelin & Pursiainen 1998, Jonsson 1998c, Rauste 1999, V. Rauste *in litt.*).

'Moult to **first-summer**' partial Mar–May, including head and sometimes parts of mantle, scapulars and to a lesser degree tertials and coverts, into adult or near-adult type. The first-years 'moult into first-summer' can be regarded as last steps of moult into first-winter, or as first step of complete moult into **second-winter**.

Moult to **second-winter** complete May–Jan. Active moult of head, upperparts (including some coverts, especially inner and median coverts), some rectrices and P1–2 late May–late Jun. Rest of coverts, secondaries and tail Aug–Dec. Primary moult reaches P3–5 Aug, P9–10 (Sep)Nov–Feb, the most advanced completing moult before southward migration (Lindholm 1997, Rauste 1999, V. Rauste *in litt.*, photos and skins).

Moult of "*taimyrensis*" on average 1–2 months later than in nominate. P1 Jun–late Jul, P2–4 Sep (moult suspended during migration), P3–6 Nov, P8 early Dec, P9–10 late Jan–early Mar. Most moult P10 late Feb–Mar, but some have only reached P5–8 by Feb. Winter head present into Mar (Filchagov *et al.* 1992a, Kennerley *et al.* 1995, King & Carey 2000, skins in MCZ, NHM).

Immature moults earlier than adult with larger amount of moult in summering areas; normally 20–40% of moult to winter plumage completed before leaving breeding sites. Primary moult reaches P6 late Jul (Buzun 2002). A second-winter had reached P8 late Jul (this individual showed grey mantle and a few inner coverts only; dark tail-bar and slightly paler mottling at tail-base and whitish underwing with scattered dark markings, most striking on lesser coverts).

Plumage similar to Caspian of 'Steppe' form *barabensis*, which is smaller generally (size of Armenian) with rounded, all-white head, slenderer and weaker bill, smaller eyes and slight bluish wash to fresh upperparts; white tertial crescents sometimes lacking or weak. Bill and legs generally deeper yellow; bill with more distinct dark red and pale markings in winter (see Geographical Variation in Caspian Gull). *Barabensis* moults 1–2 months earlier than '*taimyrensis*', adult usually completed Dec–early Jan (Filchagov *et al.* 1992a, Garner & Quinn 1997, skins in MCZ, pers. obs. in India).

Other ages poorly known; probably as nominate before developing paler grey upperpart feathers.

DESCRIPTION

Adult Almost identical to Lesser Black-backed Gull race *graellsii*. Upperwing dark slate (Kodak Grey Scale 8–11), with blacker primaries. P10 black with 11–55mm white rounded or diamond-shaped mirror, sometimes restricted to inner web; base of inner web on undersurface pale grey. P9 black, 30–35% with 2–20mm white mirror, mainly in outer web; base of inner web grey to dark slate, in some contrast to black. Rest of flight feathers as Lesser Black-backed *graellsii* or slightly paler, but blackish subterminal spot on P4–6 often more distinct. Grey base of inner web rather sharply divided from black distal part; in P9-10 at 60° angle, in P3-8 rounded, suggestion that grey merges into black (Shirihai 1996b) seems erroneous. Black in P8-10 reaches primary coverts. P7 often with narrow white tongue on inner web. P6 with 60–100mm black outer web and 35–60mm black on inner web; often with 3–6mm white tongue on inner web. P5 normally with 25–40mm black tip and 7–10mm white tongue on inner web; dark subterminal markings sometimes lacking. P4 with varying dark subterminal markings, in best-marked birds solid on both webs, but in majority restricted to 15–20mm on outer web and isolated dark spot on inner web. Less than 5% black markings on P4 (normally those with largest amount of white on P9–10, probably males). 50% have max. 6mm white 'moon' on inner web. P3 sometimes with dark subterminal spot on outer web. All primaries apart from P10 have white tips, when fresh up to 12mm. P10 4–7mm > P9. Primary coverts as rest of upperparts; in some (probably young adults) with black shaft-streaks forming drop-spots; most frequent on outer 2–3 primary coverts. Shows broad white edges to tertials and scapulars. Eye yellow to pale yellow, in 80% with fine dark peppering, creating impression of brownish eye; spotting in <10% strong enough to create darkish-looking iris at distance. 5% have pale yellow eyes (Rauste 1999, Buzun 2002, V. Rauste & M. Collinson *in litt.*). Orbital ring red, rarer orange-red or orange (5%). Bill yellow with orange to red gonys-spot, not reaching upper mandible; may show dark markings at tip (often correlated with dark markings on primary coverts, this indicating younger adults). Bill shape often similar to Caspian Gull nominate *cachinnans*; nostril triangular, but narrow; depth at distal edge 1.2–3.2mm, length 9.6–14.5mm. Bill length:bill depth at gonys 2.8–3.5. Legs yellow, occasionally with fleshy tinge (Garner 1997); probably birds of E origin. 5–10% shows greyish-tinged legs (Buzun 2002) but feet always yellow. **Adult summer** (Apr–Oct) Head white. Bare parts bright.

Adult winter (Oct–Mar) Head usually with brown spots, drops or streaks on hindneck creating dark necklace. Sometimes entire head brown-streaked; normally finely, but sometimes stronger especially on ear-coverts and around eye, where sometimes forming eye-mask (V. Rauste *in litt.*). Bill duller than in summer, sometimes with dark markings especially on upper mandible, rarely as complete but irregular bar or well-separated spots. Gonys-spot dull red, but probably never absent (*contra* Shirihai *et al.* 1996). Legs grey with yellow or (more rarely) pinkish tinge; rarely bright yellow. Many show fleshy feet and yellow-tinged tarsus.

Juvenile (fledging–Dec) Head and underbody whitish with solid dark shading on ear-coverts (creating unpatterned, rather solid dark mask) and dark streaks on crown, sometimes reaching forehead as slight spotting. Underbody brownish-grey with slight darker streaks or spots especially on flanks. Mantle and scapulars dark brown with pale sandy edges, generally browner with broader, more solid pale edges than in Lesser Black-backed Gull nominate *fuscus* (in which dark often reaches feather-edges; less often this occurs in Heuglin's), creating strongly scaly pattern. Tertials dark brown with pale edges, broadest near tip, often irregular, but in others as in Lesser Black-backed or Caspian Gull (solid dark centres and regular pale edges); rarely with faint paler subterminal markings near tip. In birds with tertial pattern similar to Herring, pale edges much narrower than in northern Herring (from within range of Heuglin's Gull), but overlapping with more southerly populations (V. Rauste *in litt.*). Rump white with dark, often dense spots or bars. Upperwing-coverts greyish-brown with pale, often buffish edges, greater coverts with variable pale barring, generally narrower than in Herring nominate *argentatus*; barring sometimes reduced to inner 50% (as in Caspian and Yellow-legged Gulls), in others broader, matching Herring or even Great Black-backed Gull. In darkest birds greater coverts almost unmarked dark brown, with only narrow pale edges, thus similar to average Lesser Black-backed. Underwing-coverts pale with narrow dark edges, axillaries whitish with dark barring as in Eurasian Curlew *Numenius arquata*. Midwing sometimes paler; matching Caspian nominate *cachinnans* and certain pale-marked Lesser Black-backed nominate *fuscus*. Darkest birds have axillaries and coverts darker greyish-brown as in Yellow-legged Gull, but normally still finely barred. Undertail-coverts pale with dark markings, especially along edges as in Caspian and Yellow-legged Gulls, in others with distinct dark spotting in mid-part. Flight feathers dark brown; P1–5 sometimes with paler bases and inner webs against dark subterminal markings and outer web, creating faint pale window. Rump white with dark spotting. Tail blackish with white (sometimes narrow) base, which has variable dark mottling. Dark bar in T1 53–70mm. T6 dark, outer web with only faint pale markings along edges; rarely pale with dark markings reduced to near tip. Eyes dark. Bill black. Legs pinkish.

First-winter (Dec–May) similar to juvenile, but head whitish with narrow brown streaks on crown and ear-coverts (often creating dark mask) and broad dark spots/streaks on hindneck, sides of neck and breast. Shows narrow white eyelids. Underbody and flanks often densely dark-spotted, contrasting with whitish mid-belly. Mantle and scapulars greyish-brown with distinct blackish subterminal markings, which may be shaped as anchors, bars, broad spots or streaks; many retain most juvenile upperparts and moult directly to adult-type mantle, scapulars and usually some coverts. These feathers as adults or slightly paler, often with narrow dark subterminal markings and shaft-streaks, and paler edges. Eye dark. Bill black with pale base and tip. Few other gulls (or birds) change their appearance as much during their first ten months as do Heuglin's Gulls *heuglini*.

First-spring (summer) (Mar–Jun) Head, underparts and tail as first-winter, but a varying number (0–100%) of feathers on mantle, scapulars and coverts (especially inner and median coverts) of greyish-type with fine dark markings. Scapulars dark brown to pale brownish-grey with pale edges and dark markings (mainly as shaft-streaks, but sometimes as anchor-markings). Tertials juvenile or blackish-brown with 2–3 paler subterminal markings, darker markings on inner web or near tip, dark shaft-streaks and broad white tip. Bill pale flesh or yellowish with dark tip and often cutting edges; rarely mainly dark. Legs fleshy-grey to yellowish-tinged.

Second-winter (Jul/Sep–Feb) at first similar to first-spring (summer), but P1–5 grey with white tips. Moult continuous throughout late summer. Dark tail-bar generally narrower than in first-years but with similar dark mottling to tail-base; rarely broader. Markings on T5–6 sometimes restricted to dark spots near tip and fine barring on basal part. Bill pale with 20–22mm black subterminal bar and pale tip (6–7mm on upper, 5–8 on lower mandible).

From Sep/Nov, upperparts, wing and tail similar to adult, but with variable number of brownish-patterned coverts with fine pale vermiculations especially on greater coverts. In less advanced birds some or all scapulars are greyish with dark patterning, as in first-spring. Primaries (of second generation) variable. P1–5 grey (from pale grey to blackish) with white tips; birds with palest ground colour show darker outer webs and subterminal markings. P6–10 similar to adult, but brownish-tinged with narrower pale edges; if present, white mirror to P10 smaller. Secondaries, tertials and primary coverts blackish-brown with pale edges. Underwing white with narrow brown tips to especially lesser and median coverts and faint barring on axillaries. Tail with dark subterminal markings, in small minority as broad blackish tail-bar similar to first-years, but often broken into several bars. Bill fleshy to greyish-yellow with black subterminal markings and sometimes cutting edges; tip whitish. Eye often yellow. Legs fleshy to dull yellow.

Second-summer similar to second-winter or adult, but a variable (usually small) number of wing-coverts brown (normally a row of greater coverts), often strongly abraded. Tail sometimes with narrow black markings especially on T5–6; may show fine black transverse barring on entire tail. Head often with narrow brown streaks especially on hindneck. Bill similar to adult, but usually with dark subterminal markings; rarely fleshy with black subterminal bar. Legs often yellow.

Third-winter similar to adult, but a few lesser coverts

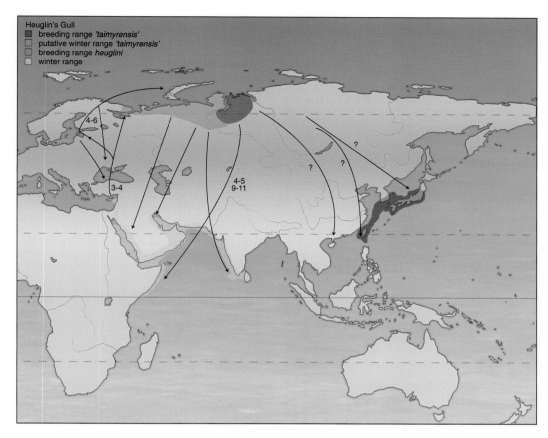

4-6

3-4

4-5
9-11

?

?

?

sometimes brown with pale edges, and primary coverts often brownish-tinged. Primaries often slightly duller, brownish-tinged with generally broader black markings on P3–4 and narrower white mirrors on P(9)10. Tail white, rarely with black markings on T4–6. Underwing white with scattered dark spots, especially on lesser coverts. Bill as adult, but often with slightly broader black subterminal bar.

Third-summer as adult, but primaries as third-winter. Orbital ring duller reddish-brown, bill often with dark subterminal markings and legs often fleshy-tinged (including foot).

Hybrids For hybridisation between Heuglin's Gull *'taimyrensis'* and Vega Gull, see latter species. There are some indications of hybridisation between Heuglin's Gull nominate *heuglini* and Lesser Black-backed Gull nominate *fuscus* in Finland, as birds showing intermediate characters are regularly observed in summer. It is still unclear if these birds are pale Lesser Black-backed Gull nominate *fuscus*, normal race *intermedius*, or hybrids (Koskinen *et al.* 2001, V. Rauste *in litt.*).

GEOGRAPHICAL VARIATION Two subspecies.
L. h. heuglini (Russian tundra between White Sea at Kola Peninsula, W Taimyr and Yamal Peninsula; often along rivers and at lakes. Winters Black Sea and Indian Ocean S to E Africa, and W to S India; probably E to

Hong Kong) Described above. Western birds darkest. Birds from N Taimyr/upper Yenisei generally paler, approaching darkest Vega Gull, generally with largest white mirror in P10, more often with white mirror on P9, dark eyes and fleshy-tinged legs, merging into *'taimyrensis'*.
L. h. 'taimyrensis' (Russian Heuglin's E of nominate *heuglini*, SW Taimyr and Yenisei to the Kara Sea. Winters mainly E Asia, but probably small numbers reach Indian Ocean S to equator). Regarded as hybrid between nominate and Vega Gull, created when Heuglin's Gull and Vega Gull come into contact at Gulf of Yenisei and Sev Taimyr. Similar to *heuglini*, but generally larger and paler with flatter forehead and heavier bill as in Herring Gull. **Adult** has paler slaty upperparts (Kodak Grey Scale 6–8) without brownish wash. Wing-tip pattern as in nominate, but black on P5 restricted (typically broadest on outer web) and P3–4 rarely with black subterminal markings, mainly restricted to outer webs (birds with extensive black may be intergrades with *heuglini*, or younger birds). P10 black with 20–55mm white mirror; P9 in 25% with 7–22mm white mirror, usually confined to inner web; P8 black with max. 20mm grey at base of inner web; P7 with dark outer web in curved division from pale basal part of inner web. White mirrors on P5–7 generally broader and more conspicuous than in nominate, penetrating onto inner web. Palest birds similar to Vega, darkest to nominate and Black-tailed Gull;

most birds are on paler side of range. Shows broad white tertial crescents and narrow white scapular crescents. Orbital ring red. Iris pale yellow, rarely dark (intergrades with nominate?). Bill as nominate, but red gonys-spot more frequently spreads to upper mandible to create impression of red bill-tip (Ujihara & Ujihara 2000). Legs bright yellow to greyish-yellow. Sometimes fleshy or pinkish, but birds with fleshy legs probably strongly influenced by gene-flow from Vega Gull (Kennerley *et al.* 1995, Yésou & Hirschfeld 1997, Panov & Monzikov 2000).

Head in winter with brown streaks, generally more distinct than in nominate; densest and broadest on hindneck (as necklace) and ear-coverts, sometimes covering whole head.

DISTRIBUTION AND MIGRATION Total population unknown. Nominate *heuglini* breeds in open tundra with bogs and marine islands in Russia between White Sea/Kola Peninsula to W Taimyr and Gydan/Yamal Peninsula, in E part of range intergrading with race *'taimyrensis'*. Breeding status in Finland uncertain. Arrives at breeding sites late May, leaving Sep/Oct.

Long-distance migrant. Nominate *heuglini* still present near breeding sites in N Russia in hundreds up to early Oct. Eventually migrates S to SE towards winter quarters. Probably scarce migrant Baltic Sea; Finnish autumn records all from S and E. In Israel, autumn passage mid-Aug–mid-Dec, peak Oct–Nov.; mainly along Mediterranean coast (flocks up to 50 Ma'agan Michael and 120 Shifdan). Scarce Eilat, where total of 35 late Oct–early Nov. Large migration Krasnowodsk, Caspian Sea, late Oct. Vanguards Persian Gulf/Oman Oct, autumn peak Nov, with many wintering more to the south. In S Oman most abundant large gull in autumn, but sometimes outnumbered by Caspian race *barabensis* (and definitely so in N Oman).

Winters sparsely E Mediterranean, N Red Sea (some tens Eilat), Black and Caspian Seas; main winter area S Red Sea, coasts of Arabian Peninsula, Gulf States and E to Pakistan/W India. Flocks of thousands include *barabensis*, especially between Gulf States and India, although outnumbering *barabensis* in S Red Sea. Scarce Nepal, Sri Lanka and along E African coast S to Dar es Salaam Nov–Mar/May. Vagrant C and S Europe, N Egypt, Maldives, Nepal, Hong Kong.

Spring migration late Feb–mid-May; most leave Oman and Bahrain by Mar. Peak in Israel mid-Mar–mid-May. At Eilat 100–300 yearly, usually associated with Lesser Black-backed Gulls; largest day-counts 43 on 20 April 1989. In early Apr 1999 daily max. 200–300 E coast of Sinai. Migration peak Arabian Gulf States late Mar–early Apr, Aral Sea Apr–early May. In spring probably regular E Mediterranean. Regular Finland, where more than 200 occur each spring, most at dumps around Tampere and Oulu; peak 32 Tampere on 5 May 2001. Adults arrive early Apr, and peak late Apr–early May. Younger birds some weeks later, with a longish 'peak' May–early Jun. Much scarcer in autumn, especially Oct–Nov. Occurrence in other parts of N and W Europe not fully understood (Glutz von Blotzheim & Bauer 1982, Cramp & Simmons 1983, Inskipp & Inskipp 1985, Bundy 1986, Meininger & Sørensen 1992, Shirihai 1996b, Topp 1997, Grimmett *et al.* 1998, Eskelin & Pursiainen 1998, Rauste 1999, H. & H. J. Lehto *in litt.*, A. Corso & V. Rauste *in litt.*, K. Thorup pers. comm.).

L. h. 'taimyrensis' breeds Russian tundra between SW Taimyr and Yenisei River to SE Yamal. Arrives breeding sites latter half of May and leaves Sep. Probably winters E Asia eastward from Japan and China S to Hong Kong (where flocks of max. 750 Jan–Feb claimed, although many *heuglini* seem to be involved). Status between Gulf States and W India uncertain; often claimed from these areas, but at most scarce—birds 'showing characters of *'taimyrensis'* (Garner 1997) too pale-backed and to my eyes represent late-moulting Caspian nominate *cachinnans*. Birds matching *'taimyrensis'* frequent W India; birds matching *'taimyrensis'* more than *heuglini* frequent E Africa down to Equator (Filchagov *et al.* 1992a, Grimmett *et al.* 1998, O. Thorup, P. S. Hansen & R. Strack pers. comm., A. Tate *in litt.*, pers. obs. in Kenya). Possi-

---

HEUGLIN'S GULL Three-year gull, resembling Lesser Black-backed Gull races *graellsii/intermedius*. Breeds tundra of N Russia, winters Middle East to Indian Ocean. Almost identical to Lesser Black-backed, but moult time and age development differs from western Lesser Black-backed.

Adult has slaty-grey upperparts; generally with white mirror on P10 only, and black markings reach P5 (rarely P4). Bill generally yellow, often duller than Lesser Black-backed. Legs yellow. Remains white-headed into Oct, when moult confined to P1–4; moults almost exclusively in winter quarters. In **winter** (Oct–Apr) head with narrow dark streaks, often confined to hindneck, but sometimes more extensive. Normally with broad dark markings on bill.

Juvenile (Aug–Dec) almost inseparable from Lesser Black-backed nominate *fuscus*, but generally greyer and colder with stronger dark mask in paler face, slightly paler inner primaries and narrower black tail-bar, reaching tips of tail-coverts. Retains mainly juvenile plumage into midwinter. Some acquire **first-winter** mantle and scapulars—greyish with distinct dark anchor-markings, but some moult directly into **first-summer** (May–Aug), where upperparts and to a lesser degree wing-coverts a mixture of juvenile/first-winter and grey feathers of adult type. Most renew secondaries in winter, secondaries now black with broad white tips contrasting with retained juvenile primaries; inner primaries often renewed as well. Tail often renewed; tail-bar blacker and more irregular than in first-year.

Second-year rather similar to adult, but with scattered browner wing-coverts, traces of black in tail and bill-tip and often no white mirror on P10.

Third-year as adult, but most with darker shaft-streaks to primary coverts and some dark markings on bill.

bly some *'taimyrensis'* overshoot migration of *heuglini* to winter in E Africa; more information needed.

MEASUREMENTS Lengths in mm; weights in g. Own data based on skins in MCZ, NHM, NNH, NRK, UZM, ZMA. *Heuglini* W Russia; Indian Ocean between Aden and India. *'Taimyrensis'* E Russia, China.

WING

L. h. heuglini

Adult male	423–469	(449.1)	19
Adult female	405–455	(428.0)	23
First-year male	438–464	(448.7)	11
First-year female	411–451	(433.0)	3

Note Stegmann (1934a) gives for 53 adults 425–490 (mean 448); largest birds E of Kara.

L. h. 'taimyrensis'

Adult male	429–476	(455.0)	20
Adult female	420–475	(439.3)	11
First-year male	441–465	(450.8)	6
First-year female	416–451	(435.9)	8

BILL

L. h. heuglini

Adult male	47.4–57.3	(54.2)	23
Adult female	44.7–54.0	(49.8)	28
First-year male	49.6–52.3	(50.9)	2
First-year female	45.6–51.4	(49.5)	5

Note Yudin & Firsova (1988) give for adult bill 49–63, Buzun (2002) 49.0-61.7, Panov & Monzikov (2000) adult male 49.2–58.8 (mean 54.7, n=15), female 47.6–57.4 (mean 51.4, n=6).

L. h. 'taimyrensis'

Adult male	49.2–64.8	(56.4)	20
Adult female	48.4–57.8	(53.1)	8
First-year male	50.3–57.9	(54.8)	6
First-year female	46.4–53.1	(50.5)	8

Note Yésou & Hirschfeld (1997) give for adult from SE Taimyr bill 51–68.

BILL DEPTH AT GONYS

L. h. heuglini

Adult male	15.8–20.0	(18.0)	23
Adult female	13.5–19.2	(16.3)	28
First-year male	15.1–17.4	(16.3)	2
First-year female	14.3–15.9	(15.5)	5

L. h. 'taimyrensis'

Adult male	15.4–20.9	(18.8)	20
Adult female	16.1–18.8	(17.2)	8
First-year male	16.0–19.3	(17.4)	6
First-year female	15.5–17.2	(16.0)	8

BILL DEPTH AT BASE OF BILL

L. h. heuglini

Adult male	16.8–21.3	(18.9)	19
Adult female	15.6–18.7	(17.2)	23
First-year male	16.0–20.1	(18.1)	2
First-year female	16.1–17.8	(17.0)	5

L. h. 'taimyrensis'

Adult male	18.5–22.4	(20.1)	20
Adult female	16.2–20.8	(18.0)	8
First-year male	16.2–20.5	(18.9)	6
First-year female	15.6–19.4	(17.3)	8

GONYS LENGTH

L. h. heuglini

Adult male	12.4–15.9	(14.7)	19
Adult female	12.3–17.1	(14.6)	23
First-year male	13.2–15.2	(14.2)	2
First-year female	12.7–15.6	(14.2)	5

L. h. 'taimyrensis'

Adult male	14.5–18.9	(16.1)	20
Adult female	13.6–17.4	(15.8)	8
First-year male	14.3–16.0	(15.0)	6
First-year female	13.6–15.8	(14.6)	8

TARSUS

L. h. heuglini

Adult male	64.0–72.0	(67.7)	19
Adult female	59.1–67.7	(63.5)	23
First-year male	67.3–68.8	(68.1)	2
First-year female	61.2–67.7	(64.3)	5

Note Yudin & Firsova (1988) give for adult 62–75. Panov & Monzikov (2000) adult male 61.2–71.2 (mean 66.4, n=15), female 60.5–69.8 (mean 64.6, n=6).

L. h. 'taimyrensis'

Adult male	65.3–77.8	(69.8)	19
Adult female	62.7–71.9	(66.7)	8
First-year male	63.1–72.8	(69.2)	6
First-year female	59.1–68.4	(64.6)	7

Note Yésou & Hirschfeld (1997) give for adult from NW Taimyr 61–79, from SE Taimyr 57–69. Panov & Monzikov (2000) adult male 64.3–73.7 (mean 68.7, n=18), female 59.7–67.7 (mean 62.8, n=8).

Weight *L. h. heuglini* adult male 900–1,300, female 745–1,055, first-year female 857 (Stegmann 1934a, Panov & Monzikov 2000, Buzun 2002, skins in UZM). *L. h. 'taimyrensis'* adult 880–1,360. Male 1,050–1,300, female 890–1,120 (Glutz von Blotzheim & Bauer 1982, Yésou & Hirschfeld 1997, Panov & Monzikov 2000).

Heuglin's Gull *Larus heuglini.* Photos refer to ssp. *heuglini* unless otherwise stated. **563. Juvenile**. Slightly larger with heavier bill than Lesser Black-backed *fuscus.* Many identical to *fuscus* in plumage, but mantle and scapulars generally with broader and more complete pale edges, creating stronger scaling. Compare 527-529. Archangelsk, NW Russia. 4 Sep 1998. *Visa Rauste.* **564. Juvenile.** Juvenile plumage kept into late autumn, appearing fresh into Dec. Almost identical to Lesser Black-backed *fuscus,* but note less patterned head, all-white belly and broader pale scaling on upperparts. Archangelsk, NW Russia. 3 Sep 1998. *Visa Rauste.* **565. Juvenile**. This individual shows rather prominent pale pattern on greater coverts. Wings proportionally shorter than in Lesser Black-backed *fuscus.* Archangelsk, NW Russia. 3 Sep 1998. *Visa Rauste.* **566. Juvenile**. Unlike Lesser Black-backed *fuscus,* inner primaries are often paler. Otherwise very similar to Lesser Black-backed *fuscus,* but generally colder-tinged. Black tail-bar narrower on average. Archangelsk, NW Russia. 1 Sep 1998. *Visa Rauste.* **567. Juvenile**. As in Lesser Black-backed, upperwing shows broad dark bars across greater coverts and secondaries. Archangelsk, NW Russia. 4 Sep 1998. *Visa Rauste.* **568. Juvenile.** Unusually dark bird, showing very broad dark tail-bar and prominent dark eye-mask. Apart from large males, which are larger and heavier than any Lesser Black-backed *fuscus,* and which sometimes give a Great Black-backed impression, such birds are impossible to identify from Lesser Black-backed, but note fresh juvenile plumage well into autumn. Archangelsk, NW Russia. 1 Sep 1998. *Visa Rauste.*

Heuglin's Gull *Larus heuglini*. Photos refer to ssp. *heuglini* unless otherwise stated. **569. Juvenile.** Underwing varies, but often with fine dark barring on pale background, or - as here - with paler greater coverts against darker lesser coverts and axillaries. Archangelsk, NW Russia. 4 Sep 1998. *Visa Rauste*. **570. 1st-winter.** Note that part of mantle and scapulars have been renewed. Shifdan, Israel. Late autumn. *Hadoram Shirihai*. **571. 1st-spring**. Note diamond-shaped mantle and scapulars, and broad pale edges to 1st-winter tertials. A less advanced individual than 572–573 and 575–578. Oulu, Finland. 26 May 1998. *Harry J. Lehto*. **572. Moulting into 1st-spring.** A few adult-type dark grey feathers present in upperparts. Archangelsk, Russia. 11 Jun 1999. *Visa Rauste*. **573. 1st-spring/summer**. The development of extensive adult-like feathers on upperparts combined with juvenile primaries are indicative for Heuglin's Gull at this age. Oulu, Finland. 1 Jun 1998. *Harry J. Lehto*. **574. 1st-spring/summer**. Note delicate barring on axillaries, often present in the species. Tampere, Finland. 29 Jun 2001. *Visa Rauste*.

Heuglin's Gull *Larus heuglini*. Photos refer to ssp. *heuglini* unless otherwise stated. **575. 1st-spring**. Note that P1 is missing; secondaries still juvenile. Mantle and scapulars as well as some inner wing-coverts of adult-type. Tampere, Finland. 29 Apr 2001. *Visa Rauste*. **576. 1st-spring/summer**. Note tail and rump pattern, dark primaries and late moult compared to Lesser Black-backed Gull ssp. *fuscus;* just P1 is shed which is typical for Heuglin's Gull; *fuscus* normally much more advanced, sometimes with all primaries renewed by spring. Oulu, Finland. 1 Jun 1998. *Harry J. Lehto*. **577. 1st-spring/summer**. Half of secondaries renewed, but all primaries juvenile. Tampere, Finland. 29 May 1999. *Visa Rauste*. **578. 1st-spring/summer**. Primaries still juvenile, whereas 50% of secondaries have been renewed. Oulu, Finland. 10 May 1999. *Henry Lehto*. **579. 2nd-summer**. Similar to 3rd-summer Lesser Black-backed *graellsii* and *intermedius*. Note scattered barred coverts in otherwise adult-looking upperparts and extensive dark bill markings. Oulu, Finland. 10 May 1999. *Henry Lehto*. **580. 3rd-summer**. As adult, but white primary tips narrower or lacking and bill still with dark subterminal markings. Legs often with greyish tinge. Oulu, Finland. 1 Jun 1998. *Harry J. Lehto*.

Heuglin's Gull *Larus heuglini*. Photos refer to ssp. *heuglini* unless otherwise stated. **581. 3rd-summer**. Lack of white mirror on P10 as well as extensive dark streaks on primary coverts and brown-tinged wing-tip indicate this age. Oulu, Finland. 1 Jun 1998. *Harry J. Lehto*. **582. 3rd- or adult summer.** Dark markings on bill indicate this age. Note similarity to Lesser Black-backed *graellsii*, but eye generally with dark peppering and bill often duller. Oulu, Finland. 1 Jun 1999. *Harry J. Lehto*. **583. Adult summer**. A larger strong-billed individual, in this aspect recalling Great Black-backed, but note paler upperparts and white mirror to just P10. Khaluf, Oman. Mar. *Hanne & Jens Eriksen*.

Heuglin's Gull *Larus heuglini.* Photos refer to ssp. *heuglini* unless otherwise stated. **584. Adult summer**. Dark markings on primary coverts in full adult are more frequent in large Asian Gulls than in other large gulls. Oulu, Finland. 2 Jun 1997. *Henry Lehto.* **585. Adult summer**. White mirror on P10 only is the rule, but a small number show small white mirror on P9. Oulu, Finland. 5 May 1998. *Visa Rauste.* **586. Adult winter**. Hindneck and parts around eyes often faintly streaked. Note fresh outer primaries, having been renewed by Jan-Feb. Shifdan, Israel. Feb. *Hadoram Shirihai.* **587. Adult winter** Bird showing largest amount of dark head-markings in winter, appearing as long, brown hindneck streaks reaching breast-sides. Note late primary moult. Shifdan, Israel. Feb. *Hadoram Shirihai.* **588. Flock.** Note moult stage in November, the primary moult to be finished Jan/Feb. Oman. 19 Nov 1998. *Per Schiermacker-Hansen.*

Heuglin's Gull. '*taimyrensis*'. This form is now generally regarded as a hybrid between Heuglin's Gull and Vega Gull.
589. Moulting into 1st-winter. Note that parts of upperparts are still juvenile at a time when Vega Gull would have shown 1st-winter mantle and scapulars. Tokyo, Honshu, Japan. 18 Feb 2001. *Ken Hatsuno*. **590. 2nd-winter with arrested moult**. Often noted as larger and heavier than *heuglini*. Chumunjin, South Korea. 11 Dec 2000. *Jon R. King*. **591. Adult winter**. Note upperpart colour intermediate between *heuglini* and Vega Gull, appearing too pale for *heuglini*. Legs dull yellow. Chumunjin, South Korea. 11 Dec 2000. *Jon R. King*. **592. Adult winter**. Note long-legged appearance and similarity to Caspian Gull regarding head-and-bill shape and eye-colour. Tokyo, Honshu, Japan. 20 Feb 2001. *Ken Hatsuno*. **593. Adult winter**. Wing-tip pattern in this individual as in *heuglini*. Honshu, Japan. Feb 2001. *Paul Doherty*. **594. Adult winter**. Note larger white mirrors on P9-10 than in *heuglini*. Honshu, Japan. Feb 2001. *Paul Doherty*.

IDENTIFICATION Length 57–61cm, wingspan 149–170cm. Pallas's Gull is the second-largest W Palearctic Gull, almost as large as Great Black-backed. Compared to the 'white-headed gulls' it has a flatter crown and heavier bill, creating a triangular head-shape, peaking far behind eye and with strongly angled hindneck. The body is fuller, sometimes making head curiously small. In settled birds, wings project moderately beyond tail-tip, enhancing impression of attenuated rear. Loosely folded tertials often create rather prominent hump. Legs longer and thinner with longer visible tibia, and upperparts paler.

In flight front-heavy with triangular head, long bill and deep breast. Jizz sometimes similar to Glaucous Gull in adults with their pale translucent primaries, showing isolated black markings. Wings longer and slenderer with more pointed tip than other large gulls. Flies ponderously with heron-like wingbeats, bill often held slightly down. Glides on angled wings with little flexing at carpal joint. Frequently catches fish by hovering and diving. When swimming sits higher on water than other large gulls.

In plumage development Pallas's is 'a small gull that has grown to a giant'.

Adult has dark eyes and broad white eyelids. The long and slender heavy bill is yellow with red and black bars and paler tip. Grey upperparts are darkest on mantle and scapulars. White wing-tip has varying amount of black. In head-view, black markings evident against translucent white primaries, at distance creating black triangle. Against dark background it disappears and the wing looks rounded. Black pattern varies, however, and in lighter-marked birds markings are narrow, at distance producing outer wing similar to Glaucous. The best-marked birds have mainly black wing-tip similar to Yellow-legged. Leading edge to outer wing and primary coverts white, so that front-viewed flying bird gives impression of an enormous Black-headed Gull. Legs greenish to yellow. In **summer** (from Feb) shows most conspicuous velvety-black hood, unmistakable among this 'King of Gulls'! In the hood white eyelids are most striking. Bare parts are at their brightest; legs deep yellow. In **winter**, head has varying dark triangle behind eye, often emphasising elongated head shape, but sometimes reduced to indistinct spot. White eyelids often remain conspicuous. Following primary moult, fresh primaries have broad white tips, creating more white than black on wing-tip. Bill duller with less red, more black than in summer, and legs duller yellow.

Juvenile has whitish to pale brown head, 'separated' from body by extensive brown spotting on hindneck and breast-sides, sometimes covering entire breast. Mantle and scapulars brown with pale scaling. Upperwing greyish-brown with darker flight feathers, faint pale window on inner hand and two broad pale wing-bars. Greater coverts uniform or just with faint darker markings. Underparts pale with white underwing, at most showing delicate scaly pattern, and dark comma on primary coverts. Blackish secondaries contrast clearly with rest of underwing – as dark rectangle – and the dark wingtip. A rather narrow clear-cut black bar against unpatterned white rump, tail-base and lower belly to undertail-coverts is conspicuous. Bill dark with paler base. Legs greyish to pink.

Unique for its size, Pallas's Gull develops grey mantle in **first-winter**, which has white head and dark eye-mask, as adult. The dark-spotted hindneck often creates brown necklace, reaching breast-sides and sometimes upper mantle. Wing as juvenile – similar to much smaller Mediterranean, with pale grey midwing and inner primaries contrasting with darker lesser coverts, secondaries and outer primaries. Bill pale with clear-cut black tip, often similar to first-year Glaucous. Legs sometimes greenish-tinged.

An ID pitfall is provided by large Caspian Gull *cachinnans*, which shares elongated head-shape and mainly white underwing, but bill less heavy, and often fully dark into winter. If present, dark eye-mask and white eyelids (especially below eye) are much weaker, barely affecting impression of mainly white head. Unlike Pallas's, inner greater coverts usually pale-barred, and mantle, scapulars, underwing-coverts and tail-coverts have fine dark pattern. The legs – although often narrow – are paler pinkish. Other large first-year gulls show darker-spotted flanks and undertail-coverts (at least edges) and always dark-pale barred greater coverts, much more extensive dark underwing-markings, barred mantle/scapulars and extra tail bars. This is true even in in second-winter large gulls, with pure grey saddle. The dark eye-mask of Pallas's Gull may superficially be matched by some Yellow-legged and Lesser Black-backed, but these – apart from other features mentioned – never show as broad white eye-lids as Pallas's. Note, that oil-polluted large gulls may exhibit what looks like a dark mask, but it is then brown and 'wrongly placed' – at ear-coverts, not as eye-mask.

First-summer similar to first-winter, but some develop dark half-hood. Wing pattern less contrasting, as dark parts bleach to brownish. Grey mantle usually 'spreads' to inner wing. Flight feathers and tail-bar bleached before spring moult.

Second-winter more like smaller than larger gulls of this age. Head as adult winter. Upperwing grey with dark wing-tip, 1–2 white mirrors, dark-centred primary coverts and alula forming several dark rows between wing-bend and tip. Black tail-bar, narrower than in first-years, often restricted to midtail. May show traces of dark lesser coverts- and secondary-bars. Underwing similar to first-years. Bill yellow to rosy with clear-cut black ring near tip and sometimes red gonys and orange tip. Legs olive-yellow to yellowish.

Second-summer similar to second-winter but with more

or less complete dark hood, duller than in adult and often white-spotted in foreparts. A few attain adult summer hood at this age. Dark on wings and tail retained well into summer, separating this age class from older birds, although often bleached. Bill similar to adult, but black terminal bar obvious.

The often extensively white-peppered hood and large amount of dark on wing-tip is shared by autumn Herring Gull, but with experience latter should not create problems. Pallas's best identified from Herring by former's dark mask in whiter head, stronger and much more contrasting bill, better-contrasting upperwing with unpatterned greater coverts, white rump to tail-base against clear-cut black tail-bar and unmarked white axillaries. **Third-winter** similar to adult winter, but with fuller black wing-tip, usually covering most of tips to 5–6 outer primaries. White mirrors on 1–2 outer primaries and white primary tips smaller than in adult. May show traces of dark tail-bar, mostly as broken spots on midtail. **Third-summer** similar to adult summer, but with reduced or no white primary tips (in P10 not reaching tip) and sometimes traces of dark in tail and primary coverts.

VOICE Not very vocal. Calls deep and short, on breeding-sites at deep *há-u*. From flocks a goose-like *ga-gaga*. A low, slightly nasal *oow*, similar to calls of Common Raven *Corvus corax* is lower than calls of other gulls. Alarm call a barking *whe-ow* (Walker 1981b, Urban *et al.* 1986, Keijl *et al.* 1995).

MOULT Adult moult to **winter** plumage complete May/Jun–Dec(Jan), starting during or shortly after breeding season. Primaries May/Jun–Dec(Jan), sometimes earlier; P1–5 have been renewed (early)late Jun/Jul, P8–9 Sep, P9–10 Oct–Dec(late Jan). Head and body late Aug–Sep.
Moult to **adult summer** partial Jan–Mar, including head and body, starting with hindcrown, ear-coverts and lower throat, leaving pale face/throat at end of moult. Summer hood assumed (Dec)Feb–late Mar (Robel & Beschow 1994, pers. obs.).
Juvenile moult to **first-winter** partial Sep–Dec, including head, body and rump. Mantle and scapulars normally renewed by Oct, but scattered juvenile feathers often present in first-winter. Sometimes moult a few inner median coverts and T1 late autumn.
Moult to **first-summer** partial Jan–Jun, including head, body, tertials and some coverts (especially lesser and median coverts), starting with inner median coverts (Jan–Feb).
Moult to **second-winter** complete May–Dec, on average one month earlier than adult. P1–2 May, P9–10 (late Sep)Nov/Dec. Secondaries generally later than primaries. One bird atypically moulted P9–10 late Jun (skin MCZ).
Moult to **second-summer** partial. Similar to adult summer, but generally one month after adult; head late Feb–early Apr.

DESCRIPTION
Adult Mantle and inner wing pale grey (Kodak Grey Scale 4–5). Marginal coverts and secondary tips white.

P6–10 whitish with black subterminal marks (max. 70mm on outer, min. 6mm on inner web) and 55–90mm white tip; P9 white with black markings on both webs before 55–90mm white tip; P8 with up to 100mm black outer web and 40–60mm black inner web; P7 with 40–60mm black subterminal spot on outer web, 30–42mm on inner web; P6 with 16–40mm black subterminal spot on both webs; P5 usually with small black spot, typically as isolated dark spot on both webs covering 15–18mm, but sometimes restricted to inner web. Primaries with 10–15mm white tips. Variation and pattern of black highly variable. In some (probably very old males), black marks much reduced or almost lacking. Alula and five outer primary coverts white, enlarging broad white leading edge to outer wing. Tail, underbody, axillaries and underwing-coverts white, rarely with faint grey bar across greater coverts. Iris dark brown. Orbital ring dark reddish-brown.
Adult summer (Jan–Aug/Sep) Hood glossy black with thick white eyelids or oval patches above and below eye, usually not joining at rear. White primary tips reduced through wear. Iris dark brown. Orbital ring red. Bill yellow to orange-yellow with 3–6mm black subterminal bar, sometimes reduced to isolated black spots or bars on both mandibles; rarely 'doubled' (skin in AMNH, photo in Barthel 1994a), small dark patch on upper mandible may be absent. Shows reddish to orange-red subterminal parts behind black bar, covering gonys and sometimes most of lower mandible. Extreme bill-tip pale yellow to orange, rarely red. Mouth and gape dull red. Legs yellow to orange-yellow.
Adult winter (Aug–Jan/Feb) Head white with dusky markings forming well-defined, often triangular patch behind eye, sometimes extending diffusely to hindcrown. The weakest-marked show faint streaks on crown and hindneck and often darker ear-spot. Conspicuous white eyelids. Hindneck white with blackish streaks or spots, densest on lower hindneck. Upperparts grey with narrow whitish fringes to most scapulars. Bill duller yellow than in adult summer with less red, but broader black subterminal bar (5–10mm). Legs dusky, greenish-yellow or yellow.
Juvenile (fledging–Sep/Oct) Head whitish with variable brown streaks behind eye, contrasting with brown hindneck and breast-sides (may form complete breast-band). Thin white eyelids above and broader below eye. Dusky crescent in front of eye. Mantle and scapulars greyish-brown to dark brown with whitish to pale buff edges, forming scaly pattern. Rump white with dark spots. Lesser coverts dark brown with pale fringes. Outer greater coverts, primary coverts and marginal coverts blackish-brown with broad pale grey to brownish-tinged edges. Inner greater coverts brown with pale grey edges; some greater coverts may show fine dark shaft-streaks. Tertials and secondaries black with whitish fringes, bases and edges, broadest on inner webs of inner secondaries. Primaries blackish-brown, P1–4 paler with clear-cut pale edges and tips, broadest on P1–2. Inner webs to all primaries with whitish bases, penetrating as white tongue towards dark tips. Underbody white with dark spots on tail-coverts, usually restricted to edges. Underwing-coverts and axillaries white with narrow, but distinct dark markings of vari-

PLATE 56. PALLAS'S GULL *Larus ichthyaetus*

A very large gull that breeds in the steppe lakes of Central Asia. Vagrant to W and N Europe, wintering in Middle East eastwards to Gulf of Bengal, also NE Africa. Could be regarded as an outsize Black-headed Gull. Almost as large as Great Black-backed Gull with flat forehead, square neck and large, parallel-edged bill. Head often smallish-looking against full, heavy body. Moderate primary projection above tail. Legs long and slender. Outside breeding season flocks with other gulls at coastlines, in estuaries and inland wetlands.

1.   **Juvenile** (Jul–Sep) Shows greyish-brown mantle and scapulars with broad, pale feather-edges, creating scaly pattern, but these parts quickly replaced by grey first-winter-type feathers. Coverts lack pale barring of other large gulls, thus similar to Common Gull. Head brownish-white with broad white eyelids, breasts-sides to hindneck greyish-brown. Bill long, slender and bicoloured. Legs grey with fleshy tinge. Tail-bar solid black, even in settled birds contrasting well with white tail-base. Underbody white, lacking dark markings of other large gulls.

2.   **First-winter** (Oct–Apr) Similar to juvenile, but head whiter with dark mask on ear-coverts and across hindneck, bill pink with black tip and mantle/scapulars grey, in contrast to rather uniform greyish-brown wing. May look short-winged and long-legged. Head flat and smallish.

3.   **Advanced first-winter** (Dec–Apr) Similar to first-winter, but parts of coverts and tertials renewed into grey, adult-like type. Note angled eye-mask extending into streaks on hindcrown. Brown streaks on hindneck create 'shawl'. Underparts pure white.

4.   **Second-winter** (Sep–Mar) Head and underparts as first-winter but bill with pale tip, and coverts now only with faint brown markings on especially lesser coverts.

5.   **Second-summer** (Feb–Sep) Head often similar to adult summer, but forehead and lores white-freckled. Upperwing still with brownish-patterned lesser coverts. Legs often duller than in adult and primaries black, at most with faint white tips.

6.   **Adult winter** (Sep–Feb) Head similar to younger winter, but upperparts grey and white primary tips always distinct (but prone to some individual variation). Swimming birds look flat-backed and often sit high in water.

7.   **Adult moulting into summer** (Jan–Mar) Acquires hood earlier than smaller hooded gulls. White primary tips may wear off to create mainly black wing-tip.

8.   **Adult summer** (Feb–Sep) Unmistakable. Complete black hood with broad white eyelids. Bill yellow with extensive red and narrower black markings. Legs bright yellow. Wing-tip often with more white than black.

1. Juvenile

2. First-winter

3. Advanced
first-winter

4. Second-winter

5. Second-summer

dult winter

Adult moult-
g into summer

8. Adult summer

PLATE 57. PALLAS'S GULL *Larus ichthyaetus*

In flight large with deep belly, slender head and bill and long, narrow wings. Flight ponderous with slow, deep wingbeats similar to Great Black-backed Gull.

1. **Juvenile moulting into first-winter** (Sep–Nov) Upperwing resembles that of much smaller Mediterranean Gull with dark leading and trailing edges to arm, paler midwing-panel and slightly paler inner primaries contrasting with dark wing-tip. Grey saddle already acquired by Sep–Oct. Head white with dark eye-mask; bill pink with black tip. Rump and tail-base unpatterned white, in contrast to distinct black tail-bar. Underbody and underwing whitish, underwing with faint dark markings (see below); lacks dark marking on undertail-coverts.

2. **First-summer** (Mar–Sep) Upperwing worn, grey of mantle spreads onto midwing, otherwise similar to first-winter.

3. **Second-winter** (Sep–Mar) Upperwing grey with extensive dark markings on distal parts of primary coverts, and black wing-tip with small white windows on P9–10. Tail still with solid black bar, but now edged white. Bill brighter than in first-winter.

4. **Third-winter** (Sep–Feb) Wing-tip rather similar to adult, but generally with more black, less white, and scattered dark markings still present on primary coverts and tail. By third-summer shows fully adult hood.

5. **Adult winter** (Sep-Feb) Head with dark markings on ear-coverts and across hindneck. Bill brightly coloured. Wing-tip whitish with black concentrated as bar across mid-part of outer primaries; white parts strongly translucent, 'isolating' black markings in head-on and side-on light.

6. **Adult summer** (Feb–Aug) Hood glossy black with white eyelids visible at long range. Bill bright yellow with extensive red markings.

Juvenile

1. Juvenile
moulting into
first-winter

2. First-summer

3. Second-winter

4. Third-winter

5. Adult winter

6. Adult summer

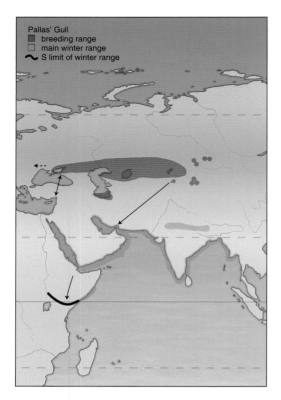

but generally darker-patterned; sometimes with incomplete dark cap, half-hood or large amount of dark on crown, ear-coverts and hindneck. Some retain first-winter head. Wing and tail similar to first-winter, but from midwinter often with a few grey coverts, starting with inner median (sometimes lesser) coverts and followed by tertials (grey, sometimes with dark centres or shaft-streaks). Bare parts as first-winter, but bill generally deeper yellow and legs greenish- to olive-yellow.

Second-winter (Jul–Apr) Head as adult winter. Upperparts grey, scapulars and tertials with white edges (broadest on tertials). Some mantle feathers may show narrow brown streaks or brown Us, sometimes doubled on back (Cramp & Simmons 1983). Shows conspicuous black markings to most or all primary coverts, forming several dark rows against pale wing-bend. Outer primary coverts black with white tips or edges, generally reduced to shaft-streaks on inner. Marginal and sometimes lesser coverts with some dark markings. Tertials grey with white edges, sometimes with dark shaft-streaks or subterminal spots. Secondaries grey with white edges and brown centres, shaft-streaks or outer webs to some or all, sometimes forming incomplete dark trailing edge to inner wing. Primaries mainly dark, P6–10 blackish with 20–30mm white mirror on inner web of P10 (sometimes also outer web), sometimes also small mirror on inner web of P9. Inner primaries gradually with less black, broader slate-grey bases; P5 with 23–30mm black tip, anchor-shaped, divided from whitish bases; P4(3) with less sharp division and smaller amount of black. Secondaries and P1–8 with white tips, only indistinct on P5–8. Underwing as adult, but with more black on wing-tip, often dark comma on tips of primary coverts and sometimes a few dark edgings to axillaries/some coverts. Tail white with black tail-bar, usually broadest in T1–3. T5 white with narrow dark spot on inner web, T6 usually all white. T1 with 27–45mm black bar (compare first-year). Orbital ring blackish. Bill yellow with black, clear-cut subterminal bar, pale ivory tip and sometimes orange to reddish tinge to gonys; sometimes as first-winter. Legs yellow to olive-yellow, rarely dusky.

Second-summer (Feb–Sep) as second-winter, but with more or less dark hood, similar to adult summer, but duller and usually heavily white-freckled, especially on lores, throat and forecrown. White primary tips gradually lost through wear. Orbital ring blackish to greyish-purple (Barthel 1994a). Bill as second-winter, but generally more orange-yellow basally. Sometimes similar to adult, but with 8–12mm black subterminal bar. Legs yellowish.

Third-winter (Jul–Apr) Head, body and wing similar to adult winter, but wing-tip more solid dark: primary pattern closer to second-winter, although blacker, normally with up to 60mm white mirror or tip to P10, max. 30mm white mirror on inner web of P9 and cleaner white bases than in second-winter, lacking dark anchor-markings or shaft-streaks. White primary tips on P5–10 narrower than in adult; primary pattern may recall Yellow-legged nominate *michahellis*. May show small dark subterminal spots to P4–5. P1–3 normally lack dark markings. Primary coverts usually with narrow dark spots or shaft-streaks. Tail usually with some dark mark-

able degree, forming dark lines, generally broadest and most obvious on tips of axillaries, lesser coverts and primary coverts (where form dark comma as in Mediterranean), sometimes also narrow markings on median coverts. Tail white with broad black subterminal bar, covering 30–40% of tail, usually extending in equal width onto T6 (which may show white outer web and is rarely all white). T1 with 58–100mm black bar. Iris dark brown. Orbital ring dark grey. Bill blackish with paler bases, especially near base of lower mandible. Legs lead-grey, brownish-grey or fleshy, rarely with yellowish or greenish tinge.

First-winter (Aug–Apr) Wing and tail as juvenile, but head with dark mask, covering eye to ear-coverts, and often broadening to streaks on rear nape. Pale-headed birds only show narrow brown streak behind eye. White crescents above and below eye emphasised by dark mask. Hindneck and sides of (sometimes entire) breast often with obvious brown spots in contrast to grey mantle, back and scapulars, on upper mantle sometimes with brown-black central blotches; a few mantle feathers may show pale edges. Rarely, juvenile mantle, scapulars and back retained. With wear, greater coverts and P1–5 generally paler, dark areas fading to brown and white tips to rectrices often disappearing with wear. From Dec often with some new uniform grey median coverts. Bill pinkish with grey or yellow tinge and broad black tip. Tip paler from winter (where rarely shows traces of red gonys-spot). Legs olive-greyish from midwinter.

First-summer (Feb–Sep) Head similar to first-winter,

PALLAS'S GULL Three-(four-)year gull, with quicker age development in first year than other large gulls. The second-largest gull, full-bodied with rather small, almost triangular head. Long, sloping forehead merges into massive bill. Shows full tertial step, but rather short primary projection beyond tail. Legs long and rather slender. Eyes dark. In flight long-winged with full body and long, sloping forehead.

Adult has pale grey upperwing with whitish outer wing showing narrow black area against white tip. Bill yellow with red and black tip. Legs yellow. In **summer** (Jan–Aug) hood jet-black with broad white eyelids. In **winter** (Sep–Jan) head white with black mask from eye to hindneck; division often angled on ear-coverts. Bill duller than in summer.

Juvenile has greyish-brown head and breast-sides and white eyelids. Upperwing resembles much smaller Mediterranean Gull with dark leading and trailing edges to inner wing contrasting with paler greater coverts and inner hand. Tail white with black bar. Underwing mainly white. Legs fleshy. Bill at first dark. In **first-winter** (Sep–Mar) head is whiter with dark mask and white eyelids similar to adult winter; develops grey saddle, which contrasts well with brown-spotted hindneck and juvenile wings. Lower body, rump and tail-base clean white lacking dark spotting of other large gulls.

Second-year shows grey upperwing with broad black tip, white mirrors on P9–10 and dark secondary bar, dark-marked primary coverts and tail-bar, the latter often incomplete. Bill yellow with black markings. In summer often develops incomplete hood, in second-summer often complete.

Third-year similar to adult, but black wing-tip usually more complete; may show scattered dark tail-markings.

ings, as isolated dark spots or streaks forming incomplete tail-bar, strongest on T1–4. Bare parts as adult winter. Some probably acquire adult plumage at this age.

Third-summer (Jan–Sep) as adult summer, but wing as third-winter (with more complete dark tip than in adult). Sometimes with less glossy, slightly white-spotted hood and narrow dark marking on primary coverts. Bare parts as adult, but orbital ring probably duller reddish-brown.

Fourth-winter (Aug–Feb) as adult winter. Birds with combination of more solid black wing-tip and a few dark-patterned rectrices should be considered 'fourth-winter type'.

Fourth-summer as adult, but sometimes with dark tail-markings. Birds with the most complete black subterminal bars around tip of bill are probably younger adults.

DISTRIBUTION AND MIGRATION Total population not estimated. Breeds barren islands in saline and fresh waters, generally in warm dry steppe areas, but also mountain lakes up to 1,700m, exceptionally higher. Often changes colonies (Dement'ev & Gladkov 1969, Hagemeijer & Blair 1997). Winters along fish-rich coasts, rivers and lakes, often on fish-ponds or reservoirs.

Estimated population European Russia/Ukraine 45,000–50,000 pairs mid-1990s, following increase of 150–200% throughout 1980s; in Ukraine just 145 pairs 1954, strong increase to 1,500 pairs in 2001. In 1987 largest colony was at Maly Zhemchuzhny Island, N Caspian: 42,000 in 1987. Several colonies >1,000 pairs in Caspian region. Future decrease expected when current reduced Caspian Sea water level is partly restored (Ecsedi 1996, Hagemeijer & Blair 1997, Ullman & Larsson 1998).

Migratory. Leaves breeding sites soon after young are fledged to gather at roosts before the late autumn migration. Cross inland Asia from breeding sites to winter quarters in Indian Ocean. Migration peak SE Kaza-

khstan mid Sep–late Oct, SE Caspian Sea Nov–Dec. Migrates Cyprus and Turkey to winter quarters along E Mediterranean coastline (Cramp & Simmons 1983, Il'icev & Zubakin 1990).

Winters E Mediterranean, Middle East, S Caspian Sea (very common), Indian Ocean from Arabian Peninsula, Gulf States, Pakistan, India and Sri Lanka to Burma. Also Turkmeniya, Azerbaijan, Iraq, Iran; Scarce Crimea, Black Sea and inland waters/rivers S of breeding range, e.g. NE Africa. Arrives late to wintering areas; peak late Dec–Mar.

In winter scarce S Turkey; max. 219 Yediker Baraji on 14 January 1997. Winter population Israel 2,200 1992/1993, before 1967 only vagrant. Largest numbers mid-Dec–mid-Mar Hulah and Beit Shean valleys and fishponds at Ma'agan Michael; max. 1,100 Beit Shean on 20 February 1993. Israeli spring passage peaks mid-Mar–early Apr, first adults, followed by immatures. Winter census N Egypt 35; 84 Suez mid-Mar probably on migration. Common Persian Gulf. Vanguards Oct, peak Jan–Mar; 600–1,000 yearly UAE; max. numbers per site 184; 570 offshore Abu Dhabi in Jan. Peak Bahrain Feb–Mar; max. flock 125 on lakes. Other counts include 100 Hamun-i-Puzak, SW Afghanistan; 100 several sites in Oman (Gulf, Masirah); 50 Iraq; flocks of 20 Nepali river systems; max. 55 Goa, India (peak Jan); and hundreds Bangladesh. Regular eastwards to W Thailand. Probably regular Yemen. Uncommon Bhutan. In NE Africa some hundreds Ethiopia, 50 Egypt and scarce S to Rift Valley Lakes of Kenya. Rare Tanzanian coast, mainly immatures Dec–Jan (Bundy & Warr 1980, Scott & Carp 1982, Inskipp & Inskipp 1985, Bundy 1986, Everett 1988, Lewis & Pomeroy 1989, Hirschfeld 1992a, Meininger & Sørensen 1992, del Hoyo et al. 1996, Porter et al. 1996a, Shirihai 1996b, Richardson & Aspinall 1997a & b, Grimmett et al. 1998, O. Amstrup, R. Strack, K. Halberg pers. comm., pers. obs.). Spring migration late Feb–Mar. Asian inland migration peaks Mar–Apr. Arrives Mongolian breeding sites Apr. In Tschany Sea, adults peak late Mar–early

Apr, immatures later. Scarce Hong Kong (max. 8 on 8 March 1994). Many immatures summer in winter range.

Regular SE Europe in increasing numbers from late 1980s, especially May–Sep. Most recorded Hungary (in 1990s regular 1–8(13) late summer, especially Horto-bagy), Bulgaria (Sep–Apr, most Black Sea), Romania and Poland (30); probably after following Dnepr River system from Ukraine. Increasing numbers in Europe linked with increase in W Palearctic breeding and win-tering populations. In Italy now regular in winter in Sicily (5–7 yearly). In Greece 16, most Jun–Sep. Vagrant Tunisia, Morocco, Canary Islands, Madeira, Denmark (2), Norway (2), Germany (4), Belgium (3), Nether-lands (2), France (1), Great Britain (1). In Africa vagrant W to Morocco and S to Uganda. In Asia Viet-nam, Korea, E China, Japan (Il'icev & Zubakin 1990, Carey *et al.* 1995, Enticott & Tipling 1997, Escedi 1998, Nankinov 2000, A. Corso *in litt.*).

MEASUREMENTS Lengths in mm; weights in g. Own data based on skins in MCZ, NHM, NNH, NRK, USNM, UZM, ZMO. Israel, Egypt, Caucasus, Caspian Sea, Ara-bian Sea, Burma, India, Himalayas. Included in adults are a few second-years, which had measurements iden-tical to adults.

WING

Adult male	470–520 (498.2)	47
Adult female	457–506 (473.4)	41
First-year male	458–502 (479.6)	12
First-year female	435–487 (457.3)	19

BILL

Adult male	56.8–72.8 (64.0)	40
Adult female	47.5–67.3 (57.5)	40
First-year male	55.9–68.8 (62.1)	12
First-year female	49.8–60.8 (55.4)	19

BILL DEPTH AT GONYS

Adult male	17.7–22.2 (20.6)	37
Adult female	16.5–20.8 (18.3)	40
First-year male	17.0–20.1 (18.4)	12
First-year female	15.1–18.3 (16.7)	19

BILL DEPTH AT BASE OF BILL

Adult male	19.7–25.0 (22.0)	37
Adult female	17.2–22.5 (19.5)	40
First-year male	18.4–23.0 (20.4)	12
First-year female	16.4–20.9 (18.3)	19

GONYS LENGTH

Adult male	14.3–19.8 (16.1)	37
Adult female	13.2–18.3 (14.9)	40
First-year male	13.2–18.8 (15.9)	12
First-year female	12.8–15.3 (14.3)	19

TARSUS

Adult male	69.7–83.8 (78.7)	39
Adult female	65.0–80.0 (72.2)	40
First-year male	69.2–80.4 (75.1)	12
First-year female	63.3–81.6 (69.5)	19

Weight Adult male 1,079–2,000, adult female 960–1,500, first-years 900–1,200 (Glutz von Blotzheim & Bauer 1982, Cramp & Simmons 1983, skins in NHM).

595

Pallas's Gull *Larus ichthyaetus.* **595. 1st-summer.** Hindneck often densely dark-spotted, creating necklace. Note overall shape and unmarked grey greater coverts. Israel. Jul 1988. *Hadoram Shirihai.*

Pallas's Gull *Larus ichthyaetus*. **596. 1st-winter**. Very large with flat crown and grotesque long, heavy and bicoloured bill. Shows broad white eyelids. Note that 1st-winter has all-grey saddle as in smaller gulls. Al Qumela, Oman. Feb. *Hanne & Jens Eriksen*. **597. 1st-winter**. Wing-pattern recalls much smaller Mediterranean Gull, but is slightly weaker. Note distinct black tail-bar. Israel. Dec 1993. *Markus Varesvuo*. **598. 1st-winter**. Note white underwing-coverts (although narrow dark lines sometimes present on lesser coverts) contrasting well with darker secondaries. Goa, India. 14 Feb 1999. *Klaus Malling Olsen*. **599. 2nd-winter**. Similar to adult, but note extensive dark markings on primary coverts and all dark-looking primaries. Compare size with Armenian Gull in background and Black-headed Gulls. Israel. Late winter. *Hadoram Shirihai*. **600. 2nd-winter**. Note wing-pattern at this age and compare to 603. Al Qumela, Oman. Feb. *Hanne & Jens Eriksen*.

Pallas's Gull *Larus ichthyaetus*. **601. 2nd-winter.** In winter shows dark mask, enhancing white eyelids. Israel, Dec. *Markus Varesvuo*. **602. 3rd-summer**. As adult summer, but generally with more extensive black in wing tip, and in this bird, black tail-markings. Goa, India. 14 Feb 1999. *Klaus Malling Olsen*. **603. 3rd-winter moulting to summer plumage**. Head moult in this species early with most showing summer hood from late Feb. Shuwaymiyah, Oman. Jan. *Hanne & Jens Eriksen*. **604. Adult summer**. Unmistakable - the king of gulls! Note velvety black hood, conspicuous white eyelids and strong, tricoloured bill. Al Qumela, Oman. Feb. *Hanne & Jens Eriksen*.

Pallas's Gull *Larus ichthyaetus.* **605. Adult summer**. Black hood combined with large size diagnostic. Note how black markings on wing-tip are surrounded by translucent white. Israel. Dec 1993. *Markus Varesvuo.* **606. Adult winter**. Note narrow black markings on the wing-tip and outer wing paler than inner wing. Ras Al Hadd, Oman. Feb. *Hanne & Jens Eriksen.* **607. Adult summer**. Bird with minimum amount of black in wing-tip. Ras Al Khabbah, Oman. Feb. *Hanne & Jens Eriksen.* **608. Adult summer.** Ras Al Khabbah, Oman. Feb. *Hanne & Jens Eriksen.*

28. BROWN-HEADED GULL
Larus brunnicephalus (Jerdon, 1840, west coast of Indian Peninsula)

Plates 58–59, Photos 609–620

IDENTIFICATION Length 41–43cm, wingspan 105–115cm. A S Asian gull often found alongside the similar Black-headed Gull, but is larger and stockier with a flatter crown, slightly stouter, drooping bill and longer legs. Swimming birds tend to raise their necks as do Slender-billed Gull, with which Brown-headed shares general shape. Wings generally longer with broader, rounder tip. Flight slower than Black-headed. Wing-tip with broad black tip; closer to Grey-headed than Black-headed Gull in showing fuller black tip with white mirrors.

Adult has black wing-tip with white mirrors similar to Common, black decreasing inwards as black tip to wing against obvious white primary bases, creating white half-moon between black wing-tip and grey upperwing. This pattern is especially striking against the light, caused by translucency of feathers, and from below contrast with pale grey underwing-coverts. Upperparts are darker grey than in Black-headed, and white trailing edge to inner wing therefore more obvious. Eyes white; bare parts similar to Black-headed, but brighter red. In **summer**, hood brown, shading to blackish at rear (most striking with wear). White eyes create 'cold' fish-eyed look, surrounded by broad white eyelids.

In **winter** head is white with dark ear-spot, often larger than in Black-headed and of more elongated shape. Legs and base of bill sometimes deep pink or raspberry.

Juvenile shares head pattern and dark eye with Black-headed, but again has different wing pattern: primaries black with white restricted to streaks on inner primaries; from below, hand looks completely dark in pale grey underwing. Black alula and primary coverts more obvious. Compared to Black-headed, lesser and median coverts darker brown with broader pale edges, creating scaly pattern. Inner and outer greater coverts often dark-centred. Bill orange-red with black tip. Eyes become paler from about 5–6 months.

Black-headed Gull may rarely show fuller dark markings on wing-tip, but never the clear-cut blackish tip of Brown-headed. Grey-headed Gull is more similar, but has darker underwings.

Many first-years undergo a very early moult of wing-coverts and often tail and secondaries in winter, before primaries. This is unique in small gulls.

First-summer similar to adult winter, but generally with more extensive head-markings, sometimes similar to first-summer Mediterranean. Retained juvenile primaries (sometimes secondaries) become paler through wear, but upperparts normally better retained as moulted in midwinter. In winter and spring, unmoulted white primary coverts contrast clearly with grey coverts to create large white patch against black wing-tip and grey inner wing. Most retain winter head; small minority with more or less adult summer hood.

Second-winter similar to adult winter, but generally with smaller white mirrors on wing-tip (frequently lacking),

dusky shaft-streaks on primary coverts and sometimes dark tail-markings.

VOICE A raucous *keear* or *geek* is deeper and gruffer than in Black-headed Gull. Also a loud wailing *ko-yek ko-yek* (Hollom *et al.* 1988, Grimmett *et al.* 1998, MacKinnon & Phillips 2000).

MOULT Adult moult to **winter** plumage complete Jun–Oct. Up to P8 renewed by early Sep; P9–10 Oct. Head and body late Jul–early Sep. Moult to **summer** plumage later than in Black-headed. Hood from (mid) late Feb, starting with crown and ear-coverts; sometimes lores. 50% of head renewed late Feb–Mar. Most with summer head late Mar; 5–7% white head-markings early Apr. Chin and throat renewed last.

Juvenile moult to **first-winter** plumage partial Aug–Sep, including head and body. 40–50% of mantle and scapulars renewed by Sep, latest on upper mantle and hind-neck. A few juvenile mantle feathers usually present Oct.

Moult to **first-summer** much earlier than in Black-headed; mostly before Apr, including larger amount of feather groups. Tertials, body and most wing-coverts mid-Oct–Mar; some still with juvenile wing late Nov; tertials Jan–Feb. By Jan/Feb, most coverts renewed, inner greater coverts and scattered lesser coverts latest. Secondaries mid-Feb–Apr (5% have not started moult first half of May). Tail from Jan, starting with T1; most-advanced birds have completed tail moult Jan, most others late Feb–early Mar. A minority still have juvenile secondaries and part of tail May–mid-Jul. Tail and upperwing-coverts often before secondaries.

Note The above description is mainly based on Thai birds (van den Berg *et al.* 1991). In Goa, India, mid-Feb secondary and tail moult seem to start slightly later: 80% had juvenile secondaries; 20% up to five new inner secondaries; >70 with juvenile tail, 25% with T1–3 renewed and 5% with whole tail renewed. Upperwing-coverts renewed: 5% had a few juvenile lesser coverts (pers. obs.). This moult of secondaries and tail supported by skins (van den Berg *et al.* 1991, Bradshaw 1993, pers. obs. in India and E China; skins in AMNH, MCZ, NHM, NRK, USNM, UZM).

DESCRIPTION
Adult Upperparts, inner primaries and secondaries medium grey (Kodak Grey Scale 4–6). P10–9 with white mirrors, on P10 30–47mm (rounded or triangular), on P9 12–40mm. Some have equal amount of white on P9–10. P8 black, in 10% with 5–15mm white mirror on inner web (mainly males). P6–10 have black tips, P8–6 pale grey inner webs; P7 black with pale grey base to inner web to 70–80mm before tip. Gradually less black on P6–4; P2–3 rarely with black to sooty-grey subtermi-

nal spots/inner webs. Bases to P5–10 white; broadest on P5–6. Bases to P1–4 grey. Primary coverts, alula and median coverts white. Secondaries grey with white tips. Underbody, axillaries and tail white, underwing-coverts pale grey. Iris white to dull yellow. Orbital ring dark. Bill dark red (rarely deep pink) with black tip. Gape orange-red. Legs dark red, crimson or deep pink.

Adult summer (Mar/Apr–Aug) Hood medium brown, darkening towards rear to form blackish border. Conspicuous white eyelids above and below eye broader than in Black-headed. With wear, hood fades and from midsummer often pale brown with obvious blackish border.

Adult winter (Aug–Mar) Head white with dark, sometimes elongated ear-spot, dark eye-crescent and variable amount of dark shading on crown and hindneck. Some have dark bar from eye to eye. Head pattern similar to Black-headed, but dark shading normally less distinct and often lacking; some white-headed apart from dark ear-spot. Dark loral spot generally broader than in Black-headed.

Juvenile (fledging–Aug) Head and upperparts similar to Black-headed, but on average with fainter brown carpal bar (although some have dark brown bar). Head and mantle greyish-brown. Lesser coverts and median coverts dark brown with broad white edges, creating scaly pattern, more obvious than in Black-headed. Greater coverts medium grey, sometimes with darker shaft-streaks on outer- and innermost. Primaries black with white to grey inner webs to P1–6, where up to 40–50mm; gradually narrower towards wing-tip, creating blackish wing-tip. P1–6 with narrow white tips (in P1 up to 8mm). Secondaries black to blackish-brown with white tips. Primary coverts usually with dark spots or shaft-streaks, broadest on outer, where often forming drop-shaped spots; rarely all white. Alula and tertials dark brown to black with white edge. Uppertail-coverts white, rarely dark-spotted. Underwing-coverts whitish. Primary coverts dark-tipped, broadest on greater. Tail white with black subterminal bar (20–40mm in T1). T5–6 white, often with narrow dark spots near tip; T6 sometimes white. Iris at first brown, but becomes paler to yellowish or medium brown in late autumn/winter (Hoogendoorn 1991a & b); some dark-eyed to Feb. Orbital ring dark. Bill orange to red with black tip. Legs orange to dull dark brown.

First-winter (Aug–Feb) as juvenile, but head, back and underbody similar to adult winter following moult (which see).

First-summer (Jan–May (Jul)) Following moult similar to adult winter, but with retained juvenile primaries and often some (rarely all) secondaries and T5–6. Outer median coverts and greater coverts often with dark shaft-streaks. Some as adult apart from a few juvenile secondaries. Most retain winter-like head, but small minority develop partial dull greyish-brown hood. Iris whitish to yellowish-brown.

Second-winter (Jul–Apr) similar to adult winter, but some show scattered dark-centred primary coverts, dark shaft-streaks on outer median coverts and greater coverts and indistinct dark tail-markings. Primaries often browner with smaller white mirrors.

GEOGRAPHICAL VARIATION Monotypic. Birds from Qinghai smaller than those from Pamir and Tibet. Measurements in Qinghai birds: wing 319–336, bill 34.8–38.5, tarsus 44.4–52.3. Adults combined; material limited (Il'icev & Zubakin 1990). Pamir population said to show intermediate characters with Black-headed Gull (del Hoyo *et al.* 1996); more information required.

DISTRIBUTION AND MIGRATION Population unknown; 1,000 pairs Pamirs, Tadjikistan, 300 pairs Karakul Lake 1977, but only 25–30 1983. Breeds between Aral Sea and C China, mainly Tibetan plateau at 3,000–4,500m, in Jun–Jul in dense colonies on islands and marshes in large cold lakes of varying salinity, often with Common Tern (Hazevoet 1987, Il'icev & Zubakin 1990, del Hoyo *et al.* 1996, Grimmett *et al.* 1998).

Autumn migration Aug–Oct. through Pamirs, Himalayas and Brahmaputra. Vagrant E China. Leaves Tibet Oct, where a few winter. Winters in flocks of hundreds along coasts, on lakes and river mouths along Indian Ocean, mainly between Pakistan, Sri Lanka and Thailand, scarcer Nepal and W Yunnan; rare, but regular Hong Kong.

Large flocks gather Thailand before migration, e.g. 2,000 Samut Sakhon 29 Mar 2003. Spring migration along Brahmaputra late Mar, in Nepal Apr (with groups of max. 35 Kosi Barrage). Arrives S Tibet mid-May. First-years summer sparsely at Bukhara, Uzbekistan (Inskipp

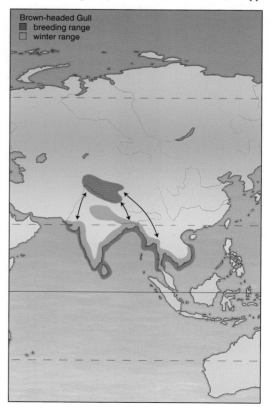

Brown-headed Gull
■ breeding range
□ winter range

PLATE 58. BROWN-HEADED GULL *Larus brunnicephalus*

Breeding range restricted to Tibetan Plateau. Winters S and SE Asia. Similar to Black-headed Gull, but slightly heavier.

1.   **First-winter** (Aug–Jan) Similar to Black-headed Gull, but bill generally darker orange-red and wing-coverts with slightly broader pale edges. Legs longer.

2.   **First-spring/summer** (Feb–Aug) Unlike other gulls, moults most of coverts, tertials and parts of secondaries and tail by midwinter, thus looking more adult. Compared to adult, settled birds show more uniform black wing-tip and eyes normally dark.

3.   **Adult winter** (Aug–Mar) Overall appearance similar to Black-headed Gull, but head slightly larger and bill slightly heavier; bare parts often brighter red or even rosy-tinged. Eyes pale. Head pattern often less extensive than in Black-headed, especially on crown. Note white mirror on P10 surrounded by black.

4.   **Adult summer** (Mar–Aug) Hood brown, often paler towards face, and when worn often in quite good contrast to black border. Pale eye largish-looking caused by both colour and white eyelids, the latter similar to Black-headed. Bill and legs dark brownish-red, often 'red-wine-coloured' or even rosy-red.

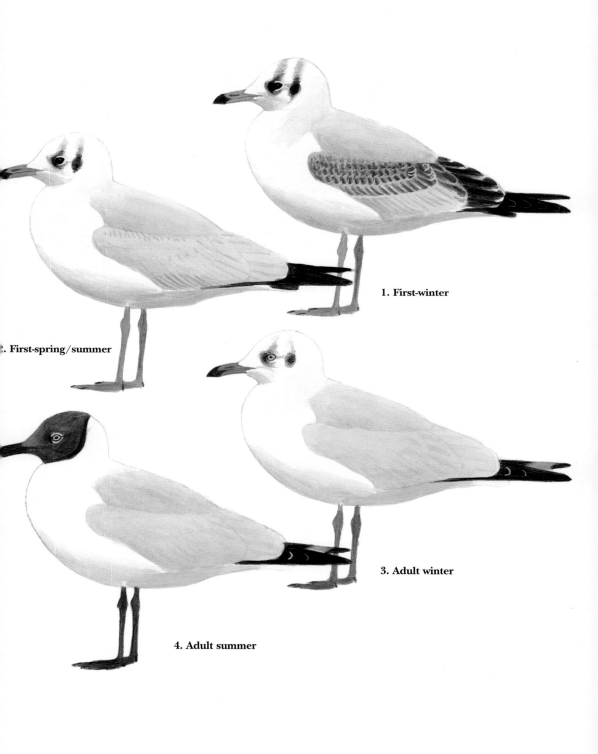

1. First-winter

2. First-spring/summer

3. Adult winter

4. Adult summer

PLATE 59. BROWN-HEADED GULL *Larus brunnicephalus*

Similar to Black-headed Gull, but with solid black wing-tip

1. **Juvenile** (Aug–Oct) Upperwing similar to Black-headed Gull, but wing-tip solid black with white restricted to streaks on inner primaries, and primary coverts dark-streaked (Black-headed invariably shows larger white areas on outer primaries, and often white, unpatterned primary coverts). Juvenile mantle and scapulars generally paler and more greyish-brown than in Black-headed. Coverts with broader pale tips and edges. Note solid dark on entire outer wing, differing from Black-headed, which shows paler outer primaries.

2. **First-winter** (early Oct–Jan) By winter some median coverts are renewed. This individual shows slightly more extensive white on inner primaries than 1.

3. **First-summer** (Jan–Aug) By Jan–Feb, most moult coverts and midtail, often also some secondaries. Moult thus much more advanced than in Black-headed Gull, which retains juvenile wing into Jun–Jul.

4. **Adult or second-winter** (Aug–Mar) Adult shows grey upperwing with white leading edge as in Black-headed, but primaries with full black tip, showing white windows on P9–10 (and occasionally P8); wing-tip pattern similar to Grey-headed or Common Gull. Dark extension of P5–6 indicates second-winter.

5. **Adult summer** (Mar–Aug) Wing-tip diagnostic from Black-headed Gull. Hood brownish with faint paler forehead, most conspicuous with wear (but also seen in worn Black-headed Gull).

6. **Adult summer** (Mar–Aug) Wing-tip pattern evident at long range.

1. Juvenile

2. First-winter

3. First-summer

4. Adult or second-winter

5. Adult summer

6. Adult summer

& Inskipp 1985, Il'icev & Zubakin 1990, Bradshaw 1993, Grimmett *et al.* 1998, J. Jansen *in litt.*).

Vagrant Bhutan, Maldives, Iran, Oman and perhaps Arabian Gulf (Porter *et al.* 1996a, Grimmett *et al.* 1998). One W Palearctic record Eilat, Israel, 12 May 1985 (Shirihai *et al.* 1987, Shirihai 1999 (discussed by Hoogendoorn 1991a & b)).

MEASUREMENTS Lengths in mm; weights in g. Own data based on skins in MCZ, NHM, NRK, USNM, UZM. Pakistan, India, Burma, Ladakh, Kashmir, Tibet, Thailand and China.

WING

Adult male	330–361 (345.4)	46
Adult female	305–349 (329.6)	47
First-year male	316–351 (332.6)	27
First-year female	301–330 (315.0)	22

BILL

Adult male	35.8–45.0 (40.4)	47
Adult female	34.1–40.8 (36.9)	48
First-year male	35.3–45.4 (40.0)	27
First-year female	33.1–40.6 (37.2)	21

BILL DEPTH AT GONYS

Adult male	9.7–12.5 (11.0)	47
Adult female	8.9–11.0 (9.8)	48

First-year male	8.8–11.6 (10.4)	27
First-year female	8.6–10.1 (9.3)	22

BILL DEPTH AT BASE OF BILL

Adult male	11.2–14.4 (12.7)	47
Adult female	10.7–12.6 (11.5)	48
First-year male	10.5–12.9 (11.7)	27
First-year female	10.1–12.7 (11.1)	22

GONYS LENGTH

Adult male	10.6–13.9 (11.9)	47
Adult female	9.3–12.7 (11.5)	48
First-year male	9.2–12.9 (11.5)	27
First-year female	9.5–12.2 (11.0)	22

TARSUS

Adult male	44.7–54.3 (51.4)	47
Adult female	43.3–53.0 (47.5)	48
First-year male	42.7–57.9 (51.0)	27
First-year female	43.7–53.9 (48.3)	22

Note *Il'icev & Zubakin (1990) give for Pamir birds: adult male 49.9–57.9 (mean 53.6, n=8), female 52.6–53.1 (mean 52.9, n=2).*

Weight 450–714 (del Hoyo *et al*, 1996)

609

Brown-headed Gull *Larus brunnicephalus*. **609. 1st-winter** (see page 424). Similar to Black-headed and Grey-headed Gulls, but note completely black and solid wing-tip and coarser dark-marked primary coverts. Kosi Barrage, Nepal. Dec 1995. *Markku Saarinen*. **610. 1st-winter**. Some lack extensive dark primary-covert markings, but note solid black wing-tip, similar to Grey-headed Gull. Bangkok, Thailand. 18 Nov 1994. *Per Schiermacker-Hansen*. **611. 1st-winter moulting into 1st-summer**. Already by mid-winter, shows active moult in coverts, secondaries and tail. Bangkok, Thailand. 30 Mar 1989. *Arnoud B. van den Berg*. **612. 1st-winter moulting into 1st-summer**. Compare with 611 and note more advanced moult. Bangkok, Thailand. 30 Mar 1989. *Arnoud B. van den Berg*. **613. Adult winter**. Compared to Black-headed Gull bill heavier with deeper red tinge, and eyes white. Goa, India. Feb 2001. *Marc Guyt*. **614. 1st- and adult winter.** Head-markings in winter sometimes differ from Black-headed Gull in being more solid on ear-coverts and hindcrown. Legs sometimes more rosy-tinged. Goa, India. 12 Feb 1999. *Klaus Malling Olsen*.

615

616

617

618

Brown-headed Gull *Larus brunnicephalus*. **615. Adult summer**. Note chocolate-brown hood and white eyes, the latter creating 'evil' look compared to Black-headed. Bombay, India. Apr 1998. *René Pop*. **616 Adult moulting from winter to summer**. Bill often stronger than in Black-headed, sometimes recalling Mediterranean Gull. Bundala, Sri Lanka. 14 Mar 1993. *Ray Tipper*. **617. Adult moulting from summer to winter**. A late moulting individual. Nanjing, China. 10 Nov 1999. *Harry J Lehto*. **618. Adult summer**. Note black wing-tip with large white mirrors on P9–10 as well as small white mirror on P8, and broad white area between black wing-tip and grey innerwing. China. May 1996. *Markku Saarinen*

619

620

Brown-headed Gull *Larus brunnicephalus*. **619. Adult summer**. Upperwing three-coloured with grey arm against white, and black-tipped outerwing. Wing-tip pattern may vaguely recall Common Gull. Bangkok, Thailand. Late Mar 2000. *Lars Hansen*. **620. Adult winter**. Head-pattern generally more extensive than in Black-headed - wing pattern most typical from both surfaces. Goa, India. Feb 2001. *Marc Guyt*.

29. GREY-HEADED GULL
Larus cirrocephalus (Vieillot, 1818, Brazil)   Plates 60–61, Photos 621–630

IDENTIFICATION   Length 39–42cm, wingspan 100–115cm. A medium-sized hooded gull, larger and stockier than Black-headed with larger head, more sloping forehead and longer, heavier bill. Breast deeper, wings longer and broader. Stands more upright on longer legs, creating taller posture; when alert has a characteristic 'head up, tail down' posture. Upperparts are darker grey and underwings grey. In flight, wings often held flatter and less angled, giving 'sail-plane' appearance during long glides. Wingbeats are slower, similar to Common Gull. May kleptoparasitise terns.
Adult has white bases to primaries and outer wing-coverts, creating broad white half-moon between coverts and black wing-tip, which shows large white mirrors on P9–10 (as in Common Gull). Combination of upperwing pattern and grey underwing (in poor light blackish-looking) only matched by Brown-headed Gull. Bill and legs dark red. The white eyes create 'fish-eye' look. In **summer (breeding)** hood pale grey with blackish border and staring pale eyes. Paleness of hood only matched by worn (or at distance moulting) Black- and Brown-headed Gulls, in which hoods are brown. In **winter**, head becomes white with faint grey markings or ear-spot and pale grey hindneck and neck-sides. Settled, almost white-headed birds may be mistaken for Slender-billed Gull, which have even more sloping forehead and slenderer, proportionately longer bill.
Juvenile has grey-brown head, mantle, scapulars and breast-sides, and pale-scaled mantle, scapulars and lesser/median coverts. Chin and throat slightly paler than rest of head. Primaries mostly black with white restricted to bases of inner and middle primaries. The dark primary coverts create a dark comma. Dark tail-bar narrow, often appearing as row of dark spots in fully spread tail. Underwing grey. Bill and legs fleshy (sometimes yellowish-tinged), the former with dark tip. **First-winter** similar to juvenile, but head and body similar to adult winter. **First-summer** as first-winter but with faded wing. Some develop adult-like, but less complete and often paler grey hood. 1st-year Grey-headed is rather similar to similar-aged Brown-headed Gull, which see. Grey-headed Gull takes one more year than Black-headed Gull to develop adult plumage but some moult directly from juvenile into adult-like plumage (D. Vangeluwe *in litt.*; see *note* below).
Second-winter similar to adult or with dark trailing edge to wing, duller dark primary pattern with narrower white mirrors on P9–10 (if present often as isolated, elongated spots) and lack of white tips. Tertials and some coverts may be dark-marked. Eye darker than in adult. Bill and legs duller flesh.
Second-summer similar to adult summer, but secondaries and eye normally darker.

VOICE Cackling and laughing calls similar to Black-headed Gull, but deeper and hoarser.
MOULT Follows common moult strategy among gulls,

although timing very variable caused by differences in breeding seasons.
Adult moult to **winter plumage** complete. In W and E Africa, Natal and Peru Jun/Oct–Nov/Mar.
In the Gambia moult to winter plumage Oct–Nov. By late Nov 90% with winter head, 10% more or less summer hood. P(8)9–10 late Nov–late Dec. By late Mar adults in summer plumage, immatures still with winter head. A few fresh juveniles present in Nov; some have only started moult of head and body.
In Equatorial E Africa, S Africa and Argentina primaries moulted Dec/Jan–late Mar/May (skins in MCZ, NHM). Head usually before primary moult has reached P3 (Cramp & Simmons 1983). Birds from Madagascar late Jan are in winter plumage and growing P9–10. Birds from Argentina have winter head Jan/Feb–May, summer head Apr–Nov.
Moult to **summer (breeding)** partial, including head and body prior to breeding season; in equatorial birds Mar–Apr, in subtropical populations late Mar–Apr (breeds May–Sep, S populations Sep–Dec). Birds from Argentina moult to summer plumage Mar–May.
Juvenile moult to **first-winter** partial (sometimes complete, see *note* below), including head, body and a variable number of tertials and coverts Aug–Jan (Argentina, tropical Africa). African birds sometimes still have parts of mantle and scapulars juvenile Jan–Mar, but Gambian birds in Jan had renewed mantle, scapulars, tertials and a variable number of coverts (ranging from none to all, thus similar to Brown-headed Gull); generally start with median coverts, ending with lesser coverts (which are often left unmoulted). Often moult tail partly at about six months; whole tail renewed in a minority before onset of primary moult (skins in NHM). Moult of coverts and tail could be regarded as first parts of moult into second-winter.
Note First-years from Senegal have been observed to moult into adult plumage. incl. tail and flight feathers, Dec–early Feb 2002 (D. Vangeluwe *in litt.*). This recently discovered moult pattern is not found in other gulls Moult to **first-summer** partial, including head and body Aug–Sep (Argentina).
Moult to **second-winter** complete. E African first-years have almost completed primary moult by Nov/Dec. A W African bird had moulted P5–6 Mar. In Argentina, head Sep–Oct. Tail moult starts Mar–Jun.
Subsequent moults probably similar to adult moult cycle, but may be somewhat advanced (Cramp & Simmons 1983).

DESCRIPTION
(race *poiocephalus*) **Adult** Mantle, scapulars, back, upperwing-coverts, secondaries and P1–5 grey (Kodak Grey Scale 5–7; coverts up to 7–8). P6–10 white with black distal part. P10 with 27–52mm white oval mirror near tip, P9 with 21–42mm white mirror. 15–20% with max. 20mm mirror on P8. P5–8 with black tip, P4 with

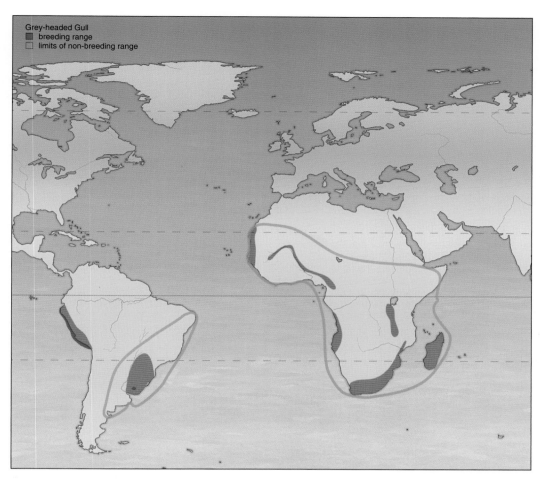

black subterminal bar. Primaries have dark inner webs. P1–8 with narrow white tips, broadest on P1–4. Underbody, tail-coverts and tail white, underbody sometimes with pinkish tinge. Underwing-coverts dark grey, rarely blackish; generally slightly paler than underside of primaries. Iris pale yellow to whitish. Orbital ring red to orange-red. Bill and legs red.

Adult summer (timing varies with breeding) Hood pale grey (Kodak Grey Scale 4–5) shading to whitish around bill. Usually with complete dark grey, brown or blackish rear border. Hindneck white. White eyelids above and below eye; sometimes indistinct whitish eye-ring, contrasting with red orbital ring. Underbody white, sometimes with slight pinkish tinge. Bill red, sometimes with dark tip. Early in breeding season, bill often darker, looking blackish at distance. Legs bright red; brighter than bill (Grant 1986b).

Adult winter Head white with dark shadings above eye and on hindneck, similar to but weaker than in Blackheaded; sometimes as shaded hood or with grey tinge to crown, hindneck or rear border of hood. Lower hindneck pale grey. Bill dull red to orange-red with variable dark tip. Legs dull red to orange, usually paler than bill (Grant 1986b).

Juvenile Head white with greyish-brown shading, darker ear-spot and eye-crescents creating partial hood. Thin white crescents above and below eye. Upper hindneck whitish, forming white hind-collar. Underparts white with grey-brown breast-sides as extension from mantle. Mantle and scapulars brown with pale featherfringes, creating scaly pattern especially on scapulars. Rump pale grey. Upperwing similar to first-year Blackheaded Gull, but slightly darker grey on inner wing; P8–10 black. White on outer webs of P1–7 largest on P4–5, creating white elongated area extending to outer primary coverts. P1–5 and their coverts grey to whitish with blackish tips joining with blackish secondary bar to form black trailing edge to wing. P6–8 with narrow white tips. Primaries with black inner webs. Outer primary coverts white, often with dark shaft-streaks. Lesser and median coverts grey-brown with pale edges. Axillaries and underwing-coverts duller and slightly paler grey than in adult. From below, underwing rather uniform apart from white outer webs to middle primaries. Tail white with narrow black subterminal bar (on T1 14–20mm), edges of rectrices often white; tail-bar looks broken and usually not extending to T5–6. Orbital ring reddish-brown. Iris brown. Gape reddish-brown. Bill

429

PLATE 60. GREY-HEADED GULL *Larus cirrocephalus*

A medium-sized gull of tropical and S Africa and S America, occurring both along coastlines and at inland lakes. Vagrant to S Europe and Middle East. Larger than Black-headed Gull, in size intermediate between Black-headed and Common Gull. Compared to Black-headed has more sloping forehead, longer neck and longer legs. Seasonal plumage developments different in different areas caused by variable breeding season.

1. **Juvenile** Plumage pattern similar to Black-headed Gull, but markings on head more diffuse and overall appearance more greyish-brown, and greater coverts darker grey. Black tail-bar narrower. Legs and bill duller and more greyish-tinged.

2. **First-winter** Head-markings and mantle/scapulars similar to adult winter, but head-streaking slightly stronger and bill-base and legs duller, more orange-tinged.

3. **Moulting into second-winter** Similar to adult, but black on wing-tip more extensive. Eye darker than in adult.

4. **Second-winter** Head in this and subsequent ages often whitish, with only faint grey markings (intermediate between Black-headed and Slender-billed Gulls). Eyes bicoloured, but not as pale as in adult. Upperparts darker grey than in Black-headed Gull, and primaries normally all dark through wear. Note that some at this age are identical to adults.

5. **Adult winter** Some show more extensive dark head pattern than 4. In adult, eyes very pale and primaries with white tips: note white mirror to P10. Legs and bill darker red than in Black-headed Gull.

6. **Adult summer** Hood grey with dark edgings. Pale eye creates cold 'fish-eyed' look. Bill dark red.

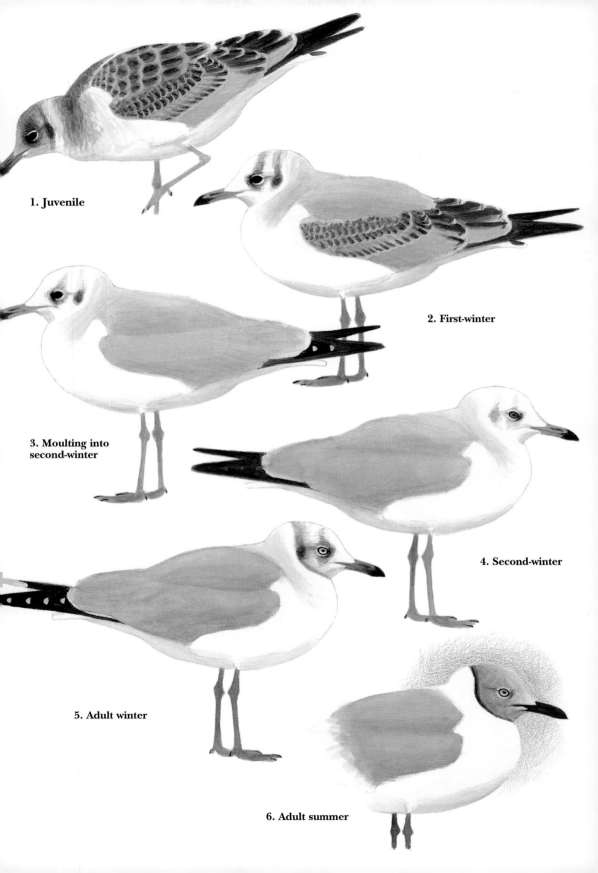

1. Juvenile

2. First-winter

3. Moulting into
second-winter

4. Second-winter

5. Adult winter

6. Adult summer

PLATE 61. GREY-HEADED GULL *Larus cirrocephalus*

Larger and slightly heavier than Black-headed Gull. Flight lazier, similar to Common Gull, but with much gliding on angled wings.

1. **Juvenile** Wing pattern similar to Black-headed Gull, but grey on upperwing darker, in better contrast to white-based primaries and their coverts. Unlike most Black-headed shows full black wingtip. Black tail-bar narrower and underwing-coverts grey, not white. From below wing-tip appears all dark unlike Black-headed Gull. Compare Brown-headed Gull.

2. **First-winter** As juvenile, but mantle and scapulars grey and head whiter with dark ear-spot and bar across crown.

3. **First-summer** Note grey coverts combined with juvenile flight feathers. May acquire all-white tail before moult of flight feathers.

4. **Second-winter** Similar to adult, but with narrower white mirrors on P9–10 and darker grey centres to secondaries.

5. **Adult winter** Black wing-tip with large white mirrors on P9–10 differs from similar Black-headed Gull, but upperwing darker grey and underwing-coverts greyish. White eye conspicuous. Bare parts darker.

6. **Adult summer** Hood greyish, eyes pale. Bill and legs dark red.

7. **Adult summer** Wing pattern conspicuous, but similar to Brown-headed Gull; hood much paler grey, lacking brown tinge of slightly smaller Brown-headed Gull.

First-winter

1. Juvenile

3. First-summer

2. First-winter

4. Second-winter

5. Adult winter

6. Adult summer

7. Adult summer

pale flesh to yellowish-flesh with black tip. Legs dull flesh or yellowish-flesh.

First-winter as juvenile, but head white with faint dark bars across crown and hindneck, often reduced to faint shading above eye and dark ear-spot, but sometimes creating half-hood. Lower hindneck pale grey. Underparts and rump white. Mantle and scapulars grey, often with a few retained juvenile feathers. Wing and tail as juvenile, but dark areas fade and white primary tips wear off. Iris sometimes pale brown. Bill acquires reddish-brown base. Legs dark orange-brown.

First-summer as first-winter, but grey on head generally more extensive. Some may acquire adult-like hood and lose pale grey on hindneck. With wear, dark juvenile areas on upperwing become very faded, especially carpal bar. White tips to flight feathers and tail disappear with wear.

Second-winter similar to adult winter, but with more (brownish) black than white on outer wing and darker secondaries. P10 black or with max. 24mm white mirror; P9 rarely with max. 10mm mirror on outer web. White primary tips reduced or lacking. Tertials and secondaries grey with dusky centres or spots, forming dark trailing edge to inner wing. Sometimes with a few brown upperwing-coverts. Tail white, rarely with traces of dark. Iris usually pale, but sometimes intermediate between juvenile and adult, looking dark at distance. Bill, orbital ring and legs dull flesh to reddish- or orange-brown. Bill black-tipped.

Second-summer similar to adult summer, but generally with more black on wing-tip, darker tertial centres and often darkish eye.

Hybrids Hybrid Grey-headed × Hartlaub's Gull *L. hartlaubii* known from S America (Cramp & Simmons 1983).

GEOGRAPHICAL VARIATION Race *poiocephalus* (Africa) described above. Birds from W Africa on average slightly smaller than E African birds. Nominate *cirrocephalus* (S America) slightly larger than *poiocephalus* (see Measurements), in adult plumage with paler upperparts and larger white mirrors on P9–10.

DISTRIBUTION AND MIGRATION Population only around 50,000 pairs, despite wide range. Breeds subtropical coasts, islands, estuaries, lakes and rivers, in Argentina also in marshes. Breeding season Transvaal May–Jun (Tarboton *et al.* 1987). Often feeds in large flocks in harbours and rubbish dumps (Tarboton *et al.* 1987, del Hoyo *et al.* 1996).

African population local and discontinuously spread, mainly around equator; colonies >2,500 pairs known Kenya, Uganda and Senegambia. S African population increasing; 200 pairs in 70 colonies mid-1990s. Banc d'Arguin, Mauritania 100 pairs (Britton 1980, Cramp & Simmons 1983, Urban *et al.* 1986, Lewis & Pomeroy 1989, Harrison *et al.* 1997). S American population around 10,000 pairs, mainly Argentina and E Pacific coast. Increase since 1920s. In Peru 1,000 pairs; rare Brazil; very rare Uruguay (del Hoyo *et al.* 1996).

Mainly resident or short-distance migrant; mainly inland breeders, which disperse to coasts outside breeding season.

Birds from Natal move up to 2,000km N along Atlantic and Indian Ocean. Birds ringed in Transvaal recovered both SE (coastal Natal to S Mozambique) and SW (mean distance 330km); also Zimbabwe, W Zambia, Botswana, Namibia and S Angola (2,000km). Large non-breeding concentrations in Africa, e.g. at Lake Chad, Lake Victoria and Lake Nakuru, where max. 8,000 Jan–Feb, and Senegambia, where very common along coastline Nov–Apr (Urban *et al.* 1986, Lewis & Pomeroy 1989, pers. obs.).

Vagrant Spain (1), Gibraltar (1), Israel (3 Eilat spring–summer 1995), Egypt, Saudi Arabia, Red Sea, Yemen. One record from Great Britain regarded as escape (Bundy 1986, Young 1991, Shirihai 1992, Mitchell & Young 1997).

S American population shows similar northward spread (see map). Mentioned as most abundant gull on Guayas River, Ecuador (Harrison 1983). Regular S to Mollendo, Peru, May–Oct. Vagrant N to Panama and Florida (record from Dec 1999 the sole one for North America—Doherty & Oddie 2001).

MEASUREMENTS Lengths in mm; weights in g. Own data based on skins in MCZ, NHM, NNH, NRK, UZM, ZMA, ZMO. *Poiocephalus*, Africa. *Cirrocephalus* Argentina, Ecuador, Peru.

WING

L. c. poiocephalus		
Adult male	308–343 (328.0)	52
Adult female	290–328 (309.9)	53
First-year male	301–319 (310.3)	7
First-year female	282–306 (293.8)	11

L. c. cirrocephalus		
Adult male	308–342 (330.4)	12
Adult female	305–335 (319.5)	12
First-year male	305–320 (314.4)	5
First-year female	300–321 (314.0)	7

BILL

L. c. poiocephalus		
Adult male	34.4–42.5 (38.0)	57
Adult female	31.2–41.3 (35.2)	49
First-year male	36.2–41.2 (39.6)	7
First-year female	30.5–38.8 (34.6)	11

L. c. cirrocephalus		
Adult male	35.2–42.6 (40.3)	12
Adult female	34.8–40.8 (37.3)	12
First-year male	35.5–42.1 (38.1)	5
First-year female	33.8–40.0 (37.2)	7

BILL DEPTH AT GONYS

L. c. poiocephalus		
Adult male	8.6–10.3 (9.6)	47
Adult female	8.4–10.2 (9.1)	47
First-year male	8.8–10.3 (9.4)	7
First-year female	7.9–9.2 (8.4)	11

L. c. cirrocephalus		
Adult male	9.5–11.3 (10.4)	11
Adult female	9.0–9.8 (9.4)	11
First-year male	8.6–10.1 (9.5)	5
First-year female	8.6–9.3 (9.0)	7

BILL DEPTH AT BASE OF BILL

L. c. poiocephalus		
Adult male	10.8–12.9 (11.8)	48
Adult female	9.5–12.6 (10.9)	47
First-year male	10.7–12.2 (11.5)	7
First-year female	8.7–10.7 (10.2)	11

L. c. cirrocephalus		
Adult male	11.0–13.9 (12.5)	11
Adult female	10.9–11.8 (11.2)	11
First-year male	10.2–13.2 (11.7)	5
First-year female	10.7–11.5 (11.2)	7

GONYS LENGTH

L. c. poiocephalus		
Adult male	9.6–12.6 (10.9)	47
Adult female	9.4–13.0 (10.6)	47
First-year male	9.5–12.2 (11.1)	7
First-year female	8.8–10.7 (10.0)	11

L. c. cirrocephalus		
Adult male	11.5–13.2 (12.2)	11
Adult female	10.0–11.9 (10.8)	11
First-year male	10.8–12.4 (11.4)	5
First-year female	10.1–11.8 (11.0)	7

TARSUS

L. c. poiocephalus		
Adult male	46.3–55.5 (51.0)	57
Adult female	43.7–53.9 (48.6)	53
First-year male	47.2–52.0 (50.2)	7
First-year female	44.0–50.7 (47.2)	11

L. c. cirrocephalus		
Adult male	50.0–59.9 (54.5)	12
Adult female	47.5–53.9 (49.8)	12
First-year male	48.7–53.8 (51.3)	5
First-year female	47.0–53.4 (50.6)	7

Weight Adult (male and female combined) E Africa 280–384, S Africa 211–377; S African female 255–355. Juvenile S Africa 280 (Cramp & Simmons 1983, Urban *et al.* 1986, skins in NHM, NNH, ZMO).

Grey-headed Gull *Larus cirrocephalus*. **621 Juvenile and adult summer.** Compared to Black-headed, shows squarer head and stronger bill. Juvenile colder brown. The Gambia. Nov 2000. *Martin Gottschling.*

Grey-headed Gull *Larus cirrocephalus*. **622. 1st-winter**. The Gambia. Nov 2000. *Martin Gottschling.* **623 1st-winter.** A worn individual. Note greyish underwing-coverts. The Gambia. Dec. *Karel Beylevelt.* **624. 1st-winter** (in background adult Hartlaub's Gull). Note that large parts of upperparts as well as tail may already have moulted into adult-type at this age. Cape Prov., South Africa. 13 Mar 1999. *Arnoud B. van den Berg.* **625. 2nd-winter**. Rather solid black wing-tip with just narrow white mirrors on P9-10 indicates this age. The Gambia. Nov 2000. *Martin Gottschling.* **626. 1st-summer.** Note square head with markings similar to Black-headed Gull, although weak in this individual, and sometimes very vague, similar to Slender-billed Gull. Darkish eye and brownish primaries indicate 1st-summer. Lake Nakuru, Kenya. 20 Mar 1992. *Ray Tipper.*

627

628

629

630

Grey-headed Gull *Larus cirrocephalus*. **627. Adult summer**. Note pale grey hood and white eyes. False Bay, South Africa. Aug. *Hanne & Jens Eriksen*. **628. Adult winter**. Upperwing appears tricoloured with solid white area between grey inner wing and black wing-tip, the latter with two broad white mirrors. Cape Prov., South Africa. 13 Mar 1999. *Arnoud B. van den Berg*. **629. Adult summer**. Note grey underwing contrasting with white underbody. False Bay, South Africa. Aug. *Hanne & Jens Eriksen*. **630. Adult summer**. Upperwing pattern, grey underwing and grey hood makes this age very distinctive. The Gambia. Nov. *Alan Tate*.

30.   BLACK-HEADED GULL
Larus ridibundus (Linnaeus, 1766, European seas)   Plates 62–63, Photos 631–650

IDENTIFICATION Length 34–39cm, wingspan 100–110cm. A small, elegant gull with a rather small, rounded head and slender bill lacking hooked tip or marked gonys-angle. The wing pattern is characteristic, with broad white leading edge and black trailing edge to outer wing – a pattern only shared with Slender-billed and Bonaparte's Gulls. From below, mid-primaries are contrastingly dark – easy to see at close range, but harder at distance, when underwing often only appears darkish with strong white leading edge. Underparts sometimes pinkish-tinged. Apart from first-years, bill and legs are red. Iris dark in all plumages.

In typically agile, fast, buoyant flight (in hard winds almost tern-like), the body looks rather short and slender with wings placed centrally on body, arm broader than pointed wing. The tail is rounded or square-ended. Feeding includes picking from water surface or from arable land, and snapping high-flying insects, often in large, dense flocks. Migrates in well-ordered rows, in calm weather at some height, in harder winds just above water surface with only short intervals of shearwatering. Often soars.

Adult summer has dark brown hood, extending less far on hindneck than in congeners, as it just penetrates to border of hindneck. However, precise shape of hood much depends on posture of bird. In early breeding season, hood and bill almost concolorous dark maroon; from midsummer, hood becomes browner and duller with darker border to head and bill brighter red with dark tip – latter also the case rest of year. During late stages of head moult in summer, many have darker neck-ring contrasting with head, which at distance may look pale grey or brown caused by wear and mixture of dark and pale feathers. Legs dark red. **Adult winter** has white head with dark ear-spot and faint variable dark bars across crown (above ear-spot) and neck. Bill bright red with dark tip, legs dark red. Acquires summer plumage Feb–mid-Mar.

Juvenile at first has ginger- to dark brown on head, upperparts and breast-sides. First fledglings of year look surprisingly dark and odd, an impression reinforced by rounded, incompletely grown wing-tips – more like odd shorebird such as Turnstone *Arenaria interpres* than a gull. Flight feathers are basically like adults, but upperwing has brown carpal bar, blackish trailing edge and dark, white-fringed tertials. Primaries have white bases, sometimes dulled by much black on outer webs. Inner primary coverts dark, outer ones usually whitish, being part of white leading edge to outer wing. Not infrequently outer greater primary coverts are dark-marked, and may create dark leading edge to outer wing (making confusion with Bonaparte's Gull possible – dark inner primary coverts then form a good distinction, as they are pale in Bonaparte's). Tail white with narrow brown-black subterminal band. Legs and bill fleshy to yellow.

From Aug, **first-winter** combines adult winter head and body with juvenile wing and tail. Bill and legs brownish-orange, the former dark-tipped. When settled, dark-centred tertials may be most eye-catching age character. Plumage is retained in **first-summer**; apart from that most have variable dark hood, duller than adult. Wings and tail very bleached by late summer, heavily worn before start of moult into **second-winter**.

Second-winter basically as adult, but some may be aged by complete black outer webs to 1–2 outermost primaries (in adult, typically only outermost primary has incomplete black outer web) and rarely dark markings on primary coverts, tertials, alula and tail. Such immature characters are, however, less frequent than in other similar-sized hooded gulls.

VOICE Very vocal in breeding colonies: a screaming, melodious *auurh* or *krriaarh*. Similar, but shorter calls (sometimes in short series) uttered outside breeding season. Also short *kek* (sometimes in short laughing series) and *kek kek kriarr*.

MOULT (own data from S Scandinavia, Netherlands)
Adult moults to **winter** plumage completely Jun–Oct. Head starts with forehead and lores early Jul, developing backwards; early Jul 5% have white forehead. Late Jul–early Aug typically with dark neck-ring as indication of remainder of summer hood; lower part of neck-ring last to be moulted. Earliest with winter head mid-Jul (small minority mid-Jun probably failed breeders); by late Aug >90% have winter head. Small minority retain summer head to early Oct, exceptionally into winter (see Aberrants) (Cramp & Simmons 1983, Holst & Ullman 1984). Coverts Jul–Aug, starting with median coverts. Average duration of primary moult three months, starting with P1 (late May)Jun. In S Scandinavia/Baltic, 10–15% shed P1 mid-Jun, 25% late Jun; 50–75% P1–3 mid-Jul, p 3–5(6) late Jul–early Aug, P7–8 late Aug. Birds from S Scandinavia/Baltic perform short-distance migration to W Europe in active wing moult (Malling Olsen 1993). Dutch birds generally more advanced by midsummer, having renewed up to P5 mid-Jul, P8–9 late Aug–mid-Sep. P10 fully grown (late Aug)late Sep–early Oct(Nov). Tail starts with T1 late Jun–early Jul; by late Aug, tail often wedge-shaped when T4–6 fully grown and T1–3 in active moult. Tail finished mid-Sep; a few rectrices rarely replaced until late winter.

Adult moult to **summer** plumage partial, including head and body. Head from late Jan–early Feb, starting with areas surrounding dark head-stripes, creating 'tiger-striped' head at early stages of moult. Hindneck generally first, forehead and chin latest. Following very mild winters, some start head moult late Dec. On other hand, head moult generally delayed some weeks following series of severe winters. Normally shows summer hood at earliest mid-Jan. In S Scandinavia by late Feb 1–5% have summer hood, 15% have hood complete behind eye, 50% show early stages of moult and 30–35% winter head. By first half of Mar most have >75% summer hood and conspicuous white blaze; 95–98% with summer hood late Mar; rarely head still moulting early May (Holst & Ullman 1984). **Juvenile** moults partially into **first-winter**, including head, body and sometimes some coverts (especially lesser and median coverts) from early Jul. Starts with mantle and scapulars, which are renewed late Aug–Sep. Scattered tertials sometimes renewed in autumn. Moult rarely delayed to Oct/Dec.

Moult to **first-summer** partial (Jan)Mar–Apr, including head, body, some wing-coverts, tertials and frequently T1 (rarer T2, very rarely also T3–4 Jan). Moult generally one month later than in adults; by mid–late Apr most have mainly winter head, often with dark neck-ring. 60–70% acquire more adult-looking summer hood (in <50% complete).

Moult to **second-winter** complete, generally 3–4 weeks earlier than in adult. Head from early Jun. 50–70% have winter head mid-Jul. Primary moult slower than in adult; P1 (early)mid-May–early Jul (>50% early Jun); >90% have renewed P3–4 mid-Jul, 75% P5–7 late Jul. P9–10 mid-Jul–late Aug(mid-Oct). Secondaries (May) Jun–late Jul, starting when primary moult has reached around P5: by late Jul most have >50% juvenile secondaries; median coverts moulted late Jul–mid-Aug. Tail late Jun–Aug, T1 sometimes earlier. Most in winter plumage mid-Aug.

Note North American breeders have adapted slightly later moult schedule, similar to Bonaparte's Gull (J. R. King pers. comm.).

DESCRIPTION

Adult Hindneck and underbody white, sometimes with slight rosy tinge, generally less clean than in Ross's and Slender-billed Gull. Narrow white crescents above and below eye usually join at rear. Upperparts and most of wing-coverts mid-grey with slight bluish wash (Kodak Grey Scale 4–5(6)). Marginal coverts and outer primary coverts white. Upperside of P7–10 white, P(9)10 with black edge of outer web, usually not reaching tip. P(4)5–10 black-tipped, dark tips of P(4)5–10 extending onto inner edge of web. P(4)5–7(8) with white extreme tip, P1–5 and secondaries with indistinct white tips; P1–5 with blackish-grey inner webs, visible from below as dark rectangle in strong contrast to white outer wing and coverts. Secondaries grey. Axillaries and lesser underwing-coverts white, median and greater coverts greyish-white. Tail white. Iris brown. Orbital ring maroon-red, rarely pink (King & Marriott 1984). Iris brown-black. Mouth and gape bright red. Legs red. Tibia 0.25–0.45 length of tarsus. **Note** black pigmentation decreases in many birds with increasing age (Allaine & Lebreton 1990).

Adult summer (Mar–Aug) Hood dark brown; when fresh blackish with maroon tinge, from Jun gradually paler and duller; rear margin normally darkest, with wear gradually creating darker neck-ring, striking during late stages of moult. Hood reaches to border of

nape and hindneck, the latter white. Eyelids white, not joining at rear. Bill dark maroon-red, sometimes black-tipped; at onset of breeding season little or no contrast with hood; brighter red with black tip later in summer, but early in breeding season sometimes with brighter red tip. Legs dark red, darkest at onset of breeding season.

Adult winter (Jul–early Mar) Head white with dark ear-spot and varying amount of dark grey shading on crown, mostly as dark grey shading from eye to eye and from ear-spot to ear-spot. Underbody white, sometimes with very pale grey wash to neck- and breast-sides. Fresh primaries with broad white tips, gradually disappearing with wear. Bill and legs bright red, the former with black tip. Legs rarely raspberry-pink.

Juvenile (fledging–Aug) Head largely buff with varying dark markings, sometimes forming partial dark hood, traces of dark cap or diffuse ear-spot; in small minority as first-winter, but browner and more diffuse. Some show greyish-brown hood with dark rear-border. Chin, throat, upper hindneck and underparts white with variable buff tinge or spots on breast-sides, sometimes forming buffish breast-band or extending onto flanks. Lower hindneck usually dark. Underwing as adult; differs in dark secondaries, often darker primaries and faint dark covert-markings at wing-bend. Lower hindneck, mantle and scapulars dark ginger-brown to buff-brown with varying pale buff to whitish edges. Lesser and median coverts brown with pale edges, greater coverts grey. Secondaries blackish with narrow white tips and edges. Tertials blackish-brown with clear-cut white edges. Primaries with broad black tips; P7–10 white, black outer webs to P(5)7–10. P1–6 grey with white tips. Better-marked birds have larger amount of dark in all primaries, thickest on mid-part of outer web; P9–10 sometimes darker on inner web and distal parts of outer web, showing traces of white mirrors and creating pattern similar to Brown-headed and Grey-headed Gulls but more diffuse (this generally most frequent in C and E Asian birds, and noted in a larger percentage from Middle East, C Asia and Xinkiang in W European population – pers. obs.). Inner primary coverts dusky, outer primary coverts in 50% white with dark edges, in rest with dark markings, especially along shafts. Alula white with dark edges. 40% have dark outer webs or subterminal spots to 2–3 outer primary coverts; <5% have black outer webs to all primary coverts (see Bonaparte's Gull). Rump and back pale grey, fading to white on uppertail-coverts. Tail white with blackish subterminal bar, broadest on midtail (19–24mm on T1) and white tip; T6 usually with dark restricted to inner web, rarely completely white. Birds with mostly white rectrices in poor state have probably lost brown on these feathers by extreme wear (K. Bengtsson *in litt.*). Iris and orbital ring dark brown. Bill dull to yellowish-flesh; outer 30% of bill blackish. Legs flesh to yellowish-flesh.

First-winter (Aug–Apr) similar to juvenile, but head, mantle and body as adult winter; may retain a few juvenile mantle feathers. Juvenile upperwing and tail gradually fade from Jan; in spring covert-bar medium brown and white tips to primaries reduced or lacking. Some wing-coverts may be new and more like in adult. Bare parts pale brownish, buffish or orange, rarely pale pink-

PLATE 62. BLACK-HEADED GULL *Larus ridibundus*

Widespread Palearctic gull. The commonest 'hooded' gull within its range, Black-headed is often abundant in large flocks near human settlements. Breeds mainly on inland lakes surrounded by reedbeds, but also in shallow lagoons. Outside breeding season, abundant in both freshwater and coastal environments. Flocks in arable lands and urban areas. Often tame.
Small, rather elegant gull with small, rounded head, slender bill, lacking marked hook or gonys-angle, and moderately long wings. Legs rather short, in settled birds with tibia normally very short-looking.

1. **Juvenile** (fledging–Aug/Sep) Head with extensive dark brown to warm buff patterning, often as diffuse hood, admixed with whitish. Head pattern usually less clear-cut than in similar species. Mantle and scapulars warm brown with pale fringes, breast-sides dark buffish. Upperwing with dark-centred lesser and median coverts, contrasting somewhat with grey greater coverts. Tertials dark brown with pale fringes. Bill at first pinkish to dull orange, somewhat varying in colour. Tip of bill black, creating bicoloured bill. Leg colour matches bill colour. Some individual plumage variation (see 2 and 3).

2. **Juvenile** A very dark brown individual, showing dark reddish-brown mantle, scapulars and head-markings. Such individuals identifiable on plumage alone, as darkness and warm coloration are never matched by other similar-plumaged species (Bonaparte's and Slender-billed Gull).

3. **Juvenile** A paler individual with restricted dark in plumage, creating head pattern similar to first-winter. Mantle and scapulars greyish-brown with broad pale edges. Such extremes are not uncommon, and may be confused with Slender-billed Gull. Note bicoloured bill, dark eyes, extensive head-markings, rounded white feathering at base of upper mandible and shortish-looking legs with only short area of tibia visible.

4. **First-winter** (Aug–Apr) Head and body as adult winter, but wing and tail as juvenile. Base of bill and legs often duller and more orange-toned than in adult.

5. **First-summer** (Apr–Aug) The majority develop partial dull blackish-brown hood, but typically retain some white feathering around base of bill. Rarely hood as complete as adult, and duller, lacking purplish gloss of fresh hood. A small minority retain head as in first-winter.

6. **Second-winter** (Aug–Mar) Most at this age indistinguishable from adult winter, but a small minority show traces of immaturity such as dark-patterned tertials (shown here) and covert-markings (especially on upper primary coverts). Otherwise as adult winter: note dark vertical head-markings (from eye to eye, and from ear-spot to ear-spot), black ear-spot and red base to bill. Legs red, often bright red.

7. **Adult winter** (Jul/Aug–Mar) Note vertical head-streaking, bright red base to bill and white tips to primaries. Often shows varying pinkish tinge to underparts year round, but rarely as extensive or as 'clean' as in Slender-billed and Ross's Gull, being more brownish and 'dirty'. Hindneck mainly whitish; in some pale grey (as shown here), although not as dark as mantle.

8. **Adult summer** (Mar–Aug) In fresh plumage, hood dark chocolate-brown and bill dark brownish-red, at distance appearing concolorous with hood. White crescents above and below eye narrow, but distinct, usually not joining at rear. From midsummer, hood duller brown (often paler around bill) and bill brighter red.

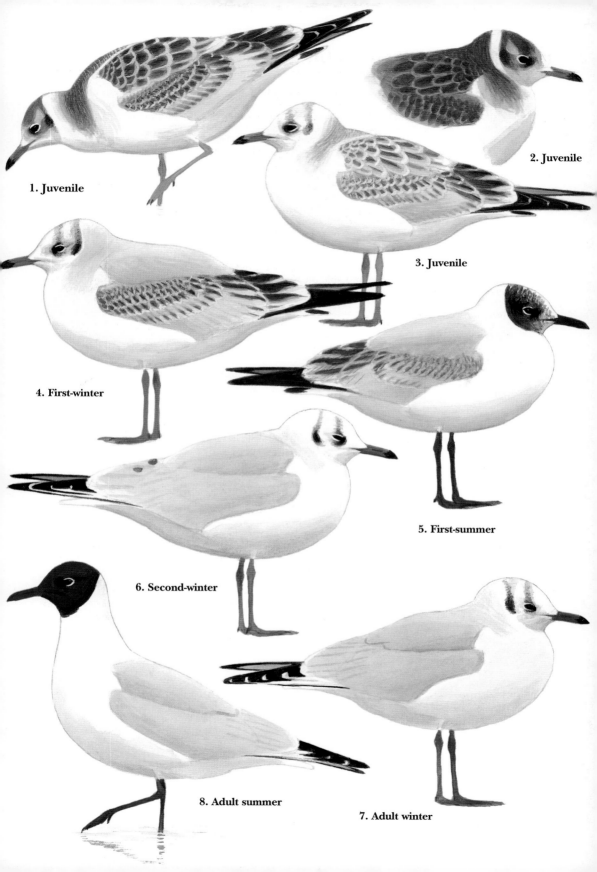

1. Juvenile

2. Juvenile

3. Juvenile

4. First-winter

5. First-summer

6. Second-winter

8. Adult summer

7. Adult winter

PLATE 63. BLACK-HEADED GULL *Larus ridibundus*

Abundant Palearctic gull. In flight a small, rather elegant gull with moderately long wings, rather short tail and rounded head. Wings placed centrally. Flight light, vaguely recalling Common Tern. On migration often in dense flocks, in light winds migrating high in air in formations.

In all plumages wing shows whitish leading edge, black trailing edge and grey inner wing, reaching mid-primaries. From below, mid-primaries darker, creating blackish wedge in contrast to white leading edge. Bill bicoloured.

1. **Juvenile** (fledging–Aug/Sep) Dark brown (often tawny) carpal bar contrasts with white outer primaries, which show dark tips. Trailing edge of wing blackish. Most birds show almost unmarked white outer primary coverts, 'elongating' white leading edge to primaries. Greater coverts, including inner primary coverts, grey. Bill and legs orange to fleshy, the former with dark tip. In first weeks after fledging often short-winged, as primaries not fully grown: looks dark with short and rounded wings compared to adult, and may be mistaken for a strange-looking shorebird.

2. **Juvenile** Pattern of outer primaries and primary coverts varies somewhat. Compared to 1, this bird shows more extensive dark along leading edge of outer wing as well as dark shaft-streaks and tips (drop-shaped) to primary coverts. Individual variation shown in spread wings below. Note grey inner primary coverts and primaries, creating impression of white along leading edge of outer wing only (not full pale centre on outer wing as in Bonaparte's Gull, which compare). Outer primaries may show even more dark than in this individual, sometimes creating blackish tip with white on inner webs turning up as white window in P9–10. May appear similar to Brown-headed Gull, which see.

3. **Juvenile moulting into first-winter** (late Aug–early Sep) In this rather pale, weakly patterned bird, head and mantle have moulted into adult-patterned first-winter (scapulars soon to follow).

4. **First-winter** (Sep–Apr) Wing and tail as juvenile (becoming slightly worn throughout winter), but head and body as adult winter.

5. **First-summer** (Apr–Aug) As worn first-winter until onset of moult in late spring, but with varying dark hood. Compared to adult, hood duller, normally speckled with white, most extensive on face. This individual has moulted central tail feathers, often the first sign of the complete moult into second- (adult) winter.

6. **First-summer** A rather worn individual with summer plumage limited to dark ring around neck. Note that with wear the full dark wedge on underwing may appear more as darker streaks, leading to confusion with Bonaparte's Gull. This individual shows rather broad markings on outer primaries, invading extensive white along leading edge of wing.

First-year wing, showing individual variation; compare lower with Brown-headed and Grey-headed Gulls

7. **Adult winter** (Jul/Aug–Mar) Head white with dark ear-spot and traces of vertical bars above eyes. Legs and bill rather deep red, the latter with black tip. The tricoloured upperwing (shared with Bonaparte's and Slender-billed Gull, which see) is visible at long range, whereas the dark wedge on mid-primaries contrasts well with the white leading edge of outer wing. In dull light and at distance, underwing may, however, look rather uniform grey.

8. **Adult summer** (Mar–Aug) Hood dark chocolate-brown, in early breeding season looking rather concolorous with bill.

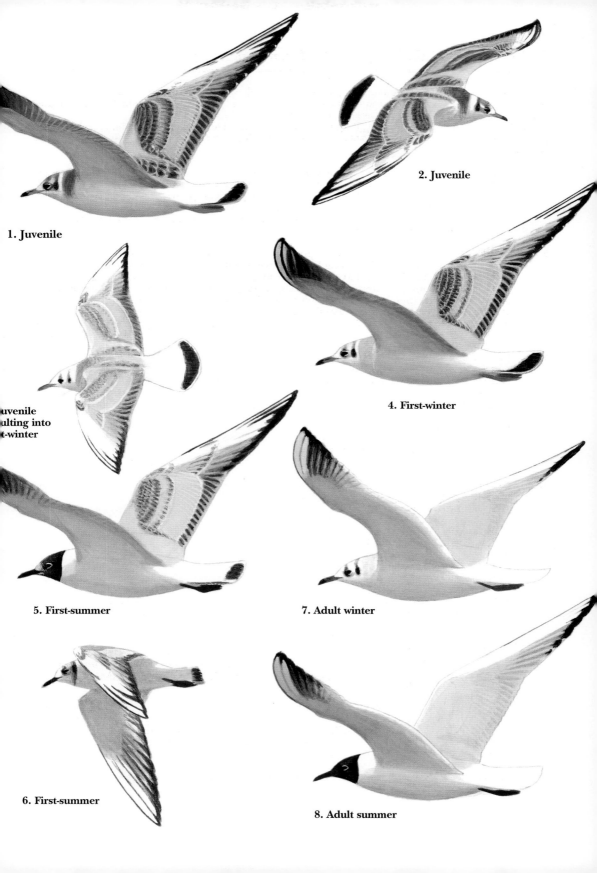

1. Juvenile

2. Juvenile

Juvenile
moulting into
first-winter

4. First-winter

5. First-summer

7. Adult winter

6. First-summer

8. Adult summer

ish; generally becomes more orange from autumn. Pink tinge to underbody absent or only very faint at this age.
First-summer (Apr–Aug) similar to first-winter, but with more or less complete hood: duller than in adult and mostly white-flecked. By May, 7% with full adult hood, 58% with white-flecked, dark hood, 24% with white head and sparse dark fleckings, 11% with winter head (Grant 1986b). Body as first-winter, but hindneck and breast off-white or grey-washed in birds retaining winter head pattern. Juvenile wing and tail parts become extremely worn from May; brown areas and secondary bar very faded by midsummer; T1(2) often white. Dark P1–5 often partly translucent, typically shadowed by dark outer webs to create slightly streaked pattern. Bill and legs as first-winter or adult.
Second-winter as adult winter, but often with black outer web to P8–10, sometimes complete on P10 (adults only with partly black on P10 and no black on outer web of P8). Frequently shows dark spots at tip of both outer and inner webs of P4 (normally in adult lacking or restricted to dark spot on outer web). 5–10% have dark spots on outer web of alula, 5–8% dark spots on outer primary coverts, <1% dark markings on tertials and T6 (K. T. Pedersen pers. comm.); a presumed adult, with only faint dark markings on T2–3 (Bowey & Pollinger 1997), may be this age-type. Bill and legs generally paler orange-red than in adult.
Second-summer as adult, apart from characters of second-winter.

Aberrants Pale individuals frequent. Some **adults** have whitish-grey upperwing similar to Slender-billed and Mediterranean Gulls (or even white). Trailing edge of primaries often brownish, but can be black as in normal birds. Others have all-white primaries or just traces of dark underside to bases of P1–5. Winter head white with faint grey or pale brown ear-spot or indications of normal pattern; sometimes all white. A pale adult followed Feb–Apr still had winter head in Apr. In **summer**, hood medium grey to pale brown, most obvious at border of hood. Bare parts sometimes brighter red than in normal birds, or even orange; may lack black bill-tip. Iris sometimes silvery or pale yellow (Königstedt 1980, Hubatsch 1988, Robel 1988, Herschmann 1991, Barthel & Königstedt 1993, Larkin 2000, P. Berg, H. J. & H. Lehto, J. Lontkowski & R. Strack *in litt.*, K. T. Pedersen pers. comm., pers. obs.). Pale individuals with whitish head and pale eyes may cause confusion with Slender-billed Gull, which see.
100% albinos are white with unusual pale—often bright red—bare parts.
First-year with greyish-white primaries, apart from black leading edge on both sides of wing known (Jörgensen 1984).
An unusually small bird (from winter), about the size of Little Gull, with all-dark bill and dull dark grey legs with a reddish tinge, has also been recorded. Wing 260mm, bill to skull 37mm, tarsus 39mm (Hedgren & Svensson 1979).
Birds with brownish-black bill rare. A bird with apparently black bill had small area of reddish-black near gape. Black-billed birds may also show darker legs than normal (Larkin 1999, H. J. Lehto & S. Carlsson *in litt.* & photos).

Very rare **melanistics** greyish-black or sooty with varying paler parts. Birds with paler lesser upperwing-coverts and blackish bill/legs known. Sooty-black adult had dark hood, pale indication of hindneck, paler centres to primary coverts and white outer webs to P9–10. Another had normal upperparts, but sooty-black greater primary coverts and lighter blackish-grey upper-tail-coverts and rump. Belly, flanks and vent greyish-black, merging into white foreneck and throat. A blackish-grey bird with black hood and white neck, white bases to all but central rectrices and 'normal' outer 3–4 primaries. This bird had pale marginal/lesser coverts and median primary coverts, creating pale leading edge to wing. Legs and bill black. Such birds may show black hood in contrast to normal individuals. Melanistics may superficially look like skuas and cause similar reaction among other gulls (Néve 1986, Walhout 1991, Thorne 1996, Hallam 1998, Holloway 1998, Orchard 1998, Pennington 1998).
Adult with dark hood in midwinter rare but regular. Several birds showed traces of darker ear-spot, others had fresh hood Nov–Dec, indicating that hood atypically may have been developed during autumn moult or as very early moult into summer; although mostly incomplete into mid-Jan. This has especially proven to be the case following series of very mild autumns and winters (in S Scandinavia more frequently winters 2000/2001 and 2001/2002 than other years) (Cowley 1989, R. Strack & A. Elkjær *in litt.*, pers. obs.). See also Moult above.
Rarely, summer hood blackish, lacking brown tinge. Such birds may have broader hood on hindneck and sometimes broader white eye-crescents; they could be multi-generation hybrids with other gulls (H. Larsson *in litt.*).

Hybrids Rare hybrid **Black-headed × Common Gull**. Compared to Black-headed larger with heavier bill; often sits higher on water. This, combined with head and bill shape, may suggest Mediterranean Gull. Bill often with dark subterminal ring. Wing pattern intermediate between Black-headed and Common Gull, with white mirrors or mid-parts of P9–10, broad black trailing edge to outer wing and traces of dark surface on P1–4. White tertial and scapular crescents may create well-defined white trailing edge to wing as in Common Gull. In summer, hood brownish, paler than in Black-headed with more distinct white eyelids. In winter, head white with dark streaks through hindneck; often with dark-streaked ear-spot. Bill typically combines characters from both species, such as Common Gull shape and Black-headed coloration. May then look similar to Mediterranean, but latter shows stronger red bill and more complete, not streaked, blackish mask.
For hybrid **Black-headed × Mediterranean Gull**, see Mediterranean Gull.

GEOGRAPHICAL VARIATION Little. Often regarded as monotypic (Cramp & Simmons 1983). Dwight (1925) separated E Asian populations as race *sibiricus*, which is accepted here as a valid subspecies (account below). Within nominate *ridibundus*, mean measurements in Baikal birds closer to European birds than series from Moscow area (Il'icev & Zubakin 1990). In Moscow birds, measurements in adult male wing 309–340 (319.1, n=66), bill 33–39 (36.2, n=90); female 288–332 (303.1, n=91), bill 30–37 (33.0, n=90). Details of measurement methods not given.

L. r. sibiricus (NE Siberia, probably grading into *ridibundus*; winters E Asia) Larger than W European *ridibundus* with proportionately longer wings, less rounded head with flatter forehead, slightly longer, deeper bill and longer legs. When settled, long wings often give impression of 'hanging hand' as in other long-winged gull taxa such as Lesser Black-backed Gull nominate *fuscus*, Iceland Gull and Common Gull race *heinei*.

Adult plumage basically as *ridibundus*, but upperparts generally paler (thus contrast between white P6–10 and grey wing less distinct), and black primary tips broader, together with narrower white primary edges creating impression of fuller black bar at trailing edge of hand, reaching P5–6 (sometimes including P4). Also, dark in mid-primaries on underwing generally deeper blackish, but this could be an effect of better contrast to generally paler plumage. Adult bare part coloration generally duller than in *ridibundus* but frequently darker red. Acquires summer head later than in W European *ridibundus* (<1% among 500 adults early–mid-Feb showed onset of head moult, rest in winter plumage—pers. obs. in Japan, Feb 2001).

First-year as *ridibundus*, but carpal bar generally paler and weaker. Black tail-bar narrower and often less clear. Unlike in *ridibundus* T5–6 sometimes all white. Combined with slightly larger size and paler coloration often recalls Slender-billed Gull (pers. obs. in E China and Japan; J. R. King *in litt.*).

Note: First-winters from Atlantic populations on average show darker, more solid markings on coverts and often primaries than seen elsewhere (e.g. Iceland, pers. obs. Mar 2004).

Measurements in mm (Dwight 1925) (11 adult males, 10 adult females): wing male 305–325 (312.4), female 280–300 (290); bill male 31–37 (36.8), female 32–38 (34.0); bill depth at base male 9–10.5 (9.7), female 8–9 (8.4); bill depth at gonys male 8.5–10 (9.3), female 8–9 (8.3); tarsus male 43–49 (46.4), female 41–46 (43.4).

DISTRIBUTION AND MIGRATION Population 2–3 million pairs. Breeds in dense colonies often of several thousands, but rarely >10,000 pairs, mostly in lakes surrounded by reedbeds with small islands; also coastal sand islands, bogs and artificial ponds. Feeds in open areas such as farmland and towns. Abundant near human settlements.

In S, W and N Europe, spread since nineteenth century, especially 1950–1980. Increase involved larger percentage of coastal breeders. Probably caused by increased amount of agricultural land and new food supplies, including scavenging opportunities in urban areas. In Denmark mainly inland breeder until strong increase in extent of breeding area; now mainly coastal. Since 1980 increase slower or population stabilised; since 1990 strong decrease S Scandinavia and Baltic. Reasons for decrease mainly change of food availability caused by more 'extensive' agriculture with limited areas of grazed land; probably also by competitive scavenging of Herring Gull.

Population late 1990s (in pairs): Sweden 135,000 (270,000 late 1960s, 135,000 mid-1980s); Denmark 112,500 (300,000 1950s, 210,000 1974–1988, since when a strong decrease); Norway 20,000–30,000; Iceland 25,000–30,000; Faeroes 250; Finland 50,000–60,000; Great Britain 150,000–300,000 (35,000–40,000 1928; steady increase since); France 38,000–40,000; Belgium 32,000; Netherlands 130,000 1999 (increase from 30,000 1920s to 90,000 1960 and 225,000 1980, since when a decrease); Germany 175,000 (380,000 1985); Poland 250,000; Estonia 50,000; Latvia 110,000 (1986); Lithuania 18,000; Belarus >200,000; Czech Republic >100,000; Hungary 20,000; Russia max. 500,000; Spain 2,000; Italy 1,000 (mainly N Adriatic, scarce and local elsewhere; only one breeding record Sicily); Bulgaria 300–500; Greece 1–5 (first bred 1987); Turkey 2,000–10,000.

First bred Iceland 1911, Greenland 1969 (50–100 early 1990s) and Newfoundland, Canada, 1977. Now scarce breeder Canada to New England W to Quebec; increase linked with Iceland increase (Finch 1978, Fredriksson 1979, Cramp & Simmons 1983, Risberg 1990, Malling Olsen 1992, Aspinall *et al.* 1993, Rheinwald 1993, Boertmann 1994, Gjershaug *et al.* 1994, Hagemeijer & Blair 1997, Handrinos & Akriotis 1997, Väisinen *et al.* 1998, Svensson *et al.* 1999, Heldbjerg 2000, Bengtsson 2001, Bijlsma *et al.* 2001, *Brit. Birds* 92: 291, A. Corso & B. Nikolov *in litt.*).

Breeding sites occupied Mar; in S Scandinavia usually late Mar. Departure from early Jul.

Northern population migratory; everywhere dispersive or partially migratory. Generally, adults stay closer to breeding grounds than younger birds, which perform the longest migration (18% North Sea birds first-years compared with 88% Adriatic birds – Glutz von Blotzheim & Bauer 1982).

British population mainly stays within Great Britain with some dispersal W to Ireland and S to N and W Africa; Iceland birds mostly migratory, moving ESE–S; ringing recovered Faeroe Islands, Great Britain and W Europe S to Spain; some (especially immatures) reach Greenland and Newfoundland. Greenland population probably winters Iceland and SE Canada, to a lesser degree Great Britain. N American winter population now several thousands, mostly confined to NE, especially Newfoundland (Glutz von Blotzheim & Bauer 1982, Cramp & Simmons 1983, Montevecchi *et al.* 1987, Boertmann 1994).

Population from Scandinavia, Baltic and W Europe winters S Scandinavia, W Europe (Great Britain to Iberian Peninsula) and N Africa; ringing recoveries S to Senegal. Northern population generally winters further N within the wintering range. Danish population showed increased tendency to winter Iberia in 1970s and 1980s, but from 1990s rarer, as S Scandinavian populations generally have wintered closer to breeding range recently (K. Bengtsson in press). 10–25% Danish birds sedentary. Some Finnish and E Baltic birds (Estonia, Latvia, Lithuania, Kaliningrad) migrate S, crossing Europe to Adriatic and E Mediterranean, where common Oct–Mar; to a lesser degree SE to Ukraine (10–250 yearly), Black Sea and Morocco. Exceptionally, Finnish

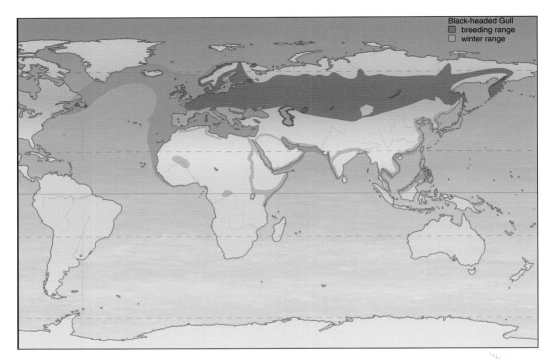

bird recovered Faeroe Islands, N and W European birds the Azores, and a Dutch bird in Labrador. W European population sedentary or short-distance migrant, wintering between Great Britain and N Africa, where joined by some C European populations (Cramp & Simmons 1983, Bowes *et al.* 1984, Lack 1986, Il'icev & Zubakin 1990, Jensen 1993).

European winter population >4 million birds; in Great Britain 3 million, of which 1.1 million in inland roosts (two-thirds of continental origin). Late autumn gatherings in Denmark max. 161,000 Aug, 63,000 Jan; in Waddenzee 80,000 Aug, 95,000 Sep; in Rheinland 70,000–80,000; in Netherlands 290,000 Jan 1975; at Bodensee, 30,000 in winter; in Spain, e.g. 75,000 around Madrid 1993 (20,000 1979–1980), 75,000 in NE and 30,000–35,000 around Gibraltar; along French W coast 1.2 million; Italy 700,000; Greece 500,000; Bulgaria max. 27,560. In N Africa max. counts 45,000 Tunisia, 13,800 Algeria; 1,000 Nouadhibou; small numbers reach further S to Nigeria. Inland wintering, associated with human activities, has increased since 1960 (Glutz von Blotzheim & Bauer 1982, Cramp & Simmons 1983, Schuster *et al.* 1983, Bowes *et al.* 1984, Lack 1986, Isenmann *et al.* 1991, Finlayson 1992, Jensen 1993, Khymyn 1993, Meschini & Frugis 1993, Shirihai 1996b, Handrinos & Akriotis 1997, Bijlsma *et al.* 2001, Mitchev & Profirov 2003).

Birds from C East Europe (Saxony, Bavaria, Czech Republic, Hungary, Slovakia, Austria) migrate S and SW to winter quarters in Adriatic, W Mediterranean and Algeria; some follow river valleys NW to North Sea. Austrian and Hungarian birds move mainly to E Mediterranean. Yugoslavian birds winter across Mediterranean; a few reach Black Sea. Russian birds move mainly SW to E Mediterranean, Black Sea and Transcaucasia. Moscow birds go mainly to Balkans; extralimitally recovered SE Caspian and Azerbaijan; some also Bodensee. C and SE Russian populations winter E Mediterranean and Middle East, probably S to E Africa. In Egypt winter counts of max. 75,000–100,000. In Israel *c.*1 million, mainly in N and W. Several thousands Arabian Gulf States: vanguards Jul, peak Dec–Mar; e.g. 13,000 UAE, max. 20,000 Bahrain Jan, tens of thousands Oman and 10,000 Iraq. In Yemen max. winter flocks 900. In NE Africa scarce Djibouti, max. 3,000 Sudan. Scarce but increasing E African Rift Valley lakes and S to Burundi and coastline of Tanzania (e.g. 550 Dar es Salaam Feb 1972) (Walker 1981a & b, Glutz von Blotzheim & Bauer 1982, Scott & Carp 1982, Cramp & Simmons 1983, Urban *et al.* 1986, Brooks *et al.* 1987, Hirschfeld 1992a, Porter *et al.* 1996b, Shirihai 1996b, Richardson & Aspinall 1997b).

Birds from NE Siberia and Kazakhstan winter Caspian Sea, Persian Gulf and Arabian Sea; locally common Indian Ocean between India and Philippines. Regular Sri Lanka. E Siberian and Kamchatka population winters Japan to S Asia; winter numbers in Hong Kong grew from 100 1970 to 15,000–20,000 mid-1990s. In Nepal, max. 150 Kosi Barrage (Glutz von Blotzheim & Bauer 1982, Inskipp & Inskipp 1985, Il'icev & Zubakin 1990, Grimmett *et al.* 1998).

In S Scandinavia, autumn migration starts with immatures late May, peaking mid-Jun–early Jul, followed by non-breeding adults early Jun. Adults peak mid-Jul–early Aug with day-counts >20,000 noted S Sweden/Baltic (Falsterbo, Ottenby) and S Danish coastline, heading for Waddenzee. Juvenile migration starts late Jun, peaks mid-Aug–mid-Sep. Slight increase in

BLACK-HEADED GULL Two-year gull. Abundant medium-sized gull of W Palearctic and E Asia. Outer wing with white leading edge, black trailing edge and grey inner parts concolorous with upperparts. Underwing with broad dark wedge on mid-primaries against white leading edge and coverts. Bill and legs generally concolorous.

Adult summer (Mar–Aug) has dark brown hood (with narrow white eyelids) and maroon to red (dark-tipped) bill and red legs. In **winter** head white with dark ear-spot and varying grey shades over crown and hindneck. Hindneck white to pale grey, paler than grey upperparts.

Juvenile (Jun–Aug) at first extensively patterned warm brown on head, breast-sides and upperparts. Juvenile wing patterned as in adult, but with brown carpal bar and black trailing edge to inner wing. Primary coverts white or dark-patterned, often with row of dark streaks. Tail white with medium-broad black bar.

First-winter (Aug–Apr) similar to adult, but juvenile wing and tail retained, and bare parts orange.

First-summer (Apr–Aug) with varying, usually incomplete, dull hood.

adult numbers Oct–Dec involves Finnish and Russian birds. Another route crosses inland Sweden towards lakes around Alingsås (day-counts >15,000), to a lesser degree Vänern/Vättern heading for Kattegat. Most winter Waddenzee, but some continue further W or S. Migration in mid-Baltic and along Danish W coast smaller. Main exodus into Great Britain mid-Sep–late Oct. C European and French populations follow large river valleys to Mediterranean and Bay of Biscay. In S Mediterranean arrival of first-years from Jul; strong increase early Nov–early Jan (Fredriksson 1966, Johansson 1990, Malling Olsen 1993, Shirihai 1996b, Strack et al. 1997).

Spring migration starts early Feb in C Europe. In Israel migration peaks late Mar–early Apr. In C Europe and S Scandinavia adult peak simultaneous; less pronounced migration of first-years into mid-May. Arrival in Baltic and S Scandinavia breeding sites highly weather-dependent; breeding sites settled late Mar, but during icy conditions delayed to late Apr; Kaliningrad sites returned to between 26 March and 23 April. Spring migration of N population peaks Baraba plains late Apr–early May. Often in large flocks in areas around breeding sites before re-occupation (Il'icev & Zubakin 1990, Malling Olsen 1993, Shirihai 1996b).

Rare but increasing visitor Nov–Jun in Caribbean region; birds ringed in Russia have been recovered in Barbados and Mexico (Ebels 2002). Vagrant S and W USA (including Finnish ringed bird recovered Texas 1998–2001), Mexico, Hawaii, Socotra, Maldives, New Guinea, Sulawesi, Wallacea, N Australia, Chad, Gabon, Mozambique, Zimbabwe, S Africa.

MEASUREMENTS Lengths in mm; weights in g. Own data based on skins in NNH, UZM, ZMA, ZMO. N and W Europe.

WING

Adult male	284–335	(306.5)	131
Adult female	280–310	(295.4)	93
First-year male	275–323	(299.2)	61
First-year female	275–312	(290.9)	53

Note Juveniles Jun–Jul: male 275–291, female 272–285.

BILL

Adult male	30.1–37.3 (33.6)	133
Adult female	28.2–35.2 (31.6)	94
First-year male	29.3–37.2 (33.1)	63
First-year female	28.3–36.3 (30.6)	55

BILL DEPTH AT GONYS

Adult male	7.4–9.3 (8.4)	131
Adult female	7.1–9.0 (7.8)	93
First-year male	6.7–8.9 (8.0)	54
First-year female	7.0–8.5 (7.5)	51

Note Juveniles Jun–Jul: male 6.4–7.3, female 6.2–7.0.

BILL DEPTH AT BASE OF BILL

Adult male	8.7–10.9 (9.7)	132
Adult female	8.3–10.1 (9.1)	94
First-year male	8.0–10.6 (9.0)	54
First-year female	7.3–10.5 (8.8)	51

Note Juveniles Jun–Jul: male 7.6–8.4, female 7.2–8.0.

GONYS LENGTH

Adult male	10.0–13.3 (11.8)	132
Adult female	9.3–12.8 (11.2)	94
First-year male	9.0–13.3 (11.3)	55
First-year female	8.7–12.9 (10.8)	49

Note Juveniles Jun–Jul: male 8.2–9.0, female 6.7–8.7.

TARSUS

Adult male	40.0–48.9 (44.2)	132
Adult female	38.0–46.6 (41.9)	100
First-year male	38.6–46.7 (43.1)	62
First-year female	36.4–46.2 (41.9)	55

Weight Adult male 186–400, female 166–350. Generally heaviest at onset of breeding season. Birds in poor condition down to 170 (male), 136 (female). Second-years 194–374, third-years 205–381. First-year male 192.5–327, female 161–352; when fledged down to 175 (male) and 151 (female) (skins in NNH, UZM, ZMA, Glutz von Blotzheim & Bauer 1982, Cramp & Simmons 1983).

Black-headed Gull *Larus ridibundus*. Photos refer to ssp. *ridibundus* unless otherwise stated. **631. Juvenile**. Note pinkish bill-base and legs and warm brown upperparts. Varberg, Halland, Sweden. 14 Aug 1999. *Klaus Malling Olsen*. **632. Juvenile**. A paler and greyer-than-average juvenile, compare with 631. Växjö, Sweden. 26 Aug 1996. *Harry J. Lehto*. **633. 1st-winter**. Note white leading edge to outer wing contrasting with grey inner-hand and black trailing edge to outer wing. Geneva, Switzerland. Apr 1997. *Don DesJardin*. **634. 1st-winter** Some birds show more extensive black in wing-tip, here with large white mirrors in P9-10. Hanstholm, North Jutland, Denmark. 10 Oct 1995. *Klaus Malling Olsen*. **635. 1st-winter**. Compared to 633-634, this bird shows the not-infrequent dark streaks to primary coverts and rather solid black wing-tip. North Jutland, Denmark. 19 Feb 1994. *Klaus Malling Olsen*.

Black-headed Gull *Larus ridibundus*. Photos refer to ssp. *ridibundus* unless otherwise stated. **636. 1st-winter**. Similar to adult, but note dark-centred median coverts and tertials as well as paler, orange-toned bill. Oman. Dec. *Hanne & Jens Eriksen*. **637. 1st-winter** ssp *sibiricus*. On average slightly larger and paler than nominate; note weaker dark upperpart markings and very narrow black tail-bar with all-white T5–6. Choshi, Japan. 11 Nov 1999. *Jon R. King*. **638. 1st-winter**. A worn individual with bleached pattern on primaries, creating semi-translucent area; compare Bonaparte's Gull. Eilat, Israel. 22 Mar 1996. *Klaus Malling Olsen*. **639. 1st-summer**. Most develop >50% dark hood at this age; compared to adult hood duller and normally with white spotting. Baden-Württemberg, Germany. 24 May 1989. *Klaus Malling Olsen*. **640. Adult winter**. Note bicoloured bill, red legs (colour as bill-base) and narrow white primary tips. California, USA. 5 Dec 1995. *Don DesJardin*.

Black-headed Gull *Larus ridibundus*. Photos refer to ssp. *ridibundus* unless otherwise stated. **641. Adult winter** ssp *sibiricus*. Compared to nominate slightly paler on upperparts. Kyoto, Honshu, Japan. 5 Feb 2001. *Klaus Malling Olsen*. **642. Adult in last stages of moult from winter to summer**. The last head feathers to change from winter to summer plumage are normally on the forehead and lores, creating a white blaze by late Feb-mid Mar. Finland. 13 Mar 1983. *Harry J. Lehto*. **643. Adult summer**. Note dark brown hood, and deep red bill which sometimes looks almost concolorous with head in early breeding season. Flevoland, Netherlands. Apr 1993. *René Pop*. **644. Adult moulting from summer to winter**. The now faded brown hood gradually disappears by mid to late summer, leaving just a dark ring around neck, which is finally moulted into winter plumage. 20 Jul 1983. *Harry J. Lehto*. **645. Adult summer**. Note white and strongly contrasting leading edge to grey wing, showing black trailing edge to primaries. Turku, Finland. 27 Mar 1993. *Harry J. Lehto*.

Black-headed Gull *Larus ridibundus*. Photos refer to ssp. *ridibundus* unless otherwise stated. **646. Adult winter**. On underwing note black mid-primaries, creating solid dark area on mid- to inner hand. Zealand, Denmark. 5 Jan 1997. *Klaus Malling Olsen*. **647. Adult summer leucistic/albinistic**. Note overall whitish impression with hood appearing 'ghostly'. This is not an infrequent abnormality in Black-headed Gull. Turku, Finland. 23 Apr 1995. *Henry Lehto*. **648. Adult winter** with Mediterranean Gull. A rare example of a bird showing blackish bill. Compare wing-pattern between the two species. Great Britain. 16 Feb 1990. *Harry J. Lehto*. **649. Adult winter** ssp. **sibiricus**. Honshu, Japan. Nov 2000. *Jon R. King*. **650. Adult winter** ssp. **sibiricus**. Compared to nominate, *sibiricus* shows on average a broader black trailing edge to outer wing. Kyoto, Honshu, Japan. 5 Feb 2001. *Klaus Malling Olsen*.

31. SLENDER-BILLED GULL

Larus genei (Brème, 1839, Sardinia)

Plates 64–65, Photos 651–664

IDENTIFICATION Length 40–44cm, wingspan 100–112cm. Similar to Black-headed Gull, but slightly larger and more graceful, with a smaller head and slimmer, more sloping forehead, flatter crown and longer bill with longer gape-line; neck longer, breast deeper, hindparts more elongated (but long tail makes primary projection rather short) and legs longer with more of tibia visible—as if the bird was wearing shorts! Always gives a white-headed impression, as there is at most a very faint grey ear-spot. Apart from some breeding birds, iris is pale, looking small and creating a beady 'fish-eyed' appearance, although this often obscured by dark orbital ring.

At rest small-headed with deep breast and long legs. When settled, shape is often more like Caspian Gull nominate *cachinnans* than Black-headed. When alert, stretches into a 'giraffe-neck' posture similar to that seen in Ruff *Philomachus pugnax*. Seen close to, the wedge of feathers on upper mandible is longer than in Black-headed (angle to cutting edge 20–45°; 35–60° in Black-headed), and reaches further than on lower mandible (as far as on lower mandible in Black-headed). Diameter of eye less than depth of bill at base, about equal in Black-headed.

Swimming bird tends to lower bill slightly, hold long neck in 90° angle towards the flat back and raise tail—in combination creating impression of an oversized swimming phalarope. Tibia often visible (rarer in Black-headed). Surface feeds, but also often wades in shallow water with small gulls and egrets, with head held high and neck stretched; in flock shepherding fish to shallow waters before plunge-diving; may also run quickly through shallow water. Other smaller gulls do not employ either of these latter two foraging methods (Baker 1984, Corso 1999).

In flight almost cigar-shaped with longer, slimmer head and neck projecting well forward of wings, deeper breast, longer wings and longer tail than Black-headed. Often feeds in flight with bill held downwards, looking hump-backed. The flight is—compared to Black-headed—lazier with slower, stiffer wingbeats, often more like a larger gull (especially Caspian Gull *cachinnans*), but has also been compared to Gull-billed Tern *Sterna nilotica*. To some observers' eyes, the shape in flight may recall an egret.

Adult has wing pattern similar to Black-headed, but with slightly paler grey upperparts, creating weaker contrast with white leading edge. On underwing, the dark inner hand may contrast better than in Black-headed, caused by paler upperparts. Head always white. Underbody often strongly flushed with pink, sometimes as strong as in adult Ross's Gull, and often sharply divided from white head (if so, diagnostic). Rosy tinge often strongest in winter. Bill dark red, darker than in Black-headed and together with white head and pale eyes creating an impression very different from Black-head-ed. In **summer,** head white and eye often darkish. Bill generally darkest in early spring, when often blackish, in strong contrast with white head, visible at long range. In **winter,** many have faint grey ear-spot and often grey shadows behind eye. The grey ear-spot may look larger than the pale eye. Bill red. Black-headed always shows stronger dark head-markings, with a large, dark ear-spot being the minimum.

Juvenile looks like bleached, white-headed Black-headed Gull, but is paler and greyer with greyish-brown upperparts (not buff and dark brown). Upperwing looks faded with paler brown carpal bar, unpatterned primary coverts and narrower, browner tail-bar. Black on outer webs of P8–10 narrower. Head whitish with dark restricted to diffuse grey, often even lacking ear-spot. Eye quickly becomes pale, reinforcing paleness of head. Bill and legs paler and more yellowish-tinged than in Black-headed, bill often uniform or at most with indistinct grey tip.

First-winter similar to juvenile, but mantle and scapulars grey as in adult. Already from Mar the plumage looks worn; head especially looks untidy with many worn feathers. Feathering at base of upper mandible has proved to be restricted in some (pers. obs. in Italy, Apr). By **first-summer,** some are worn enough to look as uniformly grey as adults when settled: the untidy plumage and pale orange bare parts are then the best field distinctions from the more fully plumaged adults. In flight, the worn juvenile wing and tail should prove age.

Second-winter similar to adult, but often with dark tertial spots and rarely dark spots/streaks on inner primary coverts. Bill paler and brighter red than in adult. An identification pitfall is provided by leucistic Black-headed Gulls, which may show similar head pattern (including only faint grey ear-spot or even white head) and brighter red bare parts than normal individuals. Jizz differences (especially bill, head and long legs), pale eyes and longer feathering at base of upper mandible are essential.

VOICE Deeper, mellower and throatier than Black-headed Gull; sometimes reminiscent of Greater Flamingo *Phoenicopterus ruber*. Long call deeper, mellower and nasal than in Black-headed, recalling larger gulls: *ka* or *kra* (Urban *et al.* 1986).

MOULT (Cramp & Simmons 1983, skins, pers. obs.) **Adult** undergoes complete moult into **winter plumage** May/Jul–Oct/Nov. Primaries mid-May–Oct. Most have reached P6–8 late Jul/mid-Aug, P8–10 mid-Sep. Most Bulgarian birds (mid-Sep) have completed primary moult; some still growing P9–10 mid-Oct/early Nov. **Adult** acquires **summer plumage** by partial moult Jan/Mar–(Apr/May), including head and parts of body. **Juvenile** acquires **first-winter** plumage by partial moult

Aug–Oct, including head, body and often parts of coverts and tertials. Moult to **first-summer** probably very restricted, at most including minor parts of head and body. In Sicily, late Apr, 80% have winter head (strongly worn) and only 20% show some head moult (pers. obs.).

Moult to **second-winter** similar to adult. Primary moult has reached P7–8 mid-Aug–early Sep and P9–10 late Sep; immature moult often advanced compared to adults; moult into second-winter may start in winter with coverts (especially median coverts) and primary coverts (Cramp & Simmons 1983, Hoogendoorn & Pop 1995).

DESCRIPTION

Adult Upperparts, secondaries and inner primaries pale grey (Kodak Grey Scale 2–4). Outer primary coverts and P7–10 white, P(2–3)4–10 with black tips, creating dark trailing edge to hand; on P4–5 black often reduces to narrow dark markings on outer web only. Outer web of P10 black, often not extending onto 20–45mm white before 7–12mm black tip (may disappear with wear); P9 may show narrow black streaks on outer web. P9–6 with 16–30mm black tips, broadest on P6–8, mostly with rounded separation from paler bases. P1–6 grey, P6 often with white inner web. White primary tips generally narrower than in Black-headed; may (almost) be absent even in fresh plumage. Secondaries with white tips. Tertials grey with diffuse whitish edges. Rump and tail white, often slightly pinkish-tinged. Shafts of rectrices white, rarely orange-straw. Iris white, pale yellow, greenish-grey or mid-brown, generally darkest at onset of breeding season. Orbital ring red to pale red, sometimes brown to blackish (especially in winter). Bill orange-red to dark red with blackish tip; by spring to summer often reddish-black to blackish. Legs dark red. Tibia 0.4–0.55 length of tarsus (compare Black-headed).

Adult summer (Jan/Mar–Jul) Head and underparts white; breast to belly often with strong pink tinge, sharply divided from head. Eye generally darker than in winter. Bill sometimes dark red to blackish.

Adult winter (Jul/Aug–Feb) Similar to adult summer, but often with faint grey ear-spot and eye-crescents. Underbody generally pinkish-tinged, in some very strong on belly and breast into midwinter. P1–5 at most with very narrow white tips, soon disappearing with wear. Eye generally pale, but sometimes dark, especially in dark-billed birds (Glutz von Blotzheim & Bauer 1992, Barthel & Königstedt 1983). Bill dark red, orange-red or orange-yellow. Legs orange-red, generally paler than bill.

Juvenile (fledging–Aug) Head white, sometimes with pale buff and grey markings, especially on ear-spot. Mantle, scapulars and sides of breast grey-brown with paler fringes, generally paler than in Black-headed with broader pale fringes. Lesser and median coverts brown with grey bases and paler fringes: grey bases to median coverts often broader, and sometimes all feathers grey. Greater coverts grey, innermost greater coverts often dark-centred with pale fringes. Tertials dark greyish-brown with pale fringes. Primary coverts (outer white, inner grey) only rarely with indistinct dark shaft-streaks.

Alula white, often with narrow dark markings. P7–10 white, P1–6 grey. Primaries with 25–35mm black tips. P10 has black outer web. P9 about 90mm black on outer part of outer webs, P1–8 with max. 80mm black on outer webs. Secondaries dark grey with broad white fringes, on both surfaces slightly paler than in Black-headed. Underwing-coverts pale grey, underside of P1–6 dark grey to blackish, contrasting well with white P7–10. Rump and tail white. Tail with dark grey to blackish-brown subterminal band, generally paler and narrower than in Black-headed (12–22mm on T6). Underbody white, sometimes with pinkish tinge. Iris dark brown, in some pale from age of fledging. Orbital ring dark. Bill greyish-orange to orange-flesh with indistinct dark tip (sometimes lacking). Legs pale orange-flesh.

First-winter (Aug–Mar/Apr) similar to juvenile, but head white with faint grey ear-spot (often lacking) and mantle/scapulars grey. Dark on upperwing fades to pale brown as winter progresses. Iris pale. Bill yellow-orange to orange (rarely red) with faint dark tip, often lacking. May show reddish orbital ring. Legs pale orange, rarely greenish-yellow.

First-summer (Feb–Sep/Oct) similar to first-winter, but head often all white. Upperwing and tail faded, appearing plain at distance. T1 often white. Bill and legs orange, by late summer often redder. Bill with blackish tip.

Second-winter (Sep–Mar) as adult winter, but often with dark markings on tertials, alula, secondaries, inner primary coverts and scattered wing-coverts. On tertials dark markings range from small spot on one feather to fuller dark patches on all (Hoogendoorn & Pop 1995). Shows 8–10mm dark outer web of P8–10 and 40–50mm dark tips to inner webs of P8–10, more diffusely divided from paler bases than in adult. P(2)3 often with dark markings near tip (rare in adult). Bill and legs often brighter red than in adult.

Variants Melanistic adult had dark grey cap on otherwise white head, dark mantle and upperwing-coverts, sooty-grey flight feathers with silvery wash and sooty underbody (pers. obs. in Israel).

DISTRIBUTION AND MIGRATION Population 75,000–125,000 pairs; scattered throughout range, seemingly fluctuating. Breeds in dense colonies on low-lying islands with mudflats and marshes in salt or saline shallow waters, often with *Salsola* or *Salicornia*. Locally in lakes.

European population 41,000–82,000 pairs late-1990s. Strong increase W Mediterranean, where first bred 1960 and where population (in pairs) at year 2000 was: Spain 1,000 (Ebro Delta first bred 1975; in 1988 429); France 900 Camargue (first bred 1970s; 70 1986, 850 1995, 566 1998); Italy 3,896; Sardinia 1,000 (first bred 1976). Greece 40 pairs; Turkey 3,000–10,000. First bred Bulgaria 1995. Marked decrease Romania where formerly common, now rare. Common Russian Black Sea, in Ukraine >35,000 (50,000); largest colonies Tendra Island 37,450 (in some years lower), also 18,000–20,000 Crimean Kerch Peninsula; Azerbaijan 450–550; Iran 3,000–5,500; Iraq 'common'; Egypt 200–400 (largest

PLATE 64. SLENDER-BILLED GULL *Larus genei*

A medium-sized gull of NW Africa, Mediterranean Basin and W Asia, occurring in scattered populations. In plumage similar to Black-headed Gull, but head white all year round. Jizz closer to a larger gull, especially Caspian Gull nominate *cachinnans*. Compared to Black-headed, head is smaller, breast deeper and hindparts more elongated. Eyes pale from early age, appearing small and beady. The bill is longer and narrower, and the feathering at base of upper bill penetrates in a 45–60° angle towards the cutting edges (more than 60° and rounded in Black-headed). Legs are longer with larger amount of tibia visible. When alert, often appears long-necked, performing 'giraffe-neck posture' similar to Ruff *Philomachus pugnax*. Wing pattern shared with Black-headed, but generally paler grey, in first-year plumage more weakly dark-marked.

1. **Juvenile** (fledging–Aug) Similar to pale-patterned Black-headed (see Plate 62, illustration 3) but head white without blackish markings (at most with weak grey ear-spot). Bill paler orange with no or restricted dark in tip (often at tip of upper mandible only). Paler yellowish-orange legs and small, beady eye, with pale iris.

2. **First-winter** (Aug–Mar/Apr) Head and body similar to adult (winter), but juvenile wing and tail retained. From midwinter often strongly worn, at distance with hardly discernible dark pattern (apart from tertials) and often with 'ragged-looking' head. Head white, at most with weak grey ear-spot, much smaller than in Black-headed, and pale iris, creating cold 'fish-eyed' look. Bill and legs paler orange.

3. **Late first-winter** (Mar–May) Often strongly worn. Note pale overall impression and long orange legs with fair amount of tibia visible. Often moults large parts of wing coverts in first-winter, unlike Black-headed Gull.

4. **Second-winter** (Sep–Mar) Similar to adult winter, but often with scattered dark markings on tertials and generally brighter red legs and bill, the latter being slightly darker at tip.

5. **Adult winter** (Sep–Mar) Some show bright red bill and legs. Upperparts pale grey with black wing-tip. White tips to primaries generally narrower than in Black-headed (but matched by eastern Black-headed race *sibiricus*).

6. **Adult summer** (Jan–Sep) Head white, body often rosy-tinged (this also the case in winter), sometimes sharply divided from head. At onset of breeding season, bill dark reddish-brown to black and eye sometimes slightly darker than in winter. Legs dark reddish-brown to dark red.

Juvenile

3. Late first-winter

2. First-winter

4. Second-winter

5. Adult winter

Adult summer

PLATE 65. SLENDER-BILLED GULL *Larus genei*

Plumage similar to Black-headed Gull, best identified on slightly larger size, more elongated (elliptical) body with longer tail, smaller, well-protruding head against deep breast and longer bill. Jizz in flight not dissimilar to Caspian Gull nominate *cachinnans*. Flight lazier than in Black-headed with slower, stiffer wingbeats.

1. **First-winter** (Aug–Apr) Plumage similar to Black-headed Gull, but on average paler with paler, generally more greyish-brown carpal bar and less full dark grey secondary bar. Head whitish, only at close range showing faint grey ear-spot. Leading edge of outer wing white, lacking black markings on outer primary coverts as in certain Black-headed wing pattern.

2. **First-winter** By late winter, wing pattern becomes worn and appears washed out compared to Black-headed.

3. **Second-winter** (Sep–Mar) As adult winter, but note faint black streaks on outer web of outer primaries and bright red bill and legs (latter, however, variable and also seen in many adult winter).

4. **Adult** Head white, in winter at most with faint grey ear-spot. Eyes small and beady. Often strongly rosy-tinged on underbody. The tricoloured wing pattern is shared with Black-headed (and Bonaparte's) Gull. Basically a white-headed Black-headed Gull with long, protruding head, longer body and tail and deep breast.

5. **Adult summer** (Feb/Mar–Jul) By early breeding season often with blackish-looking bill.

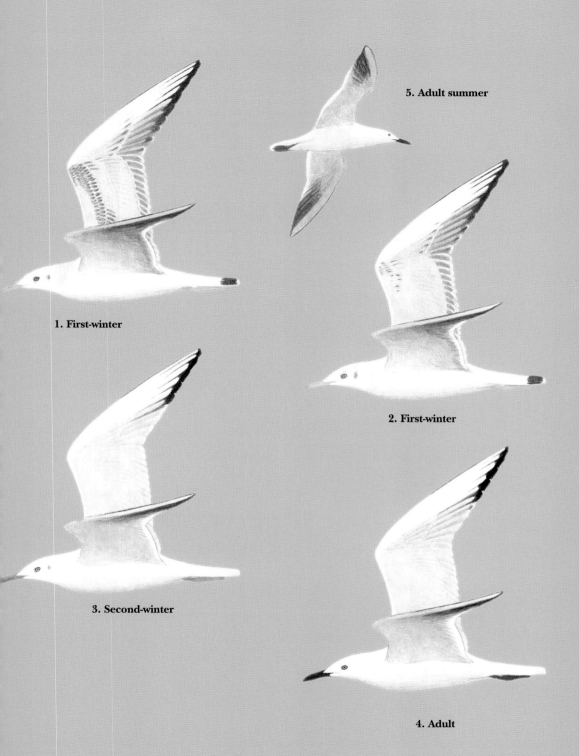

5. Adult summer

1. First-winter

2. First-winter

3. Second-winter

4. Adult

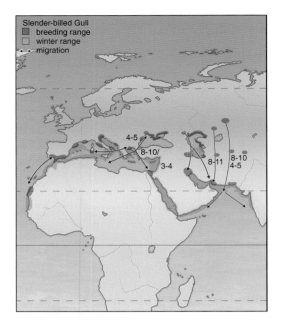

Slender-billed Gull
- ■ breeding range
- □ winter range
- ◄--► migration

4-5

8-10/

3-4

8-11

8-10
4-5

winter S Caspian Sea and Oman. Scarce in winter Spain, France, N Mediterranean, Sicily, Balkans, Black Sea, Sea of Azov and E to W India.

Black Sea birds winter Mediterranean, mainly between Egypt and Tunisia (>200 recoveries of Orlov birds Egypt/Sinai), but thousands also Greece. Along Tunisian coastline 15,848 Mar–May 1978. Ringed Black Sea birds have reached W to Tenerife and Portugal. In Israel and Egypt arrival in two waves: first mid-Jul–late Aug; second (larger) early Sep–Oct, the latter involving day-counts of max. 100 S Mediterranean coast and 140 Bardawil, N Egypt. Max. 120 winter in Bulgaria. In winter 300–500 Israel (mainly Mediterranean). In N Egypt, max. 6,000 Port Said, 6,600 Nile Delta and 140 Bardawil. In Sinai flocks of max. 100.

C Asian birds winter Arabia and Persian Gulf E to W India. Iran max. 55,000; Bahrain 8,000, UAE 1,500–2,000 (1,800 Abu Dhabi Jan 1994 considered exceptional); some thousands Oman and Iraq. Scarcer S Arabia (e.g. 500 Aden and some hundreds Yemen) and S coast of Caspian Sea, Pakistan to W India (especially Gujarat). In Mauritania, max. 2,500 winter (Erard 1958, Bundy & Warr 1980, Petersen & Sørensen 1981, Glutz von Blotzheim & Bauer 1982, Cramp & Simmons 1983, Albrecht 1986b, Ash 1988, Il'icev & Zubakin 1990, Finlayson 1992, Nankinov 1992b, Shirihai 1996b, Handrinos & Akriotis 1997, Nankinov et al. 1997).

Spring migration late Feb–May, peaking Mar–Apr. Main route along W coast of Black Sea; peak mid-Apr. Arrives Black Sea breeding sites late Mar–early May. In Greece peak mid-Mar–mid-Apr (max. 2,200). Israeli migration peaks Apr (adults); immature peak late May; spring counts at Eilat 500–3,000. Many immatures remain in winter quarters, e.g. flocks of hundreds Nile Delta and 100–150 Israel. Abundant Persian Gulf, Gulf of Oman and Arabian Sea (Cramp & Simmons 1983, Meininger et al. 1986, Nankinov 1992b, Porter et al. 1996b, Shirihai 1996b, Richardson & Aspinall 1997a & b, Handrinos & Akriotis 1997, Grimmett et al. 1998, Knaus & Balzari 1999).

Vagrant Canary Islands, Nigeria, Ethiopia, Sudan, Kenya, Sri Lanka, E Asia (Nepal to E China, Hong Kong and Japan). In N and W Europe up to year 2000: Great Britain (9) (of which two records of pairs), Germany

5,688); Tunisia 150–200; Morocco 'scarce'. Irregular N Africa and Canary Islands. Also Senegal/Mauritania 6,000–7,000; increasing, probably recent colonist (Vasiliu 1968, Glutz von Blotzheim & Bauer 1982, Urban et al. 1986, Siotkin et al. 1988, Cottridge & Vinicombe 1996, del Hoyo et al. 1996, Nankinov et al. 1996, Shirihai 1996b, Barlow et al. 1997, Hagemeijer & Blair 1997).

Leaves breeding sites Jul. At Sea of Azov, adult peaks late Jul with another wave late Oct–early Nov. Main migration Adjarkul, C Asia, late Sep; in SW Caspian Sea migration Aug–early Dec. Large autumn migration of Black Sea birds, Bosporus, Bulgaria and Greece, peaking Sep–Oct (e.g. flocks >1,000 Lake Atanassovsko, Bulgaria). At Eregli, N Turkey, 1,500 20 October–4 December 1977.

W Mediterranean birds winter S Mediterranean and NW African coast together with Mauritanian/Senegal population. Caspian birds recovered in autumn and

SLENDER-BILLED GULL Two- or three year gull. W Palearctic. Resembles Black-headed Gull, but slightly larger with small, whitish head, thinner bill and longer tail. In flight has longer, cigar-shaped body, long neck and deep, protruding breast. Settled birds have long, sloping forehead with feathering at base pointed to tip, ending near nostril. Legs long and slender with long section of tibia visible.

Adult rather similar all year; always white-headed (in winter at most with faint grey ear-spot) and often with strong rosy tinge to underbody. Wing as in Black-headed including white leading edge and black trailing edge to outer wing, and dark mid-primaries on underwing. Bill long and dark, often turning almost blackish in spring, otherwise reddish. Eyes white, but often darkening in spring.

Juvenile (Jul–Sep) like washed-out Black-headed with similar wing pattern, but brown carpal bar fainter and primary coverts lack dark stripes. Upperparts cold greyish-brown. Head white, only with faint grey ear-spot. Tail white with narrow black bar. Legs and bill pale orange-yellow, bill-tip at most with faint dark markings.

First-winter (Sep–Apr) like juvenile, but head and body as adult winter. Often strongly worn and bleached in spring (more so than Black-headed).

Second-year similar to adult, but tertials sometimes dark-marked and bill and legs generally brighter red.

(>10) (including seven – four forming two pairs – Lake Constance 1997), Switzerland (35–40; annual from 1998: spring 1997 30, including flock of 20 Les Grangettes 14 May); Poland (2), Belarus (1–2), Austria (4), Hungary (9), Sweden (2), Finland (1). Surprisingly scarce Portugal (six records up to 2000) (Stevenson 1982, Mitchell & Young 1997, Gantlett 1999, Maumary & Gysel 1998, Rogers *et al.* 2001).

MEASUREMENTS Lengths in mm; weights in g. Own data based on skins in AMNH, MCZ, NHM, NNH, USNM, UZM, ZMA. Mediterranean, Tunisia, Black and Caspian Seas, Turkey, Egypt, Iran, India, Pakistan, Senegal.

WING

Adult male	287–321 (309.8)	82
Adult female	275–316 (295.8)	55
First-year male	290–311 (300.7)	13
First-year female	273–304 (288.2)	10

BILL

Adult male	35.7–47.2 (43.3)	82
Adult female	35.6–46.9 (40.0)	52
First-year male	35.2–45.8 (41.8)	13
First-year female	35.0–43.3 (38.5)	11

BILL DEPTH AT BASE OF BILL

Adult male	10.4–13.0 (11.8)	82
Adult female	9.5–12.8 (10.9)	52
First-year male	9.7–12.5 (10.9)	13
First-year female	8.6–11.8 (10.2)	11

BILL DEPTH AT GONYS

Adult male	9.0–10.3 (9.7)	82
Adult female	7.7–10.0 (8.6)	52
First-year male	8.2–9.5 (9.0)	13
First-year female	7.2–8.9 (8.3)	11

GONYS LENGTH

Adult male	13.4–17.3 (15.6)	88
Adult female	12.4–16.3 (14.4)	53
First-year male	12.1–16.7 (14.7)	13
First-year female	10.9–15.8 (13.8)	11

TARSUS

Adult male	47.2–55.9 (52.0)	84
Adult female	44.9–53.8 (49.7)	52
First-year male	44.2–53.5 (51.0)	13
First-year female	45.0–50.5 (47.5)	11

Weight Russia: adult male 276–375, female 230–360. NW Iran: male 247–297, female 223–248. Spring adults, Italy, 276–290 (Borodulina 1960, Dolgushin 1962, Cramp & Simmons 1983, skins in UZM).

Slender-billed Gull *Larus genei*. **651. 1st-winter.** Compared to Black-headed Gull, bill longer and paler orange with indistinct darker tip, with longer extension of feathering at base of upper mandible. Note also pale eyes, faint grey ear-spot on white head and long, orange legs with parts of tibia clearly visible. Moult in wing-coverts extensive. Israel, Dec. 1993. *Markus Varesvuo.*

Slender-billed Gull *Larus genei*. **652. Juvenile**. Greyer and less heavily marked than Black-headed Gull (but see 632); note longer neck and narrow head with longer and paler bill. Turkey. 5 Jul 1998. *Per Schiermacker-Hansen*. **653. 1st-winter**. Long, pale orange legs and long bill. Jizz somewhat similar to Caspian Gull *cachinnans*. Eilat, Israel. 23 Mar 1998. *Klaus Malling Olsen*. **654. 1st-winter.** Head and upperwing-markings much fainter than in Black-headed Gull, resulting in a much paler-looking bird. Bangkok, Thailand. 9 Feb 1995. *Per Schiermacker-Hansen*. **655. 1st-winter**. Note elongated shape, deep breast, longish-looking head and long tail. Eilat, Israel. 19 Mar 1998. *Klaus Malling Olsen*. **656. Probably 2nd-summer** (worn). The bright red legs and bill suggest this age. Sardinia, Italy. Aug 2001. *Bruno D'Amicis*. **657. 1st-winter.** Some birds at this age show almost yellow legs and darker-than-average bill. Israel. Mar. *Karel Beylevelt*

Slender-billed Gull *Larus genei*. **658. Adult summer**. Note darkish-looking eye and bill in breeding season. Bill looks blackish at distance. Khaluf, Oman. Mar. *Hanne & Jens Eriksen*. **659. Adult summer**. Long neck, creating phalarope-impression, is evident; also note the darkish eye and bill and the rosy-tinged underparts (which are often conspicuous even in winter). Eilat, Israel. 22 Mar 1998. *Klaus Malling Olsen*. **660. 1st-winter**, with Black-headed Gull. Compared to latter, note larger size, longer, cigar-shaped body and rosy tinge to underparts. Siracusa, Sicily, Italy. 29 Apr 2000. *Klaus Malling Olsen*. **661. Adult.** Underwing as Black-headed Gull. Khawer, Shumay, Oman. Jan. *Hanne & Jens Eriksen*. **662. Adult summer**. Wing-pattern similar to Black-headed Gull, but note all-white head. Camargue, France. Jul 1998. *René Pop*.

Slender-billed Gull *Larus genei*. **663. Adult summer**. At distance, white head on long neck evident. When swimming, shape is reminiscent of phalarope, especially Wilson's Phalarope. France. Jul 1988. *René Pop*. **664. Adult summer**. Like white-headed, long-necked Black-headed Gull. Ebro, Spain. Jul 1988. *René Pop*.

32. BONAPARTE'S GULL
Larus philadelphia (Ord, 1815, Philadelphia, Pennsylvania)

Plates 66–67, Photos 665–679

IDENTIFICATION Length 28–30cm, wingspan 75–90cm. Like a miniature Black-headed Gull; only slightly larger than Little Gull. Small size, black bill, pale legs and whitish translucent surface to hand, which has black trailing edge as in *Sterna* tern, are diagnostic. The bill is spike-like, in longest-billed males looking long and slender, but in females short and fine as in Little. Upperparts similar to Black-headed, but slightly darker grey, with grey neck and breast-sides melting into grey on upperparts.

The larger Black-headed has orange to red, black-tipped bill, darker red or orange legs and much darker surface to inner primaries – only in worn birds are the dark areas reduced to streaks, but never looking extensively translucent as in Bonaparte's. Hindneck and breast-sides are white or very pale grey, never concolorous with mantle.

Settled Bonaparte's looks like long-winged Little Gull. Wing-tip projection beyond tail is similar to bill length (less in Little). The pale legs are generally shorter than in Black-headed, often with only tarsus visible (also tibia in Black-headed). Swimming Bonaparte's often elongates neck to create phalarope-like jizz – enhanced by quick movements while swimming.

Flight lighter, more graceful and with quicker wing-beats than Black-headed, often closer to Little Gull and *Chlidonias* terns – much as a result of Bonaparte's lighter weight. It feeds as Black-headed, but also with short dives towards surface as in Little Gull or *Chlidonias* terns, although less buoyant. Regularly hovers to pick food from water. May dive after small fish. Often forms large dense feeding flocks, reminiscent of terns.

Adult upperparts dark grey (darker than Black-headed) with stronger contrast to the white leading edge of forewing than Black-headed. From below, inner primaries are slightly greyish-tinged, but not enough to create any strong contrast with the white outer ones, and not affecting impression of full translucency. Legs orange-red to pinkish, brightest in **summer.** Hood sooty-black, and penetrates further down hindneck than chocolate-brown of Black-headed, while black bill and broader white eyelids further contribute to different appearance from latter. In **winter**, head similar to Black-headed, but generally whiter with more isolated and often larger black ear-spot. Some show faint grey shadows to crown and hindneck as in Black-headed. The grey hindneck often reaches sides of neck and breast, and 'isolates' white head from underbody – sometimes giving impression of winter Ross's Gull. Bill black and legs fleshy-pink.

Juvenile similar to Black-headed, but wing more contrasting blackish and pale with darker but generally narrower carpal bar. Head and upperparts marked with greyish-brown (not gingery-brown), often with a smart dark 'Little Gull cap' and dark ear-spot. Upperwing pale with dark edgings: carpal bar, outer primaries and whole trailing edge to wing blackish-brown in strong contrast to pale grey midwing. Two to five outer primaries have dark outer webs, creating narrow but complete dark line around white wing-tip. The primaries have white bases on outer ones, becoming greyer on inner ones, which are concolorous with secondary coverts. Outer primary coverts have dark markings as streaks or drops offsetting dark leading edge to outer wing. Underwing white with complete but narrow black trailing edge. Legs pale fleshy. From late summer moults into **first-winter**, where head and body become adult-like, but juvenile wing and tail retained. By late spring to summer of second calendar year, greater coverts often very pale and translucency of underwing most obvious. Pale impression evident in **first-summer**; most have more or less winter head; only a small percentage acquire summer hood.

First-year Black-headed differs from similar-aged Bonaparte's by larger size, orange black-tipped bill and orange legs. Upperwing has paler brown carpal bar but darker mid- and inner primaries. Shows dark-marked inner primary coverts, but often unmarked white greater primary coverts, emphasizing white leading edge to hand (although outer primary coverts are white in majority). Some first-year Black-headed show markings similar to Bonaparte's, but have darker inner primary coverts. Dark trailing edge to inner wing browner, broader and less clear-cut owing to broader pale feather-edges.

Second-year similar to adult, but larger percentage than in Black-headed have traces of immaturity, especially dark primary covert markings, dark streak on outer web of P9 (mostly white in adult) and faint dark spots on tail and secondaries.

VOICE Call is a harsh *keek* (recalling tern, but lower). In flocks a low, short *kew*, and an almost sparrow-like feeding call. Generally higher-pitched and more rasping than in Black-headed. Some calls strongly differ from Black-headed, but the composition of call series similar. Juvenile gives a high, slightly nasal squeal, *peeeur* (Sibley 2000).

MOULT (pers. obs.; skins in AMNH, LACM, NHM, USNM). In all ages generally 2–3 weeks later than in Black-headed Gull, mostly so in E populations.

Adult acquires **winter plumage** by complete moult Jul–Oct/Nov. Head and body Jul–Aug. Starts with chin, throat and forehead; most still have full hood late Jul, and most have 50–100% full hood mid-Aug. Hood rarely retained to Nov–Dec (Bent 1921, D. DesJardin *in litt.*). P1–2 early Jul; P4–6 mid-Aug; P8–9 mid-Sep. Primary moult usually completed late Sep, but some are still growing P10 by Nov.

Adult acquires **summer plumage** by partial moult, including head and body (Jan)Mar–May. Head starts

PLATE 66. BONAPARTE'S GULL *Larus philadelphia*

Small Nearctic gull, vagrant to W Palearctic. Breeds in wooded lakeland, often nesting in trees unlike other gulls. Winters along coastlines. Overall similar to Black-headed Gull, but smaller, in size intermediate between Black-headed and Little. More compact than Black-headed with narrower bill and shorter legs. Female looks very round-headed with short, spike-like bill; male may look long-billed. Plumage similar to Black-headed, but bill blackish and legs pink to orange. Bill always darker than legs (rather similar-coloured in Black-headed).

1. **Juvenile** (fledging–Aug) Head with greyish-brown cap and blackish ear-spot; head pattern more distinct than in Black-headed. Mantle and scapulars greyish-brown with pale fringes. Blackish-brown median coverts generally in strong contrast to pale grey greater coverts. Bill blackish and legs fleshy.

2. **First-winter** (Sep–Apr) Head and body as adult winter, but wing and tail as juvenile. Head white with black ear-spot and varying (often no) grey shading on crown. Grey hindneck merges into upper mantle and breast-sides. Legs paler than bill.

3. **Late first-winter/first-summer** (Feb–Aug) With wear, pale fringes to coverts lost; dark brown median coverts often in strong contrast to bleached, pale grey greater coverts. Head pattern varies; majority in their first-summer retain head similar to winter, but generally with darker vertical streaks from eye to eye and hindneck to hindneck.

4. **First-summer** (Apr–Aug) A small minority develop greyish-black hood, similar to adult summer, but duller with whitish freckling especially on lores, cheek and throat.

5. **Adult winter** (Aug–Apr) Like a small, short-legged Black-headed Gull with black bill. Note grey extension of upper mantle onto hindneck and breast-sides (often isolating white head), and large black ear-spot. Compared to Black-headed Gull, head normally with less pattern, whiter crown, more distinct black ear-spot and darker grey hindneck and upperparts. Legs pinkish.

6. **Adult summer** (Apr–Aug) Hood and bill black. White crescents above and below eyes narrow. Hood normally extends more down hindneck than in Black-headed, but this less evident in alert bird as shown here. Upperparts a tinge darker grey than in Black-headed. Legs reddish-orange.

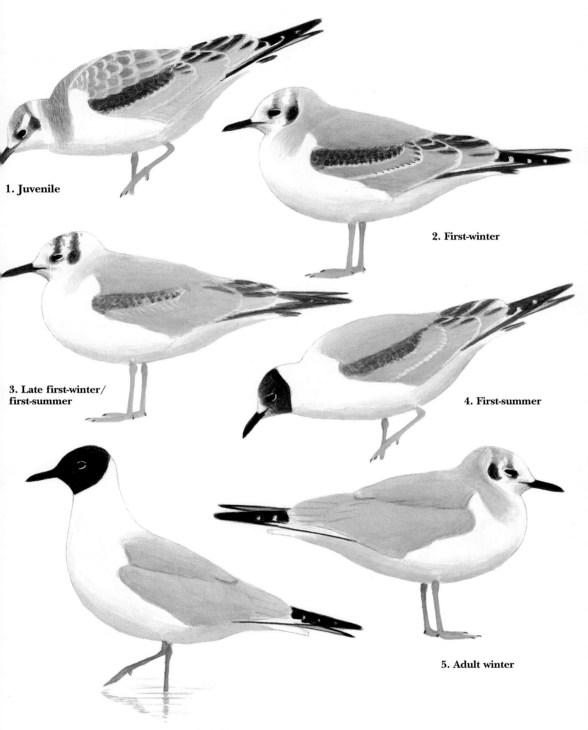

1. Juvenile

2. First-winter

3. Late first-winter/
first-summer

4. First-summer

5. Adult winter

6. Adult summer

PLATE 67. BONAPARTE'S GULL *Larus philadelphia*

Small, almost tern-like gull, in size between Black-headed and Little. Wings rather short and straight-edged. Flight similar to Black-headed, but often more elegant, recalling marsh tern *Chlidonias*. From below, outer wing white with black trailing edge, similar to many terns, dissimilar to dark inner hand of Black-headed. In head-on and side-on lighting, hand translucent, especially on outer wing. Inner primaries sometimes slightly darker grey, but never as dark as in Black-headed.

1. **Juvenile** (fledging–Aug) Blackish-brown carpal bar in contrast to grey inner wing. Leading edge of outer wing blackish, as primary coverts and outer primaries show large amount of dark. Shows complete black trailing edge to wing, on secondaries often as row of dark spots. Inner primaries rather pale, thus not in strong contrast to white area on outer wing as in Black-headed.

2. **Juvenile** (fledging–Aug) Basically, upperwing is grey, edged dark. Note fully black-streaked primary coverts, pale 'tongue' on mid-hand against dark edges and blackish-brown carpal bar. Head pattern of juvenile contrasts with smart grey cap and blackish ear-spot.

3. **First-winter** (Aug/Sep–Apr) Head and body similar to adult winter, but wing and tail juvenile. Amount of black streaking on primary coverts varies. This individual shows limited streaking, restricted to outer primary coverts – a pattern matched by certain Black-headed Gulls. Note that inner hand is pale grey, thus not in strong contrast to white leading edge of outer wing as in Black-headed, which shows darker inner primaries and their coverts. Black trailing edge to inner wing often looks broken, as secondaries show broad white edges. Dark earthy-brown carpal bar contrasts strongly with pale grey midwing-panel. Note translucent underside of primaries.

4. **First-winter** At distance similar to Little Gull, but note pale grey wing with dark edgings, not full W on upperwing.

5. **First-summer (or late first-winter)** (Feb–Aug) With wear, carpal bar and dark markings on flight feathers browner, but still in contrast to grey upperwing, as plumage generally bleaches. Some birds moult central tail feathers from May. Winter head pattern often retained in first-summer.

6. **First-summer** (Apr–Aug) A small minority develop greyish-black hood.

7. **Second-winter** (Sep–Apr) As adult, but aged by combination of dark streaks on outer primary coverts, generally more complete black on outer web of outer two primaries, traces of dark on mid-secondaries and black tail-spots. Such traces of immaturity are commoner than in Black-headed Gull.

8. **Adult winter** (Sep–Apr) Upperwing tricoloured: grey with white leading edge and black trailing edge to outer wing. Pattern as in Black-headed, but caused by darker grey ground colour, pattern of outer wing more contrasting, white leading edge being visible at long range, and often offset by translucence of outer wing. Underside of primaries white with distinct black trailing edge, inner primaries at most a tinge darker (mainly because uppersides of inner primaries are greyer than white uppersides of outer). Note black bill and ear-spot.

9. **Adult winter** From above, white leading edge against grey inner wing striking. Note white underside to hand, at most with a tinge greyer inner primaries, but never matching the blackish underside of Black-headed Gull. Note also the white crown contrasting with grey hind-neck and neck-sides, and the black ear-spot creating an 'extra eye'. May year-round show rosy tinge to underparts.

10. **Adult summer** (Apr–Aug) Head and bill black. White eye-crescents narrower than in Black-headed.

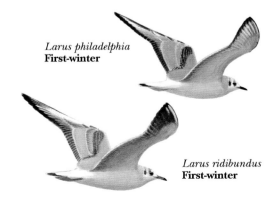

Larus philadelphia
First-winter

Larus ridibundus
First-winter

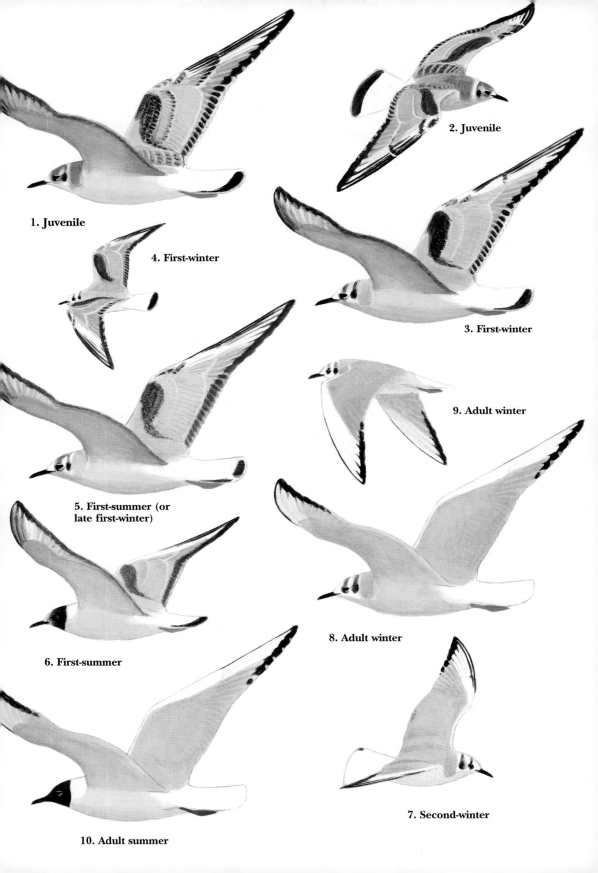

1. Juvenile

2. Juvenile

4. First-winter

3. First-winter

9. Adult winter

5. First-summer (or
late first-winter)

8. Adult winter

6. First-summer

7. Second-winter

10. Adult summer

Mar with hindneck, ear-coverts and sometimes feathers around base of bill. Last to be renewed are cheek, throat, forehead and lores. Late Mar–early Apr head white-peppered or with broad white blaze (present in 10–15% late Apr/early May); advanced birds have summer hood mid-Mar. Many W American birds have almost completed head moult late Mar (J. R. King pers. comm.).

Juvenile acquires **first-winter** plumage by partial moult Aug–Nov, including head, body and rarely some wing-coverts and tertials. Starts with mid-mantle mid-Aug; mantle sometimes juvenile until early Dec.

Moult to **first-summer** partial Apr–May, including body, scapulars, usually some wing-coverts and occasionally some tertials. Head moult often restricted to parts behind eye; <5% develop adult-like hood.

Acquires **second-winter** plumage by complete moult May–Sep. P1–4 mid-Jun/early Jul, P8–10 Aug/early Sep. Secondaries generally later than primaries. A Dutch bird took 75 days to renew all primaries (Eigenhuis 1989). Head, coverts and tail mid-Jun–early Aug; head sometimes completed late Aug.

Moult to **second-summer** similar to adult, but generally later. 50% show basically winter head late Apr, when most adults have completed head moult.

DESCRIPTION

Adult Mantle, scapulars, tertials and upperwing-coverts medium grey, darker than in Black-headed (Kodak Grey Scale (4)5–7). Flight feathers pale grey; dark tips to P(3)4–10 create black trailing edge to outer wing. Black tip to P10 11–55mm, P9–6 18–45mm, broader on P6–7. P8–10 otherwise white, P10(9) with narrow dark edges to outer web (in P9 restricted to black streak on mid-part before black tip). P1–7 with pale grey bases; P7 with white outer web. On P1–6 (7–8) black restricted to tip, often on one web only. Narrow white tips to P1–8 disappears with wear, normally absent from late winter. P10 3–6mm >P9. Tertials with white fringes. Hindneck, body, tail, tail-coverts and underwing-coverts white; tail sometimes with slight grey wash to distal part. Underbody often with slight pinkish tinge, generally stronger and more frequent than in Black-headed, especially in summer. Iris dark brown. Orbital ring and bill black. Gape orange-red to coral-red.

Adult summer (Apr–Jul/Aug) Hood greyish-black with distinct white crescents above and below eye, thickest at rear. Often with a few white feather fringes on especially lores and chin. Legs orange-red.

Adult winter (Jul–Mar) Head white with dark ear-spot (sometimes as 'extra eye' up to twice size of eye); small dark spot in front of eye and often greyish tinge to crown and hindneck, as bases of hindneck feathers are dark. Some show head similar to Black-headed with two dark bars, one above eye and one on hindneck. Sides of breast and neck greyish, varying from greyish-white to grey as mantle. Underparts white, sometimes with slight pinkish tinge. Bill sometimes with reddish or brownish base. Legs fleshy-pink.

Juvenile (fledging–Aug) Head white with blackish to greyish-brown ear-spot and cap. Mantle, scapulars, back and breast-sides pale greyish-brown to blackish-brown with paler feather-fringes; edges of tertials and tips to

scapulars cinnamon-brown, rarely buff. Marginal coverts white. Greater and median coverts pale grey, latter with pale brown subterminal bar and whitish tip. Lesser coverts blackish-brown with grey bases, when fresh with buff to off-white edges. Outer primary coverts pale grey with dark shaft-streaks and drop-spots near tip, sometimes covering whole outer web; median ones often with black subterminal spots near tips, outermost often black with white reduced to extreme tip and base of inner web. Inner greater primary coverts medium grey, lacking dark markings. Alula blackish. Primaries with 25–30mm black tips, creating black trailing edge to outer wing, on P7–10 black tips penetrate to outer webs. Extreme tips of P1–9 white, broadest on P1–4. P6–10 white, P1–5 grey. Secondaries blackish with pale tips and fringes. Tail white with black to blackish-brown subterminal bar (11–20mm on T1). T6 and tips of other rectrices white; T6 sometimes with greyer inner webs (rarely base of outer webs). Underparts and underwing white, greater under primary coverts often with dark fringes. Iris dark brown. Bill black, lower mandible usually with paler base; rarely, lower mandible brown (Alström 1993) or whole bill brownish-black. Gape flesh. Legs pale flesh, rarely dark reddish-brown.

First-winter (Aug/Sep–Apr) similar to juvenile, but head, hindneck, breast-sides, mantle, scapulars and back as adult winter, sometimes with a few retained juvenile feathers, especially scapulars. White primary tips gradually reduced through wear, often lacking in late winter (apart from innermost). Bare parts as juvenile.

First-summer (Feb–Aug) similar to first-winter, but black head-markings usually stronger, especially on ear-coverts, hindcrown and around base of bill. Most retain head similar to winter; <5% develop adult-like but dull blackish hood. May show grey hindneck and breast-sides. Wings similar to juvenile before autumn moult, but from May bleached to whitish in mid-part; carpal bar and secondaries brownish. Upperparts not dissimilar to adult White-winged Black Tern *Chlidonias leucopterus*. Tail white, usually with black markings on T4–6 retained into Jun. White primary spots and tips to rectrices usually disappear with wear. Bare parts as in first-winter.

Second-winter (Aug–Feb) as adult winter, but some with dark shaft-streaks in max. four outer greater primary coverts, sometimes broadening to drop-shaped at tip especially on outermost, which may be mainly black. May show narrow dark markings on tail (especially near tip of outer web of T6, but sometimes as broken black tail-bar) and tertials; often shows faint dark, normally broken secondary bar (W. Hoogendoorn *in litt.*). Primaries as adult, but on average with broader black tip to P10 (20–25mm), normally complete black outer web to P10 and longer black edge of P9, typically reaching black tip unlike in adult. Also more frequently with black subterminal spots on P2–4. Tips and edges of undersides of greater primary coverts often dark.

Some birds in otherwise adult plumage still show narrow dark shaft-streaks to four outer primary coverts, indicating that this character may be present in later age, or is the only immature character present in advanced second-winter.

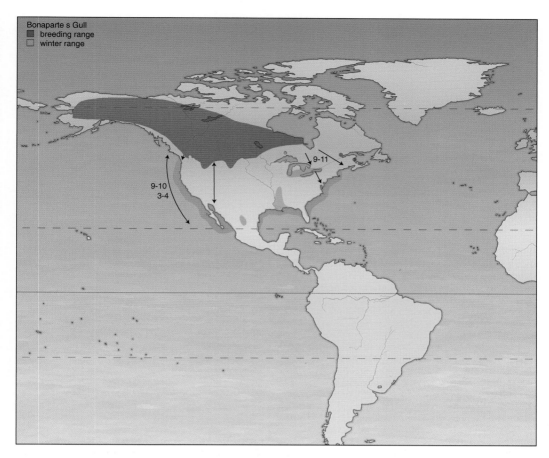

9-11

9-10
3-4

Variants Grant (1986b) mentioned juvenile with exten-sive black on upperwing, no white visible on outer upperwing, and dark carpal bar extending to almost all coverts. An aberrant first-year had blackish flight feath-ers with slightly paler tinge to P1–5, pale grey primary coverts with dark markings, pale grey greater and medi-an coverts (but in one wing two darker greater coverts), dark brown lesser coverts, with white alula and margin-al coverts (White 1999).

A leucistic bird in winter plumage had pale greyish-brown ear-spot, whitish upperparts and dark in primar-ies restricted to grey outer web to P10 and grey shading on P9 (skin USNM 417981).

A melanistic bird had an all-grey body, blackish hood with pale shading on forehead, white chin and throat, and nar-row white eye-crescent. Tail dull white; underside of wings grey as body; translucency of primaries duller than in nor-mal birds. Could at range be mistaken for a strange-look-ing Black Tern *Chlidonias niger* (Bohlen 1993).

Hybrids Putative hybrid Bonaparte's Gull × Franklin's Gull (or Laughing Gull), Oct 1992, had wing-pattern of Bonaparte's, but strong reddish bill with pronounced gonys-angle, very dark red legs and winter-head with broader dark markings than average Bonaparte's Gull (M. Reid *in litt.*)

DISTRIBUTION AND MIGRATION Population 85,000–175,000 pairs (del Hoyo *et al.* 1996), but proba-bly larger; ninefold increase in Christmas Bird Count numbers 1950–1984. Breeds in small colonies in taiga zone up to tree limit near ponds or muskeg. Nests mainly in spruces *Picea* and tamaracks *Larix*. Breeds in Canada up to 600m. Rarely breeds in reeds or on the ground (Symons 1968, Lamont 1980, Dolbeer & Bern-hardt 1986, del Hoyo *et al.* 1996).

Flocks from latter half of Jul. Migration starts Aug and peaks Sep. Alberta birds migrate W towards Washington and N Mexico, tending to continue southwards as win-ter progresses. Birds from between Saskatchewan and Mississippi initially follow two main routes: one through Great Lakes and SE to Atlantic coast, the other from St Lawrence River overland through river valleys to Bay of Fundy, New Brunswick; along former route max. 35,000 counted (Ontario) and along latter max. 30,000 count-ed in late summer. Reaches Maine Sep, Massachusetts mid-Sep–Oct. Peaks Minnesota and Michigan late Sep–mid-Nov, Atlantic coast mid-Oct–late Nov (max. 10,000 New York region, several thousands off N Car-olina). Before freeze-up large gatherings Great Lakes and Niagara Falls, max. 100,000 Niagara Falls, 148,000 Lake Erie and 150,000 Presque Isle, Pennsylvania Nov–Dec. In Mid-west, sometimes large winter flocks,

BONAPARTE'S GULL Two-year gull. Nearctic. Small and round-headed with all-black bill. Size between Black-headed and Little Gull. Shares wing pattern with Black-headed: white leading and black trailing edges to outer wing, but inner primaries paler, on underwing lacking solid dark of Black-headed. Outer wing often translucent, reinforcing pale appearance.

Adult with generally darker grey upperparts than Black-headed, thus stronger contrasting white leading edge. Bill dark but legs orange to fleshy. In **summer** (Apr–Aug) hood blackish, as bill, with narrow but contrasting white eyelids. Legs bright red. In **winter** (Aug–Apr) head white with black ear-spot; head-markings (apart from ear-spot) fainter than Black-headed, but hindneck grey, concolorous with upperparts.

Juvenile (Jul–Aug) shows dark cap and ear-spot and greyish-brown upperparts. Upperwing generally pale with dark edgings; narrow but dark carpal bar connects with dark-patterned primary coverts and black markings on outer wing. Inner part of outer wing paler than in Black-headed, appearing as long white tongue into dark-edged wing-tip.

First-winter (Sep–Apr/May) similar to adult winter, but juvenile wing and tail retained. Often strongly worn and pale from late winter.

Second-year sometimes possible to age: shows dark markings on primary coverts and tail in otherwise adult plumage.

e.g. 100,000 Nov and 35,000 Jan, Cleveland. Common E coast; winter flocks max. 4,000 Massachusetts, 1,700 New Jersey and 20,000 Cape Hatteras. In both migration seasons (rarely in winter) flocks of max. 15,000 Niagara River, Ontario and E Coast. Along W Coast common in migration seasons S to Baja California; here and in California scarce and in varying numbers in winter, sometimes almost absent.

Spring migration starts Mar. Peak California late Mar–mid-Apr (max. day-count 22,000 San Mateo), British Columbia late Apr (max. day-counts >10,000); 5,000–10,000 Kentucky Apr regarded as exceptional (Glutz von Blotzheim & Bauer 1982, Clapp & Buckley 1984, Cramp & Simmons 1983, Braune 1987).

Small but increasing numbers winter inland in North America and S to N Caribbean, Bermuda and Yucatán; in mild winters N to S Ontario; exceptionally Newfoundland and Alaska. Vagrant Greenland, Lesser and Netherlands Antilles, Panama, Hawaii, Laysan and Midway Islands, and Japan (Glutz von Blotzheim & Bauer 1982, Pratt *et al.* 1987, Hoogendoorn & Steinhaus 1990, Brazil 1991, Boertmann 1994).

European vagrancy similar to Ring-billed Gull, with most autumn records from southern part and spring records generally more to N; relatively more records towards the E of W Europe mirrors migration routes in North America. Most recorded Great Britain 105 up to 2002 (peak 11 in 1990); also Azores (5), Spain (6), Portugal (5), France (4), Netherlands (5), Iceland (11), Norway (5), with 1–3 in Belgium, Germany, Sweden, Denmark, Czech Republic and Hungary. One record Senegal, the sole African record (Hoogendoorn & Steinhaus 1990, Baillon & Dubois 1992, Cottridge & Vinicombe 1996, Mitchell & Young 1997, Rogers *et al.* 1999, 2001, A. T. Mjøs & Y. Kolbeinsson *in litt.*).

MEASUREMENTS Lengths in mm; weights in g. Own data based on skins in MCZ, NHM, NRK, USNM, UZM, ZMA, ZMO. North America.

WING

Adult male	250–278 (266.5)	70
Adult female	246–275 (262.0)	59
First-year male	248–277 (258.4)	73
First-year female	246–270 (255.6)	58

BILL

Adult male	26.9–33.2 (29.9)	70
Adult female	23.7–31.6 (28.2)	60
First-year male	26.4–32.4 (29.5)	72
First-year female	23.9–31.0 (28.1)	58

BILL DEPTH AT BASE OF BILL

Adult male	7.1–9.5 (8.2)	70
Adult female	7.0–8.8 (7.8)	59
First-year male	7.0–8.7 (7.8)	72
First-year female	6.4–8.3 (7.6)	58

BILL DEPTH AT GONYS

Adult male	6.3–8.1 (7.0)	70
Adult female	5.9–8.0 (6.5)	59
First-year male	5.9–7.6 (6.6)	72
First-year female	5.3–7.0 (6.3)	58

GONYS LENGTH

Adult male	10.1–13.4 (11.9)	70
Adult female	8.9–12.5 (11.2)	59
First-year male	9.4–13.5 (11.5)	71
First-year female	8.8–12.4 (11.1)	58

TARSUS

Adult male	32.0–37.9 (34.7)	70
Adult female	32.0–37.7 (34.4)	60
First-year male	32.1–37.6 (35.0)	72
First-year female	29.5–37.0 (33.4)	58

Weight Alaska: adult male 182–227; female 5–7% lighter. Mean in wintering birds, California 176.8 (Glutz von Blotzheim & Bauer 1982).

Bonaparte's Gull *Larus philadelphia*. **665. 1st-winter**. Note black bill, rosy-pink legs and blackish-brown lesser-coverts bar. California, USA. Dec 1992. *Don DesJardin*. **666. 1st-winters with adult** (right). Compared to Black-headed and Little Gull, winter head-markings generally more restricted, often as dark ear-spot only. Texas, USA. 26 Mar 1982. *Arnoud B. van den Berg*. **667. 1st-winter**. Note rather solid blackish-brown lesser coverts. California, USA. 4 Dec 1995. *Don DesJardin*. **668. 1st-winter.** In flight, wing appears pale, surrounded by dark. California. Nov. *Brian G. Prescott*.

Bonaparte's Gull *Larus philadelphia*. **669. 1st-winter**. Note blackish-brown leading edge to wing, dark streaks in primary coverts and whitish head against grey neck-sides. Great Britain. Winter. *George Reszeter*. **670. 1st-summer**. Most retain mainly winter-patterned head in 1st-summer, unlike Black-headed Gull. Note pale underwing with translucent hand and solid black trailing edge. Salton Sea, California, USA. 25 May 1984. *Harry J. Lehto*. **671. 1st-summer**. Note the phalarope-like posture when swimming. IJmuiden, Netherlands. 6 Aug 1988. *Arnoud B. van den Berg*. **672. Adult summer**. Note black tips to pale primaries. Canada. Jun. *Karel Beylevelt*. **673. Adult summer**. Note blackish hood and bill - summer head here exceptionally retained in winter (or perhaps developed atypically early). California, USA. 7 Dec 1993. *Don DesJardin*.

Bonaparte's Gull *Larus philadelphia*. **674. Adult winter.** Santa Barbara, California, USA. 30 Jan 1997. Note black bill, grey hind-neck and flesh-coloured legs. *Don DesJardin*. **675. Adult winter.** Certain birds have longer bill, appearing slender - indicating male. USA. 8 Nov 1982. *Thomas Grüner.* **676. Adult winter.** Note the translucent pale primaries with black trailing edge as in Arctic Tern *Sterna paradisaea*, although inner primaries slightly darker. Grey neck-sides contrast somewhat to white head. USA. 3 Nov 1982. *Thomas Grüner.* **677. Adult winter.** Same bird as 674. *Thomas Grüner.* **678. 2nd-winter.** Note faint dark markings in primary coverts and tail, suggesting this age. Lista, Vest-Ager, Norway. 18 Dec 1995. *Håkon Heggland.*

Bonaparte's Gull *Larus philadelphia*. **679. Flock**. Birds in flocks keep close together in a tern-like manner. When lit from the side, outerwing (especially along leading edge) contrasts strongly with the innerwing. Note translucent primaries with narrow, but clear-cut black trailing edge, creating primary pattern recalling Arctic Tern. USA. Feb 1993. *Philippe J. Dubois.*

33. SAUNDERS' GULL

Larus saundersi (Swinhoe, 1871, Amoy, China)

IDENTIFICATION Length 30–33cm. Wingspan unknown. A small elegant gull, confined to E Asia. In size and shape it is between Black-headed and Little Gull. Compared to Black-headed, the head is rounder and the bill much shorter and broader with a slightly hooked tip. In flight shows short, oval-shaped body, rounded head and rather narrow tail. Wing long and pointed, held angled when flying. The shape is not unlike Ross's Gull. Has characteristic feeding flight over water, low with short drops to surface to snap prey in the briefest landing before flying off, in manner of Gull-billed Tern (Brazil 1992, pers. obs.). Active flight tern-like, more buoyant than in Black-headed.

Coastal, keeping along tidelines; often gathers with other small gulls.

Adult from above somewhat similar to Little Gull; the narrow, black primary spots are only visible at close range against pale background, whereas the wing-tip looks rounded against dark background. P10 is white, at most with indistinct dark streak along outer web. From below, blackish underside of median primaries creates a panel similar to that shown by Black-headed, but more restricted and oval-shaped as it only covers mid-primaries and is surrounded by white, translucent outer and inner primaries. It therefore often looks darker and more distinct. Shows faint greyish wash to underwing-coverts, at certain angles offsetting broad white trailing edge to inner wing, not unlike Ross's Gull, and broader than in Black-headed Gull. Upperparts darker grey than Black-headed. Bill blackish and legs dark red.

Adult summer has blackish hood penetrating further behind hindneck than in Black-headed, almost reaching mantle, largely as a result of its short neck. Broad white eyelids join behind eyes as U, rather as in Franklin's Gull, visible even at long range as a 'clown-mask' in the black hood. The black bill is concolorous with the head.

Adult winter has white head with broad black ear-spot and narrow brownish or grey cap, which may be absent or very subtle. Head pattern resembles Little Gull, but black on crown generally less extensive.

Juvenile/first-winter combines head like Little Gull with heavy bill and upperpart pattern like Black-headed Gull; compared to Black-headed, carpal bar paler brown, narrower and weaker, and dark secondary bar restricted to outer or central secondaries to create blackish triangle or row of spots on outer arm. Outer primaries often have extensive white on inner webs, together with dark pattern on primary coverts forming outer wing pattern close to first-winter Bonaparte's Gull. Typically both median and greater primary coverts have black markings, creating black 'double-marking' against whitish outer wing, easy to see head-on. Black tail-bar much narrower than in Black-headed (resembling Relict Gull) and may be absent from mid-winter. Legs dark reddish-brown.

First-summer similar to first-winter, but with more extensive dark markings behind eye and on crown, often forming dark half-hood as in winter Franklin's Gull; rarely with complete hood.

Second-winter/summer as adult, but sometimes with traces of dark shaft-streaks on greater primary coverts and duller summer hood.

VOICE A harsh tern-like *kip*. Also a harsh *chao*, similar to call from marsh tern *Chlidonias* (P. Schiermacker-Hansen *in litt.*).

MOULT Adult moult to **winter** plumage complete late Jun–Sep. P1 sometimes shed mid-May (pers. obs., China).

Moult to **adult summer** partial, including head Feb–early Mar; by late Feb has almost completed head moult apart from scattered white feathers on forehead, lores and crown. The majority develop summer hood late Mar.

Juvenile moult to **first-winter** partial Aug–early Sep, including head, body and rump.

Moult to **first-summer** poorly known; may retain winter head or show blackish half-mask similar to Franklin's Gull, although some moult head completely. Sometimes parts of tail moulted Feb–May.

DESCRIPTION

Adult Hindneck, underparts, rump and tail white. Upperparts pale bluish-grey (Kodak Grey Scale (3)4–5). P10 white, sometimes with blackish inner web, narrow black stripe on outer web or narrow dark subterminal spot. P9–6 white with narrow blackish subterminal spots near tip; P7–8 usually with more extensive black inner web, creating streaked pattern from above. P1–6 pale grey, sometimes with small black subterminal spot to P6. P1–5 grey. Primaries with 10–14mm white tips. Underside of P9–7 black, with dark markings on outer web of P5–6. Secondaries pale grey with broader white tips, forming white trailing edge to inner wing. Lesser coverts and axillaries white, under median coverts whitish-grey and greater coverts medium to pale grey. Alula whitish. Iris dark brown. Bill black. Legs dark red.

Adult summer (Mar–Aug) Hood jet-black with white eyelids above and below eye, broadest (6–7mm) at rear, where joining to form conspicuous white U. Lores blackish. Hood may show slight brownish wash with wear.

Adult winter (Aug–Feb/Mar) Head white with black ear-spot. Shows varying brownish-grey cap, usually less extensive than ear-spot, often streaked, but sometimes lacking. Shows faint greyish wash to hindneck.

Juvenile (fledging–Sep) Cheek, throat and ear-coverts whitish, rest of head brownish-grey, darkest around eye, on ear-coverts, crown and ear-spot. Hindneck and mantle buffish-tinged, palest on mantle. Upper greater coverts grey, other wing-coverts brown with pale buff edges. P6–10 white, inner webs of P8–10 dark brown,

PLATE 68. SAUNDERS' GULL *Larus saundersi*

Small E Asian gull, restricted to E China with winter range reaching S to Hong Kong. Rare, world population probably not exceeding 9,000 birds. Breeds in lagoons and coastal marshes; feeds along shallow coastlines with sandy banks. World population threatened by human settlements and cultivation.
Size between Black-headed and Little Gull. Head rounded, bill short, black and strongly hooked. Legs short and dark. Wings rather long and pointed, tail narrow. Settled bird is short-legged and elongated, like a long-winged Little Gull with rounder head and much deeper, stronger bill. In flight, shows long, pointed and angled wings, short, rounded head and rather long, narrow tail. Flies elegantly, recalling Gull-billed Tern *Sterna nilotica*, with deep wingbeats and, when feeding, shallow dives towards surface. Often associates with Gull-billed Tern. Underwing similar to Black-headed Gull, showing dark mid-primaries, but white leading edge broader.

1. **First-winter** (Sep–May) Upperwing pale grey with narrow warm brown carpal bar, strong blackish pattern on primary coverts and along leading edge of outer wing, white streaks on black wing-tip and broken black secondary bar, typically strongest on outer secondaries (may gradually 'disappear' towards body). Black tail-bar narrow. Head white with faint dark cap and black ear-spot. The dark bill is short and deep.

2. **First-winter** (Sep–May) Settled birds are round-headed with short, dark and hooked bill, elongated body emphasised by long wings and short legs. Note white head with faint grey shading above eye, on hindneck and on crown (crown often is all white). Pale edges to dark-centred tertials generally broader, but more diffuse than in other similar-sized gulls. Legs dark brown.

3. **First-summer** (Apr–Aug) Similar to first-winter, but many show incomplete dark hood. Amount of dark on upperwing varies individually; this bird is a poorly marked first-summer, showing least amount of dark on upperwing. Note elongated dark triangle in mid-part of trailing edge of wing, created by only outer secondaries being dark-centred. Also note restricted dark at leading edge of outer wing compared to 1. Pattern closer to Black-headed Gull, but white leading edge to outer wing only weakly indicated.

4. **Adult winter** (Aug–Apr) Upperwing in adult pale grey with white leading edge to outer wing, full white outer primary and dark spots on outer primaries creating broken black pattern (not full black edge of Black-headed Gull). The white edge to inner wing is broader than in Black-headed and Little Gull. Head white with very small, indistinct grey cap, and black ear-spot like an 'extra eye'. Short but strong dark bill evident at rather long range.

5. **Adult summer** (Apr–Aug) Short-necked with black hood and bill; white eye-crescents conspicuous. Upperwing pattern discussed under 3; this individual shows less restricted black on wing-tip, but still appearing as row of black spots rather than full black trailing edge to outer wing. Note clean white outer primary. Underwing similar to Black-headed Gull, but note narrower dark area on underside of hand, surrounded by translucent white outer and inner primaries.

6. **Adult summer** Short broad head and bill, but rather narrow tail. Narrow dark area on underside of primaries, surrounded by white and, at tips, broken by white primary tips, is seen well in this illustration.

7. **Adult summer** Hood black, merging into short, strongly hooked blackish bill. White crescents above and below eye broad, creating 'clown-like' look. Legs short and dark reddish-brown. Wing-tip with equal amount of black and white.

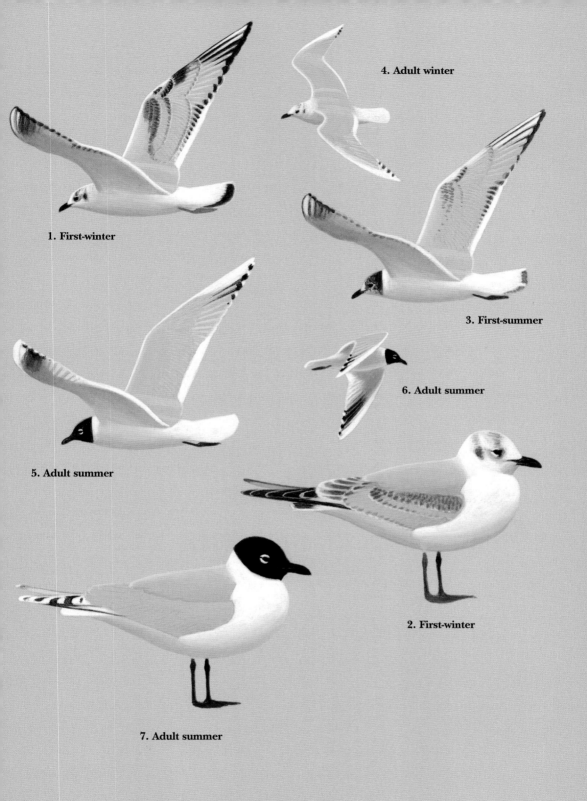

1. First-winter

4. Adult winter

3. First-summer

5. Adult summer

6. Adult summer

2. First-winter

7. Adult summer

sometimes with extensive area of white basally, outer webs blackish. P1–7 grey with darker inner webs and black to dark brown tips or subterminal spots (sometimes indistinct on P1–4), appearing as dark spots or more complete dark trailing edge to outer wing. Primaries with narrow white tips. Secondaries grey with indistinct dark spots on outer webs to create faint secondary bar. Greater and median primary coverts with dark shaft-streaks, broadening towards tip to form dark drop-shaped spots. Tertials dark with broad white edges. Underparts and rump white. Tail white with narrow dark bar (8–12mm on T1): T6 white. Rarely, whole tail white. Bill blackish to dark brown. Legs dark reddish-brown.

First-winter (Aug–Apr) Head white with greyish-brown cap, indistinct dark streaks on hindneck and dark ear-spot. Mantle and scapulars grey, often with brownish tinge. Otherwise as juvenile but, with wear, upperwing and tail become worn and faded, appearing greyish-white from May; parts of secondaries and tail often of adult type in spring (pers. obs. in China). White primary tips usually disappear through wear from Jan.

First-summer (Mar/Apr–Aug/Sep) as first-winter, but central crown to hindneck generally with more extensive blackish markings and indistinct white spotting, rarely complete hood similar to adult summer. Retained juvenile wings and tail strongly faded by midsummer.

Second-winter/summer similar to adult, but sometimes with black shaft-streaks to greater primary coverts and – in summer – duller black hood.

DISTRIBUTION AND MIGRATION Population 3,500-4,500 breeding birds, winter population 7,100-9,600 birds. Breeds coastal saltmarshes and in river deltas. Endangered by agricultural development, reclamation, construction of salt pans and shrimp ponds and environmental changes with recent decline; formerly common SE China. In China breeds in Liaoning 600–700 pairs, Hebei 25 pairs, Shandong 200 pairs, Jiangsu 300–750 pairs. All seven known colonies endangered by development or plans for agriculture. Further human disturbance includes environmental changes and egg collecting, oil pollution, coastal sewage and industrial waste. In S Korea breeding confirmed at two sites late 1990's (130 pairs), but none secure (Brazil 1991, 1992, Carey 1993, Poole 1994, del Hoyo *et al.* 1996, Moores 1998, Collar 2001).

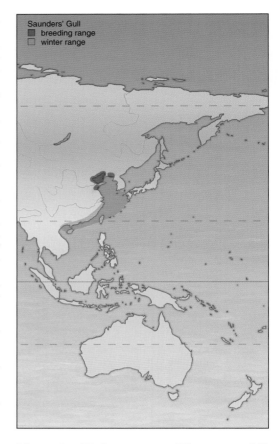

Saunders' Gull
■ breeding range
□ winter range

Migrates S and E. On passage max 68 in autumn and 85 in spring Happy Island, 5-600 Sep 1991 Qingdao, Shandong. main winter site Yansheng marshes, Jiangsú, where max 2,000 winter. Winters coastal estuaries S Japan: 1,000; mainly Kyushu, especially some tidal flats, Fu Kaoko, Daijyugarami and Shinkomori in Saga, Isahaya in Nagasaki and Shio-hama in Kumamoto; max 450 Nov–Dec at Saga-gun, Saga. Winter population peaks Dec; rapid decrease late Mar; regular N to central Honshu, China (widespread in migration and in winter E and S coasts 1,100 Shanghai S to Hong Kong (max. 200 winter); Taiwan 500, S Korea 3,500 (estuaries W

SAUNDERS' GULL Two-year gull. Very rare: breeds in a few sites along E China coast, wintering E Asia between southern Japan and Hong Kong. A small gull, in size between Black-headed and Little with rounded head, short hooked bill and long wings and tail (shape and flight may at distance suggest Ross's).

Adult has pale grey upperwing with broad white trailing edge. Wing-tip from above whitish with black confined to spots along mid-trailing edge. Underwing greyish with black patch on mid-primaries (similar to Black-headed Gull but narrower and better contrasting). Bill black, legs red. In **summer** (Apr–Aug) hood black with broad white eyelids. In **winter** (Aug–Mar) head white with narrow dark ear-spot and sometimes greyish tinge to central crown.

First-year has indistinct narrow brown carpal bar, dark wing-tip with white inner webs and narrow dark trailing edge to inner wing as spots, most extensive on outer arm, where forming blackish triangle. Primaries dark-patterned, surrounded by pale. Black tail-bar very narrow. Head as adult winter, but markings on crown sometimes more extensive.

Second-year as adult, but sometimes with dark markings on primary coverts.

and S coast, especially Asan Bay, Kum and Nakdong Estuaries, North and South Cholla. Most recorded Suncheon Bay, South Cholla (2,000 Feb 1999)) and N Vietnam (max. 200 Song Koi near Hanoi). Vagrant E Russia, Macao (Il'icev & Zubakin 1990, del Hoyo *et al.* 1996, Lopez & Mundkur 1997, Moores 1998, Collar 2001).

MEASUREMENTS Lengths in mm; weight in g. Based on Il'icev & Zubakin (1990), combined with own data from skins in MCZ, UZM.

WING

Adult male	277–297 (284.9)	11
Adult female	268–282 (276.7)	8
First-winter male	279	1

BILL

Adult male	28.0–29.0 (28.2)	11
Adult female	23.0–27.0 (25.0)	8
First-winter male	26.6	1

Note Bill depth at gonys: adult male 9.2 (1), adult female 8.6 (2), first-winter male 9.4 (1). Bill depth at base of bill: adult male 10.4 (1), adult female 9.1–9.5 (2), first-winter male 10.4 (1). Gonys length: adult male 10.7 (1), adult female 9.5–9.6 (2), first-winter male 10.6 (1) (skins in MCZ, UZM).

TARSUS

Adult male	42.0–44.0 (43.2)	11
Adult female	39.0–41.0 (40.5)	8
First-winter male	38.2	1

Weight No information.

680

Saunders' Gull *Larus saundersi.* **680. 1st-winter.** Note short, stubby and slightly hooked, black bill. Nanjing, China. 10 Nov 1999. *Harry J. Lehto.*

Saunders' Gull *Larus saundersi*. **681. 1st-winter.** Underwing pattern resembles Black-headed Gull, but dark area is slightly narrower. Note dark double-mark along wing-bend and short, dark secondary bar with dark just solid in outer part of arm. Kwaile Dao, Hebei Prov., China. Sep 1994. *Felix Heintzenberg*. **682. 1st-winter**. Dark double-mark at wing-bend, incomplete dark secondary bar and very narrow dark tail-bar clearly visible. Kwaile Dao, Hebei Prov., China. 14 Oct 2001. *Per Schiermacker-Hansen*. **683. Adult summer**. Note black hood, broad white eyelids and short, hooked bill. Hong Kong, China. April. *Alan Tate*. **684. Adult summer**. Note compact body and solid blackish oval in underwing. Underwing-coverts slightly greyish-tinged. Hebei Prov., China. May 1998. *Julian R. Hough*. **685. Adult summer**. Note pale upperwing with black-tipped primaries. Kwaile Dao, Hebei Prov., China. 17 May 1997. *Klaus Malling Olsen*.

34. MEDITERRANEAN GULL

Larus melanocephalus (Temminck, 1820, coast of Adriatic Sea) **Plate 69, Photos 686–702**

IDENTIFICATION Length 36–40cm, wingspan 92–100cm. Size of or slightly larger than Black-headed, compared to which the head is larger with a flatter crown and fuller hindneck, bill deeper with more parallel edges and stronger-hooked tip, and legs longer and darker. Some males (largest being size of Common Gull) have heaviest bill and jizz-wise may look like miniature large gull. Small females have shorter, stubbier bill and often look 'cuter' with large, rounded head and only short gape. Has shorter, fuller, bulkier body and shorter, broader wings than Black-headed, the difference in wing-shape striking in the pale- and round-winged adult. Settled bird is stocky with long legs. Relaxed bird often looks surprisingly compact and neckless with flat back. Swimming bird sits higher on water than Black-headed, showing broader, shorter neck and shorter wings.

In flight rather full-bodied with short neck, 'well-fed' belly and often shortish-looking wings. Wingbeats generally stiffer than in Black-headed and Common Gull. Often feeds on arable land, but may feed with short dips (as Little Gull) to water surface, or takes flying insects in a Black-headed Gull manner.

Adult has very pale grey upperparts, being paler and cleaner pearly-grey than in Black-headed. The pale wings have whitish, translucent primaries. A narrow black edge to outer web to P10 is normally invisible in field, so that wings appear all white in flight. Bill coral-red with black subterminal bar and often pale tip. Legs red. In **summer** has velvety black hood (dark chocolate-brown in Black-headed) and broad white eyelids creating 'clown-like' look. Hood reaches further down on hindneck than in Black-headed, but – as in other hooded species – shape of hood can change noticeably with posture. Black hood, very pale rest of plumage and bright red bare parts may superficially create tern-like impression – these characters obvious when seen alongside Black-headed, with which it often gathers. In **winter** very pale; distant flying birds in strong sunlight may recall small egrets because of the whiteness of the wings. Has varying dark mask, mostly as dark triangle behind eye, but sometimes almost lacking. Bare parts duller than in summer. Silvery-white plumage creates identification pitfall with adult Ivory Gull, but red bill and legs and dark head-markings prevent confusion; in distant flying birds, pale grey tone to plumage and different structure are best characters.

Juvenile more similar to juvenile Common than to Black-headed. Has plain head, white or washed with grey or buff; sometimes a bit darker on ear-coverts but head still distinctly paler than in juvenile Black-headed, lacking strong contrast between pale and dark feather areas of that species. Underparts whitish with variable brown or grey-brown mottling on breast and flanks. Upperparts brown, pale-scaled. Upperwing pattern like strongly marked first-year Common (and Ring-billed)

Gull, thus very different from Black-headed with better contrasts: dark carpal bar and secondaries striking against paler grey greater coverts and inner primaries. Unlike Common, outer primaries have white on inner webs forming white spots or narrow lines (outer primaries all dark in Common), visible in fully spread wing. Lesser and median coverts brown or grey-brown with whitish or buffish fringes, sometimes with blackish 'anchors', recalling pattern of juvenile Curlew Sandpiper *Calidris ferruginea*. The underwing is white with dark comma on primary coverts and dark bar across secondaries, showing up as distinct dark rectangle. The black tail-band is narrower than in Common, and tail often has broad white edges. Bill blackish. Long, dark legs create booted impression.

First-winter combines adult body and head (although often with fuller dark mask) with juvenile wing and tail from Aug–Sep. Characteristic head pattern emphasised by dark, hooked bill, although paler base may be developed from Oct.

First-year Common Gull has paler, dark-tipped bill, dark spots or streaks on head (no mask) and weaker upperwing contrast. Axillaries and underwing-coverts dark-patterned, although weakly marked birds may look more uniformly pale. Dark tail-band broader and legs pale. When juvenile upperparts are replaced (first-winter), Common also shows darker grey upperparts (even distinctly darker than Black-headed), whereas upperparts of Mediterranean are slightly paler than in Black-headed.

First-summer as first-winter, but with faded and generally paler, less contrasting upperwing. Head similar to first-winter; only small minority have traces of summer hood (rarely almost complete). Bill red to reddish with dark tip, duller than in adult. Swimming red-billed spring birds may easily pass as Black-headed Gulls, but – apart from shape – the bill is heavier, often with brighter red base. Legs darker red than in Black-headed.

Second-winter similar to adult winter, but with variable black markings on outer (3–6) primaries (as in second-winter Little). Bill pale with dark tip; sometimes similar to adult, but generally duller.

Second-summer similar to adult summer, but second-winter primary pattern retained (although often faded from May). Hood generally duller than in adult, often with a few white spots.

Third-winter/summer as adult or with faint short dark markings on outer webs of P8–10 (only P10 in adult). Legs sometimes darker than adult.

VOICE Commonest call is a very distinctive mellow *ee-ar* or *yee-ah*, whining or recalling small barking dog.

MOULT (pers. obs. in Scandinavia, France, Bulgaria) **Adult** moult to **winter** plumage complete Jun–Oct, some weeks later than Black-headed. Head from late Jul with forehead, lores and chin moulted quickly; >90%

481

PLATE 69. MEDITERRANEAN GULL *Larus melanocephalus*

Medium-sized West Palearctic gull, breeding mainly within former USSR, but with scattered populations in S, C and N Europe. Breeds coastal lagoons, especially on sand-banks, often in association with other gulls. Outside breeding season mainly coastal.

Size between Black-headed and Common Gull. Compared to Black-headed, stockier with heavier, squarer head with fuller neck, heavier, drooping bill and longer, darker legs. Young birds plumaged somewhat similar to Common Gull, older birds closer to Black-headed. Settled birds stocky with short neck and square head, older birds with shortish primary projection beyond tail and long dark legs. In flight heavy with square body, full head, drooping bill and short tail. Wings on average broader but shorter than in Black-headed and Common Gulls. Wingbeats stiffer, more powerful than in Black-headed.

1. **Juvenile moulting to first-winter** (Aug–Sep) Dark brown juvenile scapulars contrast to pale grey mantle of first-winter. Compared to 2, this individual shows stronger dark markings on greater coverts, but a tinge paler brown carpal bar, creating less contrast on upperwing. However, distinct ground pattern of brown, grey and black, even at range creating 'piebald' plumage, retained. Note long, almost blackish legs.

2. **Juvenile** (fledging–Aug/Sept) Juvenile head and mantle/scapulars present, head being rather featureless with diffuse brown mask and tinge to breast-sides, diffusely contrasting with paler face. White crescents above and below eye evident from early age. Juvenile mantle and scapulars dark brown with pale edges, and normally blacker subterminal markings, creating pattern as in juvenile *Calidris* sandpiper. Dark-centred lesser and median coverts contrast with pale grey midwing-panel on greater coverts. Legs long and dark with larger amount of tibia being visible than in Black-headed or Common Gull. Strongly hooked bill often appears all dark.

3. **First-winter** (Sep–Apr) In flight well-marked with good contrast between blackish-brown carpal bar, very pale grey mid-wing panel/inner primaries and blackish outer primaries and secondaries. At close range, note white streaking on mid-primaries. Tail-bar narrower than in Black-headed and Common Gull. First-winter head markings often strong: dark eye-mask and bill contrast clearly with white head. Long legs almost reach tip of tail. From below, white underwing-coverts and inner primaries in contrast to dark secondaries, which form distinct dark rectangle on underwing, well offset from dark outer primaries. Many show narrow dark 'comma' at tips of primary coverts. Main ID confusion is similar-aged Common Gull which, however, shows streaking on head, bicoloured bill (sometimes in Mediterranean also), weaker wing-markings with brownish tinge 'obscuring' pale and dark pattern, broader tail-bar and dark-tipped underwing-coverts and axillaries, thus creating darker, less contrasting under-wing than in Mediterranean.

4. **First-winter** (Sep–May) Clearly patterned in grey, blackish and white: head white with black-eye-mask ('zorro-mask') and broad white crescents above and below eye. Mantle and greater coverts pale grey, in contrast to dark brown lesser/median coverts and brown-centred tertials. Legs long, brown to blackish. Bill dark, often with variable paler base, from first-autumn creating bicoloured bill. This plumage mainly retained to first-summer; only a small minority develop darker hood. By summer, often strongly worn, but still contrasting.

5. **Second-winter** (Aug–Apr) From autumn of second calendar year similar to adult, but with black pattern on wing-tip and often duller base to bill and legs.

6. **Second-winter** Pale grey upperwing with narrow white trailing edge. Outer five primaries black-patterned with long black streaks to outer two primaries, creating pattern similar to second-winter Little Gull, although more distinct (comparable with dark pattern to outer wing of adult Iceland race *kumlieni* and Thayer's Gull). Note black eye-mask covering eye and bicoloured bill.

7. **Adult winter** (Aug/Sep–Mar) Head white with dark mask from around eye across hindneck. The mask varies, however, in some being restricted to grey spot behind eye. Such birds almost whitish-looking in field, at distance almost uniform whitish with broad wings (not unlike egret). Bill bright red, often slightly duller than in summer and normally with dark subterminal markings and yellowish-tinged tip.

8. **Adult summer** (Mar/Apr–Aug) Velvety black hood in contrast to white crescents above and below eye and coral-red bill. Upperwing pearly grey with very narrow black streaks on outer web of outer primary. Long legs coral-red.

9. **Adult summer** In flight pale grey with almost whitish outer wing. All flight feathers translucent. Narrow black streak on leading edge of wing only visible at very close range. Black hood contrasts strongly with coral-red bill and legs.

1. Juvenile moulting
to first-winter

3. First-winter

6. Second-winter

9. Adult summer

2. Juvenile

4. First-winter

5. Second-winter

8. Adult summer

7. Adult winter

have winter head late Aug, 100% mid-Sep. Primaries Jun–Oct; P5–7 Aug, P9–10 mid-Sep (10% mid-Oct). Tail late Jul–Sep, generally starting with T1; T6 usually mid-Sep.

Adult moult to **summer** plumage partial, mid-Feb–Apr, including head, body and sometimes P1–2. Head on average two weeks later than Black-headed, starting with crown and ear-coverts, developing downwards. Rarely moults minor areas of hindneck and ear-coverts Dec–Jan. Hood mid-Feb–early Apr. By first half Mar most have white blaze/throat. Full summer head from mid–late Mar. White feathers on forehead and throat may be present early May. Rarely, area around base of bill and lores moulted first (Cramp & Simmons 1983, Hoogendoorn *et al.* 1992, pers. obs.).

Juvenile moult to **first-winter** partial from Aug–mid-Oct. Most late Aug–mid-Sep have moulted head, mantle and scapulars, but retarded birds still have mainly juvenile head to mid-Sep and parts of mantle/scapulars (frequently all) late Sep. A few median coverts sometimes moulted Sep–Oct.

Moult to **first-summer** partial Mar–Jun, often limited. Most retain winter-patterned head and coverts; may moult T1–2 Mar–Jun. Head moult normally limited to a few feathers on hindneck; in small minority adult summer hood developed.

Moult to **second-winter** complete Jul–Oct, generally slower than adult. P1–3(6) early Jul, P9–10 late Aug–early Oct; among 300 in Bulgaria mid-Sep, 90% had completed flight feather moult. Coverts Jun–Jul, tail Jul–Aug.

Moult to **second-summer** partial, including head and body, on average 2–3 weeks later than in adult. By late Mar–early Apr many show white-spotted forehead (sometimes complete white blaze) (Hoogendoorn *et al.* 1992, R. Strack & T. Ortvad pers. comm.).

DESCRIPTION

Adult Upperparts pale grey (Kodak Grey Scale (2)3–5), shading to white on upper part of primaries. P10(9) with black line on outer web, not extending to tip and becoming brownish and very indistinct through wear. Secondaries very pale grey with tip and inner web largely white. Marginal coverts white. Underwing-coverts, neck, rump, tail and underparts white. Iris brown. Orbital ring red or orange-red. Bill red with pale tip. Gape red.

Adult summer (Mar–Jul) Hood glossy black, extending to upper hindneck. Prominent white eyelids above and below eye, in male sometimes joining behind eye, but otherwise rather squarish and not connecting (T. Hoogendoorn *in litt.*). Bill coral-red to scarlet with variable black subterminal markings, which may form 4–6mm broad bill ring, but sometimes lacking. Bill-tip red, orange, yellow or whitish. Legs scarlet to coral-red.

Adult winter (Jul/Aug–Feb) Head white with varying dark mask from behind eye to nape; often triangular, but sometimes reduced to weak grey ear-spot on otherwise white head. Crown and hindneck sometimes greyish-tinged, hindneck often with narrow dark streaks. In autumn, unmoulted primaries slightly brownish-tinged. Bill dull red to orange (rarely pink, bright red or black) with broad, complete black subterminal band or tip.

Legs dull reddish, red or orange-red; rarely black.

Juvenile (fledging–Aug/Sep) Head white or buffish, plain or with slight greyish wash to crown and ear-coverts. Eye-crescents black; has thin white crescents above and below eye. Mantle and lower hindneck grey to greyish-brown, often with fine pale fringes. Scapulars, lesser coverts and median coverts grey-brown to rusty-brown, often with darker subterminal 'anchors' and neat pale buff to whitish fringes, creating scaly pattern; sometimes with full darker centres. Greater coverts pale grey with slightly darker grey subterminal spots (sometimes weak) and whitish fringes; inner greater coverts with dark centres. Primary coverts blackish. P6–10 black with variable white tongues on median part of inner webs. P10 sometimes wholly black. P1–5 pale grey with dark subterminal spots and triangles, gradually narrowing to 20–40mm on P1–3. Secondaries black with white tips and fringes to outer webs. Tertials dark-centred with darker subterminal markings and clear-cut whitish fringes. Rump and tail white, rump sometimes with indistinct dark spots. Tail with black subterminal bar (30–38mm in T1), not extending onto T(5)6; tips to rectrices white. Rump and underbody white with pale grey, buff or brown breast and flanks (often darker-mottled). Underwing white, but with dark pattern of primaries and secondaries shining through. Under primary coverts with dark tips, creating dark comma against white coverts and primary bases. Axillaries white but sometimes with faint dark markings. Iris dark brown. Bill black, usually with some pale grey or flesh at base of lower mandible. Legs brownish-black or black.

First-winter (Aug/Sep–Apr/May) similar to juvenile, but head white with variable dark mask behind eye, sometimes clear-cut, extending from eye to nape and rear crown; in weakest-marked birds restricted to a few dark streaks behind eye or as dark ear-spot similar to winter Black-headed. White eyelids above and below often prominent, given emphasis by dark shading in front of eye and dark borders. Mantle, scapulars and back pale grey. Juvenile wing and tail fade with wear from midwinter, when carpal bar becomes gingery-brown and white flight feather tips disappear. Bare parts as juvenile; bill often paler (reddish, yellow, buff, pink or orange; rarely bright red) with dark tip from late autumn. Extreme bill-tip often reddish. Some show bill pattern similar to Black-headed; others retain black bill to first-summer. Legs as juvenile, but from late winter often greyer, olive-tinged or reddish. Gape dull flesh.

First-summer (Mar–Jul/Sep) as first-winter, but head often with more extensive dark markings near eye. <5% develop full summer hood. A few replace most inner wing-coverts and lack brown carpal bar (Grant 1986b). Upperparts more faded than in winter. Bare parts vary from blackish to adult-like, but then usually duller.

Second-winter (Sep–Apr) as adult winter but P(5)7–10 with varying black: outer webs to P8–10 black and black subterminal spots to P5–7; some just with weak dark grey markings on P9–10 (especially males). Markings mostly distinct and well defined, rarely more diluted. Primaries with white tips, narrower than in adult. Outer greater primary coverts and alula sometimes with black markings. Bill flesh or olive with dark tip or subterminal band, sometimes red with black subterminal bar and yellow-white tip. Legs similar to adult, but often with orange or blackish-brown tinge. Advanced birds as adult in second-winter apart from primary markings.

Second-summer (Apr–Aug/Oct). As second-winter, but hood as adult summer, although generally duller and often white-flecked, especially on forehead and lores. White primary tips reduced through wear from late May; black primary pattern gradually disappears during moult into adult winter. Bare parts as adult summer.

Third-winter (Oct–Feb) as adult winter; P8–10 sometimes with short dark markings on outer web (present in 25% of third-winter males and 50% of third-winter females). Rarely with dark markings on under primary coverts. Bare parts as adult; legs sometimes darker. A third-winter bird with black spots to both webs on P9–10 about 10mm from tip was probably diseased (Paterson 1985b, Grant 1986b, T. Hoogendoorn pers. comm.).

Hybrids A few instances of **Mediterranean × Black-headed Gull** recorded. Structure intermediate between the two species; often similar to Mediterranean, but bill slightly weaker and wing-tip less full, never with solid dark inner primaries from below as in Black-headed Gull.

Adult has slightly darker upperparts than Mediterranean and traces of Black-headed primary pattern (e.g. whiter P7–10, often darker upperside to P3–6 and black outer web of P10). Summer hood dark chocolate-brown, penetrating more towards hindneck than in Black-headed (but in some similar). White eye-crescents on average broader than in Black-headed. Winter head white, generally with restricted dark markings compared to Black-headed; often only faint grey ear-spot. Bare part shape and colour intermediate between the two. Bill brighter than Black-headed, less bright than Mediterranean, often with yellow tip and hint of black gonys-spot. One closely studied bird had black outer web to P10 and black spots to P7–10. Underwing white, apart from black spots at tips of P7–10, lacking solid dark area on mid-primaries of Black-headed (although this was suggested in some). White primary tips normally much broader than in Black-headed (Taverner 1970b, Köhler *et al.* 1983, Langman 2000, Leray *et al.* 1999, D. Kok *in litt.*).

Juvenile similar to Black-headed Gull, but brown on head and upperparts less ginger, and upperparts more uniform warm-brown and scaly. Primaries blackish with slight paler bases to inner ones (Langman 2000).

First-winter Head similar to Black-headed, but white eye-crescents more prominent; some have head closer to Mediterranean. Mantle/scapulars paler than in Black-headed. Upperwing similar to Mediterranean, but dark areas browner; on upperwing, inner and mid-primaries either similar to Black-headed (lacking conspicuous pale window of Mediterranean) or paler, sometimes with white markings forming white spots at bend of wing. Underwing similar to Mediterranean, but with more extensive white on inner webs of outer primaries; inner and mid-primaries not dusky as in Black-headed. Bill orange-red with black tip (bill generally duller than in Black-headed). Legs dull pale reddish (Langman 2000, A. Corso & M. Langman *in litt.* & photos).

Second-year similar to second-year Mediterranean Gull, but upperparts slightly darker and wing pattern often more like Black-headed with paler leading edge (although less prominent) and dark trailing edge to outer wing. P(7)8–10 often with black subterminal spots or tips, appearing as dark spots on underwing. Inner primaries often slightly darker (but never solid dark on underside as in Black-headed). Apparently, whitish underwing with well-spaced black spots at tips of P7–10 diagnostic, recalling Bonaparte's Gull (Langman 2000). Bill pattern as Mediterranean: red with diffuse black subterminal bars and yellowish tip, or slightly duller.

Third-year similar to second-year, but with small black subterminal spot to P10 only (Langman 2000).

Adult hybrid **Mediterranean Gull × Common Gull** generally with darker upperparts than Mediterranean; obvious white tertial and scapular crescents and broad white trailing edge to wing (as in Common), shading to grey on P1–4. (One bird had restricted black on P8–10, large white spots on P9–10 and rather extensive black tips with small white spots on P5–10.) Summer hood pale grey to blackish-grey; shape similar to Black-headed, but penetrates more towards hindneck (thus more similar to Mediterranean) and lacks brown tinge; sometimes shows paler greyish forehead and whitish eye-stripe. White eye-crescents rather squarish at corners, not connecting at rear (as in typical Mediterranean). Bill similar to Mediterranean: dull red with black subterminal ring and yellow tip; may be heavier than in Mediterranean. Sometimes larger than Mediterranean with fuller breast; floats higher on the water than Mediterranean, as does Common Gull (Hoogendoorn *et al.* 1998).

Probable first-winter hybrid had head pattern resembling Mediterranean, but with dark streaks on hindneck, breast and flanks as well as no obvious face-mask, and wing pattern closer to first-winter Common. Bill nearly all dark and legs pale reddish (Balten *et al.* 1993).

Aberrants First-winter with all-dark upperwings recorded (Edgeller 1996): had brownish-black upperwing-coverts with some black subterminal markings, clean white fringes to greater and median coverts on upperwing and white secondary tips. Tertials brownish-black with narrow white edges. Underwing with prominent broad secondary bar. Dark plumage parts appeared crisp, at a time when 'normal' Mediterranean Gulls of similar age were worn, especially on wing-coverts. Legs blackish. Plumage similar to certain first-winter Little Gulls (which see). Another first-winter showed dark 'half-hood' (similar to Franklin's), dark breast-sides and flanks and much darker upperparts than normal; tail and underwing normal (A. Corso *in litt.* & photos).

DISTRIBUTION AND MIGRATION 300,000–370,000 pairs mid-1990s (99% in former USSR). Strong increase since 1950s when estimated <40,000 pairs. Breeds along coasts and lagoons (<1% in inland waters) with sparse vegetation; generally avoids barren sand. Sometimes

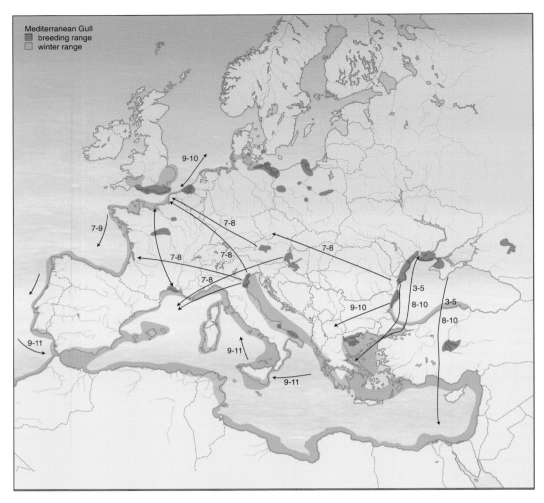

Mediterranean Gull
■ breeding range
□ winter range

coastal saltmarshes. Outside breeding season mostly coastal, often with Black-headed Gull. In Ukraine 245,000 pairs (100,000 1970). Main site Tendra Bay, Black Sea. In all large breeding sites, numbers fluctuate from year to year. In Tendra Bay (in pairs) 93,500 1961, 17,000 1974, 335,000 1983, <20,000 1993, 72,000 1998. In 1994 60,000 Golaya Pristan. From 1972 range expansion to Azerbaijan, W Caspian Sea; 28 nests 1989; probably 10,000 in good years 1990s.

Since 1940 spread in Europe. First bred Hungary 1940, Netherlands 1959 (breeding attempt in pair with Black-headed Gull 1933), E Germany 1963, Belgium 1964, France 1965, Great Britain 1968 and Italy 1978; has bred most European countries. European population around year 2000: Netherlands 1,300 (in 2001; since 1970s [when <8 pairs] steady increase; 410 pairs 1998; Most breed Delta area); Belgium 250–300; France 1,600 in 1999 (of which 1,457 Camargue); Italy 2,500–3,000 (mainly in NE); Hungary >100; Greece 2,000 (but 7,300 Alyki Kitrous Lagoon 1988); Bulgaria 100; Turkey 500–1,500. Also Germany 10–50 (1997 13 in 8 colonies; 2–7 E Germany since 1960s; one Heligoland mid-

1990s); Great Britain around 100 in 2001 (mainly Norfolk and Essex); Poland 25–30; Denmark 1–4 pairs from 2000. Irregular Austria, Switzerland, Belarus, Czech Republic and Estonia. Breeding attempt Sweden 1980 and from late 1990s, Ireland 1995 (Glutz von Blotzheim & Bauer 1982, Cramp & Simmons 1983, Il'icev & Zubakin 1990, Meininger & Bekhuis 1990, Risberg 1990, Spencer et al. 1990, Boldreghini et al. 1992, Malling Olsen 1992, Rheinwald 1993, Tucker & Heath 1994, del Hoyo et al. 1996, Hagemeijer & Blair 1997, Handrinos & Akriotis 1997, Yésou 1997, van den Berg & Bosman 1999, Ogilvie et al. 1999, 2001, Bijlsma et al. 2001, J. Dyczkowski in litt.).

Arrives at breeding sites from early Apr; laying period mainly May; leaves from late Jun, probably heading for moulting areas in W Black Sea (e.g. max. 6,000 moulting late Jul. Bourgas, Bulgaria). Migration mainly coastal; large numbers early Jul from Crimea towards Sea of Azov and moving W or SW through Turkey into mid-Nov. Some cross Turkey and Bosporus heading for E Mediterranean or follow large rivers of E and C Europe. Main migration E Mediterranean and Aegean

MEDITERRANEAN GULL Three-year gull. Breeds mainly E Mediterranean and Black Sea. Following breeding season gathers in SW Europe from Netherlands and southwards. Size between Black-headed and Common Gull. Compared to Black-headed shows larger head with flatter crown and fuller hindneck. Stronger bill with more hooked tip, longer legs and shorter wings; when settled wings only slightly longer than tail. In flight full-bodied and broad-winged.

Adult very pale, with pale grey upperwing and white wing-tip (small black line on P10 normally not visible). Bill and legs bright red. In **summer** (Mar–Jul) hood jet-black, reaching further down on hindneck than in Black-headed. Broad white eyelids form 'clown-mask'. Bill strongly contrasting coral-red. In **winter** (Aug–Mar) head white with dark shading on ear-spot and across hindneck, sometimes more extensive, giving impression of dark half-hood, but in others reduced to isolated dark markings behind eye. Very pale, almost egret-like at distance. Legs and bill bright red.

Juvenile (Jul–Aug/Sep) has greyish-brown head and breast-sides contrasting with hooked, dark bill. Mantle and scapulars brown with prominent pale scaling. Upperwing with brown carpal bar and black trailing edge to inner wing strongly contrasting with pale grey midwing and mirror on inner primaries; outer primaries and their coverts dark. Underwing white with solid dark rectangle on secondaries. Tail white with rather narrow black bar.

First-winter (Sep–May) as juvenile, but head white with distinct dark eye-mask and bar across hindneck, contrasting strongly with white crown. Bill blackish, but may develop pale base. Mantle and scapulars grey, as in adult, in contrast to juvenile wing, which is generally retained well into spring. In **first-summer** sometimes with traces of dark head, but generally similar to first-winter.

Second-year similar to adult, but with dark markings on outer five primaries, creating dark-streaked wing-tip.

Third-year as adult, but may show narrow dark markings along outer webs of outer primaries.

Sea Sep–Oct. In Bulgaria large gatherings; at Lake Atanasovsko max. 20,000–30,000 mid-Sep; among 10,000 there 13 September 1998, >95% adults, numbers quickly dropping during following week when first-year proportion became >10%. Max. 25,000 Kavarna and Kaliakra mid-late Sep (e.g. 21 Sep 1974 25,000 migrating Cape Kaliakra). In Danube Delta, Romania, max. 13,000 Oct. Main migration middle and E Mediterranean mid-Oct–late Nov, some continuing to Atlantic coast (Cramp & Simmons 1983, Finlayson 1992, *Birding World* 11: 380, pers. obs.).

Black Sea population winters sparsely S Black Sea and E Mediterranean, commoner Aegean and Adriatic Seas (but, as with C European breeders, with westward migration to France), but mainly S Mediterranean between N Egypt and NW Morocco. Winter population in Mediterranean at least 700,000, e.g. 43,000 S and E coast of Spain, 1,000 Malta, 8,000 Tunisia (mostly in SE), several thousands Apulia, Italy. Some 100,000 between Portugal and Libya. All recoveries of Greek birds are from Ukraine. Small dispersal to areas N of Mediterranean, as indicated by regular occurrence Bodensee and N to S Scandinavia (see below); probably arriving from large C European river systems as shown by ringing recoveries of birds from Orlov Island in Poland and Denmark. W Mediterranean breeding birds otherwise winter mainly around S coast of Spain (Schuster *et al.* 1983, Shirihai 1996b, Handrinos & Akriotis 1997, Ogilvie *et al.* 2002, B. Nikolov & U. Mellone *in litt.*).

Following breeding, most of W European population gathers at Le Portel, Pas-de-Calais, France, where max. 2,500 late Jul–early Sep. W European autumn birds include small numbers from Hungary, Italy and Black Sea. A bird ringed Black Sea, Jun, recovered Netherlands, Sep, and found dead Cadiz, Spain, Dec. Most first-winters stay close to breeding grounds (especially NW France and S England), older birds between S England and Morocco. No sign of W European breeders

entering Mediterranean. Increasing numbers winter N and W Europe S to France and Spain, e.g. 3,570 Llobregat Delta. Common Gibraltar Nov–Feb. In winter >1,200 Great Britain and 100 Ireland late 1990s, mainly in SW (50 & 100 E Sussex and Folkestone respectively). In France 4,000 winter of which max. 600 Le Portel, Pas-de-Calais and 1,850 Ile-de-Ré; including Mediterranean probably 8–9,000 (Cramp & Simmons 1983, Lack 1986, Powell 1990, Boldreghini *et al.* 1992, Finlayson 1992, Meininger *et al.* 1993, Hoogendoorn *et al.* 1996, McGeehan 1997b, Bijlsma *et al.* 2001, *Birding World* 11: 50).

Spring migration from late Feb, peaks Black Sea early Mar–late May, immatures last to migrate; in Crimea late Mar. In France max. 7,000 Mediterranean coast in Mar. Regular C, E and N Europe, mainly adults mid-May–mid-Jun.

Regular visitor N to Denmark (since 1980s 10–56 yearly), Sweden (yearly max. 34), Scotland (11–17 yearly); mainly adults in May and first-years Aug–Oct; a few winter. Vagrant N to Norway (28) and Finland (14), W to Azores, Madeira and Canary Islands, Africa S to Senegambia (8, Nov–Feb) and Kenya; Arabian Gulf States and Iraq (Bundy & Warr 1980, Glutz von Blotzheim & Bauer 1982, Cramp & Simmons 1983, Risberg 1990, Malling Olsen 1992, Barlow *et al.* 1997, James & Norton 1997, Tyrberg 1998, A.T. Mjøs & B. Nikolov *in litt.*).

MEASUREMENTS Lengths in mm; weights in g. Own data based on skins in AMNH, MCZ, NHM, NNH, NRK, USNM, UZM. Mediterranean, Bosporus and Great Britain.

WING

Adult male	295–320 (308.8)	42
Adult female	282–317 (302.0)	32
First-year	286–318 (299.4)	21

BILL		
Adult male	30.6–38.0 (34.6)	42
Adult female	30.7–37.0 (33.3)	33
First-year	30.3–35.5 (33.0)	16

BILL DEPTH AT BASE OF BILL

Adult male	10.4–12.4 (11.2)	42
Adult female	10.0–12.3 (10.8	32
First-year	9.9–12.0 (10.8)	21

BILL DEPTH AT GONYS

Adult male	9.4–12.0 (11.0)	42
Adult female	9.2–11.5 (10.5)	32
First-year	8.6–10.7 (9.6)	21

GONYS LENGTH

Adult male	9.9–13.3 (11.1)	42
Adult female	9.3–12.2 (10.4)	32
First-year	8.6–11.5 (9.9)	21

TARSUS

Adult male	45.7–54.7 (50.3)	42
Adult female	44.8–52.8 (48.6)	32
First-year	45.7–51.7 (49.0)	21

Weight Adult, Black Sea male 248–348, female 217–280. An adult male, Wismar, Germany 11 April, 388 (Glutz von Blotzheim & Bauer 1982).

Mediterranean Gull *Larus melanocephalus.* **686. 1st-winter**. Note dark eye-mask emphasising white eyelids and rather strong, bicoloured bill. Copt Point, Great Britain. 16 Mar 1996. *David Astins.* **687. Juvenile**. Note dark brown, pale-edged saddle of juvenile. Juvenile head shows brown tinge. Finland. Sep 1994. *Henry Lehto.* **688. 1st-winter**. Note very conspicuous wing-pattern - like very contrasting Common Gull, but cleaner grey, black and white. Pas-de Calais, France. 23 Sep 1998. *Annika Forsten.*

Mediterranean Gull *Larus melanocephalus*. **689. 1st-winter**. Slightly less contrasting than 688. Note black bill and eye-mask contrasting well with white forehead. Pas-de-Calais, France. 30 Aug 1993. *Klaus Malling Olsen*. **690. 1st-summer**. Underwing of 1st-years white with strongly contrasting dark rectangle over secondaries. Greece. 1 Jul 1986. *Per Schiermacker-Hansen*. **691. 1st-summer moulting into 2nd-winter**. Most 1st-summers retain more or less winter head, but on average more coarsely spotted. This bird shows more-than-average summer head, but still only patchy and dull. Pas-de-Calais, France. 25 Jul 1992. *Arnoud B. van den Berg*. **692. 2nd-winter**. Similar to adult, but bill on average darker and outer primaries with dark pattern, although here rather weak. Copt Point, Great Britain. 16 Mar 1996. *David Astins*. **693. 2nd-winter moulting into 2nd-summer**. By this age, summer hood as adult, here in last stages of moult into summer. Compare the more extensive dark primary markings in this bird with 692. Copt Point, Great Britain. 16 Mar 1996. *David Astins*.

Mediterranean Gull *Larus melanocephalus*. **694. 2nd-winter (almost complete).** This bird is still growing P9-10. At this age bill is variable, here rather dull with black tip. Dark eye-mask typically joins at rear with hindcrown streaking. Hanstholm, Denmark. 20 Sep 1997. *Klaus Malling Olsen*. **695. 2nd-winter.** Bird with rather extensive dark primary pattern. Pas-de-Calais, France. 23 Sep 1999. *Arnoud B. van den Berg*. **696. 2nd-winter.** Wing-tip often appears streaked as here. Pas-de-Calais, France. 7 Nov 1992. *Arnoud B. van den Berg*. **697. Adult winter (near end of moult).** Outer primaries still growing, resulting in shortish-looking body. Note bright red bill and legs. At distance, adult winters look almost white – especially in flight. Hanstholm, Denmark. 1 Oct 2000. *Klaus Malling Olsen*. **698. Adult moulting from summer to winter plumage.** Note white surround to base of bill and compare with Black-headed Gull at similar stage of moult (photo 642). Settled adults shows all-white rear. Pas-de-Calais, France. 27 Jul 1992. *Arnoud B. van den Berg*. **699. Adult summer.** Note velvety-black hood extending further down hindneck than in Black-headed Gull, 'clown-like' white eyelids and coral-red bill and legs. The white primaries add to the smart look. Netherlands. May. *Karel Beylevelt*. **700. Adult summer.** Note almost white wings in flight. Netherlands. Apr 1985. *René Pop*. **701. Adult summer.** Note pale grey wings with very narrow black outer web to P10, normally not visible in the field. Malmö, Sweden. 17 Apr 1997. *Klaus Malling Olsen*. **702. Adult summer.** Note translucency of wings. Malmö, Sweden. 17 Apr 1997. *Klaus Malling Olsen*.

699

700

701

702

35. RELICT GULL

Larus relictus (Lönnberg, 1931, Tsondol, southern Gobi)

IDENTIFICATION Length 42–46cm, wingspan unknown. Relict Gull is confined as a breeding bird to C Asia. It was given specific status 1970, having formerly been regarded as conspecific with Mediterranean Gull or aberrant Brown-headed Gull (based on a single specimen).

Relict Gull is the size of Mediterranean with similar summer head pattern, hooked bill-tip and long legs, but has different wing-tip pattern and darker bill (apart from first-years). Settled birds look small-headed with large, broad body and protruding breast. The bill is short and thick, the legs long and slender. Gait often plover-like. Feeds with quick plover-like steps ('tip-toeing'). Flight similar to Common Gull.

Adult summer has blackish-brown hood and broad white eyelids, normally joining at rear as in Saunders' and Franklin's Gulls. Upperparts silvery-grey with varying dark primary markings, ranging from black wing-tip with two white mirrors (and black extending onto P5) to less extensive black, similar to well-marked second-year Mediterranean Gull. In flight, many show noticeably more white than black on wing-tip. Settled birds show black wing-tip with white spots (rarely reduced to white markings on P10). Bill and legs dark red.

Brown-headed Gull is slightly smaller with longer, sharper-ended wing-tip, paler brown hood, narrower white eyelids (rarely meeting behind eye) and usually more complete black wing-tip, usually with two white mirrors and narrower white primary tips. The paler legs are shorter. Black-headed Gull slightly smaller, in all ages with different wing-tip, as leading edge of hand white, trailing edge black.

Adult winter has white head with dark ear-spot and sometimes isolated dark spots on crown and, more frequently, hindneck.

Juvenile/first-winter similar to Common Gull, but with darker bill and legs and narrower dark tail-bar, often restricted to midtail. Head white, often with narrow brown streaks or tinge on hindneck and sometimes faint dark ear-spot. Primary coverts and outer primaries mainly dark, forming solid dark wing-tip, often with narrow white mirror on P10. Inner primaries pale with dark subterminal spots, merging into a row of darker spots on secondaries; dark secondary bar thus fainter than in other gulls apart from Saunders'. From below underwing white with black leading edge to primaries and dark-spotted secondaries. Bill dark, sometimes slightly paler at base. Legs dark grey.

First-summer similar to first-winter, but head-markings usually more extensive, upperwing faded (contrasting with grey mantle) with dark subterminal markings on secondaries and primary coverts; outer wing brown.

Second-winter similar to adult, but has more black on wing-tip (similar to adult Common and Brown-headed Gull) and narrower white primary tips. Also, shows dark-centred primary coverts and tertials and black bill with greenish- to orange-tinged base.

Second-summer similar to adult summer, but with more black on wing-tip; P9–10 with white mirrors.

Third-winter as adult, but generally with narrower white mirrors on P9–10; some outer primary coverts dark-streaked.

VOICE Similar to Mediterranean Gull. At breeding sites a short, trisyllabic *kaw-kaw-kaw*. Also a hoarser *arr*, *arrriu* and *rwiu*, like barking dog.

MOULT Adult moult to **winter plumage** from late Jul/Aug, active moulting Aug–Sep (Heinzelberg & Dierschke 1996). Winter head by late Aug/early Sep. Primary moult reaches P7–9 early Sep. Probably finishes moult in winter quarters around Sep; last parts renewed are tail and secondaries, which are generally moulted at onset of moult to P7–8.

Moult to **first-winter** probably similar to Black-headed Gull.

Moult to **second-winter** starts with P1, median coverts and sometimes inner lesser coverts, a few secondaries and rectrices mid-May. Primary moult usually completed late Aug–Sep.

A third-year bird from 9 April was in summer plumage (Il'icev & Zubakin 1990).

DESCRIPTION

Adult Upperparts pale grey. P10 grey with white tip; sometimes with black subterminal spot near tip. P9 grey with white median part grading into grey base. P8 with black tip and outer part of outer web. P7–6 with black subterminal spots. Sometimes black subterminal spot on P5, rarely small on P4. Primaries and secondaries with white tips and grey bases. Underparts, hindneck, rump and tail white. Iris dark reddish-brown. Bill and legs dark red.

Adult summer (Apr–Aug) Head blackish-brown with dark brown or sooty tinge; darkest at rear. White eyelids above and below eye 4–7mm broad, often joining behind eye. Nape white.

Adult winter (Aug–Mar/Apr) Head white with dark ear-spot and isolated dark spots or short streaks on crown.

Juvenile (fledging–Aug) Head white with reddish-brown nape and dark streaks behind eye. Eye-crescents blackish. Mantle, scapulars and upperwing-coverts grey with broad reddish-brown subterminal spots and pale edges creating scaly pattern. Rump and underparts white. Outer webs and primary tips black, decreasing in extent to small black subterminal spots on P5–6. P6–10 black, P10 with small white spot near tip of inner web. P1–5 grey with dark subterminal spots (gradually smaller inwards) forming pale window on inner wing. Secondaries black with broad white edges and tips. All flight feathers white-tipped. Tertials dark with broad whitish edges. Lesser upperwing-coverts brown, median coverts and greater coverts grey. Underparts white, with dark tips to primary coverts and brownish wash on

492

flanks. Tail white with narrow black subterminal bar, sometimes T4–6 white. Iris dark reddish-brown. Bill dark brown. Legs dark grey.

First-winter (Aug–May) similar to juvenile, but head whitish, sometimes with distinct dark streaks on hindneck and normally with faint dark ear-spot. White crescents above and below eye narrower than in adult; shows grey crescent in front of eye. Mantle and scapulars pale grey. Bill sometimes with grey base and black tip.

First-summer (Apr–Aug) as first-winter, but sometimes with more extensive dark head-markings, rarely as incomplete hood. Before moult, coverts bleach to whitish and contrast with darker grey saddle, and primaries are brownish. Secondaries and tertials white with small brown spots. Bill orange-red with dark tip. Legs orange-red to grey (Fisher 1985).

Second-winter (Aug–Apr) similar to adult winter, but with more complete black on P9–10 and isolated white mirrors on P9–10. Shows black subterminal marking to P(5)6 and thus black trailing edge to outer wing. Tertials and primary coverts dark with broad white edges. Bill black with greenish to orange base.

Second-summer similar to adult summer, but with wing-tip pattern of second-winter.

Third-winter as adult, but black wing-markings generally stronger, white mirrors on P9–10 smaller and some outer primary coverts with black markings. Bill on average with more solid dark markings at tips.

DISTRIBUTION AND MIGRATION Population <4,000 pairs, probably <2,000 pairs. Decrease in recent years, but numbers fluctuate strongly. Breeds on small islands or shores in arid landscape, usually saline or semi-saline lakes in semi-desert at 1,000–1,500m altitude. Often with Gull-billed *Sterna nilotica* and Caspian Tern *Sterna caspia*. Prefers islands at least 100m away from shore. Threatened by human disturbance, changes in water level and predation from Caspian Gull race *mongolicus*. Changes breeding sites depending on state of water reservoirs.

Main range Mongolia and Inner Mongolia, where breeding at 2 or more sites, where replaces Brown-headed Gull. Colonies of 600 pairs Ordos Highlands and 1,115 Maowusu Desert. 2 larger colonies Ordos Plateau at Taolimiao - Alashan Nur, 581-1500 nests 1990-1993. At Anbai Nur 624 nests 1991. At both lakes 4096 birds breeding 1986. In former Russia estimated 2,200 pairs, of which 1,180 Hu-Han, but apparently

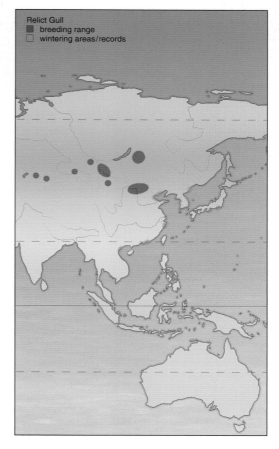

Relict Gull
■ breeding range
□ wintering areas/records

much fewer recently. At Kukan Island, Barun-Torey Lake 0-1025 pairs bred 1967-85, but none in 1992 and 1995. Small numbers W to E Kazakhstan Lakes of Balkhash and Alakol' (0-1200 pairs), where formerly more widespread (Auezov 1971, Il'icev & Zubakin 1990, Fen-Qi *et al.* 1992, Zhang & Fen-Qi 1993, del Hoyo *et al.* 1996, Gavrilov & Gavrilov 2000, Collar 2001).

Migratory, wintering in E Asia. Leaves breeding sites late Jun–Aug (a few adults probably resident), first-years from Sep. Migrates E towards Gobi Desert to main wintering range on Asian E coast between China and Vietnam, as proved by recovering of birds ringed at

RELICT GULL Three-year gull. One of the rarest gulls, breeding only inner Central Asia, wintering E Asia. Size similar to Mediterranean Gull, but head rounder (and smaller on more solid body) and bill broader, but shorter with more hooked tip. Feeds with rapid, tip-toeing gait.

Adult has pale grey upperwing with black on wing-tip, either as solid black with two white mirrors or with longer white tongues on midwing almost connecting with large white mirrors. Bill and legs red. In **summer** (Apr–Aug) hood blackish with broad white eyelids. In **winter** (Sep–Mar) head white and bill-tip sometimes dark. May get some dark spots on hindneck.

First-year superficially like Black-headed, but with much fainter dark wing-markings; dark trailing edge reduced to row of isolated dark spots. Inner primaries dark-spotted as well, creating darker wing-tip. Underside of wing-tip dark. Tail white with much narrower dark bar than in Black-headed. Head white with slight dark hindneck-streaks. Bill dark, from winter with paler base.

Second-year similar to adult, but bill generally duller with fuller black tip, wing-tip black with white mirrors and primary coverts with dark streaks.

493

PLATE 70. RELICT GULL *Larus relictus*

Very rare and local Central Asian gull. A few thousand pairs breed Central Asia, especially Mongolia. Main wintering area coast of E China. Similar to Mediterranean Gull in size and jizz, but with more rounded head and shorter, more strongly hooked bill. Legs long and dark. Settled bird shows plover-like gait with small, rounded head, long wings and long legs. Leg action while foraging rapid.

1. **First-winter** (Sep–May) Wing pattern similar to Mediterranean Gull: upperwing with large contrast between dark and pale areas; underwing white. Secondaries with paler edges, not creating strong dark rectangle on underwing as in Mediterranean. Head small, rounded and white with short, hooked black bill and large black eyes. Dark tail-bar narrow, appearing as row of black spots.

2. **First-winter** (Sep–May) Settled bird shows rounded, white head, greyish necklace and short, blackish bill. Dark-centred lesser coverts and tertials in contrast to rest of upperparts. Note long dark legs.

3. **First-summer** (May–Sep) With wear, secondary bar and tail-bar become indistinct. Moult of coverts early, often resulting in only outer wing juvenile.

4. **Second-winter** (Aug–Apr) Bill and legs dark, head with indistinct dark shading behind eye. Note primary pattern similar to Common Gull.

5. **Second-summer** (May–Sep) Note indistinct dark shading on crown and ear-coverts (sometimes traces of hood, as shown by 3). Upperparts similar to adult, but wing-tip black with only narrow white primary tips; may show dark-centred tertials as shown here. Legs dark reddish-brown. Bill either all dark or shaded with red.

6. **Adult summer** (Apr–Aug) Blackish hood shows conspicuous white eyelids, similar to Franklin's Gull. Head and legs dark red. Upperwing pattern resembles second-year Mediterranean Gull.

7. **Adult summer** Bill and legs dark reddish.

8. **Adult summer** Individual with larger amount of black on wing-tip. Note plover-like stance, rounded head and short bill. Breast protruding.

1. First-winter

3. First-summer

4. Second-winter

6. Adult summer

2. First-winter

5. Second-summer

7. Adult summer

8. Adult summer

Lake Alakol'. During migration max. 865 by Sep Happy Island and 15 Beidaihe, Hebei province, China, mainly involving first- and second-years; peak first part of Sep. In South Korea scarce wintering, max. 65 at Nakdong, but numbers fluctuate. Known from Yellow Sea shores in Apr. and regular Korea in small numbers. Vagrant Hong Kong (3), Vietnam (2) and Japan (2). Birds ringed as Relict Gull, Lake Alakol', recovered Bulgaria (Burgas) and S Turkey; although the latter two recoveries considered insufficiently documented, they indicate that the species may infrequently reach W Palearctic. There is also a claim of 14 ad. Ukraine, May 2001 (Fisher 1989, Zhang & Fen-Qi 1991, Duff *et al.* 1991, Zhang *et al.* 1991, Leader & Lam 1993, Leven & Carey 1993, Bradshaw & Rowlands 1996, del Hoyo *et al.* 1996, Heintzenberg & Dierschke 1996, Enticott & Tipling 1997, Moores 1998, Rubinic & Birizovikov 2000, Gavrilov & Gavrilov 2000, Nankinov 2001).

MEASUREMENTS in mm and g, derived from Il'icev & Zubakin (1990), Zhang & Fen-Qi (1993). Kazakhstan, Transbaikalia, China.

WING

Adult male	337–370 (347.7)	30
Adult female	322–354 (334.2)	16

BILL

Adult male	32.3–42.5 (36.9)	30
Adult female	32.0–37.0 (34.3)	16

TARSUS

Adult male	53.0–65.4 (58.5)	30
Adult female	49.0–59.0 (54.8)	13

Weight Kazakhstan, adult male 470–575, female 420–488. Transbaikalia, adult 499–695 (Il'icev & Zubakin 1990); China, two males 560, 700, one female 540 (Zhang & Fen-Qi 1991).

Relict Gull *Larus relictus.* **703. 1st-winter.** Upperwing rather similar to Mediterranean Gull, but note broken dark secondary bar, short black bill, lack of head markings and very narrow dark tail-bar. Hebei Prov., China. Sep 1999. *Thomas Sacher.* **704. 2nd-winter.** Note rounded, dove-like head and short, broad bill. Head pattern very faint, reduced to slight grey tinge as indication of ear-spot. Kwaile Dao, Hebei Prov., China. Sep 1994. *Felix Heintzenberg.* **705. Adult or 2nd-winter.** White eyelids present in slightly greyish-tinged head. Chumunjin, South Korea. 11 Dec 2000. *Jon R. King.*

Relict Gull *Larus relictus*. **706. 2nd-winter**. Note rounded head, large dark eye and narrow black markings in wing-tip. Kwaile Dao. Hebei Prov., China. Sep 1994. *Felix Heintzenberg*. **707. 2nd-winter or adult.** Small white mirrors on P9-10 and faint dark markings on primary coverts indicate this age. Chumunjin, South Korea. 11 Dec 2000. *Jon R. King*. **708. Adult winter**. White mirrors on P9-10 always extensive in adult, but somewhat varying; compare with 707. Chumunjin, South Korea. 11 Dec 2000. *Jon R. King*. **709. Adult summer**. Note broader white markings on P9-10 than 706. Summer head black with conspicuous white eyelids. Short bill adds to the Franklin's Gull impression. Kazakhstan. Jun. *Alan Tate*.

710

711

Relict Gull *Larus relictus*. **710. Adult summer**. Note short bill and conspicuous white eyelids. Kazakhstan. Jun. *Alan Tate*. **711. Adults winter**. Head in winter white with variable (but never strong) dark ear-spot, often appearing diffuse and greyish. Kwaile Dao, Hebei Prov., China. Sep 1994. *Felix Heintzenberg*.

Relict Gull *Larus relictus*. **712. Adult winter**. Bill duller than in summer, often appearing bicoloured. Chumunjin, South Korea. 11 Dec. 2000. *Jon R. King*. **713. Adults moulting from summer to winter plumage**. Note variable extent of white in wing-tip. Kwaile Dao, Hebei Prov., China. Sep 1994. *Felix Heintzenberg*.

36. LAUGHING GULL
Larus atricilla (Linnaeus, 1758, Bahamas)

Plates 71–72, Photos 714–729

IDENTIFICATION Length 36–41cm, wingspan 95–120cm. A medium-sized, slender and elegant gull, with a rather small head. About the size of Common or Mew Gull. Combination of flat crown and long, heavy, slightly drooping bill creates a vaguely fierce look. It has relatively longer wings than other similar-sized gulls and long, dark legs. Upperparts are darker than in most other medium-sized gulls apart from Franklin's (which see for fuller discussion). Flight is powerful with rather slow wingbeats on long, angled wings, giving impression of miniature large gull – in adult especially Lesser Black-backed because of dark upperparts.

Adult has dark grey upperwing (similar to Lesser Black-backed Gull race *graellsii*) with blacker wing-tip and conspicuous white trailing edge. It lacks white mirror on wing-tip, but has narrow white primary tips in fresh plumage. From below, broad black wing-tip against white underparts recalls pattern of Caspian Tern *Sterna caspia*. Legs often reddish-black, but vary from black to dark red (brightest in summer, especially in old birds). In **summer** shows sooty-black hood and white eye-crescents as two isolated white bars, creating 'sleepy' look. The hood reaches down nape. Bill red, at onset of breeding season often maroon to blackish, almost concolorous with hood. In **winter** head is white with varying dark markings, ranging from dark mask behind eye extending over nape, to faint grey wash behind eye. Bill dark with vermilion tip to upper mandible.

Juvenile has greyish-brown head and often paler face. Dark of head penetrates onto greyish breast and flanks. Upperparts are rather dark brown with narrow pale edges, contrasting with blackish flight feathers. White rump stands out against darkish-looking tail consisting of full, broad dark band (greyer base of tail only visible at close range). In flight, underwing is an important feature, being moderately dusky with strikingly darker axillaries (in heaviest-marked birds creating 'faint-marked Grey Plover' impression) visible at long range. Flight feathers are contrasting dark. Bill and legs dark.

First-winter gradually acquired in autumn, when brown head and body feathers are replaced by grey, during moult creating untidy, patchy look. Head similar to adult winter, but usually with more prominent dark mask behind eye and narrower white eye-crescents. The best-marked birds have dark hind-collar reaching crown and penetrating to breast-sides. Shows grey saddle, with wear contrasting clearly with juvenile, browner wing. Rather similar to Franklin's Gull (which see): note that an extensive half-hood as in Franklin's can be present in Laughing during head moult into first-summer, and in some well-marked first-summers; Laughing, however, always shows narrower white eyelids than Franklin's. **First-summer** similar to first-winter, but retained juvenile coverts (especially greater) very worn and faded. Some develop greyish half-hood around and behind eyes. From midsummer, moults into second-

winter, which is similar to adult but with darker greater primary coverts and alula, little or no white on primary tips and sometimes traces of dark secondary bar and tail-bar. **Second-summer** as adult summer, but hood duller (often white-spotted), all-dark primaries lacking white spots and generally duller red bare parts.

VOICE Calls a cackling, rather goose-like, laughing nasal *ha-ha-ha*, a deep *greek* and a whining *kerook* or *kiika*. Long-call first rapid, then slowing (Sibley 2000). Rather silent outside breeding season.

MOULT (*megalopterus*, North America) (own study, skins)
Adult moult to **winter plumage** complete Jun–Oct (Nov). Primaries Jul–Oct, P1 early Jul, P3–7 late Jul–late Aug, P9–10 late Sep–early Oct(mid-Nov). Outer secondaries late Sep/early Oct. Coverts Jul–mid-Sep. Head from Jun, starting with chin, lores and throat, followed by forehead; may still show full summer hood early Jul; most-advanced birds attain winter head late Jul, majority in Aug, but traces of summer hood common first half of Sep; <0.5% with summer hood Oct.
Moult to **adult summer** plumage partial late Feb–early Apr, including head and body. Starts with ear-coverts and hindneck, ending with chin and throat; scattered white feathers on lores and forehead often present early May. A few wing-coverts may be moulted (Cramp & Simmons 1983).
Juvenile moult to **first-winter** partial mid-Aug–Dec, including head and body, starting with mantle, followed by head, breast, flanks, mantle and scapulars Sep–Oct; 50% of mantle/scapulars usually renewed late Sep. Some median coverts (greater coverts) may be moulted late Sep–Nov, sometimes before main body moult. Rarely, all upperwing-coverts (except a few greater coverts) moulted Oct–Dec. Parts of upperwing usually renewed in autumn; rarely complete on upperwing-coverts. In some, juvenile upperwing retained through first year (skins in UZM, ZMA).
Moult to **first-summer** partial (Dec)Mar–May, including head, body, some lesser and greater coverts and some or all median coverts. Scattered coverts sometimes from mid-Dec. Occasionally, some rectrices moulted in winter; a bird early Jun had renewed whole tail apart from T4, another in May had white tail (Hoogendoorn 1996); but most retain most of juvenile tail into Jul. Most of head and body Mar–Apr.
Moult to **second-winter** complete May–Oct. On average earlier than in adult; P1 mid-May; P9–10 and primary coverts generally Oct. Greater coverts May–Jul; some have renewed all coverts late Jun, but majority Aug–Sep. Subsequent moults as adult.
In *atricilla*, adult moult to summer plumage earlier than in *megalopterus*: by mid–late Mar >99% Aruba and Trinidad/Tobago had summer hood. Moult to winter

500

plumage later, most still with summer head early Aug and active head moult Sep. Primary moult later; P3–5 (rarely none) renewed late Aug–late Sep when most *megalopterus* moult P8–10 (skins in AMNH, USNM, H. J. Lehto & K. Beylevelt *in litt.*, pers. obs.).

DESCRIPTION

(*L. a. megalopterus*) **Adult** Upperparts dark grey (Kodak Grey Scale (7)8–10). P9–10 black; P8–6 black with grey wedge on inner webs; P1–6 dark grey, P6 with 25–50mm wide black outer part against dark grey bases; P5 often with some black near tip, sometimes forming subterminal bar; P1–8 and secondaries with white tips, broadest on P1–4; reduced with wear from late spring (less so on innermost). Primary coverts dark grey; a few outer greater primary coverts sometimes with black spots. Underside of outer primaries black, rest of primaries dark grey, gradually becoming paler toward whitish inner secondaries. Underwing-coverts pale grey to whitish. Neck, underbody and tail white. Iris dark brown. Orbital ring, mouth and gape red. Legs dull red or blackish-brown, rarely scarlet or with slight pinkish tinge to tarsus.

Adult summer (Mar–Aug/Sep) Hood sooty-black (Kodak Grey Scale 12–15), 60–70mm from base of bill over crown to hindneck. In fresh feathers sometimes with indistinct white dots on forehead and crown, which soon wear off. Prominent white eyelids above and below eyes do not join at rear. Underbody sometimes rosy-tinged while breeding. Bill dull red to blackish-brown, at onset of breeding season often blackish or maroon, concolorous with hood. Bill may be clouded with black or with black subterminal bar, tip often red to scarlet. Bill sometimes brighter red, especially in midsummer – probably indicating older birds (van den Berg & Pop 1982, skins in ZMA).

Adult winter (Aug/Sep–Mar) Head white with varying grey patch on ear-coverts, often extending over hindcrown and nape as elongated grey patch; sometimes as dark flecking. Dark on head diffusely demarcated, and sometimes reduced to slight greyish wash behind eyes. May show slight grey wash above eye. Eye-crescents before eye black. Eyelids white, highlighted by grey eye-surroundings. Underbody white, sometimes with pale grey wash to lower hindneck and breast-sides. P1–8 with white tips, most conspicuous when fresh. Bill black or blackish-brown with vermilion tip to culmen, rarely extending to gonys (and rarely absent). Legs black to dark grey, often with brownish wash.

Juvenile (fledging–Sep/Oct) Head to hindneck greyish-brown with pale-tinged forehead, lores, chin and throat, and dark tinge to rear ear-coverts to nape. Eye-crescents before eye blackish. White eyelids narrower than in adult. Mantle, scapulars and tertials dark brown with prominent pale fringes, broadest on scapulars, creating scaly pattern; but often worn off by Sep. May show pale subterminal spots especially on lower scapulars. Back uniform grey. Upperwing with lesser and median coverts dark brown with pale fringes and sometimes paler grey bases. Greater coverts grey-brown with whitish fringes; outermost sometimes with dark spots near tip of outer web. Inner greater coverts sometimes paler subterminally. Secondaries black with narrow white fringes and broad white tips. Primaries and primary coverts blackish, P1–5 sometimes very slightly paler. P1–8 with narrow white fringes at tips. Grey fringes at webs of P5–7 increase inwards. Breast and flanks greyish-brown, belly to undertail-coverts dull off-white. Underwing with blackish primaries and secondaries. Underwing-coverts dull white with dusky grey markings, on axillaries forming dark armpit, sometimes extending to inner median coverts and lesser coverts in contrast to paler greater coverts (in well-marked birds with darker tips); <1% lack dark armpit. Tips of primary coverts dark, forming 'double comma'. Rump and uppertail-coverts white. Tail black with thin white fringes and tips. Bases to outer webs of rectrices grey, inner webs whitish. Iris dark. Bill black, often with some brown at base. Legs blackish to dark brown.

First-winter (Aug/Nov–Mar) Similar to juvenile, but head, underbody, mantle/scapulars and sometimes a few inner wing-coverts (especially median coverts) as adult, although head-markings often stronger: head mainly grey with whitish forehead, lores, chin and throat, and almost blackish ear-coverts, often extending over nape and hindcrown to above eye. White throat may penetrate to below and behind ear-coverts. Brown-grey markings on underbody generally more extensive. Bare parts as juvenile.

First-summer (Mar–Aug/Sep(Oct)) Similar to first-winter, but head generally paler with more prominent and isolated dark patch behind eye. Some get incomplete, white-flecked, dull dark grey hood, most prominent behind eye (rarely as adult summer, but duller). Underparts with less grey on hindneck, breast and flanks. Most upper juvenile wing-coverts fade to pale brown by spring. White fringes to flight feathers and tail reduced or lacking. Bill dark, sometimes with reddish at tip of culmen. Legs blackish.

Second-winter (Jul–Apr) As adult, but sometimes with stronger grey wash on hindneck, breast-sides and flanks. Upperparts similar to adult, but white primary tips narrower; lacking on P7–10. Black on outer webs of some secondaries forms indistinct or broken secondary bar. Primary coverts dark brown with dark shaft-streaks broadening towards tip (compare adult). Alula blackish. Tertials usually with dark markings. Underwing as adult; sometimes with a few dark-centred coverts (especially primary coverts). Tail rarely with greyish base and grey or black subterminal spots forming broken dark tail-bar, especially on T2–4. Bare parts similar to adult winter, but less frequently with dull red tip to upper mandible.

Second-summer (Mar–Oct) similar to adult summer, but hood often duller, sometimes slightly white-flecked. Underparts sometimes with grey clouding on breast-sides and flanks. Primaries blackish without white fringes (may be very faint). Bill dull red, often with black or red patches near tip. Legs dull red to blackish-brown.

Third-winter (Aug–Mar) as adult winter; small minority with dark spots on one or two tertials and dark shaft-streaks on primary coverts.

Hybrids Has paired with Grey-headed Gull in Senegal (Wilds 1986).

PLATE 71. LAUGHING GULL *Larus atricilla*

Slender, medium-sized gull from Eastern USA and West Indies. Slender-bodied with rather small head and long, drooping bill. Wing proportionally longer than in similar-sized gull, creating jizz rather similar to immature Lesser Black-backed or Black-tailed Gull. In all ages shows dark head-markings, greyish tinge to underbody, rather conspicuous white eyelids and long, slender, dark legs. Although rather localised, abundant where present, especially along coastlines. Often attracted by human activities.

1. **Juvenile** (Aug–Sep/Nov) In fresh juvenile plumage, head, breast and flanks brown and upperparts prominently scaled. Face dull with narrow white eyelids, creating sleepy look.

2. **Juvenile moulting into first-winter** (Sep/Oct) During moult into grey first-winter, typically piebald-looking with head and underbody a mixture of grey and brown. By mid-autumn, upperparts also typically a mixture of juvenile scaly and first-winter grey feathers. Face becomes paler from autumn, and head-markings better developed.

3. **First-winter** (Sep–Mar) Head in this bird rather well marked, in others whiter with weaker dark markings. Mantle/scapulars (and usually scattered coverts) of first-winter type contrast well with otherwise juvenile wing, which abrades to pale brown during winter. Black bill and legs retained.

4. **First-summer** (Mar–Aug) Similar to first-winter, but often with traces of dark hood (sometimes similar to half-hood of winter Franklin's Gull, which see). Covert moult somewhat variable; in this bird some lesser and greater juvenile coverts retained, being extremely worn and faded.

5. **Second-winter** (Sep–Mar/Apr) Second-winter and older birds show strong greyish tinge to hindneck and breast-sides, which gives Laughing a characteristic dull impression unique to Northern Hemisphere gulls. Note dark blue-grey upperparts. Second-winters still show blackish legs and bill and the folded wings look all black.

6. **Adult winter** (Sep–Mar) Similar to second-winter, but note clear white primary tips and vermilion-red tip to upper mandible. Head-markings often paler than shown here, and then in rather good contrast to grey breast-sides. Legs blackish to reddish-brown.

7. **Adult moulting from winter to summer plumage** (Mar/early May) Hood starts to develop at the nape moving towards the forehead, resulting in fine white flecking often present as last stages of winter plumage into early May.

8. **Adult summer** (Mar/Apr–Sep) Note narrow white eyelids in blackish hood and dark red, drooping bill. Blue-grey upperparts and long, black hand with only narrow white primary tips suggest Lesser Black-backed Gull. Legs dark (sometimes bright) red.

1. Juvenile

2. Juvenile moulting into first-winter

3. First-winter

4. First-summer

5. Second-winter

6. Adult winter

7. Adult moulting from winter to summer plumage

8. Adult summer

PLATE 72. LAUGHING GULL *Larus atricilla*

Flying Laughing Gulls are medium-sized like Common or Ring-billed Gull, but the long, dark wings, short tail, smallish-looking head with drooping bill and slender body create jizz closer to Lesser Black-backed or Black-tailed Gull. The dark overall appearance reinforces the Lesser Black-backed impression, but could also suggest a skua/jaeger Stercorariidae.

1. **Juvenile** (Aug–Sep/Nov) Upperparts including head at distance dark brown with blacker flight feathers, lacking clear window. Rump white against all-dark tail.

2. **Juvenile moulting into first-winter** (Oct–Nov) Face contrasts well with brownish breast and flanks. Underwing-coverts pale with dark tips, but axillaries dark, creating distinct dark armpit.

3. **First-winter** (Oct–Mar/Apr) Similar to juvenile, but mantle, scapulars and a variable number of coverts (here median) dark bluish-grey, from midwinter in contrast to worn juvenile feathers.

4. **First-summer** (Apr–Aug) Similar to first-winter, but note strongly bleached lesser and greater coverts and dark half-hood. Primaries often strongly faded before moult.

5. **Second-winter** (Sep–Mar/Apr) Dull grey appearance typical of birds more than two years old. Similar to adult, but primaries lack white tips, upper primary coverts dark-streaked and bill all black. Note extensive black at tip of underwing, as in Lesser Black-backed or Black-tailed Gull.

6. **Second-summer** (Apr–Aug) Similar to adult, but bill darker, hood duller and there are traces of immature primary coverts and rectrices.

7. **Adult winter** (Sep–Mar/Apr) Adult shows dark bluish-grey upperparts with black wing-tip; at close range white primary tips are visible. Against the dark upperparts, white tail and trailing edge to wing contrast surprisingly strongly. Head slender with long, dark, drooping bill (with vermilion-red stripe on upper mandible only visible at close range). Black mask penetrates over crown and ear-coverts.

8. **Adult summer** (Apr–Aug) Hood often smallish-looking in slender head, offset by long, dark red bill.

1. Juvenile

2. Juvenile moulting
into first-winter

3. First-winter

4. First-summer

6. Second-summer

5. Second-winter

7. Adult winter

8. Adult summer

Winter hybrid **Laughing × Black-headed Gull,** probably adult, had weaker and paler red bill than Laughing, but still with drooping tip. Upperpart colour intermediate between Black-headed and Laughing Gull (Sibley 1994). Primary pattern similar to Black-headed, but with black subterminal markings on P9–10 (isolating large white spot near tip), with extension of grey halfway to tip of P6–8 and broader white primary tips than Laughing. Underwing with dark primaries; white outer webs of bases and broad white tips to P9–10 and narrow white spot on central outer web of P8.

Presumed adult hybrid **Laughing** (or Herring) × **Ring-billed Gull** had size of Ring-billed with darker upperparts, more black on wing-tip (with faint white spot on P10), strong dark ear-spot (as indication of adult summer hood of Laughing), dark eyes and long greyish legs, proportionately longer and thicker than in any gull smaller than Herring Gull (Sibley 1994).

GEOGRAPHICAL VARIATION Two subspecies

L. a. megalopterus (north-east America) described. Variation within breeding range very small. Birds from New York have on average longer wings, but weaker bill than birds from Florida (Hanners & Patton 1985, Evans *et al.* 1993, skins in USNM).

L. a. atricilla (Caribbean, Venezuela and Surinam) generally smaller than *megalopterus* in wing and tarsus, to a lesser degree bill. At onset of breeding season, bill and legs normally almost blackish (rarer in *megalopterus*). Adult tends to have more black on primaries, including more complete black markings on P5 (normally only weak dark spot on outer web in *megalopterus*) (Cramp & Simmons 1983, skins).

DISTRIBUTION AND MIGRATION Population 400,000 pairs (del Hoyo *et al.* 1996). Breeds coastal marshes of North America N to Maine. Widespread in nineteenth century, but eliminated from much of breeding range until protection 1913; since then increased. Recent population increase between Maine and Delaware; largest colonies 18,000 pairs Stone Harbour, New Jersey, and 20,680 Wreck Island, Virginia. Max. 80,000 Louisiana. Locally a pest near airports. Recent decline Florida, where 50,000 late 1980s.

Leaves breeding sites late Jul–Aug. Medium-distance migrant. N population performs longest migration, wintering mainly S USA, C and S America north of equator. First-years from Galveston, Texas, migrate to W

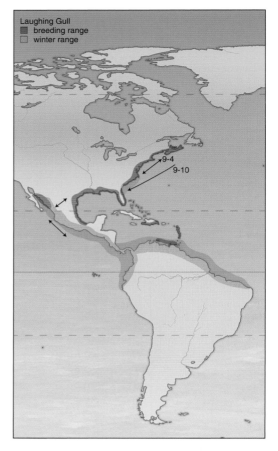

Laughing Gull
■ breeding range
□ winter range

9-4
9-10

Mexico and C America. Main migration E Coast Sep–Nov, where tens of thousands New Jersey. Autumn hurricanes may drive migration N as did hurricanes in 1958 and hurricane 'Gladys' Oct 1968, which brought thousands to Newfoundland and Nova Scotia. Regular Great Lakes and N to Newfoundland/Nova Scotia (especially summer). Common wintering Mexican Gulf (max. 30,000 Galveston, Texas). Winters sparsely N to Mid-west, along American E Coast N to New York and also in Baja California. Scattered records most of N America W to Hawaii (where regular, e.g. influx of 10

LAUGHING GULL Three-year gull. Abundant in E North America and Caribbean. Medium-sized, slender, with long, dark and drooping bill and long, dark legs. Upperwing dark, combined with slenderness of wings suggesting miniature Lesser Black-backed Gull.

Adult has dark grey upperwing with pointed black outer wing and narrow but prominent white trailing edge to inner wing. Legs dark. In **summer** (Mar–Aug/Sep) hood blackish with brownish tinge; shows prominent white eyelids. Bill dark, often as dark as hood, but sometimes red (especially after young fledged). In **winter** (Sep–Mar) head white with dark ear-coverts and hindneck markings, sometimes reduced to weak grey ear-coverts. Sides to neck and breast grey. Bill black, often with red tip to upper mandible.

Juvenile (Aug–Oct) greyish-brown with strongly scaled saddle. Upperwing greyish-brown with darker flight feathers, creating impression of all-dark wing. Underwing with dark spotting and often solid dark axillary-markings. Tail almost fully black, in contrast to white rump.

First-winter (Sep–Mar) develops from autumn, when grey on head, forebody and saddle intermixes with retained brown juvenile parts to create piebald pattern. Wing, tail and bare parts as juvenile.

winter 1987/1988). Winters S to Peru, Chile and N Brazil. Spring migration mid-Mar–mid-May; max. flocks 30,000 S Texas mid-May (>80% first-years). Casual E to Great Plains and N to Greenland (Mills 1969, Cramp & Simmons 1983, Hoogendoorn & Steinhaus 1990, Belant & Dolbeer 1993, Sibley 1993, Boertmann 1994, Enticott & Tipling 1997, M. Jørgensen *in litt.*).

In W Palearctic infrequent vagrant. Great Britain and Atlantic between France and NW Africa: up to year 2001, Great Britain 96, France 22, Spain 23, Portugal 3, Gibraltar 4, Azores 1, Netherlands 4, Belgium 1, Germany 4, Iceland 9, Norway 3, Denmark 3, Sweden 5, Finland 1, Austria 1, Italy 1, Greece 1, Canary Islands 1, Morocco 6, W Africa S to Senegambia 5. In Europe, occurrence generally more westerly than other Nearctic gulls. Probably arrives in winter, birds gradually moving N in spring; some first-years in autumn following Transatlantic crossing. Has been observed displaying with Black-headed Gull in Great Britain. Also vagrant Pacific Ocean SE to Australia, Japan (Pratt *et al.* 1987, Fisher & Fisher 1989, Baillon & Dubois 1992, Higgins & Davies 1996, Mitchell & Young 1997, van den Berg & Bosman 1999, Rogers *et al.* 2001).

MEASUREMENTS Lengths in mm; weights in g. Own data based on skins in AMNH, NHM, NNH, NRK, USNM, UZM, ZMA. *Atricilla* West Indies, Suriname. *Megalopterus* USA, Mexico, Ecuador.

WING

L. a. atricilla		
Adult male	302–332 (314.0)	64
Adult female	276–326 (306.7)	52
First-year male	295–336 (313.8)	15
First-year female	293–303 (296.5)	10
L. a. megalopterus		
Adult male	314–358 (330.8)	108
Adult female	303–344 (322.3)	92
First-year male	309–338 (321.3)	26
First-year female	296–326 (312.3)	25

Note Adults from New York: male 315–391, female 300–338; Florida male 274–354, female 261–345 (Hanners & Patton 1985, Evans et al. 1993).

BILL

L. a. atricilla		
Adult male	35.1–43.1 (39.2)	65
Adult female	34.4–40.9 (36.8)	45
First-year male	36.7–43.2 (39.7)	12
First-year female	33.3–37.6 (36.0)	10
L. a. megalopterus		
Adult male	35.8–46.2 (40.8)	108
Adult female	30.3–41.7 (39.0)	92
First-year male	37.2–44.2 (40.5)	26
First-year female	33.0–42.9 (37.6)	25

BILL DEPTH AT BASE OF BILL

L. a. atricilla		
Adult male	11.1–13.5 (12.5)	64
Adult female	9.9–13.0 (11.1)	42
First-year male	9.5–13.1 (11.4)	12
First-year female	9.4–10.6 (10.3)	10
L. a. megalopterus		
Adult male	11.0–14.0 (12.8)	104
Adult female	10.0–13.3 (11.7)	90
First-year male	10.6–13.4 (12.3)	26
First-year female	9.9–12.6 (11.5)	25

BILL DEPTH AT GONYS

L. a. atricilla		
Adult male	9.7–11.6 (10.5)	64
Adult female	8.3–11.0 (9.9)	43
First-year male	8.3–11.1 (10.2)	12
First-year female	8.5–10.1 (9.5)	10
L. a. megalopterus		
Adult male	9.7–12.4 (11.1)	104
Adult female	9.3–11.2 (10.3)	78
First-year male	9.3–11.5 (10.4)	26
First-year female	9.1–10.8 (9.9)	25

Note Adults from New York, male 8.0–12.5 (mean 11.2, n=65), female 9.0–11.5 (mean 10.1, n=38) (Evans et al. 1993). Florida male 10.5–13.5 (mean 11.6, n=86), female 9.8–12.2 (mean 10.8, n=79) (Hanners & Patton 1985, Evans et al. 1993).

GONYS LENGTH

L. a. atricilla		
Adult male	10.5–13.6 (11.8)	64
Adult female	9.7–13.6 (11.4)	43
First-year male	9.9–13.2 (11.5)	12
First-year female	10.0–12.5 (11.1)	10
L. a. megalopterus		
Adult male	11.1–14.1 (12.5)	104
Adult female	10.0–13.6 (11.9)	78
First-year male	10.3–13.8 (11.8)	26
First-year female	7.9–13.0 (11.2)	25

TARSUS

L. a. atricilla		
Adult male	43.1–52.4 (48.2)	64
Adult female	41.2–47.7 (44.3)	43
First-year male	42.9–52.0 (47.1)	12
First-year female	42.8–45.3 (43.9)	10
L. a. megalopterus		
Adult male	46.0–57.7 (51.9)	108
Adult female	43.5–52.9 (50.1)	97
First-year male	46.3–55.7 (51.1)	26
First-year female	41.0–52.1 (48.3)	25

Weight *L. a. atricilla* (Lesser Antilles) breeding adult male 205–275, female 219–275. First-years 200–366 (skins in UZM, ZMA). *L. a. megalopterus* (Florida) adult male 249–366(400), female 203–371. First-year male 137–352, first-year female 140–272 (Cramp & Simmons 1983, Hanners & Patton 1985, Urban *et al.* 1986, skins in USNM).

Laughing Gull *Larus atricilla*. Photos refer to ssp. *megalopterus* unless otherwise stated. **714. Juvenile at start of moult to 1st-winter**. Mantle and scapulars greyish brown with pale edges, creating slightly scaly pattern. Note greyish-brown head to breast, slender and slightly drooping dark bill and long dark legs. Juveniles show slightly scaled saddle, soon to be moulted into 1st-winter plumage. Cape May, New Jersey, USA. Sep 1998. *Julian R. Hough*. **715. 1st-winter**. As juvenile, but mantle and scapulars grey, by winter in stronger contrast to juvenile parts of wing. Cape May, New Jersey, USA. 28 Sep 1989. *Klaus Malling Olsen*. **716. 1st-winter**. Some birds moult parts of wing-coverts to grey, adult-type in autumn. Florida, USA. Apr 1998. *Don DesJardin*. **717. Juvenile moulting into 1st-winter**. Note brown wings with darker flight feathers, white trailing edge to inner wing and white rump in strong contrast to black tail. Appears long-winged in flight. Cape May, New Jersey, USA. 25 Sep 1989. *Klaus Malling Olsen*. **718. 1st-winter**. Note dark-patterned underwing with diagnostic dark 'armpits'. Cape May, New Jersey, USA. 1 Oct 1989. *Klaus Malling Olsen*.

Laughing Gull *Larus atricilla*. Photos refer to ssp. *megalopterus* unless otherwise stated. **719. Juvenile.** Head, breast and flanks greyish-brown in contrast to dark 'armpits'. Note slender outline. Martha's Vineyard, Massachusetts, USA. 14 Sep 1997. *Klaus Malling Olsen*. **720. 2nd-winter.** Similar to adult, but note traces of dark tail-bar and dark primary coverts. Cape Henlopen, Delaware, USA. 31 May 1989. *Harry J. Lehto*. **721. 1st-summer.** Hood at this age incomplete. Florida, USA. Apr 1995. *Don DesJardin*. **722. 2nd-summer**. 2nd-summers basically like adult, but note slightly browner primaries as well as solid dark centres to primary coverts. Virginia, USA. 10 Jun 1998. *Harry J. Lehto*. **723. 2nd-summer.** Compared to adult, hood duller and slightly pale-freckled and wing-tip solid dark, lacking white primary tips of adult. Bill and legs darker and duller than in full adult. Maryland, USA. 17 May 1994. *Klaus Malling Olsen*. **724. Adult summer.** Note velvety black hood, dark red bill and legs, and narrow white primary tips. White eyelids conspicuous, but not joining at rear. Florida, USA. Apr 1995. *Don DesJardin*.

Laughing Gull *Larus atricilla*. Photos refer to ssp. *megalopterus* unless otherwise stated. **725. Adult summer** ssp. *atricilla*. By early breeding season, bill often blackish in this ssp., more frequent than in *megalopterus*. Aruba, Lesser Antilles. Mar. *Karel Beylevelt*. **726. Adult summer** ssp. *atricilla*. All Laughing Gulls shows solid dark undersurface of wing-tip. Aruba, Lesser Antilles. Late Mar. *Karel Beylevelt*. **727. Adult moulting to summer**. Note black wing-tip, with narrow white primary tips, otherwise dark grey upperparts and broad white trailing edge to inner wing. Texas, USA. 24 Feb 1982. *Arnoud B. van den Berg*. **728. Adult winter**. Head white with faint dark markings, ranging from solid dark eye-mask to faint grey ear-spot. Hindcrown often slightly spotted. Note rather broad white tips to fresh primaries. Bill blackish with red spot near tip of upper mandible. Florida, USA. Jan 1999. *Harry J. Lehto*. **729. Adult winter.** Variation in winter head evident in this flock. Note strong, drooping black bill, dark grey upperparts and long, dark legs. Brownsville, Texas, USA. 1 Dec 1988. *Anders Blomdahl*.

510

37. FRANKLIN'S GULL
LARUS PIPIXCAN (WAGLER, 1831, MEXICO) PLATES 73–74, PHOTOS 730–741

IDENTIFICATION Length 32–38cm, wingspan 85–92cm. A small and dark-mantled gull, similar to Laughing, but smaller and more compact with shorter, less pointed wings and shorter legs with barely visible tibia, fuller, rounder head and heavier but shorter and less drooped bill. Size as Black-headed Gull or slightly smaller. Jizz-wise a 'Little Gull' version of Laughing with shape similar to Mediterranean. Moves very quickly while feeding; almost like a small shorebird. Unique moult cycle results in fresh-looking plumage most of year.

Dark mantle makes confusion likely only with Laughing. Apart from in summer plumage, head pattern differs as Franklin's has a conspicuous blackish, more clear-cut half-hood and broader white eyelids almost joining at rear, like goggles. Underwing white with only limited black markings on outer primaries. Pattern of wing-tip of adults also different from Laughing in showing solid white areas. In North America, mainly seen inland, thus less coastal than Laughing. Behaves as Laughing, but often picks food from surface in flight (rare in Laughing). Flight buoyant, similar to Bonaparte's Gull, but appears shorter-winged with rounder wing-tip and stubbier head. Sometimes similar to Little Gull.

Adult has upperparts and upperwing dark grey as Laughing, but broader white trailing edge to arm and different pattern to wing-tip, with white outer half to outer primaries except for limited black markings near tips (showing much broader white tips than in Laughing with white band bordering black markings – Laughing invariably shows solid black wingtip). Settled birds show striking white, black-spotted wing-tip. Tail grey-centred, not white as in congeners, but grey may be difficult to see. Legs bright red, but darker in winter.

Moults completely twice a year (the only gull to do so): following breeding season Jul–Oct and before northbound migration Nov–Apr. Therefore, wing should never appear strongly worn, and white primary tips always obvious. **Adult summer** has black hood (shape as Mediterranean Gull) with broad white eyelids, giving impression of near complete eye-ring. Bill and legs bright red (usually darker in Laughing). In **winter** has broad black half-hood; retains broad white eyelids, in dark half-hood most obvious behind eyes. Bill dark, often with reddish tip. Legs dark red or blackish.

Juvenile similar to Laughing, but with conspicuous black half-hood, as in adult winter but less contrasting owing to brownish or grey hindneck. Underparts pure white, lacking full darker breast-band, grey flanks and dark axillaries of Laughing. Thus it shows contrast between white underparts and dark upperparts, unlike similar-aged Laughing. When fresh, most primaries have small white tips. Inner primaries mainly grey, often creating slight pale window lacking in Laughing. Tail white with much narrower black band than Laughing, centrally placed, as tips and edges of tail are white. Pale scaling on upperparts narrower and weaker than in Laughing. Bill black. **First-winter** similar to juvenile, but

head, mantle and scapulars as adult winter. Frequently some upperwing-coverts are renewed, reducing brown carpal bar. Complete moult Jan–Apr to **first-summer** plumage. A few arrest moult and only renew a few inner primaries; juvenile outer wing then brownish through wear. **First-winter** similar to Laughing Gull of same age, but shows dark half-hood and thick, prominent white eyelids, prominent white-tipped primaries and grey-centred tail with narrow black band, pale window on inner wing (both surfaces) and narrower pale fringes to coverts. **First-summer** similar to first-winter, but tail lacks black markings, and upperwing grey with black distal part of outer primaries, white tips to primaries and broad white trailing edge to secondaries.

Second-winter as adult, but with more black/less white on wing-tip, black markings reaching P5. Outer primaries often all dark, with only narrow white tips and sometimes indistinct white patch on outer web of P10. This wing-tip pattern approaches adult Laughing, but black still less extensive, especially on underwing. Often with a few brownish-tinged upperwing-coverts. Frequent intermediates safest to assign to 'second-winter/adult type'. Certain out-of-range birds (e.g. two in Europe) retained first-winter plumage in their second-summer. Legs and bill as adult winter.

VOICE Nasal and laughing, but hollow-sounding, less penetrating, but higher-pitched than in Laughing Gull. Feeding call a short *krruk* or a low chuckling, often doubled: *wee-a wee-a...* or *keek-keek...* The common call on breeding sites is a louder, rather musical and plaintive *po-lee*, recalling Eurasian Curlew *Numenius arquata*. Long-call descending and accelerating with each note rising, the series having much greater pitch change than Laughing Gull. First-years have a harsh call resembling that of Sandwich Tern *Sterna sandvicensis* (Cramp & Simmons 1983, Farrand 1983, Sibley 2000).

MOULT The only gull undergoing two complete moults yearly.

Adult moult to **winter** plumage complete Jun–Sep/Oct. P1–6 Jul, P3–7 Aug, P8–10 Sep–Oct (moult sometimes finished mid-Sep). Secondaries moulted when primary moult reaches P4–5. Head and body starts early Jul with chin, throat and forehead. Normally attains winter head in Aug; may show summer hood into Oct.

Adult moult to **summer** plumage complete Nov/Dec–May. Primary moult starts again Nov/early Dec; P1–5 late Dec–early Jan, P(1)4–9 late Jan/late Feb. Advanced birds have renewed P10 late Jan; most complete primary moult late Feb–Mar, but some still actively moulting P(9)10 by May. If moult delayed, it is often suspended Mar–May (around P6–8), and thus reflected in subsequent moult. Tail Jan–Feb; moult irregular, but often starts with T6, then inwards (opposite to commonly used strategy in Laridae of moult into adult summer). Head from Jan, starting with chin, throat and forehead. Summer hood attained (late Jan–)early Apr;

PLATE 73. FRANKLIN'S GULL *Larus pipixcan*

Breeds locally in freshwater lakes in Central North American states; winters South America. Migration concentrated, often in dense flocks of thousands in W Mexican Gulf and Central America.
Has two complete moults a year, and plumage never strongly worn (note that out-of-range birds may show restricted moult). Resembles Laughing Gull with similar colour above, but smaller and 'cuter' with more compact shape, rounder, larger head and shorter, smallish-looking bill. Jizzwise a 'Little Gull version of Laughing Gull'. In all ages shows conspicuous white eyelids, joining at rear, creating curious 'clown-like' look, unlike 'sleepy' look of Laughing; moreover, hindneck and underbody never grey. Legs and bill shorter than in Laughing, flight more graceful.

1. **Juvenile** (Aug–Sep) Compared to Laughing Gull, head better marked with brown half-hood, broad eyelids and brown wash on underbody reduced to breast-sides. Upperparts more brownish-tinged with broader pale tertial edges than in Laughing. Shorter wings, on average with broader white primary tips than in Laughing.

2. **Juvenile moulting into first-winter** (Sep) First signs of moult are (as in Laughing Gull) on mantle and scapulars. Note diagnostic winter head pattern with solid brown half-hood and broad white eyelids.

3. **First-winter** (Sep–Apr) From first-winter Laughing Gull by strong head-markings, shorter bill and white hindneck and underparts (at most with slight brownish tinge on neck-sides).

4. **First-summer** (Apr–Aug) Following complete moult, fresh-looking with dark blue-grey upperparts and white tips to fresh black primaries. Similar-aged Laughing has strongly worn flight feathers and parts of coverts. Note also rounded head with black half-mask and white eyelids joining at rear; certain first-summer Laughing may show similar head pattern, but have narrower eyelids (usually not joining at rear, and producing sleepy versus alert look), slenderer head and (usually) longer, more drooping bill. Second-winter (Sep–Apr) similar, but on average with broader white primary tips.

5. **Second-summer** (Apr–Aug) Similar to adult, but sometimes with white forehead and duller bare parts.

6. **Adult winter** (Aug–Mar/Apr) Note blackish half-hood, all-white hindneck and underparts, more white than black in folded wing and dark reddish-brown legs. Like Laughing, bill black with red tip to upper mandible.

7. **Adult summer** (Apr–Aug) Bill and legs bright red. Hood similar to Laughing, but eyelids broader. Often shows rosy tinge to underparts.

1. Juvenile

2. Juvenile moulting into first-winter

3. First-winter

4. First-summer

5. Second-summer

6. Adult winter

7. Adult summer

PLATE 74. FRANKLIN'S GULL *Larus pipixcan*

Plumage rather similar to Laughing Gull, but Franklin's is smaller (about size of or smaller than Black-headed Gull) and more compact with shorter, rounder wings, rounder, larger head and slightly longer tail.

1. **Juvenile** (Aug–Sep) Similar to Laughing Gull, but upperparts generally paler with broader pale feather-edges, thus appearing slightly scaled at distances at which Laughing looks uniform. Note slightly paler inner primaries, broader white trailing edge to inner wing and only narrow black tail-bar not reaching tail-sides. Tail slightly greyish-tinged. White forehead against dark eye-mask often conspicuous at distance.

2. **First-winter** (Sep–Apr) Similar to juvenile, but note grey mantle/scapulars and white hindneck.

3. **First-winter** First-year shows white underwing-coverts, hindneck and underbody; compare Laughing, which shows strong grey or brown tinge to underbody and dark armpits. Black and white winter head pattern unique. Note large head and 'cute' look compared to Laughing.

4. **Second-winter** (Sep–Apr) At this age upperparts may approach darkness of Laughing with similar black primary tips, but note broader white trailing edge to wing including central primaries and grey tail in contrast to white rump – a diagnostic tail pattern retained in all older birds. While certain birds at this age may appear indistinguishable from adult, narrow black shaft-streaks on primary coverts age the bird shown here.

5. **Second-summer** (Apr–Aug) From this age shows very characteristic tricoloured upperparts with narrow black wing-tip isolated from grey upperwing by white (a pattern strangely similar to that found in similar-aged Pallas's Gulls). Grey on upperparts coloured as in Laughing Gull or a tinge paler.

6. **Adult winter** (Aug–Mar) Dark half-hood present throughout winter. Note upperwing pattern, in this individual showing least amount of black on wing-tip, as black bar surrounded by white; wing pattern shown in 6–8 depicts the individual variation in amount of black on wing-tip.

7. **Adult summer** (Apr–Aug) Some birds show rosy tinge to underparts almost as strong as in Ross's and Slender-billed Gull. Note 'tricoloured head': black hood, white eyelids and coral-red bill. The diagnostic primary pattern shows through on underwing, as white parts are strongly translucent. This individual shows maximum amount of black on wing-tip for adult.

8. **Adult summer** Bird with 'average' amount of black on wing-tip.

1. Juvenile

4. Second-winter

2. First-winter

3. First-winter

5. Second-summer

Adult winter

7. Adult summer

8. Adult summer

may show a few white feathers on chin into (late) May (skins in MCZ, M. Reid *in litt.*).

Juvenile moult to **first-winter** plumage partial Jul–Oct, including head, body and a few inner wing-coverts. Starts with mantle late Jul. Most have renewed 50% of mantle and scapulars early Sep, 80–100% by Nov. Timing variable: some have not started moult early Oct, others have completed moult mid-Sep (skins in MCZ).

Moult to **first-summer** complete; timing variable. Primaries generally from Jan–Feb; up to P5–8 Mar–early Apr. Most have reached P8 early Apr–mid-May; often arrest moult at this stage before moulting again Jul. Primary moult slower than in other gulls, each new feather fully or almost fully grown before adjacent one renewed. A bird from mid-Jun had new P9, but old P10 and P8 (skin in NHM). Rarely, primary moult not started Jul. Secondaries Mar–Apr. Mantle and scapulars late summer to autumn. Most moult some coverts (especially median coverts) and secondaries Jan–Apr. Tail from early–mid-Feb, generally completed by late Mar; T3–5 sometimes Apr–early May. Summer hood generally not attained until May.

Moult to **second-winter** complete Jul–Oct. Similar to adult moult, but if primary moult arrested, P8–10 moulted late Jul–Sep.

Moult to **second-summer** similar to adult, but primaries generally later, often arrested at P5–8. Birds from Feb had not yet started primary moult, birds from Apr–late May had old P8–10 or active moult on P9–10; two specimens had reached P5 early Dec. Tail often Feb–Mar (skins in MCZ).

Note Several birds from W Palearctic and Australia had arrested moult to winter plumage in flight feathers (as terns) or no sign of moult. This was probably caused by their longer than usual migration or provoked by weak condition. Out-of-range birds may therefore show different moult than described above (Hoogendoorn & van IJzendoorn 1994, pers. obs.).

DESCRIPTION

Adult Mantle, back, scapulars and upperwing-coverts dark grey (Kodak Grey Scale (6)7–9), as in Laughing Gull, but generally more bluish-tinged. Secondaries and P1–5 dark grey with broad white tips, forming white trailing edge to wing. Outer primaries greyish at base but with large white outer part, increasing from P5 to P10, dividing grey coverts from black subterminal markings on P7–10 (sometimes even P6, in other cases only P8–10). Large white tips to outer primaries. P10 very variable, in some with up to 100mm white tip (when black subterminal marking restricted or absent and white tip connected to basal white of feather), in others with dark subterminal markings, generally broadest on inner web; some with white mirror on inner web or both webs. Outer web of P10 predominantly black. P9 with 35–112mm white tip and only faint dark spot near tip of inner web; sometimes more black on inner web. Black subterminal bars on P8 25–60mm, on P7 17–35mm. P6 often with dark markings, as elongated shaft-streak or isolated spot, and white 'moon' between black subterminal markings and grey bases. P5 sometimes with narrow dark markings. Some (second-years?) have more black on wing-tip, similar to second-winter. Rump and

uppertail-coverts white. Tail grey with white sides, caused by grey on T1–3(4) (darkest on T1). Underparts white with pinkish tinge, generally strongest in spring (where often obvious). Eye dark. Orbital ring bright red. Gape scarlet.

Adult summer (Apr–Aug) Hood slaty-black (Kodak Grey Scale 15–17) with thick white eyelids below and above eye, joining behind eye, where up to 4–5mm broad. Length of hood 55–70mm (bill-base to crown). Bill red, usually with dark subterminal spot or thin, Z-shaped bar up to 6mm. Extreme tip sometimes yellow. Legs vary from bright red to blackish.

Adult winter (Aug–Mar) Head white with blackish half-hood; distinct white eyelids as in summer. Bill usually dark red or blackish with red or orange tip and with black subterminal markings. Legs dark red or blackish.

Juvenile (fledging–Sep/Oct) Forehead, lores, chin, throat and eye-crescents below and above eye whitish (latter usually not joining at rear). Has clear-cut, dark half-hood formed mainly by uniform dark grey-brown crescents in front of eye, ear-coverts, hindcrown and nape (where often streaked). Hindneck pale brown. Mantle, back and scapulars dark brown with white to pale cinnamon fringes, broadest on scapulars. Carpal bar on upperwing brownish with pale fringes. Greater coverts uniform brownish-grey. Secondaries and tertials grey-brown with blackish centres and broad white tips. P8–10, outer primary coverts and alula blackish with grey on inner webs of primaries increasing inwards from P7–8 and black decreasing to subterminal bar on P4–5. Shows white fringes and tips to primaries, 3–6mm broad, increasing inwards. Tail pale grey with black subterminal bar, broadest in centre (in T1 20–28mm). T5–6 white. Underwing-coverts white; underside of greater primary coverts dusky-marked. Underparts, rump and uppertail-coverts white, breast-sides with faint brownish wash. Bill blackish, sometimes paler at base. Legs blackish.

First-winter (Aug–Feb) similar to juvenile, but half-hood stronger blackish-brown and white eyelids broader, joining at rear. Often shows dark spots on forehead and lores. Hindneck and sometimes breast-sides pale grey, mantle and scapulars dark grey. Scapulars sometimes with narrow brown shaft-streaks – rarely solid brown. Belly sometimes with weak pink tinge. Wings as juvenile but through wear paler; pale tertial fringes and white tips reduced or lacking. Bill and legs as juvenile; legs sometimes reddish-brown or dull dark pinkish-grey.

First-summer (Apr–Aug) Head and body similar to first-winter, but dark half-hood often blackish. May show dull partial summer hood. Upperwing dark grey with broad white trailing edge to secondaries and white tips to primaries (broadest on P1–5, where covering up to 50% of inner web). P8–10 with black outer web; black decreases to subterminal mark on P(4)5–6, thus similar to adult, but dark markings brownish-tinged and broader, more diffusely divided from grey bases. Outer greater primary coverts dark brown with paler edges. Alula often blackish. Dark markings form dusky extension of black wing-tip at leading edge of outer wing. Dark centres on some secondaries form incomplete dark secondary bar. Tail as adult winter, but sometimes darker-shaded towards tip and with dark shaft-streaks. Sometimes with dark subterminal spots forming indis-

tinct bar on midtail. Bill and legs blackish, bill sometimes with reddish base.

A minority have only partial or arrested moult to first-
summer with variable number of juvenile outer primaries and their coverts retained.

Second-winter (Aug–Feb) similar to adult, but primaries with fuller dark markings: P9–10 invariably with
strong dark markings; white mirror on P10 small and
restricted to near tip of inner web. P5 with max. 15mm
black subterminal spot. Primaries with small area of
white to pale grey dividing black on P5–10 from grey
bases. Primaries usually with obvious white tips, increasing inwards. Primary coverts grey with indistinct dusky
centres or shaft-streaks, usually drop-shaped at tip.
Often shows a few brown-tinged upperwing-coverts. Eye
and orbital ring dark. Bill black to brown with
10–15mm red or orange tip. Legs blackish or dull red.
Second-summer as adult summer, but often with white-
flecked hood (especially forehead, lores and chin),
immature markings from second-winter, often dark tip
to folded wing and darker red base to bill.

Aberrants Leucistic bird (Texas, Nov 2002) had greyish-
brown head-markings and whitish upperparts, apart
from slightly darker saddle. Adult lacking white eyelids
known (Texas, spring) (M. Reid *in litt.*).

Hybrids Has paired with Grey-headed Gull in Senegal
and S Africa; breeding unsuccessful (Erard *et al.* 1984,
Hockey *et al.* 1988). Suspected hybrids with Ring-billed
Gull and Bonaparte's Gull, see those species.

DISTRIBUTION AND MIGRATION Nearctic. Population *c.*350,000 pairs in 25 colonies. Breeds freshwater
marshes in inland prairies. Strong decline; may have
decreased by 90% 1960–2000; Salt Plain National
Wildlife Refuge, Oklahoma, population 3 million 1950,
15,000 1990 (Greij 1993, del Hoyo *et al.* 1996).

Long-distance migrant, wintering mainly S of equator.
Leaves breeding sites from early Jul. Migrates over narrow corridor through central USA and NE Mexico (Ver-
acruz), some crossing on wider front between Mississippi
and Rocky Mountains, settling in fields and lakes, e.g.
30,000 Lake Reel, Saskatchewan, Jul, 300,000–400,000
Kansas and 37,840 Say Reservoir Oct; max. flocks of
4,000 Texas Nov. A few E to Lakes Erie and Ontario; very
scarce migrant W and E Coast; exceptionally dozens
Cape May, New Jersey, Nov 1998. In California on average 20 records yearly. Most have left C USA by late Oct,
prairie region/SE USA late Nov. Scarce in winter Mexican Gulf (max. 31 on Christmas Bird Count, Texas).
Migration peak Costa Rica Oct–Nov. Winters Pacific
coast, mainly between Peru and Chile, scarce N to
Guatemala/Mexican Gulf and W to Galapagos. Vanguards late Sep (mostly immatures); main arrival mid-
Oct–mid-Nov. Common Oct–Apr; largest counts >1 million off C Peru, Nov 1972. Also Andes of Peru and
Bolivia. Large numbers recently found Córdoba, C
Argentina, Mar; occasional flocks in puna zone of C Peru
(around 4,000m), Oct–Dec and May, suggest frequent
inland migration. Leaves winter quarters Mar–Apr. Large
numbers gather Punta Arenas and Limón, Costa Rica,
Apr–mid-May; rare along Caribbean Gulf coast. Spring

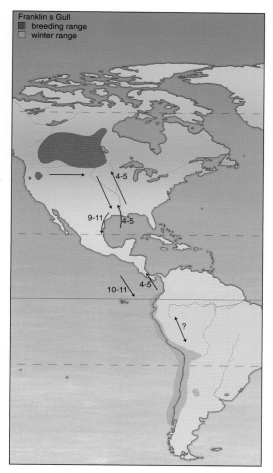

Franklin s Gull
■ breeding range
□ winter range

migration peak Kansas/Minnesota mid-Apr–mid-May;
max. 400,000. Scarce California; flock of 32 24 May 1988
exceptional. In Texas last migrants early Jun (Plenge
1974, Schulenberg 1980, Stiles & Skutch 1989, Fjeldså &
Krabbe 1990, Hoogendoorn & Steinhaus 1990, van den
Berg & Bosman 1999, R. V. Laux, M. Reid *in litt.*).
Vagrant Caribbean and S America S to Magellan strait
and Patagonia, Falklands and Tristan da Cunha. In
Pacific W to Hawaii (influx 1988 >25; 12 records before;
most May; a few Apr and one Jun) and Japan, N to Alas-
ka/N Canada and SE to Australia (7). In Africa vagrant
Senegambia (7), S Africa (probably regular), Mozambique (2). Vagrant W Palearctic, (mainly older) birds
probably arriving directly from winter quarters in S
America. First-years mainly recorded from Iberia and
southwards late in year, suggesting arrival after Transatlantic passage. Records well spread throughout year;
most summer records from N Europe: up to 2001 Great
Britain 41 (most May–Aug); Spain 6; Madeira 1; Italy 1;
France 12; Belgium 2; Netherlands 3; Germany 3; Norway 4; Sweden 7; Iceland 3; Finland 1; Hungary 1; Israel
1; Greenland 4 (Grandjean 1981, Cramp & Simmons
1983, Hoogendoorn & Steinhaus 1990, Baillon &
Dubois 1992, Boertmann 1994, Higgins & Davies 1996,

FRANKLIN'S GULL Two- or three-year gull. Breeds prairies of N America, winters S America. Similar to Laughing Gull, but smaller (often smaller than Black-headed Gull) with shorter, stubbier bill, shorter legs and shorter, rounder wings. Always with solid dark half-hood and broad white eyelids. Unlike other gulls moult complete twice a year, resulting in always fairly fresh plumage, but also in 'unexpected' moult timing compared to other gulls.

Adult has grey upperwing, the colour of Laughing, but with broad white trailing edge to wing connecting to white primary bases, isolating narrow black markings on primary tips. In **summer** (Apr–Aug) hood blackish with broad white eyelids, connecting behind eye. Bill bright red. Legs dark. May show rosy tinge to underparts. In **winter** (Aug–Mar) shows full blackish half-hood reinforcing broad white eyelids, and contrasting with white crown and face. Bill black, often with red tip to upper mandible. Hindneck to breast-sides white.

Juvenile (Aug–Sep) similar to Laughing, but face, crown and eyelids white in contrast to blackish-brown half-hood. Tail greyish-white with narrow black tail-bar, underwing clean white.

First-winter (Sep–Apr) similar to juvenile, but head and saddle of adult type.

Second-year similar to adult, but black wing-tip markings generally fuller, sometimes with little white between black tips and grey upperwing.

Cottridge & Vinicombe 1996, Mitchell & Young 1997, Rogers *et al.* 1999, Geiregat & Stomphorst 2000, M. Carter *in litt.*).

MEASUREMENTS Lengths in mm; weights in g. Own data based on skins in MCZ, NHM, NRK, USNM, UZM. N, C and S America, Greenland.

WING

Adult male	277–310	(288.9)	76
Adult female	269–300	(282.3)	62
First-year male	272–297	(285.2)	29
First-year female	255–295	(279.7)	30

BILL

Adult male	28.4–34.6	(31.3)	78
Adult female	25.8–33.1	(29.7)	63
First-year male	27.5–33.4	(30.7)	29
First-year female	27.0–33.4	(30.0)	30

BILL DEPTH AT BASE OF BILL

Adult male	9.1–11.6	(10.2)	78
Adult female	8.6–10.8	(9.6)	64
First-year male	8.3–11.0	(9.9)	29
First-year female	8.2–10.2	(9.2)	30

BILL DEPTH AT GONYS

Adult male	7.8–9.8	(8.9)	78
Adult female	7.9–9.3	(8.3)	64
First-year male	7.7–8.9	(8.6)	29
First-year female	6.7–8.7	(8.0)	30

GONYS LENGTH

Adult male	9.3–11.8	(10.3)	78
Adult female	8.3–11.2	(10.1)	64
First-year male	8.4–10.7	(9.4)	29
First-year female	7.4–11.2	(9.0)	30

TARSUS

Adult male	39.2–46.3	(42.3)	78
Adult female	37.3–44.3	(41.1)	64
First-year male	37.2–45.3	(41.4)	29
First-year female	36.5–45.1	(40.8)	30

Weight Adult (Minnesota, Atlanta) summer: male 220–335, female 250–325. In winter generally 230–375. Greenland specimen 201 (skins in LACM, UZM; Cramp & Simmons 1983).

Franklin's Gull *Larus pipixcan*. **730. 1st-winter**. Note rounded shape, short legs and dark half-mask. Invariably shows conspicuous white eyelids, stronger than in other North American gulls. Ventura, California, USA. 23 Dec 1994. *Don DesJardin*. **731. Juvenile**. Note white underbody, and clear-cut black tail-bar surrounded by white. Tendency to show pale window in outer wing; compare Laughing Gull photos 715-717. Alberta, Canada. 25 Jul 1999. *Jon R. King*.

Franklin's Gull *Larus pipixcan*. **732. 1st-summer**. Note variation in head-pattern. Black primaries with narrow white tips indicate this age. Arica. Chile. May 1980. *Arnoud B. van den Berg*. **733. Adult winter.** Note very broad white primary tips, creating equal amount of white and black in folded wing-tip. Bill short and stubby and half-mask solid, surrounding broad white eyelids. Cabo Frio, Peru. Nov 1997. *Rob Williams*. **734. 2nd-summer**. Full summer hood indicates this age, but wing-tip more solid black than expected. British Columbia, Canada. 16 Jun 2001. *Bruce Mactavish*. **735. 2nd-winter**. Note characteristic head-pattern and rather slender, black bill. Cheddar, Somerset, Great Britain. Mar 2000. *Steve Young*.

Franklin's Gull *Larus pipixcan*. **736. Adult summer.** White eyelids very broad at rear, where usually joining or almost so. Compare with Laughing Gull in background, the latter showing longer, darker bill, narrower white eye-lids and all-dark primaries. Texas, USA. May. *David Astins*. **737. Adult summer**. Note large amount of white in wing-tip of this individual, and compare 734. Texas, USA. May. *David Astins*. **738. Adult winter** Note broad white trailing edge to dark grey upperwing, joining with extensive white middle parts of primaries. Black in wing-tip surrounded by white. Galapagos. *Alan Tate*. **739. 2nd- or adult winter**. Individual with more extensive black in wing-tip than 736, possibly 2nd-winter. Paracas, Peru. Nov. *Hanne & Jens Eriksen*.

740

741

Franklin's Gull *Larus pipixcan*. **740. Adult and 2nd-summers**.
Note variation of wing-tip pattern, birds with solid black wing-
tip matching 2nd-summer. Canada. Jul. *Bruce Mactavish*. **741.**
1st-winter. Vancouver, Canada. 25 Aug 1998. *René Pop*.

38. LITTLE GULL

Larus minutus (Pallas, 1776, rivers of Siberia)

IDENTIFICATION Length 25–27cm, wingspan 75–80cm. The world's smallest gull, about two-thirds the size of Black-headed and much more compact than other small gulls. Large, rounded head, short, slim bill and compact shape create a confiding gentle look. Short legs make settled bird look even smaller than it really is. Wings proportionately shorter and broader than in other gulls with rounded (adult) or pointed (first-year) tip. Bill and crown dark in all plumages. In summer associated with fresh water but in winter mainly marine.

Flight buoyant, recalling marsh tern *Chlidonias*; feeds with 'yo-yo' movements towards water surface like marsh tern (and regularly associates with them) or 'patters' at surface like storm petrel. Wingbeats quick and fluttering; deeper and slower in head-wind, when it advances slowly, often with short, abrupt dips towards surface. Often migrates low over water in dense tern-like flocks, but may fly high in calm weather. In hard side- and tail-winds, flight is surprisingly rapid with almost shearwater-like turns – an adaptation to its mainly pelagic winter habitat. Swimming bird looks neckless and sits high on water like a cork.

Adult has blackish underwing and pale grey upperwing, bordered entirely by distinct white, which emphasizes rounded wing-tip. Contrast between pale upperparts and black underwing creates 'negative image' compared to dark-backed gulls, making distant birds easy to pick out among terns and smaller gulls. Underbody may show slight rosy tinge. Legs red and bill black. In **summer** hood is jet-black, more square-cut than in Black-headed and reaching further down onto nape. Has black bill and lacks white eye-crescents of most other hooded gulls. In **winter,** head white with dark cap and ear-spot, the former sometimes reduced by late winter. Often shows extensive grey wash on sides of neck and breast, concolorous with upperparts.

Juvenile has head similar to adult winter, but more extensive dark crown and ear-spot. Saddle blackish-brown with prominent pale scales, showing up as transverse barring. Dark of upperparts extends onto breast-sides (creating marking similar to juvenile Black Tern), sometimes covering entire breast. Upperwing with obvious black W as in first-year Black-legged Kittiwake and Ross's Gull, created by dark outer primaries and dark diagonal bar over wing-coverts, but also a faint dark secondary bar (lacking in congeners), offsetting white rump and tail-base. There is some variation, and some have much more extensively marked upperparts (see Aberrants). Wing-tip narrower, more pointed than in adult. Tail with near-complete black band, unlike first-year Ross's, which shows projecting central tail with triangular black patch, not reaching sides of tail. Compared to Ross's Gull and Black-legged Kittiwake, Little furthermore smaller and more compact with more extensively dark wing-tip, square-cut tail and smart dark

cap. Underwing white, with black tips to outer primaries, creating trailing edge to outer wing as in many terns. Legs reddish-flesh. In autumn gradually moults into **first-winter**, which combines adult head and body with juvenile wings and tail. Upper mantle often black to early Nov, but upperparts grey from Dec. **First-summer** similar to first-winter, but head with varying dark markings, ranging from dull adult-like hood to head pattern basically as in winter, but with broader markings behind eye. By late spring, outer wing becomes duller and browner through wear; outer primaries contrast with black carpal bar, and upperwing W then less evident, most obvious on inner wing. Tail-bar often incomplete with white feathers in midtail, in spring regularly with strange-looking combination of all-white (renewed) tail but still juvenile wing.

Second-winter similar to adult winter, but with black markings near tips of P6–10 (similar to second-winter Mediterranean). Underwing two-toned with grey coverts and blackish primaries. Underwing can be quite pale greyish, when confusion with adult winter Ross's possible, but Ross's (which see) shows wedge-shaped tail, white trailing edge that does not reach outermost primaries and no dark cap. Some Little show dark-patterned tertials, secondaries and primary coverts.

Second-summer similar to second-winter, but hood as adult summer.

Third winter/summer as adult, but birds with grey instead of black underwing coverts probably this age.

VOICE Short calls similar to Black Tern *Chlidonias niger*: *kek-kek-kek*, sometimes deeper when alarmed, recalling Jackdaw *Corvus monedula*. In display a rhythmical, high-pitched *kjaae-ki… kjaae-ki…*, which is sometimes heard during spring migration and at breeding sites after breeding (H. J. Lehto *in litt.*).

MOULT (pers. obs., N, W and C Europe) **Adult** moult complete into **winter plumage** Jul–Nov. Head and body Jul–Aug, earliest in failed breeders. Most of head renewed by early Sep; neck/hindneck feathers often still growing by Oct. Small minority mid-Sep have only started head moult, probably Russian birds, which may delay primary moult to Sep (Ginn & Melville 1983). Flight feathers Jul–Nov; in most-advanced birds, >50% of primary moult finished before migration from Baltic/N Germany. 20–25% have completed primary moult late Sep; >50% have reached P6–8 Sep, P9 early Nov; P10 often growing late Nov (skins in NHM, UZM, ZMA).

Adult moult to **summer** plumage partial Mar–May, including head and body (sometimes only partial on upperparts); head early–mid-Apr, starting with forehead and chin. Forehead sometimes white-spotted into early May.

Juvenile moult to **first-winter** plumage partial Aug–Oct, including head, underparts, mantle, most scapulars and in Oct sometimes 1–2 tertials. Starts with mid-mantle Aug. In Sep 30–50% of mantle and scapulars are renewed. Mantle grey in 65–75% early Oct, 85–100% late Oct; last to be moulted are hindneck and upper mantle, which are unmoulted in 90% at end Oct. Delayed moult frequent: specimen from 23 November had only two grey mantle feathers (skin in ZMA); <1% still fully juvenile by Nov. T1–2 often Jan–Mar (as first step of moult into second-winter). Baker (1993) states that whole tail may be renewed in first autumn; we have not seen this.

Moult to **first-summer** partial Mar–May, including head and body. Head moult mostly incomplete and birds with winter head in first-summer not uncommon. Lesser coverts and some primary coverts early May. Tail moult continues (see above); by mid-May–mid-Jun, >50% have renewed T1–2 (in 10% even up to T5–6; small minority have completed tail moult in May).

Moult to **second-winter** complete Jun–Sep(Nov) (but see above for moult of tail, which starts even earlier), earlier than in adults. Primaries from Jun; may finish primary moult early Aug. Majority in S Scandinavia/Germany have renewed flight feathers and tail early Sep; in small minority T(3)5–6 and P9–10 not renewed until late Sep (early Nov). Head, body and coverts Jul–Aug. A few with traces of summer hood early Sep. Lesser coverts sometimes late Sep.

Subsequent moults similar to adults; in autumn sometimes earlier (Cramp & Simmons 1983).

DESCRIPTION

Adult Upperwing pale grey (Kodak Grey Scale 4–5) with white tips to flight feathers, broadest on P10 (in adult male 21–32mm, adult female 18–26mm). P1–7 with 10–15mm white tips. Median coverts pale grey to white. Scapulars with faint or no whitish crescents. Tail white with 0–4mm fork. Breast to belly white, often with variable pink tinge, sometimes including rump and tail. Axillaries pale to medium grey. Underwing-coverts and primaries blackish to dark grey (Kodak Grey Scale 11–15); rarely medium grey especially on greater (probably younger adults), creating underwing in distant birds similar to Ross's Gull. Iris blackish-brown. Orbital ring red. Bill black to dark reddish-brown, rarely with bluish-grey base to lower mandible. Gape red, orange-red or pale orange.

Adult summer (Apr–Aug/Sep) Hood velvety black extending to upper neck. Pink tinge on breast and belly at its strongest (especially breast). Legs scarlet.

Adult winter (Aug–Mar/Apr) Head white with grey to blackish cap (sometimes indistinct by midwinter), eye-crescents and ear-spot. Black cap sometimes extends to hindneck or connects with ear-spot. Dark cap and ear-spot create white supercilium in between. Often shows grey breast-sides as extension of mantle. Legs dull red to fleshy.

Juvenile (fledging–Sep/Oct) Head somewhat similar to adult winter, but dark markings more extensive and browner-tinged. Mantle, back and scapulars blackish-brown to black with whitish or creamy fringes creating strong pale scaling or barring especially on scapulars. Lower scapulars generally pale grey. Inner lesser coverts

pale grey. Primary coverts, tertials, median coverts and to a varying degree lesser coverts blackish-brown (with neat pale fringes), creating strong dark midwing-bar, connecting with dark P6–10 to form distinct dark W on upperwing. Greater coverts pale to mid-grey with narrow pale edges. Lesser and greater coverts may be darker to create broader dark carpal areas (see Aberrants below). Primaries with black outer webs and tips. Inner webs of P6–8 white, generally reduced on P8–10, where sometimes dark. P1–5 pale grey with white tips and dark subterminal spots on P(3)4–5, sometimes bordered with white against greyer bases. Rarely all primaries dark or only P7–10 dark (Young 1990). Secondaries dark with pale tips and edges forming dark secondary bar, varying from (typically) ill-defined to strong. Shows dark spot on inner secondary, where body and wing meet, on both surfaces. Underwing white with black tips to P6–10 and black outer web on P10. Rump and uppertail-coverts white, in 1–5% with brown or blackish tips. Tail white with black subterminal bar, broadest on midtail (16–23mm on T1). T5–6 sometimes white. Underparts white with variable dark brown, buffish- or yellowish-brown suffusion to breast-sides (often forming breast-band), sometimes also to flanks. Iris dark brown to black. Orbital ring and bill black. Gape fleshy. Legs greyish-flesh, pale flesh or reddish, rarely greyish-brown.

First-winter (Aug–Apr) similar to juvenile, but head white with dark grey to blackish eye-crescents, ear-spot and crown, generally darkest on ear-coverts. Crown grey, sometimes weakly marked. May show grey hindneck and sides of neck and breast as extension of mantle colour. Breast-sides generally paler yellowish-buff than in juvenile, rarely continuing across breast. Mantle, back and scapulars pale grey, often with retained juvenile feathers on especially upper mantle and scapulars into Nov. Wing and tail as juvenile but, with wear, white terminal spots on primaries and terminal fringe on tail reduced or lacking. Legs as juvenile; sometimes pale orange.

First-summer (Mar–Oct) similar to first-winter, but in about 50% with more or less dull black, brown or grey hood; normally with some white feathers on forehead; in 20–30% reduced to half-hood behind eye. 10–20% have winter head. Hindneck white. May show pink flush to underparts and lose grey on breast-sides. By summer, wings become worn and faded (from late May, P6–10 often brownish). Tail normally with white T1 from May; sometimes whole tail renewed in spring. Legs dull red to dull reddish-brown. Birds in transition from first-summer to second-winter have patchy grey and white underwing.

Second-winter (Aug–Apr) similar to adult winter, but outer web of P10–6(5) with varying black outer webs or subterminal spots; sometimes black spots on P9–10 only. Best-marked birds have distinct black lines or spots on outer webs of P5–10, normally reduced to subterminal spots on P5–7. May show blackish-brown markings on primary coverts, alula, inner secondaries and tertials (sometimes extensive, especially on tertials). Underwing two-toned with pale grey coverts and dark grey/blackish bases to flight feathers. Small minority show pale bases to flight feathers from surface as well.

PLATE 75. LITTLE GULL *Larus minutus*

The smallest of the world's gulls. Size about that of Black Tern *Chlidonias niger*. Breeds in colonies in freshwater lakes, surrounded by reedbeds, often together with Black-headed Gull and marsh terns *Chlidonias*, wintering mainly at sea, basically in North Atlantic and Mediterranean. A small, elegant, compact gull with large, rounded head and narrow bill, creating 'cute' look. Wings and legs short. Buoyant flight is similar to marsh terns, including frequent 'yo-yo'movements towards water surface. Migrates in dense flocks, often associated with terns and small gulls.

1. **Juvenile** (fledging–Sep) Distinct head pattern with smart dark cap and dark ear-coverts. Upperparts densely barred in blackish-brown and white. Dark and pale wing pattern retained throughout first winter. Bill blackish. Legs fleshy.

2. **First-winter** (Sep–Apr/May) Head and body similar to adult winter, but otherwise as juvenile.

3. **First-summer** (Apr/May–Aug) Somewhat variable. Whereas some individuals develop hood similar to adult (although less deep black, and usually with whitish freckling in front), others remain basically as first-winter. Dark on upperwing often bleached, thus browner than in autumn/winter.

4. **First-summer**: An individual showing head pattern similar to first-winter.

5. **Second-winter** (Sep–Mar/Apr) Similar to adult winter, but with variable dark pattern on outer primaries.

6. **Adult winter** (Sep–Mar/Apr) Head with smart dark cap and blackish ear-spot. Primaries with broad white tips.

7. **Adult summer** (Apr–Aug) Blackish hood and bill. Lacks white eye-crescents of other hooded gulls. Legs bright red. Upperparts pale grey with white primary tips. Underparts white, often with rosy tinge. The extensive black on underwing often shows though in settled birds.

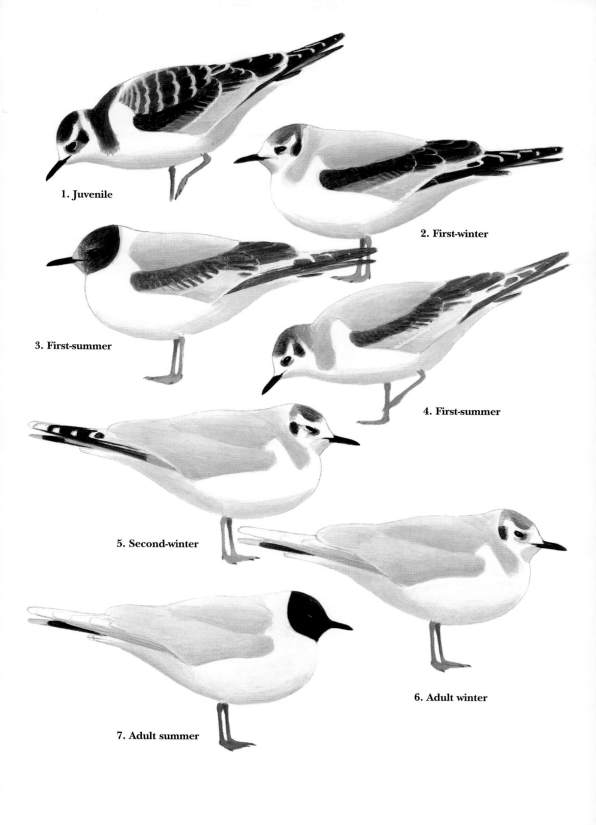

1. Juvenile

2. First-winter

3. First-summer

4. First-summer

5. Second-winter

6. Adult winter

7. Adult summer

PLATE 76. LITTLE GULL *Larus minutus*

In flight small and compact with large head and rather short wings, being pointed in first-years, but otherwise with slightly rounded tip. Always identified by small size, compact shape and distinct wing pattern.

1. **Juvenile** (fledging–Aug/Sep) Wing pattern striking: broad blackish W across wing, and dark-centred secondaries creating dark trailing edge (similar to juvenile Common Tern *Sterna hirundo*). Head with dark cap and ear-spot. Blackish-and-white juvenile upperparts retained into Sep, when gradually exchanged for first-winter upperparts (last on hindneck and upper mantle). Underwing white with dark trailing edge to outer primaries and dark inner secondaries. Tail short, slightly forked with black tail-bar.

2. **First-winter** (Sep–Apr) Juvenile wing pattern retained, but often bleached. Amount of dark on outer wing is more extensive than in 1, showing variation in first-years.

3. **First-summer** (Apr–Aug) Some develop partial dark hood. Wing pattern retained into midsummer. Central tail often moulted to adult type in spring, as shown in this individual.

4. **Second-winter** (Aug–Apr) Similar to adult winter, but note dark pattern on outer wing (similar to second-winter Mediterranean Gull) and two-toned underwing with pale axillaries and coverts against dark primaries.

5. **Adult winter** (Sep–Mar/Apr) Head with dark cap and ear-spot. Adults shows blackish underwing and pale grey upperwing, both surfaces with white trailing edge.

6. **Adult winter** Note short wings, large head and short tail. Adults may show slight rose tinge to underbody all year.

7. **Adult summer** (Apr–Aug) Full blackish hood. Underbody either white or rosy-tinged.

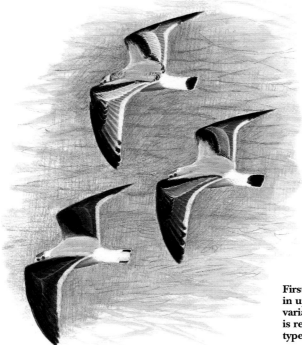

First-winters, showing variation in upperwing pattern; lower variant rare. Note, that mid-tail is regularly moulted into adult type in First-winter.

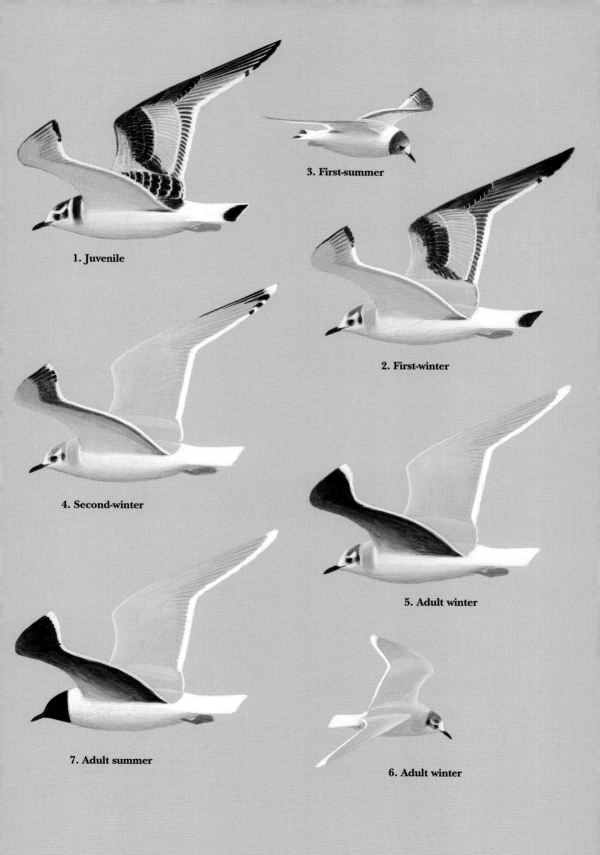

1. Juvenile

3. First-summer

2. First-winter

4. Second-winter

5. Adult winter

7. Adult summer

6. Adult winter

Axillaries white. Underwing sometimes as adults or with partly 'adult pattern' mixed with second-winter characters.

Second-summer (Mar–Oct) Head similar to adult summer, but hood generally duller, rarely incomplete or lacking. Wing pattern as second-winter, but faded with wear. Legs dull red.

Third-winter (Aug–Apr) as adult winter; birds with black outer web to P10 and/or dark streaks on outer primary coverts, and grey (not black) underwing-coverts, probably this age.

Third-summer as adult, apart from characters mentioned under third-winter.

Aberrants First-year sometimes with more extensive dark on upperwing. May have brownish-black upperwing-coverts, often with narrow white tips to greater and primary coverts; others have black carpal bar enlarged by dark brown lesser and greater coverts, often with broader dark primary tips from below. Very dark birds have all upperwing-coverts and flight feathers blackish, the former with white tips and edges (Martin 1982, Grant 1986a, Harris *et al.* 1989, Young 1990, Spanoghe 1997, Larsson 1999b; T. Ortvad & G. de Smet pers. comm.; pers. obs.).
Adult with white eyelids (May; H. & H. J. Lehto *in litt.*) could be atypically late moulting bird.

GEOGRAPHICAL VARIATION Not fully documented. Breeding males from Siberia on average have longer wings than in other populations (mean 230.6), but sample restricted.

DISTRIBUTION AND MIGRATION Probably some tens of thousands of pairs, mainly in former USSR. Breeds on grassy islands, sandbanks and reedbeds in fresh shallow lowland lakes, often together with Black-headed Gull and marsh terns. In E Baltic in brackish water. On migration along shores, on reservoirs and lagoons, lakes and at sea. Winters at sea and along sandy or muddy beaches (Il'icev & Zubakin 1990, Hagemeijer & Blair 1997).
European population around 2000 (in pairs) 25,000–34,000: Russia 11,000–14,000; Sweden 1,100 (90–125 early 1990s); Norway 60–100 (first bred 1976; recent increase, e.g. 50 pairs Pasvik Valley, Sørvaranger 2002–2003); Finland 8,000–10,000 (first bred 1879; strong increase in recent decades); Poland 0–30; Latvia 700–3,000; Estonia 1,000–2,000; Belarus 1,800–2,300; Lithuania 100–200; Ukraine 100–200. Netherlands 5–40 (61) (first bred 1942, after which irregular and often unsuccessful, but regular 1975–1988 on Lauwersmeer; since then most records Waddenzee and Delta area). Irregular Great Britain, Germany, Denmark (1940–1950s >50–75 pairs W/N Jutland; since 1980 irregular), Iceland (first bird 2003), C Europe and Romania. Exceptional France. General decrease in S part of breeding range, increase in N Scandinavia and Baltic since 1970, now breeds N to Barents Sea and Kola, N Russia, where locally common. Breeding attempt Iceland 2003 (Cramp & Simmons 1983, Tucker & Heath 1994, del Hoyo *et al.* 1996, Hagemeijer & Blair 1997, Svensson *et al.* 1999, Bijlsma *et al.* 2001, M. Gün-

ther & Y. Kolbeinsson *in litt.*).
Recently spread to N America. First record 1919–1922, since 1987 regular. First bred Canada 1962, USA 1975; subsequent breeding records in many states (Glutz von Blotzheim & Bauer 1982, Godfrey 1986, del Hoyo *et al.* 1996).
Migratory. Arrives breeding sites late Apr–late May, leaves from late Jul. Population from Fennoscandia and W Russia migrates W and SW to main wintering grounds W Mediterranean and Atlantic coast N to Brittany; Finnish and Baltic birds recovered W to Great Britain and E to Adriatic/Black Sea, extralimitally Kazakhstan.
In autumn usually coastal, but thousands (mainly second-years and adults) gather N German lakes and low wetlands to moult before further migration; leave early–mid-Sep, max. 40,000, mouth of Vistula River, N. Poland, 14 Sep 1990. Migration in N and W Europe: large migration S Baltic, to a lesser degree Swedish Great Lakes (mainly first-years). Large migration Swedish and Danish Baltic coastline (N to Gotland), where on average 13,000 pass yearly. Most observed from coast in strong E–S winds combined with rain and low visibility. First-years start Jul and peak mid-Aug–mid-Sep. Migration route of northern (Finnish?) populations passes mid-Baltic, max. 1,350 at Björn, Uppland, on 16–18 August 1996. Head SW across Swedish lakes (Mälaren–Vänern) to N Kattegat. Adults much scarcer along this route, but flocks of max. 200 noted mid–late Oct. First-years otherwise generally head S across C Europe.
Adult migration in S Baltic starts late Aug, peaks mid-Oct–early Nov. Visible migration greatly dependent on weather; best years around 6,000 Scania and Öland, Sweden, respectively. Best autumns 1994 (with unsurpassed peak mid-Sep) and 2000 following hard SSE winds and poor visibility. In Sweden max. day-counts 3,565 at Öland on 16 August 1994 (31% adult, 8% second-years, 61% first-years), 3,309 at Segerstad on 7 November 2000 and 1,614 at Sandhammaren on 29 October 2000 (1,223 adults, 115 second-years and 148 first-years). At Gedser, SE Denmark, 4,000 in best season (Glutz von Blotzheim & Bauer 1982, Koop 1985, Breife 1987, Jensen 1993, Darefeldt & Johansson 1994, Dahlgren *et al.* 1995, Lindberg & Lötberg 1997, Arinder 2001, pers. obs.).
Max. 1,100 Angus, Scotland late Jul–Oct suggests arrival via Swedish Great Lakes and N Kattegat. Gathers at moulting sites in N Great Britain before heading W and S late Sep–Oct (see below); situation similar to German. Along Danish W coast regular; day-counts >600 in strong SSW winds. Large passage Dutch W coast and Belgium (late Jul)Aug–mid-Oct (max. 10,000 Netherlands; mainly first-years into early Oct, followed by adults). Peak Oct–Nov; max. day-counts 2,238 Netherlands and 1,435 Zeebrugge, Belgium. Probably arrives after large-scale inland migration W from S part of breeding range. Peak of mainly adults Pas-de-Calais, NW France, Oct–Nov (daily max. 3,500). Regular C European lakes. In Bodensee peak late Aug–late Sep. Max. 280, mainly first-years (Hutchinson & Neath 1978, Cramp & Simmons 1983, Schuster *et al.* 1983, Malling Olsen 1992, Murray 1994, Green 2003).

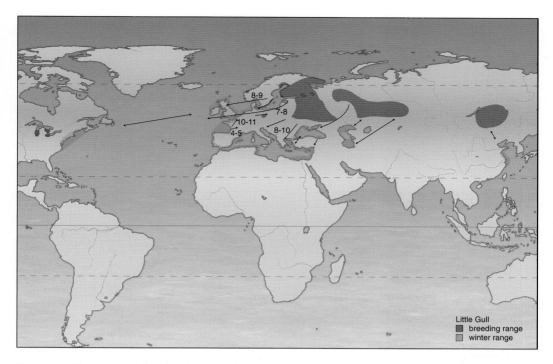

Little Gull
■ breeding range
▫ winter range

European migrant population heads W for Atlantic Ocean between Irish Sea and Morocco (some further S to Nigeria and Angola) to offshore wintering sites; >600 seen from land in onshore winds Wicklow, Ireland, Jan. British winter population 1,000; largest European winter count 5,000–10,000 N Brittany late Dec 1974. Around 1,500 winter Dutch Waddenzee (exceptionally 10,000). Scarce Baltic Sea in winter; in Sweden max. day-counts 190 Öland and 482 E Scania Dec–Feb, more irregular Swedish Great Lakes in mild winters or before freeze-up; max. 215 Vänersborg on 4 March 1992 (>90% adults) (Glutz von Blotzheim & Bauer 1982, Åkerman 1986, Breife 1987, Darefeldt & Johansson 1994, Bijlsma et al. 2001, Green 2003).

In spring, flocks over 1,000 regular, Camargue and W France (max. 1,350 Apr; in May mainly first-years, 3–5,000 Brittany 20 Apr 1980). At Gibraltar and Cap Gris Nez, France, peak late Mar–late Apr. Of 2,225 Cap Gris Nez 88% adult, 1% second-years, 11% first-years, followed by larger numbers of first-years in May. Large passage N Netherlands (max. 30,000 in one year) mid-Apr–mid-May; most 4,008 30 April–2 May 1976. Several thousands Apr–May Krammer-Volkerak, SW Netherlands. Along Merseyside coast, NW England, peak second half of Apr (max. day-count 680); >90% leave before mid-May, probably mainly heading for Finland, where migration peak concentrated first weeks May. In spring 1987 large passage (4,136) Heligoland, Germany: peak late Apr–early May; 1,410 on 5 May. Mainly adults in Apr, from late month increasing numbers of first-years: on 5 May 78–80% (16–18% second-years, 4% adults). Largest German influx 30 Apr 1998: 21,000 Schleswig-Holstein. In Switzerland, max. 1,300 Préverenges on 30 Apr 1999. Influxes caused by strong SE winds. Bodensee peak similar timing to above-mentioned, with adults passing late Apr–early May; from early May dominance by first- and second-years: of 145 on 5 May only four adults. In S Scandinavia, following SSE winds, flocks of max. 200 late Apr–early May in Denmark and Scania (but 4,000 in one day May 2003) (where mainly adults; first- and second-years dominant from mid-May). First-years summer in small groups C and N European lakes and Great Britain (Woutersen 1980, Glutz von Blotzheim & Bauer 1982, Cramp & Simmons 1983, Schuster et al. 1983, Whittington 1987, Moritz 1988, Messenger 1993, Meininger 1995, Dubois et al. 2000, H. J. Lehto & M. Günther in litt.).

C Siberian population migrates via Aral, Caspian and Black Seas to E Mediterranean. Common migrant N and W coast of Black Sea and Turkey (Anatolia, Bosporus, Dardanelles) Aug–Sep. Max. 30,000 Romania, early Aug. Max. counts Bulgaria and Bosporus 2,500 mid-Aug–early Sep. Fewer cross inland Turkey. Some hundreds winter Black Sea and Balik Gölü, Turkey; 2,000–5,000 Greece. In Mediterranean intermix with W population. Recovery of bird from Barabinsk, C Siberia, in Belgium (Erard 1960, Cramp & Simmons 1983, Handrinos & Akriotis 1997).

Many winter E Mediterranean. In Nile Delta survey Dec–Jan 1989/1990 of 52,769 counted 47,316 were at Lake Manzala 7–8 January 1990 (largest number ever counted). Only a few hundreds there late 1970s and 1980s suggests recent change in winter quarters. Along Israeli Mediterranean coast max. flocks of 460 Jan–Feb, mostly following strong onshore winds. Israeli winter population 2,000–4,000, mainly first-years. In W Mediterranean, max. 1,300 noted off E coast of Spain, 900 Tunisia, hundreds Oran, Algeria and max. 100

LITTLE GULL Three-year gull. The smallest gull, only the size of a *Chlidonias* tern. Compared to other gulls more compact with shorter (in adult rounded) wings and tail, but relatively larger head. Flight similar to *Chlidonias* tern, often with similar 'yo-yo'movements when feeding. Sits high in water, where appears 'neckless'.

Adult has pale grey upperwing with complete white trailing edge reaching rounded outer wing; underwing blackish in strong contrast to upperwing. Bill black and legs dark reddish-brown. In **summer** (Apr–Aug) hood velvety black; lacks white eyelids of other hooded gulls. Underparts often slightly rosy-tinged. In **winter** (Aug–Mar) head white with narrow dark cap and prominent dark ear-spot.

Juvenile (Jul–Sep) has blackish, pale-barred upperparts and broad black W on upperwing (sometimes extending to all coverts); shows grey trailing edge to inner wing and solid black tail-bar. Underwing white with black trailing edge to pointed outer wing.

First-winter (Sep–Apr) develops grey saddle and gets paler head; black on upper mantle often retained into Oct–Nov.

First-summer (Apr–Aug) similar to first-winter, but dark W bleached, head often with incomplete hood and midtail often white.

Second-year similar to adult, but with black markings on up to five outer primaries and bicoloured underwing, as paler coverts contrast with darker flight feathers, the latter similar to adult. Often shows complete dark hood in second summer.

Tripoli. Strong movements at Gibraltar during easterly gales. Abundant winterer in Caspian Sea (Bourne 1957, Bundy 1976, Cramp & Simmons 1983, Finlayson 1992, Meininger & Sørensen 1993, Shirihai 1996b).

Spring migration of C Siberian population timed similar to westerly; off Port Said 5,000 late Mar 1990; in E Mediterranean generally largest numbers Apr (max. 2,000 certain Greek sites), sometimes May (e.g. 5,000 Evros Delta, May 1968). Flocks of first-years often summer (Cramp & Simmons 1983, Meininger & Sørensen 1993, Handrinos & Akriotis 1997).

Movements and winter quarters of E population less known; probably winters Sea of Okhotsk and Japan S to China. Erard (1960) suggests that main wintering zone is Sea of Okhotsk. According to Il'icev & Zubakin (1988) China holds three widely separated wintering areas, in NW China, NE China and along the E China Sea coast.

Migration of N American population associated with Bonaparte's Gull. Max. 25 Niagara Falls/New England, E Coast, and max. day-count 112, N Carolina, winter and spring, and 50 Lake Ontario, spring. In autumn, max. 10 per day New York, Sep. In winter small numbers between Massachusetts and New York. Vagrant to most states W to California. Autumn arrival to N America probably associated with W movements from W Palearctic. In Iceland 164 up to 2001, most May–Jun (first-summer) and Sep (adults). Vagrant Greenland, Arabian Gulf (e.g. seven, UAE), Afghanistan, India, Taimyr, Canary Islands, Azores, Bermuda, Caribbean, tropical Africa S to Sierra Leone, Nigeria and Kenya (largest number 60 Jan 1979 Lake Turkana could indicate unknown winter area) (Cramp & Simmons 1983, Urban *et al.* 1986, Péturson 1987, Boertmann 1994, del Hoyo *et al.* 1996).

MEASUREMENTS Lengths in mm; weights in g. Own data based on skins in NHM, NNH, UZM, ZMA, ZMO. Netherlands, W Europe, Russia, Siberia and Middle East.

WING

Adult male	214–239 (225.6)	76
Adult female	211–236 (221.5)	59
First-year male	215–234 (220.8)	44
First-year female	209–228 (217.3)	46

TAIL PROFILE (differences between T1 and T6)

Adult	0–5 (2.2)	120
First-year	3–10 (6.8)	90

BILL

Adult male	21.5–26.7 (23.2)	70
Adult female	21.1–24.2 (22.9)	51
First-year male	20.0–24.0 (23.0)	43
First-year female	19.8–25.1 (22.0)	43

BILL DEPTH AT BASE OF BILL

Adult male	5.7–7.5 (6.5)	69
Adult female	5.4–7.1 (6.2)	54
First-year male	5.6–7.0 (6.3)	44
First-year female	5.3–6.8 (6.1)	42

BILL DEPTH AT GONYS

Adult male	4.8–6.0 (5.3)	69
Adult female	4.7–5.9 (5.2)	54
First-year male	4.8–5.8 (5.2)	42
First-year female	4.6–5.4 (5.0)	40

GONYS LENGTH

Adult male	8.2–10.4 (9.5)	69
Adult female	8.2–10.2 (9.3)	52
First-year male	6.6–10.8 (9.2)	45
First-year female	6.5–10.1 (8.7)	41

TARSUS

Adult male	23.7–29.0 (25.8)	70
Adult female	23.6–29.4 (25.2)	52
First-year male	22.5–28.8 (25.7)	45
First-year female	23.1–27.0 (25.1)	40

Weight Adult male 82–127, female 68–133, first-year 66–121 (Glutz von Blotzheim & Bauer 1982, Cramp & Simmons 1983, skins in NNH, UZM, ZMA).

Little Gull *Larus minutus*. **742. Juvenile**. Note extensive black cap, ear-spot and pale-scaled saddle. Liverpool, Merseyside, Great Britain. Sep 1994. *Steve Young*. **743. Juvenile moulting into 1st-winter**. By 1st-autumn acquires grey saddle. Note short, slender bill, large head and black cap. IJmuiden, Netherlands. 10 Oct 1988. *Arnoud B. van den Berg*. **744. Juvenile** with Black-headed Gull juvenile. Compare size and upperpart pattern between the two species. Vesanto, Finland. 12 Jul 1997. *Harry J. Lehto*. **745. Juvenile**. Note extensive black W in upperwing, and dark-centred secondaries, creating dark bar. Liverpool, Merseyside, Great Britain. Sep 1994. *Steve Young*. **746. 1st-summer**. Many 1st-summers attain more or less winter head-pattern. Finland. 18 May 1997. *Henry Lehto*.

Little Gull *Larus minutus*. **747. 1st-winter**. Variant with extensive dark upperwing-coverts and darker-than-average flight-feathers, thus showing largely dark upperwing in strong contrast to grey saddle. Mid-tail has been renewed in spring. Liverpool, Merseyside, Great Britain. Apr 1992. *Steve Young*. **748. 1st-summer**. Some develop summer hood at this age, but compared to adult duller and with variable amount of white. Juvenile wing-pattern retained. Liverpool, Merseyside, Great Britain. Jun 1992. *Steve Young*. **749. 1st-summer.** A small percentage develops full summer hood at this age. Liverpool, Merseyside, Great Britain. Jun 1992. *Steve Young*. **750. Adult winter**. Note narrow dark cap and white, unmarked primary tips (with dark undersurface showing through). IJmuiden, Netherlands. 29 Nov 1982. *Arnoud B. van den Berg*. **751. 1st-summer moulting to 2nd-winter**. As moult into 2nd-winter advances, juvenile wing-pattern gradually lost. Liverpool, Merseyside, Great Britain. Sep 1994. *Steve Young*. **752. 2nd-summer**. Note dark pattern on 4 (in some up to 5) outermost primaries, diagnostic of this age. Finland. 15 May 1991. *Henry Lehto*.

753

754

755

756

Little Gull *Larus minutus.* **753. 2nd-summer or older.** Faint dark markings in outer wing could indicate 2nd-summer with minimum amount of dark, or an older bird. Note white lines around trailing edge and tip of wing. Solu, Finland. 10 May 1998. *Harry J. Lehto.* **754. 2nd-summer.** Pale grey instead of blackish underwing-coverts typical for this age. Finland. 8 May 1997. *Harry J. Lehto.* **755. Adult summer.** Note full black hood, black bill and lack of white eyelids. Wing-projection above tail rather short. Liverpool, Merseyside, Great Britain. Jun. *Steve Young.* **756. Adult summer.** Note velvety-black underwing in strong contrast to white trailing edge and primary tips. Vesanto, Finland. 11 Jul 1998. *Harry J. Lehto.*

Little Gull *Larus minutus*. **757. Adult summer**. Adults show rounded, short wings, which are pale grey on upper surface with white edgings. Finland. 10 Jul 1998. *Harry J. Lehto*. **758. Adult winter**. Note white wing-tip and dark cap and ear-spot. Liverpool, Merseyside, Great Britain. Oct. *Steve Young*. **759. Adult winters.** Note contrast between blackish underwing and pale grey upperwing. Netherlands. Jan 1983. *René Pop*. **760. Adult near end of moult to winter** (P9–10 still growing). Certain adults show paler underwing-coverts than 754, but underwing still very contrastingly dark. Constanta, Romania. 12 Oct 2000. *Annika Forsten*.

39. SABINE'S GULL

Larus sabini (Sabine, 1819, Sabine islands near Melville Bay, west coast of Greenland)

Plates 77–78, Photos 761–774

IDENTIFICATION Length 27–35cm, wingspan 90–100cm. A small, slender, elegant gull, only slightly larger than Little, but with smaller head, larger, longer and more pointed wings, and more forked tail. Often initially suggests Black-legged Kittiwake (as it is seen from land during premium sea-watching days in most places – see also below) but is smaller and has lighter, more tern-like flight with deeper, more powerful wing-beats. Flight path direct and low over sea, rarely performing shearwatering as typical of kittiwakes in hard winds. Wings are usually more angled and plumage shows stronger contrasts – a small dark gull with very prominent white trailing edge to inner wing will mostly prove to be Sabine's. Feeding birds often pick food from surface – as Little Gull, but even more agile, often with surprising turns. In tundra, catches insects, both on foot and in flight. Settled bird is small-headed with short, dark bill, attenuated rear and short legs (at distance like dark elongated Little Gull). Swimming birds sometimes pick food from surface. Often very tame.

Upperparts diagnostic: wings three-coloured, divided in triangles: coverts grey (adult) or brown (juvenile), wing-tip black and inner primaries and secondaries gleaming white, as white as tail. Another reliable character is dark bar on greater underwing-coverts, together with grey outer primaries and strongly translucent white secondaries, creating a 'ghost version' of the diagnostic upperwing pattern – especially in head- and side-views. This dark bar may be absent in adults, but is often surprisingly eye-catching in juveniles.

Distant birds at sea may be difficult to separate from first-year Black-legged Kittiwake. Distant Black-legged Kittiwake may 'lose' black W, e.g. in strong tail-view; and rare variants with all-dark coverts or limited carpal bar exist. Black-legged Kittiwake is larger with larger, fuller head, white crown sharply divided from grey mantle (offset by black neck-bar, but note that a few winter birds lack neck-bar and show slightly greyish-tinged crown); also shows slight grey tinge to trailing edge of wing (darker than white tail) and performs much more shearwatering in hard winds. First-summer Black-legged Kittiwake is often mentioned as an ID pitfall, but is very worn and faded at a time when Sabine's is fresh-looking. See also Red-legged Kittiwake.

Adult has bluish-grey mantle and coverts, slightly darker than in Black-legged Kittiwake. White tail has short fork. Bill dark with yellow tip. Legs black. Moult differs from other Northern Hemisphere gulls; Sabine's undergoes complete moult in autumn/winter and partial one in spring, similar to long-distance migrant terns and skuas. **Adult summer** has dark slate hood with black hind-rim, hood often looking all black at a distance. Small head makes hood look smaller than in other hooded gulls, and hood normally retained into mid-Oct (other hooded gulls winter-headed from Aug). Blackish outer primaries have white tips. **Adult winter** has white

head with dark 'half-mask' from behind eye broadening across nape. A few have mask reduced to dark ear-spot or hindcrown, but never as distinct hindneck-bar of juvenile Black-legged Kittiwake, which is situated much lower, at junction with mantle.

Juvenile has continuous area of brownish to grey-brownish on coverts, scapulars, breast-sides, mantle and neck to central crown, creating half-hooded impression. Often surprisingly dark when viewed head-on, and even from behind dark head-markings may create impression of hood. Forehead paler and narrow white eye-ring sometimes distinct. Upperpart feathers and coverts delicately scaled with pale and variably darker subterminal lines (visible at close range); in some also slightly darker shaft-streak visible. In strong sunlight, brown parts look greyer; in poorer light, dark brown and dark against very conspicuous white trailing edge to inner wing, at distance upperwing may resemble that of Common Redshank *Tringa totanus*. Black tail-bar emphasises fork of tail and 'restricts' white tail-base and rump to white square behind mantle and lower back. Bill black and legs flesh. Juvenile plumage retained during autumn migration.

First-winter similar to adult winter, but juvenile upperparts – especially coverts – often retained in spring. Primary tips with limited (if any) white. Bill dark and legs dark grey. '**First-summer**' similar, but sometimes with incomplete (rarely almost complete) dark hood. Tail often with scattered dark markings at tip. Bill dark; pale tip narrower than in adult, if present.

Second-winter as adult winter, but sometimes with traces of immaturity and generally more worn outer primaries.

VOICE Most frequent calls are a harsh *kirrr* similar to Arctic Tern *Sterna paradisaea* and a call similar to Black-headed Gull; from juvenile a high, plaintive twitter, *vihihihi*. Also a very short, clicking or snapping *tseet* (Urban *et al.* 1986, Sibley 2000).

MOULT Adult moult to **winter** plumage partial Jul–Nov in Northern Hemisphere, limited to head and body only. Starts with a few body feathers (rarely head) Jul. In Aug–early Oct >90% with full summer hood: small minority with scattered white feathers especially on forehead and throat (throat rarely white from Aug; lower part of black neck-ring sometimes moulted with chin and throat). 1% of birds with 50% summer head feathers Aug–early Oct; by mid-Oct up to 50% of birds have 50% summer head feathers: rest of head moulted late Oct/early Nov. Winter head normally acquired quickly after arrival in winter quarters. Two among 52 on 12 October, South Africa, and four birds Mauritania Nov had winter head (skins in NNH). Delayed migrants, such as late autumn Northern Hemisphere birds, rarely show summer head in Nov.

PLATE 77. SABINE'S GULL *Larus sabini*

Small, elegant High Arctic gull with almost circumpolar distribution. Breeds in loose colonies in High Arctic tundra. Winters at sea. Long-distance migrant, wintering in southern oceans. Between breeding quarters and wintering range pelagic, mainly observed in autumn after gales.
Body size between Little and Black-headed Gull. Compared to Little smaller-headed, but longer-winged. Moult differs from other gulls. Summer and juvenile plumage retained more or less into late autumn, then moulted out in winter quarters.

1. **Juvenile** (fledging–Nov/Dec) Crown, hindneck and breast-sides greyish-brown, merging into greyish-brown upperparts. Mantle, scapulars and coverts with delicate dark and pale scaling. Head small and rounded with short black bill against white face. Legs short and fleshy. Wings long. Settled birds appear very dark and elongated; swimming birds on high waves sometimes look like driftwood.

2. **Juvenile** Some birds are more strongly brownish-tinged than 1; note also individual variation in head-markings, this individual showing broad white 'face'. A few birds show pale base to lower mandible, as here. Sometimes a few mantle feathers/scapulars are moulted in autumn.

3. **First-winter** (Jan–May) Head and body similar to adult winter, but note retained (and strongly bleached and worn) upperwing-coverts, fleshy-grey legs and narrower white primary tips than in adult. Also, bill black, lacking yellow tip of adult summer. This plumage is acquired by partial moult of head and body in winter. A few first-summers may not moult wing-coverts and head in spring, and therefore may look like first-winter. However, second-summer is normally similar to adult, apart from dark head (dull and generally incomplete; often white-freckled) and dark bill.

4. **Second-winter** (Oct/Nov–Mar/Apr) Head white with extensive slaty-grey bar across crown and ear-coverts, contrasting with grey hindneck. Head-markings may be less extensive than shown, in some restricted to narrow dark bar across hindneck, contrasting with white lower hindneck. Bill black. Upperparts medium grey. Legs dark. Adult winter similar, but bill-tip yellow and white primary tips much broader.

5. **Adult summer** (Apr–Oct) Hood slaty-grey with blackish rear border. Bill black with yellow tip. Note broad white tips to primaries.

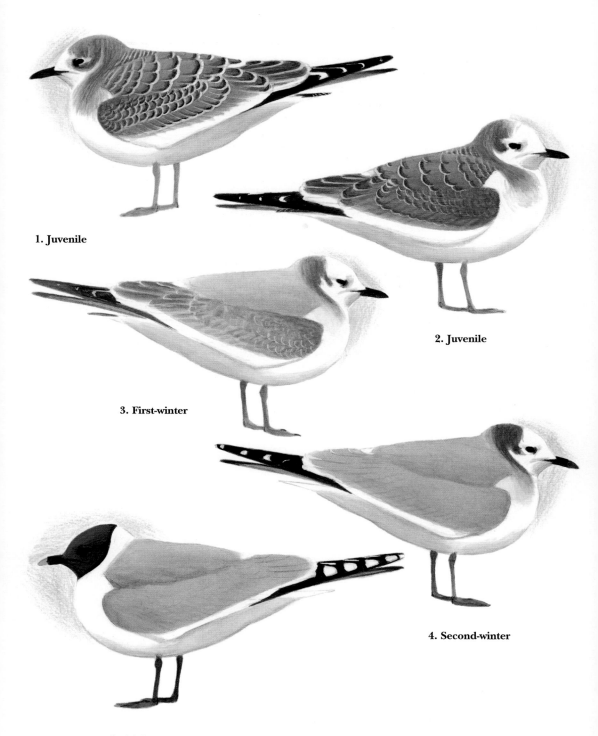

1. Juvenile

2. Juvenile

3. First-winter

4. Second-winter

5. Adult summer

PLATE 78. SABINE'S GULL *Larus sabini*

In flight slightly larger than Little Gull, with longer, 'fuller' wings (showing broad arm), small head, slender body and forked tail. A small, elegant gull, in hard winds performing low, tern-like flight with deep, powerful wingbeats. On migration, keeps low and direct between waves, with direct flight-path, rarely shearwatering. Diagnostic wing pattern divides upperparts into triangles of black, white and grey. Appears dark in front with white hind-parts including shining white, translucent secondaries and inner primaries.

Distinctive but mainly observed from land in hard onshore winds, so beware confusion with first-year Black-legged Kittiwake (see Plate 82, caption 3 for latter).

1. **Juvenile** (fledging–Dec/Jan) Distinctly patterned mud-brown, black and white. Greyish-brown crown and neck-sides blend into similar-coloured upperparts. Head often looks hooded at distance. Leading edge of outer wing black, trailing edge to inner wing broad, triangular and gleaming white. Rump and tail-base white, creating white area against black tail-bar on forked tail. Against dark background, black tail-bar disappears to give very short-tailed illusion. Underwing mirrors pattern of upperwing, offset by grey greater covert bar and translucent broad white trailing edge to wing. Fully juvenile throughout autumn, unlike other small gulls.

2. **Juvenile** Note grey crown blending into grey mantle. A slightly greyer individual with restricted dark upperpart-markings. Note small head and forked tail.

3. **First-winter** (Jan–May) Similar to juvenile, but note grey saddle against unmoulted brown wing-coverts. Compared to juvenile, head-markings greyer and more restricted.

4. **First-summer** (Apr–Sep) In autumn, some birds moult not only mantle and scapulars, but also coverts. Similar to adult winter, but note all-black bill, worn tail and fleshy legs. Complete moult in winter includes flight feathers (as in Franklin's Gull).

5. **Adult winter** (Nov–Mar/Apr) Distinctly patterned grey, black and white. Note blackish-grey hind-crown-bar. Bill sometimes similar to adult summer, but often black. General wing pattern resembles juvenile, but with grey mantle, scapulars and upperwing-coverts and unmarked white tail (against dark background appearing longer than in juvenile as tips lack black bar). Grey bar on greater underwing-coverts generally narrower than in juvenile, and sometimes lacking. White primary tips stronger than in younger birds.

6. **Adult summer** (Apr–Oct/Nov) Slaty-black hood retained well into autumn, but from Aug sometimes white-spotted. Compared to other hooded gulls, hood looks curiously small, as head is disproportionately small against large wings.

7. **Adult summer** (Apr–Oct/Nov) Elegant with small head, large wings and forked tail. Sometimes shows narrow white markings on outer primaries.

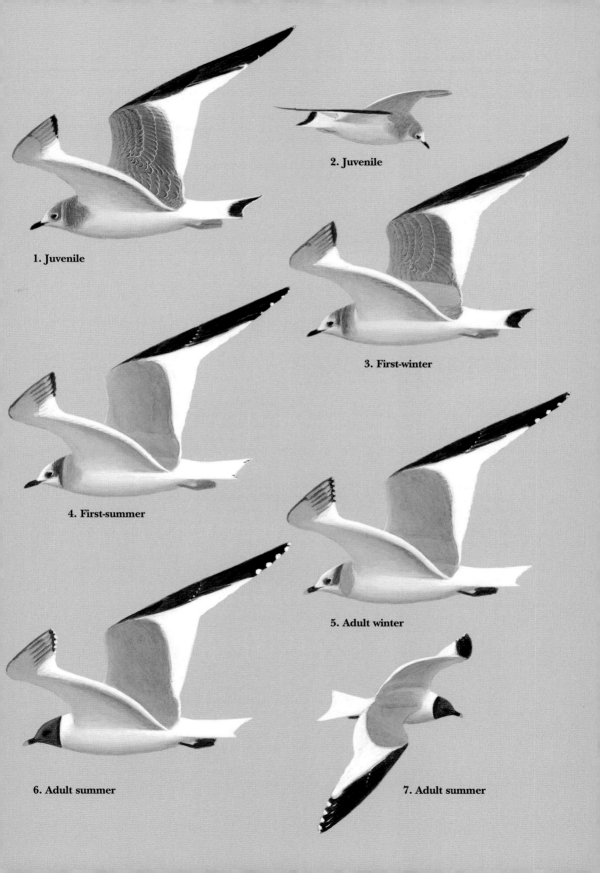

1. Juvenile

2. Juvenile

3. First-winter

4. First-summer

5. Adult winter

6. Adult summer

7. Adult summer

Adult moult to **summer** plumage complete Dec–early Apr, overlapping with moult from summer to winter, including head and body, prior to spring migration. Head from late Mar. Most have full summer hood early Apr. Flight feather moult starts (late Nov)Dec; P1–2 usually mid-Dec, P9–10 Mar–Apr. Secondaries/tail moulted when about P5 renewed. Californian autumn birds moult slightly earlier with P1–2 mid-Oct and head frequently from Sep (J. R. King pers. comm.).

Juvenile moult to **first-winter** complete (or almost so) Nov–Apr, including head and body. On migrating stopovers small minority have renewed scattered mantle and scapulars (rarely lesser coverts) late Sep, but most retain juvenile plumage to Dec/Jan. Moult limited to part of head and body, sometimes whole mantle/scapulars and most of head. Main moult Feb/Mar, including flight feathers and (most of) tail, starting with P1 Feb; P4–5 Mar–Apr; P9–10 May; retarded birds grew P1 Apr and P5 Aug. Secondaries and tail Mar–May.

Moult to **first-summer** at most very limited, restricted to parts of head (if any moult at all) Apr–May. Two Israeli first-summers (mid-Jun/early Aug) were in worn juvenile plumage apart from a few grey mantle feathers (Lambert 1975, Cottridge & Vinicombe 1996, Shirihai 1999).

Moult to **second-winter** similar to adult; P1–2 frequently moulted prior to autumn migration.

DESCRIPTION

Adult Nape, underbody, rump, uppertail-coverts and tail white. Mantle, scapulars, back, most lesser coverts and median coverts, tertials and inner secondaries medium grey, often with slight bluish tinge (Kodak Grey Scale 6–9(10)). Outer secondaries, most greater coverts, outermost median coverts and lesser coverts, P1–5 and their coverts white. Alula and outer primary coverts black, latter often with narrow white tips. P6–10 black with 7–15mm white tips, often partly worn off late summer and autumn (may be absent on P7–10). Some with narrow white lines on inner webs of outer P7–10, sometimes visible in fully spread wing. P1–5 white. P5 with variable amount of black on half of outer web and base of inner web (often lacking in adult male). P4 sometimes with some black on base of outer web. At rest, white outer wing-coverts normally visible as white division between grey coverts and black primaries. Tertials grey with white fringes. Tail with slight fork. 1% with orange shaft to T1. Underwing white with variable grey bar on greater coverts (may be absent). Iris blackish-brown, orbital ring red. Bill black with clear-cut 10–14mm broad yellow to orange-yellow tip. Gape and mouth bright red. Legs dark grey to blackish.

Adult summer (Apr–Oct) Hood blackish-grey (Kodak Grey Scale 10–14) with darker rear border; broadest and most diffuse on nape. Underbody sometimes with slight pinkish tinge in spring (Cramp & Simmons 1983).

Sexes similar: some females have paler grey hood and broader, more diffuse black border; some males have narrow white fringes to lower edge of black border (skins; see also Grant 1986b photo 169). White primary tips max. 14mm in males, <10mm in females. Yellow tip

of bill on average broader in males (max. 14mm; in females <12mm) (skins). Rarely, tip to upper mandible dark.

Adult winter (Nov/Dec–Apr) Head white with black eye-crescent and blackish-grey nape to upper hindneck, often extending to rear ear-coverts, neck-sides and hindcrown as dark triangle behind eye, broadest at rear; sometimes limited to dark streak behind eye, forming ear-spot or dark bar over hindcrown. Central crown sometimes dark-streaked. Lower hindneck white, often with dark mottling. Upperwing as adult summer, but before primary moult outer primaries browner through wear with restricted or no white tips. Legs sometimes reddish-brown or pinkish-grey.

Juvenile (fledging–Feb/Apr) Forehead, lores, chin and throat white, when fresh often tinged greyish-brown. Eye-ring whitish, eye-crescents before eye blackish. Crown and breast-sides greyish-brown, when fresh with narrow pale fringes; brown on breast-sides sometimes extensive. Some have paler head with whitish lores and forehead, pale greyish-brown crown and broader pale eye-surroundings; such birds may become almost white-headed in winter. Mantle, back, scapulars, lesser coverts, median coverts and inner greater coverts medium brown to brownish-grey with black subterminal crescents and gingery to white fringes, broadest on scapulars, lower mantle and back (pattern similar to certain juvenile *Calidris* sandpipers). Darker shaft-streak also sometimes visible. Inner median coverts sometimes slightly paler greyish-brown or with grey bases, matching colour of adult but lacking bluish tinge (normally in birds with palest head-markings). Tertials and inner secondaries grey-brown with broad whitish fringes. Other secondaries, P1–4/5, inner primary coverts and outer greater coverts white. Alula and outer primary coverts blackish with distinct but narrow white edges. P5–10 black with narrow white tips or fringes and white inner webs increasing inwards to wholly white on P4–5 as white inners on spread wing. Outer web of P5(4) sometimes with indistinct black to dark grey spots. P5–10 with white inner webs, increasing inwards to wholly white on P4–5, showing as white lines in spread outer wing. Underbody and underwing white; greater coverts dark grey, forming dark bar on underwing, generally more distinct than in adults and, although sometimes faint, never absent apart from on innermost coverts. From below, P5–10 medium grey with narrow darker tips. Median and primary coverts sometimes dark-tipped. Tail white with black band (on T1 16–34mm), generally broadest in midtail. All rectrices have narrow whitish tips and fringes, broadest in midtail. T6 white with black terminal spot near tip of inner (and sometimes outer) web. Iris brown. Orbital ring black. Bill black, sometimes with grey, yellowish to pinkish-tinged base to lower mandible or yellowish-tinged tip. Gape flesh. Legs pale pinkish-grey to greyish-brown.

First-winter (Dec–Mar/Apr) similar to juvenile with head and body similar to adult winter, and variable amount of wing-coverts grey as in adult (especially inner, but sometimes all); some birds, however, show juvenile coverts throughout first summer. Black on wing and tail browner through wear, and primaries with narrower white tips than in adult, often none. Bill dark,

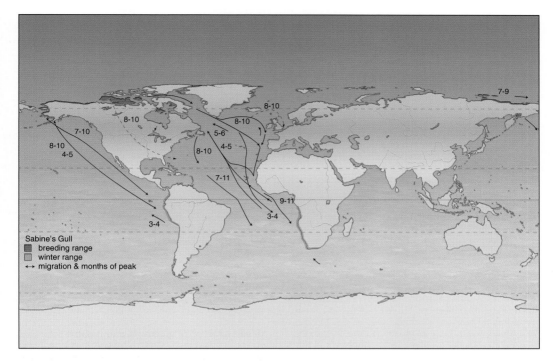

Sabine's Gull
■ breeding range
▨ winter range
← → migration & months of peak

sometimes with indistinct paler-tinged tip. Legs grey, rarely black.

First-summer (Apr–Sep/Oct) Head as adult winter, but majority have darker hindneck and greyish wash to breast-sides; dark markings sometimes browner than in adult winter. A few develop adult-like hood, but duller than in adult, at most with white speckling. Upperparts as first-winter; retained juvenile feathers become strongly worn and faded, and lose patterning. Tertials often with dusky subterminal marks. Primaries similar to adult, with white tips 0–8mm; may show extensive black on P5 and black markings on P3–4. Tail white, sometimes with dark spots, especially T5–6; rarely juvenile tail retained. Bill black or with darker yellow, narrower tip than in adult. Legs dark grey to fleshy (Yésou 1997, Shirihai 1999).

Second-winter (Oct–Apr) as adult winter, but generally with browner primaries, normally lacking white tips. Upperparts sometimes brownish-tinged. Some show dark spots in tail, tertials and alula. Bill similar to adult, but yellow tip generally less extensive and clear-cut.

Second-summer (Apr–Oct) as adult summer; birds with pale-spotted hood and immature traces of second-winter probably this age (may be advanced first-summer).

GEOGRAPHICAL VARIATION Monotypic. Birds from E Siberia/W Alaska said to show darker mantle than other populations (Cramp & Simmons 1983) and sometimes treated as subspecies *woznesenskii*. We found differences negligible and variation clinal; therefore regard the species as monotypic (as do Il'icev & Zubakin 1990). Certain E Siberian birds the palest in studied series (skins in MCZ). Average wing length in adult male E Siberia 282.9, Alaska 281.2, Greenland

279.5; female E Siberia 274.0, Alaska 270.2, Greenland and W Europe 268.4. Tarsus adult male E Siberia mean 33.9, Alaska 33.7, Greenland and N Atlantic 32.1; adult female E Siberia 31.9, Alaska 31.8, Greenland and N Atlantic 31.5. All measurements overlap; combined in measurements below.

DISTRIBUTION AND MIGRATION Total population <100,000 pairs, most in Canada and Arctic Russia W to Taimyr; also 100–200 pairs Greenland (e.g. 40 Henrik Krøyers Holme, NE Greenland). Irregular Spitsbergen, where 2–5 pairs (max. four pairs Moffen Island). Breeds Arctic tundra with bogs and small ponds, normally alongside Arctic Tern *Sterna paradisaea*. Present on breeding sites late May–early Sep, juveniles to Oct (Salomonsen 1967, Cramp & Simmons 1983, Forchhammer & Maagaard 1991, Yésou 1991a, Isaksen & Bakken 1995, del Hoyo *et al.* 1996).

Long-distance migrant, mainly pelagic. Adults leave breeding sites late Jul–Aug, followed by juveniles a few weeks later. Often in medium-sized flocks, but closer to land usually as wind-blown singletons or small groups, usually juveniles. Canadian breeders migrate E, and eventually S between Greenland and Canada before heading SE. Very scarce American E Coast and Great Lakes in autumn. Migration heads towards Bay of Biscay, where flocks of several hundreds sometimes present. A minority migrate inland North America, heading for wintering areas in Pacific; records from Florida.

Peak N Atlantic late Aug–early Sep (adults), mid-Sep–mid-Oct (juveniles); stragglers to early Dec, exceptional later in winter. Max. France 2,000+ in autumn 1981 and 1993; 1,000 Brittany on 25 August 1965 (with large flocks of Grey Phalaropes *Phalaropus fulicarius*).

Frequently blown away from migration routes by gales, reaching North Sea. Annual occurrence in NW Europe varies; in Great Britain annual average of 124 1968–1997. Recent North Atlantic peaks: 704 Great Britain 1987 (250 15–16 October, mostly SW England, with exceptional dominance of adults) and 187 Denmark in same year (second-best year); 850 Les Sables d'Olonne, Vendée, France, 7 September 1995. Large influx autumn 1997 in NW Europe: 1,300 Great Britain, including 890 Ireland (830 late Aug, with 347 at Brandon Head, Ireland, 28 August), 141 Sweden, 440 Denmark (Scandinavian peak latter half of Sep (104/515 records in respective countries up to 1997)), 220 Netherlands (40 on 12 October) and 14 Belgium. Much scarcer Norway with some hundreds recorded in total, and Iceland (43 records up to 2001).

Elsewhere: Finland (4), Estonia (20); Germany, Poland (13); most mid-Oct–early Nov, generally later than in W Europe, suggesting arrival via seabird migration route directly from White Sea, Russia (Harrison 1983, Hume & Christie 1989, Lewington et al. 1991, del Hoyo et al. 1996, Bunch 1997, van Dongen et al. 1997, Fraser et al. 1997, 1999a & b, Elkins & Yésou 1998, SOF 2003).

From Bay of Biscay follows Canary/Senegal current upwellings to wintering grounds in cold upwellings off SW Africa, especially cool Benguela current, Namibia. Common winterer S Africa S to Cape Town (flocks up to 1,000), much scarcer Indian Ocean. Immatures present all year in winter quarters. Winters regularly N to Canary current; very irregular in N Atlantic and rare W Coast of N America; most reports not verified (Lambert 1975, Dunn 1983, Harrison 1983, Sinclair et al. 1993, van den Berg & Bosman 1999, Duquet 2002).

Timing of Siberian and Alaskan migration slightly earlier, with small groups California from late Jul. Pass Bering Sea and N Pacific coast in small flocks between Washington state and California (in Sep–Oct daily max. 2,000 off Washington, 430 California) to main winter areas: Humboldt current off Peru (flocks up to 1,000). Scarcer N to Ecuador and Colombia, mainly during migration. Accidental S to Chile. Spring migration Apr–May small in E Atlantic; peak off W Africa first half of May heading directly for Arctic breeding grounds in mid-Atlantic; 220 off Dakar, Senegal, 21–28 April 1992. Pacific migration peaks Apr (Glutz von Blotzheim & Bauer 1982, Cramp & Simmons 1983, Harrison 1983, Marr & Porter 1992).

Vagrant C Europe (e.g. 4 Hungary, of which one adult), Mediterranean, Bulgaria, Israel (2, Eilat, Jun–Aug), Jordan, Egypt, UAE, the Gambia, Congo, Cameroon, Mozambique, Somalia. W Pacific (Japan, Korea, Sumatra and Australia (minimum six), S Indian Ocean (Prince Edward Island, Isles Crozet). (Glutz von Blotzheim & Bauer 1982, Urban et al. 1986, Lewington et al. 1991, Higgins & Davies 1996, Attila 1998, Johnstone & Storr 1998, Shirihai 1999).

MEASUREMENTS Lengths in mm; weights in g. Own data based on skins in NHM, NNH, NRK, USNM, UZM, ZMA, ZMO. Greenland, North America, E Siberia, California, Mauritania (Apr–Nov). Juveniles Greenland, W Europe Aug–Nov.

WING

Adult male	264–298 (279.1)	78
Adult female	248–290 (269.2)	52
Juvenile	242–271 (257.2)	65

FORK (difference between T1 and T6)

Adult male	16–29 (22.0)	59
Adult female	14–23 (20.0)	21
Juvenile	19–29 (23.1)	64

BILL

Adult male	24.2–29.7 (26.2)	76
Adult female	21.8–26.8 (25.0)	52
Juvenile	20.4–28.4 (23.4)	60

BILL DEPTH AT BASE OF BILL

Adult male	7.2–9.6 (8.6)	76
Adult female	7.4–9.0 (8.1)	52
Juvenile	6.3–8.2 (7.2)	63

BILL DEPTH AT GONYS

Adult male	7.1–8.6 (7.9)	76
Adult female	6.9–8.0 (7.4)	52
Juvenile	5.6–7.4 (6.5)	60

GONYS LENGTH

Adult male	8.7–11.8 (10.1)	76
Adult female	7.9–11.4 (9.8)	52
Juvenile	6.1–9.8 (8.0)	64

TARSUS

Adult male	28.9–36.2 (32.9)	77
Adult female	26.3–34.5 (31.7)	52
Juvenile	27.3–36.0 (30.7)	65

Weight Breeding: Alaska, Canada, Greenland adult male 140–218, female 138–226 (Glutz von Blotzheim & Bauer 1982, Cramp & Simmons 1983, skins in USNM, UZM, ZMA). Non-breeding: two adult males and an adult female, Mauritania, Nov–Dec, 215–245, S Africa male 164–174, female 168–170. Juvenile Canada, W Europe 118–210 (Glutz von Blotzheim & Bauer 1982, Urban *et al.* 1986, skins in NNH, UZM).

Sabine's Gull *Larus sabini*. **761. Juvenile**. Note large wings with diagnostic brown, black and white triangles. From behind, extensive dark head-markings often create hooded appearance. Halland, Sweden. Sep 1997. *Felix Heintzenberg*. **762. Juvenile**. Rather dark, short-legged and long-winged. Note delicate pale scaling on upperparts. Halland, Sweden. Sep 1997. *Felix Heintzenberg*.

Sabine's Gull *Larus sabini*. **763. Juvenile.** White trailing edge and tail-base often contrasts strongly to rather dark plumage. White face only, hindneck being dark and concolorous with mantle. Halland, Sweden. Sep 1997. *Felix Heintzenberg*. **764. Juvenile at the beginning of moult to 1st-winter**. A paler individual than 762, having moulted one scapular to uniform grey. Flevoland, Netherlands. Oct 1991. *René Pop*.

Sabine's Gull *Larus sabini*. **765. Juvenile**. Swimming birds look attenuated with long wings. Scania, Sweden. Sep 1997. *Felix Heintzenberg*. **766. Juvenile**. Upperwing-pattern is mirrored on underwing, emphasised by translucency of white flight feathers and by solid dark line across greater coverts. Båstad, Scania, Sweden. 5 Oct 1997. *Klaus Malling Olsen*. **767. 1st-summer/2nd-winter**. Dull flight feathers, lacking white primary tips, and dull, pale-flecked hood indicates this age. Algarve, Portugal. 1 Sep 2001. *Ray Tipper*. **768. Adults, summer and moulting into summer**. Note small-headed appearance; compare wing-pattern of flying bird with 764. Agadir, Morocco. 30 Apr 1998. *Arnoud B. van den Berg*. **769. Putative 2nd-summer**. The faint pale tip to bill and dull hood are indicative of this age. Farmoor, Great Britain. Sep 2001. *George Reszeter*.

545

Sabine's Gull *Larus sabini*. **770. Putative 2nd-summer**. Same as 769. Upperwing diagnostic with grey, white and black triangles. Farmoor, Great Britain. Sep 2001. *George Reszeter*. **771. Adult summer**. Note broad yellow bill-tip, slaty grey, black-edged hood and broad white primary tips. Alaska, USA. Jul. *Karel Beylevelt*. **772. Adult summer**. Wing-pattern, deeply forked white tail and small dark hood makes the species easily recognised at this age. Greenland. Jul. *Knud Falk*. **773. Adult winter**. Note dark half-hood. Great Britain. Dec 1996. *M. S. Wallen*. **774. Adult winter**. Dark half-hood sometimes appears as dark bar across hindneck, divided from mantle by white hind-collar. Cape Prov., South Africa. Nov 2000. *R. J. Lowe*.

40. IVORY GULL

Pagophila eburnea (Phipps, 1774, Spitsbergen)

IDENTIFICATION Length 40–43cm, wingspan 108–120cm. A High Arctic, mainly white gull. In shape it is the polar bear among the gulls, being slightly larger but much stockier and fuller-bodied than Common Gull, with a shorter neck, full chest and dark short thick legs. The eyes are dark. At rest, the noticeably short legs produce a somewhat pigeon-like impression. Has a rolling gait.

In flight heavy, rather long-tailed with long, broad-based wings and powerful (almost skua-like) wingbeats. Often hangs legs slightly in flight. Soars on flat wings. Often remarkably confiding and approachable. Quite aggressive, sometimes chasing large gulls away. Obtains most food by scavenging, but also picks from surface while 'pattering'. In breeding range sometimes feeds on Polar Bear *Thallassarctos maritimus* droppings. Prefers to sit on ice and rocks instead of swimming.

Adult all-white with faint creamy tinge. Bill greyish to greenish with variable yellow tip. Legs dark. Within gulls, all-white plumage is only shared with fully albinistic individuals of other species, which are identified by less stocky appearance and longer, paler legs (bare parts never black in 100% albinos). Leucistic gulls have traces of otherwise dark plumage parts. The flight feather moult of Ivory differs from other gulls, with outer wing moulting at a time when other gulls are moulting inner wing.

Juvenile white with dusky dirty face, black tips to primaries, tail feathers and outer wing-coverts and varying dark spots to head and body. In best-marked birds, dark covers most of upperparts and to a lesser degree underbody, and face looks almost blackish. Least-marked birds only have black tips to primaries and rectrices. Bill dark greyish with pale tip; legs black. Plumage is retained in **first-winter,** where dark is generally reduced (especially on face and mantle) and bill becomes paler with broader pale tip. In **first-summer,** dusky face and dark spots on coverts and inner wing further reduced or lacking. Moults directly to **second-winter** plumage, which is either as adult or with a few dark spots on marginal coverts, greater primary coverts and alula.

VOICE Grating, similar to Common Tern *Sterna hirundo: kriiääh* and sometimes a melancholy *psieooe.* Juvenile sometimes gives a short *pyot.*

MOULT (skins in NHM, UZM, ZMO, photos, supplied by Bent 1921, Stresemann & Stresemann 1966, de Korte 1972, Tomkovic 1986, Il'icev & Zubakin 1990, Howell 2001). Adapted to High Arctic environments, only performing one yearly, complete moult.

Adult undergoes complete moult Feb–Jul/Aug. Moult suspended during breeding season, completed late summer–early autumn. P1 Mar, P6–7 May/early Jul. Moult then suspended with P6–8. P9–10 in earliest late Jul/early Aug (earliest finishers probably failed breeders). Small minority have not completed primary moult before mid-Oct. Extremely worn bird had not started primary moult early Jul. Conversely, one grew P9–10 Mar. Tail Jun–Jul. Head and body moult hard to recognise owing to white plumage; head and body moult into summer plumage mentioned by Dwight (1925), but not supported by skin studies.

Juvenile plumage retained until complete moult into **second-winter** or **adult** plumage Apr–Oct. Head and body late Apr–early Jun; rarely a few head and body feathers renewed in first-autumn. Primary moult rarely completed as early as early Jun, but mainly by late Sep.

DESCRIPTION

Adult white, with only faint ivory cast to especially upperparts. Primary shafts white to straw-yellow. Iris blackish-brown, orbital ring dark red. Bill grey with blue to green tinge and yellow to orange (sometimes reddish-tinged) tip, orange most frequent on lower mandible. Gape lilac, flesh or orange-flesh. In summer, bill colour often brighter than in winter.

Sexes alike, but male larger and heavier, on average with broader yellow bill-tip (male 15–21mm, female 13–18mm).

Juvenile (fledging–May/Jul) white. Head with variable dusky to blackish forehead, lores and chin, sometimes behind eye. Narrow white crescents above and below eye, most prominent in front of eye. Crown, nape, hindneck, ear-coverts, mantle, scapulars and sometimes breast with dark spots. Tertials with black crescents. Wing-coverts, alula, rump and secondaries with small, black subterminal spots (in secondaries most frequent on outer). Primaries with black crescents at tips, decreasing in size inwards to small subterminal markings on P1–5. Tail with narrow black subterminal bar forming thin, often broken tail-band. Underwing-coverts with dark markings on median coverts, most frequent on outer wing. Iris dark brown, orbital ring black. Bill black with yellow tip. Gape pinkish-orange. By Dec–Feb with gradually less dark in face and finer dark markings on breast (especially centre) and upperwing-coverts (where sometimes lacking). Bill grey with greenish to bluish tinge and yellow to pinkish-yellow tip. May show orange on lower mandible or along cutting edges. From midwinter, bill becomes paler and dark may be reduced to subterminal spots near tip of especially

IVORY GULL Two-year gull. High Arctic, rare outside Arctic areas. Size similar to Common Gull, but stockier with fuller plumage, short dark legs and grey, yellow-tipped bill.
Adult all white.
First-year with dusky face and varying black markings on body and tips of flight feathers and tail.

PLATE 79. IVORY GULL *Pagophila eburnea*

Medium-sized, stocky gull of the High Arctic. Shows dense plumage, rather large, full head and short dark legs. Flight rather strong and direct with powerful wingbeats. Often confident.

1.   **Juvenile** (fledging–Apr) Juvenile plumage basically retained throughout first winter. Upperparts and face delicately dark-spotted with dark trailing edge to wing (often lacking or weak on secondaries) and narrow dark tail-bar. Face dirty-looking. Bill dark grey with yellow tip.

2.   **Juvenile** A less patterned individual than 1, with only fine dark peppering on upperparts and indistinct dark spots on secondaries and tail.

3.   **Juvenile** White with dark smudging on face, grey yellow-tipped bill and fine dark peppering on upperparts. Primaries and tail black-tipped.

4.   **Adult** All white with dark eye and bill and grey yellow-tipped bill.

5.   **Adult** All white. Shape, short black legs and bicoloured bill distinguish this species from albinos of other gulls. See text for details.

548

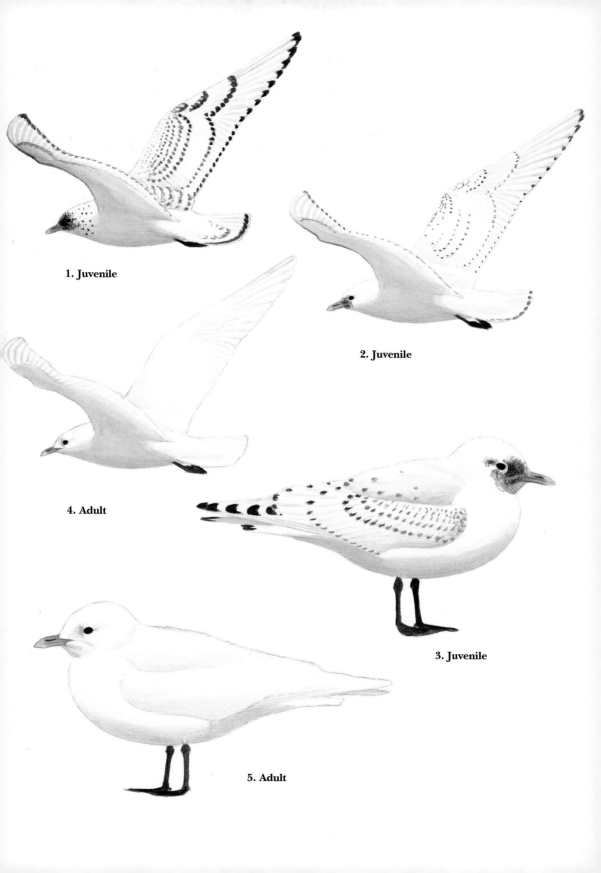

1. Juvenile

2. Juvenile

4. Adult

3. Juvenile

5. Adult

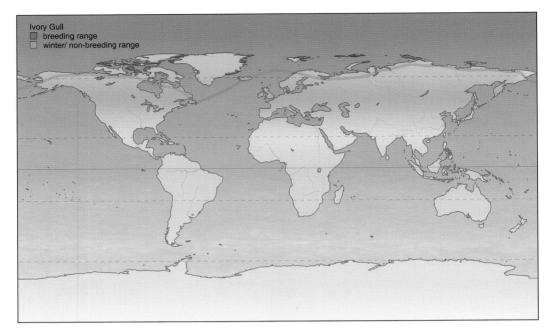

Ivory Gull
□ breeding range
□ winter/ non-breeding range

lower mandible. By Mar–Sep, dark markings further reduced, and dusky mask and black spots may almost be absent apart from dark-tipped primaries and rectrices. Bill often as adult, but generally more uniform greyish-yellow.

Second-winter (Aug–Apr) as adult winter, but sometimes with a few dark spots on median coverts (especially near carpal joint), primary coverts and alula. Also, black spot near eye and sometimes black orbital ring indicates this age (B. Mactavish *in litt.*).

DISTRIBUTION AND MIGRATION Total population around 9,000 pairs, maybe up to 25,000 pairs. Ranges further N than any other bird. Breeds High Arctic on sea-cliffs, isolated rock peaks above snow or ice and in barren tundra. Lives on fish, carcasses and locally the kills and droppings of polar bear (Haney 1993, del Hoyo *et al.* 1996).

Russian Arctic population 1,000–1,500 pairs, of which 1,000 Novaya Zemliya (700 Domashny Island). Also NE Canada 1,500; Greenland (100–200) 350–1,250 (of which 250 NE Greenland); Franz Josef Land 2,000–2,500; Spitsbergen 200–1,000. Russian and probably Spitsbergen population decreasing, probably caused by climate changes through warmer temperatures (Glutz von Blotzheim & Bauer 1982, Cramp & Simmons 1983, Mehlum & Fjeld 1987, de Korte & Volkov 1993, Tucker & Heath 1994, del Hoyo *et al.* 1996).

Leaves breeding sites Aug–Oct. S movements along E Greenland (max. 1,500 on 1–2 September 1975); regular migration Taimyr, Bering Sea, and Barrow, Alaska, Sep–early Nov. Ringing proves random spread within High Arctic, most wintering along pack-ice and drift-ice zone. Present in winter range Sep–Mar; main arrival Oct–Nov. Main wintering range around Baffin Island,

in Davis Strait and Labrador Sea (35,000 Mar 1978), Greenland Sea S to Angmagssalik and Bering Sea; fewer Nova Scotia (max. 166 in one winter) and Newfoundland (exceptionally several hundreds Jan 1998); more accidental further S along N American east coast to New Jersey and inland N America.

Spring migration late Feb–early Jun, in E Barents Sea peak late Apr–mid-May. Around 1,000 on drift-ice W of Qeqertarsuaq, W Greenland, on 8 May 1979; 100 Newfoundland on 21 April 1988 during NE gales. In Novaya Zemliya arrival mid-May–early Jun. Abundant whole year in drift-ice areas of W Greenland and Labrador Stream. Recoveries of Greenland birds from Bear Island and Labrador, where some immatures summer. Small SW migration along N Norwegian coast probably responsible for European records (Kampp & Kristensen 1980, Glutz von Blotzheim & Bauer 1982, Orr & Parsons 1982, Renaud & McLaren 1982, Cramp & Simmons 1983, Il'icev & Zubakin 1990, Boertmann 1994).

Vagrant W Palearctic, up to around year 2000: Great Britain at least 121 including records in 2002; Iceland 258 (up to 2001, of which 50% first-winter Oct–May; in 1995 94, of which 50 on 24 March N of Horn); Norway 65; probably regular winter visitor Faeroe Islands. Elsewhere in N Europe Denmark 6, Sweden 20, Finland 25 (22 before 1972), Germany 5, France 3, Netherlands 3, Channel Islands 1, Estonia 1, Poland 1, Switzerland 1, Italy 2. General W Palearctic decrease in recent decades, probably caused by climatic change through warmer average temperatures, but several records winter 2001-2002 in UK. (Bloch & Sørensen 1984, Péturson 1987, Visser & van der Wal 1987, Il'icev & Zubakin 1990, BLIKI 1994, Frainsson & Péturson 1997, Mitchell & Young 1997, Argeloo 1999, Rogers *et al.* 2001, *Brit. Birds* 91: 48, A. T. Mjøs & Y Kolbeinsson *in litt.*).

MEASUREMENTS. Lengths in mm; weights in g. Own data based on skins in NRK, UZM, ZMA, ZMO. Greenland, Spitsbergen, Iceland.

WING

Adult male	325–366 (347.5)	56
Adult female	313–351 (331.8)	44
First-year male	323–356 (343.4)	51
First-year female	315–345 (328.1)	35

Note Adult male with both wings 315mm (ZMA, late Aug not in moult), and juv. female with both wings 300 (6/11) omitted.

BILL

Adult male	31.2–40.0 (34.2)	68
Adult female	29.1–36.5 (31.9)	45
First-year male	30.5–38.7 (33.8)	43
First-year female	28.8–34.3 (31.2)	35

BILL DEPTH AT GONYS

Adult male	10.0–13.1 (11.9)	62
Adult female	9.5–11.7 (10.6)	42
First-year male	10.3–12.5 (11.3)	44
First-year female	9.0–11.7 (10.4)	34

BILL DEPTH AT BASE OF BILL

Adult male	11.8–15.2 (13.5)	61
Adult female	11.1–13.2 (12.2)	42
First-year male	11.1–14.8 (12.7)	44
First-year female	10.6–13.3 (11.8)	35

GONYS LENGTH

Adult male	10.4–14.9 (12.8)	59
Adult female	10.0–13.1 (11.8)	42
First-year male	10.2–13.9 (12.3)	44
First-year female	9.6–13.1 (11.5)	35

TARSUS

Adult male	32.5–40.3 (36.6)	67
Adult female	29.6–39.2 (34.1)	45
First-year male	32.4–39.6 (36.0)	44
First-year female	29.1–39.8 (33.8)	35

Weight Adult: male Apr–Aug. 500–687, female 448–583. Svalbard breeders, mean adult male 546.8, female 455.3. Weakened first-winters down to 322.5. Two first-year males 560–598 (de Korte 1972, Glutz von Blotzheim & Bauer 1982, Cramp & Simmons 1983, Norderhaug 1989, skins in ZMA, UZM).

Ivory Gull *Pagophila eburnea*. **775. Juvenile**. Note short black legs and white plumage with black speckling. Stellendam, Netherlands. 12 Feb 1990. *Arnoud B. van den Berg*.

Ivory Gull *Pagophila eburnea*. **776. Juvenile**. A slightly more well-marked bird with more extensive dark face than 775. New-foundland, Canada. 7 Jan 1998. *Bruce Mactavish*. **777. Juvenile**. Same as 775. Note white, black-tipped primaries and scattered black spotting on upperparts. Stellendam, Netherlands. 12 Feb 1990. *Arnoud B. van den Berg*. **778. Juvenile.** Note dark face and black spotting on upperparts. Juvenile plumage retained in 1st-winter. Vadsø, Finnmark, Norway. 31 Mar 1987. *Tomi Muukonen*. **779. Juvenile**. A rather weakly patterned bird, with extensive black markings just on primary coverts. Newfoundland, Canada. 18 Jan 1998. *Bruce Mactavish*. **780. Juvenile**. More densely patterned bird - note how broad black tips to greater coverts form black commas in upperwing. Tail-bar always very narrow. Newfoundland, Canada. 7 Jan 1998. *Bruce Mactavish*.

Ivory Gull *Pagophila eburnea*. **781. Juvenile and adult**, with Glaucous Gull. Often feeds on carcasses. Adult white with dark eyes and grey, yellow-tipped bill. Newfoundland, Canada. 18 Jan 1998. *Bruce Mactavish.* **782. Adult.** Note grey bill with yellowish tip. Spitsbergen, Norway. Jul 1999. *Jan Eske Schmidt.* **783. Adult**. All-white in flight. See main text for identification from full albinos of other gulls. Spitsbergen, Norway. Late Jul 1999. *Jan Eske Schmidt.*

784

785

Ivory Gull *Pagophila eburnea.* **784. Adult.** Newfoundland, Canada. Jan 1998. *Bruce Mactavish.* **785. Adult.** All white. The black legs contrast strongly with plumage in flight; large black eye is also prominent. Newfoundland, Canada. 18 Jan 1998. *Bruce Mactavish.*

554

41. ROSS'S GULL

Rhodostethia rosea (MacGillivray, 1824, Melville Peninsula, Canada)

Plates 80–81, Photos 786–794

IDENTIFICATION Length 29–31cm, wingspan 90–100cm. A beautiful, High Arctic small gull. Its enigmatic life and genuine beauty make it a most sought-after species, and its discovery outside its breeding range is always a revelation. Ross's Gull is only slightly larger than Little Gull, compared to which it has a slightly longer, cigar-shaped body, longer and more angled, pointed wings with long hand and longer wedge-shaped tail with projecting central tail feathers, in flight shaped similar to juvenile Long-tailed Skua *Stercorarius longicaudus*. Rounded head, large eye and short bill create a very gentle look, in winter emphasised by black eye-patch. The legs are very short. Feeds in a leisurely, buoyant flight like Little or Sabine's Gull or a small tern, with surface-dipping but fewer 'yo-yo' movements, more hovering and frequent surface-plunging. Often picks food from surface like phalaropes. Travelling flight strong, but with deep and powerful wingbeats. Settled bird bears some resemblance to *Streptopelia* dove with its rounded head, short bill, deep breast and elongated shape. Swimming bird shows attenuated rear end with long wings and tail.

Adult has pale grey upperparts and upperwing. White trailing edge to wing broader than on Little, broadest in midwing. It does not extend onto outer primaries and around wing-tip as in Little. The white trailing edge is shaped as a broad white triangle, unlike the narrower but evenly broad trailing edge of Little. Underwing mid-grey (may look blackish in poor light, when Ross's may be overlooked as adult Little – Dunn 1984). In fact, upper- and underwing are of the same coloration, but upperwing normally looks clearly paler. Very narrow black outer web on outermost primaries is invisible apart from against pale background at very close range. Bill black, legs orange-red.

During tail moult in late summer, certain smaller gulls have wedge-shaped, but shorter, tail. Some second-year Little (or Little near end of moult into third-winter or adult winter) have dark on upperwing confined to markings on outer two primaries, creating dark line at leading edge of wing. When present, this is more obvious than in Ross's. Little also has shorter, more rounded wings with narrower white trailing edges reaching wing-tip, square-cut, shorter tail, and smart dark cap.

Adult summer has white head with a narrow, complete black neck-ring dividing whitish head from pink or rosy underbody (rarely whitish). **Adult winter** has white to pale grey head with large-looking dark eye and faint dark ear-spot. Often with distinct grey smudge from hindneck to breast-sides and regularly also on crown, separated from white face. Underparts whitish, generally less rosy-tinged than in summer. Legs duller orange than in breeding season.

Juvenile/first-winter shares black W on upperwing with Little Gull and Black-legged Kittiwake, but on inner wing it connects over back . Unlike both, Ross's shows white trailing edge to wing that eats into black on wing-tip. Outer primaries have black tips, creating black line against broad white 'tongue' on wing-tip. This extensive white area is joined to broad white trailing edge on inner wing, white areas being broadest on midwing. On underwing, broad white trailing edge contrasts somewhat to pale grey underwing-coverts, sometimes creating rather strong contrast, as in Sabine's Gull. Long wedge-shaped tail is white with black tips to midtail feathers only – these look strangely isolated from rest of tail ('as some extra extension').

In Little Gull, pale trailing edge to wing does not extend to outer primaries (Ross's rarely also shows darker outer primaries), and pale trailing edge to inner wing dulled by grey secondary bar. Underwing whitish with narrow white trailing edge and black trailing edge to outer hand, lacking contrast of Ross's. Tail shorter with complete black bar.

On closed wing Ross's shows prominent broad white primary edges (especially on inner primaries) and often some isolated dark primary spots, unlike Little, which shows a complete dark outer edge to closed wing. Ross's at rest shows a prominent pale area on primaries just extending beyond tertials and the dark of wing-tip formed by outer primaries. **Juvenile** has dark brown cap and head-markings, often extending to breast-sides, and dark, pale-edged mantle feathers. Upperparts similar to juvenile Little Gull, but browner. **First-winter** has head and upperparts similar to adult winter, with grey smudge to hindneck and breast-sides and hint of dark ear-spot. White head may stand out against grey neck-sides and hindneck. Crown may also be smudged with grey, but lacks distinctive dark crown-patch of most Little.

First-summer similar to first-winter, but head and tail similar to adult summer; neck-ring normally less complete and tail sometimes with a few black-tipped feathers. Underparts often with slight rose tinge, less extensive than in adult summer.

Second-winter as adult winter, but some have traces of dark carpal bar (especially in autumn) on upperwing and dark patches on tail. Rarely with grey V-markings on primary tips.

Second-summer as adult summer, but sometimes aged by characters mentioned under second-winter as well as incomplete or even largely absent black neck-ring. Some probably retain winter-like plumage. Such birds (including several seen well into Jun far out of normal breeding range) may be retarded.

VOICE Higher-pitched and more melodious than in most Laridae, similar to calls of terns. Generally silent outside breeding season. Call at breeding site is a short, dry *a-dac a-dac a-dac* or *de-urrr de-urr*, sometimes barking, thus bearing resemblance to Black-legged Kittiwake. A short high-pitched *kew*, similar to Black Tern *Chlidonias*

PLATE 80. ROSS'S GULL *Rhodostethia rosea*

A small High Arctic gull. Breeds on Arctic tundra, winters in Arctic environments, but yearly straggler to temperate waters. Slightly larger than Little Gull, but with much longer wings and tail, appearing very accentuated when settled. Dense plumage, large rounded head and very small, black bill give settled birds a pigeon-like appearance. In most plumage distinctive – and very appealing; certain plumages need to be separated from especially Little Gull.

1. **Juvenile** (Jul–Aug) Head, breast and flanks mainly brown with complex white mask. Upperparts buff-scaled. Legs fleshy. This plumage is almost solely observed in the High Arctic, and exchanged for first-winter by early autumn.

2. **First-winter** (Sep–Apr/May) Head and body similar to adult winter. Black carpal bar and pale grey upperparts shared with Little Gull; told by elongated shape (with long primary projection) and pale grey head with largish-looking eye (caused by dark eye-surroundings); shows faint grey ear-spot and short pinkish legs. Little Gull shorter with smart dark cap and larger ear-spot, but shorter primary projection.

3. **First-summer** (May–Aug) Combines adult-looking head and body with retained juvenile wing. Compared to adult, pink flush to body less extensive, and often lacking. Legs bright red.

4. **Adult winter** (Sep–Apr) Head similar to first-winter. Shows variable pink tinge to underparts, varying from weak to as strong as in adult summer. Adult upperparts uniform pale grey, only with very narrow black outer web on P10.

5. **Adult summer** (Apr–Aug) Head white (often with pinkish flush), sharply divided from pink underbody by distinct black neck-ring.

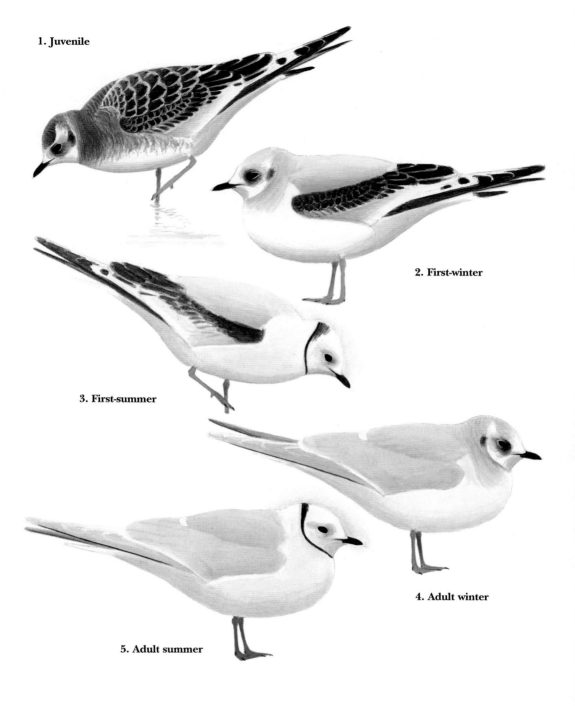

1. Juvenile

2. First-winter

3. First-summer

4. Adult winter

5. Adult summer

PLATE 81. ROSS'S GULL *Rhodostethia rosea*

Small, elegant gull, only slightly larger than Little Gull, but with proportionately much longer wings and longer, wedge-shaped tail. Appears neckless, head and body creating short oval. Flight tern-like and buoyant.

1.	**Juvenile** (Jul–Aug) Brown head and body soon moulted into first-winter. Wing pattern, however, retained throughout first winter. Upperwings with dark W as in Little Gull, but outer parts narrower, caused by more solid white area on outer wing (creating white wedge); therefore shows narrower black trailing edge to outer wing than Little. Also, secondaries white, creating white trailing edge to hindwing. Underwing coverts pale grey. Tail wedge-shaped with black tip, not complete bar.

2.	**First-winter** (Sep–Apr/May) Head and body as adult winter; juvenile wings and tail retained.

3.	**First-summer** (Apr–Aug) Head and body often similar to adult summer (but may retain winter head pattern throughout first summer). With wear, dark W on upperwing fades to brownish. Central tail moulted in early summer, resulting in adult-looking tail from Jun.

4.	**Second-winter** (Sep–Apr) As adult: whitish head against grey necklace, varying pinkish flush to underbody, pale grey upperparts and broad white trailing edge to wing, forming narrow triangle. Underwing-coverts grey, generally coloured as upperparts, but typically darker-looking (but never blackish as in Little) in field. This bird represents a rare immature stage with broader black outer web to P10 than in adult, as well as narrow black tips to outer primaries. This pattern still not matched by second-year Little, which shows more solid dark markings on outer wing.

5.	**Adult winter** (Sep–Apr) See caption under 4. Note almost uniform pale grey upperwing with rather broad white trailing edge. The very narrow black outer web to P10 normally invisible in field (but may be observed at <50m against pale background). Some birds less pink than shown here, sometimes with white underbody; conversely, some show pink flush to tail and secondaries also.

6.	**Adult winter** Note neckless, oval body shape, narrow wedge-shaped tail and angled, pale wings with broader white trailing edge than in Little Gull.

7.	**Adult summer** (Apr–Aug/Sep) Narrow, distinct black neck-ring separates head from body.

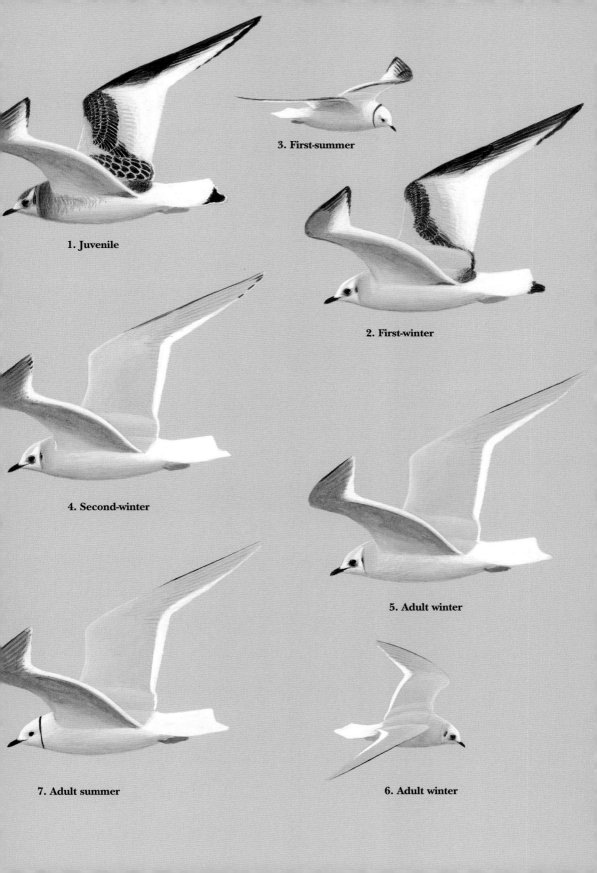

1. Juvenile

3. First-summer

2. First-winter

4. Second-winter

5. Adult winter

7. Adult summer

6. Adult winter

niger, is heard in winter. A series of short, tern-like notes, *kik-kik-kik-kik...*, is given in alarm (Densley 1979, Sibley 2000).

MOULT Adult moult to **winter** plumage complete late Jun/Jul–early Oct, and often advanced by mid–late Jul. Head starts in failed breeders late Jun, sometimes while breeding. Winter head acquired Sep, rarely early Oct. Primaries late Jun–late Sep. Advanced birds have moulted P5 mid-Jul; 80–90% have completed primary moult late Sep; a few early Oct have only reached P5. Tail starts with T1–2 late Jun and is completed late Aug/Sep (rarely, tail moult has not started Oct when primary moult finished). Coverts Jul–Aug (Densley 1979, Il'icev & Zubakin 1990, skins in MCZ, USNM, P. Yésou *in litt.*). Moult to **adult summer** partial Feb–Apr, including head and body. Adult normally in summer plumage from mid-Apr. Out-of-range birds often have delayed moult, and may not be representative (Cramp & Simmons 1983, Asker 1984, pers. obs.).

Juvenile moult to **first-winter** partial Aug–Sep, including head and mantle, most of hindneck and scapulars and parts of underbody. Rarely retains most of juvenile hindneck into spring.

Moult to **first-summer** partial Feb–May, including head, body and tail; T1–4 normally earliest. Onset of tail moult could be regarded as first steps of moult into second-winter, but is often completed by spring before onset of rest of moult into second-winter.

Moult to **second-winter** complete late Jun–Oct, starting with lesser and median coverts and P1; P10 first half of Oct (late Nov). Head and body late Aug–early Sep; traces of neck-ring and very worn secondaries sometimes present late Nov. Moult also includes juvenile parts of tail which had not been renewed in previous moult (Meltofte *et al.* 1981, Cramp & Simmons 1983).

DESCRIPTION

Adult Mantle, scapulars, upperwing-coverts and P5–10 pale grey (Kodak Grey Scale 3–4(5)). P1–4 greyish-white to white, secondaries white, with grey bases, forming broad white trailing edge to wing; P1–4 and secondaries sometimes with slightly rosy tinge. P10 with black outer edge to outer web, often only up to 18–40mm before tip. Breast to undertail-coverts, axillaries and inner wing-coverts white with variable grey, pink or rosy tinge. Underwing-coverts and underside of P5–10 mid-grey (Kodak Grey Scale 4–5). Marginal coverts, rump and tail white, sometimes with pinkish tinge. Iris blackish-brown. Orbital ring red. Bill blackish, gape red. Legs orange-red to red.

Adult summer (Mar–Sep) Head white, divided from breast by complete black neck-ring; broadest – and sometimes more diffuse – on nape. Crown sometimes greyish. Rarely whole head with slight pink tinge. Underparts normally strongly rosy-tinged, especially early in breeding season; in late breeding season, rosy tinge strongest on flanks, belly and undertail-coverts. Underbody rarely white. Legs red.

Sexes similar; females tend to show broader neck-ring on nape (3–10mm *versus* 1–6mm in males) and some have grey rather than jet-black neck-ring on nape, often with white spots (Densley 1991, skins in UZM, ZMO).

Adult winter (Aug–Mar/Apr) Head white with pale greyish wash on crown and hindneck. Has faint dark ear-spot, often as dark crescent, where summer neck-ring present. Breast-sides and sometimes central breast often greyish. Dark feathers around eye, especially in front. Has very fine stiff black hairs, 3–6mm long, creating blackish eye-crescent and emphasizing dark eye. Legs generally duller orange-tinged than in adult summer (Densley 1979).

Juvenile (fledging–Oct) Head with blackish-brown to brown crescents in front of eye, ear-spot, crown (may reach eye to upper lores) and hindneck. Shows thin white line below and behind eye. Dark crown (often with indistinct sandy edges) frequently connected with brown breast-sides by dark hindneck. Lores and broad patch behind eye whitish. Mantle and scapulars dark brown with greyish-brown, buff or golden feather-edges, creating scaly pattern, strongest on scapulars. Uppertail-coverts and lower rump white with narrow black to brown tips. Underbody white; flanks and breast-sides (sometimes continuing as diffuse band across central breast) greyish-brown, indistinctly mottled paler. Upper lesser coverts pale grey, lower lesser and median coverts blackish-brown, forming clear-cut carpal bar. Greater coverts pale grey to white. Secondaries white, innermost with small black markings. Alula and outer primary coverts blackish with narrow pale edges, inner primary coverts grey. Outer web and 30–50% of basal part of inner web of P8–10 black (rest of inner web white); sometimes with narrow white area on outer web near tip of P8(9). P(5)6–7 similar but with white patch on outer web proximal to black tip. Black tip on inner web of P3–10 black, broadest on P10 (19–22mm) and on P9–7 (20–24mm). P1–(5)6 white, with narrow black tips (max. 10mm; often reduced to subterminal spots on P3–4; often lacking on P1–2). In general, narrower dark primary tips than Little Gull. Marginal coverts white. Underwing-coverts pale grey, sometimes similar to adult. Secondaries white. Tail white with broad black subterminal spot on elongated central pairs (22–36mm on T1), decreasing to small terminal marks on T4. T5–6 white, T5 sometimes with dark mottling. Black tail-markings may be restricted to T1–2, whole tail rarely white (skin in USNM). Iris and orbital ring brown to blackish. Bill blackish, sometimes with reddish-brown base. Gape flesh. Legs brown, dull flesh or dull red.

First-winter (Aug–Apr) Head and body as adult winter, but upperparts may retain juvenile feathers, especially on lower back. Rest of plumage as juvenile.

First-summer (Mar–Sep) Head and body similar to adult summer, wing pattern similar to first-winter before moult in late summer. May retain winter head in first-summer (probably weakened birds); others attain hindneck portion of neck-ring or show dark spotting as indication of neck-ring. May show a few dark-tipped feathers below eye (skin in ZMO). Tail white, frequently with dark spots especially on T1–2 (second-generation feathers). By late summer, wing becomes worn and dark areas fade to brownish. Bare parts as first-year; orbital ring sometimes reddish.

Second-winter (Aug–Apr) similar to adult winter, but primary coverts often dark-streaked or -centred (espe-

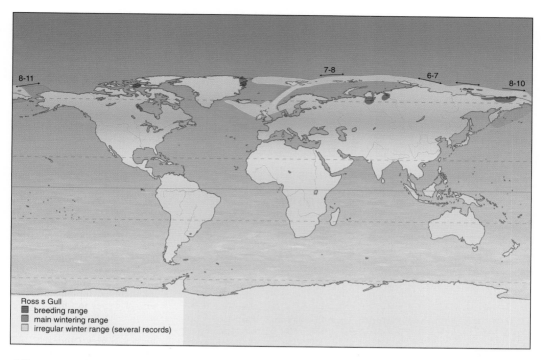

Ross s Gull
- breeding range
- main wintering range
- irregular winter range (several records)

cially outer ones). Rarely with darker grey tips or inner webs on P6–10. May retain partial carpal bar into Nov/Dec. Extremely worn secondaries frequent in autumn (as well as in spring), probably a result of physical abnormality. Underwing often paler grey than in adult; sometimes with some dark-tipped greater primary coverts. Rectrices sometimes with brownish shafts, rarely with faint dark edges to especially T1–2. Legs as adult; sometimes with dark tibia and reddish-grey tarsus (Densley 1979, Il'icev & Zubakin 1990, Moerbeek 1993, skins in NRK, USNM, UZM).

Second-summer (Mar–Sep) as adult summer, apart from differences outlined under second-winter. Some (probably weakened birds) show poorly developed neck-ring and only have slight or no rosy tinge to underparts. Some retain wholly or partly winter head pattern. Brownish tinge to neck-ring probably indicates this age. Some also show dark grey spots to P6–10, grey spots on median and greater coverts and grey tips to T1–2. Shafts of rectrices sometimes brownish. Two birds (May, Denmark) in this plumage had very worn secondaries. At least two birds retaining winter plumage in W Europe (May, Jul) lacked rosy tinge to plumage (Il'icev & Zubakin 1990, Densley 1991, Moerbeek 1993, R. Christensen pers. comm.).

DISTRIBUTION AND MIGRATION Population 45,000–55,000 (maybe 100,000) birds. Breeds High Arctic marshy tundra and deltas with low willows. Main population between Khatanga to Kolyma; largest colony 12,000 pairs Cherskii, Kolyma Delta. Populations in N America and Greenland small and probably not permanent. Has bred Svalbard. Arrives breeding grounds late May–early Jun, leaves late Jul–Aug (Cramp & Simmons

1983, Boertmann 1994).

Highly arctic outside breeding season, normally associated with permanent ice. Autumn migration starts late Jul; late summer migration in Arctic Ocean takes birds both W and E along coast or edge of pack ice. W movements from Siberia towards Franz Josef Land and Spitsbergen, reaching ocean off W Greenland, where 1,000 Jul–Sep 1980 in pack-ice between NE Greenland and Franz Josef Land, probably mainly non-breeders. Noted in groups in midsummer, Taimyr. Main migration E to Bering Sea. Autumn migration well studied Barrow, Alaska; yearly totals max. 38,000 Aug–Nov, peak late Sep–mid-Oct (max. 4,300 29 September 1976). Fluctuation in numbers depends on ice and wind conditions; most seen in years with strong NW winds. Winters Beaufort, Bering and Okhotsk Seas. In Japan irregular, but late Jan 2001 influx of >100 N Hokkaido. Spring migration poorly known (Meltofte *et al.* 1981, Glutz von Blotzheim & Bauer 1982, Hjort *et al.* 1995, del Hoyo *et al.* 1996, Hjort & Elander 1996).

Regular but scarce visitor further S in Europe, with records up to and including year 2002: Great Britain 83 (yearly max. 8), Iceland 37, Sweden 17 Norway 11, Denmark 10, Finland 5, Netherlands 12. Vagrant to most other European countries S to Spain, Macedonia and Italy. Most recorded in severe Arctic winters, although a good scatter throughout year, e.g. most Icelandic birds in spring–summer; mainly adults (Glutz von Blotzheim & Bauer 1982, Elkins 1987, Péturson 1987, BLIKI 1994, Cottridge & Vinicombe 1996, Mitchell & Young 1997, Rogers *et al.* 1999, Y Kolbeinsson *in litt.*).

Vagrant USA S to Illinois, Massachusetts, Oregon; also Pribilofs, Hokkaido and Manchuria.

ROSS'S GULL Two-year gull. A beautiful, High Arctic breeder, which in winter may reach temperate waters. Superficially similar to Little, but with longer wings (especially outer wing) and longer, wedge-shaped tail. Flight more buoyant. Always appears large-eyed and very short-billed.

Adult has grey upperwing with broad white trailing edge to inner wing, being broadest at border between arm and hand; outer wing grey with very narrow black line on P10. Underbody rosy. In **summer** (Apr–Sep) head white with distinct black neck-bar against rosy underbody. In **winter** head shows dark ear-spot, and neck-sides become grey.

First-year shows black carpal bar and outer primaries, similar to Little, but carpal bar narrower and extensive whitish tongue on outer wing, isolating black trailing edge to outer wing. Secondaries are white; shows conspicuous white trailing edge to wing. Tail with black spot near tip. Head as adult winter, thus paler with larger eye than in Little. In **first-summer** often develops adult head pattern and white tail.

MEASUREMENTS Lengths in mm; weights in g. Own data based on skins in NHM, NMNH, NRK, USNM, UZM, ZMA, ZMO. Alaska, Greenland, E Siberia. Juvenile/first-winter from late Aug.

WING

Adult male	242–282	(264.9)	59
Adult female	239–279	(257.6)	59
First-year male	238–267	(252.4)	32
First-year female	239–260	(248.3)	21

TAIL WEDGE (differences in length between T1 and T6)

Adult	18–42	(27.9)	70
First-year	17–33	(25.8)	41

BILL

Adult male	16.5–22.4	(19.6)	60
Adult female	16.2–22.3	(19.2)	61
First-year male	18.3–22.1	(20.1)	30
First-year female	18.2–21.4	(19.6)	19

BILL DEPTH AT BASE OF BILL

Adult	6.0–7.9	(6.8)	115
First-year	5.8–7.7	(6.5)	52

Note Male and female identical.

BILL DEPTH AT GONYS

Adult	5.3–7.6	(6.0)	118
First-year	5.0–6.5	(5.8)	52

Note Male and female identical.

GONYS LENGTH

Adult male	6.1–8.0	(7.1)	60
Adult female	5.6–8.0	(7.0)	61
First-year	5.5–8.0	(6.7)	53

TARSUS

Adult male	27.8–33.6	(30.5)	62
Adult female	26.3–32.9	(29.9)	63
First-year	28.4–32.8	(30.6)	31
First-year	26.8–32.9	(30.1)	21

Weight Adults 200–250. Mean weight in dead birds 187.5; one specimen 148. Adult male 138–190, female 124–145. Adult Alaska late Sep 213. First-winter male Oct 237, first-winter female late Sep 195 (Densley 1979, Cramp & Simmons 1983, Il'icev & Zubakin 1990, skins in USNM).

786

Ross's Gull *Rhodostethia rosea.* **786. Juvenile** (see page 562). Overall impression pale brown with weak pale markings on head and scaly upperparts. Kolyma, NE Russia. Jul 1993. *Werner Suter.* **787. 1st-winter.** Extensive white in outer wing isolates black trailing edge to outer wing. Note black-tipped, diamond-shaped tail, white head, dark ear-spot and grey neck-sides. Uthaug, Norway. 22 Jan 2000. *Morten Vang.* **788. 1st-summer.** 1st-year wing-pattern retained. Compare with Little Gull, 745-746, and note white trailing edge to inner wing of Ross's, large pale area near primary tips and diamond-shaped tail. Mid-tail often renewed resulting in all-white tail in 1st-summer. Note black neck-ring contrasting with grey neck-sides. Chukotka, NE Russia. Late Jun 1992. *Jan Unosson.* **789. 2nd- or adult winter**. Many birds in winter almost lack rosy tinge. Note pale head, short reddish legs and long wings. Skagen, Denmark. Early Jun 1995. *Hanne & Jens Eriksen.* **790. 2nd- or adult winter**. Same as 789. Note oval body-shape, long tail and broad white trailing edge to inner wing. Skagen, Denmark. 2 Jun 1995. *Per Schiermacker-Hansen.* **791. Adult winter**. Note long, slender wings, diamond-shaped tail, grey underwing-coverts and broad white trailing edge to inner wing. Even in winter some birds are strongly rosy-tinged. Thorsminde, West Jutland, Denmark. 1 Feb 1984. *Klaus Malling Olsen.* **792. Adult summer**. White head separated from rosy underbody by complete black neck-ring. Broad white trailing edge to inner wing contrasts with grey coverts on both wing-surfaces. Chukotka, NE Russia. Late Jun 1992. *Graham Bell.*

793

794

Ross's Gull *Rhodostethia rosea*. **793. Adult summer**. Almost pigeon-like with rounded head and very short bill, adult in summer plumage is among the finest of all gulls. Note very narrow black outer web to P10, barely visible under normal circumstances in the field. Kolyma, NE Russia. Jun 1992. *Jan Unosson.* **794. Adult summer.** Kolyma, Almost neck-less in flight. Strong rosy tinge to underparts and grey underwings are visible at long range. NE Russia. Jul. *Hanne & Jens Eriksen.*

42. BLACK-LEGGED KITTIWAKE
Rissa tridactyla (Linnaeus, 1758, Great Britain)

Plate 82, Photos 795–811

IDENTIFICATION Length 38–40cm, wingspan 93–120cm. A coastal to pelagic medium-sized gull, similar to Common and Mew Gull in size and adult plumage, but more compact with a broader arm, slenderer, pointed hand and shorter, dark legs. In calm winds, flight is quicker with stiffer, mechanical wingbeats. As a true pelagic, well adapted to severe winds: in strong head-winds almost fights against wind with stiff wingbeats on sharply angled wings alternating with shearwatering during wave-passing. In tail-winds and calm weather often flies high and direct, e.g. large flocks between feeding grounds and hear··· ··es. Breeds in enormous colonies on sea-cliffs, locally on buildings. **Adult** has three-toned upperwing, paler than in Common and lacking clear white trailing edge. Mantle and coverts grey, primary-bases whitish and extreme wing-tip black – 'dipped in ink'. Tip is conspicuous against pale background, offset by translucent primaries, but disappears against dark background, wing looking rounded with paler distal parts. As in Common, the large dark eyes bestow a gentle appearance. In **summer** head is white, bill cold yellow, legs black to brownish. In early autumn, amount of black on wing-tip limited during primary moult; wing-tip then looks pale and rounded. From autumn, **adult winter** has pale grey shading on neck, often as slightly darker ear-spot, reaching onto hindneck as half-hood.
Juvenile is three-coloured – grey, black and white. Conspicuous black carpal W on upperwing contrasts strongly with grey coverts/mantle and greyish-white trailing edge to inner wing. Head white with black ear-spot and neck-boa. Tail with black bar emphasising slight tail-fork. Bill black. Legs dark, often brownish-tinged. From midwinter, **first-winter** is similar, but black neck-boa may almost disappear giving way to grey wash, which may include crown. Dark ear-spot becomes greyer and weaker. Birds with weakest head pattern look different from 'classic' juveniles, and may create ID pitfall with the smaller, slenderer Sabine's Gull, which has darker mantle, uniform coverts (see Aberrants), gleaming white trailing edge to inner wing and, in juvenile, dark crown concolorous with mantle. In distant flying Black-legged Kittiwakes, black carpal W may 'disappear', making all coverts looks evenly dark, in low sun sometimes brownish-tinged. Then look for white crown – and also black neck-boa; normally present well into winter.
Black carpal W shared with the much smaller Little and Ross's Gulls. Little has shorter wings, dark cap, much weaker bill and dark secondary bar, creating darker, less contrasting upperwing. Ross's has longer, wedge-shaped tail with dark central spot (not complete tail-bar) and greyish tinge to underwing.
From Mar, plumage becomes worn, bill paler-based and legs sometimes unexpectedly pale. From Apr, **first-summer** is very worn with extremely abraded flight and tail feathers (from midsummer often reduced to spikes as only shafts retained). During moult to second-winter

often odd-looking with barely visible dark tail-bar and much abraded, brownish outer primaries. Flight then weak and laboured with quick stiff wingbeats.
Second-winter similar to adult, but with dark-patterned bill. Also, has more extensive black wing-tip, dark spots on up to seven outer primaries, alula and primary coverts and rarely dark tertial spots. Some have winter head in summer. Most-advanced birds indistinguishable from adults.

VOICE At breeding sites very vocal, with a shrill, nasal *keti-waeek*, almost laughing. Also a gruff *kek-kek-kek*. In flight a short nasal *kja!*

MOULT (*tridactyla*), pers. obs. in S Scandinavia, Iceland. **Adult** moult to **winter** plumage complete May–Dec. P1 late May (Denmark) to mid-Jul (Spitsbergen – de Korte 1972); most have renewed P3–4(6) late Jul–mid-Aug, P(5)8–10 (late Aug)mid-Sep–late Oct; retarded birds P10 Dec(Jan). Secondaries at time of P5–6 or later; many have strongly worn secondaries Oct when most primary moult completed. Tail from late Jun simultaneous with P1–4. T1–2 generally late Aug–early Oct, followed by T4–5; a few have not started tail moult early Oct. Head and body moult Aug–Sep; 50% with summer head mid-Aug, 1–5% early Oct.
Adult moult to **summer** plumage partial Mar–Apr, including head and body. Summer head attained mid-Mar; in N Norway, 5% still with traces of winter head in mid-May (pers. obs.).
Juvenile moults partial to **first-winter** (Aug)Oct–Dec (Jan), normally very limited on head and body (especially crown to hindneck); sometimes rump. Usually no sign of moult recognisable apart from scattered new feathers on hindneck.
Moult to **first-summer** plumage partial mid-Jan–May, including head and body. Some rectrices frequently renewed spring (e.g. all but T6 mid-May – Cottle 1987, pers. obs.).
Moult to **second-winter** complete May/Jun (when flight feathers and tail are extremely worn)–Oct(Nov). Body and coverts May–Jul; late Jul most of carpal bar normally moulted. Wing earlier and often slower than in adult. P1 sometimes mid-Apr; in some moult reaches P6–7 late Apr–late May; P7–8 Sep; P8–10 early Oct. A few still grow P9–10 late Jan (Holst & Ullman 1984, skin in UZM). Secondaries start when primary moult has reached P5–7. Tail (late Mar)late Apr–Sep starting with T1. T4–5(6) Jul–Aug; tail completed (late Jul) Aug–Sep; small minority have 1–2 juvenile rectrices early Oct.
Subsequent moults as adult; moult to third-winter sometimes starts with P1–2 mid-May.

DESCRIPTION
Adult Mantle and upperwing-coverts grey (Kodak Grey Scale 6–7). Flight feathers with grey bases, fading to

PLATE 82. BLACK-LEGGED KITTIWAKE *Rissa tridactyla*

Pelagic, medium-sized gull, breeding in enormous colonies in the Northern Hemisphere. Abundant along N Pacific and Atlantic coastline. Size of Common Gull with large head and rather short bill. Appears stocky when settled, with short dark legs. Flies with quick stiff wing-beats, in hard winds performing much shearwatering on angled wings. Handles gales better than most gulls.

1. **Juvenile** Unmistakable. Legs are generally browner than in adult.

2. **Juvenile/first-winter** (Aug–Apr) Upperparts with black W across wing, contrasting with pale grey forewing and greyish-white trailing edge to wing. Tail white, slightly forked with black bar. Head diagnostic: white against black neck-boa and black ear-spot. Appears broad-necked. At distance, dark inner part of W may 'merge' with grey coverts, producing upperwing recalling Sabine's Gull, but trailing edge never gleaming white; crown white.

3. **First-winter** From autumn, many show more diffuse head pattern, as black neck-boa disappears and hindneck becomes greyer, but note large-looking head with white forehead and crown. Underwing contrast never as strong as in Sabine's Gull.

4. **First-winter** Some show narrower carpal bar and lose black neck-boa from midwinter. From late in first-winter (and into one year of age) often strongly worn with bleached W on wing and extremely worn secondaries and tail. Distinguished from Sabine's Gull by larger size, fuller body, larger head, but slightly smaller wings with hand notably slender and pointed.

5. **Late first-winter/first-summer** (Apr–Aug) Often much abraded. Bill turns pale-based from Mar. This bird shows head pattern common from midwinter, where black neck-boa is moulted into grey hindneck, which may penetrate onto crown to create head pattern reminiscent of Sabine's Gull. Note large head. Legs in this bird represent a not uncommon type with paler legs (fleshy, brown or sometimes dull red).

6. **Second winter** (Sep–Mar) In second-winter, head develops grey hindneck and ear-spot. Legs sometimes 'non-black', especially in younger birds. Note full black wing-tip.

7. **Second-winter** (Sep–Mar) As adult winter, but on average with more black on wing-tip, slight dark markings on primary coverts, and grey cutting-edges and tip to bill.

8. **Adult winter** (Sep–Mar) In winter head has greyish tinge to hindneck and blackish ear-spot. Note solid black wing-tip ('dipped in ink'), conspicuous against pale background (but 'disappearing' against dark background). Primaries otherwise translucent.

9. **Adult summer** (Mar–Aug) Upperwing appears slightly three-toned with paler outer- than inner wing and black wing-tip.

10. **Adult summer** (Mar–Aug) Head white and bill bright yellow, similar to adult summer Common and Mew Gulls, but note short black legs and full black wing-tip.

Pacific race *pollicaris* slightly darker, in adult more uniform on upperparts with on average one more primary black. First-year shows broader black neck-boa. See below.

R.t. pollicaris

R.t. tridactyla

4. First-winter

2. Juvenile/first-winter

3. First-winter

8. Adult winter

7. Second-winter

9. Adult summer

1. Juvenile

5. Late first-winter/first-summer

6. Second-winter

10. Adult summer

white at trailing edge and distal primary part to create white limit to black primary tip. P10 has black outer web. Black tips to P7–10, on P10 70–75mm, on P9 45–70mm black tip to outer web, on P8 35–55mm black tip to outer web (compare second-winter). P6 with isolated black spot near tip (in small minority covering both outer and inner web). Sometimes isolated black spot even on P5. Fresh P6–8 with narrow white tips. Tail and underparts white. Bill lemon-yellow to yellow. Gape orange. Eye blackish-brown. Orbital ring orange-red to red. Legs black to dark grey or dark brown (see Aberrants).

Adult summer (Mar–Aug) Head white. Legs black.

Adult winter (Jul–Mar) Head white with dark ear-spot. Hindneck with medium grey tinge, sometimes extending to hindcrown. Legs generally browner than in summer.

Juvenile (fledging–Aug) Head white with black ear-spot, blackish hind-collar and faint grey wash around eye. Mantle, scapulars and lesser and greater coverts grey with narrow pale tips. Median coverts and P6–10 black, creating black carpal W. Some inner coverts and tertials with black shaft-streaks (generally broader on tertials). Alula and primary coverts black. Black on outer wing and tip of outer wing decreases to subterminal spot on P4–5. Narrow white primary tips decrease inwards to subterminal spot on P4–5. P1–5 pale grey to whitish, gradually becoming paler from P3 and inwards. Inner greater coverts and tertials grey with broad dark edges. Secondaries white, often with faint grey wash. Underparts white, apart from exposed black tips of outer primaries, creating black trailing edge to outer wing; P10 black. Shows variable amount of dark speckles on marginal coverts on outer wing. Rump and tail white, tail with black bar, in T1 19–24mm. T6 often white or with small black terminal spot on inner web near tip. Bill and gape blackish, legs blackish to dark sepia-brown.

First-winter (Aug–Feb) similar to juvenile, but head pattern generally faded. By Jan–Feb 75–80% have reduced, broken black hind-collar (juvenile head retained in 15–20%); small minority show grey crown and ear-coverts, creating grey half-hood. Juvenile head may be present into late May (pers. obs.). Bill has paler greyish-yellow base from mid-Feb; black tip and cutting edges retained. Legs dark brown to black, sometimes fleshy.

First-summer (Mar–Aug) often extremely worn (Apr) Jun–Aug. Head similar to first-winter, but with fainter grey markings. Wing faded; carpal bar reduced and faded to dark brown. Primaries extremely worn, less contrasting than in first-winter; sometimes, with wear, pale tips. Tail shows abraded dark bar, often as isolated dark spots, most extensive in midtail. Secondaries very worn before moult; worn, spike-like secondaries noted from Apr, the rule Jun–Jul. Bill pale to dirty yellow with dark tips, base and cutting edges.

Second-winter (Aug–Mar) similar to adult, but black on outer webs of P(8)9–10 more extensive; Outer web of P9 with 50–150mm black, sometimes also on inner web (and as dark spots at base). P8 with 40–70mm black tip to outer web. P5 with max. 20mm black subterminal spots on both webs; in about 10% grey as in adult. 10%

have narrow dark subterminal spot on P4 (uniform grey in adult). P1–6 with narrow white tips. Shows blackish central part of alula and some primary coverts; sometimes darker grey centres to tertials; small minority show distinct black spots on two tertials. Lesser upperwing-coverts frequently darker (traces of juvenile feathers). Tail white, but sometimes with a few black spots. Bill yellow, often with dark shading near tip and base and dark cutting edges. Legs dark, in general paler brown-tinged than in adults, and frequently with paler tarsus.

Some indistinguishable from adults; most constant features being dark pattern to P5 and dark patches on alula/primary coverts.

Second-summer (Mar–Sep) similar to adult but, before moult, from midsummer shows wing pattern of second-winter. May have faint grey shading to mid-crown and hindneck.

Third-winter/summer as adult; birds with faint dark shaft-streaks on primary coverts and dark tail-spots could be second-winters (Il'icev & Zubakov 1990).

Aberrants Juveniles with complete blackish upperwing-coverts recorded (K. Mullarney *in litt.*, pers. obs.). Juvenile with restricted black coverts much rarer, in extreme cases lacking dark covert-bar (two among 20,000 Denmark, autumn and winter – pers. obs. cited in Grant 1986b).

Adults with orange-red, rarely bright red legs rare but regular in N Atlantic (Meininger 1977, Grant 1986b, Hammer 1986, Robinson 1991, J.-K. Jensen, H. J. Lehto, R. Strack, L. Strandgaard and P. Yésou *in litt.*). Probably never scarlet-red as in Red-legged Kittiwake.

A leucistic second-winter bird all white, with only faint grey wash to primary tips, faint grey ear-spot, greyish-yellow bill with faint dark tip and pale flesh legs (Stone 1984, K. Mullarney *in litt.*). Three leucistic birds (skins in UZM) had very pale grey upperparts. Of other leucistic specimens, an adult shows pale brown wing-tip (P6 all-white). A first-winter showed very pale grey carpal bar, outer primaries and tail-bar. Another first-winter bird white with faint grey wash to scapulars and tail-bar, coloured as adult Glaucous Gull. Bare parts probably paler than usual, although difficult to see in skins. One first-winter, however, showed dark tip to pale bill.

Also recorded is a possibly melanistic bird with blackish plumage except for a uniform grey patch in centre of each wing, a dirty-white tail and normal bare parts. Another melanistic silvery-grey bird (similar to dark morph Northern Fulmar *Fulmarus glacialis*, but with white wing-bend) has been seen (King 1988).

Dwarf specimen (NNH 3428), in mm: first-winter female 21.2 has wing 268, bill 31.6, bill depth at gonys 8.3, bill depth at base of bill 10.3, gonys length 10, tarsus 29.0.

GEOGRAPHICAL VARIATION Moderate. Two subspecies.

R. t. tridactyla (Atlantic, W Europe and N Russia to Taimyr) described.

R. t. pollicaris (N Pacific, Bering Sea and S to Japan) larger and darker than nominate. Populations from islands N of NE Siberia said to be intermediates (Il'icev

& Zubakin 1990), combining upperwing pattern of *pollicaris* with coloration of nominate. More research needed. **Adult** has broader black primary tips, covering both outer and inner webs: 67–90mm on P9–10, 47–75mm on P8, 32–60mm on P7 and 15–26mm black subterminal spot on P6. P5 in 70% with black subterminal markings, often as isolated spots on both webs, but sometimes restricted to outer web. Unlike adult nominate often shows black subterminal markings on P4. Inner webs to primaries darker grey than nominate, creating less three-toned upperwing. Mantle colour as nominate or slightly darker (Kodak Grey Scale (6)6.5–8). **Adult summer** as nominate; **adult winter** generally has blacker and broader ear-spot, often continuing along sides of neck to extend over hindneck to mid-crown, forming an extensive blackish-grey area. In some, dark markings on ear-spot and hindcrown isolated from dark hindneck-bar, and some show as restricted dark markings as nominate. Hind toe longer and generally better developed than in nominate.

Complete moult into winter plumage later than in nominate, but timing rather variable, generally earliest in Alaska (where timing of moult similar to nominate), latest in Kamchatka and NE Siberia. Most moult P1–2 late Jun. Generally P2–4(7) renewed Aug, but some have not started any moult by mid-Aug (St Paul, Pribilofs, skins in LACM). Most reach P5–9 Sep–Oct. Advanced birds complete primary moult late Aug, but normally much later; many NE populations have only reached P5–7 Jan, P6–7 Mar–Apr, P10 mid-May (skins in MCZ, USNM). Sometimes show winter head mid-Aug. Partial moult to summer plumage in Apr.

Juvenile differs from nominate in much broader, darker head-markings with complete sooty-black bar from ear to ear merging into greyer crown. 45–60mm black neck-boa often reaches hindneck and upper mantle as large irregular blackish spots; may be retained in first-summer. Median coverts blacker, forming even more conspicuous black W on upperwing. Uppertail-coverts often dark-barred (absent or at most very faint in nominate). In **first-winter** (from late Oct) neck-bar sometimes similar to nominate. Seems to resist sun-bleach and wear better than nominate, as plumage in much better condition in first-summer, when some show grey streaks on crown and solid dark-grey neck-boa on hindneck.

Moult to second-winter later than nominate: P1–4 late May–late Jun, P5–8 Jun–Jul, P6–9 late Aug–late Sep, P10 early Oct. One had renewed P1–3 late Mar (Il'icev & Zubakov 1990). Tail Jul, often starting T2 and 6 simultaneously; tail may be renewed by late Jul.

Subsequent moult on average later than in nominate. Shows winter head from late Aug.

DISTRIBUTION AND MIGRATION

Population (both races) 6–7 million pairs; globally by far the most abundant gull. Breeds in colonies of >100,000 pairs on high sea-cliffs with narrow ledges, nominate locally on buildings, flat rocks and sandy sites up to 20km inland. Otherwise pelagic, but during moult locally in flocks of thousands on sandy beaches. Takes fish, invertebrates and small marine animals.

Tridactyla (in pairs): Greenland 100,000–200,000 (mainly W Greenland); 300,000 arctic Canada–New England; increasing up to 1990. Old World population increased steadily 1900–1970s, since then stable. European population 2.5–3.5 million mid-1990s: main population Great Britain 500,000; Norway 600,000; Faeroe Islands 300,000; Iceland 630,000; Spitsbergen 300,000; Bear Island 200,000; European Russia 60,000–70,000 (of which 45,000 Murmansk Coast). Increased Great Britain up to 1980 (annual growth rate 2% 1969–1979). France 5,680 1997 (785 in 1970). In Germany colony on Heligoland re-established 1938, in 1981 2,650. Denmark 540–600 (four colonies N Jutland; first bred 1941). Sweden 25–34 pairs Nidingen, Bohuslän. Recent decrease Faeroe Islands and Iceland; increase Norway. Extension of breeding range S in early 1970s to Portugal (15 1978) and Spain (200–210 1980; first bred 1975) (Møller 1978, Glutz von Blotzheim & Bauer 1982, Cramp & Simmons 1983, Bercena *et al.* 1984, Brown & Nettleship 1984, Asbirk 1988, Chapdelaine & Brosseau 1989, Risberg 1990, Lloyd *et al.* 1991, Malling Olsen 1992, del Hoyo *et al.* 1996, Gardarsson 1996, Hagemeijer & Blair 1997).

Disperse from colonies to sea Jul–Aug (adults first), mostly gathering at upwellings by continental shelf and at rich fish banks. Several thousands moult along Danish W coast from Jul, mainly Aug–Sep. Generally, northernmost population winters to N, southern population moves further S. Greenland birds remain in Davis Strait into Oct–Nov before heading for main wintering areas in Atlantic between 65–40°N (few recoveries from Europe), where mainly offshore; 2,500 Pointe-au-Rére, Quebec, 11 January 1987 exceptional. Also in W Atlantic, between 65–40°N. Returns to breeding sites Jan–early Mar in S part of breeding range, Mar–Apr in Arctic breeding sites.

Many young birds disperse WSW from Barents and Norwegian Seas to NW Atlantic (large gatherings around Nova Scotia) W to Greenland, Davis Strait and Newfoundland, where gatherings up to 25,000. Sometimes large numbers further S, especially following gales. Rare in other parts of C and S USA.

Most of British population reaches the Atlantic by moving N around Scotland, e.g. 80,000 Aberdeen 29 October 1969. Birds move S slowly to Bay of Biscay, to a lesser degree coasts off NW Africa S to Mauritania (where up to 100 daily Dec, Cape Blanc to St Louis, Senegal). Most recoveries of British birds in Bay of Biscay Oct–Nov, where joining populations from N Norway. Main wintering ground Sargasso Sea to the Azores (Coulson 1966, Glutz von Blotzheim & Bauer 1982, Cramp & Simmons 1983, Hazevoet 1985, *Amer. Birds* 41: 258).

European population normally well offshore, but large movements along coasts following gales. Up to 1 million winter around Iceland. Along North Sea coasts tens of thousands, mainly (Sep)Oct–Jan (max. day-counts 15,000 Kattegat, 35,500 Danish NW Coast, 11,000 Netherlands and 13,165 N France). Hundreds of thousands gather North Sea and Skagerrak following breeding season, e.g. >100,000 late autumn Netherlands and max. 315,000 Denmark, mostly well offshore in Skagerrak and North Sea Aug–Nov. Adults dominate, but in winter sometimes up to 40% first-years. Small migration

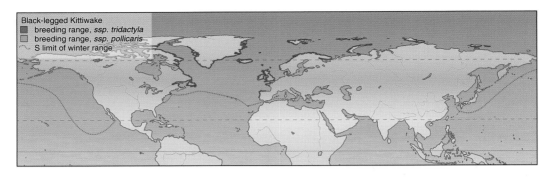

of mainly first-years from White Sea towards Baltic; max. 83 (80 juv.) 21 October 1990 Söderarm, Uppland, must have arrived following land-crossing from White Sea; influxes also noted after strong westerlies in Baltic E to Finland. In C Europe flocks up to 45 recorded inland Germany Feb. Regular but scarce, Mediterranean and Adriatic Sea; scattered records further S and E to Israel and Black Sea (Sutter 1953, Pulliainen 1962, Glutz von Blotzheim & Bauer 1982, Risberg 1990, Malling Olsen 1992, Breife *et al.* 1993, Jensen 1993, Shirihai 1996b, Portier 1999, Bijlsma *et al.* 2001, pers. obs.).

In general, dispersal most marked during immaturity, as indicated by British birds from all directions away from ringing sites: mean recovery distances 1,200km in first autumn, 2,100km in second and 2,600km in third; only 800 km in fourth year and older. Many European and Icelandic first- and second-years (fewer Canadian) summer in Greenland. During immaturity often summers within winter range. Ringed British birds recovered E to E Mediterranean and Ukraine. Two Novaya Zemliya first-years recovered Kamchatka (Glutz von Blotzheim & Bauer 1982, Cramp & Simmons 1983, Lyngs 2003).

Vagrant tropical African coastline S to S Africa, Gulf of Mexico, West Indies, Surinam, S Mediterranean, N Red Sea, Oman, UAE, Black and Caspian Seas, Baluchistan, Kirgizia, Mongolia, India, Hong Kong. In N America has reached Michigan (Glutz von Blotzheim & Bauer 1982, Cramp & Simmons 1983, Bundy 1986, Shirihai 1996b).

Pollicaris: E Kamchatka 1.6 million pairs, Alaska 1,250,000 pairs (but only 650,000 1990s, following Exxon Valdez oil spill 1989). Winters S to California

and Japan, rarely N to Alaska. Vagrant Gulf of Mexico, Peru, Hawaii, Korea and Hong Kong (Glutz von Blotzheim & Bauer 1982, Cramp & Simmons 1983, Haase 1993, del Hoyo *et al.* 1996).

MEASUREMENTS Lengths in mm; weights in g. Own data. *Tridactyla* from skins in NNH, UZM, ZMA. N Atlantic, W Europe. First-years from mid-Aug, when fully grown. *Pollicaris* from skins in AMNH, LACM, MCZ, MVZ, NHM, NRK, USNM, UZM. Alaska, Aleutians, Pribilof Islands, Sakhalin, W USA, Hawaii. Adult May–Jun, Juv. Aug–Sep.

WING

R. t. tridactyla

Adult male	297–332 (314.0)	93
Adult female	279–328 (307.5)	97
First-year male	290–322 (307.8)	60
First-year female	289–322 (300.6)	38

Note *Juvenile wing down to 270 late Jul–early Aug.*

R. t. pollicaris

Adult male	301–346 (325.8)	79
Adult female	300–341 (320.0)	72
First-year male	294–343 (315.0)	27
First-year female	284–330 (310.1)	27

FORK (difference between T1 and T6)

Adult male	3–15 (7.3)	90
Adult female	3–17 (7.7)	80
First-year male	8–18 (12.7)	47
First-year female	8–20 (12.6)	38

BLACK-LEGGED KITTIWAKE Three-year gull. Medium-sized gull, in size similar to Common Gull, but with fuller head, more pointed wings and short dark legs. Breeds in enormous colonies on cliffs in northern oceans, rest of year mainly pelagic. Flies with stiffer, quicker wingbeats than Common, in hard winds with much shearwatering.

Adult has grey inner wing, becoming slightly paler on outer wing; shows all-black, 'dipped-in-ink' wing-tip. Legs normally blackish. Bill yellow. Head in **summer** (Apr–Sep) white, in **winter** grey-shaded with dark ear-spot.

Juvenile grey, black and white with prominent black W on upperwing contrasting with greyish-white trailing edge to inner wing. Tail slightly forked, white with black bar. Head white with prominent black ear-spot and black hind-collar.

First-winter (Oct–May) as juvenile, but black hind-collar sometimes lost; bill bicoloured from spring. Often very worn on especially secondaries and tail in spring; black tail-bar then reduced to spots.

Second-year as adult, but generally with more solid black on wing-tip and sometimes dark-patterned tertials and primary coverts. Bill often less clean with dark tinge to tip and cutting edges.

570

Note R. t. tridactyla and *pollicaris* identical in this respect.

BILL

R. t. tridactyla

Adult male	30.9–41.6 (35.3)	111
Adult female	30.5–37.7 (34.0)	90
First-year male	28.8–38.7 (34.3)	61
First-year female	27.7–36.5 (32.9)	41

Note Bill down to 27.0 in juveniles into early Aug. One first-winter male with bill 42.2 omitted from the sample.

R. t. pollicaris

Adult male	35.6–44.1 (38.6)	90
Adult female	32.0–42.4 (37.9)	74
First-year male	34.2–43.0 (37.9)	27
First-year female	30.0–40.0 (36.2)	27

BILL DEPTH AT BASE OF BILL

R. t. tridactyla

Adult male	12.0–15.3 (13.2)	101
Adult female	10.6–14.4 (12.6)	85
First-year male	10.0–14.4 (12.1)	58
First-year female	9.0–12.8 (11.0)	39

R. t. pollicaris

Adult male	10.6–15.9 (14.1)	90
Adult female	10.5–15.1 (13.6)	73
First-year male	9.0–14.3 (12.8)	27
First-year female	8.4–14.2 (11.9)	27

BILL DEPTH AT GONYS

R. t. tridactyla

Adult male	9.5–12.3 (10.8)	101
Adult female	8.5–12.0 (10.4)	86
First-year male	8.5–11.0 (9.8)	59
First-year female	8.0–10.4 (9.2)	38

R. t. pollicaris

Adult male	10.1–13.4 (11.5)	90
Adult female	9.9–12.7 (11.0)	73
First-year male	9.0–11.8 (10.0)	27
First-year female	8.6–11.2 (9.7)	27

GONYS LENGTH

R. t. tridactyla

Adult male	10.1–13.8 (12.3)	100
Adult female	10.0–14.4 (12.1)	83
First-year male	8.9–13.3 (11.7)	58
First-year female	8.9–13.8 (11.1)	39

Note Juveniles with <10mm found into early Sep (early Oct). Gonys-angle best developed in males.

R. t. pollicaris

Adult male	11.2–16.8 (13.4)	90
Adult female	10.3–16.4 (12.9)	74
First-year male	9.7–14.5 (12.5)	27
First-year female	8.5–13.4 (11.6)	27

TARSUS

R. t. tridactyla

Adult male	29.8–36.9 (32.1)	110
Adult female	28.8–34.4 (31.4)	86
First-year male	30.1–36.0 (32.6)	57
First-year female	28.4–32.8 (31.1)	36

R. t. pollicaris

Adult male	31.6–39.2 (35.3)	90
Adult female	31.0–38.6 (34.2)	72
First-year male	31.5–38.3 (34.3)	27
First-year female	30.7–36.9 (33.8)	27

Weight *R. t. tridactyla*: Adult breeding: male 305–512, female 305–525. Birds washed ashore (Netherlands) adult: male 230–424, female 220–397. Juvenile/first-winter 220–400 (Cramp & Simmons 1983, Hario 1986, skins in UZM, ZMA). *R. t. pollicaris*: Alaska adult: male 429–497, female 370–532, first-winter females 312–418, first-summer 383. Emaciated adult female 250 (skins in LACM, MVZ, USNM, Dec–Jul).

Black-legged Kittiwake *Rissa tridactyla*. Photos refer to ssp. *tridactyla* unless otherwise stated. **795. Juvenile** (see page 571). Note black hind-collar bar, ear-spot and extensive black on wing-coverts. IJmuiden, Netherlands. 13 Aug. 1987. *Arnoud B. van den Berg.* **796. Juvenile/1st-winter.** Large white head is in good contrast to black hind-collar. This species seemingly retains most of juvenile plumage in 1st-winter, as indicated by pale-edged, grey mantle and scapulars, identical to juvenile in photo 795. Gilleleje, Denmark. 23 Jan 1993. *Klaus Malling Olsen.* **797. Juvenile /1st-winter.** More advanced bird, having moulted hindneck and parts of crown; greyer than in 796. IJmuiden, Netherlands. Jan 1979. *René Pop.* **798. Juvenile/1st-winter.** Note diagnostic combination of broad black W on upperwing, black hind-collar bar and white crown. Gilleleje, Denmark. 23 Jan 1993. *Klaus Malling Olsen.* **799. 1st-summer**. With wear, black W on upperwing may bleach and thus appear less distinct. Many 1st-summers - between May and Sep - are extremely worn, especially on secondaries and tail, which may lose black bar. Hirtshals, North Jutland, Denmark. 19 May 1998. *Klaus Malling Olsen.* **800. 2nd-winter**. Similar to adult, but note traces of dark along cutting-edge of bill and a few dark-centred coverts. Gilleleje, Denmark. 23 Jan 1993. *Klaus Malling Olsen.* **801. Adult winter** with reddish legs. Generally regarded as black-legged, this species may - especially in younger ages - show paler legs, mainly brownish, but sometimes reddish. In such cases, the red coloration normally has an orange tinge, and legs are never as bright red as in Red-legged Kittiwake, which see. Brouwersdam, Netherlands. Jan 1985. *René Pop.* **802. Adult summer**. Breeds in enormous colonies on sea-cliffs. Note complete, but narrow black wing-tip. Stora Ekkerøy, Finnmark, Norway. Jun. *Hanne & Jens Eriksen.*

798

800

801

802

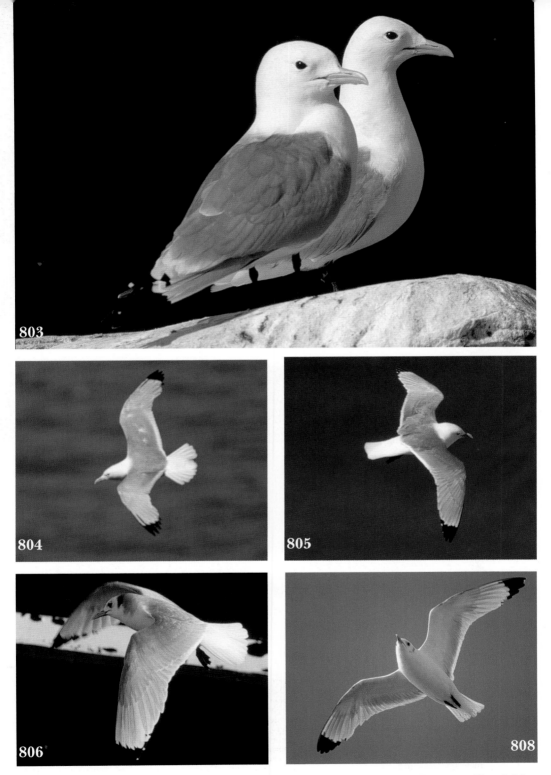

803

804

805

806

808

Black-legged Kittiwake *Rissa tridactyla*. Photos refer to ssp. *tridactyla* unless otherwise stated. **803. Adult summer**. Short dark legs and complete black wing-tip differ from Common Gull. Bulbjerg, Denmark. Jun. *Hanne & Jens Eriksen*. **804. 2nd-summer**. Dark streaking in outer primaries indicates this age. Newfoundland, Canada. 9 Jul 1997. *Bruce Mactavish*. ➡

805. Adult summer. Note bull-necked appearance. Upperwing appears slightly tricoloured with grey inner wing, paler outer wing and complete, dipped-in-ink wing-tip. Bulbjerg, Denmark. 13 May 1995. *Klaus Malling Olsen*. **806. Adult winter**. Note how black in wing-tip may disappear against dark background, creating impression of shorter and rounder wing. Against pale background, black wing-tip conspicuous and enhanced by translucence of primaries. This individual shows the typical winter-head with dark ear-spot and grey tinge rather than streaking on hindneck. Gilleleje, Denmark. 23 Jan 1993. *Klaus Malling Olsen*. **807. Adult summer**. Note black, 'dipped-in-ink' wing-tip and dark legs. Bulbjerg, Denmark. Jun. *Hanne & Jens Eriksen*. **808. Adult summer** ssp. *pollicaris*. Although difficult to discern here, the Pacific ssp. generally shows more extensive black in wing-tip. Bering Strait, NE Russia. Jun. *Hanne & Jens Eriksen*. **809. 1st-summer, adult summer and probably 2nd-summer** ssp. *pollicaris*. Note darker upperparts than in *tridactyla*. Right-hand bird shows the typical very extensive and almost black hindneck pattern of this ssp. Homer, Alaska. Aug 1998. *R. J. Lowe*. **810. Adult moulting into winter**, ssp. *pollicaris*. Generally stronger-billed than *tridactyla*. Choshi, Japan. 11 Nov 1999. *Jon R. King*. **811. Adult moulting into winter**, ssp. *pollicaris*. Note almost sooty-black ear-spot and hindneck. Generally moults later than *tridactyla*; this bird grows P7 at a time when most *tridactyla* have almost finished primary moult. Choshi, Japan. 16 Nov 1999. *Jon R. King*.

IDENTIFICATION Length 35–40cm, wingspan 84–92cm. Red-legged Kittiwake is endemic to Bering Sea and the Aleutians. It is similar to Black-legged Kittiwake, but slightly smaller. Compared to Black-legged it shows larger, squarer head with steeper forehead and often flatter crown. The eyes are larger and the bill shorter and blunter with more strongly hooked tip. The wings are longer and slenderer with narrower, more pointed hand. The tail is slightly shorter, resulting in a very long wing-projection in settled birds. The slightly shorter legs are red. Both wing-surfaces are darker.
Flight similar to Black-legged, but sometimes with faster wingbeats and gliding on even more angled wings (Kaufman 1989). Outside breeding season generally more pelagic than Black-legged Kittiwake.
Adult has more uniform, slightly darker grey upperwing with more conspicuous white trailing edge than Black-legged (intermediate between Black-legged Kittiwake and Common Gull) – a difference surprisingly easy to see even at long range. Black wing-tip broader and less clear-cut against grey primary bases, lacking paler silvery-grey of Black-legged (but weaker in latter's race *pollicaris*, with which range overlaps). The leading edge to outer wing is black, unlike Black-legged also including marginal coverts. From below, primaries greyish and much darker than in Black-legged (lacking its translucency) and contrasts well with paler inner wing. When settled, white tertial crescents are most obvious against dark grey upperparts. The legs are scarlet, strong enough to create pinkish hue to white belly.
Note that very rarely Black-legged Kittiwake has reddish legs, but often with an orange tinge lacking in Red-legged, and probably never as bright scarlet as in Red-legged.
In **summer** head is white, but in **winter** it shows dusky-grey eye-crescents, ear-spot and nape, often as a prominent black crescent on ear-coverts, and sometimes a complete grey hindneck-bar. Crown generally whiter than in Black-legged.
Juvenile is the only juvenile gull with an all-white tail. It is rather similar to adult, with head-markings as in adult winter. Upperparts dark grey with black outer 4–5 primaries, primary coverts and alula, and contrasting white triangle at trailing edge of wing, created by white inner primaries and secondaries and bearing some resemblance to wing-markings of smaller, neater Sabine's or even Ross's Gull. White trailing edge is broader than in adult; dark hindneck-bar compounds impression of Sabine's, but latter is smaller with larger, fuller wings and smaller head. Underwing-coverts are pale grey. Bill is black; legs blackish to dusky-brown.
First-winter similar to juvenile, but dark hind-collar often reduced to darker spots or elongated dark spot on ear-coverts.
First-summer has white head and grey hindneck. Juvenile wing and tail fades, these parts being retained well into May. Bill-base yellow. Legs brownish-yellow.

Second-winter similar to adult, but often with dark markings on primary coverts, alula and some lesser coverts, broader black wing-tip markings (including outer webs of three outer primaries) and ofter broader white trailing edge to wing.

VOICE Higher-pitched than in Black-legged Kittiwake; a high, falsetto squeal *suWEEEr*, repeated (Sibley 2000).

MOULT (skins in LACM, NHM, USNM) **Adult** moult to **winter plumage** complete Jul–Nov; timing similar to Black-legged Kittiwake race *pollicaris*. P1–2(3) Jul, P3–5 Sep, P9–10 Nov; a weakened bird from California had active moult on P9–10 mid-Mar. Head and body mid-Aug–Sep.
Moult to **adult summer** similar to Black-legged Kittiwake race *pollicaris*.
Juvenile moult to **first-winter** partial Aug–Oct, including head and body; sometimes restricted to hindneck (Il'icev & Zubakin 1990).
Moult to **first-summer** very limited (or absent) on head and body Apr–late May; could be regarded as first steps of complete moult into **second-winter** Apr–Sep, starting with body and P1 late Apr; by late May up to P4 has been renewed, by late Jul P6, by mid-Aug P7–8 and at least 50% of coverts and secondaries renewed; P9–10 early Sep. Lesser coverts moulted after median coverts and greater coverts. Tail Jul–Aug.

DESCRIPTION
Adult Upperparts dark grey (Kodak Grey Scale (7)8–9.5), primaries dark grey with black tips to P6–10. P9–10 have black outer web (sometimes P10 only); black tip to outer web of P10 covers 60–85mm, on P9 60–80mm (sometimes with sooty-grey base to outer web); P8 has 55–65mm black outer and 45–53mm black inner web. P7 has 35–50mm black outer and 30–40mm black inner web. P6 has 16–30mm black spot on both webs, and narrow white tongue on inner web. P5 has 5–20mm black subterminal spot on outer web, sometimes including inner web and tip, but in most as isolated dark spot. P1–9 have 2–6mm white to pale grey tips. Secondaries grey with white tips, creating distinct white trailing edge to inner wing. White scapular crescents 15–22mm. Underwing-coverts pale grey, marginal coverts and primary coverts darker grey, especially at tips, creating faint grey crescents. Tail white; sometimes with faint brown wash (*fide* Il'icev & Zubakin 1990, but not supported by skin studies). Bill yellow; iris blackish; orbital ring red; legs and feet bright red to scarlet.
Adult summer (Mar–Aug) Head and underbody white, rarely with faint grey cast to crown. Orbital ring, gape and mouth red. Bill yellow to lemon-yellow, generally colder yellow than in Black-legged Kittiwake.
Adult winter (Sep–Apr) Similar to adult summer, but head with dark ear-coverts (sometimes as elongated crescent) to hindneck, merging into grey mottling on

crown, blackish eye-crescents and greyish shading to hindneck. Orbital ring and gape duller. Bill greenish-yellow.

Juvenile (fledging–Sep) Head similar to adult winter, but with darker half-collar and ear-coverts (less contrasting than in juvenile Black-legged Kittiwake). Crown and hindneck with indistinct dark spotting. Upperparts dark grey with narrow pale fringes to upper lesser and median coverts. P(6)7–10, outer primary coverts and alula black. P4 with grey outer web, P5–6 with black subterminal spot near tip. P1–4 white, often with pale grey tips and inner webs, broadest on P1–2, together with white secondaries forming white triangular trailing edge to inner wing, similar to Sabine's Gull. In some, secondary shafts brown (Il'icev & Zubakin 1990). Underwing and axillaries greyish-white, except for darker grey outer primaries and primary coverts. Underbody, uppertail-coverts and tail white. Bill blackish to blackish-brown. Legs blackish-brown to medium brown.

First-winter (Aug–May) similar to juvenile, but head greyish-washed with fainter and narrower grey hindneck and weaker ear-spot; black half-collar reduced or lacking.

First-summer (Mar–Sep) similar to first-winter, but worn primaries fade to greyish-brown. Head white with grey hindneck and sometimes grey spots on crown and ear-coverts. Bill brownish-yellow to yellow; in some similar to adult, but often with darker tip and cutting edges. Legs brownish-yellow to dark brown, sometimes red.

Second-winter (Aug–Apr) similar to adult winter, but generally with broader, fuller black wing-tip; P9–10 often all dark, P8 with solid black outer web. Some dark-centred upper primary coverts, alula and lesser coverts. White trailing edge to inner wing and P1–5 often broader. Underwing often with dark markings on primary and marginal coverts. May show greyish cast to sides of head (Il'icev & Zubakin 1990). Legs yellowish-orange.

Second-summer (Mar–Sep) similar to adult summer, but head greyish-tinged and grey ear-spot often present. Before moult into adult-like third-winter shows second-winter characters described above.

Third-winter (Sep–Apr) as adult; birds with dark shaft-streak or outer web of outer primary coverts probably this age.

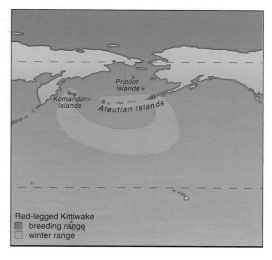

Red-legged Kittiwake
breeding range
winter range

POPULATION AND MIGRATION Population 100,000 pairs. Endemic Bering Sea and Aleutians. Breeds locally on vertical sea-cliffs on remote islands, often with Black-legged Kittiwake race *pollicaris*.

Breeds only in 6–7 colonies. Main population St George Island, Pribilofs (57,000 pairs mid-1990s; formerly 220,000). Komandor Islands population increased from 5,000 pairs 1978 to 17,000 1992. Buldir Island 6,600 pairs, 200 pairs Bogoslof Island (Beadle 1990, del Hoyo *et al.* 1996).

General decrease, considered vulnerable. Low hatching success probably caused by increased large gull population and great increase in commercial trawling causing diminishing food supply. Protecting buffer zone around nesting areas recommended (Collar *et al.* 1994, Perennou *et al.* 1994, del Hoyo *et al.* 1996).

Sedentary or slightly migratory, moving S just ahead of advancing ice or far offshore. Probably leaves Bering Sea in winter as only a few winter records here. In winter well spread N Pacific between Alaska and N Japan but rare in extralimital areas. Vagrant inland Alaska, Yukon, Nevada and S to Oregon (Sonobe 1982, Kaufman 1989).

MEASUREMENTS Lengths in mm; weights in g. Own data based on skins in LACM, MCZ, NHM, USNM, UZM. Bering Sea, Pribilof Islands, Alaska, Jul–Sep.

RED-LEGGED KITTIWAKE Three-year gull. Confined to remote islands in N Pacific; rarely observed outside breeding range. Superficially like Black-legged Kittiwake, but smaller with larger, rounder head, larger eyes, shorter bill and longer wings. All plumages rather similar, sharing pale grey underwing and white tail. Flight slightly lighter with quicker wingbeats than Black-legged. Legs never blackish.

Adult has dark grey upperwing with prominent white trailing edge; black 'dipped-in-ink' wing-tip slightly broader than in Black-legged, especially on leading edge. Legs bright coral-red. In **winter** acquires broad dark ear-spot, more elongated than in Black-legged and often extending narrowly across hindneck.

First-year rather similar to adult; the only first-year gull with all-white tail. Leading edge of wing, including primary coverts, dark brown, rest of wing as adult, but white trailing edge broader; wing pattern may resemble smaller Sabine's Gull. Bill dark. Head similar to adult winter, but with narrow dark bar across hindneck. Legs fleshy to dull red.

Second-year similar to adult, but wing-coverts with darker markings and white trailing edge broader.

PLATE 83. RED-LEGGED KITTIWAKE *Rissa brevirostris*

Range restricted to N Pacific. Resembles Black-legged Kittiwake, but with shorter, more strongly hooked bill and longer, narrower wings.

1. **Juvenile/first-winter** (Aug–Apr) Upperwing resembles Sabine's Gull with similar broad white trailing edge to wing. Lacks strong covert-markings of Black-legged and has uniform white tail.

2. **Juvenile/first-winter** Note more contrasting underwing than in Black-legged Kittiwake, with pale grey underwing-coverts, better-defined white trailing edge and darker underside of hand.

3. **First-summer** (Mar–Sep) Like Black-legged Kittiwake but with shorter, stronger-hooked bill. Most have bright red legs, but some fleshy as shown here.

4. **Second-winter** (Aug–Mar) Upperwing darker, more uniform grey than Black-legged Kittiwake with broader black wing-tip (but this matched by Pacific race *pollicaris* of Black-legged) and more distinct white trailing edge. Dark ear-spot generally blacker than in Black-legged.

5. **Adult winter** (Aug–Mar) Note darker grey underwing with longer black tip than in Black-legged.

6. **Adult winter** Upperparts darker and more uniform than in Black-legged Kittiwake. Legs are bright red. Although rare variants of Black-legged may show dull red, they probably never match the brightness of Red-legged.

7. **Adult summer** (Apr–Sep) Bright red legs often evident even at some distance.

8. **Adult summer** Note large head and very short, bright yellow bill, creating even gentler impression than in Black-legged.

1. Juvenile/first-winter

2. Juvenile/first-winter

4. Second-winter

5. Adult winter

7. Adult summer

3. First-summer

6. Adult winter

8. Adult summer

WING		
Adult male	294–329 (313.3)	37
Adult female	292–330 (311.0)	39
First-year	297–308 (302.8)	4

FORK (difference between T1 and T6)

Adult	6–13 (11.4)	65
First-year	5–11 (8.0)	4

BILL		
Adult male	27.2–31.2 (29.0)	36
Adult female	25.7–30.4 (27.8)	39
First-year	26.7–29.8 (28.3)	4

BILL DEPTH AT BASE OF BILL		
Adult male	11.4–14.0 (12.9)	37
Adult female	10.7–13.1 (12.2)	40
First-year	10.7–11.5 (11.0)	4

BILL DEPTH AT GONYS		
Adult male	9.0–12.6 (10.7)	37
Adult female	9.5–12.4 (10.3)	40
First-year	8.6–10.1 (9.4)	4

GONYS LENGTH		
Adult male	8.2–11.4 (9.6)	37
Adult female	6.8–10.8 (9.0)	40
First-year	8.3–10.5 (9.0)	4

TARSUS		
Adult male	28.2–31.7 (30.0)	37
Adult female	26.8–32.8 (29.7)	40
First-year	29.0–31.0 (29.9)	4

Weight Alaska adult (Jun–Aug) male 355–490, female 317–415 (skins in LACM, USNM).

Red-legged Kittiwake *Rissa brevirostris*. **812. Adult summer**. Note bright red legs and very short bill with hooked tip. Upperparts darker grey and black wing-tip broader than in Black-legged Kittiwake. Komander Islands. Jun. *Jan Unosson*.

Red-legged Kittiwake *Rissa brevirostris*. **813. Adult summer** with Black-legged Kittiwakes, ssp. *pollicaris*. Komander Islands. Mid-June. *Jan Unosson.* **814. Adult summers** with Black-legged Kittiwakes, ssp. *pollicaris*. St. Paul. Jun 1991. *Karel Beylevelt.*

Red-legged Kittiwake *Rissa brevirostris*. **815. Adults summer** with Black-legged Kittiwake ssp. *pollicaris*. Note dark grey upperwing and red legs. Pribilofs, Alaska, USA. Jun 1994. *Peter Scova Righini*. **816. 1st-summer**. Note black outer primaries and duller legs than adult. Komander Islands. June. *Alan Tate*. **817. Adult summer** with Black-legged Kittiwake, ssp. *pollicaris*. Red-legged is smaller with darker grey, more uniform upperwing and darker surface to primaries than Black-legged Kittiwake. St. Paul, Alaska, USA. Jul. *Paul Doherty*. **818. 1st-summer** with Black-legged Kittiwake, ssp. *pollicaris*. Note very broad white trailing edge to wing of 1st-years, compared to adult and all Black-legged Kittiwakes, as well as black outer primaries. Combined, these characters may bear reminiscence to upperwing of Sabine's Gull. Also note shorter tail and smaller size of Red-legged compared to Black-legged Kittiwake. St Paul, Alaska, USA. Jul. *Paul Doherty*. **819. 1st-summer and adult summers**. Upperwing darker grey than in Black-legged, lacking tricoloured impression of Black-legged, as outer wing is concolorous with inner wing. St. Paul, Alaska, USA. Jul. *Paul Doherty*.

582

APPENDIX OF ADDITIONAL SPECIES

Three more species, all from South America, have reached North America recently.

BAND-TAILED GULL
Larus belcheri

Photo 820

Length 48-52cm, wingspan 120cm.

Smaller than American Herring Gull and Kelp Gull. About the size of California Gull, but with head and bill shape recalling much larger gull. Notably, bill stout and heavy with bulbous tip.

Adult shows brownish-black upperwing, lacking white mirror, but with broad white trailing edge to inner wing. Ground coloration almost as dark as in Kelp Gull. Tail white with broad black band (as in adult Black-tailed Gull). Heavy bill is yellow with broad black bar and full red tip. Eyes dark. Orbital ring red. Legs yellow. In **breeding** plumage head is white. In **non-breeding** plumage it acquires full brownish hood, comparable to dark hood of 'hooded' gulls in summer plumage, but more diffusely divided from white underbody. Shows narrow pale eyelids.

Juvenile Head sooty-brown, rest of underparts greyish-brown with paler lower belly. Mantle and scapulars dark with white edges, creating scaly pattern. Greater coverts and tertials dark brown, only with faint pale patterning. Tail black, contrasting with pale rump; shows white edges to rectrices. Upperwing in flight brown with full dark outer wing, lacking pale window. Secondaries darker with white tips. Bill yellow with black tip. Legs dark brown to dull fleshy.

First-winter Similar to juvenile, but mantle and scapulars greyish-brown with narrow dark markings and dark hood, thus even more contrasting, being the darkest part of bird, and in very strong contrast to the yellow, black-tipped bill.

820. **Band-tailed Gull** *Larus belcheri*. **Immature.** Arica, Chile. May 1980. *Arnoud B. van den Berg*

Second-winter Mantle and scapulars blackish, contrasting with browner wing-coverts. Dark hood as in adult, but more diffusely offset against whitish underparts. Bill similar to adult, but red in tip less extensive.

Distribution Breeds S America with some N spread following breeding season. Vagrant Florida and California.

GREY GULL
Larus modestus

Photo 821

Length 45cm. Characteristically dark, rather small gull, normally unmistakable.

Adult Lead-grey. Flight feathers black with white trailing edge to inner wing. Lacks white tips to tertials. Tail grey with black bar and white tips. Bill and legs black. **Adult breeding** has greyish-white to white head, sharply divided from grey body. **Adult breeding** has dark greyish head, almost concolorous with rest of plumage. Shows narrow white eyelids and sometimes paler face.

Juvenile Browner than adult winter. Mantle and scapulars greyish-brown with narrow pale edges. Wing-coverts and tertials slightly darker with pale edges. Tail black, contrasting slightly with greyish-brown rump, which again is concolorous with mantle. Flight feathers blackish. Bill and legs blackish.

First-winter Similar to juvenile, but more faded, and with more uniform greyish-brown mantle and scapulars, often in some contrast to worn wing.

Second-winter Similar to adult winter, but on average browner.

Distribution Breeds Nov–Jan in harsh desert away from coast in W South America. Feeds along coast, often associated with fishing activities. Vagrant Louisiana (but record not finally accepted – Doherty & Oddie 2001).

821. Grey Gull *Larus modestus*. 1st- and 2nd-summer. Chile. May 1980. *Arnoud B. van den Berg.*

SWALLOW-TAILED GULL
Creagrus furcatus

Photos 822-823

Length 55–60cm, wingspan 124–139cm.
Unmistakable, medium-sized gull with wing pattern resembling Sabine's Gull, but much larger with more extensive white/less dark on wing.
Adult Shows tricoloured upperparts similar to

822. **Swallow-tailed Gull** *Creagrus furcatus*. **Juvenile**. Galapagos, Ecuador. 30 Jan 1981. *Arnoud B. van den Berg.*

Sabine's Gull, but grey on coverts more restricted, as greater coverts white. Most of midwing, entire trailing edge to inner wing and inner part of outer wing white, more extensively so than in Sabine's Gull; only outer primaries black, but tips to mid-primaries also black to create short black trailing edge to outer wing. Tail white, deeply forked. Bill dark with hooked, yellow tip. Eye dark. Orbital ring yellow. Legs fleshy. **Adult breeding** has dark greyish hood, somewhat diffusely divided from grey neck-sides and upper breast. **Adult non-breeding** has white head with broad dark eye-mask, enlarging the large, dark eyes.

Juvenile Head with broad dark mask, most extensive before eye; also shows dark ear-spot. Upper-parts blackish to brown with broad white feather-edges, creating strongly scaled pattern; in flight looks like an enormous 'ghostly' Sabine's Gull, but the more strongly forked tail has narrower, greyish-brown tail-bar.

First-winter Similar to juvenile, but saddle grey and coverts often strongly worn; head brownish with extensive black eye-mask as juvenile.

Distribution Confined to Galapagos Islands, breeding all year. Vagrant California (2); could be escapes or ship-assisted.

823. Swallow-tailed Gull *Creagrus furcatus*. **Adult summer**. Galapagos, Ecuador. 30 Jan 1981. *Arnoud B. van den Berg.*

ESCAPES

Furthermore, **Silver Gull** *Larus novaehollandiae* from Australia has been noted as an escape in Great Britain. It is a pale gull, when settled recalling Slender-billed Gull, but slightly larger with **adult** wing pattern resembling Brown-headed Gull. The upperparts are pale grey with black wing-tip, white mirrors on P9–10 and white bar dividing wing-tip from grey inner wing (as faint version of Grey-headed and Brown-headed Gulls). From below shows black wing-tip with white mirrors and long white tongues 'eating' into wing-tip. Head is all white, eyes pale, bill and legs red.

REFERENCES

Includes works cited and consulted

Åberg, O. (1979) Gråtrut med missbildad näbb. *Anser* 18: 209.

Abraham, D. M. & C. D. Ankney (1984) Partitioning of foraging habitat by breeding Sabine's Gulls and Arctic Terns. *Wilson Bull.* 96: 161-712.

Abrams, C. (1999) The Slender-billed Gull in Kent. *Birding World* 12: 201-204.

Acfield, D. L.& J. Miller (1987) Herring Gull showing characters of *L. a. armenicus* in Britain. *Brit. Birds* 80: 631-632.

Adolfsson, K. & Cherrug, S. (1995) Fåglar i Skåne 1994. *Anser* suppl 38.

Adriaens, P. (1996) Ringsnavelmeeuw te Kluizen in april 1994. *Dutch Birding* 18: 238-240.

Adriaens, P. & Mactavish, B. (in press). Identification of American Herring Gull. *Dutch Birding.*

Ainsley, D. G. *et al.* (1993) *Beached marine birds and mammals of the North American West Coast: a revised guide to census and identification, with supplement keys to beached sea turtles and sharks.* PRBO Int. Biol. Res., California.

Åkerman, J. (1986) Dvärgmåsen *Larus minutus* på Öland. *Calidris* 15: 25-42.

Albrecht, J. S. M. (1986a) Herring Gulls nesting on rooftops in Istanbul. *OSME Bull.* 16: 14-15.

Albrecht, J. S. M. (1986b) Notes on the birds of Eregli, Turkey 1976–1978. *Sandgrouse* 8: 74-92.

Albrektsson, T. & R. Berndtsson (1965) Amerikansk skrattmås *Larus atricilla* observerad i Göteborgs fiskehamn. *Vår Fågelvärld* 24: 289-293.

Alder, L. & C. M. James (1950) Bonaparte's Gull in Sussex. *Brit. Birds* 43: 134-135.

Ålind, P. (1986) Dags för...Långnäbbad mås. *Calidris* 15: 47-49.

Allaine, D. & J. D. Lebreton (1990) The influence of age and sex on wing-tip pattern in adult Black-headed Gull *Larus ridibundus. Ibis* 132: 560-567.

Aloussy, O. *et al.* (1982) Une Mouette de Sabine à Genève. *Nos Oiseaux* 36: 241.

Alström, P. (1981) Tärnmås eller tretåig mås – förväxlingsrisk! *Vår Fågelvärld* 40: 116-117.

Alström, P. (1984) Sabine's Gulls in winter in Sweden. *Brit. Birds* 77: 122.

Alström, P. (1993) Fältbestämning av trädmås. *Vår Fågelvärld* 53: 39-40.

Alvarez, G. (1992) Conservation programme for Audouin's Gull in the Chafarinas Islands. *Avocetta* 16: 63-66.

Alvarez, G. (1994) Ecología y situación de la Gaviota de Audouin en España. *Quercus* 100: 4-11.

Anderson, D. A. (1978) A Franklin's Gull from the Marshall Islands. *Micronesica* 14: 361-362.

Andersson, R., K. Nilsson & H. Hirsimäki (1993) Trädmås på Getterön 1 februari 1990. *Vår Fågelvärld* 53: 38.

Andresen, K. & L. Thomas (1986) The moult of Glaucous Gull *Larus hyperboreus* and Iceland Gull *Larus glaucoides* in Disko, Greenland. *Bird Study* 33: 49-50.

Andrews, I. J. (1995) *The birds of the Hashemite Kingdom of Jordan.* Privately published (I. J. Andrews).

Andrews, I. J., F. Khoury & H. Shirihai (1999) Jordan Bird Report 1995–97. *Sandgrouse* 21: 10-35.

Andrle, J. F. (1969) "Thayer's" Gull in the Niagara Frontier Region. *Auk* 86:106-109.

Andrle, R. F. (1972) Another probable hybrid of *Larus marinus* and *L. argentatus. Auk* 89: 669-671.

AOU (1998) *Check-list of North American birds.* Seventh edition. American Ornithologists' Union, Washington, D.C.

Appleby, R. H. & D. J. Britton (1979) Mediterranean Gulls in Yorkshire. *Naturalist* 104: 135-143.

Aquilar, J. S., A. Monboilliu & A. M. Paterson, eds. (1993) *Status and conservation of seabirds: ecogeography and Mediterranean action plan.* Madrid.

Argeloo, M. (1999) Ivoormeeuw langs Nederlandse en Duitse kust in mei–juni 1997. *Dutch Birding* 20: 275-278.

Arinder, M., ed. (2001) *Fåglar i Skåne 2000.* Skånes ornitologiska Förening, Lund.

Armstrong, R. H. (1980) *A guide to the birds of Alaska.* Alaska Northwest Publishing Company, Anchorage.

Artyukhin, Yu. B. & Burkanov, V. N. 1999. Morskie ptitsy i mlekopitayushchie Dal' nego Vostoka Rossii: polevoy opredelitel'. AST Publ., Moscow.

Asbirk, S. (1988) Ynglebestanden af Ride *Rissa tridactyla* i Danmark 1977–87. *Dansk Orn. Foren. Tidsskr.* 82: 133-134.

Ash, J. S. (1988) Some observations in South Yemen in 1984 and a selected bibliography of the region. *Sandgrouse* 10: 85-90.

Ashford, R. (1986) A mystery gull at Malindi. *East Afr. Nat. Hist. Soc. Bull.* 16: 7.

Asker, S. (1984) Rosenmås *Rhodostethia rosea* för första gången anträffad i Sverige. *Vår Fågelvärld* 43: 189-192.

Aspinall, S. J., J. H. Taverner & E. J. Wiseman (1993) History of Black-headed Gull colonies in Hampshire and neighbouring counties. *Brit. Birds* 86: 103-114.

Attila, S. (1998) A fecskesirály (*Larus sabini*) újabb előfordulása Magyarországon. *Túzok* 3: 164-167.

Auezov, E. M. (1971) Taxonomic evaluation and systematic status of *Larus relictus. Zool. J. Acad. Sci. Moscow* 50: 235-242.

Baillon, F. (1989) New wintering records of Audouin's Gulls *Larus audouinii* Payr. in Senegambia. *Oiseau et R.F.O.* 59: 296-304.

Baillon, F. & P. J. Dubois (1992) Nearctic gull species in Senegal and the Gambia. *Dutch Birding* 14: 49-50.

Baker, K. (1993) *Identification guide to European non-passerines.* BTO Guide 24, Norfolk.

Baker, N. E. (1984) Feeding techniques of Slender-billed Gull. *OSME Bull.* 12: 6-7.

Baker, R. R. (1980) The significance of the Lesser Black-backed Gull to models of bird migration. *Bird Study* 27: 41-50.

Bakewell, D. N., G. J. Carey, D. G. Duff, J. Palfery, A. Parker & M. D. Williams (1989) Observations of Relict Gulls *Larus relictus* on passage at Beidaihe, People's Republic of China. *Forktail* 4: 77-87.

Bakker, T., R. Offereins & R. Winters (2000) Caspian Gull identification gallery. *Birding World* 13: 60-74.

Bakker, T., K. van Dijken & E. Ebels (2001) Glaucous-winged Gull at Essaouira, Morocco, in January 1995. *Dutch Birding* 23: 271-274.

Balsh, L. G. (1980a) A brief guide to the identification and status of Asian species in Alaska. *Birding* 12: 12-22.

Balsh, L. G. (1980b) Some notes on Red-legged Kittiwake identification. *Birding* 12: 78-82.

Balten, B., E. Ebels & W. Hoogendoorn (1994) Mystery photographs 54. *Dutch Birding* 16: 267.

Banks, R. C. (1986) Subspecies of the glaucous gull, *Larus hyperboreus* (Aves: Charadriiformes). *Proc. Biol. Soc. Washington* 99: 149-159.

Barlow, C., T. Wacher & T. Disley (1997) *A field guide to birds of the Gambia and Senegal.* Pica Press, Robertsbridge.

Barnes, J. A. G. (1961) The winter status of Lesser Black-backed Gull. *Bird Study* 31: 161-170.

Barrett, R. T. & O. J. Runde (1980) Growth and survival of nestling Kittiwakes *Rissa tridactyla* in Norway. *Orn. Scand.* 11: 228-235.

Barry, C. 2002. Late winter gulling in Eire - a seasonal selection. *Birding World* 15: 72-73.

Batty, C., Lowe, T. & Millington, R. 2003. Winter gull gallery: 2002/2003. *Birding World* 16: 114-125.

Barth, E. K. (1966) Mantle colour as a taxonomic feature in *Larus argentatus* and *Larus fuscus. Nytt Mag. Zool.* 13: 56-82.

Barth, E. K. (1967) Standard body measurements in *Larus argentatus, L. fuscus, L. canus* and *L. marinus. Nytt Mag. Zool.* 15: 5-34.

Barth, E. K. (1968a) Geographical variation in mantle colour, body measurements, and eggs in *Larus argentatus, L. fuscus, L. canus* and *L. marinus.* Universitetsforlaget, Oslo.

Barth, E. K. (1968b) The circumpolar systematics of *Larus argentatus* and *Larus fuscus* with special reference to the Norwegian populations. *Nytt Mag. Zool.* 15 Suppl 1: 1-50.

Barth, E. K. (1975) Taxonomy of *Larus argentatus* and *Larus fuscus* in north-western Europe. *Orn. Scand.* 6: 49-63.

Barthel, P. H. (1987) Foto-Folge 1: Schwalbenmöwe *Larus sabini. Limicola* 1: 98-101.

Barthel, P. H. (1991) Rätselvogel 23. *Limicola* 5: 131-133.

Barthel, P. H. (1994a) Die Bestimmung von Fischmöwe *Larus ichthyaetus. Limicola* 8: 64-78.

Barthel, P. H. (1994b) Rätselvogel 43. *Limicola* 8: 270-271.

Barthel, P. H. (1997) Kurzhinweise zur Bestimmung der Korallenmöwe *Larus audouinii. Limicola* 11: 285-286.

Barthel, P. H. & D. G. W. Königstedt (1993) Die Kennzeichen der Dünnschnabelmöwe *Larus genei. Limicola* 7: 165-178.

Beadle, D. (1990) The Pribilof Islands. Birding in the Bering Sea. *Birding World* 3: 202-207.

Beaman, M. (1986) Turkey: Bird Report 1976–1981. *Sandgrouse* 8: 1-41.

Beaman, M. (1994) *Palearctic birds: a checklist of the birds of Europe, North Africa and Asia north of the foothills of the Himalayas.* Harrier Publications, Stonyhurst.

Beaman, M. & S. Madge (1998) *The handbook of bird identification for Europe and the Western Palearctic.* A & C Black, London.

Beaubrun, P.-C. (1989) Status of Yellow-legged Gull (*Larus cachinnans*) in Morocco and in the Western Mediterranean. In J. S. Aquilar, X. Mobaillou & A. M. Paterson (1989) *Estatus y conservación de aves marinas.* Proc. Second Medit. Gull Symp., Calvea 21–26 March 1989. SEO/Birdlife/Medmaravis.

Beaudoin, J.-C. (1979) Une Mouette de Franklin (*Larus pipixcan*) à Angers, Maine-et-Loire: première donnée française. *Oiseau & R.F.O.* 49: 45-49.

Behle, W. K. & R. K. Selander (1953) The plumage cycle of the California Gull (*Larus californicus*) with notes on colour changes of soft parts. *Auk* 70: 239-260.

Belant, J. L. & A. Dolbeer (1993) Migration and dispersal of Laughing Gulls in the United States. *J. Field Orn.* 64: 557-565.

Bell, D. G. (1992) Hybridization and sympatry in the Western/Glaucous-winged Gull complex. Dissertation, University of California, Berkeley.

Bell, D. G. (1996) Genetic differentiation, geographic variation and hybridization in gulls of the *Larus glaucescens–occidentalis* complex. *Condor* 98: 527-546.

Bell, D. G. (1997) Hybridization and reproductive performance in gulls of the *Larus glaucescens–occidentalis* complex. *Condor* 99: 585-594.

Bengtsson, K. (1994) Dansk fann italienare i Hörte – ny art/ras för Skåne! *Anser* 33: 43-44.

Bengtsson, K. (1995) Upplevelser och upptäckter i Västafrika. *Anser* 34: 137-140.

Bengtsson, K. (1996) Udda ornitologi – bland levande och döda måsfåglar. *Anser* 35: 189-195.

Bengtsson, K. (1998) Burhållna måsfåglar – utvärdering av försök. *Vår Fågelvärld* 58: 41.

Bengtsson, K. (2001) Skrattmåsen i Skåne 2000. *Anser* 40: 15-21.

Bengtsson, K. 2003. Ålderskaraktärer för fiskmås - går det att åldersbestämma subadulta fiskmåsar? *Anser* 42: 73-92.

Bengtsson, K. & K. T. Pedersen (1998) Östliga fiskmåsars *Larus canus* uppträdande i Öresundsregionen. *Orn. Svecica* 8: 145-156.

Bent, A. C. (1921) Life histories of North American gulls and terns. *U.S. Natn. Mus. Bull.* 113.

Bentz, G. 2000. Corportement d' un jeune Goeland argenté *Larus argentatus* leucistique. *Ornithos* 7: 88-89.

Bercena, F., A. M. Teixeira & A. Bermejo (1984) Breeding seabird populations in the Atlantic sector of the Iberian peninsula. Pp.363-370 in J. P. Croxall, P. G. H. Evans & R. W. Schreiber, eds. *Status and conservation of the world's seabirds.* ICBP Techn. Publ. 2, Cambridge, UK.

van den Berg, A. B. (1983) Yellow-legged gull at IJmuiden in October 1982 and its identification. *Dutch Birding* 4: 15.

van den Berg, A. B & C. A. W. Bosman (2001) Zeldzame vogels van Nederland. *Avifauna van Nederland* 1. Second edition. GMB Uitgeverij, Haarlem.

van den Berg, A. B. & E. J. Maasen (1983) Kleine en Grote Burgermeesters te IJmuiden in winter von 1982/83. *Dutch Birding* 5: 92-98.

van den Berg, A. B. & R. Pop (1982) Laughing Gull with flame-scarlet bill and legs. *Dutch Birding* 4: 55.

van den Berg, A. B., W. Hoogendoorn & K. Mullarney (1991) Wing and tail moult in first-year Brown-headed Gulls wintering in Thailand. *Dutch Birding* 13: 58-63.

Bergman, G. (1982) Why are the wings of *Larus f. fuscus* so dark? *Orn. Fennica* 59: 77-83.

Bermejo, A. (1999) First compilation of the references of the gull complex: *Larus argentatus/smithsonianus/michahellis/cachinnans/armenicus/fuscus.* Privately published.

Berndt, R. & R. Rahne (1968) Erstnachweis der Ringschnabelmöwe (*Larus delawarensis*) in Europa. *J. Orn.* 109: 438-440.

Bertault, Y., P. J. Dubois & J.-F. Fremont (1988) Some comments on the Armenian Gull in Turkey. *OSME Bull.* 20: 20-21.

Bevanger, K. & P. G. Thingstad (1990) Decrease in some central Norwegian populations of the northern subspecies of the Lesser Black-backed Gull (*Larus fuscus fuscus*) and its possible causes. *Fauna Norv. ser. C Cinclus* 13: 19-32.

Bijlsma, R., F. Hustings & K. (C. J.) Camphuysen (2001) Algemene en schaarse vogels van Nederland. *Avifauna van Nederland* 2. GMB Uitgeverij, Haarlem.

Billett, D. & P. J. Grant (1971) Franklin's Gull in Hampshire: a species new to Britain and Ireland. *Brit. Birds* 64: 310-313.

Bjurenståhl, P. (1986) En förmodad hybrid vittrut × gråtrut vid Räfsnäs. *Fåglar i Uppland* 13: 76-79.

Blackpoel, H., L. G. Naranjo & G. D. Tessier (1984) Immature Little Gull in South America: a first record for the continent. *Amer. Birds* 38: 372-373.

Blake, E. R. (1977) *Manual of Neotropical birds* 1. University of Chicago, Chicago.

Blanchon, J.-J., P. Dubois & P. Yésou (1983) Observations de Goélands à bec cerclé *Larus delawarensis* sur le litoral atlantique français. *Alauda* 51: 148-150.

Blick, M. A. (1979) Franklin's Gull in Cleveland. *Brit. Birds* 72: 478-479.

BLIKI (1994) *Skrá yfir íslenska fugla* (2. útgáfa juni 1994). Reykjavik.

Bloch, D. & S. Sørensen (1984) *Yvirlit yvir Føroya fuglar.* Føroyar Skúlabokagrannur, Thorshavn.

Blokpoel, H. & G. D. Tessier (1986) The Ring-billed Gull in Ontario: a review of a new problem species. *Canad. Wildl. Serv. Occas. Pap.* 57: 1-34.

Blokpoel, H., P. J. Blancher & P. M. Fetterolf (1985) On the plumage of nesting Ring-billed Gulls of different ages. *J. Field Orn.* 56: 113-124.

Blomdahl, A., Breife, B. & Holmström, N. 2003. *Flight Identification of European Seabirds.* Christopher Helm, London.

Blomquist, L. (1992) Ett magnifikt dvärgmåssträck. *Vår Fågelvärld* 51: 38-39.

Blomquist, S. & M. Elander (1981) Sabine's Gull *Xema sabini,* Ross's Gull *Rhodostethia rosea* and Ivory Gull *Pagophila eburnea*–gulls in the Arctic. *Arctic* 34: 122-140 & 388.

Blume, C. A. (1961) Iagttagelser af Gråmåge og Hvidvinget Måge. *Dansk Orn. Foren. Tidsskr.* 59: 54-56.

Boertmann, D. (1994) An annotated checklist to the birds of Greenland. *Medd om Grønland. Bioscience* 38.

Boertmann, D. (2001) The Iceland Gull complex in Greenland. *Brit. Birds* 94: 547-548.

Bohlen, H. D. (1993) Melanistic Bonaparte's Gull in central Illinois. *Amer. Birds* 47: 378.

Boldreghini, P., P. L. Meininger & R. Santolini (1992) Preliminary results of ringing Mediterranean Gulls *Larus melanocephalus* breeding in the Netherlands, Belgium and Italy. *Avocetta* 16: 73-74.

Bos, E. & P. de Heer (1982) Ring-billed Gulls on Canary Islands in March 1982. *Dutch Birding* 4: 90-91.

Boulva, J. (1975) Observations d'un Goéland à bec cerclé *Larus delawarensis* en Bretagne. *Alauda* 43: 195.

Bourne, W. R. P. (1957) Manx Shearwaters, Little Gulls and other seabirds wintering off the Algerian coast. *Ibis* 99: 117-118.

Bourne, W. R. P. (1972) Large gulls with grey wing-tips. *Brit. Birds* 65: 265.

Bourne, W. R. P. (1984) The birds of Madeira in the winter. *Bocagiana* (Funchal) 76: 1-6.

Bourne, W. R. P. (1988) Ornithological observations at the sea around Arabia. *OSME Bull.* 20: 7-11.

Bourne, W. R. P. (1991) Armenian Gulls. *OSME Bull.* 26: 49-50.

Bourne, W. R. P. (1992) What gull is that? *Oman Bird News* 12: 4.

Bourne, W. R. P. (1996) The large white-headed gulls wintering around the southern coasts of Asia. *Sea Swallow* 45: 86-91.

Bourne, W. R. P. & G. Bundy (1990) Records of Brown-headed Gulls *Larus brunnicephalus* and Grey-headed Gull *L. cirrocephalus* around Arabia. *Sandgrouse* 12: 37-42.

Bourne, W. R. P. & G. Bundy (1993) Post-juvenile moult and western limit of Brown-headed Gull. *Dutch Birding* 15: 173-176.

Bourne, W. R. P. & W. F. Curtis (1986) South Atlantic bird islands. *Sea Swallow* 35: 24-34.

Bowes, A., P. C. Lack & M. R. Fletcher (1984) Wintering gulls in Britain, January 1983. *Bird Study* 31: 161-170.

Bowey, K. & B. Pollinger (1997) Aberrant tail pattern of adult Black-headed Gull. *Brit. Birds* 90: 229.

Bowey, K., P. Davidson & K. Robson (1995) Common Gull in juvenile plumage in late February. *Brit. Birds* 88: 34.

Bradley, R. (1986) The breeding biology of Audouin's Gull in the Chafarinas Islands. In Medmaravis & X. Monbailliu, eds. *Mediterranean marine avifauna*. Springer-Verlag (NATO ASI Ser G 12: 221-30), Berlin.

Bradshaw, C. (1990) Laughing Gull identification. *Birding World* 3: 417-418.

Bradshaw, C. (1993) Brown-headed Gulls in Uzbekistan in May 1985. *Dutch Birding* 15: 69-70.

Bradshaw, C. & A. Rowlands (1996) Relict Gull numbers at Beidaihe, China, in autumn 1992. *Dutch Birding* 18: 247.

Braune, B. M. (1987) Body morphometrics and molt of Bonaparte's Gull in the Quoddy region, New Brunswick, Canada. *Condor* 89: 150-157.

Brazil, M. A. (1991) *The birds of Japan*. Christopher Helm, London.

Brazil, M. A. (1992) The threatened Saunders's Gull of east Asia. *Birding World* 5: 72-74.

Breife, B. (1985) Albinistisk havstrut. *Vår Fågelvärld* 44: 285.

Breife, B. (1987) Dvärgmåsens *Larus minutus* uppträdande på Öland vintertid 1981–86. *Calidris* 16: 61-66.

Breife, B. (1993) Ung dvärgmås eller tretåig mås? *Calidris* 22: 24.

Breife, B., N. Holmström & L. Blomquist (1993) Sjöfågelboken – fältbestämnus av sträckande sjöfåglar. *Vår Fågelvärld* suppl. 18.

Brewer, A. D. & A. Salvadori (1978) Second annual report on non-game bird banding in Ontario, 1965–1970. *Ontario Bird Banding* 11: 30-99.

Britton, D. J. (1979) Identification of Bonaparte's Gull. *Brit. Birds* 72: 339-340.

Britton, D. J. (1987) Mystery photographs 121. *Brit. Birds* 80: 16-17.

Britton, P. M., ed. (1980) *Birds of East Africa: their habitat, status and distribution*. East Afr. Nat. Hist. Soc., Nairobi.

Brooke, R. K. & J. Cooper (1979) The distinctiveness of southern African *Larus dominicanus* (Aves: Laridae). *Durban Mus. Novit.* 12: 27-37.

Brooks, D. J., M. I. Evans, R. P. Martins & R. F. Porter (1987) The status of birds in North Yemen and the records of the OSME Expedition in autumn 1985. *Sandgrouse* 9: 4-66.

Brown, B. J. (1979) Franklin's Gull in Suffolk. *Brit. Birds* 72: 479-482.

Brown, R. G. B. (1967) Species isolation between the Herring Gull *Larus argentatus* and Lesser Black-backed Gull *Larus fuscus. Ibis* 109: 310-317.

Brown, R. G. B. & Nettleship, D. N. (1984) The seabirds of northeastern North America: their present status and conservation requirements. Pp.85-100 in J. P. Croxall, P. G. H. Evans & R. W. Schreiber, eds. *Status and conservation of the world's seabirds*. ICBP Techn. Publ. 2, Cambridge, UK.

Bruns, H. (1985) Weisse Möwen. *Orn. Mitt.* 37: 58-61.

Bruns, H. (1988) Zur feldornithologischen Unterscheidung unausgefarbter Heringsmöwen (*Larus fuscus*) und Mantelmöwen (*L. marinus*). *Orn. Mitt.* 40: 215-226.

Buckingham, D. L. (1998) Variation and occurrence of *intermedius* Lesser Black-backed Gull in southern England. *Brit. Birds* 91: 60-62.

Buckley, P. A. & F. G. Buckley (1984) Seabirds of the north and middle Atlantic coasts of the United States: their status and conservation. Pp.101-133 in J. P. Croxall, P. G. H. Evans & R. W. Schreiber, eds. *Status and conservation of the world's seabirds*. ICBP Techn. Publ. 2, Cambridge, UK.

Bulteel, G. (1983) Geelpootmeeuwen *Larus cachinnans michahellis*, in Vlaanderen. *Wielewaal* 49: 165-181.

Bunch, M. J. (1997) Sabinemågeinvasionen – en foreløbig status. *DOF Nyt* 2/4: 4-5.

Bundy, G. (1976) *The birds of Libya*. BOU, London.

Bundy, G. (1986) Notes on seabirds in south-eastern Arabia. *Sandgrouse* 7: 9-42.

Bundy, G. & E. Warr (1980) A check-list to the birds of the Arabian Gulf States. *Sandgrouse* 1: 4-49.

Burger, J. & R. Brownstein (1968) The status of Bonaparte's Gull in New York State. *Kingbird* 18: 9-20.

Burke, P. (1995) A probable first-winter Nelson's Gull. *Birders J.* 4: 41-44.

Burneleau, G. (1987) Remarques sur la livrée post-nuptiale des Goélands Leucophées (*Larus cachinnans*) "Adultes". *Trajhasse* 16: 29-35.

Burton, N. H. K., Musgrave, A. J., Rehfisch, M. M., Sutcliffe, A. & Waters, R. 2003. Numbers of wintering gulls in the United Kingdom, Channel Islands and Isle of Man: a review of the 1993 and previous Winter Gull Roost Surveys. *Brit. Birds* 96: 376-401.

Busuttill, S. & D. Flumm (1998) Seawatching at Ras Beirut, Lebanon, in spring 1997. *Sandgrouse* 20: 142-143.

Buturlin, S. A. (1906) The breeding-grounds of the Rosy Gull. *Ibis* 8(6): 131-139, 333-337, 661-666.

Buturlin, S.A. (1934) *Larus taimyrensis armenicus* subsp. nov. *Ibis* 13(4): 171-172.

Buturlin, S. A. & G. P. Dement'ev (1934) *Complete guide to the birds of the USSR*. All-Union Coop. Unit Publ., Moscow and Leningrad.

Buzun, V. (1993) Armenian Gull *Larus armenicus* Buturlin, 1934: Morpho-biometrical and behavioural distinctions with indication of taxonomical status. In Russian, *Russ. J. Orn.* 2: 471-490.

Buzun, V.A. (2002) Descriptive update on gull taxonomy: West Siberian Gull. *Brit. Birds*: 216-232.

Cade, M. (1982) Plumage variability of immature Common and Ring-billed Gulls. *Brit. Birds* 75: 580.

Calladine, J. (1987) The Bonaparte's Gull at Ogston. *Twitching* 1: 103-105.

Carey, G. (1993) Saunders's Gull heading for extinction? *Dutch Birding* 15: 68-69.

Carey, G. J. & P. R. Kennerley (1996) "Mew" Gull: the first record for Hong Kong and the identification and systematics of Common Gull forms in East Asia. *Hong Kong Bird Rep.* 1995: 134-149.

Carey, G. J., D. A. Diskin, V. A. Picken & P. J. Leader (1995) Systematic list. *Hong Kong Bird Rep.* 1994: 16-91.

Carlsson, L. (1991) Tretåiga måsens uppträdande på Öland. *Calidris* 20: 131-135.

Carrera, E., M.-R. Nebot & F.-X. Vila Grasa (1981) Comentaris sobre els deplacaments erràtics de la població catalana de Gavià Argentat (*Larus argentatus michahellis*). *Bull. Inst. Cat. Hist. Nat.* 47 (Sec. Zool. 4): 143-153.

Carrera, E., J. Trias, A. Bermejo, E. de Juana & J. Varela (1987) Etude biométrique des populations ibériques et nord-africaines du Goéland leucophée *Larus cachinnans*. *Oiseau et R.F.O.* 57: 32-38.

Catley, G. P. (1982) Second-winter Common Gull with prominent tail band. *Brit. Birds* 75: 88-89.

Cederroth, C. (1995) Gulfotad trut. En nygammal art i trutflockarna. *Vår Fågelvärld* 54/6-7: 14-22.

Chabrcyk, G. & J. C. Coulson (1976) Survival and recruitment in the Herring Gull. *J. Anim. Ecol.* 44: 187-203.

Chandler, R. J. (1989) Mystery photographs. Grey-headed Gull. *Brit. Birds* 82: 258-260.

Chapdelaine, G. & P. Brosseau (1989) Size and trends of Black-legged Kittiwake (*Rissa tridactyla*) populations in the Gulf of St. Lawrence (Quebec) 1975–1985. *Amer. Birds* 43: 21-24.

Chartier, B. & F. Cooke (1980) Ross's Gulls *Rhodostethia rosea* nesting at Churchill, Manitoba, Canada. *Amer. Birds* 34: 839-841.

Chown, D. J. & P. G. Akers (1989) Inland Mediterranean Gulls. *Brit. Birds* 92: 271.

Christensen, J. O. (1990) *Status of breeding populations of gulls and terns in Denmark 1988*. DOF, Copenhagen.

Christensen, K. & E. Søby (1998) Fugle i Danmark 1996. Årsrapport over observationer. *Dansk Orn. Foren. Tidsskr.* 92: 201-249.

Christensen, S. (1971) Feltbestemmelse af ung Svartbag, Sølvmåge og Sildemåge. *Feltornitologen* 13: 64-66.

Chu, P. C. (1998) A phylogeny of the gulls (Aves: Laridae) inferred from osteological and integumentary characters. *Cladistics* 14: 1-43.

Chylarecki, P. (1993b) New Herring Gull taxonomy. *Brit. Birds* 86: 316-318.

Chylarecki, P. & K. Eigenhuis (1993) Identification of *argentatus* Herring Gull. *Birding World* 6: 166-167.

Chylarecki, P. A. & A. Sikora (1991) Yellow-legged Gulls in Poland: a comment. *Dutch Birding* 13: 145-148.

Clapp, R. B. & P. A. Buckley (1984) Status and conservation of seabirds in the southeastern United States. Pp.135-155 in J. P. Croxall, P. G. H. Evans & R. W. Schreiber, eds. *Status and conservation of the world's seabirds*. ICBP Techn. Publ. 2, Cambridge, UK.

Clarke, T. (1999) Autumn 1998 on the Azores. *Birding World* 12: 205-212.

Clasper, B. (1989) Ring-billed Gull displaying to Common Gull. *Brit. Birds* 82: 446-447.

Close, D. H. (1981) The Kelp Gull in South Australia. *S. Austral. Orn.* 28: 155-156.

Clugston, D. L. (1983) Franklin's Gull in Ayrshire. *Scot. Birds* 12: 258-259.

Collar, N.J. (ed) (2001) *Threatened Birds of Asia. The Birdlife International Red Data Book*. Birdlife International, Cambridge

Collar, N. J., M. J. Crosby & A. J. Stattersfield (1994) *Birds to watch 2: the world list of threatened birds*. BirdLife International (Conserv. Ser. 4), Cambridge, UK.

Collinson, M. (2001) Genetic relationships among the different races of Herring Gull, Yellow-legged Gull and Lesser Black-backed Gull. *Brit. Birds* 94: 523-528.

Colston, P., P. Alström & I. Lewington (1992) *A field guide to the rare birds of Europe*. HarperCollins, London.

Conover, M. R. (1983) Recent changes in Ring-billed and California Gull populations in the western United States. *Wilson Bull.* 95: 362-383.

Conover, M. R. & B. C. Thompson (1984) Inland breeding by the Glaucous-winged Gull. *J. Field Orn.* 55: 380-382.

Cornell, C., K. Tutt & I. McLaren (1995) Yellow-legged Gull in Nova Scotia. *Birders J.* 4: 302-304.

Cornier, C. & G. Savard (1994b) Second-winter Slaty-backed Gull *Larus schistisagus* at Chicoutima. *Birders J.* 3: 286-288.

Cornier, C. & C. Savard (1994a) A Slaty-backed Gull at Sague-nay/Lake St. Jean. First record for Quebec. *Birders J.* 3: 54-56.

Cornwallis, L. & R. F. Porter (1982) Spring observations of the birds of North Yemen. *Sandgrouse* 4: 1-36.

Corso, A. (1999) Slender-billed Gull. *Alula* 5: 138-141.

Costa, H. & Comité Português de Raredades da SPEA (1997) Aves de ocorrência rara ou acidental em Portugal. Relatório do comité Português de raredades referente ao ano de 1995. *Pardela* 5: 1-20.

Cottaar, F. (2004) Geelpootmeeuwcomplex van IJmuiden: in hoeverre zijn Geelpootmeeuwen echte Geelpootmeeuwen? *Dutch Birding* 26: 36-42.

Cottaar, F. & K. Verbeek (1994) Geelpootmeeuw gepaard met Kleine Mantelmeeuw broedend te IJmuiden. *Dutch Birding* 16: 231-239.

Cottle, N.W. (1987) Spring moult of Kittiwake. *Brit. Birds* 80: 633-634.

Cottridge, D. & K. Vinicombe (1996) *Rare birds in Britain and Ireland: a photographic record*. HarperCollins Publishers/Birding World.

Coues, E. (1862) Revision of the gulls of North America; based upon specimens in the Museum of the Smithsonian Institution. *Proc. Acad. Nat. Sci. Philadelphia* 14: 291-312.

Coulson, J. C. (1959) The plumage and leg colour of the Kittiwake and comments on the non-breeding population. *Brit. Birds*. 52: 189-196.

Coulson, J. C. (1966) The movements of the Kittiwake. *Bird Study* 13: 107-115.

Coulson, J. C. & C. S. Thomas (1985) Changes in the biology of the Kittiwake *Rissa tridactyla*: a 31-year study of a breeding colony. *J. Anim. Ecol.* 54: 9-26.

Coulson, J. C., N. Duncan & P. Monaghan (1980) Variation in Herring Gulls. *Brit. Birds* 73: 230-231.

Coulson, J. C., N. Duncan, C. S. Thomas & P. Monaghan (1981) An age-related difference in the bill-depth of Herring Gull *Larus argentatus*. *Ibis* 123: 449-502.

Coulson, J. C., C. S. Thomas & W. Wright (1982) Variation in the wing tip pattern of the Herring Gull in Britain. *Bird Study* 29: 111-120.

Coulson, J. C., C. S. Thomas, J. E. L. Butterfield, N. Duncan, P. Monaghan & C. Shedden (1983) The use of head and bill length to sex live gulls. *Ibis* 125: 549-557.

Coulson, J. C., J. Butterfield, N. Duncan, S. Kearsey, P. Monaghan & C. Thomas (1984a) Origin and behaviour of Great Black-backed Gulls wintering in northeast England. *Brit. Birds* 77: 1-11.

Coulson, J. C., P. Monaghan, J. E. L. Butterfield, N. Duncan, K. Ensor, C. Shedden & C. Thomas (1984b) Scandinavian Herring Gulls wintering in Britain. *Orn. Scand.* 15: 79-88.

Cowley, E. (1989) Black-headed Gull in summer plumage in December. *Brit. Birds* 82: 565.

Cramp, S. & K. E. L. Simmons, eds. (1983) *The birds of the western Palearctic*, Vol. 3. Oxford University Press, Oxford.

Crawford, R. J. M., J. Cooper & P. A. Shelton (1982) Distribution, population size, breeding and conservation of the Kelp Gull in southern Africa. *Ostrich* 53: 164-177.

Crochet, P-A. (1998) Structure génétique des populations chez le Goéland leucophée, phylogéographie et phylogénie chez les laridés. Ph.D. thesis, Montpellier.

Crochet, P-A., J-D Lebreton & Bonhomme, F. (2002) Systematics of large white-headed gulls: patterns of mitochondrial DNA variation in Western Europe, *Auk* 119:603-620.

Dahlgren, L., A. Lundquist, A. Ståhl, M. Wallin & A. Waldenström (1995) Fåglar på Öland 1994. *Calidris* suppl 15.

Darefeldt, G. & B. Johansson (1994) Vänersborgsviken. Högklassig sträcklokal i inlandet. *Vår Fågelvärld* 53/4: 8-16.

Davenport, L. J. (1985) British status of northern Lesser Black-backed Gulls. *Brit. Birds* 78: 668-669.

Davies, M. (1978) Identification of hybrid or leucistic gull. *Brit. Birds* 71: 80-82.

Davies, R. H, P. G. Akers & I. F. Tew (1984) Ring-billed Gull displaying in West Glamorgan. *Brit. Birds* 77: 208.

De Benedictis, P. (1980) Gleanings from the technical literature. *Birding* 12: 74-76.

De Benedictis, P. (1987) Gleanings from the technical literature. *Birding* 19: 29-32.

De Benedictis, P. (1990) Gleanings from the technical literature. Thayer's Gull. *Birding* 22: 197-200.

De Mesel, D. (1990) Geelpootmeeuwen *Larus cachinnans michahellis*, in Belgie: een analyse van ringgegevens. *Gerfaut* 80: 25-26.

Dean, A. R. (1984) Origin and distribution of British Glaucous Gulls. *Brit. Birds* 77: 165-166.

Dean, A. R. (1987) Seasonality of Herring Gulls in the west Midlands. *Brit. Birds* 80: 632-633.

Dean, A. R. (1988) Mystery photographs. *Brit. Birds* 81: 23-25.

Dean, A. R. (1990) Mystery photographs. *Brit. Birds* 83: 561-564.

Dean, T. (1994) Yellow-legged Gull. *Birders J.* 3: 148-152.

Debruyne, R. (1982) Volwassen Kleine Mantelmeeuw met vleeskleurig roze poten. *Dutch Birding* 4: 92.

Delin, H. & L. Svensson (1988) *Photographic guide to the birds of Britain and Europe*. Hamlyn, London.

Dement'ev, G. P. (1940) *Materialy k avifaune Korjakskjoj Zeml.* Moscow.

Dement'ev, G. P. & N. A. Gladkov, eds. (1969) *The birds of the Soviet Union*, 3. Jerusalem. Israel Program for Sci. Transl.

Dennis, J. V. (1981) A summary of banded North American birds encountered in Europe. *North Amer. Bird Band.* 6: 88-96.

Dennis, J. V. (1986) European encounters of birds ringed in North America. *Dutch Birding* 8: 41-44.

Dennis, M. K. (1992) Yellow-legged Herring Gulls in Essex. *Brit. Birds* 85: 246.

Dennis, M. K. (1995) Yellow-legged Gulls along the River Thames in Essex. *Brit. Birds* 88: 8-14.

Densley, M. (1977) Ross's Gulls in Britain. *Scot. Birds* 9: 334-342.

Densley, M. (1979) Ross's Gulls in Alaska. *Brit. Birds* 72: 23-28.

Densley, M. (1991) Ross's Gulls in Siberia. *Dutch Birding* 13: 168-175.

Densley, M. (1992) Magnificent obsession. *Birds Illustrated* 1/3: 77-80.

Deutsch, A., S. Pleines, G. Sennert & K. Hubatsch (1996) Die Heringsmöwe (*Larus fuscus*) als Sommergast in Nordrhein-Westphalen. *Charadrius* 32: 206-219.

Devillers, P. (1982) *Larus canus heinei* en Belgique. *Gerfaut* 72: 107-110.

Devillers, P. (1983) Yellow-legged Herring Gulls on southern North Sea coasts. *Brit. Birds* 76: 91-92.

Devillers, P. & R. Potvliege (1981) Le Goéland leucophée, *Larus cachinnans michahellis* en Belgique. *Gerfaut* 71: 659-666.

Devillers, P., G. McCaskie & J. R. Jehl (1971) The distribution of certain large gulls (*Larus*) in southern California. *California Birds* 2: 11-26.

Diggin, J. (2001) The American Herring Gulls in County Cork. *Birding World* 14: 62-66.

Dittami, J., W. Bock, M. Taborsky, R. van den Elzen & E. Vogel-Millesi, eds. (1994) Research notes on avian biology: selected contributions from the 21st International Ornithological Congress. *J. Orn.* 135, suppl. 44.

Doherty, P. (1990) Quizbird 28. *Birding World* 3: 347, 358-359.

Doherty, P. (1992) Armenian Gull and California Gull. *Birding World* 5: 117-118.

Doherty, P. & W. E. Oddie (2001) *Gulls: a video guide to the gulls of Europe, Asia and North America.* Bird Images Videos. Yorkshire.

Dolbeer, R. A. & G. E. Bernhardt (1986) Early-winter population trends of gulls in western Lake Erie, 1950–1984. *Amer. Birds* 40: 1097-1102.

Dolgushin, I. A. (1962) Lariformes. Pp.246-327 in *Pticy Kasakhstana*, 2. Alma Ata.

van Dongen, R. M. & P. W. W. de Rouw (1987) Kleine Kokmeeuw te IJmuiden in augustus 1985. *Dutch Birding* 9: 55-59.

van Dongen, R. M., R. Hofland & P. W. W. de Rouw (1997) Recente meldingen Nederland oktober–november 1997. *Dutch Birding* 19: 309-314.

Donnelly, B. G. (1974) The Lesser Black-backed Gull *Larus fuscus* in southern and central Africa. *Bull. Brit. Orn. Club* 94: 63-68.

Douhan, B. (1988) Skrattmåsen i Uppland. *Fåglar i Uppland* 15: 29-42.

Dowdall, J. F. & A. McGeehan (1989) Galway's Thayer's Gull. *Dutch Birding* 11: 175-178.

Drennan, M., D. C. Folger & C. Treyball (1987) Common Black-headed Gull on Petit Manan Island, Maine. *Amer. Birds* 41: 195-196.

Dröge, F. (1990) Ivoormeeuw te Stellendam in februari 1990. *Dutch Birding* 12: 238-241.

Drost, R. (1938) Geschlechtsunderschiede am Schnabel der Silbermöwen *Larus a. argentatus. Orn. Monatsb.* 46: 129-131.

Drury, W. H. & J. A. Kadlec (1974) The current status of the Herring Gull population in the north-eastern United States. *Bird-Banding* 45: 297-306.

Dubois, P. J. (1985) Considérations sur le Goéland d'Armenique *Larus armenicus* Buturlin en Israel. *Alauda* 53: 226-228.

Dubois, P. J. (1987) Notes on the "Cantabrican Herring Gull". *Proc 4th Intern. Ident. Meeting*, Eilat, November 1986: 41-42.

Dubois, P. J. (1994) Identification du Goéland à ailes blanches *Larus glaucoides. Ornithos* 1: 84-90.

Dubois, P. J. (1995) A propos du Goéland de Kumlien *Larus glaucoides kumlieni. Ornithos* 2: 45.

Dubois, P. J. (1997a) Identification of North American Herring Gull. *Brit. Birds* 90: 314-324.

Dubois, P. J. (1997b) Putative Glaucous × Herring Gulls. *Birding World* 10: 276-278.

Dubois, P. J. (2001) Atlantic Islands Yellow-legged Gulls – an identification gallery. *Birding World* 14: 293-304.

Dubois, P. J., Le Maréchal, P., Olioso, G. & Yésou, P. (2000). *L' Inventaire des Oiseaux de France: avifaune de la France métropolitaine*. Nathan, Paris.

Dubois, P. J. & T. Stawarczyk (1991) Yellow-legged Gulls in Poland: a reply to Chylarecki & Sikora. *Dutch Birding* 13: 182-183.

Dubois, P. J. & P. Yésou (1984) Identification of juvenile Yellow-legged Herring Gulls. *Brit. Birds* 73: 344-348.

Dubois, P. J., M. Skajug & T. Stawarczyk (1990) Occurrence of Yellow-legged Gulls in Poland. *Dutch Birding* 12: 14-17.

Duff, D. G., D. N. Bakewell & M. D. Williams (1991) The Relict Gull *Larus relictus* in China and elsewhere. *Forktail* 6: 43-65.

Duflon, J.-M. *et al.* (1988) Le Goéland railleur, *Larus genei*, une nouvelle acquistion pour l'avifaune suisse et pour le lac Léman. *Nos Oiseaux* 39: 418-419.

Dufourny, H. (1997) Rapport de la Commission d'Homologations Année 1994. *Aves* 35: 73-96.

Dummigan, K. A. (1978) Head pattern of Sabine's Gull. *Brit. Birds* 71: 129.

Dunn, J. (1983) Sabine's Gull in Britain in winter. *Brit. Birds* 76: 91.

Dunn, J. L. (1997) Video 1: The Large Gulls of North America. *The Advanced Birding video series.* Peregrine.

Dunn, P. J. (1984) Underwing of adult Ross's Gull. *Brit. Birds* 77: 23-24.

Duquet, M. (2002) Présence hivernale de la Mouette de Sabine *Larus sabini* en France. *Ornithos* 9: 65-67.

Dvorak, M. (1991) Die ersten Brutnachweise der Weisskopfmöwe (*Larus cachinnans michahellis*) in Österreich und ihre Brutverbreitung im Binnenland Mitteleuropas. *Egretta* 34: 1-15.

Dwight, J. (1925) The gulls Laridae of the world: their plumages, moults, relationships and distribution. *Bull. Amer. Mus. Nat. Hist.* 52: 63-401.

Ebels, E.B. (2002) Transatlantic vagrancy of Palearctic species to the Caribbean region. *Dutch Birding* 24:202-210

Ebels, E. B., P. Knolle & J. M. van Muiswinkel (1996) Kaspische Geelpootmeeuw bij Geldermalsen in december 1991. *Dutch Birding* 18: 302-304.

Ebels, E., P. Adriaens & J. R. King (2001) Identification and ageing of Glaucous-winged Gull and hybrids. *Dutch Birding* 23: 247-270.

Eber, G. (1958) Zum Einflug der Dreizehenmöwe in Spätwinter 1957 nach Westdeutschland. *Vogelwelt* 79: 9-15.

Ecsedi, Z. (1996) Great Black-headed Gulls in Europe. *Birding World* 9: 303-312.

Edgeller, M. J. (1996) First-year Mediterranean Gull with all dark wings. *Dutch Birding* 18: 241-242.

Editors (1990) Herring Gulls resembling Thayer's. *Birding World* 3: 94-95.

Editors (1999) DB Actueel. Heuglins Meeuw in Groningen: nieuw voon Nederland? *Dutch Birding* 21: 239-240.

Eggenhuizen, A. H. V. (1987) Common Gull with retained juvenile plumage. *Brit. Birds* 80: 628.

Eggenhuizen, G. & G. W. J. van Gool (1984) Kleine Burgermeester met twee korte handpennen. *Limosa* 57: 154-155.

Eigenhuis, K. J. (1989) Kleine Kokmeeuw te IJmuiden van juni 1988 tot januari 1989. *Dutch Birding* 145-151.

Eigenhuis, K. J. (1990a) Occurrence of Yellow-legged Gull in Poland. *Dutch Birding* 12: 193-194.

Eigenhuis, K. J. (1990b) Russische Stormmeeuwen in Nederland. *Dutch Birding* 12: 191-192.

Eigenhuis, K. J. (1991) Yellow-legged Gulls in Poland. *Dutch Birding* 13: 209-210.

Eigenhuis, K. J. (1993) Identification of *argentatus* Herring Gull. *Birding World* 6: 167.

Ekberg, S. & L. Nilsson (1994) *Skånes Fåglar del 1*. Signum. Lund.

Elkins, N. (1987) Origin of Arctic gulls in Britain and Ireland. *Brit. Birds* 80: 635-637.

Elkins, N & P. Yésou (1998) Sabine's Gull in Western France and southern Britain? *British Birds* 91: 386-397, 582

Enevoldsen, E., A. S. Frich, K. Malling Olsen & S. E. Pedersen (1984) Rosenmågen i Thorsminde. *Fugle* 4/2: 25.

Enticott, J. & D. Tipling (1997) *Photographic handbook of the seabirds of the world*. New Holland, London.

Erard, C. (1958) Sur les zones de reproduction et d'hivernage et les migrations de Göeland railleur. *Alauda* 26: 86-104.

Erard, C. (1960) Sur l'aire de reproduction, les zones d'hivernages et le migrations de la Mouette Pygmée *Larus minutus* Pallas. *Alauda* 28: 196-228.

Erard, C., J.-J. Guillou & J. Mayaud (1984) Sur l'identité spécifique de certains laridés nicheurs au Sénégal. *Alauda* 52: 184-188.

Erskine, A. J. (1963) The Black-headed Gull (*Larus ridibundus*) in eastern North America. *Audubon Field Notes* 17: 334-338.

Escalante, R. (1970) *Aves marinas del Rio de la Plata*. Barreiro y Ramos S.A. Montevideo.

Escedi, Z. 1998. A halászsirály (*Larus ichthyaetus*) európai és magyarországi helyzete. *Partimadár* 6/7: 15-24.

Escott, C. (1997) Photo-quiz Solution. *Birders' Journal*. 6: 204.

Eskelin, T. & J. Pursiainen (1998) The status of "Lesser Black-backed Gulls" of *heuglini*, *graellsii* and *intermedius* type in Finland. *Alula* 3/2: 42-54.

Evans, D. R., E. M. Hooper & C. R. Griffin (1993) Discriminating the sex of Laughing Gulls by linear measurements. *J. Field Orn.* 64: 472-476.

Evans, L. (1994) Ivory Gulls in Britain and Ireland. *Birding World* 7: 10-14.

Everett, M. (1988) Selected spring observations from the Suez Canal and the Gulf of Suez. *OSME Bull.* 20: 3-5.

Evers, P., H. Swinkels & T. Cuypers (1996) Ringsnavelmeeuw in Belgisch-Nederlands: Maasplassenbegied in januari 1995. *Dutch Birding* 18: 240-241.

Faber, M., J. Betleja, R. Gwiazda & P. Malczyk (2001) Mixed colonies of large white-headed gulls in southern Poland. *Brit. Birds* 94: 529-535.

Faber, M. & Neubauer, G. (2002) Herring, Yellow-legged and Pontic Gulls wintering in inland Poland. *Dutch Birding* 24:350-357.

Farrand, J., ed. (1983) *The Audubon Society master guide to birding 2: gulls to dippers*. Alfred A. Knopf, New York.

Fasola, M. & L. Canova (1991) Nest habitat selection by eight syntopic species of Mediterranean gulls and terns. *Col. Waterbirds* 15: 168-178.

Fen-Qi, H. & Z. Yun-Sun (1992) Colonial breeding of the Brown-headed Gull and the Relict Gull from the Ordos highlands of Inner Mongolia, China. *Orient Bird Club Bull.* 16: 39.

Fen-Qi, H., Z. Yun-Sun, W. Yong & G. Tie-Jun (1992) The distribution of the Relict Gull *Larus relictus* in Maowusu Desert, Inner Mongolia, China. *Forktail* 7: 151-154.

Filchagov, A. V. (1993) The Armenian Gull in Armenia. *Brit. Birds* 86: 550-560.

Filchagov, A. V. (1994) Contact zones of *Larus argentatus–cachinnans–fuscus* Gull complex in Eastern Europe and Northern Asia. In J. Dittima, W. Bock, M. Taborsky, R. van den Elzen & E. Vogel-Millesi, eds. Research notes on avian biology 1994: selected contributions from the 21st International Ornithological Congress. *J. Orn.* 135, suppl. 44.

Filchagov, A. V. (1996) Colonization of the central part of the East-European plain by *Larus argentatus–cachinnans*. *Ibis* 138: 148-150.

Filchagov, A. V. & V. Y. Semashko (1987) Distribution and ecology of the West-Siberian Herring Gull (*Larus argentatus heuglini* Bree, 1987) in the Kola peninsula. *Byull. Mosk. Ob-va Ispyt. Prirody Otd. Biol.* 92(3): 37-42.

Filchagov, A. V., P. Yésou & V. I. Grabovsky (1992a) Le Goéland du Taimyr *Larus heuglini taimyrensis*; répartition et biologie estivales. *Oiseau et R.F.O.* 62: 128-148.

Filchagov, A. V., V. V. Bianchi, A.E. & V. Y. Semashko (1992b) Relations between Lesser Black-backed Gull *Larus fuscus* and West-Siberian Gull *L. heuglini*, in the contact zone. *Zool. Zh.* 71(10): 148-152.

Finch, D. W. (1978) Black-headed Gulls nesting in Newfoundland. *Amer. Birds* 32: 312.

Finlayson, C. (1992) *Birds of the strait of Gibraltar*. T. & A. D. Poyser, London.

Firsova, L. V. (1985) Variability of plumages in the Slaty Black-backed Gull *Larus schistisagus*, Stejneger. *Proc.18th Intern. Orn. Congress* 2: 1100.

Firsova, L. W. & A. V. Levada (1982) Ornithological finds at the south of Koryak plateau. *Ornitologiya* 17: 112-118.

Fisher, D. J. (1985) Observations on Relict Gull in Mongolia. *Dutch Birding* 7: 117-120.

Fisher, D. (1989) Relict Gulls in Japan. *Birding World* 2: 216-217.

Fisher, D. J. & A. Quinn (1980) Identification of an unusual Common Gull. *Brit. Birds* 73: 310-312.

Fisher, K. & L. Fisher (1989) Laughing Gull *Larus atricilla*: a new species to Australia. *Austral. Bird Watcher* 13: 34-35.

Fjeldså, J. & J.-K. Jensen (1985) "Invasion" af Hvidvingede og Kumlien's Måger *Larus glaucoides* og *kumlieni* på Nolsø på Færøerne. *Dansk Orn. Foren. Tidsskr.* 79: 103-106.

Fjeldså, J. & N. Krabbe (1990) *Birds of the High Andes*. Zoological Museum of Copenhagen and Apollo Books, Svendborg.

Flegg, J. J. M. & C. J. Cox (1972) Movement of Black-headed Gulls from colonies in England and Wales. *Bird Study* 19: 228-240.

Flensted, K. (1985) Racer af Sølvmåge i Danmark. Københavns Universitet. PhD thesis.

Flore, B.-O. (1997) Die Korallenmöwe *Larus audouinii*, eine neue Art für Deutschland. *Limicola* 11: 281-285.

Forchhammer, M. & L. Maagaard (1991) Breeding biology of Sabine's Gull *Larus sabini* in northeastern Greenland. *Dansk Orn. Foren. Tidsskr.* 85: 53-62.

Forsman, D. (1995) Suuntana Suomi? Mustapäälokki. *Alula* 1: 28-31.

Forsten, A. (1995) Mustanmerenlokki Paimiossa 24.10-2.11 1994. *Alula* 1: 38-40.

Forsten, A. (2000) Den östliga silltruten (*Larus f. heuglini*) i första sommardräkt. Fyra silltrutraser, samt grått och kaspisk trut. *Fåglar i Uppland* 27: 12-22.

Fouquet, M. & F. Demée (1989) Aves nuevas para España: Gaviota Guanaguanare *Larus atricilla*. *Garcilla* 1989: 14-5.

Fox, G. A., C. R. Cooper & J. P. Ryder (1981) Predicting the sex of Herring Gulls by using external measurements. *J. Field Orn.* 52: 1-9.

Franck, D. & W. Epprecht (1959) Zur Kopfgefiedermauser der Lachmöwe in Frühjahr. *Orn. Beob.* 56: 101-109.

Franzmann, N. E. (1973) Gulbenet Sølvmåge (*Larus argentatus omissus*) ynglende på Christansø. *Feltornitologen* 15: 209.

591

Fraser, P. A., P. G. Lansdown & M. J. Rogers (1999a) Report on scarce migrant birds in Britain in 1996. *Brit. Birds* 92: 3-35.

Fraser, P. A., P. G. Lansdown & M. J. Rogers (1999b) Report on scarce migrant birds in Britain in 1997. *Brit. Birds* 92: 618-658.

Frede, M. & H. Langbehn (1997) A contribution to the identification and distribution of the Armenian Gull. *Alula* 3: 102-108.

Fredriksson, S. (1966) Höststräcket vid Åsjön åren 1962–1966. *Fåglar på Västkusten* 1965/66: 19-24.

Fredriksson, S. (1968) Fågelsträcket via Ålandasjön åren 1962–1967. *Vår Fågelvärld* 27: 309-326.

Fredriksson, S. (1979) Skrattmåsen *Larus ridibundus* i Sverige. *Vår Fågelvärld* 38: 173-200.

Frings, H., M. Frings, J. Jumper, R.-G. Busnel, J. Giban & P. Gramet (1958) Reactions of American and French species of *Corvus* and *Larus* to recorded communication signals tested reciprocally. *Ecology* 39: 126-131.

Fritze, E. (1976) Ringing of Herring Gulls (*Larus argentatus*) and Greater Black-backed Gulls (*Larus marinus*) of Copenhagen Dump. *Ring* 86-87: 22-24.

Gallissa, E. C. I. (1987) *Invernada de gaviotas y charranes en la Peninsula Iberica*. Sociedad Española de Ornitologia, Madrid.

Gantlett, S. J. M. (1991) The rise and fall of Thayer's Gull. *Birding World* 4: 84-86.

Gantlett, S. (1999) 1998: the Western Palearctic year. *Birding World* 12: 13-30.

Garcia, E. F. J. (1987) Juvenile Herring Gull with aberrant white wing markings. *Brit. Birds* 80: 630-631.

Gardarsson, A. (1996) Ritubyggdir. *Bliki* 17: 1-16.

Gardner, M. (1987) Pink colouration of Little Gull *Brit. Birds* 80: 628.

Garner, M. (1990) The Galway Thayer's Gull. *Birding World* 3: 84-86.

Garner, M. (1997) Large white-headed gulls in the United Arab Emirates. *Emirates Bird Report* 19: 94-103.

Garner, M. (1999) Identification of alleged juvenile Pontic Gull in the Netherlands in September 1997. *Dutch Birding* 21: 40-41.

Garner, M. & A. McGeehan (1997) Dumb gulls. *Birding World* 10: 101-102.

Garner, M. & A. McGeehan (1998) Identification of juvenile and first-winter Thayer's Gull. *Birding World* 11: 94-101.

Garner, M. & D. Quinn (1997) Identification of Yellow-legged Gulls in Britain. *Brit. Birds* 90: 25-63.

Garner, M., D. Quinn & B. Glover (1997) Identification of Yellow-legged Gulls in Britain Part 2. *Brit. Birds* 90: 369-383.

Garner, M., Y. Kolbeinsson & B. Mactavish (2000) Identification of first-winter Kumlien's Gull and the "Whitby Gull". *Birding World* 13: 116-119.

Garve, E., D. Königstedt & H. Langbehn (1987) Die Feldkennzeichen von *Larus cachinnans*. *Orn. Mitt.* 39: 301-308.

Gaston, A. J. & R. Decker (1985) Interbreeding of Thayer's Gull *Larus thayeri* and Kumlien's Iceland Gull *Larus glaucoides kumlieni* on Southampton Island, Northwest Territories. *Canad. Field-Nat.* 99: 257-259.

Gaston, A. J. & R. D. Elliot (1990) Kumlien's Gull, *Larus glaucoides kumlieni*, on Coats Island, Northwest Territories. *Canad. Field-Nat.* 104: 477-479.

Gavrilov, N. N. (1993) Distribution, numbers and dynamics of the breeding sites of colonial waterfowl in the Volga Delta in the North Caspian Sea. Abstract of candidate thesis, Moscow.

Gavrilov, E. I. & A. E. Gavrilov (2000) Possible ringing recoveries of Relict Gull in Bulgaria and Turkey. *Dutch Birding* 22: 219-221.

Geiregat, N. & D. Stomphorst (2000) Franklin's Meeuw(en) in België en Nederland. *Dutch Birding* 22: 58-59.

Géroudet, P. (1989) Réflexions sur la genées et l'evolution des mouvements postnuptieaux chez les Goélands leucophées de Méditerranée occidentale. *Nos Oiseaux* 40: 167-172.

Géroudet, P. (1992a) L'alimentation et le repos chez les Goélands leucophées, *Larus cachinnans*, du Léman. *Nos Oiseaux* 41: 293-304.

Géroudet, P. (1992b) Les classes d'age (1989–1990), et les comportements juvéniles chez les Goélands leucophées *Larus cachinnans* du Léman. *Nos Oiseaux* 41: 397-403.

Gibbins, C. N. 2003. Phenotypic variability of Caspian Gull. *Birding Scotland* 6: 59-74.

Gilbert, M. (1987) The first twitchable Slender-billed Gulls since 1971. *Twitching* 1: 120-121.

Ginn, H. B. & D. S. Melville (1983) *Moult in birds*. BTO, Tring.

Gjershaug, J. O., P. G. Thingstad, S. Eldøy & S. Byrkjeland (1994) *Norsk fugleatlas: hekkefuglenes utbredelse og bestandsstatus i Norge*. Norsk Orn. Foren., Klæbu.

Gloe, P. (1987) Zwergmöwen (*Larus minutus*) – Vorkommen 1979–1985 an der Meldorfer Bucht (Westküste Schleswig-Holstein). *Seevögel* 8: 41-44.

Gloe, P. (1996) Schwarzkopfmöwen (*Larus melanocephalus*) an der Meldorfer Bucht (Westküste Schleswig-Holstein). *Orn. Mitt.* 48: 3-8.

Glutz von Blotzheim, U. N. & K. M. Bauer (1982) *Handbuch der Vögel Mitteleuropas*, vol. 8/I. Akademische Verlagsgesellschaft, Wiesbaden.

Godfrey, W. E. (1986) *The birds of Canada*. Ottawa.

Goethe, F. (1963) Verhaltensunterschiede zwischen europäischer Forme des Silbermöwengruppe (*Larus argentatus*) im südlichen deutschen Nordseegebiet. *Vogelwarte* 21: 1-25.

Goetz, R. E., W. M. Ridder & P. Snetsinger (1986) Slaty-backed Gull winters in the Mississippi River. *Amer. Birds* 40: 207-216.

Golley, M. (1991) Thayer's Gull status and identification. *Birding World* 4: 124-125.

Golley, M. (1994) Double take. *Birdwatch* 113/3: 40-44.

Golley, M. & M. Elliott (1993) Identification of *argenteus* Herring Gulls. *Birding World* 6: 32-38.

Gosselin, M. & N. David (1975) Field identification of Thayer's Gull (*Larus thayeri*) in eastern North America. *Amer. Birds* 29: 1059-1066.

Goutner, V. (1987) Vegetation preferences by colonies of Mediterranean Gull (*Larus melanocephalus*) and Gull-billed Terns (*Gelochelidon nilotica*) in the Evros Delta (Greece). *Seevögel* 8: 29-31.

Goutner, V. (1992) Habitat use in Yellow-legged Gull (*Larus cachinnans michahellis*) coastal wetland colonies of north-east Greece. *Avocetta* 16: 81-85.

Graham, D. J. (1984) A sighting of a Black-legged Kittiwake in Saint Lucia. A first record for the Lesser Antilles. *Amer. Birds* 38: 256.

Grandjean, P. (1981) Præriemåge *Larus pipixcan* ved Færøerne 1976. *Dansk Orn. Foren. Tidsskr.* 75: 146-147.

Grant, P. J. (1980) Field identification of Ring-billed Gull. Pp.126-132 in J. T. R. Sharrock, ed. *The frontiers of bird identification*. MacMillan, London.

Grant, P. J. (1981a) Mystery bird 4: Mediterranean Gull. *Dutch Birding* 2: 60-61.

Grant, P. J. (1981b) Mystery photographs. Franklin's Gull. *Brit. Birds* 74: 298-299.

Grant, P. J. (1981c) On identification and ageing of Great Black-backed Gull. *Dutch Birding* 2: 58-59.

Grant, P. J. (1982a) Mystery photographs. Laughing Gull. *Brit. Birds* 75: 375-376.

Grant, P. J. (1982b) Mystery photographs. Audouin's Gull *Brit. Birds* 75: 575-576.

Grant, P. J. (1982c) Common Gull with retained juvenile plumage. *Brit. Birds* 75: 578-579.

Grant, P. J. (1982d) *Gulls – a guide to identification*. T. & A. D. Poyser, Calton.

Grant, P. J. (1983) Yellow-legged Herring Gulls in Britain. *Brit. Birds* 76: 192-194.

Grant, P. J. (1984a) Mystery Photographs. Laughing Gull. *Dutch Birding* 6: 13-14.

Grant, P. J. (1984b) Photospot 1: Sooty Gull and White-eyed Gull. *Brit. Birds* 77: 149-150.

Grant, P. J. (1984c) Mystery photographs. Laughing or Franklin's Gull. *Brit. Birds* 77: 350-352.

Grant, P. J. (1985) Photospot 14: Ross's Gull. *Brit. Birds* 78: 393.

Grant, P. J. (1986a) Mystery photographs. Little Gull. *Brit. Birds* 79: 119-120.

Grant, P. J. (1986b) *Gulls – a guide to identification.* Second edition. T. & A. D. Poyser, Calton.

Grant, P. J. (1987a) Sabine's Gulls in winter. *Brit. Birds* 80: 75-77.

Grant, P. J. (1987b) Notes on Armenian Herring Gull. P.43 in *Proc. 4th Intern. Ident. Meeting,* Eilat, November 1986.

Grant, P.J. & K. Mullarney (1989) *The new Approach to Identification.* Witley Press, Norfolk.

Grant, P. J. (1989a) Quizbird. *Birding World* 2: 366-367.

Grant, P. J. (1989b) Ross's Gull. *Dutch Birding* 11: 89-92.

Grant, P. J. & R. A. Hume (1981) Herring Gull with characters of Mediterranean race in Kent. *Brit. Birds* 74: 350-351.

Green. S. R. 2003. The status and occurrence of Little Gulls in Angus. *Birding Scotland* 6: 118-119.

Greij, E. (1993) Prairie birds. *Birder's World* 1993: 6.

Grell, M. B. (1998) *Fuglenes Danmark.* Gads Forlag, Copenhagen.

Grenon, F. & R. Storms (2001) Alberta's first Slaty-backed Gull. *Birders J.* 10: 110-113.

Gribble, F. C. (1976) Census of Black-headed Gull colonies in England and Wales in 1973. *Bird Study* 23: 139-140.

Grimmett, R., C. Inskipp & T. Inskipp (1998) *Birds of the Indian subcontinent.* Christopher Helm (A&C Black), London.

Groot Koerkamp, G. (1987) Common Gull with pale iris. *Brit. Birds* 80: 628-629.

Groot Koerkamp, G. & E. B. Ebels (1997) Pontische Geelpootmeeuw bij Zutphen in september–november 1988. *Dutch Birding* 19: 280-283.Gross, A. O. (1964) Albinism in the Herring Gull. *Auk* 81: 551-552.

Gruber, D. (1995) Die Kennzeichen und das Vorkommen der Weisskopfmöwe *Larus cachinnans* in Europa. *Limicola* 9: 121-165.

Gruber, D. (1996) Erstnachweis einer beringten Steppen-Weisskopfmöwe (*Larus cachinnans cachinnans*) in Niedersachsen. *Vogelkd. Ber. Niedersachsen* 28: 44-46.

Gruber, D. (1999) Identification of juvenile and immature Baltic Gull. *Dutch Birding* 21: 129-147.

Gustafson, M. E. & P. G. Peterjohn (1994) Adult Slaty-backed Gulls. Variability in mantle colour and comments on identification. *Birding* 26: 243-249.

Guyot, I. (1981) *Oiseaux de mer richeurs des côtes françaises méditerraniens.* Parc National Régional de Corse, Ajaccio.

Guyot, I. & D. Miege (1980) *Observations sur les oiseaux de mer nicheurs en Corse, saison 1980.* Parc National Régional de Corse, Ajaccio.

Haase, B. J. M. (1993) Sight record of Black-legged Kittiwake in Peru. *Amer. Birds* 47: 382-383.

Haase, B. 1996. Kelp Gull *Larus dominicus* - a new breeding species for Ecuador. *Cotinga* 5: 73-74.

Haffer, J. (1982) Systematik und Taxonomie der *Larus argentatus*-Artengruppe. Pp.502-515 in U. N. Glutz von Blotzheim & K. M. Bauer, eds. *Handbuch der Vögel Mitteleuropas,* Vol. 8/1. Akademische Verlagsgesellschaft, Wiesbaden.

Haftorn, S. (1971) *Norges fugler.* Universitetsforlaget, Oslo.

Hagemeijer, W. J. M. & M. J. Blair, eds. (1997) *The EBCC atlas of European breeding birds: Their distribution and abundance.* T. & A. D. Poyser, London.

Hallam, N. J. (1998) Melanistic Black-headed Gulls. *Brit. Birds* 91: 561.

van der Ham, N. (1981) Waarneming van Ross' Meeuw te Camperduin in januari 1981. *Dutch Birding* 3: 16-17.

Hamer, K. C., D. R. Thompson, A. J. Rundle, S. A. Lewis & F. M. Stewart (1994) Mesopelagic fish eaten by Yellow-legged Herring Gulls *Larus argentatus atlantis* in the Azores. *Seabird* 16: 30-33.

Hammer, U. (1986) Dreizehenmöwen (*Rissa tridactyla*) mit roten Fussen. *Orn. Mitt.* 38: 20.

Handrinos, G. & T. Akriotis (1997) *The birds of Greece.* Christopher Helm (A&C Black), London.

Haney, J. C. (1993) Ivory Gull: a closer look. *Birding* 25: 330-338.

Hanners, A. & S. R. Patton (1985) Sexing Laughing Gulls using external measurements and discriminant analysis. *J. Field Orn.* 56: 158-164.

Hario, M. (1984) Onset and pattern of primary moult in the Lesser Black-backed Gull *Larus f. fuscus* – a comparison with the Herring Gull *L. argentatus. Orn. Fennica* 61: 19-23.

Hario, M. (1985a) Factors affecting the breeding success of gulls in the Gulf of Finland. *Suomen Riista* 32: 23-31.

Hario, M. (1985b) Mustanmerenlokki *Larus melanocephalus* ensi kerran Suomessa. *Lintumies* 20: 160-162.

Hario, M. (1986) *Itämeren lokkilinnut.* Lintutieto.

Hario, M. (1990) Breeding failure and feeding conditions of Lesser Black-backed Gulls *Larus f. fuscus* in the Gulf of Finland. *Orn. Fennica* 67: 113-129.

Hario, M. (1992) Myyttiten *heuglini* – tietoja ja otaksumia. *Lintumies* 27: 113-117.

Hario, M. (1994) Reproductive performance of the nominate Lesser Black-backed Gull under the pressure of Herring Gull predation. *Orn. Fennica* 71: 1-10.

Hario, M. (1997) Keltajalkaisten harmaalokkie esiintymisestä Suomenlahdella. *Alula* 3: 10-15.

Hario, M. & E. Rudbäck (1996) High frequency of chick diseases in nominate Lesser Black-backed Gulls *Larus f. fuscus* from the Gulf of Finland. *Orn. Fennica* 73: 63-77.

Hario, M. & E. Rudbäck (1999) Dying in the midst of plenty – the third-chick fate in nominate Lesser Black-backed Gulls *Larus f. fuscus. Orn. Fennica* 76: 71-77.

Hario, M. & J. Uuksulainen (1993) Mercury load according to moulting areas on primaries of the nominate race of the Lesser Black-backed Gull. *Orn. Fennica* 70: 32-39.

Hario, M., K. Himberg, T. Hollmen & E. Rudbäck (2000) Polychlorinated biphenyls in diseased Lesser Black-backed Gull (*Larus fuscus fuscus*) chicks from the Gulf of Finland. *Environ. Pollution* 107: 53-60.

Harris, A., L. Tucker & K. Vinicombe (1989) *The Macmillan field guide to bird identification.* Macmillan, London and Basingstoke.

Harris, A., H. Shirihai & D. Christie (1996) *The Macmillan birder's guide to European and Middle Eastern birds.* Macmillan, London and Basingstoke.

Harris, M. P. (1962) Difficulties in the ageing of the Herring Gull and the Lesser Black-backed Gull. *Bird Study* 9: 100-103.

Harris, M. P. (1962) Recoveries of ringed Great Black-backed Gulls. *Bird Study* 9: 192-197.

Harris, M. P. (1964a) Measurements and weight of Great Blackbacked Gulls. *Brit. Birds* 57: 71-75.

Harris, M. P. (1964b) Recoveries of ringed Herring Gulls. *Bird Study* 11: 183-191.

Harris, M. P. & P. H. Jones (1969) Sexual differences in measurements of Herring and Lesser Black-backed Gulls. *Bird Study* 16: 121-135.

Harrison, J. A., D. G. Allan, L. G. Underhill, M. Herremans, A. J. Tree, V. Parker & C. J. Brown, eds. (1997) *The atlas of southern African birds,* Vol. 1: Non-passerines. BirdLife South Africa.

Harrison, P. (1983) *Seabirds – an identification guide.* Croom Helm, London.

Harrison, P. (1987) *Seabirds of the world: a photographic guide.* Christopher Helm, London.

Harrop, H. R. (1993) Mystery photographs. *Brit. Birds* 86: 268-269.

Harrop, H. & M. Mellor (1993) Kumlien's Gull in Shetland – the fourth Scottish record. *Scot. Birds* 17: 63-64.

Hart, C. (1986) Laughing Gull in Greece in August 1984. *Dutch Birding* 8: 62-63.

Harvey, W. G. (1981) Field identification of Great Black-headed Gull. *Brit. Birds* 74: 523-524.

Harz, I. M. Harz & U. Wietschke (1994) Die Fischmöwe *Larus ichthyaetus* – eine neue Art für Deutschland. *Limicola* 8: 49-50.

Hastings, R. (1988) Quizbird 8: Silver Gull. *Birding World* 1: 306, 327-328.

Haupt, H. & R. Kaminski (1995) Sind Silbermöwe und Weisskopfmöwe einige Arten? *Falke* 42: 68-73.

van der Have, T. M., V. M. van den Berk, J. P. Cronau & M. J. Langeveld (1989) Importance of the Cukurova deltas, southern Turkey, for migrating waders and other waterbirds in spring. *Sandgrouse* 11: 76-88.

Hazevoet, C. J. (1985) Bird records from Mauritania in December 1984. *Dutch Birding* 7: 26-27.

Hazevoet, C. J. (1987) Breeding range of Brown-headed Gull. *Dutch Birding* 9: 176-177.

Hedgren, S. (1990) Sjöfågelsträcket vid Faludden hösterna 1988 och 1989. *Bläcku* 16: 3-10.

Hedgren, S. & L. Larsson (1973) Vittrut *Larus hyperboreus*, vitvingad trut *L. glaucoides* eller missfärgad annan trut – svårigheter vid fältbestämning av ljusvingade trutar. *Vår Fågelvärld* 32: 173-198.

Hedgren, S. & L. Svensson (1979) Identification of an abnormal Black-headed Gull. *Brit. Birds* 72: 33-36.

Hedgren, S., E. Hjalmarsson & J. Pettersson (1993) Fåglar på Gotland 1992. *Bläcku* 19: 47-73.

de Heer, P. (1981) Over herkenning van Geetpootmeeuw en Voorkommen in Nederland. *Dutch Birding* 3: 131-139.

de Heer, P. (1982a) On Great Black-backed Gull with orange legs. *Dutch Birding* 4: 9.

de Heer, P. (1982b) Over status van Baltische Kleine Mantelmeeuw in Nederland. *Dutch Birding* 4: 55.

Heidrich, P., D. Rostow & M. Wink (1996) Differenzierung von Gelb- und Schwarzschnabeltauchern und Grossmöwen des Silbermöwenkomplexes. *J. Orn.* 137: 281-294.

Hein, K. (1994a) Schwarzkopfmöwe, *Larus melanocephalus* als Dauergast in einem Stadtpark in Kiel. *Falke* 41: 61-63.

Hein, K. (1994b) Hybrid zwichen Sturmmöwe *Larus canus* und Lachmöwe *Larus ridibundus*. *Falke* 41: 64.

Hein, K. & Martens, S. 1988. Messmethoden zur Geschlechtsbestimmung bei der Lachmöwe (*Larus ridibundus*). *Die Vogelwarte* 34: 189-200.

Hein, K. & Martens, S. 2002. Biometrie, Färbung und Wanderungen von in Schleswig-Holstein ind Hamburg gefangenden Sturmmöwen (*Larus canus canus* und *L. c. heinei = L. c. major*). *Corax* 19: 49-65.

Heintzenberg, F. & J. Dierschke (1996) Large numbers of Relict Gulls on Happy Island, China, in August–September 1994. *Dutch Birding* 18: 59-63.

Helbig, A. J. (1994) Genetische Differenzierung von Möwen und Sturmtauchern: ein Kommentar. *J. Orn.* 135: 609-615.

Heldbjerg, H. (2000) De danske Hættemåger på retur. Dyr i Natur og Museum. *Zool. Mus. Tidsskr.* 1/2000: 28-31.

Hémery, G., E. Pasquet & J. C. Thibault (1988) Réflexions sur les populations d'oiseaux marins en France. *Alauda* 56: 1-7.

Herroelen, P. (1981) Eerste ringvondst van een zuidelijke Geelpootzilveurmeeuw *Larus cachinnans/michahellis* in Nederland. *Wielewaal* 47: 129-130.

Herschmann, W. (1991) Lachmöwenalbino bei Pirna. *Falke* 38: 203.

Heubeck, M. (2002) The decline of Shetland's Kittiwake population. *Brit. Birds* 95:118-122.

Hickling, R. A. O. (1977) Wintering gulls of England and Wales, 1973. *Bird Study* 24: 79-88.

Hickling, R. A. O. (1984) Lesser Black-backed Gull numbers at British inland roosts in 1979/90. *Bird Study* 31: 157-160.

Higgins, P. J. & S. J. F. Davies, eds. (1996) *Handbook of Australian, New Zealand and Antarctic birds*, vol. 3: snipe to pigeons. Oxford University Press, Oxford.

Hilmarsson, J.O. (1999) *Islenskur Fuglavisir.* Idunn, Reykjavik.

Hirschfeld, E. (1991) Rare birds in Bahrein in 1989 and 1990. *OSME Bull.* 26: 20-25.

Hirschfeld, E. (1992a) *Birds of Bahrain.* Hobby Publishing, Dubai.

Hirschfeld, E. (1992b) More gulls with bill bands. *Birding World* 5: 116.

Hirschfeld, E. & M. Ullman (1985) Förekomsten av vittrut *Larus hyperboreus* i Skåne. *Anser* 24: 103-114.

Hjort, C. (1980) Ross's Gull *Rhodostethia rosea* breeding in Peary Land, North Greenland, 1979. *Dansk Orn. Foren. Tidsskr.* 74: 75-76.

Hjort, C. & M. Elander (1996) Freeze up at Barrow. *Vår Fågelvärld* 55/1: 13-15.

Hjort, C., N. Kjellén & A. Hedenström (1995) Rosenmåsens

ambulerande tillvaro. *Vår Fågelvärld* 54/1: 28-29.

Hockey, P. A. R. & Rarities Committee (1988) Rare birds in Southern Africa, 1986–87. *Bokmakierie* 40: 111-114.

Hoffman, W. (1979) Answer to snap judgment 5 (Vega Gull). *Continental Birdlife* 1: 146-147.

Hoffman, W., J. A. Wiens & J. M. Scott (1978) Hybridization between gulls (*Larus glaucescens* and *L. occidentalis*) in the Pacific Northwest. *Auk* 95: 441-458.

Hogg, A. (1991) The Thayer's-type gull at Ayr. *Birding World* 4: 82-83.

Hollom, P. A. D., R. F. Porter, S. Christensen & I. Willis (1988) *Birds of the Middle East and North Africa.* T. & A. D. Poyser, Calton.

Holloway, J. (1998) Reaction of other birds to melanistic Black-headed Gull. *Brit. Birds* 91: 561.

Holst, O. & M. Ullman (1984) Några måsar med avvikande ruggningsmönster. *Anser* 23: 215-218.

Holt, D. W., J. Lortie, B. Nikula & R. Humphrey (1986) First record of Common Black-headed Gulls breeding in the United States. *Amer. Birds* 40: 204-206.

Hoogendoorn, W. (1982) Ring-billed Gull in Morocco in August 1982. *Dutch Birding* 4: 91-92.

Hoogendoorn, W. (1988) Franklin's Meeuw in Nederlands-Belgisch grensgebied in juni–july 1987. *Dutch Birding* 10: 71-77.

Hoogendoorn, W. (1991a) Gull records from the northern Egyptian Red Sea coasts in January and February 1989. *OSME Bull.* 26: 32-36.

Hoogendoorn, W. (1991b) Record of Brown-headed Gull in Israel in May 1985. *Dutch Birding* 13: 104-106.

Hoogendoorn, W. (1993) First record of Laughing Gull in Chile. *Amer. Birds* 47: 156-157.

Hoogendoorn, W. (1995a) Meerdags verblijf van Vorkstaartmeeuwen in Nederland. *Dutch Birding* 17: 11-15.

Hoogendoorn, W. (1995b) The Audouin's Gull in northern France. *Birding World* 8: 263-265.

Hoogendoorn, W. (1996) Mystery photographs 57: Laughing Gull *Dutch Birding* 18: 317-319.

Hoogendoorn, W. & E. J. van IJzendoorn (1994) Pre-breeding moult in Franklin's Gulls in the Western Palearctic. *Dutch Birding* 16: 61-64.

Hoogendoorn, W. & E. J. Mackrill (1987) Audouin's Gulls in south-western Palearctic. *Dutch Birding* 9: 99-107.

Hoogendoorn, W. & R. Pop (1995) Kennzeichen der Dünnschnabelmöwe *Larus genei* in zweiten Winter- und zweiten Sommerkleid. *Limicola* 9: 15-24.

Hoogendoorn, W. & P. van Scheepen (1998) Status van Baltische Mantelmeeuw in Nederland. *Dutch Birding* 20: 6-10.

Hoogendoorn, W. & G. R. Steinhaus (1990) Nearctic gulls in the Western Palearctic. *Dutch Birding* 12: 109-164.

Hoogendoorn, W., A. B. van den Berg & K. Mullarney (1991) Brown-headed Gulls with mirrors on three primaries. *Dutch Birding* 13: 63-65.

Hoogendoorn, W., D. J. Moerbeek, P. L. Meininger & C. M. Berrevoets (1992) Spring head moult in Mediterranean Gull in north-western France. *Dutch Birding* 14: 207-214.

Hoogendoorn, W., K. J. Eigenhuis & J. van 't Hof (1993) Herring Gull with much restricted black marks on wing-tip at IJmuiden. *Dutch Birding* 15: 262-264.

Hoogendoorn, W., G. R. Steinhaus, D. J. Moerbeek & A. B. van den Berg (1995) Large number of Mediterranean Gulls in Boulonnais in summer 1995. *Dutch Birding* 17: 151-152.

Hoogendoorn, W., N. C. Moores & T. Morioka (1996) The occurrence and field identification of adult Herring Gulls with yellow legs in Japan. *Birder* 10: 64-73.

Hoogendoorn, W., K. Malling Olsen, A. T. Mjøs, B. Nyberg, M. Vang & T. R. Østerås (1998) Hybridmåke ved Stjørdal i april 1993. *Vår Fuglefauna* 21: 85-87.

Hoogendoorn, W., Adriaens, P., Cederroth, C., De Smet, G. & Lindholm, A. 2003. Three American Herring Gulls at Porto, Portugal, in March-April 2001. *Dutch Birding* 25: 235-245.

Hoogendoorn, W., Laó, C. A. O., Camberlain, P., Johansson, C. & Lowe, R. 2003. Interesting gull records at Porto, Portugal, in March-April 2001. *Dutch Birding* 25: 246-247.

Horton, N., T. Brough, M. R. Fletcher, J. B. A. Rochard & P. I. Stanley (1984) The winter distribution of foreign Black-headed Gulls in the British Isles. *Bird Study* 31: 171-186.

Hosey, G. R. & F. Goodridge (1980) Establishment of territories in two species of gulls on Walney Island, Cumbria. *Bird Study* 27: 73-80.

Howell, S. N. G. (1998) Shades of gray: the catch 22 of Thayer´s Gulls. *Birders J.* 7: 305-309.

Howell, S. N. G. (1999) A basic understanding of moult: what, why, when, and how much? *Birders J.* 8: 296-300.

Howell, S. N. G. (2000) Moult and age of first-year "white-winged" gulls. *Brit. Birds* 93: 99-100.

Howell, S. N. G. (2001) A new look at moult in gulls. *Alula* 7: 2-11.

Howell, S. N. G. & C. Corben (2000a) Molt cycles and sequences in the Western Gull. *Western Birds* 31: 38-49.

Howell, S. N. G. & C. Corben (2000b) Retarded wing moult in Black-legged Kitiwakes. *Western Birds* 31:121-125.

Howell, S. N. G. & M. T. Elliott (2001) Identification and variation of winter adult Thayer's Gulls with comments on taxonomy. *Alula* 4/2001: 130-144.

Howell, S. & J. King (1997) Glib style, a half truth seen? *Birding World* 10: 270-271.

Howell, S. N. G. & J. R. King (1998) Tail-pattern variation in first-year Herring Gull. *Western Birds* 29: 63-64.

Howell, S. N. G. & J. R. King (1999) First prebasic molt in Herring, Thayer's and Glaucous-winged Gulls. *J. Field Orn.* 70: 543-554.

Howell, S. N. G. & B. McKee (1998) Variation of second-year Mew Gulls. *Birders J.* 7: 210-213.

Howells, R. J. (1986) Ring-billed Gulls displaying in West Glamorgan. *Brit. Birds* 79: 42.

del Hoyo, J., A. Elliott & J. Sargatal, eds. (1996) *Handbook of the birds of the world*, vol. 3. Lynx Edicions, Barcelona.

Hubatsch, K. (1988) Eine weitere leuzistische Lachmöwe *Larus ridibundus* mit Ohrfleck. *Limicola* 2: 221-222.

Hüe, F. & R. Etchécopar (1970) *Les oiseaux du Proche et du Moyen Orient.* Boubée, Paris.

Hume, R. A. (1976) The pattern of Mediterranean Gull records at Blackpill, West Glamorgan. *Brit. Birds* 69: 503-505.

Hume, R. A. (1978a) Herring Gulls in Israel. *Brit. Birds* 71: 181-191.

Hume, R. A. (1978b) Identification of hybrid gulls. *Brit. Birds* 71: 279.

Hume, R. A. (1978c) Variations in Herring Gulls at a Midland roost. *Brit. Birds* 71: 338-345.

Hume, R. A. (1980) Identification and ageing of Glaucous and Iceland Gulls. Pp.170-182 in J. T. R. Sharrock, ed. *The frontiers of bird identification.* Macmillan, London.

Hume, R. A. (1982) Ring-billed Gull in West Glamorgan. Pp.184-191 in J. T. R. Sharrock & P. J. Grant, eds. *Birds new to Britain and Ireland.* T. & A. D. Poyser, Calton.

Hume, R. A. (1983a) Herring Gulls in Israel. *Brit. Birds* 76: 189-191.

Hume, R. A. (1983b) Mystery photographs. *Brit. Birds* 76: 530-532.

Hume, R. A. & D. A. Christie (1989) Sabine's Gull and other seabirds after the October 1987 storm. *Brit. Birds* 82: 191-208.

Humphrey, P. S. & K. C. Parkes (1959) An approach to the study of moults and plumages. *Auk* 76: 1-31.

Hutchinson, C. D. & B. Neath (1978) Little Gulls in Britain and Ireland. *Brit. Birds* 71: 563-582.

van IJzendoorn, E. J. (1982) Mystery photographs 9. *Dutch Birding* 4: 131.

van IJzendoorn, E. J. (1989) Reuzenzwartkopmeeeuw in IJselmeergebied in zomers van 1974–76. *Dutch Birding* 11: 5-8.

van IJzendoorn, E. J. & J. Mulder (1981) Atypical first-winter Iceland Gull at IJmuiden in February 1981. *Dutch Birding* 3: 56-57.

van IJzendoorn, E. J. & G. J. Oreel (1981) Second-winter Iceland Gull at IJmuiden from January to March 1981. *Dutch*

Birding 3: 13-15.

Il'icev, V. D. & V. A. Zubakin (1988) *Ptitsy SSSR: Chaykovye* [Birds of the USSR: Lari] Nauka, Moscow.

Il'icev, V. D. & V. A. Zubakin (1990) *Handbuch der Vögel Sowjetunion,* Vol.6/1. A. Ziemsen Verlag, Wittenberg Lutherstadt.

van Impe, J. (1969) Sur la migration d'automne de *Larus minutus* Pallas dans le sud-est de la Roumanie. *Alauda* 37: 79-80.

Ingolfsson, A. (1969) Sexual dimorphism of large gulls (*Larus* ssp.). *Auk* 86: 732-737.

Ingolfsson, A. (1970a) Hybridization of Glaucous Gulls (*Larus hyperboreus*) and Herring Gulls (*L. argentatus*) in Iceland. *Ibis* 112: 340-381.

Ingolfsson, A. (1970b) The moult of remiges and rectrices in Great Black-backed Gulls *Larus marinus* and Glaucous Gulls *L. hyperboreus* in Iceland. *Ibis* 112: 83-92.

Ingolfsson, A. (1987) Hybridization of Glaucous and Herring Gulls in Iceland. *Stud. Avian Biol.* 10: 131-140.

Ingolfsson, A. (1993) The variably plumaged gulls of Iceland. *Auk* 110: 409-410.

Inskipp, C. & T. Inskipp (1985) *A guide to the birds of Nepal.* Croom Helm, London.

Iron, J. & R. Pittaway (2001) Molts and plumages of Ontario's Heermann's Gull. *Ontario Birds* 19: 65-78.

Isaksen, K. & V. Bakken, eds. (1995) *Seabird populations in the northern Barents Sea.* Medd. no. 135, Norsk Polarinstitutt, Oslo.

Isenmann, P. (1973) Biometrische Untersuchungen an der Gelbfüssigen Silbermöwe *Larus argentatus michahellis* an der Camargue. *Vogelwarte* 27: 16-24.

Isenmann, P. (1976) Contribution et de l'ecologie du Goéland Argenté à Pieds Jaunes (*Larus argentatus michahellis*) en Camargue. *Rev. Ecol. (Terre Vie)* 30: 551-563.

Isenmann, P., J.-D. Lebreton & R. Brandl (1991) The Black-headed Gull in Europe. *Acta XX Congr. Int. Orn.,* Christchurch: 2384-2389.

Jaberg, C. & S. Wohlhauser (1989) Mouette de Sabine *Xema sabini* sur le lac de Neuchatél. *Nos Oiseaux* 40: 222-223.

James, D. (1995) Picking a gull-friend. *Wingspan* 5/2: 34-37.

James, S. L. & J. Norton (1997) Mediterranean Gull at Ramtha tip – the first record for the United Arab Emirates. *Emirates Bird Report* 19: 123-124.

Jansen, F. H. & A. Remeeus (1978) Naar een definitieve vestiging van de Zwartkopmeeuw *Larus melanocephalus* in Nederland? *Limosa* 51: 88-106.

Jehl, J. R. (1971) A hybrid Glaucous × Herring Gull from San Diego. *California Birds* 2: 27-32.

Jehl, J. R. (1987a) A review of "Nelson's Gull" *Larus nelsoni.* Bull. Brit. Orn. Club 107: 86-91.

Jehl, J. R. (1987b) Geographical variation and evolution in the California Gull *Larus californicus.* *Auk* 104: 421-428.

Jehl, J. R. & R. C. Frohling (1965) Two probable hybrid gulls from New Jersey. *Auk* 82: 498-500.

Jehl, J. R., F. S. Todd, M. A. E. Rumboll & D. Schwartz (1978) Notes on the avifauna of South Georgia. *Gerfaut* 68: 534-550.

Jensen, F. P. (1993) *Fuglene i de danske farvande: resultater af landsdækkende undersøgelser 1987–91.* Miljøministeriet/Skov- & Naturstyrelsen, København.

Jiquet, F. (2002) Taxonomy of the Kelp Gull *Larus dominicanus* Lichtenstein inferred from biometrics and wing plumage pattern, including two previously undescribed subspecies. *Bull. brit. Orn. Club* 122: 50-70.

Jiquet, F., A. Jamarillo & I. Sinclair (2001) Identification of Kelp Gull. *Birding World* 14: 112-125.

Jiquet, F. & Defos Du Rau, P. 2003. Hybride probable Mouette rieuse *Larus ridibundus* X Goeland cendré *Larus canus.* *Ornithos* 10: 44-45.

Johansen, H. (1960) Die Vogelfauna Westsibiriens III Teil 9. *J. Orn.* 101: 316-339.

Johansen, H. (1961) Die Superspecies *Larus canus.* *Vogelwarte* 21: 152-156.

Johansson, B. (1990) Sträckräckningar i Vänern och Vättern juli/augusti 1990. Privately published.

Johnson, E. D. H., J. F. Monk & J. C. M. Robertson (1990) Grey-headed Gull in Algeria in April 1981. *Dutch Birding* 12: 71-72.

Johnston, D. W. (1955) The Glaucous Gull in Western North America south of its breeding range. *Condor* 58: 134-162.

Johnston, D. W. (1956) The annual reproductive cycle of the California Gull, I. Criteria of age and the testis cycle. *Condor* 58: 134-162.

Johnston, D. W. (1961) Timing of annual molt in the Glaucous Gulls of Northern Alaska. *Condor* 63: 474-478.

Johnstone, R. E. & G. M. Storr (1998) *Handbook of Western Australian birds*, Vol. 1. Non-passerines. Western Australian Museum, Perth.

Joiris, C. (1978) Le Goéland argenté portugais *L. a. lusitanius* nouvelle forme de Goéland argenté à pattes jaunes. *Aves* 15: 17-18.

Jönck, M. (1993) Die Dünnschnabelmöwe *Larus genei*, eine neue Art für Deutschland. *Limicola* 7: 172-174.

Jonsson, L. (1986) Liten havsfågelbok 2: dvärgmås och tretåig mås. *Bläcku* 12: 61-64.

Jonsson, L. (1996) "Gulfotade" trutar. Räkna med både Medelhavstrut och Kaspisk trut! *Vår Fågelvärld* 55/8: 12-26.

Jonsson, L. (1998b) Baltic Lesser Black-backed Gull *Larus fuscus fuscus* – moult, ageing and identification. *Birding World* 11: 295-317.

Jonsson, L. (1998c) Yellow-legged Gulls and Yellow-legged Herring Gulls in the Baltic. *Alula* 3: 74-100.

Jonsson, L. & B. Mactavish (2001) American Herring Gulls at Niagara Falls and Newfoundland. *Birders J.* 10: 90-107.

Jönsson, P. E. & O. Wennberg (1981) Präriemåsen *Larus pipixcan* påträffad i Sverige. *Vår Fågelvärld* 40: 263-269.

Jörgensen, J. (1982) Fiskmås i andra sommardräkt med stjärtband. *Calidris* 11: 281.

Jörgensen, J. (1984) Black-headed Gull with aberrant underwing pattern. *Brit. Birds* 77: 358-359.

Jørgensen, O. H. (1973) Some results of Herring Gull ringing in Denmark 1958–1969. *Dansk Orn. Foren. Tidsskr.* 67: 53-63.

de Juana, E. & J. M. Varela (1993) The world breeding population of the Audouin's Gull *Larus audouinii*. Pp.71-85 in J. S. Aquilar, X. Monbailliu & A. M. Paterson, eds. *Status and conservation of seabirds: ecogeography and Mediterranean action plan. Proc II Medit. Seabird Symp. Mallorca.* Sociedad Española de Ornithologia/Birdlife/Medmaravis.

de Juana, E., J. Varela & H.-H. Witt (1984) The conservation of seabirds in the Chafarinas Islands. Pp.363-370 in J. P. Croxall, P. G. H. Evans & R. W. Schreiber (1984) *Status and conservation of the world's seabirds*. ICBP Techn Pub 2, Cambridge, UK.

de Juana, E., P. M. Bradley, J. M. Varela & H.-H. Witt (1987) Sobre los movimientos migratorios de la Gaviota de Audouin (*Larus audouinii*). *Ardeola* 34: 15-24.

Jukema, J. (1987) Kleden van leucistische Zilvermeeuw. *Dutch Birding* 9: 25-28.

Juvaste, R. (1994a) Selkälokkitiedustelu 1994. *Siipirikko* 21: 3-7.

Juvaste, R. (1994b) Rääkkylän ja kesälahden selkävesilinnustoselvitykset. *Siipirikko* 21: 8-28.

Kampp, K. & R. M. Kristensen (1980) Ross's Gull *Rhodostethia rosea* breeding in Disko Bay, West Greenland, 1979. *Dansk Orn. Foren. Tidsskr.* 74: 65-74.

Kasparek, M. (1992) *Die Vögel der Türkei*. Max Kasparek Verlag, Heidelberg.

ten Kate, C. G. B. (1946) *Larus ichthyaetus* Pallas, nieuw voor de Nederlandse lijst. *Limosa* 19: 52-55.

Kaufman, K. (1988) Answer to June photo Quiz. *Birding* 20: 257-260.

Kaufman, K. (1989) The practiced eye: Black-legged Kittiwake and Red-legged Kittiwake. *Amer. Birds* 43: 3-6.

Kaufman, K. (1990) *A field guide to advanced birding*. Houghton Mifflin, Boston.

Kaufman, K. (1991) Answers to October photo quiz. *Birding* 23: 360-363.

Kaufman, K. (1992) Answers to the June photo quiz. *Birding* 24: 250-253.

Kaufman, K. (1993) The practiced eye: identifying the Common Black-headed Gull. *Amer. Birds* 47: 1156-1159.

Kay, G. T. (1947) The Glaucous Gull in winter. *Brit. Birds* 40: 369-373.

Kay, G. T. (1950) The Iceland Gull in winter. *Brit. Birds* 43: 399-402.

Kehoe, C. (1991) Identification pitfalls and the Yellow-legged Gull at Seaforth. *NW Reg. Bird Report* 1991.

Kehoe, C. (1992) A possible Ring-billed Gull × Common Gull. *Birding World* 5: 312-313.

Kehoe, C. (1993a) Patterns of recognition. *Birdwatch* 2: 40-45.

Kehoe, C. (1993b) Where to watch white-winged gulls. *Birdwatch* 2: 14-17.

Kehoe, C. & M. Elliott (1992) Ring-billed Gull confusion risks. *Birdwatch* (1992)1: 44-48.

Keijl, G. O., T. M. van der Have & P. S. Ruiters (1995) Great Black-headed Gull in Tunisia in February 1994. *Dutch Birding* 17: 17-18.

Kennerley, P. R. (1987) Iris, leg and mantle colour of Mongolian Yellow-legged Gull. *Dutch Birding* 9: 29.

Kennerley, P. R. (1990) Birds new to Hong Kong. Relict Gull at Mai Po: the first record for Hong Kong. *Hong Kong Bird Rep.* 1989: 80-91.

Kennerley, P. R. (1991) Ageing of first- and second-winter Common Gulls. *Hong Kong Bird Rep.* 1989: 194.

Kennerley, P. R., W. Hoogendoorn & M. L. Chalmers (1995) Identification and systematics of large white-headed gulls in Hong Kong. *Hong Kong Bird Rep.* 1994: 127-156.

Kennerley, P. R. (1979) Goéland atricille *Larus atricilla* au Maroc. *Alauda* 47: 214-215.

Kerautret, L. (1981) Une Mouette de Franklin (*Larus pipixcan*) dans le Pas-de-Calais. *Oiseau et R.F.O.* 51: 337-339.

Khymyn, M. (1993) *The atlas of wintering birds in Lutsk District (1988/89–1991/92)*. Bird World, Lutsk.

Kilbane, T. (1989) Thayer's Gull at Galway – a new Western Palearctic bird. *Birding World* 2: 125-127.

Kilpi, M. (1984) Seasonal movements and dispersal of Finnish Herring Gulls *Larus argentatus*. *Ann. Zool. Fenn.* 21: 253-257.

Kilpi, M. (1988) Breeding and movements of Herring Gull *Larus argentatus* in the northern Baltic: strategies for reproduction and survival of a successful species. Thesis, Helsinki.

Kilpi, M. & M. Hario (1986) Wing-tip pattern and possible affinities of coastal Finnish Herring Gulls *Larus argentatus*. *Orn. Fennica* 63: 42-54.

Kilpi, M. & P. Saurola (1983a) Geographic distribution of breeding season recoveries of adult and immature *Larus marinus*, *L. argentatus* and *L. fuscus* ringed in Finland. *Orn. Fennica* 60: 117-125.

Kilpi, M. & P. Saurola (1983b) Pre-breeding movements of coastal Finnish Herring Gulls. *Ann. Zool. Fenn.* 20: 245-254.

Kilpi, M. & P. Saurola (1984) Migration and wintering strategies of juvenile and adult *Larus marinus*, *L. argentatus* and *L. fuscus*. *Orn. Fennica* 61: 1-8.

Kilpi, M. & P. Saurola (1985) Movements and survival areas of Finnish common gulls *Larus canus*. *Ann. Zool. Fenn.* 22: 157-168.

King, B. (1988) Possibly melanistic Kittiwake in Cornwall. *Brit. Birds* 81: 181-182.

King, B. & P. G. Marriott (1984) Pink Black-headed Gulls. *Brit. Birds* 77: 615.

King, J. R. (2001) Field identification of adult *californicus* and *albertaensis* California Gulls. *Birders Journal* 11: 245-261.

King,. J. R. (1997) Thayer's Gulls age. *Birders Journal* 6: 232.

King, J. R. (1995) Western Gulls with yellow legs. *Birders Journal* 9: 200-205.

King, J. & H. Shirihai (1996) Identification and ageing of Audouin's Gull. *Birding World* 9: 52-61.

King, J. R. & G. J. Carey (1999) Slaty-backed Gull. Hybridization and variation in adult upperparts colour. *Birders J.* 8: 88-93.

King, J. R. & G. Carey (2000) Gulls in Japan. *Birding World* 13: 160-163.

King, J. R. & S. N. G. Howell (1998) Identification and molt of hybrid Glaucous-winged Gulls. *Western Birds* 29: 484-485.

King, J. R. & S. N. G. Howell (1999) Variation in iris colour of adult Thayer's Gull. *Western Birds* 30: 55-56.

Kirwan, G. (1993) Western Palearctic news: Yemen. *Birding World* 6: 142.

Kirwan, G., R. P. Martins, K. M. Morlan & D. A. Showler (1996) The status of birds in Socotra and Ábd Al-Kuri. *Sandgrouse* 17: 83-101.

Kist, J. (1961) "Systematische" Beschouwingen naar aanleiding van de waarneming van Heuglins Geelpootzilvermeeuw *Larus cachinnans heuglini* Bree in Nederlands. *Ardea* 49: 1-51.

Kitson, A. R. (1980) *Larus relictus*: a review. *Bull. Brit. Orn. Club* 100: 178-185.

Kitson, A. R. (1982) A pink Black-headed Gull. *Brit. Birds* 75: 536.

Klein, R. (1994) Silbermöwe *Larus argentatus* und Weisskopfmöwe *Larus cachinnans* auf Mülldeponien in Mecklenburg – erste Ergebnisse einer Ringfundanalyse. *Vogelwelt* 115: 267-286.

Klein, R. & A. Buchheim (1997) Die westlische Schwartzmeerkuste als Kontaktgebiet zweier Formen der *Larus cachinnans*-Gruppe. *Vogelwelt* 118: 61-70.

Klein, R. & D. Gruber (1997) Die Bestimmung und taxonomische Stellung der in Mitteleuropa auftretenden Weisskopfmöwen. *Limicola* 11: 49-75.

Klimashkin, O. V., Khokhlov, V. & Il'yukh, M. P. 2003. Gnezdovaya ekologiya chaykovykh ptits Tsentral' nogo Predkavkaz' ya. Russian Bird Conservation Union, Stavropol'.

Knaus, P. & C. A. Balzari (1999) Seltene Vogelarten und ungewöhnliche Vogelbeobachtungen in der Schweiz im Jahre 1998. *Orn. Beob.* 96: 157-182.

de Knijff, P., E. Denkers, N. D. van Swelm & M. Kuiper, on behalf of Port of Rotterdam Gull Study Group (2001) Genetic affinities within the Herring Gull *Larus argentatus* assemblage revealed by AFLP genotyping. *J. Molec. Evol.* 52: 85-93.

Knolle, P., J. Jansen & P. Palmen (1997) Pontische Geelpootmeeuwen bij Enschede en in Noord-Limburg. *Dutch Birding* 19: 319-320.

Knox, A. (1985) Glaucous × Herring Gull hybrids. *Brit. Birds* 78: 246-247.

Knudsen, B. (1976) Colony turnover and hybridization in some Canadian arctic gulls. *Pacific Seabird Group* 3: 27.

Koerkamp, N. J. (1991) Waarnemingen van oostelijke Stormmeeuwen in Nederland. *Dutch Birding* 13: 25-27.

Kohl, I. (1959) Contributions to systematic studies of the Black Sea's Herring Gulls. *Aquila* 65: 127-143.

Köhler, D., P. Kneis & G. Mauersberger (1983) Gestalt und Verhalten zweier Bastarde *Larus melanocephalus* × *L. ridibundus*. *Mitt. Zool. Mus. Berlin* 59, Suppl. *Ann. Orn.* 7: 27-46.

Kolbeinsson Y., G. Thrainsson, G. Pétursson (2004) Sjaldgaefir Fuglar á Islandi 2001. *Bliki* 25 (in press)

Kompanje, E. J. O. & J. N. J. Post (1990) Oostelijke Stormmeeuwen *Larus canus heinei* in Nederland en West-Europa. *Limosa* 63: 2-6.

Kompanje, E. J. O. & J. N. J. Post (1993) Nieuwe vondsten van Russische Stormmeeuw in Nederland. *Dutch Birding* 15: 254-258.

Königstedt, D. (1980) Ein weiterer Beitrag zur Feldkennzeichnung der Dünnschnabelmöwe *Larus genei*. *Beitr. Vogelkunde* 26: 285-294.

Königstedt, B. & D. Königstedt (1980) Die Feldkennzeichen der Dünnschnabelmöwe. *Falke* 27: 238-242.

Königstedt, D. & H. Langbein (1988) Rätselvogel 3. *Limicola* 1: 31-33.

Koop, B. (1985) Rast und Zug der Zwergmöwe (*Larus minutus*) am Grossen Plöner See 1982–1984. *Corax* 11: 70-78.

de Korte, J. (1972) Birds observed and collected by "De Nederlandse Spitsbergen Expeditie" in West and East Spetsbergen, 1967 and 1968–'69; second part. *Beaufortia* 19: 197-232.

de Korte, J. & A. Volkov (1993) Large colony of Ivory Gull *Pagophila eburnea* at Domastiny Island, Severnaya Zemlja. *Sula* 7: 107-110.

Koskinen, K., H. Kettunen & M. Kangasniemi (2001) Tuhkaselkälokkien esiintymisestä Tampereella. *Linnut* 36: 27-30.

Köth, T. (1985) Zur Altersklassifizierung nestjunger Dreizehen-möwen (*Rissa tridactyla*) auf Helgoland. *Seevögel* 6: 141-144.

Kovsar, A. F. (1982) Reliktovaja cajka (Lönnbergmöwe). Pp.407-411 in *Pticy Kazakhstana* 5. Alma Ata.

Kozlova, E. V. (1938) Field observations of the breeding of the Herring Gull *Larus argentatus ponticus* on the Caspian Sea. *Ibis* 14(2): 245-253.

Kraft, M. (1994) Ornithologisches Protokoll einer Reise auf Zypern vom 2. bis 16. April 1993. *Orn. Mitt.* 46: 173-182.

Krauss, W. (1959) Wanderungen der bayerischen Lachmöwen. *Anz. Orn. Ges. Bayern* 5: 363-375.

Krauss, W. (1965) Beiträge zum Zugverhalten und Überwintern der Lachmöwe in Bayern, speziell in München. *Anz. Orn. Ges. Bayern* 7: 379-428.

van Kreuningen, J. (1980) Great Black-backed Gull with orange legs. *Dutch Birding* 2: 14.

Kumari, E. (1978) On the distribution dynamics of the Herring Gull in the Baltic area within the past 125 years. *Ornitoloogi-line Kogumik* 9: 11-43.

Kumlien, L. (1879) Contributions to the natural history of Arctic America. *U.S. Natn. Mus. Bull.* 15: 1-179.

Kuschert, H. (1979) Die Silbermöwe (*Larus argentatus*) in Schleswig-Holstein: ein Beitrag zur Diskussion über ihre taxonomische Stellung. *Abh. Geb. Vogelkunde* 6: 87-112.

Kwater, E. (1992) Pennsylvania's first Mew Gull, with notes on its racial identification. *Pennsylvania Birds* 6: 8-9.

Lack, P. (1986) *The atlas of wintering birds in Britain and Ireland*. BTO & Irish Wildb. Cons., Poyser. London.

Lambert, K. (1975) Schwalbenmöwen-Beobachtungen *Xema sabini* (Sabine 1819) in Südsommer 1972–1973 im Südafrikanischen Winterquartier. *Beitr. Vogelkunde* 21: 410-415.

Lamont, S. M. (1980) Atypical nest of Bonaparte's Gull. *Blue Jay* 38: 44-45.

Lange, P., ed. (1995) Årsrapport over fugleobservationer i Danmark 1984–87. Medd. 21 fra Rapportgruppen, DOF.

Langman, M. (2000) Hybrid Mediterranean × Black-headed Gulls. *Birding Scotland* 3: 56-65.

Larkin, P. (1999) Black-headed Gull with black bill. *Brit. Birds* 92: 612.

Larkin, P. (2000) Identification of aberrant hybrid Mediterranean × Black-headed Gull. *Brit. Birds* 93: 114.

Larsson, H. (1995) Fler Medelhavstrutar i Skåne. *Anser* 34: 7-11.

Larsson, H. (1999a) Fältbestämning av "kaspisk trut" *Larus argentatus cachinnans* höstetid. *Anser* 38: 153-168.

Larsson, H. (1999b) Udda dvärgmås. *Anser* 38: 226.

Larsson, H. & J. Lorentzon (1998) Dräkten hos unga trutar. *Vår Fågelvärld* 58/1: 40-41.

Lauro, A. J. & B. J. Spencer (1980) A method for separating juvenal and first-winter Ring-billed Gull *Larus delawarensis* and Common Gull *L. canus. Amer. Birds* 34: 111-116.

Leader, P. J. & C. Y. Lam (1993) Monthly summaries. *Hong Kong Bird Rep.* 1992: 6-13.

Lehman, P. (1980) The identification of Thayer's Gull in the field. *Birding* 12: 198-210.

Lehman, P. (1983a) Point-counterpoint ID points: Reddish Egret, Laughing/Franklin's Gulls, Royal/Elegant Terns. *Birding* 15: 228-230.

Lehman, P. (1983b) Point-counterpoint: some thoughts on Thayer's Gull and *Sterna* terns. *Birding* 15: 107-108.

Lehman, P. (1994) Franklin's vs. Laughing Gulls. A "new" problem arises. *Birding* 26: 126-127.

Lehman, P. (1999) The spread of Kelp Gull. *Birding World* 12: 253.

Lehto, H., A. McGeehan & H. Vasamies (1998) Photonews. *Alula* 3/2: 68-70.

Leray, A., Yésou, P., Beaudouin, J. C. & Fossé, A. 1999. Un hybride Mouette rieuse X Mouette mélanocéphele a élevé deux jeunes en Maine-et-Loire en 1998. *Ornithos* 6: 40-45.

Leven, M. R. & G. J. Carey (1993) Systematic list. *Hong Kong Bird Rep.* 1993: 14-74.

Lewis, A. & D. Pomeroy (1989) *A bird atlas of Kenya*. A.A. Balkema. Rotterdam.

Lewis, R. H. (1996) First North Carolina record of Yellow-legged Gull. *Chat* 60/4: 153-156.

Liebers, D. & V. Dierschke (1997) Variability of field characters in adult Pontic Yellow-legged Gulls. *Dutch Birding* 19: 277-280.

Liebers. D. & A. J. Helbig (1999) Phänotypische Charakterisierung und systematische Stellung der Armeniermöwe *Larus armenicus. Limicola* 13: 281-320.

Liebers, D., A. J. Helbig & P. de Knijff (2001) Genetic differentation and phylogeography of gulls in the *Larus cachinnans–fuscus* group (Aves: Charadriiformes). *Molec. Ecology* 10: 2447-2462.

Lindberg, N. & U. Lötberg (1997) Rekordsträck av dvärgmås. *Fåglar i Uppland* 24: 18-20.

Lindholm, A. (1997) Obin lauden *heuglini* – lokit. The *heuglini* gulls in the Bay of Ob. *Alula* 3: 126-128.

Lloyd, C., M. L. Tasker &. K. Partridge (1991) *The status of seabirds in Britain and Ireland.* T. & A. D. Poyser, London.

Lobley, G. R. (1997) Photospot: White-eyed and Sooty Gulls at the Red Sea Coast of Saudi Arabia. *Sandgrouse* 19: 18-21.

Lock, A. R. (1988) Recent increases in the breeding population of Ring-billed Gulls, *Larus delawarensis*, in Atlantic Canada. *Canad. Field-Nat.* 102: 627-633.

Lohmann, M. (1988) Weisskopfmöwe *Larus cachinnans*, brütete 1987 auch am Chiemsee. *Anz. orn. Ges. Bayern* 27: 296-297.

Lonergan, P. (1999) Another Thayer's Gull in Ireland. *Birding World* 12: 38-39.

Lonergan P. & K. Mullarney (2004) Identification of American Herring Gulls in a Western European context. *Dutch Birding* 26: 1-36.

Lönnberg, E. (1919) Hybrid gulls. *Ark. Zool.* 12: 1-22.

Lönnberg, E. (1933) Some remarks on the systematic status of yellow-legged Herring gulls. *Ibis* 33: 47-50.

Lopez, H. & T. Mundkur, eds. (1997) *The Asian Waterfowl Census 1994–1996. Results of the coordinated waterfowl census and an overview of the status of wetlands.* Wetlands International, Kuala Lumpur.

Lucas, Z. (1997) A Black-tailed Gull on South Island, Nova Scotia. *Birders Journal* 6: 207-207.

Ludwig, J. P. (1974) Recent changes in the Ring-billed Gull population and biology in the Laurentian Great Lakes. *Auk* 91: 575-594.

Lyngs, P. 2003. Migration and winter ranges of birds in Greenland. *Dansk Orn. Foren. Tidsskr.* 97: 1-167.

MacKinnon, J. & K. Phillips (2000) *A field guide to the birds of China.* Oxford University Press, Oxford.

Mackrill, E. J. (1987) Mystery photographs 24. Audouin's Gull. *Dutch Birding* 9: 113-115.

Mackrill, E. J. (1989a) Audouin's Gulls in Senegal in January 1989. *Dutch Birding* 11: 122-123.

Mackrill, E. J. (1989b) First-year plumages of Audouin's Gull. *Brit. Birds* 82: 73-77.

MacPearson, A. H. (1961) Observations on Arctic *Larus* gulls and on the taxonomy of *L. thayeri* Brooks. *Arctic Inst. N. Amer. Tech. Pap.* 7: 1-40.

Mactavish, B. (1995) Yellow-legged Gull in St. John's Newfoundland. *Birders J.* 4: 294-300.

Mactavish, B. (1998) A Black-tailed Gull in Newfoundland. *Birders J.* 7: 157-159.

Madge, S. C. (1978) Apparent immature Glaucous × Herring Gull hybrids. *Brit. Birds* 71: 272-274.

Madge, S. C. (1983) Iris colour of Mongolian Yellow-legged Gull. *Dutch Birding* 5: 91.

Madge, S. C. (1985) Iris colour of Mongolian Yellow-legged Gull. *Dutch Birding* 7: 145.

Madge, S. C. (1990) Eine Armeniermöwe *Larus (cachinnans) armenicus* ohne schwarze Schnabelzeichnung. *Limicola* 4: 216-217.

Madge, S. C. (1992) Yellow-legged Gulls with bill bands. *Birding World* 5: 67-68.

Madge, S. C. (1996) Races apart. *Birdwatch* 9: 28-33.

Makatsch, W. (1952) *Die Lachmöwe.* Neue Brehm-Bücherei 56. Geest & Portig, Leipzig.

Malius, J. (1989) Thayer's Gull in Ireland in March 1989. *Dutch*

Birding 11: 81-83.

Mallalieu, M. & T. N. Hodge (1981) Yellow-legged Herring Gulls in North Kent. *Brit. Birds* 74: 351-353.

Malling Olsen, K. (1984) Sabinemågen – stormfuld gæst fra det høje nord. *Fugle* 3/4: 18-19.

Malling Olsen, K. (1986a) De store hvide måger. *Fugle* 5/1: 26-27.

Malling Olsen, K. (1986b) När ruggar tärnmåsen till vinterdräkt? *Vår Fågelvärld* 45: 286-287.

Malling Olsen, K. (1991a) Fältbestämning av tärnmås. *Fåglar i Uppland* 18: 185-193.

Malling Olsen, K. (1991b) Fältbestämning av vittrut och vitvingad trut – samt något om avvikande trutar, thayertrut och kumlientrut. *Fåglar i Stockholmstrakten* 20: 145-157.

Malling Olsen, K. (1992) *Danmarks fugle – en oversigt.* DOF, København.

Malling Olsen, K. (1993) Sträcket av måsar och tärnor vid Falsterbo sommaren och hösten 1991 och 1992. *Anser* 32: 253-262.

Malling Olsen, K. (1997) Fältbestämning av trädmås *Larus philadelphia. Roadrunner* 3/1: 6-11.

Malling Olsen, K. & H. Larsson (1993) Fältbestämning av ringnäbbad mås och fiskmås. *Fåglar i Uppland* 20: 85-96.

Malling Olsen, K. & H. Larsson (1995a) Svarthuvad mås, en allt mer regelbunden raritet. *Vår Fågelvärld* 54/4: 34-38.

Malling Olsen, K. & H. Larsson (1995b) *Terns of Europe and North America.* Christopher Helm (A&C Black), London.

Malling Olsen, K. 2003. Die Bestimmung der Ringschnabelmöwe *Larus delawarensis. Limicola* 17: 105-131.

Marion, L., P. Yésou, P. J. Dubois & P. Nicolau-Guillaumet (1985) Coexistence progressive de la reproduction de *Larus argentatus* et de *Larus cachinnans* sur les côtes atlantiques françaises. *Alauda* 53: 81-89.

Mark, D. M. (1981) Thayer's Gulls from Western Christmas Bird counts: a cautionary note. *Amer. Birds* 35: 898-900.

Marr, T. & R. Porter (1992) Spring seabird passage off Senegal. *Birding World* 5: 391-394.

Martin, J. P. (1982) Unusual upperwing pattern of Little Gull. *Brit. Birds* 75: 88.

Martins, R. P. (1989) Turkey Bird Report 1982–6. *Sandgrouse* 11: 1-42.

Mauer, K. (1984) Atypische Stormmeeuwen op Schiermonnikoog in augustus 1983. *Dutch Birding* 6: 57.

Maumary, L. & S. Gysel (1998) Seltene Vogelarten und ungewöhnlische Vogelbeobachtungen in der Schweiz im Jahre 1997. *Orn. Beob.* 95: 259-281.

Maunder, J. E. & W. Threlfall (1972) The breeding biology of the Black-legged Kittiwake in Newfoundland. *Auk* 89: 789-816.

Mayaud, N. (1931) Notes et remarques sur le passage des Mouettes de Sabine *Xema sabini* (Sabine) sur les côtes ouest de la France. *Alauda* 3: 106-109.

McDermot, P. (1994) Franklin's Gull in County Kerry – a species new to Ireland. *Irish Birds* 5: 203-204.

McGeehan, A. (1983) Ross's Gulls in Northern Ireland. *Irish Birds* 2: 309-317.

McGeehan, A. (1997a) Next stop North America? *Birders Journal* 6: 186-195.

McGeehan, A. (1997b) Thayer's Gull in Belfast. *Dutch Birding* 20: 47-48.

McGeehan, A. & M. Garner (1997) The Thayer's Gull in Belfast. *Birding World* 10: 93-100.

McGeehan, A. & R. Millington (1998) The adult Thayer's Gull in Donegal. *Birding World* 11: 102-108.

McGill, A. R. (1955) The two large gulls in eastern Australia. *Emu* 43: 65-66.

McGowan, R. Y. & A. C. Kitchener (2001) Historical and taxonomic review of the Iceland Gull *Larus glaucoides* complex. *Brit. Birds* 94: 191-195.

McInerny, C., Sweeney, J. & Votier, S. 2002. Winter gull watching in the Glasgow area. *Birding Scotland* 5: 71-87.

McKenzie, P. M. (1990) First summer record of the Common Black-headed Gull for Puerto Rico. *Amer. Birds* 44: 1092-1093.

Meeus, H. & M.-L. Meeus (1984) Leg colour of immature Yellow-legged Herring Gulls *Larus cachinnans* at the Bosphorus. *Wielewaal* 50: 68-69.

Meeus, H. & M.-L. Meeus (1985) On bill colour of immature Yellow-legged Herring Gulls *Larus cachinnans* at the Bosphorus. *Wielewaal* 51: 57-59.

Mehlum, F. & P. E. Fjeld (1987) Catalogue of seabird colonies in Svalbard. *Norsk Polarinst Rapp.* 35.

Meininger, P. L. (1977) Waarneming van een Drieteenmeeuw *Rissa tridactyla* met rode poten. *Limosa* 50: 146.

Meininger, P. L. (1995) Little Gulls breeding in south-western Netherlands. *Dutch Birding* 17: 152-154.

Meininger, P. L. & J. P. Bekhuis (1990) The Mediterranean Gull *Larus melanocephalus* as breeding bird in the Netherlands and Europe. *Limosa* 63: 121-134.

Meininger, P. L. & U. G. Sørensen (1992) Armenian Gulls *Larus armenicus* in Egypt 1989/90, with notes on the winter distributions of large gulls. *Avocetta* 16: 89-92.

Meininger, P. L. & U. G. Sørensen (1993) Egypt as a major wintering area of Little Gulls. *Brit. Birds* 86: 407-411.

Meininger, P. L., U. G. Sørensen & G. A. M. Atta (1986) The breeding birds of the lakes in the Nile Delta. *Sandgrouse* 7: 1-20.

Meininger, P. L., P. Raevel & W. Hoogendoorn (1993) Occurrence of Mediterranean Gull at le Portel in north-western France. *Dutch Birding* 15: 45-54.

Meininger, P. L., P. A. Wolf, D. A. Hadoud & M. F. A. Essghaier (1996) Notes on the coastal birds of Libya, July 1993. *Sandgrouse* 18: 53-60.

Meltofte, H. & J. Faldborg (1987) Forekomsten af måger og terner på Blåvandshuk 1963–77. *Dansk Orn. Foren. Tidsskr.* 81: 137-166.

Meltofte, H., C. Edelstam, G. Granström, J. Hammar & C. Hjort (1981) Ross's Gulls in the Arctic pack-ice. *Brit. Birds* 74: 316-320.

Melville, D. S. (1990) Notes on the identification of adult Slaty-backed Gulls. *Hong Kong Bird Rep.* 1989: 144-150.

Melville, D. S. (1991) Yellow-legged Herring Gulls in Essex. *Brit. Birds* 84: 342-343.

Meschini, E. & S. Frugis, eds. (1993) Atlante degli uccelli nidificanti in Italia. *Suppl. Ric. Biol. Selvaggina* 20: 1-344.

de Mesel, D. (1990) Geetpootmeeuwen, *Larus cachinnans michahellis*, in Belgie. Een analyse van ringgegevens. *Giervalk* 80: 25-56.

Messenger, D. (1993) Spring passage of Little Gulls across Northern England. *Brit. Birds* 86: 397-406.

Michev, T. & Profirov, L. 2003. Mid-winter numbers of waterbirds in Bulgaria (1977-2001). Pensoft, Sofia–Moscow.

Mierauskas, P., E. Greimas & V. Buzun (1991) A comparison of morphometrics, wing-tip pattern & vocalizations between Yellow-legged Herring Gulls (*Larus argentatus*) from eastern Baltic and *Larus cachinnans*. *Act. Orn. Lituanica* 4: 3-26.

Mierauskas, P., E. Greimas & V. Buzun (1992) Taxonomic status of yellow-legged Herring Gulls in eastern Baltic. *Act. Orn. Lituanica* 4: 91-94.

Migot, P. (1985) Le Goéland argenté *Larus argentatus argenteus* Brehm en Bretagne: caractéristiques biométriques des individus (annexe). *Alauda* 55: 67-69.

Mikkola, K. (1970) Identification of albino Herring Gulls. *Orn. Fennica* 47: 172-176.

Millington, R. (1991) Six-in-a-row Quizbird No. 4. Solution. *Birding World* 4: 181-182.

Millington, R. (1993) Identification and status of Kumlien's Gull. *Birding World* 6: 101-106.

Millington, R. 2002. Pipits, dippers, gulls and more - the best winter sightings. *Birding World* 15: 62-71.

Millington, R. & M. Garner (1998) American Herring Gulls in another age. *Birding World* 11: 109-112.

Millington, R. & M. Garner (1999) Winter gulls gallery. *Birding World* 12: 62-68.

Mills, E. L. (1969) Hurricane "Gladys" and its ornithological effect on the Maritime Provinces. *Nova Scotia Bird Soc. Newsl.* 11: 6-16.

Milon, P., J.-J. Petter & G. Randrianasolo (1973) *Faune de Madagascar 35: Oiseaux.* Tananarive & Paris.

Mitchell, D. & S. Young (1997) *Photographic handbook of the rare birds of Britain and Europe.* New Holland, London.

Mjøs, A. T. & M. Garner (2000) The Thayer's Gull in Norway. *Birding World* 13: 10-11.

Mjøs, A. T. & K. E. Solheim (1995) Europas østligste funn av ringnebbsmåke i Vardø – och litt om artens hekkestatus, opptreden i Norge og kjennetegn i felt. *Vår Fuglefauna* 18: 147-153.

Moerbeek, D. J. (1993) Ross' Meeuw te IJmuiden in november 1992. *Dutch Birding* 15: 7-12.

Moerbeek, D. J. & W. Hoogendoorn (1993) Ringsnavelmeeuw in Belgisch-Nederlands grensgebied in april 1992. *Dutch Birding* 15: 249-254.

Møller, A. P. (1978) Mågernes yngleudbredelse, bestandsstørrelse og -ændringer i Danmark med supplerende oplysninger om forholdene i det øvrige Europa. *Dansk Orn. Foren. Tidsskr.* 72: 15-39.

Monaghan, P. (1983) The geographical variation of the Herring Gull within Britain and in northern Europe: a biometrical approach. *Ibis* 125: 412-417.

Monaghan, P. & N. Duncan (1979) Plumage variation in known-age Herring Gulls. *Brit. Birds* 72: 100-103.

Monroe, B. L., Jr. (1988) Summary of highest counts of individuals for Canada and the United States. *Amer. Birds* 42: 1184-1190.

Monroe, B. L., Jr. (1989) Summary of highest counts of individuals for Canada and the United States. *Amer. Birds* 43: 1213-1220.

Montevecchi, W. A., D. K. Cairns, A. E. Burger, R. D Elliot & J. Wells (1987) The status of the Common Black-headed Gull in Newfoundland and Labrador. *Amer. Birds* 41: 197-203.

Monzikov, D. G. & E. N. Panov (1996) Allopatric hybridization of gull complex *Larus argentatus–cachinnans–fuscus*: structure of a mixed colony. *Uspekhi sovremenzoy biologii* 116(3): 369-383.

Moore, C. C. (1982) Notes on a first-year Iceland Gull (*Larus glaucoides*) at Peniche (Portugal). *Cyanopica* 2: 42-43.

Moore, C. C. (1994) The first record of American Herring Gull for Portugal. *Airo* 5: 32-34.

Moore, C. C. (1996) Ship-attending movements of Atlantic Yellow-legged Gulls in Portuguese waters. *Dutch Birding* 18: 18-22.

Moores, N. (1998) Saunders's Gull colony in South Korea: first nesting records outside the People's Republic of China. *Orient. Bird Club Bull.* 28: 42-43.

Morgan, P. G. D. (1989) Unusual plumage of Lesser Black-backed Gull. *Brit. Birds* 82: 220-221.

Moritz, D. (1988) Ungewöhnlich starkes Auftreten der Zwergmöwe *Larus minutus* in Frühjahr 1987 bei Helgoland. *Limicola* 2: 109-112.

Moynihan, M. (1959) A revision of the family Laridae (Aves). *Amer. Mus. Novit.* 1928.

Mulder, J. & J. de Ridder (1985) Kelp Gull in Kenya in January 1984. *Dutch Birding* 7: 138-139.

Mullarney, K. (1982) Mystery photographs 6: Ring-billed Gull. *Dutch Birding* 4: 20-22.

Mullarney, K. (1990) American Herring Gulls in Ireland. *Birding World* 3: 96-100.

Mullarney, K. (2000) Monthly Marathon: Audouin's Gull. *Brit. Birds* 93: 405-406.

Mullarney, K. (2001) Monthly Marathon: Little Gull. *Brit. Birds* 94: 54-55.

Müller, A (1996) Hinweise zur Bestimmung von Grossmöwen (*Larus* spec.). *Charadrius* 32: 135-148.

Murphy, R. C. (1936) *Oceanic birds of South America,* Vol. 1/II. American Museum of Natural History, New York.

Murray, R., ed. (1994) *Scottish Bird Report 1993.* Scottish Ornithologists' Club, Edinburgh.

Muse, C. S. & D. Muse (1980) First record of a gull *Larus atricilla* for the Samoan Islands. *Amer. Birds* 34: 848-849.

Nankinov, D. N. (1992a) The nesting by the Herring Gull

(*Larus argentatus*) in the towns and villages of Bulgaria. *Avocetta* 16: 93-94.

Nankinov, D. N. (1992b) Status and migration of the Slender-billed Gull (*Larus genei*) in Bulgaria. *Avocetta* 16: 95-97.

Nankinov, D. 1989. On the migration of the Mediterranean Gull (*Larus melanocephalus*) in Bulgaria. Pp. 173-179 in Aquilar, J. S., Monmailliu, X. & Paterson, A. M. (eds.): Status and conservation of seabirds. Proc. II. Mediterr. Seabirds Symp. 25-26.3.1989, Calviá.

Nankinov, D. 1998. First addition to the list of birds of Bulgaria. *Riv. Ital. Orn.* 68: 183-187.

Nankinov, D. 2000. Fie Fischmöwe *Larus ichthyaetus* aus Gast in Bulgaria. *Orn. Mitt.* 52: 422-423.

Nankinov, D. 2001. Die Lönnbergmöwe *Larus relictus*: Eine Neue Art für die Fauna des westlichen Paleatktis. *Orn. Mitt.* 53: 120-121.

Nankinov, D. N., K. Popov & S. Kirilev (1996) Die Dünnschnabelmöwe *Larus genei* – ein neuer Brutvogel an den Bulgarischen Schwarzmeerkuste. *Limicola* 10: 199-201.

Nankinov, D. N., Simeonov, S. D., Michev, T. M., & Ivanov, B. E. 1997. Fauna Bulgarica [The fauna of Bulgaria], vol. 26. Aves. Part II. Academic Publishing House "Prof. Marin Drinov" & "Pensoft", Sofia.

Neubauer, G. & R. Millington (2000) Caspian Gull identification revisited. *Birding World* 13: 462-465.

Néve, G. (1986) Observation d'une Mouette rieuse (*Larus ridibundus*) mélanique. *Aves* 23: 63-64.

Néve, G. (1988) Observation d'un Goéland atypique, hybride possible argenté × Goeland bourgmestre *Larus argentatus × hyperboreus*. *Aves* 25: 136-138.

Nicholson, E. M. (1975) Field characters of Audouin's Gull. *Brit. Birds* 68: 297-298.

Nicolau-Guillaumet, P. (1977) Mise au point et réflexions sur la répartition des Goélands argentés *Larus argentatus* en France. *Alauda* 45: 53-73.

Nightingale,T. & M. Hill (1993) *Birds of Bahrain*. Immel Publ., London.

Nikander, P. J. (1993) Tringa 10 Määrityskilpailu jäsenille. *Tringa* 20: 140-141.

Nikander, P. J. (1996) Nuorit isot lokit. Juvenile large gulls. *Alula* 2: 8-15.

Nikolov, S. & Nikolov, B. 2003. Great Black-headed Gull *Larus ichthyaetus*. *Acrocephalus* 24: 42.

Nikula, B. (1993) Common Black-headed Gull. *Birding* 25: 54-60.

Nisbet, I. C. T. (1978) Recent changes of gull populations in the western North America. *Ibis* 120: 129-130.

Noordhuis, R. & A. L. Spaans (1992) Interspecific competition for food between Herring *Larus argentatus* and Lesser Black-backed Gulls *Larus fuscus* in the Dutch Wadden Sea area. *Ardea* 80: 115-132.

Norderhaug, M. (1989) *Svalbards fugler*. Dreyer, Oslo.

Oddie, B. (1994) Possible Common Gull × Mediterranean Gull hybrid. *Dutch Birding* 16: 72.

Oddie, B. & P. Doherty (1995) *A Bird Images video guide: the gulls of Britain*. Bird Images.

Ogilvie, M. & the Rare Breeding Birds Panel (2001) Rare breeding birds in the United Kingdom in 1999. *Brit. Birds* 94: 344-381.

Ogilvie, M. & the Rare Breeding Birds Panel (2002) Rare Breeding Birds in the United Kingdom in 2000. *Brit. Birds* 95: 542-583.

Oliver, P. J. (1981) Herring Gull with yellow legs nesting in London. *Brit. Birds* 74: 353.

Olsson, V. (1983) Om mystiska truten i Kåseberga. *Anser* 22: 95-96.

Olsson, V. (1988) Flyttnings- och spridningsförhållanden hos havstrutar *Larus marinus* och grårutar *Larus argentatus* från Gryts skärgård, Östergötland. *Vår Fågelvärld* 47: 246-256.

Olthoff, M. (1997) Lachmeeuw in Groningen in augustus–september 1997. *Dutch Birding* 20: 107-110.

Onnen, J. (1981) Erstnachweis einer adulten Mittelmeer-Silbermöwe (*Larus argentatus michahellis*) an der deutschen Nordsee-Küste. *Vogelwarte* 31: 111-112.

Orchard, M. J. (1998) Presumed melanistic Black-headed Gull. *Brit. Birds* 91: 561-562.

Oro, D. & A. Martinez (1994) Migration and dispersal of Audouin's Gull *Larus audouinii* from the Ebro Delta colony. *Ostrich* 65: 225-230.

Oro, D., L. Jover & X. Ruiz (1996a) Influence of trawling activities on the breeding ecology of a threatened seabird, Audouin's Gull *Larus audouinii*. *Mar. Ecol. Prog. Ser.* 139: 19-29.

Oro, D., X. Genovart, X. Ruiz, J. Jiménez & J. García-Gans (1996b) Differences in diet, population size and reproductive performance between two colonies of Audouin's Gull *Larus audouinii* affected by a trawling moratorium. *J. Avian Biol.* 27: 245-251.

Orr, C. D. & J. L. Parsons (1982) Ivory Gulls *Pagophila eburnea*, and ice-edges in Davis Strait and the Labrador Sea. *Canad. Field-Nat.* 96: 323-328.

Osborn, K. (1985) Possible "Eastern" Common Gull on Fair Isle. *Brit. Birds* 78: 454.

Palmer, R. S. (1962) *Handbook of North American birds*, vol. 1. Yale University Press, New Haven.

Palmgren, R. (1918) Om bastardering mellan måsarter i Högholmens zoologiska trädgård sommaren 1918. – *Larus glaucus* Brünn hane × *L. fuscus* L. hona. *Medd. Sol. Fauna Flora Fenn.* 45: 44-46.

Paludan, K. (1953) Nogle resultater af Københavns zoologiske museums ringmærkning af *Larus argentatus*. *Vidensk. Medd. Dansk Naturh. Foren.* 115: 181-204.

Panov, E. N. & D. G. Monzikov (2000) Status of the form *barabensis* within the "*Larus argentatus–cachinnans–fuscus* complex". *Brit. Birds* 93: 227-241.

Panov, N., V. I. Grabovsky & L. Y. Zykova (1991) Biology of nesting behaviour and taxonomy of *Larus cachinnans* 3. Specificity of communication signals. *Zool. Zh.* 70: 73-89.

Paterson, A. M. (1985a) Identificación de campo de las gaviotas *Larus glaucoides* y *Larus hyperboreus*. *Garcilla* 65: 42-46.

Paterson, A. M. (1985b) Unusual wing-tip pattern of third-year Mediterranean Gull. *Brit. Birds* 78: 195.

Paterson, A. M., A. Martinez-Vilalta & J. I. Diez (1992) Partial breeding failure of Audouin's Gull in two Spanish colonies in 1991. *Brit. Birds* 85: 97-100.

Patten, S. & A. R. Weisbrod (1974) Sympatry and interbreeding of Herring and Glaucous-winged Gulls in south-eastern Alaska. *Condor* 76: 343-344.

Pedersen, K. (1983) Sorthovedet Måge. *Fugle* 5/3: 2.

Pedersen, K. T., E. B. Fritze & S. P. Kharitonov (2000) Migration patterns of Common Gulls *Larus canus* ringed in the non-breeding season in Copenhagen and the surrounding area. *Ringing & Migration* 20: 97-106.

Pedrozzi, V. & X. Ruiz (1995) On the current status of Audouin's Gull *Larus audouinii* in the Mediterranean. P.40 in M. L. Tasker, ed. *Threats to seabirds: Proc 5th Intern Seabird Group Conf.* Sandy.

Peltomäki, J. (2000) Finland next – Ring-billed Gull. *Alula* 6: 2-6.

Pennington, M. (1997) Glaucous and Herring Gull hybridization. *Birding World* 10: 352.

Pennington, M. G. (1998) Another melanistic Black-headed Gull. *Brit. Birds* 91: 563.

Pepin, D. & M. Duquet (1989) Une Mouette mélanocephale *Larus melanocephalus* en Franche-Comté. *Nos Oiseaux* 40: 181-182.

Perennou, C., T. Mundkur, D. A. Scott, A. Folkestad & L. Kvenild (1994) *The Asian waterfowl census 1987–91: distribution and status of Asian waterfowl*. AWB Publ. 86/IWRB Publ. 24, Kuala Lumpur & Slimbridge.

Petersen, Æ. (1998) *Islenskir Fuglar*. Vaka-Helgafell, Reykjavik.

Petersen, B. S. (1984) Rekrutteringsområdet for Sølvmågerne *Larus argentatus* i Øresund med særligt henblik på ændringer i nyere tid. *Dansk Orn. Foren. Tidsskr.* 78: 15-24.

Petersen, I. & U. G. Sørensen (1981) Migration studies from the eastern part of the lagoon "Sabkhet el Bardawil" on the north coast of the Sinai Peninsula, 7–30 September 1980.

Privately published, Copenhagen.

Peterz, M. & T. Rönnertz (1980) Iakttagelser rörande flyktsätt hos några havsfåglar. *Anser* 19: 167-173.

Peterz, M., B. Oldén & P. E. Jönsson (1988) Havsfågelräkning från färjor i Kattegatt. *Pelagicus* 3: 17-40.

Péturson, G. (1987) Flækingsfuglar á Íslandi: Máfar. *Náttúrfredingurinn* 57: 57-79.

Pforr, M. & A. Limbrunner (1981) *The breeding birds of Europe: a photographic handbook*, Vol. 1. Hollowbrook, London.

Phillips, N. R. (1982) Observations on the birds of North Yemen. *Sandgrouse* 4: 37-59.

Pierotti, P. (1987) Isolating mechanisms in seabirds. *Evolution* 41: 559-570.

Pineau, O., Y. Kayser, M. Sali, A. Gueye &. H. Hafner (2001) The Kelp Gull at Banc d'Arguin – a new Western Palearctic bird. *Birding World* 14: 110-111.

Pittaway, R. (1999) Taxonomic history of Thayer's Gull. *Ontario Birds* 17: 2-13.

Plata, W. & B. Kotlarz (1992) Pierwsza obserwacja mewy cienkodziobej *Larus genei* w Polsce. *Notatki Orn.* 33: 153-155.

Plenge, M. A. (1974) Notes on some birds in west-central Peru. *Condor* 76: 326-330.

Pleske, T. (1928) Birds of the Eurasian tundra. *Mem. Boston Soc. Nat. Hist.* 6: 111-285.

Plomp, M. (2001) *Onze meeuwen en Sterns.* Plomp Digital Videos.

Poelmans, W. (1992) Nearctic gulls in the western Palearctic. *Dutch Birding* 14: 52.

Poole, C. (1994) More Saunders's Gull colonies found in north China. *Orient. Bird Club Bull.* 19: 19.

Poor, H. H. (1946) Plumage and soft-parts variations in the Herring Gull. *Auk* 63: 135-151.

Portenko, L. A. (1939) Fauna Anadyrskogo kraja pticy. *Trudy Inst polarn Zemled zivotnovod i promysl choz* 5: 5-209; 6: 5-197.

Porter, R. F., R. P. Martins, K. D. Shaw & I. Sørensen (1996a) The status of non-passerines in southern Yemen and the records of the OSME survey in spring 1993. *Sandgrouse* 17: 22-53.

Porter, R. F., S. Christensen & P. Schiermacker-Hansen (1996b) *Field guide to the birds of the Middle East.* T.& A. D. Poyser, London.

Portier, N. (1999) Autumn seawatching in northern France in the 1990s. *Birding World* 12: 334-338.

Post, P. W. & R. H. Lewis (1995a) The Lesser Black-backed Gull in the Americas: occurrence and subspecies identity. Part 1: taxonomy, distribution, and migration. *Birding* 27: 283-290.

Post, P. W. & R. H. Lewis (1995b) Lesser Black-backed Gull in the Americas. Part 2. *Birding* 27: 370-390.

Powell, C. (1990) Mediterranean Gulls at Folkestone. *Birding World* 3: 239-241.

Pratt, H. D., P. L. Bruner & D. G. Berrett (1987) *A field guide to Hawaii and the tropical Pacific.* Princeton University Press, Princeton.

Preiswork, G. (1981a) Protocol of the observation of an Iceland Gull *Larus glaucoides* at Porto (Portugal). *Cyanopica* 2: 35-39.

Preiswork, G. (1981b) Protocol of the observation of a Laughing Gull *Larus atricilla* at Porto (Portugal). *Cyanopica* 2: 40-42.

Price, J., S. Orvege & A. Price (1995) *The summer atlas of North American birds.* Academic Press. London.

Pulliainen, E. (1962) The invasions of the Kittiwake into Finland in February and March 1959 and 1962. *Orn. Fennica* 39: 81-96.

Pyle, P. (1997) First year Slaty-backed Gull. *Birders J.* 6: 251.

Pyzhianov, S. V. & I. I. Tubitsyn (1992) Variability of phenotypic characters in the Mongolian subspecies of the Herring Gull. Pp.18-20 in A. V. Zubakin & A. N. Khoklov, eds. *The Herring Gull and related forms: distribution, systematics, ecology.* Russian Academy of Sciences, North Caucasian Department, Stavropol.

Radford, M. C. (1962) British ringing recoveries of the Black-headed Gull. *Bird Study* 9: 42-55.

Ramadan-Jadari, G. & M. Ramadan-Jadari (1997) Notes on some breeding birds in Lebanon. *Sandgrouse* 19: 122-125.

Rand, A. L. (1942) *Larus kumlieni* and its allies. *Canad. Field-Nat.* 56: 123-126.

Rasmussen, B. (1998) Kaspisk Måge – forekommer regelmæssigt i Danmark. *Pica* 10/1: 4-11.

Rattiste, K. (1993) Distribution of the West Estonian Common Gull *Larus canus* in the nonbreeding period. *Orn. Fennica* suppl 3: 61-62.

Rauste, V. (1999) Kennzeichen und Mauser von "Baltischen Heringsmöwen" *Larus (fuscus) fuscus* und "Tundramöwen" *L. (fuscus) heuglini. Limicola* 12: 105-128, 153-188.

Redman, P. S. (1981) Yellow-legged Herring Gulls in France and Britain. *Brit. Birds* 74: 349-350.

Redshaw, K. (1972) Slender-billed Gull in Kent. *Brit. Birds* 65: 395-397.

Ree, V. (1974) Kanadisk hettemåke observert i Norge. *Sterna* 13: 109-115.

Reichholf, J. (1987) Erste Brut der Weisskopfmöwe *Larus cachinnans* in Bayern. *Anz. orn. Ges. Bayern* 26: 270.

Renaud, W. E. & P. L. McLaren (1982) Ivory Gull (*Pagophila eburnea*) distribution in late summer and autumn in eastern Lancaster Sound and western Baffin Bay. *Arctic* 35: 118-125.

Rendall, A. (1991) Eine Ringschnabelmöwe *Larus delawarensis* in Bayern. *Limicola* 5: 248-250.

Rheinwald, G. (1993) *Atlas der Verbreitung und Häufigkeit der Brutvögel Deutschlands Kartierung um 1985.* Schriftenreihe des DDA 12. Berlin.

Richards, K. C. & F. B. Gill (1976) The 1974 mystery gull at Brigantine, New Jersey. *Birding* 8: 325-328.

Richardson, C. (1990) *The birds of the United Arab Emirates.* Dubai & Warrington, Cheshire.

Richardson, C. & S. Aspinall (1997a) Systematic list of the birds reported in 1994. *Emirates Bird Report* 19: 20-85.

Richardson, C. & S. Aspinall (1997b) 1995 international waterfowl census. *Emirates Report Bird* 19: 89-93.

Richardson, C., S. Aspinall & M. Verhage (1997) Abu Dhabi islands breeding bird survey. *Emirates Bird Report* 19: 104-112.

Ridgley, R. & Greenfield, P. 2001. The Birds of Ecuador, Vol. I: Status, Distribution and Taxonomy. Cornell University Press, Ithaca and Christopher Helm, London.

Rigbäck, L. (1988) Vittruten *Larus hyperboreus* på Öland. *Calidris* 17: 83-92.

Rinnhofer, G. (1985) Feldornithlogische Kennzeichen unausgefärbter Zwergmöwen. *Falke* 32: 298-300.

Risberg, L. (1990) Sveriges Fåglar. *Vår Fågelvärld* suppl 14. Stockholm.

Ritter, M. & E. Fuchs (1980) Das Zugverhalten der Lachmöwe nach schweizerischen Ringfunden. *Orn. Beob.* 77: 219-229.

Robel, D. (1988) Leuzistische Lachmöwe *Larus ridibundus* mit Ohrfleck. *Limicola* 2: 29-30.

Robel, D. & R. Beschow (1994) Eine Fischmöwe *Larus ichthyaetus* in Brandenburg. *Limicola* 8: 51-62.

Roberts, T. J. (1991) *The birds of Pakistan*, Vol. 1. Oxford University Press. Oxford.

Robinson, P. (1991) "Red-legged" Kittiwake on Scilly. *Birding World* 4: 258-259.

Rogers, M. J. & the Rarities Committee (1999) Report on rare birds in Great Britain in 1998. *Brit. Birds* 92: 554-609.

Rogers, M. J. & the Rarities Committee (2000) Report on rare birds in Great Britain in 1999. *Brit. Birds* 93: 512-567.

Rogers, M. J. & the Rarities Committee (2001) Report on rare birds in Great Britain in 2000. *Brit. Birds* 94: 452-503.

Rogers, M. J. & The Rarities Committee (2002) Report on rare birds in Great Britain in 2001. *Brit. Birds* 95: 476-528.

Rogers, M. J. & the Rarities Committee (2003) Report on rare birds in Great Britain in 2002. *Brit. Birds* 96: 542-609.

Roggeman, W. (1970) The migration of *Larus ridibundus* ringed as chick in the north of Belgium. *Gerfaut* 60: 301-321.

Rönnertz, T. (1981) Sotvingad mås *Larus atricilla* ny art för Öland. *Calidris* 10: 260-261.

Rooke, K. B. (1949) Herring Gull with yellow legs in Dorset. *Brit. Birds* 42: 29-30.

Rosche, L. O. & R. L. Hannikman (1989) A wintering Sabine's Gull in Ohio, with comments on the winter status of this species in the ABA area. *Birding* 21: 241-246.

Rose, D. M. & D. A. Scott (1994) *Waterfowl population estimates.* IWRB Pulb. 29, Internatn. Wildfowl Res. Bur., Slimbridge.

Rosenzweig, M. (1989) Birdwatching in the Sinai. *OSME Bull.* 22: 10-19.

Rubunic, B. & Berezovikov, N. 2002. The fluctuations of breeding numbers of Relict Gull *Larus relictus* on Lake Alakol (SE Kazakhstan): a review of surveys for 1968-2001. *Acrocephalus* 23: 185-188.

Rufray, X. & Cramus, P. 2002. Note: Car des mélanisme chez les Larides. *Ornithos* 9: 168-169.

Rumbao, E. M. (1997) Estudio de la población y la ecologia trófica de la Gaviota Patiamarilla, *Larus cachinnans* Pallas, en Galicia. Thesis. Universidade de Santiago de Compostela.

Ruttledge, R. F. (1974) Unprecedented numbers of Little Gulls in Ireland. *Brit. Birds* 67: 166-167.

Ruttledge, R. F. (1990) Exceptional influx of Little Gulls on the North Wicklow coast. *Irish Birding News* 1/2: 73-74.

Ryder, J. P. (1978) Sexing Ring-billed Gulls externally. *Bird-Banding* 49: 218-222.

Ryttman, H., H. Tegelström & H. Jansson (1981) Genetiska undersökningar av artssammanband mellan grårtut *Larus argentatus* och silltrut *Larus fuscus*. *Vår Fågelvärld* 40: 239-248.

Salomonsen, F. (1967) *Grønlands fugle.* Rhodos, København.

Sangster, G. (1999) Trends in systematics. Relationship among gulls: new approaches. *Dutch Birding* 21: 207-218.

Satat, N. & B. Laird (1992) The Armenian Gull. *Birding World* 5: 32-36.

Schaaning, H. T. L. (1916) Bidrag til Novaja Zemljas fauna. *Dansk Orn. Foren. Tidsskr.* 10: 145-190.

Schiermacker-Hansen, P. (1998) Middelhavssølvmåge *Larus cachinnans*. *Strømstæren* 1998/3: 9-27.

Schiermacker-Hansen, P. & C. C. Tofte (1999) Middelhavssølvmåge *Larus cachinnans*. *DOF Nyt* 3/1999: 6-9.

Schnell, G. D., G. L. Worthen & M. E. Douglas (1985) Morphometric assessment of sexual dimorphism in skeletal elements of California Gulls. *Condor* 87: 483-493.

Schreiber, R. W. & P. J. Mock (1988) Christmas Bird Counts as indices of the population status of Brown Pelicans and three gull species in Florida. *Amer. Birds* 41: 1334-1339.

Schrijvershof, P. & R. Schrijvershof (1988) Ringsnavelmeeuw te Europoort in juli 1986. *Dutch Birding* 10: 20-24.

Schulenberg, T. S. (1980) A Franklin's Gull *Larus pipixcan* in southeastern Peru. *Giervalk* 70: 403-404.

Schuster, S. *et al.* (1983) *Die Vögel des Bodenseegebietes.* Ornithologische Arbeitsgemeinschaft Bodensee, Konstanz.

Schütt, R. (1979) Zum Vorkommen der Zwergmöwe (*Larus minutus*) im Lübecker Raum. *Corax* 7: 43-64.

de Schutter, G. (1989) Die Bestimmung der Grossmöwen in Belgien. *Orn. Mitt.* 41: 230-253.

Schweizer, M. 2003. Die Postjuvenilmauser der Mittelmeermöwe *Larus michahellis*. *Limicola* 17: 169-187.

Scott, J. M. (1971) Interbreeding of the Glaucous-winged and Western Gull in the Pacific northwest. *California Birds* 2: 129-133.

Scott, J. M. & E. Carp (1982) A midwinter survey of wetlands in Mesopotamia, Iraq. *Sandgrouse* 4: 60-76.

Serra, G., Melaga, L. & Baccetti, N. (eds.). 2001. Piano d'azione nazionale per il Gabbiano corso (*Larus audouinii*). *Quad. Cons. Natura.*

Sharrock, J. T. R. (1974) *Scarce migrant birds in Britain and Ireland.* T. & A. D. Poyser, Berkhamsted.

Sharrock, J. T. R. (1983) Rare breeding birds in the United Kingdom in 1981. *Brit. Birds* 67: 67-79.

Sharrock, J. T. R. & C. Davies (2000) The European Bird Report. *Brit. Birds* 93: 114-128.

Sharrock, J. T. R. & P. J. Grant, eds. (1982) *Birds new to Britain and Ireland.* T.& A. D. Poyser, Calton.

Shaw, T.-H. (1936) The birds of Hopeh province. *Fan Memorial Institute of Biology, Peking, Zool Sinica* B15: Fascicle I.

Sheldon, B. & R. Fredriksson (1994) Långnäbbad mås – ny art för Uppland! *Fåglar i Uppland* 21: 98-100.

Shepherd, K. B. & S. C. Votier (1993) Common Gull showing characters apparently consistent with North American race.

Brit. Birds 86: 220-223.

Shirihai, H. (1992) Grey-headed Gulls in Israel and their identification. *Dutch Birding* 14: 1-7.

Shirihai, H. (1996a) Identification and ageing of Audouin's Gull. *Birding World* 9: 52-61.

Shirihai, H. (1996b) *The birds of Israel.* Academic Press, London.

Shirihai, H. (1999) Fifty species new to Israel, 1979–1998, their discovery and documentation, with tips on identification. *Sandgrouse* 21: 45-105.

Shirihai, H., A. Jönsson & N. Sebba (1987) Brown-headed Gull in Israel in May 1985. *Dutch Birding* 9: 120-122.

Shitega, Y. (1993) Common Gull – an attempt to examine the subspecies of Common Gull occurring in Japan. *Birder* 7: 36-41.

Sibley, C. G. & B. L. Monroe Jr. (1990) *Distribution and taxonomy of birds of the world.* Yale University Press, New Haven.

Sibley, C. G. & B. L. Monroe (1995) *A supplement to the distribution and taxonomy of birds of the world.* Yale University Press, New Haven.

Sibley, D. (1993) *The birds of Cape May.* Cape May Bird Observatory, New Jersey.

Sibley, D. (1994) A guide to finding and identifying hybrid birds. *Birding* 26: 162-177.

Sibley, D. (2000) *The North American bird guide.* Pica Press., London.

Sick, H. (1979) Notes on some Brazilian birds. *Bull. Brit. Orn. Club* 99: 115-120.

Sinclair, I. (1993) Gull identification in southern Africa. *Bird. South Africa* 45: 3-7.

Sinclair, I., P. Hockey & W. Tarboton (1993) *Birds of southern Africa.* New Holland, London.

Siotkin, V. D. *et al.* (1988) *Colonial waterbirds of southern Ukraine – Charadriiformes.* Naukova Dumka, Kiev.

Skovgaard, P. (1932) Hvidehavsmaagen (*Larus argentatus omissus*) Suschkin, ny for Danmarks fauna. *Danske Fugle* 4: 17.

Small, A. (1987) Ring-billed Gull: first for Ecuador and the Galapagos. *Amer. Birds* 41: 390.

Small, B. (2001) The juvenile Caspian Gull in Suffolk. *Birding World* 14: 385.

Smith, A. E. (1989) Black-headed Gull in summer plumage in winter. *Brit. Birds* 82: 565.

Smith, G. (1999) The Ivory Gull in Suffolk. *Birding World* 12: 480-481.

Smith, N. G. (1966) Evolution of some arctic gulls (*Larus*): an experimental study of isolating mechanisms. *Orn. Monogr.* 4.

Smith, N. G. (1967) Visual isolation in gulls. *Sci. Amer.* 217: 94-102.

Smith, N. G. (1991) Arctic gulls 32 years later: a reply to Snell. *Col. Waterbirds* 12: 12-23.

Smith, P. H. (1987) The changing status of Little Gulls in North Merseyside, England. *Seabird* 10: 12-21.

Smith, R. D. (1988) Age and sex-related differences in biometrics and moult of Kittiwakes. *Ringing & Migration* 9: 44-48.

Snell, R. R. (1989) Status of *Larus* gulls at Home Bay, Baffin Island. *Col. Waterbirds* 12: 12-23.

Snell, R. R. (1991a) Conflation of the observed and the hypothesized: Smith's 1961 research in Home Bay, Baffin Island. *Col. Waterbirds* 14: 196-202.

Snell, R. R. (1991b) Intraspecific allozyme differentiation among North American white-headed *Larid*-gulls. *Auk* 108: 319-328.

Snell, R. R. (1991c) Variably plumaged Icelandic Herring Gulls reflect founders not hybrids. *Auk* 108: 329-341.

Snell, R. R. (1993) Variably plumaged Icelandic Herring Gulls: high intraspecific variation in a founder population. *Auk* 110: 410-413.

Snell. R. R. & W. E. Godfrey (1991) Geographical variation in the Iceland Gull (*Larus glaucoides*). Abstract Number 156. American Ornithologists' Union Meeting. Montreal.

SOF. 2003. *Sällsynta fåglar i Sverige.* 2: a uppl. Stockholm.

Sonobe, K., ed. (1982) *A field guide to the birds of Japan.* Wild Bird Society of Japan, Tokyo.

Sørensen, S. & J.-K. Jensen (1994) Sjældne fugle på Færøerne i

1990, 1991 og 1992. *Dansk Orn. Foren. Tidsskr.* 88: 33-38.

Southern, W. E. (1974a) Florida distribution of Ring-billed Gulls from the Great Lakes Region. *Bird-Banding* 45: 341-352.

Southern, W. E. (1974b) Seasonal distribution of Great Lakes region Ring-billed Gulls. *Jack-Pine Warbler* 52: 154-179.

Southern, W. E. (1980) Comparative distribution and orientation of North American Gulls. Pp.449-498 in J. Burger, B. L. Olla & H. E. Winn, eds. *Behaviour of marine animals* 4. Plenum Press, New York.

Southern, W. E. (1987) Gull research in the 1980s: symposium overview. *Stud. Avian Biol.* 10: 1-7.

Southern, W. E. & F. R. Moore (1974) Range extremes for Ring-billed Gulls from the Great Lakes region. *Inland Bird Band News* 46: 83-87.

Spanoghe, G. (1997) Zwergmöwen *Larus minutus* mit dunklen Oberflügeln. *Limicola* 11: 296-298.

Spear, L. B. (1987) Hybridization of the Glaucous and Herring Gull at the Mackenzie Delta, Canada. *Auk* 104: 123-125.

Spencer, B. J. & A. J. Lauro (1984) Separating first basic Ring-billed and Common Gull. *Dutch Birding* 6: 55-57.

Spencer, R. J. & the Rare Breeding Birds Panel (1990) Rare breeding birds in the United Kingdom in 1988. *Brit. Birds* 83: 353-390.

Spitzer, G. (1976) Zur Biometrie Adriatischer Silbermöwen *Larus argentatus michahellis*. *Vogelwarte* 28: 206-212.

Stanley, P. I., T. Brough, M. R. Fletcher, N. Horton & J. B. A. Rochard (1981) The origins of Herring Gulls wintering inland in southeast England. *Bird Study* 28: 123-132.

Stegemann, L. (1991) Yellow-legged Gulls with flesh-coloured legs. *Dutch Birding* 13: 176-177.

Stegmann, B. K. (1934a) Über die Formen der grossen Möwen subgenus *Larus* und ihre gegenseitige Beziehungen. *J. Orn.* 72: 340-380.

Stegmann, B. K. (1934b) Eine neue Form von *Xema sabini*. *Orn. Monatsb.* 42: 25-26.

Stegmann, B. K. (1935) Die paläarktischen Formen der Sturmmöwe. *Orn. Monatsb.* 43: 20-21.

Stegmann, B. (1960) Zur Systematik das Rassenkreises *L. argentatus*. *J. Orn.* 101: 489-499.

Stejneger, L. (1885) Results of Ornithological Exploration in the Commander Islands and in Kamtschatka. *Bull. U.S. Natn. Mus.* 29.

Stepanyan, L. S. (1975) *Sostav i raspredelenie ptic fauna SSSR.* Ne-vorob'inye, Moscow.

Stepanyan, L. S. (1990) *Conspectus of the ornithological fauna of the USSR.* Nauka, Moscow.

Stevenson, T. (1982) Further records of Slender-billed Gull *Larus genei* at Lake Turkana. *Scopus* 6: 22-23.

Stiles, F. G. & A. F. Skutch (1989) *A guide to the birds of Costa Rica.* Christopher Helm, London.

Stone, C. W. (1984) The pitfall of a white Kittiwake. *Brit. Birds* 77: 484-485.

Strack, R., M. Funch, H. Johansen & M. Rasmussen (1997) *Ishøj Fuglestation 1994–96.* DOF, Copenhagen.

Strang, C. A. (1977) Variation and distribution of Glaucous Gulls in western Alaska. *Condor* 79: 170-175.

Strangeman, P. J. (1982) Bill colour of winter adult Common Gull. *Brit. Birds* 75: 289-290.

Strann, K. B. & W. Vader (1992) The nominate Lesser Black-backed Gull *Larus fuscus fuscus*: a gull with a tern-like feeding biology, and the recent decrease in North Norway. *Ardea* 80: 133-142.

Stresemann, V. (1963) Zeitraum und Verlauf der Handschwingen-Mauser paläarctischer Möwen, Seeschwalben und Limicolen. *J. Orn.* 104: 424-435.

Stresemann, E. & N. W. Timofeeff-Ressovsky (1947) Artentstehung in geographischen Formenkreisen I. Der Formkreis *Larus argentatus–cachinnans–fuscus*. *Biol. Zentralbl.* 66: 57-76.

Stresemann, V. & E. Stresemann (1966) Die Mauser der Vögel. *J. Orn.* 107. Sonderdruck.

Stugart, G. W. (1977) A method of externally sexing gulls. *Bird-Banding* 48: 118-121.

Størkersen, Ø. R. (1986) Pink Black-headed Gulls. *Brit. Birds* 79:

211-212.

Sushkin, P. P. (1925) *List and distribution of the birds of the Russian Altai and adjacent parts of northwestern Mongolia, with a description of new or imperfectly known forms.* In Russian. Academy of Sciences of the USSR, Leningrad.

Suter, W. (1990) Comments on the breeding range of the Armenian Gull. *OSME Bull.* 25: 12-15.

Sutherland, M. P. (1983) Presumed hybrid Glaucous × Herring Gulls in Kent. *Brit. Birds* 76: 83-85.

Sutter, E. (1956) Über das gehäufte Auftreten der Dreizehenmöwe in der Schweiz im Winter 1954/55. *Orn. Beob.* 53: 81-93.

Sutton, G. M. (1968) Review of: Smith, N. G. (1966) Evolution in some arctic gulls: an experimental study of isolating mechanisms. *Ornithological Monographs* 4. *Auk* 85:142-145.

Svensson, L., P. J. Grant, K. Mullarney & D. Zetterström (1999) *Collins bird guide.* Collins, London.

Svensson, S., M. Svensson & M. Tjernberg (1999) *Svensk fågelatlas.* SOF, Lunds Universitet.

Sweeney, J. J. (1981) Glaucous Gull with unusually small bill. *Brit. Birds* 74: 524.

Symens, D., G. Driessens & P. Buys (1988) Eerste waarmening van een Franklins Meeuw in België en Nederland. *Oriolus* 54: 170-174.

Symons, R. D. (1968) Atypical nesting of Bonaparte's Gull in Saskatchewan. *Blue Jay* 26: 70-74.

Tarboton, W. R., M. I. Kemp & A. C. Kemp (1987) *Birds of the Transvaal.* Transvaal Museum, Pretoria.

Taverner, J. H. (1970a) Mediterranean Gulls nesting in Hampshire. *Brit. Birds* 63: 67-79.

Taverner, J. H. (1970b) A presumed hybrid Mediterranean × Black-headed Gull in Hampshire. *Brit. Birds* 63: 380-382.

Taverner, P. A. (1933) A study of the Kumlien's Gull. *Canad. Field-Nat.* 47: 88-90.

Teyssèdre, A. (1983) Etude comparée de quatre populations de Goélands argentés à pattes jaunes d'Europe occidentale. *Oiseau et R.F.O.* 53: 43-52.

Teyssèdre, A. (1984) Comparaison acoustique de *Larus argentatus argenteus*, *L. fuscus graellsii*, *L. cachinnans* (?) *michahellis* et du Goélands argenté à pattes jaunes cantabrique. *Behaviour* 88: 13-33.

Thiede, W. (1995) Die Grossmöwen Zyperns. *Orn. Mitt.* 47: 3-8.

Thomas, L. & K. Andreasen (1986) Wingbeat rates of Glaucous and Iceland Gulls. *Brit. Birds* 79: 42.

Thorne, R. H. F. (1996) Melanistic Black-headed Gull. *Brit. Birds* 89: 570.

Thrainsson, G. L. & G. Péturson (1997) Sjaldgæfir fuglar á Íslandi 1995. *Bliki* 18: 23-50.

Threlfall, W. & D. D. Jewer (1978) Notes on the standard body measurements of two populations of Herring Gull *Larus argentatus*. *Auk* 95: 749-753.

Tjernberg, M. (1976) Dvärgmås och tretåig mås vid Skatudden den 18 okt. 1975. *Fåglar i Uppland* 3: 5.

Tomkovic, P. S. (1986) Materialy pa biologii beloj cajki na ostrove Gréem-Bell (Zemlya Franca-Josifa). *Aktualnye problemy ornitologii Moscow.* 34-39.

Topp, A. (1997) Photonews. *Alula* 3: 130-131.

Tostain, O. & J.-L. Dujardin (1989) Mise en place d'une aire d'hivernage néotropicale de laridés holarctiques: *Larus pipixcan*, *Larus ridibundus* et *Larus fuscus*. *Alauda* 57: 189-215.

Tove, M. H. (1985) First Utah records of Thayer's and Mew Gulls, with comments on their regional distribution and status. *Western Birds* 16: 147-160.

Tove, M. H. (1993) Field separation of Ring-billed, Mew, Common, and Kamtchatka Gulls. *Birding* 25: 387-401.

Tove, M. H. & D. L. Fischer (1988) Recent changes in the status of wintering gull populations in Utah. *Amer. Birds* 42: 182-190.

Tucker, G. M. & M. F. Heath (1994) *Birds in Europe: their conservation status.* BirdLife International, Cambridge, UK.

Tucker, V. (1985) Origin of British Glaucous Gulls. *Brit. Birds* 78: 355-356.

Tuomainen, J. (1998) Kuopion seudun selkälokit. *Siivekäs* 19: 4-

14.

Tyrberg, T. (1998) Fågelrapport för 1997. *Fågelåret* 1997: 89-139.

Udvardy, M. D. F. & T. Säll (1987) A Ring-billed Gull on the Galapagos Islands. *Western Birds* 18: 175-176.

Ujihara, O. & U. Michinka (2000) *Kamome Shikibetu hand book*. Tokyo.

Ujihara, O. & M. Ujihara (1992) Kamome Shikbetsu Gaido. *Nihon no Seibustu* 6, special issue. Bun-ichi Sogo Shuppan, Tokyo.

Ullman, M. (1983) Ljus trut i Kåseberga hamn. *Anser* 22: 43-47.

Ullman, M. (1992) Vilken fågel? – hybrid vittrut × gråtrut. *Vår Fågelvärld* 51/1: 25, 51.

Ullman, M. (1993) Vilken fågel? *Vår Fågelvärld* 52/8: 7.

Ullman, M. (1997) "Kaspisk trut" och "medelhavstrut". *Vår Fågelvärld* 56/8: 37.

Ullman, M. (1998) Dvärgmåsen genomför fågelvärldens metamorfos. *Vår Fågelvärld* 57/1: 2-3.

Ullman, M. & H. Larsson (1998) Favorit i repris: Svarthuvad Mås. *Vår Fågelvärld* 57/3: 28-31.

Urban, E. K., C. H. Fry & S. Keith (1986) *The birds of Africa*, Vol. 3. Academic Press, London.

Väisinen, R. A., E. Lammi & P. Koskimies (1998) *Muuttuva pesimällinnusto*. Otava, Helsinki.

Vanderpoel, J. (1997) *The large gulls of North America*. The Advanced Video Series, 1. Peregrine Video Productions.

Varela, J. M. & E. de Juana (1987) Comparación de los plumajes neoptiles de *Larus audouinii* y *Larus cachinnans michahellis*. *Ardeola* 34: 113-122.

Vasiliu, G. D. (1968) Systema Avium Romaniae. *Alauda* (suppl.):1-120.

Vaughan, H. (1991) Common Gulls with pale irides. *Brit. Birds* 84: 342.

Vauk, G. & J. Prüter (1987) *Möwen. Arten, Bestände, Verbreitung, Probleme*. Ottendorf.

Vaurie, C. (1962) The status of *Larus relictus* and of other hooded gulls from central Asia. *Auk* 79: 303-309.

Vaurie, C. (1965) *The birds of the Palearctic fauna: non-passeriformes*. Witherby, London.

Veen, J. (1980) Breeding behaviour and breeding success of a colony Little Gulls *Larus minutus* in the Netherlands. *Limosa* 53: 73-83.

Verbeek, N. A. M. (1977) Timing of primary moult in adult Herring Gulls and Lesser Black-backed Gulls. *J. Orn.* 118: 87-93.

Verbeek, N. A. M. (1993) *Glaucous-winged Gull. The Birds of North America* No 59. Academy of Natural Sciences of Philadelphia.

Vercruijsse, H. (1995) In Frankrijk geringde Geelpootmeeuw gepaard met Zilvermeeuw op Neeltje Jans in 1992–94. *Dutch Birding* 17: 246-247.

Vermeer, K. (1963) The breeding biology of the Glaucous-winged Gull (*Larus glaucescens*) on Mandarte Island, B.C. *Occas. Pap. Brit. Colum. Prov. Mus.* 13: 1-104.

Vernon, J. D. R. (1969) Spring migration of the Common Gull in Britain and Ireland. *Bird Study* 16: 101-107.

Vernon, J. D. R. (1970) Feeding habitats and food of the Black-headed and Common Gulls. Part I. Feeding habits. *Bird Study* 17: 287-296.

Vernon, J. D. R. (1972) Feeding habitats and food of the Black-headed and Common Gulls. Part II: Food. *Bird Study* 19: 173-186.

Verrall, K. (1977) Laughing Gull in Argyllshire. *Scot. Birds* 9: 38.

Versluys, M. & J. Fokkema (1990) Franklins Meeuw in Brandemeer in juni 1988. *Dutch Birding* 12: 65-69.

Veysey, C. M. (1971) Colour of soft parts of immature Glaucous Gull. *Brit. Birds* 64: 458-460.

Vinicombe, K. E. (1971) Sabine's Gull hawking flying insects inland. *Brit. Birds* 64: 503-504.

Vinicombe, K. E. (1973) A second Ring-billed Gull in Glamorgan. *Brit. Birds* 66: 513-516.

Vinicombe, K. E. (1981) Yellow-legged Herring Gulls in Britain. *Brit. Birds* 74: 352-353.

Vinicombe, K. (1984) Mystery photographs. Herring Gull. *Brit. Birds* 77: 245-247.

Vinicombe, K. E. (1985) Ring-billed Gulls in Britain and Ireland. *Brit. Birds* 78: 327-337.

Vinicombe, K. E. (1988) Identification pitfalls and assessment problems 9: Ring-billed Gull. *Brit. Birds* 81: 126-134.

Vinicombe, K. (1995) Nice race, shame about the legs. *Birdwatch* 1995: 24-29.

Vinicombe, K. & P. J. Hopkin (1993) The Great Black-backed Gull in Britain. *Brit. Birds* 86: 201-205.

Visser, C. & C. A. van der Wal (1987) Ivoormeeuw op Schiermonnikoog in februari 1987. *Dutch Birding* 9: 60-62.

van der Vliet, R. E., J. van der Laan & CDNA (2001) Rare birds in the Netherlands in 2000. *Dutch Birding* 23: 315-347.

van der Vliet, R. E., J. van der Laan & CDNA (2002) Rare birds in the Netherlands in 2001. *Dutch Birding* 24: 325-349.

Voipio, P. (1954) Über die gelbfüssigen Silbermöwen Nordwesteuropas. *Acta Soc. Fauna Flora Fenn.* 71: 1-56.

Voipio, P. (1968) Zur Verbreitung der *argentatus*- und *cachinnans*- Möwen. *Orn. Fennica* 45: 73-83.

Voipio, P. (1972) Silbermöwen der *Larus argentatus cachinnans*-Gruppe als Besiedler des baltischen Raumes. *Ann. Zool. Fenn.* 9: 131-136.

Voipio, P. (1993) Differences in ecological properties in the herring gull (*Larus argentatus*) as a basis for explaining and predicting colonization events – a case history in retrospect. *Ann. Zool. Fenn.* 30: 3-15.

Voous, K. H. (1959) Geographical variation of the Herring Gull *Larus argentatus* in Europe and North America. *Ardea* 47: 176-187.

Voss, M. (1986) Zur Bürzelfärbung junger Dreizehenmöwen (*Rissa tridactyla*). *Seevögel* 7: 12.

Walhout, J. (1991) Melanistische Kokmeeuw bij Borsele in juni 1989. *Dutch Birding* 13: 141-142.

Walker, D. (1991a) Albino Herring Gulls. *Birding World* 4: 88.

Walker, D. (1991b) The Dungeness Thayer's-type Gull. *Birding World* 4: 213.

Walker, D. (1995) Status of Yellow-legged Gulls at Dungeness. *Brit. Birds* 88: 5-7.

Walker, D. 2003. The Audouin's Gull in Kent - a new British bird. *Birding World* 16: 199-202.

Walker, F. J. (1981a) Notes on the birds of northern Oman. *Sandgrouse* 2: 33-55.

Walker, F. J. (1981b) Notes on the birds of Dhofar. *Sandgrouse* 2: 56-85.

Wallace, D. I. M. (1964) Studies on less familiar birds. 128. Slender-billed Gull. *Brit. Birds* 57: 241-247.

Wallace, D. I. M. (1980) Identification of some scarce or difficult Western Palearctic species. Pp.133-145 in J. T. R. Sharrock, ed. *The frontiers of bird identification*. Macmillan, London.

Wallander, J. & J. Mogren (1983) Ringnäbbad mås *Larus delawarensis* för första gången anträffad i Sverige. *Vår Fågelvärld* 42: 431-433.

Walters, J. (1978) The primary moult in four gull species near Amsterdam. *Ardea* 66: 32-47.

Wannhoff, U. (1996) Ornithologische Beobachtungen auf den Kommandeur-Inseln. *Limicola* 10: 281-303.

Watson, F. J. (1983) Head shapes and postures of Slender-billed and Black-headed Gulls. *Brit. Birds* 76: 137-138.

Watson, F. J. (1983) Leg and bill colours of Ring-billed Gulls. *Brit. Birds* 76: 576.

Watson, P. S. (1981) Seabird observations from commercial trawlers in the Irish Sea. *Brit. Birds* 75: 82-90.

Weber, J. W. (1981) The *Larus* gulls of the Pacific Northwest's interior, with taxonomic comments on several forms 1. *Continental Birdlife* 2: 1-10.

Webster, M. A. (1968) Gulls of the south China coast. *Hong Kong Bird Rep.* 1967: 31-33.

Weir, D. N., R. Y. McGowan, A. C. Kitchener, S. McOrist, B. Zonfrillo & M. Heubeck (1995) Iceland Gulls from the "Braer" disaster, Shetland 1993. *Brit. Birds* 88: 15-25.

Weir, D. N., A. C. Kitchener & R. Y. McGowan (2000) Hybridization and changes in the distribution of Iceland gulls (*Larus glaucoides/kumlieni/thayeri*). *J. Zool. Lond.* 252: 517-530.

Welch, G. & H. Welch (1984) Birds seen on an Expedition to Djibouti. *Sandgrouse* 6: 1-23.

Weseloh, D. V. (1981) A probable Franklin's × Ring-billed Gull pair nesting in Alberta. *Canad. Field-Nat.* 95: 474-476.

Weseloh, D. V. & P. Mineau (1986) Apparent hybrid Common × Black-headed Gull nesting in Lake Ontario. *Amer. Birds* 40: 18-20.

von Westernhagen, W. (1966) Dünnschnabelmöwe in Südwesteuropa. *Orn. Mitt.* 18: 217-220.

White, M. (1999) An unusual plumage of Bonaparte's Gull. *Birders J.* 8: 38-39.

White, R. (1988) Ross's Gull in Cornwall and Devon. *Birding World* 1: 83-85.

White, R. & C. Kehoe (1992) Ring-billed gull tracking. *Birding World* 5: 446.

Whittington, P. (1987) Little Gull Influx. *BTO News* 159: 3.

Wiegant, W. M., A. de Bruin & CDNA (1998) Rare birds in the Netherlands in 1996. *Dutch Birding* 20: 145-167.

Wiegant, W. M., A. de Bruin & CNDA (1999) Rare birds in the Netherlands in 1998. *Dutch Birding* 21: 309-320.

Wilds, C. (1986) "Mystery photographs 92": Franklin's Gull or Laughing Gull. *Brit. Birds* 79: 343-348.

Wilds, C. & D. Czaplak (1994) Yellow-legged Gulls *Larus cachinnans* in North America. *Wilson Bull.* 106: 344-356.

Williams, M. D., G. J. Carey, D. G. Duff & Xu Weishu (1992) Autumn bird migration at Beidaihe, China 1986–1990. *Forktail* 7: 3-55.

Williams, R. B. (1986) Black-headed Gull in summer plumage in January. *Brit. Birds* 79: 658-659.

Williamson, S. L. & L. J. Peyton (1963) Interbreeding of Glaucous-winged and Herring Gulls in the Cook Inlet region, Alaska. *Condor* 65: 24-28.

Wilson, J. (1990) Thayer's Gull in County Cork. *Birding World* 3: 91-93.

Wink, M., U. Kahl & P. Heidrich (1994) Lassen sich Silber-, Weisskopf- und Heringsmöwe (*Larus argentatus, L. cachinnans* & *L. fuscus*) molekulargenetisch unterscheiden? *J. Orn.* 135: 73-80.

Winkler, D. W. (1996) *California Gull. The Birds of North America* No. 259. Academy of Natural Sciences of Philadelphia, Philadelphia.

Winter, J. (1985) Partial albinism in a melanistic Mew Gull. *Western Birds* 16: 187-188.

Winters, R. (1999) Baltische Mantelmeeuw op Schiermonnikoog in oktober 1992. *Dutch Birding* 21: 23-26.

Wirdheim, A. (1997) Havsfågelhösten. Fantastiska studier men också ond, utdragen död. *Vår Fågelvärld* 56/7: 16-27.

Witt, H.-H. (1977) On the biology of Audouin's Gull *Larus audouinii* – breeding and feeding. *J. Orn.* 118: 134-155.

Witt, H.-H. (1982) Diet and breeding distribution of Audouin's Gull *Larus audouinii* in comparison with Yellow-legged Gull *Larus argentatus michahellis*. *Seevögel* 3: 87-91.

Witt, H.-H., J. Crespo, E. de Juano & J. Varela (1981) Comparative feeding ecology of Audouin's Gull and the Herring Gull *Larus argentatus* in the Mediterranean. *Ibis* 123: 519-526.

Woutersen, K. (1980) Migrating Little Gulls in the Netherlands. *Brit. Birds* 73: 192-193.

Wynne-Edwards, V. C. (1935) On the habits and distribution of birds of the North Atlantic. *Proc. Boston Soc. Nat. Hist.* 40: 233-346.

Yésou, P. (1985a) Atypical Common Gulls. *Dutch Birding* 7: 106.

Yésou, P. (1985b) Separating Ring-billed and Common Gulls. *Dutch Birding* 7: 105-106.

Yésou, P. (1991a) Reproduction de la Mouette de Sabine *Larus sabini* dans l'estuaire de la Taimyra, Sibérie. *Oiseau et R.F.O.* 61: 142-148.

Yésou, P. (1991b) The sympatric breeding of *Larus fuscus, L. cachinnans* and *L. argentatus* in western France. *Ibis* 133: 256-263.

Yésou, P. (1994) Contribution à l'étude avifaunistique de la Péninsule du Taïmyr. *Alauda* 62: 247-252.

Yésou, P. (2001a) Phenotypic variation and systematics of Mongolian Gull. *Dutch Birding* 23: 65-81.

Yésou, P. (2001b) The systematics of the *Larus fuscus–cachinnans–argentatus* complex of forms: a review. P.76 in G. Tellini Florenzano, F. Barbagli & N. Baccetti, eds. Atti XI Convegno Italiano di Ornitologgia. *Avocetta* 25.

Yésou, P. (2002) Systematics of *Larus argentatus - cachinnans - fuscus* complex revisited. *Dutch Birding* 24: 271-299.

Yésou, P. (2003) Les goélands du complexe *Larus argentatus-cachinnans-fuscus*: où en est la systematique?. *Ornithos* 10: 144-181.

Yésou, P. & P. J. Dubois (1993) Do flesh-coloured legs really occur in *adult* Yellow-legged Gulls? *Dutch Birding* 15: 24.

Yésou, P. & A. Filchagov (1993) Bare part colouration, head/eye contrast and kin recognition in gulls: the situation in Palearctic forms of the *Larus argentatus–Larus fuscus* group. *Colonial Waterbird Soc. Bull.* 17: 61.

Yésou, P. & E. Hirschfeld (1997) Which large gulls from the *Larus fuscus–cachinnans–argentatus* complex of (sub)species occur in Bahrein? *Sandgrouse* 19: 111-121.

Yésou, P. & P. Triblet (1995) The Common Gull in Senegal. *Malimbus* 17: 26-27.

Yésou, P., A. Filchagov & P. Dubois (1994a) An answer to Chylerecki's comment on the "new Herring Gull taxonomy". *Brit. Birds* 87: 73-78.

Yésou, P., M. Fouquet & O. Girard (1994b) Mediterranean Gull breeding in its first year. *Dutch Birding* 16: 60-61.

Yésou, P. & Sultana, J. (eds.) (2000) *Monitoring and Conservation of Birds, Mammals and Sea Turtles of the Mediterranean and Black Seas.* Environment Protection Department, Malta.

Young, D. (1990) Unusual upperwing pattern of Little Gull. *Brit. Birds* 83: 503-504.

Young, R. (1991) The Grey-headed Gull in Hertfordshire. *Birding World* 4: 46-47.

Yudin, K. A. & Firsova, L. V. (1988) The Herring Gull. In V.D. Il'icev & V.A. Zubakin (eds) Birds of USSR, Moscow.

Zetterström, D. (1989) Sotvingad mås sedd vid Falsterbo. *Anser* 28: 273-275.

Zhang, Y.-S. & He Fen-Qi (1993) A study of the breeding of the Relict Gull *Larus relictus* in Ordos, Inner Mongolia, China. *Forktail* 8: 125-132.

Zhang, Y.-S., L. Chang-Jiang, T. Lu & B. He (1991) Recent records of the Relict Gull *Larus relictus* in western Nei Mongol autonomous region, China. *Forktail* 6: 66-67.

Zimmer, K. J. (1985) *The western birdwatcher.* Prentice-Hall Inc. Englewood, New Jersey.

Zimmer, K. J. (1991) The impossible identification zone: plumage variation in "Kumlien's" Iceland Gull. *Birding* 23: 254-269.

Zimmer, K. J. (2000) Birding in the American West: A Handbook. Cornell University Press.

Zimmermann, D. A., D. A. Turner & D. J. Pearson (1996) *Birds of Kenya and northern Tanzania.* Christopher Helm, London.

Zimmermann, S. T. & I. L. Jones (1991) Birding the Pribilof Islands, Alaska. *Birding* 23: 271-280.

Zink, R. M., S. Rohwer, A. V. Andreev & D. L. Dittmann (1995) Trans-Beringia comparisons of mitochondrial DNA differentiation in birds. *Condor* 97: 639-649.

Zubakin, V. A., Panov, E. N., Fil'chagov, A. V. & Khokhlov, A. N. (eds.) 1992. Serebristaya chayka. Rasprostranenie, sistematika, ekologiya [The Herring Gull and related forms: Distribution, systematics, ecology]. Stavropol' Pedagogical Institute.

Zwart, F. (1984) Over een Kleine Burgermeester *Larus glaucoides* op Terschelling. *Limosa* 57: 115-116.

INDEX

All species are listed both under their common and scientific names. Numbers in roman text refer to page numbers, while those in italics refer to the plates and those in bold to the photographic plates. All subspecies recognised as valid in this work, but not synonyms, are included. Subspecies are presented in alphabetical order under the scientific name of the respective species. Page numbers for subspecies refer to the description of that subspecies within the 'Geographical variation' section of each species account. The index covers only the species accounts, not the introductory chapters.